studysync®

Teacher's Edition

Grade 12 | Volume 2

studysync.com

Send all inquiries to:
BookheadEd Learning, LLC
610 Daniel Young Drive
Sonoma, CA 95476

ISBN 978-1-94-973936-7

1 2 3 4 5 6 LKV 24 23 22 21 20 19

A

Grade 12

Volume 2 Contents

Authors and Advisors

DR. DOUGLAS FISHER

Dr. Douglas Fisher is Professor of Educational Leadership at San Diego State University and a teacher leader at Health Sciences High & Middle College having been an early intervention teacher and elementary school educator. He is the recipient of a Christa McAuliffe award for excellence in teacher education and is a member of the California Reading Hall of Fame. He is a renowned speaker and author of numerous articles and books and is President of the International Literacy Association (ILA) Board.

DR. TIMOTHY SHANAHAN

Dr. Timothy Shanahan is Distinguished Professor Emeritus at the University of Illinois at Chicago where he is Founding Director of the UIC Center for Literacy. He was Director of Reading for Chicago Public Schools, and, among other awards, received the William S. Gray Citation for Lifetime Achievement and the Albert J. Harris Award for outstanding research on reading disability from the International Literacy Association (ILA). He is the author/editor of more than 200 publications and books, and his research emphasizes the connections between learning to read and learning to write, literacy in the disciplines, and improvement of reading achievement.

DR. MICHELLE H. MARTIN

Dr. Michelle H. Martin is the Beverly Cleary Endowed Professor for Children and Youth Services in the Information School at the University of Washington and from 2011-2016 was the inaugural Augusta Baker Endowed Chair in Childhood Literacy at the University of South Carolina. She published Brown Gold: Milestones of African-American Children's Picture Books, 1845-2002 (Routledge, 2004), and is the founder of Read-a-Rama, a non-profit that uses children's books as the springboard for year-round and summer camp programming.

CATLIN TUCKER

Catlin Tucker is a Google Certified Innovator, bestselling author, international trainer, and frequent Edtech speaker, who teaches in Sonoma County where she was named Teacher of the Year in 2010. Her books Blended Learning in Grades 4-12 and Blended Learning In Action are both bestsellers. She is currently in the doctoral program at Pepperdine University, and writes the Techy Teacher column for ASCD's Educational Leadership.

JEFF ANDERSON

Jeff has inspired writers and teachers with the power and joy of the writing process. His particular area of interest is in making editing and grammar in context a meaning-making experience for students and teachers. He has written five books on writing and teaching writing. More recently, he has taken up writing middle grade novels, including Zack Delacruz: Me and My Big Mouth, which was selected for the Keystone State Reading List in Pennsylvania.

DR. PATRICIA MORALES

Dr. Patricia Morales is founder of ellservices©, consultant, and a professional development provider in English as a Second Language (ESL), Bilingual Education, and Dual Language Education. She is also an independent educational consultant at the Teaching and Learning Division of the Harris County Department of Education in Houston, Texas. She has taught university courses focusing on language acquisition and pedagogy, and continues to prepare thousands of teachers pursuing certifications in bilingual education and English as a Second Language in Texas.

JESSICA ROGERS

Jessica Rogers is a Lecturer at Baylor University and founder of Rogers Education Consulting, which specializes in Balanced Literacy professional development. She has over fifteen years experience in education, including teaching ESL, inclusion, gifted and talented, self-contained classrooms, mentoring teachers, and designing and implementing professional development. Her passion is making abstract educational theory and cutting-edge techniques practical for the classroom teacher.

GERRIT JONES-ROOY

Gerrit Jones-Rooy is Director of Literacy at Collegiate Academies in New Orleans as well as a 9th grade teacher. Previously he worked as a Staff Developer for the Reading and Writing Project, leading work across the country as well as in Saudi Arabia, Colombia, Poland and Thailand. He is the author or co-author of several Teachers College units including "Turning Every Kid into a Reader, Really" and "All About Books: Writing in Non-fiction."

DR. MARCELA FUENTES

Dr. Marcela Fuentes is an Assistant Professor of Creative Writing and Latinx Literature at Texas A&M University. She is a graduate of the Iowa Writers' Workshop, and was the 2016-2017 James C. McCreight Fellow in Fiction at the Wisconsin Institute for Creative Writing. She co-founded The Iowa Youth Writing Project, a nonprofit dedicated to promoting writing programs and events for K-12 students in the Iowa City area.

J. SCOTT BROWNLEE

J. Scott Brownlee is a Career & Talent Development Consultant at UT-Austin's McCombs School of Business, and a core faculty member for Brooklyn Poets, a NYC-based literary nonprofit. The author of four books of poetry, he received the Texas Institute of Letters 2015 Bob Bush Award for Best First Book of Poetry, as well as the 2014 Robert Phillips Prize from Texas Review Press.

DR. LYNNE KNOWLES

Dr. Lynn Knowles spent the majority of her 28-year teaching career at Flower Mound High School in Texas, where she served as English department chair and taught English II pre-AP and Humanities, as well as AP Capstone. She holds a bachelor's degree in Journalism from The University of Texas, a master's in Humanities from the University of Texas at Dallas, and a Ph.D. in Rhetoric from Texas Woman's University.

RICHARD ORLOPP

Richard Orlopp moved to Texas after graduating from Rutgers University with degrees in English and Journalism. He never left. He has taught English for the past 17 years and currently teaches AP Literature and Composition and International Baccalaureate seniors at Coppell High School.

WENDY MASSEY

Wendy Massey has taught high school for 20 years now. She has experience teaching grades 9-12 but primarily has taught English II Pre-AP and PSAT/SAT Prep. She has served several years now as the English department co-chair; in addition, she has served on the curriculum writing team for her district and has been the Academic Decathlon language coach.

MUHAMMAD SHIMAL

Mr. Shimal has been teaching for eleven years now. His teaching experience spans high school to college classes domestically and internationally. He current ly teaches English Language AP/Dual Credit for Juniors and College Prep classes for Seniors. He holds a Bachelor's degree in English Language and Literature, a Masters degree in Linguistics, and is currently finishing his PhD in English at the University of Texas at San Antonio.

VALENTINA GONZALES

Valentina Gonzalez is a Professional Development Specialist for English Language Learners in Texas, coaching teachers in ELL strategies and leading professional development at the state and national level. She has a natural love of language stemming from her experience as an immigrant from Serbia, Yugoslavia. Her years in education include roles as a classroom teacher, ESL Specialty Support Teacher, and ESL Facilitator. She holds a bachelor's degree in Interdisciplinary Studies from The University of Houston, and a master's in Educational Administration from Lamar University.

UNIT 4

Sculpting Reality

What is the power of story?

Unit titles and essential questions provide a thematic link for all texts in the unit.

A **Thematic Option**

The thematic option provides 30 days of integrated reading and writing instruction with a series of short texts connected to a common theme.

B **Novel Study Option**

Each novel study option provides 30 days of comparative texts with integrated reading and writing instruction.

Thematic Selections

Genre Focus
POETRY

Novel Study Choices

The Importance of Being Earnest
DRAMA
Oscar Wilde

Wuthering Heights
FICTION
Emily Brontë

Pride and Prejudice
FICTION
Jane Austen

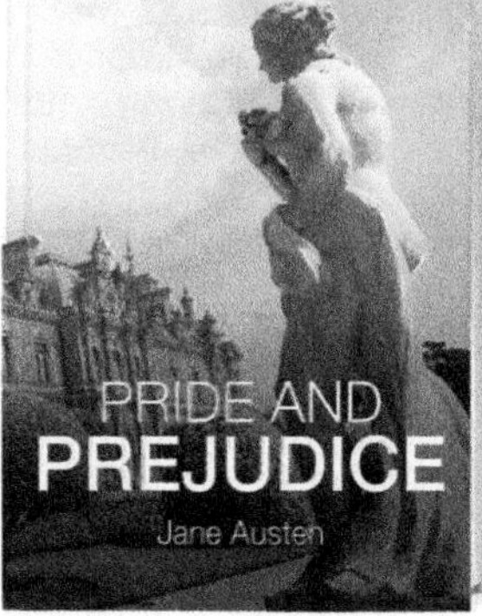

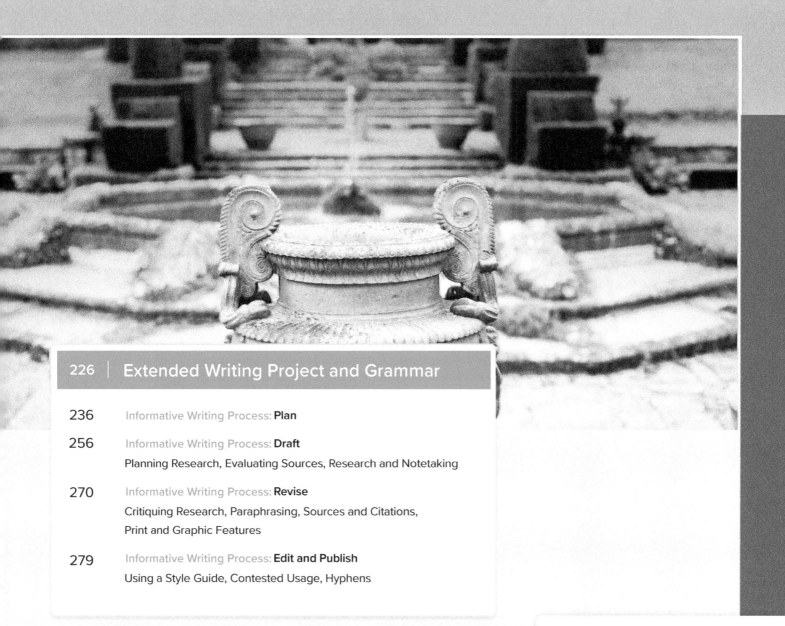

English Language Learner Resources offer instruction using texts written at four distinct levels that serve as structural and thematic models of authentic texts in the unit.

End-of Unit Assessments gauge students' understanding of key instuctional content and mastery of standards covered in the unit.

Author Biographies

CHARLOTTE BRONTË

When she was a twenty-year-old schoolteacher, Charlotte Brontë (1816–1855) self-financed the publication of a volume of poems she and her two younger sisters had written, using pseudonyms to disguise their gender. Although only two copies of the book sold, Brontë was not dismayed. She refused to let publishers ignore her. Her persistence paid off when a year later her novel Jane Eyre was published and became a runaway success.

ELIZABETH BARRETT BROWNING

The most esteemed female poet of the English-speaking world during the 19th century, Elizabeth Barrett Browning (1806–1861) spent her childhood engrossed in literature. Before she was a teenager, Browning had read the works of Shakespeare, Homer, and Milton—as well as the Old Testament in its original Hebrew. Her voracious appetite for words evolved into a career as a poet. Browning's works included passionate admonishments of the social injustices of her time, including the American slave trade, British child labor, and women's oppression.

WANDA COLEMAN

Known as "the L.A. Blueswoman," Wanda Coleman (1946–2013) called Southern California home for her whole life. She was pleased to be described as uncompromising by literary critics, and her poetry often explored African American identity in the context of racism and economic hardship. Coleman's first poems were printed in a local newspaper when she was just thirteen years old. In addition to other poetry, she went on to publish essays, screenplays, and fiction for the rest of her life.

CHARLES DICKENS

Widely considered the greatest novelist of the Victorian era, Charles Dickens (1812–1870) was forced to leave school at the age of twelve and sent to work in a London factory, after his father was sent to debtor's prison. This early experience led Dickens to take an interest in the lives of working-class people, a theme which he explored throughout his fiction. Dickens's novels—many of them serialized in popular magazines—were immensely popular and appealed to people from all walks of life, from factory workers to Queen Victoria herself.

JOAN DIDION

For California-born journalist and author Joan Didion (b. 1934), writing is synonymous with experience. She wrote in *The White Album* (1979), "We tell ourselves stories in order to live." Didion has reported on and written about a wide range of subjects, from the evolving American cultural landscape to personal narratives about the deaths of her husband and daughter. In 2015, Didion appeared in an advertisement for the French fashion label Céline, demonstrating her enduring status as a style icon.

ROSS GAY

American author Ross Gay (b. 1974) grew up outside Philadelphia and played college football before becoming a renowned poet and professor. He currently writes and teaches in Indiana, where he also tends to the Bloomington Community Orchard. Gay helped start the publicly owned orchard in 2010, which is maintained by volunteers and shares its harvest with the community. In his poetry, Gay strives to explore and create compassion.

JOHN KEATS

When John Keats (1795–1821) abandoned his training as an apothecary and surgeon to become a poet, it was not at the encouragement of the literary community. In fact, Keats, who after his lifetime would be considered among the most beloved English poets, was first received by critics as "unintelligible." Keats is best known for a series of odes, and he only wrote poetry seriously for about six years before succumbing to tuberculosis. His friend Percy Bysshe Shelley wrote the epic poem *Adonais* (1821) as an elegy for Keats in the days after his death.

YUSEF KOMUNYAKAA

Yusef Komunyakaa (b. 1947) spent his youth in Bogalusa, Louisiana, daydreaming of the world outside his rural town and was often found listening to his mother's waist-high wooden radio. He revered jazz and blues music especially and mentions the music of Louis Armstrong, Otis Redding, Thelonious Monk and others among his sixteen collections of poetry. He served in the U.S. Army during the Vietnam War and currently lives and works in New York.

URSULA K. LE GUIN

American author Ursula K. Le Guin (1929–2018) published children's books, short story collections, poetry, screenplays, essays, and novels in her lifetime. Early in her career, she faced years of rejection and first found success in the genres of fantasy and science fiction. "We read books to find out who we are," wrote Le Guin in *The Language of the Night* (1979). Her most popular novels exhibited how the genre of science fiction could reflect real issues of human nature and the environment.

WILLIAM WORDSWORTH

William Wordsworth (1770–1850) published *Lyrical Ballads* with Samuel Taylor Coleridge in 1798, introducing Romanticism to English poetry with poems like Wordsworth's "Lines Composed a Few Miles above Tintern Abbey" and Coleridge's "The Rime of the Ancient Mariner." Wordsworth's love for the natural world was nurtured in his youth, when he lived in a house along the River Derwent in Northern England. The exploration of human connection to nature imbued his writings throughout his lifetime.

PERCY BYSSHE SHELLEY

English poet Percy Bysshe Shelley (1792–1822) was a literary icon of the Romantic era, which emphasized the importance of the imagination. He received an upper-class education and traveled throughout Europe as a young man. In addition to writing poetry and plays, Shelley also wrote political pamphlets, some of which he distributed with hot air balloons. He was married to Mary Shelley, the author of the novel Frankenstein (1818). Just before his thirtieth birthday, the poet drowned off the coast of Italy while sailing.

HEID E. ERDRICH

A member of the Turtle Mountain Band of Ojibwe, Heid E. Erdrich (b. 1963) was raised in North Dakota by an Ojibwe mother and German American father who taught at the nearby Bureau of Indian Affairs boarding school. The author of several poetry collections, she explores themes of history, biology, motherhood, and spirituality in her writing. Erdrich co-edited the anthology Sister Nations: Native American Women on Community, a collection of fiction, prose, and poetry that celebrates the rich and diverse writing of contemporary Native American women.

UNIT 5

Fractured Selves

What causes individuals to feel alienated?

A

Thematic Option

The thematic option provides 30 days of integrated reading and writing instruction with a series of short texts connected to a common theme.

B

Novel Study Option

Each novel study option provides 30 days of comparative texts with integrated reading and writing instruction.

Students learn to identify features of the unit's literary focus and then analyze those features at the end of the unit.

Every lesson in the Thematic units features integrated scaffolding and differentiation for all levels of English Language Learners. Approaching grade-level readers, and Beyond grade-level readers.

Thematic Selections

Genre Focus
ARGUMENTATIVE TEXT

Novel Study Choices

1984
FICTION
George Orwell

Frankenstein
DRAMA
Mary Shelley

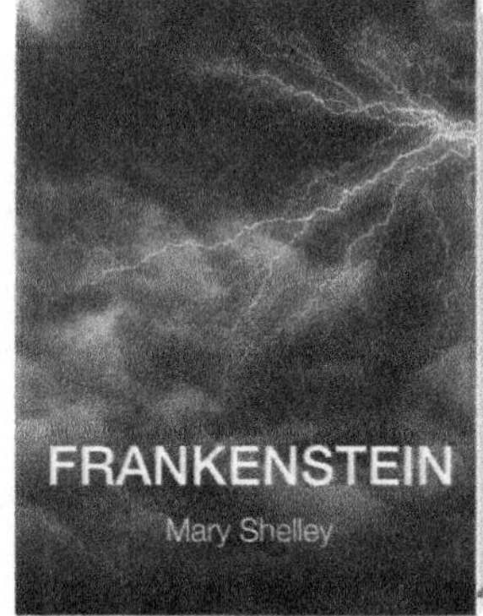

The Bluest Eye
FICTION
Toni Morrison

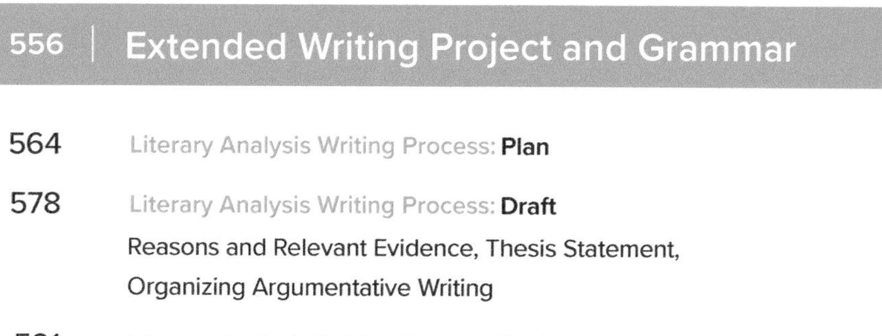

556 | Extended Writing Project and Grammar

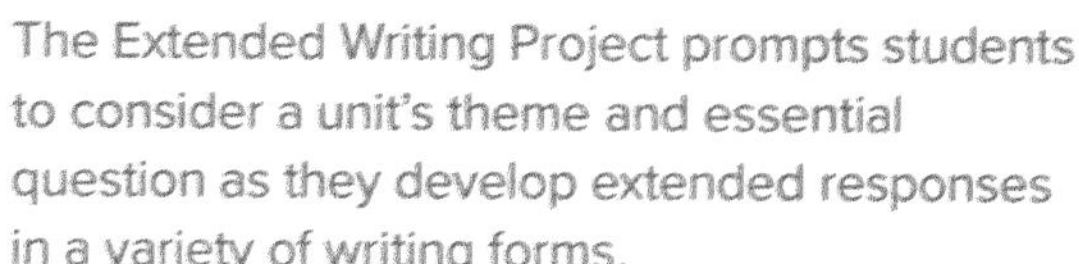

The Extended Writing Project prompts students to consider a unit's theme and essential question as they develop extended responses in a variety of writing forms.

602 | English Language Learner Resources

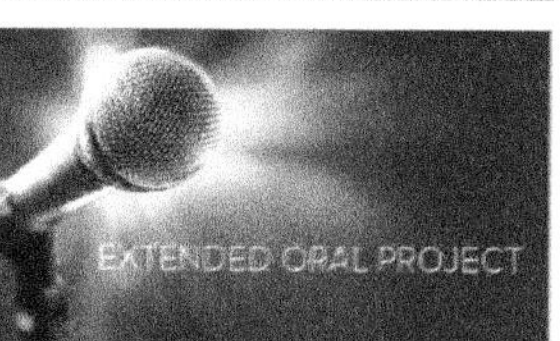

634 | End-of-Unit Assessment

Author Biographies

FAREENA AREFEEN

High schooler Fareena Arefeen was Houston's Youth Poet Laureate in 2016. Her one-year term included delivering public readings in the area and representing her city's youth, and she received a book deal and a scholarship to college. Arefeen, who moved to Texas from Bangladesh with her mother and sister, sees a mission beyond personal recognition in her role. "I want to tell other immigrants, like me, that their stories matter," she says. She plans to attend New York University.

MARCI CALABRETTA CANCIO-BELLO

Miami-based poet Marci Calabretta Cancio-Bello (b. 1989) was born in South Korea and adopted as a baby to a family in upstate New York. The idea for a poem published in her award-winning collection *Hour of the Ox* (2016) came to Cancio-Bello in the process of researching her Korean heritage. She became fascinated to learn about the dying art of pearl diving, and wondered if she could be descended from its early practitioners.

WINSTON CHURCHILL

Twice the prime minister of the United Kingdom, Winston Churchill (1874–1965) led a successful Allied strategy with the United States and the Soviet Union to defeat Nazi Germany in World War II. He won the Nobel Prize for Literature in 1953 "for his mastery of historical and biographical description as well as for brilliant oratory in defending exalted human values." He remains one of the most quoted figures in English-speaking history and is credited for coining the word *summit* in 1950.

LUCILLE CLIFTON

American poet Lucille Clifton (1936–2010) is known for her concise language, carefully wrought lines, and the complexity she draws through straightforward images. Her poems confront and celebrate African American experience, capturing the lives of heroes and everyday characters alike. Clifton's work received many awards in her lifetime, and in 1987 she earned the distinction of the first author to ever have two books of poetry nominated for the Pulitzer Prize in the same year.

ALICE MOORE DUNBAR-NELSON

The writer Alice Moore Dunbar-Nelson (1875–1935) was born in New Orleans. Her African American, Anglo, Creole, and Native American heritage offered Dunbar-Nelson, according to her writing, a racially ambiguous appearance, which in turn allowed her mobility among various social classes and ethnicities. Dunbar-Nelson published poetry, plays, fiction, essays, and journalism in her lifetime. She is also one of the few African American diarists of the 20th century in the published record.

T.S. ELIOT

Author of "The Waste Land," which is widely considered the most influential work of 20th-century literature, T. S. Eliot (1888–1965) was born in St. Louis, Missouri. After earning his undergraduate degree at Harvard, Eliot moved to England, becoming a British citizen in 1927. He worked as a bank clerk as well as a literary critic and publisher. His poetry was noted as radical and innovative in style, as he gave expression to the dissatisfaction his generation felt in the wake of World War I.

KATHERINE MANSFIELD

Katherine Mansfield (1888–1923) was born in New Zealand and died in France at the age of thirty-four from tuberculosis. In her brief life, she was known as a pioneer of the modernist short story. Mansfield was very prolific in her final years, and at the time of her death much of her work had yet to be published. Upon hearing the news of her death, her friend and contemporary Virginia Woolf wrote in her diary, "I was jealous of her writing—the only writing I have ever been jealous of."

GEORGE ORWELL

"What I have most wanted to do," wrote the English author George Orwell (1903–1950), "is make political writing into an art." Born in Myanmar (known as Burma at the time) and raised in England, Orwell knew he wanted to be a writer from a young age. His experiences working as a colonial police officer in India and fighting in the Spanish Civil War inform many of his stories and essays, which critique social inequality and totalitarianism.

LILLIAN SMITH

American author Lillian Smith (1897–1966) critiqued the values upheld by her community of white Southerners in the era of Jim Crow, stating, "segregation is evil." Her 1944 novel *Strange Fruit*, which features an interracial love story, was so controversial that the United States Postal Service refused to mail it. She was an early and ardent supporter of the Civil Rights Movement and continued to write until her death from cancer in 1966.

TENESSEE WILLIAMS

American playwright Tennessee Williams (1911-1983) grew up in Columbus, Mississippi and St. Louis, Missouri, and recalls a childhood scarred by his parents' tense marriage. He began to write during this time, and would later base characters like Amanda Wingfield in *The Glass Menagerie* and Big Daddy in *Cat on a Hot Tin Roof* on his mother and father. Williams' plays are known for transforming American theater by bringing forth characters more dark and complex than had ever been seen before.

WILLIAM CARLOS WILLIAMS

The American modernist poet William Carlos Williams (1883–1963) worked as a family doctor in Rutherford, New Jersey, scribbling lines on his prescription blanks in between patient visits. He crafted the language in his poems to mirror the patterns of everyday speech, which he saw as a distinctly American project. In his epic poem *Paterson,* Williams writes, "Any poem that has any worth expresses the whole life of the poet."

VIRGINIA WOOLF

The work of Virginia Woolf (1882–1941) received renewed attention long after her lifetime in the second wave of feminism in the 1970s. Woolf was a prominent writer of essays and modernist novels in London during the period between World War I and World War II. Woolf's fiction employed stream-of-consciousness and female-driven narrative. Her book-length essay *A Room of One's Own* (1929) argued for the importance of creating space for women writers in a male-dominated literary tradition.

UNIT 6

Times of Transition

How are we shaped by change?

A
Thematic Option

The thematic option provides 30 days of integrated reading and writing instruction with a series of short texts connected to a common theme.

B
Novel Study Option

Each novel study option provides 30 days of comparative texts with integrated reading and writing instruction.

Thematic Selections

Genre Focus
FICTION

Independent Reads provide opportunities to focus on reading comprehension and skills application.

Students read and reflect on a self-selected text that corresponds to the unit's theme and essential question and then self-select a format for a written response.

Novel Study Choices

Death and the King's Horseman
DRAMA
Akinwande Oluwole Babatunde 'Wole' Soyinka

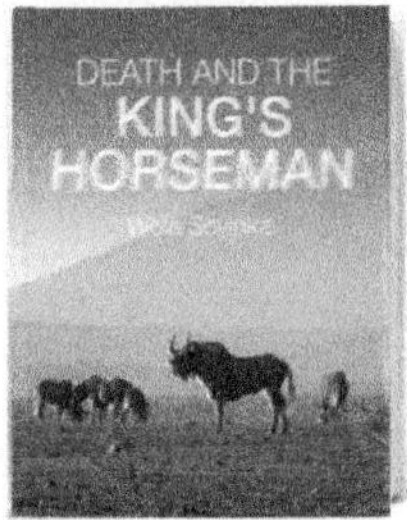

The Kite Runner
FICTION
Khaled Hosseini

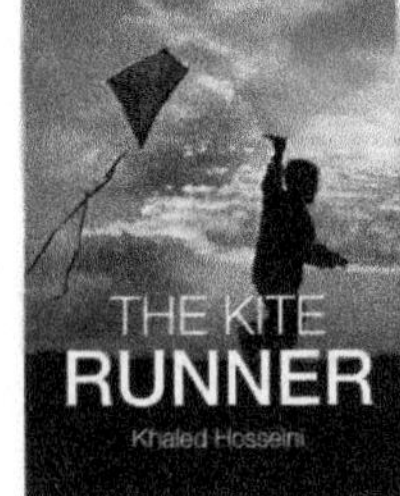

A Bend in the River
FICTION
V.S. Naipaul

Heart of Darkness
FICTION
Joseph Conrad

Grammar instruction is embedded in the Extended Writing Project to reinforce the connection between grammar concepts and writing proficiency. Hundreds of additional grammar lessons are also available in the StudySync Skills library.

In the Extended Oral Project, students apply the structure and approach of the Extended Writing Project to an oral presentation.

UNIT 6

Author Biographies

LEILA ABOULELA

Leila Aboulela (b. 1964) is a Sudanese writer of short stories and novels. She was born in Cairo, Egypt; was raised in Khartoum, Sudan; and has lived much of her adult life in Aberdeen, Scotland. All of her literary works carefully portray the faith and values of her characters, which often feature people who practice Islam and must negotiate ethical dilemmas. Aboulela sees fiction as a "gentle way of passing on information" about Islam to non-Muslim readers.

CHIMAMANDA NGOZI ADICHIE

Chimamanda Ngozi Adichie (b. 1977) writes short stories, novels, and essays and splits her time between Nigeria and the United States. Her education has included studies in medicine, communication, political science, African history, and creative writing. Adichie's family lived in the house once owned by the notable Nigerian author Chinua Achebe, a literary figure Adichie credits as her inspiration for becoming a writer.

MAHZARIN R. BANAJI

Harvard psychologist Mahzarin R. Banaji (b. 1956) was born and raised in Secunderabad, India, and moved to the United States to pursue her PhD at Ohio State University. Banaji is best known for her work exploring the concept of implicit bias, or the prejudice that results from stereotypes and attitudes built in to our society. Along with her work at Harvard, Banaji runs the website Project Implicit, which aims to spread awareness of the role implicit bias plays in our daily lives.

RITA DOVE

American author Rita Dove (b. 1952) served as the United States Poet Laureate from 1993 to 1995, and as the Poet Laureate of Virginia from 2004 to 2006. In addition to poetry, she writes plays and fiction. Over the course of Dove's career, one major change in her approach to writing has been her sense of an audience. When she began writing, she did not yet have readers; now, after numerous publications and awards, she writes knowing that many people will read the ideas and perspectives she puts forth.

JAMAICA KINCAID

Jamaica Kincaid (b. 1949) moved from St. John's, Antigua, at the age of sixteen to work as an au pair in Manhattan, and has lived in New York ever since. Her early writing career began as a journalist for a girls' magazine, and as her talent was recognized, she became a staff writer for *The New Yorker.* Critics often struggle to categorize her work, which is by turns both political and personal, and like the human experience itself: complex, beautiful, and resonant.

JHUMPA LAHIRI

Jhumpa Lahiri (b. 1967) says, "While I am American by virtue of the fact that I was raised in this country, I am Indian thanks to the efforts of two individuals." Lahiri's parents infused her Rhode Island childhood with the language, values, and traditions of their Bengali Indian origins, and the family took frequent trips to Kolkata, the capital of West Bengal. Lahiri's fiction and essays often feature characters who navigate multiple cultural identities, modeled after her own Indian American experience.

JAWAHARLAL NEHRU

Activist, lawyer, and politician Jawaharlal Nehru (1889–1964) was repeatedly imprisoned for civil disobedience in the 1920s and 1930s. A leader of the movement to establish Indian independence from the British administration, Nehru worked closely with Mahatma Gandhi and was recognized as his successor by the end of World War II. Named the first prime minister of India in 1947, Nehru went on to model the new government into a secular republic with democratic values.

BEN OKRI

Ben Okri (b. 1959) spent part of his childhood in London and part in his home of Nigeria, where he experienced the Biafran War firsthand. He was once again living in London when he polished the final draft of *The Famished Road* (1991), which made Okri the youngest ever winner of the Man Booker Prize for Fiction. In prose and in verse, Okri's attention to the music of language and the art of storytelling reflect his lifelong love of literature and deep connection to his Urhobo culture.

ZADIE SMITH

Author Zadie Smith (b. 1975) grew up in London with a Jamaican mother and an English father. She liked to sing, dance, and write from an early age. When she was fourteen, Smith changed the spelling of her first name, Sadie, to its current spelling with a Z. Smith pitched her first novel to an agent while she was still in college in Cambridge, England; *White Teeth* (2000) became an instant bestseller. She writes fiction and essays and works as a professor of creative writing in New York City.

DEREK WALCOTT

The poetry of Derek Walcott (1930–2017) celebrates his Caribbean heritage and interrogates the influence of colonialism. Walcott was raised in the British colony of Saint Lucia in the West Indies, where he trained as a painter and began publishing poems at age fourteen. He later lived between Trinidad, New York City, Boston, and Saint Lucia as a poet, playwright, and professor. Walcott defined poetry as a form of survival, cohering the "fragmented memory" of individual and cultural histories.

EHUD LAVSKI AND YAEL NATHAN

Together, writer Ehud Lavski and illustrator Yael Nathan publish EL Comics, a science fiction–infused series of webcomics they describe as having "twisted endings." Lavski lives in Los Angeles and works primarily in film and television as a scriptwriter. Nathan lives in Tel Aviv and works in a wide range of design fields, producing images for graphic and interface design in addition to creating classical animation, character design, and illustration.

Bring Literature to Life

- Instructional choice from thematic units, novel studies, and teacher-created units.
- Interchangeable print and digital use.
- A continuously growing library of over 1,600 classic & contemporary texts.

Student Print Edition

Novel Options

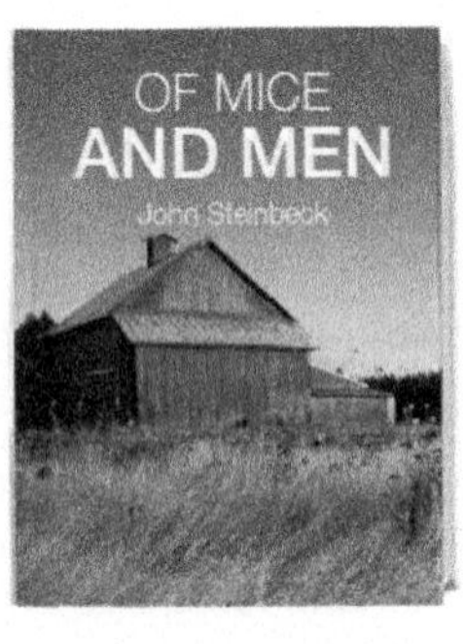

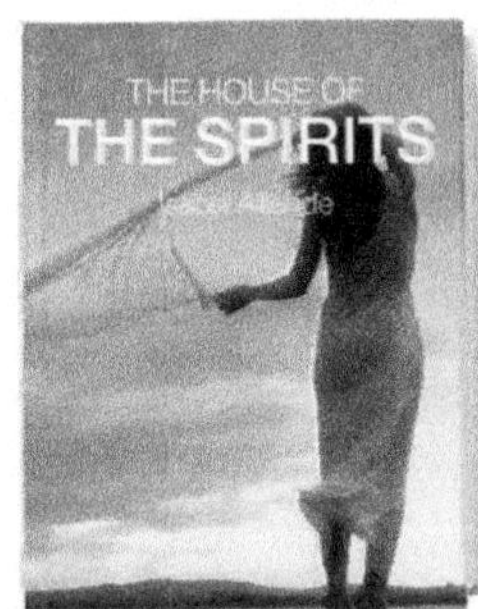

- Extensive writing and research practice.
- Automatically embedded scaffolds so ALL students reach their potential.
- Data-driven assessment to track progress and inform instruction.

Teacher Print Edition

Data Driven Assesment

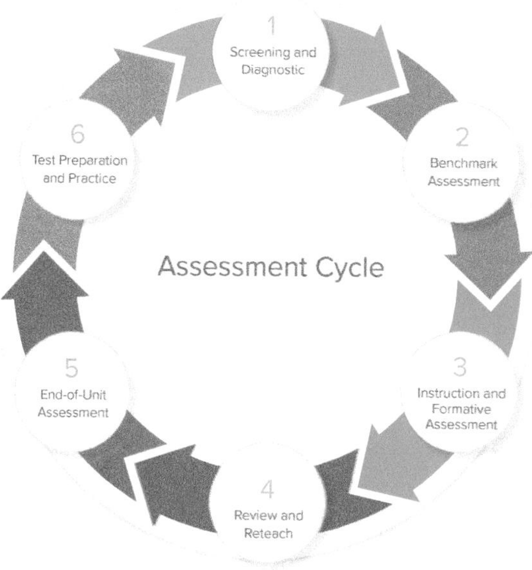

Comprehensive Student and Teacher Digital Experience

Pick Your Path

StudySync provides four curricular options to enhance your teaching experience in print and online.

1 Thematic Units

These units contain several text types from a variety of genres. Selections include multiple paired readings to challenge students to compare within and across genres.

2 Novel Studies

Each unit has at least three novel study options. Teachers can choose a whole- class novel study or employ a more independent, student-choice model.

3 Unit Creator

Build the units you want using StudySync's Unit Creator and library of thousands of texts and instructional materials.

4 American or British Literature

Teachers in Grades 11 and 12 can choose an optional chronological format to American and British literature.

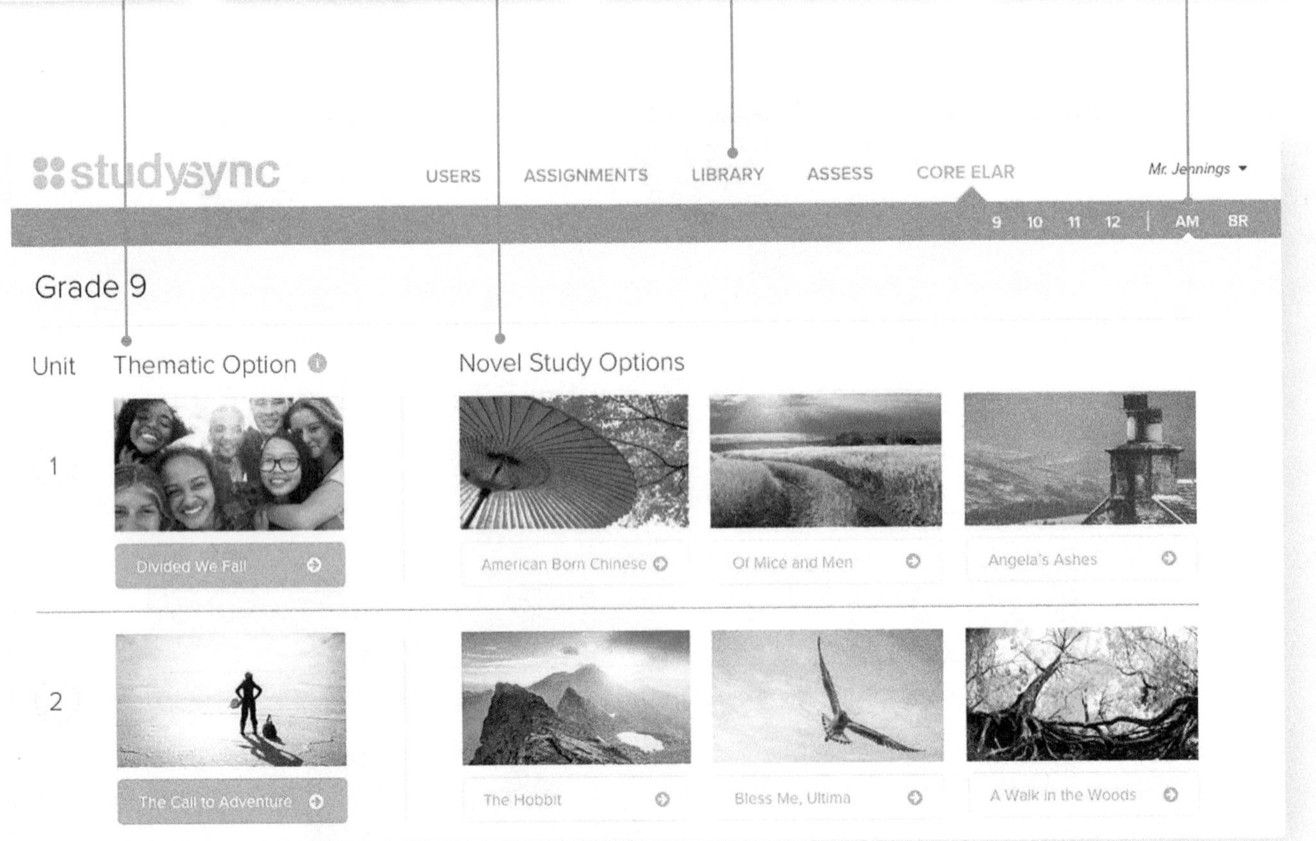

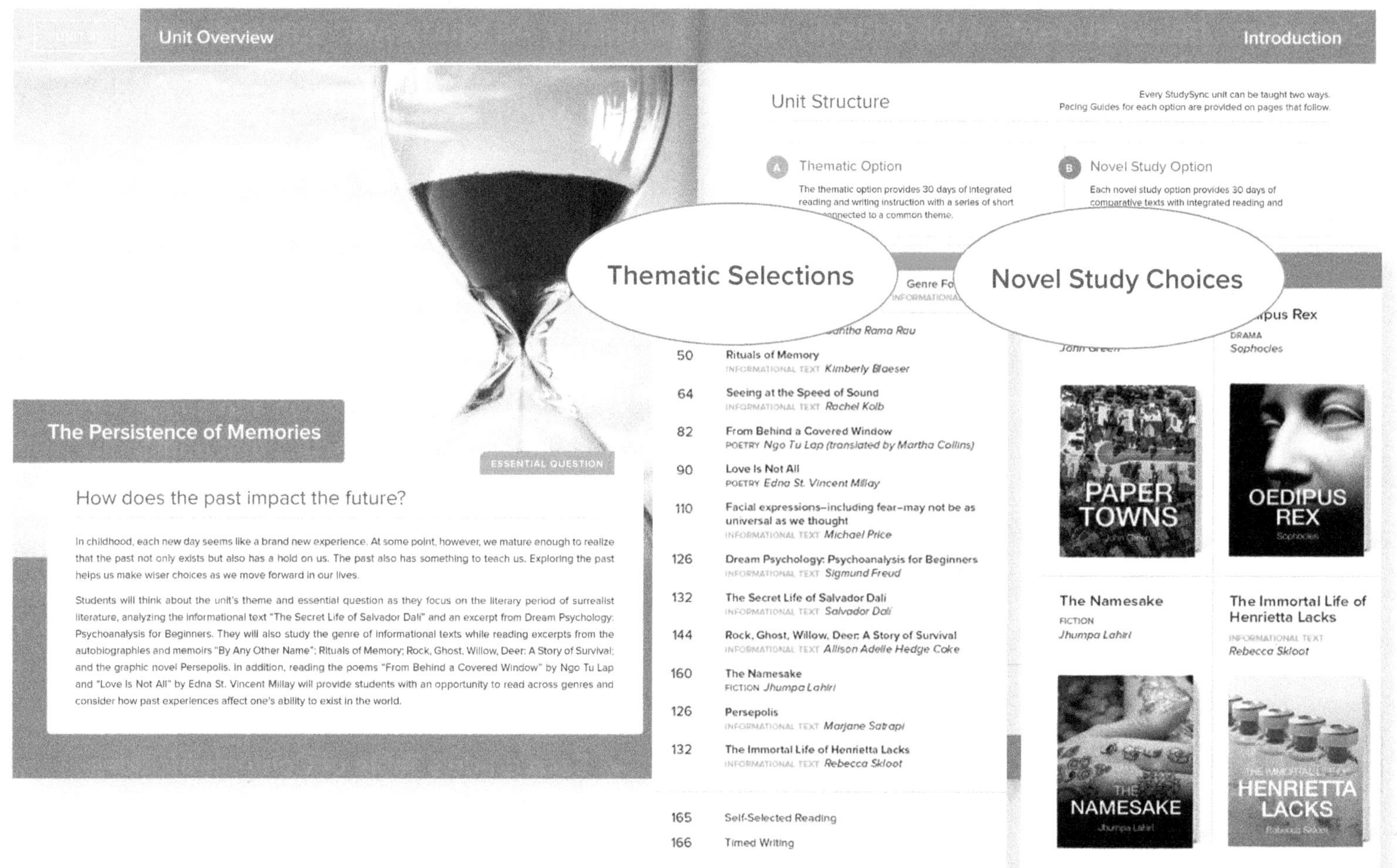

Unit Overview
Introduction
Unit Structure
Every StudySync unit can be taught two ways. Pacing Guides for each option are provided on pages that follow.
Thematic Option
The thematic option provides 30 days of integrated reading and writing instruction with a series of short
Novel Study Option
Each novel study option provides 30 days of comparative texts with integrated reading and
Thematic Selections
Novel Study Choices
The Persistence of Memories
ESSENTIAL QUESTION
How does the past impact the future?
In childhood, each new day seems like a brand new experience. At some point, however, we mature enough to realize that the past not only exists but also has a hold on us. The past also has something to teach us. Exploring the past helps us make wiser choices as we move forward in our lives.
Students will think about the unit's theme and essential question as they focus on the literary period of surrealist literature, analyzing the informational text "The Secret Life of Salvador Dali" and an excerpt from Dream Psychology: Psychoanalysis for Beginners. They will also study the genre of informational texts while reading excerpts from the autobiographies and memoirs "By Any Other Name"; Rituals of Memory; Rock, Ghost, Willow, Deer: A Story of Survival; and the graphic novel Persepolis. In addition, reading the poems "From Behind a Covered Window" by Ngo Tu Lap and "Love Is Not All" by Edna St. Vincent Millay will provide students with an opportunity to read across genres and consider how past experiences affect one's ability to exist in the world.
50 Rituals of Memory INFORMATIONAL TEXT Kimberly Blaeser
64 Seeing at the Speed of Sound INFORMATIONAL TEXT Rachel Kolb
82 From Behind a Covered Window POETRY Ngo Tu Lap (translated by Martha Collins)
90 Love Is Not All POETRY Edna St. Vincent Millay
110 Facial expressions—including fear—may not be as universal as we thought INFORMATIONAL TEXT Michael Price
126 Dream Psychology: Psychoanalysis for Beginners INFORMATIONAL TEXT Sigmund Freud
132 The Secret Life of Salvador Dali INFORMATIONAL TEXT Salvador Dali
144 Rock, Ghost, Willow, Deer: A Story of Survival INFORMATIONAL TEXT Allison Adelle Hedge Coke
160 The Namesake FICTION Jhumpa Lahiri
126 Persepolis INFORMATIONAL TEXT Marjane Satrapi
132 The Immortal Life of Henrietta Lacks INFORMATIONAL TEXT Rebecca Skloot
165 Self-Selected Reading
166 Timed Writing
DRAMA Sophocles
PAPER TOWNS
OEDIPUS REX
The Namesake
FICTION
Jhumpa Lahiri
The Immortal Life of Henrietta Lacks
INFORMATIONAL TEXT
Rebecca Skloot
THE NAMESAKE
HENRIETTA LACKS

StudySync's high school curriculum is designed for maximum flexibility. Each unit offers both a Thematic and several Novel Study unit options. All of these options offer 30 days of instruction on the same standards and can be used interchangeably.

This variety of options means that teachers can create more than 4,000 different combinations of Thematic and Novel Study units that satisfy the standards in each grade level, adapting the curriculum to the unique requirements of their school and classroom.

Amplify Student Voices

StudySync helps students think critically and thoughtfully. All StudySync students see themselves in their curriculum. StudySync encourages students to develop their own unique voices while they grow as readers, writers, and future leaders in college and career settings.

- StudySync's curriculum is centered around students. Lesson activities and the digital platform enable teachers to easily facilitate peer review and other on and offline collaborative approaches that transform classrooms into workshops of great reading and writing.
- The Table of Contents for every grade features at least 50% of texts written by female authors and at least 50% of texts written by authors from diverse backgrounds.
- Each grade's Table of Contents includes stories about extraordinary young people. Whether it's NFL linebacker Shaquem Griffin or poet Sara Abou Rashed, students will learn how other young people like them are changing the world today.

- Integrated media such as StudySyncTV and SkillsTV models collaborative and academic conversations, providing students the roadmap they need to develop their own voices.
- Unique media like the “What’s Next” podcast series helps teachers meet multimedia and digital literacy standards with high-quality resources that are relevant to the lives of today’s students.
- Blast lessons help students understand the most important issues in today’s world. Teachers have access to a brand new Blast article - leveled for 3 different Lexiles - every single school day, helping them deliver a fresh, relevant learning experience every year.

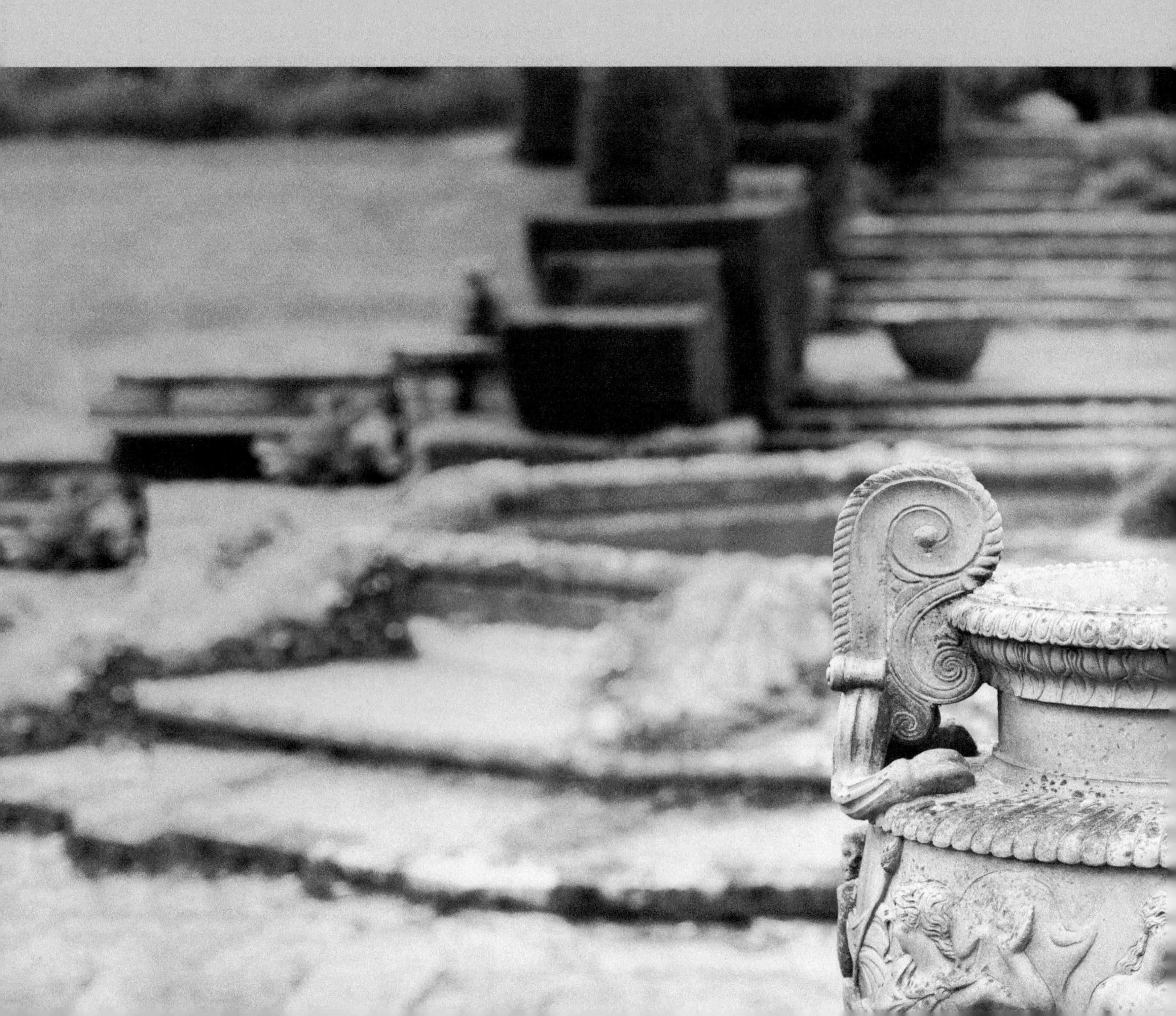

Sculpting Reality

What is the power of story?

UNIT 4

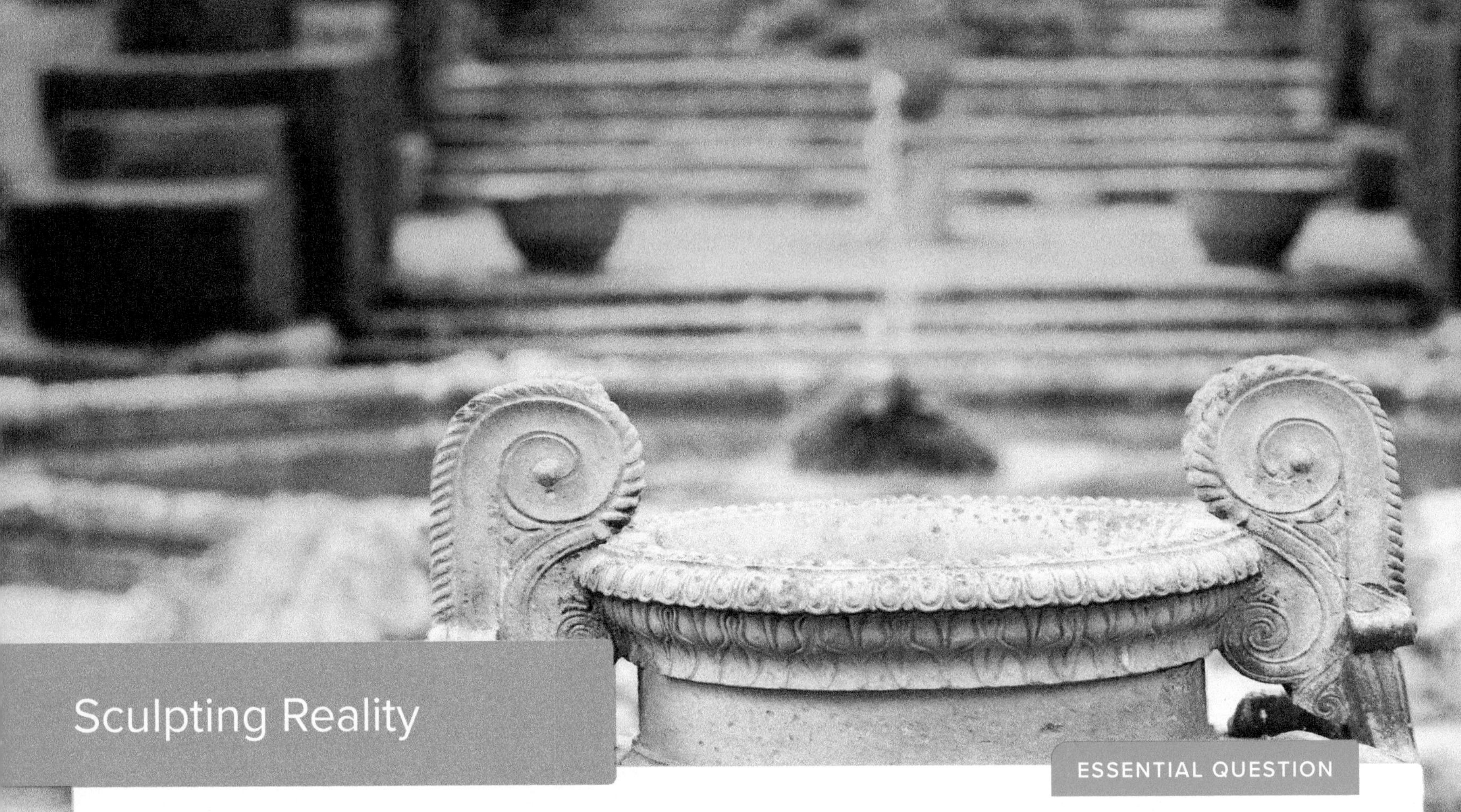

Sculpting Reality

ESSENTIAL QUESTION

What is the power of story?

From *Cinderella* to *Harry Potter*, everyone has a favorite story. Stories have the power to sweep audiences into fantasy worlds and help them see their own worlds in new or clearer ways.

How can stories teach us important lessons? How can stories change our hearts and minds? What do readers learn by reading about fictional characters and events? What do stories teach us about ourselves and our society?

In this unit, students will think about the theme and essential question as they focus on Romanticism and Victorianism. They will explore examples of Romantic literature, including the poems "Ozymandias," "Ode on a Grecian Urn," and "Lines Composed a Few Miles Above Tintern Abbey." They will also review Victorian literature through the poem "The Cry of the Children" as well as excerpts from the seminal classics A *Tale of Two Cities* and *Jane Eyre*. In addition, students will study the genre of poetry while reading poems from other literary periods, including "Facing It," "Stung," "Catalog of Unabashed Gratitude," and "Dear Mama." Furthermore, the nonfiction texts "Jabberwocky Baby," "Freedom," and "Why I Write" encourage students to think about the power of storytelling in other areas of life.

Students will begin this unit as readers, and they will finish as writers, as they apply what they have learned about story elements to their own argumentative research writing projects.

Unit Structure

Every StudySync unit can be taught two ways.
Pacing Guides for each option are provided on pages that follow.

Thematic Option

The thematic option provides 30 days of integrated reading and writing instruction with a series of short texts connected to a common theme.

Novel Study Option

Each novel study option provides 30 days of comparative texts with integrated reading and writing instruction.

Thematic Selections

Genre Focus: POETRY

Novel Study Choices

The Importance of Being Earnest
DRAMA
Oscar Wilde

Wuthering Heights
FICTION
Emily Brontë

Pride and Prejudice
FICTION
Jane Austen

Jane Eyre
FICTION
Charlotte Brontë

Sculpting Reality

(tv) StudySyncTV or SkillsTV Episode

Pacing Guide

Days	Readings	Skill and Standard Instruction	Skill Practice and Spiraling
1	Essential Question **The Big Idea: What is the power of story?** p. 20	• Literary Focus: Romanticism • Recognizing Genre • Academic Vocabulary	
2-3	**Ozymandias** (tv) p. 32	• Media	• Theme • Language, Style, and Audience • Literary Analysis Writing • Collaborative Conversations
4-7	PAIRED READINGS **Facing It** p. 48 **Ode on a Grecian Urn** p. 58	• Poetic Elements and Structure • Figurative Language	• Theme • Literary Analysis Writing
8-12	**Lines Composed a Few Miles Above Tintern Abbey on Revisiting the Banks of the Wye on a Tour, July 13, 1798** p. 76	• Context Clues • Figurative Language (tv) • Analyzing Romanticism	• Textual Evidence • Literary Analysis Writing • Collaborative Conversations
13	**Stung** p. 98		• Textual Evidence • Summarizing • Poetry Writing
14-15	**Catalog of Unabashed Gratitude** p. 106		• Textual Evidence • Summarizing • Point of View • Personal Response Writing

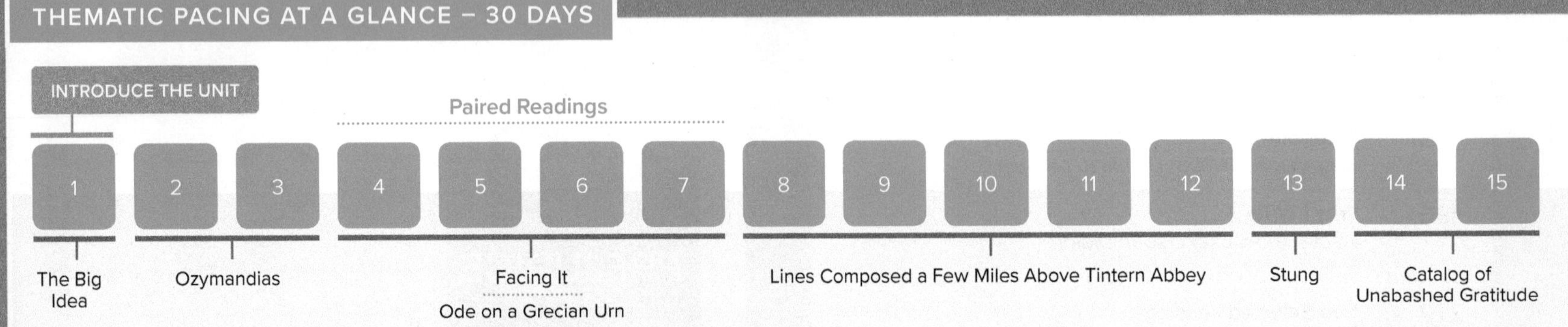

Days	Readings	Skill and Standard Instruction	Skill Practice and Spiraling
16-17	**The Cry of the Children** p. 128	• Literary Focus: Victorianism	• Summarizing • Poetry Writing
18	**A Tale of Two Cities** tv p. 140		• Literary Analysis Writing • Collaborative Conversations
19-22	PAIRED READINGS **Jane Eyre** p. 150 **Jabberwocky Baby** p. 160 **Dear Mama** p. 170	• Analyzing Victorian Literature • Language, Style, and Audience	• Theme • Poetic Elements and Structure • Narrative Writing
23-26	PAIRED READINGS **Freedom** p. 186 **Why I Write** p. 196	• Summarizing • Author's Purpose and Point of View tv • Figurative Language	• Compare and Contrast • Informative Writing • Collaborative Conversations
27	**Self-Selected Reading and Response** p. 222	• Independent Reading	• Personal Response Writing
28	**Timed Writing** p. 224		• Timed Writing

Review and Assessment See page p. 318.

Days	Review and Assessment	Skill Practice and Assessment
29	**Skills Review** p. 318	Students will have the opportunity to complete one or more Spotlight Skill lessons in order to improve understanding and further practice skills from the unit that they found most challenging.
30	**End-of-Unit Assessment** p. 319	For more details, please see the End-of-Unit Assessment information for Grade 12 Unit 4 on p. 319.

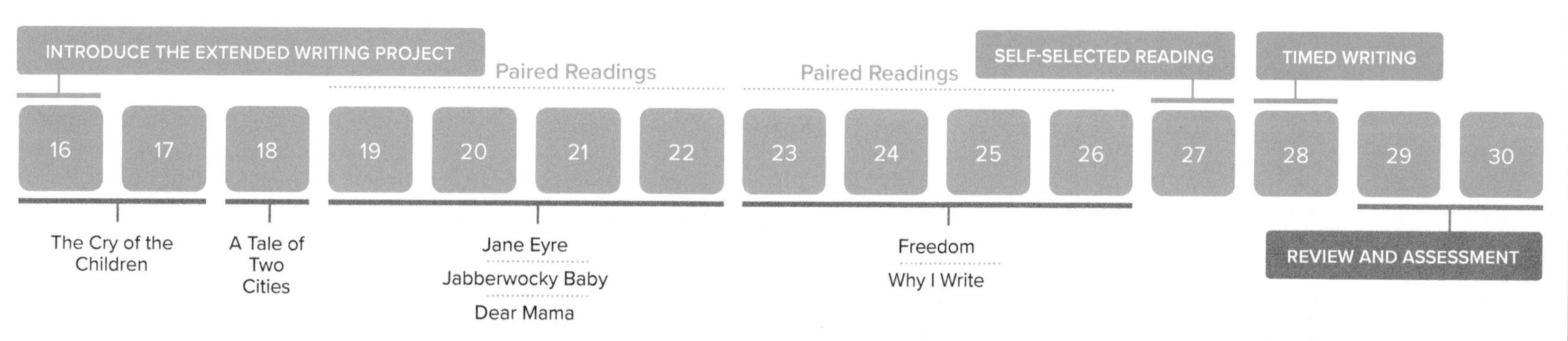

Extended Writing Project and Grammar

Pacing Guide

In the second half of the unit, students continue exploring texts that address the unit's Essential Question and begin crafting a longer composition to share their own ideas about the Essential Question in the Extended Writing Project. The writing project will take your students through the writing process to produce a research essay.

Extended Writing Project Prompt

How can we better value nature through our daily behaviors?

Think of a daily behavior that the average person may not know is damaging to nature. For example, people may not think about reducing their use of plastic bags when cleaning up after their dogs or may not consider the consequences of constantly upgrading their phones and other technology. Research your topic and structure your essay to be clear, informative, and convincing. Then, write an informative research essay, using both informative text structures and source materials to support your claim and make your informative essay convincing.

Days	Extended Writing Project and Grammar	Skill and Standard Instruction	Connect to Mentor Texts
16	**Research Writing Process: Plan** p. 236		
17-20	**Research Writing Process: Draft** p. 256	• Planning Research • Evaluating Sources • Research and Notetaking	
21-24	**Research Writing Process: Revise** p. 270	• Critiquing Research • Paraphrasing • Sources and Citations • Print and Graphic Features	
25-26	**Research Writing Process: Edit and Publish** p. 279	• Using a Style Guide • Contested Usage • Hyphens	Additional grammar lessons can be found in the StudySync Skills Library.

Research

The following lessons include opportunities for research:

- Blast **Sculpting Reality** Research Links*
- Blast **Making Waves** Research Links*
- Independent Read **Facing It** Write
- Independent Read **The Cry of the Children** Beyond the Book
- Independent Read **A Tale of Two Cities** Beyond the Book
- Independent Read **Jane Eyre** Developing Background Knowledge
- Independent Read **Jabberwocky Baby** Beyond the Book
- Blast **Anecdotal Arguments** Research Links*
- Close Read **Why I Write** Beyond the Book

*See the teacher lesson plan online

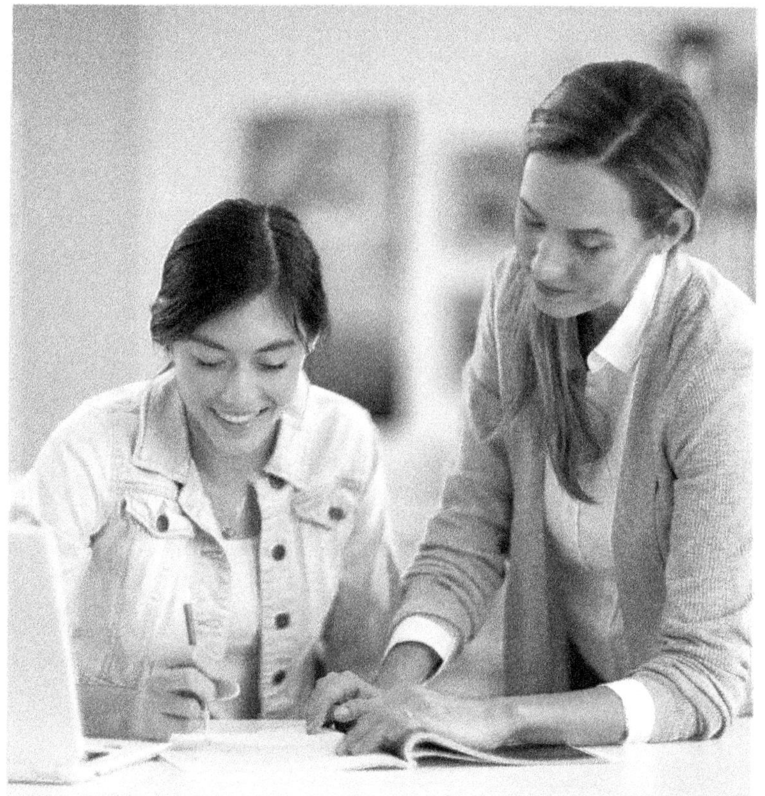

Self-Selected Reading Prompt

After reading a self-selected text, students will respond to the following argumentative prompt:

"Four score and seven years ago our fathers brought forth on this continent, a new nation, conceived in liberty, and dedicated to the proposition that all men are created equal." More than 150 years have passed since Abraham Lincoln said this line, and most people can still identify it as a quote from the Gettysburg Address after hearing the first few words. That shows how powerful words can be.

How can a text change the way you think?

Choose the most powerful and memorable lines from the selection you've just read in the previous lesson. What makes this line interesting to you? Why might this line be appealing to a wide audience? Write a response in which you identify a powerful line (or lines) and explain why it is memorable.

Timed Writing Prompt

Students will respond to the following ACT-style argumentative prompt:

Write a unified, coherent essay about teaching history through diction.

In your essay, be sure to:

- clearly state your own perspective on the issue and analyze the relationship between your perspective and at least one other perspective
- develop and support your ideas with reasoning and examples
- organize your ideas clearly and logically
- communicate your ideas effectively in standard written English

NOVEL STUDY OPTION 1

THE IMPORTANCE OF BEING EARNEST

Oscar Wilde

At-a-Glance

Author
Oscar Wilde

Genre
Drama

Publication Year
1895

Text Complexity
N/A

Themes & Topics

Comedy

Satire

Manners

Leaving his country home to visit London, John Worthing inhabits the made-up persona of Ernest. But when he falls for his friend Algernon's cousin, Gwendolen, as Ernest, he must find a way to keep his artifices from unraveling. This play pioneered modern farce with absurd situations, social deception and embarrassment, and speedy, vicious wordplay.

The precise epigrams of Oscar Wilde (1854–1900) expressed a frank, modern aesthetic with fierce wit. Wilde is remembered most frequently for *The Importance of Being Earnest*, *The Picture of Dorian Gray,* and the poem *The Ballad of Reading Gaol*, written while Wilde served a prison sentence for homosexuality, which was forbidden by law in Victorian England.

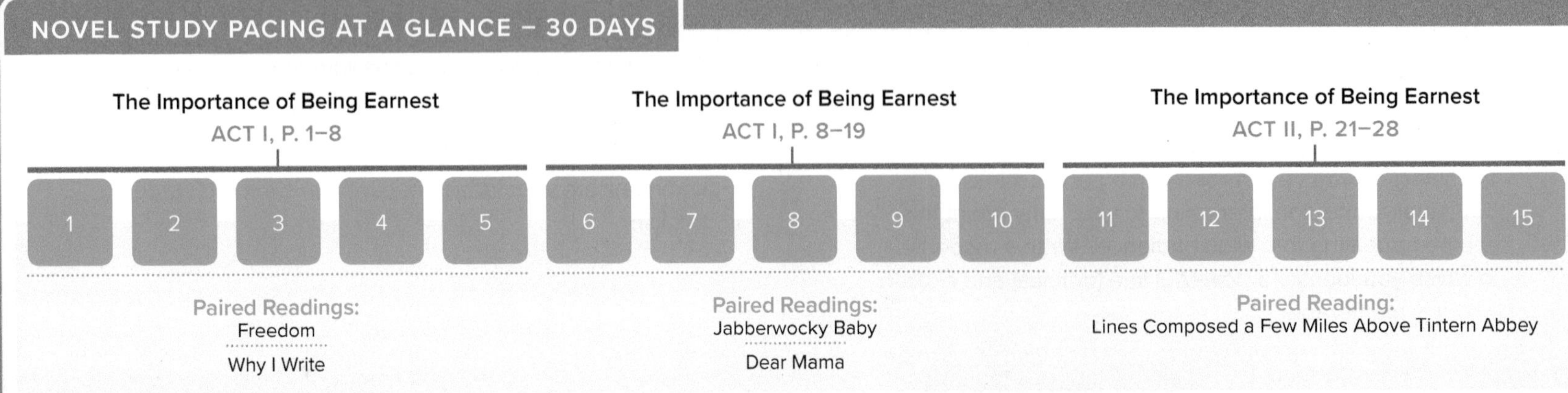

Pacing Guide: The Importance of Being Earnest

Days	Readings	Paired Readings	Skill and Standard Instruction	Skill Practice and Spiraling
1-5	**The Importance of Being Earnest** Act I, p. 1–8	Freedom Why I Write	• Summarizing • Author's Purpose and Point of View (tv) • Figurative Language	• Compare and Contrast • Informative Writing • Collaborative Conversations
6-10	**The Importance of Being Earnest** Act I, p. 8–19	Jabberwocky Baby Dear Mama	• Language, Style, and Audience	• Poetic Elements and Structure • Narrative Writing
11-15	**The Importance of Being Earnest** Act II, p. 21–28	Lines Composed a Few Miles Above Tintern Abbey	• Context Clues • Figurative Language (tv)	• Textual Evidence • Literary Analysis Writing
16-19	**The Importance of Being Earnest** Act II, p. 28–42	Ozymandias (tv)	• Media	• Literary Analysis Writing • Collaborative Conversations
20-23	The Importance **of Being Earnest** Act III, p. 43–54	Facing It Ode on a Grecian Urn	• Poetic Elements and Structure • Figurative Language	• Theme • Literary Analysis Writing
24-28	Culminating Writing Task	Recommended for instruction with this unit's Culminating Writing Task.	• Planning Research • Evaluating Sources • Research and Notetaking • Critiquing Research • Paraphrasing	• Sources and Citations • Print and Graphic Features • Using a Style Guide • Contested Usage • Hyphens

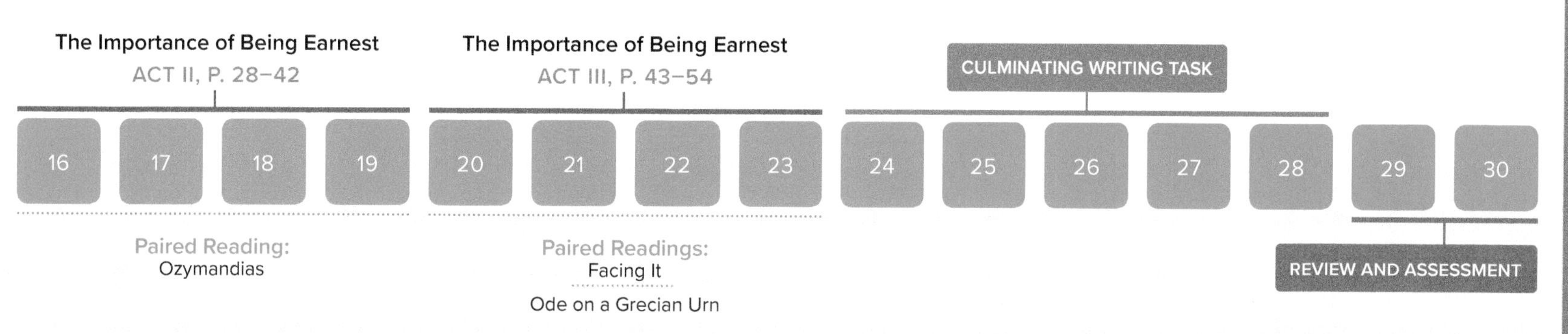

Unit Overview

WUTHERING HEIGHTS

Emily Brontë

At-a-Glance

Author
Emily Brontë

Genre
Fiction

Publication Year
1847

Text Complexity
880L

Themes & Topics

Love

Betrayal

Supernatural

Kindly Mr. Earnshaw brings a dark-haired orphan home to the manor house of Wuthering Heights, but Earnshaw's son Hindley mistreats the boy, who falls in love with Cathy, the daughter. When Earnshaw dies and Cathy is engaged to a rich neighbor, the orphan Heathcliff goes away to become very wealthy—and returns to enact an elaborate revenge on his tormentors.

Emily Brontë (1818–1848) grew up in the parsonage of Howarth, Yorkshire, in the close company of another famous English novelist, sister Charlotte, the author of *Jane Eyre*. Doomed by severe poverty and primitive sanitation, all the Brontë children died young, Emily at thirty. *Wuthering Heights* was her only published book, but it remains a classic and indelible work of English literature.

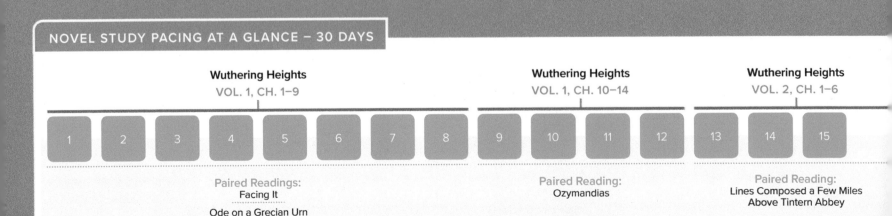

NOVEL STUDY PACING AT A GLANCE – 30 DAYS

Reading	Days	Paired Reading(s)
Wuthering Heights VOL. 1, CH. 1–9	1, 2, 3, 4, 5, 6, 7, 8	Paired Readings: Facing It; Ode on a Grecian Urn
Wuthering Heights VOL. 1, CH. 10–14	9, 10, 11, 12	Paired Reading: Ozymandias
Wuthering Heights VOL. 2, CH. 1–6	13, 14, 15	Paired Reading: Lines Composed a Few Miles Above Tintern Abbey

Pacing Guide: Wuthering Heights

Days	Readings	Paired Readings	Skill and Standard Instruction	Skill Practice and Spiraling
1-8	**Wuthering Heights** Volume 1, Ch. 1–9	Facing It Ode on a Grecian Urn	• Poetic Elements and Structure • Figurative Language	• Theme • Literary Analysis Writing
9-12	Wuthering Heights Volume 1, Ch. 10–14	Ozymandias tv	• Media	• Literary Analysis Writing • Collaborative Conversations
13-16	**Wuthering Heights** Volume 2, Ch. 1–6	Lines Composed a Few Miles Above Tintern Abbey	• Context Clues • Figurative Language tv	• Textual Evidence • Literary Analysis Writing
17-19	Wuthering Heights Volume 2, Ch. 7–14	Jabberwocky Baby Dear Mama	• Language, Style, and Audience	• Poetic Elements and Structure • Narrative Writing
20-23	**Wuthering Heights** Volume 2, Ch. 15–20	Freedom Why I Write	• Summarizing • Author's Purpose and Point of View tv • Figurative Language	• Compare and Contrast • Informative Writing • Collaborative Conversations
24-28	**Culminating Writing Task**	Recommended for instruction with this unit's Culminating Writing Task.	• Planning Research • Evaluating Sources • Research and Notetaking • Critiquing Research • Paraphrasing	• Sources and Citations • Print and Graphic Features • Using a Style Guide • Contested Usage • Hyphens

Unit Overview

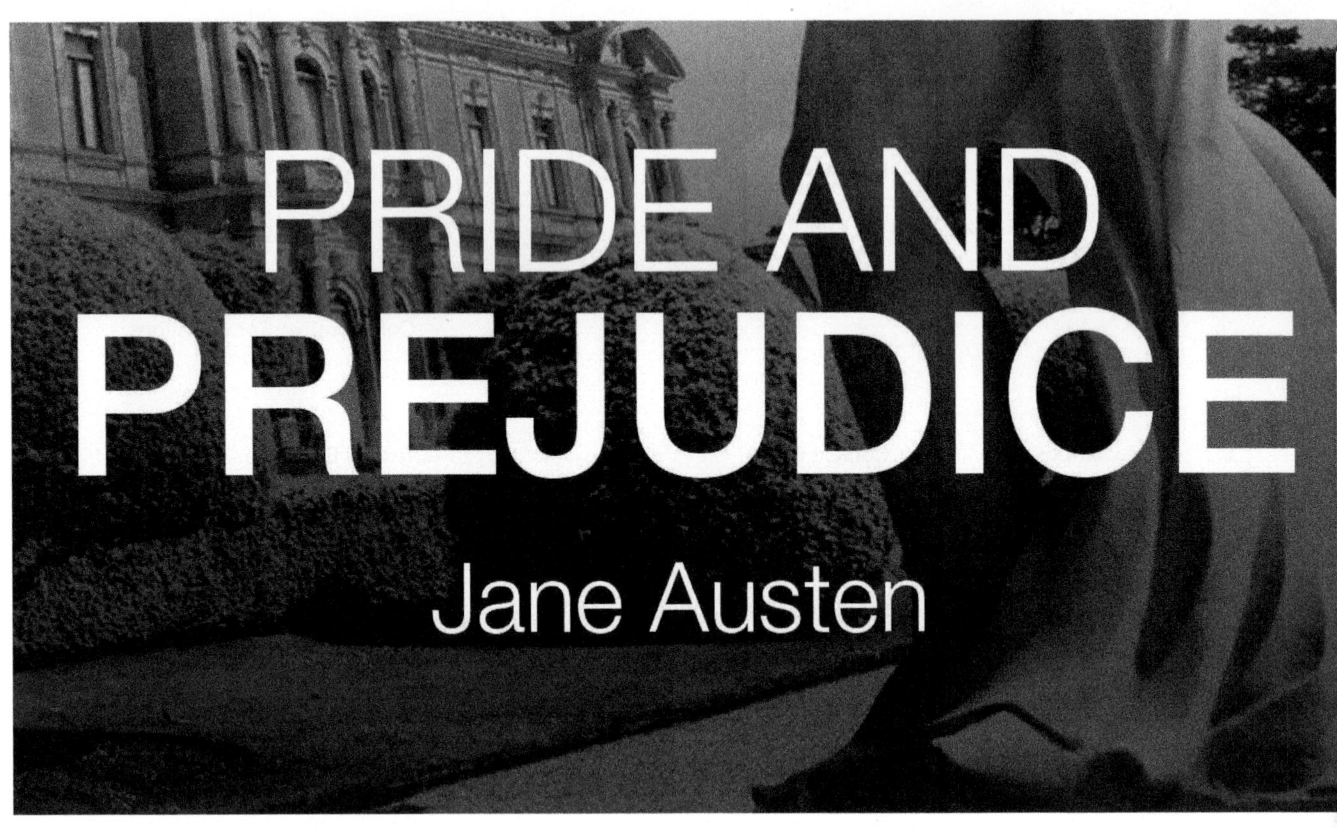

At-a-Glance

Author
Jane Austen

Genre
Fiction

Publication Year
1813

Text Complexity
1070L

Themes & Topics

Love

Money

Marriage

Revolution—in America, then France—is the background for the story of the Bennet daughters, Jane, Elizabeth, and Lydia, along with their suitors. Illustrating the dilemmas of an English middle class dependent on marrying up to keep from slipping down, *Pride and Prejudice* features proposals, deceptions, and revelations in the dramas of the domestic and everyday.

Jane Austen (1775–1817), daughter of a rector at a country parish, began writing as a teenager. Her novels *Sense and Sensibility*, *Pride and Prejudice*, *Mansfield Park* and *Emma* won their author mass popularity and acclaim during her lifetime, but she retained a relative measure of anonymity. Her final two novels were published posthumously, including the work said to be her most autobiographical, *Persuasion*.

NOVEL STUDY PACING AT A GLANCE – 30 DAYS

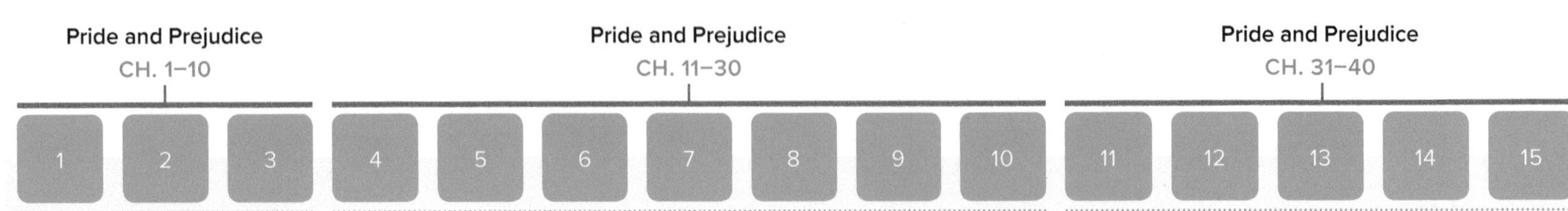

Pacing Guide: Pride and Prejudice

Days	Readings	Paired Readings	Skill and Standard Instruction	Skill Practice and Spiraling
1-3	**Pride and Prejudice** Ch. 1–10	Ozymandias (tv)	• Media	• Literary Analysis Writing • Collaborative Conversations
4-10	**Pride and Prejudice** Ch. 11–30	Jabberwocky Baby Dear Mama	• Language, Style, and Audience	• Poetic Elements and Structure • Narrative Writing
11-15	**Pride and Prejudice** Ch. 31–40	Lines Composed a Few Miles Above Tintern Abbey	• Context Clues • Figurative Language (tv)	• Textual Evidence • Literary Analysis Writing
16-19	**Pride and Prejudice** Ch. 41–50	Facing It Ode on a Grecian Urn	• Poetic Elements and Structure • Figurative Language	• Theme • Literary Analysis Writing
20-23	**Pride and Prejudice** Ch. 51–61	Freedom Why I Write	• Summarizing • Author's Purpose and Point of View (tv) • Figurative Language	• Compare and Contrast • Informative Writing • Collaborative Conversations
24-28	**Culminating Writing Task**	Recommended for instruction with this unit's Culminating Writing Task.	• Planning Research • Evaluating Sources • Research and Notetaking • Critiquing Research • Paraphrasing	• Sources and Citations • Print and Graphic Features • Using a Style Guide • Contested Usage • Hyphens

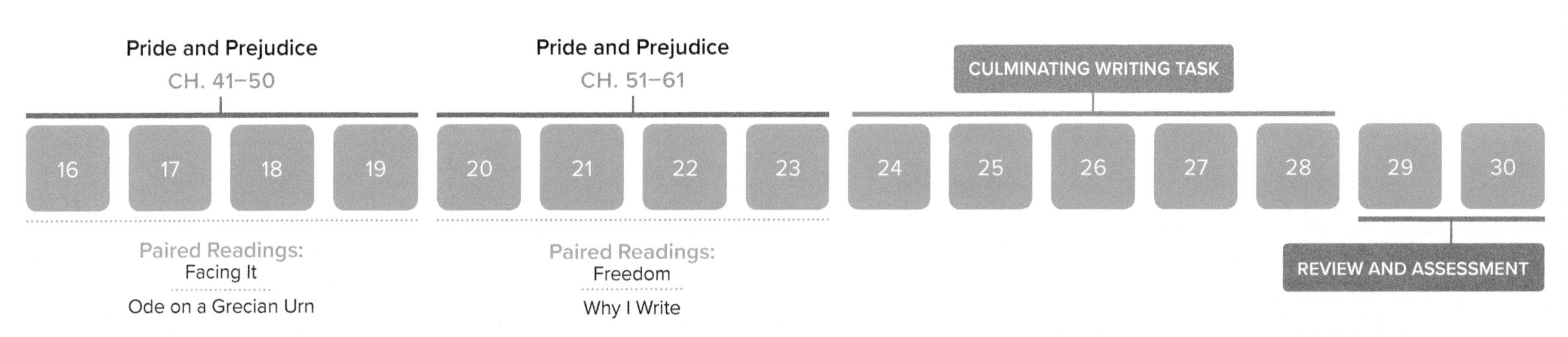

NOVEL STUDY OPTION 4

JANE EYRE

Charlotte Brontë

At-a-Glance

Author
Charlotte Brontë

Genre
Fiction

Publication Year
1847

Text Complexity
890L

Themes & Topics

Coming of Age

Marriage

Victorian England

Jane is hired by the mysterious Mr. Rochester to teach a child in his care he says is not his. Stranger yet are the footsteps in the house after dark; a guest is attacked and a fire nearly kills Mr. Rochester, who proposes marriage to the governess. But there is a secret hidden somewhere, and it will come out no matter who tries to stop it.

Charlotte Brontë (1816–1855) was raised in a parsonage at Howarth, Yorkshire, in conditions so poor two of her sisters died. As children, her siblings—including Emily, author of *Wuthering Heights*—imagined fantasy worlds which gave birth to their famous novels. The longest living of all her siblings, Brontë died at 39 from an illness associated with her pregnancy.

NOVEL STUDY PACING AT A GLANCE – 30 DAYS

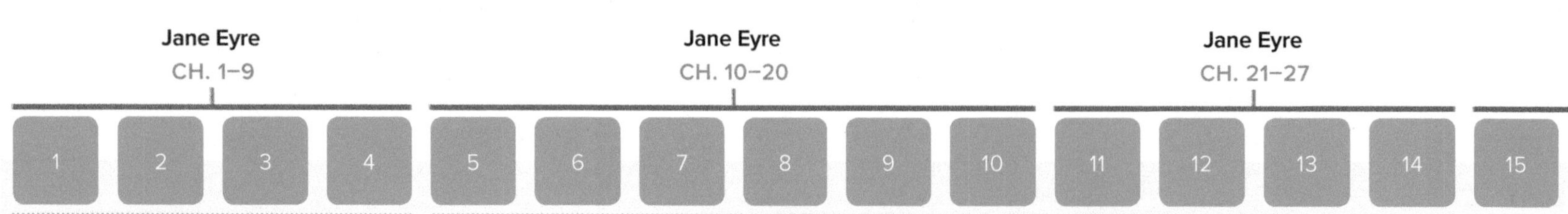

Paired Reading:
Lines Composed a Few Miles Above Tintern Abbey

Paired Reading:
Ozymandias

Paired Readings:
Facing It
Ode on a Grecian Urn

Pacing Guide: Jane Eyre

Days	Readings	Paired Readings	Skill and Standard Instruction	Skill Practice and Spiraling
1-4	**Jane Eyre** Ch. 1–9	Lines Composed a Few Miles Above Tintern Abbey	• Context Clues • Figurative Language (tv)	• Textual Evidence • Literary Analysis Writing
5-10	**Jane Eyre** Ch. 10–20	Ozymandias (tv)	• Media	• Literary Analysis Writing • Collaborative Conversations
11-14	**Jane Eyre** Ch. 21–27	Facing It Ode on a Grecian Urn	• Poetic Elements and Structure • Figurative Language	• Theme • Literary Analysis Writing
15-18	Jane Eyre Ch. 28–33	Jabberwocky Baby Dear Mama	• Language, Style, and Audience	• Poetic Elements and Structure • Narrative Writing
19-23	**Jane Eyre** Ch. 34–38	Freedom Why I Write	• Summarizing • Author's Purpose and Point of View (tv) • Figurative Language	• Compare and Contrast • Informative Writing • Collaborative Conversations
24-28	**Culminating Writing Task**	Recommended for instruction with this unit's Culminating Writing Task.	• Planning Research • Evaluating Sources • Research and Notetaking • Critiquing Research • Paraphrasing	• Contested Usage • Hyphens • Sources and Citations • Print and Graphic Features • Using a Style Guide

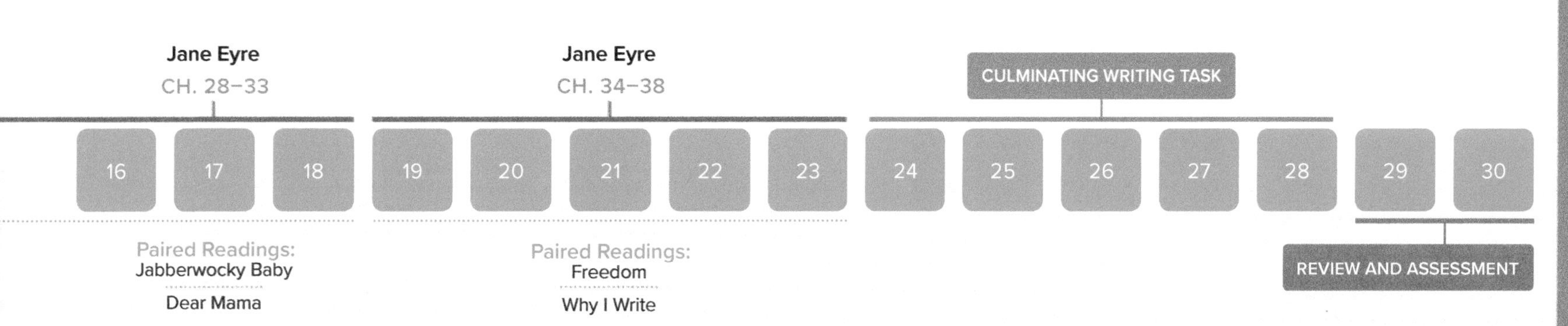

Integrated Scaffolding

ELL and Approaching grade-level students receive scaffolds for every lesson, whether in the Thematic, Novel Study or ELL Resources sections of the unit. Specific scaffolds are intentionally designed to support the needs of English Language Learners and Approaching grade-level students in the ELA classroom. Other scaffolds exist as part of the many standard features in the StudySync digital platform and can be strategically utilized to support students' comprehension and engagement.

English Language Learner Resources

Both Thematic and Novel Study units include English Language Learner resources designed to match the thematic focus, text structures, and writing form of the unit. ELL resources include two leveled texts and an extended oral project.

ELL Texts	Differentiated Text Levels	Skill and Standard Instruction
 	BEGINNING N/A I 160 words INTERMEDIATE N/A I 165 words ADVANCED N/A I 182 words ADVANCED HIGH N/A I 185 words Use this text in place of or as an extension to "Ozymandias."	• Sight Vocabulary and High-Frequency Words • Generating Questions • Language Structures • Analyzing and Evaluating Text • Spelling Patterns and Rules
 	BEGINNING 1000L I 1030 words INTERMEDIATE 1080L I 1035 words ADVANCED 1140L I 1050 words ADVANCED HIGH 1260L I 1061 words Use this text in place of or as an extension to *A Tale of Two Cities*.	• Classroom Vocabulary • Using Prereading Supports • Analyzing Expressions • Visual and Contextual Support • Main and Helping Verbs
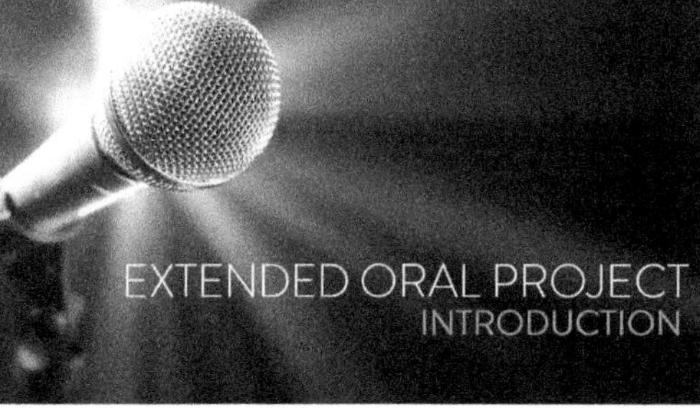 	In this Extended Oral Project, students will write and deliver an informative presentation. This may be assigned in place of this unit's EOP.	• Acquiring Vocabulary • Connecting Words

Focus on English Language Proficiency Levels

- ADVANCED HIGH
- ADVANCED
- INTERMEDIATE
- BEGINNING

ELL Resources provide targeted support for four levels of proficiency: Beginning, Intermediate, Advanced, and Advanced High. Instruction and scaffolds, as well as the texts themselves, are differentiated based on these levels.

Additional differentiated scaffolds include visual glossaries, speaking and writing frames, and suggested grouping for peer and teacher support. Lessons also include suggested extension activities to challenge Advanced and Advanced High students as they progress through the year.

Assessment

DAYS 29-30

Assessment in StudySync is built upon a recursive cycle that includes assessment, instruction, and review. Screening, placement, and benchmark assessments help teachers establish baselines and determine scaffold needs. Throughout the course of instruction, teachers regularly assess student progress using formative and summative measures, and use the individualized data from those assessments to guide choices about instruction, review, remediation, and enrichment to bring all students to standards mastery and College and Career Readiness.

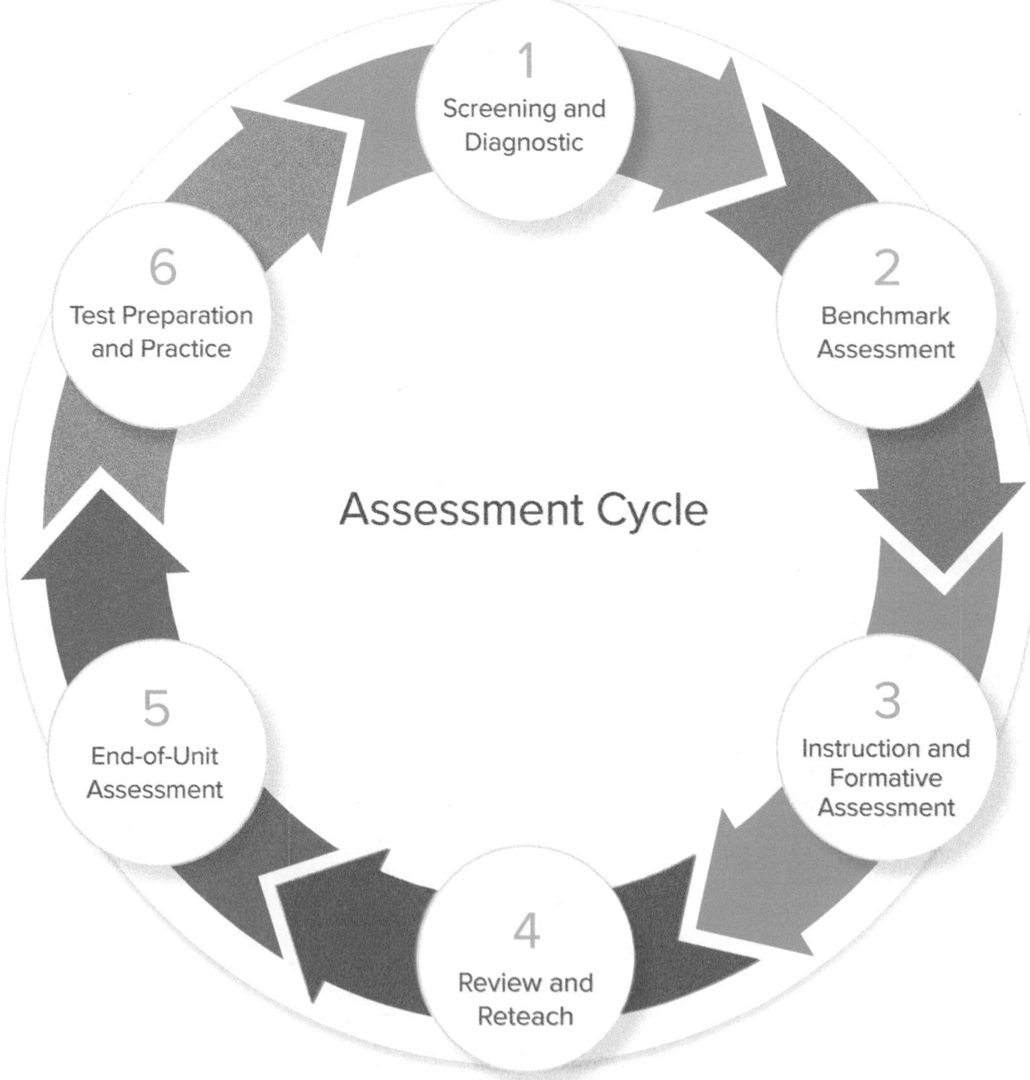

What's Next?

Assessment results can be viewed by item, standard, and skill to monitor mastery and make decisions for upcoming instruction.

- ✓ Reteach skills that students have not yet mastered, using Spotlight Skills or the Test Preparation and Practice book.
- ✓ Revise your teaching plan to provide more or less explicit instruction into a skill or text, using Beyond the Book activities for enrichment.
- ✓ Regroup students and levels of scaffolding based on standards progress.

Review

Spotlight Skills Review

A review day before the end-of-unit assessment gives you an opportunity to review difficult concepts with students using Spotlight Skill lessons. Spotlight Skills are targeted lessons that provide you resources to reteach or remediate without assigning additional readings. Every Core ELA Skill lesson has a corresponding Spotlight Skill lesson. Spotlight Skills can be assigned at any point in the year, but the end of each unit provides a natural moment to pause, review data collected throughout the unit, and reteach skills students have not yet mastered.

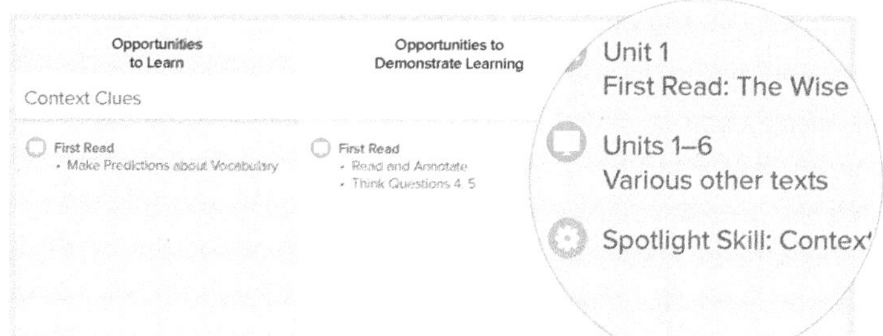

Progress Monitoring

The Progress Monitoring charts that appear before every text in this unit identify standards and associated Spotlight Skills. On review day, you may want to give preference to reteaching skills that are not revisited in later units. You can see where skills are covered again in the Opportunities to Reteach column.

StudySync Gradebook

As students submit assignments on StudySync, their mastery of skills and standards is tracked via the gradebook. The gradebook can be sorted and viewed in a variety of ways. Sorting by assignment shows overall student performance, while sorting by standards or by skill lessons displays student progress toward mastery goals.

	First Read	Skill: Text	Close Read
MAX SCORE	10	2	12
STUDENT			
Tate O'Brien	10	2	9
Olivia Adams	8	1	11

Skills Library

Spotlight Skills are located in the Skills section of the StudySync Library. You can assign Spotlight Skills to individual students or groups of students. Search tools allow you to search by skill type or name.

End-of-Unit Assessment

Assessed Reading Skills

- Author's Purpose and Point of View
- Context Clues
- Figurative Language
- Language, Style, and Audience
- Poetic Elements and Structure
- Summarizing
- Textual Evidence

Assessed Revising, Editing, and Writing Skills

- Critiquing Research
- Evaluating Sources
- Paraphrasing
- Planning Research
- Print and Graphic Features
- Research and Notetaking
- Sources and Citations
- Using a Style Guide

Unit Preview

Introduce the Unit

As a class, watch the unit preview and discuss the questions below.

- What two words would you use to describe this video?
- What key words or images from the video do you think will be most important to this unit?

Instructional Path

Big Idea Blast

Objectives: After exploring background information and research links about a topic, students will respond to a question with a 140-character response.

Literary Period: Romanticism

Objectives: After an initial reading about Romanticism, students will be able to identify and describe characteristics of the literary period.

Skill: Recognizing Genre

Objectives: After learning about the genre of poetry, students will be able to identify and describe characteristics of different types of poetry, including sonnets, odes, free verse, blank verse, and dramatic monologues.

Skill: Academic Vocabulary

Objectives: After learning the meanings of ten academic vocabulary words, students will be able to recognize and use them in a variety of contexts.

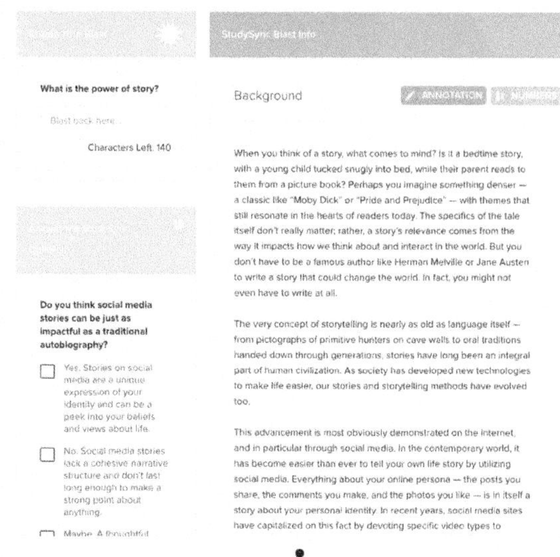

Blast: Sculpting Reality

What is the power of story?

TEXT TALK

Why does the author say the specifics of a story don't really matter?

A story's relevance comes from the way it impacts how we think about the world. The details of the story are not really relevant.

How have social media sites capitalized on the facts about online personal identity?

They have made specific video types like "stories" to share life as it happens.

What does writer Ian Bogost say about the "stories" trend?

He says that in contemporary culture everything gets framed as a story even when it's clearly not.

Create Your Own Blast

SCAFFOLDS

Ask students to write a 140-character Blast after they complete the QuikPoll.

Use the scaffolds below to differentiate instruction for your ELL English Language Learners.

ELL **BEGINNING** Write a response using the word bank to complete the sentence frame.

INTERMEDIATE Write a response using the sentence frame.

ADVANCED, ADVANCED HIGH Write a response using the sentence starter.

BEGINNING		INTERMEDIATE	ADVANCED, ADVANCED HIGH
Word Bank		Sentence Frame	Sentence Starter
describing showing changing	experience life belief	The power of storytelling is in ____ a(n) ____.	• The power of storytelling is . . .

Introduction to Romanticism

Introduction

This informational text offers historical and cultural background about the society that gave rise to Romanticism. Romantic poets like William Wordsworth, Lord Byron, and John Keats were rejecting ideals of the Enlightenment that emphasized science, order, and modernization, turning instead to the freedom of nature. During the Romantic period, poets wrote of the importance of deep reflection and connection to the natural world. They were daunted by a society in which the Industrial Revolution had engendered deep inequality and poor health. The antidote, Romantic poets proclaimed, was nature.

"They believed the peacefulness and untouched beauty of the natural world enriched the soul."

NOTES

1 Think of all the technology you use today compared with what your parents had. You can watch movies on a screen that fits in your pocket. You can buy almost any product or service without having to leave your home. You can summon a virtual assistant with a word or phrase. There are so many things you are able to do that your parents could not when they were your age. New technology also creates new problems, however. Cyberbullying, catfishing, piracy, internet addiction, and other problems were rare or nonexistent in the past. Some people may even question if all this technology is good for us. This is not the first time people have felt this way. The literary period known as **Romanticism** was born from concerns about modernization, and the movement continued through the 1800s. The works of the Romanticists resonate with many readers today.

A Time of Upheaval

2 Romanticism emerged in the late 1700s, when society was being transformed by two major events: the Industrial Revolution and the Enlightenment. The Industrial Revolution was a transition from an economy based on farming and handmade goods to one based on manufacturing. This change was possible thanks to inventions like steam engines and weaving machines. These developments tended to move people away from nature. People began to leave the countryside and come to the cities, which quickly became overcrowded and polluted. A class of ultra-wealthy industrialists rose to power, while factory workers lived and labored in poor, unsafe, and unhealthful conditions. The Romantic poet Lord Byron, in his narrative poem *The Corsair,* questioned whether the Industrial Revolution really represented progress:

3 Such hath it been — shall be — beneath the sun
The many still must labor for the one.

4 While the Industrial Revolution changed how people lived and worked, the Enlightenment changed how they thought. The Enlightenment was an intellectual movement that championed the power of **reason**. People felt empowered to overturn old social structures. People showed skepticism towards religion. They began to replace monarchies with democracies. They believed science and civilization could conquer nature.

First Read

Literary Focus: Romanticism

Introduce the Text

As a class, watch the video preview and have students read the introduction in pairs to make connections to the video preview. Ask students:

- What information from the video was new to you and what information did you already know?
- What are some examples of recent texts, art, or ideas that could be considered Romantic?

ELL SPEAKING FRAMES

- I didn't know that ____. I already knew that ____.
- I think ____ could be considered Romantic.

TEXT TALK

1. Which movements did Romanticism oppose?

(See paragraphs 4 and 5: Romanticism was a response to the Industrial Revolution and the Enlightenment.)

SELECTION VOCABULARY

Romanticism / Romanticismo *noun* a movement in the arts and literature that originated in the late 18th century, emphasizing inspiration, subjectivity, and the primacy of the individual COGNATE

reason / la razón *noun* the power of the mind to think, understand, and form judgments by a process of logic COGNATE

Bridal Procession on the Hardangerfjord, by Adolph Tidemand and Hans Gude, 1848

5 The Industrial Revolution and the Enlightenment brought many benefits to society, but they also brought problems. Some people worried that the growing gap between humans and the natural world could be harmful. They worried that the focus on cold logic and materialism would result in the neglect of human emotions and spirit. From these concerns sprang the Romantic movement in arts and letters.

Nature vs. Science

6 Romanticism values emotions over reason, individualism over **conformity**, and freedom over order. Romantics opposed the mass-production and cold efficiency of the Industrial Revolution. They sought to get away from it by embracing nature. They believed the peacefulness and untouched beauty of the natural world enriched the soul. Not surprisingly, Romanticism contributed to the formation of the environmentalist movement. Although modern environmentalism is connected to fields of science like **ecology** and biology, the Romantics were generally opposed to science, as it was a product of the Enlightenment. Enlightenment thinkers imposed rules of science and order upon the natural world. They wanted to understand and even tame nature. Enlightenment thinkers believed that nature could be improved by putting it in organized gardens. Romantics believed that true enlightenment could be found in the wilderness; "civilizing" nature would corrupt it just as civilization can corrupt humanity. As Romantic poet William Wordsworth wrote in "The Tables Turned":

7 Our meddling intellect
Mis-shapes the beauteous forms of things;
— We murder to dissect.

8 Romantic distrust toward science can also be seen in another work by a famous Romantic writer, Mary Wollstonecraft Shelley's *Frankenstein*.

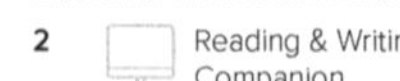

TEXT TALK

2. What are some of the characteristics of Romanticism?

   (See paragraph 6 Romanticism usually holds nature in high regard and searches for truth and beauty. Classical Greek influences are also common.)

SELECTION VOCABULARY

conformity / conformidad ***noun*** behavior in accordance with socially accepted conventions or standards COGNATE

ecology / ecología ***noun*** the branch of biology that deals with the relations of organisms to one another and to their physical surroundings COGNATE

NOTES

The Poetic Quest

9 Romanticism prized creativity, and so followers made great contributions to various forms of art. Poetry was particularly esteemed. Wordsworth called poetry a "spontaneous overflow of powerful feelings" and considered it "the language really used" by people. Percy Bysshe Shelley, husband of Mary Wollstonecraft Shelley, claimed "poets are the unacknowledged legislators of the World." Prominent Romantic poets saw it as their responsibility to guide people in a search for truth and beauty. They wrote poems that can be interpreted as allegories for the quest to guide other Romantics. John Keats's poetry is an example of how imagination can allow one to search for beauty and truth without leaving home.

John Keats, a British poet, one of the most important writers of Romanticism

10 Major Concepts

- **The Preeminence of Nature —** As the Industrial Revolution began to transform Britain into a nation of cities and factories, Romantics sought inspiration in the beauty of the natural world, the lives of ordinary workers, and the innocence of childhood. This first generation of Romantic poets included William Wordsworth, William Blake, and Samuel Taylor Coleridge.
- **The Quest for Truth and Beauty —** A second generation of English Romantics inherited many of the enthusiasms and value of their predecessors. During their tragically brief lives, Romantic poets such as Lord Byron, Percy Bysshe Shelley, and John Keats each pursued the ideals of truth and beauty.

Style and Form

11 English Romantic Poetry

- Although Romantics stressed emotion and the freedom of the human spirit, they still wrote poetry in a structured poetic form to create meaning.
- Nature was an important feature of Romantic poetry and a source of inspiration.

TEXT TALK

3. What role did poets play in Romanticism?

(See paragraph 9: Poets were respected and considered themselves leaders and guides for the movement.)

- Romantic poetry involved **contemplation** and reflection on the part of the speaker.
- Romantic poets often allude to the art, literature, and culture of the ancient Greeks.

12 Romanticism can be embodied in the idiom "stop and smell the roses." Modern life can be hectic. Honking traffic and ringing smartphones can make a person feel stressed. Many people benefit from putting aside part of the day for self-reflection and enjoying the outdoors. Romanticism remains popular not only because of the sheer volume of the movement's contributions to art but also because people still need to be reminded not to neglect their emotional well-being. What aspects of modern life do you think Romantics would approve or disapprove of?

SELECTION VOCABULARY

contemplation / la contemplación *noun* deep reflective thought COGNATE

Reading Comprehension

Have students complete the digital reading comprehension questions ✓ when they finish reading.

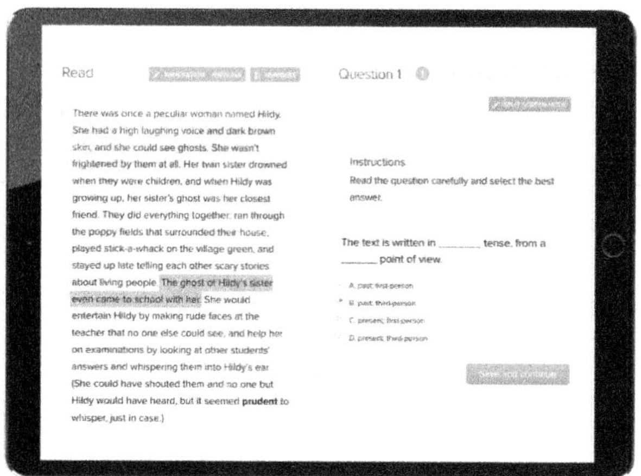

ANSWER KEY

QUESTION 1: D

QUESTION 2: C

QUESTION 3: B

QUESTION 4: C

QUESTION 5: B

QUESTION 6: A

QUESTION 7: A

QUESTION 8: D

QUESTION 9: *See first chart.*

QUESTION 10: *See second chart.*

Definition	Word
behavior in accordance with socially accepted conventions or standards	conformity
a movement in the arts and literature that originated in the late 18th century, emphasizing inspiration, subjectivity, and the primacy of the individual	Romanticism
deep reflective thought	contemplation
the branch of biology that deals with the relations of organisms to one another and to their physical surroundings	ecology

Beliefs	Author or Poet	Beliefs	Author or Poet
Viewed poetry as a "spontaneous overflow of powerful feelings" and "the language really used" by people	William Wordsworth	Viewed poetry as a "spontaneous overflow of powerful feelings" and "the language really used" by people	William Wordsworth

Think Questions

Circulate as students answer Think Questions independently. Scaffolds for these questions are shown on the opposite page.

QUESTION 1: Textual Evidence

The Industrial Revolution involved the growth of factories and cities, and the Enlightenment focused on the use of science and reason. The Romantics believed people should focus on nature, imagination, and emotion.

QUESTION 2: Textual Evidence

Wordsworth believed the scientific quest for understanding was destructive toward the things it studied.

QUESTION 3: Textual Evidence

Beauty is a concept related to emotion and imagination, not to reason or science.

QUESTION 4: Context Clues

Conformity means "being similar to others." The text says Romanticism valued "individualism over conformity," so I think *individualism* must be an antonym of *conformity.*

QUESTION 5: Context Clues

Ecology means "the study of the environment." From words like *biology*, I know that *-logy* is used to describe fields of study. *Ecology* could be translated as "the study of habitats," or the study of the environment and nature.

Literary Period

Read "Introduction to Romanticism." After you read, complete the Think Questions below.

THINK QUESTIONS

1. Why were followers of Romanticism unhappy about the Industrial Revolution and the Enlightenment?
2. What might William Wordsworth have meant when he wrote "Our meddling intellect / Mis-shapes the beauteous forms of things; / — We murder to dissect"?
3. How is the Romantic poets' interest in beauty related to other ideas of Romanticism?
4. Use context clues to determine the meaning of the word **conformity**. Write your best definition here, along with the words and phrases that were most helpful in determining the word's meaning. Then, check a dictionary to confirm your understanding.
5. The word **ecology** likely stems from the Greek *oikos*, meaning "house or habitation," and *logos*, meaning "word or account." With this information in mind, write your best definition of the word *ecology* as it used in this text. Cite any words or phrases that were particularly helpful in coming to your conclusion.

Think Questions

SCAFFOLDS

Use the scaffolds below to differentiate instruction for your ELL English Language Learners and A Approaching grade-level learners.

ELL **BEGINNING** Write a response using the word bank and sentence frames.

INTERMEDIATE Write a response using the sentence frames.

ADVANCED, ADVANCED HIGH Write a response using the Text-Dependent Question Guide.

A **APPROACHING** Write a response using the Text-Dependent Question Guide.

BEGINNING	INTERMEDIATE	APPROACHING / ADVANCED, ADVANCED HIGH
Word Bank	**Sentence Frames**	**Text-Dependent Question Guide**
emotion scientific environment reason opposite factories words an idea	1. Romantics were unhappy about the Industrial Revolution because it involved the growth of ____ and cities. They did not like the Enlightenment because it focused on the use of science and ____.	1. • What did the followers of Romanticism dislike about the Industrial Revolution? • What did the followers of Romanticism dislike about the Enlightenment? • What did the Romantics believe that people should do?
	2. William Wordsworth believed that the ____ effort to understand harmed the things that science studied.	2. • How does the word ***dissect*** provide a clue for what Wordsworth is talking about? • Why does Wordsworth believe that this thing is destructive?
	3. The Romantic poets believed that beauty is an ____ connected with ____ and imagination.	3. • What did the Romantics value most? • How are these things related to beauty?
	4. The word *conformity* means "being the same as others." The text says Romanticism valued "individualism over conformity," so I think *individualism* has a meaning that is ____ to the meaning of *conformity*.	4. • Read: "Romanticism values emotions over reason, individualism over **conformity,** and freedom over order." • Which three things did Romantics not prefer? • How might conformity be related to the other two things they did not prefer? How might conformity be related to individualism?
	5. *Ecology* means "the study of the environment." From ____ like *biology*, I know that -logy is used to describe fields of study. *Ecology* could be translated as "the study of habitats," or the study of the ____ and nature.	5. • What are the meanings of the two roots of ***ecology?*** • Put the two meanings together. What do you think this combination means? • How does ***biology*** provide a context clue?

Skill: Recognizing Genre

Introduce the Genre: Poetry

Watch the Concept Definition video  and read the following definitions with your students.

Poetry is writing that uses qualities of language to evoke feelings in addition to simply conveying meaning. These qualities of language include sound, symbolism, imagery, and rhythm. **Symbolism** is the use of concrete objects to represent abstract ideas or qualities. **Imagery** is descriptive language used to appeal to the reader's senses. **Rhythm** is the pattern of unstressed and stressed syllables in a line of poetry.

Poetry can appear in a variety of different forms. Some poems are **closed form** and have regular rhyme and rhythm. Other poems are **free verse** and have no regular rhyme or rhythm.

All types of poetry share certain characteristics. Poems are meant to be read aloud so the reader can hear aspects of sound, rhythm, meter, and voice. Poems often have multiple meanings. To interpret multiple meanings of a poem, a reader must examine the literal meaning of the poem in conjunction with the figurative meanings that arise from analyzing the rhythm, sound, images, and symbols.

TURN AND TALK

- What is your favorite poem? Do you know what form of poetry it is?
- What about this poem makes you like it?

Your Turn

Ask students to complete the Your Turn activity.

Description	Literary Genre
a formal, ceremonious poem that celebrates the rebirth associated with springtime	ode
a poem that uses punctuation and white space to affect the reader's understanding of the poem	free verse
a poem written in the form of a speech delivered by a speaker revealing his inner thoughts about life and love	dramatic monologue
a short, rhyme-structured poem of 14 lines that reflects on love lost	sonnet
a poem that does not rhyme but uses consistent iambic pentameter to explore the relationship between authorship and nature	blank verse

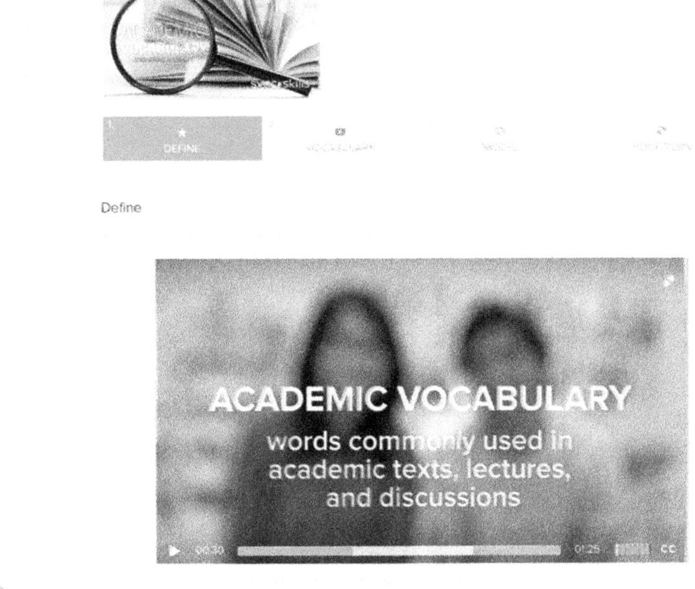

Skill: Academic Vocabulary

Introduce the Terms

albeit / no obstante *conjunction* although

convince / convencer *verb* to cause someone to believe or agree that something is true COGNATE

devote / consagrar *verb* to give entirely to a specific person, activity, or cause

exploit / explotar *verb* to draw from; to make the best use of COGNATE

invoke / invocar *verb* to cite as an authority or reminder in order to support an idea COGNATE

levy / el impuesto *noun* a charge imposed and collected by the government or other authority

likewise / también *adverb* also

nonetheless / sin embargo *adverb* despite what has just been said

notwithstanding / no obstante *preposition* Despite, or in spite of; regardless of

reluctance / la reticencia *noun* a certain degree of unwillingness

Practice Using Vocabulary

Divide the vocabulary words into two lists. Pair students and give each student one half of the list. Challenge students to have a casual conversation with each other that uses every word on their list. Students should aim to insert their vocabulary words in a way that sounds natural. You may wish to turn this activity into a game, allowing partners to award each other points if they effectively use each word on their list.

Your Turn

Ask students to complete the Your Turn activities.

Your Turn 1

QUESTION 1: A **QUESTION 2:** A **QUESTION 3:** B **QUESTION 4:** B **QUESTION 5:** A

Your Turn 2

QUESTION 1: D **QUESTION 2:** B **QUESTION 3:** D **QUESTION 4:** A **QUESTION 5:** A

Your Turn 3

See digital teacher's edition for sample answers.

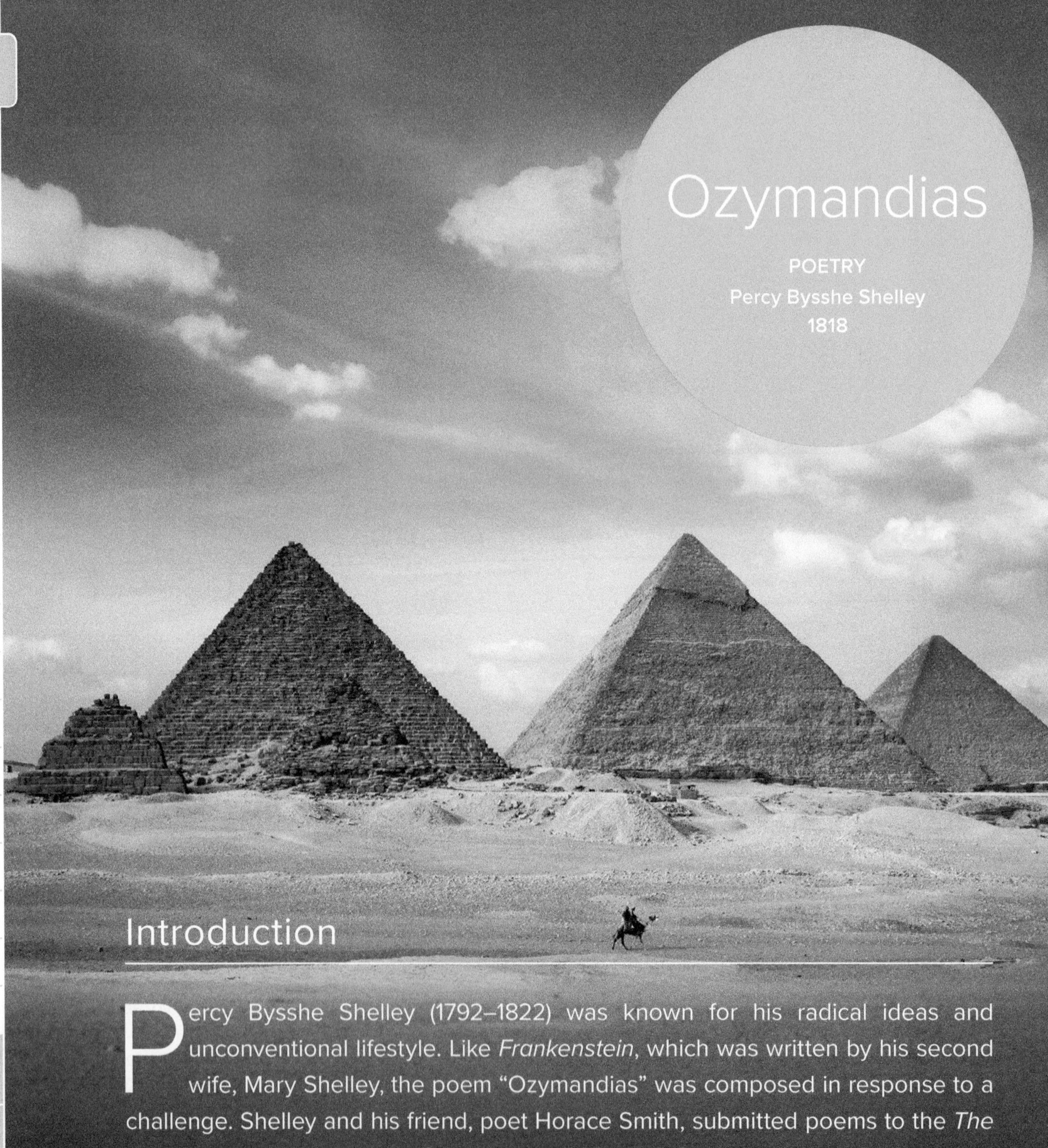

Ozymandias

POETRY
Percy Bysshe Shelley
1818

Introduction

Percy Bysshe Shelley (1792–1822) was known for his radical ideas and unconventional lifestyle. Like *Frankenstein*, which was written by his second wife, Mary Shelley, the poem "Ozymandias" was composed in response to a challenge. Shelley and his friend, poet Horace Smith, submitted poems to the *The Examiner* on the occasion of the statue of Pharaoh Rameses II being transported from Egypt to London. Shelley's 14-line sonnet appeared in the paper first in January of 1818. The imaginative poet invented a traveler and a sculptor's inscription, evoking the ancient relic's ruin as a metaphor for the fall of dynasties and the limitations of tyrants.

The English Romantic poet Percy Bysshe Shelley wrote this poem in response to the statue of Pharaoh Ramses II being transported from Egypt to London. The speaker in the poem meets a traveler who describes seeing a statue in a state of disrepair. The legs of the statue were standing, but the trunk was missing and its head lay half-buried in the sand. On its face, the statue wore a haughty sneer, conveying that the sculptor understood how to accurately capture a tyrant's features. The pedestal of the statue carried an inscription: "my name is Ozymandias . . . look on my works . . . and despair." Looking around, one would see nothing but boundless desert in every direction.

ELL Proficiency-leveled summaries and summaries in multiple languages are available digitally.

 Audio and audio text highlighting are available with this text.

CONNECT TO ESSENTIAL QUESTION

What is the power of story?

In this famous sonnet by English Romantic poet Percy Bysshe Shelley, the speaker of the poem meets a traveler from Egypt. The traveler's description of ancient ruins tells an ironic story about the ravages of time and the legacies of powerful rulers.

Entry Point

As students prepare to read "Ozymandias," share the following information with them to provide context.

- ✓ Percy Bysshe Shelley is an important poet also known for his essay "Defence of Poetry," which helped define the Romantic movement. In that essay, Shelley argues that people recognize beauty through the combination of logical thought and imagination, and the synthesis forms the basis for civilization.
- ✓ Shelley was born into a wealthy aristocratic family. He was heir to his grandfather's estate and a seat in Parliament, but was disinherited and expelled from Oxford because he was an atheist and refused to declare himself Christian.
- ✓ Shelley was nineteen when he eloped with sixteen-year-old Harriet Westbrook, but a few years later he fell in love and ran away with Mary Godwin (who wrote *Frankenstein*). They married after Harriet committed suicide in 1816. Shelley drowned in a sailing accident a few weeks before he would have turned thirty.

Instructional Path

The print teacher's edition includes essential point-of-use instruction and planning tools. Complete lesson plans and program documents appear in your digital teacher account.

First Read: Ozymandias

Objectives: After an initial reading and discussion of the poem, students will be able to identify and describe the setting and other literary elements that contribute to the poem's meaning.

Skill: Media

Objectives: After rereading and discussing a model of close reading, students will be able to analyze multiple interpretations of a poem evaluating how each version interprets the source text.

Close Read: Ozymandias

Objectives: After engaging in a close reading and discussion of "Ozymandias," students will be able write a short response that evaluates how the video "A Strange Relativity" interprets Percy Bysshe Shelley's ideas about the tyranny of time.

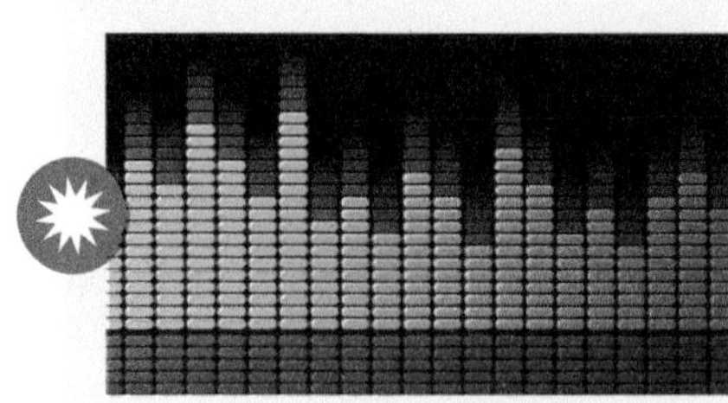

Blast: Making Waves

Objectives: After exploring background information and research links about a topic, students will respond to a question with a 140-character response.

Progress Monitoring

Opportunities to Learn	Opportunities to Demonstrate Learning	Opportunities to Reteach
Media		
Skill: Media	Skill: Media • Your Turn Close Read • Skills Focus • Write	Unit 5 Skill: Media - The Glass Menagerie Unit 6 Skill: Media - Honesty on Social Media Spotlight Skill: Media

First Read

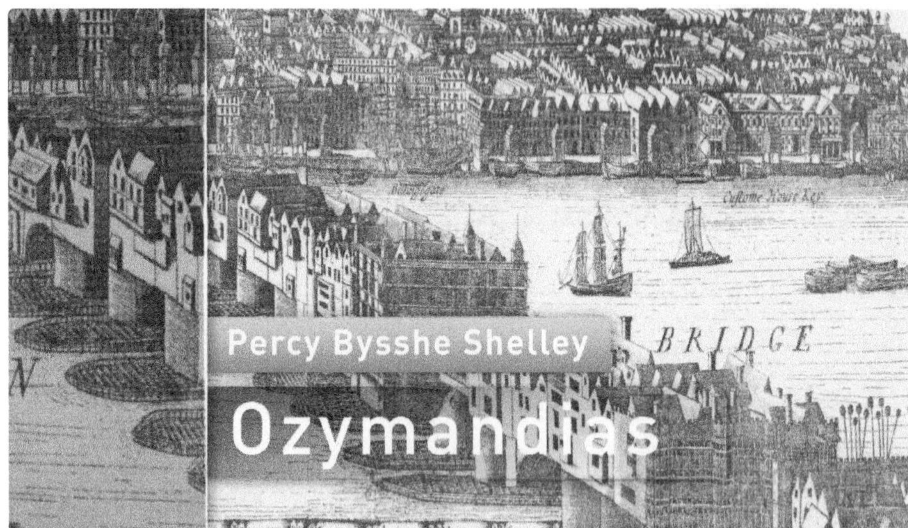

Introduce the Text

As a class, watch the video preview and have students read the introduction in pairs to make connections to the video preview.

To activate prior knowledge and experiences, ask students:

- What image was your favorite from the video? Why? What other images could you imagine using in this video?
- What do we know about ancient civilizations? How do we know this?

SPEAKING FRAMES

- My favorite image from the video was ____.
- Another image I could imagine using in this video is ____.
- We know ____ about ancient civilizations.

Access Complex Text

LEXILE: N/A **WORD COUNT:** 112

The following areas may be challenging for students, particularly ELL English Language Learners and A Approaching grade-level learners.

Prior Knowledge	Connection of Ideas
• Students may be unfamiliar with the Pharaoh Ramesses II and the rise and fall of his empire. • Explain to students that Ozymandias is a Greek form of the name Ramesses II, the pharaoh who ruled Egypt during the thirteenth century B.C., and that much of our knowledge of Ramesses II is derived from the large-scale monuments he built to glorify his reign.	• Students need to analyze how descriptions and images work together to imply a meaning, and then infer the overall meaning of the poem. • Remind students to annotate descriptions or images they find striking or important while they read. After reading, they can review their annotations as they infer the general meaning of the poem.

 SCAFFOLDS  ENGLISH LANGUAGE LEARNERS  APPROACHING GRADE LEVEL  BEYOND GRADE LEVEL

These icons identify differentiation strategies and scaffolded support for a variety of students. See the digital lesson plan for additional differentiation strategies and scaffolds.

"Look on my works, ye Mighty, and despair!"

I met a traveller from an antique land
Who said: 'Two vast and trunkless legs of stone
Stand in the desert. Near them, on the sand,
Half sunk, a shattered **visage**[1] lies, whose frown,
And wrinkled lip, and sneer of cold command,
Tell that its sculptor well those passions read
Which yet survive, stamped on these lifeless things,
The hand that **mocked** them and the heart that fed.
And on the **pedestal** these words appear—
"My name is Ozymandias, king of kings:
Look on my works, ye Mighty, and **despair**!"
Nothing beside remains. Round the decay
Of that **colossal** wreck, boundless and bare
The lone and level sands stretch far away.

Statue of Ramesses II. Egyptian civilisation. New Kingdom, Dynasty XIX. Aswan, Nubian Museum

Skill: Media

Dr. Kalanithi expresses a desire to accomplish something in the time he has left.

This reminds me of how the once colossal accomplishment in "Ozymandias" is now a ruin.

Shelley, Percy Bysshe. "Ozymandias." The Examiner, 1 Feb. 1818, pp. 73.

1. **visage** face

Developing Background Lnowledge and Cultural Awareness

Find out what your students already know about Ramesses II.

1. In small groups, have students do a five-minute online search of keywords related to Ramesses II and his building of monuments.
2. On the board, collate the various types of information students learned. Ask one student to volunteer to create an instant summary.

Discuss with students: Is it important to have an impact on history, and to be remembered? What are the possible benefits and dangers of wanting to make your mark? Consider Rameses II as well as other famous historical figures: are they all remembered positively for their legacies? Why or why not?

Media

What does the student note about Dr. Kalanithi's relationship with time?

Dr. Kalanithi's relationship with time seems to resonate with how Shelley treats the same theme in his sonnet. Dr. Kalanithi also seems concerned by what his accomplishments will mean in the face of time.

SELECTION VOCABULARY

visage / el rostro *noun* the face or outward appearance of a person

mock / burlarse *verb* made fun of someone or something, especially by imitating a behavior

pedestal / el pedestal *noun* the support or base of a tall object, such as a column or statue COGNATE

despair / desesperar *verb* to lose or give up hope that things will improve COGNATE

colossal / colosal *adjective* huge or very great in size COGNATE

TEXT TALK

What did the traveler see?

See line 2: The traveler saw a broken statue.

Where was the traveler when he saw this?

See lines 3 and 14: The traveler saw this in the desert.

Who was Ozymandias?

See lines 10 and 11: He was an Egyptian pharaoh.

How did researching Ramses II and discussing his legacy deepen your understanding of "Ozymandias"?

Answers will vary.

Think Questions

Circulate as students answer Think Questions independently. Scaffolds for these questions are shown on the opposite page.

QUESTION 1: Textual Evidence

The traveler describes "two vast and trunkless legs of stone" and the "shattered visage" of the statue and, beyond that, a "boundless and bare" desert.

QUESTION 2: Textual Evidence

It refers to the city or civilization Ozymandias created in his lifetime. Ozymandias is so proud of his "works" that he brags about them, as if they were eternal, in the inscription under a larger-than-life statue of himself.

QUESTION 3: Textual Evidence

The speaker would agree because the speaker understands that kings die and nothing, even a great monument or statue, lasts forever, so living in the present moment, the way the dying doctor does, is the only reasonable choice.

QUESTION 4: Context Clues

A *pedestal* is the base on which a statue stands because that's where you would normally see an inscription. A synonym for *pedestal* is "platform."

QUESTION 5: Context Clues

I think *colossal* means larger-than-life because the word refers to "vast and trunkless legs of stone [that]/ Stand in the desert." The word comes from the Greek word "kolossus," which means "gigantic statue."

First Read

Read "Ozymandias." After you read, complete the Think Questions below.

THINK QUESTIONS

1. How does the traveler in the poem describe the statue and the area that surrounds it? Cite specific details from the text to support your response.
2. In the inscription on the pedestal, what does the term *works* refer to? Use specific details from the text to support your answer.
3. In the video "A Strange Relativity: Altered Time for Surgeon-Turned-Patient," Paul Kalanithi explains that "clocks are now kind of irrelevant to me." Do you think the speaker of "Ozymandias" would agree with this opinion about time? Use evidence from the poem to support your response.
4. Use context to determine the meaning of the word **pedestal** as it is used in line 9 of the poem "Ozymandias." Write your definition of *pedestal* here and tell how you determined its meaning. Then write a synonym for this term. Check your inferred meaning of *pedestal* in a dictionary. Consult a print or digital dictionary, or a thesaurus to verify the synonym you wrote.
5. Use context to determine the meaning of the word **colossal** as it is used in line 13 of the poem "Ozymandias." Check the etymology and part of speech of the word in a general or specialized dictionary, or in another reference. Then write the definition of *colossal* here and explain how it is derived from the Greek.

Think Questions

SCAFFOLDS

Use the scaffolds below to differentiate instruction for your ELL English Language Learners and A Approaching grade-level learners.

ELL **BEGINNING** Write a response using the word bank and sentence frames.

INTERMEDIATE Write a response using the sentence frames.

ADVANCED, ADVANCED HIGH Write a response using the Text-Dependent Question Guide.

A **APPROACHING** Write a response using the Text-Dependent Question Guide.

BEGINNING	INTERMEDIATE	APPROACHING / ADVANCED, ADVANCED HIGH
Word Bank	**Sentence Frames**	**Text-Dependent Question Guide**
statue platform Ozymandias wreck base big desert forever	The traveller says the ____ is broken into pieces. The surrounding area is ____.	1. • Which words and phrases relate something about the statue? • Where does the traveler see the statue? • How do you know this?
	The term *works* refers to things ____ built.	2. • Read what the traveler says about the inscription on the pedestal. • Is *works* used here as a noun or a verb? • Which details in the poem help you determine what the term *works* refers to?
	I think the speaker of "Ozymandias" would agree with this opinion. The speaker knows that kings die and nothing lasts ____.	3. • Watch the video "A Strange Relativity: Altered Time for Surgeon-Turned-Patient." • Why does Paul Kalanithi say "clocks are now kind of irrelevant to me"? What is his opinion about time? • How does the poem also explore the concept of time?
	A *pedestal* is the ____ on which a statue stands. A synonym for *pedestal* is ____.	4. • Read: "And on the **pedestal** these words appear." • What is this line about? • What does that tell me about the meaning of the word *pedestal*?
	Colossal describes the ____ of the statue. The statue is also described as "vast." This is a clue that *colossal* means very ____.	5. • Read: "Nothing beside remains. Round the decay/Of that **colossal** wreck." • What was the wreck described as *colossal*? • Which other words or phrases are context clues for *colossal*?

Reading Comprehension

Have students complete the digital reading comprehension questions when they finish reading.

ANSWER KEY

QUESTION 1: C
QUESTION 2: B
QUESTION 3: C
QUESTION 4: A

QUESTION 5:
See chart below.

First	Second	Third	Fourth
The story is situated as a fable-like tale from a wise traveler	The poet renders images of crumbling, fading, and decay	The reader realizes what this crumbling statue originally symbolized	The poet lends his own voice as a contrast to the vain boast of the proclamations of Ozymandias.

Connect and Extend OPTIONAL

CONNECT TO EXTENDED WRITING PROJECT

Students can use "Ozymandias" in their informative essays to inspire their ideas about the power and nature and the importance of its lasting effect on human life.

BEYOND THE BOOK

Game: How would you respond?

Put students in groups of six. Give each group a stack of twelve index cards. Instruct students to:

- Write a real-life scenario on one index card then write an age between three and their current age on a second card.
- Mix the scenario cards in one stack and mix the age cards in a second stack.
- Draw a real-life scenario card and an age card from each stack then act out how you think a child would respond to that situation at that age.

Select the "best performance" and have the student who has been selected by each group perform their reaction for the class.

To reflect, ask students:

- When do people become more logical and less emotional?
- What behavior is common for younger children? What does this reveal?

Skill: Media

Use the Checklist to analyze Media in "Ozymandias." Refer to the sample student annotations about Media in the text.

••• CHECKLIST FOR MEDIA

In order to identify multiple interpretations of a story, drama, or poem, do the following:

- ✓ note the similarities and differences in different media, such as the live production of a play or a recorded novel or poetry
- ✓ evaluate how each version interprets the source text
- ✓ consider how, within the same medium, a story can have multiple interpretations if told by writers from different time periods and cultures
- ✓ consider how stories told in the same medium will likely reflect the specific objectives as well as the respective ideas, concerns, and values of each writer

To analyze multiple interpretations of a story, drama, or poem, evaluating how each version interprets the source text, consider the following questions:

- ✓ What medium is being used, and how does it affect the interpretation of the source text?
- ✓ What are the main similarities and differences between the two (or more) versions?
- ✓ If each version is from a different time period and/or culture, what does each version reveal about the author's objectives and the time period and culture in which it was written?

SKILL VOCABULARY

medium / el medio *noun* a form of communication, such as television, the Internet, and radio COGNATE

media / los medios *noun* the plural form of the word medium; a means of sending a communication to an intended audience COGNATE

Skill: Media

Introduce The Skill

Watch the Concept Definition video ▶ and read the following definition with your students.

Media is the plural form of the word *medium*. A **medium** is a means of sending a communication to an intended audience. Throughout most of human history, people communicated through three main media: speech, writing, and visual arts such as drawing, painting, and sculpture. But in the 19th century media options suddenly exploded. The invention of photography, and then the telegraph and the telephone, changed the world. Within a century radio, motion pictures, and television followed.

Stories and ideas change as they are translated from one medium to another. A dialogue between two characters in a novel, for example, becomes very different when it is delivered by actors in a film—with close-ups, sound effects such as music, and other elements unique to the medium of film itself.

Today new media are being invented at a much faster pace than ever before, and each of these forms of online communication has its own "language" and creates its own experience.

TURN AND TALK

1. Have you read a book and also seen the film adaptation? How were they similar or different?
2. Have you watched the news on TV only to get a different interpretation through another medium?

SPEAKING FRAMES

- A book I read was ____. The film adaptation was [similar/different] because ____.
- At first, I thought I understood the [topic/themes/conflict] but then I learned ____. when I watched a different medium.

Your Turn

Ask students to complete the Your Turn Activity.

QUESTION 1

A. Incorrect. While Dr. Kalanithi was a young and respected neurosurgeon with a terminal illness, he does not imply that Egyptian rulers were also struck down by illness.

B. Correct. Dr. Kalanithi's medical training did not extend his life or make him invincible. Much like the powerful Egyptian pharaohs, his time on earth is also temporary.

C. Incorrect. Dr. Kalanithi's words do not focus on the disease itself, but rather on how time seems to change due to the disease.

D. Incorrect. Neither the video nor the poem focus on the themes of financial and personal stress.

QUESTION 2

A. Incorrect. This is not the purpose for the video, and it is not the main reason scenes from Thanksgiving were included.

B. Incorrect. While this might be a valid sentiment, it is not the main reason scenes from Thanksgiving were included.

C. Correct. Dr. Kalanithi mentions being grateful for the moments he has with his family and is mindful that his terminal illness may prevent him attending the celebrations to come.

D. Incorrect. Family is not a main theme that is addressed in the video.

Skill: Media

Reread lines 9–14 of "Ozymandias" and watch the StudySyncTV episode. Then, using the Checklist on the previous page, answer the multiple-choice questions below.

YOUR TURN

1. In the clip, Dr. Kalanithi describes his relationship with time. How do his words reflect the theme shown in these lines of "Ozymandias"?

   - A. Even a doctor, someone in a position of power, or on a "pedestal," can be struck down by illness, much like the rulers of ancient Egypt.
   - B. Medical training, like the "king of kings," wants to show power over the future, but time extends beyond all of us.
   - C. Cancer, like the decay mentioned in the poem, cause "despair" and a "colossal wreck" for all of its victims.
   - D. Being a surgeon, like "the colossal wreck," often results in financial and personal stress, causing pain over time.

2. What is the most likely reason the video included scenes from Dr. Kalanithi and his family enjoying a Thanksgiving meal?

   - A. The video is a tribute to Dr. Kalanithi's family and friends, and the memories they share.
   - B. The video was made to remind Dr. Kalanithi's family and friends to live each day to the fullest.
   - C. The video evokes the idea of gratitude for the time we have on earth, even if that time is short.
   - D. The video uses the scenes to underscore one of the themes of the importance of family.

Close Read

Reread "Ozymandias." As you reread, complete the Skills Focus questions below. Then use your answers and annotations from the questions to help you complete the Write activity.

SKILLS FOCUS

1. Identify a detail that contributes to an overall theme in the poem and write a sentence that explains why you chose it.
2. All sonnets contain a volta, which means "turn" in Italian. More specifically, a volta is a turning point in which there is a shift in language, style, meaning or tone. Highlight the volta in "Ozymandias" and explain how it represents a turning point.
3. The words on the pedestal of Ozymandias' statue are "My name is Ozymandias, king of kings: / Look on my works, ye Mighty, and despair!" How does the video of Dr. Kalanithi influence or change your reading of these words?
4. Most of this sonnet repeats the story told by "a traveller." What is the power of this story "from an antique land?" Why is the narrator of the poem repeating what he heard the traveller say?

WRITE

LITERARY ANALYSIS: The scholar and literary critic Donald H. Reiman has stated that Shelley "dedicated his efforts to the destruction of tyranny in all its forms." In the video "A Strange Relativity," Dr. Paul Kalanithi invokes "Ozymandias" while reflecting on his new relationship with time, which he describes as "peculiar and free." Write a short essay indicating whether you find evidence of a philosophy of destroying the tyranny of time in "Ozymandias." How accurate is the interpretation put forth in the video? Remember to use textual evidence to support your claim.

Close Read

Skills Focus

QUESTION 1: Theme

The poem shows how eventually even powerful people are defeated by time and their monuments are reclaimed by nature, just like everything else.

QUESTION 2: Language, Style, and Audience

See line 13. The shortest sentence is blunt and sad. It reveals that what remains of Ozymandias is broken and abandoned. The tone changes from awe to sad irony: the statue is now a "colossal wreck."

QUESTION 3: Media

See line 10. The video reminds me time is the ruler over us all, no matter title or circumstance.

QUESTION 4: Essential Question

See line 1–2. The poem reports the observations of a "traveller" who describes a broken and abandoned statue that once memorialized Ozymandias' rule. Ironically, by repeating the description, the narrator of the poem helps the traveler's story, Ozymandias' statue, and the poet's own words live on through time.

CHECK FOR SUCCESS

If students struggle ask the following questions:

1. What is one of the themes in Shelley's poem?
2. What is one detail Shelley includes to discuss this theme?

Writer's Notebook

Connect to Literary Period: Give students time to reflect on how "Ozymandias" demonstrates the conventions and characteristics of this unit's literary period, Romanticism, by freewriting in their Writer's Notebooks.

ELL Beginning & Intermediate

Remind students of the unit's literary period, Romanticism. Encourage students to draw their connections or allow students to write in their native language. Circulate around the room, prompting students for their thoughts as they respond orally or through pantomime.

Advanced & Advanced High

Allow students to share their connections orally in pairs or small groups before freewriting.

StudySyncTV

Project the StudySyncTV episode and pause at the following times to prompt discussion:

1:42 How do students use textual evidence to characterize Ozymandias in the poem?

3:33 How does learning about Ramesses II help the students interpret the poem?

5:25 What does the group think Shelley was trying to say about the legacy of a tyrant compared with the legacy of an artist? How did they reach this conclusion?

Collaborative Conversation

SCAFFOLDS

Break students into collaborative conversation groups to discuss the Close Read prompt. Ask students to use the StudySyncTV episode as a model for their discussion. Remind them to reference their Skills Focus annotations in their discussion.

The scholar and literary critic Donald H. Reiman has stated that Shelley "dedicated his efforts to the destruction of tyranny in all its forms." In the video "A Strange Relativity," Dr. Paul Kalanithi invokes "Ozymandias" while reflecting on his new relationship with time, which he describes as "peculiar and free." Write a short essay indicating whether you find evidence of a philosophy of destroying the tyranny of time in "Ozymandias." How accurate is the interpretation put forth in the video? Remember to use textual evidence to support your claim.

Use the scaffolds below to differentiate instruction for your ELL English Language Learners and A Approaching grade-level learners.

ELL **BEGINNING, INTERMEDIATE** Use the discussion guide and speaking frames to facilitate the discussion with support from the teacher.

ADVANCED, ADVANCED HIGH Use the discussion guide and speaking frames to facilitate the discussion in mixed-level groups.

A **APPROACHING** Use the discussion guide to facilitate the discussion in mixed-level groups.

APPROACHING

ADVANCED, ADVANCED HIGH

BEGINNING, INTERMEDIATE

Discussion Guide	Speaking Frames
1. What is tyranny? Is it positive or negative? Why?	• Tyranny is when ____. • Tyranny is [positive/negative] because ____ .
2. What do you think Shelley thought about tyrants?	• Shelley thought tyrants were ____. • I know this because ____.
3. How is time and our relationship to it described in Shelley's poem and Dr. Kalanithi's video?	• Shelley describes time as ____. • Dr. Kalanithi describes time as ____.

Review Prompt and Rubric

Before students begin writing, review the writing prompt and rubric with the class.

LITERARY ANALYSIS: The scholar and literary critic Donald H. Reiman has stated that Shelley "dedicated his efforts to the destruction of tyranny in all its forms." In the video "A Strange Relativity," Dr. Paul Kalanithi invokes "Ozymandias" while reflecting on his new relationship with time, which he describes as "peculiar and free." Write a short essay indicating whether you find evidence of a philosophy of destroying the tyranny of time in "Ozymandias." How accurate is the interpretation put forth in the video? Remember to use textual evidence to support your claim.

ELL PROMPT GUIDE

A

- What is tyranny? Is it positive or negative? Why?
- What do you think Shelley thought about tyrants?
- How is time and our relationship to it described in Shelley's poem and Dr. Kalanithi's video?
- How is this description similar to how Shelley views tyrants in his poem?

An additional rubric item for Language and Conventions appears in your digital teacher and student accounts.

Score	Theme	Media
4	The writer clearly analyzes and explains how the poem reflects Shelley's ideas about tyranny and time. The writer provides exemplary analysis, using relevant textual evidence.	The writer clearly evaluates how the video "A Strange Relativity" interprets the theme of tyranny and time in "Ozymandias," providing exemplary analysis and using relevant textual evidence.
3	The writer analyzes and explains how the poem reflects Shelley's ideas about tyranny and time. The writer provides sufficient analysis, using relevant textual evidence most of the time.	The writer sufficiently evaluates how the video "A Strange Relativity" interprets the theme of tyranny and time in "Ozymandias," providing analysis and using relevant textual evidence.
2	The writer begins to analyze or explain how the poem reflects Shelley's ideas about tyranny and time, but the analysis is incomplete. The writer uses relevant textual evidence only some of the time.	The writer begins to evaluate how the video "A Strange Relativity" interprets the theme of tyranny and time in "Ozymandias," using relevant textual evidence some of the time, but the analysis is incomplete.
1	The writer attempts to analyze or explain how the poem reflects Shelley's ideas about tyranny and time, but the analysis is not successful. The writer uses little or no relevant textual evidence.	The writer attempts to evaluate how the video "A Strange Relativity" interprets the theme of tyranny and time in "Ozymandias," but the analysis is not successful. The writer uses little or no relevant textual evidence.
0	The writer does not provide a relevant response to the prompt or does not provide a response at all.	The writer does not provide a relevant response to the prompt or does not provide a response at all.

Write

SCAFFOLDS

Ask students to complete the writing assignment using text evidence to support their answers.

Use the scaffolds below to differentiate instruction for your ELL English Language Learners and A Approaching grade-level learners.

ELL **BEGINNING** With the help of the word bank, write a response using paragraph frame 1.

INTERMEDIATE With the help of the word bank, write a response using paragraph frames 1 and 2.

ADVANCED, ADVANCED HIGH Write a response of differentiated length using the sentence starters.

A **APPROACHING** Write a response of differentiated length using the sentence starters.

BEGINNING

INTERMEDIATE

ADVANCED, ADVANCED HIGH

APPROACHING

Word Bank	Paragraph Frame 1	Paragraph Frame 2	Sentence Starters
eternal tyranny time accomplishments statue	Ozymandias is so proud of his rule, that he has a ____ created to document the good of his "works" for all to see. He is proud of his ____ and seems to brag about them as if they were ____ in an inscription under a larger-than-life statue of himself. The poem's ending illustrates how the belief in his eternal rule is wishful thinking and that ____ is really the only ruler over us all. While describing the destruction of ____ with Ramesses II's broken statue, Shelley also fights back against the tyranny of time by writing a poem that reminds us of this Egyptian king.	Dr. Kalanithi, considers his relationship with time as well given his terminal diagnosis and ____. He is concerned by ____. Dr. Kalanithi's relationship with time resonates with ____.	• Ozymandias is so . . . • He has a statue created to . . . • He is proud of his . . . • The poem's ending illustrates . . . • Dr. Kalanithi considers his relationship with time . . . • He is concerned by . . .

Peer Review

Rate

Respond to the following with a point rating that reflects your opinion.

	1	2	3	4
Ideas				
Evidence				
Language and Conventions				

Submit

Students should submit substantive feedback to two peers using the review instructions below.

- How well does this response answer the prompt?
- How well does the writer support his or her ideas with evidence from the poem and video?
- How well does the writer explain Shelley's relationship with time and Dr. Kalanithi's interpretation of it?
- What does the writer do well in this response? What does the writer need to work on?

Remember that your comments are most useful when they are kind and constructive.

ELL **SENTENCE FRAMES**

A

- You were able to (completely / partly / almost) ____ answer the prompt because ____.
- You could support your response with evidence from the poem and video by ____.
- You were able to (completely/partly/mostly) explain Shelley's relationship with time and Dr. Kalanithi's interpretation of it.
- You might also say ____ in your response.

Facing It

POETRY
Yusef Komunyakaa
1988

Introduction

The poetry of Yusef Komunyakaa (b. 1947) sheds light on some of the deepest and darkest elements of the human experience. He draws on his own background, exploring the intersection between African American culture and war. In his collection of poetry *Dien Cai Dau* (Vietnamese for "crazy"), Komunyakaa writes of his experience as a correspondent and editor during the Vietnam War (1955–1975) in a conversational style. "Facing It," one of the poems included in this collection, shows Komunyakaa reflecting on his first visit to the Vietnam Veterans Memorial.

In this poem, the speaker talks about visiting the Vietnam Veterans Memorial. Looking upon it, his reflection fades into the memorial's black granite. He promised himself he wouldn't cry, but as the tears come, he tries to steel himself. Catching his eyes in the black-mirrored surface, he sees how angry they look. Overwhelmed, he turns to look away, and then again, turns back to face it. Reading through the list of names, he's surprised his own name isn't up there. He touches the name of an old friend of his and remembers the explosion that killed him. Other images are reflected upon the granite's surface—a woman's blouse, a bird flying past, a veteran missing an arm. The speaker reflects that the man lost his arm inside the stone. After these visitors leave, the names always remain.

ELL Proficiency-leveled summaries and summaries in multiple languages are available digitally.

Audio and audio text highlighting are available with this text.

COMPARING WITHIN AND ACROSS GENRES

Both "Facing It" by Yusef Komunyakaa and "Ode on a Grecian Urn" by John Keats explore the connections between life, death, and art.

"Facing It" tells the story of a war veteran who visits the Vietnam Veterans Memorial in Washington, D.C. In the poem, reality blurs with memory as the speaker tries to make sense of the tremendous loss of human life that resulted from the war.

Entry Point

As students prepare to read "Facing It ," share the following information with them to provide context.

- ✓ Maya Lin, a Chinese American architect and artist, designed the memorial when she was a college student. Her design won a national competition.
- ✓ The two granite walls of the memorial form a V shape, with one wall pointing toward the Washington Monument and the other wall pointing toward the Lincoln Memorial.
- ✓ The monument lies in a space dug out of the ground; Lin intended the carved-out area to symbolize a wound.
- ✓ The names of the fallen soldiers engraved on the walls are sometimes traced onto paper by visitors, especially members of the soldiers' families and veterans of the war who served with the honorees.

Instructional Path

The print teacher's edition includes essential point-of-use instruction and planning tools. Complete lesson plans and program documents appear in your digital teacher account.

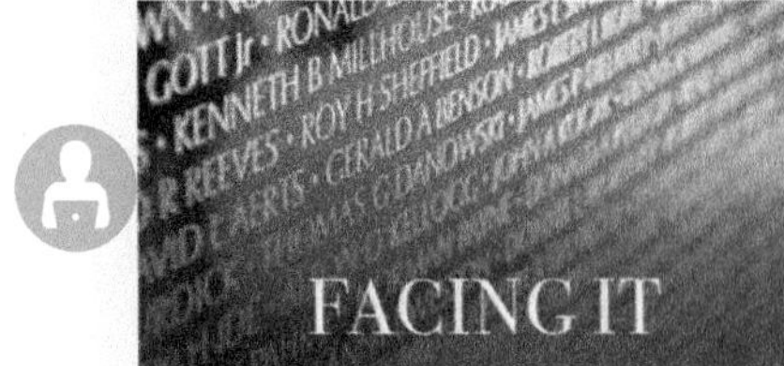

Independent Read: Facing It

Objectives: After reading the text, students will write a poem that demonstrates their understanding of how a person reacts to seeing a memorial.

Independent Read

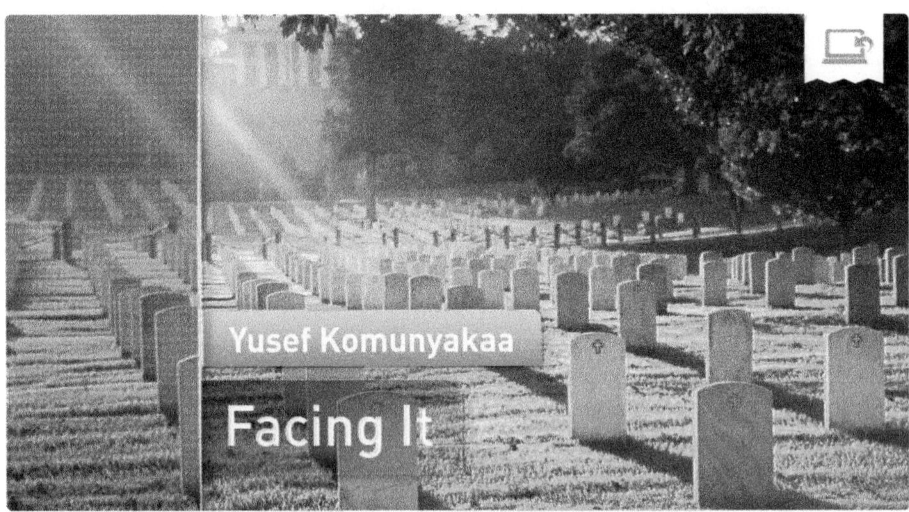

Introduce the Text

As a class, watch the video preview and have students read the introduction in pairs to make connections to the video preview.

- What other images could you imagine using in this video?
- What is the difference between a poem and a story?

Access Complex Text

LEXILE: N/A **WORD COUNT:** 168

The following areas may be challenging for students, particularly 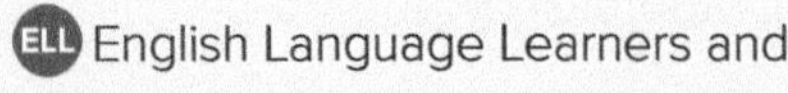 English Language Learners and Approaching grade-level learners.

Purpose	Prior Knowledge
• Students may find the content of this poem unsettling. Explain that the poem is an elegy. In an elegy, the speaker reflects on a serious topic such as a death. • Discuss why this poem was written and what ideas and feelings the poet wanted to express.	• Students may wonder how the poet is connected to the Vietnam War. Explain that Komunyakaa wrote for a U.S. military newspaper in Vietnam. He earned a medal — the Bronze Star — for his writing. • Students may not be familiar with the Vietnam Veterans Memorial. Show them a picture and explain that it consists of black granite walls bearing the names of U.S. military personnel killed or missing in Vietnam.

Facing It

> "I go down the 58,022 names, / half-expecting to find / my own in letters like smoke."

NOTES

My black face fades,
hiding inside the black granite.
I said I wouldn't
dammit: No tears.
I'm stone. I'm flesh.
My clouded **reflection** eyes me
like a bird of prey, the **profile** of night
slanted against morning. I turn
this way—the stone lets me go.
I turn that way—I'm inside
the Vietnam Veterans **Memorial**
again, **depending** on the light
to make a difference.
I go down the 58,022 names,
half-expecting to find
my own in letters like smoke.
I touch the name Andrew Johnson;
I see the booby trap's white flash.
Names shimmer on a woman's blouse
but when she walks away
the names stay on the wall.
Brushstrokes flash, a red bird's
wings cutting across my stare.
The sky. A plane in the sky.
A white vet's **image** floats
closer to me, then his pale eyes
look through mine. I'm a window.

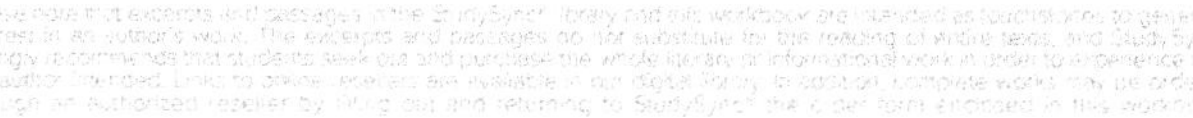

Reading & Writing Companion 13

Developing Background Knowledge and Cultural Awareness

Have students find images of the Vietnam Veterans Memorial.

1. Have students work in small groups to do a five-minute online search for images of the memorial.
2. Encourage students to find images that provide a variety of perspectives: near and far, with and without people, during the day and in the evening, and so on.

Discuss with students: Why do you think humans build and visit memorials? What is the purpose of memorials? How do they help us understand or connect with history? How might we think differently if we did not build memorials?

TEXT TALK

How is the speaker feeling in the first few lines of the poem?

See lines 1–4: The speaker is fighting back tears and is very emotional.

How are the speaker's memories of the war triggered by what he sees at the memorial?

See lines 17–18: The speaker sees the name Andrew Johnson and is reminded of an explosion during the war.

In the lines about the "white vet," what does the speaker mean when he says "his pale eyes look through mine" and "he's lost his right arm inside the stone"?

See lines 25–29: The white vet, who lost an arm in the war, is standing next to the speaker. The speaker sees the vet's reflection in the wall, including his eyes.

SELECTION VOCABULARY

reflection / el reflejo *noun* a visual portrayal of something in a mirror or other shiny surface COGNATE

profile / el perfil *noun* an outline or silhouette

memorial / el monumento conmemorativo *noun* an object (e.g. statue) that serves to preserve the memory of something

depend / depender *verb* to rely on someone or something for support, maintenance, or help COGNATE

image / la imagen *noun* a visual representation of a person or thing COGNATE

Prepare for Advanced Courses

Author's Syntax

Use the activity below to differentiate instruction for your B Beyond grade level learners.

Reread lines 3–4 of the poem. Direct students to the author's use of punctuation to create caesuras, or breaks in the flow of a line of verse. Have students review the text, focusing on where the author uses punctuation and line breaks to vary the length of his phrases and his sentences. Ask students:

- How does the author's use of caesuras, or breaks in the flow of sound, affect the reading of this poem?
- What does the use of these breaks in sound reveal about the speaker's emotions?
- How does the author's use of caesuras serve the purpose of his poem?

He's lost his right arm
inside the stone. In the black mirror
a woman's trying to erase names:
No, she's brushing a boy's hair.

 WRITE

POETRY: In the poem "Facing It," the speaker describes his experience at the Vietnam Veterans Memorial. Write a poem that expresses your thoughts and feelings as you imagine yourself at the site of a memorial that you have personally visited or that you have researched.

TEXT TALK

How did researching the Vietnam Memorial and thinking about the purpose of memorials deepen your understanding of "Facing It"?

Answers will vary.

 Ask each Beyond grade-level student to write one additional discussion question. Then, have one or two students facilitate a discussion, using their questions to guide the conversation.

Writer's Notebook

Connect to Essential Question: Give students time to reflect on how "Facing It" connects to the unit's essential question "What is the power of story?" by freewriting in their Writer's Notebooks.

CHECK FOR SUCCESS

If students are still struggling to respond to the prompt, ask them scaffolded questions, such as:

- How is the speaker's experience in the Vietnam War like a story?
- What parts of this story does the speaker remember as he looks at the memorial?

Reading Comprehension OPTIONAL

Have students complete the digital reading comprehension questions ✓ when they finish reading.

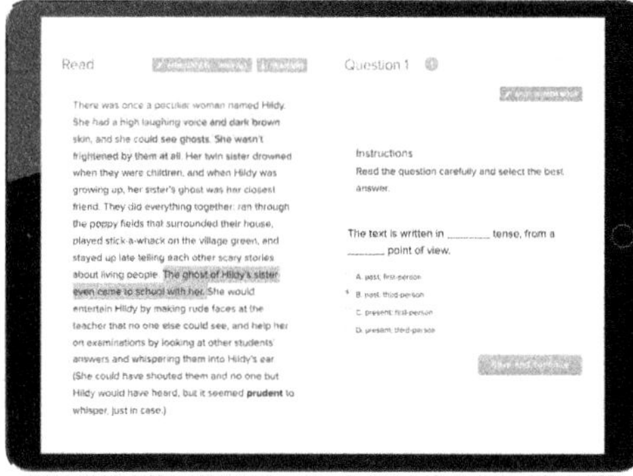

ANSWER KEY

QUESTION 1: C
QUESTION 2: B
QUESTION 3: C
QUESTION 4: D

QUESTION 5:
See chart below.

Definition	Word
A picture or representation of something	image
A visual portrayal of something in a mirror	reflection
Relying for support, maintenance, or help	depending
An object (e.g. statue) that serves to preserve the memory of something	memorial
An outline or silhouette	profile

Connect and Extend OPTIONAL

CONNECT TO EXTENDED WRITING PROJECT

Students can find inspiration from Yusef Komunyakaa for their informative essays. Have them work to convey specific emotions or ideas through the connotations of their words.

BEYOND THE BOOK

Art: Making a Memorial

Architect Maya Lin received high praise for her Vietnam Veterans Memorial. She intended it to be "an interface, between our world and the quieter, darker, more peaceful world beyond." Ask students to design their own memorial honoring one or more persons who have died. Encourage them to write a statement that tells the following information:

- why the person or persons should be remembered
- what the memorial looks like, including what it is made of
- where it should be placed
- how people should respond to it.

Students can submit a drawing or a computer model to show what they envision. Once students have completed their memorials, they can share them with the class.

Collaborative Conversation

SCAFFOLDS

Post the writing prompt to generate a discussion in small groups. Ask students to first break down the prompt before they discuss relevant ideas and textual evidence.

In the poem "Facing It," the speaker describes his experience at the Vietnam Veterans Memorial. Write a poem that expresses your thoughts and feelings as you imagine yourself at the site of a memorial that you have personally visited or that you have researched.

Use the scaffolds below to differentiate instruction for your ELL English Language Learners and A Approaching grade-level learners.

ELL **BEGINNING, INTERMEDIATE** Use the discussion guide and speaking frames to facilitate the discussion with support from the teacher.

ADVANCED, ADVANCED HIGH Use the discussion guide and speaking frames to facilitate the discussion in mixed-level groups.

A **APPROACHING** Use the discussion guide to facilitate the discussion in mixed-level groups.

APPROACHING
ADVANCED, ADVANCED HIGH
BEGINNING, INTERMEDIATE

Discussion Guide	Speaking Frames
1. In the first few lines of the poem, the speaker is ____.	• Check lines 1–4.
2. The speaker sees ____ and remembers ____	• Check lines 17–18 and 22–24.
3. The speaker sees the white veteran ____.	• Check lines 25–29.

Text to World

Use the activity below to differentiate instruction for your B Beyond grade level learners.

In lines 3–4, the speaker reveals mixed emotions about his visit to the Vietnam Veterans Memorial:

I said I wouldn't,

dammit: No tears.

Have students conduct informal research about the controversies that surrounded the construction of the Vietnam Veterans Memorial.

Ask students:

- What were the divisive issues that emerged around the design and building of the Vietnam Veterans Memorial?
- How does the public reaction to the Vietnam Veterans Memorial in the 1980s compare with public reaction to the memorial today?
- What is your own reaction to the memorial? Would you consider it to be a fitting and successful memorial? Why or why not?

Review Prompt and Rubric

Before students begin writing, review the writing prompt and rubric with the class.

POETRY: In the poem "Facing It," the speaker describes his experience at the Vietnam Veterans Memorial. Write a poem that expresses your thoughts and feelings as you imagine yourself at the site of a memorial that you have personally visited or that you have researched.

ELL A

PROMPT GUIDE

- Which memorial will you write about?
- What image do you see in your mind when you think about the memorial?
- How does the memorial make you feel?

Score	Poetry Composition	Language and Conventions
4	The writer clearly writes a poem expressing thoughts and feelings about visiting a memorial.	The writer demonstrates a consistent command of grammar, punctuation, and usage conventions. Although minor errors may be evident, they do not detract from the fluency or the clarity of the essay.
3	The writer sufficiently writes a poem expressing thoughts and feelings about visiting a memorial.	The writer demonstrates an adequate command of grammar, punctuation, and usage conventions. Although some errors may be evident, they create few (if any) disruptions in the fluency of the writing or the clarity of the essay.
2	The writer begins to write a poem expressing thoughts and feelings about visiting a memorial, but the poem is incomplete.	The writer demonstrates a partial command of grammar, punctuation, and usage conventions. Some distracting errors may be evident, at times creating minor disruptions in the fluency or clarity of the writing.
1	The writer attempts to write a poem expressing thoughts and feelings about visiting a memorial, but the attempt is not successful.	The writer demonstrates little or no command of grammar, punctuation, and usage conventions. Serious and persistent errors create disruptions in the fluency of the writing and sometimes interfere with meaning.
0	The writer does not provide a relevant response to the prompt or does not provide a response at all.	Serious and persistent errors overwhelm the writing and interfere with the meaning of the response as a whole, making the writer's meaning impossible to understand.

Write

SCAFFOLDS

Ask students to complete the writing assignment using text evidence to support their answers.

Use the scaffolds below to differentiate instruction for your ELL English Language Learners and A Approaching grade-level learners.

ELL **BEGINNING** With the help of the word bank, write a response using paragraph frame 1.

INTERMEDIATE With the help of the word bank, write a response using paragraph frames 1 and 2.

ADVANCED, ADVANCED HIGH Write a response of differentiated length using the sentence starters.

A **APPROACHING** Write a response of differentiated length using the sentence starters.

BEGINNING / INTERMEDIATE			ADVANCED, ADVANCED HIGH / APPROACHING
Word Bank	**Paragraph Frame 1**	**Paragraph Frame 2**	**Sentence Starters**
footsteps person Lincoln inside small	Walking into the ____ Memorial, I think about the ____ it honors. The large statue makes me feel ____, and the sound of my ____ echoes off the marble ceiling. Standing ____ here, all people are equal.	The great man ____. Relaxed and thoughtful, ____, After a long and brutal war, he is ____. As I walk back down the steps outside, I ____. Lincoln will always be here for us, and we ____.	• Walking into the . . . Memorial, • I think about . . . • The large statue . . . • The sound of my footsteps . . . • Standing . . . here, all people . . . • As I walk back down the steps outside . . .

Peer Review

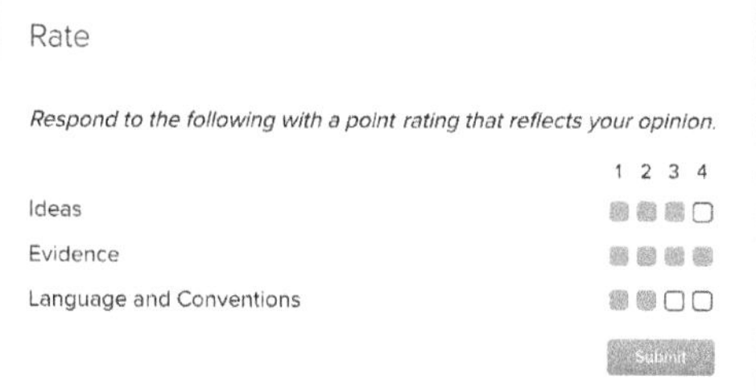

Students should submit substantive feedback to two peers using the review instructions below.

- How well does this poem address the prompt?
- Which of the thoughts or feelings did you find to be most interesting? Why?
- What does the writer do well in this poem? What does the writer need to work on?

Remember that your comments are most useful when they are kind and constructive.

SENTENCE FRAMES

A

- You were able to (completely / partly / almost) ____ answer the prompt.
- You could answer the prompt more completely by including ____ in your poem.
- I thought differently about memorials after reading ____ in your poem.
- My favorite part of your poem is ____.

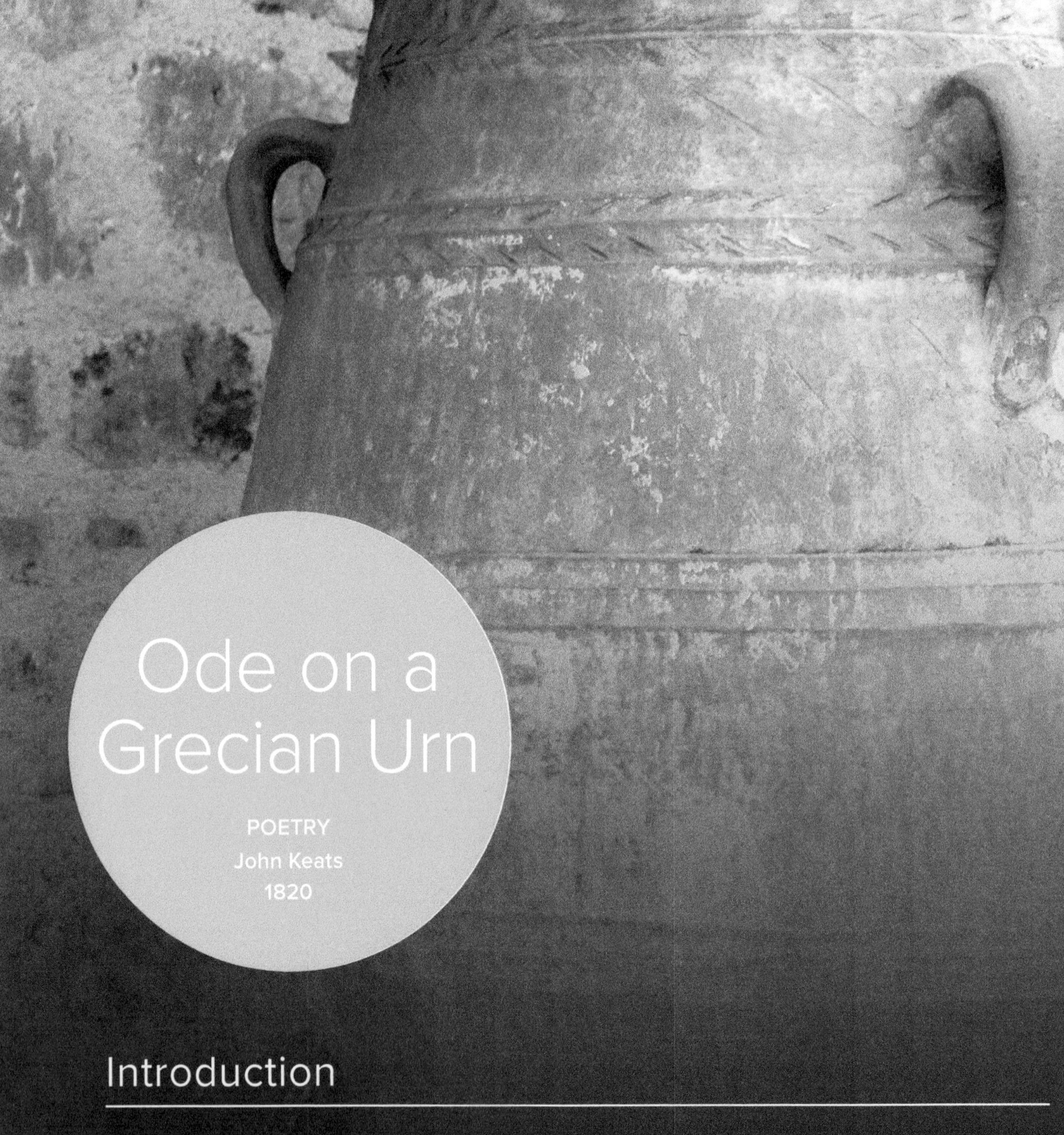

Ode on a Grecian Urn

POETRY
John Keats
1820

Introduction

What is the relationship between art and life, between beauty and truth? The Romantic poet John Keats (1795–1821) only lived to be 25 years old, having grown up in England and dying from tuberculosis in a bedroom that overlooked the Piazza di Spagna in Rome. "Ode on a Grecian Urn" was written only a year before his death, and like much of Keats's work it examines the relationships between life, death, beauty, and truth with depth and lyrical insight.

The speaker looks upon a Grecian urn, marveling at the pictures upon its side. Speaking to it, he thinks it knows how to tell a story even better than his poetry can. One of the pictures is a young man playing a pipe beneath the trees. The speaker addresses him, saying that imagined melodies are even sweeter than those heard out loud. He envies the youth, because he will never grow old, the trees will not go bare, nor will the beauty of his lover ever fade. Looking at another picture, the speaker sees priests leading a cow to sacrifice. His mood turns darker, thinking how that town will stay silent forever, with no one to explain why it is so desolate on this day. In the final stanza, the speaker addresses the urn itself—how it will remain when he and everyone he knows is dead. The urn will continue teaching its lesson, that truth and beauty are one and the same, for all of eternity.

Proficiency-leveled summaries and summaries in multiple languages are available digitally.

Audio and audio text highlighting are available with this text.

COMPARING WITHIN AND ACROSS GENRES

Both "Facing It" by Yusef Komunyakaa and "Ode on a Grecian Urn" by John Keats explore the connections between life, death, and art.

In "Ode on a Grecian Urn," the speaker praises an ancient vase. The decorations on the vase tell a story about life, love, and happiness that has been captured in time through art. The poem reflects on the timelessness of art and ends with a statement about truth and beauty that is still discussed and debated today.

Entry Point

As students prepare to read "Ode on a Grecian Urn," share the following information with them to provide context.

- ✓ Ancient Greece is known for producing magnificent works of art, including pottery. This art form can be traced to the city of Corinth in the seventh century B.C. Athenian artisans were known for painting narrative scenes on pots. These scenes were typically based on Greek mythology, including stories of Hercules, Zeus, Athena, and other important figures.
- ✓ In Keats's day, excavations in the Mediterranean region uncovered many Greek urns, sparking interest throughout Europe in all things classical.
- ✓ Keats left school when he was fifteen to apprentice with a surgeon-apothecary. He became a licensed apothecary in 1816, but he pursued poetry instead and never practiced medicine. His first poetry collection was published in 1817, when he was only twenty-two.

Instructional Path

The print teacher's edition includes essential point-of-use instruction and planning tools. Complete lesson plans and program documents appear in your digital teacher account.

First Read: Ode on a Grecian Urn

Objectives: After an initial reading and discussion of the poem, students will be able to identify and analyze structural and poetic elements to determine the poem's meaning.

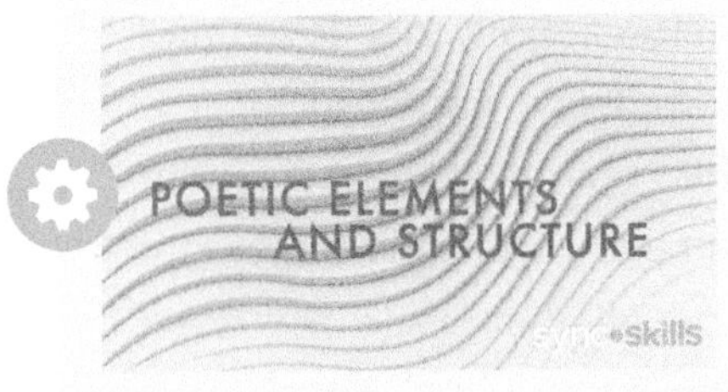

Skill: Poetic Elements and Structure

Objectives: After rereading and discussing a model of close reading, students will be able to analyze how poetic elements and structure help convey meaning.

Skill: Figurative Language

Objectives: After rereading and discussing a model of close reading, students will be able to analyze the meaning and purpose of figurative language in a text.

Close Read: Ode on a Grecian Urn

Objectives: After engaging in a close reading and discussion of "Ode on a Grecian Urn," students will be able to identify how poets use figurative language as well as poetic elements and structure to develop a theme by comparing and contrasting two poems from different literary time periods.

Progress Monitoring

Opportunities to Learn	Opportunities to Demonstrate Learning	Opportunities to Reteach
Poetic Elements and Structure		
Skill: Poetic Elements and Structure	Skill: Poetic Elements and Structure • Your Turn Close Read • Skills Focus • Write	Unit 5 Skill: Poetic Elements and Structure - The Love Song of J. Alfred Prufrock Spotlight Skill: Poetic Elements and Structure
Figurative Language		
Skill: Figurative Language	Skill: Figurative Language • Your Turn Close Read • Complete Vocabulary Chart • Skills Focus • Write	Unit 4 Skill: Figurative Language – Lines Composed A Few Miles Above Tintern Abbey Unit Skill: Figurative Language – Why I Write Spotlight Skill: Figurative Language

First Read

Introduce the Text

As a class, watch the video preview  and have students read the introduction in pairs to make connections to the video preview.

To activate prior knowledge and experiences, ask students:

- What do you think this poem is going to be about?
- What painting, sculpture, or other artistic object has especially inspired or impressed you? Why?

ELL SPEAKING FRAMES

- I think this poem will be about ____.
- I really like a piece of art called ____. I like it because ____.

Access Complex Text

LEXILE: N/A WORD COUNT: 373

The following areas may be challenging for students, particularly ELL English Language Learners and A Approaching grade-level learners.

Genre	Connection of Ideas	Specific Vocabulary
• An ode is a type of lyric poem that is often serious with a formal style and tone. • Explain that many odes celebrate people or objects. These odes normally use apostrophe, which is to address a personified thing or an absent person.	• Students might need some context to understand the poem's details. The speaker addresses the ode and describes what is depicted on it. • Students will need to understand the connection between stanzas to trace the theme of the poem.	• The poem includes many words not commonly used today, such as "thou" and "Sylvan historian." • Students should use context clues and a dictionary to help define any unfamiliar words.

 SCAFFOLDS

 ENGLISH LANGUAGE LEARNERS  APPROACHING GRADE LEVEL  BEYOND GRADE LEVEL

These icons identify differentiation strategies and scaffolded support for a variety of students. See the digital lesson plan for additional differentiation strategies and scaffolds.

"More happy love! more happy, happy love!"

NOTES

Skill: Poetic Elements and Structure

In the tradition of odes, the speaker of "Ode on a Grecian Urn" uses formal language to address the urn directly. In contrast, the speaker of the contemporary elegy "Facing It" expresses the rawness of his emotions through the use of vernacular language.

Skill: Figurative Literature

Keats personifies the urn by calling it a "sylvan historian." Komunyakaa says his face is "hiding" inside the stone of the wall, which is also personification. It's as if he is a part of the wall even as he stands looking at it.

Thou still unravish'd bride of quietness,
Thou **foster**-child of silence and slow time,
Sylvan[1] historian, who canst thus express
A flowery tale more sweetly than our rhyme:
What leaf-fring'd legend haunts about thy shape
Of deities or mortals, or of both,
In Tempe[2] or the dales of Arcady?[3]
What men or gods are these? What maidens loth?
What mad pursuit? What struggle to escape?
What pipes and timbrels? What wild ecstasy?

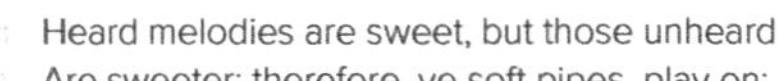

Ancient Greek urn

Heard melodies are sweet, but those unheard
Are sweeter; therefore, ye soft pipes, play on;
Not to the sensual ear, but, more endear'd,
Pipe to the spirit ditties of no tone:
Fair youth, beneath the trees, thou canst not leave
Thy song, nor ever can those trees be bare;
Bold Lover, never, never canst thou kiss,
Though winning near the goal—yet, do not grieve;
She cannot fade, though thou hast not thy bliss,
For ever wilt thou love, and she be fair!

Ah, happy, happy boughs! that cannot shed
Your leaves, nor ever bid the Spring adieu;
And, happy melodist, unwearied,
For ever piping songs for ever new;
More happy love! more happy, happy love!
For ever warm and still to be enjoy'd,
For ever panting, and for ever young;
All breathing human passion far above,

1. **Sylvan** of the woods
2. **Tempe** a beautiful valley in Arcadia
3. **Arcady** Arcadia, a mountainous region in Greece, traditionally considered an ideal rustic landscape

Developing Background Knowledge and Social Emotional Learning

Find out what your students already know about ancient Greece.

- Tell students to take a few minutes to brainstorm images related to ancient Greek urns.
- In small groups, have students do a quick online search of images. Choose one or two to project and discuss as a class.
- Discuss with students: Have you ever given special value to a piece of art (a painting, sculpture, song, book, etc.)? What experiences, ideas, or memories made that artwork valuable to you? Why do you think humans give special meaning to specific works of art?

Poetic Elements and Structure

What does the reader notice about how the language in the two poems is different?

The reader notices that "Ode on a Grecian Urn" uses formal language and "Facing It" uses vernacular language.

Figurative Literature

How is the poet's use of personification different in each poem?

Keats uses personification to imply that the urn can tell stories of the past, whereas Komunyakaa's use of personification reflects the speaker's fractured self.

SELECTION VOCABULARY

foster / adoptivo/a ***adjective*** indicator of parental care though an adult not related by blood or legal ties

sylvan / silvano/a ***adjective*** related to woods or forests COGNATE

TEXT TALK

What does the phrase "deities or mortals" refer to?

See lines 5–7: It means "gods or humans," and it refers to images on the urn.

What are some of the negative characteristics of people who love, according to stanza 3?

See lines 29 and 30: Sorrow, hot foreheads, and dry mouths.

Skills Focus

QUESTION 4: Theme

These lines reflect the theme of the power of art and beauty because people will die, but the urn will still exist and its beauty will comfort people in the future as it does now.

Prepared for Advanced Courses

Use the activity below to differentiate instruction for your B Beyond grade level learners.

Author's Word Choice

Reread lines 26-27.

Direct students to reread the poem, noting the use of words, such as for ever, that denote immeasurable expanses of time. Ask students:

- What meanings or emotions are amplified by the author's repeated use of these words?
- How does the author's use of these words support the themes developed in this text?

NOTES

That leaves a heart high-sorrowful and cloy'd,
A burning forehead, and a parching tongue.

Who are these coming to the sacrifice?
To what green altar, O mysterious priest,
Lead'st thou that heifer lowing at the skies,
And all her silken flanks with garlands drest?
What little town by river or sea shore,
Or mountain-built with peaceful citadel,
Is emptied of this folk, this pious morn?
And, little town, thy streets for evermore
Will silent be; and not a soul to tell
Why thou art **desolate**, can e'er return.

O Attic shape![4] Fair attitude! with brede
Of marble men and maidens overwrought,
With forest branches and the trodden weed;
Thou, silent form, dost tease us out of thought
As doth eternity: Cold **Pastoral**![5]
When old age shall this **generation** waste,
Thou shalt remain, in midst of other woe
Than ours, a friend to man, to whom thou say'st,
"Beauty is truth, truth beauty,"—that is all
Ye know on earth, and all ye need to know.

4. **Attic shape** in the simple, graceful style characteristic of Attica, the region in Greece where Athens was located
5. **Pastoral** a work depicting the life of shepherds, or simple rural life in general

TEXT TALK

According to the final stanza, what will survive long after the people of Keats's time are dead?

See lines 45–50: The urn will continue to exist; as the poem puts it, "Thou shalt remain."

B Ask each Beyond grade-level student to write one additional discussion question. Then, have one or two students facilitate a discussion, using their questions to guide the conversation.

SELECTION VOCABULARY

desolate / desolado/a *adjective* very lonely and sad COGNATE

pastoral / pastoral *adjective* having to do with country life COGNATE

generation / la generación *noun* all the people living at the same time or of approximately the same age COGNATE

Reading Comprehension OPTIONAL

Have students complete the digital reading comprehension questions when they finish reading.

ANSWER KEY

QUESTION 1: B
QUESTION 2: C
QUESTION 3: A
QUESTION 4: D
QUESTION 5: B

Connect and Extend OPTIONAL

CONNECT TO EXTENDED WRITING PROJECT

Students can use "Ode on a Grecian Urn" as inspiration for their Extended Writing Project. Have students think about the descriptions of nature and beauty in the poem. Encourage students to use their feelings about nature to help them choose a topic for their essay.

BEYOND THE BOOK

Art: Everyone's a Critic

The speaker in "On a Grecian Urn" praises the object's figures and its value to generation after generation. Identify a work of art that appeals to you. It might be a painting, drawing, sculpture, fountain, mural, building, or installation. Write a brief essay of art criticism that assesses the piece. In your paper, you should:

- include a photo of the piece
- describe what it looks like in words
- explain why it is well done
- explain what the work inspires in viewers
- tell what the work says to you
- include something the artist has said about the work, if possible

You might choose to give your opinion in a video, rather than a paper. This could require you to collaborate with classmates.

Think Questions

Circulate as students answer Think Questions independently. Scaffolds for these questions are shown on the opposite page.

QUESTION 1: Textual Evidence

The urn itself can express a "flowery tale" because of the images and scenes depicted on it.

QUESTION 2: Textual Evidence

The "Bold Lover" should not grieve because his beloved will always be young and beautiful, even though she may be inaccessible to him.

QUESTION 3: Textual Evidence

The urn is a constant reminder of the ability of human beings to create wonderful and lasting objects—things that are examples of "truth" and "beauty." Even when people grow old, even when people experience "other woe," the urn is a reminder that humans can rise above misfortune.

QUESTION 4: Context Clues

There are several nature images in this part of the poem, such as "a flowery tale" and "leaf-fring'd legend." I think that *sylvan* probably has to do with nature, especially plants, and might specifically involve forests.

QUESTION 5: Word Meaning

Definition number 3 most closely matches the meaning of the word *desolate* in the poem. The stanza refers to towns that are "emptied of this folk" and "silent," so *desolate* probably means "deserted and bleak."

First Read

Read "Ode on a Grecian Urn." After you read, complete the Think Questions below.

THINK QUESTIONS

1. In the first stanza of the poem, what is it that can express "A flowery tale more sweetly than our rhyme"?
2. In the second stanza, Keats writes of the "Bold Lover" who can never kiss his beloved. Why, according to the poem, should he not grieve?
3. In what sense is the urn "a friend to man"? Explain what Keats means by this phrase, using textual evidence from the poem to support your response.
4. Use context clues to determine the meaning of the word **sylvan** as it is used in stanza 1. Write your definition of *sylvan* here and explain which clues helped you determine the word's meaning.
5. Read the following dictionary entry:

   des•o•late /ˈde-sə-lət, ˈde-zə-/ *adjective*
   Adjective

   1. lacking the items that make people feel welcome in a place
   2. very lonely and sad
   3. (of a place) deserted and bleak

   Which of these definitions most closely matches the meaning of **desolate** as it is used in stanza 4? Write the correct definition of *desolate* here and explain which clues helped you figure it out.

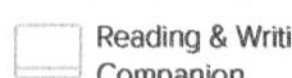

SCAFFOLDS

Think Questions

Use the scaffolds below to differentiate instruction for your ELL English Language Learners and A Approaching grade-level learners.

ELL **BEGINNING** Write a response using the word bank and sentence frames.

INTERMEDIATE Write a response using the sentence frames.

ADVANCED, ADVANCED HIGH Write a response using the Text-Dependent Question Guide.

A **APPROACHING** Write a response using the Text-Dependent Question Guide.

BEGINNING	INTERMEDIATE	APPROACHING / ADVANCED, ADVANCED HIGH
Word Bank	**Sentence Frames**	**Text-Dependent Question Guide**
grieve plants or forests human beings beautiful truth nature images Grecian urn kiss sweetly beauty	The poet says that the ____ is a beautiful object that can tell stories. It is the object that can tell a "flowery tale more ____ than our rhyme."	1. • Is the speaker addressing a thing or a person? • What clues in the poem and title tell me to what or whom he is speaking? • What images does the speaker see?
	The poem says the lover should not ____ because the woman will always be young and ____. Even though he cannot ____ her, she will never grow old and ugly.	2. • What will the Bold Lover do "for ever"? • What will always be true of the woman in the image? • How do these answers help me answer the question?
	The urn is a reminder that ____ can create beautiful, lasting objects that tell stories. The urn shows us that ____ and ____ are the same.	3. • What will happen to "this generation"? • What does the phrase "other woe" mean? • How can the urn help humans through hard times?
	There are lots of ____ in the first stanza of the poem. I think *sylvan* has to do with ____.	4. • Read: "**Sylvan** historian, who canst thus express A flowery tale more sweetly than our rhyme: What leaf-fring'd legend haunts about thy shape..." • What images from nature appear in these lines? • What do those images tell me about the meaning of the word *sylvan*?
	Desolate as used in the poem matches definition #____.	5. • Read: "And, little town, thy streets for evermore Will silent be; and not a soul to tell Why thou art **desolate**, can e'er return." • Is "desolate" lacking items? (#1) • Is "desolate" lonely and sad? (#2) • Is "desolate" deserted and bleak? (#3)

Skill: Poetic Elements and Structure

Introduce the Skill

Watch the Concept Definition video and read the following definition with your students.

Poetic structure describes the organization of words and lines in a poem as well as its rhyme scheme and meter. Poems consist of words that are divided into **lines.** A group of lines is called a **stanza.**

Other elements of poetry that contribute to structure include rhyme and rhythm. **Rhyme** is the repetition of the same or similar vowel sounds. The **rhyme scheme** of a poem is the pattern formed by the rhyming words at the end of lines. **Rhythm** is the pattern of unstressed and stressed syllables in a line of poetry. A regular pattern is called **meter,** and it gives a line of poetry a predictable rhythm.

The poet's choice of **poetic form**, or arrangement and style of a poem, will help determine the structure. Common forms include haiku, limerick, and sonnet, each with its own rules. Poetry without a consistent meter, rhyme, or stanza length is called **open form**.

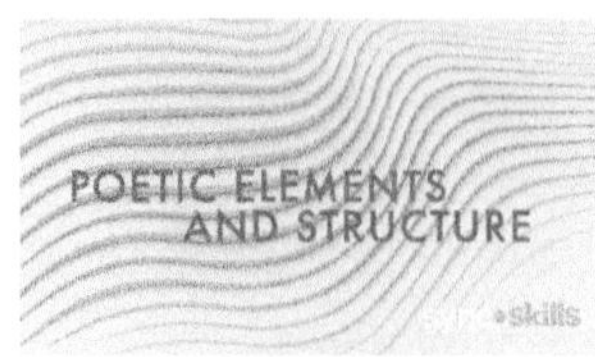

Skill: Poetic Elements and Structure

Use the Checklist to analyze Poetic Elements and Structure in "Ode on a Grecian Urn." Refer to the sample student annotations about Poetic Elements and Structure in the text.

••• CHECKLIST FOR POETIC ELEMENTS AND STRUCTURE

In order to analyze a poet's choices concerning how to structure specific parts of a poem, note the following:

- ✓ the form and overall structure of the poem
- ✓ the rhyme, rhythm, and meter, if present
- ✓ lines and stanzas in the poem that suggest its meanings and aesthetic impact
- ✓ how the poet began or ended the poem
- ✓ if the poet provided a comedic or tragic resolution
- ✓ poetic terminology, such as the following:
  - **ode:** a type of lyric poem that is serious with an elevated tone and style that usually celebrates a person, a quality, or an object, or expresses a private meditation
  - **apostrophe:** a figure of speech in which an idea, personified object, or absent person is directly addressed (Nearly all odes include an apostrophe.)
  - **elegy:** a poem that laments a death or some other great loss

To analyze how an author's choices concerning how to structure specific parts of a poem contribute to its overall structure and meaning as well as its aesthetic impact, consider the following questions:

- ✓ How does the poet structure the poem? What is the structure of specific parts?
- ✓ How do the poet's choices contribute to the poem's overall structure, meaning, and aesthetic impact?
- ✓ How does the poem reflect a specific literary time period and culture?
- ✓ How is this poem different from the poetry of other literary time periods and cultures?

TURN AND TALK

1. What is the difference between poetry and prose?
2. Why is this difference important to understand when analyzing poetry?

ELL SPEAKING FRAMES

- Poetry is ____. Prose is ____.
- The difference is important because ____.

SKILL VOCABULARY

poetic structure / la estructura poética ***noun*** the organization of words and lines as well as the rhyme and meter of a poem COGNATE

rhyme scheme / el patrón de rima ***noun*** the pattern formed by the rhyming words at the end of lines in a poem

poetic form / la forma poética ***noun*** the particular set of rules guiding the arrangement of words and lines in a poem COGNATE

open form / la forma abierta ***noun*** poetic form without consistent meter, rhyme, or stanza length

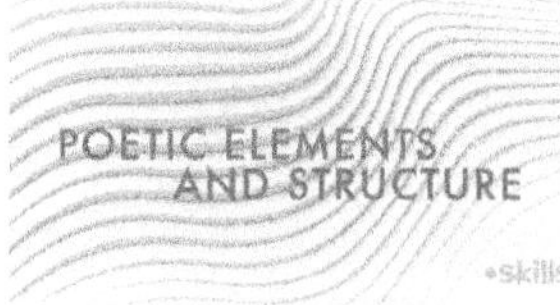

Skill: Poetic Elements and Structure

Reread lines 1–10 of "Ode on a Grecian Urn" and lines 1–16 of "Facing It." Then, using the Checklist on the previous page, answer the multiple-choice questions below.

YOUR TURN

1. Based on the excerpts from "Ode on a Grecian Urn" and "Facing It," a reader can assume that over time, there has been a trend for poetry to become—
   - A. less rigid in structure.
   - B. more consistent in rhyme scheme.
   - C. less like an elegy.
   - D. more likely to use apostrophe.

2. How does the rhyme scheme in "Ode on a Grecian Urn" contribute to its meaning?
   - A. The consistent repetition of sounds moves the reader through the speaker's positive contemplations.
   - B. The use of a traditional structure makes the speaker seem less excited about the urn.
   - C. The internal rhyming sounds help the reader connect the speaker's flowing contemplations.
   - D. The use of rhyming couplets highlights how the speaker is singing the urn's praises.

3. Compare the rhyme scheme in "Facing It" to that of "Ode on a Grecian Urn." How is the rhyme scheme different, and how does it contribute to the meaning of the poem?
   - A. The absence of a rhyme scheme in "Facing It" makes the poem flow more naturally and feel more somber, which reflects how war makes the speaker feel.
   - B. The absence of a rhyme scheme in "Facing It" means the poem's language is often harder to understand, which reflects how the speaker feels about war.
   - C. The absence of a rhyme scheme in "Facing It" puts all of the emphasis on the visual aspects of the poem, which parallels how the speaker interacts with the wall.
   - D. The absence of a rhyme scheme in "Facing It" means punctuation and line spacing stop the reader at particular points, which mimics how the speaker interacts with the wall.

Your Turn

Ask students to complete the Your Turn Activity.

QUESTION 1

A. Correct. "Facing It" is free verse and looser in structure than "Ode on a Grecian Urn."

B. Incorrect. "Facing It" has no apparent rhyme scheme, but "Ode on a Grecian Urn" has a clear rhyme scheme.

C. Incorrect. "Facing It" is lamenting lives lost and can be considered an elegy.

D. Incorrect. "Ode on a Grecian Urn" uses apostrophe, but "Facing It" does not.

QUESTION 2

A. Correct. The consistent rhyme scheme encourages readers to move from line to line, reflecting the speaker's interest and excitement about the urn.

B. Incorrect. The poem's details support the idea that the speaker is excited about the urn.

C. Incorrect. The poem's rhyme scheme consists of end rhymes.

D. Incorrect. The poem does not use rhyming couplets.

QUESTION 3

A. Incorrect. The absence of a rhyme scheme does not make the poem flow more naturally.

B. Incorrect. The poem's language is not hard to understand.

C. Incorrect. The absence of a rhyme scheme does not put *all* of the emphasis on the visual aspects of the poem.

D. Correct. The poem focuses on punctuation to move the reader through the poem, which stops the reader at specific points. This stopping and starting is how the speaker interacts with the wall.

Skill: Figurative Language

Introduce the Skill

Watch the Concept Definition video and read the following definition with your students.

Figurative language is language used for descriptive effect, often to illustrate or imply ideas indirectly. Types of figurative language include simile, metaphor, and personification. A **simile** uses the words *like* or *as* to compare two seemingly unlike things. A **metaphor** directly compares two seemingly unlike things without using *like* or *as*. **Personification** is a **figure of speech** in which an animal, object, force of nature, or an idea is given human qualities.

When reading prose, and especially poetry, readers use **context**—including when and where a text was written, for example—to analyze the impact of word choice and to help determine or interpret the meaning of figurative words and phrases.

Skill: Figurative Language

Use the Checklist to analyze Figurative Language in "Ode on a Grecian Urn." Refer to the sample student annotations about Figurative Language in the text.

••• CHECKLIST FOR FIGURATIVE LANGUAGE

In order to determine the meaning of figurative language in context, note the following:

- ✓ words that mean one thing literally and suggest something else
- ✓ similes, metaphors, or personification
- ✓ figures of speech, including
  - paradoxes, or a seemingly contradictory statement that when further investigated or explained proves to be true, such as
    - > a character described as "a wise fool"
    - > a character stating, "I must be cruel to be kind"
  - hyperbole, or exaggerated statements not meant to be taken literally, such as
    - > a child saying, "I'll be doing this homework until I'm 100!"
    - > a claim such as, "I'm so hungry I could eat a horse!"

In order to interpret figurative language in context and analyze its role in the text, consider the following questions:

- ✓ Where is there figurative language in the text and what seems to be the purpose of the author's use of it?
- ✓ Why does the author use a figure of speech rather than literal language?
- ✓ What impact does exaggeration or hyperbole have on your understanding of the text?
- ✓ Where are there examples of paradoxes and how do they affect the meaning in the text?
- ✓ Which phrases contain references that seem contradictory?
- ✓ Where are contradictory words and phrases used to enhance the reader's understanding of the character, object, or idea?
- ✓ How does the figurative language develop the message or theme of the literary work?

TURN AND TALK

1. What is an example of figurative language you have read or heard?
2. Why do you think writers might use figurative language instead of saying an idea directly?

SPEAKING FRAMES

- I read/heard figurative language in ____. The figurative language was ____.
- Writers use figurative language because ____.

SKILL VOCABULARY

simile / el símil *noun* a figure of speech that uses the words like or as to compare two seemingly unlike things COGNATE

metaphor / la metáfora *noun* a figure of speech that compares two seemingly unlike things but implies a comparison instead of stating it directly with the words like or as COGNATE

personification / la personificación *noun* a figure of speech in which an animal, object, force of nature, or an idea is given human form or qualities COGNATE

Skill: Figurative Language

Reread lines 41–50 of "Ode on a Grecian Urn" and lines 14–23 of "Facing It." Then, using the Checklist on the previous page, answer the multiple-choice questions below.

YOUR TURN

1. Which phrase is a simile?
   - A. "Thou, silent form"
   - B. "Beauty is truth"
   - C. "Brushstrokes flash"
   - D. "letters like smoke"

2. The phrase "a friend to man" in line 48 of "Ode on a Grecian Urn" can best be described as an example of—
   - A. personification.
   - B. paradox.
   - C. hyperbole.
   - D. simile.

3. Which statement best explains what the phrase "a friend to man" means in line 48 of "Ode on a Grecian Urn"?
   - A. The urn is "a friend to man" because it teaches people that nature is a source of timeless beauty.
   - B. The urn is "a friend to man" because it teaches people that there is beauty in truth and truth in beauty.
   - C. The scenes depicted on the urn are "a friend to man" because they stop us from forgetting important historical moments.
   - D. The scenes depicted on the urn are "a friend to man" because they show us that there is value in telling stories of the past.

Your Turn

Ask students to complete the Your Turn Activity.

QUESTION 1

A. Incorrect. Similes must compare two objects, and this phrase does not.

B. Incorrect. Although this phrase compares two objects, it is a metaphor rather than a simile because it does not use the word *like* or *as*.

C. Incorrect. Similes must compare two objects, and this phrase does not.

D. Correct. This phrase compares two objects using the word *like.*

QUESTION 2

A. Correct. The phrase addresses the urn as if it were a human being.

B. Incorrect. A paradox is a statement that contradicts itself but still seems correct.

C. Incorrect. Hyperbole is exaggeration, which is not present in this phrase.

D. Incorrect. A simile compares two objects using *like* or *as,* which is not the case in this phrase.

QUESTION 3

A. Incorrect. The urn does not symbolize only the beauty of nature in the poem.

B. Correct. The final three lines of the poem show that the urn is "a friend to man" because it tells us that "Beauty is truth, truth beauty."

C. Incorrect. The speaker imagines what the scenes on the urn are depicting, so they cannot be "important historical moments."

D. Incorrect. The urn itself is "a friend to man," not just the depictions on it.

Close Read

Skills Focus

QUESTION 1: Figurative Language

See Lines 3–4: Keats uses personification to describe the urn as a "sylvan historian" who tells "a flowery tale." These lines reveal that the speaker views the urn as a better storyteller than a poet.

QUESTION 2: Poetic Structure

See Lines 8–10: Keats structures the stanza as a series of questions to show that the speaker does not know the story being told on the urn. This gives the urn an air of mystery and increases the reader's curiosity.

QUESTION 3: Theme

See Lines 11–14: The speaker claims that "unheard" melodies are better than songs that can be heard. This idea develops the poem's theme that the objects of beauty created by the imagination will live on long after those who created them.

QUESTION 4: Theme See Lines 46–48.

QUESTION 5: Connect to Essential Question

See Lines 25–34: The speaker is intensely curious about the scenes on the urn and asks many questions about them. He compares one of the scenes to life on earth, preferring the portrait of endless "happy love" to the "high-sorrowful" hearts that exist in reality.

Close Read

Reread "Ode on a Grecian Urn." As you reread, complete the Skills Focus questions below. Then use your answers and annotations from the questions to help you complete the Write activity.

SKILLS FOCUS

1. Identify figurative language that the poet uses to describe the urn in the first stanza. What does this example of figurative language reveal about the speaker's view of the urn?
2. Notice all the question marks and the repetition of the word *What* in the first stanza. What is the effect of the poet's choice to structure the stanza this way? What does this structure suggest about the urn?
3. Highlight a section of the second stanza of "Ode on a Grecian Urn" that describes the difference between heard and unheard music. Explain how this distinction helps develop the poem's theme.
4. Identify a section of the fifth stanza that focuses on the passage of time and explain how this section reflects the poem's theme.
5. In "Ode on a Grecian Urn," the speaker views three different stories on an urn, and each has a different emotional impact. What is the power of these stories over the speaker? Support your answer with textual evidence.

WRITE

LITERARY ANALYSIS: "Ode on a Grecian Urn" is a famous ode devoted to an ancient Greek urn. "Facing It" is an elegy written by a contemporary American poet about a visit to the Vietnam Veterans Memorial. Write an essay that analyzes how these texts use figurative language as well as poetic elements and structure to express ideas about art, culture, and society. Support your analysis with textual evidence from "Ode on a Grecian Urn."

Writer's Notebook

Connect to Essential Question: Give students time to reflect on how "Ode on a Grecian Urn" connects to the unit's essential question "What is the power of story?" by freewriting in their Writer's Notebooks.

Beginning & Intermediate

Read aloud the unit's essential question: "What is the power of story?" Encourage students to draw their connections or allow students to write in their native language. Circulate around the room, prompting students for their thoughts as they respond orally or through pantomime.

Advanced & Advanced High

Allow students to share their connections orally in pairs or small groups before freewriting.

Collaborative Conversation

SCAFFOLDS

Break students into collaborative conversation groups to discuss the Close Read prompt. Ask students to use the StudySyncTV episode as a model for their discussion. Remind them to reference their Skills Focus annotations in their discussion.

"Ode on a Grecian Urn" is a famous ode devoted to an ancient Greek urn. "Facing It" is an elegy written by a contemporary American poet about a visit to the Vietnam Veterans Memorial. Write an essay that analyzes how these texts use figurative language as well as poetic elements and structure to express ideas about art, culture, and society. Support your analysis with textual evidence from "Ode on a Grecian Urn."

Use the scaffolds below to differentiate instruction for your ELL English Language Learners and A Approaching grade-level learners.

ELL **BEGINNING, INTERMEDIATE** Use the discussion guide and speaking frames to facilitate the discussion with support from the teacher.

ADVANCED, ADVANCED HIGH Use the discussion guide and speaking frames to facilitate the discussion in mixed-level groups.

A **APPROACHING** Use the discussion guide to facilitate the discussion in mixed-level groups.

APPROACHING
ADVANCED, ADVANCED HIGH
BEGINNING, INTERMEDIATE

Discussion Guide	Speaking Frames
1. What poetic structure do you see in "Ode on a Grecian Urn"?	• The poem uses a ____.
2. What figurative language do you see in "Ode on a Grecian Urn"?	• An example of figurative language is ____. • The poet uses this language because ____.
3. What poetic structure do you remember from "Facing It"?	• The poem uses a ____.
4. What figurative language do you remember from "Facing It"?	• An example of figurative language is ____. • The poet uses this language because ____.
5. What ideas about society do you see in each poem?	• "Ode on a Grecian Urn" says that society is ____. • "Facing It" says that society is ____.

Text to World

Use the activity below to differentiate instruction for your B Beyond grade level learners.

Reread lines 17–22. Ask students:

- In the text, what are some of the things that the "bold lover" will never obtain? And what will he never lose?
- In your life, what are some of the goals you have obtained, and what did you learn from that experience?
- What are some of your goals that remain, and what do you hope to gain from obtaining them?
- Would you agree that there is value in wanting something, even if one is likely never to obtain it? Explain your response.

Review Prompt and Rubric

Before students begin writing, review the writing prompt and rubric with the class.

LITERARY ANALYSIS: "Ode on a Grecian Urn" is a famous ode devoted to an ancient Greek urn. "Facing It" is an elegy written by a contemporary American poet about a visit to the Vietnam Veterans Memorial. Write an essay that analyzes how these texts use figurative language as well as poetic elements and structure to express ideas about art, culture, and society. Support your analysis with textual evidence from "Ode on a Grecian Urn."

PROMPT GUIDE

- How is the structure of each poem similar and different?
- How is the figurative language of each poem similar and different?
- How do the poems look at art, culture, and society?

Score	Figurative Language	Poetic Elements and Structure	Language and Conventions
4	The writer clearly analyzes the figurative language in the poems. The writer provides exemplary analysis, using relevant textual evidence.	The writer clearly analyzes poetic elements and structure in the poems. The writer provides exemplary analysis, using relevant textual evidence.	The writer demonstrates a consistent command of grammar, punctuation, and usage conventions. Although minor errors may be evident, they do not detract from the fluency or the clarity of the essay.
3	The writer analyzes the figurative language in the poems. The writer provides sufficient analysis, using relevant textual evidence most of the time.	The writer analyzes the poetic elements and structure in the poems. The writer provides sufficient analysis, using relevant textual evidence most of the time.	The writer demonstrates an adequate command of grammar, punctuation, and usage conventions. Although some errors may be evident, they create few (if any) disruptions in the fluency of the writing or the clarity of the essay.
2	The writer begins to analyze the figurative language, but the analysis is incomplete. The writer uses relevant textual evidence only some of the time.	The writer begins to analyze poetic elements and structure, but the analysis is incomplete. The writer uses relevant textual evidence only some of the time.	The writer demonstrates a partial command of grammar, punctuation, and usage conventions. Some distracting errors may be evident, at times creating minor disruptions in the fluency or clarity of the writing.
1	The writer attempts to analyze the figurative language, but the analysis is not successful. The writer uses little or no relevant textual evidence.	The writer attempts to analyze poetic elements and structure, but the analysis is not successful. The writer uses little or no relevant textual evidence.	The writer demonstrates little or no command of grammar, punctuation, and usage conventions. Serious and persistent errors create disruptions in the fluency of the writing and sometimes interfere with meaning.
0	The writer does not provide a relevant response to the prompt or does not provide a response at all.	The writer does not provide a relevant response to the prompt or does not provide a response at all.	Serious and persistent errors overwhelm the writing and interfere with the meaning of the response as a whole, making the writer's meaning impossible to understand.

Write

SCAFFOLDS

Ask students to complete the writing assignment using text evidence to support their answers.

Use the scaffolds below to differentiate instruction for your ELL English Language Learners and A Approaching grade-level learners.

ELL **BEGINNING** With the help of the word bank, write a response using paragraph frame 1.

INTERMEDIATE With the help of the word bank, write a response using paragraph frames 1 and 2.

ADVANCED, ADVANCED HIGH Write a response of differentiated length using the sentence starters.

A **APPROACHING** Write a response of differentiated length using the sentence starters.

BEGINNING / INTERMEDIATE		INTERMEDIATE	ADVANCED, ADVANCED HIGH / APPROACHING
Word Bank	**Paragraph Frame 1**	**Paragraph Frame 2**	**Sentence Starters**
rhyme powerful structure modern organized	The poem "Ode on a Grecian Urn" uses a traditional poetic ____. The lines have meter, and the words at the end of the lines ____. The structure of this poem suggests that art should be ____. "Facing It" is much more ____. This poem does not use meter or rhyme. This poem expresses ____ ideas without using a traditional structure.	Both poems use ____. "Ode on a Grecian Urn" uses figurative language that ____. The reader might need to ____. "Facing It" uses language that is ____. The images are ____.	• "Ode on a Grecian Urn" uses a ____ poetic structure to . . . • "Facing It" uses ____ to . . . • Both poems use ____ to . . . • The poems use structure similarly/differently because . . . • The poems express similar/different ideas about art, culture, and society . . . • Ultimately, the two poems . . .

Peer Review

Rate

Respond to the following with a point rating that reflects your opinion.

	1	2	3	4
Ideas				
Evidence				
Language and Conventions				

Submit

Students should submit substantive feedback to two peers using the review instructions below.

- How well does this response answer the prompt?
- How well does the writer analyze figurative language and poetic elements and structure?
- What did the writer do well in this response? What does the writer need to work on?

Remember that your comments are most useful when they are kind and constructive.

ELL A **SENTENCE FRAMES**

- You (completely / partly) ____ answered the prompt because ____.
- You could answer the prompt more completely by ____.
- Your analysis of the figurative language was ____.
- Your analysis of poetic elements and structure was ____.
- When you wrote ____, I changed my opinion because ____.
- One idea you expressed well is ____.
- One section that could be improved is ____.

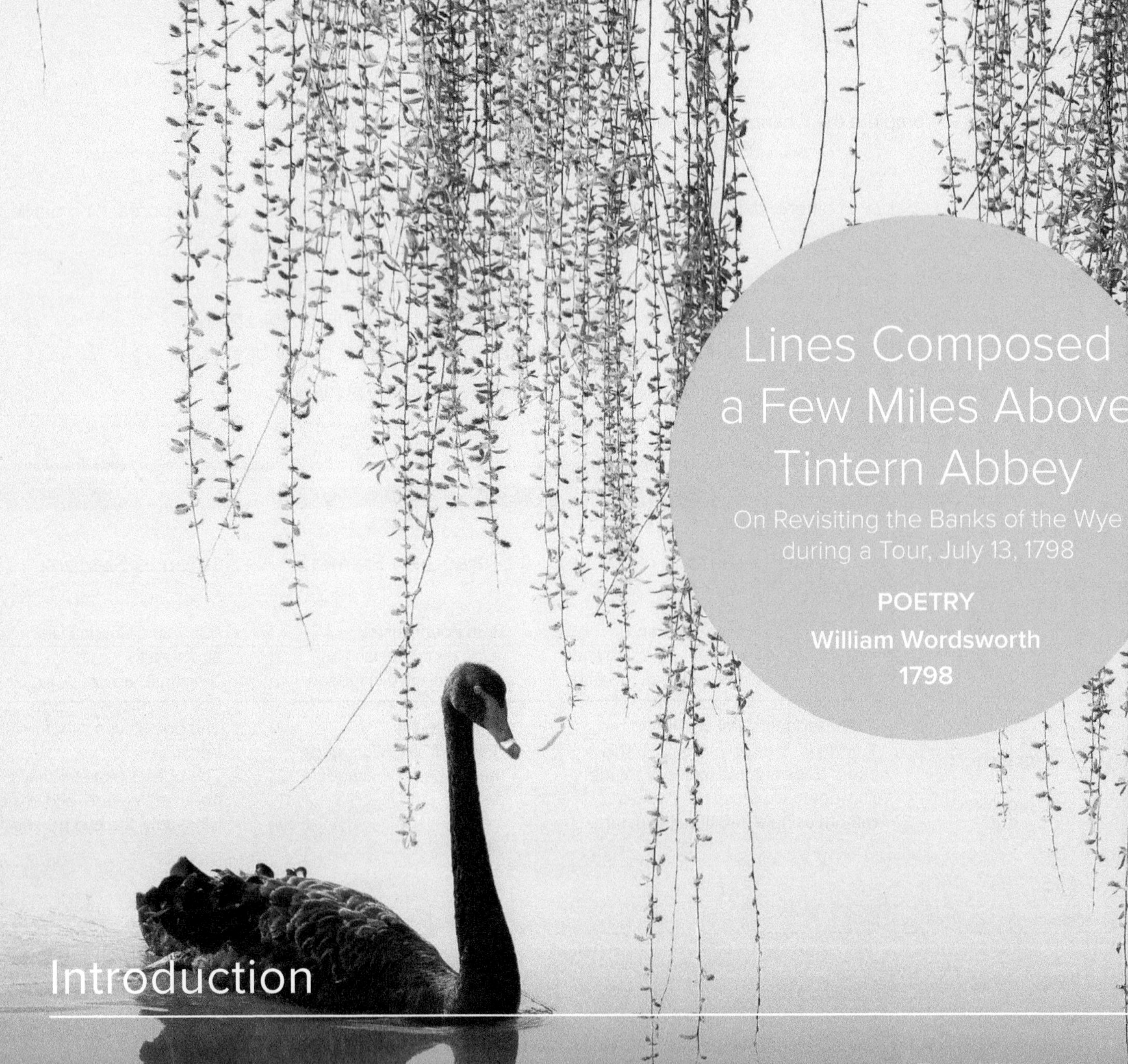

Lines Composed a Few Miles Above Tintern Abbey

On Revisiting the Banks of the Wye during a Tour, July 13, 1798

POETRY

William Wordsworth

1798

Introduction

William Wordsworth (1770–1850) gave "Lines Composed a Few Miles above Tintern Abbey, On Revisiting the Banks of the Wye during a Tour, July 13, 1798" one of literature's most specific titles, recalling his thoughts at a particular place that left a deep impression on him, by the Wye River near Wales. It was a place of peace in a life sometimes troubled by tragedy: the early death of both parents, the loss of two young children, and his separation from his beloved sister, to whom the poem is addressed. Meditating on the natural world around Tintern Abbey, Wordsworth also explores the way nature can soothe the soul in a world growing ever busier and less peaceful.

It's been five summers separated by five long winters since the speaker visited Tintern Abbey. In the opening stanza, he describes the beauty of the countryside bathed in summer. This scenery has sustained and restored him through long years in the city—memories returning to him more as feelings of calm and tranquility. When he first came to these woods, he explored them so fervently, it was as if he was running from something, rather than seeking something he loved. Now being older, he looks upon nature with a newfound maturity—gleaning a deeper, subtler meaning from his surroundings. In the final stanza, the speaker addresses his sister—the dear friend he's had a falling out with. He offers nature a prayer —since nature never betrays those who love her—asking the moon to shine upon his sister. If she suffers solitude or grief, he hopes that she remembers what pleasures nature brings.

Proficiency-leveled summaries and summaries in multiple languages are available digitally.

Audio and audio text highlighting are available with this text.

CONNECT TO ESSENTIAL QUESTION

What is the power of story?

This poem is among the most famous works by William Wordsworth. The speaker of the poem revisits an old childhood haunt, the beautiful landscape surrounding Tintern Abbey. Nature serves as a source of inspiration as the speaker reflects on his own personal story and philosophy of life.

Entry Point

As students prepare to read "Lines Composed A Few Miles Above Tintern Abbey," share the following information with them to provide context.

- ✓ William Wordsworth was a key figure in the Romantic movement in literature. Many now trace the beginning of the movement to his publication of *Lyrical Ballads* with fellow poet Samuel Taylor Coleridge in 1798.
- ✓ Wordsworth's decision to write poetry in the common language of the people drew harsh criticism from establishment critics. Though it's difficult to imagine from a contemporary perspective, he and other Romantic poets were considered radical poets at the time.
- ✓ Wordsworth's sister Dorothy, just one year younger than him and a poet herself, was a close lifelong confidant and partner whom Wordsworth addresses in this poem as "my dear, dear Friend."

Instructional Path

The print teacher's edition includes essential point-of-use instruction and planning tools. Complete lesson plans and program documents appear in your digital teacher account.

First Read: Lines Composed A Few Miles Above Tintern Abbey

Objectives: After an initial reading and discussion of the poem, students will be able to identify and describe images and ideas and explain how they relate to the themes of the poem.

Skill: Context Clues

Objectives: After rereading and discussing a model of close reading, students will be able to use context clues such as definition, examples, comparison and contrast to clarify the meaning of words.

Skill: Figurative Language

Objectives: After rereading and discussing a model of close reading, students will be able to analyze the speaker's use of figurative language—such as sensory metaphors, hyperbole, and paradoxes—and the impact that it has on the meaning and message in "Lines Composed a Few Miles Above Tintern Abbey."

Close Read: Lines Composed A Few Miles Above Tintern Abbey

Objectives: After engaging in a close reading and discussion of "Lines Composed a Few Miles Above Tintern Abbey," students will be able to write a short response that analyzes and evaluates the figurative language used by Wordsworth to heighten the emotional effect and convey the message of the poem.

Skill: Analyzing Romanticism

Objectives: After reading and discussing a model of close reading, students will be able to explain how a text from the unit reflects the literary period of Romanticism.

Progress Monitoring

Opportunities to Learn	Opportunities to Demonstrate Learning	Opportunities to Reteach
Context Clues		
Skill: Context Clues	Skill: Context Clues • Your Turn Close Read • Complete Vocabulary Chart • Skills Focus • Write	Unit 6 Skill: Context Clues – The Mysterious Anxiety of Them and Us Spotlight Skill: Context Clues
Figurative Language		
Skill: Figurative Language	Skill: Figurative Language • Your Turn Close Read • Complete Vocabulary Chart • Skills Focus • Write	Unit 4 Skill: Figurative Language – Why I Write Unit 5 Skill: Figurative Language – Shooting an Elephant Spotlight Skill: Figurative Language

First Read

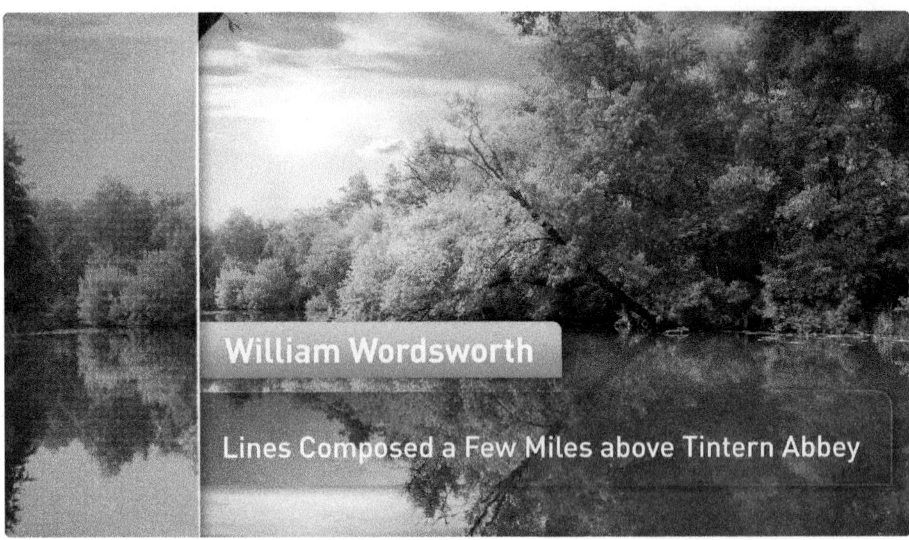

William Wordsworth
Lines Composed a Few Miles above Tintern Abbey

Introduce the Text

As a class, watch the video preview  and have students read the introduction in pairs to make connections to the video preview.

To activate prior knowledge and experiences, ask students:

- What other images could you imagine using in this video?
- Do you have a place, in nature or elsewhere, that is a place of peace or special significance for you? Why is this place meaningful to you?

ELL SPEAKING FRAMES

- I can imagine using an image of ___ in this video.
- I (do / do not) have a special place. It is meaningful because ___.

Access Complex Text

LEXILE: N/A WORD COUNT: 1,228

The following areas may be challenging for students, particularly 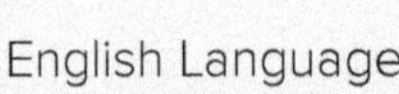 English Language Learners and A Approaching grade-level learners.

Purpose	Prior Knowledge
• Explain to students that Wordsworth was a literary pioneer who defied the conventions of his time and insisted that poetry should express deep feelings about common people and everyday experiences rather than be written by and for the wealthy nobility. • Have students discuss how the poem demonstrates Wordsworth's belief about the purpose of poetry.	• Tintern Abbey, founded in 1131, has inspired poets for centuries. This poem, however, focuses on the surrounding area. The full title of the poem is "Lines Composed a Few Miles Above Tintern Abbey, On Revisiting the Banks of the Wye during a Tour. July 13, 1798" • Have students work in groups to analyze the sensory details about the setting.

 SCAFFOLDS  ENGLISH LANGUAGE LEARNERS  APPROACHING GRADE LEVEL  BEYOND GRADE LEVEL

These icons identify differentiation strategies and scaffolded support for a variety of students. See the digital lesson plan for additional differentiation strategies and scaffolds.

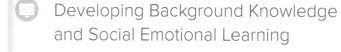

O sylvan Wye! thou wanderer thro' the woods, How often has my spirit turned to thee!

Five years have past; five summers, with the length
Of five long winters! and again I hear
These waters, rolling from their mountain-springs
With a soft inland murmur.—Once again
Do I behold these steep and lofty cliffs,
That on a wild secluded scene impress
Thoughts of more deep seclusion; and connect
The landscape with the quiet of the sky.
The day is come when I again **repose**
Here, under this dark sycamore, and view
These plots of cottage-ground, these orchard-tufts,
Which at this season, with their unripe fruits,
Are clad in one green hue, and lose themselves
'Mid groves and copses. Once again I see
These hedge-rows, hardly hedge-rows, little lines
Of sportive wood run wild: these pastoral farms,
Green to the very door; and wreaths of smoke
Sent up, in silence, from among the trees!
With some uncertain notice, as might seem
Of vagrant dwellers in the houseless woods,
Or of some Hermit's cave, where by his fire
The Hermit sits alone.

These beauteous forms,
Through a long absence, have not been to me
As is a landscape to a blind man's eye:
But oft, in lonely rooms, and 'mid the din
Of towns and cities, I have owed to them,
In hours of weariness, sensations sweet,

Artist David Cox the elder, Walter de Clare, 'Tintern Abbey,' circa 1840

NOTES

Skill: Figurative Language

The speaker repeats "length" and "long" to make a hyperbole about how difficult is has been to be away from this place.

"Soft inland murmur" is a sensory metaphor suggesting that the sounds of nature are calling to the speaker.

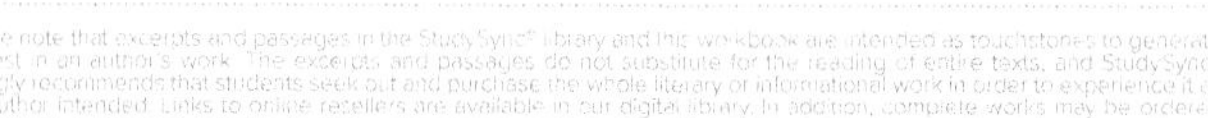

Developing Background Knowledge and Social Emotional Learning

Have your students conduct an image search of the setting of the poem.

1. Tell students to take a few minutes to brainstorm images related to the area surrounding Tintern Abbey and the River Wye.
2. In small groups, have students do a quick online search of images. Choose one or two to project and discuss as a class.

Discuss with students: Do you have a place that you associate with positive memories, feelings, or ideas? How did that place become important to you? Why do you think humans assign significance to places? What role do these places have in our memories and emotions?

Figurative Language

In the first annotation, what does the reader note?

The reader notes that the speaker uses hyperbole to express that his absence from nature has been challenging. The speaker also uses figurative language to express his feelings toward the natural landscape.

SELECTION VOCABULARY

repose / el reposo *noun* a state of tranquility or sleep COGNATE

Context Clues

How does the reader use context clues to first determining a word's part of speech?

The reader notices that *Burthen* is preceded by the article "the" and followed by the preposition "of," so it is probably a noun.

NOTES

Felt in the blood, and felt along the heart;
And passing even into my purer mind
With **tranquil** restoration:—feelings too
Of unremembered pleasure: such, perhaps,
As have no slight or trivial influence
On that best portion of a good man's life,
His little, nameless, unremembered, acts
Of kindness and of love. Nor less, I trust,
To them I may have owed another gift,
Of aspect more sublime; that blessed mood,
In which the burthen of the mystery,
In which the heavy and the weary weight
Of all this unintelligible world,
Is lightened:—that serene and blessed mood,
In which the affections gently lead us on,—
Until, the breath of this corporeal frame
And even the motion of our human blood
Almost suspended, we are laid asleep
In body, and become a living soul:
While with an eye made quiet by the power
Of harmony, and the deep power of joy,
We see into the life of things.

If this
Be but a vain belief, yet, oh! how oft—
In darkness and amid the many shapes
Of joyless daylight; when the fretful stir
Unprofitable, and the fever of the world,
Have hung upon the beatings of my heart—
How oft, in spirit, have I turned to thee,
O **sylvan**[1] Wye![2] thou wanderer thro' the woods,
How often has my spirit turned to thee!

And now, with gleams of half-extinguished thought,
With many recognitions dim and faint,
And somewhat of a sad perplexity,
The picture of the mind revives again:
While here I stand, not only with the sense
Of present pleasure, but with pleasing thoughts
That in this moment there is life and food
For future years. And so I dare to hope,
Though changed, no doubt, from what I was when first

Skill: Context Clues

Burthen is preceded by the article "the" and followed by the preposition "of," so it is probably a noun.

The repetition of "in which" suggests that "burthen of the mystery" is related to "the heavy and the weary weight."

1. **Sylvan** wooded
2. **Wye** the river along whose banks Wordsworth walked during his visit

Skills Focus

QUESTION 4: Essential Question

The speaker is reminiscing about his younger days. The joyous times are preserved because he cherishes them. The memories are powerful because he can rely on them, even in more challenging times.

TEXT TALK

What does the speaker consider the "best portion of a good man's life"?

See lines 34–36: The man's little, unremembered acts of kindness and love.

SELECTION VOCABULARY

tranquil / tranquilo / a ***adjective*** peaceful and quiet COGNATE

sylvan / silvano / a ***adjective*** related to woods or forests COGNATE

NOTES

I came among these hills; when like a roe
I bounded o'er the mountains, by the sides
Of the deep rivers, and the lonely streams,
Wherever nature led: more like a man
Flying from something that he dreads, than one
Who sought the thing he loved. For nature then
(The coarser pleasures of my boyish days
And their glad animal movements all gone by)
To me was all in all.—I cannot paint
What then I was. The sounding **cataract**[3]
Haunted me like a passion: the tall rock,
The mountain, and the deep and gloomy wood,
Their colours and their forms, were then to me
An appetite; a feeling and a love,
That had no need of a remoter charm,
By thought supplied, not any interest
Unborrowed from the eye.—That time is past,
And all its aching joys are now no more,
And all its dizzy raptures. Not for this
Faint[4] I, nor mourn nor murmur; other gifts
Have followed; for such loss, I would believe,
Abundant recompense. For I have learned
To look on nature, not as in the hour
Of thoughtless youth; but hearing oftentimes
The still sad music of humanity,
Nor harsh nor grating, though of ample power
To chasten and **subdue**.—And I have felt
A presence that disturbs me with the joy
Of elevated thoughts; a sense sublime
Of something far more deeply interfused,
Whose dwelling is the light of setting suns,
And the round ocean and the living air,
And the blue sky, and in the mind of man:
A motion and a spirit, that impels
All thinking things, all objects of all thought,
And rolls through all things. Therefore am I still
A lover of the meadows and the woods
And mountains; and of all that we behold
From this green earth; of all the mighty world
Of eye, and ear,—both what they half create,
And what perceive; well pleased to recognise
In nature and the language of the sense

Skill: Figurative Language

The speaker uses contradictory language, describing a positive feeling, "joy" as something "that disturbs." Wordsworth uses a paradox to illustrate the intense impact that nature has on him.

3. **cataract** waterfall
4. **Faint** to lose heart; to become depressed

Figurative Language

What does the reader note in the second annotation?

The reader notes that the poet uses a paradox to express the intensity of his emotions.

TEXT TALK

How has the speaker "learned / To look on nature" in adulthood?

See lines 90–104: He sees it "not as in the hour / Of thoughtless youth," but as a deep, sublime sense of connectedness.

SELECTION VOCABULARY

cataract / la catarata *noun* a waterfall COGNATE

subdue / dominar *verb* to force or coerce into loyalty or obedience

Skills Focus

QUESTION 3: Figurative Language

A metaphor is used to compare the mind to a mansion. Connecting abstract ideas, like mind and memory, to a physical place helps readers understand that good memories can live inside us as if in a large home that we can return to.

Prepare for Advanced Courses

Use the activity below to differentiate instruction for your B Beyond grade level learners.

Analyze for Enrichment

Reread the following lines, each of which begins a section of the text: Ask students:

line 1:
Five years have past; five summers, with the length

line 51:
If this

and line 114:
Nor perchance,

- What is the mood in each of the three sections of this poem, and how does the author's descriptive language develop that mood?
- What is the author's purpose in each section?
- In what ways does the mood support the purpose of each section?

The anchor of my purest thoughts, the nurse,
The guide, the guardian of my heart, and soul
Of all my moral being.

Nor perchance,
If I were not thus taught, should I the more
Suffer my genial spirits to decay:
For thou art with me here upon the banks
Of this fair river; thou my dearest Friend,
My dear, dear Friend; and in thy voice I catch
The language of my former heart, and read
My former pleasures in the shooting lights
Of thy wild eyes. Oh! yet a little while
May I behold in thee what I was once,
My dear, dear Sister! and this prayer I make,
Knowing that Nature never did betray,
The heart that loved her; 'tis her privilege,
Through all the years of this our life, to lead
From joy to joy: for she can so inform
The mind that is within us, so impress
With quietness and beauty, and so feed
With lofty thoughts, that neither evil tongues,
Rash judgments, nor the sneers of selfish men,
Nor greetings where no kindness is, nor all
The dreary intercourse of daily life,
Shall e'er prevail against us, or disturb
Our cheerful faith, that all which we behold
Is full of blessings. Therefore let the moon
Shine on thee in thy solitary walk;
And let the misty mountain-winds be free
To blow against thee: and, in after years,

When these wild ecstasies shall be matured
Into a sober pleasure; when thy mind
Shall be a mansion for all lovely forms,
Thy memory be as a dwelling-place
For all sweet sounds and harmonies; oh! Then,
If solitude, or fear, or pain, or grief,

Should be thy portion, with what healing thoughts
Of tender joy wilt thou remember me,
And these my exhortations! Nor, perchance—
If I should be where I no more can hear
Thy voice, nor catch from thy wild eyes these gleams
Of past existence—wilt thou then forget
That on the banks of this delightful stream
We stood together; and that I, so long

TEXT TALK

What does the speaker tell his sister to remember in the final stanza?

See lines 140–161: He wants her to remember sweet sounds and harmonies, to remember him and this poem, and to remember their visit to Tintern Abbey together.

How did discussing images of Tintern Abbey and the River Wye and discussing emotional associations to places deepen your understanding of the poem?

Answers will vary.

NOTES

A worshipper of Nature, hither came
Unwearied in that service: rather say
With warmer love—oh! with far deeper zeal
Of holier love. Nor wilt thou then forget,
That after many wanderings, many years
Of absence, these steep woods and lofty cliffs,
And this green pastoral landscape, were to me
More dear, both for themselves and for thy sake!

Reading Comprehension OPTIONAL

Have students complete the digital reading comprehension questions when they finish reading.

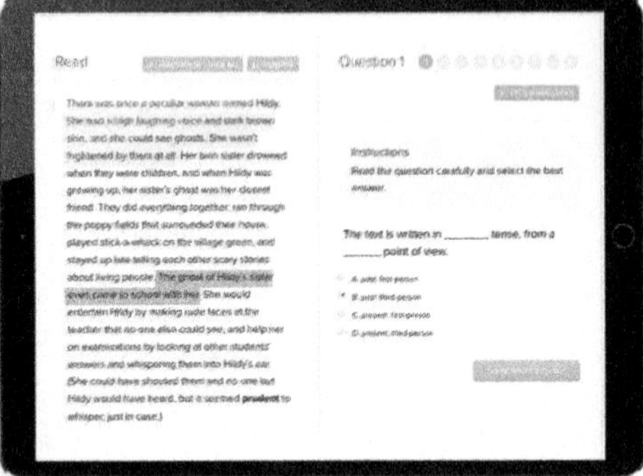

ANSWER KEY

QUESTION 1: D
QUESTION 2: A
QUESTION 3: C
QUESTION 4: B
QUESTION 5: A
QUESTION 6: D
QUESTION 7: A
QUESTION 8: B
QUESTION 9: *See first chart.*
QUESTION 10: *See second chart.*

Definition	Word
Related to woods or forests	sylvan
Serene and placid	tranquil
The state of being at rest	repose
A waterfall	cataract
To bring under mental or emotional control	subdue

First	Second	Third	Fourth
"Five years have past; five summers, with the length / Of five long winters!"	"Thou wanderer thro' the woods, / How often has my spirit turned to thee!"	"In nature and the language of the sense / The anchor of my purest thoughts"	"wilt thou then forget / That on the banks of this delightful stream / We stood together"

Connect and Extend OPTIONAL

CONNECT TO EXTENDED WRITING PROJECT

Students can use "Lines Composed a Few Miles Above Tintern Abbey" to inform their ideas about the value of nature when writing their informative essays.

BEYOND THE BOOK

Writing: A Special Place

This poem expresses the author's remembering the good and bad of a place that is special to him. Students will reflect on a place that is special to them.

Ask students to:

- Generate a list of places that hold a lot of memories to them.
- Choose one of the places and write three special memories of the place.
- Write a poem, dedicating a stanza to each memory, add a final stanza to reflect on the place as a whole.
  - > What senses are activated by the memory?
  - > Who is present?
  - > How do you feel about this memory?
- Set the writing to music or create a visual for the poem.
- Share with classmates.

To reflect, ask students:

- What memories created powerful poems?
- How are poems useful in documenting emotions?

First Read

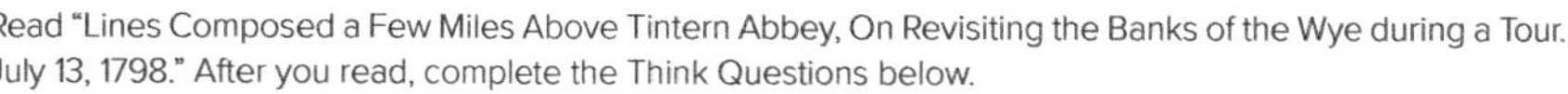

Read "Lines Composed a Few Miles Above Tintern Abbey, On Revisiting the Banks of the Wye during a Tour. July 13, 1798." After you read, complete the Think Questions below.

THINK QUESTIONS

1. What is the effect of the opening eight lines of the poem in light of the poem's title? In what way do these lines clarify the author's relationship to the countryside around Tintern Abbey? Explain using textual evidence to support your answer.
2. Based on the second stanza, did the speaker in the poem forget the countryside around Tintern Abbey when he was away from it? Explain, using textual evidence to support your answer.
3. In the third stanza, the author mentions "the fretful stir / Unprofitable, and the fever of the world." What is he referring to with these words? Cite any other relevant quotes or passages from the poem in your answer.
4. In describing the beauties of nature in the fourth stanza, the author mentions "deep rivers and lonely streams" as well as the "sounding cataract." Using context clues, define *cataract*. Write your definition here, and explain how you inferred it.
5. Use context clues to determine the definition of **subdue** as it is used in the poem. Write your definition of *subdue* here, and explain how you inferred it.

Think Questions

Circulate as students answer Think Questions independently. Scaffolds for these questions are shown on the opposite page.

QUESTION 1: Textual Evidence

The title says he is "Revisiting the Banks of the Wye," and the following lines confirm that since he says five years have past and now, "Once again / Do I behold these steep and lofty cliffs." It seems like he has a deep connection to the countryside around Tintern Abbey.

QUESTION 2: Textual Evidence

No, it seems like the opposite is the case. Despite a long absence, he has not forgotten the countryside around Tintern Abbey. He has thought of it "oft, in lonely rooms, and 'mid the din / Of towns and cities."

QUESTION 3: Textual Evidence

He refers to the sadness caused by disconnection from nature that goes with city life. He says in the third stanza "How oft, in spirit, have I turned to thee" which sounds like when he says how oft he "owed to them, / In hours of weariness, sensations sweet." He expresses how he turns to nature when city life has kept him disconnected.

QUESTION 4: Context Clues

In line 3 the author hears "These waters, rolling from their mountain-springs." The "sounding cataract" is also water he hears, like a fast river or waterfall. Since he mentions tall rocks and mountains, I infer that it is a waterfall.

QUESTION 5: Context Clues

Because it describes "still sad music," it must be somber or sorrowful, so I think "subdue" relates to that. The next line contrasts this feeling with "disturbs me with the joy / Of elevated thoughts." So "subdue" must mean to "dampen or restrain" his feelings.

SCAFFOLDS

Think Questions

Use the scaffolds below to differentiate instruction for your ELL English Language Learners and A Approaching grade-level learners.

ELL **BEGINNING** Write a response using the word bank and sentence frames.

INTERMEDIATE Write a response using the sentence frames.

ADVANCED, ADVANCED HIGH Write a response using the Text-Dependent Question Guide.

A **APPROACHING** Write a response using the Text-Dependent Question Guide.

BEGINNING	INTERMEDIATE	APPROACHING / ADVANCED, ADVANCED HIGH
Word Bank	**Sentence Frames**	**Text-Dependent Question Guide**
forgotten deep waterfall revisiting lonely five living memories dampen or restrain	The title says he is "____ the Banks of the Wye," and the speaker says ____ years have past. He has good ____ of the landscapes. It seems like he has a ____ connection to the countryside around Tintern Abbey.	1. • What information do the first eight lines convey? • What does the author say about the landscape? • How do his descriptions relate to the title?
	The speaker has not ____ these views of the landscape. He often thought of them when ____.	2. • What does the speaker say in the second stanza about his absence from the countryside around Tintern Abbey? • What feelings does he express toward it? • What textual evidence shows that he remembers the abbey?
	The "fever of the world" has to do with the sadness and loneliness of ____ in a city.	3. • Read the third stanza (lines 51–59), then reread lines 26–29. • How do these passages express similar ideas? • What is the author referring to in these passages?
	The rushing water of the **cataract** makes it sound to me like a ____.	4. • Read: "The sounding **cataract** / Haunted me like a passion: the tall rock, / The mountain, and the deep and gloomy wood, / Their colours and their forms, were then to me / An appetite;" • How does this relate to "again I hear / These waters, rolling from their mountain-springs / With a soft inland murmur" in lines 2–4? • What is a kind of rolling water that you can hear?
	He says the sadness of humanity can still **subdue** him. I think that means to ____.	5. • Read: "The still sad music of humanity, / Nor harsh nor grating, though of ample power / To chasten and **subdue**." • What effect might sad music have on somebody? • If it is neither "harsh nor grating," what other effect could that sad music have on a person's feelings?

CONTEXT CLUES
»skills

Skill: Context Clues

Use the Checklist to analyze Context Clues in "Lines Composed a Few Miles Above Tintern Abbey, On Revisiting the Banks of the Wye during a Tour. July 13, 1798." Refer to the sample student annotations about Context Clues in the text.

••• CHECKLIST FOR CONTEXT CLUES

In order to use context as a clue to the meaning of a word or phrase, note the following:

- ✓ clues about the word's part of speech
- ✓ clues in the surrounding text about the word's meaning
- ✓ words with similar denotations that seem to differ slightly in meaning
- ✓ signal words that cue a type of context clue, such as:
  - *comparably*, *related to*, or *similarly* to signal a comparison context clue
  - *on the other hand*, *however*, or *in contrast* to signal a contrast context clue
  - *by reason of*, *because*, or *as a result* to signal a cause-and-effect context clue

To determine the meaning of a word or phrase as they are used in a text, consider the following questions:

- ✓ What is the meaning of the overall sentence, paragraph, or text?
- ✓ How does the position of the word in the sentence help me define it?
- ✓ How does the word function in the sentence? What clues help identify the word's part of speech?
- ✓ What clues in the text suggest the word's definition?
- ✓ What do I think the word means?

To verify the preliminary determination of the meaning of the word or phrase based on context, consider the following questions:

- ✓ Does the definition I inferred make sense within the context of the sentence?
- ✓ Which of the dictionary's definitions makes sense within the context of the sentence?

V SKILL VOCABULARY

context clue / la clave del contexto *noun* a hint in the surrounding text that can help a reader infer the meaning of an unfamiliar word, phrase, or description

figurative language / el lenguaje figurativo *noun* expressions used for descriptive or rhetorical effect that are not literally true but that express some truth beyond the literal level COGNATE

Skill: Context Clues

Introduce the Skill

Watch the Concept Definition video ▶ and read the following definition with your students.

Context clues are hints in the text preceding or following an unfamiliar word, phrase, or description that help clarify its meaning. When trying to figure out the meaning of an unknown word or phrase, a reader might check the surrounding text for one of these specific types of context clues: definition, example, comparison, contrast, and cause and effect. A reader can also analyze the general context to draw conclusions about **nuanced,** or more subtle, meanings, such as the ones expressed through **imagery** (sensory descriptions that help readers visualize the text) and **figurative language** (expressions used for descriptive or rhetorical effect that are not literally true but that express some truth beyond the literal level).

TURN AND TALK

1. How do you approach unfamiliar words or phrases in a text?
2. How could you use context clues to determine the meaning of the word?

SPEAKING FRAMES

- When I come across an unfamiliar word or phrase in a text I ____.
- Context clues can help me ____.

Your Turn

Ask students to complete the Your Turn Activity.

QUESTION 1

A. Incorrect. *Former* is not an adverb, and does not modify the verbs *catch* and *read*.

B. Incorrect. *Former* is used to describe a noun, so it is an adjective.

C. Correct. *Former* is an adjective used to describe Wordsworth's past heart, and the past pleasures he received from the Wye River.

D. Incorrect. While *former* is used as an adjective, it is used to describe *heart* and *pleasure*, not *wild eyes*.

QUESTION 2

Part A

A. Incorrect. While the poet's relationship to the Wye River may have changed, context clues suggest that the place remains intact.

B. Incorrect. Based on context clues, *former* is used to describe Wordsworth's "heart" and the "pleasures" he experienced.

C. Correct. *Former* is used to describe the poet's previous thoughts and feelings about a place that held a significant role for him.

D. Incorrect. Based on context clues, *former* is not used to describe a frame or core, rather to describe Wordsworth's "heart" and "pleasures."

Part B

A. Incorrect. This line shows that the poet is talking about and to his "dearest Friend," but it does not help the reader understand the meaning of *former*.

B. Incorrect. This line does not help the reader understand the meaning of *former*.

C. Incorrect. This line tells what Wordsworth's sister's eyes are like, but there are no words that help the reader understand the meaning of *former*.

D. Correct. The speaker sees in his sister's eyes "what I was once," which helps the reader understand that *former* means something in the past.

Lines Composed a Few Miles above Tintern Abbey

Skill: Context Clues

Reread lines 115–138 of "Lines Composed a Few Miles Above Tintern Abbey, On Revisiting the Banks of the Wye during a Tour. July 13, 1798." Then, using the Checklist on the previous page, answer the multiple-choice questions below.

YOUR TURN

1. What clues could you use to accurately determine the part of speech of the word *former*?

   - A. *Former* is used twice to modify the verbs that the speaker uses such as catch and read. It must be an adverb.
   - B. *Former* is used twice following the pronoun my, suggesting that the speaker possesses it. It must be a noun.
   - C. *Former* is used twice, once to describe heart and once to describe pleasure. It must be an adjective.
   - D. *Former* is used twice following the pronoun my and to describe wild eyes. It must be an adjective.

2. This question has two parts. First, answer Part A. Then, answer Part B.

   Part A: Based on context clues in the poem, what is most likely the meaning of the word *former*?

   - A. Something that is now destroyed or has changed form
   - B. A person that forms, or makes, something
   - C. Something that in the past used to have a particular role
   - D. A frame or core around which an electrical coil can be wound

   Part B: Which line from the poem BEST supports the answer to Part A?

   - A. "Of this fair river; thou my dearest Friend,"
   - B. "My dear, dear Friend; and in thy voice I catch"
   - C. "Of thy wild eyes. Oh! yet a little while"
   - D. "May I behold in thee what I was once,"

SKILL VOCABULARY

nuanced / con matices *adjective* having subtle shades of meaning

imagery / la imaginería *noun* descriptive or figurative language in a work of literature used to appeal to the reader's senses COGNATE

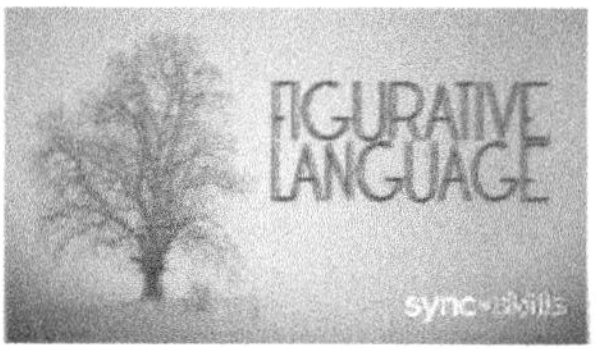

Skill:
Figurative Language

Use the Checklist to analyze Figurative Language in "Lines Composed a Few Miles Above Tintern Abbey, On Revisiting the Banks of the Wye during a Tour. July 13, 1798." Refer to the sample student annotations about Figurative Language in the text.

••• CHECKLIST FOR FIGURATIVE LANGUAGE

In order to determine the meaning of a figure of speech in context, note the following:

✓ words that mean one thing literally and suggest something else
✓ similes, metaphors, or personification
✓ figures of speech, including
  • paradoxes, or a seemingly contradictory statement that when further investigated or explained proves to be true, such as:
    > a character described as "a wise fool"
    > a character stating "I must be cruel to be kind"
  • hyperbole, or exaggerated statements not meant to be taken literally, such as:
    > a child saying " I'll be doing this homework until I'm 100!"
    > a claim such as, "I'm so hungry I could eat a horse!"
  • sensory metaphors, or comparisons that emphasize the senses such as:
    > A character being compared to a light "When she walked in, she lit up the entire room."
    > A place described using language related to taste "The visit to the restaurant was bittersweet."

In order to interpret a figure of speech in context and analyze its role in the text, consider the following questions:

✓ Where is there a figure of speech or figurative language in the text and what seems to be the purpose of it?
✓ What impact does exaggeration or hyperbole have on your understanding of the text?
✓ How does the figurative language develop the message or theme?

SKILL VOCABULARY

figurative language / el lenguaje figurativo *noun* expressions used for descriptive or rhetorical effect that are not literally true but that express some truth beyond the literal level COGNATE

simile / el símil *noun* a figure of speech that uses the words like or as to compare two seemingly unlike things COGNATE

metaphor / la metáfora *noun* a figure of speech that compares two seemingly unlike things but implies a comparison instead of stating it directly with the words like or as COGNATE

Skill: Figurative Language

Introduce the Skill

Watch the Concept Definition video and read the following definition with your students.

Figurative language is language used for descriptive effect, often to illustrate or imply ideas indirectly. Types of figurative language include simile, metaphor, and personification. A **simile** uses the words *like* or *as* to compare two seemingly unlike things. A **metaphor** directly compares two seemingly unlike things without using *like* or *as*. **Personification** is a **figure of speech** in which an animal, object, force of nature, or an idea is given human qualities.

When reading prose, and especially poetry, readers use **context**—including when and where a text was written, for example—to analyze the impact of word choice and to help determine or interpret the meaning of figurative words and phrases.

TURN AND TALK

1. Have you ever had to describe a difficult, humorous, or mind-boggling story to a friend, but the literal details didn't do the story justice? What kind of words or expressions did you use?
2. How does figurative language help an author or poet convey ideas in a more powerful manner? Explain.

SPEAKING FRAMES

- Literal details [did / did not] do my story justice because ____.
- The [words / expressions] I used to tell my story were ____.
- Figurative language can help an author or poet by ____.

Your Turn

Ask students to complete the Your Turn Activity.

QUESTION 1

A. Incorrect. The author's words do not suggest that the speaker, in his youth, liked to observe animal movements and behavior in nature.

B. Correct. The speaker uses animal-focused figurative language to show that when he was a boy, he felt, as does an animal, that nature was a place of instinct and spontaneity rather than a place for spiritual reflection. The speaker sees it as the latter now.

C. Incorrect. The author's words do not express a negative tone about the sometimes immature and superficial behaviors of boyhood.

D. Incorrect. The author's words do not convey that the speaker regrets losing the adeptness and ability to live comfortably in nature that he had earlier in his life.

QUESTION 2

A. Incorrect. The word choice does not suggest that the more mature speaker still holds the views that he held as a boy.

B. Incorrect. The word choice does not emphasize that nature and humanity are cruel and disagreeable.

C. Incorrect. The word choice does not convey the negative viewpoint that harmony between nature and humanity is impossible.

D. Correct. The word choice conveys that the speaker can now see a connection between nature and one's spiritual life that results in a deeper appreciation of nature—one which is different from his relationship with nature during his "thoughtless youth."

Skill: Figurative Language

Reread lines 64–95 of "Lines Composed a Few Miles Above Tintern Abbey, On Revisiting the Banks of the Wye during a Tour. July 13, 1798." Then, using the Checklist on the previous page, answer the multiple-choice questions below.

YOUR TURN

1. The author uses references to animals in phrases such as "like a roe," "bounded o'er the mountains," and "glad animal movements" to—

   - ○ A. suggest that the speaker used to enjoy watching the movements of the animals in their natural environment, and that he continues to enjoy it during this second visit.
   - ○ B. convey that in his youth, the speaker experienced nature in the way an animal lives in the natural world, with feeling and instinct rather than intellectual thought.
   - ○ C. express a negative tone about the behaviors of boyhood, which can be immature and superficial compared to the way the speaker is now approaching nature.
   - ○ D. help readers understand that the speaker, now more mature, wishes he still had the ability to live comfortably in nature, as animals do.

2. The speaker says that he now has "other gifts." His use of the phrases "hearing oftentimes / The still sad music of humanity, / Nor harsh nor grating . . ." is an effective description of one of these gifts because it—

   - ○ A. suggests in a positive way that although the speaker has matured, he still has the views of nature he held as a youth.
   - ○ B. emphasizes the viewpoint that humanity, like nature, is at times cruel and disagreeable but yet should be viewed as a gift.
   - ○ C. conveys that the speaker believes that a sense of harmony between nature and humanity is impossible.
   - ○ D. shows that the speaker has gained a deeper appreciation of nature, one in which he recognizes a connection between nature and one's spiritual life.

SKILL VOCABULARY

personification / la personificación ***noun*** a figure of speech in which an animal, object, force of nature, or an idea is given human form or qualities COGNATE

figure of speech / la figura literaria ***noun*** a word or phrase not meant to be taken literally, but rather used for effect

context / el contexto ***noun*** the set of facts or circumstances that surround a situation or event COGNATE

Lines Composed a Few Miles above Tintern Abbey

3. Identify the paradox from the statements below.
   - A. "And all its aching joys are now no more,"
   - B. "Wherever nature led: more like a man"
   - C. "Have followed; for such loss, I would believe"
   - D. "An appetite; a feeling and a love"

Your Turn

Ask students to complete the Your Turn Activity.

QUESTION 3

A. Correct. This statement appears to be contradictory, but is accurate given the content and context of Wordsworth's ideas conveyed in the poem.

B. Incorrect. The statement is a metaphor, not a paradox.

C. Incorrect. This statement is not a paradox.

D. Incorrect. Rather, this statement affirms the paradox in Answer A.

SkillsTV

Project the SkillsTV episode and pause at the following times to prompt discussion:

1:01 What descriptive details do the students first notice in the poem? What mood does this descriptive language suggest?

2:01 How do the students use context clues to make connections between Wordsworth's use of figurative language and the speaker's attitude toward nature?

3:06 How does Wordsworth set up a contrast using figurative language?

Close Read

Skills Focus

QUESTION 1: Context Clues

See Lines 17–22: This gives a sense of isolation and solitude, but not loneliness. Hermits choose to be alone, and are often treated as wise, so the imagery of hermits creates a tone of admiration rather than pity.

QUESTION 2: Figurative Language

See Lines 11–14: I'm visualizing how the green of the farm and orchard blend with the colors of the woods. The elements of nature blend together. These visual details help me understand the feeling the speaker has of becoming one with nature.

QUESTION 3: Figurative Language See Lines 141–147.

QUESTION 4: Essential Question See Lines 61–73.

CHECK FOR SUCCESS

If students struggle to respond to Skills Focus Question #1, ask:

1. What does the poet describe in lines 17–22?
2. What do you visualize from the description and sensory details?
3. How is this related to the idea of being connected to nature?

Close Read

Reread "Lines Composed a Few Miles Above Tintern Abbey, On Revisiting the Banks of the Wye during a Tour. July 13, 1798." As you reread, complete the Skills Focus questions below. Then use your answers and annotations from the questions to help you complete the Write activity.

SKILLS FOCUS

1. Find an example of imagery that reflects the thoughts and feelings of the speaker. Use context clues to determine the nuanced meaning of the image.
2. Choose a passage that helps you visualize the landscape. Explain how the descriptions and sensory metaphors deepen your understanding of the message of the poem.
3. Locate an example of figurative language, such as hyperbole, paradox, metaphor, or simile in the poem. Explain how it contributes to the overall meaning of the poem.
4. Throughout the poem, the speaker experiences nature while also remembering his youth. What effect do the memories of younger days have on the poem? What is the power of this story over the speaker's current experience?

WRITE

LITERARY ANALYSIS: The essence of Romantic poetry is the precise choice of language that invokes the emotional response of the individual in relation to nature. Wordsworth revolutionized the literary form by exploiting the power of words to reveal the emotional depth of everyday experiences. Write an essay in which you analyze and evaluate Wordsworth's use of figurative language to contribute to the poem's message and emotional effect. Use context clues to analyze language and ideas that might be challenging.

Writer's Notebook

Connect to Literary Period: Give students time to reflect on how "Lines Composed a Few Miles Above Tintern Abbey" demonstrates the conventions and characteristics of this unit's literary period, Romanticism, by freewriting in their Writer's Notebooks.

Beginning & Intermediate

Remind students of the unit's literary period, Romanticism. Encourage students to draw their connections or allow students to write in their native language. Circulate around the room, prompting students for their thoughts as they respond orally or through pantomime.

Advanced & Advanced High

Allow students to share their connections orally in pairs or small groups before freewriting.

Collaborative Conversation

SCAFFOLDS

Break students into collaborative conversation groups to discuss the Close Read prompt. Ask students to use the StudySyncTV episode as a model for their discussion. Remind them to reference their Skills Focus annotations in their discussion.

The essence of Romantic poetry is the precise choice of language that invokes the emotional response of the individual in relation to nature. Wordsworth revolutionized the literary form by exploiting the power of words to reveal the emotional depth of everyday experiences. Write an essay in which you analyze and evaluate Wordsworth's use of figurative language to contribute to the poem's message and emotional effect. Use context clues to analyze language and ideas that might be challenging.

Use the scaffolds below to differentiate instruction for your ELL English Language Learners and A Approaching grade-level learners.

ELL **BEGINNING, INTERMEDIATE** Use the discussion guide and speaking frames to facilitate the discussion with support from the teacher.

ADVANCED, ADVANCED HIGH Use the discussion guide and speaking frames to facilitate the discussion in mixed-level groups.

A **APPROACHING** Use the discussion guide to facilitate the discussion in mixed-level groups.

APPROACHING
ADVANCED, ADVANCED HIGH
BEGINNING, INTERMEDIATE

Discussion Guide	Speaking Frames
1. What is the message and emotional effect of the poem?	• The message of "Lines Composed a Few Miles Above Tintern Abbey" is ____. • William Wordsworth wants the reader to feel ____.
2. How does Wordsworth use figurative language to communicate the message and emotional effect of the poem?	• The language he uses is ____. • An example of this is when he says "____."
3. How does Wordsworth use imagery to communicate the message and emotional effect of the poem?	• He uses imagery related to ____. • An example of this is in lines ____, where he says "____."

Text to World

Use the activity below to differentiate instruction for your B Beyond grade level readers.

Reread lines 9–11. Remind students that Wordsworth is returning to a natural place that has, in important ways, remained the same as it was on his previous visit five years prior. Have students conduct informal research on how the natural landscape in their communities, in their state, and in our country is changing. Ask students:

- What are the locations in your community, state, and country where one could go to "repose" in nature?
- How have those areas changed over the past 5–10 years?
- How do you predict these locations will change in the next 5–10 years?

Review Prompt and Rubric

Before students begin writing, review the writing prompt and rubric with the class.

LITERARY ANALYSIS: The essence of Romantic poetry is the precise choice of language that invokes the emotional response of the individual in relation to nature. Wordsworth revolutionized the literary form by exploiting the power of words to reveal the emotional depth of everyday experiences. Write an essay in which you analyze and evaluate Wordsworth's use of figurative language to contribute to the poem's message and emotional effect. Use context clues to analyze language and ideas that might be challenging.

PROMPT GUIDE

- What is interesting about Wordsworth's use of language in this poem?
- Why do you think he made these decisions?
- What ideas is he expressing with his word choice and figurative language?

An additional rubric item for Language and Conventions appears in your digital teacher and student accounts.

Score	Context Clues	Figurative Language
4	The writer provides an exemplary analysis of the language and ideas in Wordsworth's poem using context clues consistently in the response.	The writer clearly analyzes and explains how Wordsworth's use of figurative language contributes to the poem's message and emotional effect. The writer provides exemplary analysis, using relevant textual evidence.
3	The writer provides a sufficient analysis of the language and ideas in Wordsworth's poem using context clues occasionally in the response.	The writer analyzes and explains how Wordsworth's use of figurative language contributes to the poem's message and emotional effect. The writer provides sufficient analysis, using relevant textual evidence most of the time.
2	The writer begins to analyze the language and ideas in Wordsworth's poem, but has limited use of context clues in the response.	The writer begins to analyze or explain how Wordsworth's use of figurative language contributes to the poem's message and emotional effect, but the analysis is incomplete. The writer uses relevant textual evidence only some of the time.
1	The writer attempts to analyze the language and ideas in Wordsworth's poem, but the analysis is not successful. The writer uses little or no context clues in the response.	The writer attempts to analyze or explain how Wordsworth's use of figurative language contributes to the poem's message and emotional effect, but the analysis is not successful. The writer uses little or no relevant textual evidence.
0	The writer does not provide a relevant response to the prompt or does not provide a response at all.	The writer does not provide a relevant response to the prompt or does not provide a response at all.

Write

SCAFFOLDS

Ask students to complete the writing assignment using text evidence to support their answers.

Use the scaffolds below to differentiate instruction for your ELL English Language Learners and A Approaching grade-level learners.

ELL **BEGINNING** With the help of the word bank, write a response using paragraph frame 1.

INTERMEDIATE With the help of the word bank, write a response using paragraph frames 1 and 2.

ADVANCED, ADVANCED HIGH Write a response of differentiated length using the sentence starters.

A **APPROACHING** Write a response of differentiated length using the sentence starters.

BEGINNING / INTERMEDIATE / ADVANCED, ADVANCED HIGH / APPROACHING

Word Bank	Paragraph Frame 1	Paragraph Frame 2	Sentence Starters
nature imagery simpler nostalgia time	In "Lines Composed a Few Miles Above Tintern Abbey," William Wordsworth expresses feelings of ____ and love for ____ using figurative language and imagery. One example of this is in the first four lines. He describes how much ____ has passed and uses nature ____. This makes the reader think of ____ times in the past.	Another example can be found in the way he describes the ____ in ____. He uses ____ words and imagery: "____." The language and imagery here is raw and powerful and has ____. It is evident that the natural world ____. His message about ____ has ____ on the reader.	• Wordsworth expresses feelings of . . . • An example of this is . . . • The figurative language in ____ makes the reader think of . . . • Imagery such as ____ helps the poem to . . .

Peer Review

Rate

Respond to the following with a point rating that reflects your opinion.

	1	2	3	4
Ideas				
Evidence				
Language and Conventions				

Submit

Students should submit substantive feedback to two peers using the review instructions below.

- How well does this response answer the prompt?
- How well does the writer analyze Wordsworth's language and ideas using context clues?
- How well does the writer interpret the poet's use of figurative language?
- Which sentence in the writer's response changed your thinking about the poem?
- What does the writer do well in this response? What does the writer need to work on?

ELL A **SENTENCE FRAMES**

- You (completely/partly/almost) ____ answered the prompt because ____.
- You could answer the prompt more completely by ____.
- You (completely / partly / almost) ____ analyzed Wordsworth's language using context clues when ____ .
- I think your interpretation of Wordsworth's figurative language is ____.
- The sentence about ____ really made me think of the poem as ____.
- One idea you expressed well is ____.
- One idea that needs clarification is ____.

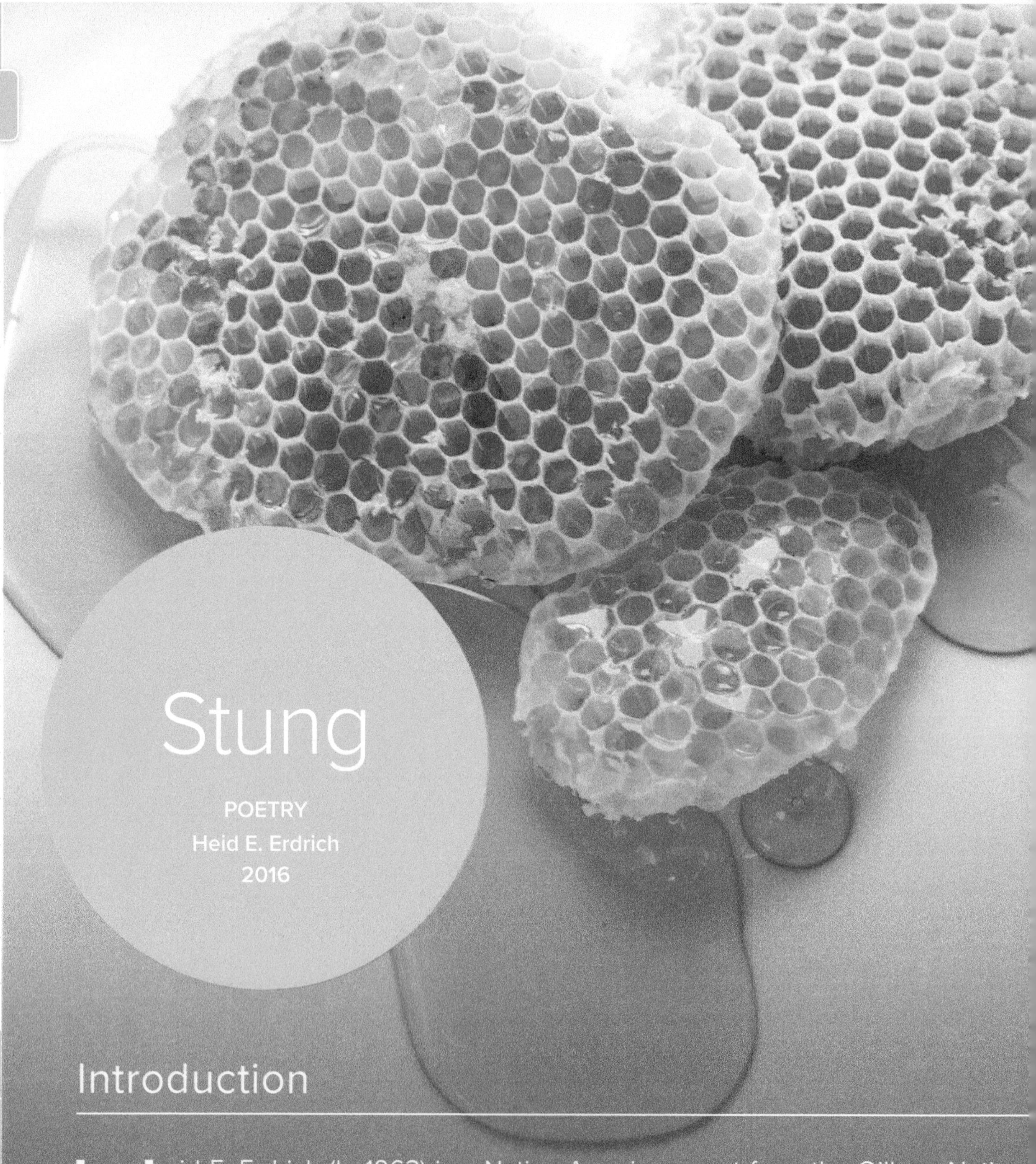

Stung

POETRY

Heid E. Erdrich

2016

Introduction

Heid E. Erdrich (b. 1963) is a Native American poet from the Ojibwe Nation. Aside from penning five full-length collections of poetry, Erdrich teaches for the MFA program at Augsburg College. In "Stung," Erdrich's speaker details an unexpected encounter with a bee.

The speaker laments over the bee that just stung her finger. Picking a flower, the speaker had surprised the sleeping bee, and there was no warning for either of them. The bee clutched the speaker's finger for just a moment before she was flung to the ground. The gold of her stripes is a true yellow, not just a trick of the evening light, which makes the speaker's white roses look gold. As the speaker sees the bee twitching on the ground, she mourns the bee's short life. It was cold outside and the bee was probably just trying to survive—unaware that the speaker, in an act of love, picks a rose every evening.

 Proficiency-leveled summaries and summaries in multiple languages are available digitally.

 Audio and audio text highlighting are available with this text.

CONNECT TO ESSENTIAL QUESTION

What is the power of story?

Native American poet Heid E. Erdrich tells a story about a common occurrence: getting stung by a bee. This poem demonstrates how an everyday experience can reveal the unintended harm humans can cause in the natural world.

Entry Point

As students prepare to read "Stung," share the following information with them to provide context.

- ✓ Heid E. Erdrich is a member of the Ojibwe Nation, one of the largest indigenous ethnic groups north of the Rio Grande. They are also known as the Chippewa. Erdrich grew up in Wahpeton, North Dakota, as one of seven siblings. Her sister, Louise Erdrich, is also a well-known author. Both draw upon Native American traditions in their writing.
- ✓ In addition to writing poetry, Heid Erdrich writes short stories and nonfiction. She also promotes the work of other Native American writers as an editor and writing teacher.

Instructional Path

The print teacher's edition includes essential point-of-use instruction and planning tools. Complete lesson plans and program documents appear in your digital teacher account.

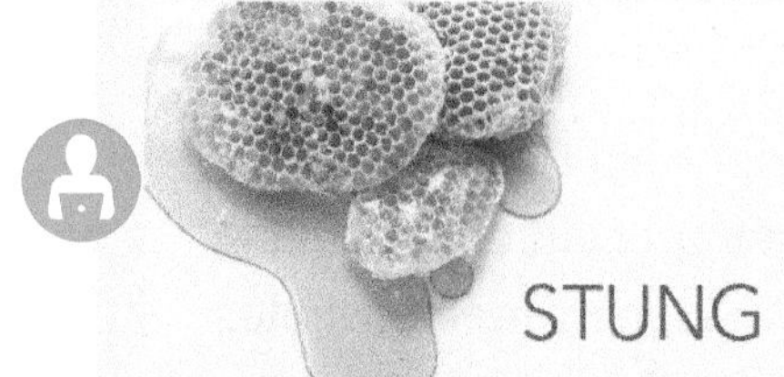

Independent Read: Stung

Objectives: After reading "Stung," students will write a short poem that uses well-chosen details to describe an encounter with an animal.

Independent Read

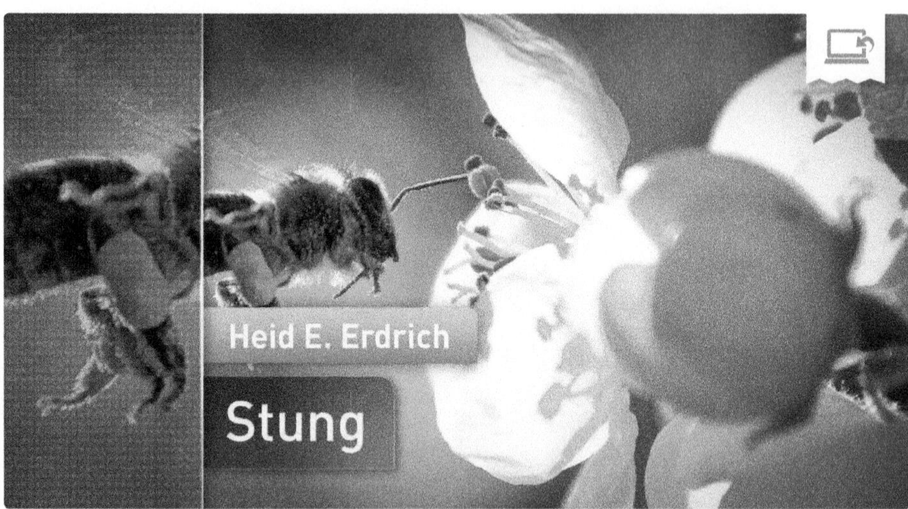

Introduce the Text

As a class, watch the video preview and have students read the introduction in pairs to make connections to the video preview.

- What key words or images from the video do you think will be most important to the poem you are about to read?
- When have you had a memorable encounter with an animal?

ELL SPEAKING FRAMES

- A key word or image that seemed important is ____.
- I encountered a/an ____. It was memorable because ____.

Access Complex Text

LEXILE: N/A **WORD COUNT:** 120

The following areas may be challenging for students, particularly ELL English Language Learners and A Approaching grade-level learners.

Genre	Connection of Ideas
• The poem is written in free verse and thus does not rhyme or follow a steady meter. Students may struggle to understand this poetic form. • Remind students to read the poem as if it were a paragraph. Guide them to connect ideas across line breaks instead of stopping at the end of each line.	• The poet uses simple language to describe a common occurrence: getting stung by a bee. Students may wonder why the author chose to commemorate such an event in a poem. • Remind students that poets choose their language carefully to develop mood and theme. Guide students to identify concrete details that reveal the speaker's attitude toward the bee.

In the cold, she hardly had her wits to buzz.

She couldn't help but sting my finger,
clinging a moment before I flung her
to the ground. Her gold is true, not the trick
evening light plays on my roses.
She curls into herself, stinger twitching,
gilt wings folded. Her whole life just a few weeks,
and my pain **subsided** in a moment.
In the cold, she hardly had her wits to buzz.
No warning from either of us:
she sleeping in the richness of those petals,
then the hand, my hand, cupping the bloom
in devastating force, crushing the petals for the scent.
And she **mortally** threatened, wholly unaware
that I do this daily, alone with the gold last light,
in what seems to me an act of love.

WRITE

POETRY: Write a poem about your own encounter with a bee or another animal. Include details that make clear the kind of encounter it was: frightening, awe-inspiring, or comical, for example. You can model your poem after Erdrich's, writing 15 lines of free verse. And like her, you can include lines from the perspective of the animal. After your first draft, evaluate your details to make sure they are well-chosen, and replace words that are too general.

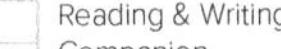

SELECTION VOCABULARY

gilt / bañado/a en oro *adjective* covered with gold

subside / disminuir *verb* to wear off or go away

mortally / mortalmente *adverb* to an extreme or severe degree COGNATE

Developing Background Knowledge and Cultural Awareness

1. In small groups, have students do a five-minute online search of keywords related to bees, bee stings, and bee life spans.
2. On the board, collate the various types of information students learned. Ask one student to volunteer to create an instant summary.

Discuss with students: All over the world, humans and cultures value animals in different ways. While some cultures assign animals spiritual and religious value, others simply show respect for wildlife, and still others show little regard for the natural world. Why do you think humans and cultures treat the animal world so differently? How would someone's cultural background change the way they react when they accidentally damage nature?

TEXT TALK

What happens to the speaker at the beginning of the poem?

See line 1: She gets stung by a bee.

What does the speaker do that causes this to happen?

See lines 10 and 11: The bee was inside a flower when the speaker squeezed that flower in her hand.

How did researching bees and thinking about the different cultural views of the animal world deepen your understanding of the poem?

Answers will vary.

Writer's Notebook

Connect to Essential Question: Give students time to reflect on how "Stung" connects to the unit's essential question, "What is the power of story?" by freewriting in their Writer's Notebooks.

Reading Comprehension OPTIONAL

Have students complete the digital reading comprehension questions ✓ when they finish reading.

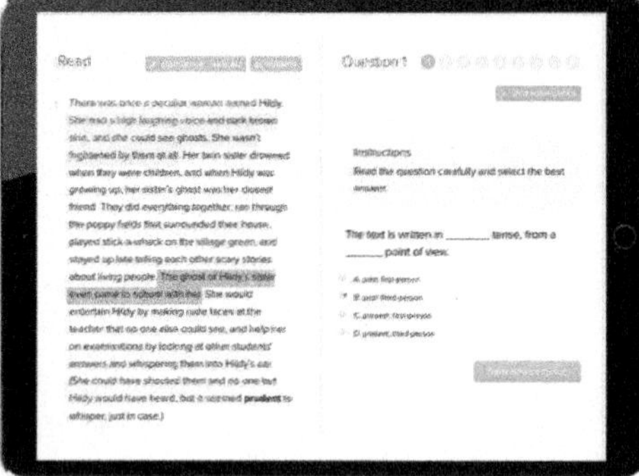

ANSWER KEY

QUESTION 1: D
QUESTION 2: D
QUESTION 3: B
QUESTION 4: A

QUESTION 5:
See chart below.

First	Second	Third	Fourth
The bee sleeps inside of the flower.	The speaker cups the flower in their hand.	The bee stings the speaker.	The bee dies.

Connect and Extend OPTIONAL

CONNECT TO EXTENDED WRITING PROJECT

Students can find inspiration from Heid Erdrich for their informative essay. Have them work to describe the natural world and detail its value.

BEYOND THE BOOK

Performance: Pantomimed Encounters

Heid Erdrich does a good job of showing what it feels like when a person interacts with a frightened bee. Challenge students to act out, alone or in pairs, the encounter with an animal they wrote about. The audience can guess what animal is being portrayed, how the person feels, and where the scene takes place.

Ask these questions to get students to reflect:

- Did the performer(s) convincingly portray the person and the animal?
- Did the encounter seem realistic?
- How was the pantomime similar to and different from the poem?

Collaborative Conversation

SCAFFOLDS

Post the writing prompt to generate a discussion in small groups. Ask students to first break down the prompt before they discuss relevant ideas and textual evidence.

Write a poem about your own encounter with a bee or another animal. Include details that make clear the kind of encounter it was—frightening, awe-inspiring, or comical, for example. You can model your poem after Erdrich's, writing 15 lines of free verse. And like her, you can include lines from the perspective of the animal. After your first draft, evaluate your details to make sure they are well-chosen, and replace words that are too general.

Use the scaffolds below to differentiate instruction for your ELL English Language Learners and A Approaching grade-level learners.

ELL **BEGINNING, INTERMEDIATE** Use the discussion guide and speaking frames to facilitate the discussion with support from the teacher.

ADVANCED, ADVANCED HIGH Use the discussion guide and speaking frames to facilitate the discussion in mixed-level groups.

A **APPROACHING** Use the discussion guide to facilitate the discussion in mixed-level groups.

APPROACHING
ADVANCED, ADVANCED HIGH
BEGINNING, INTERMEDIATE

Discussion Guide	Speaking Frames
1. What animal did you encounter? What happened?	• I encountered a / an ____. • I encountered this animal when I ____.
2. What kind of encounter was it? Why?	• The encounter was ____. • The experience made me feel ____ because ____.
3. What precise details can you include to describe the encounter?	• A detail I can use is ____. • This detail will help readers understand ____.

Text to World

Use the activity below to differentiate instruction for your B Beyond grade level learners.

Reread lines 13 and 15:

And she mortally threatened

and

in what seems to me an act of love.

Have students conduct informal research about issues that arise when humans and wildlife share habitats, focusing on the impact human behavior has on wildlife.

Ask students:

- What type of wildlife are commonly found in areas where humans reside?
- In what ways are wildlife "mortally threatened" by well-intentioned human behavior?

Review Prompt and Rubric

Before students begin writing, review the writing prompt and rubric with the class.

POETRY: Write a poem about your own encounter with a bee or another animal. Include details that make clear the kind of encounter it was—frightening, awe-inspiring, or comical, for example. You can model your poem after Erdrich's, writing 15 lines of free verse. And like her, you can include lines from the perspective of the animal. After your first draft, evaluate your details to make sure they are well-chosen, and replace words that are too general.

PROMPT GUIDE

- What animal did you encounter? What happened?
- What kind of encounter was it? Why?
- What precise details can you include to describe the encounter?

Score	Poetry	Language and Conventions
4	The writer composes a strong poem that effectively engages the reader and uses well-chosen details to describe an encounter with an animal.	The writer demonstrates a consistent command of grammar, punctuation, and usage conventions. Although minor errors may be evident, they do not detract from the fluency or the clarity of the essay.
3	The writer composes a poem that engages the reader and uses mostly well-chosen details to describe an encounter with an animal.	The writer demonstrates an adequate command of grammar, punctuation, and usage conventions. Although some errors may be evident, they create few (if any) disruptions in the fluency of the writing or the clarity of the essay.
2	The writer composes a poem that sometimes engages the reader and uses some well-chosen details to describe an encounter with an animal.	The writer demonstrates a partial command of grammar, punctuation, and usage conventions. Some distracting errors may be evident, at times creating minor disruptions in the fluency or clarity of the writing.
1	The writer composes a poem that does not effectively engage the reader and uses few well-chosen details to describe an encounter with an animal.	The writer demonstrates little or no command of grammar, punctuation, and usage conventions. Serious and persistent errors create disruptions in the fluency of the writing and sometimes interfere with meaning.
0	The writer does not provide a relevant response to the prompt or does not provide a response at all.	Serious and persistent errors overwhelm the writing and interfere with the meaning of the response as a whole, making the writer's meaning impossible to understand.

Write

Ask students to complete the writing assignment using text evidence to support their answers.

Use the scaffolds below to differentiate instruction for your ELL English Language Learners and A Approaching grade-level learners.

ELL **BEGINNING** With the help of the word bank, write a response using paragraph frame 1.

INTERMEDIATE With the help of the word bank, write a response using paragraph frames 1 and 2.

ADVANCED, ADVANCED HIGH Write a response of differentiated length using the sentence starters.

A **APPROACHING** Write a response of differentiated length using the sentence starters.

BEGINNING: Word Bank, Paragraph Frame 1 | INTERMEDIATE: Word Bank, Paragraph Frame 1, Paragraph Frame 2 | ADVANCED, ADVANCED HIGH / APPROACHING: Sentence Starters

Word Bank	Paragraph Frame 1	Paragraph Frame 2	Sentence Starters
dog bird sunny rainy scratching chirping flash shadow laugh jump	I once met a / an ____. It was a ____ day. I was ____. Suddenly, I heard ____. Then I saw ____. In the end, ____.	I once met a / an ____. It was a ____ day. I was ____. Suddenly, I heard ____. Then I saw ____. It made me think of ____. I will remember ____. I felt ____. In the end, ____.	• I once met . . . when I was . . . • Suddenly I heard . . . • Then I saw . . . • It made me think of . . . • I will remember . . . • In the end . . .

Peer Review

Rate

Respond to the following with a point rating that reflects your opinion.

	1	2	3	4
Ideas				
Evidence				
Language and Conventions				

Submit

Students should submit substantive feedback to two peers using the review instructions below.

- How well does this response answer the prompt?
- How well does the writer use well-chosen details to describe the encounter?
- What does the writer do well in this response? What does the writer need to work on?

Remember that your comments are most useful when they are kind and constructive.

ELL **SENTENCE FRAMES**

A
- You were able to (completely / partly / almost) ____ answer the prompt.
- You could answer the prompt more completely by ____.
- A strong detail you included was ____.
- My favorite part of your response is ____.

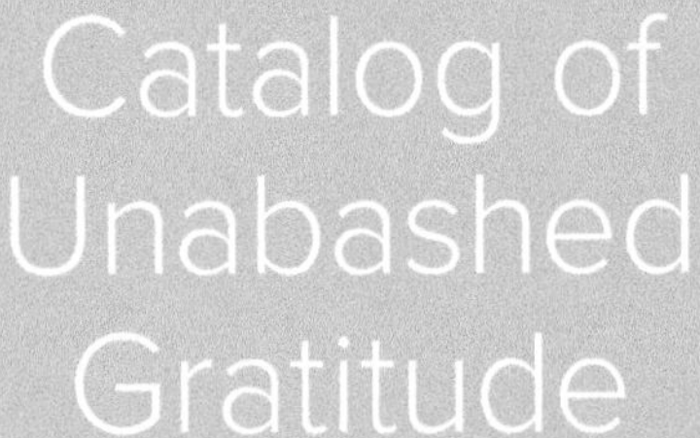

Catalog of Unabashed Gratitude

POETRY

Ross Gay

2015

Introduction

Written by poet Ross Gay (b. 1974), "Catalog of Unabashed Gratitude" is a tribute to both the marvelous and the mundane in modern life. Central to the poem is a community orchard in Bloomington, Indiana, a one-acre piece of land that is holds importance to Gay—he helped build it and now serves on the board of its non-profit organization. "Catalog of Unabashed Gratitude" was published in a 2015 poetry collection of the same title. The book was a finalist for the 2015 National Book Award for Poetry and winner of the 2016 National Book Critics Circle Award for Poetry. Gay, a professor of English, currently teaches at Indiana University.

Waking up from a dream of a robin dancing like a matador, the speaker feels compelled to give a full accounting of all the things he's grateful for. He recalls hauling manure to plant a community garden. Two years later, he watched a barefoot baby tamp the earth around a newly planted apple tree. From there, the poem takes off in all directions, giving gratitude for things big and small, happy and sad. He's grateful that his friend survived a suicide attempt and that his middle-aged team beat a group of teenagers in 3-on-3 basketball. Gratitude for cups of tea, for the bees he keeps and the honey they make, and for all the love in his life. Lastly, he expresses gratitude for little acts of kindness—strangers helping strangers, helping an old woman off the ground, stopping traffic to rescue a turtle in the road, and the man who stayed up all night to protect his peach tree from frost.

Proficiency-leveled summaries and summaries in multiple languages are available digitally.

Audio and audio text highlighting are available with this text.

CONNECT TO ESSENTIAL QUESTION

What is the power of story?

This award-winning poem by contemporary poet Ross Gay presents a catalog of events from the speaker's life, some tragic and some lovely. Throughout this dramatic monologue, the speaker is able to tell a story of gratitude that triumphs over all his experiences.

Entry Point

As students prepare to read "Catalog of Unabashed Gratitude," share the following information with them to provide context.

- Ross Gay is an American poet and professor of English. Born in Ohio in 1974, he grew up in Pennsylvania. He has published several books of poetry and has taught at several colleges and universities. As of 2018, he is a professor at Indiana University in Bloomington, Indiana.
- Gay describes himself as an eager gardener with a deep interest in the land. He was one of the founders of the Bloomington Community Orchard, the basis for "Catalog of Unabashed Gratitude," a nonprofit organization which focuses on food justice—that is, ensuring that all people have the healthy, nutritious food they need.
- Gay once told an interviewer "I'm always writing joyful poems," although he describes himself as having been "gloomy" and "sullen" as a boy.

Instructional Path

The print teacher's edition includes essential point-of-use instruction and planning tools. Complete lesson plans and program documents appear in your digital teacher account.

Independent Read: Catalog of Unabashed Gratitude

Objectives: After reading the text, students will write a short response that examines the speaker's argument and explains if they are in agreement with his message about gratitude.

Independent Read

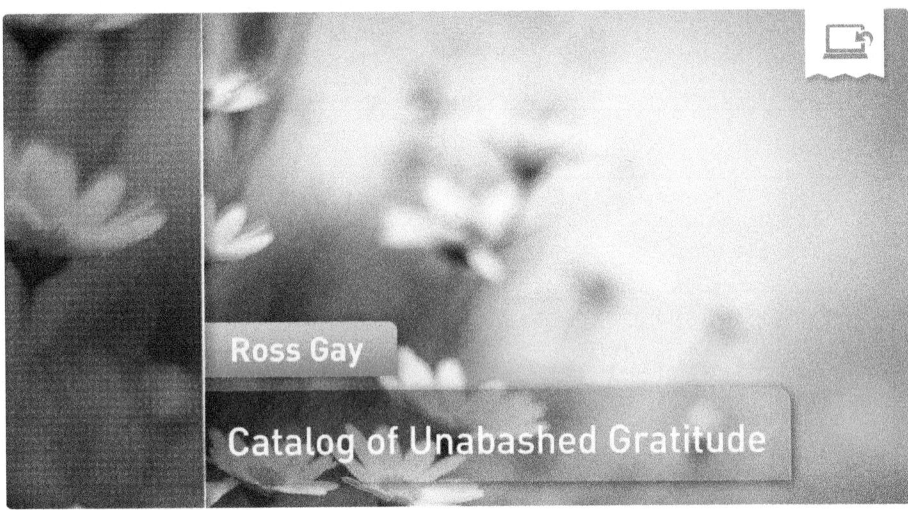

Introduce the Text

As a class, watch the video preview and have students read the introduction in pairs to make connections to the video preview.

- What part of the video was most interesting to you? Why?
- When in your life have you felt gratitude? What was that like?

ELL SPEAKING FRAMES

- The most interesting part of the video was ____.
- I felt gratitude when ____. It felt like ____.

Access Complex Text

LEXILE: N/A **WORD COUNT:** 1,927

The following areas may be challenging for students, particularly ELL English Language Learners and A Approaching grade-level learners.

Purpose	Connection of Ideas
• Remind students that authors always have a purpose in their writing, and may express more than one purpose. Ask them to analyze the poem for the author's multiple purposes, whether explicitly stated or not. • In addition to describing the joys of building a community orchard, this poem encourages readers to feel gratitude even in small things.	• The poem connects a variety of ideas and images, from vignettes of people interacting with each other in the orchard to scenes from the poet's childhood. • The ideas in the poem center on the image of the orchard and the steady growth of the trees, flowers, and fruit it contains.

“Friends, will you bear with me today, for I have awakened”

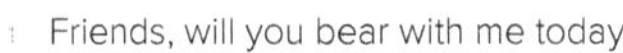

Friends, will you bear with me today,
for I have awakened
from a dream in which a robin
made with its shabby wings a kind of veil
behind which it shimmied and stomped something from the south
of Spain, its breast aflare,
looking me dead in the eye
from the branch that grew into my window,
coochie-cooing my chin,
the bird shuffling its little talons left, then right,
while the leaves bristled
against the plaster wall, two of them drifting
onto my blanket while the bird
opened and closed its wings like a matador
giving up on murder,
jutting its beak, turning a circle,
and flashing, again,
the ruddy bombast of its breast
by which I knew upon waking
it was telling me
in no **uncertain** terms
to bellow forth the tubas and sousaphones,
the whole rusty brass band of gratitude
not quite dormant in my belly—
it said so in a human voice,
“Bellow forth”—
and who among us could ignore such odd
and **precise** counsel?

Hear ye! hear ye! I am here
to holler that I have hauled tons—by which I don't mean lots,
I mean *tons* — of cowshit
and stood ankle deep in swales of maggots
swirling the spent beer grains
the brewery man was good enough to dump off

 SELECTION VOCABULARY

uncertain / incierto/ a *adjective* not known or defined COGNATE

precise / preciso/ a *adjective* clearly defined and accurate COGNATE

Developing Background Knowledge and Social Emotional Learning

1. Generate a list (on the board or on paper) of things students are grateful for, but maybe take for granted or don't acknowledge.
2. Have students discuss why these are important, and why some things are taken for granted.

Discuss with students: Gratitude is an emotion that can be easy to ignore. However, a 2012 study published in *Personality and Individual Differences* showed that people who express gratitude also report feeling healthier and happier than the average person. Why do you think it might be important to experience and express gratitude? How might gratitude support and encourage other positive emotions and feelings?

Prepare for Advanced Courses

Use the activity below to differentiate instruction for your B Beyond grade level learners.

Author's Word Choice

Reread stanza 1, in which a robin, “in no uncertain terms” and “in a human voice” commands the speaker to “bellow forth . . . the whole rusty brass band of gratitude.” Ask students:

- What language does the author use to anthropomorphize the robin? (Remind students that anthropomorphizing is a way of describing something that makes the animal or object seem or act like a human.)
- How does the language used to describe the robin set a mood for the poem?
- What does this anthropomorphism suggest about the speaker's beliefs about nature?
- What are other examples of anthropomorphosis, and how do these examples further define the speaker's attitude toward nature?

NOTES

holding his nose, for they smell very bad,
but make the compost writhe giddy and lick its lips,
twirling dung with my pitchfork
again and again
with hundreds and hundreds of other people,
we dreamt an orchard this way,
furrowing our brows,
and hauling our wheelbarrows,
and sweating through our shirts,
and two years later there was a party
at which trees were sunk into the well-fed earth,
one of which, a liberty apple, after being watered in
was tamped by a baby barefoot
with a bow hanging in her hair
biting her lip in her joyous work
and friends this is the realest place I know,
it makes me squirm like a worm I am so grateful,
you could ride your bike there
or roller skate or catch the bus
there is a fence and a gate twisted by hand,
there is a fig tree taller than you in Indiana,
it will make you gasp.
It might make you want to stay alive even, thank you;

and thank you
for not taking my pal when the engine
of his mind dragged him
to swig fistfuls of Xanax and a bottle or two of booze,
and thank you for taking my father
a few years after his own father went down thank you
mercy, mercy, thank you
for not smoking meth with your mother
oh thank you thank you
for leaving and for coming back,
and thank you for what inside my friends'
love bursts like a throng of roadside goldenrod
gleaming into the world,
likely hauling a shovel with her
like one named Aralee ought,
with hands big as a horse's,
and who, like one named Aralee ought,
will laugh time to time til the juice
runs from her nose; oh
thank you
for the way a small thing's wail makes

TEXT TALK

About how long did it take for the people of the neighborhood to build the community orchard?

See lines 40–45: About two years. The poet says "we dreamed" an orchard, and "two years later" there was a party.

Catalog of Unabashed Gratitude

the milk or what once was milk
in us gather into horses
huckle-buckling across a field;

and thank you, friends, when last spring
the hyacinth bells rang
and the crocuses flaunted
their upturned skirts, and a quiet roved
the beehive which when I entered
were snugged two or three dead
fist-sized clutches of bees between the frames,
almost clinging to one another,
this one's tiny head pushed
into another's tiny wing,
one's forelegs resting on another's face,
the translucent paper of their wings fluttering
beneath my breath and when
a few dropped to the frames beneath:
honey; and after falling down to cry,
everything's glacial shine.

And thank *you*, too. And thanks
for the corduroy couch I have put you on.
Put your feet up. Here's a light blanket,
a pillow, dear one,
for I can feel this is going to be long.
I can't stop
my gratitude, which includes, dear reader,
you, for staying here with me,
for moving your lips just so as I speak.
Here is a cup of tea. I have spooned honey into it.

And thank you the tiny bee's shadow
perusing these words as I write them.
And the way my love talks quietly
when in the hive,
so quietly, in fact, you cannot hear her
but only notice barely her lips moving
in conversation. Thank you what does not scare her
in me, but makes her reach my way. Thank you the love
she is which hurts sometimes. And the time
she misremembered elephants
in one of my poems which, oh, here
they come, garlanded with morning glory and wisteria
blooms, trombones all the way down to the river.

TEXT TALK

What does the poet discover inside the beehive? How does that make him feel?

See lines 83–95: The poet discovers several bunches of dead bees, and this discovery makes him unhappy.

SELECTION VOCABULARY

peruse / examinar *verb* to read thoroughly

NOTES

Thank you the quiet
in which the river bends around the elephant's
solemn trunk, polishing stones, floating
on its gentle back
the flock of geese flying overhead.

And to the quick and gentle flocking
of men to the old lady falling down
on the corner of Fairmount and 18th, holding patiently
with the softest parts of their hands
her cane and purple hat,
gathering for her the contents of her purse
and touching her shoulder and elbow;
thank you the cockeyed court
on which in a half-court 3 vs. 3[1] we oldheads
made of some runny-nosed kids
a shambles, and the 61-year-old
after flipping a reverse lay-up off a back door cut
from my no-look pass to seal the game
ripped off his shirt and threw punches at the gods
and hollered at the kids to admire the pacemaker's scar
grinning across his chest; thank you
the glad accordion's wheeze
in the chest; thank you the bagpipes.

And you, again, you, for the true kindness
it has been for you to remain awake
with me like this, nodding time to time
and making that noise which I take to mean
yes, or, *I understand*, or, *please go on*
but not too long, or, *why are you spitting*
so much, or, *easy Tiger*
hands to yourself. I am excitable.
I am sorry. I am grateful.
I just want us to be friends now, forever.
Take this bowl of blackberries from the garden.
The sun has made them warm.
I picked them just for you. I promise
I will try to stay on my side of the couch.

And thank you the baggie of dreadlocks I found in a drawer
while washing and folding the clothes of our murdered friend;

1. **half-court 3 vs. 3** an informal way of playing basketball where each team has three players and they only use half the court

TEXT TALK

What happens to the woman who falls on the corner of Fairmount and 18th?

See lines 124–130: She is helped up by a group of men who ensure that she is all right.

the photo in which his arm slung
around the sign to "the trail of silences"; thank you
the way before he died he held
his hands open to us; for coming back
in a waft of incense or in the shape of a boy
in another city looking
from between his mother's legs,
or disappearing into the stacks after brushing by;
for moseying back in dreams where,
seeing us lost and scared
he put his hand on our shoulders
and pointed us to the temple across town;

and thank you to the man all night long
hosing a mist on his early-bloomed
peach tree so that the hard frost
not waste the crop, the ice
in his beard and the ghosts
lifting from him when the warming sun
told him *sleep now*; thank you
the ancestor who loved you
before she knew you
by smuggling seeds into her braid for the long
journey, who loved you
before he knew you by putting
a walnut tree in the ground, who loved you
before she knew you by not slaughtering
the land; thank you
who did not bulldoze the ancient grove
of dates and olives,
who sailed his keys into the ocean
and walked softly home; who did not fire, who did not
plunge the head into the toilet, who said *stop,*
don't do that; who lifted some broken
someone up; who volunteered
the way a plant birthed of the reseeding plant
is called a *volunteer*, like the plum tree
that marched beside the raised bed
in my garden, like the arugula that marched
itself between the blueberries,
nary[2] a bayonet, nary an army, nary a nation,
which usage of the word volunteer
familiar to gardeners the wide world

2. **nary** an alternate way to say "not," usually suggesting "not a single one" of what it describes

TEXT TALK

Why is the man spraying a peach tree? Why does the poet thank him?

See lines 184–190: Spraying the tree protects its blossoms from freezing; the poet thanks the man for helping nature and giving of himself.

NOTES

made my pal shout "Oh!" and dance
and plunge his knuckles
into the **lush** soil before gobbling two strawberries
and digging a song from his guitar
made of wood from a tree someone planted, thank you;

thank you zinnia, and gooseberry, rudbeckia
and pawpaw, Ashmead's kernel, cockscomb
and scarlet runner, feverfew and lemonbalm;
thank you knitbone and sweetgrass and sunchoke
and false indigo whose petals stammered apart
by bumblebees good lord please give me a minute . . .
and moonglow and catkin and crookneck
and painted tongue and seedpod and johnny jump-up;
thank you what in us rackets glad
what gladrackets us;

and thank you, too, this knuckleheaded heart, this pelican heart,
this gap-toothed heart flinging open its gaudy maw
to the sky, oh clumsy,
oh giddy, oh dumbstruck,
oh rickshaw, oh goat twisting
its head at me from my peach tree's highest branch,
balanced impossibly gobbling the last fruit,
its tongue working like an engine,
a lone sweet drop tumbling by some miracle
into my mouth like the smell of someone I've loved;
heart like an elephant screaming
at the bones of its dead;
heart like the lady on the bus
dressed head to toe in gold, the sun
shivering her shiny boots, singing
Erykah Badu to herself
leaning her head against the window;

and thank you the way my father one time came back in a dream
by plucking the two cables beneath my chin
like a bass fiddle's strings
and played me until I woke singing,
no kidding, singing, smiling,
thank you, thank you,
stumbling into the garden where
the Juneberry's flowers had burst open
like the bells of French horns, the lily
my mother and I planted oozed into the air,

SELECTION VOCABULARY

lush / exuberante ***adjective*** growing plentifully

labor / trabajar ***verb*** to work with great effort

the bazillion ants **labored** in their earthen workshops
below, the collard greens waved in the wind
like the sails of ships, and the wasps
swam in the mint bloom's viscous swill;

and you, again you, for hanging tight, dear friend.
I know I can be long-winded sometimes.
I want so badly to rub the sponge of gratitude
over every last thing, including you, which, yes, awkward,
the suds in your ear and armpit, the little sparkling gems
slipping into your eye. Soon it will be over,

which is precisely what the child in my dream said,
holding my hand, pointing at the roiling sea and the sky
hurtling our way like so many buffalo,
who said *it's much worse than we think,*
and sooner; to whom I said
no duh child in my dreams, what do you think
this singing and shuddering is,
what this screaming and reaching and dancing
and crying is, other than loving
what every second goes away?
Goodbye, I mean to say.
And thank you. Every day.

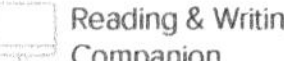

WRITE

PERSONAL RESPONSE: Write a personal response in which you examine the speaker's argument and state whether you agree or disagree with his message about gratitude. Remember to cite relevant textual evidence and include original commentary to support your response.

TEXT TALK

How did reflecting on the importance of experiencing and expressing gratitude deepen your understanding of the poem?

Answers will vary.

B Ask each Beyond grade-level student to write one additional discussion question. Then, have one or two students facilitate a discussion, using their questions to guide the conversation.

Writer's Notebook

Connect to Essential Question: Give students time to reflect on how "Catalog of Unabashed Gratitude" connects to the unit's essential question "What is the power of story?" by freewriting in their Writer's Notebooks.

CHECK FOR SUCCESS

If students are still struggling to respond to the prompt, ask them scaffolded questions, such as:

- What story or stories is the poet telling in "Catalog of Unabashed Gratitude"?
- How might the poet expect the reader to respond to these stories?

Reading Comprehension OPTIONAL

Have students complete the digital reading comprehension questions ✓ when they finish reading.

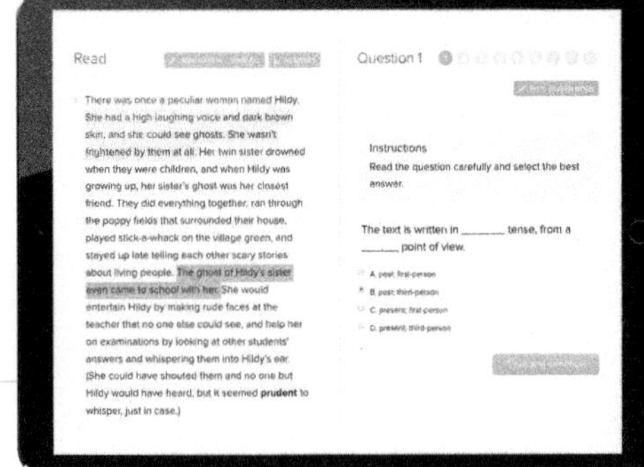

ANSWER KEY

QUESTION 1: D
QUESTION 2: B
QUESTION 3: A
QUESTION 4: B
QUESTION 5: A
QUESTION 6: C
QUESTION 7: B
QUESTION 8: B
QUESTION 9: *See first chart.*
QUESTION 10: *See second chart.*

Definition	Word
Growing plentifully	lush
Not known or defined	uncertain
Read thoroughly	peruse
Done with difficulty	labored
Accurate or exact	precise

First	Second	Third	Fourth
to bellow forth the tubas and sousaphones / the whole rusty brass band of gratitude	And thank you, too. And thanks / for the corduroy couch I have put you on.	and thank you to the man all night long / hosing a mist on his early-bloomed	which is precisely what the child in my dream said, / holding my hand, pointing at the roiling sea and the sky

Connect and Extend OPTIONAL

CONNECT TO EXTENDED WRITING PROJECT

Students can find inspiration from Ross Gay for their informative essay. Have them illustrate their ideas about nature with specific examples.

BEYOND THE BOOK

Advertisement: Catalog of Gratitude

The general meaning of *catalog* is an organized list. A particular meaning of *catalog* is a publication showing photos and written descriptions of items for sale; for example, a clothing or fashion catalog. Challenge students to revisit their discussion of things they are grateful for and create a printed catalog depicting these things and describing why they inspire gratitude. It might be difficult to come up with a visual image for an abstract source of gratitude, such as recovery from illness, but encourage students to try.

Have students reflect by asking them:

- Which items in the catalogue were the most unusual or surprising?
- What insights have you gained about gratitude from assembling the catalog?

Collaborative Conversation

Post the writing prompt to generate a discussion in small groups. Ask students to first break down the prompt before they discuss relevant ideas and textual evidence.

Write a personal response in which you examine the speaker's argument and state whether you agree or disagree with his message about gratitude. Remember to cite relevant textual evidence and include original commentary to support your response.

Use the scaffolds below to differentiate instruction for your ELL English Language Learners and A Approaching grade-level learners.

ELL **BEGINNING, INTERMEDIATE** Use the discussion guide and speaking frames to discuss with support from the teacher.

ADVANCED, ADVANCED HIGH Use the discussion guide and speaking frames to discuss in mixed-level groups.

A **APPROACHING** Use the discussion guide to discuss in mixed-level groups.

APPROACHING
ADVANCED, ADVANCED HIGH
BEGINNING, INTERMEDIATE

Discussion Guide	Speaking Frames
1. What does it mean to have gratitude? Do you agree with the poet's idea of what gratitude is? Why or why not?	• Gratitude means ____. • I agree/disagree with the poet because ____.
2. What connections can you make between the poem and the times you have felt gratitude?	• The poem reminds me of when ____. • This poem connects to ____.
3. How has the poem changed the way you think about gratitude?	• The poem made me realize that ____. • At first I thought ____, but now I think ____.

Text To World

Use the activity below to differentiate instruction for your B Beyond grade level learners.

Reread stanza 2, in which the speaker extols his community orchard.

Have students conduct informal research on public spaces in their neighborhood and in their state. (Consider parks and gardens, recreation and community centers, libraries, and playfields.)

Ask students:

- What public spaces are available in your community and in your state?
- What are the benefits of the public space in your community and in your state?
- Which public spaces do you enjoy the most and why?

Time permitting, students could create one stanza of gratitude about one of their favorite public spaces, modeled after stanza 2 of "Catalog of Unabashed Gratitude."

Review Prompt and Rubric

Before students begin writing, review the writing prompt and rubric with the class.

PERSONAL RESPONSE: Write a personal response in which you examine the speaker's argument and state whether you agree or disagree with his message about gratitude. Remember to cite relevant text evidence and include original commentary to support your response.

PROMPT GUIDE

- What does the poet say about gratitude?
- According to the poet, when should people show gratitude?
- Do you agree with the poet about gratitude? Why or why not?

Score	Personal Response	Language and Conventions
4	The writer clearly explains his or her agreement or disagreement with the author, using relevant textual evidence as needed.	The writer demonstrates a consistent command of grammar, punctuation, and usage conventions. Although minor errors may be evident, they do not detract from the fluency or the clarity of the essay.
3	The writer sufficiently explains his or her agreement or disagreement with the author, using relevant textual evidence most of the time.	The writer demonstrates an adequate command of grammar, punctuation, and usage conventions. Although some errors may be evident, they create few (if any) disruptions in the fluency of the writing or the clarity of the essay.
2	The writer begins to explain his or her agreement or disagreement with the author, but the explanation is incomplete. The writer uses relevant textual evidence only some of the time.	The writer demonstrates a partial command of grammar, punctuation, and usage conventions. Some distracting errors may be evident, at times creating minor disruptions in the fluency or clarity of the writing.
1	The writer attempts to explain his or her agreement or disagreement with the author, but the explanation is not successful. The writer uses little or no relevant textual evidence.	The writer demonstrates little or no command of grammar, punctuation, and usage conventions. Serious and persistent errors create disruptions in the fluency of the writing and sometimes interfere with meaning.
0	The writer does not provide a relevant response to the prompt or does not provide a response at all.	Serious and persistent errors overwhelm the writing and interfere with the meaning of the response as a whole, making the writer's meaning impossible to understand.

Write

Ask students to complete the writing assignment using text evidence to support their answers.

Use the scaffolds below to differentiate instruction for your ELL English Language Learners and A Approaching grade-level learners.

ELL **BEGINNING** With the help of the word bank, write a response using paragraph frame 1.

INTERMEDIATE With the help of the word bank, write a response using paragraph frames 1 and 2.

ADVANCED, ADVANCED HIGH Write a response of differentiated length using the sentence starters.

A **APPROACHING** Write a response of differentiated length using the sentence starters.

BEGINNING / INTERMEDIATE	BEGINNING / INTERMEDIATE	INTERMEDIATE	ADVANCED, ADVANCED HIGH / APPROACHING
Word Bank	**Paragraph Frame 1**	**Paragraph Frame 2**	**Sentence Starters**
attention fallen gratitude smaller men	Ross Gay says that people should feel ____ as they go through their day. He says that people should feel grateful for big things, but also for ____ things. For instance, he felt thankful when he saw some ____ help a woman who had ____. Gay says that if you pay ____ you will often feel gratitude.	I agree with Gay that gratitude is ____. But I think he is wrong when he says that ____. It can be hard to feel ____ when ____. Still, I think the poet ____.	• Gay says that gratitude means . . . • Gratitude is important because . . . • Gay says people should feel grateful when . . . • I think Gay is right when he says . . . • I wonder why Gay says . . . • The poem changed my thinking because . . .

Peer Review

Students should submit substantive feedback to two peers using the review instructions below.

- How well does this response address the prompt?
- Which of the writer's points led you to think differently about the text?
- What does the writer do well in this response? What does the writer need to work on?

Remember that your comments are most useful when they are kind and constructive.

Rate

Respond to the following with a point rating that reflects your opinion.

1 2 3 4

Ideas

Evidence

Language and Conventions

Submit

ELL A **SENTENCE FRAMES**

- You (completely / partly / almost) ____ answered the prompt.
- You could add to your answer by ____.
- I wasn't sure what you meant when ____.
- I changed my mind about the text when you said ____.
- The best part of your response is ____.

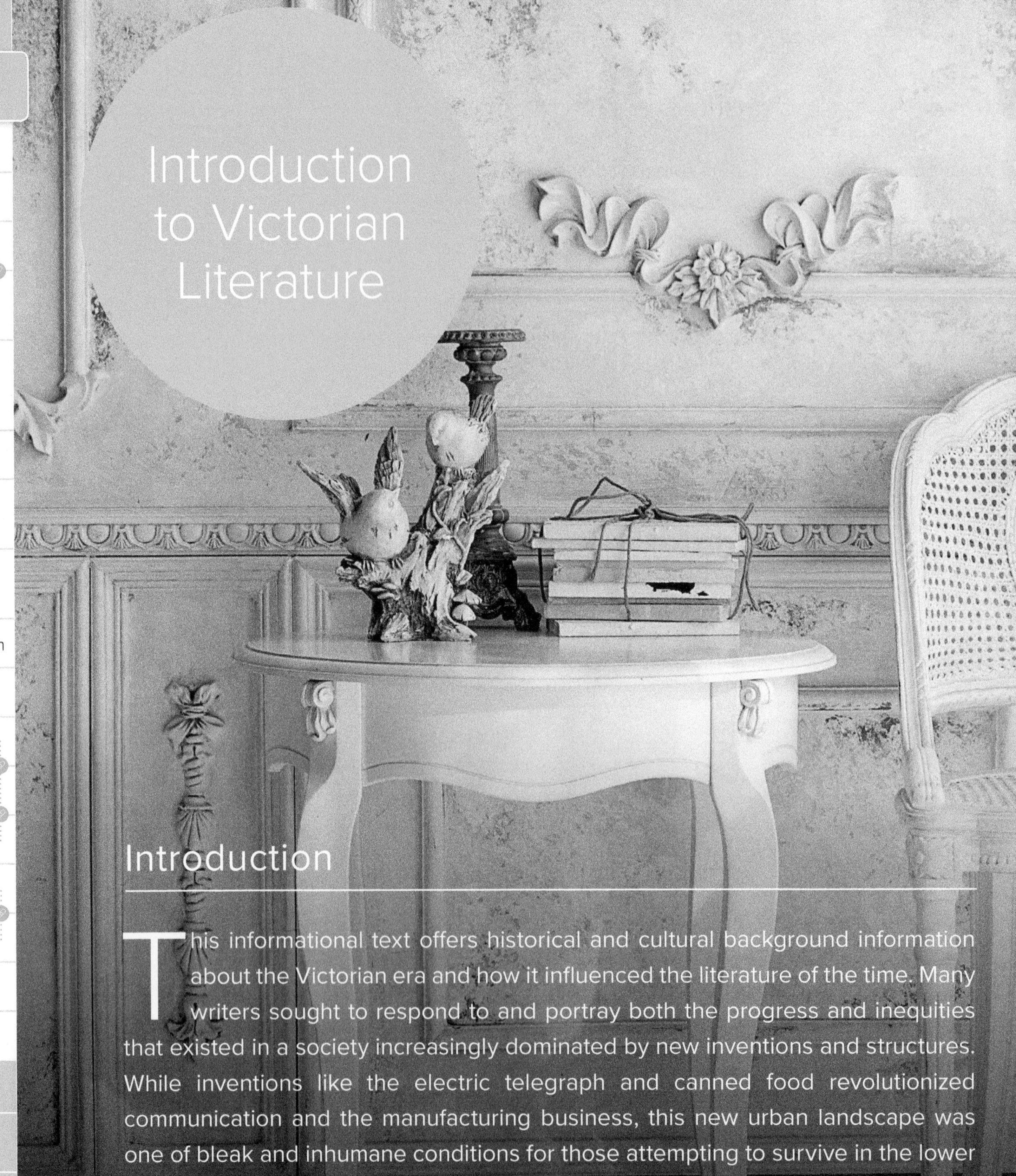

Introduction to Victorian Literature

Introduction

This informational text offers historical and cultural background information about the Victorian era and how it influenced the literature of the time. Many writers sought to respond to and portray both the progress and inequities that existed in a society increasingly dominated by new inventions and structures. While inventions like the electric telegraph and canned food revolutionized communication and the manufacturing business, this new urban landscape was one of bleak and inhumane conditions for those attempting to survive in the lower classes of society. Victorian literature was marked by realism, a commitment by writers to portray both the good and the bad that existed in a world marked by modernization.

"Amidst all the progress, some people were being left behind."

NOTES

1 If you've ever attended a comic-book convention or even seen pictures of one, you may have noticed a particular type of cosplayer. They'll wear top hats, vests, and goggles, often decorated with clockwork gears. These people are taking part in steampunk subculture. They enjoy fashion, artwork, and media set in a fictionalized, sci-fi version of the nineteenth century. Much of the steampunk aesthetic borrows directly from the culture and ideals of nineteenth century England. This time period was called the Victorian Age and, as any steampunk fan will attest, it continues to fascinate people today.

The Victorian Age

A portrait of Queen Victoria of Great Britain (1819–1901). Queen Victoria was one of the most famous British monarchs, reigning from 1837 to 1901, a period which established Great Britain as one of the world's leading powers.

2 The Victorian Age, like other time periods in England, derives its name from the monarch of the time, Queen Victoria. During her reign, from 1837 to 1901, the British empire expanded to cover over one-fifth of the earth. Almost one in four people were subjects of Queen Victoria. Much of this was made possible by the first Industrial Revolution. Steam-powered locomotives and ships made it possible for merchants and military to travel all over the world, even to the Arctic and Antarctic. The rise of factories created a need for raw materials to import and customers to buy the exported manufactured goods. Factories also created a demand for workers, and cities swelled as people left the countryside to seek work.

First Read

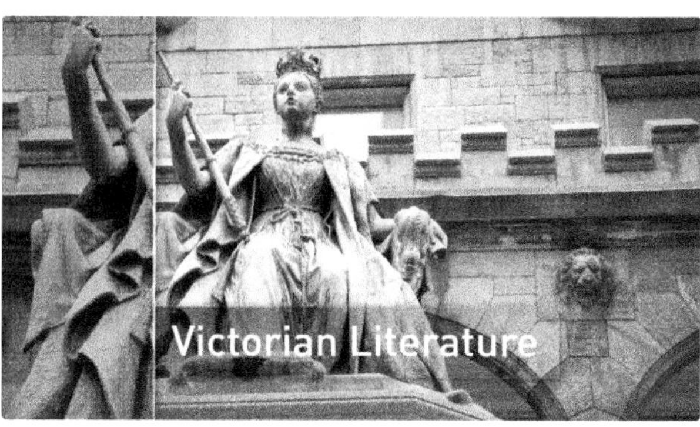

Introduce the Text

As a class, watch the video preview and have students read the introduction in pairs to make connections to the video preview. Ask students:

- What parts of the video related to information you already knew, and what parts gave new information?
- What books, movies, or TV shows do you know that take place in the Victorian Age?

ELL SPEAKING FRAMES

- I already knew ____. I didn't know ____.
- ____ takes place in the Victorian Age.

Instructional Path

The print teacher's edition includes essential point-of-use instruction and planning tools. Complete lesson plans and program documents appear in your digital teacher account.

Literary Focus: Victorian Literature

Objectives: After an initial reading about Victorian Literature, students will be able to identify and describe characteristics of the literary period.

NOTES

3 Cities were not only growing in population and land area, they were becoming taller as well. As techniques for producing cast iron improved, iron-framed building began to replace wooden and brick structures. This stronger building material, as well as steam-powered elevators, allowed taller buildings to be erected. Communication also improved during this time. The electric telegraph was invented in 1837 and quickly spread through the British empire. Even continents were linked with **transoceanic** cables. In 1876, the next great step in communication revolutionized the way people spoke to each other: the telephone. By the end of Victoria's reign, radio was being developed. Other Victorian developments included photography, vaccination, and canned food.

4 Not everything was progress and comfort, however. For most, city life was unpleasant. Until unions began to form, most workers were severely underpaid and overworked. Men, women, and even very young children were made to work in dangerous conditions, like deep mine shafts or buildings with little-to-no fire safety measures. Scientists like Louis Pasteur would not develop the germ theory, the understanding that many diseases are caused by microorganisms and not the wrath of gods or influence of witches, until the 1860s. His process of pasteurization made food safer, but it still took time for people to understand the importance of good hygiene and sanitation. People did not realize the effects of burning coal or dumping chemicals into rivers, so cities were filthy and polluted, and sickness was not uncommon. Society was rushing to reap the benefits of new technology, but people were slower to adapt to the risks and dangers technology brought with it.

The Age of the Novel

5 The Victorians did not invent the novel, nor could they be said to have popularized the form. Novels were common during Romanticism, but Romantics viewed them as **inferior** to poetry. Indeed most novels were written by women, who were also treated as lesser. In the Victorian Age, however, novels reigned supreme. While Romantics styled themselves as elites, changes in the Victorian Age made literature available to everyone. A growing middle class and education reforms ensured more people were literate. New technology made it cheaper to produce books, newspapers, and magazines. People who couldn't afford even those were still able to read, thanks to the 1850 Public Libraries Act, which allowed libraries to stop charging **subscriptions** and loan books for free. Reading was now a hobby for the common person, and novels became the common genre, as they often emphasize enjoyability over artistry. Writing was no longer a leisure activity for the wealthy: it was a booming business and more people were writing than ever before.

6 Literary magazines were profitable and gave authors a large audience. Many writers therefore tailored their work to be suitable for publishing in **periodicals**. As a result, the serial novel became a popular trend during the Victorian Age. Just as a TV series differs from a movie by telling a story over the course many

TEXT TALK

What technology came from the Victorian Age?

See paragraphs 2 and 3: Steam engines, telegraphs and telephones, and other innovations came from the Victorian Age.

What kinds of people were reading?

See paragraph 5: Almost everyone was reading. Literacy, inexpensive publishing, and a growing middle class meant more people were reading than ever before.

SELECTION VOCABULARY

transoceanic / transoceánico/a ***adjective*** crossing an ocean COGNATE

inferior / inferior ***adjective*** lower in rank or position; closer to the bottom of a group COGNATE

subscription / la suscripción ***noun*** a regular ongoing payment for a service or product COGNATE

periodical / el periódico ***noun*** a magazine or newspaper published at regular intervals COGNATE

episodes, a serial novel is released a chapter at a time instead of all at once. Some authors, including Charles Dickens, would not even have a complete story planned when they began publishing chapters. Instead, they would use the reactions of their readers to decide how to shape the rest of the story.

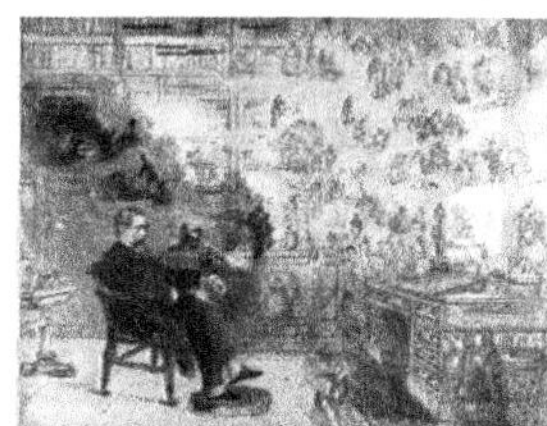

Dickens' Dream. British writer Charles Dickens sleeping on a chair and dreaming about the characters of his novels.

Subgenres: Social-Problem and Regionalist Novels

7 Although the Industrial Revolution caused problems like poverty and poor living conditions, it also brought solutions. Increased literacy and improved printing technology made it possible to reach and inform far more people than ever before of the social problems that plagued the Victorian Age. Social-problem, or "Condition of England," novels became a common subgenre. Works of realistic fiction such as Dickens's *Hard Times* and *Oliver Twist* revealed the poverty and exploitation of London's lower classes. Dickens also drew attention to the corruption in the legal system with his novel *Bleak House*. And poet Elizabeth Barrett Browning's 1857 *Aurora Leigh* was a groundbreaking critique of Victorian views toward women.

8 Another subgenre that found great success in the Victorian Age was the regionalist novel. Like the Romantics, many nineteenth century people wanted an escape from city life, so novels focusing on the people and landscape of the countryside appealed to a wide audience. While Romanticism idealized nature and pastoral regions, Victorian regionalist writing tended to be more realistic. Regionalist novels were usually set in real locations and often referred to natural or physical landmarks. The character of the people was included as well, through the use of local dialect, unique political or social values, and **parodies** of local residents. Emily Brontë's *Wuthering Heights* was notable for its brutal depiction of life on the Yorkshire moors in Northern England. Brontë's sister, Charlotte Brontë, wrote *Jane Eyre*, which features a strong woman in conflict due to social issues common in Yorkshire.

9 **Major Concepts**

- **The Rise of Realism**—The literary movement of realism gained prominence in the late nineteenth and early twentieth centuries. Realism seeks to

SELECTION VOCABULARY

parody / la parodia *noun* humorous or satirical mimicry COGNATE

TEXT TALK

How did regionalist novels differ from Romantic works?

See paragraph 8: Romantic writing saw nature as beautiful, but regionalist writing was more realistic and often grim.

NOTES

portray life as it is really lived, good and bad. Realistic fiction often focuses on middle- and working-class conditions and characters. Social reform is a frequent goal of realistic writing.

- **Victorian Social Classes—**Through literature, writers depicted the condition of England in a socially realistic way. They examined the different social classes, from the very rich to the growing middle class to the poorest peasants. Victorian stories spoke out on behalf of the poor and helpless and also recounted stories about social progress and lifting oneself up to the middle class.

Style and Form

10 **Victorian Novels**

- Many Victorian novelists used realism to portray practical problems and convey stories that had a moral message for their readers.
- A common topic that novelists wrote about was the "condition of England." Victorian literature depicted contemporary life and often provided criticism of social problems caused by industrialism.
- The protagonists of Victorian novels lead difficult lives but often succeed in the end through hard work, perseverance, love, and luck.
- Because many were originally published in serial format, Victorian novels can be long and sprawling. They usually contain frequent cliffhangers that writers used to keep their readers interested and wanting to read the next installment.

11 **Victorian Poetry**

- Far less idealistic about nature than the Romantics, Victorian poets were more concerned with the realities of life, including the suffering caused by industry and technological **advancement**.
- Victorian poetry contemplated questions of morality and emphasized ideals such as truth, justice, and love.
- Notable features of Victorian poetry include sensory elements and imagery as well as sentimentality to convey experiences and struggles of religion, science, nature, and romance.

12 The Victorian Age was a time of rapid changes in society. Social hierarchies, technology, the roles of women, and many other aspects of life were undergoing transformations. Amidst all the progress, some people were being left behind. During this period people sought to find a balance and decide which parts of the past should be held onto and which should be relinquished for the future. Anyone who is dealing with transition can find something relatable in Victorian literature. How is the modern world similar to the Victorian era?

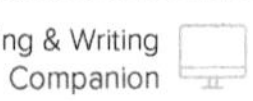

TEXT TALK

What can you learn by studying literature from the Victorian Age?

Answers will vary, but should indicate that students will gain a deeper understanding of the culture and the prevailing values and beliefs.

SELECTION VOCABULARY

advancement / el progreso *noun* gradual improvement or growth or development

B Ask each Beyond grade-level student to write one additional discussion question. Then, have one or two students facilitate a discussion, using their questions to guide the conversation.

Reading Comprehension

Have students complete the digital reading comprehension questions when they finish reading.

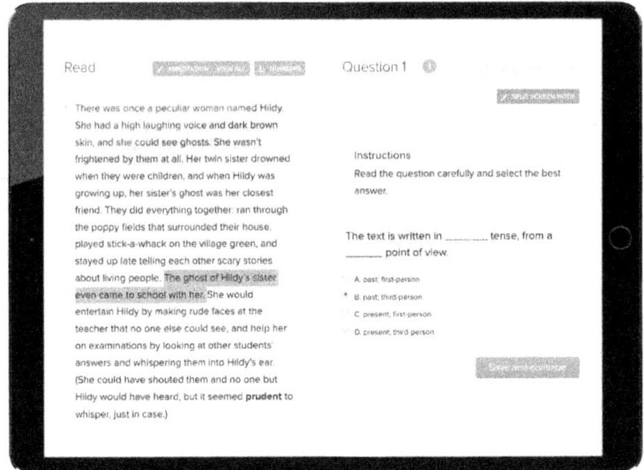

ANSWER KEY

QUESTION 1: B
QUESTION 2: C
QUESTION 3: A
QUESTION 4: D
QUESTION 5: C
QUESTION 6: A
QUESTION 7: A
QUESTION 8: A
QUESTION 9: *See first chart.*
QUESTION 10: *See second chart.*

Definition	Word
Development or improvement	advancement
Crossing an ocean	transoceanic
An imitation or version of a person or something that is often humorous	parodies
A magazine or newspaper published at regular intervals	periodicals

First	Second	Third	Fourth
"This time period was called the Victorian Age and, as any steampunk fan will attest, it continues to fascinate people today."	"As techniques for producing cast iron improved, iron-framed building began to replace wooden and brick structures."	"Like the Romantics, many nineteenth-century people wanted an escape from city life, so novels focusing on the people and landscape of the countryside appealed to a wide audience."	"Social hierarchies, technology, the roles of women, and many other aspects of life were undergoing transformations."

Think Questions

Circulate as students answer Think Questions independently. Scaffolds for these questions are shown on the opposite page.

QUESTION 1: Textual Evidence

The Industrial Revolution brought about better technology, communication, and scientific knowledge. It also led to pollution and poverty.

QUESTION 2: Textual Evidence

Novels became popular because books were cheaper to produce and more people were reading. Writing and publishing became profitable, and novels had the broadest appeal and made the most money.

QUESTION 3: Textual Evidence

Romantics wrote to inspire people with beauty, but Victorians wanted to entertain and educate readers. Social-problem novels especially tried to draw attention to problems in life.

QUESTION 4: Context Clues

The text says that writers for literary magazines made their writing suitable for *periodicals*. The text also compares serial novels to TV episodes. Magazines and TV shows are both released in regular intervals, so I think *periodical* means "a written work published in issues over time."

QUESTION 5: Greek and Latin Affixes and Roots

Transoceanic means "crossing oceans." The text says that transoceanic cables linked continents. Continents are separated by oceans, so this detail supported my conclusion.

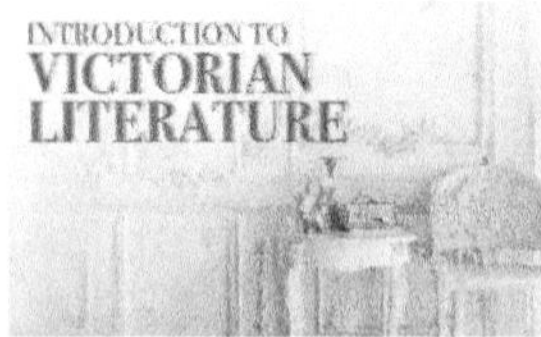

Literary Period

Read "Introduction to Victorian Literature." After you read, complete the Think Questions below.

THINK QUESTIONS

1. What were some benefits and problems of the Industrial Revolution? Cite textual evidence to support your response.
2. Why did novels become so popular during the Victorian Age? Explain, citing textual evidence to support your response.
3. What were the goals of Victorian writers? How did they differ from those of the Romantics? Cite textual evidence to support your explanations.
4. Use context clues to determine the meaning of the word **periodicals**. Write your best definition here, along with the words and phrases that were most helpful in determining the word's meaning. Then, check a dictionary to confirm your understanding.
5. The word **transoceanic** uses the Latin prefix *trans-*, meaning "across." With this information in mind, write your best definition of the word *transoceanic* as it is used in this text. Cite any words or phrases that were particularly helpful in coming to your conclusion.

SCAFFOLDS

Think Questions

Use the scaffolds below to differentiate instruction for your ELL English Language Learners and A Approaching grade-level learners.

ELL **BEGINNING** Write a response using the word bank and sentence frames.

INTERMEDIATE Write a response using the sentence frames.

ADVANCED, ADVANCED HIGH Write a response using the Text-Dependent Question Guide.

A **APPROACHING** Write a response using the Text-Dependent Question Guide.

BEGINNING	INTERMEDIATE	APPROACHING / ADVANCED, ADVANCED HIGH
Word Bank	**Sentence Frames**	**Text-Dependent Question Guide**
realism crossing technology reforms pollution issues nature social-problem continents easier serial	The Industrial Revolution brought benefits like ____. It also brought problems like ____.	1. • What benefits did the Industrial Revolution bring? • What problems did the Industrial Revolution cause?
	More people were reading because of educational ____. Books were ____ to produce.	2. • What made people able to read novels? • What made it easier to produce novels? • Why did most people like novels more than other types of writing?
	Romantics idealized ____, but Victorians were interested in ____. ____ novels tried to draw attention to problems in life.	3. • What did Victorian writers try to do? • What did Romantic writers try to do? • How do the goals of Victorians and Romantics differ?
	The text says that ____ novels were published a chapter at a time in periodicals. I think *periodical* means "a written work published in ____ over time."	4. • Read: "Literary magazines were profitable and gave authors a large audience. Many writers therefore tailored their work to be suitable for publishing in **periodicals**." • How often are magazines published? • What does that tell you about the meaning of *periodicals*?
	Transoceanic means "____ oceans." The text says that transoceanic cables linked ____.	5. • Read: "The electric telegraph was invented in 1837 and quickly spread through the British empire. Even continents were linked with **transoceanic** cables." • What word parts make up the word *transoceanic*? • What does that tell you about the meaning of *transoceanic*?

The Cry of the Children

POETRY
Elizabeth Barrett Browning
1843

Introduction

Elizabeth Barrett Browning (1806–1861), was a popular and celebrated British poet of the Victorian era. She spent much of her life indoors, isolated from the outside world due to her chronic poor health and weak lungs. Following a prolonged and romantic exchange of letters, she married Victorian poet Robert Browning in 1845. She is perhaps best known for her poem "How Do I Love Thee?" from her collection titled *Sonnets from the Portuguese*. However, she was passionately moved by the suffering of others and addressed these darker thoughts and concerns in her poetry as well. "The Cry of the Children" exposes the grueling and unethical working conditions many children were forced to endure in industrialized England. Browning first published "The Cry of the Children" in 1843. Shortly thereafter, Parliament enacted massive and much-needed reforms to child labor laws.

The speaker asks if anyone else can hear these children crying. While other young animals are singing happily, these children weep bitter tears. The children are sad because they have a long miserable life ahead of them. Their friend Alice died the previous year and to them, her grave looked comfortable. The speaker beseeches them to go play in the fields, but the children are too tired and would rather sleep. They've been working long hours in the coal mines and factories. The speaker prays that these children will taste some sweetness and tells them to pray to God for help, but they wonder how God could ever hear them over the din of the factory floor. Besides, the only prayer they know is "Our Father," and when they look up to heaven, they can see nothing through their tears. The speaker calls upon the nation for help, because a child's cry is even worse than the wrath of man.

Proficiency-leveled summaries and summaries in multiple languages are available digitally.

Audio and audio text highlighting are available with this text.

CONNECT TO ESSENTIAL QUESTION

What is the power of story?

Elizabeth Barrett Browning is remembered for her love poetry, but Barrett Browning also wrote extensively about the social issues of her time. This poem is a protest poem that expresses a strong condemnation of child labor practices during the Industrial Revolution.

Entry Point

As students prepare to read "The Cry of the Children ," share the following information with them to provide context.

- When the Industrial Revolution began in the late 1700s, many children went to work in mills, mines, and factories.
- Children were preferred by mine and factory owners for two reasons: first, they could be paid very little; second, their small size enabled them to fit into crevices in mines or between large machines in factories. The work was dangerous, and the hours were long. Children lost fingers and limbs, and suffered permanent damage to their health.
- While the system of child labor was brutal, many people supported it. The low pay for child workers translated to cheaper prices for goods. Schools for children in low-income communities were inadequate or nonexistent. And children had always worked on farms, and some saw no distinction between farm labor and factory work.

Instructional Path

The print teacher's edition includes essential point-of-use instruction and planning tools. Complete lesson plans and program documents appear in your digital teacher account.

Independent Read: The Cry of the Children

Objectives: After reading "The Cry of the Children" students will write a short response poem that raises awareness of certain important and unjust issues using figurative language to persuade their readers to take action.

Independent Read

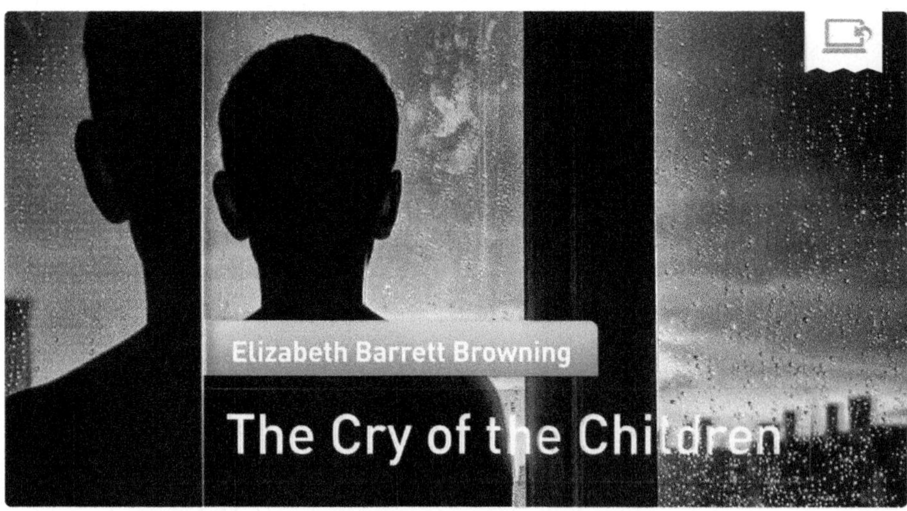

Introduce the Text

As a class, watch the video preview and have students read the introduction in pairs to make connections to the video preview.

- In your opinion, what current situations in your community or the world are unjust to children?
- Why do you find these issues important to your generation or community?

ELL SPEAKING FRAMES

- An unjust situation for children in my (community / world) is ____.
- These (issues / situations) are important to to my (community / generation) because ____.

Access Complex Text

LEXILE: N/A **WORD COUNT:** 1,326

The following areas may be challenging for students, particularly ELL English Language Learners and A Approaching grade-level learners.

Specific Vocabulary	Prior Knowledge
• Word forms such as *lieth* and *ere* (*lies* and *before*) are common in the poetry of Barrett Browning's time, but may be unfamiliar to modern readers. • Barrett Browning was writing in the 1840s, and some of her vocabulary is now considered archaic. For example, *kirk-chime* refers to the ringing of church bells. Discuss with students the meanings of archaic terms.	• Though child labor is uncommon in the modern developed world, it was a fact of life among the lower classes in the 1840's, and continues to be a cause for concern in many underdeveloped parts of the world today. • Some reformers pushed back against the custom of hiring very young workers in factories and mines, but many people accepted child labor as a given.

"... how long, O cruel nation,
Will you stand, to move the world,
on a child's heart,—"

NOTES

"Pheu pheu, ti prosderkesthe m ommasin, tekna;"
[[Alas, alas, why do you gaze at me with your eyes, my children.]]—Medea.
Do ye hear the children weeping, O my brothers,
Ere the sorrow comes with years?
They are leaning their young heads against their mothers,—
And that cannot stop their tears.
The young lambs are bleating[1] in the meadows;
The young birds are chirping in the nest;
The young fawns are playing with the shadows;
The young flowers are blowing toward the west—
But the young, young children, O my brothers,
They are weeping bitterly!
They are weeping in the playtime of the others,
In the country of the free.

Do you question the young children in the sorrow,
Why their tears are falling so?
The old man may weep for his to-morrow
Which is lost in Long Ago—
The old tree is leafless in the forest—
The old year is ending in the frost—
The old wound, if stricken, is the sorest—
The old hope is hardest to be lost:
But the young, young children, O my brothers,
Do you ask them why they stand
Weeping sore before the bosoms of their mothers,
In our happy Fatherland?

Illustration from *The Life and Adventures of Michael Armstrong, the Factory Boy*, by Frances Trollope, Auguste Hervieu [illustrator], 1876

1. **bleating** the sound of a sheep or goat crying out

Developing Background Knowledge and Cultural Awareness

1. Elizabeth Barrett Browning is known for her love poems, but she also wrote literature that tackled major issues of the day, including a book-length poem *Aurora Leigh*.
2. Virginia Woolf said the following about Browning's writing: "Aurora Leigh, with her passionate interest in social questions, her conflict as an artist and woman, her longing for knowledge and freedom, is the true daughter of her age."
3. Have students use their knowledge of the Victorian age to discuss the possible meaning of the quotation.

Discuss with students: In the United States, the Fair Labor Standards Act of 1938 prohibits "oppressive child labor." In other parts of the world, however, children are coerced into mentally and physically harmful forced labor occupations. What parts of childhood do we need to protect and guarantee for all children? Why is it important to do so?

NOTES

They look up with their pale and sunken faces,
And their looks are sad to see,
For the man's grief **abhorrent,** draws and presses
Down the cheeks of infancy—
"Your old earth," they say, "is very dreary;"
"Our young feet," they say, "are very weak!"
Few paces have we taken, yet are weary—
Our grave-rest is very far to seek!
Ask the old why they weep, and not the children,
For the outside earth is cold—
And we young ones stand without, in our bewildering,
And the graves are for the old!"

"True," say the children, "it may happen
That we die before our time!
Little Alice died last year her grave is shapen
Like a snowball, in the rime.
We looked into the pit prepared to take her—
Was no room for any work in the close clay:
From the sleep wherein she lieth none will wake her,
Crying, 'Get up, little Alice! it is day.'
If you listen by that grave, in sun and shower,
With your ear down, little Alice never cries;
Could we see her face, be sure we should not know her,
For the smile has time for growing in her eyes ,—
And merry go her moments, **lulled** and stilled in
The shroud, by the kirk-chime!
It is good when it happens," say the children,
"That we die before our time!"

Alas, the wretched children! they are seeking
Death in life, as best to have!
They are binding up their hearts away from breaking,
With a **cerement** from the grave.
Go out, children, from the mine and from the city—
Sing out, children, as the little thrushes[2] do—
Pluck you handfuls of the meadow-cowslips[3] pretty
Laugh aloud, to feel your fingers let them through!
But they answer, "Are your cowslips of the meadows
Like our weeds anear the mine?
Leave us quiet in the dark of the coal-shadows,
From your pleasures fair and fine!

2. **thrushes** common songbirds
3. **cowslips** certain wildflowers

TEXT TALK

What happened to Alice? How does the poem view what happened to her?

See stanza 4: Alice died; the poem says this is a blessing because she no longer has to experience the miseries of work.

How do the children in the poem say they would react if they saw meadows?

See stanza 6: The children would not delight in the view but would want to fall asleep in the meadows.

SELECTION VOCABULARY

abhorrent / aborrecible ***adjective*** causing disgust or hatred COGNATE

lulled / arrullar ***verb*** to calm or soothe

cerement / la mortaja ***noun*** a cloth used to wrap the dead

"For oh," say the children, "we are weary,
And we cannot run or leap—
If we cared for any meadows, it were merely
To drop down in them and sleep.
Our knees tremble sorely in the stooping—
We fall upon our faces, trying to go;
And, underneath our heavy eyelids drooping,
The reddest flower would look as pale as snow.
For, all day, we drag our burden tiring,
Through the coal-dark, underground—
Or, all day, we drive the wheels of iron
In the factories, round and round.

"For all day, the wheels are droning, turning,—
Their wind comes in our faces,—
Till our hearts turn,—our heads, with pulses burning,
And the walls turn in their places
Turns the sky in the high window blank and reeling—
Turns the long light that droppeth down the wall,—
Turn the black flies that crawl along the ceiling—
All are turning, all the day, and we with all!—
And all day, the iron wheels are droning;
And sometimes we could pray,
'O ye wheels,' (breaking out in a mad moaning)
'Stop! be silent for to-day!' "

Ay! be silent! Let them hear each other breathing
For a moment, mouth to mouth—
Let them touch each other's hands, in a fresh wreathing
Of their tender human youth!
Let them feel that this cold metallic motion
Is not all the life God fashions or **reveals**—
Let them prove their inward souls against the notion
That they live in you, or under you, O wheels!—
Still, all day, the iron wheels go onward,
As if Fate in each were stark;
And the children's souls, which God is calling sunward,
Spin on blindly in the dark.

Now tell the poor young children, O my brothers,
To look up to Him and pray—
So the blessed One, who blesseth all the others,
Will bless them another day.
They answer, "Who is God that He should hear us,
While the rushing of the iron wheels is stirred?

Prepare For Advanced Courses

Use the activity below to differentiate instruction for your B Beyond grade level learners.

Author's Word Choice

Notice the repetition of "all day" and "round" in the final four lines of stanza 6.

> *For, all day, we drag our burden tiring,*
> *Through the coal-dark, underground—*
> *Or, all day, we drive the wheels of iron*
> *In the factories, round and round*

Direct students to reread stanzas 6 and 7 to find other instances of repetition in the voices of the children as they describe their existence.

Ask students:

- How does the author's use of repetition in the children's dialogue affect the mood of the poem?
- What emotions are evoked in the reader by the repetition of words in stanzas 6 and 7?
- How does the repetition support the author's purpose for this text?

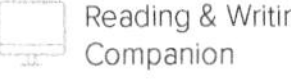

SELECTION VOCABULARY

reveal / revelar *verb* to make something previously hidden known COGNATE

TEXT TALK

According to the poet, what do the children think about the possibility that God will hear their cries? Why?

See stanzas 9–11: The children feel abandoned by God; humans do not pay attention to their cries, and they worry God may not either.

When we sob aloud, the human creatures near us
Pass by, hearing not, or answer not a word!
And we hear not (for the wheels in their **resounding**)
Strangers speaking at the door:
Is it likely God, with angels singing round Him,
Hears our weeping any more?

"Two words, indeed, of praying we remember;
And at midnight's hour of harm,—
'Our Father,' looking upward in the chamber,
We say softly for a charm.
We know no other words, except 'Our Father,'
And we think that, in some pause of angels' song,
God may pluck them with the silence sweet to gather,
And hold both within His right hand which is strong.
'Our Father!' If He heard us, He would surely
(For they call Him good and mild)
Answer, smiling down the steep world very purely,
'Come and rest with me, my child.'

"But, no!" say the children, weeping faster,
"He is speechless as a stone;
And they tell us, of His image is the master
Who commands us to work on."
"Go to!" say the children,—"up in Heaven,
Dark, wheel-like, turning clouds are all we find!
Do not mock us; grief has made us unbelieving—
We look up for God, but tears have made us blind."
Do ye hear the children weeping and disproving,
O my brothers, what ye preach?
For God's possible is taught by His world's loving—
And the children doubt of each.

And well may the children weep before you;
They are weary ere they run;
They have never seen the sunshine, nor the glory
Which is brighter than the sun:
They know the grief of man, without its wisdom;
They sink in the despair, without its calm—
Are slaves, without the liberty in Christdom,—
Are martyrs, by the pang without the palm,—
Are worn, as if with age, yet unretrievingly
No dear remembrance keep,—
Are orphans of the earthly love and heavenly:
Let them weep! let them weep!

TEXT TALK

How does analyzing the quotation by Virginia Woolf in relation to Barrett Browning's poem deepen your understanding of the text?

Answers will vary.

SELECTION VOCABULARY

resounding / resonante *adjective* resonating or echoing COGNATE

palpitation / la palpitación *noun* a strong or irregular heart beat often caused by anxiety or stress COGNATE

They look up, with their pale and sunken faces,
And their look is dread to see,
For they think you see their angels in their places,
With eyes meant for Deity[4];—
"How long," they say, "how long, O cruel nation,
Will you stand, to move the world, on a child's heart,—
Stifle down with a mailed heel its **palpitation**,
And tread onward to your throne amid the mart?[5]
Our blood splashes upward, O our tyrants,
And your purple shews your path;
But the child's sob curseth deeper in the silence
Than the strong man in his wrath!"

4 **Deity** divine nature
5 **mart** marketplace

WRITE

POETRY: This is a protest poem written to call attention to the terrible conditions endured by children who worked in British coal mines in the nineteenth century—conditions that endangered their souls as well as their health. Think about a cruel situation you would like to end. Perhaps you can find information about modern-day child labor or envision a way to help homeless students succeed in school. Write a poem, as Elizabeth Barrett Browning did, to raise awareness of the issue and persuade the reader that the situation should not be tolerated. Be sure to describe the situation as you see it, using figurative language to stir the sympathies of your readers and persuade them to take action.

TEXT TALK

How did discussing the importance of the Fair Labor Standards Act of 1938 deepen your understanding of the text?

Answers will vary.

B Ask each Beyond grade-level student to write one additional discussion question. Then, have one or two students facilitate a discussion, using their questions to guide the conversation.

Writer's Notebook

Connect to Literary Period: Give students time to reflect on how "The Cry of the Children" demonstrates the conventions and characteristics of this unit's literary period, Victorian Literature, by freewriting in their Writer's Notebooks.

CHECK FOR SUCCESS

If students are still struggling to respond to the prompt, ask them scaffolded questions, such as:

- How does Barrett Browning express idealism in her poem?
- What problems does she perceive in British society of her time?

Reading Comprehension OPTIONAL

Have students complete the digital reading comprehension questions ✓ when they finish reading.

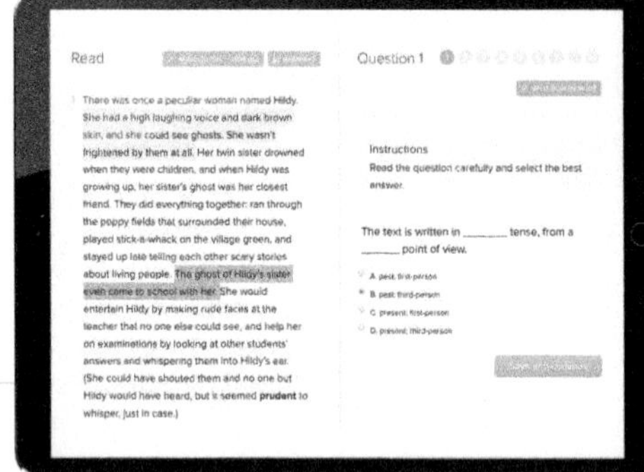

ANSWER KEY

QUESTION 1: B
QUESTION 2: A
QUESTION 3: D
QUESTION 4: C
QUESTION 5: D
QUESTION 6: B
QUESTION 7: D
QUESTION 8: A
QUESTION 9: *See first chart.*
QUESTION 10: *See second chart.*

The speaker	The children
"Let them touch each other's hands, in a fresh wreathing / Of their tender human youth!"	"Our knees tremble sorely in the stooping— / We fall upon our faces, trying to go;"
"They are weeping in the playtime of the others, / In the country of the free."	"When we sob aloud, the human creatures near us / Pass by, hearing not, or answer not a word!"
"The old tree is leafless in the forest— / The old year is ending in the frost—"	"And they tell us, of His image is the master / Who commands us to work on."

First	Second	Third	Fourth
The children rest their heads against their mothers.	The children plead with Alice to get up.	The children say they would rather sleep in the meadow than play.	The children doubt whether or not God can hear their pleas.

Connect and Extend OPTIONAL

CONNECT TO EXTENDED WRITING PROJECT

Students can use the the alienation from nature the child workers experience in "The Cry of the Children" to inspire their informative essays on the importance of nature.

BEYOND THE BOOK

Storytelling: The Industrial Revolution Revealed in Primary Sources

This poem articulates Browning's outrage with children working during the Industrial Revolution. Students will find, analyze, and discuss primary sources about child labor from the Industrial Revolution.

Ask students to:

- Conduct informal research on child labor during the Industrial Revolution using primary sources exclusively.
- Choose three different primary sources (e.g. photograph, letters, documents) that explain what life was like for a child.
- Analyze the sources and make inferences about the child's life.
- Weave these sources together in a journal entry through the perspective of a child.
- Share the story with the class.

To reflect, ask students:

- How can studying primary sources help shed light on the past?
- How is reading a primary source document different from reading a history book on a topic?

Collaborative Conversation

SCAFFOLDS

Post the writing prompt to generate a discussion in small groups. Ask students to first break down the prompt before they discuss relevant ideas and textual evidence.

This is a protest poem written to call attention to the terrible conditions endured by children who worked in British coal mines in the nineteenth century—conditions that endangered their souls as well as their health. Think about a cruel situation you would like to end. Perhaps you can find information about modern-day child labor or envision a way to help homeless students succeed in school. Write a poem, as Elizabeth Barrett Browning did, to raise awareness of the issue and persuade the reader that the situation should not be tolerated. Be sure to describe the situation as you see it, using figurative language to stir the sympathies of your readers and persuade them to take action.

Use the scaffolds below to differentiate instruction for your ELL English Language Learners and A Approaching grade-level learners.

ELL **BEGINNING, INTERMEDIATE** Use the discussion guide and speaking frames to facilitate the discussion with support from the teacher.

ADVANCED, ADVANCED HIGH Use the discussion guide and speaking frames to facilitate the discussion in mixed-level groups.

A **APPROACHING** Use the discussion guide to facilitate the discussion in mixed-level groups.

APPROACHING
ADVANCED, ADVANCED HIGH
BEGINNING, INTERMEDIATE

Discussion Guide	Speaking Frames
1. What is the problem that the poet describes in the text?	• The poem tells about children who ____. • The poet says that this is a problem because ____.
2. What are the lives of these children like?	• The children spend their time ____. • The children say they want to ____ instead of ____.
3. What does the poet want the reader to think or to do?	• The poet wants the reader to ____. • My evidence for this is ____.

Ethical Issues

Use the activity below to differentiate instruction for your B Beyond grade level learners.

Reread lines 10–12.

They are weeping bitterly!
They are weeping in the playtime of the others,
In the country of the free.

Have students consider the irony of a situation in which children are forced to work "in the country of the free."

Ask students:

- What dilemmas or controversies are involved with child labor?
- How have these dilemmas or controversies changed from the time of the poem, 1843, to the present?
- What social rules or norms are violated?

Review Prompt and Rubric

Before students begin writing, review the writing prompt and rubric with the class.

POETRY: This is a protest poem written to call attention to the terrible conditions endured by children who worked in British coal mines in the nineteenth century—conditions that endangered their souls as well as their health. Think about a cruel situation you would like to end. Perhaps you can find information about modern-day child labor or envision a way to help homeless students succeed in school. Write a poem, as Elizabeth Barrett Browning did, to raise awareness of the issue and persuade the reader that the situation should not be tolerated. Be sure to describe the situation as you see it, using figurative language to stir the sympathies of your readers and persuade them to take action.

PROMPT GUIDE

- What cruel or unjust situation for children do you know about?
- What makes this situation cruel or unjust?
- What images could you use in a poem to help people learn about this situation?

Score	Poetry	Language and Conventions
4	The writer clearly describes the unjust situation, raises awareness, and consistently uses figurative language effectively to stir the sympathies of the reader to take action.	The writer demonstrates a consistent command of grammar, punctuation, and usage conventions. Although minor errors may be evident, they do not detract from the fluency or the clarity of the essay.
3	The writer sufficiently describes the unjust situation, raises awareness, and uses figurative language to stir the sympathies of the reader to take action.	The writer demonstrates an adequate command of grammar, punctuation, and usage conventions. Although some errors may be evident, they create few (if any) disruptions in the fluency of the writing or the clarity of the essay.
2	The writer begins to describe the unjust situation, but the description is incomplete. The writer uses figurative language only some of the time to stir the sympathies of the reader to take action.	The writer demonstrates a partial command of grammar, punctuation, and usage conventions. Some distracting errors may be evident, at times creating minor disruptions in the fluency or clarity of the writing.
1	The writer attempts to describe the unjust situation, but the description is not successful. The writer uses little or no figurative language.	The writer demonstrates little or no command of grammar, punctuation, and usage conventions. Serious and persistent errors create disruptions in the fluency of the writing and sometimes interfere with meaning.
0	The writer does not provide a relevant response to the prompt or does not provide a response at all.	Serious and persistent errors overwhelm the writing and interfere with the meaning of the response as a whole, making the writer's meaning impossible to understand.

Write

SCAFFOLDS

Ask students to complete the writing assignment using text evidence to support their answers.

Use the scaffolds below to differentiate instruction for your ELL English Language Learners and A Approaching grade-level learners.

ELL **BEGINNING** With the help of the word bank, write a response using paragraph frame 1.

INTERMEDIATE With the help of the word bank, write a response using paragraph frames 1 and 2.

ADVANCED, ADVANCED HIGH Write a response of differentiated length using the sentence starters.

A **APPROACHING** Write a response of differentiated length using the sentence starters.

BEGINNING / INTERMEDIATE	BEGINNING / INTERMEDIATE	INTERMEDIATE	ADVANCED, ADVANCED HIGH / APPROACHING
Word Bank	**Paragraph Frame 1**	**Paragraph Frame 2**	**Sentence Starters**
crash hurting a bruise crying angry sobs change sad despair pay attention	It makes me ____. The people are ____. You can hear the ____. You will see ____ on their faces. It hurts like ____ to watch it. We need to ____.	It makes me ____. The people are ____. You can hear the ____. You will see ____ on their faces. It hurts like ____ to watch it. We need to ____. I believe ____. People can ____. We can make a difference by ____	• I wish . . . • I feel like crying when . . . • The people . . . • I believe that I must . . . • I can see . . . , and I can hear . . . • We can speak up for . . . . . .

Peer Review

Rate

Respond to the following with a point rating that reflects your opinion.

	1	2	3	4
Ideas				
Evidence				
Language and Conventions				

Submit

Students should submit substantive feedback to two peers using the review instructions below.

- How well does this response identify an unjust situation and explain why it is important to fix the problem?
- Which examples of figurative language in the poem are most effective?
- What does the writer do well in this response? What does the writer need to work on?

Remember that your comments are most useful when they are kind and constructive.

ELL A **SENTENCE FRAMES**

- You (completely / mostly / partly) ____described an unjust situation.
- You (fully / partly) ____ explained why it is important to fix the problem.
- One good example of figurative language was ____.
- My favorite part of your poem is ____.
- One part of the poem that can benefit from figurative language is ____.

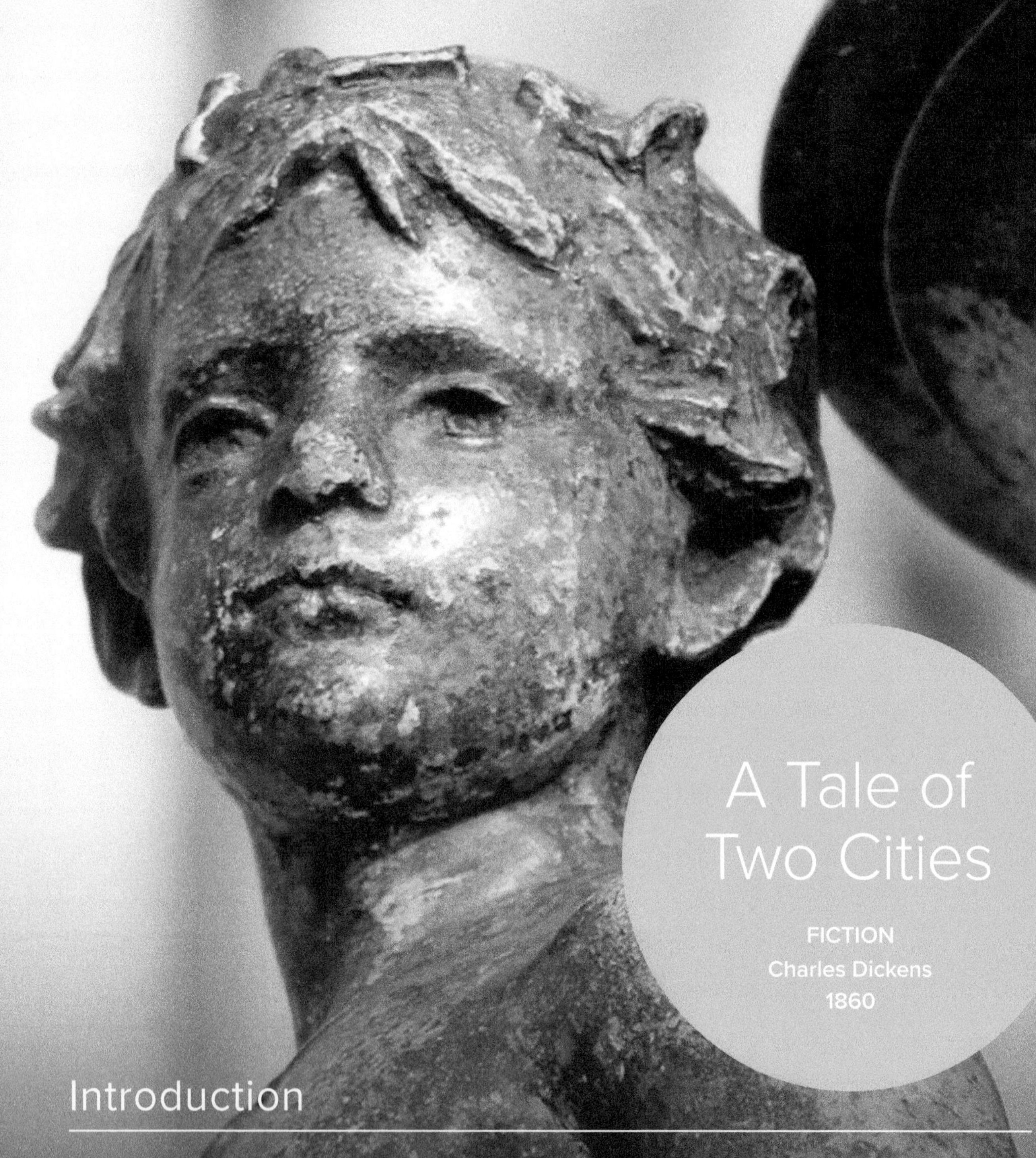

A Tale of Two Cities

FICTION
Charles Dickens
1860

Introduction

A *Tale of Two Cities* is an 1859 novel by Charles Dickens (1812–1870), one of the greatest and most popular writers of the Victorian era. Mixing fact and fiction, the story is set during the French Revolution near the end of the 18th century. Through this period of crisis and contradiction are intertwined human tales of suffering, justice, and courageous sacrifice. The novel opens with a rhythmic recitation of contrasts and similarities between the two titular settings, London and Paris.

The year 1775 was the best of times and it was the worst of times. Large-jawed kings sat on the thrones of both England and France, and it felt as if things were going to go on as they were forever. In England, apart from a recent message from the kingdom's American subjects, things were quiet. France, too, was rolling along, with plenty of money and good guidance from its spiritual leaders. Peasants who refused to kneel respectfully were punished accordingly, and the guillotine was already under construction. However, the Revolution was already brewing silently. Likewise, trouble was brewing in England, as daring burglaries and highway robberies were the norm. People were cautioned about going out at night, while masked thieves challenged men along the road or held hostages in drawing rooms. All these things were going on in 1775, while the little people planned and the kings continued to rule with divine right.

 Proficiency-leveled summaries and summaries in multiple languages are available digitally.

 Audio and audio text highlighting are available with this text.

CONNECT TO ESSENTIAL QUESTION

What is the power of story?

The first chapter of *A Tale of Two Cities* begins with the one of the most quoted and memorable openings in English literary history. The rest of the chapter sets the historical background for the events that will unfold before and during the French Revolution. Through this masterpiece, Charles Dickens uses the power of story to champion the poor and fight for social justice.

Entry Point

As students prepare to read *A Tale of Two Cities*, share the following information with them to provide context.

- ✓ Charles Dickens is among the best-known English writers in history. His characters and stories appeal to a wide variety of readers. These elements likely stem from Dickens's own experiences.
- ✓ His family was middle class, but his father's irresponsible financial habits often put them on the brink of ruin. At age 12, Dickens temporarily left school to work in a factory because his father had been sent to prison for debt.
- ✓ Dickens often included political and social messages in his works. *Hard Times*, for example, criticizes industrialization, *A Christmas Carol* encourages charity, and *Oliver Twist* sheds light on poverty.

Instructional Path

The print teacher's edition includes essential point-of-use instruction and planning tools. Complete lesson plans and program documents appear in your digital teacher account.

A TALE OF TWO CITIES

Independent Read: A Tale of Two Cities

Objectives: After reading an excerpt from *A Tale of Two Cities*, students will demonstrate their understanding of the author's development of the novel's beginning by explaining its dualities in a short written response.

Independent Read

Introduce the Text

As a class, watch the video preview and have students read the introduction in pairs to make connections to the video preview.

- How does the information from this video connect with what you already know?
- What are some examples of fictional stories that are inspired by real historical events?

ELL SPEAKING FRAMES

- I already knew about ___.
- ___ takes place during ___.

Access Complex Text

LEXILE: 1610 **WORD COUNT:** 1003

The following areas may be challenging for students, particularly ELL English Language Learners and A Approaching grade-level learners.

Specific Vocabulary	Prior Knowledge
• This text uses archaic and unfamiliar words that may prove challenging for students. • Encourage students to look for synonyms, antonyms, and other context clues in the text to infer word meaning.	• The text makes references to a number of people, places, and events that may be unfamiliar to contemporary American readers. • Encourage students to do some research on the French Revolution and the period leading up to it. Have students share their findings with the class.

"It was the best of times, it was the worst of times . . ."

NOTES

Chapter I
The Period

Charles Dickens

1 It was the best of times, it was the worst of times, it was the age of wisdom, it was the age of foolishness, it was the epoch of belief, it was the epoch of incredulity, it was the season of Light, it was the season of Darkness, it was the spring of hope, it was the winter of despair, we had everything before us, we had nothing before us, we were all going direct to Heaven, we were all going direct the other way—in short, the period was so far like the present period, that some of its noisiest **authorities** insisted on its being received, for good or for evil, in the superlative degree of comparison only.

2 There were a king with a large jaw and a queen with a plain face, on the throne of England; there were a king with a large jaw and a queen with a fair face, on the throne of France. In both countries it was clearer than crystal to the lords of the State preserves of loaves and fishes[1], that things in general were settled for ever.

3 It was the year of Our Lord one thousand seven hundred and seventy-five. Spiritual revelations were conceded to England at that favoured period, as at this. Mrs. Southcott[2] had recently attained her five-and-twentieth blessed birthday, of whom a prophetic private in the Life Guards had heralded the sublime appearance by announcing that arrangements were made for the swallowing up of London and Westminster. Even the Cock-lane ghost[3] had

1. **the lords of the State preserves of loaves and fishes** the aristocrats who manage the royal food supply
2. **Mrs. Southcott** Joanna Southcott, a woman who claimed to be a religious prophet
3. **Cock-lane Ghost** a reference to a purported haunting in a house on Cock Lane in London that attracted mass public attention

Developing Background Knowledge and Cultural Awareness

Guide students to do a brief online search related to *A Tale of Two Cities* and the French Revolution.

1. In small groups, have students do a five-minute online search of keywords related to *A Tale of Two Cities* and the French Revolution.
2. On the board, collate the various types of information students learned. Ask one student to volunteer to create an instant summary.

Discuss with students: The excerpt describes the divisions between rich and poor, between oppressor and oppressed, that existed leading up to the French Revolution. When else in history have such divisions existed? What causes people to lose empathy for each other across such divisions? What could close this distance?

SELECTION VOCABULARY

authority / la autoridad *noun* a person in whom power and clout is vested COGNATE

TEXT TALK

What are the two cities mentioned in the title?

See paragraphs 2–4: The text discusses England and France. The cities are most likely London and Paris.

Prepare for Advanced Courses

Use the activity below to differentiate instruction for your (B) Beyond grade level learners.

Author's Syntax

Reread the parallel structure used in the phrases that make up paragraph 1. Remind students that parallel structure is the use of a repeated pattern of words within a text.

Ask students:

- What is the purpose of this first paragraph, and how does the author's syntax support this purpose?
- How does the author's use of syntax in the first and second paragraphs develop mood and tension?
- How does the author's use of syntax in the first two paragraphs—specifically the use of "It was" at the beginning of many phrases and sentences—develop the narrative voice?

NOTES

been laid only a round dozen of years, after rapping out its messages, as the spirits of this very year last past (supernaturally deficient in originality) rapped out theirs. Mere messages in the earthly order of events had lately come to the English Crown and People, from a congress of British subjects in America: which, strange to relate, have proved more important to the human race than any communications yet received through any of the chickens of the Cock-lane brood.

4 France, less favoured on the whole as to matters spiritual than her sister of the shield and trident, rolled with **exceeding** smoothness down hill, making paper money and spending it. Under the guidance of her Christian pastors, she entertained herself, besides, with such humane achievements as sentencing a youth to have his hands cut off, his tongue torn out with pincers, and his body burned alive, because he had not kneeled down in the rain to do honour to a dirty procession of monks which passed within his view, at a distance of some fifty or sixty yards. It is likely enough that, rooted in the woods of France and Norway, there were growing trees, when that sufferer was put to death, already marked by the Woodman, Fate, to come down and be sawn into boards, to make a certain movable framework with a sack and a knife in it[4], terrible in history. It is likely enough that in the rough outhouses of some tillers of the heavy lands **adjacent** to Paris, there were sheltered from the weather that very day, rude carts, bespattered with **rustic** mire, snuffed about by pigs, and roosted in by poultry, which the Farmer, Death, had already set apart to be his tumbrils[5] of the Revolution. But that Woodman and that Farmer, though they work unceasingly, work silently, and no one heard them as they went about with muffled tread: the rather, forasmuch as to entertain any suspicion that they were awake, was to be atheistical and traitorous.

5 In England, there was scarcely an amount of order and protection to justify much national boasting. Daring burglaries by armed men, and highway robberies, took place in the capital itself every night; families were publicly cautioned not to go out of town without removing their furniture to upholsterers' warehouses for security; the highwayman in the dark was a City tradesman in the light, and, being recognised and challenged by his fellow-tradesman whom he stopped in his character of "the Captain," gallantly shot him through the head and rode away; the mall was waylaid by seven robbers, and the guard shot three dead, and then got shot dead himself by the other four, "in consequence of the failure of his ammunition:" after which the mall was robbed in peace; that magnificent potentate, the Lord Mayor of London, was made to stand and deliver on Turnham Green, by one highwayman, who despoiled the illustrious creature in sight of all his retinue[6]; prisoners in

4. **a certain movable framework with a sack and a knife in it** the guillotine
5. **tumbrils** the type of cart used during the French Revolution to take prisoners to the guillotine
6. **retinue** entourage

TEXT TALK

What happened to the Lord Mayor of London?

See paragraph 5: He was robbed by a highwayman.

What does the answer to the previous question tell you about the setting of the novel?

Lawlessness and burglaries were a widespread problem.

SELECTION VOCABULARY

exceeding / extraordinario/ a ***adjective*** exceptional

adjacent / contiguo ***adjective*** having a common boundary or edge; abutting, touching

rustic / rústico/ a ***adjective*** related to rural living COGNATE

requisition / el requerimiento ***noun*** the state of being required

London gaols fought battles with their turnkeys[7], and the majesty of the law fired blunderbusses in among them, loaded with rounds of shot and ball; thieves snipped off diamond crosses from the necks of noble lords at Court drawing-rooms; musketeers went into St. Giles's, to search for contraband goods, and the mob fired on the musketeers, and the musketeers fired on the mob, and nobody thought any of these occurrences much out of the common way. In the midst of them, the hangman, ever busy and ever worse than useless, was in constant **requisition**; now, stringing up long rows of miscellaneous criminals; now, hanging a housebreaker on Saturday who had been taken on Tuesday; now, burning people in the hand at Newgate by the dozen, and now burning pamphlets at the door of Westminster Hall; to-day, taking the life of an atrocious murderer, and to-morrow of a wretched pilferer who had robbed a farmer's boy of sixpence.

6 All these things, and a thousand like them, came to pass in and close upon the dear old year one thousand seven hundred and seventy-five. Environed by them, while the Woodman and the Farmer worked unheeded, those two of the large jaws[8], and those other two of the plain and the fair faces[9], trod with stir enough, and carried their divine rights with a high hand. Thus did the year one thousand seven hundred and seventy-five conduct their Greatnesses, and myriads of small creatures—the creatures of this chronicle among the rest—along the roads that lay before them.

7. **turnkeys** guards
8. **those two of the large jaws** the kings of England and France
9. **those other two of the plain and the fair faces** the queens of England and France

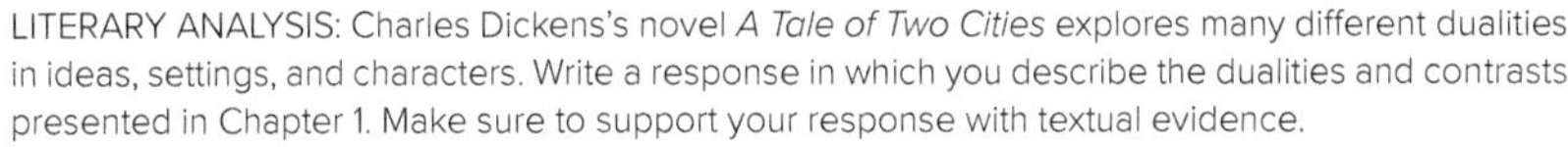

WRITE

LITERARY ANALYSIS: Charles Dickens's novel *A Tale of Two Cities* explores many different dualities in ideas, settings, and characters. Write a response in which you describe the dualities and contrasts presented in Chapter 1. Make sure to support your response with textual evidence.

TEXT TALK

How did discussing the French Revolution and divisions between people throughout history deepen your understanding of the text?

Answers will vary.

Ask each Beyond grade-level student to write one additional discussion question. Then, have one or two students facilitate a discussion, using their questions to guide the conversation.

Writer's Notebook

Connect to Literary Period: Give students time to reflect on how *A Tale of Two Cities* demonstrates the conventions and characteristics of this unit's literary period, Victorian Literature, by freewriting in their Writer's Notebooks.

CHECK FOR SUCCESS

If students are still struggling to respond to the prompt, ask them scaffolded questions, such as:

- What kind of people, places, and events does the text describe?
- Are the descriptions positive or negative?

Reading Comprehension OPTIONAL

Have students complete the digital reading comprehension questions ✓ when they finish reading.

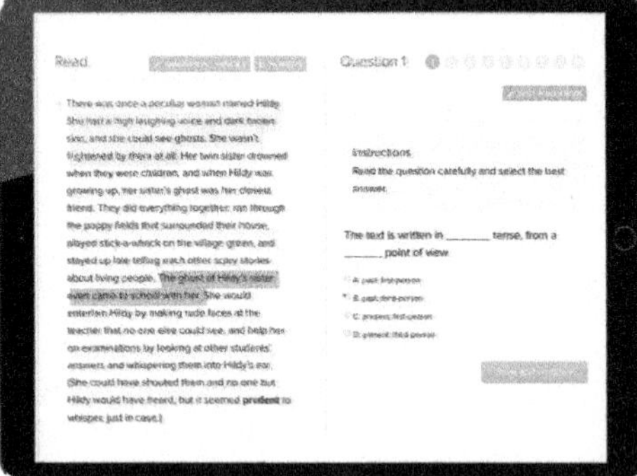

ANSWER KEY

QUESTION 1: B
QUESTION 2: D
QUESTION 3: A
QUESTION 4: B
QUESTION 5: A
QUESTION 6: C
QUESTION 7: D
QUESTION 8: C
QUESTION 9: *See first chart.*
QUESTION 10: *See second chart.*

First	Second	Third	Fourth
"It was the best of times, it was the worst of times, it was the age of wisdom, it was the age of foolishness,"	"Even the Cock-lane ghost had been laid only a round dozen of years, after rapping out its messages, as the spirits of this very year last past"	"But that Woodman and that Farmer, though they work inceasingly, work silently, and no one heard them as they went about with muffled tread:"	"Thus did the year one thousand seven hundred and seventy-five conduct their Greatnesses, and myriads of small creatures—the creatures of this chronicle among the rest—along the roads that lay before them."

Synonym	Word
need	requisition
pastoral	rustic
expert	authority
considerable	exceeding
bordering	adjacent

Connect and Extend OPTIONAL

CONNECT TO EXTENDED WRITING PROJECT

Students can find inspiration in the urban depictions in *A Tale of Two Cities*. Ask students to consider how experiences in nature can help alleviate some of the ills and stresses of life in urban settings, such as London or Paris.

BEYOND THE BOOK

Activity: Build The Setting

In Chapter 1, Dickens sets up the time period and locations for the reader. Students will create either France or England, using all aspects of setting.

Ask students to:

- Choose either France or England and reread the text, paying attention to all the details.
- Conduct informal research on the chosen location and the time.
  - > When does the story take place?
  - > What is the physical geography and location to the rest of the world?
  - > What are the people like? How do they dress? What is the weather? How do they socialize?
  - > What major historical events are occuring in the location at the time of the novel?
- Create a visual display of the setting chosen.
- Share with classmates, explaining the specific details that express the setting.

To reflect, ask students:

- Besides where and when, what elements make up the setting of a story?
- How will the characters' lives be affected by the setting?

StudySyncTV

Project the StudySyncTV episode  and pause at the following times to prompt discussion:

studysync

3:05 How does the group use the rhythm of the language to determine the meaning of the passage?

4:15 How do the students make connections between the text and society?

6:04 How do the students use the metaphor of the pendulum and textual evidence to draw conclusions about the text?

Collaborative Conversation

Post the writing prompt to generate a discussion in small groups. Ask students to first break down the prompt before they discuss relevant ideas and textual evidence. Ask students to use the StudySyncTV episodes as a model for discussion.

Charles Dickens's novel *A Tale of Two Cities* explores many different dualities in ideas, settings, and characters. Write a response in which you describe the dualities and contrasts presented in Chapter 1. Make sure to support your response with textual evidence.

Use the scaffolds below to differentiate instruction for your ELL English Language Learners and A Approaching grade-level learners.

ELL **BEGINNING, INTERMEDIATE** Use the discussion guide and speaking frames to facilitate the discussion with support from the teacher.

ADVANCED, ADVANCED HIGH Use the discussion guide and speaking frames to facilitate the discussion in mixed-level groups.

A **APPROACHING** Use the discussion guide to facilitate the discussion in mixed-level groups.

APPROACHING
ADVANCED, ADVANCED HIGH
BEGINNING, INTERMEDIATE

Discussion Guide	Speaking Frames
1. What are the dualities in ideas in *A Tale of Two Cities?*	• Pairs of contrasting ideas include ____.
2. How are the cities similar and different?	• Paris and London are similar because ____. • Paris and London are different because ____.
3. How do the people mentioned in *A Tale of Two Cities* show contrasts?	• Examples of contrasts in the people include ____.

Review Prompt and Rubric

Before students begin writing, review the writing prompt and rubric with the class.

LITERARY ANALYSIS: Charles Dickens's novel *A Tale of Two Cities* explores many different dualities in ideas, settings, and characters. Write a response in which you describe the dualities and contrasts presented in Chapter 1. Make sure to support your response with textual evidence.

PROMPT GUIDE

- What are the contrasts in ideas?
- What are the contrasts in settings?
- What are the contrasts in characters?

Score	Literary Analysis	Language and Conventions
4	The writer clearly explains dualities in the text, using relevant textual evidence as needed.	The writer demonstrates a consistent command of grammar, punctuation, and usage conventions. Although minor errors may be evident, they do not detract from the fluency or the clarity of the essay.
3	The writer sufficiently explains dualities in the text, using relevant textual evidence most of the time.	The writer demonstrates an adequate command of grammar, punctuation, and usage conventions. Although some errors may be evident, they create few (if any) disruptions in the fluency of the writing or the clarity of the essay.
2	The writer begins to explain dualities in the text, but the explanation is incomplete. The writer uses relevant textual evidence only some of the time.	The writer demonstrates a partial command of grammar, punctuation, and usage conventions. Some distracting errors may be evident, at times creating minor disruptions in the fluency or clarity of the writing.
1	The writer attempts to explain dualities in the text, but the explanation is not successful. The writer uses little or no relevant textual evidence.	The writer demonstrates little or no command of grammar, punctuation, and usage conventions. Serious and persistent errors create disruptions in the fluency of the writing and sometimes interfere with meaning.
0	The writer does not provide a relevant response to the prompt or does not provide a response at all.	Serious and persistent errors overwhelm the writing and interfere with the meaning of the response as a whole, making the writer's meaning impossible to understand.

Write

SCAFFOLDS

Ask students to complete the writing assignment using text evidence to support their answers.

Use the scaffolds below to differentiate instruction for your ELL English Language Learners and A Approaching grade-level readers.

ELL **BEGINNING** With the help of the word bank, write a response using paragraph frame 1.

INTERMEDIATE With the help of the word bank, write a response using paragraph frames 1 and 2.

ADVANCED, ADVANCED HIGH Write a response of differentiated length using the sentence starters.

A **APPROACHING** Write a response of differentiated length using the sentence starters.

BEGINNING / INTERMEDIATE		INTERMEDIATE	ADVANCED, ADVANCED HIGH / APPROACHING
Word Bank	**Paragraph Frame 1**	**Paragraph Frame 2**	**Sentence Starters**
crime punishments kings problems France	In Chapter 1 of *A Tale of Two Cities*, Charles Dickens compares and contrasts England with ____ The countries are alike because they both have ____ . Both countries also suffer from ____. The French people suffer because of unfair ____, and the English suffer because of ____.	A piece of evidence that shows how the countries are similar is that ____. A piece evidence that shows how the countries are different is that ____. By comparing and contrasting these two nations, Dickens suggests ____. For example, ____.	• In *A Tale of Two Cities*, Dickens describes . . . • In France, . . . • In England, . . . • Both countries are similar because . . . • The countries are different because . . . • People in both countries are . . .

Peer Review

Rate

Respond to the following with a point rating that reflects your opinion.

	1	2	3	4
Ideas				
Evidence				
Language and Conventions				

Submit

Students should submit substantive feedback to two peers using the review instructions below.

- How well does this response answer the prompt?
- Does the writer explain the dualities and contrasts in ideas, settings, and characters?
- What new insights did you get from the writer's response? Are there any ideas that need more consideration?
- What does the writer do well in this response? What does the writer need to work on?

Remember that your comments are most useful when they are kind and constructive.

ELL **SENTENCE FRAMES**

- You were able to (completely / partly / almost) ____ answer the prompt.
- You could answer the prompt more completely by . . .
- I liked your idea that . . .
- An idea that could be better explained is . . .
- My favorite part of your response is . . .

Jane Eyre

FICTION

Charlotte Brontë

1847

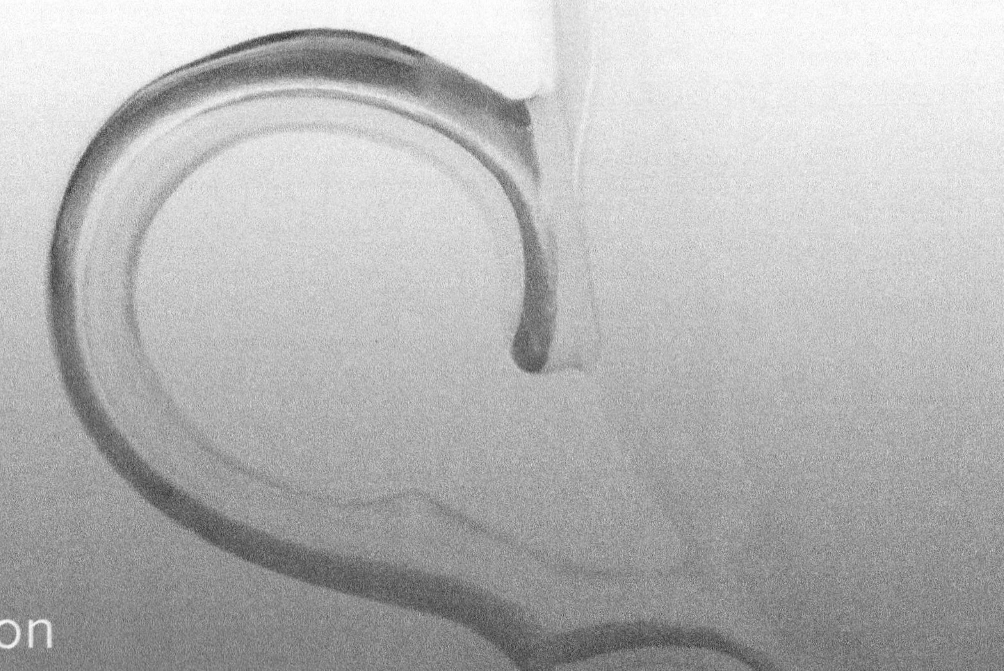

Introduction

Charlotte Brontë (1816–1855) is one of the best-known English novelists of the 19th century. Many of her works, including *Jane Eyre*, were published under the pseudonym Currer Bell in order to disguise her sex, as female authors were not commonly accepted in England during this time period. In *Jane Eyre*, the novel's protagonist, Jane, grows up as an orphan and regularly feels like an outcast. Eventually, she takes a job caring for a young girl, Adèle, at Thornfield Hall. In this excerpt from the novel, Jane has recently arrived at Thornfield Hall and begun her new job. She describes her feelings toward Adèle, the work, and her larger desires for life.

Arriving at Thornfield Hall, Jane is presented with the possibility of a long career. Mrs. Fairfax is even-tempered and kind, and her daughter Adele, while not especially talented, quickly becomes an obedient student. Jane likes Adele and Mrs. Fairfax, but something in her cries out for more. Often, in her free time, Jane finds herself in the attic, looking out over field and hill, longing for the life beyond—a life she has heard about but never experienced. Restlessness is part of her nature and the only relief she can find is to pace the attic, lost in daydreams. Jane believes that human beings are dissatisfied with tranquility and speaks of the little rebellions growing in the hearts of people who long to revolt against their lot in life. Lastly, she adds that women too—not just men—long to use their given faculties to the fullest, and suffer from stagnation, just as men would.

Proficiency-leveled summaries and summaries in multiple languages are available digitally.

Audio and audio text highlighting are available with this text.

COMPARING WITHIN AND ACROSS GENRES

The excerpt from the novel Jane Eyre by English writer Charlotte Brontë and the essay "Jabberwocky Baby" by African American poet Wanda Coleman are paired together to provide different perspectives on what it feels like to be held back by society's restrictions and expectations. In addition, this comparison includes Coleman's poem "Dear Mama," giving students the opportunity to read both literary and nonfiction works by the same writer.

Entry Point

As students prepare to read "Jane Eyre," share the following information with them to provide context.

- ✓ Published in 1847, *Jane Eyre* tells the story of a governess who falls in love with her pupil's guardian, Mr. Rochester. Right before they marry, it is revealed that Rochester has a secret wife he keeps locked in the house. He explains that he was tricked into marrying a Jamaican heiress, Bertha, who developed a mental illness shortly following their union.
- ✓ The characters in *Jane Eyre* are heavily influenced by the gender-based and colonial power dynamics that are a product of the novel's historical setting. In 1966, Jean Rhys wrote *Wide Sargasso Sea*, a feminist and anticolonial version of *Jane Eyre* that is told from Bertha's perspective. In this version of the story, Bertha is declared mentally ill by her husband, whose unfaithfulness and emotional abuse begin early in their marriage. Jean Rhys explores the power dynamics between men and women and postcolonial themes, such as racism, displacement, and assimilation.

Instructional Path

The print teacher's edition includes essential point-of-use instruction and planning tools. Complete lesson plans and program documents appear in your digital teacher account.

Independent Read: Jane Eyre

Objectives: After reading an excerpt from *Jane Eyre*, students will write a short argumentative response that analyzes textual evidence to argue whether or not Jane Eyre was content at Thornfield Hall.

Skill: Analyzing Victorian Literature

Objectives: After reading and discussing a model of close reading, students will be able to explain how a text from the unit reflects the literary period of Victorianism.

Independent Read

Introduce the Text

As a class, watch the video preview and have students read the introduction in pairs to make connections to the video preview.

- What kind of story are you about to read? How can you tell?
- Have you ever felt like you don't fit in? Why?

ELL **SPEAKING FRAMES**

- I think the story will be ____. A clue was ____.
- I once felt like I did not fit in with ____. I felt this way because ____.

Access Complex Text

LEXILE: 1280 **WORD COUNT:** 781

The following areas may be challenging for students, particularly ELL English Language Learners and A Approaching grade-level learners.

"... they must have action; and they will make it if they cannot find it."

NOTES

1 The promise of a smooth career, which my first calm introduction to Thornfield Hall seemed to pledge, was not belied on a longer acquaintance with the place and its inmates. Mrs. Fairfax turned out to be what she appeared, a **placid**-tempered, kind-natured woman, of competent education and average intelligence. My pupil was a lively child, who had been spoilt and indulged, and therefore was sometimes wayward; but as she was committed entirely to my care, and no injudicious interference from any quarter ever thwarted my plans for her improvement, she soon forgot her little freaks, and became obedient and teachable. She had no great talents, no marked traits of character, no peculiar development of feeling or taste which raised her one inch above the ordinary level of childhood; but neither had she any deficiency or vice which sunk her below it. She made reasonable progress, entertained for me a **vivacious**, though perhaps not very profound, affection; and by her simplicity, gay prattle[1], and efforts to please, inspired me, in return, with a degree of attachment sufficient to make us both content in each other's society.

Illustration of Charlotte Bronte

2 This, *par parenthèse*[2], will be thought cool language by persons who entertain solemn doctrines about the angelic nature of children, and the duty of those charged with their education to conceive for them an idolatrous devotion: but I am not writing to flatter parental egotism, to echo cant[3], or prop up humbug[4]; I am merely telling the truth. I felt a **conscientious** solicitude for Adèle's welfare and progress, and a quiet liking for her little self: just as I cherished towards Mrs. Fairfax a thankfulness for her kindness, and a pleasure in her

1. **gay prattle** pleasant and empty conversation
2. **par parenthèse** incidentally
3. **echo cant** a monotonous, rhythmic chant that has two "sides" calling in tandem
4. **prop up humbug** support deceptive or false speech or action

Developing Background Knowledge and Cultural Awareness

Find out what your students already know about the author.

1. In small groups, have students do a five-minute online search of keywords related to Charlotte Bronte.
2. On the board, collate the various types of information students learned. Ask one student to volunteer to create an instant summary.

Discuss with students: Charlotte Bronte and her sisters had to use male pseudonyms to have their first novels published. While for different reasons, people still choose to use pseudonyms today. Why might someone want to hide their identity behind a new name? What advantages and disadvantages are there to changing who you are in the public eye, especially when writing or communicating something?

TEXT TALK

What does Jane think of her student?

See paragraph 1: Jane thinks Adèle was spoiled at first, but now she thinks she is pleasant and unremarkable.

SELECTION VOCABULARY

placid / plácido/a *adjective* calm and peaceful; not easily emotional COGNATE

vivacious / vivaz *adjective* energetic and happy; lively COGNATE

conscientious / concienzudo/a *adjective* characterized by extreme care and great effort COGNATE

Prepare for Advanced Courses

Use the activity below to differentiate instruction for your B Beyond grade level learners.

Analyze for Enrichment

Reread paragraph 5.

Although this text comes from literature, ask students to reread it as if it were a piece of argumentative writing.

Ask students:

- What is the thesis of Jane's argument about the condition and character of women?
- What reasons does Jane give to support her position?
- How do Jane's current experiences at Thornfield Hall support or undermine her argument?
- How does Jane's presentation of this argument both reveal aspects of her character and suggest themes for the novel?

NOTES

society proportionate to the tranquil regard she had for me, and the moderation of her mind and character.

3 Anybody may blame me who likes, when I add further, that, now and then, when I took a walk by myself in the grounds; when I went down to the gates and looked through them along the road; or when, while Adèle played with her nurse, and Mrs. Fairfax made jellies in the storeroom, I climbed the three staircases, raised the trap-door of the attic, and having reached the leads, looked out afar over sequestered field and hill, and along dim sky-line—that then I longed for a power of vision which might overpass that limit; which might reach the busy world, towns, regions full of life I had heard of but never seen—that then I desired more of practical experience than I possessed; more of intercourse with my kind, of acquaintance with variety of character, than was here within my reach. I valued what was good in Mrs. Fairfax, and what was good in Adèle; but I believed in the existence of other and more vivid kinds of goodness, and what I believed in I wished to behold.

4 Who blames me? Many, no doubt; and I shall be called discontented. I could not help it: the restlessness was in my nature; it **agitated** me to pain sometimes. Then my sole relief was to walk along the corridor of the third storey, backwards and forwards, safe in the silence and solitude of the spot, and allow my mind's eye to dwell on whatever bright visions rose before it—and, certainly, they were many and glowing; to let my heart be heaved by the exultant movement, which, while it swelled it in trouble, expanded it with life; and, best of all, to open my inward ear to a tale that was never ended—a tale my imagination created, and narrated continuously; quickened with all of incident, life, fire, feeling, that I desired and had not in my actual existence.

5 It is in vain to say human beings ought to be satisfied with tranquillity: they must have action; and they will make it if they cannot find it. Millions are condemned to a stiller doom than mine, and millions are in silent revolt against their lot. Nobody knows how many rebellions besides political rebellions ferment in the masses of life which people earth. Women are supposed to be very calm generally: but women feel just as men feel; they need exercise for their faculties, and a field for their efforts, as much as their brothers do; they suffer from too rigid a restraint, too absolute a **stagnation**, precisely as men would suffer; and it is narrow-minded in their more privileged fellow-creatures to say that they ought to confine themselves to making puddings and knitting stockings, to playing on the piano and embroidering bags. It is thoughtless to condemn them, or laugh at them, if they seek to do more or learn more than custom has pronounced necessary for their sex.

TEXT TALK

How does Jane describe herself?

See paragraph 4: Jane describes herself as restless and agitated.

What do women need, according to Jane?

See paragraph 5: Women need freedom to exercise their minds and make their own choices beyond the domestic sphere.

How did researching the author help you better understand Jane's feelings in this excerpt?

Answers will vary.

SELECTION VOCABULARY

agitate / agitar *verb* to cause excitement, anger, or general disturbance COGNATE

stagnation / el estancamiento *noun* the state of being still or without movement

WRITE

In this excerpt, Jane mentions many positive and negative aspects of her current situation at Thornfield Hall. Considering the evidence, is Jane content with her current situation? Using textual evidence to support your claim, write a response of at least 300 words arguing whether or not Jane is happy at Thornfield Hall.

Writer's Notebook

Connect to Literary Period: Give students time to reflect on how *Jane Eyre* demonstrates the conventions and characteristics of this unit's literary period, Victorian Literature, by freewriting in their Writer's Notebooks.

CHECK FOR SUCCESS

If students are still struggling to respond to the prompt, ask them scaffolded questions, such as:

- What feelings or ideas are revealed in this excerpt?
- How do Jane's desires reflect Victorian issues?

Reading Comprehension OPTIONAL

Have students complete the digital reading comprehension questions when they finish reading.

ANSWER KEY

QUESTION 1: B
QUESTION 2: D
QUESTION 3: A
QUESTION 4: D

QUESTION 5:
See chart below.

Definition	Word
failure to develop or advance	stagnation
lively and animated	vivacious
upset or disturbed	agitated
doing one's work or duty well	conscientious
calm and peaceful	placid

Connect and Extend OPTIONAL

CONNECT TO EXTENDED WRITING PROJECT

Students can find inspiration from *Jane Eyre* for their informative essays. Have students review the last paragraph of the excerpt and analyze the claim the narrator makes about social restrictions on women. Ask students to consider what makes the writing persuasive and compelling.

BEYOND THE BOOK

Graphic Story: Dreams vs. Reality

In this excerpt Jane is describing her surroundings, but shares how she is bored and desires more action in her life. Students will create a graphic story, or short comic book, showing the contrast between Jane Eyre's reality and what she is longing for.

Ask students to:

- Create a T-Chart: for the first column, select textual evidence that explains Jane Eyre's reality, and, for the second column, select textual evidence that explains her wishes.
- Use the details in the T-chart to inspire a graphic story, or short comic book, that shows Jane Eyre going through the motions of her life while dreaming about what could be.
- Share their stories with classmates explaining what textual evidence inspired each decision.

Collaborative Conversation

SCAFFOLDS

Post the writing prompt to generate a discussion in small groups. Ask students to first break down the prompt before they discuss relevant ideas and textual evidence.

In this excerpt, Jane mentions many positive and negative aspects of her current situation at Thornfield Hall. Overall, is Jane happy with her current situation? Why or why not? Argue your case in an essay of at least 300 words. Include multiple pieces of textual evidence to make your argument convincing.

Use the scaffolds below to differentiate instruction for your ELL English Language Learners and A Approaching grade-level learners.

ELL **BEGINNING, INTERMEDIATE** Use the discussion guide and speaking frames to facilitate the discussion with support from the teacher.

ADVANCED, ADVANCED HIGH Use the discussion guide and speaking frames to facilitate the discussion in mixed-level groups.

A APPROACHING Use the discussion guide to facilitate the discussion in mixed-level groups.

APPROACHING
ADVANCED, ADVANCED HIGH
BEGINNING, INTERMEDIATE

Discussion Guide	Speaking Frames
1. What does Jane like about her life at Thornfield Hall?	• Jane likes ____. • The text shows that ____.
2. What does Jane dislike about her life at Thornfield Hall?	• Jane dislikes ____. • The text shows that ____.
3. What are Jane's overall feelings about her life at Thornfield Hall?	• Overall, I think Jane feels ____. • The text shows that ____.

Ethical Issues

Use the activity below to differentiate instruction for your B Beyond grade level learners.

Reread the final sentence of the excerpt:

It is thoughtless to condemn them, or laugh at them, if they seek to do more or learn more than custom has pronounced for their sex.

Ask students:

- What dilemmas or controversies are involved with the way women are treated in 19th century England?
- From the perspective of an English citizen of the 1800s, what social rules or norms are being violated?
- From your 21st century perspective, what social rules or norms are being violated?

Review Prompt and Rubric

Before students begin writing, review the writing prompt and rubric with the class.

ARGUMENTATIVE In this excerpt, Jane mentions many positive and negative aspects of her current situation at Thornfield Hall. Overall, is Jane happy with her current situation? Why or why not? Argue your case in an essay of at least 300 words. Include multiple pieces of textual evidence to make your argument convincing.

 PROMPT GUIDE

- What does Jane like about her life at Thornfield Hall?
- What does Jane dislike about her life at Thornfield Hall?
- What are Jane's overall feelings about her life at Thornfield Hall?
- What textual evidence can you use to convince others of your claim?

Score	Argument	Language and Conventions
4	The writer clearly states a claim and provides strong support, using sufficient and relevant textual evidence in the argumentative response.	The writer demonstrates a consistent command of grammar, punctuation, and usage conventions. Although minor errors may be evident, they do not detract from the fluency or the clarity of the essay.
3	The writer states a claim and provides support, using relevant textual evidence most of the time.	The writer demonstrates an adequate command of grammar, punctuation, and usage conventions. Although some errors may be evident, they create few (if any) disruptions in the fluency of the writing or the clarity of the essay.
2	The writer states a claim and attempts to provide support, but the support is insufficient. The writer uses relevant textual evidence only some of the time in the argumentative response.	The writer demonstrates a partial command of grammar, punctuation, and usage conventions. Some distracting errors may be evident, at times creating minor disruptions in the fluency or clarity of the writing.
1	The writer attempts to state a claim but fails to provide support. The writer uses little or no relevant textual evidence in the argumentative response.	The writer demonstrates little or no command of grammar, punctuation, and usage conventions. Serious and persistent errors create disruptions in the fluency of the writing and sometimes interfere with meaning.
0	The writer does not provide a relevant response to the prompt or does not provide a response at all.	Serious and persistent errors overwhelm the writing and interfere with the meaning of the response as a whole, making the writer's meaning impossible to understand.

Write

SCAFFOLDS

Ask students to complete the writing assignment using text evidence to support their answers.

Use the scaffolds below to differentiate instruction for your ELL English Language Learners and A Approaching grade-level learners.

ELL **BEGINNING** With the help of the word bank, write a response using paragraph frame 1.

INTERMEDIATE With the help of the word bank, write a response using paragraph frames 1 and 2.

ADVANCED, ADVANCED HIGH Write a response of differentiated length using the sentence starters.

A **APPROACHING** Write a response of differentiated length using the sentence starters.

BEGINNING / INTERMEDIATE	BEGINNING / INTERMEDIATE	INTERMEDIATE	ADVANCED, ADVANCED HIGH / APPROACHING
Word Bank	**Paragraph Frame 1**	**Paragraph Frame 2**	**Sentence Starters**
freedom student restless calm land	Jane describes her first days at Thornfield Hall as ____. Jane cares for her ____. She enjoys looking out at the ____ around the estate. Jane also feels ____. She wishes that women had more ____. Overall, I think Jane is / is not happy with her situation at Thornfield Hall.	Although Jane likes / dislikes some parts about her life at Thornfield Hall, the text shows that she feels ____ about the experience overall. For example, Jane's reflections show that she ____. A quotation from the text that supports this idea is ____.	• Janes feels . . . about her life at Thornfield Hall. • Jane likes . . . • Jane dislikes . . . • Some textual evidence that supports this idea is . . . • This shows that Jane feels . . .

Peer Review

Students should submit substantive feedback to two peers using the review instructions below.

- How well does this response answer the prompt?
- Does the writer include strong and sufficient supporting textual evidence?
- What does the writer do well in this response? What does the writer need to work on?

Remember that your comments are most useful when they are kind and constructive.

Rate

Respond to the following with a point rating that reflects your opinion.

1 2 3 4

Ideas

Evidence

Language and Conventions

Submit

SENTENCE FRAMES

A

- You were able to (completely / partly / almost) ____ answer the prompt.
- You could answer the prompt more completely by ____.
- Some strong textual evidence you included is ____.
- Your idea about ____ needs more support.

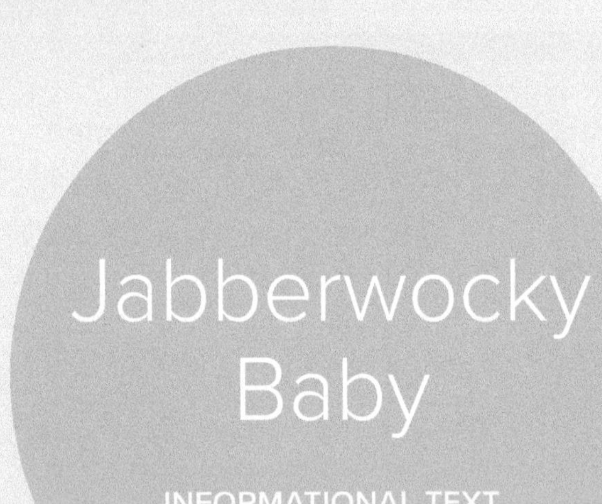

Jabberwocky Baby

INFORMATIONAL TEXT
Wanda Coleman
2005

Introduction

Wanda Coleman (1946–2013) was a nationally renowned poet who frequently wrote about the complexities of growing up and living as a black woman in the city of Los Angeles. "Jabberwocky Baby" is from Coleman's *The Riot Inside Me*, a collection of writings on art, politics, race, and class—and on the practice of writing itself. Here, she investigates the alienation she endured as a book-loving African American child growing up in 1950s and 60s, and how the topsy-turvy surreality of Lewis Carroll's works reflected her own adolescence and came to have a profound effect on her poetry.

Wanda Coleman says she grew up in an environment of "intellectual loneliness." Like other awkward children, Coleman found escape through reading, but she did not have many books. She quickly devoured her parents' magazines and covertly began dipping into the adults-only books her mother kept hidden. When she was ten, her cousin gave her a copy of *Alice's Adventures in Wonderland,* and Coleman fell in love with Lewis Carroll's poetry. While commonly regarded as nonsense, it made perfect sense to Coleman, since the world she lived in—1960s Los Angeles—was itself an upside -down world. While her white teachers told her that police were there to help, her parents were often too afraid to ask them for directions. At the time, being black in L.A. meant confronting one dehumanizing injustice after another; and Coleman recalls how, even as a free citizen, a black person was wise to avoid certain places after sundown.

Proficiency-leveled summaries and summaries in multiple languages are available digitally.

Audio and audio text highlighting are available with this text.

COMPARING WITHIN AND ACROSS GENRES

Before reading Wanda Coleman's poem "Dear Mama," students will read the essay "Jabberwocky Baby," by the poet. In this essay, Coleman recalls her own struggles to fit into a society that discriminated against her and describes finding solace in literature, particularly in the works of prominent Victorian writer, Lewis Carroll. Students can draw comparisons between this essay and the excerpt from Jane Eyre, in which the heroine struggles under restrictive Victorian social norms.

Entry Point

As students prepare to read "Jabberwocky Baby," share the following information with them to provide context.

- ✓ The title "Jabberwocky, Baby" refers to Lewis Carroll's poem "Jabberwocky," which appears in *Through the Looking-Glass*, the sequel to *Alice's Adventures in Wonderland*. "Jabberwocky" is considered one of the greatest nonsense poems written in English, telling the tale of the mythical Jabberwock, and using many words of Carroll's own creation. At least one of those words, *chortle*, has found its way into regular English usage, as a combination of chuckle and snort.
- ✓ *Alice's Adventures in Wonderland* has achieved worldwide adoration since its publication in 1865, spawning film, TV, and stage adaptations and introducing readers to such memorable characters as the Cheshire Cat, the White Rabbit, and the Mad Hatter.
- ✓ Wanda Coleman, who is known as "the L.A. Blueswoman" and "the unofficial poet laureate of Los Angeles," highlights social inequalities in her writing, emphasizing their absurdity. Perhaps this is why Alice's adventures in nonsensical worlds "made perfect sense" to Coleman.

Instructional Path

The print teacher's edition includes essential point-of-use instruction and planning tools. Complete lesson plans and program documents appear in your digital teacher account.

Jabberwocky Baby

Independent Read: Jabberwocky Baby

Objectives: After reading the text, students will write a short response explaining the personal meaning, key ideas and impact of a work of art, using relevant textual evidence in their response.

Independent Read

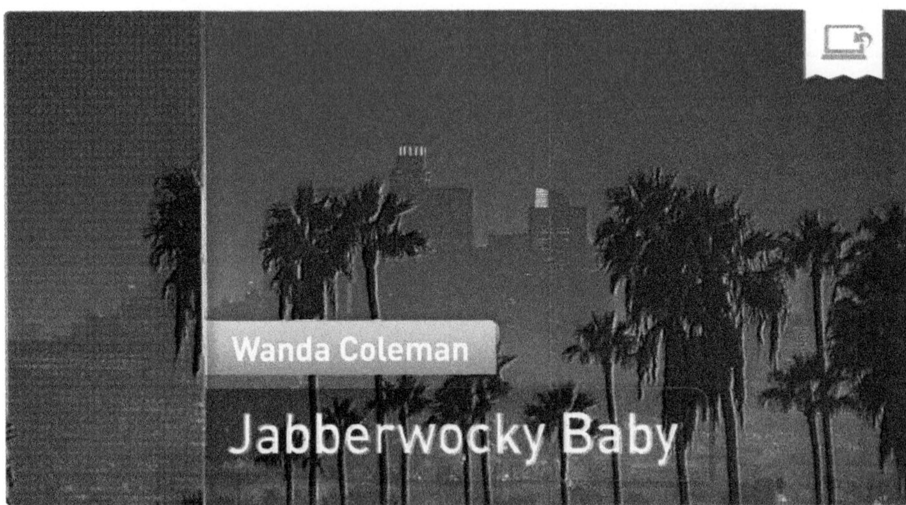

Introduce the Text

As a class, watch the video preview and have students read the introduction in pairs to make connections to the video preview.

- How do the images, words, and music in this video make you feel?
- Do you have a particular book or work of art that was meaningful to you as a child? What made it meaningful?
- In what ways does the book or work of art still impact you today?

Access Complex Text

LEXILE: 1290 **WORD COUNT:** 2580

The following areas may be challenging for students, particularly ELL English Language Learners and A Approaching grade-level learners.

Organization

- Tell students that this excerpt is organized like a memoir, in which the author narrates an event from her childhood while occasionally inserting thoughts from the time when she was writing it.
- Explain to students that they can note these changes by paying attention to when verbs shift between past and present tense.

Prior Knowledge

- Students may not be familiar with many of the works mentioned by Coleman in this excerpt.
- Have students work in groups to identify the works mentioned. Assist them as needed to understand the difficulty level of the works Coleman read at different ages.

"My reading appetite had no limits."

NOTES

1 The stultifying intellectual loneliness of my 1950s and '60s upbringing was dictated by my looks—dark skin and unconkable kinky hair. Boys gawked at me, and girls tittered behind my back. Black teachers shook their heads in pity, and White teachers stared in amusement or in wonder. I found this **rejection** unbearable and, encouraged by my parents to read, sought an escape in books, which were usually hard to come by. There were no colored-owned bookstores in our neighborhood. The libraries discouraged Negro readers.

2 My reading appetite had no limits. At six or seven I was slogging through Papa's **dull** issues of *National Geographic* and Mama's tepid copies of *Reader's Digest* and her favorite murder mysteries. At age ten I consumed the household copy of the complete works of Shakespeare, and while the violence was striking—and *Hamlet* engrossing, particularly Ophelia—I was too immature to fully appreciate The Bard until frequent rereadings during my mid-teens. In high school I would read Plato's *Dialogues*, Aristotle's *Metaphysics*, Machiavelli's *The Prince*, and Alexander Pope, and my teachers would complain to my parents that I was reading the wrong kind of literature, that my "little learning" was "a dangerous thing."

3 One Christmas, around age ten, I received Johanna Spyri's *Heidi* as a well-intended gift. I had long exhausted our teensy library, including my father's collections of *Knight*, *Esquire*, and *Playboy* (kept in the garage), and had begun sneaking through my mother's dresser drawers to scarf on unexpurgated Henry Miller. But between my raids on the adults-only stuff, there were only the Sunday funnies (*Brenda Starr*), comic books (*Archie*, *Little Lulu*), and *Heidi*, reread in desperation until I could quote chunks of the text, **mentally** squeezing it for what I imagined to be hidden underneath. One early-spring day, my adult first-cousin Rubyline came by the house with a nourishing belated Christmas gift: an illustrated one-volume edition of *Alice's Adventures in Wonderland* and *Through the Looking-Glass*. (Later, on my twelfth birthday, she would also give me my first *Roget's*, which I still use.)

4 In love with poetry since kindergarten, my "uffish" vows were startlingly renewed with *Alice*. Saved, I promptly retired *Heidi* and steeped myself in

SELECTION VOCABULARY

rejection / el rechazo *noun* state of being unaccepted

dull / aburrido/a *adjective* lacking in liveliness or animation; lacking in interest

mentally / mentalmente *adverb* with or in one's mind COGNATE

Developing Background Knowledge and Cultural Awareness

Find out what images come to mind when your students think of Lewis Carroll.

1. Tell students to take a few minutes to brainstorm images related to *Alice's Adventures in Wonderland* and *Through the Looking-Glass* by Lewis Carroll.
2. In small groups, have students do a quick online search of images. Choose one or two to project and discuss as a class.

Discuss with students: Research shows a correlation between home libraries and academic success for students. What are some reasons why some children might have less access to books than others? What could individuals, schools, and organizations do to change this inequality?

TEXT TALK

Why were books hard to come by when Coleman's parents encouraged her to read?

See paragraph 1: There were no black-owned bookstores in her neighborhood and libraries discouraged black readers. Her family also did not have money for books.

Why does Coleman sneak around trying to read "adults-only stuff"?

See paragraph 3: She had exhausted what little there was to readily read and so she goes looking for anything interesting she can find.

Prepare for Advanced Courses

Use the activity below to differentiate instruction for your B Beyond grade level learners.

Analyze for Enrichment

Reread the first sentence of paragraph 1.

Ask students:

- How, specifically, did the prejudice and racism of the 1950s and '60s influence the author's intellectual isolation? (Consider not only her and her family's access to texts, but also the content of the texts she was able to acquire before her twelfth birthday.)
- How do the author's experiences with literature before her twelfth birthday and experiences in her childhood world of Los Angeles support her uncommon position that "Jabberwocky" makes "perfect sense"?

TEXT TALK

What are some examples of the hypocrisy Coleman experienced growing up?

Answers will vary, but should include an understanding of how those who were in service to the community—doctors, teachers, policemen—treated black people in hypocritical ways.

How does identifying the answer to question 2 deepen your understanding of Coleman's relationship to reading?

Answers will vary.

How did discussing access to books deepen your understanding of the text?

Answers will vary.

B Ask each Beyond grade-level student to write one additional discussion question. Then, have one or two students facilitate a discussion, using their questions to guide the conversation.

NOTES

Alice to an iambic spazz. "Jabberwocky" is one of only about a dozen poems I've ever loved enough to memorize (among the others are Poe's "Raven," Service's "Cremation of Sam McGee," Byron's "Prisoner of Chillon," Coleridge's "Rime of the Ancient Mariner," Henley's "Invictus," and E.A. Robinson's "Richard Cory").

5 Lewis Carroll's influence on my poetry is easily **discerned**. I occasionally allude to characters from *Alice* (the White Rabbit, the Cheshire Cat, and my favorite, the Red Queen), dot poems with references to his memorable lines and phrases, and have even written a poem in homage ("Black Alice Laments," in *Mercurochrome*). In one of my poetic fugues, I imagine my own mad tea party, to which I invite deceased surrealist writers and artists whom I admire ("The Ron Narrative Reconstructions," in *Bathwater Wine*).

6 Many have referred to Carroll's rhymes as nonsense, but in my childhood world—Los Angeles in the '50s—they made perfect sense. It was a city where up was down and down was up. Black adults were always scrounging for money, regardless of how good or how bad they were. White people laughed at things that were not funny. Distances were deceptive and maps untrustworthy. My parents were constantly getting lost and were frightened of asking the police or fireman for assistance, those same authorities White teachers said were friendly and there to protect and serve us. Smiling White adults were instantly and incomprehensibly nasty to us the moment our parents were not around. Waiters, waitresses, and drive-in car hops were hostile, always got our orders wrong, served our food cold, or made us wait until they had attended to everyone else beforehand. Store clerks refused to take our money unless we asked for the correct amount first. White doctors and nurses would never touch us with their bare hands, and seldom with gloves on. White ministers smiled while calling us heathens and pickaninnies. Black and Mexican children were **chastised** or ignored for behavior that earned White children recognition and praise. All White people lied. Nothing was what it seemed. We were free citizens, yet there were places in the city that we could not visit after sundown.

7 The daily upheavals in my reality made the Looking-Glass world seem not only logical but somewhere I wished I could go for vacation.

SELECTION VOCABULARY

discern / discernir *verb* to perceive or recognize COGNATE

chastise / regañar *verb* to scold

Jabberwocky Baby

WRITE

PERSONAL RESPONSE: Write a short personal response about a poem or any other work of art that saved you from a painful situation, as "Jabberwocky" saved Wanda Coleman by mirroring her nonsensical reality as a black child in Los Angeles. Choose details about this work of art carefully so that they point to key ideas that you absorbed. What impact did the work have on you? Perhaps a character in the work reminded you of yourself, or the setting was bleaker than anything you ever imagined. Consider if there was a line that sounded so true, it would not leave your head. Keep your response near 300 words.

Writer's Notebook

Connect to Essential Question: Give students time to reflect on how "Jabberwocky, Baby" connects to the unit's essential question "What is the power of story?" by freewriting in their Writer's Notebooks.

CHECK FOR SUCCESS

If students are still struggling to respond to the prompt, ask them scaffolded questions, such as:

- How does Coleman connect her story to the stories of *Alice in Wonderland* and *Through the Looking-Glass*?
- What does this connection reveal about the story Coleman tells of her life growing up in Los Angeles?

Reading Comprehension OPTIONAL

Have students complete the digital reading comprehension questions ✓ when they finish reading.

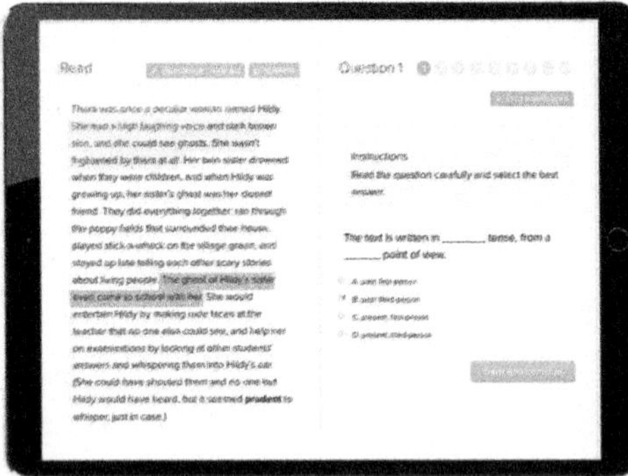

ANSWER KEY

QUESTION 1: C
QUESTION 2: B
QUESTION 3: D
QUESTION 4: C
QUESTION 5: A
QUESTION 6: B
QUESTION 7: D
QUESTION 8: D
QUESTION 9:
See first chart.
QUESTION 10:
See second chart.

Synonym	Word
scold	chastise
intellectually	mentally
recognize	discern
boring	dull
disapproval	rejection

First	Second	Third	Fourth
"Black teachers shook their heads in pity, and White teachers stared in amusement or in wonder."	"At six or seven I was slogging through Papa's dull issues of *National Geographic* and Mama's tepid copies of *Reader's Digest* and her favorite murder mysteries."	"It was a city where up was down and down was up. Black adults were always scrounging for money, regardless of how good or how bad they were. White people laughed at things that were not funny."	"The daily upheavals in my reality made the Looking-Glass world seem not only logical but somewhere I wished I could go for vacation."

Connect and Extend OPTIONAL

CONNECT TO EXTENDED WRITING PROJECT

Students can use the themes of individualism and self-reliance in "Jabberwocky, Baby" to inform the writing of their informative essays on the value of nature and the individual's relation to it.

BEYOND THE BOOK

In "Jabberwocky, Baby," the author describes how books, specifically Lewis Carroll's works, like *Alice in Wonderland* and "Jabberwocky" had a profound impact on her.

Have students conduct informal research about Carroll's works, and the messages or key ideas his works inspired.

To reflect, ask students:

- What themes or ideas does Carroll discuss? What do his characters confront or experience?
- What can we learn about life from his stories?

Collaborative Conversation

SCAFFOLDS

Post the writing prompt to generate a discussion in small groups. Ask students to first break down the prompt before they discuss relevant ideas and textual evidence.

Write a short personal response about a poem or any other work of art that saved you from a painful situation, as "Jabberwocky" saved Wanda Coleman by mirroring her nonsensical reality as a black child in Los Angeles. Choose details about this work of art carefully so that they point to key ideas that you absorbed. What impact did the work have on you? Perhaps a character in the work reminded you of yourself, or the setting was bleaker than anything you ever imagined. Consider if there was a line that sounded so true, it would not leave your head. Keep your response near 300 words.

Use the scaffolds below to differentiate instruction for your ELL English Language Learners and A Approaching grade-level learners.

ELL **BEGINNING, INTERMEDIATE** Use the discussion guide and speaking frames to facilitate the discussion with support from the teacher.

ADVANCED, ADVANCED HIGH Use the discussion guide and speaking frames to facilitate the discussion in mixed-level groups.

A **APPROACHING** Use the discussion guide to facilitate the discussion in mixed-level groups.

APPROACHING
ADVANCED, ADVANCED HIGH
BEGINNING, INTERMEDIATE

Discussion Guide	Speaking Frames
1. Think about a poem or work of art that is meaningful to you. What is a poem or work of art that saved you from a painful situation?	• Some works of art that are meaningful to me are ____. • A work of art that saved me from a painful situation is ____.
2. What details and key ideas were important to you?	• The details that were important are ____. • The key ideas that were important are ____.
3. Was there a memorable character, setting, or line? What impact did the work have on you?	• Something memorable from the work was ____. • It impacted me by ____.

Ethical Issues

Use the activity below to differentiate instruction for your B Beyond grade level learners.

Reread the final sentence of paragraph 1:

The libraries discouraged Negro readers.

Have students discuss the irony of that sentence. Then direct students to reread the text, identifying other statements that evidence how the author's world was one of irony and contradiction.

Ask students:

- What dilemmas or controversies are involved in the contradictions that the author describes?
- How did those contradictions influence or define the ethics of the dominant culture in the 1950s and '60s?
- What social rules or norms were violated by the contradictions the author describes?

Review Prompt and Rubric

Before students begin writing, review the writing prompt and rubric with the class.

PERSONAL RESPONSE: Write a short personal response about a poem or any other work of art that saved you from a painful situation, as "Jabberwocky" saved Wanda Coleman by mirroring her nonsensical reality as a black child in Los Angeles. Choose details about this work of art carefully so that they point to key ideas that you absorbed. What impact did the work have on you? Perhaps a character in the work reminded you of yourself, or the setting was bleaker than anything you ever imagined. Consider if there was a line that sounded so true, it would not leave your head. Keep your response near 300 words.

PROMPT GUIDE

- What is a poem or work of art that saved you from a painful situation?
- What details do you remember from the work of art?
- What key ideas did you learn from it?
- What impact did it have on you?

Score	Personal Response	Language and Conventions
4	The writer uses details to clearly explain the key ideas, personal meaning, and impact of the work of art, using relevant textual evidence in the personal response.	The writer demonstrates a consistent command of grammar, punctuation, and usage conventions. Although minor errors may be evident, they do not detract from the fluency or the clarity of the essay.
3	The writer sufficiently uses details to explain the key ideas, personal meaning, and impact of the work of art, using relevant textual evidence in the personal response most of the time.	The writer demonstrates an adequate command of grammar, punctuation, and usage conventions. Although some errors may be evident, they create few (if any) disruptions in the fluency of the writing or the clarity of the essay.
2	The writer begins to use details to explain the key ideas, personal meaning, and impact of the work of art, using some relevant textual evidence, but the explanation is incomplete.	The writer demonstrates a partial command of grammar, punctuation, and usage conventions. Some distracting errors may be evident, at times creating minor disruptions in the fluency or clarity of the writing.
1	The writer attempts to explain the personal meaning and impact of the work of art, but the explanation is not successful. The writer uses little or no relevant textual evidence.	The writer demonstrates little or no command of grammar, punctuation, and usage conventions. Serious and persistent errors create disruptions in the fluency of the writing and sometimes interfere with meaning.
0	The writer does not provide a relevant response to the prompt or does not provide a response at all.	Serious and persistent errors overwhelm the writing and interfere with the meaning of the response as a whole, making the writer's meaning impossible to understand.

Write

SCAFFOLDS

Ask students to complete the writing assignment using text evidence to support their answers.

Use the scaffolds below to differentiate instruction for your ELL English Language Learners and A Approaching grade-level learners.

ELL **BEGINNING** With the help of the word bank, write a response using paragraph frame 1.

INTERMEDIATE With the help of the word bank, write a response using paragraph frames 1 and 2.

ADVANCED, ADVANCED HIGH Write a response of differentiated length using the sentence starters.

A **APPROACHING** Write a response of differentiated length using the sentence starters.

BEGINNING — INTERMEDIATE | ADVANCED, ADVANCED HIGH — APPROACHING

Word Bank

the poem ____
meaningful
the setting
get through
friendship
the book ____
important
a character
overcome
self-reliance

Paragraph Frame 1

A work of art that saved me from a painful situation is ____. This work was very ____ to me. One key idea that I absorbed from it was the importance of ____. A detail that I remember is ____. It impacted me by ____. ____ helped me ____ that difficult situation.

Paragraph Frame 2

I remember in particular ____. In my life at that time I was ____. The work of art ____.

Sentence Starters

- A work of art that saved me from a painful situation is . . .
- This work of art was . . .
- Some details that I remember are . . .
- These details helped me absorb . . .
- The work impacted me by . . .
- It helped me . . .

Peer Review

Rate

Respond to the following with a point rating that reflects your opinion.

	1	2	3	4
Ideas				
Evidence				
Language and Conventions				

Submit

Students should submit substantive feedback to two peers using the review instructions below.

- How well does this response answer the prompt?
- How well does the writer describe the meaning, importance, and impact of the work?
- What does the writer do well in this response? What does the writer need to work on?

Remember that your comments are most useful when they are kind and constructive.

ELL **SENTENCE FRAMES**

A

- You were able to (completely / partly / almost) ____ answer the prompt.
- You could answer the prompt more completely by ____.
- You were able to (completely / partly / almost) ____ describe the meaning, importance and impact of the work.
- My favorite part of your responses is ____.

Dear Mama

POETRY
Wanda Coleman
1987

Introduction

Wanda Coleman (1946–2013) was recognized as the unofficial poet laureate of Los Angeles, and was once nominated for state poet laureate of California. Her artistic interests spanned many genres of literature as well as performance art. Coleman was known for writing in colloquial English and from the perspectives of those who are often ignored and oppressed: the poor, women of color, and the underclass. In this poem, "Dear Mama," the speaker marvels at her changing relationship with her mother, and deals with the daunting realization of what mortality means for both mother and child.

Addressing her mother, the speaker wonders when they became friends. It happened gradually, after the speaker went through her childish rebellion and began to grow into an adult. She guesses that this is what most young people go through. Now, as her mother is getting older, the speaker is filled with fright, thinking of being in the world without her mother. Beyond all rational feelings, she wants to protect and care for her mother, knowing there's not much she can do. She has begun to treasure every moment, because every moment counts. She also finds herself laughing more with her mother and saving every word her mother says. She recognizes that all these words will one day be priceless; that her memories of happy times spent with her mother will be the only way to ward off sadness when she's gone.

Proficiency-leveled summaries and summaries in multiple languages are available digitally.

Audio and audio text highlighting are available with this text.

COMPARING WITHIN AND ACROSS GENRES

After comparing the theme of social restrictions explored in the excerpt from Jane Eyre and Wanda Coleman's essay "Jabberwocky Baby," students will read Coleman's poem "Dear Mama." This poem showcases Coleman's poetic style and demonstrates how her love of literature that she describes in her essay led to her becoming a poet.

Entry Point

As students prepare to read "Dear Mama," share the following information with them to provide context.

- ✓ Wanda Coleman (1946-2013) was born in Los Angeles and much of her poetry is informed by the racism and poverty she experienced in the Watts neighborhood of Los Angeles during her childhood. Encouraged by her parents, she read widely and began writing poetry at age 5. At age 13, she published her first poems in a local newspaper.
- ✓ Before becoming a professional poet, Coleman had a number of different jobs, including as a journalist and television writer. She shared an Emmy award in 1976 as a member of the writing team for the soap opera *Days of Our Lives.*
- ✓ Coleman published a number of collections of poetry and fiction throughout her life and received numerous awards and grants for her work. Coleman was also a gifted public speaker, performing her work in rock clubs, prisons, institutions, and college campuses throughout the United States and overseas.

Instructional Path

The print teacher's edition includes essential point-of-use instruction and planning tools. Complete lesson plans and program documents appear in your digital teacher account.

First Read: Dear Mama

Objectives: After an initial reading and discussion of the poem, students will be able to identify and discuss the speaker's point of view as well as possible themes.

Skill: Language, Style, and Audience

Objectives: After rereading and discussing a model of close reading, students will be able to analyze the meaning and impact of the poet's word choice and language.

Close Read: Dear Mama

Objectives: After engaging in a close reading and discussion of "Dear Mama," students will be able to analyze the language and style of the poem and draw inspiration from it to compose a letter of their own.

Progress Monitoring

Opportunities to Learn	Opportunities to Demonstrate Learning	Opportunities to Reteach
Language, Style, and Audience		
Skill: Language, Style, and Audience	Skill: Language, Style, and Audience • Your Turn Close Read • Complete Vocabulary Chart • Skills Focus • Write	Unit 5 Skill: Language, Style, and Audience - The Love Song of J. Alfred Prufrock Unit 6 Skill: Language, Style, and Audience - Commencement Address at the New School Spotlight Skill: Language, Style, and Audience

First Read

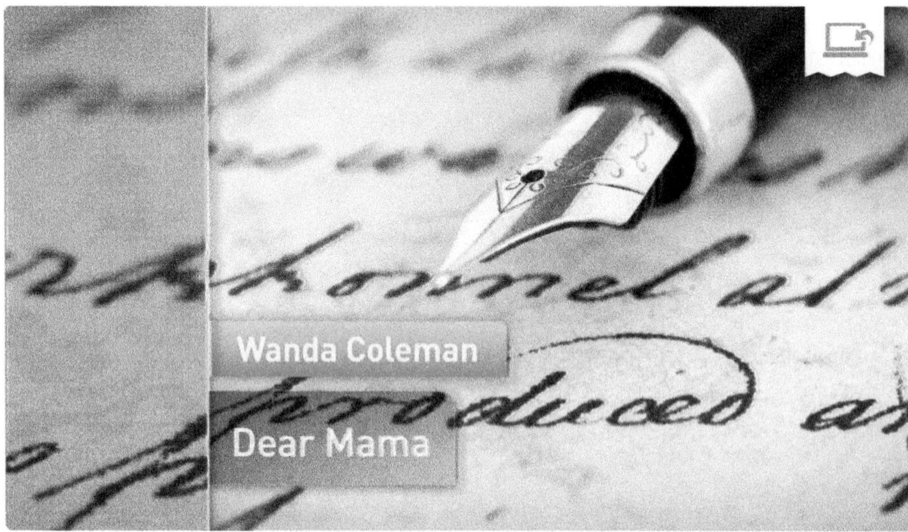

Introduce the Text

As a class, watch the video preview  and have students read the introduction in pairs to make connections to the video preview.

To activate prior knowledge and experiences, ask students:

- What part of the video stood out to you the most?
- Describe a time when you had a serious disagreement with a family member. How was the situation resolved?

ELL SPEAKING FRAMES

- The part of the video that stood out was ____.
- I disagreed with a family member when ____. The disagreement ended when ____.

Access Complex Text

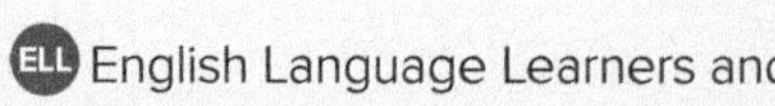 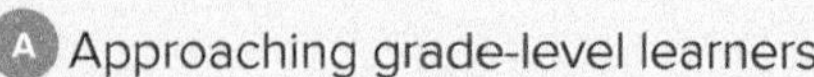

LEXILE: 720 WORD COUNT: 137

The following areas may be challenging for students, particularly ELL English Language Learners and A Approaching grade-level learners.

Connection of Ideas	Specific Vocabulary
• Students may have difficulty connecting the figurative language in the last stanza of the poem to the content of the other stanzas. • If students struggle to connect these ideas, have partners discuss the last stanza and how it might relate to the theme of the poem.	• "Spanish eight" in line 20 is likely unfamiliar to students. • Explain that "spanish eight" refers to the Spanish silver dollar used in many countries from about 1600 to the mid-1800s. People sometimes broke a coin into eight pieces to use for smaller purchases. Pirates considered the coins valuable treasure because they were accepted in so many countries.

SCAFFOLDS

 ENGLISH LANGUAGE LEARNERS  APPROACHING GRADE LEVEL  BEYOND GRADE LEVEL

These icons identify differentiation strategies and scaffolded support for a variety of students. See the digital lesson plan for additional differentiation strategies and scaffolds.

"The thought stark and irrevocable / of being here without you / shakes me."

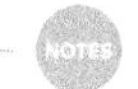

when did we become friends?
it happened so gradual i didn't notice
maybe i had to get my run out first
take a big bite of the honky world and choke on it
maybe that's what has to happen with some uppity youngsters
if it happens at all

and now
the thought **stark** and **irrevocable**
of being here without you
shakes me

Skill: Language, Style, and Audience

The poet uses unusual syntax—placing the adjectives stark and irrevocable after the noun they modify (thought)—perhaps as a way of slowing the reader down to allow them to absorb the seriousness of the situation.

beyond love, fear, regret or anger
into that **realm** children go
who want to care for/protect their parents
as if they could
and sometimes the lucky ones do

into the realm of making every moment
important
laughing as though laughter wards off death
each word given
received like **spanish eight**[1]

treasure to bury within
against that shadow day
when it will be the only coin i possess
with which to buy peace of mind

From *Heavy Daughter Blues* by Wanda Coleman. Copyright © Wanda Coleman, 1991.

1. **spanish eight** a currency coin used in Spain

Developing Background Knowledge and Social Emotional Learning

Have students prepare to analyze the poem by discussing part of the fourth stanza.

1. Share with students the following quotation from the poem: "the realm of making every moment / important / laughing as though laughter wards off death."
2. In small groups, have students discuss the meaning of the quotation and how it relates to something in their lives or to something they've read or learned about.

Discuss with students: Have you ever experienced a moment that you wished would never end? In what ways do you remember that moment? What effect does it have on you when you return to it? If you shared that moment with another person, how did it shape your feelings towards that person?

Language, Style, and Audience

How does the reader evaluate the author's use of descriptive language?

The reader explains that the poet uses descriptive language to show the speaker's feelings. She thinks the language is effective because it shows the power of the relationship.

SELECTION VOCABULARY

realm / el terreno *noun* a region or domain with its own particular set of rules

spanish eight / el real de a 8 *noun* a silver coin worth eight Spanish reales (a unit of currency) that was minted in the Spanish Empire in the late 1400s

TEXT TALK

How does the speaker try to reassure and prepare herself for what she knows is inevitable?

See lines 16-20: The speaker wants to spend meaningful time with her mother to create good memories.

Why do you think the speaker had to feel distant from her mother before she felt close to her?

Think Questions

Circulate as students answer Think Questions independently. Scaffolds for these questions are shown on the opposite page.

QUESTION 1: Textual Evidence

When the speaker's mother dies, she will "buy peace of mind" with the happy memories that she shared with her mother. The speaker wants to make "every moment / important" and remember all the "laughing."

QUESTION 2: Textual Evidence

When the speaker was younger, she did not consider her mother to be a friend. The speaker blames this on having been "uppity." Now she says the thought "of being here without you / shakes me."

QUESTION 3: Textual Evidence

The simile "like spanish eight" in line 20 compares the times the speaker spends with her mother to valuable old coins. The speaker uses the metaphor "that shadow day" in line 22 to refer to the day her mother will die.

QUESTION 4: Context Clues

I think the word *irrevocable* means "not able to be taken back." The context clue "being here without you," which seems to refer to the mother's death, suggests this meaning because death cannot be undone.

QUESTION 5: Greek and Latin Roots and Affixes

I think a realm is a kind of place that is controlled by someone or something. The poem talks about children going to a realm where they can feel as if they can protect their parents.

First Read

Read "Dear Mama." After you read, complete the Think Questions below.

THINK QUESTIONS

1. Why will the speaker eventually need "to buy peace of mind"? Explain, citing textual evidence to support your response.

2. How does the speaker's relationship with her mother change over the course of her life? Be specific, and be sure to cite textual evidence in order to back up your assertions.

3. Explain how the author uses simile and metaphor in the last two stanzas of the poem. Cite lines from the text that help support your explanation.

4. Use context clues to determine the meaning of **irrevocable** as it is used in "Dear Mama." Write your definition of *irrevocable* here, along with the words or phrases that helped you determine its meaning. Then check a print or an online dictionary to confirm your understanding.

5. The word **realm** stems from the Latin word *regimen*, meaning control. With this information in mind, explain how that meaning connects to how you think the word is used in this poem. Write your explanation and definition of *realm* here, along with any words or phrases that helped you come to your conclusions.

Think Questions

SCAFFOLDS

Use the scaffolds below to differentiate instruction for your ELL English Language Learners and A Approaching grade-level learners.

ELL **BEGINNING** Write a response using the word bank and sentence frames.

INTERMEDIATE Write a response using the sentence frames.

ADVANCED, ADVANCED HIGH Write a response using the Text-Dependent Question Guide.

A **APPROACHING** Write a response using the Text-Dependent Question Guide.

BEGINNING	INTERMEDIATE	APPROACHING / ADVANCED, ADVANCED HIGH
Word Bank	**Sentence Frames**	**Text-Dependent Question Guide**
mother laughter without dies permanent friendly memories taken place values appreciate going to	The speaker will need peace of mind after her mother ____. The speaker will feel peace if she has good ____ of spending time with her mother. These memories will include ____.	1. • What does "peace of mind" mean? • What event in the future is the speaker worried about? • What will help her get peace of mind after the event happens?
	When the speaker was younger, she was not ____ with her mother. After the speaker had trouble, she began to ____ her mother more.	2. • What word does the speaker use to describe her current relationship with her mother? • What was their relationship like when the speaker was younger? • What caused that change to happen?
	"Like spanish eight" is a simile that shows how much the speaker ____ the time she spends with her mother. "That shadow day" is a metaphor for the day the speaker's ____ dies.	3. • What two things does the speaker compare in lines 18–20? • What event does the speaker refer to as "that shadow day"? • What do these comparisons reveal about the speaker's feelings?
	The speaker talks about being ____ her mother after she dies. This is a clue that *irrevocable* means unable to be ____ back because death is ____.	4. • Read: "the thought stark and **irrevocable** of being here without you shakes me" • What event is being described in these lines? Is it permanent or temporary? • What does that tell you about the meaning of the word *irrevocable*?
	I think a realm is a kind of ____ that is controlled by someone or something. The poem talks about children ____ a realm where they can feel as if they can protect their parents.	5. • Read: "into that **realm** children go who want to care for/protect their parents" • What do the context clues *into* and *go* tell you about the noun *realm*? • How might a realm be controlled by someone or something?

Reading Comprehension OPTIONAL

Have students complete the digital reading comprehension questions when they finish reading.

ANSWER KEY

QUESTION 1: D
QUESTION 2: A
QUESTION 3: A
QUESTION 4: C
QUESTION 5:
See second chart.

Synonym	Word
domain	realm
coins	Spanish eight
unalterable	irrevocable
bare	stark

Connect and Extend OPTIONAL

CONNECT TO EXTENDED WRITING PROJECT

Students can use "Dear Mama" as inspiration for their Extended Writing Project. Have students think about the descriptions of relationships, memory, and time in the poem. Encourage students to connect these topics to nature to help them choose a focus for their essay.

BEYOND THE BOOK

I Remember When . . .

The speaker in "Dear Mama" reflects on the value of memories. Have students choose a single photograph or create a collage of photographs that reflect an important time in their lives. Ask students to write a brief narrative in prose or poetry to provide contextual details.

Display the photographs and narratives. To reflect, ask students:

- What do the photographs and words make you think about?
- How does the work of others connect to your own life?

Skill: Language, Style, and Audience

Use the Checklist to analyze Language, Style, and Audience in "Dear Mama." Refer to the sample student annotations about Language, Style, and Audience in the text.

••• CHECKLIST FOR LANGUAGE, STYLE, AND AUDIENCE

In order to determine an author's style and possible intended audience, do the following:

- ✓ identify and define any unfamiliar words or phrases that have multiple meanings
- ✓ identify any particularly unusual, difficult, or effective syntax
- ✓ identify language that is particularly fresh, engaging, or beautiful
- ✓ analyze the surrounding words and phrases as well as the context in which the specific words are being used
- ✓ note the audience—both intended and unintended—and possible reactions to the author's word choice and style
- ✓ examine your reaction to the author's word choice and how the author's choice affected your reaction

To analyze the impact of a specific word choice on meaning including words with multiple meanings or language that is particularly fresh, engaging, or beautiful, consider the following questions:

- ✓ How does the author's use of fresh, engaging, or beautiful language enhance or change what is being described? How would a specific phrase or sentence sound different or shift in meaning if a synonym were used?
- ✓ How does the rhyme scheme, meter, and other poetic language affect the meaning?
- ✓ How does word choice, including different possible meanings from other countries, help determine meaning?
- ✓ How would the text be different with other words or different syntax? How does the author's use of varied syntax influence the meaning of the text?

Skill: Language, Style, and Audience

Introduce the Skill

Watch the Concept Definition video and read the following definition with your students.

Authors use language to convey meaning or to affect the way their audience thinks and perceives. An **audience** is the intended reader or listener. Readers can analyze an author's style to better understand the tone and meaning of a text.

Style refers to the way an author uses language (words, sentences, paragraphs) to achieve a purpose. One element of style is word choice. **Word choice** is a technique in which writers choose specific words for precise meaning or to convey a certain tone. **Syntax** refers to word order, or the arrangement of words, phrases, or clauses to create well-formed sentences. **Meaning** is a reader's interpretation of the text's deeper messages, themes, or ideas. **Tone** expresses a writer's **attitude** (or thoughts and feelings) toward his or her subject. Tone can be described, for example, as formal, casual, conversational, ironic, sad, bitter, humorous, or serious.

SKILL VOCABULARY

style / el estilo *noun* a way of expressing something that is characteristic of the person or time period COGNATE

word choice / la elección de palabras *noun* specific words chosen for precise meaning or to generate an emotional response

tone / el tono *noun* the writer's or speaker's attitude toward his or her subject matter COGNATE

TURN AND TALK

1. What words and phrases would you use to create a sad tone?
2. How might those words and phrases affect your audience?

SPEAKING FRAMES

- A word like ____ creates a sad tone.
- This word might make the audience feel ____.

Your Turn

Ask students to complete the Your Turn Activity.

QUESTION 1

Part A

A. Incorrect. The speaker does not compare death to “spanish eight.”

B. Incorrect. The speaker does not compare protection to “spanish eight.”

C. Correct. The speaker compares words “given” and “received” to “spanish eight.”

D. Incorrect. The speaker does not compare inner peace to “spanish eight.”

Part B

A. Incorrect. The poem mentions “peace of mind,” but the simile is not about the difficulty of finding inner peace.

B. Correct. The simile shows how much the speaker values time with her mother.

C. Incorrect. The simile does not stress that money cannot buy happiness.

D. Incorrect. There are no details in the text about the speaker’s inheritance.

QUESTION 2

A. Incorrect. This is one probable meaning, but there is another.

B. Incorrect. This is one probable meaning, but there is another.

C. Incorrect. Nothing in the original implies that anything “must” be done.

D. Correct. Depending on the syntax, either of these meanings can be considered probable.

Skill: Language, Style, and Audience

Reread lines 16–24 of “Dear Mama.” Then, using the Checklist on the previous page, answer the multiple-choice questions below.

YOUR TURN

1. This question has two parts. First, answer Part A. Then, answer Part B.

   Part A: What does the speaker compare to “spanish eight” in these lines?

   - A. death
   - B. protection
   - C. conversation
   - D. inner peace

   Part B: The poet uses this figurative language to—

   - A. suggest that inner peace, like treasure, is hard to find.
   - B. show how much the speaker values time with her mother.
   - C. stress that money cannot buy happiness in times of grief.
   - D. hint that the speaker is interested in money she will inherit.

2. A verb is missing from lines 19–20. Which of these sentences, with alternative syntax, best retains a probable intended meaning of the sentence?

   - A. “Each word is given and received like spanish eight.”
   - B. “Each word given is received like spanish eight.”
   - C. “Each word must be received like spanish eight.”
   - D. Both A and B can be probable intended meanings.

SKILL VOCABULARY

attitude / la actitud ***noun*** a state involving beliefs and feelings that causes a person to think or act in a certain way COGNATE

audience / la audiencia ***noun*** the people who read a written text, listen to an oral response or presentation, or watch a performance COGNATE

meaning / el significado ***noun*** what is meant by a word; the general message of a text or idea

Close Read

Reread "Dear Mama." As you reread, complete the Skills Focus questions below. Then use your answers and annotations from the questions to help you complete the Write activity.

SKILLS FOCUS

1. The poet uses informal language in the first stanza before switching to more elevated language in the second stanza. Identify an example of elevated language in the second stanza. Then evaluate the effect of this shift in style.
2. Highlight details in the poem that help reveal the poem's theme and explain how these details relate to the poem's theme.
3. A lyric poem is a short poetic form meant to express a state of mind, a thought process, or a particular feeling of a speaker. Identify a detail that shows the speaker's emotion, and explain why this poem is characteristic of lyric poetry.
4. "Dear Mama" and "Jabberwocky Baby" discuss the power stories and memories have in our relationships with families. Using textual evidence from the last two stanzas of "Dear Mama," explain how the speaker imagines she will use memories of her mother.

WRITE

CORRESPONDENCE: Using Coleman's poem as a model, write a letter (in prose or poetry) to someone important to you and include enough details for the reader to understand why this person is important in your life. Title the letter "Dear ___" and begin the body with a question, as Coleman does with "when did we become friends?" Answer the question in your letter and use figurative language to express the unique relationship you have with the person you are writing to.

Close Read

Skills Focus

QUESTION 1: Language, Style, and Audience

See Lines 7–10. *Stark* and *irrevocable* signal that the speaker is discussing a serious topic. This is an effective shift away from the more casual tone in the first stanza.

QUESTION 2: Theme

See Lines 12–15. The use of *as if* and *lucky* shows that it is almost impossible to control a parent's future. This helps me understand the poem's theme of enjoying time with a parent (or anyone important to you) while you can.

QUESTION 3: Poetic Elements and Structure

See Lines 21–24. The poem tracks the speaker's thought process as she ponders her relationship with her mother and how she will find comfort after her mother's death.

QUESTION 4: Connect to Essential Question

See Lines 16–24.The speaker imagines keeping all the "important" moments she spends with her mother as buried "treasure." They will spend time "laughing," even though death is inevitable. After her mother is gone, the speaker will use these happy memories to bring her some "peace of mind."

Writer's Notebook

Connect to Essential Question: Give students time to reflect on how "Dear Mama" connects to the unit's essential question "What is the power of story?" by freewriting in their Writer's Notebooks.

Beginning & Intermediate

Read aloud the unit's Essential Question: "What is the power of story?" Encourage students to draw their connections or allow students to write in their native language. Circulate around the room, prompting students for their thoughts as they respond orally or through pantomime.

Advanced & Advanced High

Allow students to share their connections orally in pairs or small groups before freewriting.

Collaborative Conversation

Break students into collaborative conversation groups to discuss the Close Read prompt. Ask students to use the StudySyncTV episode as a model for their discussion. Remind them to reference their Skills Focus annotations in their discussion.

Using Coleman's poem as a model, write a letter (in prose or poetry) to someone important to you and include enough details for the reader to understand why this person is important in your life. Title the letter "Dear ___" and begin the body with a question, as Coleman does with "when did we become friends?" Answer the question in your letter and use figurative language to express the unique relationship you have with the person you are writing to.

Use the scaffolds below to differentiate instruction for your ELL English Language Learners and A Approaching grade-level learners.

ELL **BEGINNING, INTERMEDIATE** Use the discussion guide and speaking frames to facilitate the discussion with support from the teacher.

ADVANCED, ADVANCED HIGH Use the discussion guide and speaking frames to facilitate the discussion in mixed-level groups.

A **APPROACHING** Use the discussion guide to facilitate the discussion in mixed-level groups.

APPROACHING
ADVANCED, ADVANCED HIGH
BEGINNING, INTERMEDIATE

Discussion Guide	Speaking Frames
1. Who is an important person in your life?	• An important person is ____. • This person is important because ____.
2. What question would you like to ask that person?	• A question I would like to ask is ____. • I would like to ask that question because ____.
3. What figurative language can you use to describe your unique relationship?	• Our relationship is unique because ____. • Figurative language I can use to describe our relationship is ____.

Multiple Perspectives

Use the activity below to differentiate instruction for your B Beyond grade level learners.

Reread stanza 1. Ask students:

- What can you infer about the speaker's perspective on how "youngsters" see their parents versus how adult children see their parents?
- How does the speaker's perspective as a youngster inhibit or delay the friendship between mother and child?
- How does the speaker's perspective as an adult child change the roles the speaker assumes while interacting with the mother?
- Now in your late teens, do you see yourself more aligned with the perspective of a "youngster" or of an adult child? In what ways?

Review Prompt and Rubric

Before students begin writing, review the writing prompt and rubric with the class.

CORRESPONDENCE: Using Coleman's poem as a model, write a letter (in prose or poetry) to someone important to you and include enough details for the reader to understand why this person is important in your life. Title the letter "Dear ___" and begin the body with a question, as Coleman does with "when did we become friends?" Answer the question in your letter and use figurative language to express the unique relationship you have with the person you are writing to.

PROMPT GUIDE

- Who is an important person in your life?
- What question would you like to ask that person?
- What figurative language can you use to describe your unique relationship?

Score	Language, Stle, and Audience	Language and Conventions
4	The writer effectively composes a letter, providing enough details for the audience to understand the person's importance. The writer uses figurative language clearly and effectively to express the unique relationship.	The writer demonstrates a consistent command of grammar, punctuation, and usage conventions. Although minor errors may be evident, they do not detract from the fluency or the clarity of the essay.
3	The writer composes a letter, providing sufficient details for the audience to understand the person's importance. The writer uses some figurative language to express the unique relationship.	The writer demonstrates an adequate command of grammar, punctuation, and usage conventions. Although some errors may be evident, they create few (if any) disruptions in the fluency of the writing or the clarity of the essay.
2	The writer attempts to compose a letter, but there is not enough detail for the audience to understand the person's importance. The writer uses some figurative language to express the unique relationship.	The writer demonstrates a partial command of grammar, punctuation, and usage conventions. Some distracting errors may be evident, at times creating minor disruptions in the fluency or clarity of the writing.
1	The writer attempts to compose a letter, but the composition severely lacks details. The writer uses little to no figurative language to express the unique relationship.	The writer demonstrates little or no command of grammar, punctuation, and usage conventions. Serious and persistent errors create disruptions in the fluency of the writing and sometimes interfere with meaning.
0	The writer does not provide a relevant response to the prompt or does not provide a response at all.	Serious and persistent errors overwhelm the writing and interfere with the meaning of the response as a whole, making the writer's meaning impossible to understand.

Write

SCAFFOLDS

Ask students to complete the writing assignment using text evidence to support their answers.

Use the scaffolds below to differentiate instruction for your ELL English Language Learners and A Approaching grade-level learners.

ELL **BEGINNING** With the help of the word bank, write a response using paragraph frame 1.

INTERMEDIATE With the help of the word bank, write a response using paragraph frames 1 and 2.

ADVANCED, ADVANCED HIGH Write a response of differentiated length using the sentence starters.

A **APPROACHING** Write a response of differentiated length using the sentence starters.

BEGINNING INTERMEDIATE	BEGINNING INTERMEDIATE	INTERMEDIATE	ADVANCED, ADVANCED HIGH APPROACHING
Word Bank	**Paragraph Frame 1**	**Paragraph Frame 2**	**Sentence Starters**
times together grow up strangers separated hearts happy peas in a pod fish out of water sad special	Dear ____, When did we ____? We were ____. Our ____ were like ____. But now we ____. It makes me feel ____.	Dear ____, When did we ____? We were ____. Our ____ were like ____. But now we ____. It makes me feel ____. I remember when ____. Our relationship was ____. But over time we ____.	• When did we . . . ? • I remember when . . . • But now we . . . • It makes me feel . . .

Peer Review

Rate

Respond to the following with a point rating that reflects your opinion.

	1	2	3	4
Ideas				
Evidence				
Language and Conventions				

Submit

Students should submit substantive feedback to two peers using the review instructions below.

- How well does this response answer the prompt?
- How well does the writer use details to help the audience understand the importance of the person?
- How well does the writer use figurative language to convey the unique relationship?
- What did the writer do well in this response? What does the writer need to work on?

Remember that your comments are most useful when they are kind and constructive.

SENTENCE FRAMES

A

- You (completely / partly) ____ answered the prompt because ____.
- You could answer the prompt more completely by ____.
- Some strong details you used were ____.
- I particularly liked the figurative language you used to describe ____.
- One idea you expressed well is ____.
- One area that could be improved is ____.

Freedom

ARGUMENTATIVE TEXT

Ursula K. Le Guin

2014

Introduction

Ursula K. Le Guin (1929–2018) was an American author who wrote science fiction and fantasy novels. She has been described as one of America's greatest science fiction writers and a great influence to many others. Some of Le Guin's best known works include *The Left Hand of Darkness* and *The Dispossessed*. Her science fiction novels and short stories often deal with themes related to anthropology, the environment, gender, and religion. This speech was given as an acceptance of the 2014 National Book Foundation Medal for Distinguished Contribution to American Letters award, which Le Guin received when she was 84 years old.

Upon receiving a National Book Foundation award in 2014, Ursula K. Le Guin shared it with her fellow sci-fi writers—all those who have watched realists being celebrated for so long. Le Guin believes that the future will be difficult and require thinkers who can imagine alternatives to the present—visionaries that can imagine a larger reality. Most importantly, we will need writers who understand the difference between commodity and art. Le Guin disparages the practice of writing solely to meet market demands as irresponsible. She describes how even her own publishers put profits first, ceding control to sales departments. She also sees her fellow writers accepting constraints on what they write. Ultimately, the profit motive is in conflict with art, and although capitalism seems inescapable, Le Guin believes that anything can be resisted.This resistance often begins through art.

Proficiency-leveled summaries and summaries in multiple languages are available digitally.

Audio and audio text highlighting are available with the text.

COMPARING WITHIN AND ACROSS GENRES

Read together, the informational texts "Freedom" by Ursula K. Le Guin and "Why I Write" by Joan Didion help students explore the power and responsibility of storytelling. Originally given as an acceptance speech for an award, "Freedom" challenges an audience of readers and writers alike to consider what is lost when creativity gives way to marketing and other financial concerns.

Entry Point

As students prepare to read "Freedom," share the following information with them to provide context.

✓ Ursula K. Le Guin (1929–2018) was the daughter of an anthropologist and a writer. Growing up in that environment had a significant impact on her life. Both in the characters she created and themes she explored, Le Guin showed an interest in the ways in which culture and society affect people. Le Guin used the fantastic settings of science fiction to examine the human condition and criticize the shortcomings of society.

✓ Some of her works that explore these concepts are:

- *The Left Hand of Darkness*, which examines gender by telling the story of a race of androgynous humans who can switch between being male and female.
- *Dispossessed*, which shows the flaws of two opposite worlds: one capitalist and the other anarchic.
- *The Lathe of Heaven*, which asks what would happen if a person had the power to change reality. Even with such power, bringing world peace proves far from simple.

Instructional Path

The print teacher's edition includes essential point-of-use instruction and planning tools. Complete lesson plans and program documents appear in your digital teacher account.

Independent Read: Freedom

Objectives: After reading "Freedom" students will demonstrate their understanding of the effects of the profit motive in book publishing on society in a group discussion.

Blast: Anecdotal Arguments

Objectives: After exploring background information and research links about a topic, students will respond to a question with a 140-character response.

Independent Read

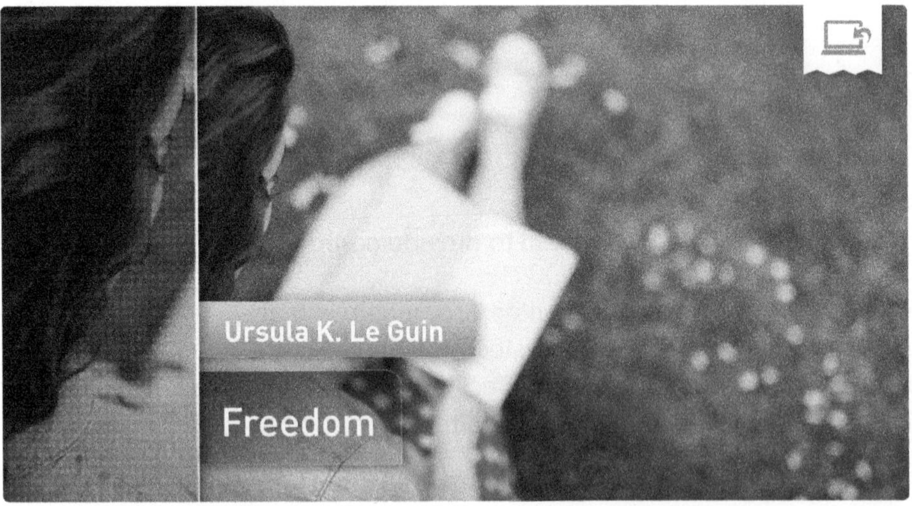

Introduce the Text

As a class, watch the video preview  and have students read the introduction in pairs to make connections to the video preview.

- What part of the video stood out to you the most?
- What do you think of fantasy and science fiction?
- In what ways do fantasy and science fiction explore the human condition and issues in society? Can you think of any examples from a text or movie to share?

ELL **SPEAKING FRAMES**

- The part of the video that stood out was ____.
- I think that fantasy and science fiction are ____.
- Fantasy and science fiction explore the human condition and issues in society by ____.
- An example I can think of is ____.

Access Complex Text

LEXILE: 1320 **WORD COUNT:** 423

The following areas may be challenging for students, particularly 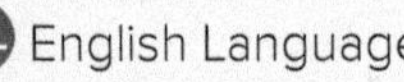 English Language Learners and  Approaching grade-level learners.

"Resistance and change often begin in art. Very often in our art, the art of words."

1 To the givers of this beautiful reward, my thanks, from the heart. My family, my agents, my editors, know that my being here is their doing as well as my own, and that the beautiful reward is theirs as much as mine. And I rejoice in accepting it for, and sharing it with, all the writers who've been excluded from literature for so long—my fellow authors of fantasy and science fiction, writers of the imagination, who for fifty years have watched the beautiful rewards go to the so-called realists.

2 Hard times are coming, when we'll be wanting the voices of writers who can see alternatives to how we live now, can see through our fear-stricken society and its obsessive technologies to other ways of being, and even imagine real grounds for hope. We'll need writers who can remember freedom—poets, visionaries—realists of a larger reality.

3 Right now, we need writers who know the difference between production of a market **commodity** and the practice of an art. Developing written material to suit sales strategies in order to maximise corporate profit and advertising revenue is not the same thing as responsible book publishing or authorship.

4 Yet I see sales departments given control over editorial. I see my own publishers, in a silly panic of **ignorance** and greed, charging public libraries for an e-book six or seven times more than they charge customers. We just saw a profiteer try to punish a publisher for **disobedience**, and writers threatened by corporate fatwa. And I see a lot of us, the producers, who write the books and make the books, accepting this—letting commodity profiteers sell us like deodorant, and tell us what to publish, what to write.

5 Books aren't just commodities; the profit **motive** is often in conflict with the aims of art. We live in capitalism, its power seems inescapable—but then, so did the divine right of kings. Any human power can be resisted and changed by human beings. Resistance and change often begin in art. Very often in our art, the art of words.

Developing Background Knowledge and Cultural Awareness

1. Present students with the following statement: Making money is more important than artistic freedom.
2. Have students raise their hands as to whether they a) strongly disagree; b) disagree; c) agree; d) strongly agree. Assign each response a corner of the room, and have students go to their respective corners to explain their positions.
3. Have one student from each group be the spokesperson to explain the group's response.

Discuss with students: What is the role of the artist in today's society? Does art lose its power when it starts to be popular and make money for the artist? Does money change art?

TEXT TALK

Whom does Le Guin refer to as "realists of a larger reality," and why?

See paragraph 2: She refers to writers of science fiction and fantasy as "realists of a larger reality" because she believes that writers can imagine a better world.

What do "profiteers" do?

See paragraph 4: They overcharge libraries and bully publishers and writers.

SELECTION VOCABULARY

commodity / la mercancía ***noun*** an article of commerce; a raw or primary material or product that can be bought and sold

ignorance / la ignorancia ***noun*** lack of knowledge about something COGNATE

disobedience / la desobediencia ***noun*** refusal to follow rules or law COGNATE

motive / el motivo ***noun*** a reason for doing something, especially one that is hidden COGNATE

proceeds / la recaudación ***noun*** the total amount of money received, usually from an event or activity

Prepare for Advanced Courses

Use the activity below to differentiate instruction for your B Beyond grade level learners.

Analyze for Enrichment

Reread paragraph 6, in which the author brings together her claim that those "who live by writing and publishing" want, should demand, and do deserve greater freedom in the creation of their art.

Remind students that arguments require strong reasons to support their claims.

Ask students:

- What reasons are presented in support of the author's claim?
- What specific evidence has the author offered to support her reasons?
- Does the evidence the author provides effectively support her claim? Support your response with evidence from the text or your own suggestions for revisions to the text.

6 I've had a long career as a writer, and a good one, in good company. Here at the end of it, I don't want to watch American literature get sold down the river. We who live by writing and publishing want and should demand our fair share of the **proceeds**; but the name of our beautiful reward isn't profit. Its name is freedom. Thank you.

WRITE

DISCUSSION: In her acceptance speech, Ursula K. Le Guin argues passionately against the profit motive in book publishing. Think about the effects of the profit motive on society. Do you think its effects are good, bad, or neutral overall? What are the positive aspects of the profit motive and what are the negative aspects? What can be done to prevent those pursuing profit from exploiting other members of society? To prepare for the discussion, use the graphic organizer to write down your ideas about these questions. After your discussion, you will write a reflection.

TEXT TALK

Why is this speech titled "Freedom"?

See paragraph 6: Le Guin says that authors write for freedom, not money.

How did discussing the relationship between art and money deepen your understanding of the text?

Answers will vary.

Writer's Notebook

Connect to Essential Question: Give students time to reflect on how "Freedom" connects to the unit's essential question "What is the power of story?" by freewriting in their Writer's Notebooks.

CHECK FOR SUCCESS

If students are still struggling to respond to the prompt, ask them scaffolded questions, such as:

- Does a desire for profit help or hurt art?
- How are stories and art affected when profit is a consideration?

Reading Comprehension OPTIONAL

Have students complete the digital reading comprehension questions when they finish reading.

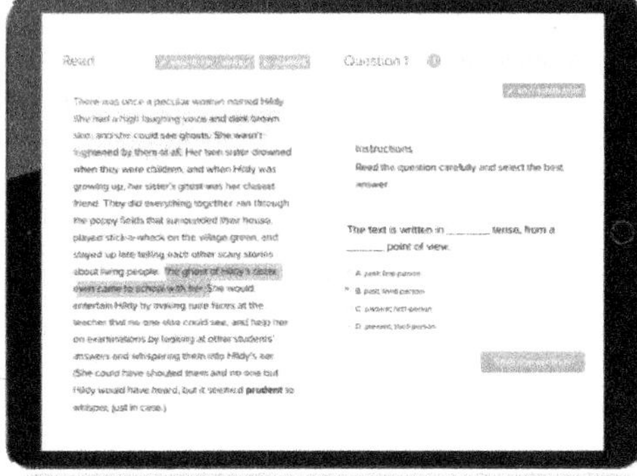

ANSWER KEY

QUESTION 1: A
QUESTION 2: C
QUESTION 3: A
QUESTION 4: D
QUESTION 5: *See chart below.*

Definition	Word
Lack of knowledge or information	ignorance
Money obtained from an activity	proceeds
Refusal to obey rules or someone in authority	disobedience
Reason for doing something	motive
A product that can be bought and sold	commodity

Connect and Extend OPTIONAL

CONNECT TO EXTENDED WRITING PROJECT

Students can find inspiration from "Freedom" for their informative essays. Encourage students to analyze how Le Guin makes a claim and uses evidence throughout her speech to inform the reader.

BEYOND THE BOOK

Interview: My Favorite Author

Ursula Le Guin expresses her disdain for publishers excessively profiting from the authors' work and explains that writing is not about the financial reward, it is about freedom. Students will choose their favorite author and interview them on why they write and how they feel about publishers.

Ask students to:

- Choose a favorite author.
- Generate a list of questions they can use to interview this author that will uncover why they write, what their long-term goals are, and how they feel about the publishing process.
- Choose the top three questions and send them to the author via social media, their blog, or email.
- Present questions and/or answers with the class.

To reflect, ask students:

- What information was the most surprising?
- Should authors be focused on profit or the art?

Collaborative Conversation

SCAFFOLDS

Post the writing prompt to generate a discussion in small groups. Ask students to first break down the prompt before they discuss relevant ideas and textual evidence.

In her acceptance speech, Ursula K. Le Guin argues passionately against the profit motive in book publishing. Think about the effects of the profit motive on society. Do you think its effects are good, bad, or neutral overall? What are the positive aspects of the profit motive and what are the negative aspects? What can be done to prevent those pursuing profit from exploiting other members of society? To prepare for the discussion, use the graphic organizer to write down your ideas about these questions. After you discussion, you will write a reflection in the space below.

Use the scaffolds below to differentiate instruction for your ELL English Language Learners and A Approaching grade-level learners.

ELL **BEGINNING, INTERMEDIATE** Use the discussion guide and speaking frames to facilitate the discussion with support from the teacher.

ADVANCED, ADVANCED HIGH Use the discussion guide and speaking frames to facilitate the discussion in mixed-level groups.

A **APPROACHING** Use the discussion guide to facilitate the discussion in mixed-level groups.

APPROACHING
ADVANCED, ADVANCED HIGH
BEGINNING, INTERMEDIATE

Discussion Guide	Speaking Frames
1. What are the benefits of the profit motive in society?	• The desire for money helps society by ____. • An example of this would be ____.
2. How does the profit motive harm society?	• The desire for money harms society by ____.
3. Do you think the profit motive is overall beneficial, neutral, or harmful?	• I think the profit motive is ____.

Multiple Perspective

Use the activity below to differentiate instruction for your B Beyond grade level learners.

Reread paragraph 5. Here the author suggests that the perspectives of those who are motivated by profit conflict with those who are motivated by art. Ask students:

- What is the author's perspective on the role of "the art of words"?
- How is the author's perspective on writing different from people who focus on the profit of that writing? Use both the text and your understanding of our capitalist economy to support your response.
- Based on the text and your own experiences, do you share the author's perspective that American literature is at risk of getting "sold down the river"? Why or why not?

Review Prompt and Rubric

Before students begin writing, review the writing prompt and rubric with the class.

REFLECTION: As you write, make sure to

- evaluate how well everyone followed the rules when making decisions affecting the group
- evaluate your own participation in the discussion
- identify a specific goal for improving your contributions to future discussions

ELL PROMPT GUIDE

A
- What are the benefits of the profit motive in society?
- How does the profit motive harm society?
- Do you think the profit motive is overall beneficial, neutral, or harmful for society?

Score	Reflection	Language and Conventions
4	The writer clearly reflects on his or her own participation. The writer consistently refers to specific examples from the discussion.	The writer demonstrates a consistent command of grammar, punctuation, and usage conventions. Although minor errors may be evident, they do not detract from the fluency or the clarity of the essay.
3	The writer reflects on his or her own participation. The writer refers to specific examples from the discussion most of the time.	The writer demonstrates an adequate command of grammar, punctuation, and usage conventions. Although some errors may be evident, they create few (if any) disruptions in the fluency of the writing or the clarity of the essay.
2	The writer begins to reflect on his or her own participation. The writer refers to specific examples from the discussion some of the time.	The writer demonstrates a partial command of grammar, punctuation, and usage conventions. Some distracting errors may be evident, at times creating minor disruptions in the fluency or clarity of the writing.
1	The writer attempts to reflect his or her own participation. The writer refers to few, if any examples from the discussion.	The writer demonstrates little or no command of grammar, punctuation, and usage conventions. Serious and persistent errors create disruptions in the fluency of the writing and sometimes interfere with meaning.
0	The writer does not provide a relevant response to the prompt or does not provide a response at all.	Serious and persistent errors overwhelm the writing and interfere with the meaning of the response as a whole, making the writer's meaning impossible to understand.

Write

SCAFFOLDS

Ask students to complete the writing assignment using text evidence to support their answers.

Use the scaffolds below to differentiate instruction for your ELL English Language Learners and A Approaching grade-level learners.

ELL **BEGINNING** With the help of the word bank, write a response using paragraph frame 1.

INTERMEDIATE With the help of the word bank, write a response using paragraph frames 1 and 2.

ADVANCED, ADVANCED HIGH Write a response of differentiated length using the sentence starters.

A **APPROACHING** Write a response of differentiated length using the sentence starters.

BEGINNING | INTERMEDIATE | ADVANCED, ADVANCED HIGH | APPROACHING

Word Bank	Paragraph Frame 1	Paragraph Frame 2	Sentence Starters
made a connection to discussed gave an example refuted explained understanding freedom use text evidence apply society	My best contribution was when I ____. I plan to ____ to improve my contributions in future discussions.	I think that my best contribution helped other students to ____. My goal for future discussions will help me ____.	• My best contribution to the discussion was when I . . . • To improve my contributions to future discussions, I plan to . . . • I think that my best contribution helped other students to . . . • My goal for future discussions will enable me to . . .

Peer Review

Students should submit substantive feedback to two peers using the review instructions below.

- How well does the writer refer to specific examples from the discussion?
- What does the writer do well in this reflection? What does the writer need to work on?

Remember that your comments are most useful when they are kind and constructive.

Rate

Respond to the following with a point rating that reflects your opinion.

	1	2	3	4
Ideas				
Evidence				
Language and Conventions				

Submit

SENTENCE FRAMES

A

- You were able to (completely / partly / almost) ____ answer the prompt.
- You could answer the prompt more completely by ____.
- My favorite part of your responses is ____.

Why I Write

INFORMATIONAL TEXT
Joan Didion
1976

Introduction

Joan Didion (b. 1934) is an American novelist, journalist, playwright, and essayist who was a finalist for the Pulitzer Prize in 2005 for her memoir, *The Year of Magical Thinking*. Didion's literary heroes include Ernest Hemingway, Henry James, and George Eliot. Her writing is known for its focus on sentence structure and the influence of media. Didion was born in California, attended UC Berkeley, and currently lives in New York City. The essay "Why I Write" was first published in the *New York Times Book Review* in 1976.

Joan Didion believes that writing is a way of imposing oneself upon people, asking them to listen and pay attention. No matter how nicely it is disguised, writing is still an aggressive act. Didion recalls her years at Berkeley, where she dabbled with the world of intellectual ideas, but only learned that she didn't have a mind for the abstract. Rather, she veers towards the specific—specific imagery, moods, facts. In order to graduate Berkeley, Didion had to do a summer intensive on Milton and, although she wrote over 10,000 words about him that summer, all she remembers is the rancid butter in the train car she used to ride up to school. She still had many years to go before she discovered what she was meant to be: a writer. Now, her novels unfold in the same way, because she writes to discover precisely what she is thinking, what is in front of her, and what it means.

 Proficiency-leveled summaries and summaries in multiple languages are available digitally.

 Audio and audio text highlighting are available with this text.

COMPARING WITHIN AND ACROSS GENRES

 Like "Freedom" by Ursula K. LeGuin, the essay "Why I Write" inspires the audience to consider why and how writers tell the stories they do. Didion uses anecdotes from her own life and writing process to communicate her view that writing is a hostile act that conveys a writer's ideas into a reader's most private space: his or her mind. Given the power to change readers' hearts and minds, what responsibilities do writers have?

Entry Point

As students prepare to read "Why I Write," share the following information with them to provide context.

- ✓ Joan Didion's career began in 1956 when she graduated from the University of California, Berkeley, and moved to New York City to work for *Vogue*. She became an editor at *Vogue* and worked there until 1963, during which time she also wrote her first novel.
- ✓ While she has written novels and screenplays, she is best known for her nonfiction work in the form of memoirs and literary journalism. Writers of literary journalism focus on factual information, but they present that information using literary writing techniques. This type of writing often reads like a story, even if it is about real-life events.
- ✓ Didion is described as a New Journalist. Unlike the type of journalism readers expect in a newspaper that relies on only the facts, New Journalism writers like Didion express how they feel or what they experience in a situation.

Instructional Path

The print teacher's edition includes essential point-of-use instruction and planning tools. Complete lesson plans and program documents appear in your digital teacher account.

First Read: Why I Write

Objectives: After an initial reading and discussion of the essay, students will be able to identify and restate its key ideas and details.

Skill: Summarizing

Objectives: After rereading and discussing a model of close reading, students will be able to objectively summarize a text.

Skill: Author's Purpose and Point of View

Objectives: After rereading and discussing a model of close reading, students will be able to determine an author's purpose and point of view in a text.

Skill: Figurative Language

Objectives: After rereading and discussing a model of close reading, students will be able to analyze the meaning and purpose of figurative language in a text.

Close Read: Why I Write

Objectives: After engaging in a close reading and discussion of "Why I Write," students will be able to summarize a text as well as analyze the author's purpose, point of view, and use of figurative language.

Progress Monitoring

Opportunities to Learn	Opportunities to Demonstrate Learning	Opportunities to Reteach

Summarizing

Opportunities to Learn	Opportunities to Demonstrate Learning	Opportunities to Reteach
Skill: Summarizing	Skill: Summarizing • Your Turn Close Read • Skills Focus	Unit 5 Skill: Summarizing - A Cup of Tea Units 6 Skill: Summarizing - Commencement Address at the New School Spotlight Skill: Summarizing

Author's Purpose and Point of View

Opportunities to Learn	Opportunities to Demonstrate Learning	Opportunities to Reteach
Skill: Author's Purpose and Point of View	Skill: Author's Purpose and Point of View • Your Turn Close Read • Skills Focus • Write	Unit 5 Skill: Author's Purpose and Point of View - Shooting an Elephant Spotlight Skill: Author's Purpose and Point of View

Figurative Language

Opportunities to Learn	Opportunities to Demonstrate Learning	Opportunities to Reteach
Skill: Figurative Language	Skill: Figurative Language • Your Turn Close Read • Complete Vocabulary Chart • Skills Focus • Write	Unit 5 Skill: Figurative Language - Shooting an Elephant Spotlight Skill: Figurative Language

First Read

Introduce the Text

As a class, watch the video preview  and have students read the introduction in pairs to make connections to the video preview.

To activate prior knowledge and experiences, ask students:

- What part of the video stood out to you the most?
- Do you have a favorite writer or literary hero? Who is it? Why?

ELL SPEAKING FRAMES

- The part of the video that stood out was ____.
- A writer I like is ____. I like this writer because ____.

Access Complex Text

LEXILE: 1140 WORD COUNT: 2,587

The following areas may be challenging for students, particularly  English Language Learners and  Approaching grade-level learners.

Organization	Specific Vocabulary
• "Why I Write" does not follow the traditional organization of an expository essay with a clear thesis statement in the first paragraph. Students may struggle to identify and connect familiar structural elements of informational texts in the essay. • Encourage students to keep the title of the essay in mind as they follow Didion's ideas from paragraph to paragraph.	• Difficult vocabulary, such as *baroque*, and anachronistic slang, such as *ball*, may be unfamiliar to students. • Vocabulary, such as *bevatron* (a particle accelerator) reflects the 1950s when Didion was at college, and may require explanation or visual support.

 SCAFFOLDS  ENGLISH LANGUAGE LEARNERS  APPROACHING GRADE LEVEL  BEYOND GRADE LEVEL

These icons identify differentiation strategies and scaffolded support for a variety of students. See the digital lesson plan for additional differentiation strategies and scaffolds.

Like many writers I have only this one “subject,” this one “area”: the act of writing.

1 Of course I stole the title from this talk, from George Orwell. One reason I stole it was that I like the sound of the words: Why I Write. There you have three short **unambiguous** words that share a sound, and the sound they share is this:

2 *I*

3 *I*

4 *I*

5 In many ways writing is the act of saying *I*, of **imposing** oneself upon other people, of saying *listen to me, see it my way, change your mind*. It's an aggressive, even a hostile act. You can disguise its aggressiveness all you want with veils of subordinate clauses and qualifiers and tentative subjunctives, with ellipses and evasions—with the whole manner of intimating rather than claiming, of alluding rather than stating—but there's no getting around the fact that setting words on paper is the tactic of a secret bully, an invasion, an imposition of the writer's sensibility on the readers' most private space.

6 I stole the title not only because the words sounded right but because they seemed to sum up, in a no-nonsense way, all I have to tell you. Like many writers I have only this one “subject,” this one “area”: the act of writing. I can bring you no reports from any other front. I may have other interests: I am “interested,” for example, in marine biology, but I don't flatter myself that you would come out to hear me talk about it. I am not a scholar. I am not in the least an intellectual, which is not to say that when I hear the word “intellectual” I reach for my gun, but only to say that I do not think in **abstracts**. During the years when I was an undergraduate at Berkeley, I tried, with a kind of hopeless late-adolescent energy, to buy some temporary visa into the world of ideas, to forge for myself a mind that could deal with the abstract.

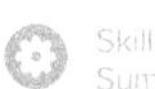

Skill: Summarizing

Didion continues to explain the essay title's significance by clarifying that she's explaining what she knows best—writing—by using only her personal knowledge, rather than abstract ideas about the nature of writing.

7 In short I tried to think. I failed. My attention veered inexorably back to the specific, to the tangible, to what was generally considered, by everyone I knew then and for that matter have known since, the peripheral. I would try to

SELECTION VOCABULARY

unambiguous / inequívoco/ a ***noun*** having or exhibiting a single clearly defined meaning

impose / imponer ***verb*** to force something unwelcome or unfamiliar to be accepted COGNATE

abstract / la abstracción ***noun*** something that exists in theory or as an idea COGNATE

Developing Background Knowledge and Social Emotional Learning

Guide students as they analyze and discuss a relevant quotation:

1. Share with students the following quotation from Joan Didion's essay: “I write entirely to find out what I'm thinking, what I'm looking at, what I see and what it means.”
2. In small groups, have students discuss the quotation's meaning, and how it relates to something in their own lives or to something they've read or learned about.

Discuss with students: What things do you do to better understand your own thoughts and feelings? How do you create meaning in your life? What other things might you do to better understand yourself?

Summarizing

What does the reader note about paragraph 6?

Didion writes about writing because it's what she knows best, and she uses personal experience instead of abstract knowledge.

TEXT TALK

What reason does Didion give for saying writing is “a hostile act”?

See paragraph 5: She says it's hostile because writers impose their ideas on “reader's most private space.”

Author's Purpose and Point of View

What does the reader note about paragraph 10?

Didion's purpose is to explain why she writes, but her point of view about writing is odd: she writes to discover what she thinks.

contemplate the Hegelian dialectic and would find myself concentrating instead on a flowering pear tree outside my window and the particular way the petals fell on my floor. I would try to read linguistic theory and would find myself wondering instead if the lights were on in the bevatron[1] up the hill. When I say that I was wondering if the lights were on in the bevatron you might immediately suspect, if you deal in ideas at all, that I was registering the bevatron as a political symbol, thinking in shorthand about the military-industrial complex and its role in the university community, but you would be wrong. I was only wondering if the lights were on in the bevatron, and how they looked. A physical fact.

8 I had trouble graduating from Berkeley, not because of this inability to deal with ideas—I was majoring in English, and I could locate the house-and-garden imagery in *The Portrait of a Lady* as well as the next person, "imagery" being by definition the kind of specific that got my attention—but simply because I had neglected to take a course in Milton. For reasons which now sound baroque I needed a degree by the end of that summer, and the English department finally agreed, if I would come down from Sacramento every Friday and talk about the cosmology of *Paradise Lost*, to certify me proficient in Milton. I did this. Some Fridays I took the Greyhound bus, other Fridays I caught the Southern Pacific's City of San Francisco on the last leg of its transcontinental trip. I can no longer tell you whether Milton put the sun or the earth at the center of his universe in *Paradise Lost*, the central question of at least one century and a topic about which I wrote 10,000 words that summer, but I can still recall the exact **rancidity** of the butter in the City of San Francisco's dining car, and the way the tinted windows on the Greyhound bus cast the oil refineries around Carquinez Straits into a grayed and obscurely sinister light. In short my attention was always on the periphery, on what I could see and taste and touch, on the butter, and the Greyhound bus. During those years I was traveling on what I knew to be a very shaky passport, forged papers: I knew that I was no legitimate resident in any world of ideas. I knew I couldn't think. All I knew then was what I couldn't do. All I knew was what I wasn't, and it took me some years to discover what I was.

Skill: Author's Purpose and Point of View

Didion's purpose is to explain why she writes, but her point of view about her own profession is odd: she writes to "find out" what she thinks. To help the reader understand this, she uses specific questions about what interests her.

9 Which was a writer.

10 By which I mean not a "good" writer or a "bad" writer but simply a writer, a person whose most absorbed and passionate hours are spent arranging words on pieces of paper. Had my credentials been in order I would never have become a writer. Had I been blessed with even limited access to my own mind there would have been no reason to write. I write entirely to find out what I'm thinking, what I'm looking at, what I see and what it means. What I want and what I fear. Why did the oil refineries around Carquinez Straits

1. **bevatron** a particle accelerator

TEXT TALK

What does Didion remember best about the time in her life when she commuted from Sacramento to Berkeley to talk about Milton? What doesn't she remember?

See paragraph 8: She remembers sensory details, like the taste of the butter and the view through the window when she was commuting, but does not remember what Milton wrote in *Paradise Lost*.

SELECTION VOCABULARY

rancidity / la rancidez ***noun*** the state of having a strong and unpleasant scent or flavor (as of old cooking oil) COGNATE seem sinister to me in the summer of 1956? Why have the night lights in the bevatron burned in my mind for twenty years? *What is going on in these pictures in my mind?*

NOTES

11 When I talk about pictures in my mind I am talking, quite specifically, about images that shimmer around the edges. There used to be an illustration in every elementary psychology book showing a cat drawn by a patient in varying stages of schizophrenia. This cat had a shimmer around it. You could see the molecular structure breaking down at the very edges of the cat: the cat became the background and the background the cat, everything interacting, exchanging ions. People on hallucinogens describe the same perception of objects. I'm not a schizophrenic, nor do I take hallucinogens, but certain images do shimmer for me. Look hard enough, and you can't miss the shimmer. It's there. You can't think too much about these pictures that shimmer. You just lie low and let them develop. You stay quiet. You don't talk to many people and you keep your nervous system from shorting out and you try to locate the cat in the shimmer, the grammar in the picture.

12 Just as I meant "shimmer" literally I mean "grammar" literally. Grammar is a piano I play by ear, since I seem to have been out of school the year the rules were mentioned. All I know about grammar is its infinite power. To shift the structure of a sentence alters the meaning of that sentence, as definitely and inflexibly as the position of a camera alters the meaning of the object photographed. Many people know about camera angles now, but not so many know about sentences. The arrangement of the words matters, and the arrangement you want can be found in the picture in your mind. The picture dictates the arrangement. The picture dictates whether this will be a sentence with or without clauses, a sentence that ends hard or a dying-fall sentence, long or short, active or passive. The picture tells you how to arrange the words and the arrangement of the words tells you, or tells me, what's going on in the picture. *Nota bene*[2]:

Skill: Figurative Language

Didion uses a simile here to highlight the power of how sentences are constructed. She compares sentence structure to a camera, which seems to imply that a writer is like a photographer.

13 It tells you.

14 You don't tell it.

15 Let me show you what I mean by pictures in the mind. I began *Play It as It Lays* just as I have begun each of my novels, with no notion of "character" or "plot" or even "incident." I had only two pictures in my mind, more about which later, and a technical intention, which was to write a novel so elliptical and fast that it would be over before you noticed it, a novel so fast that it would scarcely exist on the page at all. About the pictures: the first was of white space. Empty space. This was clearly the picture that dictated the

2. **nota bene** "observe carefully," a Latin phrase used to draw attention to what is written next

Skills Focus

QUESTION 4: Compare and Contrast

Didion's act of writing is like practicing an art. Didion is like an artist who starts painting without knowing what the picture will become. Like Le Guin, Didion does not write to make money; she writes to create.

Figurative Language

What does the reader note about Didion's simile?

Didion compares sentence structure to a camera to highlight the power of sentences.

Prepare for Advanced Courses

Use the activity below to differentiate instruction for your B Beyond grade level learners.

Author's Syntax

Reread paragraph 12:

> *To shift the structure of a sentence alters the meaning of that sentence, as definitely and inflexibly as the position of a camera alters the meaning of the object photographed.*

Use the sentence above as a starting point to locate and discuss instances in the essay where the author chose to place a single word or a short sentence on a separate line.

Ask students:

- How does the placement of these short lines of text support the author's message? How do they affect the reader's perception of the essay?
- How would the impact of this essay differ if the author had taken those short lines of text and connected them to the preceding paragraphs?
- In your opinion, was the author's placement of these short lines an effective choice? Why or why not?

Skills Focus

QUESTION 2: Figurative Language

Didion uses imagery to convey the extreme heat of the airport. She uses figurative language when she says, "I lived in that airport for several years." Didion did not actually live in the airport but imagined it in vivid detail while she wrote the book.

Skills Focus

QUESTION 5: Connect to Essential Question

Didion writes stories to better understand what she sees and thinks. She writes to answer questions, even though many of those questions are about her own characters. She blends real events with invented ones to find structure and understanding.

NOTES

narrative intention of the book—a book in which anything that happened would happen off the page, a "white" book to which the reader would have to bring his or her own bad dreams—and yet this picture told me no "story," suggested no situation. The second picture did. This second picture was of something actually witnessed. A young woman with long hair and a short white halter dress walks through the casino at the Riviera in Las Vegas at one in the morning. She crosses the casino alone and picks up a house telephone. I watch her because I have heard her paged, and recognize her name: she is a minor actress I see around Los Angeles from time to time, in places like Jax and once in a gynecologist's office in the Beverly Hills Clinic, but have never met. I know nothing about her. Who is paging her? Why is she here to be paged? How exactly did she come to this? It was precisely this moment in Las Vegas that made *Play It as It Lays* begin to tell itself to me, but the moment appears in the novel only **obliquely**, in a chapter which begins:

16 "Maria made a list of things she would never do. She would never: walk through the Sands or Caesar's alone after midnight. She would never: ball at a party, do S-M unless she wanted to, borrow furs from Abe Lipsey, deal. She would never: carry a Yorkshire in Beverly Hills."

17 That is the beginning of the chapter and that is also the end of the chapter, which may suggest what I meant by "white space."

18 I recall having a number of pictures in my mind when I began the novel I just finished, *A Book of Common Prayer*. As a matter of fact one of these pictures was of that bevatron I mentioned, although I would be hard put to tell you a story in which nuclear energy figured. Another was a newspaper photograph of a hijacked 707 burning on the desert in the Middle East. Another was the night view from a room in which I once spent a week with paratyphoid, a hotel room on the Colombian coast. My husband and I seemed to be on the Colombian coast representing the United States of America at a film festival (I recall invoking the name "Jack Valenti" a lot, as if its reiteration could make me well), and it was a bad place to have fever, not only because my indisposition offended our hosts but because every night in this hotel the generator failed. The lights went out. The elevator stopped. My husband would go to the event of the evening and make excuses for me and I would stay alone in this hotel room, in the dark. I remember standing at the window trying to call Bogota (the telephone seemed to work on the same principle as the generator) and watching the night wind come up and wondering what I was doing eleven degrees off the equator with a fever of 103. The view from that window definitely figures in *A Book of Common Prayer*, as does the burning 707, and yet none of these pictures told me the story I needed.

19 The picture that did, the picture that shimmered and made these other images **coalesce**, was the Panama airport at 6 A.M. I was in this airport only once, on

SELECTION VOCABULARY

obliquely / indirectamente ***adverb*** in a way that is slanted or not communicated directly

coalesce / fusionarse ***verb*** to come together to form one group or mass

a plane to Bogota that stopped for an hour to refuel, but the way it looked that morning remained superimposed on everything I saw until the day I finished *A Book of Common Prayer*. I lived in that airport for several years. I can still feel the hot air when I step off the plane, can see the heat already rising off the tarmac at 6 A.M. I can feel my skirt damp and wrinkled on my legs. I can feel the asphalt stick to my sandals. I remember the big tail of a Pan American plane floating motionless down at the end of the tarmac. I remember the sound of a slot machine in the waiting room. I could tell you that I remember a particular woman in the airport, an American woman, a *norteamericana*, a thin *norteamericana* about 40 who wore a big square emerald in lieu of a wedding ring, but there was no such woman there.

20 I put this woman in the airport later. I made this woman up, just as I later made up a country to put the airport in, and a family to run the country. This woman in the airport is neither catching a plane nor meeting one. She is ordering tea in the airport coffee shop. In fact she is not simply "ordering" tea but insisting that the water be boiled, in front of her, for twenty minutes. Why is this woman in this airport? Why is she going nowhere, where has she been? Where did she get that big emerald? What derangement, or disassociation, makes her believe that her will to see the water boiled can possibly prevail?

21 "She had been going to one airport or another for four months, one could see it, looking at the visas on her passport. All those airports where Charlotte Douglas's passport had been stamped would have looked alike. Sometimes the sign on the tower would say "Bienvenidos" and sometimes the sign on the tower would say "Bienvenue," some places were wet and hot and others dry and hot, but at each of these airports the pastel concrete walls would rust and stain and the swamp off the runway would be littered with the fuselages of cannibalized Fairchild F-227's and the water would need boiling.

22 "I knew why Charlotte went to the airport even if Victor did not.

23 "I knew about airports."

24 These lines appear about halfway through *A Book of Common Prayer*, but I wrote them during the second week I worked on the book, long before I had any idea where Charlotte Douglas had been or why she went to airports. Until I wrote these lines I had no character called "Victor" in mind: the necessity for mentioning a name, and the name "Victor," occurred to me as I wrote the sentence. *I knew why Charlotte went to the airport* sounded incomplete. *I knew why Charlotte went to the airport even if Victor did not* carried a little more narrative drive. Most important of all, until I wrote these lines I did not know who "I" was, who was telling the story. I had intended until that moment that the "I" be no more than the voice of the author, a nineteenth-century omniscient narrator. But there it was:

Skills Focus

QUESTION 3: Summarizing

The first and last paragraphs of the essay are connected by the letter "I." The first paragraph uses the essay's title to introduce the letter "I." The last paragraph discusses the "I" of the author versus the "I" of the narrator in a novel.

25 "I knew why Charlotte went to the airport even if Victor did not.

26 "I knew about airports."

27 This "I" was the voice of no author in my house. This "I" was someone who not only knew why Charlotte went to the airport but also knew someone called "Victor." Who was Victor? Who was this narrator? Why was this narrator telling me this story? Let me tell you one thing about why writers write: had I known the answer to any of these questions I would never have needed to write a novel.

TEXT TALK

Who is the "I" in this sentence from Didion's novel *A Book of Common Prayer*: "'I knew why Charlotte went to the airport even if Victor did not.'"?

See paragraph 27: Didion says the *I* is not herself, the author, but a made-up narrator.

How did discussing the quotation deepen your understanding of "Why I Write"?

Answers will vary.

B Ask each Beyond grade-level student to write one additional discussion question. Then, have one or two students facilitate a discussion, using their questions to guide the conversation.

Reading Comprehension OPTIONAL

Have students complete the digital reading comprehension questions when they finish reading.

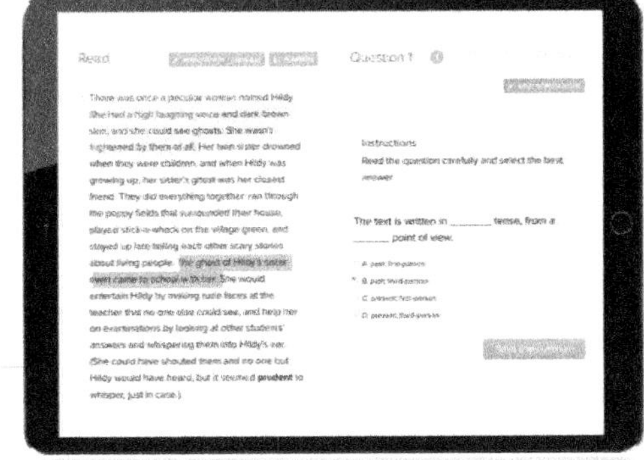

ANSWER KEY

QUESTION 1: B
QUESTION 2: B
QUESTION 3: A
QUESTION 4: A
QUESTION 5: D
QUESTION 6: C
QUESTION 7: B
QUESTION 8: D
QUESTION 9: *See first chart.*
QUESTION 10: *See second chart.*

unambiguous	Not open to more than one interpretation
imposing	Grand and impressive in appearance
abstracts	Things that exist in thought or as an idea but do not have a physical or concrete existence.
rancidity	Having an unpleasant flavor or odor because of decomposition

First	Second	Third	Fourth
The author chose the title because it best describes her skills.	The author tried to engage with big ideas while in college but constantly found herself distracted by the details around her.	During her last class in college, the author realized how much her thoughts were drawn to the specifics of her environment.	The author embraces her life as a writer because it helps her discover herself.

Connect and Extend OPTIONAL

CONNECT TO EXTENDED WRITING PROJECT

Students can use "Why I Write" as inspiration for their Extended Writing Project. Have students think about Didion's use of specific examples to help readers better understand complex statements and ideas. Encourage students to research and describe specific examples in their essays.

BEYOND THE BOOK

The Power of Images

In "Why I Write," Didion explains that she thinks in images, preferring a "physical fact" to an abstract idea. Have students choose an image by doing online research. This image could be a photograph, a piece of art, a drawing, a company's logo, or anything visual that a student finds interesting or intriguing. Once students have chosen their image, encourage them to write a short story inspired by the image. Have students present their images and stories to the class or in small groups.

Think Questions

Circulate as students answer Think Questions independently. Scaffolds for these questions are shown on the opposite page.

QUESTION 1: Textual Evidence

All three words in the title sound like *I*, and Didion says, "writing is the act of saying *I*" because writers force their readers to look at things from the writer's perspective.

QUESTION 2: Textual Evidence

She says she tried to learn to think and deal with the abstract, but her "attention veered inexorably back to the specific, to the tangible." She was able to focus on concrete details, but not ideas.

QUESTION 3: Textual Evidence

Didion makes this comparison to explain that she does not know the rules of grammar. Just like someone who "plays by ear" plays notes until it sounds right, she arranges words until the sentence sounds right.

QUESTION 4: Word Meaning

Definition number 2 most closely matches the meaning of the word in paragraph 6. I figured this out because the phrase "world of ideas" provides a context clue to *abstract* being something theoretical.

QUESTION 5: Context Clues

I think *coalesce* means "merge" because Didion is explaining how one picture made all the other images come together to form the plot of her novel.

First Read

Read "Why I Write." After you read, complete the Think Questions below.

THINK QUESTIONS

1. What reason does Didion give for "stealing" the title of her essay? Use textual evidence to support your answer.
2. How does Didion describe her experience as an English major at UC Berkeley? Use textual evidence to support your answer.
3. Explain what Didion means when she writes "Grammar is a piano I play by ear." Be specific, quoting details or passages from the text.
4. Read the following dictionary entry:

   abstract
   ab•stract /ab'strakt,'ab,strakt/

   noun

   1. a summary of the contents of a book, article, or study
   2. a theoretical concern or consideration about something

   verb

   3. to isolate or remove

   adjective

   4. existing in thought or concept but not physical or tangible

   Which definition most closely matches the meaning of **abstract** as it is used in the text? Write the best definition of *abstract* in your own words, along with a brief explanation of how you figured it out.
5. What is the meaning of the word **coalesce** as it is used in paragraph 20? Write your best definition of *coalesce* here, along with a brief explanation of how you figured out its meaning.

SCAFFOLDS

Think Questions

Use the scaffolds below to differentiate instruction for your ELL English Language Learners and A Approaching grade-level learners.

ELL **BEGINNING** Write a response using the word bank and sentence frames.

INTERMEDIATE Write a response using the sentence frames.

ADVANCED, ADVANCED HIGH Write a response using the Text-Dependent Question Guide.

A **APPROACHING** Write a response using the Text-Dependent Question Guide.

BEGINNING	INTERMEDIATE	APPROACHING / ADVANCED, ADVANCED HIGH
Word Bank	**Sentence Frames**	**Text-Dependent Question Guide**
ideas rules merge meaning stole I arrange story things sound	Didion says she ____ the title because she liked the way the words ____ and because "writing is the act of saying ____."	1. • What does Didion like about the title? • What ideas does the title express? • What text evidence supports your answer?
	Didion struggled with abstract ____ and got distracted by real ____.	2. • What does Didion say she struggled with at UC Berkeley? • What distracted Didion while she was at Berkeley? • What did Didion learn about herself because of her struggles?
	Didion does not know the ____ of grammar. She does know how to ____ words to create ____.	3. • Does Didion know the rules of grammar? • What does Didion know how to do? • How is this a clue to the meaning of the idiom *play by ear*?
	Abstract as used in the essay matches definition #____.	4. • Read: "I do not think in **abstracts**. During the years when I was an undergraduate at Berkeley, I tried, with a kind of hopeless late-adolescent energy, to buy some temporary visa into the world of ideas, to forge for myself a mind that could deal with abstract." • Does "abstract" refer to a summary? (#1) • Does "abstract" refer to a theoretical concern? (#2) • Does "abstract" refer to removing something? (#3)
	Different images coalesce into one ____. This gives me a clue that *coalesce* means ____.	5. • Read: "Sometimes a picture that shimmers makes other images • **coalesce**, or combine and blend in a novel." • What action is being described in this paragraph? • What does that tell me about the meaning of the word *coalesce*?

Skill: Summarizing

Introduce the Skill

Watch the Concept Definition video and read the following definition with your students.

When you **summarize** a text, you briefly state the main points and most important details in your own words. Summarizing can help you organize, explain, and remember concepts in an informational text or the events that take place in a story.

To summarize, you must decide what is most important as you read. Ask the basic questions: *who, what, when, where, why,* and *how.* Using your own words, write your answers to these questions from an **objective** point of view, without inserting your own feelings and opinions.

Summarizing is sometimes confused with paraphrasing. When you **paraphrase,** you do not condense a text to its most important details. Instead, you restate the entire text in your own words. A summary is much shorter than the original text, while a paraphrase may be the same length as the original text.

Skill: Summarizing

Use the Checklist to analyze Summarizing in "Why I Write." Refer to the sample student annotations about Summarizing in the text.

••• CHECKLIST FOR SUMMARIZING

In order to determine how to write an objective summary of a text, note the following:

- ✓ answers to the basic questions *who, what, where, when, why,* and *how*
- ✓ in literature or nonfiction, note how two or more themes or central ideas are developed over the course of the text, and how they interact and build on one another to produce a complex account
- ✓ stay objective, and do not add your own personal thoughts, judgments, or opinions to the summary

To provide an objective summary of a text, consider the following questions:

- ✓ What are the answers to basic *who, what, where, when, why,* and *how* questions in literature and works of nonfiction?
- ✓ Does my summary include how two or more themes or central ideas are developed over the course of the text, and how they interact and build on one another in my summary?
- ✓ Is my summary objective, or have I added my own thoughts, judgments, and personal opinions?

TURN AND TALK

1. When you are trying to tell a friend about a movie, TV show, or book, what information is most important for you to share?
2. Why is it important to share this information?

SPEAKING FRAMES

- It is important for me to share ____, ____, and ____ when I am trying to tell a friend about a movie, TV show, or book.
- This information is important because ____.

SKILL VOCABULARY

summarize / resumir *verb* to restate briefly the most important points in a text

objective / objetivo/a *adjective* undistorted by emotion or personal bias COGNATE

paraphrase / parafrasear *verb* to restate the author's words in your own words COGNATE

Skill: Summarizing

Reread paragraph 15 of "Why I Write." Then, using the Checklist on the previous page, answer the multiple-hoice questions below.

YOUR TURN

1. The following sentence is a student's summary of this paragraph: "Didion starts writing a novel without planning any of the characters or plot events." How does this summary need to be improved?
   - A. The summary needs to include the important points about the images Didion had in mind and their role in her creation of *Play It as It Lays*.
   - B. The summary needs to include details about the minor actress that Didion used as inspiration for her main character in *Play It as It Lays*.
   - C. The summary needs to explain the role of white space in Didion's conception of the novel *Play It as It Lays*.
   - D. The summary needs to explain why Didion wanted the action to take place off the page in the novel *Play It as It Lays*.

2. If you were to write a summary of this essay, what two central ideas do you notice in this paragraph that are repeated from the beginning of the essay?
   - A. Didion always starts her writing process without having in mind who her characters will be or what events will be in plot.
   - B. Didion uses her personal experience to discuss the writing process and is interested in specifics rather than the abstract.
   - C. Didion writes elliptical novels that move quickly and uses personal experiences as inspiration.
   - D. Didion wants readers to use their own experiences to understand the point of her novels.

Your Turn

Ask students to complete the Your Turn Activity.

QUESTION 1

A. Correct. The student's summary only includes information from the very beginning of the paragraph.

B. Incorrect. The student's summary should include important points from the entire paragraph, not just details about the minor actress.

C. Incorrect. The student's summary should include important points from the entire paragraph, not just details about the importance of white space in the novel.

D. Incorrect. The student's summary should include important points from the entire paragraph, and the paragraph does not explain why Didion wanted the action to occur off the page.

QUESTION 2

A. Incorrect. This is the first time Didion mentions writing without having the characters or events planned.

B. Correct. These are central ideas in this paragraph and in paragraphs 1–3.

C. Incorrect. Didion only discusses the elliptical nature of *Play It as It Lays* in this paragraph.

D. Incorrect. Didion only mentions that the "reader would have to bring his or her own bad dreams" in this paragraph.

QUESTION 3

A. Incorrect. This summary inaccurately recounts only some of the paragraph's main ideas and is not objective.

B. Incorrect. This is not a complete summary of the paragraph and is not objective.

C. Incorrect. This sentence summarizes the main points of the paragraph but not in an objective way.

D. Correct. This summarizes the main points of the paragraph in an objective way.

3. Which statement does not present any bias in its summary of paragraph 15?

   - A. Didion begins writing a novel by first thinking of the narrative intention; *Play It as It Lays* is intended to be elliptical and fast, and it focuses on the uneventful moment of a woman in a casino being paged.
   - B. Didion describes her writing process by explaining how she came up with the strange idea for *Play It as It Lays*; she watched a woman being paged in a casino and wanted to know more details about the woman's life.
   - C. Didion has an interesting writing process because she does not plan the characters and plot; in *Play It as It Lays*, for example, she started the novel with only an image of white space and of a woman she saw being paged in a casino in her mind.
   - D. Didion begins writing a novel because of images in her mind, instead of planning the characters and plot; she began *Play It as It Lays*, for example, with the images in her mind of white space and a woman she saw being paged in a casino.

Skill: Author's Purpose and Point of View

Use the Checklist to analyze Author's Purpose and Point of View in "Why I Write." Refer to the sample student annotations about Author's Purpose and Point of View in the text.

••• CHECKLIST FOR AUTHOR'S PURPOSE AND POINT OF VIEW

In order to identify author's purpose and point of view, note the following:

- ✓ whether the writer is attempting to establish trust by citing his or her experience or education
- ✓ whether the evidence the author provides is convincing and that the argument or position is logical
- ✓ what words and phrases the author uses to appeal to the emotions
- ✓ the author's use of rhetoric, or the art of speaking and writing persuasively, such as the use of repetition to drive home a point as well as allusion and alliteration
- ✓ the author's use of rhetoric to contribute to the power, persuasiveness, or beauty of the text

To determine the author's purpose and point of view, consider the following questions:

- ✓ How does the author try to convince me that he or she has something valid and important for me to read?
- ✓ What words or phrases express emotion or invite an emotional response? How or why are they effective or ineffective?
- ✓ What words and phrases contribute to the power, persuasiveness, or beauty of the text? Is the author's use of rhetoric successful? Why or why not?

Skill: Author's Purpose and Point of View

Introduce the Skill

Watch the Concept Definition video and read the following definition with your students.

Author's purpose is the author's reason for writing. Authors typically write for one or more of the following purposes: to entertain, to inform, to persuade, or to explain something to readers. The **author's point of view** refers to the way the author looks at a topic or a subject, and his or her attitude toward it. In order to fully understand an author's purpose for writing, it is often necessary to identify the author's point of view on the subject he or she has chosen to write about, including how it is conveyed or expressed in the text. Sometimes an author's point of view is directly stated. When it is implied, the reader will need to look at textual evidence to infer the author's point of view.

TURN AND TALK

1. Think of an informational text you have read recently. What was the author's purpose in this text?
2. What was the author's point of view? How could you tell?

SPEAKING FRAMES

- I read an informational text about ____. The author's purpose was to ____.
- The author's point of view was ____. I could tell because ____.

SKILL VOCABULARY

author's purpose / el propósito del autor *noun* an author's reason for writing, such as to entertain, to inform, or to persuade

author's point of view / el punto de vista del autor *noun* the way an author looks at a topic or subject, and his or her attitude toward it

Your Turn

Ask students to complete the Your Turn Activity.

QUESTION 1

Part A

A. Correct. Didion explains a specific example from how she wrote one of her novels to show how she writes to understand what she thinks.

B. Incorrect. There is no evidence to support this statement.

C. Incorrect. Didion discusses narrative point of view, but she does not do so to indicate that she writes to experiment with point of view.

D. Incorrect. This is the opposite of what Didion says in these paragraphs; she writes without having any characters in mind.

Part B

A. Incorrect. This is a sentence from Didion's novel and does not show Didion's point of view in this essay.

B. Incorrect. This evidence explains why Didion added Victor to the sentence in one of her novels and does not show Didion's point of view in this essay.

C. Incorrect. This evidence does not show Didion's point of view in this essay.

D. Correct. This evidence shows why Didion writes her novels.

QUESTION 2

A. Incorrect. "I knew about airports" is a sentence from Didion's novel, not Didion telling the reader of the essay that she knows about airports.

B. Correct. Didion uses examples to show her process for writing *A Book of Common Prayer* to show "why writers write."

C. Incorrect. Didion tells how two of her characters came to be, but there are not enough details for the reader to relate to these characters.

D. Incorrect. Didion's purpose in discussing *A Book of Common Prayer* is to illustrate her process, not how all writers write; in addition, Didion's writing process includes very little planning.

Why I Write

Skill: Author's Purpose and Point of View

Reread paragraphs 22–27 of "Why I Write." Then, using the Checklist on the previous page, answer the multiple-choice questions below.

YOUR TURN

1. This question has two parts. First, answer Part A. Then, answer Part B.

Part A: Which statement best explains the stance Didion is expressing about her motivations for writing?

- A. Didion writes because she wants to learn the answers to questions.
- B. Didion writes to explain her knowledge in subjects important to her.
- C. Didion writes to experiment with new forms of narrative point of view.
- D. Didion writes because she has specific characters that she wants to describe.

Part B: Which evidence best supports your answer to Part A?

- A. "'I knew about airports.'" (paragraph 23)
- B. "*I knew why Charlotte went to the airport* sounded incomplete." (paragraph 24)
- C. ". . . that the 'I' be no more than the voice of the author, a nineteenth-century omniscient narrator." (paragraph 24)
- D. ". . . had I known the answer to any of these questions I would never have needed to write a novel." (paragraph 27)

2. How does Didion establish trust with her audience in these paragraphs?

- A. Didion tells the reader that she knows a lot about airports in an important part of her novel *A Book of Common Prayer.*
- B. Didion uses examples from her own writing process to make a claim about writers more generally.
- C. Didion explains how she comes up with her characters so that the reader can better relate to them.
- D. Didion describes how she planned her novel *A Book of Common Prayer* to show how all

SkillsTV

Project the SkillsTV episode and pause at the following times to prompt discussion:

1:01 What descriptive details do the students first notice in the poem? What mood does this descriptive language suggest?

2:01 How do the students use context clues to make connections between Wordsworth's use of figurative language and the speaker's attitude toward nature?

3:06 How does Wordsworth set up a contrast using figurative language?

3. Why does Didion focus on the word "I" in paragraph 27?

- A. Didion uses the word to highlight that her writing is based exclusively on her personal experiences.
- B. Didion likes using the word because she believes it creates a useful distance between herself and her audience.
- C. Didion repeats the word throughout the essay as a way to illustrate the detailed planning that goes into her novels.
- D. Didion repeats the word throughout the essay to remind her audience of the argument she introduced at the beginning.

QUESTION 3

A. Incorrect. This is the opposite of what Didion implies in paragraph 24.

B. Incorrect. This is not supported by paragraph 24 and is the opposite of what Didion says about the word "I" and the act of writing in the beginning of the essay.

C. Incorrect. The essay makes clear that Didion's writing process does not include detailed planning.

D. Correct. Didion explains her interest in the word "I" in the first paragraph and continues to refer to its significance throughout.

Skill: Figurative Language

Introduce The Skill

Watch the Concept Definition video and read the following definition with your students.

Figurative language is language used for descriptive effect, often to illustrate or imply ideas indirectly. Types of figurative language include simile, metaphor, and personification. A **simile** uses the words *like* or *as* to compare two seemingly unlike things. A **metaphor** directly compares two seemingly unlike things without using *like* or *as*. **Personification** is a **figure of speech** in which an animal, object, force of nature, or an idea is given human qualities.

When reading prose, and especially poetry, readers use **context**—including when and where a text was written, for example—to analyze the impact of word choice and to help determine or interpret the meaning of figurative words and phrases.

Skill:
Figurative Language

Use the Checklist to analyze Figurative Language in "Why I Write." Refer to the sample student annotations about Figurative Language in the text.

••• CHECKLIST FOR FIGURATIVE LANGUAGE

In order to determine the meaning of figurative language in context, note the following:

- ✓ words that mean one thing literally and suggest something else
- ✓ similes, metaphors, or personification
- ✓ figures of speech, including
  - paradoxes, or a seemingly contradictory statement that when further investigated or explained proves to be true, such as
    - > a character described as "a wise fool"
    - > a character stating, "I must be cruel to be kind"
  - hyperbole, or exaggerated statements not meant to be taken literally, such as
    - > a child saying, "I'll be doing this homework until I'm 100!"
    - > a claim such as, "I'm so hungry I could eat a horse!"

In order to interpret figurative language in context and analyze its role in the text, consider the following questions:

- ✓ Where is there figurative language in the text and what seems to be the purpose of the author's use of it?
- ✓ Why does the author use a figure of speech rather than literal language?
- ✓ What impact does exaggeration or hyperbole have on your understanding of the text?
- ✓ Where are there examples of paradoxes and how do they affect the meaning in the text?
- ✓ Which phrases contain references that seem contradictory?
- ✓ Where are contradictory words and phrases used to enhance the reader's understanding of the character, object, or idea?
- ✓ How does the figurative language develop the message or theme of the literary work?

TURN AND TALK

1. What is an example of figurative language you have read or heard?
2. Why do you think a writer of an informational text would use figurative language?

SPEAKING FRAMES

- I read/heard figurative language in ____. The figurative language was ____.
- A writer of an informational text would use figurative language to ____.

V SKILL VOCABULARY

simile / el símil ***noun*** a figure of speech that uses the words like or as to compare two seemingly unlike things COGNATE

metaphor / la metáfora ***noun*** a figure of speech that compares two seemingly unlike things but implies a comparison instead of stating it directly with the words like or as COGNATE

personification / la personificación ***noun*** a figure of speech in which an animal, object, force of nature, or an idea is given human form or qualities COGNATE

Skill: Figurative Language

Reread paragraph 12 of "Why I Write." Then, using the Checklist on the previous page, answer the multiple-choice questions below.

YOUR TURN

1. This question has two parts. First, answer Part A. Then, answer Part B.

Part A: Which type of figurative language does Didion use in this section of the text?

- ○ A. simile
- ○ B. paradox
- ○ C. onomatopoeia
- ○ D. personification

Part B: Why does Didion use this type of figurative language?

- ○ A. Didion uses contradictions when describing sentences to highlight the strangeness of language.
- ○ B. Didion gives human qualities to the picture to make it seem the picture writes instead of her.
- ○ C. Didion compares camera angles to novels to highlight the control an author has.
- ○ D. Didion uses words that imitate sounds to give a musical quality to her writing.

Your Turn

Ask students to complete the Your Turn Activity.

QUESTION 1

Part A

A. Incorrect. Didion does not make a comparison using "like" or "as."

B. Incorrect. There are no contradictory terms appearing together.

C. Incorrect. There are no words that imitate sounds.

D. Correct. Didion personifies the picture in her mind by giving it the human characteristic of being able to speak: "It tells you."

Part B

A. Incorrect. Didion does not use contradictory terms to describe sentences.

B. Correct. Didion describes the picture as the one who is doing the action of telling, which makes it seem as though Didion herself has little control over her own writing.

C. Incorrect. Didion does not compare camera angles to novels.

D. Incorrect. Didion does not use words that imitate sounds.

Close Read

Skills Focus

QUESTION 1: Author's Purpose and Point of View

See Paragraph 7. Didion's view is that writing helps her discover her own thoughts and ideas. These details support the author's purpose because they tell the reader why Didion writes and suggest Didion's view that writing is a form of self-discovery.

QUESTION 2: Figurative Language See Paragraph 16.

QUESTION 3: Summarizing See Paragraph 24.

QUESTION 4: Compare and Contrast See Paragraph 13.

QUESTION 5: Connect to Essential Question

See Paragraph 17.

CHECK FOR SUCCESS

If students struggle to respond to Skills Focus Question #1, ask students the following questions:

- Which words and phrases show Didion's opinion of writing?
- What is Didion's purpose for writing this essay?
- Which sentence could be used as evidence to show Didion's purpose?

Close Read

Reread "Why I Write." As you reread, complete the Skills Focus questions below. Then use your answers and annotations from the questions to help you complete the Write activity.

SKILLS FOCUS

1. Identify details that show Didion's view of writing. Explain how these details support the author's purpose and point of view.
2. Reread paragraph 16, in which Didion describes an experience that inspired her writing. How does Didion use figurative language in this paragraph to help her audience understand why she found this experience inspiring?
3. Reread the introduction and conclusion. What key information and central ideas do these paragraphs contain that would be useful when summarizing this essay?
4. In "Freedom," author Ursula K. Le Guin warns that greed may have a negative impact on creativity in the publishing industry. Le Guin writes, "Right now, we need writers who know the difference between production of a market commodity and the practice of an art." Identify textual evidence in "Why I Write" that supports the idea that writing can be "the practice of an art." Write a sentence that compares the writers' ideas.
5. In "Why I Write," Joan Didion explains what motivates her to write, and how this purpose influences her process. What is the power of a story over Didion, as an author? Support your answer with textual evidence.

WRITE

EXPLANATORY ESSAY: Write a short paper analyzing what you learn about Joan Didion's writing style and point of view from this essay. Why does she write? What does she believe about herself? Her statements are not always simple or obvious, so you will have to look closely at how Didion's content and style, particularly her use of figurative language, interact to develop her point of view. Pay special attention to the last sentence, which seems to achieve the purpose of asserting why she writes. Be sure to explain your understanding of this sentence in your analysis. Use textual evidence from the essay to support your points.

Writer's Notebook

Connect to Essential Question: Give students time to reflect on how "Why I Write" connects to the unit's essential question "What is the power of story?" by freewriting in their Writer's Notebooks.

Beginning & Intermediate

Read aloud the unit's essential question: "What is the power of story?" Encourage students to draw their connections or allow students to write in their native language. Circulate around the room, prompting students for their thoughts as they respond orally or through pantomime.

Advanced & Advanced High

Allow students to share their connections orally in pairs or small groups before freewriting.

Collaborative Conversation

SCAFFOLDS

Break students into collaborative conversation groups to discuss the Close Read prompt. Ask students to use the StudySyncTV episode as a model for their discussion. Remind them to reference their Skills Focus annotations in their discussion.

Write a short paper analyzing what you learn about Joan Didion's writing style and point of view from this essay. Why does she write? What does she believe about herself? Her statements are not always simple or obvious, so you will have to look closely at how Didion's content and style, particularly her use of figurative language, interact to develop her point of view. Pay special attention to the last sentence, which seems to achieve the purpose of asserting why she writes. Be sure to explain your understanding of this sentence in your analysis. Use textual evidence from the essay to support your points.

Use the scaffolds below to differentiate instruction for your ELL English Language Learners and A Approaching grade-level learners.

ELL **BEGINNING, INTERMEDIATE** Use the discussion guide and speaking frames to facilitate the discussion with support from the teacher.

ADVANCED, ADVANCED HIGH Use the discussion guide and speaking frames to facilitate the discussion in mixed-level groups.

A APPROACHING Use the discussion guide to facilitate the discussion in mixed-level groups.

APPROACHING
ADVANCED, ADVANCED HIGH
BEGINNING, INTERMEDIATE

Discussion Guide	Speaking Frames
1. What does Didion believe about herself?	• She believes she is not a ____ because ____. • She believes the act of writing is ____ because ____.
2. What is Didion's writing style like? When does she use figurative language?	• Didion's writing style is ____. • She uses figurative language when ____.
3. How does the last sentence convey Didion's purpose?	• The last sentence suggests Didion writes because ____.

Text to World

Use the activity below to differentiate instruction for your B Beyond grade level learners.

Reread paragraph 9, which comprises only one sentence: "Which was a writer." Have students reflect on this essay as Didion's journey to discover something she was not (an "intellectual") and something she was (a writer). Ask students:

- What experiences led the author to believe she would never be able to reside in "the world of ideas"?
- What experiences led the author to know that she is a writer?
- What experiences have shaped you? How have they helped you understand your own identity?

Review Prompt and Rubric

Before students begin writing, review the writing prompt and rubric with the class.

EXPLANATORY ESSAY: Write a short paper analyzing what you learn about Joan Didion's writing style and point of view from this essay. Why does she write? What does she believe about herself? Her statements are not always simple or obvious, so you will have to look closely at how Didion's content and style, particularly her use of figurative language, interact to develop her point of view. Pay special attention to the last sentence, which seems to achieve the purpose of asserting why she writes. Be sure to explain your understanding of this sentence in your analysis. Use textual evidence from the essay to support your points.

ELL **PROMPT GUIDE**

A

- What does Didion believe about herself?
- What is Didion's writing style like? When does she use figurative language?
- How does the last sentence convey Didion's purpose in "Why I Write"?

Score	Author's Point of View	Figurative Language	Language and Conventions
4	The writer clearly analyzes the development of Didion's point of view in the essay. The writer provides exemplary analysis, using relevant textual evidence.	The writer clearly analyzes Didion's use of figurative language. The writer provides exemplary analysis, using relevant textual evidence.	The writer demonstrates a consistent command of grammar, punctuation, and usage conventions. Although minor errors may be evident, they do not detract from the fluency or the clarity of the essay.
3	The writer analyzes the development of Didion's point of view in the essay. The writer provides sufficient analysis, using relevant textual evidence most of the time.	The writer analyzes Didion's use of figurative language. The writer provides sufficient analysis, using relevant textual evidence most of the time.	The writer demonstrates an adequate command of grammar, punctuation, and usage conventions. Although some errors may be evident, they create few (if any) disruptions in the fluency of the writing or the clarity of the essay.
2	The writer begins to analyze the development of Didion's point of view in the essay, but the analysis is incomplete. The writer uses relevant textual evidence only some of the time.	The writer begins to analyze Didion's use of figurative language, but the analysis is incomplete. The writer uses relevant textual evidence only some of the time.	The writer demonstrates a partial command of grammar, punctuation, and usage conventions. Some distracting errors may be evident, at times creating minor disruptions in the fluency or clarity of the writing.
1	The writer attempts to analyze the development of Didion's point of view in the essay, but the analysis is not successful. The writer uses little or no relevant textual evidence.	The writer attempts to analyze Didion's use of figurative language, but the analysis is not successful. The writer uses little or no relevant textual evidence.	The writer demonstrates little or no command of grammar, punctuation, and usage conventions. Serious and persistent errors create disruptions in the fluency of the writing and sometimes interfere with meaning.
0	The writer does not provide a relevant response to the prompt or does not provide a response at all.	The writer does not provide a relevant response to the prompt or does not provide a response at all.	Serious and persistent errors overwhelm the writing and interfere with the meaning of the response as a whole, making the writer's meaning impossible to understand.

Write

SCAFFOLDS

Ask students to complete the writing assignment using text evidence to support their answers.

Use the scaffolds below to differentiate instruction for your ELL English Language Learners and A Approaching grade-level learners.

ELL **BEGINNING** With the help of the word bank, write a response using paragraph frame 1.

INTERMEDIATE With the help of the word bank, write a response using paragraph frames 1 and 2.

ADVANCED, ADVANCED HIGH Write a response of differentiated length using the sentence starters.

A **APPROACHING** Write a response of differentiated length using the sentence starters.

BEGINNING / INTERMEDIATE	BEGINNING / INTERMEDIATE	INTERMEDIATE	ADVANCED, ADVANCED HIGH / APPROACHING
Word Bank	**Paragraph Frame 1**	**Paragraph Frame 2**	**Sentence Starters**
discovery answers pictures figurative language figure out	Joan Didion writes novels based on ____ she sees in her mind. She writes to ____ what she thinks. She uses ____ to show the kinds of images she sees. The last sentence of the essay states that she writes to find out ____. This shows that Didion believes the goal of writing is ____.	Didion explains that she does not think in ____. She prefers to focus on ____, such as ____. This led her to become a writer because she uses ____ to ____. Evidence from the essay that supports this idea is ____. Didion uses figurative language to ____. For example, she writes, ____. This example is ____.	• I learned that Didion views writing as . . . • Didion's writing style is . . . • One thing Didion believes about herself is . . . • Didion uses figurative language to . . . • An example of this is . . . • From the last sentence, I can infer that . . . • The last sentence is important because . . .

Peer Review

Rate

Respond to the following with a point rating that reflects your opinion

	1	2	3	4
Ideas				
Evidence				
Language and Conventions				

Submit

Students should submit feedback to two peers using the review instructions below.

- How well does this response answer the prompt?
- How well does the writer analyze Didion's writing style and figurative language?
- How well does the writer analyze the development of Didion's point of view?
- How well does the writer support his or her points with textual evidence?
- What did the writer do well in this response? What does the writer need to work on?

Remember that your comments are most useful when they are kind and constructive.

ELL A **SENTENCE FRAMES**

- You (completely / partly) ____ answered the prompt because ____.
- You could answer the prompt more completely by ____.
- Your explanation of Didion's point of view was ____.
- Your explanation of Didion's figurative language was ____.
- Your use of textual evidence was ____.

Blast: Matter, Mood, and Moment

What more about the subject matter are you in the mood to read in this moment?

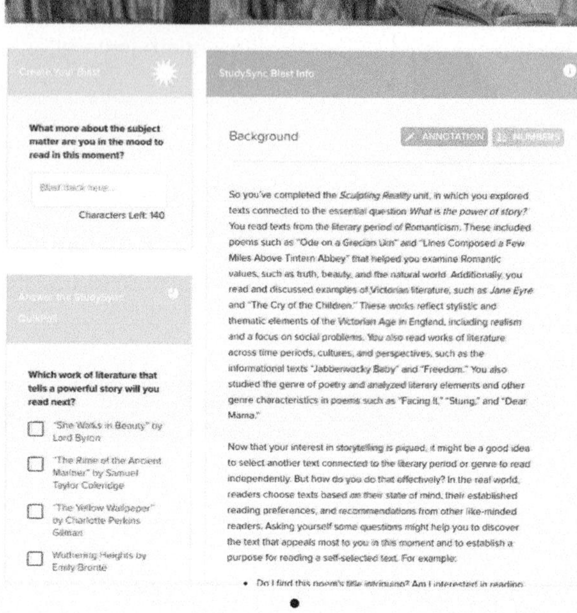

TEXT TALK

What did you think of the *Sculpting Reality* unit? What is your opinion of Romantic or Victorian literature based on the unit's selections?

Answers will vary.

What is one strategy you can use for self-selecting a new text? How does it work?

Answers will vary.

Create Your Own Blast

SCAFFOLDS

Ask students to write a 140-character Blast after they complete the QuikPoll.

Use the scaffolds below to differentiate instruction for your ELL English Language Learners.

ELL **BEGINNING** Write a response using the word bank to complete the sentence frame.

INTERMEDIATE Write a response using the sentence frame.

ADVANCED, ADVANCED HIGH Write a response using the sentence starter.

BEGINNING	INTERMEDIATE	ADVANCED, ADVANCED HIGH
Word Bank	Sentence Frame	Sentence Starter
subject matter genre video preview time period poster	I am in the mood to read ____. The ____ made me want to read this text.	• I am in the mood to read . . . • The reasons I selected this text include . . .

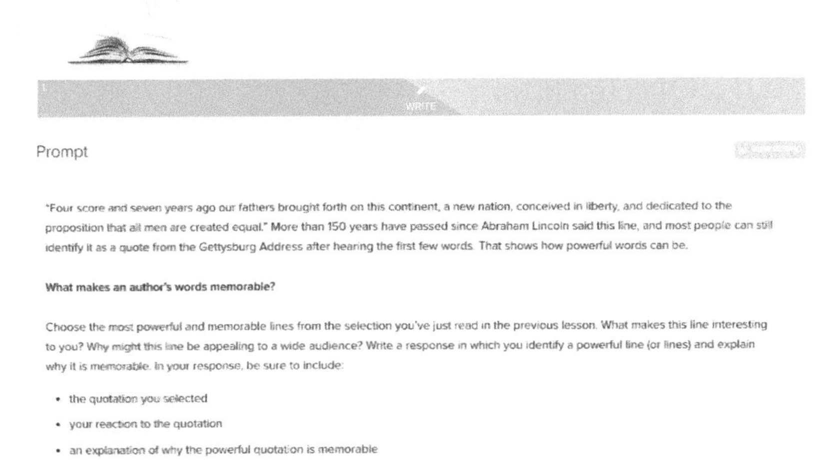

Self-Selected Response
WRITE
Prompt
"Four score and seven years ago our fathers brought forth on this continent, a new nation, conceived in liberty, and dedicated to the proposition that all men are created equal." More than 150 years have passed since Abraham Lincoln said this line, and most people can still identify it as a quote from the Gettysburg Address after hearing the first few words. That shows how powerful words can be.
What makes an author's words memorable?
Choose the most powerful and memorable lines from the selection you've just read in the previous lesson. What makes this line interesting to you? Why might this line be appealing to a wide audience? Write a response in which you identify a powerful line (or lines) and explain why it is memorable. In your response, be sure to include:
• the quotation you selected
• your reaction to the quotation
• an explanation of why the powerful quotation is memorable

Self-Selected Response

Introduce the Prompt

Read aloud the prompt. Ask students to discuss:

- What is the prompt asking you to do?
- Why might it be a good idea to think about your own reactions to a text before choosing a line?

Write

SCAFFOLDS

Ask students to complete the writing assignment using text evidence to support their answers.

Use the scaffolds below to differentiate instruction for your ELL English Language Learners and A Approaching grade-level readers.

ELL **BEGINNING** With the help of the word bank, write a response using paragraph frame 1.

INTERMEDIATE With the help of the word bank, write a response using paragraph frames 1 and 2.

ADVANCED, ADVANCED HIGH Write a response of differentiated length using the sentence starters.

A **APPROACHING** Write a response of differentiated length using the sentence starters.

BEGINNING / INTERMEDIATE	BEGINNING	INTERMEDIATE	ADVANCED, ADVANCED HIGH / APPROACHING
Word Bank	**Paragraph Frame 1**	**Paragraph Frame 2**	**Sentence Starters**
happy theme sad character surprised imagery develops relatable shows emotional	I read the text (title) ____ by ____. The most memorable line is "____." When I read this line, I felt ____. This line is interesting because it ____. Many people like this line because it ____. This line is more memorable than others because ____.	I read the text (title) ____ by ____. The most memorable line is "____." When I read this line, I felt ____. This line is interesting because it ____. Many people like this line because it ____. This line is more memorable than others because ____. The line reminds me of ____. I will think of this line when ____.	• I read the text . . . by . . . • The most memorable line is . . . • I felt . . . while reading this line . . . • A word or phrase that I would describe my reaction to this line is . . . • This line is more interesting than other lines because . . . • This line would also be appealing to others because . . .

Timed Writing Recommendations

Issue	Suggestion
Students don't finish their essays in the time allowed.	• Remind students of the time remaining and give suggestions of what they should be working on at that point. • Set and track writing goals for struggling students.
Students struggle to start their essays.	• Revisit and remodel the planning process. • Provide students with sentence starters for particular genres or sentence types.
Students spend too much time planning.	• Suggest students limit their planning to 5–10 minutes. • Have students identify several "buzzwords" from the prompt to use in their thesis and commentary.
Students don't understand the prompt.	• Have students rewrite the prompt using their own words. • Encourage students to use context clues to determine the meaning of unfamiliar language.
Students get nervous or stressed about writing.	• Provide students with strategies that help prevent or counter stress, such as stretching and breathing exercises, or limiting how often they look at the clock or track their peers' progress.
Students focus too much on editing and do not make progress on their writing.	• Advise students to use their knowledge of their own common errors to prioritize their editing. • Remind students to focus on specific areas, such as sentence structure or comma usage.
Students get stuck as they are writing.	• Recommend that students pause to reread the prompt and their response to that point. • Have students identify the types of challenges they encounter and brainstorm solutions to those problems that they can implement moving forward.
Your classroom spans a wide variety of abilities.	• Have several students share strategies or reflections with the rest of the class. • Create a classroom "resume" that lists each student's strengths so that students can consult with peers for their writing.

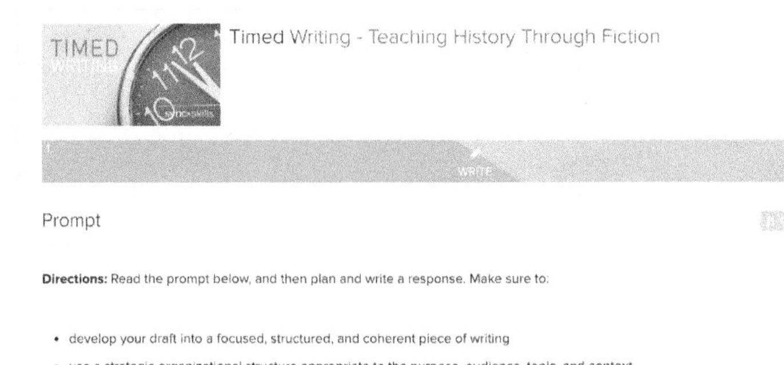

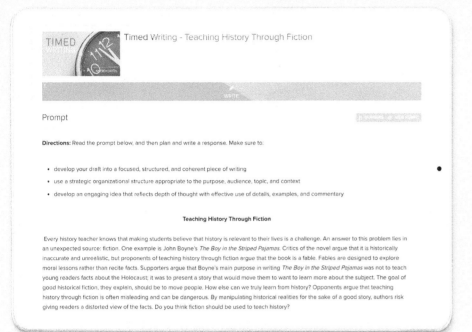

Timed Writing - Teaching History Through Fiction

Prompt

Directions: Read the prompt below, and then plan and write a response. Make sure to:

- develop your draft into a focused, structured, and coherent piece of writing
- use a strategic organizational structure appropriate to the purpose, audience, topic, and context
- develop an engaging idea that reflects depth of thought with effective use of details, examples, and commentary

Teaching History Through Fiction

Every history teacher knows that making students believe that history is relevant to their lives is a challenge. An answer to this problem lies in an unexpected source: fiction. One example is John Boyne's *The Boy in the Striped Pajamas*. Critics of the novel argue that it is historically inaccurate and unrealistic, but proponents of teaching history through fiction argue that the book is a fable. Fables are designed to explore moral lessons rather than recite facts. Supporters argue that Boyne's main purpose in writing *The Boy in the Striped Pajamas* was not to teach young readers facts about the Holocaust; it was to present a story that would move them to want to learn more about the subject. The goal of good historical fiction, they explain, should be to move people. How else can we truly learn from history? Opponents argue that teaching history through fiction is often misleading and can be dangerous. By manipulating historical realities for the sake of a good story, authors risk giving readers a distorted view of the facts. Do you think fiction should be used to teach history?

Timed Writing

Ask students to complete the writing assignment.

Note: To replicate the testing environment, turn off scaffolds, but allow ELL students to ask clarifying questions about unknown words or phrases in the prompt before they begin writing.

CLARIFYING QUESTIONS

- What does the word ____ mean in the prompt?
- I do not know what the phrase ____ means. Can you explain it to me?
- What does it mean in the instructions when it says ____?

Write

SCAFFOLDS

Use the scaffolds below to differentiate instruction for your ELL English Language Learners and A Approaching grade-level learners.

ELL **BEGINNING, INTERMEDIATE, ADVANCED, ADVANCED HIGH** Use the sentence starters to organize and write your response.

A **APPROACHING** Write a response of differentiated length using the sentence starters.

BEGINNING, INTERMEDIATE, ADVANCED, ADVANCED HIGH

APPROACHING

Purpose of Sentence	Sentence Starters
To state your thesis or claim	• I believe ____ because I think it's important to . . . • My opinion on ____ is . . .
To introduce evidence	• For example, . . . • One reason that supports my claim is . . .
To explain your evidence	• ____ shows that . . . • This reason is important because . . .
To include a counter argument	• Some people might argue ____. However, . . . • A reason against my opinion is ____, but . . .
To conclude your essay	• To summarize . . . • Overall, the most important point to remember is . . .

Extended Writing Project

The Extended Writing Project (EWP) in Grade 12, Unit 4 focuses on research and informative writing. Students consider the following question—How can we better value nature through our daily behaviors?—as they write an essay on a topic related to nature that utilizes strong sources to convince readers. The unit's selections about the influence of storytelling provide a context for students, and the multiple pieces of fiction in the unit serve as mentor texts for students to analyze. Specific skill lessons teach developing ideas, organization, and conventions, while other skill lessons on evaluating sources, critiquing research, and sources and citations focus on characteristics of the genre and help students develop their research skills. Directed revision leads students through the process of revising for clarity, development, organization, word choice, and sentence fluency. Throughout the EWP, students have the opportunity to practice, using created student writing, authentic texts, and their own work.

CONNECT TO ESSENTIAL QUESTION

What is the power of story?

The texts in this unit showed students that stories have great power. In an informative essay, students will use source materials to support their claim about valuing nature.

Audio and audio text highlighting are available in select lessons in the Extended Writing Project.

Extended Writing Project Prompt

How can we better value nature through our daily behaviors?

Think of a daily behavior that the average person may not know is damaging to nature. For example, people may not think about reducing their use of plastic bags when cleaning up after their dogs or may not consider the consequences of constantly upgrading their phones and other technology. Research your topic, and structure your essay to be clear, informative, and convincing. Then, write an informative research essay, using both informative text structures and source materials to support your claim and make your informative essay convincing.

These icons identify differentiation strategies and scaffolded support for a variety of students. See the digital lesson plan for additional differentiation strategies and scaffolds.

Instructional Path

Informative Writing Process: Plan

Objectives: After learning about genre characteristics and craft, students will analyze a sample Student Model and plan a meaningful informative research essay in response to a prompt.

Skill: Planning Research

Objectives: After reading and discussing a model of student writing, students will prepare to write a research paper by generating and refining questions for formal inquiry and developing a research plan.

Skill: Evaluating Sources

Objectives: After reading and discussing a model of student writing, students will develop their drafts by examining sources for accuracy, credibility and reliability.

Skill: Research and Notetaking

Objectives: After reading and discussing a model of student writing, students will develop their drafts by taking notes on research and synthesizing the sources.

Informative Writing Process: Draft

Objectives: After reading a Student Model draft and reviewing a writing checklist, students will draft a meaningful informative research essay in response to a prompt.

The print teacher's edition includes essential point-of-use instruction and planning tools. Complete lesson plans and program documents appear in your digital teacher account.

Skill: Critiquing Research

Objectives: After reading and discussing a model of student writing, students will develop their drafts by critiquing their research.

Skill: Paraphrasing

Objectives: After reading and discussing a model of student writing, students will paraphrase select sources in order to integrate information into the text while maintaining the flow of ideas in their informative research essays.

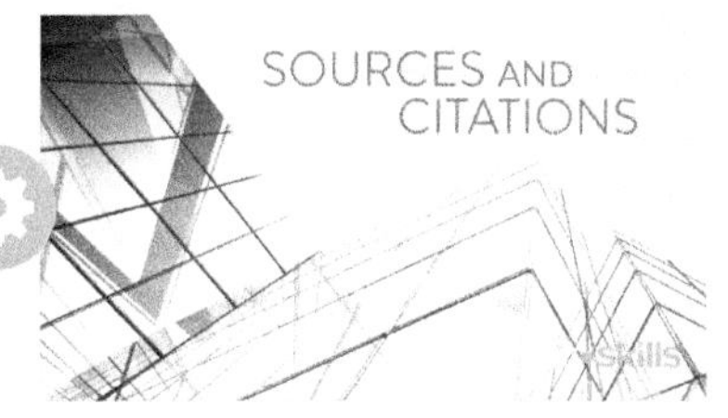

Skill: Sources and Citations

Objectives: After reading and discussing a model of student writing, students will develop their drafts by displaying academic citations and citing source materials in the appropriate format.

Skill: Print and Graphic Features

Objectives: After reading and discussing a model of student writing, students will develop their drafts by adding print and graphic features to their research essays.

Informative Writing Process: Revise

Objectives: Students will use a revision guide to revise the draft of their informative research essay for clarity, development, organization, style, diction, and sentence fluency.

Skill: Using a Style Guide

Objectives: After reading and discussing a model of student writing, students will develop their drafts by using a style guide, as appropriate, to improve their command of standard English conventions, syntax, and MLA citations.

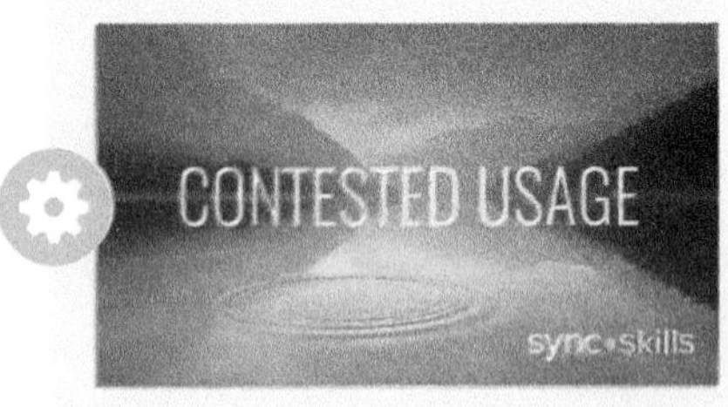

Grammar: Contested Usage

Objectives: After learning about contested usage and seeing how it occurs in text examples, students will practice using contested usage correctly.

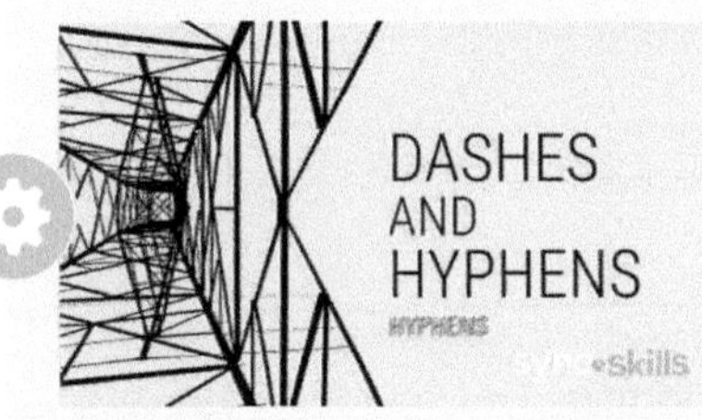

Grammar: Hyphens

Objectives: After learning about hyphens and seeing how they are used in text examples, students will practice using hyphens correctly.

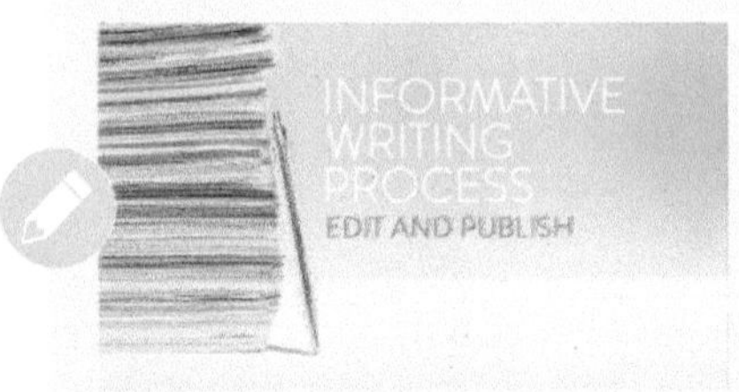

Informative Writing Process: Edit and Publish

Objectives: After seeing an example of editing in the Student Model and reviewing an editing checklist, students will edit and publish the final draft of their informative research essay.

Progress Monitoring

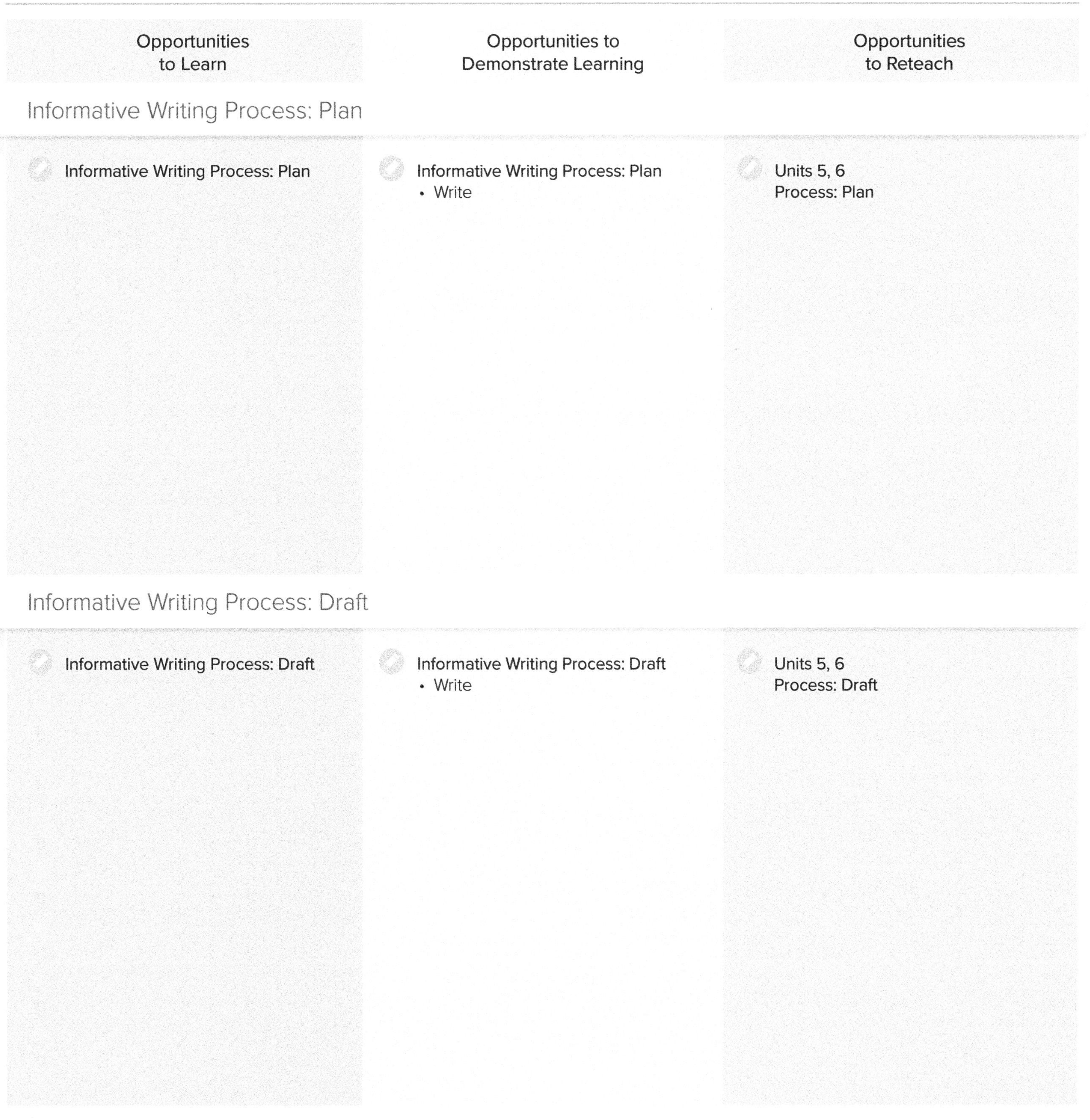

Opportunities to Learn	Opportunities to Demonstrate Learning	Opportunities to Reteach
Informative Writing Process: Plan		
Informative Writing Process: Plan	Informative Writing Process: Plan • Write	Units 5, 6 Process: Plan
Informative Writing Process: Draft		
Informative Writing Process: Draft	Informative Writing Process: Draft • Write	Units 5, 6 Process: Draft

Opportunities to Learn	Opportunities to Demonstrate Learning	Opportunities to Reteach
Informative Writing Process: Revise		
Informative Writing Process: Revise	Informative Writing Process: Revise • Write	Units 5, 6 Process: Revise
Informative Writing Process: Edit and Publish		
Informative Writing Process: Edit and Publish	Informative Writing Process: Edit and Publish • Write	Unit 5 Process: Edit and Publish Unit 6 Process: Edit and Present
Planning Research		
Skill: Planning Research	Skill: Planning Research • Your Turn Informative Writing Process: Draft	Spotlight Skill: Planning Research

Opportunities to Learn	Opportunities to Demonstrate Learning	Opportunities to Reteach
Evaluating Sources		
Skill: Evaluating Sources	Skill: Evaluating Sources • Your Turn Informative Writing Process: Draft	Unit 6 Skill: Evaluating Sources Spotlight Skill: Evaluating Sources
Research and Notetaking		
Skill: Research and Notetaking	Skill: Research and Notetaking • Your Turn Informative Writing Process: Draft	Spotlight Skill: Research and Notetaking

Opportunities to Learn	Opportunities to Demonstrate Learning	Opportunities to Reteach
Critiquing Research		
Skill: Critiquing Research	Skill: Critiquing Research • Your Turn Informative Writing Process: Revise	Spotlight Skill: Critiquing Research
Paraphrasing		
Skill: Paraphrasing	Skill: Paraphrasing • Your Turn Informative Writing Process: Revise	Spotlight Skill: Paraphrasing
Sources and Citations		
Skill: Sources and Citations	Skill: Sources and Citations • Your Turn Informative Writing Process: Revise	Unit 6 Skill: Sources and Citations Spotlight Skill: Sources and Citations

Opportunities to Learn	Opportunities to Demonstrate Learning	Opportunities to Reteach
Print and Graphic Features		
Skill: Print and Graphic Features	Skill: Print and Graphic Features • Your Turn Informative Writing Process: Revise	Spotlight Skill: Print and Graphic Features
Using a Style Guide		
Skill: Using a Style Guide	Skill: Using a Style Guide • Your Turn Informative Writing Process: Edit and Publish	Unit 5 Skill: Using a Style Guide Spotlight Skill: Using a Style Guide
Contested Usage		
Grammar: Contested Usage	Grammar: Contested Usage • Your Turn Informative Writing Process: Edit and Publish	Grammar: Prepositions – Prepositions and Prepositional Phrases
Hyphens		
Grammar: Hyphens	Grammar: Hyphens • Your Turn Informative Writing Process: Edit and Publish	Grammar: Dashes and Hyphens

Informative Writing Process: Plan

Introduce the Extended Writing Project

- What is the prompt asking you to do?
- What are the five characteristics of informative writing?
- Which characteristics of informative writing will you need to learn more about in order to respond to the prompt?

DIFFERENTIATED QUESTIONS

- What does **consider** mean?
- What are some things your community can do to protect nature?
- How can you persuade your readers to support your claim?

Informative Writing Process: Plan

PLAN | DRAFT | REVISE | EDIT AND PUBLISH

As the Industrial Revolution transformed Britain in the 18th and 19th centuries, the English Romantic poets sought inspiration in the beauty of the natural world. Romanticism's passionate defense of and nostalgia for nature have continued to this day, represented in environmental movements.

WRITING PROMPT

How can we better value nature through our daily behaviors?

Think of a daily behavior that the average person may not know is damaging to nature. For example, people may not think about reducing their use of plastic bags when cleaning up after their dogs or may not consider the consequences of constantly upgrading their phones and other technology. Research your topic, and structure your essay to be clear, informative, and convincing. Then, write an informative research essay, using both informative text structures and source materials to support your claim and make your informative essay convincing. Be sure to include the following elements:

- an introduction that clearly expresses your thesis on a topic related to daily behaviors and their impact on nature
- a clear thesis statement that informs and engages the reader
- a clear and logical informative text structure
- a formal style with an appropriate register and purposeful vocabulary, tone, and voice
- a conclusion that wraps up your ideas
- a works cited page

Writing to Sources

As you gather ideas and information from the texts in the unit, be sure to:

- use evidence from multiple sources, and
- avoid overly relying on one source.

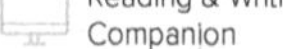

Introduction to Informative Writing

Informative research writing examines a researchable topic and presents information supported by evidence from a variety of reliable sources. The characteristics of informative research writing include:

- a clear thesis statement that presents a claim about your topic
- supporting details from a variety of sources
- a text structure that organizes ideas in a clear, impactful, and convincing manner
- a conclusion that rephrases the thesis
- in-text citations and a works cited page

As you continue with this Extended Writing Project, you'll receive more instruction and practice in crafting each of the characteristics of informative research writing to create your own research paper.

Review the Rubric

Have students examine the "Informative Writing Rubric - Grade 12" grading rubric. Inform students that this is the same rubric that will be used to evaluate their completed Informative Extended Writing Project.

Read and Annotate

As students read, have them use the Annotation Tool to identify and label the genre characteristics of informative writing, including:

- a thesis statement
- supporting details
- text structure
- a conclusion
- in-text citations and a works cited page

When students finish reading, ask them to share their annotations in small groups.

ANNOTATION GUIDE

Find the following sentences in the Student Model. Then, use the Annotation Tool to label each sentence as an example of a thesis statement, supporting fact, or quotation.

- With more and more damage being done to the environment, we need to take action to reduce the harmful daily burdens we place on the environment due to our behaviors, habits, and choices.
- Americans recycle nearly 70 million tons of material per year (Albeck- Ripka).
- This was because China is the largest processor of recycled materials in the world.
- A plastic soft drink bottle takes about 450 years to biodegrade (New Hampshire Department of Environmental Services).
- "Plastic pollution is surpassing crisis levels in the world's oceans, and I'm proud Seattle is leading the way and setting an example for the nation by enacting a plastic straw ban"
- "Come forth into the light of things; let nature be your teacher."

READ AND ANNOTATE

Pair students with on-grade-level peers to complete the annotation activity.

Before you get started, read this informative research essay that one student, Rishal, wrote in response to the writing prompt. As you read the Model, highlight and annotate the features of informative research writing that Rishal included in his essay.

STUDENT MODEL

Nurture Nature

A Damaging Relationship

1 Did you know that it takes on average 66 days to establish a habit? Yet, in today's fast-paced world, many people do not stop and think about how their daily habits impact the environment around them. Although nature isn't always a consideration when going through our daily routine, even the smallest decisions and behaviors can have a lasting impact on the environment, either positively or negatively. Humans did not always have such a damaging relationship with the environment. The great civilizations of the past, such as ancient Greece, celebrated nature instead of trying to dominate it. Things started to change during the Industrial Revolution. Nonetheless, during the 1800s, Romantic writers praised nature and were skeptical of industrial development. Two-hundred years later, the environment is rarely something we think about while going through our daily lives. With more and more damage being done to the environment, we need to take action to reduce the harmful daily burdens we place on the environment due to our behaviors, habits, and choices.

An Unexpected Truth

2 One of the daily behaviors that is unexpectedly damaging to the environment is recycling. This common, well-meaning habit isn't as good for the environment as people tend to think. When people think about how to reduce the amount of trash in their community, they usually think mainly of recycling.

TEXT TALK

Purpose

Where does Rishal introduce the thesis statement in his informative research essay?

See paragraph 1: Rishal introduces the thesis statement at the end of the first paragraph.

Word Choice

What is an example in Rishal's essay of the formal word choice that is appropriate for informative research writing?

Answers will vary. Sample answer: In paragraph 1, Rishal says, "The great civilizations of the past, such as ancient Greece, celebrated nature instead of trying to dominate it."

NOTES

28% OF AMERICANS LIVE IN AREAS SEEN TO **STRONGLY ENCOURAGE** RECYCLING

% OF US ADULTS WHO SAY PEOPLE IN THEIR LOCAL COMMUNITY ______ RECYCLING AND RE-USE

STRONGLY ENCOURAGE	ENCOURAGE BUT ARE NOT OVERLY CONCERNED	DO NOT ENCOURAGE
28%	48%	

As this graph demonstrates, almost 80% of U.S. communities encourage recycling, according to data collected by the Pew Research Center. Many cities and towns have recycling containers in public places, and some even provide them individually to homes and office buildings. Recently, however, recycling has become a less helpful option for improving the environment.

A New Challenge

3 Americans recycle nearly 70 million tons of material per year (Albeck-Ripka). Previously, most of this material went to China for processing. This was because China is the largest processor of recycled materials in the world. All that changed in 2018. China announced that it would temporarily stop accepting recycled material from other countries. China produced enough recyclable material within its own borders to meet its needs. It threatened to make the changes permanent.

4 What this meant was that the United States suddenly had to figure out what to do with tons and tons of materials collected for recycling. There are too few factories in our country to process such a large quantity of recyclables. Other nations such as Indonesia and Vietnam have such factories, but they can handle only a fraction of the amount that China used to process. The Los Angeles Times Editorial Board said of the situation in California: "Bales of mixed paper (cereal boxes, junk mail and the like) and plastics are piling up in warehouses up and down the state." Some communities have even started depositing their recyclables in landfills.

TEXT TALK

Focus

What ideas does Rishal address in his opening paragraphs?

See paragraphs 2 and 3: Rishal provides information about recycling and says that people usually think first of recycling when trying to reduce the quantity of trash in nature.

Organization

How does Rishal transition to the supporting ideas for his thesis?

See paragraphs 2–4: Rishal provides explanation of his thesis by adding examples, details, and data points to explain the issue with recycling.

An Inefficient Process

5 As the NBC News footage of a recycling plant shows (watch the news footage in the Plan lesson on the StudySync site), recycling even a fraction of these 70 million tons is not a clean and easy process. In these ten seconds of video, we hear considerable sound pollution, see piles of waste being moved around by machinery, and clouds of exhaust pouring out of a factory in Seattle, Washington. This short glimpse into the process gives us a sense of how wasteful even recycling can be.

A Simple Solution

6 Yet, what are we to do with our trash if recycling is no longer the best answer?

7 The answer is simple: We must produce less trash.

8 Where do we start?

9 When looking where to start trash reduction programs, we need look no further than plastic. Many people do not even bother recycling plastics and other trash and just throw them in the garbage. The garbage is taken to landfills. While landfills may seem like a viable solution, some parts of the United States are running out of space for landfills. For example, the Northeast has to pay neighboring states to accept its trash because the region no longer has adequate space to manage its own landfills (Lakeshore Recycling Services).

10 Plastic trash takes the longest to biodegrade, or break down. For example, a plastic shopping bag takes at least ten years to break down. A plastic soft drink bottle takes about 450 years to biodegrade (New Hampshire Department of Environmental Services). When people don't throw plastic waste into a recycle bin or even a garbage can, nature can be seriously harmed. For instance, fish mistake the plastic for food and die after eating it. Huge sections of the Pacific Ocean are covered with plastic trash that has drifted out to sea and been collected together by currents. This, in combination with climate change, has created huge "dead zones" where there is little life near the ocean's surface. All of the marine life near the surface suffers from a lack of oxygen. The plastic also blocks out sunlight, interfering with photosynthesis in tiny plants called phytoplankton. These plants form the base of the oceanic food chain.

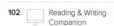

TEXT TALK

Sentence Fluency

Choose one sentence that states an idea effectively. Why do you think the sentence is so effective?

Answers will vary. Sample answer: I think the sentence in paragraph 7 "The answer is simple: We must produce less trash" is strong. It clearly restates the thesis in a visible way.

Elaboration

Why does Rishal focus on the reduction of plastic waste as opposed to other types of waste?

See paragraph 10 Rishal points out that plastic waste takes longer to biodegrade than other types of waste, and this idea connects to the thesis at the end of paragraph 1.

11 Another problem with plastic is that it does not recycle well. Most plastics can be recycled into lower-quality material that is only useful for cheap products like synthetic fabric and bumper stickers (Somerville). In addition, factories that recycle plastics require a great deal of energy, often generating greenhouse gases and other pollution. Although we should continue to recycle as much paper as we have factory space for, recycling plastic is much less efficient.

A Growing Community

12 Some people have already started working on the problem. As the graph below shows, approximately 75% of U.S. adults are concerned for the environment, and 20% consistently take action as a result of that concern. This is a community that must keep growing, and effective strategies for trash reduction are already emerging.

MOST AMERICANS REPORT CONCERN FOR THE ENVIRONMENT; ONE-IN-FIVE TRY TO ACT ON THAT CONCERN ALL THE TIME

% OF US ADULTS WHO SAY THEY ARE ________ ABOUT HELPING THE ENVIRONMENT AS THEY GO ABOUT THEIR DAILY LIVES.

PARTICULARLY CONCERNED
NOT PARTICULARLY CONCERNED
76%

% OF US ADULTS WHO SAY THEY LIVE IN WAYS TO HELP PROTECT THE ENVIRONMENT...

ALL THE TIME
SOME OF THE TIME
NOT TOO OFTEN
NOT AT ALL
20%
63%

13 One of the most effective strategies is banning stores from giving out plastic shopping bags. In Kenya, a ban on plastic bags has resulted in cleaner waterways and a less contaminated food supply chain (Watts). After the state of California banned plastic shopping bags, there was a drop in the amount of litter on beaches. Manufacturers of plastic shopping bags have lobbied heavily against these laws. Another campaign against plastic involves plastic straws. Seattle has banned plastic straws and plastic utensils in restaurants. "Plastic pollution is surpassing crisis levels in the world's oceans, and I'm proud Seattle is leading the way and setting an example for the

TEXT TALK

Evidence

What types of support does Rishal use to support his thesis statement in the second half of the essay?

Answers will vary. Sample answer: In paragraph 10, Rishal uses a fact about how plastic biodegrades. In paragraph 13, he uses a quotation.

Conventions

Where does Rishal use a hyphen to create a compound adjective?

Answers will vary. Sample answer: Rishal uses a hyphen in paragraph 11 to create the compound adjective *lower-quality*.

nation by enacting a plastic straw ban," Seattle Public Utilities General Manager Mami Hara said (CBS News). The city was inspired by a similar ban in Great Britain. India has announced it will institute the same type of ban in several years. Each community that takes action against plastic waste inspires other communities to do the same.

A Huge Difference

14 We can make a huge difference if we all change our daily routines. Individuals can take easy and immediate action and make better decisions when it comes to their impact on nature, especially when it comes to recycling. For example, when you order carry-out, ask that no plastic utensils or straws be included.

15 Staying informed will help you adjust your daily routines to respond to new facts and discoveries in the field. By sharing your research and the strategies you've implemented, you can support your friends and family members in understanding the problem and help them value nature in a more sustainable, beneficial manner.

16 Nature needs to be nurtured. Nature provides us with food, water, and the air we breathe. Yet, in return, some of our choices and behaviors damage it. Nature should be a source of inspiration. We need to be advocates for nature, just as the Romantic writers were. William Wordsworth said it best: "Come forth into the light of things; let nature be your teacher."

Works Cited

Albeck-Ripka, Livia. "Your Recycling Gets Recycled, Right? Maybe, or Maybe Not." *The New York Times*, 29 May 2018, www.nytimes.com/2018/05/29/climate/ Recycling-landfills-plastic-papers.html. Accessed 20 Oct. 2018.

Anderson, Monica. "For Earth Day, Here's How Americans View Environmental Issues." *Pew Research Center*, 20 Apr. 2017, http://www.pewresearch.org/fact-tank/2017/04/20/for-earth-day-heres-how-americans-view-environmental-issues/. Accessed 31 Dec. 2018.

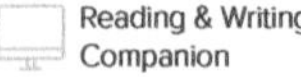

CBS News. "Seattle Becomes First U.S. City to Ban Plastic Utensils and Straws." *CBS News*, 2 Jul. 2018, www.cbsnews.com/news/seattle-becomes-first-u-s-city-to-ban-plastic-utensils-and-straws/. Accessed 20 Oct. 2018.

Dean, Signe. "Here's How Long It Really Takes to Break a Habit, According to Science." *Science Alert*, 9 Jun. 2018, www.sciencealert.com/how-long-it-takes-to-break-a-habit-according-to-science. Accessed 21 Nov. 2018.

Desilver, Drew. "Perceptions and Realities of Recycling Vary Widely From Place to Place." *Pew Research Center*, 7 Oct. 2016, http://www.pewresearch.org/fact-tank/2016/10/07/perceptions-and-realities-of-recycling-vary-widely-from-place-to-place/ft16-10-05recyclingencouraged/. Accessed 31 Dec. 2018.

Lakeshore Recycling Services. "Roundup of Successful Waste Reduction Campaigns by Cities." *Lakeshore Recycling Services*, 25 Apr. 2018. www.lrsrecycles.com/ roundup-successful-waste-reduction-campaigns-cities/. Accessed 31 Dec. 2018.

Los Angeles Times Editorial Board. "California Has a Recycling Crisis." *The Los Angeles Times*, 26 May 2018, www.latimes.com/opinion/editorials/la-ed-recycling-crisis-20180526-story.html. Accessed 20 Oct. 2018.

NBC News X Press. "Recycling Center." *NBC News X Press*, 25 Jun. 2018. https://www.nbcnewsarchivesxpress.com/contentdetails/1937321. Accessed 23 Nov. 2018.

New Hampshire Department of Environmental Services. "Approximate Time It Takes Garbage to Decompose in Its Environment." New Hampshire Department of Environmental Services, 23 Mar. 2017, www.des.nh.gov/organization/ divisions/water/wmb/coastal/trash/documents/marinedebris.pdf. Accessed 7 Jan. 2019.

Scientific American. "'Dead' Sea of Plastic Bottles." *Scientific American*, www.scientificamerican.com/article/dead-sea-of-plastic-bottles/. Accessed 2 Oct. 2018.

Somerville, Madeleine. "Yes, You Recycle. But Until You Start Reducing, You're Still Killing the Planet." *The Guardian,* 19 May 2016, www.theguardian.com/lifeandstyle/ 2016/jan/19/eco-friendly-living-sustainability-recycling-reducing-saving-the-planet. Accessed 20 Oct. 2018.

Watts, Jonathan. "Eight Months On, Is the World's Most Drastic Plastic Bag Ban Working?" *The Guardian,* 25 Apr. 2018, https://www.theguardian.com/world/2018/apr/25/nairobi-clean-up-highs-lows-kenyas-plastic-bag-ban. Accessed 20 Oct. 2018.

WRITE

When writing, it is important to consider your audience and purpose so you can write appropriately for them. Reread the prompt to determine your purpose for writing.

To begin, review the questions below and then select a strategy, such as brainstorming, journaling, reading, or discussing, to generate ideas.

- **Topic:** What topic about the human impact on nature do you find most interesting?
- **Purpose:** What is your reason for writing? What message do you want to express?
- **Audience:** Who is your audience? How will knowing your audience help you write a better essay?
- **Questions:** What do you want to learn about your topic? What questions do you want to research?

Response Instructions

Use the questions in the bulleted list to write a one-paragraph research summary. Your summary should include possible research questions based on the prompt.

This is your first step in writing an informative research essay. As you progress through this Extended Writing Project, you will develop a research plan and will have opportunities to critique your research plan at each step of the writing process. If necessary, you will be able to implement changes. For example, as you begin reviewing sources, you may find that your major research question is too broad. If so, you can modify your major research question and then refocus and revise your research plan as needed.

Write

Circulate as students use the questions in the bulleted list to plan their writing. See the instructions for scaffolding and differentiation that follow.

CHECK FOR SUCCESS

If students struggle to come up with answers for the questions in the lesson, work with students to provide an answer to one question and then help them build from there.

For example, start by asking students, "How do you feel about nature?" or "What do you like about nature?" Once students have answered one question, help them to work through a second question until they've begun to build some momentum. It may be helpful to start with a different question than the one that's listed first in the lesson.

Review Prompt and Rubric

Before students begin writing, review the writing prompt and rubric with the class.

Response Instructions

Use the questions in the bulleted list on the previous page to write a one-paragraph research summary. Your summary should include possible research questions based on the prompt.

This is your first step in writing an informative research essay. As you progress through this Extended Writing Project, you will develop a research plan and will have opportunities to critique your research plan at each step of the writing process. If necessary, you will be able to implement changes. For example, as you begin reviewing sources, you may find that your major research question is too broad. If so, you can modify your major research question and then refocus and revise your research plan as needed.

Score	Plan	Language and Conventions
4	The writer responds to the questions, and the writing is clear and focused.	The writer demonstrates a consistent command of grammar, punctuation, and usage conventions. Although minor errors may be evident, they do not detract from the fluency or clarity of the writing.
3	The writer responds to the questions, but the writing is not always clear or focused.	The writer demonstrates an adequate command of grammar, punctuation, and usage conventions. Although some errors may be evident, they create few (if any) disruptions in the fluency or clarity of the writing.
2	The writer responds to the questions, but the writing is somewhat unclear and unfocused.	The writer demonstrates a partial command of grammar, punctuation, and usage conventions. Some distracting errors may be evident, at times creating minor disruptions in the fluency or clarity of the writing.
1	The writer responds to the questions, but the writing is very unclear and unfocused.	The writer demonstrates little or no command of grammar, punctuation, and usage conventions. Serious and persistent errors create disruptions in the fluency of the writing and sometimes interfere with meaning.
0	The writer does not provide a relevant response to the prompt or does not provide a response at all.	Serious and persistent errors overwhelm the writing and interfere with the meaning of the response as a whole, making the writer's meaning impossible to understand.

Write

Use the scaffolds below to differentiate instruction for your ELL English Language Learners and A Approaching grade-level learners.

ELL **BEGINNING, INTERMEDIATE** With the help of the word bank, write a response using the paragraph frame.

ADVANCED, ADVANCED HIGH Write a response using the sentence starters.

A APPROACHING Write a response using the sentence starters.

BEGINNING / INTERMEDIATE		ADVANCED, ADVANCED HIGH / APPROACHING
Word Bank	**Paragraph Frame**	**Sentence Starters**
about pollution essay nature teacher magazine gardening	A topic about the impact of people on nature that interests me is ____. My audience will be my ____. I want to give my audience this message: ____. I want to learn ____. I can use this research question: ____? I can answer my research question by reading books and online ____. I can use ____ to share the information that I find.	• The topic about the impact of people on nature that I find most interesting is . . . • My audience is . . . • The message I want to express to my audience is . . . • What I want to learn about my topic is . . . • To focus my research, I can use this research question: . . . • Sources I can use to answer my question include . . . • I can share the information I find by . . .

Peer Review

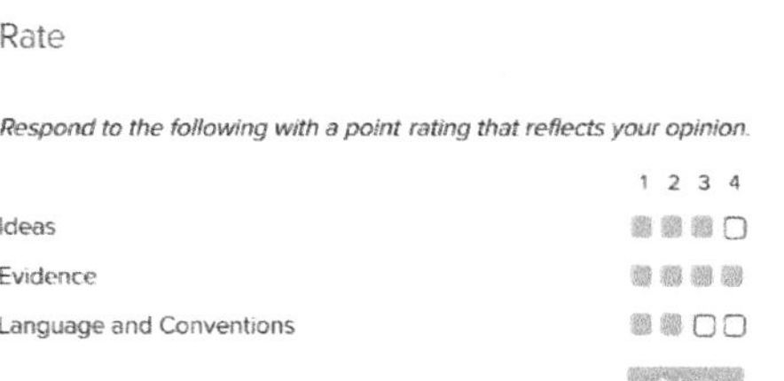

Students should submit substantive feedback to two peers using the review instructions below.

- How well does this response answer the prompt questions?
- Which answer interested you the most?
- Are there any ideas that could be improved on? How so?

ELL A SENTENCE FRAMES

- The response does a good job of answering the prompt question ____.
- I thought the answer ____ was interesting.
- I think you could improve the idea ____ by (adding / clarifying / describing) ____.

Skill: Planning Research

Introduce the Skill

Watch the Concept Definition video and read the following definition with your students.

Inquiry refers to the questioning process writers and researchers use in search of information or knowledge. Your search may be for a **formal** purpose, such as a research report, or for an **informal** purpose, such as learning about the life of an author whose work you enjoy reading.

When you write a formal research report, one of your first steps is to identify a **major research question**. You can use this question to guide your research process, and to develop a thesis or claim that is the answer to your question.

Once you have formulated your major research question, you should develop a **research plan**, or a series of steps you can follow to find information that will help you answer your question.

Later in the research process, you might find that you will need to **modify** your research question, making changes to improve it, and revise and refocus your research plan.

Skill:
Planning Research

••• CHECKLIST FOR PLANNING RESEARCH

In order to conduct a short or more sustained research project to answer a question or solve a problem, do the following:

- select a topic or problem to research
- think about what you want to find out and what kind of research can contribute to the project
- start to formulate your major research question by asking open-ended questions that begin "How. . .?" and "Why. . .?" and then choose a question that you are interested in exploring
- synthesize multiple sources on the subject to look at information from different points of view, while demonstrating understanding of the subject under investigation

In order to conduct a short or more sustained research project to answer a question or solve a problem, consider the following questions:

- Does my major research question allow me to explore a new issue, an important problem worth solving, or a fresh perspective on a topic?
- Can I research my question within my given time frame and with the resources available to me?
- Have I synthesized multiple sources on the question or problem, looking for different points of view?
- Have I demonstrated understanding of the subject under investigation in my research project?

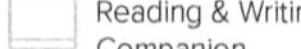

TURN AND TALK

Turn to a partner and discuss the last time you needed to find the answer to a question. What resources did you use for an informal search? Did you stop at the first source you encountered, or did you spend time looking for a reliable source?

SPEAKING FRAMES

- I had a question about ____.
- To find the answer, I looked ____.
- I (did / did not) stop at the first source, which was ____.
- I (did / did not) spend time looking for ____.

SKILL VOCABULARY

inquiry / la indagación ***noun*** the process of questioning in a search for information or knowledge

formal / formal ***adjective*** relating to a way of doing something according to established norms and requirements COGNATE

informal / informal ***adjective*** relating to a way of doing something in a casual manner COGNATE

YOUR TURN

Read the research questions below. Then, complete the chart by sorting the questions into the correct category. Write the corresponding letter for each question in the appropriate column.

Research Questions	
A	Why do people choose to spend time outdoors?
B	Why did the bald eagle become an endangered species?
C	How does pollution lead to microplastics in the ocean or carcinogens in the air?
D	What are major pollutants in the world today?
E	How has America treated wild animals throughout its history?
F	How does pollution affect air and water quality in the U.S.?
G	Does hiking make people live longer?
H	How are endangered species currently being protected in the U.S.? What can be improved?
I	How does spending time outdoors or in nature affect people's health and mood?

Topic	Too Narrow	Appropriate	Too Broad
Endangered Species			
Pollution			
Spending Time Outdoors			

Your Turn

Ask students to complete the Your Turn activity.

Topic	Too Narrow	Appropriate	Too Broad
Endangered Species	B	H	E
Pollution	C	F	D
Spending Time Outdoors	G	I	A

SKILL VOCABULARY

major research question/ la pregunta principal de investigación ***noun*** a question that a writer uses to guide the research process and develop a thesis or claim

research plan/ el plan de investigación ***noun*** a series of steps a person can follow to find information to answer a research question

modify / modificar ***verb*** to make minor changes in order to make something better COGNATE

Your Turn

Ask students to complete the Your Turn activity. Answers will vary.

Process	Plan
Research Question	How can people reduce food waste in their lives? What effect would that have on the environment?
Step 1	Look up articles and resources about the food supply, how food waste happens, and why it is problematic.
Step 2	Find out more about what impact food waste has on the environment.
Step 3	Search for solutions to the problem of food waste, including ways people can reduce it in their own lives.
Step 4	Find out more about what initiatives are already taking place to address food waste and its environmental impact.

YOUR TURN

Develop a research question for formal research. Then, write a short plan for how you will go about doing research for your essay.

Process	Plan
Research Question	
Step 1	
Step 2	
Step 3	
Step 4	

Writer's Notebook

Divide students into pairs, and ask them to imagine they are writing a research essay about their partner. Their essay can focus, for example, on their partner's early childhood, a memorable event in his or her life, or his or her experiences playing an instrument. Have students use a graphic organizer to draft a research question and a plan for finding the information they need.

TURN AND TALK

Allow students to share their research questions and plans orally in pairs or small groups before writing.

Skill:
Evaluating Sources

CHECKLIST FOR EVALUATING SOURCES

Once you gather your sources, identify the following:

- where information seems inaccurate, biased, or outdated
- where information strongly relates to your task, purpose, and audience
- where information helps you make an informed decision or solve a problem

In order to conduct advanced searches to gather relevant, credible, and accurate print and digital sources, use the following questions as a guide:

- Are there specific terms or phrases that I can use to adjust my search?
- Can I use *and*, *or*, or *not* to expand or limit my search?
- Can I use quotation marks to search for exact phrases?
- Is the material published by a well-established source or expert author?
- Is the material up-to-date or based on the most current information?
- Is the material factual, and can it be verified by another source?
- Are there discrepancies between the information presented in different sources?

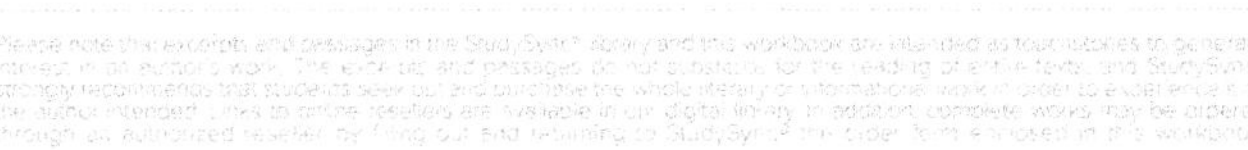

Skill: Evaluating Sources

Introduce the Skill

Watch the Concept Definition video and read the following definition with your students.

One important step in the research process is gathering and evaluating sources of information. Evaluating a source involves examining the source to determine whether it is reliable, credible, accurate, and useful for your purpose.

- A source is **reliable** if it provides consistently accurate and up-to-date information.
- A source is **credible** if it is trustworthy and supported by evidence.
- A source is **accurate** if its information is factual and can be verified.
- A source is useful if it directly supports your task and is suitable for your audience.

Avoid sources that contain omissions or discrepancies in the information and data provided. **Discrepancies** may mean that a source is inaccurate or biased.

If you find that a source is faulty or does not suit your purpose, you may need to adjust your search. Adding specific terms and punctuation can expand or limit your search results to provide new sources.

TURN AND TALK

Turn to your partner and discuss the last article you read online. How did you determine whether or not the information came from a credible source?

SPEAKING FRAMES

- The last article I read online was ____.
- I found the article on ____.
- I knew the source (was / was not) credible because ____.

SKILL VOCABULARY

reliable source / la fuente confiable *noun* a source that is known for providing consistently good and up-to-date information

credible source / la fuente confiable *noun* a source that is trustworthy and believable

accurate source / la fuente precisa *noun* a source based on factual information that can be verified

discrepancy / la discrepancia *noun* a noticeable difference or mismatch between two or more facts or sources COGNATE

Your Turn

Ask students to complete the Your Turn activity.

Credible and Reliable	Not Credible or Reliable
A	B
C	D
E	F

YOUR TURN

Read the sentences below. Then, complete the chart by sorting the sentences into two categories: those that are credible and reliable and those that are not. Write the corresponding letter for each sentence in the appropriate column.

	Sentences
A	The article was published recently and uses up-to-date information.
B	The text uses only one viewpoint or relies on opinions instead of cited sources.
C	The text includes many viewpoints that are properly cited.
D	The article was published many years ago and uses statistics that may be outdated.
E	The article includes clear arguments and counterarguments that are supported by factual information.
F	The website is a personal blog or social media website.

Credible and Reliable	Not Credible or Reliable

Writer's Notebook

Ask students to do a quick internet search on a topic of their choosing, such as their favorite band, sports team, or author. Have them identify one source that they believe is credible and accurate. Have them identify one source that they believe is not credible or accurate, due to bias, omission, faulty reasoning, or some other problem. Ask students to write a short paragraph to explain their reasoning.

TURN AND TALK

Allow students to share their reasons orally in pairs or small groups before freewriting.

YOUR TURN

Complete the chart below by filling in the title and author of a source for your informative research essay and answering the questions about this source.

Questions	Answers
Source Title and Author:	
Reliability: Has the source material been published in a well-established book or periodical or on a well-established website? Is the source material up-to-date or based on the most current information?	
Accuracy: Is the source based on factual information that can be verified by another source? Are there any discrepancies between this source and others?	
Credibility: Is the source material written by a recognized expert on the topic? Is the source material published by a well-respected author or organization?	
Should I use this source in my research essay?	

Your Turn

Ask students to complete the Your Turn activity. Answers will vary.

Source Title and Author:	• The *Los Angeles Times*: "It's been a year since California banned single-use plastic bags. The world didn't end." by Los Angeles Times Editorial Board
Reliability: Has the source material been published in a well-established book or periodical or on a well-established website? Is the source material up-to-date or based on the most current information?	• Yes, *The Los Angeles Times* is a well-established newspaper. • Yes, the article was published in November 2017.
Accuracy: Is the source based on factual information that can be verified by another source? Are there any discrepancies between this source and others?	• The article is an editorial, or opinion piece, but does rely on statistics to back up its arguments.
Credibility: Is the source material written by a recognized expert on the topic? Is the source material published by a well-respected author or organization?	• Yes, *The Los Angeles Times* is well respected, but I can't ignore that this is an opinion piece, so there may be biases.
Should I use this source in my research essay?	• I do not think I am going to use this source in my essay. It is too clearly advocating for one opinion, and though it uses many facts to back up its claims, I would have to verify a lot of what it says with another source in order to fully trust the information.

Skill: Research and Notetaking

Introduce the Skill

Watch the Concept Definition video and read the following definition with your students.

When doing research, you need to gather information from a variety of sources including books, scholarly articles, videos, and online publications, in order to get different points of view on a topic. You should find **reliable** sources that contain information that is **relevant**, or appropriate and logically related to your research. Look for sources that have the most up-to-date information. When researching online, look for sites that are connected to schools or with government agencies, such as NASA.

As you read and take notes for your research, **synthesize** the information you gather. Synthesizing is the process of merging, or joining together, new information with information you have already found in order to reach a new understanding. As you acquire more information and review your notes, you may see connections and contradictions. Synthesizing notes from various sources may cause you to modify your thinking, **refocus** the research plan, and consider new conclusions.

Skill: Research and Notetaking

••• CHECKLIST FOR RESEARCH AND NOTETAKING

In order to conduct short as well as more sustained research projects to answer a question (including a self-generated question) or solve a problem, note the following:

- answer a question for a research project, or think of your own question that you would like to have answered
- look up your topic in an encyclopedia to find general information
- find specific, up-to-date information in books and periodicals or on the Internet. If appropriate, conduct interviews with experts to get information
- narrow or broaden your inquiry when appropriate
  - > if you find dozens of books on a topic, your research topic may be too broad
  - > if it is difficult to write a research question, narrow your topic so it is more specific
- synthesize your information by organizing your notes from various sources to see what your sources have in common and how they differ

To conduct short as well as more sustained research projects to answer a question (including a self-generated question) or solve a problem, consider the following questions:

- What is my research question?
- Where could I look to find information?
- How does new information I have found affect my research question?
- How can I demonstrate my understanding of the subject I am investigating?

TURN AND TALK

Turn to your partner and discuss your researching strategies. When you want to research something you heard in a news report, where do you go to find more information?

SPEAKING FRAMES

- I learn about news by ____.
- When I want to research more about a news story, I ____.

SKILL VOCABULARY

reliable / confiable *adjective* trustworthy and of good quality

relevant / relevante *adjective* appropriate and logically related to the topic COGNATE

synthesize / sintetizar *verb* to merge new information with other information previously gained through reading in order to reach a new understanding COGNATE

refocus / cambiar el enfoque *verb* to focus on something new or different; change direction

YOUR TURN

Read each point from Rishal's note cards below. Then, complete the chart by sorting the points into two categories: those that support re-examining our relationship with recycling and those that support reducing waste consumption. Write the corresponding letter for each point in the appropriate column.

	Points
A	Source 5: Processing plastic for re-use provides low-quality material that can be used only for cheap products.
B	Source 3: A plastic soft drink bottle takes about 450 years to biodegrade, or break down.
C	Source 6: The Northeastern United States has run out of room for landfills.
D	Source 8: As NBC News footage of a recycling plant shows, recycling even a fraction of these 70 million tons is not a clean and easy process.
E	Source 4: The situation after China's ban on foreign garbage: "bales of mixed paper (cereal boxes, junk mail and the like) and plastics are piling up in warehouses up and down the state."
F	Source 7: "Plastic pollution is surpassing crisis levels in the world's oceans."

Re-examine Our Relationship with Recycling	Reduce Waste Consumption

WRITE

Use the questions in the checklist to locate sources and synthesize the information about one point or idea related to your topic in a paragraph for your draft.

Your Turn

Ask students to complete the Your Turn activity.

Re-examine Our Relationship with Recycling	Reduce Waste Consumption
A	B
D	C
E	F

Write

Ask students to complete the writing assignment.

ELL REWRITE CHECKLIST

A Sources

- ☐ Which sources give information on the same topic?
- ☐ How are the ideas in those sources related?
- ☐ How can I clarify which information comes from which source?

Synthesis of Ideas

- ☐ How does the information in each source change or refine what I have learned?
- ☐ How can I combine information from multiple sources to make a point?

Writer's Notebook

Ask students for examples of unreliable sources. Have them explain why these sources are unreliable. Then, ask them to think of a time when unreliable information caused a problem for them or their friends and family members. Ask them to write a brief reflection about how they decide whether information is unreliable.

ELL TURN AND TALK

Allow students to share their ideas orally in pairs or small groups before writing.

Informative Writing Process: Draft

WRITE

Ask students to complete the writing assignment.

CHECK FOR SUCCESS

If students struggle to begin drafting their essays, ask them the following questions:

- What is your thesis statement or claim?
- What are your main ideas about the topic?
- What textual evidence from sources supports your main ideas?

DRAFT CHECKLIST

Purpose and Focus

☐ Have I made my thesis or claim clear to readers?

Organization

☐ Does the order of ideas in my essay make sense?

Evidence and Elaboration

☐ Have I provided sufficient evidence and elaboration?

Informative Writing Process: Draft

PLAN | DRAFT | REVISE | EDIT AND PUBLISH

You have already made progress toward writing your informative research essay. You have developed a research plan; selected a major research question; and located, evaluated, and synthesized information from a variety of sources. Before you begin drafting, you should take a moment to critique your research plan and implement any changes needed. For example, now that you have done your background reading and research, you may want to refine your thesis or claim or clarify the points you plan to make in your essay.

Now it is time to draft your informative research essay.

WRITE

Use your plan and other responses in your Binder to draft your essay. You may also have new ideas as you begin drafting. Feel free to explore those new ideas as you have them. You can also ask yourself these questions to ensure that your writing is focused and organized and you have elaborated on your ideas:

Draft Checklist:

☐ **Purpose and Focus:** Have I made my claim clear to readers? Will they understand the purpose of my research? Have I included only relevant information and details and nothing extraneous that might confuse my readers?

☐ **Organization:** Does the organizational structure in my essay make sense? Will readers be engaged by the organization and interested in the way I present information and evidence?

☐ **Evidence and Elaboration:** Have I provided sufficient evidence and elaboration? Will my readers be able to follow my ideas and details?

Before you submit your draft, read it over carefully. You want to be sure that you've responded to all aspects of the prompt.

Peer Review

Students should submit substantive feedback to two peers using the review instructions below.

- Has the writer clearly expressed his or her ideas? Are there any places where the ideas could be clarified or improved?
- What suggestions can you make to help the writer improve the use of information from sources in the research essay?

SENTENCE FRAMES

- You clearly stated your idea that ____. You could clarify your idea that ____.
- You could improve your use of sources by ____.

Here is Rishal's informative research essay draft. As you read, notice how Rishal develops his draft to be focused and organized, so it has relevant evidence and elaboration to support his claim. As he continues to revise and edit his informative research essay, he will find and improve weak spots in his writing, as well as correct any language or punctuation mistakes.

STUDENT MODEL: FIRST DRAFT

Nurture Nature

~~Although nature isn't always a consideration when going through our daily routine, even the smallest decisions and behaviors can have a lasting impact on the environment, either positively or negatively. Modern society seems more focused on economic gain and "progress" at the expense of the environment. The great civilizations of the past, such as anchent Greece, celebrated nature instead of trying to dominate it. In the 1800s, Romantic writers praised nature and were sceptical of industrial development. With more and more damage being done to the environment, we need to take action to reduce the amount of trash that is dumped in the natural world.~~

A Damaging Relationship

Did you know that it takes on average 66 days to establish a habit? Yet, in today's fast-paced world, many people do not stop and think about how their daily habits impact the environment around them. Although nature isn't always a consideration when going through our daily routine, even the smallest decisions and behaviors can have a lasting impact on the environment, either positively or negatively. Humans did not always have such a damaging relationship with the environment. The great civilizations of the past, such as ancient Greece, celebrated nature instead of trying to dominate it. Things started to change during the Industrial Revolution. Nonetheless, during the 1800s, Romantic writers praised nature and were skeptical of industrial development. Two-hundred years later, the environment is rarely something we think about while going through our daily lives. With more and more damage being done to the environment, we need to take action to reduce the harmful daily burdens we place on the environment due to our behaviors, habits, and choices.

Skill: Print and Graphic Features

Rishal adds a heading to signal to his readers what the paragraph will be about. As he rereads his draft, he will continue to add headings to help organize his information effectively.

ELL SPEAKING FRAMES

- Rishal added ___ because ___.
- He also added a ___ to his second paragraph.
- This thinking will help Rishal by ___.

Analyze Student Model

Have students discuss the questions in the lesson as well as the Student Model draft. Ask:

- How does Rishal organize his informative research essay draft?
- How does Rishal reveal the focus of his research in his informative research essay draft?
- How does Rishal use evidence and elaboration in his informative research essay draft?
- How can you organize, reveal the focus of, and use evidence and elaboration in your own informative research essay?

Encourage students to share ideas for their own informative research essays based on the questions in the lesson.

ELL SPEAKING FRAMES

- The writer uses ___ organization to ___.
- The focus of the writer's essay is ___. This helps readers because ___.
- The writer reveals this focus when ___. I think this is effective because ___.
- The writer uses ___ example when he elaborates on his ideas, which helps him ___.
- An idea that I have for my essay is ___.

Print and Graphic Features

Discuss the Model

1. The Model shows how Rishal changed his second paragraph to include a print or graphic feature. What did he add and why? Rishal added a visual showing how common recycling is because he was concerned the paragraph was too general and thought his audience might need additional exposure to the topic.
2. What else does Rishal do to improve the second paragraph? He added an effective heading.
3. How will this thinking help Rishal revise or add other print and graphic features in this text and others? Answers will vary, but should indicate an understanding of how print and graphic features can enhance and improve how information is conveyed to an audience.

Critiquing Research

Discuss the Model

1. Why does Rishal revise his research question? He was worried that his research question framed his essay as being too strongly against recycling, so he revises his question to clarify that reduction is a more viable solution.
2. What is Rishal's critique of his sources? Rishal confirms that his sources are reputable and reliable.
3. How does Rishal refocus his thesis? He adjusts his thesis from "With more and more damage being done to the environment, we need to take action to reduce the amount of trash that is dumped in the natural world." to "One of the daily behaviors that is unexpectedly damaging to the environment is recycling. However, this common, well-meaning habit isn't as good for the environment as people tend to think."
4. How do Rishal's critique and changes improve his essay? Answers will vary. Sample answer: Rishal modifies his major research question to refocus his thesis and adds a source to connect ideas, which allows him to paraphrase without plagiarizing.

SPEAKING FRAMES

- Rishal revises his research question because ____. He changes it to ____.
- Rishal confirms that his sources are ____.
- Rishal refocuses his thesis by ____.
- Rishal's critique and changes improve his essay by ____.

DESIGN A GRAPHIC ORGANIZER

Before students write their draft, have them think about the Student Model (and process) and the prompt. Challenge students to create an original graphic organizer to help plan their thoughts before beginning their draft. Students can share/compare their graphic organizers with their peers.

NOTES

When people think about how to reduce the amount of trash in their community, they usually think first of recycling. Many cities and towns have recycling containers in public places, and some even provide them individually to homes and office buildings. Americans recycle nearly 70 million tons of material per year (Albeck-Ripka).

~~We must produce less trash. When looking where to start trash reduction programs, we need look no further than plastic. Fish mistake the plastic for food and die after eating it. Plastic trash takes practically forever to biodegrade. When people are too lazy to be responsible and throw plastic waste into a recycle bin or even a garbage can, defenseless creatures are forced to suffer! Huge sections of the Pacific Ocean are covered with plastic trash that has drifted out to sea and been collected together by currents. Gross! This, in combination with climate change, has created huge hypoxic areas where there is little life near the ocean's surface. The plastic also interferes with the photosynthesis of phytoplankton, which form the base of the oceanic trophic pyramid.~~

Skill: Critiquing Research

As he revises, Rishal thinks about how to synthesize and integrate information from multiple sources. In this paragraph, he adds relevant information from the New Hampshire Department of Environmental Services.

Plastic trash takes the longest to biodegrade, or break down. For example, a plastic shopping bag takes at least ten years to break down. A plastic soft drink bottle takes about 450 years to biodegrade (New Hampshire Department of Environmental Services). When people don't throw plastic waste into a recycle bin or even a garbage can, nature can be seriously harmed. For instance, fish mistake the plastic for food and die after eating it. Huge sections of the Pacific Ocean are covered with plastic trash that has drifted out to sea and been collected together by currents. This, in combination with climate change, has created huge "dead zones" where there is little life near the ocean's surface. All of the marine life near the surface suffers from a lack of oxygen. The plastic also blocks out sunlight, interfering with photosynthesis in tiny plants called phytoplankton. These plants form the base of the oceanic food chain.

Another problem with plastic is that it does not recycle well. Most plastics can be recycled into awful material that is only fairly awful and only good for cheap products like sinthetick fabric and bumper stickers (*The Guardian*). And, factories that recycle plastics require a great deal of energy, often with greenhouse gases and other

pollution. Although we should continue to recycle as much paper as we have factory space for, recycling plastic is much less effishient.

For example, the Northeast has to pay nayboring states to accept its trash. It's run out of room for it (Lakeshore Recycling Services). Many people do not even bother recycling plastics and other trash and just throw them in the garbage. The garbage is taken to landfills. It's now at the point that some parts of the United States are running out of space for landfills.

~~All of this means that our top priority should be programs that reduce the amount of plastic waste and some people have already started work on the problem because one of the most effective strategies is banning stores from giving out plastic shopping bags. In Kenya, a ban on plastic bags has resulted in cleaner waterways and a less contaminated food supply chain. After the state of California banned plastic shopping bags, there was a drop in the amount of litter on beaches. Manufacturers of plastic shopping bags have lobbyed heavily against these laws. Another campaign against plastic involves plastic straws. Seattle has banned plastic straws and plastic utensils in restaurants. Plastic pollution is serpassing crisis levels in the world's oceans, and I'm proud Seattle is leading the way and setting an example for the nation by enacting a plastic straw ban, Seattle Public Utilities General Manager Mami Hara said. The city was inspired by a similar ban in Great Britain. India has announced it will institute the same type of ban in several years. Each community that takes action against plastic waste inspires other communities to do the same.~~

One of the most effective strategies is banning stores from giving out plastic shopping bags. In Kenya, a ban on plastic bags has resulted in cleaner waterways and a less contaminated food supply chain (Watts). After the state of California banned plastic shopping bags, there was a drop in the amount of litter on beaches. Manufacturers of plastic shopping bags have lobbied heavily against these laws. Another campaign against plastic involves plastic straws. Seattle has banned plastic straws and plastic utensils in restaurants. "Plastic pollution is surpassing crisis levels in the world's oceans, and I'm proud Seattle is leading the way and setting an example for the nation by enacting a plastic straw ban," Seattle Public Utilities

Skill: Paraphrasing

Rishal realizes that he forgot to use quotation marks in a citation. Since the statement from Mami Hara is a direct quotation, not a paraphrase, he puts quotation marks around it.

Skill: Sources and Citations

Even though Rishal attributed the statement about Seattle's plastic straw ban to Mami Hara, he needs to cite the source of the remark. So he inserts a parenthetical citation. Since the source is electronic, he doesn't have to include a page number.

Paraphrasing

Discuss the Model

1. **The Model shows how Rishal updates the *Los Angeles Times* citation. What does he note about the citation? What does he decide to do as a result?** He notes that the information in the first sentence seems challenging for his audience and does not match the vocabulary in his essay. He chooses to paraphrase the sentence to integrate this information into his essay using his own words.
2. **What else does he choose to include?** He chooses to quote the article directly because the second sentence seems more appropriate for his audience.
3. **How do these changes improve his informative research essay?** Answers will vary, but should include an understanding of how paraphrasing information and integrating it allow Rishal to maintain a logical flow of ideas and the original meaning of the source. Rishal also avoids plagiarism by correctly citing both the paraphrased and quoted material.

ELL **SPEAKING FRAMES**

- Rishal notes ____.
- As a result, he decides to ____.
- He chooses to include ____.
- These changes improve his essay by ____.

Sources and Citations

Discuss the Model

1. What revisions did Rishal make to his in-text citations? He added a necessary citation for paraphrased information. He also added quotation marks around a direct quote as well as a citation for the source the quote came from.
2. What revisions did Rishal make to his works cited list? He corrected the format of the publication title as well as the format of the publication date for each of his sources.
3. What is the difference between paraphrasing and plagiarism? How do citations help prevent plagiarism? Answers will vary, but should indicate that all information, whether paraphrased or quoted, should be given a proper citation to credit the original author.

ELL SPEAKING FRAMES

- Rishal revised his in-text citations by ____.
- Rishal revised his works cited list by ____.
- Having proper citations is important because ____.

General Manager Mami Hara said (CBS News). The city was inspired by a similar ban in Great Britain. India has announced it will institute the same type of ban in several years. Each community that takes action against plastic waste inspires other communities to do the same.

As individuals, we shouldn't rely on our local leaders do all the work on waste. We can make a huge difference if we all change our daily routines. Take a reusable bag to the store when you shop. If you forget to take a reusable bag to the store when you shop, ask for a paper bag. You can also make a difference when you order carry out. When you order carry out, ask that no plastic utensils or straws be included. Support businesses that use biodegradable containers instead of plastic. Tell your friends and family members about the problem, and share ways to fix it with them.

Nature needs to taken care of. Nature should be a source of inspiration. We need to be advocates for nature, just as the Romantic writers were. William Wordsworth said it best: "Come forth into the light of things; let nature be your teacher."

Works Cited

Albeck-Ripka, Livia. "Your Recycling Gets Recycled, Right? Maybe, or Maybe Not," *The New York Times*, 29 May 2018, www.nytimes.com/2018/05/29/climate/ recycling-landfills-plastic-papers.html

CBS News. "Seattle Becomes First U.S. City to Ban Plastic Utensils and Straws," 2 Jul. 2018. www.cbsnews.com/news/seattle-becomes-first-u-s-city-to-ban-plastic-utensils-and-straws

Lakeshore Recycling Services. "Roundup of Successful Waste Reduction Campaigns by Cities." Blog, 4/25/2018. www.lrsrecycles.com/roundup-successful-waste-reduction-campaigns-cities/

"California Has a Recycling Crisis." *Los Angeles Times Editorial Board*, 5/26/2018. www.latimes.com/opinion/editorials/la-ed-recycling-crisis-20180526-story.html

NBC News Archives Xpress. "Recycling Center." Accessed on Nov. 23, 2018. https://www.nbcnewsarchivesxpress.com/contentdetails/1937321

Scientific American. "'Dead' Sea of Plastic Bottles." Accessed 2 Oct. 2018. www.scientificamerican.com/article/dead-sea-of-plastic-bottles/

Somerville, Madeleine. "Yes, You Recycle. But Until You Start Reducing, You're Still Killing the Planet." *The Guardian*, 19 May 2016, www.theguardian.com/lifeandstyle/ 2016/jan/19/eco-friendly-living-sustainability-recycling-reducing-saving-the-planet

Watts, Jonathan. "Eight Months On, Is the World's Most Drastic Plastic Bag Ban Working?" *The Guardian*, 4/25/2018, www.theguardian.com/world/2018/apr/25/nairobi-clean-up-highs-lows-kenyas-plastic-bag-ban.

Skill: Critiquing Research

Introduce the Skill

Watch the Concept Definition video and read the following definition with your students.

While doing research to answer a question you should **critique**, or evaluate, your research process and make changes as needed. For instance, if you cannot find enough information to answer the **major research question** you are using to develop a thesis or claim, you might **modify**, or make adjustments to improve the question. For example, you may need to expand the topic. You can also **assess** and evaluate a source by asking yourself questions about a writer's background or the reliability of a website. If you begin to notice that your sources do not agree, you should look for more reliable sources of information that contain correct and up-to-date information. Similarly, if your perspective changes as you learn more about your topic, you may need to revise your thesis or claim to reflect your new understanding. By critiquing the research process at each step, you can identify needs and make changes that will result in a successful outcome.

Skill: Critiquing Research

••• CHECKLIST FOR CRITIQUING RESEARCH

In order to conduct short or sustained research projects to answer a question or solve a problem, drawing on several sources, do the following:

- narrow or broaden the question or inquiry as necessary when researching your topic
- use advanced search terms effectively when looking for information online, such as using unique terms that are specific to your topic (i.e., "daily life in Jamestown, Virginia" rather than just "Jamestown, Virginia")
- assess the strengths and limitations of each source in terms of the task, purpose, and audience
- synthesize and integrate information from multiple sources to maintain a flow of ideas, and avoid overly relying on one single source
- quote or paraphrase the information you have found without plagiarizing, or copying your source
- provide information about your sources in a bibliography or another standard format for citations

To evaluate and use relevant information while conducting short or sustained research projects, consider the following questions:

- Did I narrow or broaden my research inquiry as needed?
- Have I successfully synthesized and integrated information from multiple sources on my topic to maintain a flow of ideas and avoided overly relying on one single source?
- Did I quote or paraphrase information without plagiarizing?

TURN AND TALK

Turn to your partner and discuss whether you have ever had to change your focus part way through writing a paper. How did making that change improve your essay?

SPEAKING FRAMES

- I had to rewrite a paper on ____.
- I had to change ____ to ____.
- This changed improved ____.

SKILL VOCABULARY

critique / criticar ***verb*** to evaluate COGNATE

major research question / la pregunta principal de investigación ***noun*** a question that a writer uses to guide the research process and develop a thesis or claim

modify / modificar ***verb*** to make minor changes in order to make something better COGNATE

assess / evaluar ***verb*** to estimate the quality, ability, or significance of; to evaluate

YOUR TURN

Choose the best answer to each question.

1. Below is the introduction from a student's draft, which explains why conservation is important. As he researches, the student discovers that restoration ecology may be more effective for saving endangered species. How should he replace his underlined thesis statement?

   Biodiversity is the variety of life in an environment. A healthy ecosystem needs to be biodiverse. When one species go extinct, other species often follow. Scientists had not realized that extinction occurs until late in the eighteenth century, so the concept was still relatively new to Romantics. Even so, they realized the threat extinction posed to nature, and so they began the conservation movement to protect rare plants and animals. <u>Conservation has been successful in rescuing many species, but it is important to maintain efforts to protect the environment.</u>

   - ○ A. Conservation has been ineffective in preventing extinction in many cases.
   - ○ B. Humans are the primary cause of extinction in the modern world.
   - ○ C. Biodiversity is essential to our understanding of how environments work.
   - ○ D. However, it is not enough to conserve; damaged ecosystems need to be restored.

2. Rishal came across the following information and source in his research about recycling. What should he do?

   Recycled products contain the energies of previous products, and their previous uses will determine the characteristic of the new product that will be made from the recycled material.

   Source: www.conspiracy.blog.com

   - ○ A. Modify his research question.
   - ○ B. Consider if the source is appropriate.
   - ○ C. Rewrite his thesis using the new information.
   - ○ D. Revise his research plan.

WRITE

Use the questions in the checklist to critique your research process to determine whether you need to modify your major research question, revise your research plan, or change any other aspect of your informative research essay.

Your Turn

Ask students to complete the Your Turn activity.

QUESTION 1

A. Incorrect. This thesis does not support restoration ecology.

B. Incorrect. The topic is conservation versus restoration, not causes of extinction.

C. Incorrect. Biodiversity is the goal of restoration, but this thesis does not address the topic directly.

D. Correct. This thesis argues that restoration should replace conservation.

QUESTION 2

A. Incorrect. This source provides information about recycling, so it seems to suit his purpose.

B. Correct. This information seems unusual and the source is a blog, so it may not be accurate information.

C. Incorrect. This information may support his thesis, but it seems unreliable.

D. Incorrect. He should check the source and compare it to others before revising his plan.

Write

Ask students to complete the writing assignment.

REWRITE CHECKLIST

Major Research Question

- ☐ Is your research question too narrow?
- ☐ Is your research question too broad?
- ☐ How can you revise your research question to make it specific and engaging?

Sources

- ☐ Are your sources reputable and reliable?
- ☐ Did you modify your research question? Do you need to modify your sources?

Thesis

- ☐ Has my thinking changed?
- ☐ Can you state your thesis or claim in a more precise and detailed way?

Skill: Paraphrasing

Introduce the Skill

Watch the Concept Definition video and read the following definition with your students.

When you **quote**, you repeat or copy from a text or speech exactly as it was written and indicate the original author. When you **paraphrase**, you restate something in your own words while retaining the meaning and the order of the original text.

Paraphrasing is sometimes confused with summarizing. When you **summarize**, you provide a brief statement of the main ideas and most important details in a text. In contrast, when you paraphrase, you do not condense the text. Instead, you restate the entire text in your own words.

When you write you must use sources ethically, and that means giving proper credit to avoid **plagiarism**, or taking another person's words or ideas and presenting them as your own. You must always credit your sources when you quote or paraphrase with citations. A **citation** is a reference to an outside source, including source information that is quoted or paraphrased.

Skill: Paraphrasing

••• CHECKLIST FOR PARAPHRASING

In order to integrate information into your research essay, note the following:

- make sure you understand what the author is saying after reading the text carefully; note:
  - > any words or expressions that are unfamiliar
  - > words and phrases that are important to include in a paraphrase to maintain the meaning of the text
- avoid plagiarism by acknowledging all sources for both paraphrased and quoted material, and avoid overly relying on any one source
- integrate information selectively to maintain a logical flow of ideas

To integrate information into your research essay, consider the following questions:

- Do I understand the meaning of the text? Have I determined the meanings of any words in the text that are unfamiliar to me?
- Does my paraphrase of the text maintain the text's original meaning? Have I missed any key points or details?
- Have I avoided plagiarism by acknowledging all my sources for both paraphrased and quoted material and avoided overly relying on any one source?
- Did I integrate information selectively to maintain a logical flow of ideas?

TURN AND TALK

Turn to your partner and discuss whether you have ever had to paraphrase something for someone else, like a series of events in a story or instructions for making or fixing something. Why is paraphrasing an important skill? Is it important to be accurate and keep things in a logical order when you paraphrase? Why?

SPEAKING FRAMES

- I had to paraphrase (a series of events in a story/ instructions) when ___.
- Paraphrasing is an important skill because ___.
- It is important to be accurate and keep things in a logical order when paraphrasing because ___.

V SKILL VOCABULARY

quote / citar *verb* to use an author's exact words and place them within quotation marks

paraphrase / parafrasear *verb* to restate the author's words in your own words COGNATE

summarize / resumir *verb* to restate briefly the most important points in a text

YOUR TURN

Read the quotation below from one of Rishal's sources for his informative research essay. Then, answer the multiple-choice questions.

"Portland keeps an impressive seventy percent of its waste out of landfills. The city cooperates with more than three dozen independent haulers of trash and recycling, which actually makes this milestone even more impressive." (Lakeshore Recycling Systems)

1. What is incorrect about this paraphrase of the quotation from Lakeshore Recycling Systems?

"Portland works with three dozen independent haulers to keep an impressive seventy percent of its waste out of landfills."

- ○ A. It is incorrect because it summarizes the information, rather than paraphrasing it.
- ○ B. It is incorrect because it quotes much of the text directly, rather than paraphrasing it.
- ○ C. It is incorrect because the original meaning of the text is not maintained.
- ○ D. It is incorrect because key points are missing, and this alters the original meaning.

2. What would be the most accurate and complete paraphrase of the source?

- ○ A. The city of Portland works with various companies to keep seventy percent of its waste away from landfills.
- ○ B. The city of Portland has many recycling programs to support waste disposal, which is helpful to residents.
- ○ C. Thirty-six companies that specialize in waste management and recycling move over 50% of waste into landfills.
- ○ D. 70% of waste is kept out of landfills in Oregon thanks to the city of Portland's excellent recycling program.

WRITE

Use the questions in the checklist to paraphrase and integrate information from a source into a paragraph of your informative research essay.

SKILL VOCABULARY

plagiarism / el plagio *noun* the taking of another person's words or ideas and presenting them as the writer's own

citation / la cita *noun* a quotation from or reference to an outside source

Your Turn

Ask students to complete the Your Turn activity.

QUESTION 1

A. Incorrect. This sentence does not summarize the information.

B. Correct. This sentence does not paraphrase enough because it quotes the source almost directly.

C. Incorrect. This sentence repeats the text directly.

D. Incorrect. This sentence repeats the text directly.

QUESTION 2

A. Correct. This is an accurate and complete paraphrase of the source.

B. Incorrect. This is not an accurate or complete example of a paraphrasing of this source.

C. Incorrect. This is not an accurate or complete example of a paraphrasing of this source.

D. Incorrect. This is not an accurate or complete example of a paraphrasing of this source.

Write

Ask students to complete the writing assignment.

REWRITE CHECKLIST

Key Ideas and Details from Source(s)

- ☐ Do I understand the meaning of the text?
- ☐ Have I determined the meanings of any words from the text that are unfamiliar to me?
- ☐ Does my paraphrase of the text maintain its original meaning? Have I missed any key points or details?

Integrating Information

- ☐ Did I integrate information selectively to maintain a logical flow of ideas?
- ☐ Have I avoided plagiarism by acknowledging all my sources for both paraphrased and quoted material and avoided overly relying on any one source?

Skill: Sources and Citations

Introduce the Skill

Watch the Concept Definition video and read the following definition with your students.

A **source** is a person, text, or other medium from which information is obtained for research. **Primary sources** contain information that comes from first-hand accounts. **Secondary sources** are written later and are based on primary sources. Authors must give credit when using a source to avoid **plagiarism**, the practice of taking someone else's work or ideas and passing them off as one's own.

To credit sources, writers use citations. A **citation** is a reference to or a quotation from an outside source. It is required whenever authors quote another person's writing or refer to someone else's ideas. Types of citations include parenthetical citations, footnotes, and endnotes. In a **parenthetical citation** the writer gives credit to the source by using parentheses at the end of the sentence that contains the researched information. **Footnotes** are inserted at the bottom of a page, and **endnotes** are included at the end of a research paper or nonfiction book. A **bibliography** is a list of all the books and sources used to research a paper, placed at the end of the text.

Skill: Sources and Citations

CHECKLIST FOR SOURCES AND CITATIONS

In order to gather relevant information from multiple authoritative print and digital sources and to cite the sources correctly, do the following:

- gather information from a variety of print and digital sources, using search terms effectively to narrow your search
- find information on authors to see if they are experts on a topic
- avoid relying on any one source, and synthesize information from a variety of books, publications, and online resources
- quote or paraphrase the information you find, and cite it to avoid plagiarism
- integrate information selectively to maintain a logical flow of ideas in your essay, using transitional words and phrases
- include all sources in a bibliography, following a standard format:
    - > Halall, Ahmed. *The Pyramids of Ancient Egypt*. New York: Central Publishing, 2016.
    - > for a citation, footnote, or endnote, include the author, title, and page number

To check that you have gathered information and cited sources correctly, consider the following questions:

- Did I cite the information I found using a standard format to avoid plagiarism?
- Did I include all my sources in my bibliography?

TURN AND TALK

Turn to your partner and discuss why it is important to have a common format for citations. How does including citations help readers and writers?

SPEAKING FRAMES

- Having a common format for citations is important because ____.
- Citations help readers ____.
- Citations help writers ____.

SKILL VOCABULARY

primary source / la fuente primaria *noun* a source written by a person who actually experienced the event he or she recorded

secondary source / la fuente secundaria *noun* a source that summarizes, describes, or interprets primary sources

parenthetical citation / la documentación parentética *noun* credit given to a source in parentheses at the end of the sentence that contains the researched information COGNATE

YOUR TURN

Choose the best answer to each question.

1. Below is a section from a previous draft of Rishal's research paper. What change should Rishal make to improve the clarity of his citations?

> According to Megan Forbes on the National Oceanic and Atmospheric Administration (NOAA) Ocean Podcast episode "Garbage Patches: How Gyres Take Our Trash Out to Sea," there are at least three major patches of "concentrated (and mostly plastic) marine debris" in our oceans (Forbes).

- ○ A. Add the page number after the author in the parentheses.
- ○ B. Remove the citation in parentheses after the quotation.
- ○ C. Remove the quotation marks around the cited material.
- ○ D. No change needs to be made.

2. Below is a section from a previous draft of Rishal's works cited page in the MLA format. Which revision best corrects his style errors?

> Thompson, James. *Landfill Waste Costs Continued to Rise in 2016. Solid Waste Environmental Excellence Protocol*, 12 Jan. 2017. https://nrra.net/sweep/cost-to-landfill-waste-continues-to-rise-through 2016/

- ○ A. Thompson, James. "Landfill Waste Costs Continued to Rise in 2016." Solid Waste Environmental Excellence Protocol, 12 Jan 2017. https://nrra.net/sweep/cost-to-landfill-waste-continues-to-rise-through-2016/
- ○ B. *Landfill Waste Costs Continued to Rise in 2016*. by James Thompson. *Solid Waste Environmental ExcellenceProtocol*, 12 Jan 2017. https://nrra.net/sweep/cost-to-landfill-waste-continues-to-rise-through-2016/
- ○ C. "Landfill Waste Costs Continued to Rise in 2016." by James Thompson. *Solid Waste Environmental Excellence Protocol*, 12 Jan. 2017. https://nrra.net/sweep/cost-to-landfill-waste-continues-to-rise-through-2016/
- ○ D. Thompson, James. "Landfill Waste Costs Continued to Rise in 2016." *Solid Waste Environmental Excellence Protocol*, 12 Jan. 2017, https://nrra.net/sweep/cost-to-landfill-waste-continues-to-rise-through-2016/. Accessed 31 Dec. 2018.

WRITE

Use the questions in the checklist to create or revise your in-text citations and works cited list.

SKILL VOCABULARY

footnote / la nota al pie *noun* a note inserted at the bottom of a page, identifying a source

endnote / la nota final *noun* a note at the end of a research paper or non-fiction book, identifying a source

bibliography or works cited / la bibliografía o los trabajos citados *noun* an alphabetized list of sources that appears at the end of a research paper or nonfiction book

Your Turn

Ask students to complete the Your Turn activity.

QUESTION 1

A. Incorrect. Since this is an online podcast, a page number is not needed.

B. Correct. Rishal has already included the author in the text introducing the quotation, so he does not need to repeat it in parentheses.

C. Incorrect. Since this is a direct quote and not a paraphrase, quotation marks are required.

D. Incorrect. Rishal needs to remove one of the double references to the author, Forbes.

QUESTION 2

A. Incorrect. This citation incorrectly puts the publication in regular type rather than italics.

B. Incorrect. This citation incorrectly puts the article title in italics and incorrectly places the author's name.

C. Incorrect. This citation correctly puts the article title in quotation marks but incorrectly places the author's name.

D. Correct. This citation correctly puts the article title in quotation marks, changes the period after the date to a comma, and adds the date that the article was accessed on.

Write

Ask students to complete the writing assignment.

ELL REWRITE CHECKLIST

A Internal, or In-Text, Citations

- ☐ Is there quoted or paraphrased information in your essay?
- ☐ Did you include a parenthetical citation?
- ☐ Is this citation also in your works cited list?

Works Cited

- ☐ Does your works cited list follow the most up-to-date MLA guidelines?
- ☐ Do your citations vary according to the type of source (e.g., book, periodical, website)?

Skill: Print and Graphic Features

Introduce the Skill

Watch the Concept Definition video and read the following definition with your students.

Texts, both in print and online, often use more than words to communicate information. When writing informative texts, using print and graphic features can help aid your readers' comprehension and provide additional information.

Print features are text elements—such as titles, headings, and boldface terms—that help organize information or call out specific sections of a text. **Graphic features** are visual elements—such as photographs, drawings, maps, charts, graphs, and diagrams—that convey information more efficiently and effectively than prose alone can accomplish. You may even consider including **multimedia**—content that combines multiple forms of media, like photographs and audio—to add interest and variety.

Writers need to think critically about when and how to use print and graphic features. Unnecessary or unrelated additions may clutter your writing and confuse your readers. However, using these features strategically can help you better communicate and engage with your readers.

Extended Writing Project

Skill: Print and Graphic Features

••• CHECKLIST FOR PRINT AND GRAPHIC FEATURES

First, reread your draft and ask yourself the following questions:

- To what extent would including formatting, graphics, or multimedia be effective in achieving my purpose?
- Which formatting, graphics, or multimedia seem most important in conveying information to the reader?
- How is the addition of the formatting, graphics, or multimedia useful in aiding comprehension?

To include formatting, graphics, and multimedia, use the following questions as a guide:

- How can I use formatting to better organize information? Consider adding:
  - > titles
  - > headings
  - > subheadings
  - > bullets
  - > boldface and italicized terms
- How can I use graphics to better convey information? Consider adding:
  - > charts
  - > graphs
  - > tables
  - > timelines
  - > diagrams
  - > figures and statistics
- How can I use multimedia to add interest and variety? Consider adding a combination of:
  - > photographs
  - > art
  - > audio
  - > video

128  Reading & Writing Companion

TURN AND TALK

Turn to your partner and discuss a print feature and a graphic feature you have seen in informational text. How can these features be helpful to readers?

ELL SPEAKING FRAMES

- An example of a print feature is ____.
- An example of a graphic feature is ____.
- These features can be helpful because ____.

V SKILL VOCABULARY

print features / la característica de la publicación ***noun*** text elements such as titles, headings, or boldface terms

graphic features / la característica gráfica ***noun*** visual elements such as photographs, drawings, maps, charts, graphs, or diagrams

multimedia / multimedia ***adjective*** using several communications media at the same time COGNATE

YOUR TURN

Choose the best answer to each question.

1. Reread the paragraph from Rishal's draft. Which of the following headings best represents the content of the passage and would help his audience focus on the main idea?

> We must produce less trash. When looking where to start trash reduction programs, we need look no further than plastic. Fish mistake the plastic for food and die after eating it. Plastic trash takes practically forever to biodegrade. When people are too lazy to be responsible and throw plastic waste into a recycle bin or even a garbage can, defenseless creatures are forced to suffer! Huge sections of the Pacific Ocean are covered with plastic trash that has drifted out to sea and been collected together by currents. Gross! This, in combination with climate change, has created huge hypoxic areas where there is little life near the ocean's surface. The plastic also interferes with the photosynthesis of phytoplankton, which form the base of the oceanic trophic pyramid.

- ○ A. Stop the Plastics Lobby Today
- ○ B. The Most Harmful Everyday Material
- ○ C. Oceans are not Landfills
- ○ D. Climate Change and Recycling

2. Rishal also considers adding an image, graph, or table to help his audience understand how extensive plastic waste is. Which of the following graphic elements would be most helpful to readers?

- ○ A. An image of a water bottle floating in the ocean, with wildlife nearby
- ○ B. A table depicting the increase in recycling facilities worldwide
- ○ C. A graphic displaying the effect of climate change on the world's oceans
- ○ D. An image showing large quantities of plastic waste in the ocean

WRITE

Use the questions in the checklist to add at least three headings, two graphics, and one piece of multimedia to your research essay.

Your Turn

Ask students to complete the Your Turn activity.

QUESTION 1

A. Incorrect. There is no information in the passage relevant to the plastics lobby.

B. Correct. The paragraph focuses on the harmful effects of everyday plastic on the environment.

C. Incorrect. This heading does not represent the main idea of the paragraph.

D. Incorrect. This heading does not represent the content of the paragraph.

QUESTION 2

A. Incorrect. This image would not be the most helpful to his audience in understanding how harmful plastic waste can be.

B. Incorrect. This table would not be the most helpful to his audience in understanding how harmful plastic waste can be.

C. Incorrect. A graphic displaying the effect of climate change would be irrelevant.

D. Correct. This image would be the most helpful to readers.

Write

Ask students to complete the writing assignment.

ELL REWRITE CHECKLIST

A Considering adding formatting, such as

- ☐ Headings
- ☐ Subheadings
- ☐ Bullets to create a list structure
- ☐ Boldface and italicized terms to emphasize technical terms or important ideas

Considering adding graphics, such as

- ☐ charts
- ☐ graphs
- ☐ timelines
- ☐ diagrams

Consider adding multimedia, such as

- ☐ video

Informative Writing Process: Revise

Review Revision Guide

Break the class into five groups, and assign each group a category of the revision guide. Ask:

- What is the purpose of this section of the guide?
- How did it improve Rishal's writing?
- How will it help to improve your writing?

Allow groups to share their ideas with the class.

SPEAKING FRAMES

- I think (clarity / development / organization / word choice / sentence fluency) improved Rishal's writing by ____.
- I think (clarity / development / organization / word choice / sentence fluency) will improve my writing because ____.

Informative Writing Process: Revise

PLAN | DRAFT | REVISE | EDIT AND PUBLISH

You have written a draft of your informative research essay. You have also received input from your peers about how to improve it. Now you are going to revise your draft.

 REVISION GUIDE

Examine your draft to find areas for revision. Keep in mind your purpose and audience as you revise for clarity, development, organization, and style. Use the guide below to help you review.

Review	Revise	Example
	Clarity	
Reread the concluding paragraph of your informative research essay.	Make sure you rephrase your thesis or claim in a new way to remind readers of the purpose of your research and topic.	Nature needs to ~~taken care of~~ be nurtured. Nature provides us with food, water, and the air we breathe. Yet, in return, some of our choices and behaviors damage it. Nature should be a source of inspiration. We need to be advocates for nature, just as the Romantic writers were. William Wordsworth said it best: "Come forth into the light of things; let nature be your teacher."

Review	Revise	Example
	Development	
Highlight a key detail used to support your claim.	Strengthen your essay by supporting key details with evidence from reputable sources. Make sure to include any additional sources in your works cited list.	Plastic trash takes ~~practically forever~~ the longest to biodegrade, or break down. For example, a plastic shopping bag takes at least ten years to break down. A plastic soft drink bottle takes about 450 years to biodegrade (New Hampshire Department of Environmental Services). When people ~~are too lazy to be responsible and~~ don't throw plastic waste into a recycle bin or even a garbage can, ~~defenseless creatures are forced to suffer!~~ nature can be seriously harmed.
	Organization	
Review your body paragraphs. Are they organized? Does information flow from one paragraph to the next? Identify and annotate any sentences within and across paragraphs that don't flow in a clear and logical way.	Rewrite the sentences so they appear in a clear and logical order.	For example, the Northeast has to pay nayboring states to accept its trash~~. It's run out of room for it~~ because the region no longer has adequate space to manage its own landfills (Lakeshore Recycling Services). ~~Many people do not even bother recycling plastics and other trash and just throw them in the garbage. The garbage is taken to landfills. It's now at the point that some parts of the United States are running out of space for landfills.~~

Revise

Students should start this activity with a copy of their drafts either printed on paper or open in a word-processing program, such as Google Docs. Allow students time to revise their drafts using the instructions in the revision guide. Once students have finished revising their essay, have them submit their work.

CHECK FOR SUCCESS

Circulate around the room to spend time with individual students. Ask:

- What category are you working on?
- Why are you revising this specific section?
- How are you revising it?
- How does this change support your purpose?
- Does this change make your writing appropriate for your audience?

If students struggle while revising their drafts, choose an exemplary revision to share with the class while the student talks through the process. You could also invite a student to share a dilemma in the revision process and allow the class to offer feedback or suggestions.

SENTENCE FLUENCY

Revise your draft, focusing on sentence fluency. Identify sentences in your essay that sound choppy, are repetitive, or do not logically flow. Rewrite the sentences to improve the fluency.

SENTENCE FLUENCY

Tell students to revise their drafts using the revision guide, focusing on sentence fluency. In addition, have students make revisions that focus on organization, as practiced in the previous unit.

Write

Ask students to complete their writing assignment.

REVISION CHECKLIST

- ☐ Read aloud your essay.
- ☐ Identify a paragraph or series of sentences that sound choppy or repetitive.
- ☐ Use strategies such as combining or shortening sentences, reordering sentences, and adding transition words or phrases to the sentences to increase fluency.

Review	Revise	Example
Style: Word Choice		
Identify any weak adjectives or verbs.	Replace weak adjectives and verbs with strong, descriptive adjectives and verbs.	~~Tell your friends and family members about the problem, and share ways to fix it with them.~~ By sharing your research and the strategies you've implemented, you can support your friends and family members in understanding the problem and help them value nature in a more sustainable, beneficial manner.
Style: Sentence Fluency		
Read aloud your writing and listen to the way the text sounds. Does it sound choppy? Or does it flow smoothly with rhythm, movement, and emphasis on important details and events?	Rewrite a key passage, making your sentences longer or shorter to achieve a better flow of writing. Remove repetitive phrases.	We can make a huge difference if we all change our daily routines. ~~Take a reusable bag to the store when you shop. If you forget to take a reusable bag to the store when you shop, ask for a paper bag. You can also make a difference when you order carry out. When you order carry out, ask that no plastic utensils or straws be included.~~ Individuals can take easy and immediate action and make better decisions when it comes to their impact on nature, especially when it comes to recycling. For example, when you order carry-out, ask that no plastic utensils or straws be included.

WRITE

Use the revision guide, as well as your peer reviews, to help you evaluate your informative research essay to determine places that should be revised both within and between sentences.

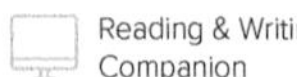

Skill:
Using a Style Guide

••• CHECKLIST FOR USING A STYLE GUIDE

In order to make sure that your writing conforms to the guidelines in a style manual, do the following:

- Determine which style guide you should use before you write your draft.
  - > Follow the guidelines chosen by a teacher, for example.
  - > Familiarize yourself with that guide, and check your writing against the guide when you edit.
- Use the style guide for the overall formatting of your paper, citation style, bibliography format, and other style considerations for reporting research.
- As you draft, use an additional style guide, such as *Artful Sentences: Syntax as Style* by Virginia Tufte, to help you vary your syntax, or the grammatical structure of sentences.
  - > Use a variety of simple, compound, complex, and compound-complex sentences to convey information.
  - > Be sure to punctuate your sentences correctly.
  - > Follow standard English language conventions to help you maintain a formal style for formal papers.

To edit your work so that it conforms to the guidelines in a style manual, consider the following questions:

- Have I followed the conventions for spelling, punctuation, capitalization, sentence structure, and formatting, according to the style guide?
- Have I varied my syntax to make my information clear for readers?
- Do I have an entry in my works cited or bibliography for each reference I used?
- Have I followed the correct style, including the guidelines for capitalization and punctuation, in each entry in my works cited or bibliography?

TURN AND TALK

Turn to your partner and discuss the references you consult when writing a research paper. How can using a style guide improve your informative research essay?

ELL SPEAKING FRAMES

- I usually consult ____ when I write a research paper.
- Using a style guide can help improve my informative research essay by ____.

Skill: Using a Style Guide

Introduce the Skill

Watch the Concept Definition video and read the following definition with your students.

When you write, one of your goals is to match your style to the writing discipline. A **style guide** is a manual for writing and formatting text following conventions, specifically how to apply syntax and language conventions.

Syntax refers to the orderly arrangement of words and phrases to create well-formed sentences in a language. The principles of syntax fall into two interconnected classes: parts of speech and structural elements. **Parts of speech** are types of words that have particular roles in a sentence. The most common parts of speech are nouns, pronouns, verbs, modifiers (such as adjectives and adverbs), prepositions, and conjunctions. **Structural elements** include phrases and clauses that are created by groups of words.

Language **conventions** are rules for spelling, punctuation, capitalization, grammar, sentence structure, and formatting that make writing clear and understandable.

Different disciplines, or fields of study, use different styles. Using a style guide creates consistency and helps ensure that a piece of writing meets the expectations of a particular discipline. Here are several common style guides:

- Modern Language Association (MLA): used in literature and the humanities.
- Chicago Manual of Style: used in the humanities and social sciences.
- APA (American Psychological Association): used in the social sciences.
- *A Manual for Writers* by Kate Turabian: adapts the Chicago style for students.

Your Turn

Ask students to complete the Your Turn activity.

In a Style Guide	Not in a Style Guide
C	A
E	B
G	D
I	F
J	H

Write

Ask students to complete the writing assignment.

REWRITE CHECKLIST

In-Text Citations

- ☐ How do I cite my sources in a text?
- ☐ What if the source I'm using doesn't have a specific author?
- ☐ What if I am citing a television documentary as one of my sources?

Formatting a Bibliography

- ☐ Which sources do I include?
- ☐ What is the format for a source citation in a bibliography?
- ☐ How should I order my sources?

Quotation Marks

- ☐ Should I always use an open quote and a close quote when quoting a text?
- ☐ Should I use quotation marks if I am summarizing or paraphrasing a source?
- ☐ Should I use quotation marks for a block quote?

Varied Syntax and Sentence Structure

- ☐ Have I varied my syntax to make my information clear for readers?
- ☐ Have I used the style guide to confirm the rules for sentence structure and conventions?

YOUR TURN

Read the types of information below. Then, complete the chart by sorting them into two categories: those that are found in a style guide and those that are not. Write the corresponding letter for each type of information in the appropriate column.

Types of Information			
A	a list of possible research topics	**F**	the definition of a word
B	how to select a thesis	**G**	when to use italics
C	how to cite internet sources	**H**	synonyms for a word
D	how to write an outline	**I**	when to use a hyphen
E	how to format a bibliography	**J**	proper punctuation for quotations

In a Style Guide	Not in a Style Guide

WRITE

Use the checklist to help you choose a convention that you have found challenging to follow. Use a credible style guide to check and correct any errors related to that convention in your research essay.

SKILL VOCABULARY

style guide / la guía de estilo ***noun*** a set of standards for the writing and formatting of documents COGNATE

syntax/ la sintaxis ***noun*** word order, or the way in which the elements of language (words, phrases, clauses, etc.) are arranged to create well-formed sentences COGNATE

conventions / la norma ***noun*** spelling, punctuation, capitalization, and grammar that help make writing and speaking clear and understandable

Grammar: Contested Usage

For most formal writing, it is probably advisable to follow the traditional rules of grammar. In most cases, following the rules will improve both the clarity and effectiveness of your communication. However, there are a number of grammar "rules" that can be broken if you do it deliberately to improve the effectiveness of your writing.

Contested Rules	Text
• Never begin a sentence with *And* or *But*. • A paragraph must always consist of more than one sentence. • Never end a sentence with a preposition. • Dialogue should be set off by quotation marks.	And now Miss Emily had gone to join the representatives of those august names where they lay in the cedar-bemused cemetery among the ranked and anonymous graves of Union and Confederate soldiers who fell at the battle of Jefferson. A Rose for Emily, by William Faulkner

People, and even references, often disagree about word usage. For one thing, new words enter the language all the time. An example of a current debate regarding usage involves the word *literally*. This word is sometimes used to emphasize a statement or description that is not literally true or possible. Some sources argue against this usage, explaining that it is illogical to use the word *literally* to mean "figuratively." And yet, even Mark Twain used the word *literally* to describe things that could not be literally true. For instance:

Text	Contested Usage
And when the middle of the afternoon came, from being a poor poverty-stricken boy in the morning, Tom was literally rolling in wealth. The Adventures of Tom Sawyer, by Mark Twain	The character Tom Sawyer was not literally tumbling around in piles of money.

If you are unsure whether it is acceptable to break a rule or if you want to resolve questions you may have about usage, you can always check a reference work on the subject. Several worth recommending are Merriam-Webster's *Dictionary of English Usage*, Bryan A. Garner's *Garner's Modern American Usage*, and Theodore Bernstein's *Miss Thistlebottom's Hobgoblins*. The *Merriam-Webster Dictionary* online also includes a Usage Guide for words that have been the subject of contested usage. For instance, if you look up the word *affect*, you will find a Usage Guide on the different uses of the word *affect* versus *effect*.

Grammar: Contested Usage

Introduce the Skill

Review the image and definition for contested usage as a class.

- word usage - the rules governing how to use words
- grammar usage - the rules governing how to use grammar
- contested usage - usage rules that are debated

Discuss the Model

1. What are some contested grammar usage rules? Never begin a sentence with *And* or *But*; a paragraph must always contain more than one sentence.
2. How can you find answers to questions about usage? You can check a reference work on the relevant subject, like the *Merriam-Webster Dictionary* online Usage Guide.

Your Turn

Ask students to complete the Your Turn activities.

QUESTION 1

A. Incorrect.

B. Correct. The second sentence ends with the preposition *of.*

QUESTION 2

A. Correct. *Ginormous* was originally a slang term that eventually entered the dictionary.

B. Incorrect.

QUESTION 3

A. Incorrect.

B. Correct. The last part of the sentence would be easier to read if the writer applied the traditional rules of grammar.

QUESTION 4

A. Incorrect.

B. Correct. Traditional grammar rules state that dialogue should be set off by quotation marks.

YOUR TURN

1. What rule of usage has been deliberately broken in the sentence below?

> Dost thou love life? Then do not squander time, for that is the stuff life is made of.
> —Benjamin Franklin

○ A. Never begin a sentence with *Then*.
○ B. Never end a sentence with a preposition.

2. What evidence or source justifies the use of the word *ginormous* in the sentence below?

> Can you really eat that ginormous sandwich?

○ A. The dictionary includes the word *ginormous* and recommends it for informal and humorous contexts.
○ B. Most grammar resources tell users to avoid using slang in formal writing.

3. Does the following sentence break the rules of grammar in an effective way?

> Knowledge of a particular time in history will help you better understand what an essay written during that time period is about.

○ A. Yes, the sentence ends with a preposition, which makes the last part of the sentence "what an essay written during that time period is about" clear and easy to read.
○ B. No, it would be clearer and more effective to follow the rules of grammar and change the last part of the sentence to "the content of an essay written during that time period."

4. Read the dialogue below. What rule of grammar does this excerpt violate?

> What is it, Papa?
>
> It's a treat. For you.
>
> What is it?
>
> Here. Sit down.
>
> from *The Road*, by Cormac McCarthy

○ A. Every line of dialogue needs to identify the speaker.
○ B. Dialogue needs to be set off by quotation marks.

Extended Writing Project

Grammar: Hyphens

Hyphens are mostly used to combine words, but they can also be used to divide words.

Rule	Text
You may use a hyphen in a compound adjective that precedes a noun.	That **yearned-for** golden age became even more golden in the imaginations of later medieval writers, who enhanced Geoffrey's legend. Unsolved Mysteries of History
Usually, hyphens are not needed to join a prefix to a word, but there are a few exceptions. • Use a hyphen after any prefix joined to a proper noun or a proper adjective. • Use a hyphen after the prefixes *all-*, *ex-* (meaning "former"), and *self-*. • Generally, hyphens are used to avoid confusion, such as in words beginning with *re-* that could be mistaken for another word. • Use a hyphen after the prefix *anti-* when it is joined to a word beginning with *i-*.	No complete parallel for the Cadbury fortification has been found anywhere else in **post-Roman** Britain. Conversation with Geoffrey Ashe
Hyphens can be used to create compound nouns by joining words and giving them a unified meaning.	She had once been a lowly **maid-of-all-work** just like Amelia. After the Ball
Hyphenate any compound word that is a spelled-out cardinal number (such as *twenty-one*) or ordinal number (such as *twenty-first*) up to *ninety-nine* or *ninety-ninth*. Hyphenate any spelled-out fraction.	She was **forty-six** years old, of average height and bearing, with an unremarkable face. American Jezebel

Grammar: Hyphens

Introduce the Skill

Review the image and definition for hyphens as a class.

- hyphen (word division) - punctuation that shows a division of a word at the end of a line
- hyphen (compounds) - punctuation that indicates a compound adjective or noun

Discuss the Model

1. What are some of the different uses for hyphens? Hyphens can be used in divided words, compound adjectives, prefixes, compound nouns, and numbers.
2. What determines whether a compound adjective has a hyphen? If the compound adjective comes before the noun it modifies, then it has a hyphen.

Your Turn

Ask students to complete the Your Turn activities.

QUESTION 1

A. Incorrect.

B. Incorrect.

C. Incorrect.

D. Correct. Cardinal numbers should be hyphenated, and additional information should be set off by a dash.

QUESTION 2

A. Incorrect.

B. Incorrect.

C. Correct. A hyphen should be used to add *anti-* to a word beginning with *i*.

D. Incorrect.

QUESTION 3

A. Incorrect.

B. Incorrect.

C. Incorrect.

D. Correct. No hyphens are needed in this sentence.

YOUR TURN

1. How should this sentence be changed?

   The world's population is growing at an alarming rate—fast enough to double in only forty-three years!

   - A. The world's population is—growing at an alarming rate—fast enough to double in only forty-three years!
   - B. The world's population is growing at an alarming rate—fast enough to double in only forty three years!
   - C. The world's population is growing at an alarming rate-fast enough to double in only forty-three years!
   - D. No change needs to be made to this sentence.

2. How should this sentence be changed?

   The op-ed article—the one printed in the local paper—suggested that anti intellectual attitudes were threatening democracy.

   - A. The op—ed article—the one printed in the local paper—suggested that anti intellectual attitudes were threatening democracy.
   - B. The op-ed article-the one printed in the local paper-suggested that anti intellectual attitudes were threatening democracy.
   - C. The op-ed article—the one printed in the local paper—suggested that anti-intellectual attitudes were threatening democracy.
   - D. No change needs to be made to this sentence.

3. How should this sentence be changed?

   John F. Kennedy was president of the United States from 1961 to 1963.

   - A. John F. Kennedy was president of the United States from 1961-to-1963.
   - B. John F. Kennedy was president of the United-States from 1961 to 1963.
   - C. John-F.-Kennedy was president of the United States from 1961 to 1963.
   - D. No change needs to be made to this sentence.

Extended Writing Project

Informative Writing Process: Edit and Publish

PLAN | DRAFT | REVISE | EDIT AND PUBLISH

You have revised your informative research essay based on your peer feedback and your own examination.

Now, it is time to edit your informative research essay. When you revised, you focused on the content of your essay. You probably critiqued your research and made sure you paraphrased sources correctly and avoided plagiarism. When you edit, you focus on the mechanics of your essay, paying close attention to things like grammar and punctuation.

Use the checklist below to guide you as you edit:

- ☐ Have I followed all the rules for hyphens?
- ☐ Can I defend any contested usage I have chosen? (Consult a style guide, such as *Artful Sentences: Syntax as Style* by Virginia Tufte, as appropriate.)
- ☐ Do I have any sentence fragments or run-on sentences?
- ☐ Have I spelled everything correctly?

Notice some edits Rishal has made:

- Hyphenated a compound adjective preceding a noun
- Corrected spelling errors
- Corrected a citation to match the MLA style
- Started a sentence with a conjunctive adverb, instead of the conjunction *and*

Informative Writing Process: Edit and Publish

Practice with Student Model (Optional)

Provide groups with a different section of Rishal's draft. Each group should practice editing Rishal's Model using the checklist in the lesson. Has he:

- ☐ followed all the rules for hyphens?
- ☐ used contested usage only when needed to make the writing clearer and more effective?
- ☐ corrected any sentence fragments or run-on sentences?
- ☐ spelled everything correctly?

After the groups have finished, call on volunteers from each group to make edits until all the mistakes have been found and edited, pausing to discuss points of disagreement.

SPEAKING FRAMES

- Rishal (did/did not) follow the rules for hyphens when he wrote ____.
- Rishal chose a contested usage when he wrote ____.
- ____ is an example of a (run-on sentence/sentence fragment) that Rishal (has/has not) corrected.
- ____ is spelled incorrectly. The correct spelling is ____.

WRITE

After students finish editing, suggest, if there's time, that they set their essays aside for a few minutes and that they then proofread them one more time. Once they have completed their writing, they should submit their work.

CHECK FOR SUCCESS

If students struggle to edit successfully, help them determine where edits are needed and what changes need to be made.

Direct students to the grammar lessons in this unit if they are uncertain about the rules for specific concepts.

READ ALOUD

Encourage students to read their essays aloud to themselves or to a partner in order to catch any remaining mistakes.

READ ALOUD

Encourage students to read their essays aloud to themselves or to an on-grade-level peer in order to catch any remaining mistakes.

PLAY CRITIC

Have students review their writing for any potential weaknesses or places in which they might have gone in different directions. Invite them to operate as their own critics—how might their conclusion resolve their essay differently? How might someone with an opposing point of view challenge a point made in their essay? What other piece of evidence might have been included in their research essay? Have students critically analyze an aspect of their own work from an outsider's perspective.

Another problem with plastic is that it does not recycle well. Most plastics can be recycled into ~~awful~~ lower-quality material that is only useful for cheap products like ~~sinthetick~~ synthetic fabric and bumper stickers (~~*The Guardian*~~ Somerville). ~~And~~ In addition, factories that recycle plastics require a great deal of energy, often generating greenhouse gases and other pollution. Although we should continue to recycle as much paper as we have factory space for, recycling plastic is much less ~~effishient~~ efficient.

WRITE

Use the questions in the checklist, as well as your peer reviews, to help you evaluate your informative research essay to determine areas that need editing. Then, edit your informative research essay to correct those errors.

Once you have made all your corrections, you are ready to publish your work. You can distribute your writing to family and friends, hang it on a bulletin board, or post it on your blog. If you publish online, share the link with your family, friends, and classmates.

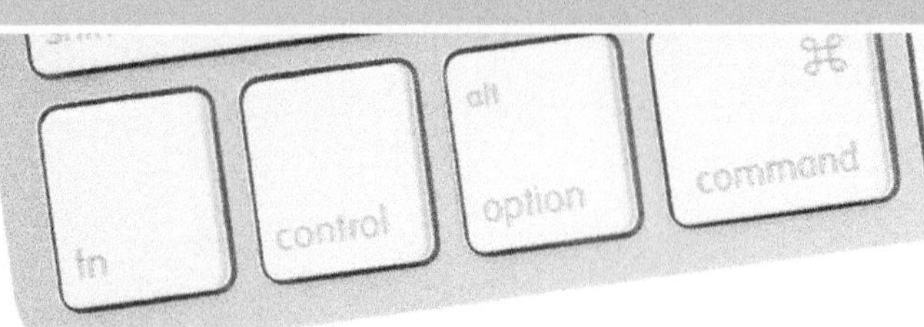

English Language Learner Resources

studysync

USERS ASSIGNMENTS

GRADE 12 › UNIT

Sculpting Reality

Core ELA
Grade 12
30 Days

Unit Overview

Integrated Reading and Writing

Extended Writing Project

ELL Resources

Novel Study

End-of-Unit Assessment

Instructional Path

Add to

A Golden Coin

A Modern Man from the 1800s: The Influential Life of Charles Dickens

Skill: Classroom Vocabulary

After learning classroom vocabulary words, students will be able to recognize and use them in a variety of contexts. Words include: *although, artistic, content, embarrassed, finally, guest, normal, rather, surprised,* and *unless.*

Teacher Resources: Lesson Plan

Assign Preview

Skill: Using Prereading Supports

After reading and discussing a model, students will be able to create a graphic organizer for taking notes while listening to or reading a text.

Teacher Resources: Lesson Plan

Assign Preview

Lessons in the English Language Learner Resources section offer explicit ELL instruction. These lessons share a thematic and genre focus with all other lessons in the Core ELA unit.

The twenty ELL Resources in this section are developed around two texts and an Extended Oral Project. Each text is written at four distinct levels, which serve as structural and thematic models of authentic texts in the Integrated Reading and Writing section of the unit.

ELL lessons modify the routines used with texts in the Integrated Reading and Writing section. Explicit vocabulary instruction is emphasized, and reading and writing Skills lessons focus strongly on language acquisition and reading comprehension.

The Extended Oral Project can be used in place of or as an extension to the Extended Writing Project. In this unit, students will plan and present an informational presentation. Throughout these lessons, students will interact with texts and their peers as readers, writers, speakers, and listeners to maximize comprehension and provide multiple access points for every learner.

Focus on English Language Proficiency Levels

ADVANCED HIGH
ADVANCED
INTERMEDIATE
BEGINNING

ELL Resources provide targeted support for four levels of proficiency: Beginning, Intermediate, Advanced, and Advanced High. Instruction and scaffolds, as well as the texts themselves, are differentiated based on these levels.

Additional differentiated scaffolds include visual glossaries, speaking and writing frames, and suggested grouping for peer and teacher support. Lessons also include suggested extension activities to challenge Advanced and Advanced High students as they progress through the year.

ELL Resources

ELL TEXTS

A Golden Coin

- Skill: Sight Vocabulary and High-Frequency Words
- Skill: Generating Questions
- First Read
- Skill: Language Structures
- Skill: Analyzing and Evaluating Text
- Skill: Spelling Patterns and Rules
- Close Read

A Modern Man from the 1800s: The Influential Life of Charles Dickens

- Skill: Classroom Vocabulary
- Skill: Using Prereading Supports
- First Read
- Skill: Analyzing Expressions
- Skill: Visual and Contextual Support
- Skill: Main and Helping Verbs
- Close Read

EXTENDED ORAL PROJECT

- Introduction
- Skill: Acquiring Vocabulary
- Plan
- Skill: Connecting Words
- Practice
- Present

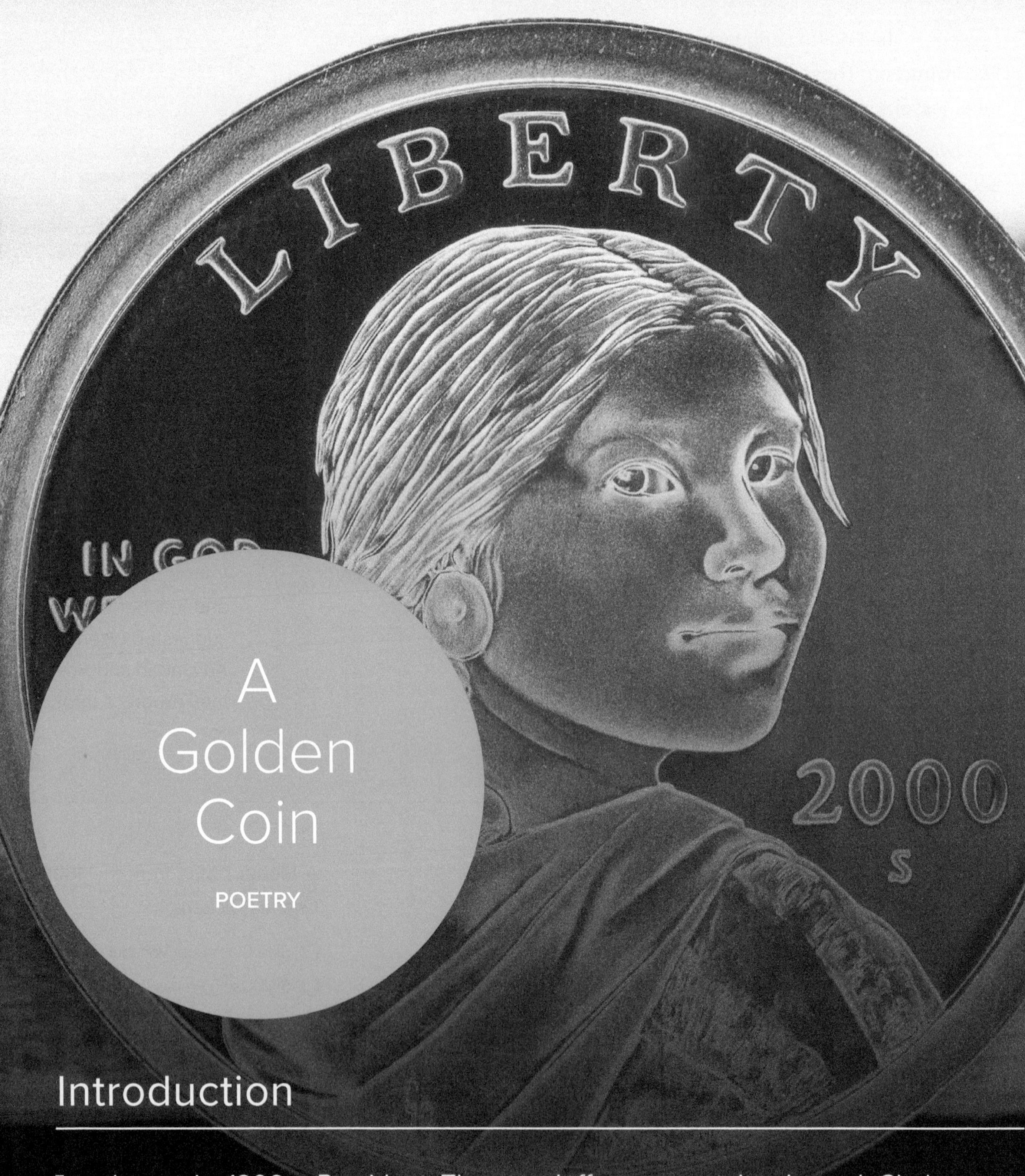

A Golden Coin

POETRY

Introduction

In the early 1800s, President Thomas Jefferson sent Lewis and Clark on an expedition to explore the unknown western part of the country. Fortunately they hired a Native American woman to guide them. How did she help? How is she remembered today?

The speaker looks through his grandfather's antique coin box. One of these coins shows a Native American woman with an infant tied to her back: Sacagawea of the Shoshone tribe. The speaker believes that Sacagawea deserves a recognition greater than an image on a coin. She was an ambassador, a peacemaker, and a counselor. She led Lewis and Clark out West on their great expedition of America. She was a guide and translator, speaking the different languages of the tribes they met. She endured danger and discomfort, all while carrying a baby. On the back of the coin is a soaring bird, perhaps a symbol for Sacagawea, who some people called "bird woman."

Proficiency-leveled summaries and summaries in multiple languages are available digitally.

Audio and audio text highlighting are available with this text.

CONNECT TO ESSENTIAL QUESTION

What is the power of the story?

In this poem, the speaker finds a coin that bears the image of Sacagawea, the young Native American woman who helped Lewis and Clark explore the American West in the early 1800s. How does putting a person's image on a coin help preserve his or her legacy and honor his or her life story?

Core ELA Connections

Texts	Theme	Genre
Ozymandias	The narrator gives a fervent plea to remember Sacagawea of the Shoshone tribe. This poem explores the relationship between sacrifice and honor.	"A Golden Coin" is a poem that asks the reader to examine how society pays tribute to our heroes.

Differentiated Text Levels

ELL LEVEL	BEGINNING	INTERMEDIATE	ADVANCED	ADVANCED HIGH
WORD COUNT	160	165	182	185
LEXILE	N/A	N/A	N/A	N/A

Instructional Path

The print teacher's edition includes essential point-of-use instruction and planning tools. Complete lesson plans and program documents appear in your digital teacher account.

Skill: Sight Vocabulary and High-Frequency Words

DIGITAL ONLY

Objectives: Students will be able to learn and recognize sight vocabulary and high-frequency words in English.

Objectives: Students will be able to recognize sight vocabulary and high-frequency words when listening and reading, and produce sight vocabulary and high-frequency words when speaking and writing.

Skill: Generating Questions

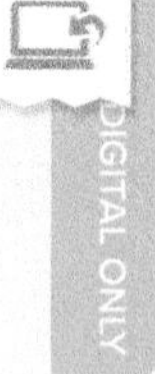

Objectives: Students will be able to learn and practice the skill of generating questions when reading a new text.

Objectives: Students will be able to generate questions before, during, and after reading.

First Read: A Golden Coin

Objectives: Students will be able to perform an initial reading of a text using the strategy of generating questions.

Objectives: Students will be able to demonstrate comprehension of a text by generating questions and by responding to questions orally and in writing using textual evidence.

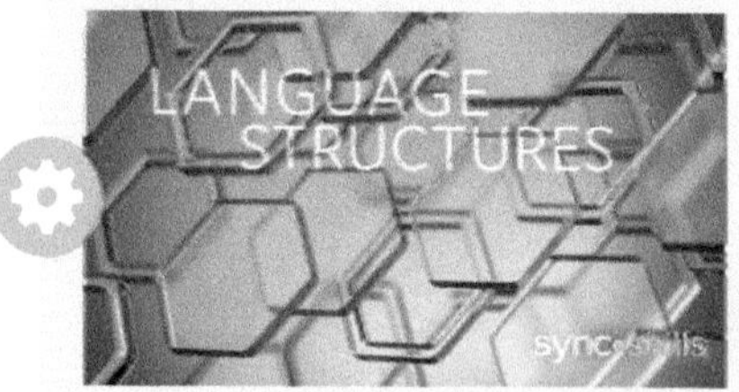

Skill: Language Structures

Objectives: Students will be able to recognize the adjective + noun language structure.

Objectives: Students will be able to use the adjective + noun language structure when speaking.

Skill: Analyzing and Evaluating Text

Objectives: Students will be able to analyze and evaluate a text to understand the author's purpose and message.

Objectives: Students will be able to analyze and evaluate a text to understand the author's purpose and message when speaking.

Skill: Spelling Patterns and Rules

Objectives: Students will be able to recognize and apply spelling patterns and rules.

Objectives: Students will be able to recognize spelling patterns and rules when reading and apply spelling patterns and rules when writing.

Close Read: A Golden Coin

Objectives: Students will be able to perform a close reading of a text in order to analyze and evaluate text.

Objectives: Students will be able to analyze and evaluate text to participate in a collaborative conversation and write a short constructed response.

Progress Monitoring

Opportunities to Learn	Opportunities to Demonstrate Learning	Opportunities to Reteach
Sight Vocabulary and High-Frequency Words		
Skill: Sight Vocabulary and High-Frequency Words	Skill: Sight Vocabulary and High-Frequency Words • Your Turn First Read • Sight Vocabulary and High-Frequency Words	Spotlight Skill: Sight Vocabulary and High-Frequency Words
Generating Questions		
Skill: Generating Questions	Skill: Generating Questions • Your Turn First Read • Practice Prereading Skill • Read and Annotate • Text Talk • Think Questions 1–3	Spotlight Skill: Generating Questions
Language Structures		
Skill: Language Structures	Skill: Language Structures • Your Turn Close Read • Complete Vocabulary Chart • Skills Focus • Collaborative Conversation	Spotlight Skill: Language Structures
Analyzing and Evaluating Text		
Skill: Analyzing and Evaluating Text	Skill: Analyzing and Evaluating Text • Your Turn Close Read • Skills Focus • Peer Review and Reflect	Spotlight Skill: Analyzing and Evaluating Text
Spelling Patterns and Rules		
Skill: Spelling Patterns and Rules	Skill: Spelling Patterns and Rules • Your Turn Close Read • Write	Spotlight Skill: Spelling Patterns and Rules

First Read

Introduce the Text

As a class, watch the video preview and have students read the introduction in pairs to make connections to the video preview. Ask students verious "wh" questions such as:

- What did you see in the video? How does it make you feel?
- What do you think the text will be about?
- Is there something in the video or introduction that surprised you?

Practice Prereading Skill

Remind students that Generating Questions:

Deepens your understanding of the text. Before reading, preview the title and other visual elements to generate questions about what you want to learn about the text. During reading, ask questions about unfamiliar words and confusing passages. After reading, ask questions about the main idea or message and connect the text to bigger ideas.

Have students work in small, on-level groups to choral read or listen to the audio of the poem. Remind students to generate questions before, during, and after reading.

As students are working in small groups, circulate to listen for sample questions like:

- Can you explain the reference to Lewis and Clark in the sixth stanza?
- How old was Sacagawea?

ELL **Beginning & Intermediate**

SPEAKING FRAMES

- I saw ____. I feel ____.
- I think the text will be about ____.
- I was surprised by ____.

Activate Prior Knowledge and Experiences OPTIONAL

Find out what your students already know about tributes to public figures.

Have students make connections while practicing their oral language by discussing what they know about tributes to public figures. Ask students to share where their background knowledge came from. For example, did their ideas come from a movie, friend, television show, book, or family member?

VOCABULARY

antique
very old and valuable

counselor
a person who gives advice and helps others

tribute
something that shows respect and admiration for someone

endure
suffer pain or difficulty over a period of time

survivor
someone who lives through very difficult circumstances

READ

Sleeping in grandfather's **antique** coinbox
are silver men of fame
long past Presidents.

Golden coins, mixed in, show bearded men,
names known only to history teachers.
Half hidden, a coin shows a golden woman,
sleeping infant tied to her back.
Despite her coinbox destiny,
her **tribute** should be greater.

"She deserves better," I say.
"Sacagawea of the Shoshone tribe,
this **survivor**.
She was an admirable ambassador,
a peacemaker,
a gentle guide,
and a **counselor**."

AUDIO TEXT HIGHLIGHTING

Allow students to use the audio text highlight feature to follow along as they read. Alternatively, you may wish to work directly with students or group them in twos or threes for partner reading or choral reading.

Preteach Vocabulary

Model the following word and example for the class.

1. The word *counselor* means "someone who gives advice and helps others."
2. When I hear the word *counselor*, I think of an adult that I trust.
3. For example: If I need help with a personal problem, I may talk to the school *counselor* to ask if he or she can help me solve my problem.
4. A *counselor* might help me make decisions about further education or my future career.

Continue this exercise with each word in the glossary, calling on individuals or groups of students to share out.

Beginning

PRETEACH VOCABULARY

Beginning students may benefit from additional practice or visual cues that help reinforce meanings in context. Ask students multiple-choice questions with obvious correct answers such as the following.

- Which item would you see in an **antique** shop?
  a. a piano
  b. a cell phone
- Where does a **counselor** work?
  a. a grocery store
  b. a school
- Who has to **endure** very cold winters?
  a. people who live in the north
  b. people who live in the south
- Which characteristic describes a **survivor**?
  a. someone who gives up
  b. someone who continues to try
- Which **tribute** would you use to honor your grandparents?
  a. a handwritten poem
  b. a gift certificate

Students may also benefit from seeing images related to the correct multiple-choice responses. For example, present an image of a piano or a snowy landscape.

Sight Vocabulary and High-Frequency Words Focus

Remind students of the sight vocabulary and high-frequency words that they studied at the beginning of the unit. Point out that some of the words may be useful as they think about and discuss the text. For example:

- among (*Among* all the coins . . .)
- box (The *box* contains . . .)
- check (I can *check* my response by . . .)
- decided (We *decided* to . . .)
- finally (After many years, Sacagawea *finally* got . . .)

NOTES

Could you
endure floods,
cold, heat,
swarms of mosquitos like hungry armies?

Could you
be resourceful in the face of starvation,
all with a baby on your back?

She was young,
friend to Clark, adviser to Lewis.
She led them west,
speaking to the natives in their languages. They trusted her.
A woman and infant, journeying with white men, means peace.

I turn the coin over. I see a golden bird in full flight,
perhaps an eagle, perhaps a dove,
perhaps a symbol for the Shoshone
called, by some, "bird woman."

TEXT TALK

Have students discuss the questions in small groups. Circulate around the room and check for understanding.

1. What is the poem about?
2. Who are people in the poem?
3. What event takes place in the poem?
4. How does the poem make you feel?

All Levels

SPEAKING FRAMES

Giving Information:

- This poem is about ____.
- The people in the poem are ____.
- The event described in the poem is ____.
- The poem makes me feel ____.

Asking for Information:

- Can you explain ____?
- What do you think about ____?
- Do you agree with ____?

First Read

Read "A Golden Coin." After you read, complete the Think Questions below.

THINK QUESTIONS

1. **Who is the subject of the poem?**

   The subject of the poem is ______.

2. **Why does the speaker think that Sacagawea deserves better?**

   The speaker thinks Sacagawea deserves better because ______

   ______.

3. **How did Sacagawea help Lewis and Clark? Include a line from the poem to support your response.**

   In line ______ Sacagawea helped Lewis and Clark

   by ______.

4. **Use context to confirm the meaning of the word *antique* as it is used in "A Golden Coin." Write your definition of *antique* here.**

   Antique means ______.

   A context clue is ______.

5. **What is another way to ask if someone could *endure* floods, cold, and heat like Sacagawea did?**

   Like Sacagawea, a person could ______?

Think Questions

Circulate as students answer Think Questions independently. Answers will vary.

QUESTION 1: Comprehension

The subject of the poem is Sacagawea of the Shoshone tribe.

QUESTION 2: Comprehension

The speaker thinks that Sacagawea's image on a rare coin is not an adequate tribute. She was "an admirable ambassador, a peacemaker, a gentle guide, and a counselor."

QUESTION 3: Comprehension

Answers will vary, but may include the following examples:

- "She led them west, / speaking to the natives in their languages."
- "A woman and infant, journeying with white men, means peace."

Student responses should provide an example from the text and an explanation of how their example shows Sacagawea helped Lewis and Clark.

QUESTION 4: Language

In the first stanza, the context clues "grandfather's" and "long past" tell me that *antique* items are taken care of and kept for a long time. A definition for *antique* is "old and valuable."

QUESTION 5: Language

Could you ***survive*** through floods, cold, and heat like Sacagawea?

Skill: Language Structures

Introduce the Skill

Watch the Concept Definition video and read the definition for Language Structures.

TURN AND TALK

1. What are language structures?
2. Why is it helpful to understand how sentences are structured?
3. What can you do if you are struggling to understand language structures?

Beginning & Intermediate

SPEAKING FRAMES

- Language structures are ____.
- It is helpful because ____.
- I can identify ____ in a sentence, which tells me ____.

Advanced & Advanced High

SPEAKING FRAMES

- Language structures are ____. For example, ____.
- It is helpful to understand the structure of a sentence in order to ____.
- If I struggle, I can identify ____ in a sentence. This tells me ____.

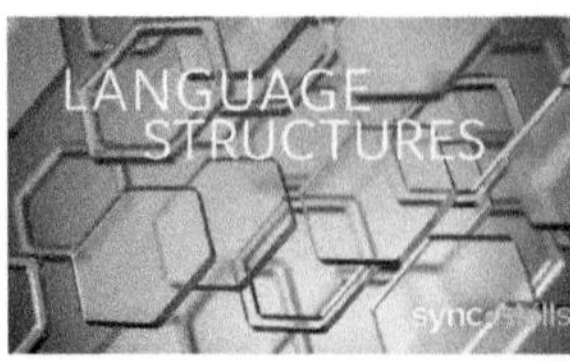

Skill: Language Structures

★ DEFINE

In every language, there are rules that tell how to **structure** sentences. These rules define the correct order of words. In the English language, for example, a **basic** structure for sentences is subject, verb, and object. Some sentences have more **complicated** structures.

You will encounter both basic and complicated **language structures** in the classroom materials you read. Being familiar with language structures will help you better understand the text.

••• CHECKLIST FOR LANGUAGE STRUCTURES

To improve your comprehension of language structures, do the following:

✓ Monitor your understanding.

- Ask yourself: Why do I not understand this sentence? Is it because I do not understand some of the words? Or is it because I do not understand the way the words are ordered in the sentence?

✓ Break down the sentence into its parts.

- In English, adjectives almost always come before the noun. Example: He had a **big dog**.
  - > A **noun** names a person, place, thing, or idea.
  - > An **adjective** modifies, or describes, a noun or a pronoun.
  - > If there is more than one adjective, they usually appear in the following order separated by a comma: quantity or number, quality or opinion, size, age, shape, color. Example: He had a **big, brown dog**.
  - > If there is more than one adjective from the same category, include the word *and*. Example: He had **a brown and white dog**.
- Ask yourself: What are the nouns in this sentence? What adjectives describe them? In what order are the nouns and adjectives?

✓ Confirm your understanding with a peer or teacher.

V SKILL VOCABULARY

structure / la estructura *verb* the arrangement or ordering of parts COGNATE

basic / básico/a *adjective* relating to a base; fundamental COGNATE

complicated / complicado/a *adjective* composed of many different parts; difficult to understand, complex COGNATE

language structure / la estructura del lenguaje *noun* the order of words in a sentence

YOUR TURN

Read each phrase in the chart below. Then complete the chart by sorting the words and images into the adjective, noun, and image columns.

Words and Images	
A	ambassador
B	gentle
C	[image of a smiling person pointing to a path]
D	armies
E	admirable
F	[image of many military people eating in a cafeteria]
G	guide
H	[image of a smiling teenage ambassador, wearing a coat with shiny pins, standing in front of a foreign flag]
I	hungry

Phrase	Adjective	Noun	Image
"She was an admirable ambassador. . ."			
". . .a peacemaker, a gentle guide, and a counselor."			
". . .swarms of mosquitos like hungry armies?"			

Your Turn

Ask students to complete the Your Turn Activity.

Phrase	Adjective	Noun	Image
"She was an admirable ambassador . . . "	admirable	ambassador	
" . . . a peacemaker, a gentle guide, and a counselor."	gentle	guide	
" . . . swarms of mosquitos like hungry armies?"	hungry	armies	

Discuss the Skill Model

1. How does the student use her knowledge of language structures?

   The student uses her knowledge of language structures to better understand the images in "A Golden Coin."

2. In the student's first annotation, what do the adjectives describe?

   The adjectives in the first sentence describe the quality or color of each noun.

3. Why doesn't the student understand the highlighted phrases in her second annotation?

   She doesn't understand the adjectives in the her second annotation because they do not have a literal meaning.

4. How does the student confirm her understanding of the adjectives in the second annotation?

   The student confirms her understanding by discussing her ideas with her teacher.

Beginning & Intermediate

Have students use the speaking frames and helpful terms to participate in the group discussion. If beginning students are hesitant to participate in a discussion, encourage them by prompting with *yes* or *no* questions.

Advanced & Advanced High

Have students use the speaking frames to participate in the group discussion.

SPEAKING FRAMES

- The student uses her knowledge of language structures to ____.
- The adjectives in the first sentence describe ____.
- She does not understand because ____.
- The student confirms her understanding by ____.

HELPFUL TERMS FOR DISCUSSION

- images
- idea
- discuss
- adjective
- noun
- quality
- understand
- literal
- meaning

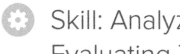

Skill: Analyzing and Evaluating Text

Introduce the Skill

Watch the Concept Definition video and read the definition for Analyzing and Evaluating Text.

TURN AND TALK

1. What does it mean to analyze and evaluate a text?
2. What should a reader do when the author's message and purpose are not stated directly?
3. What does the reader learn from this process?

Beginning & Intermediate

SPEAKING FRAMES

- Analyzing and evaluating a text means ___.
- The reader can ___.
- The reader learns how to ___.

Advanced & Advanced High

SPEAKING FRAMES

- Analyzing and evaluating a text means ___.
- When the message or purpose is not stated directly, ___.
- By analyzing and evaluating the text, ___.

Skill: Analyzing and Evaluating Text

DEFINE

Analyzing and **evaluating** a text means reading carefully to understand the author's **purpose** and **message**. In informational texts, authors may provide information or opinions on a topic. They may be writing to inform or persuade a reader. In fictional texts, the author may be **communicating** a message or lesson through their story. They may write to entertain, or to teach the reader something about life.

Sometimes authors are clear about their message and purpose. When the message or purpose is not stated directly, readers will need to look closer at the text. Readers can use textual evidence to make inferences about what the author is trying to communicate. By analyzing and evaluating the text, you can form your own thoughts and opinions about what you read.

••• CHECKLIST FOR ANALYZING AND EVALUATING TEXT

In order to analyze and evaluate a text, do the following:

✓ Look for details that show why the author is writing.

- Ask yourself: Is the author trying to inform, persuade, or entertain? What are the main ideas of this text?

✓ Look for details that show what the author is trying to say.

- Ask yourself: What is the author's opinion about this topic? Is there a lesson I can learn from this story?

✓ Form your own thoughts and opinions about the text.

- Ask yourself: Do I agree with the author? Does this message apply to my life?

SKILL VOCABULARY

analyze / analizar *verb* to consider in detail and discover essential features or meaning COGNATE

evaluate / evaluar *verb* to judge or decide; to estimate the quality of COGNATE

purpose / el propósito *noun* the reason for writing or speaking COGNATE

message / el mensaje *noun* verbal or written piece of information COGNATE

communicate / comunicar *verb* to express thoughts or feelings COGNATE

YOUR TURN

Read lines 4–20 of "A Golden Coin." Then, using the Checklist on the previous page, answer the multiple-choice questions.

from **"A Golden Coin"**

Golden coins, mixed in, show bearded men,
names known only to history teachers.
Half hidden, a coin shows a golden woman,
sleeping infant tied to her back.
Despite her coinbox destiny,
her tribute should be greater.

"She deserves better," I say.
"Sacagawea of the Shoshone tribe,
this survivor.
She was an admirable ambassador,
a peacemaker,
a gentle guide,
and a counselor."

Could you
endure floods,
cold, heat,
swarms of mosquitos like hungry armies?

Discuss the Skill Model

1. What does the student locate in the second stanza?

   The student locates the main idea.

2. What does the student decide to locate next?

   The student decides to analyze and evaluate lines from the text to determine the author's purpose.

3. Why does the student highlight facts about Sacagawea?

   The student thinks the author's purpose is to educate the reader using facts about Sacagawea's life.

4. How does the student's second annotation support the main idea of the poem?

   The highlighted facts about Sacagawea's life strengthen the main idea that this historical figure deserves a better tribute.

ELL **Beginning & Intermediate**

Have students use the speaking frames and helpful terms to participate in the group discussion. If beginning students are hesitant to participate in a discussion, encourage them by prompting with *yes* or *no* questions.

Advanced & Advanced High

Have students use the speaking frames to participate in the group discussion.

SPEAKING FRAMES

- The student locates the ____.
- The student decides to ____ in order to determine ____.
- The student highlights facts because ____.
- The student's second annotation ____.

HELPFUL TERMS FOR DISCUSSION

- analyze
- educate
- main idea
- author's purpose
- evaluate
- strengthen
- deserve
- historical figure
- reader

1. What is the message or lesson of this poem?

   - ○ A. Only images of presidents should be on silver United States coins.
   - ○ B. Students would benefit from more facts about historical figures.
   - ○ C. The Shoshone tribe became a well-known tribe in history.
   - ○ D. Mosquitos are a big problem in the United States.

2. A detail that best supports this conclusion is—

   - ○ A. "Golden coins, mixed in, show bearded men, names known only to history teachers."
   - ○ B. "She deserves better," I say.
   - ○ C. "She was an admirable ambassador, a peacemaker, a gentle guide, and a counselor."
   - ○ D. "Could you endure floods, cold, heat, swarms of mosquitos like hungry armies?"

3. Which line from the poem suggests that the poet is trying to relate to the reader?

   - ○ A. "Sleeping in grandfather's antique coinbox are silver men of fame long past Presidents."
   - ○ B. "Golden coins, mixed in, show bearded men, names known only to history teachers."
   - ○ C. "Sacagawea of the Shoshone tribe, this survivor."
   - ○ D. "Could you endure floods, cold, heat, swarms of mosquitos like hungry armies?"

Your Turn

Ask students to complete the Your Turn Activity.

QUESTION 1: B. Correct. The poet includes several facts about Sacagawea.

QUESTION 2: C. Correct. This line shows examples of facts about Sacagawea.

QUESTION 3: D. Correct. The poet wants the reader to try to relate to the obstacles in Sacagawea's life.

Close Read

WRITE

INFORMATIONAL: In the poem "A Golden Coin," the author claims that Sacagawea's "tribute" should be greater than a coin in a coinbox. How does Sacagawea's life merit a greater tribute? Write a paragraph in which you explain why Sacagawea's life deserves to be celebrated and remembered. Pay attention to and edit for *ea* and *a+consonant+e* spelling rules.

Use the checklist below to guide you as you write.

- ☐ Why is Sacagawea considered an important historical figure?
- ☐ What details about Sacagawea's life should be celebrated?
- ☐ How should Modern Americans remember Sacagawea?

Use the sentence frames to organize and write your argument.

Modern Americans should remember Sacagawea because ____________________.

Sacagawea should be celebrated because ____________________.

For example, ____________________.

Sacagawea should be remembered as a symbol of ____________________

because she was "____________________."

I ____________________ with the poet because ____________________

____________________.

Close Read

Complete Skills Focus

To prepare students to complete the Skills Focus, remind them of the Reading Skill Analyzing and Evaluating Text. Tell students that one way you can analyze and evaluate a text is by looking for details that show what the author is trying to say. Direct students to the Skills Focus and remind them to track as you read aloud.

Identify lines of text evidence to support the author's main idea.

Have students complete the Skills Focus in groups of three. Have each group analyze lines of text evidence.

- Divide the poem into three sections.
- Have each group member search their section of the poem for details that support the main idea.
- Have group members analyze and evaluate each chosen line.
- Have group members discuss how the details they found support the author's main idea.

Allow students to reread the text and mark down their ideas using the annotation tool, adding an exclamation point (!) to note things they want to remember or that surprise them, and a question mark (?) to note things that confuse them.

Prompt students to work cooperatively to complete their assigned tasks. Circulate around the room and monitor groups as they work.

Collaborative Conversation

Group students into pairs. Prompt each student to explain their chosen lines from the text to their partner.

- How did you decide which lines from the text supported the author's main idea?
- How did discussing your ideas with other students help to confirm your understanding?

Collaborative Conversation

SCAFFOLDS

ELL **BEGINNING, INTERMEDIATE** Use the word bank to participate in the group discussion.

ADVANCED Use the speaking frames to participate in the group discussion.

BEGINNING, INTERMEDIATE	ADVANCED
Word Bank	**Speaking Frames**
• helped me understand • analyze and evaluate • text evidence • identify • author's main idea • support	• My group ____ and ____ to determine ____. • Discussing the text with other students helped me because ____.

Write

Informational Prompt: In the poem "A Golden Coin," the author claims that Sacagawea's "tribute" should be greater than a coin in a coinbox. How does Sacagawea's life merit a greater tribute? Write a paragraph in which you explain why Sacagawea's life deserves to be celebrated and remembered. Pay attention to and edit for "ea" and "a + consonante + e" spelling rules.

ELL **BEGINNING** Write a response using the paragraph frames and word banks.

INTERMEDIATE Write a response using the paragraph frames.

INTERMEDIATE

BEGINNING

Paragraph Frames

Modern Americans should celebrate and remember Sacagawea because ____. Sacagawea should be celebrated because ____. For example, ____. Sacagawea should be remembered as a symbol of ____ because she was "____." I ____ with the poet because ____.

Word Bank

- deserve
- history
- Lewis and Clark
- obstacles
- peace

A Modern Man

INFORMATIONAL TEXT

Introduction

Charles Dickens is probably best known for being an author of novels like *A Christmas Carol* and *Oliver Twist*. However, his influence in our society today expands well beyond the pages of a book. Charles Dickens inspired people to make changes by using his talent of writing. For example, his works have inspired improvements for people with disabilities, people living in poverty, as well as the conditions of communities suffering from pollution. Although Dickens will always be known for his entertaining writing, today we have him to thank for many of society's advancements.

A Modern Man from the 1800s: The Influential Life of Charles Dickens

Charles Dickens is a well-known author who is famous for the line "Bah! Humbug!" Surprisingly, several of his novels led to major changes in society in 19th-century England. When Charles Dickens wrote *The Pickwick Papers*, he inadvertently named a disease that people are now diagnosed with and treated for. A popular Dicken's novel, *Oliver Twist*, inspired many wealthy citizens to donate food, clothing, and money to the less fortunate. Furthermore, this novel also led to the creation of "ragged schools" in poor neighborhoods, to give needy children access to education. Dickens's most famous story, *A Christmas Carol*, essentially defined the holiday season as we know it today. Back in the 1800s, Christmas was not a holiday—it was his story that turned the season into a time for family and presents. Lastly, with Bleak House, Dickens brought attention to the importance of hygiene and cleanliness, inspiring many English citizens to start cleaning up the filthy conditions in their communities. Charles Dickens used his writing to inspire positive changes that are still important today.

ELL Proficiency-leveled summaries and summaries in multiple languages are available digitally.

Audio and audio text highlighting are available with this text.

CONNECT TO ESSENTIAL QUESTION

What is the power of the story?

This informational text explains how the fictional works of Charles Dickens influenced the people and ideas of the 19th century and beyond. How can stories change the world?

Core ELA Connections

Texts	Theme	Genre
A Tale of Two Cities	Charles Dickens' novels have influenced society in several ways throughout many generations. This text highlights literature's effect on community involvement and improvement.	"A Modern Man from the 1800s: The Influential Life of Charles Dickens" is an informational text that explains how four of his novels inspired positive change.

Differentiated Text Levels

ELL LEVEL	BEGINNING	INTERMEDIATE	ADVANCED	ADVANCED HIGH
WORD COUNT	1030	1035	1050	1061
LEXILE	1000L	1080L	1140L	1260L

Instructional Path

The print teacher's edition includes essential point-of-use instruction and planning tools. Complete lesson plans and program documents appear in your digital teacher account.

Skill: Classroom Vocabulary

Objectives: Students will be able to learn and recognize classroom vocabulary words in English.

Objectives: Students will be able to recognize classroom vocabulary words when listening and reading, and produce classroom vocabulary words when speaking and writing in a variety of contexts.

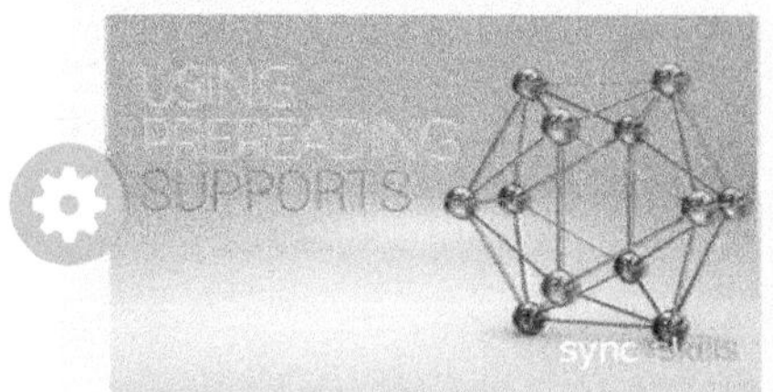

Skill: Using Prereading Supports

Objectives: Students will be able to learn and practice the skill of using prereading supports when reading a new text.

Objectives: Students will be able to read a new or unfamiliar text using prereading supports, such as graphic organizers, illustrations, and topic vocabulary.

First Read: A Modern Man from the 1800s: The Influential Life of Charles Dickens

Objectives: Students will be able to perform an initial reading of a text using the strategy of using prereading supports.

Objectives: Students will be able to use prereading supports and demonstrate comprehension by responding to questions using textual evidence.

Skill: Analyzing Expressions

Objectives: Students will be able to analyze expressions.

Objectives: Students will be able to analyze expressions when reading and speaking.

Skill: Visual and Contextual Support

Objectives: Students will be able to use visual and contextual support before and during reading.

Objectives: Students will be able to use visual and contextual support before and during reading to better understand a text and to discuss observations when speaking.

Skill: Main and Helping Verbs

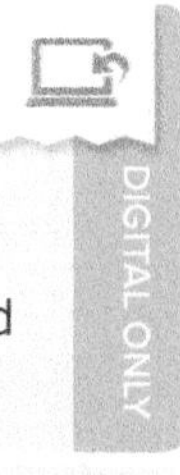

Objectives: Students will be able to recognize main and helping verbs.

Objectives: Students will be able to recognize main and helping verbs when reading and use main and helping verbs when writing.

Close Read: A Modern Man from the 1800s: The Influential Life of Charles Dickens

Objectives: Students will be able to perform a close reading of a text in order to analyze visual and contextual supports.

Objectives: Students will be able to demonstrate analysis of visual and contextual supports by participating in a collaborative conversation and writing a short constructed response.

Progress Monitoring

Opportunities to Learn	Opportunities to Demonstrate Learning	Opportunities to Reteach
Classroom Vocabulary		
Skill: Classroom Vocabulary	Skill: Classroom Vocabulary • Your Turn First Read • Classroom Language Focus	Spotlight Skill: Classroom Vocabulary
Using Prereading Supports		
Skill: Using Prereading Supports	Skill: Using Prereading Supports • Your Turn First Read • Pre-Teach Vocabulary • Practice Prereading Skill	Spotlight Skill: Using Prereading Supports
Analyzing Expressions		
Skill: Analyzing Expressions	Skill: Analyzing Expressions • Your Turn	Spotlight Skill: Analyzing Expressions
Visual and Contextual Support		
Skill: Visual and Contextual Support	Skill: Visual and Contextual Support • Your Turn Close Read • Skills Focus • Collaborative Conversation	Spotlight Skill: Visual and Contextual Support
Main and Helping Verbs		
Skill: Main and Helping Verbs	Skill: Main and Helping Verbs • Your Turn Close Read • Write	Spotlight Skill: Main and Helping Verbs

First Read

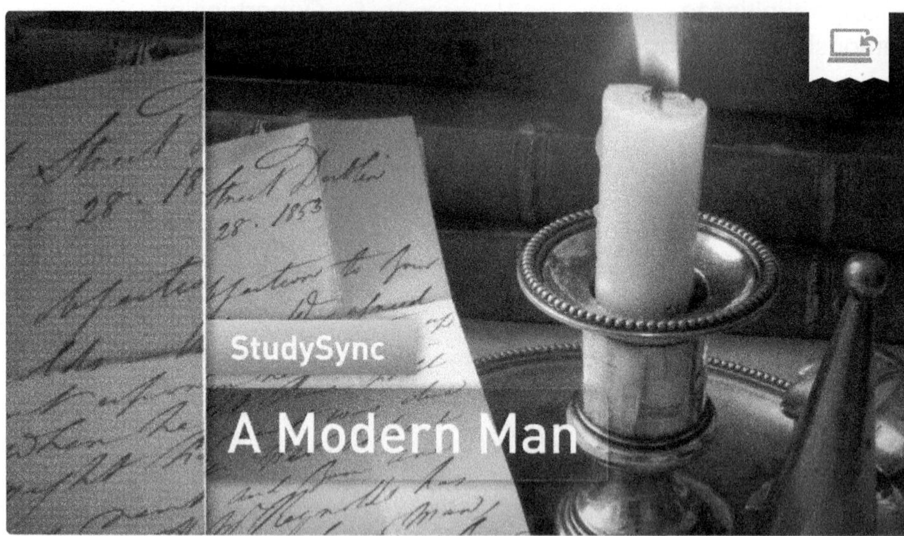

Introduce the Text

As a class, watch the video preview and have students read the introduction in pairs to make connections to the video preview. Ask students various "wh" questions such as:

- What did you see in the video? How does it make you feel?
- What do you think the text will be about?
- Is there something in the video or introduction that surprised you?

Practice Prereading Skill

Remind students that Using Prereading Supports:

Helps you prepare to read a text. Graphic organizers can be used to write down notes about the text you are reading and to show the connections between the ideas in the text.

Have students work in small, on-level groups to choral read or listen to the audio of the text. Remind students to create a graphic organizer first.

As students are working in small groups, circulate to listen for sample questions like:

- That is an important detail to write down.
- This line explains the main idea.
- These ideas are connected.

ELL Beginning & Intermediate

SPEAKING FRAMES

- I saw ____. I feel ____.
- I think the text will be about ____.
- I was surprised by ____.

Activate Prior Knowledge and Experiences OPTIONAL

Find out what your students already know about Charles Dickens.

Have students make connections while practicing their oral language by discussing what they know about Charles Dickens. Ask students to share where their background knowledge came from. For example, did their ideas come from a movie, friend, television show, book, or family member?

A Modern Man from the 1800s: The Influential Life of Charles Dickens

 VOCABULARY

influence
to have an effect on someone or something

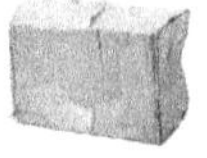

condition
a state of something, especially regarding its quality and usually at a particular time

pollution
an undesirable state of the natural environment being contaminated with harmful substances as a consequence of human activities

industrialization
the process of building factories and large businesses in a country, city, or region

READ

A Modern Man from the 1800s: The Influential Life of Charles Dickens

1 "Bah! Humbug!" Perhaps you have heard someone say this phrase around the holiday season. This person is probably tired of waiting in long lines at the store, hearing the same songs on the radio, and spending money on gifts for others. We often call this person a "scrooge."

2 Scrooge was originally a character in Charles Dickens's famous novel *A Christmas Carol*. This reference is extremely popular in modern-day society even though the novel it comes from was written in 1843. Today, Dickens is well-known for his literature, but he has **influenced** society in many other ways as well. Using his talent for writing, Charles Dickens was able to help his readers understand the issues threatening England during the 19th century. Without his influence, our lives would have been very different today. Charles Dickens was a writer living in the 1800s, but he is considered a modern man for improving society as we know it.

3 Four of Charles Dickens's novels in particular inspired great change in 19th-century England. We still see this change today. The following novels helped improve the lives of people with disabilities, lend a helping hand to those living in poverty, reignite the Christmas spirit, and create **pollution** laws.

AUDIO TEXT HIGHLIGHTING

Allow students to use the audio text highlight feature to follow along as they read. Alternatively, you may wish to work directly with students or group them in twos or threes for partner reading or choral reading.

Preteach Vocabulary

Model the following word and example for the class.

1. The word *pollution* means "the presence of something harmful or poisonous in one's environment"
2. When I hear the word *pollution*, I think of garbage on the beach.
3. For example: if I see garbage on the beach, I worry that the *pollution* will go into the ocean and harm the fish.
4. This is an example of *pollution* because it is harmful to the environment.

Continue this exercise with each word in the glossary, calling on individuals or groups of students to share out.

Beginning

PRETEACH VOCABULARY

Beginning students may benefit from additional practice or visual cues that help reinforce meanings in context. Ask students multiple-choice questions with obvious correct answers such as the following:

- Which person is liely to **influence** a child?
  a. an older sibling
  b. a weather reporter
- How can people prevent **pollution**?
  a. watch a movie
  b. pick up trash
- What is a person's typical **condition** after running?
  a. bored
  b. tired
- What is an effect of **industrialization**?
  a. People move to cities from farms.
  b. People move from cities to farms.

Students may also benefit from seeing images related to the correct multiple-choice responses. For example, present an image of pollution or a large city.

Classroom Vocabulary Focus

Remind students of the classroom vocabulary that they studied earlier in the unit. Point out that some of the words may be useful as they think about and discuss the text. For example:

- although (*Although* Dickens was a writer, he also . . .)
- content (I think the *content* of the novels . . .)
- rather (It is *rather* interesting that . . .)
- surprised (I was *surprised* to learn . . .)

NOTES

The Pickwick Papers, 1836

4 *The Pickwick Papers* was the first novel that Charles Dickens published. In this story, a character named Joe is an overweight boy who has trouble staying awake. He falls asleep at random times, no matter what he is doing. When Dickens wrote about Joe's disability in 1836, there was not a name for it. However, over 100 years later, doctors decided that Joe's sleeping problem described in *The Pickwick Papers* was an actual medical **condition**. In fact, today, when people experience the same symptoms as Joe, they are often diagnosed with "Pickwickian Syndrome." Thanks to Charles Dickens, this disability has a name. Pickwickian Syndrome was recognized as a legitimate condition thanks to Dickens's novel. Now people can get the help they need.

Oliver Twist, 1837

5 In *Oliver Twist*, the main character is a poor, hungry orphan who steals in order to survive. This popular story shocked many people in 19th-century England. The upper class, or members of society who had money, didn't know that children were living like this on the streets of England in real life. Inspired by the novel *Oliver Twist*, many wealthy people realized that charity begins at home. The upper class began to donate food, clothing, and money to help those in need. In addition, Charles Dickens's story led to the creation of "ragged schools." These were schools that were built in poor communities. These schools helped to educate children who previously had no access to a school. Today, all students can receive an education in the public school system, no matter if they are rich or poor.

Brook Street Ragged and Industrial School, Hampstead Road, London

A Christmas Carol, 1843

6 Arguably Dickens's most famous story, *A Christmas Carol*, defined the holiday season as we know it. Throughout the early 1800s in England, Christmas was not celebrated like it is today. In fact, most people worked on Christmas day. People didn't think of Christmas as a time with family, for getting presents, or eating food. However, that all changed after Charles Dickens wrote *A Christmas Carol* in 1843. His novel showed Christmas as a party with loved ones, a

Mr. Fezziwig's Ball from A Christmas Carol, 1843. Artist: John Leech

TEXT TALK

Have students discuss the questions in small groups. Circulate around the room and check for understanding.

1. What is the text about?
2. What is the author mainly discussing?
3. What are some examples that the author gives?
4. Does the text change the way you think about the topic?

ELL **All Levels**

SPEAKING FRAMES

Giving Information:

- This text is about ____.
- The author is discussing ____.
- Some examples the author gives about ____ include ____.
- This text makes me think _____.

Asking for Information:

- Can you explain ____?
- What do you think about ____?
- Why do you think _____?
- Is ____ important?

lavish feast, and even snow! Once this novel became popular, the celebration of Christmas changed and became more like the holiday season we know today. For this reason, Charles Dickens is known as "The Man Who Invented Christmas."

7 Similar to Dickens's novel *The Pickwick Papers*, *A Christmas Carol* also inspired members of society to view people with disabilities more positively. In *A Christmas Carol*, a character named Tiny Tim has a physical disability that prevents him from walking without his crutches. Tiny Tim touched the hearts of many due to his kind nature and loving spirit. This fictional character really inspired a man named William Treloar. Treloar decided to open a college and hospital in England for people with disabilities. Thanks to Dickens's writing, more people like William Treloar started to accept and help people with disabilities. Through his writing, Dickens encouraged society to develop resources for people with disabilities. This idea is still popular today. Now, it is easy to find and support charities and events for people with disabilities. One example is the Special Olympics.

***Bleak House*, 1852**

8 Charles Dickens wrote the novel *Bleak House* in 1852. In this story, a character named Jo is a sweeper who cleans the polluted streets of England. Like *Oliver Twist*, this book inspired many citizens of England to address the filthy living conditions in their own communities. Thanks to *Bleak House*, the conditions of the roads and neighborhoods greatly improved. Also, this book brought attention to the importance of hygiene and cleanliness worldwide.

9 Dickens helped with the pollution problem in the streets of England, but a man named Charles Babbage wanted his help with a different kind of pollution: noise pollution. Babbage was an inventor and engineer who lived in London. He had a problem with the excessive noise coming from the street musicians outside of his home. Since Babbage knew that Charles Dickens was such an inspirational man, he enlisted his help in this fight against noise. Sure enough, actions spoke louder than words, or in this case, noise. Working together, Dickens and Babbage helped pass a law against noise disturbances. Babbage even wrote a book about his quest to end unnecessary noise in the streets of England. In Babbage's book, Dickens wrote about his own experience with noise. In one line, he wrote that he was "daily interrupted, harassed, worried, wearied, driven nearly mad, by street musicians." This law against excessive street noise is still enforced today.

10 If Charles Dickens had not written his famous novels, our world would be very different today. His works inspired charity, education, acceptance, celebration, cleanliness, and even some peace and quiet. Dickens's legacy can inspire us to speak up about the issues affecting our modern-day society. Charles Dickens was an author living in 19th-century England, but his relevance still lives strong today.

Think Questions

Circulate as students answer Think Questions independently. Answers will vary.

QUESTION 1: Comprehension

Charles Dickens is a writer. He lived in the 19th century.

QUESTION 2: Comprehension

A *Christmas Carol* changed the way people celebrate Christmas. The novel also inspired members of society to help and respect people with disabilities.

QUESTION 3: Comprehension

Answers will vary, but may include the following examples:

- "His works inspired charity, education, acceptance, celebration, cleanliness, and even some peace and quiet."
- "Dickens's legacy can inspire us to speak up about the issues affecting our modern-day society."

Student responses should provide an example from the text and an explanation that describes how Dickens had a positive impact on society.

QUESTION 4: Language

Pickwickian Syndrome is a condition that leads to sleeping problems. A definition for *condition* is "a state of being."

QUESTION 5: Language

Someone has caused change to happen in society.

First Read

Read "A Modern Man from the 1800s: The Influential Life of Charles Dickens." After you read, complete the Think Questions below.

THINK QUESTIONS

1. Who is Charles Dickens? When did he live?

   Charles Dickens is ______________________________.

   He lived ______________________________.

2. Write two or three sentences describing how *A Christmas Carol* affected society.

   A Chistmas Carol affected society ______________________________

   ____

   ______________________________.

3. How did Dickens help make the world a better place? Include a line from the text to support your response.

   In paragraph __________ Dickens ______________________________

4. Use context to confirm the meaning of the word *condition* as it is used in "A Modern Man from the 1800s: The Influential Life of Charles Dickens." Write your definition of *condition* here.

   Condition means ______________________________.

   A context clue is ______________________________.

5. What is another way to say that someone has "influenced" society?

   Someone has ______________________________.

A Modern Man from the 1800s: The Influential Life of Charles Dickens

Skill: Analyzing Expressions

DEFINE

When you read, you may find English expressions that you do not know. An **expression** is a group of words that communicates an idea. Three types of expressions are idioms, sayings, and figurative language. They can be difficult to understand because the meanings of the words are different from their **literal**, or usual, meanings.

An **idiom** is an expression that is commonly known among a group of people. For example, "It's raining cats and dogs" means it is raining heavily. **Sayings** are short expressions that contain advice or wisdom. For instance, "Don't count your chickens before they hatch" means do not plan on something good happening before it happens. **Figurative** language is when you describe something by comparing it with something else, either directly (using the words *like* or *as*) or indirectly. For example, "I'm as hungry as a horse" means I'm very hungry. None of the expressions are about actual animals.

••• CHECKLIST FOR ANALYZING EXPRESSIONS

To determine the meaning of an expression, remember the following:

- ✓ If you find a confusing group of words, it may be an expression. The meaning of words in expressions may not be their literal meaning.
  - Ask yourself: Is this confusing because the words are new? Or because the words do not make sense together?
- ✓ Determining the overall meaning may require that you use one or more of the following:
  - context clues
  - a dictionary or other resource
  - teacher or peer support
- ✓ Highlight important information before and after the expression to look for clues.

Skill: Analyzing Expressions

Introduce the Skill

Watch the Concept Definition video ▶ and read the definition for Analyzing Expressions.

TURN AND TALK

1. Why do you think people use expressions when they speak?
2. What are some expressions you already know?
3. What is a new expression you have heard recently?

ELL Beginning & Intermediate

SPEAKING FRAMES

- I think people use expressions because ____.
- I know the expression "____."
- I heard someone say "____."

ELL Advanced & Advanced High

SPEAKING FRAMES

- Expressions can help ____ and are also ____.
- I know the expression "____," which means ____.
- Recently, I heard someone use the phrase "____."

SKILL VOCABULARY

expression / la expresión *noun* a phrase used to express an idea COGNATE

literal / literal *adjective* describing the usual meaning of a word COGNATE

idiom / el modismo *noun* a phrase or expression used to convey a meaning that is different from its literal definition

saying / el dicho *noun* an expression that contains advice or wisdom

figurative / figurado/a *adjective* not literal; using figures of speech

Discuss the Skill Model

1. Which phrases does the student not understand?

   The student does not understand some of the expressions, like "charity begins at home" and "actions speak louder than words."

2. How does the student analyze these expressions?

   The student discusses context clues with his teacher and peers.

3. What context clue did the student use in the first annotation? What does the student infer?

   English people were surprised that those living close to home were affected. The student infers that "charity begins at home" means that people should help others close to them.

4. What context clue did the student use in the second annotation? What does the student conclude?

   Dickens and Babbage did not just talk about the problem, they worked to pass a law to fix the issue with noise pollution. The student concludes that the expression "actions spoke louder than words" must mean that doing something is better than talking about doing something."

ELL

Beginning & Intermediate

Have students use the speaking frames and helpful terms to participate in the group discussion. If beginning students are hesitant to participate in a discussion, encourage them by prompting with *yes* or *no* questions.

Advanced & Advanced High

Have students use the speaking frames to participate in the group discussion.

SPEAKING FRAMES

- The student does not understand ____.
- The student uses ____.
- In the first annotation, the student uses ____. He infers that ____ means ____.
- In the second annotation, the student explains ____. He concludes that ____ means ____.

HELPFUL TERMS FOR DISCUSSION

- charity
- issue
- context clues
- pass
- expressions
- surprised

YOUR TURN

Read the conversations in the chart below. Then use the context clues to match the correct meaning to the excerpts.

Meanings	
A	Do not criticize other people for doing the same bad things that you have done.
B	Things that other people have always seem better than the things that you have.
C	You can give a person knowledge and resources, but you cannot force them to do something.

Excerpts	Meaning
Alex: "I already told you how to make a grilled cheese sandwich. Everything you need is in the kitchen. It's easy." Donny: "No, I can't do it. Just do it for me." Alex: "I guess **you can lead a horse to water but you can't make him drink**, huh?"	
Kerry: "You're so lucky to have a sister!" Linda: "What? No, I would rather have a little brother like you do!" Kerry: "I guess **the grass is always greener on the other side.**"	
Dan: "Gary said I cheated at a card game last night. Then he got quiet when I explained that he was caught cheating on a test last week." Samantha: "He needs to learn that **people who live in glass houses should not throw stones!**"	

Your Turn

Ask students to complete the Your Turn Activity.

The meaning of each expression should appear in this order: C, B, A.

A Modern Man from the 1800s: The Influential Life of Charles Dickens

Skill: Visual and Contextual Support

DEFINE

Visual support is an image or an object that helps you understand a text. **Contextual support** is a **feature** that helps you understand a text. By using visual and contextual supports, you can develop your vocabulary so you can better understand a variety of texts.

First, preview the text to identify any visual supports. These might include illustrations, graphics, charts, or other objects in a text. Then, identify any contextual supports. Examples of contextual supports are titles, headers, captions, and boldface terms. Write down your **observations**.

Then, write down what those visual and contextual supports tell you about the meaning of the text. Note any new vocabulary that you see in those supports. Ask your peers and your teacher to **confirm** your understanding of the text.

••• CHECKLIST FOR VISUAL AND CONTEXTUAL SUPPORT

To use visual and contextual support to understand texts, do the following:

- ✓ Preview the text. Read the title, headers, and other features. Look at any images and graphics.
- ✓ Write down the visual and contextual supports in the text.
- ✓ Write down what those supports tell you about the text.
- ✓ Note any new vocabulary that you see in those supports.
- ✓ Create an illustration for the reading and write a descriptive caption.
- ✓ Confirm your observations with your peers and teacher.

Skill: Visual and Contextual Support

Introduce the Skill

Watch the Concept Definition video and read the definition for Visual and Contextual Support.

TURN AND TALK

1. What is visual support? What is an example?
2. What is contextual support? What is an example?
3. How can visual and contextual supports help you if you are struggling to understand a text?

Beginning & Intermediate

SPEAKING FRAMES

- Visual support is ____. For example, ____.
- Contextual support is ____. For example, ____.
- These features can help you ____.

Advanced & Advanced High

SPEAKING FRAMES

- Visual support is ____. For example, ____.
- Contextual support is ____. For example, ____.
- These features can help you understand a text because ____.

SKILL VOCABULARY

visual / visual *adjective* relating to the use of color, lines, and perspective in still and moving images such as illustrations and film

support / el apoyo *noun* a person or thing that offers assistance

contextual / contextual *adjective* depending on the circumstances or situation that something is in COGNATE

feature / la característica *noun* a prominent attribute or aspect of something

observation / la observación *noun* a statement or thought about things one hears or sees COGNATE

confirm / confirmar *verb* to establish validity; to verify, to prove COGNATE

Discuss the Skill Model

1. How does the student preview the text?

   The student reads the title and scans the headers and images.

2. What does the student notice about the headers?

   She notices that the headers are written in italics and are in order by date.

3. How does the student use the image in the second annotation?

   The student uses the image to compare a modern-day Christmas to a Christmas in the 1800s.

4. How does identifying these features help the reader?

   Answers will vary, but should indicate an understanding of how these text features prepare her to read and comprehend the text.

ELL Beginning & Intermediate

Have students use the speaking frames and helpful terms to participate in the group discussion. If beginning students are hesitant to participate in a discussion, encourage them by prompting with *yes* or *no* questions.

Advanced & Advanced High

Have students use the speaking frames to participate in the group discussion.

SPEAKING FRAMES

- The student looks at ____ and ____.
- The student notices ____.
- The student uses the image in order to ____.
- Visual and contextual supports help ____.

HELPFUL TERMS FOR DISCUSSION

- header
- order
- image
- prepare
- italics
- title

YOUR TURN

Read the examples below. Then, complete the chart by sorting the examples into those that are visual supports and those that are contextual supports.

	Examples
A	graphics
B	titles
C	boldface terms
D	captions
E	headers
F	photographs
G	illustrations
H	charts

Visual Supports	Contextual Supports

Your Turn

Ask students to complete the Your Turn Activity.

Visual Supports	Contextual Supports
illustrations	headers
graphics	titles
charts	captions
photographs	boldface terms

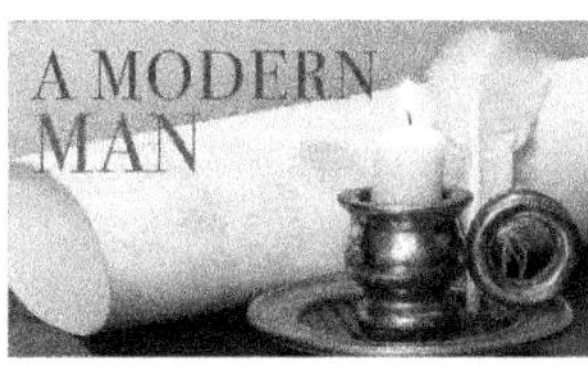

Close Read

WRITE

PERSONAL NARRATIVE: The author of "A Modern Man from the 1800s: The Influential Life of Charles Dickens" claims that Charles Dickens has influenced modern society in several ways. How has an author or piece of fiction influenced you in your personal life? Describe a time when you acted or thought differently after reading a piece of literature. Pay attention to and edit for main and helping verbs.

Use the checklist below to guide you as you write.

- ☐ What author or piece of fiction has influenced you to change?
- ☐ How did you think or act before you read the story?
- ☐ How did you think or act afterward? Why?

Use the sentence frames to organize and write your personal narrative.

I (acted / thought) ____________ differently after reading ____________.

I was influenced by____________.

The (lesson / theme / main idea) ____________ of the text ____________.

Before I read the story, I ____________.

After I read the story, I ____________.

The story changed the way I ____________.

Close Read

Complete Skills Focus

To prepare students to complete the Skills Focus, remind them of the Reading Skill Visual and Contextual Supports. Tell students that one way to better understand ideas in a text is to analyze the visual and contextual supports while you are reading. Direct students to the Skills Focus and remind them to track as you read aloud.

Identify visual and contextual supports that help you understand the topics presented in the article.

Have students complete the Skills Focus in pairs. Ask one partner to focus on the visual supports and the other partner to focus on the contextual supports.

- Have partners explain their findings to each other.
- Have partners discuss how each visual or contextual support helped them to understand the ideas in the text.

Allow students to reread the text and mark down their ideas using the annotation tool, adding an exclamation point (!) to note things they want to remember or that surprise them, and a question mark (?) to note things that confuse them.

Prompt students to work cooperatively to complete their assigned tasks. Circulate around the room and monitor groups as they work.

Collaborative Conversation

Place pairs together into groups of four. Prompt groups to discuss which visual and contextual supports helped them to understand the text.

- What visual and contextual supports did you analyze?
- How did the visual and contextual supports connect to the text?
- How did analyzing the visual and contextual supports improve your understanding of the text?

Collaborative Conversation

BEGINNING, INTERMEDIATE Use the word bank to participate in the group discussion.

ADVANCED Use the speaking frames to participate in the group discussion.

BEGINNING, INTERMEDIATE	ADVANCED
Word Bank	**Speaking Frames**
• connection • detail • helped me understand • image • now I understand • subtitle	• I analyzed ____. • The visual support connected to ____. • The contextual support connected to ____. • Analyzing the visual and contextual supports helped me ____.

Write

PERSONAL NARRATIVE PROMPT: The author of "A Modern Man from the 1800s: The Influential Life of Charles Dickens" claims that Charles Dickens has influenced modern society in several ways. How has an author or piece of fiction influenced you in your personal life? Tell the story of a time when you acted or thought differently after reading a piece of literature. Pay attention to and edit for main and helping verbs.

ELL **BEGINNING** Write a response using the paragraph frames and word banks.

INTERMEDIATE Write a response using the paragraph frames.

INTERMEDIATE
BEGINNING

Paragraph Frames	Word Bank	
I (acted / thought) ____ differently after reading ____. I was influenced by ____. The (lesson / theme / main idea) ____ of the text ____. Before I read the story, I ____. After I read the story, I ____. The story changed the way I ____.	• encourage • feel • important	• plot • teach

In the Extended Oral Project, students plan, draft, practice, and deliver an oral presentation that ties into the theme of the unit and spans informative, argumentative, and narrative genres. Lessons provide explicit instruction to prepare students for the unique challenges of an oral presentation and to help break down the genre characteristics of each prompt. At each step in the process, students focus in-depth on specific writing and speaking skills as they brainstorm, organize, and refine their presentation. Students also receive discussion prompts and frames to guide them in providing effective peer feedback as they practice and discuss in small group before presenting to the class on the final day.

CONNECT TO ESSENTIAL QUESTION

What is the power of the story?

In this unit, students practiced effective collaborative communication skills: making predictions, and comparing and contrasting, while reading and analyzing two texts about supporting traditions and questioning beliefs. Now students will apply those skills to work together in writing and participating in a debate.

Developing Effective Presentations

Form	Language and Conventions	Oral Language Production
Students may struggle with the structure and logic of a formal argument, such as providing reasons and evidence to support their claims.	Students should be encouraged to experiment with more than one type of sentence to help show readers connections between their ideas and provide sentence variety.	Students may make mistakes when they transfer grammatical forms from their native languages into English. Remind students to monitor their use of pronouns when discussing gender and quantity.

SCAFFOLDS

ENGLISH LANGUAGE LEARNERS

Vocabulary, discussion, and peer and teacher support in the Extended Oral Project is differentiated for Beginning, Intermediate, Advanced, and Advanced High English Language Learners. See individual lesson plans for additional scaffolding and and support.

Instructional Path

All Extended Oral Project lessons lesson plans appear in your digital teacher account.

Introduction

Objectives: Students will be able to identify the components of an informative presentation in order to brainstorm and plan their own presentations.

Objectives: Students will be able to record ideas for an informative presentation in writing.

Skill: Acquiring Vocabulary

Objectives: Students will be able to use a graphic organizer to make connections between words and acquire new vocabulary for their informative presentations.

Objectives: Students will be able to brainstorm new words to use in writing their informative presentations.

Plan

Objectives: Students will be able to plan and write a first draft of their presentation

Objectives: Students will be able to organize their first draft using an outline.

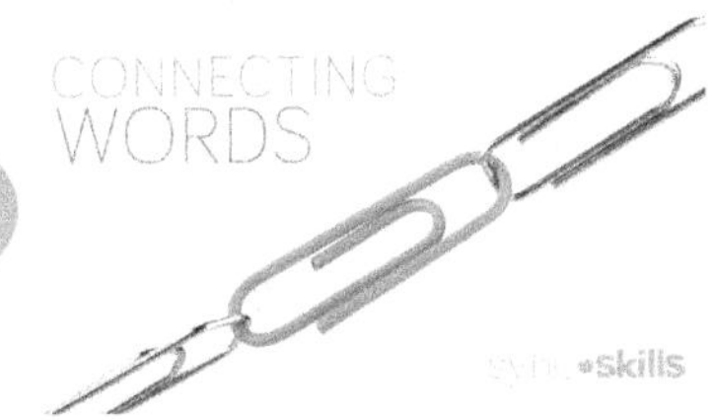

Skill: Connecting Words

Objectives: Students will be able to apply knowledge of connecting words to revise their informative presentations.

Objectives: Students will be able to combine phrases, clauses, and sentences with connecting words orally and in writing.

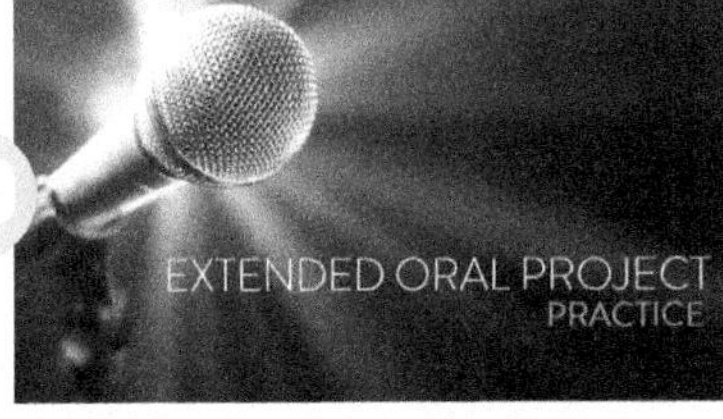

Practice

Objectives: Students will be able to practice and revise their informative presentations based on peer feedback.

Objectives: Students will be able to practice their informative presentations orally and make revisions in writing.

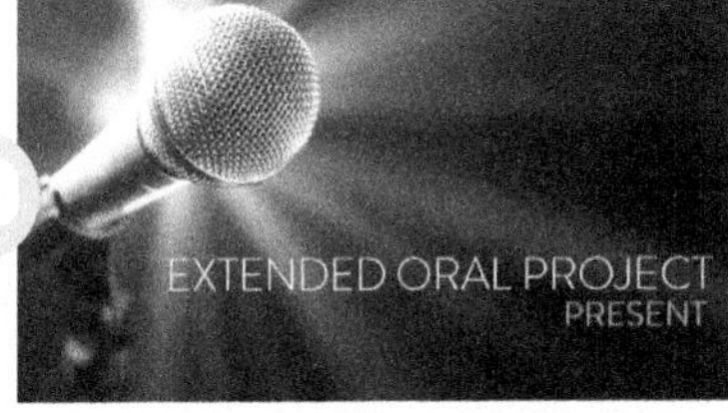

Present

Objectives: Students will be able to observe and perform an informative presentation in order to give and receive peer feedback.

Objectives: Students will be able to use connecting words in an oral presentation and give peer feedback orally and in writing.

Spotlight Skills Review

A review day before the end-of-unit assessment gives you an opportunity to review difficult concepts with students using Spotlight Skills lessons. Spotlight Skills are targeted lessons that provide you resources to reteach or remediate without assigning additional readings. Every Core ELA Skill lesson has a corresponding Spotlight Skill lesson. Spotlight Skills can be assigned at any point in the year, but the end of each unit provides a natural moment to pause, review data collected throughout the unit, and reteach skills students have not yet mastered.

Progress Monitoring

The Progress Monitoring charts that appear before every text in this unit identify standards and associated Spotlight Skills. On review day, you may want to give preference to reteaching skills that are not revisited in later units. You can see where Skills are covered again in the Opportunities to Reteach column.

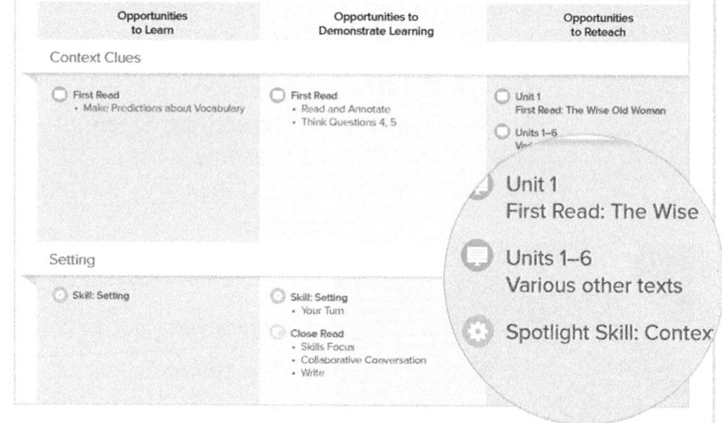

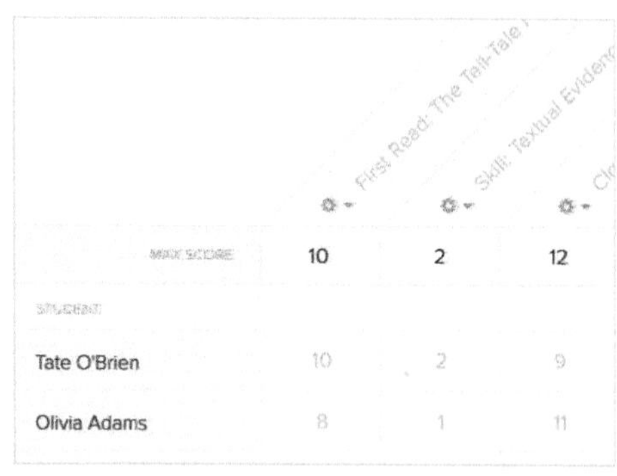

StudySync Gradebook

As students submit assignments on StudySync, their mastery of skills and standards is tracked via the gradebook. The gradebook can be sorted and viewed in a variety of ways. Sorting by assignment shows overall student performance, while sorting by standards or by Skill lessons displays student progress toward mastery goals.

Skills Library 

Spotlight Skills are located in the Skills section of the StudySync Library. You can assign Spotlight Skills to individual students or groups of students. Search tools allow you to search by Skill type or name.

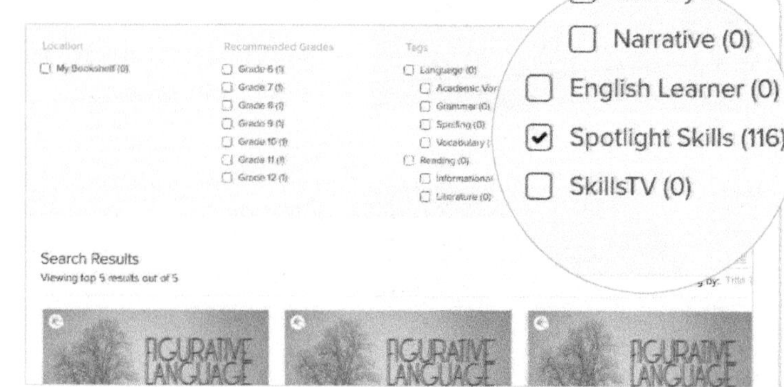

End-of-Unit Assessment

The end-of-unit assessment can be found in two places. The digital version of the assessment can be assigned from the Online Assessment tab inside your ConnectED account. The paper-based version of the assessment can be printed from the End-of-Unit Assessment tab inside this unit in your StudySync account.

Assessment Section	Content	Assessed Skills	
READING	Metaphors Are Our Friends Genre: Non-fiction Word Count: 500 Lexile: 1100	• Context Clues • Summarizing • Textual Evidence	• Figurative Language • Author's Purpose and Point of View
	Aurora Leigh: An excerpt from *Book Nine* Genre: Poetry Word Count: 1000 Lexile: N/A	• Textual Evidence • Figurative Language • Language, Style, and Audience	• Poetic Elements and Structure
	Testing the Limits Genre: Fiction Word Count: 829 Lexile: 1200	• Context Clues • Textual Evidence	• Language, Style, and Audience • Figurative Language
	The Walrus and the Carpenter Genre: Poetry Word Count: 605 Lexile: N/A	• Textual Evidence • Language, Style, and Audience	• Figurative Language • Poetic Elements and Structure
REVISING and **EDITING**	Student Passage #1	• Contested Usage	• Hyphens
	Student Passage #2	• Statements • Examples	• Transitions • Evidence Use
WRITING	Prompt: Research Report	• Research Report	

What's Next?

Assessment results can be viewed by item, standard, and skill to monitor mastery and make decisions for upcoming instruction.

RETEACH skills that students have not yet mastered, using Spotlight Skills or the Test Preparation and Practice book.

REVISE your teaching plan to provide more or less explicit instruction into a skill or text, using Beyond the Book activities for enrichment.

REGROUP students and levels of scaffolding based on standards progress.

Fractured Selves

What causes individuals to feel alienated?

UNIT 5

Fractured Selves

ESSENTIAL QUESTION

What causes individuals to feel alienated?

During the twentieth century, a century with two world wars, many authors and artists wanted their work to reflect reality.

What does more realistic literature tell us about modern life? Why did life become increasingly solitary during that time period? How did World War I and World War II change the way people viewed and experienced their lives? Why do people sometimes feel alienated?

In this unit, students will think about the theme and essential question as they focus on Modernist art and literature. They will explore examples of Modernist poetry such as "The Great Figure" and "The Love Song of J. Alfred Prufrock." They will also read the Modernist short stories "A Cup of Tea" and "The New Dress" along with an excerpt from the play *The Glass Menagerie*. The poems "miss rosie," "The Idler," "Hurricane Season," and "Pearl Divers' Daughters" also allow students to consider how feelings of alienation can result from a variety of situations. Furthermore, the nonfiction texts *A Room of One's Own*, "Be Ye Men of Valour," *Killers of the Dream*, and "Shooting an Elephant" encourage students to think about the power of the written word to reflect important historical events and the alienation that individuals experience.

Students will begin this unit as readers, and they will finish as writers, as they apply what they have learned about story elements to their own literary analysis essays.

Unit Structure

Every StudySync unit can be taught two ways.
Pacing Guides for each option are provided on pages that follow.

A Thematic Option

The thematic option provides 30 days of integrated reading and writing instruction with a series of short texts connected to a common theme.

B Novel Study Option

Each novel study option provides 30 days of comparative texts with integrated reading and writing instruction.

Thematic Selections

Genre Focus
ARGUMENTATIVE TEXT

Novel Study Choices

1984
FICTION
George Orwell

Frankenstein
FICTION
Mary Shelley

The Bluest Eye
FICTION
Toni Morrison

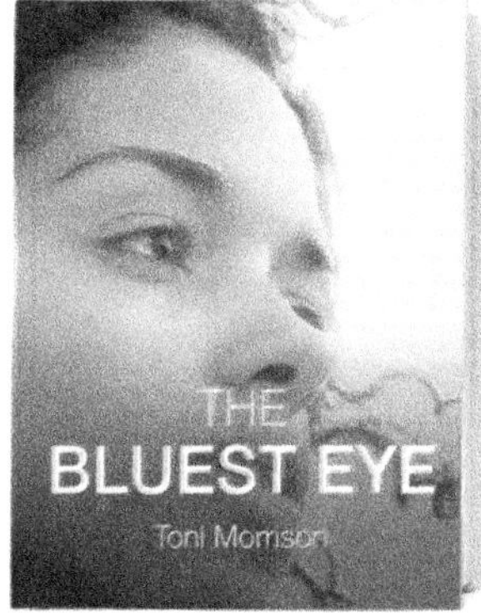

Fractured Selves

(tv) StudySyncTV or SkillsTV Episode

Pacing Guide

Days	Readings	Skill and Standard Instruction	Skill Practice and Spiraling
1	Essential Question **The Big Idea: What causes individuals to feel alienated?** p. 338	• Literary Focus: Modernism • Recognizing Genre • Academic Vocabulary	
2-5	PAIRED READINGS **The Great Figure** p. 352 **The Love Song of J. Alfred Prufrock** (tv) p. 362	• Language, Style, and Audience (tv) • Poetic Elements and Structure • Compare and Contrast	• Textual Evidence • Literary Analysis Writing • Collaborative Conversations
6-9	PAIRED READINGS **miss rosie** p. 384 **The Idler** (tv) p. 392 **A Cup of Tea** (tv) p. 402	• Word Patterns and Relationships • Summarizing	• Theme • Point of View • Comparative Writing • Collaborative Conversations
10-12	**The Glass Menagerie** p. 426	• Dramatic Elements and Structure • Media	• Textual Evidence • Comparative Writing
13-14	**A Room of One's Own** p. 452		• Central or Main Idea • Informational Text Structure • Author's Purpose and Point of View • Argumentative Writing
15-16	**The New Dress** p. 462		• Textual Evidence • Theme • Language, Style, and Audience • Narrative Writing

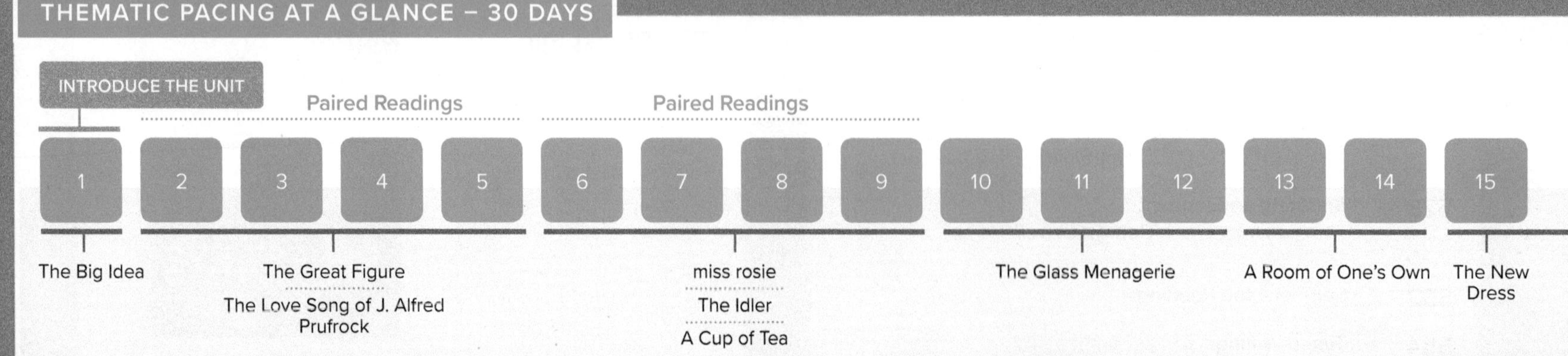

Days	Readings	Skill and Standard Instruction	Skill Practice and Spiraling
17	Hurricane Season p. 476		• Textual Evidence • Point of View • Literary Analysis Writing
18-21	Be Ye Men of Valour p. 486	• Informational Text Structure (tv) • Central or Main Idea • Word Meaning	• Textual Evidence • Rhetorical Analysis Writing
22	The Pearl Divers' Daughters p. 508		• Point of View • Theme • Informative Writing
23-26	PAIRED READINGS **Killers of the Dream** p. 518 **Shooting an Elephant** p. 528	• Author's Purpose and Point of View • Connotation and Denotation • Figurative Language • Analyzing Modernism	• Textual Evidence • Summarizing • Rhetorical Analysis Writing
27	**Self-Selected Reading and Response** p. 552	• Independent Reading	• Personal Response Writing
28	**Timed Writing** p. 554		• Timed Writing

Review and Assessment See page 634.

Days	Review and Assessment	Skill Practice and Assessment
29	**Skills Review** p. 634	Students will have the opportunity to complete one or more Spotlight Skill lessons in order to improve understanding and further practice skills from the unit that they found most challenging.
30	**End-of-Unit Assessment** p. 635	For more details, please see the End-of-Unit Assessment information for Grade 12 Unit 5 on page 635.

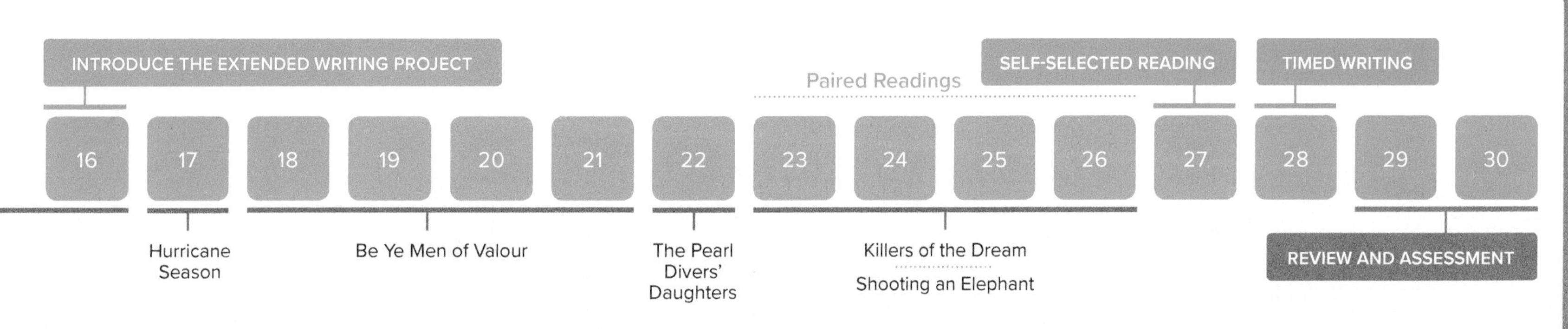

Extended Writing Project and Grammar

Pacing Guide

In the second half of the unit, students continue exploring texts that address the unit's Essential Question and begin crafting a longer composition to share their own ideas about the Essential Question in the Extended Writing Project. The writing project will take your students through the writing process to produce a literary analysis essay.

Extended Writing Project Prompt

Why is alienation such a common theme in Modernist literature?

Consider all the texts you have read in this unit, and reflect on how alienation impacts those who experience it. Then, select three characters or speakers from the texts. Write a literary analysis essay to examine how the authors explore the theme of alienation through these three characters or speakers. In your conclusion, synthesize the ideas in these texts about alienation in the modern world.

Days	Extended Writing Project and Grammar	Skill and Standard Instruction	Connect to Mentor Texts
16	**Literary Analysis Writing Process: Plan** p. 564		
17-20	**Literary Analysis Writing Process: Draft** p. 578	• Reasons and Relevant Evidence • Thesis Statement • Organizing Argumentative Writing	• Be Ye Men of Valour • Killers of the Dream
21-23	**Literary Analysis Writing Process: Revise** p. 591	• Introductions • Transitions • Conclusions	• Be Ye Men of Valour • Killers of the Dream
24-26	**Literary Analysis Writing Process: Edit and Publish** p. 600	• Using a Style Guide • Commonly Misspelled Words • Pronoun Case and Reference	Additional grammar lessons can be found in the StudySync Skills Library.

Research

The following lessons include opportunities for research:

Blast **Behind the Screen** Research Links*

Independent Read **The Great Figure** Developing Background Knowledge

Blast **All the Lonely People** Research Links*

Independent Read **miss rosie** Text to World (Beyond)

Independent Read **A Room of One's Own** Developing Background Knowledge

Blast **Power to the Poets** Research Links*

Independent Read **The Pearl Divers' Daughters** Write

Independent Read **Killers of the Dream** Beyond the Book

Close Read **Shooting an Elephant** Beyond the Book

*See the teacher lesson plan online

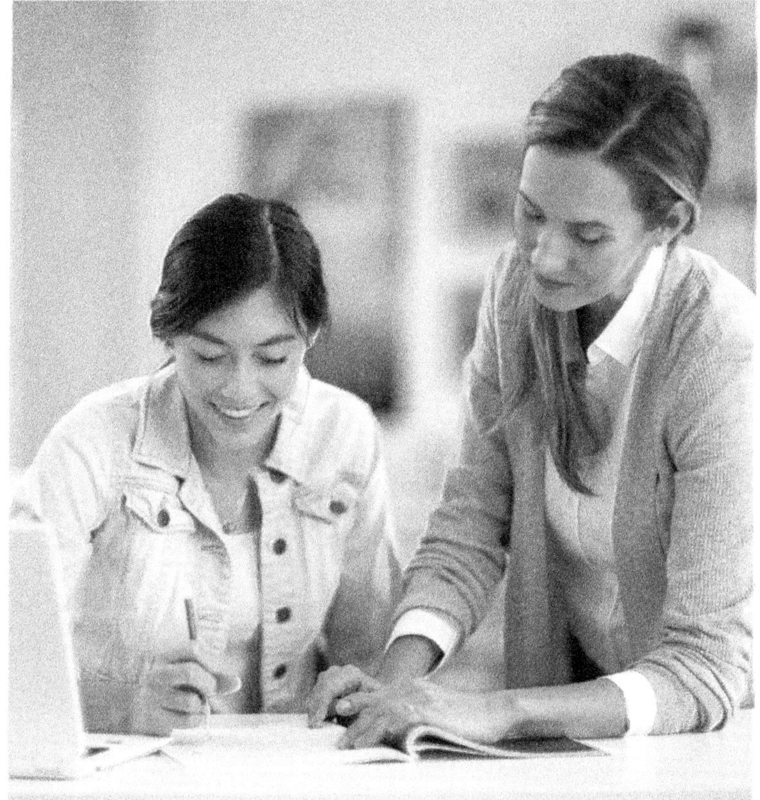

Self-Selected Reading Prompt

After reading a self-selected text, students will respond to the following informative prompt:

The first films were just shots of people doing ordinary things, demonstrating the new technology. Among the first to actually tell a story was Le Voyage dans la lune, or A Trip to the Moon, by Georges Méliès. It was based on a novel by Jules Verne. From the beginning of film history, writing has inspired movies.

How would you adapt a text to film?

Imagine you were tasked with using this text to inspire a film—it could be a movie or documentary. What would your film be about? What aspects of the text (e.g., topic, themes, characters, style, setting, etc.) would you use to inspire your film?

Timed Writing Prompt

Students will respond to the following SAT-style rhetorical analysis prompt:

Write an essay in which you explain how the author builds an argument to persuade their audience that violent movies are negatively impacting our society.

In your essay, analyze how the author uses one or more of the features in the directions that precede the passage (or features of your own choice) to strengthen the logic and persuasiveness of their argument. Be sure that your analysis focuses on the most relevant features of the passage.

Unit Overview

1984

George Orwell

At-a-Glance

Author
George Orwell

Genre
Fiction

Publication Year
1949

Text Complexity
1090L

Themes & Topics

Dystopia

Science Fiction

Totalitarianism

On Airstrip One (once Great Britain) in the alliance of Oceania, the "future" year is 1984 (the final digits reversed from 1948, when the book was written). It's a world divided between three dictatorial powers constantly at war. Revising history and the meaning of words to control thought, there is no love in Oceania except for Big Brother. When a co-worker at the Ministry of Truth passes Winston Smith a love note, his descent into subversive "thoughtcrime" begins.

Critic and journalist George Orwell (1903–1950) covered poverty and war in books like *Down and Out in Paris and London* and *Homage to Catalonia* but is best known for the novels *Animal Farm* and *1984*. Both depict collective dystopias run by vicious, controlling regimes, a condition for which the word 'Orwellian' has been coined.

NOVEL STUDY PACING AT A GLANCE – 30 DAYS

Text	Days	Paired Reading(s)
1984 PT. 1, CH. I–III	1, 2, 3, 4, 5	Paired Readings: The Great Figure; The Love Song of J. Alfred Prufrock
1984 PT. 1, CH. IV–PT. 2, CH. IV	6, 7, 8, 9, 10, 11	Paired Reading: The Glass Menagerie
1984 PT. 2, CH. V–VIII	12, 13, 14, 15	Paired Reading: Be Ye Men of Valour

Pacing Guide: 1984

Days	Readings	Paired Readings	Skill and Standard Instruction	Skill Practice and Spiraling
1-5	**1984** Part 1, Ch. I–III	The Great Figure The Love Song of J. Alfred Prufrock (tv)	• Language, Style, and Audience (tv) • Poetic Elements and Structure • Compare and Contrast	• Textual Evidence • Literary Analysis Writing • Collaborative Conversations
6-11	**1984** Part 1, Ch. IV– Part 2, Ch. IV	The Glass Menagerie	• Dramatic Elements and Structure • Media	• Textual Evidence • Comparative Writing
12-15	**1984** Part 2, Ch. V–VIII	Be Ye Men of Valour	• Informational Text Structure (tv) • Central or Main Idea • Word Meaning	• Textual Evidence • Rhetorical Analysis Writing
16-18	**1984** Part 2, Ch. IX–X	miss rosie The Idler A Cup of Tea (tv)	• Word Patterns and Relationships • Summarizing	• Theme • Point of View • Comparative Writing • Collaborative Conversations
19-23	**1984** Part 3, Ch. I–VI	Shooting an Elephant	• Author's Purpose and Point of View • Connotation and Denotation • Figurative Language	• Textual Evidence • Rhetorical Analysis Writing
24-28	**Culminating Writing Task**	Recommended for instruction with this unit's Culminating Writing Task.	• Reasons and Relevant Evidence • Thesis Statement • Organizing Argumentative Writing • Introductions • Transitions • Conclusions • Using a Style Guide	• Commonly Misspelled Words • Pronoun Case and Reference

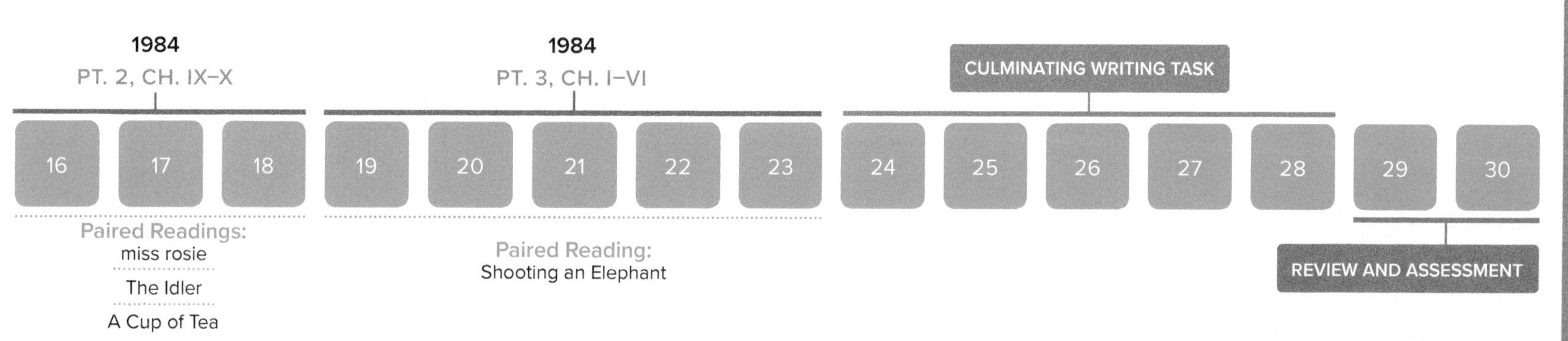

FRANKENSTEIN

Mary Shelley

At-a-Glance

Author
Mary Shelley

Genre
Fiction

Publication Year
1818

Text Complexity
1170L

Themes & Topics

Horror

Supernatural

Revenge

Studying at a college in Germany, Victor Frankenstein successfully re-animates a creature assembled from the parts of corpses. Quickly horrified by his own creation, Victor abandons it and tries to return to a normal life—but the creature soon seeks revenge on its creator. Shelley's novel was at once the genesis of three genres that have left an indelible mark on storytelling: horror, science-fiction, and Gothic literature.

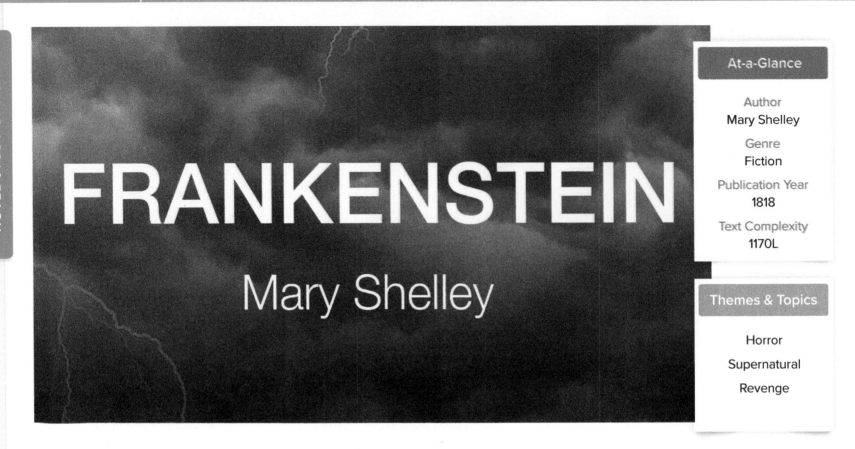

Daughter of political philosophers William Godwin and Mary Wollstonecraft, Mary Shelley (1797–1851) wrote *Frankenstein* when she was only 19 years old. She famously came up with the idea for *Frankenstein* in a ghost story-writing contest with her husband, Percy Shelley, and the poet Lord Byron, the three of them trapped indoors on a rainy summer holiday.

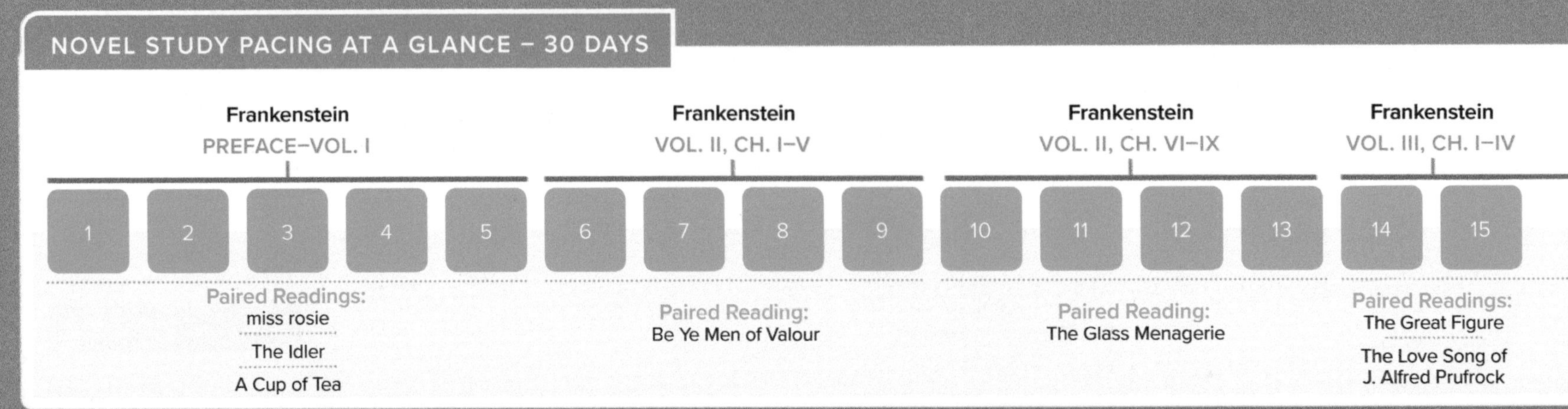

Days	Readings	Paired Readings	Skill and Standard Instruction	Skill Practice and Spiraling
1-5	**Frankenstein** Preface – Volume I	miss rosie The Idler A Cup of Tea (tv)	• Word Patterns and Relationships • Summarizing	• Theme • Collaborative Conversations
6-9	**Frankenstein** Volume II, Chapters I–V	Be Ye Men of Valour	• Informational Text Structure (tv) • Central or Main Idea • Word Meaning	• Textual Evidence • Rhetorical Analysis Writing
10-13	**Frankenstein** Volume II, Chapters VI–IX	The Glass Menagerie	• Dramatic Elements and Structure • Media	• Textual Evidence • Comparative Writing
14-18	**Frankenstein** Volume III, Chapters I–IV	The Great Figure The Love Song of J. Alfred Prufrock (tv)	• Language, Style, and Audience (tv) • Poetic Elements and Structure • Compare and Contrast	• Textual Evidence • Literary Analysis Writing • Collaborative Conversations
19-23	**Frankenstein** Volume III, Chapters V–VII	Shooting an Elephant	• Author's Purpose and Point of View • Connotation and Denotation • Figurative Language	• Textual Evidence • Rhetorical Analysis Writing
24-28	**Culminating Writing Task**	Recommended for instruction with this unit's Culminating Writing Task.	• Reasons and Relevant Evidence • Thesis Statement • Organizing Argumentative Writing • Introductions • Transitions • Conclusions • Using a Style Guide	• Commonly Misspelled Words • Pronoun Case and Reference

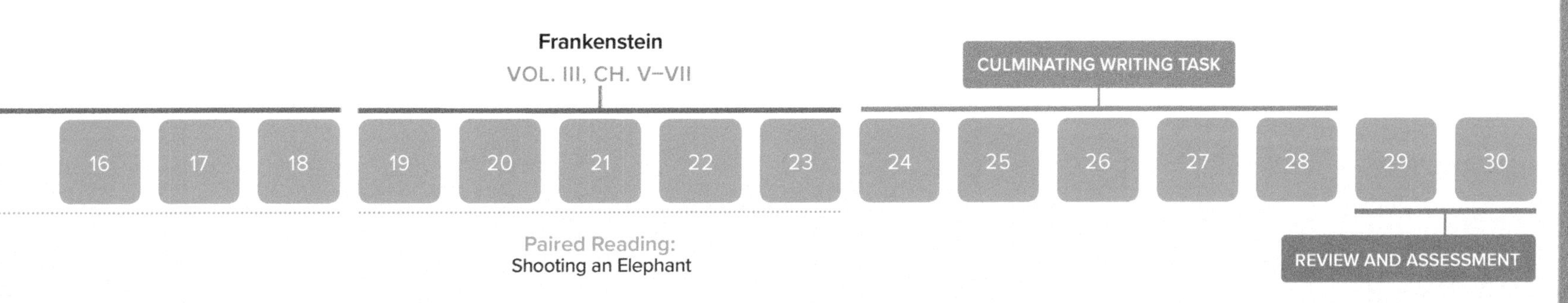

THE BLUEST EYE

Toni Morrison

At-a-Glance

Author
Toni Morrison

Genre
Fiction

Publication Year
1970

Text Complexity
920L

Themes & Topics

Coming of Age

Racism

African Americans

Pecola grows up poor in foster care, and her white classmates call her “ugly” for her dark skin. At home, she fantasizes of having blue eyes like the dolls of her childhood. Narrated by her foster sister, Claudia MacTeer, the novel explores Pecola’s roots and her struggles to transcend a young life shaped by instability, abuse, and a persistent sense of inferiority.

Toni Morrison (b. 1931) is the Nobel Prize-winning author of *The Bluest Eye, Song of Solomon,* and *Beloved*. Her novels are frequently cited among the greatest works of contemporary literature and have earned her many honors, including the Presidential Medal of Freedom. Retiring from teaching at Princeton in 2006, she remains on the board of *The Nation* magazine.

Pacing Guide: The Bluest Eye

Days	Readings	Paired Readings	Skill and Standard Instruction	Skill Practice and Spiraling
1-4	**The Bluest Eye** Pt 1 (Foreword, P. ix–xii; P. 3–32	miss rosie The Idler A Cup of Tea (tv)	• Word Patterns and Relationships • Summarizing	• Theme • Collaborative Conversations
5-9	**The Bluest Eye** P. 33–58	Be Ye Men of Valour	• Informational Text Structure (tv) • Central or Main Idea • Word Meaning	• Textual Evidence • Rhetorical Analysis Writing
10-13	**The Bluest Eye** P. 59–93	The Glass Menagerie	• Dramatic Elements and Structure • Media	• Textual Evidence • Comparative Writing
14-18	**The Bluest Eye** P. 94–153	The Great Figure The Love Song of J. Alfred Prufrock (tv)	• Language, Style, and Audience (tv) • Poetic Elements and Structure • Compare and Contrast	• Textual Evidence • Literary Analysis Writing • Collaborative Conversations
19-23	**The Bluest Eye** P. 154–206	Shooting an Elephant	• Author's Purpose and Point of View • Connotation and Denotation • Figurative Language	• Textual Evidence • Rhetorical Analysis Writing
24-28	Culminating Writing Task	Recommended for instruction with this unit's Culminating Writing Task.	• Reasons and Relevant Evidence • Thesis Statement • Organizing Argumentative Writing • Introductions • Transitions • Conclusions • Using a Style Guide	• Commonly Misspelled Words • Pronoun Case and Reference

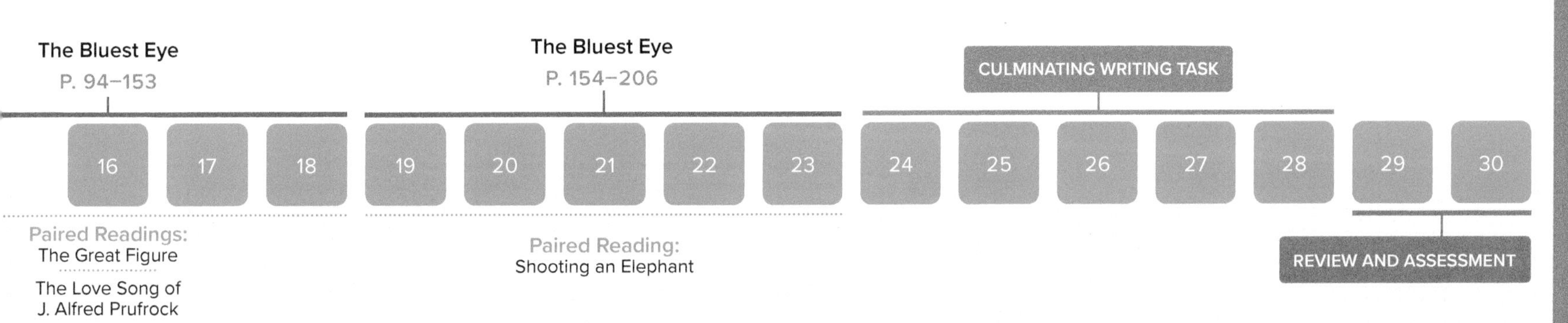

Integrated Scaffolding

ELL and Approaching grade-level students receive scaffolds for every lesson, whether in the Thematic, Novel Study or ELL Resources sections of the unit. Specific scaffolds are intentionally designed to support the needs of English Language Learners and Approaching grade-level students in the ELA classroom. Other scaffolds exist as part of the many standard features in the StudySync digital platform and can be strategically utilized to support students' comprehension and engagement.

English Language Learner Resources

Both Thematic and Novel Study units include English Language Learner resources designed to match the thematic focus, text structures, and writing form of the unit. ELL resources include two leveled texts and an extended oral project.

ELL Texts	Differentiated Text Levels	Skill and Standard Instruction
	BEGINNING 770L I 609 words INTERMEDIATE 900L I 640 words ADVANCED 1010L I 695 words ADVANCED HIGH 1110L I 747 words Use this text in place of or as an extension to "The Love Song of J. Alfred Prufrock."	• Sight Vocabulary and High-Frequency Words • Using Prereading Supports • Language Structures • Supporting Evidence • Spelling Patterns and Rules
	BEGINNING 620L I 288 words INTERMEDIATE 900L I 607 words ADVANCED 980L I 676 words ADVANCED HIGH 1100L I 713 words Use this text in place of or as an extension to "The New Dress."	• Classroom Vocabulary • Making Connections • Analyzing Expressions • Visual and Contextual Support • Negatives and Contractions
EXTENDED ORAL PROJECT INTRODUCTION	In this Extended Oral Project, students will write and perform a monologue. This may be assigned in place of this unit's EWP.	• Acquiring Vocabulary • Sentence Types

Focus on English Language Proficiency Levels

ADVANCED HIGH
ADVANCED
INTERMEDIATE
BEGINNING

ELL Resources provide targeted support for four levels of proficiency: Beginning, Intermediate, Advanced, and Advanced High. Instruction and scaffolds, as well as the texts themselves, are differentiated based on these levels.

Additional differentiated scaffolds include visual glossaries, speaking and writing frames, and suggested grouping for peer and teacher support. Lessons also include suggested extension activities to challenge Advanced and Advanced High students as they progress through the year.

Assessment

DAYS 29-30

Assessment in StudySync is built upon a recursive cycle that includes assessment, instruction, and review. Screening, placement, and benchmark assessments help teachers establish baselines and determine scaffold needs. Throughout the course of instruction, teachers regularly assess student progress using formative and summative measures, and use the individualized data from those assessments to guide choices about instruction, review, remediation, and enrichment to bring all students to standards mastery and College and Career Readiness.

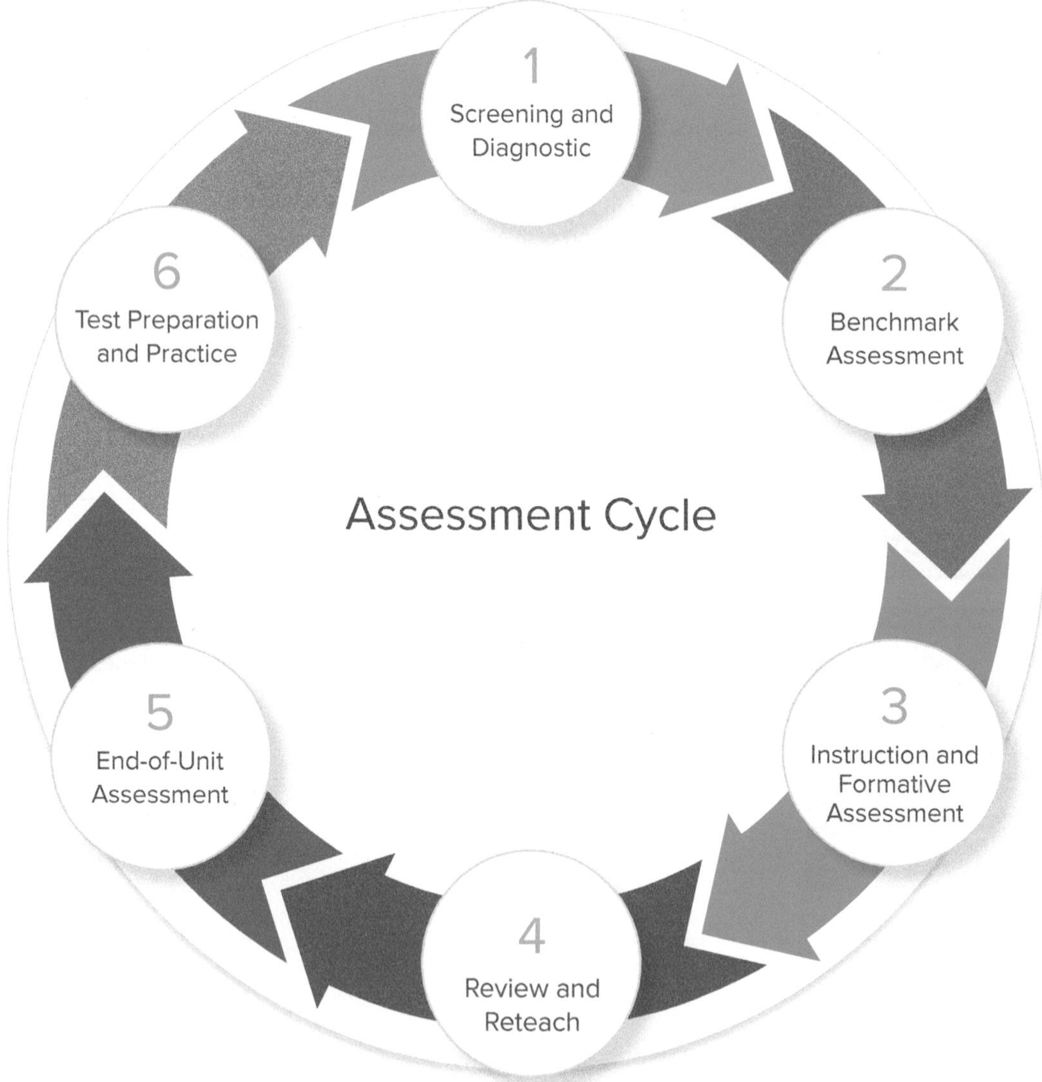

What's Next?

Assessment results can be viewed by item, standard, and skill to monitor mastery and make decisions for upcoming instruction.

- ✓ Reteach skills that students have not yet mastered, using Spotlight Skills or the Test Preparation and Practice book.
- ✓ Revise your teaching plan to provide more or less explicit instruction into a skill or text, using Beyond the Book activities for enrichment.
- ✓ Regroup students and levels of scaffolding based on standards progress.

Review

Spotlight Skills Review

A review day before the end-of-unit assessment gives you an opportunity to review difficult concepts with students using Spotlight Skills lessons. Spotlight Skills are targeted lessons that provide you resources to reteach or remediate without assigning additional readings. Every Core ELA Skill lesson has a corresponding Spotlight Skill lesson. Spotlight Skills can be assigned at any point in the year, but the end of each unit provides a natural moment to pause, review data collected throughout the unit, and reteach skills students have not yet mastered.

Progress Monitoring

The Progress Monitoring charts that appear before every text in this unit identify standards and associated Spotlight Skills. On review day, you may want to give preference to reteaching skills that are not revisited in later units. You can see where skills are covered again in the Opportunities to Reteach column.

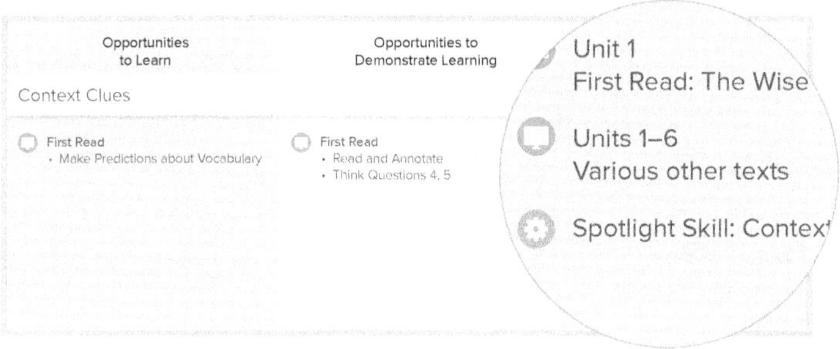

StudySync Gradebook

As students submit assignments on StudySync, their mastery of skills and standards is tracked via the gradebook. The gradebook can be sorted and viewed in a variety of ways. Sorting by assignment shows overall student performance, while sorting by standards or by skill lessons displays student progress toward mastery goals.

Skills Library

Spotlight Skills are located in the Skills section of the StudySync Library. You can assign Spotlight Skills to individual students or groups of students. Search tools allow you to search by skill type or name.

End-of-Unit Assessment

Assessed Reading Skills

- ✓ Author's Purpose and Point of View
- ✓ Central or Main Idea
- ✓ Compare and Contrast
- ✓ Dramatic Elements and Structure
- ✓ Figurative Language
- ✓ Informational Text Structure
- ✓ Poetic Elements and Structure
- ✓ Summarizing
- ✓ Word Meaning
- ✓ Word Patterns and Relationships

Revising, Editing, and Writing Skills

- ✓ Commonly Misspelled Words
- ✓ Introductions and Conclusions
- ✓ Organizing Argumentative Writing
- ✓ Pronoun Case and Reference
- ✓ Reasons and Relevant Evidence
- ✓ Thesis Statement
- ✓ Transitions
- ✓ Using a Style Guide

Unit Preview

Introduce the Unit

As a class, watch the unit preview and discuss the questions below.

- What two words would you use to describe this video?
- What key words or images from the video do you think will be most important to this unit?

Instructional Path

Big Idea Blast

Objectives: After exploring background information and research links about a topic, students will respond to a question with a 140-character response.

Literary Focus: Modernism

Objectives: After an initial reading about Modernism, students will be able to identify and describe characteristics of the literary period.

RECOGNIZING GENRE

Skill: Recognize Genre

Objectives: After learning about the genre of argumentative writing, students will be able to identify and describe characteristics of argumentative texts.

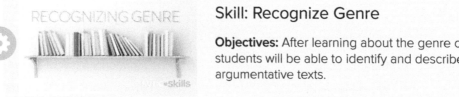

Skill: Academic Vocabulary

Objectives: After learning the meanings of ten academic vocabulary words, students will be able to recognize and use them in a variety of contexts.

DIGITAL ONLY

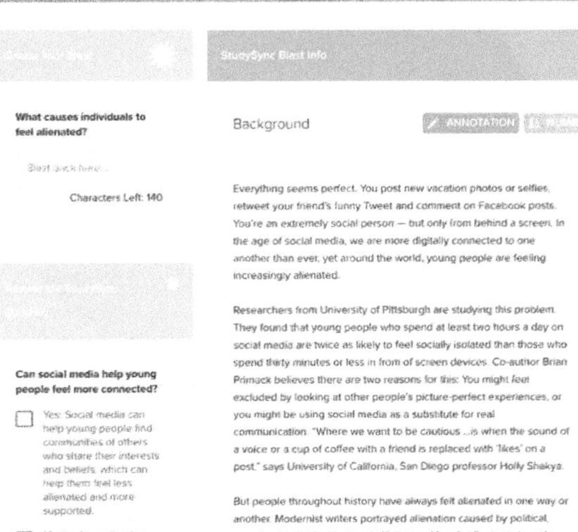

Blast: Fractured Selves

What causes individuals to feel alienated?

TEXT TALK

What did researchers at the University of Pittsburgh find? (Researchers found that young people who spend at least two hours a day on social media are twice as likely to feel isolated than those who have 30 minutes or less of screen time.)

How could schools work to combat loneliness? (School programs could teach students how to build and maintain friendships as well as how to reframe negative responses in social situations.)

Why are some immigrants drawn to their home countries? (Immigrants are drawn to where people speak their language and they feel a connection with the culture.)

Create Your Own Blast

SCAFFOLDS

Ask students to write a 140-character Blast after they complete the QuikPoll.

Use the scaffolds below to differentiate instruction for your ELL English Language Learners.

BEGINNING Write a response using the word bank to complete the sentence frame.

INTERMEDIATE Write a response using the sentence frame.

ADVANCED, ADVANCED HIGH Write a response using the sentence starter.

BEGINNING		INTERMEDIATE	ADVANCED, ADVANCED HIGH
Word Bank		**Sentence Frame**	**Sentence Starter**
social media transition hostility	inadequate disconnected unwelcome	People feel alienated because ___ makes them feel ___.	• People feel alienated because . . .

Introduction to Modernist Art and Literature

Introduction

This informational text provides readers with historical and cultural background information about the early 20th century and the formation of Modernism. "Introduction to Modernist Art and Literature" explains how the onset of the Great War and the breakdown of colonialism led to unprecedented work among artists who were intent on defying old rules and values. Modernist painters, such as Pablo Picasso, and writers, such as T.S. Eliot, were disillusioned by the manipulation of power and technology and the dreadful effects that these had on society. Modernists attempted to deal with their frightening reality by creating work that challenged age-old institutions and principles.

"Inspiring heroes and happy endings were no longer a requirement for good writing."

NOTES

1 Throughout the history of storytelling, animals have been used to impart lessons to audiences. There are the trickster gods of various cultures, like the western Native Americans' Coyote, India's Hanuman the monkey, and Anansi the spider from West Africa. Aesop used animal characters so frequently in his fables that it became a defining characteristic of the genre. More recent stories with animal characters are Rudyard Kipling's collection *The Jungle Book*, published in 1894, and George Orwell's *Animal Farm*, published in 1945. Despite the surface similarities, however, these stories send remarkably different messages. In *The Jungle Book*, Mowgli, a human raised by wolves, learns to obey the "law of the jungle" and find his place in their social order. In *Animal Farm*, a group of farm animals overthrow the human farmers and try to set up their own society. Under the guise of furthering equality, the cunning pigs compete with each other to take over and create a horrifying dictatorship. In less than fifty years, popular books went from praising the virtues of societies to sharp condemnations of their oppressive elements. This sudden change reflects the cultural revolution of Modernism, a movement that broke all the rules by creating new aesthetic forms that reconciled—or broke from—the past.

A Shrinking Empire

2 Rudyard Kipling and George Orwell are two of Britain's best known writers. Both were born in India and lived in British colonies for parts of their childhoods and adult lives. Both experienced British **imperialism** firsthand, but they had completely opposite opinions of it. This difference can be attributed to the dominant cultures of their generations. Kipling was born in 1865, and so his views are representative of the late Victorian era. Kipling thought imperialism fueled growth and progress and, like many in the Victorian era, he sincerely believed that the British were civilizing the world. He became known as a strong supporter of British colonialism.

SELECTION VOCABULARY

imperialism / el imperialismo *noun* a policy of extending the power of a country by acquiring new land, often through military force or political maneuvering COGNATE

First Read

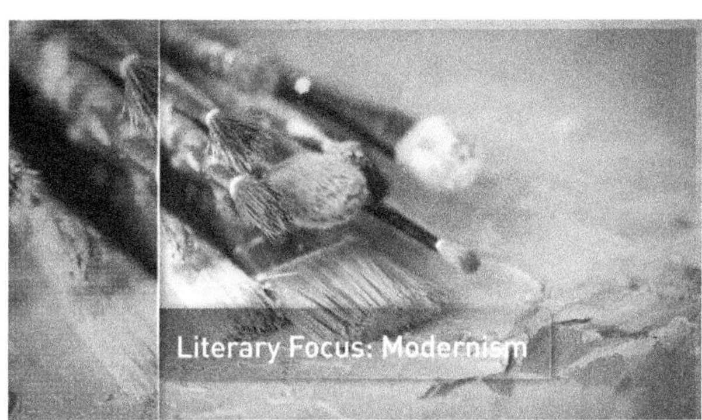

Introduce the Text

As a class, watch the video preview and have students read the introduction in pairs to make connections to the video preview. Ask students:

- How do the images, words, and music in this video make you feel?
- What questions do you have after reading the introduction?

SPEAKING FRAMES

- The video made me feel ____.
- I would like to know ____.

Storming of Delhi, Thomas H. Sherratt & Matthew Somerville Morgan (1857). Depiction of the Sepoy uprising (1857–1858) against British rule, known as the Indian Mutiny.

3 Orwell was born in 1903. He didn't witness the explosive growth of the British Empire or see how it brought new resources and wealth to the United Kingdom. Instead, he witnessed its human costs. As a young man, Orwell worked for the Indian Imperial Police in Burma (now Myanmar). He saw growing resentment from the Burmese people living under British rule. He saw how the British empire took advantage of their labor and resources while enforcing a social hierarchy where the colonists were on top and the indigenous people were on the bottom. Orwell was so ashamed of the role he played in this injustice that he eventually resigned from his job and turned to writing.

4 When the British Empire peaked in the early twentieth century, it controlled about a quarter of the world's population. In the coming decades, however, its control would begin to shrink. The shrinking of the empire began close to home. All but six of the counties of Ireland, Britain's first colony, broke off from the United Kingdom to form the Irish Free State in 1922. India and Pakistan followed in 1947, then Sri Lanka and Burma in 1948, Ghana in 1957, to name a few. Several factors allowed these countries to free themselves from British rule. There was a growth in nationalism and a desire for independence within the colonies. There was also a growing distaste for imperialism among the British. More and more people living under British rule were siding with George Orwell in the belief that "civilizing the world" while pillaging its resources and exploiting indigenous people was wrong. A key part of the Modernist movement was a rebellion against older traditions, and this was due to a strong sense of disillusionment, particularly after World War I.

World at War

5 The United Kingdom of Great Britain and Northern Ireland was the strongest empire of the time leading up to World War I, but not the only one. France, having recovered from a series of revolutions and regime changes, began competing with Britain for control of Africa. Russia, the Ottoman Empire, and Austro-Hungarian Empire competed for control of eastern Europe. In the middle of all of this, Germany gained power with such rapidity that Great

TEXT TALK

What factors caused the British Empire to shrink?

See paragraph 4: A rise in nationalism in the colonies, a growing distaste for imperialism by the British, and warfare caused the British Empire to shrink.

Why was World War I so shocking to people?

See paragraph 5: The enormous scale of the war and new weapons made it much more brutal than anyone expected.

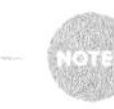

Britain made alliances with Russia and France, despite their being historical enemies. Borders shifted, governments rose and fell, and alliances formed and broke. When a Serbian assassin killed Archduke Franz Ferdinand of Austria-Hungary, it sparked a **conflagration**. Country after country declared war to support their allies or oppose their enemies. World War I had begun.

Battle of Ypres, (1915) by Achille Beltrame.
The effects of poison gases in World War I.

6 The Great War, as it was called at the time, was brutal. Young soldiers had grown up on stories of glorious charges into the enemy line to fight with rifles and bayonets. They were unprepared for machine guns and mustard gas. They did not expect to spend weeks hiding in filthy trenches while listening to the sounds of gunshots and explosions. By the end of the war in 1919, 8.5 million soldiers were dead. More people were killed in WWI than in every previous European conflict combined. The scale of the bloodshed and destruction disillusioned a generation of artists and thinkers who would be central to Modernism. The Central Powers, consisting of the German, Austro-Hungarian, and Ottoman Empires, had all broken up. The Russian Empire also dissolved and was replaced by the Soviet Union. Germany suffered two economic crises while trying to pay reparations, which led to feelings of resentment. This fueled extremism, leading to the rise of Adolf Hitler and the Second World War.

7 World War II was even more brutal than its predecessor, leaving 40–50 million dead. The United Kingdom was among the victors, but it had suffered immensely from the war. Germany used a tactic they called *Blitzkrieg*, literally "lightning war." From September 1940 to May 1941, the German Air Force, or *Luftwaffe*, conducted nighttime bombing raids targeting London and other major British cities. By targeting civilians, they had hoped to demoralize Britain and force them out of the war. Germany failed to kill the British spirit, but they did do severe damage to their cities and infrastructure. Also, with so many young people dead, the government needed to organize a way to care

SELECTION VOCABULARY

conflagration / la conflagración *noun* a war or conflict COGNATE

for the unemployed, the sick, and the elderly. Under the Labour Party, the UK government created a system of national health care. Between this and rebuilding, the United Kingdom had little money left for running an empire. Most of the remaining colonies of the British Empire gained independence in quick succession. Some of the British felt embarrassed by this loss of stature, but others were relieved to be finished with imperialism.

A New World

8 The seeds of Modernism began to sprout before the First World War, but it was between the wars that the movement truly flourished. War had not only devastated the world physically; it was a shock to the psyche as well. The British—as well as Continental Europeans—began to question whether imperialism was really spreading civilization. They also realized that the world was not as beautiful or polite as the Romantics and Victorians had claimed. Improved technology had promised better communication and more productive lives, but it was used to create unimaginable destruction during the war. Put simply, everything people thought they knew was wrong. Modernism was a search for a new way to look at the world. Modernists felt that the old forms of art depicting Western civilization needed to be recreated in order to still have meaning. Their movement was a rebellion against old traditions and conventions.

Modernist painter Pablo Picasso posing with paintings and ceramics.

9 Modernism took hold in visual arts before it spread to literature. Artists became less interested in trying to create realistic depictions of the world around them. Cubism, developed by Georges Braque and Pablo Picasso, rejected conventions of perspective, foreshortening, modeling, and chiaroscuro, or contrasting light and shade. Instead, Cubists used sharp, geometric angles to create a fragmented vision of the world. They would

TEXT TALK

Why was Modernism so focused on breaking traditions and conventions?

See paragraph 8: The great changes in society and people's perspectives made old traditions seem irrelevant.

NOTES

show multiple sides of a subject at the same time, creating a new view of reality. **Surrealism** also became popular. Surrealist art, influenced by Sigmund Freud and his system of psychoanalysis, intentionally defied reason by combining dreamlike images and reality. Other Modernist art movements include Futurism, Expressionism, Constructivism, de Stijl, and Abstract Expressionism. These various movements did not try to capture a visual scene; they tried to capture movement, thought, emotion, and other abstractions that can't normally be portrayed on a canvas.

10 The artistic and literary communities of Modernism mingled frequently. Gertrude Stein, a writer and leader of the Modernist movement, hosted artists in her Paris salon such as Picasso, Braque, and Henri Matisse, and writers like Ernest Hemingway, F. Scott Fitzgerald, Ezra Pound, and Sherwood Anderson. It was inevitable that Modernist rebellions would spread to the written word. For example, Imagist poetry, which presents an image and lets the reader interpret it freely, has parallels to the Cubist method of presenting a subject from multiple perspectives. Futurism, an artistic movement that captured dynamic movement in a single image, can be compared to stream-of-consciousness writing. **Stream of consciousness**, pioneered by Virginia Woolf and James Joyce, mimics the free-flowing thoughts, feelings, and memories of a person's internal monologue. This style often seems chaotic and ignores strict rules of grammar, since a person's thoughts are not normally as clean and ordered as most prose writing.

11 Modernist writers also broke the rules when it came to themes and subject matter. They would openly discuss sexuality, criticize religion, and violate other taboos. Nothing was off-limits, and this openness was refreshing for many. Many people were reeling from the horrors of war and experiencing a sense of **alienation** from modern life. The public related to stories of flawed protagonists who were overwhelmed by despair. Inspiring heroes and happy endings were no longer a requirement for good writing. This can be seen clearly in T.S. Eliot's poem *The Waste Land*, which reflects the widespread feelings of disillusionment and disgust following World War I. Modernist writers broke away from traditional literary forms and values to create the classics of a new literature, wherein reality might be redefined not by fidelity to exterior appearances but by the patterns of myth or the flow of the subconscious mind.

12 **Major Concepts**

- **Class, Colonialism, and War** – In the first half of the century, Britain's power was challenged by conflict between the upper and lower classes, resistance to colonialism abroad, and the outbreak of World War I. British writers responded to the profound changes in Britain's life and culture. In World War II, the British and the other Allies defeated the Axis powers, but

V SELECTION VOCABULARY

surrealism / el surrealismo *noun* a 20th century movement of artists and writers (developing out of dadaism) who used fantastic images and incongruous juxtapositions in order to represent unconscious thoughts and dreams COGNATE

stream of consciousness / el flujo de conciencia *noun* a person's thoughts, feelings, and reactions to events, perceived as a continuous flow

alienation / la alienación *noun* the experience of being alone or apart from a group; estrangement COGNATE

TEXT TALK

What does stream of consciousness imitate?

See paragraph 10: It mimics the flow of thoughts in a person's mind.

B Why did people between World War I and World War II turn to art to make sense of the modern world?

postwar Britain dismantled its colonial empire. These years brought a deep sense of disillusionment that permeated British writing.

- **Women's Rights –** Women comprised another disaffected group who began to seek greater political power. The suffrage movement in Britain, which had long been working peacefully to secure votes for women, took a bold new direction, and British suffragettes used unusual publicity stunts to call attention to their demands. The British government finally relented and gave women over thirty the right to vote in 1918; ten years later, the voting age was lowered to twenty-one.

13 **Style and Form**

Modernist Literature

- Modernist writing was about breaking traditions, both literary and social. For instance, poets used free verse instead of rhyme and meter, and writers challenged social norms regarding social class and women's traditional roles.
- Modernist writers did not view reality as a recognizable constant; rather, reality depended on each person's fragmented or subjective perception of it. "Look within," suggested Virginia Woolf. Woolf and other writers, including Katherine Mansfield and James Joyce, concentrated on writing about "an ordinary mind on an ordinary day."
- Sigmund Freud's system of psychoanalysis contributed to the focus on the internal life of a character and spurred Surrealism and related literary innovations, and his influence is felt in stream-of-consciousness writing focusing on the internal psychological struggles within characters.

14 The twentieth century was a traumatic time for many. Technology, philosophy, international relations: almost every aspect of life was turned on its head. Modernism was a new movement for a new world. The old rules had lost their credibility, so artists and writers needed to find new ways to view and comprehend reality. Modernist writers pioneered new ways of thinking and opened the way for the variety of styles and techniques that writers use today. What are some examples of writers, filmmakers, musicians, and artists who break conventions today?

Reading Comprehension

Have students complete the digital reading comprehension questions ✓ when they finish reading.

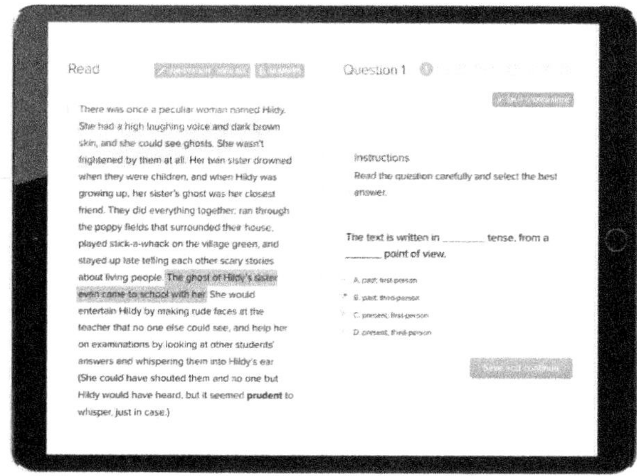

ANSWER KEY

QUESTION 1: D	**QUESTION 5:** D	**QUESTION 9:**
QUESTION 2: A	**QUESTION 6:** A	*See first chart.*
QUESTION 3: B	**QUESTION 7:** A	**QUESTION 10:**
QUESTION 4: B	**QUESTION 8:** B	*See second chart.*

Definition	Word
A style of writing that mimics human thought	stream of consciousness
Art that focuses on the machinations and imagery of dreams	Surrealism
A system of governance in which one country rules another	imperialism
Isolation from one's community	alienation
A destructive fire, or a war	conflagration

First	Second	Third	Fourth	Fifth
Animal Farm and *The Jungle Book* represent some of the ideals of two very different artistic generations.	George Orwell quit his job with the British police force in India because of his guilt as a colonizer.	The end of WWI led to a change in the distribution of political power throughout Europe.	Writers became inspired by Modernist painters.	British women fought for their right to vote, and won suffrage in 1918.

Think Questions

Circulate as students answer Think Questions independently. Scaffolds for these questions are shown on the opposite page.

QUESTION 1: Textual Evidence

Rudyard Kipling was in favor of imperialism and optimistic about society, which was a common view of late Victorian England. George Orwell opposed imperialism and was critical of society, which reflects the attitudes of Modernism. In just fifty short years, the most popular literature changed "from praising the virtues of societies to making sharp condemnations of their oppressive elements"

QUESTION 2: Textual Evidence

The devastation of the wars "disillusioned a generation of artists and thinkers", so the Modernist movement actively rebelled against traditions and conventions.

QUESTION 3: Textual Evidence

Modernist literature might not follow grammar rules and discuss topics that were formerly taboo.

QUESTION 4: Context Clues

The text says Kipling and Orwell both lived in British colonies and experienced imperialism. *Imperialism* must be related to countries with colonies. I checked a dictionary, which defines it as "the practice of extending the power and dominion of a nation by taking territories or controlling other areas."

QUESTION 5: Word Patterns and Relationships

Alienation means "the feeling of being separate or cut off from others." The text says people felt alienated in modern life.

Literary Period

Read "Introduction to Modernist Art and Literature." After you read, complete the Think Questions below.

THINK QUESTIONS

1. How do the lives and writings of Rudyard Kipling and George Orwell reflect the change in attitudes in the early twentieth century? Use evidence from the text to support your answer.
2. How did the World Wars shape the Modernist movement? Use evidence from the text to support your answer.
3. What are some of the ways Modernism broke conventions? Use evidence from the text to support your answer.
4. Use context clues to determine the meaning of the word imperialism. Write your best definition here, along with the words and phrases that were most helpful in determining the word's meaning. Then, check a dictionary to confirm your understanding.
5. The word alienation likely stems from the Latin alienatus, meaning "separated." With this information in mind, write your best definition of the word alienation as it is used in this text. Cite any words or phrases that were particularly helpful in coming to your conclusion.

Think Questions

SCAFFOLDS

Use the scaffolds below to differentiate instruction for your ELL English Language Learners and A Approaching grade level readers.

ELL **BEGINNING** Write a response using the word bank and sentence frames.

INTERMEDIATE Write a response using the sentence frames.

ADVANCED, ADVANCED HIGH Write a response using the Text-Dependent Question Guide.

A **APPROACHING** Write a response using the Text-Dependent Question Guide.

BEGINNING	INTERMEDIATE	APPROACHING / ADVANCED, ADVANCED HIGH
Word Bank	**Sentence Frames**	**Text-Dependent Question Guide**
Victorian forbidden India separation imperialism grammar disillusionment Modernism traditions colonies opposed isolation	Question 1 Rudyard Kipling was in favor of ____ and optimistic about society, which was a common view of late ____ England. George Orwell ____ imperialism and was critical of society, which reflects the attitudes of ____.	1. • When did Rudyard Kipling live, and what were his beliefs? • When did George Orwell live, and what were his beliefs? • How did views change when Modernism began?
	Question 2 The devastation of the wars created ____, so the Modernist movement actively rebelled against ____.	2. • What was notable about World Wars I and II? • How did people react to the wars? • How do people's feelings connect to Modernism's goals?
	Question 3 Modernist literature might not follow rules of ____ and discuss topics that were formerly ____.	3. • What are the characteristics of Modernism? • What are common characteristics of earlier movements? • How is Modernism different from earlier movements?
	Question 4 The text mentions that Kipling and Orwell were both born in ____ and they experienced imperialism. *Imperialism* must be related to countries with ____.	4. • Read: "Rudyard Kipling and George Orwell are two of Britain's best known writers. Both were born in India and lived in British colonies for parts of their childhoods and adult lives. Both experienced British **imperialism** firsthand . . ." • What do Kipling and Orwell have in common? • What does that tell me about the meaning of the word **imperialism**?
	Question 5 *Alienation* means ____. The text says people felt alienated due to the ____ of modern life.	5. • Read: "Many people were reeling from the horrors of war and experiencing a sense of **alienation** from modern life. The public related to stories of flawed protagonists who were overwhelmed by despair. Inspiring heroes and happy endings were no longer a requirement for good writing." • Is **alienation** a positive or negative feeling? • What feelings might the changes of the twentieth century have caused? • What smaller word can you find in **alienation**?

Skill: Recognize Genre

Introduce the Genre: Argumentative

Watch the Concept Definitions video  and read the following definition with your students.

Argumentative text presents a writer or speaker's **claim**, or position on a debatable issue or problem, and attempts to persuade others to agree with it. In order to support the claim, the writer or speaker constructs an argument made up of **reasons** why the claim is valid and **evidence** in the form of details, facts, examples, statistics, and expert opinions. An argument also includes **rhetorical appeals** called logos (logic), **pathos** (emotion), and **ethos** (ethics). Logical appeals include sound reasons and evidence, emotional appeals attempt to provoke strong feelings, and ethical appeals establish the writer or speaker's credibility.

A typical argumentative **text structure**, or organizational pattern, includes an engaging introduction that builds to a claim, body paragraphs that include reasons and evidence, and a strong conclusion that restates the claim and leaves a lasting impression. Effective arguments also include a **counter argument**, or a section in which the writer or speaker acknowledges a point made by the opposition and makes a **rebuttal**, or an attempt to disprove it.

Argumentative writing can take many forms, including essays, speeches, editorials, and letters. Any time a person puts pen to paper to express an opinion and convince others to share it, he or she is writing an argument.

Your Turn

Ask students to complete the Your Turn activity.

See digital teacher's edition for sample answers.

TURN AND TALK

- Think of a memorable advertisement you have seen on television, online, or in person. What methods did the advertisement use to persuade the audience?
- Was the ad effective? Why or why not?

ELL SPEAKING FRAMES

- I saw an advertisement for ____.
- The advertisement persuaded by ____.
- I do / do not think it was effective because ____.

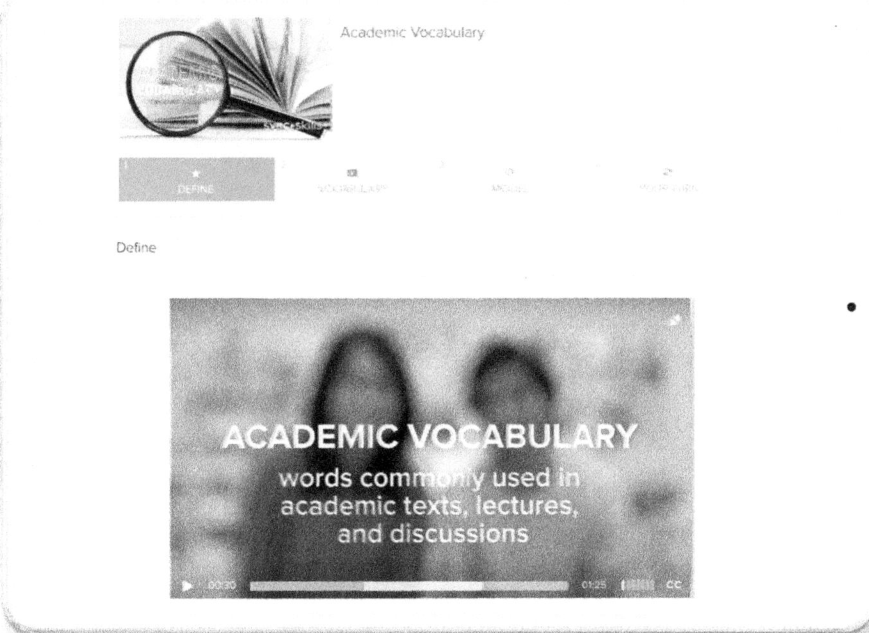

Skill: Academic Vocabulary

Introduce the Terms

atmosphere / la atmósfera ***noun*** a particular environment or surrounding influence COGNATE

compose / compilar ***verb*** to be made up of

depart / partir ***verb*** to move away from a place into another direction; to leave

dull / aburrido/a ***adjective*** lacking in liveliness or animation; lacking in interest

host / el/la anfitrión/a ***noun*** a person who invites guests to a social event

passage / el paso ***noun*** the act of passing from one state or place to the next

relief / el alivio ***noun*** the feeling that comes when something distressful or burdensome is removed or reduced

serious / serio/a ***adjective*** grave in manner or disposition; thoughtful; solemn COGNATE

substantial / considerable ***adjective*** fairly large

waver / vacilar ***verb*** to pause or hold back in uncertainty or unwillingness; to be unsure

Practice Using Vocabulary

Pair students and assign each pair a word from the list. Prompt them to draw an image or comic strip that communicates the meaning of the word using only pictures. Then, have partners share their image with the group.

Your Turn

Ask students to complete the Your Turn activities.

Your Turn 1

See digital teacher's edition for sample answers.

Your Turn 2

QUESTION 1: C **QUESTION 2:** B **QUESTION 3:** D **QUESTION 4:** A **QUESTION 5:** A

Your Turn 3

See digital teacher's edition for sample answers.

The Great Figure

POETRY

William Carlos Williams

1921

Introduction

In contrast to modernist writers who left America for Europe, such as Ezra Pound and T. S. Eliot, William Carlos Williams (1883–1963) sought to write in and embrace a uniquely American vernacular. "The Great Figure" is the final poem in his collection *Sour Grapes*, published in 1921. In his autobiography, Williams wrote that the poem stems from a real event: "I heard a great clatter of bells and the roar of a fire engine passing the end of the street down Ninth Avenue. I turned just in time to see a golden figure 5 on a red background flash by." Charles Henry Demuth, a friend of the poet, used the poem as inspiration for his painting *I Saw the Figure Five in Gold* (1928), which is now housed at the Metropolitan Museum of Art.

Looking through the rain and the shimmering lights of the darkened city, the speaker glimpsed the figure 5, painted in gold on a red fire truck. The truck moved with weight and urgency. It seemed tense and paid no heed to the gong clanks and siren howls and rumbling wheels that filled the darkened city.

ELL Proficiency-leveled summaries and summaries in multiple languages are available digitally.

Audio and audio text highlighting are available with this text.

COMPARING WITHIN AND ACROSS GENRES

What causes individuals to feel alienated?

"The Great Figure" by William Carlos Williams and "The Love Song of J. Alfred Prufrock" by T. S. Eliot are examples of poetry by two of the most well-known authors of Modernism.

"The Great Figure" is a very short poem that relies on images. The speaker concisely describes the sights and sounds of the sudden appearance of a fire engine on a dark and rainy night.

Entry Point

As students prepare to read "The Great Figure," share the following information with them to provide context.

- ✓ William Carlos Williams practiced medicine and wrote poetry in his hometown of Rutherford, New Jersey, from 1910 until his death in 1963. Williams published numerous volumes of poetry during his long career, as well as novels, short stories, essays, and a play.
- ✓ Many of Williams's poems follow the principles of Imagism that Ezra Pound, Williams's lifelong friend and a central figure in Modernist art and literary circles, outlined in the March 1913 issue of *Poetry*. Pound believed Imagist poems should carefully observe and describe events, emotions, feelings, or concrete objects, and avoid generalizations or abstractions.

Instructional Path

The print teacher's edition includes essential point-of-use instruction and planning tools. Complete lesson plans and program documents appear in your digital teacher account.

Independent Read: The Great Figure

Objectives: After reading "The Great Figure," students will write a short response that demonstrates their understanding of sensory details through a personal narrative.

Independent Read

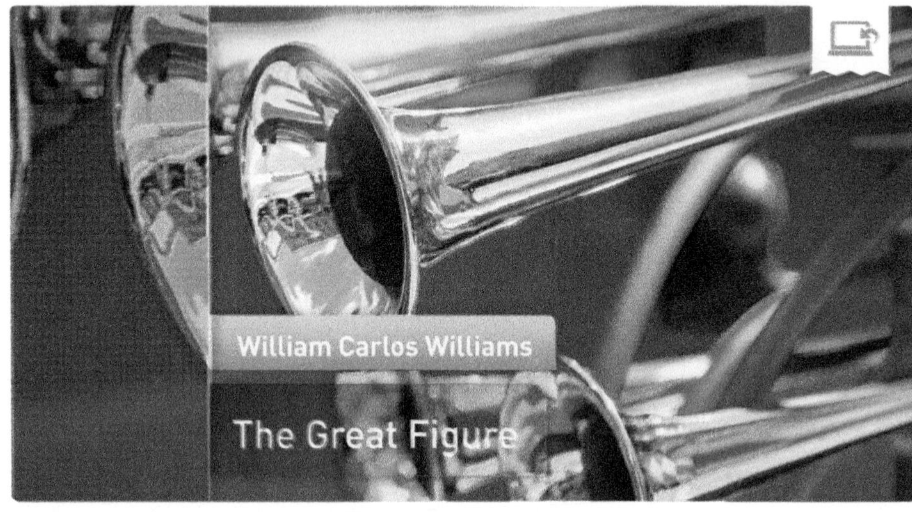

Introduce the Text

As a class, watch the video preview and have students read the introduction in pairs to make connections to the video preview.

- What kind of poem are you about to read? How can you tell?
- What information does the video provide that the introduction does not?

ELL SPEAKING FRAMES

- I am about to read a poem that ___________.
- I know this because ________________.
- The video ________________.

Access Complex Text

LEXILE: N/A **WORD COUNT:** 35

The following areas may be challenging for students, particularly ELL English Language Learners and A Approaching grade-level learners.

Genre	Sentence Structure
• Explain to students that "The Great Figure" is an example of an Imagist poem. • Imagist poems usually describe a single image, prioritizing sensory details over other poetic elements, such as meter or rhyme.	• "The Great Figure" is a very short poem with very little punctuation. • Guide students through the poem line by line, highlighting which lines have single words, which lines are single phrases, and what these structural choices might mean.

"Among the rain / and lights / I saw the figure 5"

NOTES

Among the rain
and lights
I saw the figure 5
in gold
on a red
firetruck
moving
with weight and **urgency**
tense
unheeded
to **gong** clangs
siren howls
and wheels rumbling
through the dark city.

I Saw the Figure 5 in Gold, by Charles Demuth (1928) was inspired by William Carlos Williams' poem, "The Great Figure."

Williams, William Carlos. "The Great Figure." *Sour Grapes*. Boston: The Four Seas Company, 1921.

SELECTION VOCABULARY

urgency / la urgencia *noun* something that requires quick action COGNATE

tense / tenso/a *adjective* tight or rigid muscles COGNATE

unheeded / desatendido/a *adjective* understood or noticed but ignored

gong / el gong *noun* a saucer-shaped bell that makes a loud, deep sound when it is struck by a padded hammer COGNATE

Developing Background Knowledge and Social Emotional Learning

1. In small groups, have students do a five-minute online search of Imagism.
2. On the board, collate the main principles of Imagism. How does Imagism connect to what you know about Modernism? Why is "The Great Figure" an example of Imagism?

Discuss with students: What is a moment in your life that you think of often? What specific image sticks in your mind about that moment? What emotions do you associate with that image? What artistic medium would you choose to communicate the power of that image to others?

TEXT TALK

What words are used to describe how the "firetruck" looks?

See lines 3–6: It is "red" with a "gold" "figure 5" on it.

What words are used to describe how the "firetruck" sounds?

See lines 11–14: There is a "gong" that "clangs" with a howling "siren" and "rumbling" "wheels."

How did researching Imagism help you better understand the poem?

Answers will vary.

How did discussing the power of communicating an image help you better understand the poem?

Answers will vary.

Ask each Beyond grade-level student to write one additional discussion question. Then, have one or two students facilitate a discussion, using their questions to guide the conversation.

Prepare for Advanced Courses

Use the activity below to differentiate instruction for your B Beyond grade level learners.

Author's Syntax

Have students write the poem as a single sentence without line breaks. Then have them add punctuation to the poem according to standard grammatical rules. Finally, have them break up the sentence into two or more smaller sentences.

Ask students:

- Why do you think Williams chose to present the poem in this manner?
- What effect do the syntax and line breaks have on the meaning of the poem?

WRITE

PERSONAL NARRATIVE: Write about a seemingly minor event that affected you enough that you continue to remember it. Your response can be a poem, short story, or personal narrative. Be sure to provide specific details about the sights and sounds of the event, as Williams does in "The Great Figure." You may also include your thoughts and emotions about the event and why you continue to remember it.

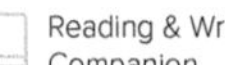

Writer's Notebook

Connect to Literary Focus: Give students time to reflect on how "The Great Figure" demonstrates the conventions and characteristics of this unit's literary focus, Modernism, by freewriting in their Writer's Notebooks.

CHECK FOR SUCCESS

If students are still struggling to respond to the prompt, ask them scaffolded questions, such as:

1. What were some common stylistic choices of Modernist writers?
2. Which of these stylistic choices is reflected in the poem?

Reading Comprehension OPTIONAL

Have students complete the digital reading comprehension questions ✔ when they finish reading.

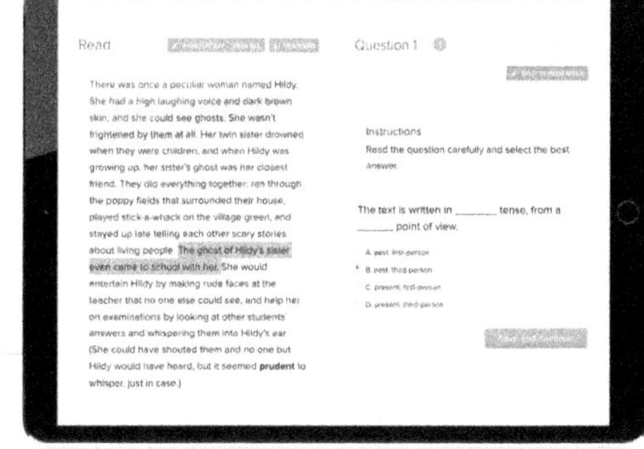

ANSWER KEY

QUESTION 1: D
QUESTION 2: A
QUESTION 3: D
QUESTION 4: C
QUESTION 5: *See chart below.*

Synonym	Word
worried	tense
ignored	unheeded
alarm	gong
insistence	urgency

Connect and Extend OPTIONAL

CONNECT TO EXTENDED WRITING PROJECT

Students might want to use "The Great Figure" as one of the texts they focus on in their literary analysis. Encourage students to think about whether this poem explores the theme of alienation.

BEYOND THE BOOK

Reading versus Reality

Imagist poets focused on describing in words events that are normally experienced with our other senses, such as sight and sound. Put students in small groups to discuss the following questions:

- How is reading "The Great Figure" different than seeing a fire engine pass by in real life?
- Did the poem make you think differently about the experience of seeing a fire engine? Why or why not?
- What are some other events that are different in real life compared with reading about them?

Invite groups to share their ideas to foster a class discussion about experiencing events versus reading about them.

Collaborative Conversation

SCAFFOLDS

Post the writing prompt to generate a discussion in small groups. Ask students to first break down the prompt before they discuss relevant ideas and textual evidence.

Write about a seemingly minor event that affected you enough that you continue to remember it. Your response can be a poem, short story, or personal narrative. Be sure to provide specific details about the sights and sounds of the event, as Williams does in "The Great Figure." You may also include your thoughts and emotions about the event and why you continue to remember it.

Use the scaffolds below to differentiate instruction for your ELL English Language Learners and A Approaching grade-level learners.

ELL **BEGINNING, INTERMEDIATE** Use the discussion guide and speaking frames to facilitate the discussion with support from the teacher.

ADVANCED, ADVANCED HIGH Use the discussion guide and speaking frames to facilitate the discussion in mixed-level groups.

A **APPROACHING** Use the discussion guide to facilitate the discussion in mixed-level groups.

APPROACHING
ADVANCED, ADVANCED HIGH
BEGINNING, INTERMEDIATE

Discussion Guide	Speaking Frames
1. What is a minor event that you remember well?	• I remember when ____.
2. What is something specific that you remember seeing during this event?	• I remember seeing ____.
3. What is something specific that you remember hearing during this event?	• I remember hearing ____.

Text to World

Use the activity below to differentiate instruction for your B Beyond grade level learners.

The poem is written from the perspective of someone seeing a firetruck "among the rain." Have students imagine how this poem would have been different if it had been written from the perspective of the truck driver. Ask students: Reread lines 1–4:

- What words, images, and details would the truck driver's poem share with this poem?
- What words, images, and details would be unique to the truck driver's poem?
- Why do you think William Carlos Williams chose to write this poem from the perspective of someone outside of the firetruck? How does this perspective strengthen the themes and images of the poem?

Review Prompt and Rubric

Before students begin writing, review the writing prompt and rubric with the class.

PERSONAL NARRATIVE: Write about a seemingly minor event that affected you enough that you continue to remember it. Your response can be a poem, short story, or personal narrative. Be sure to provide specific details about the sights and sounds of the event, as Williams does in "The Great Figure." You may also include your thoughts and emotions about the event and why you continue to remember it.

ELL A PROMPT GUIDE

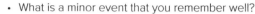

- What is a minor event that you remember well?
- What is something specific that you remember seeing during this event?
- What is something specific that you remember hearing during this event?

Score	Personal Narrative	Language and Conventions
4	The writer is able to skillfully convey the sensory details of the experience.	The writer demonstrates a consistent command of grammar, punctuation, and usage conventions. Although minor errors may be evident, they do not detract from the fluency or the clarity of the essay.
3	The writer is able to clearly convey the sensory details of the experience.	The writer demonstrates an adequate command of grammar, punctuation, and usage conventions. Although some errors may be evident, they create few (if any) disruptions in the fluency of the writing or the clarity of the essay.
2	The writer is able to convey some sense of the experience but may not include enough specific details.	The writer demonstrates a partial command of grammar, punctuation, and usage conventions. Some distracting errors may be evident, at times creating minor disruptions in the fluency or clarity of the writing.
1	The writer attempts to convey some sense of the experience, but a lack of details and an illogical structure interfere with the reader's ability to understand.	The writer demonstrates little or no command of grammar, punctuation, and usage conventions. Serious and persistent errors create disruptions in the fluency of the writing and sometimes interfere with meaning.
0	The writer does not provide a relevant response to the prompt or does not provide a response at all.	Serious and persistent errors overwhelm the writing and interfere with the meaning of the response as a whole, making the writer's meaning impossible to understand.

Write

SCAFFOLDS

Ask students to complete the writing assignment using text evidence to support their answers.

Use the scaffolds below to differentiate instruction for your ELL English Language Learners and A Approaching grade level readers.

ELL **BEGINNING** With the help of the word bank, write a response using paragraph frame 1.

INTERMEDIATE With the help of the word bank, write a response using paragraph frames 1 and 2.

ADVANCED, ADVANCED HIGH Write a response of differentiated length using the sentence starters.

A **APPROACHING** Write a response of differentiated length using the sentence starters.

BEGINNING			ADVANCED, ADVANCED HIGH
INTERMEDIATE			APPROACHING
Word Bank	**Paragraph Frame 1**	**Paragraph Frame 2**	**Sentence Starters**
refreshing loudly visited glitter warm	I remember the first time I ____ the beach. The day was bright and ____. The ocean water was cool and ____. The sunlight sparkled like ____ spread on top of the ocean as far as the eye could see. I could hear the seagulls calling ____ as I swam through the blue water.	This day I spent at the beach was ____. I spent the entire day feeling ____. This one day has stayed in my memory because ____.	• I remember a time when . . . • The day was . . . • I heard . . . • I saw . . . • I felt . . . • It was a . . . moment because . . . • I remember this moment because . . .

Peer Review

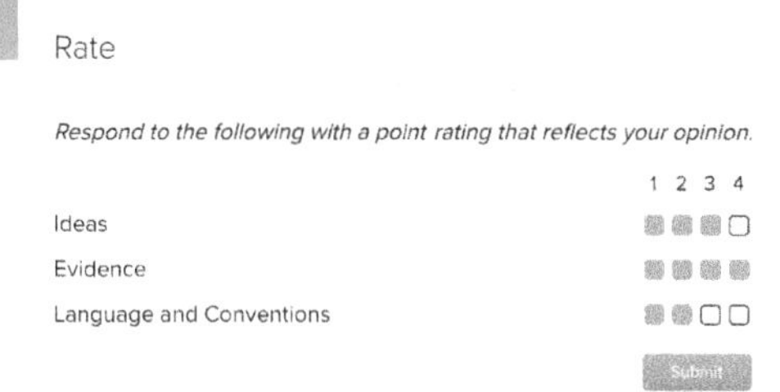

Students should submit substantive feedback to two peers using the review instructions below.

- How well does this response answer the prompt?
- Does the writer use specific sensory details to describe the event?
- What does the writer do well in this response? What does the writer need to work on?

Remember that your comments are most useful when they are kind and constructive.

ELL **SENTENCE FRAMES**

A

- You were able to (completely / partly / almost) ____ answer the prompt.
- You could answer the prompt more completely by . . .
- You could add more details when you describe . . .
- My favorite part of your response was . . .

The Love Song of J. Alfred Prufrock

POETRY
T.S. Eliot
1915

Introduction

studysync

Born in St. Louis to an old New England family, T. S. Eliot (1888–1965) was educated at Harvard, the Sorbonne, and Oxford, and received the Nobel Prize for Literature in 1948 for his boldly innovative and influential style. "The Love Song of J. Alfred Prufrock" demonstrates Eliot's characteristic stream of consciousness and versatility with diction. The poem marked a shift in poetic tradition from Romantic verse and Georgian lyrics to Modernism. Filled with allusions to other written works, Elliot takes the reader on a sentimental journey of a gentleman as he questions his life and worth.

Prufrock invites the reader to come take a walk with him, through a damp foggy day, to visit the cheap hotels and restaurants he knows. There's something important he needs to talk about. The yellow fog descends and rubs up against the window panes, but there is still plenty of time to address the important questions. Prufrock wonders "Do I dare?" considering whether to go back downstairs, afraid people will judge him for his baldness or thinness. There's something important he must ask but does not want to "disturb the universe." He thinks of how to begin, then wonders whether he's too presumptuous. He procrastinates, hoping to postpone the moment until after tea and cake. He reconsiders, thinking it's "no great matter"; he admits he was afraid. Now, he's old and envisioning himself with rolled-up pants. He walks along the beach, amidst the mermaids who won't sing to him. He lies down in the sea only to be woken up and then to drown.

Proficiency-leveled summaries and summaries in multiple languages are available digitally.

Audio and audio text highlighting are available with this text.

COMPARING WITHIN AND ACROSS GENRES

In "The Love Song of J. Alfred Prufrock," the speaker meanders through memory lane, lost in thoughts, regrets, and sensory details. Like "The Great Figure," Eliot's poem describes an often overwhelming urban landscape, and depicts the speaker's isolation and disillusion in a stream-of-consciousness style, making the poem one of Modernism's foundational texts.

Entry Point

As students prepare to read "The Love Song of J. Alfred Prufrock," share the following information with them to provide context.

- ✓ "The Love Song of J. Alfred Prufrock" was T. S. Eliot's first publication, printed in *Poetry* magazine in 1915. It was also the first poem in Eliot's first book of poems, titled *Prufrock and Other Observations* (1917).
- ✓ Although Eliot had several committed supporters, especially Ezra Pound, some critics disliked the stream-of-consciousness style and Eliot's disregard for traditional poetic structures; one critic said that the text bore "no relation to poetry."
- ✓ Today, the poem is widely known, and Eliot is seen as a foundational author of Modernism. Modernist poets often experimented with or ignored meter and rhyme; although "Prufrock" has many rhymes, it does not follow a traditional rhyme scheme.

Instructional Path

The print teacher's edition includes essential point-of-use instruction and planning tools. Complete lesson plans and program documents appear in your digital teacher account.

First Read: The Love Song of J. Alfred Prufrock

Objectives: After an initial reading and discussion of the poem, students will be able to identify details and poetic elements that support central themes in the poem.

Skill: Language, Style, and Audience

Objectives: After rereading and discussing a model of close reading, students will be able to analyze the meaning and impact of the poet's word choice and language.

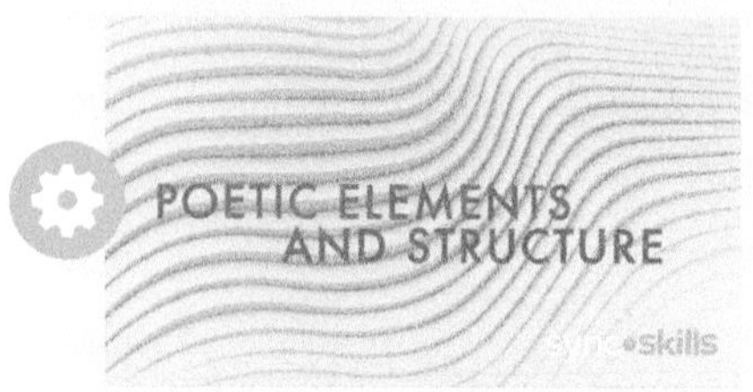

Skill: Poetic Elements and Structure

Objectives: After rereading and discussing a model of close reading, students will be able to analyze how poetic elements and structure help convey meaning.

Skill: Literary Periods

Objectives: After rereading and discussing a model of close reading, students will be able to compare and contrast how two poems reflect the themes and style of the Modernist literary period.

Close Read: The Love Song of J. Alfred Prufrock

Objectives: After engaging in a close reading and discussion of "The Love Song of J. Alfred Prufrock," students will be able to identify how poets use figurative language as well as poetic elements and structure to develop a theme by comparing and contrasting two poems from different literary time periods.

Blast: All The Lonely People

Objectives: After exploring background information and research links about a topic, students will respond to a question with a 140-character response.

Progress Monitoring

Opportunities to Learn	Opportunities to Demonstrate Learning	Opportunities to Reteach
Language, Style, and Audience		
Skill: Language, Style, and Audience	Skill: Language, Style, and Audience • Your Turn Close Read • Vocabulary Chart • Skills Focus	Unit 6 Skill: Language, Style, and Audience-Commencement Address at the New School Spotlight Skill: Language, Style, and Audience
Poetic Elements and Structure		
Skill: Poetic Elements and Structure	Skill: Poetic Elements and Structure • Your Turn Close Read • Skills Focus	Spotlight Skill: Poetic Elements and Structure
Literary Periods		
Skill: Literary Periods	Skill: Literary Periods • Your Turn Close Read • Writer's Notebook • Skills Focus • Write	Spotlight Skill: Literary Periods

First Read

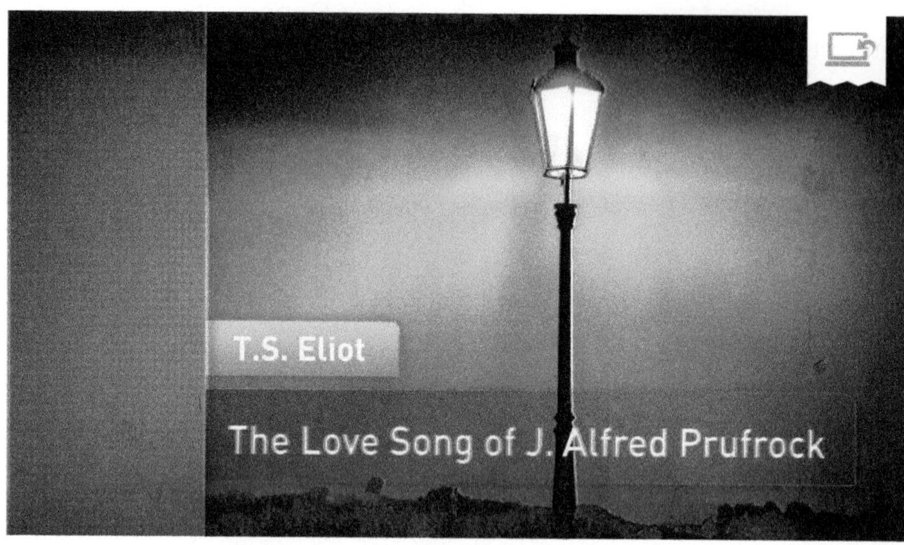

T.S. Eliot
The Love Song of J. Alfred Prufrock

Introduce the Text

As a class, watch the video preview  and have students read the introduction in pairs to make connections to the video preview.

To activate prior knowledge and experiences, ask students:

- Based on the video, what do you think will be most challenging about reading this poem?
- When have you wanted to do something but felt you did not have the courage or drive to do so?

ELL SPEAKING FRAMES

- The poem might be challenging because ____.
- I remember when I wanted to ____. I did not do that because ____.

Access Complex Text

LEXILE: N/A WORD COUNT: 1,145

The following areas may be challenging for students, particularly 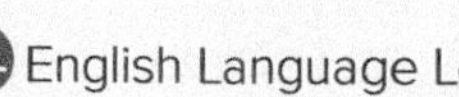 English Language Learners and Approaching grade-level learners.

Connection of Ideas	Sentence Structure	Genre
• The poem might seem random to students at first. Help them draw connections between each stanza. • Explain that interjections such as "the women come and go / Talking of Michelangelo" support the poem's meaning.	• Some sentences are very long and hard to follow. Help students trace the flow of ideas by connecting pronouns with their antecedents. • Ask students to consider how Eliot uses punctuation to structure the flow of ideas.	• Explain that the first six lines are an epigraph, or a short quotation that appears at the beginning of a literary work. • The epigraph comes from Canto XXVII of Dante's *Inferno* (the first part of *The Divine Comedy*), written in the early 1300s.

 SCAFFOLDS

 ENGLISH LANGUAGE LEARNERS  APPROACHING GRADE LEVEL  BEYOND GRADE LEVEL

These icons identify differentiation strategies and scaffolded support for a variety of students. See the digital lesson plan for additional differentiation strategies and scaffolds.

"I should have been a pair of ragged claws Scuttling across the floors of silent seas."

NOTES

Skill: Poetic Elements and Structure

Eliot begins the poem with an epigraph that is in another language. This epigraph is most likely from another literary work. Eliot assumes that his reader can read this other language or is familiar with the work.

"The Love Song of J. Alfred Prufrock"

S'io credesse che mia risposta fosse
A persona che mai tornasse al mondo,
Questa fiamma staria senza piu scosse.
Ma perciocche giammai di questo fondo
Non torno vivo alcun, s'i'odo il vero,
Senza tema d'infamia ti rispondo.

Let us go then, you and I,
When the evening is spread out against the sky
Like a patient **etherized** upon a table;
Let us go, through certain half-deserted streets,
The muttering retreats
Of restless nights in one-night cheap hotels
And sawdust restaurants with oyster-shells:
Streets that follow like a **tedious** argument
Of **insidious** intent
To lead you to an overwhelming question . . .
Oh, do not ask, "What is it?"
Let us go and make our visit.

In the room the women come and go
Talking of Michelangelo[1].

The yellow fog that rubs its back upon the window-panes,
The yellow smoke that rubs its muzzle on the window-panes
Licked its tongue into the corners of the evening,
Lingered upon the pools that stand in drains,
Let fall upon its back the soot that falls from chimneys,
Slipped by the terrace, made a sudden leap,

T.S. Eliot

1. **Michelangelo** Michelangelo di Lodovico Buonarroti Simoni (1475–1564), Renaissance artist and sculptor, whose most famous works include David and the ceiling of the Sistine Chapel in Rome

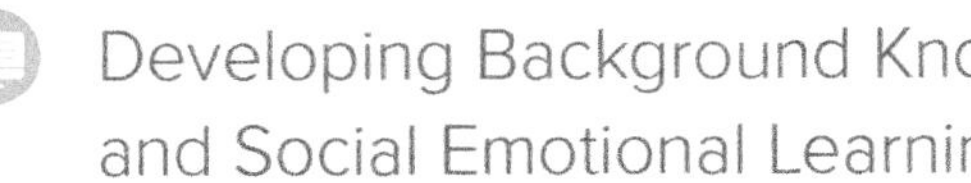

Developing Background Knowledge and Social Emotional Learning

1. Generate a list (on the board or on paper) of any information or ideas your students have about the title "The Love Song of J. Alfred Prufrock."
2. Have students discuss what they expect from a poem called a "love song" and what kind of person they envision would be named J. Alfred Prufrock.

Discuss with students: Think of a time when you doubted yourself in a key moment. Why do you think people tend to doubt themselves, especially in moments when they risk being rejected? Have you ever felt too insecure to take action or say something? What actions could you take to increase your confidence and take more risks?

Poetic Elements and Structure

What does the reader notice about the poem's epigraph?

It is probably from a literary work in another language, and Eliot assumes the reader will be familiar with this work.

SELECTION VOCABULARY

etherized / anestesiar *verb* unconscious due to ether gas, in preparation for surgery

tedious / tedioso/a *adjective* boring, long, and slow COGNATE

insidious / insidioso/a *adjective* intended to deceive or entrap someone COGNATE

TEXT TALK

What animal is the basis for the images in lines 21–28? How do you know?

See lines 21–28: The imagery draws on a cat; it rubs its back, licks with its tongue, and falls asleep.

Literary Periods

What does the reader notice about the figurative language in both poems?

The reader notices that both poems use figurative language to describe cities that are are not very pretty.

Poetic Elements and Structure

What does Eliot use to give details about Prufrock's appearance?

Eliot uses repetition and rhyming couplets.

And seeing that it was a soft October night,
Curled once about the house, and fell asleep.

And indeed there will be time
For the yellow smoke that slides along the street,
Rubbing its back upon the window panes;
There will be time, there will be time
To prepare a face to meet the faces that you meet
There will be time to murder and create,
And time for all the works and days of hands
That lift and drop a question on your plate;
Time for you and time for me,
And time yet for a hundred indecisions,
And for a hundred visions and revisions,
Before the taking of a toast and tea.

In the room the women come and go
Talking of Michelangelo.

And indeed there will be time
To wonder, "Do I dare?" and, "Do I dare?"
Time to turn back and descend the stair,
With a bald spot in the middle of my hair—
(They will say: "How his hair is growing thin!")
My morning coat, my collar mounting firmly to the chin,
My necktie rich and modest, but asserted by a simple pin—
(They will say: "But how his arms and legs are thin!")
Do I dare
Disturb the universe?
In a minute there is time
For decisions and revisions which a minute will reverse.

For I have known them all already, known them all:
Have known the evenings, mornings, afternoons,
I have measured out my life with coffee spoons;
I know the voices dying with a dying fall
Beneath the music from a farther room.
So how should I presume?

And I have known the eyes already, known them all—
The eyes that fix you in a formulated phrase,
And when I am formulated, sprawling on a pin,
When I am pinned and wriggling on the wall,
Then how should I begin
To spit out all the butt-ends of my days and ways?
And how should I presume?

Skill: Literary Periods

The city continues to be an unpleasant place. Eliot's poem has a somewhat negative outlook on people as well with words like "prepare a face" and "murder." Neither Eliot nor Williams uses a consistent rhyme scheme in their poems.

Skill: Poetic Elements and Structure

Eliot uses repetition and rhyming couplets to give details about Prufrock's appearance. He is dressed well, but he worries about what people say about him, imagining they focus on his "bald spot" and thin arms and legs.

And I have known the arms already, known them all—
Arms that are braceleted and white and bare
(But in the lamplight, downed with light brown hair!)
Is it perfume from a dress
That makes me so digress?
Arms that lie along a table, or wrap about a shawl.
And should I then presume?
And how should I begin?

. . .

Skill: Poetic Elements and Structure

The metaphor shows that Prufrock feels he should have been a creature at the bottom of the sea. The "lonely men" that Prufrock sees support the sense of isolation. Each line ends in "s" and the "s" sound is repeated throughout.

Shall I say, I have gone at dusk through narrow streets
And watched the smoke that rises from the pipes
Of lonely men in shirt-sleeves, leaning out of windows?

I should have been a pair of ragged claws
Scuttling across the floors of silent seas.

. . .

And the afternoon, the evening, sleeps so peacefully!
Smoothed by long fingers,
Asleep . . . tired . . . or it **malingers**.
Stretched on the floor, here beside you and me.
Should I, after tea and cakes and ices,
Have the strength to force the moment to its crisis?
But though I have wept and fasted, wept and prayed,
Though I have seen my head (grown slightly bald) brought in upon a platter,
I am no prophet—and here's no great matter;
I have seen the moment of my greatness flicker,
And I have seen the eternal Footman[2] hold my coat, and snicker,
And in short, I was afraid.

And would it have been worth it, after all,
After the cups, the marmalade, the tea,
Among the porcelain, among some talk of you and me,
Would it have been worth while,
To have bitten off the matter with a smile,
To have squeezed the universe into a ball
To roll it toward some overwhelming question,
To say: "I am Lazarus[3], come from the dead,
Come back to tell you all, I shall tell you all"—

2. **Footman** domestic servant dedicated to reception and service of guests
3. **Lazarus** Biblical figure raised from the dead by Jesus Christ

Poetic Elements and Structure

What does the reader note about Eliot's metaphor and word choice?

Eliot's metaphor and word choice show how isolated Prufrock feels.

Skills Focus

QUESTION 2: Language, Style, and Audience

The poet evokes the senses of sight, touch, and smell in this stanza. This choice is effective because it helps the audience connect with the speaker as readers try to imagine what the speaker sees, feels, and smells.

Skills Focus

QUESTION 3: Poetic Elements and Structure

The poet uses repetition to give some structure to this long, stream-of-consciousness type of sentence. Some words rhyme, but the pattern is not perfect. These choices make these lines hard to follow, which reflects the confusion between the "I" and "you" of the poem.

SELECTION VOCABULARY

malinger / fingir estar enfermo *verb* pretend to be sick or tired, especially to avoid work

TEXT TALK

What is the setting of lines 93–104?

The setting is a tea party or a dining table. The speaker mentions teacups and marmalade.

Skills Focus

QUESTION 4: Literary Period

Prufrock becomes overwhelmed by being lost in thoughts, regrets, and memories. He keeps questioning whether it would "have been worth it," and then becomes frustrated because he can't say what he means. The speaker in "The Great Figure" also becomes lost in the sensory experience of the fire truck. This disillusionment and feeling of being lost in personal thought is often reflected in Modernist works.

Skills Focus

QUESTION 5: Connect to Essential Question

Prufrock's insecurities result in alienation. He realizes his lack of "greatness" and feels Death, "the eternal Footman," close behind him. Then, he hears mermaids singing to each other but not to him. The "Love Song" is for love he has lost or never had.

Language, Style, and Audience

What observation does the reader make about allusions in the poem?

The reader explains the allusion to Shakespeare's *Hamlet* and how Prufrock compares and contrasts himself with Shakespeare's characters.

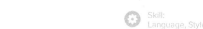

If one, settling a pillow by her head,
Should say: "That is not what I meant at all;
That is not it, at all."

And would it have been worth it, after all,
Would it have been worth while,
After the sunsets and the dooryards and the sprinkled streets,
After the novels, after the teacups, after the skirts that trail along the floor—
And this, and so much more?—
It is impossible to say just what I mean!
But as if a magic lantern threw the nerves in patterns on a screen:
Would it have been worth while
If one, settling a pillow or throwing off a shawl,
And turning toward the window, should say:
"That is not it at all,
That is not what I meant, at all."

. . .

No! I am not Prince Hamlet, nor was meant to be;
Am an attendant lord, one that will do
To swell a progress, start a scene or two,
Advise the prince; no doubt, an easy tool,
Deferential, glad to be of use,
Politic, cautious, and meticulous;
Full of high sentence, but a bit obtuse;
At times, indeed, almost ridiculous—
Almost, at times, the Fool[4].

I grow old . . . I grow old . . .
I shall wear the bottoms of my trousers rolled.

Shall I part my hair behind? Do I dare to eat a peach?
I shall wear white flannel trousers, and walk upon the beach.
I have heard the mermaids singing, each to each.

I do not think that they will sing to me.

I have seen them riding seaward on the waves
Combing the white hair of the waves blown back
When the wind blows the water white and black.

We have lingered in the chambers of the sea
By sea-girls wreathed with seaweed red and brown
Till human voices wake us, and we drown.

Skill: Language, Style, and Audience

The speaker's allusion to Shakespeare's Hamlet effectively shows that he views himself as absurd and awkward. He was not "meant to be" a prince like Hamlet, but instead thinks of himself as "the Fool."

4. **the Fool** character in a Tarot deck—a counterpart to the Joker in a deck of playing cards—depicted by an illustration of a young man at the edge of a cliff

TEXT TALK

How did discussing things you do not have the courage to do deepen your understanding of "The Love Song of J. Alfred Prufrock"?

Answers will vary.

Reading Comprehension OPTIONAL

Have students complete the digital reading comprehension questions when they finish reading.

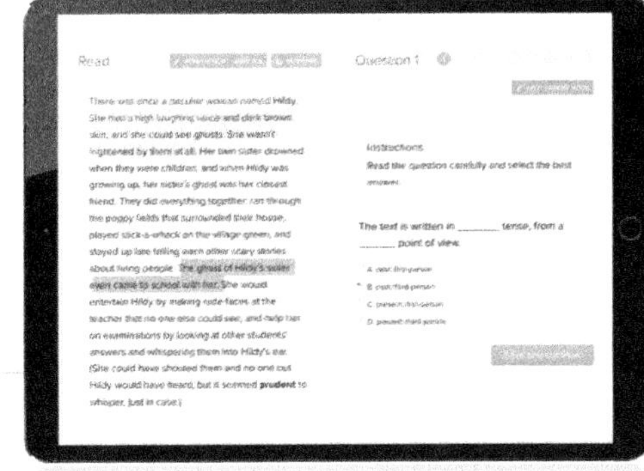

ANSWER KEY

QUESTION 1: C
QUESTION 2: B
QUESTION 3: D
QUESTION 4: B
QUESTION 5: C
QUESTION 6: C
QUESTION 7: A
QUESTION 8: D
QUESTION 9: C
QUESTION 10: *See chart below.*

First	Second	Third	Fourth
Let us go then, you and I,	Do I dare/ Disturb the universe?	Shall I part my hair behind? Do I dare to eat a peach?	We have lingered in the chambers of the sea

Connect and Extend OPTIONAL

CONNECT TO EXTENDED WRITING PROJECT

Students can use "The Love Song of J. Alfred Prufrock" as a mentor text for their Extended Writing Project. They may identify examples of Prufrock's alienation and synthesize a statement about it as they craft their own literary analysis essay.

BEYOND THE BOOK

Activity: Group Character Analysis

Prufrock is on a journey of self-discovery in this poem. He is upset about not being able to muster the strength to ask a love interest a serious question. Have students find evidence of his character traits and select songs that reflect these traits. Ask students to:

- Reread the poem and find three moments that reflect Prufrock's personality.
- Write each action on a post-it note.
- In small groups of 4 to 5, combine the post-it notes and group similar pieces of evidence together.
- Use a thesaurus and/or a list of character traits to decide what each grouping of post-it notes reveals about Prufrock.
- As a group, select three songs that should be on his music playlist.
- Write a brief explanation for each song and why it might apply to Prufrock.
- Share ideas with classmates.

To make students reflect, have them discuss these questions:

- Were there songs that were common among more than one group? If so, what traits did these songs reflect?
- What revealed more about Prufrock's traits—his actions or his words?

Think Questions

Circulate as students answer Think Questions independently. Scaffolds for these questions are shown on the opposite page.

QUESTION 1: Textual Evidence

The lines "In the room the women come and go / Talking of Michelangelo" are repeated, suggesting a theme of culture and art. The question "Do I dare?" is also repeated, which suggests that the speaker is uncertain.

QUESTION 2: Textual Evidence

He is beginning to grow bald ("With a bald spot in the middle of my hair"), and people notice that his limbs are scrawny ("his arms and legs are thin"). It seems that he is growing old and weaker.

QUESTION 3: Textual Evidence

The poem's events seem to be Prufrock's memories or imagination. He could be walking through a city ("half-deserted streets"), possibly toward the ocean ("walk upon the beach"). Prufrock thinks about his life and regrets what he has not done.

QUESTION 4: Context Clues

I think *malingers* must have something to do with being lazy or unwilling to do something. The context clue "stretched on the floor" supports this meaning.

QUESTION 5: Context Clues

I think *deferential* means "acting like a servant." I arrived at this meaning because the speaker is talking about himself as "cautious"and an "attendant" to a prince, who would be in charge.

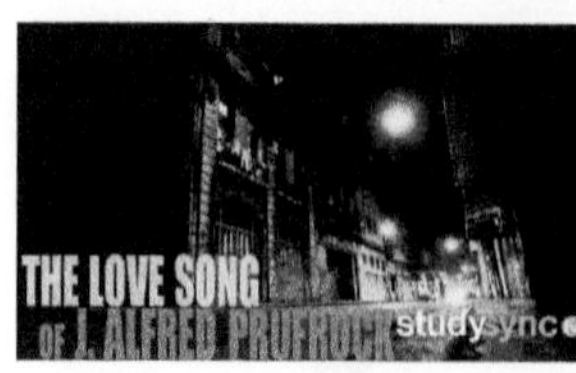

First Read

Read "The Love Song of J. Alfred Prufrock." After you read, complete the Think Questions below.

THINK QUESTIONS

1. What phrases or lines are repeated in the poem? What do these repetitions tell you about the speaker of the poem? Support your response with evidence from the text.
2. How is the speaker's appearance described? What can you infer about Prufrock from these descriptions? Support your response with evidence from the text.
3. Write two or three sentences summarizing the events of the poem. What seems to occur in the time span of the poem? Use evidence from the text to support your response.
4. Use context clues to determine the meaning of the word **malingers** as it is used in "The Love Song of J. Alfred Prufrock." Write your definition of *malingers* here and explain how you arrived at this definition.
5. Use context clues to determine the meaning of the word **deferential** as it is used in "The Love Song of J. Alfred Prufrock." Write your definition of *deferential* here and explain how you arrived at this definition.

SCAFFOLDS

Think Questions

Use the scaffolds below to differentiate instruction for your ELL English Language Learners and A Approaching grade level readers.

ELL **BEGINNING** Write a response using the word bank and sentence frames.

INTERMEDIATE Write a response using the sentence frames.

ADVANCED, ADVANCED HIGH Write a response using the Text-Dependent Question Guide.

A **APPROACHING** Write a response using the Text-Dependent Question Guide.

BEGINNING | INTERMEDIATE | APPROACHING / ADVANCED, ADVANCED HIGH

Word Bank	Sentence Frames	Text-Dependent Question Guide
pretends Prince Hamlet imagination Michelangelo hair city tired thin servant culture	Lines that are repeated are "In the room the women come and go / Talking of ____." This repetition tells me that the theme might relate to art and ____.	1. • What do you notice about lines 19 and 20, and lines 41 and 42? • Who was Michelangelo? Why was he important? • What do these lines suggest about a possible theme of the poem?
	The speaker is starting to lose his ____. He describes his arms and legs as ____.	2. • What is happening to the speaker's hair? • What is happening to his arms and legs? • Does the speaker like these changes? • What does the speaker think the changes mean?
	The poem takes place mostly in the memories or ____ of the speaker. He might be taking a walk from a ____ to the ocean.	3. • Is the speaker by himself or with someone? How do you know? • Lines 7–19 refer to streets, hotels, and restaurants. Where can you find these things? • The last stanzas talk about waves and seaweed. Where can you find these things? • How does the setting change from the beginning to the end of the poem?
	The evening is described as ____ and "stretched on the floor." This gives me a clue that *malingers* means ____ to be unable to do something.	4. • Read: "And the afternoon, the evening, sleeps so peacefully! / Smoothed by long fingers, / Asleep . . . tired . . . or it **malingers**. / Stretched on the floor, here beside you and me." • What adjectives does the speaker use? • What action does the speaker describe? • What does that tell me about the meaning of the word *malingers*?
	The speaker says he is not ____, but he might be a prince's attendant. This suggests that *deferential* means "acting like a ____."	5. • Read: "Advise the prince; no doubt, an easy tool, / **Deferential**, glad to be of use" • Whom does the speaker describe? • What action does the speaker describe? • What does that tell me about the meaning of the word *deferential*?

Skill: Language, Style, and Audience

Introduce the Skill

Watch the Concept Definition video and read the following definition with your students.

Authors use language to convey meaning or to affect the way their **audience** thinks and perceives. An audience is the intended reader or listener. Readers can analyze an author's style to better understand the tone and meaning of a text.

Style refers to the way an author uses language (words, sentences, paragraphs) to achieve a purpose. One element of style is word choice. **Word choice** is a technique in which writers choose specific words for precise meaning or to convey a certain tone. **Meaning** is a reader's interpretation of the text's deeper messages, themes, or ideas. **Tone** expresses a writer's **attitude** (or thoughts and feelings) toward his or her subject. Tone can be described, for example, as formal, casual, conversational, ironic, sad, bitter, humorous, or serious.

Skill: Language, Style, and Audience

Use the Checklist to analyze Language, Style, and Audience in "The Love Song of J. Alfred Prufrock." Refer to the sample student annotations about Language, Style, and Audience in the text.

••• CHECKLIST FOR LANGUAGE, STYLE, AND AUDIENCE

In order to determine an author's style and possible intended audience, do the following:

- ✓ identify language that is particularly fresh, engaging, or beautiful
- ✓ analyze the surrounding words and phrases as well as the context in which the specific words are being used
- ✓ note the audience—both intended and unintended—and possible reactions to the author's word choice and style
- ✓ note any allusions the author makes to texts written by other authors
- ✓ examine your reaction to the author's word choice and how the author's choice affected your reaction

To analyze the impact of a specific word choice on meaning including words with multiple meanings or language that is particularly fresh, engaging, or beautiful, consider the following questions:

- ✓ How does the author's use of fresh, engaging, or beautiful language enhance or change what is being described? How would a specific phrase or sentence sound different or shift in meaning if a synonym were used?
- ✓ How does the rhyme scheme, meter, and other poetic language affect the meaning?
- ✓ How does word choice, including different possible meanings from other countries, help determine meaning?
- ✓ How does the author use poetic techniques, multiple meaning words, and language that appeals to emotions to craft a message or idea?
- ✓ How would the text be different if another type of technique or other words were used?

TURN AND TALK

1. Who is your favorite author?
2. What is it about the way your favorite author uses language that affects you?

SPEAKING FRAMES

- My favorite author is ____.
- His/her language makes me feel ____.

SKILL VOCABULARY

style / el estilo *noun* a way of expressing something that is characteristic of the person or time period COGNATE

tone / el tono *noun* the writer's or speaker's attitude toward his or her subject matter COGNATE

attitude / la actitud *noun* a state involving beliefs and feelings that causes a person to think or act in a certain way COGNATE

Skill: Language, Style, and Audience

Reread Lines 105–116 of "The Love Song of J. Alfred Prufrock." Then, using the Checklist on the previous page, answer the multiple-choice questions below.

YOUR TURN

1. What is the most likely interpretation of "But as if a magic lantern threw the nerves in patterns on a screen"?
   - A. Prufrock can explain himself so clearly that it is like being able to read words on a screen.
   - B. Prufrock's emotions are so clear to him that it is like seeing his nervous system on a screen.
   - C. Prufrock's nervousness is so intense that it seems his nerves are being projected onto a screen.
   - D. Prufrock sees himself as a magician who can make patterns seem to appear and change on a screen.

2. Which statement best evaluates how the author's use of language affects the reader's perception of Prufrock in these lines?
   - A. The author's choice to use repetition emphasizes Prufrock's uncertainty about how to communicate what he is trying to say.
   - B. The author's choice to include a sentence that asks a question is effective because the purpose of the poem is to make a request of readers.
   - C. The language in line 113 helps readers understand that Prufrock is lying in bed as he writes the poem.
   - D. The author's lists in lines 107 and 108 are distracting because readers do not know enough about the events he is referencing.

Your Turn

Ask students to complete the Your Turn Activity.

QUESTION 1

A. Incorrect. Prufrock is unable to explain himself clearly throughout the poem.

B. Incorrect. Prufrock's emotions are not clear to him.

C. Correct. Prufrock feels as though "a magic lantern," or a kind of projector, is showing his nerves on a screen.

D. Incorrect. The reference to "a magic lantern" does not mean Prufrock sees himself as a magician.

QUESTION 2

A. Correct. The repetition of words and phrases in the poem helps readers understand the poet's stream of consciousness style, which imitates the flow of thoughts.

B. Incorrect. The purpose of this poem is not to make a request of readers. The question further emphasizes Prufrock's indecisiveness.

C. Incorrect. The language in this line does not refer to the setting of the poem.

D. Incorrect. The lists in lines 107 and 108 reference the memories shared between Prufrock and the woman he loves.

SkillsTV

Project the SkillsTV episode and pause at the following times to prompt discussion:

0:14 Why does the student say language, style, and audience is "social media in a nutshell"? Is she right?

1:59 How do the students determine the effect of the poem's language and style on readers' perceptions? What aspects of the poem, if any, did they overlook in their discussion?

2:10 Discuss the allusion to Shakespeare's *Hamlet*. Do you agree this is an example of "how language, style, and audience come together"? Why or why not?

Skill: Poetic Elements and Structure

Introduce the Skill

Watch the Concept Definition video and read the following definition with your students.

Poetic structure describes the organization of words and lines in a poem as well as its rhyme scheme and meter. Poems consist of words that are divided into **lines**. A group of lines is called a **stanza**.

Other elements of poetry that contribute to structure include rhyme and rhythm. **Rhyme** is the repetition of the same or similar vowel sounds. The **rhyme scheme** of a poem is the pattern formed by the rhyming words at the end of lines. **Rhythm** is the pattern of unstressed and stressed syllables in a line of poetry. A regular pattern is called **meter**, and it gives a line of poetry a predictable rhythm.

The poet's choice of **poetic form**, or arrangement and style of a poem, will help determine the structure. Common forms include haiku, limerick, and sonnet, each with its own rules. Poetry without a consistent meter, rhyme, or stanza length is called **open form**.

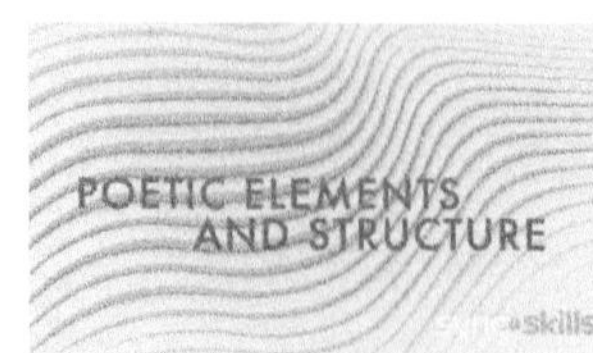

Skill: Poetic Elements and Structure

Use the Checklist to analyze Poetic Elements and Structure in "The Love Song of J. Alfred Prufrock." Refer to the sample student annotations about Poetic Elements and Structure in the text.

••• CHECKLIST FOR POETIC ELEMENTS AND STRUCTURE

In order to analyze a poet's choices concerning how to structure specific parts of a poem, note the following:

- ✓ the form and overall structure of the poem
- ✓ the rhyme, rhythm, and meter, if present
- ✓ lines and stanzas in the poem that suggest its meanings and aesthetic impact
- ✓ how the poet began or ended the poem
- ✓ if the poet provided a comedic or tragic resolution

To analyze how an author's choices concerning how to structure specific parts of a poem contribute to its overall structure and meaning as well as its aesthetic impact, consider the following questions:

- ✓ How does the poet structure the poem? What is the structure of specific parts?
- ✓ How do the poet's choices contribute to the poem's overall structure, meaning, and aesthetic impact?

TURN AND TALK

1. What are some poetic forms that you know about?
2. What is your favorite poem? Why do you like it?

ELL SPEAKING FRAMES

- A poetic form I know about is ____.
- My favorite poem is ____. I like it because ____.

V SKILL VOCABULARY

poetic structure / la estructura poética ***noun*** the organization of words and lines as well as the rhyme and meter of a poem COGNATE

rhythm / el ritmo ***noun*** the pattern of unstressed and stressed syllables in a line of poetry

meter / la métrica ***noun*** a regular pattern of unstressed and stressed syllables in a line of poetry

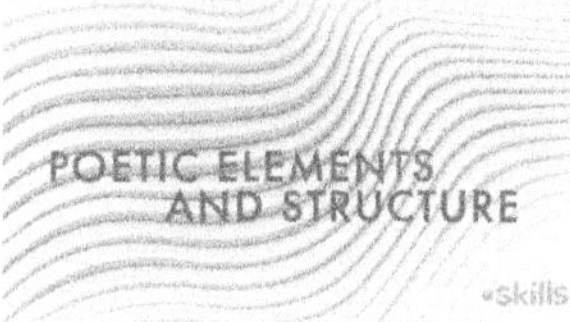

Skill: Poetic Elements and Structure

Reread lines 127–138 of "The Love Song of J. Alfred Prufrock." Then, using the Checklist on the previous page, answer the multiple-choice questions below.

YOUR TURN

1. This question has two parts. First, answer Part A. Then, answer Part B.

   Part A: Which statement best describes the rhyme scheme of these lines?

   - A. Eliot mainly uses couplets with some lines that break the pattern.
   - B. Eliot does not use a consistent rhyme scheme, even though some words rhyme.
   - C. Eliot follows a traditional rhyme scheme of *aabba*, which is usually found in sonnets.
   - D. Eliot uses blank verse to allude to the work of famous English poets who came before him.

   Part B: Which statement explains why Eliot would choose to use the rhyme scheme in Part A?

   - A. Eliot wanted to write a poem that completely rejected traditional poetic structures.
   - B. Eliot wanted to align himself with famous English writers like Shakespeare and Milton.
   - C. Eliot wanted to draw the reader's attention to the lines that do not fit the rhyme scheme.
   - D. Eliot wanted to help the reader follow the poem's conclusion by using a set rhyme scheme.

2. Which statement best explains a possible reason Eliot ended the poem as he did?

   - A. After focusing on Prufrock's regrets and insecurities, Eliot ended the poem on a hopeful note.
   - B. Prufrock is mostly unable to take action, but Eliot ends the poem with Prufrock in love.
   - C. The poem's conclusion offers Eliot's answer to Prufrock's question about how to begin.
   - D. Eliot wanted to highlight that Prufrock is unable to change by the poem's conclusion.

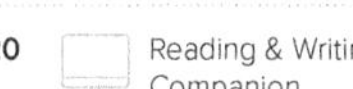

SKILL VOCABULARY

rhyme / la rima ***noun*** the repetition of the same or similar sounds in a poem

rhyme scheme / el patrón de rima ***noun*** the pattern formed by the rhyming words at the end of lines in a poem

poetic form / la forma poética ***noun*** the particular set of rules guiding the arrangement of words and lines in a poem COGNATE

open form / la forma abierta ***noun*** poetic form without consistent meter, rhyme, or stanza length

Your Turn

Ask students to complete the Your Turn Activity.

QUESTION 1

Part A

A. Correct. Most of the lines are rhyming couplets, although lines 129-131 all rhyme, line 133 does not rhyme with another line, and line 132 rhymes with line 136, which does not make a couplet because the lines are not one after the other.

B. Incorrect. Most of the lines are rhyming couplets.

C. Incorrect. Eliot does not use *aabba*.

D. Incorrect. Eliot does not use blank verse.

Part B

A. Incorrect. Although Eliot experiments with the rhyme scheme, he mainly uses the couplet, which is a traditional poetic structure.

B. Incorrect. The rhyme scheme of these final lines does not overtly align the poem with poems by Milton and Shakespeare.

C. Correct. The lines that don't fit the pattern ("me," "waves," "seas") are emphasized and support Prufrock's feelings throughout the poem of being alone and overwhelmed.

D. Incorrect. The poem does not follow a set rhyme scheme in these lines.

QUESTION 2

A. Incorrect. The poem's ending is not hopeful.

B. Incorrect. Although the last lines use the pronoun "we," these lines do not support the idea that Prufrock is successful in love.

C. Incorrect. This answer is not supported by the text.

D. Correct. The poem ends with "we drown," which could be Prufrock and the "you" of the poem being drowned by reality ("human voices wake us"), a reference to the inevitability of death, or Prufrock drowning in his questions, inabilities, and insecurities. The finality indicates that Prufrock does not grow or change by the end of the poem.

Skill: Literary Periods

Introduce the Skill

Watch the Concept Definition video and read the following definition with your students.

A **literary period** refers to a historical time and place in which a group of writers who share ideas write similar texts about a number of issues. These shared ideas can include subjects such as writing style, science, philosophy, art, politics, or culture. Sometimes a literary period or **movement** is instigated by the **historical period** in which it occurs. For example, Romanticism, which among other issues celebrated the rights of the individual, began at about the same time as the French Revolution, an event that signaled the beginning of the end for many absolute monarchies. Knowledge of the literary period in which a text was written can help provide context for the ideas and events covered in the text.

Skill: Literary Periods

Use the Checklist to analyze Literary Periods in "The Love Song of J. Alfred Prufrock." Refer to the sample student annotations about Literary Periods in the text.

••• CHECKLIST FOR LITERARY PERIODS

In order to build knowledge of eighteenth-, nineteenth-, and early-twentieth-century foundational works of American literature, note the following:

- ✓ reference materials that summarize the features of eighteenth-, nineteenth-, and early-twentieth-century foundational works of American literature
- ✓ the emergence of any specific literary periods during this span of time
- ✓ two or more foundational works of literature written during the same literary period
- ✓ how two or more texts from the same period treat similar themes or topics
- ✓ common themes, styles, word choice, language, and other text features

To demonstrate knowledge of eighteenth-, nineteenth-, and early-twentieth-century foundational works of American literature, and how two or more texts from the same period treat similar themes or topics, consider the following questions:

- ✓ What specific literary periods arose in America during the eighteenth, nineteenth, and early twentieth centuries?
- ✓ How do authors working in one or more of these literary periods treat similar themes and topics?

TURN AND TALK

Use the following questions to discuss literary periods with your students.

- What are some important events that happened in the early twentieth century?
- What do you already know about the literary period of Modernism?

Have students share out their answers with the class.

SPEAKING FRAMES

- An event in the early twentieth century was ____. It was important because ____.
- I know that Modernist writers often ____.

SKILL VOCABULARY

literary period / el periodo literario *noun* a historical time and place in which a group of writers who share ideas write similar texts about a number of issues COGNATE

movement / el movimiento *noun* an organized effort to promote shared social, political, or artistic idea, or to attain a goal COGNATE

historical period / el período histórico *noun* a period or time in history in which events occurred, identified by such things as geography, society, wars, or political events during particular decades, centuries, or eras COGNATE

Skill: Literary Periods

Reread lines 7–18 of "The Love Song of J. Alfred Prufrock." Then, using the Checklist on the previous page, answer the multiple-choice questions below.

YOUR TURN

1. What theme, common to the literary period of Modernism, do you see in these lines from both poems?

   - A. The chaos of modern life can sometimes make one feel isolated and overwhelmed.
   - B. One should be fearful of the technology and industrialization at the center of modern life.
   - C. Those who are tasked with protecting others grow accustomed to chaotic experiences.
   - D. The world seems forever dark and cold to those who are too afraid to love.

2. Which statement best compares the use of sentence structure in both poems?

   - A. Both poems reject traditional punctuation to allow readers to follow the flow of ideas.
   - B. Both poems experiment with sentence structure to show the positive outlook of the speaker.
   - C. Both poems use a combination of very short and very long sentences to highlight main ideas.
   - D. Both poems use long and fragmented sentence structure to show new thoughts entering the text.

Your Turn

Ask students to complete the Your Turn Activity.

QUESTION 1

A. Correct. The images and noises of the fire engine create a sense of chaos in the "dark city," and Prufrock's concern about "an overwhelming question" is drowned in "restless nights" and "tedious" streets.

B. Incorrect. A fear of technology is not a prevalent theme in either poem.

C. Incorrect. This theme is not prevalent in either poem.

D. Incorrect. This could possibly be a theme in Eliot's poem, but it does not apply to "The Great Figure."

QUESTION 2

A. Incorrect. This statement is not true of either poem; "The Great Figure" has very little punctuation, but it does not reject punctuation entirely.

B. Incorrect. Both poets are experimenting with sentence structure, but "the positive outlook of the speaker" does not apply to either poem.

C. Incorrect. This statement is not true of both poems.

D. Correct. Eliot's poem uses long, fragmented sentences, and Williams's entire poem is one long sentence fragmented by the line breaks.

Close Read

Skills Focus

QUESTION 1: Language, Style, and Audience

See lines 7–9. The speaker compares the evening to a patient who is about to have surgery. This word choice is unusual and creates a mood of unease.

QUESTION 2: Language, Style, and Audience

See lines 68–75.

QUESTION 3: Poetic Elements and Structure

See lines 96–104.

QUESTION 4: Literary Period

See lines 105–110.

QUESTION 5: Connect to Essential Question

See lines 129–131.

CHECK FOR SUCCESS

If students struggle to respond to Skills Focus Question #1, ask students the following questions:

1. What image does Eliot compare the evening to?
2. Is this a positive or a negative image? How do you know?
3. How does the image make you feel? Why?

Close Read

Reread "The Love Song of J. Alfred Prufrock." As you reread, complete the Skills Focus questions below. Then use your answers and annotations from the questions to help you complete the Write activity.

SKILLS FOCUS

1. Highlight a section in the beginning of the poem in which the speaker uses multiple meanings or engaging language to describe the evening. Describe the effect the poet's word choice has on the reader's understanding of the scene.
2. Identify a section in which the poet includes a description that evokes at least one of the five senses. Explain why this description is effective and how it shapes your perception of the text.
3. Identify a section in which the poet uses unconventional sentence or poetic structure. Explain why this unconventional structure is effective and how it shapes your perception of the text.
4. Highlight a section in which the speaker is shown to be overwhelmed. Using your memory of "The Great Figure," explain how the speaker's behavior reflects the poem's literary period.
5. The title "The Love Song of J. Alfred Prufrock" might seem misleading after reading the poem. Identify two moments in which the speaker of the poem expresses a feeling of alienation. What causes his alienation? Why is this poem called a "Love Song"?

WRITE

LITERARY ANALYSIS: Some critics claim that the speaker in "The Love Song of J. Alfred Prufrock" describes an atmosphere that is his own personal hell. What evidence in the poem do you find to support this claim? What is it about Prufrock's existence that seems hellish, and how does that existence help define this poem as a Modernist poem? Write a response that answers these questions, using evidence from the text to support your ideas.

Writer's Notebook

Connect to Literary Focus: Give students time to reflect on how "The Love Song of J. Alfred Prufrock" demonstrates the conventions and characteristics of this unit's literary focus, Modernism, by freewriting in their Writer's Notebooks.

Beginning & Intermediate

Remind students of the unit's literary focus, Modernism. Encourage students to draw their connections or allow students to write in their native language. Circulate around the room, prompting students for their thoughts as they respond orally or through pantomime.

Advanced & Advanced High

Allow students to share their connections orally in pairs or small groups before freewriting.

StudySyncTV

Project the StudySyncTV episode and pause at the following times to prompt discussion:

1:33 What contradiction do the students find in the first few lines of stanza 2? How does this contradiction help them move the discussion forward?

2:50 What textual evidence do group members use to determine that Prufrock is a member of the upper class?

4:58 What evidence does Christina use to support her contention that Prufrock and the woman he is speaking about "never got together"? How might this assertion affect the way the group perceives the poem?

Collaborative Conversation

Break students into collaborative conversation groups to discuss the Close Read prompt. Ask students to use the StudySyncTV episode as a model for their discussion. Remind them to reference their Skills Focus annotations in their discussion.

Some critics claim that the speaker in "The Love Song of J. Alfred Prufrock" describes an atmosphere that is his own personal hell. What evidence in the poem do you find to support this claim? What is it about Prufrock's existence that seems hellish, and how does that existence help define this poem as a Modernist poem? Write a response that answers these questions, using evidence from the text to support your ideas.

Use the scaffolds below to differentiate instruction for your ELL English Language Learners and A Approaching grade-level learners.

ELL **BEGINNING, INTERMEDIATE** Use the discussion guide and speaking frames to facilitate the discussion with support from the teacher.

ADVANCED, ADVANCED HIGH Use the discussion guide and speaking frames to facilitate the discussion in mixed-level groups.

A **APPROACHING** Use the discussion guide to facilitate the discussion in mixed-level groups.

APPROACHING
ADVANCED, ADVANCED HIGH
BEGINNING, INTERMEDIATE

Discussion Guide	Speaking Frames
1. What does it mean to be in your own personal hell?	• To be in your own personal hell means ____. • I know this because ____.
2. What is it about Prufrock's existence that seems hellish?	• Prufrock is unhappy when ____. • It is like being in hell because ____.
3. What evidence in the poem do you find to support this claim?	• One piece of textual evidence that supports this claim is ____. • This supports the claim because ____.
4. How does Prufrock's existence reflect themes of Modernism?	• Prufrock's existence connects to Modernism because ____.

Review Prompt and Rubric

Before students begin writing, review the writing prompt and rubric with the class.

LITERARY ANALYSIS: Some critics claim that the speaker in "The Love Song of J. Alfred Prufrock" describes an atmosphere that is his own personal hell. What evidence in the poem do you find to support this claim? What is it about Prufrock's existence that seems hellish, and how does that existence help define this poem as a Modernist poem? Write a response that answers these questions, using evidence from the text to support your ideas.

PROMPT GUIDE

- What does it mean to be in your own personal hell?
- What is it about Prufrock's existence that seems hellish?
- What evidence in the poem do you find to support this claim?
- How does Prufrock's existence reflect themes of Modernism?

Score	Literary Periods	Language and Conventions
4	The writer clearly explains Prufrock's hellish existence and how that existence connects to Modernism. The writer provides exemplary analysis, using relevant textual evidence.	The writer demonstrates a consistent command of grammar, punctuation, and usage conventions. Although minor errors may be evident, they do not detract from the fluency or the clarity of the essay.
3	The writer explains Prufrock's hellish existence and how that existence connects to Modernism. The writer provides sufficient analysis, using relevant textual evidence most of the time.	The writer demonstrates an adequate command of grammar, punctuation, and usage conventions. Although some errors may be evident, they create few (if any) disruptions in the fluency of the writing or the clarity of the essay.
2	The writer begins to explain Prufrock's hellish existence and how that existence connects to Modernism, but the explanation is incomplete. The writer uses relevant textual evidence only some of the time.	The writer demonstrates a partial command of grammar, punctuation, and usage conventions. Some distracting errors may be evident, at times creating minor disruptions in the fluency or clarity of the writing.
1	The writer attempts to explain Prufrock's hellish existence and how that existence connects to Modernism, but the explanation is not successful. The writer uses little or no relevant textual evidence.	The writer demonstrates little or no command of grammar, punctuation, and usage conventions. Serious and persistent errors create disruptions in the fluency of the writing and sometimes interfere with meaning.
0	The writer does not provide a relevant response to the prompt or does not provide a response at all.	Serious and persistent errors overwhelm the writing and interfere with the meaning of the response as a whole, making the writer's meaning impossible to understand.

Write

SCAFFOLDS

Ask students to complete the writing assignment using text evidence to support their answers.

Use the scaffolds below to differentiate instruction for your ELL English Language Learners and A Approaching grade level readers.

ELL **BEGINNING** With the help of the word bank, write a response using paragraph frame 1.

INTERMEDIATE With the help of the word bank, write a response using paragraph frames 1 and 2.

ADVANCED, ADVANCED HIGH Write a response of differentiated length using the sentence starters.

A **APPROACHING** Write a response of differentiated length using the sentence starters.

BEGINNING | INTERMEDIATE | ADVANCED, ADVANCED HIGH | APPROACHING

Word Bank	Paragraph Frame 1	Paragraph Frame 2	Sentence Starters
dare body unhappy self-image indecisive	The speaker in "The Love Song of J. Alfred Prufrock" seems to be very unhappy. He has a poor self-image and worries about what others think of him. This is reflected in his description of his aging body. He is also very indecisive. He asks several times "Do I dare?"	Some textual evidence that supports this analysis is ____. This shows that the speaker is ____ because ____. Another quotation from the poem that shows that the speaker is ____ is ____. Prufrock's feelings of ____ reflect a common theme of Modernist literature.	• The speaker of "The Love Song of J. Alfred Prufrock" is . . . • Part of the speaker's life that seems hellish is . . . • Textual evidence that supports this idea is . . . • This shows that . . .

Peer Review

Students should submit feedback to two peers using the review instructions below.

- How well does this response answer the prompt?
- How well does the writer connect Prufrock's hellish existence to Modernism?
- How well does the writer support his or her points with textual evidence?
- Which sentence in the writer's response made you think differently about the text?
- What did the writer do well in this response? What does the writer need to work on?

Rate

Respond to the following with a point rating that reflects your opinion.

	1	2	3	4
Ideas				
Evidence				
Language and Conventions				

Submit

ELL A **SENTENCE FRAMES**

- You (completely / partly / almost) ____ answered the prompt because ____.
- The best evidence you used was ____.
- After I read your response, I understood ____.
- One good point you made was ____.
- One idea that needed clarification was ____.

miss rosie

POETRY
Lucille Clifton
1987

Introduction

Twice a finalist for the Pulitzer Prize in Poetry, American poet and educator Lucille Clifton (1936–2010) was born in Depew, New York. In addition to offering acute insight into family dynamics, community, and the African American experience, Clifton's work is often heralded for its exploration of the enduring strength and dignity peculiar to those who live on the margins of society. One such poem, "miss rosie," tells the story of someone who, on the surface, appears to be just another homeless woman, forlorn and forgotten. But as we learn from the speaker, rarely is life so cut and dry.

The speaker sees a homeless woman, who is wrapped in rags, "like garbage," and smells of old potato peels. Wearing an old man's shoes, with toes busted out, the woman seems to be waiting for her mind to come back. The speaker continues looking at this disheveled, miserable woman, awed by the fact that she used to be called the Georgia Rose, and that one day long ago, she used to be the best- looking woman in the state. In the end, the speaker stands up for her.

COMPARING WITHIN AND ACROSS GENRES

What causes individuals to feel alienated?

The poems "miss rosie" and "The Idler" and the short story "A Cup of Tea" all explore ideas about wealth and poverty.

In "miss rosie" by Lucille Clifton, the speaker focuses on a homeless woman, and the value of human worth.

Proficiency-leveled summaries and summaries in multiple languages are available digitally.

Audio and audio text highlighting are available with this text.

Entry Point

As students prepare to read "miss rosie," share the following information with them to provide context.

- ✓ Lucille Clifton was born Thelma Lucille Sayles on June 27, 1936. She attended Howard University and graduated from State University of New York. Her first book of poetry was published in 1969. Clifton was the poet laureate of Maryland from 1979 to 1985, and won the Ruth Lilly Poetry Prize in 2007.
- ✓ Much of Clifton's work focuses on the struggles and strengths of African Americans, especially those in the inner city. She celebrates the everyday and the ordinary, while revealing the complexities of life. Her poems can be gritty, but they carry a message of hope. As judges noted when awarding her the Ruth Lilly Poetry Prize, "One always feels the looming humaneness around Lucille Clifton's poems—it is a moral quality that some poets have and some don't."
- ✓ Lucille Clifton's poetry is noted for its brevity. She says a lot with few words, and eliminates things like capitalization and punctuation.

Instructional Path

The print teacher's edition includes essential point-of-use instruction and planning tools. Complete lesson plans and program documents appear in your digital teacher account.

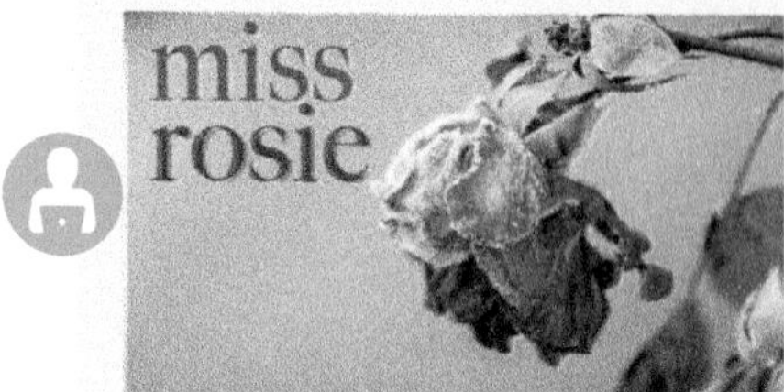

Independent Read: miss rosie

Objectives: After reading "miss rosie" students will write a short response that demonstrates how the poem's dramatic structure contributes to the poem's meaning and message.

Independent Read

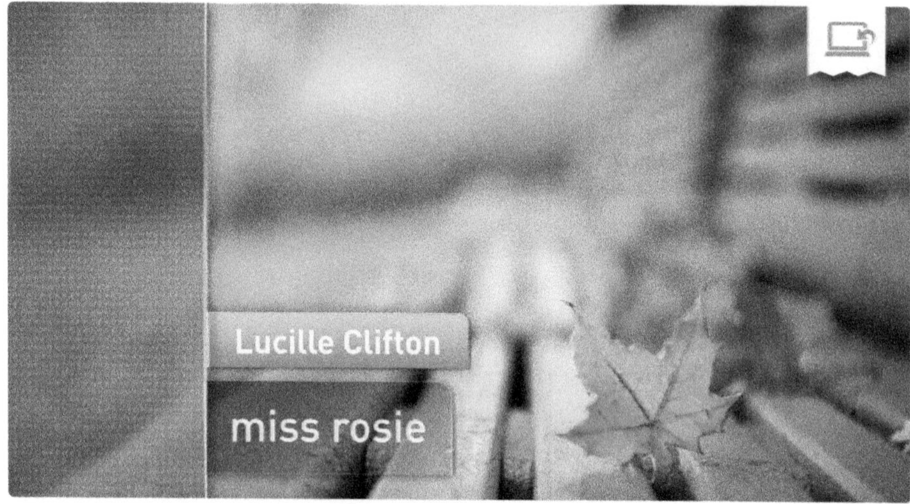

Introduce the Text

As a class, watch the video preview and have students read the introduction in pairs to make connections to the video preview.

- How do the images, words, and music in this video make you feel?
- How do you feel when you see or think about a homeless person?

ELL SENTENCE FRAMES

- The images made me feel ____.
- The words and music made me feel ____.
- Seeing or thinking about homeless people makes me feel ____.

Access Complex Text

LEXILE: N/A **WORD COUNT:** 82

The following areas may be challenging for students, particularly ELL English Language Learners and A Approaching grade-level learners.

Purpose	Connection of Ideas
• Students might not recognize the tone of the speaker in the poem, and the shift in tone in the last two lines. • Remind students that tone is the speaker's attitude toward the subject and that tone can be determined by analyzing word choice.	• Students may be challenged to determine the meaning of the last three lines of the poem. • Have students work together in a collaborative conversation, discussing the meaning of the last three lines.

"through your destruction / i stand up"

NOTES

when i watch you
wrapped up like garbage
sitting, surrounded by the smell
of too old potato peels
or
when i watch you
in your old man's shoes
with the little toe cut out
sitting, waiting for your mind
like next week's grocery
i say
when i watch you
you wet brown bag of a woman
who used to be the best looking gal in georgia
used to be called the Georgia Rose
i stand up
through your destruction
i stand up

WRITE

LITERARY ANALYSIS: The poem "miss rosie" follows a dramatic structure in telling a story about a homeless woman. Write a short response in which you analyze the effect the dramatic structure has on the meaning of the poem. In your essay, consider and respond to questions such as the following: What story does this poem tell? What relationship does the speaker of the poem have with Miss Rosie? How would the story be different if Miss Rosie were telling her own story? What message is being conveyed by this story? Remember to use textual evidence to support your response.

Developing Background Knowledge and Cultural Awareness

1. Share with students the following quotation by Lucille Clifton: "All of our stories become The Story. If mine is left out, something's missing."
2. In small groups, have students discuss the quotation's meaning, and how it relates to something in their own lives or to something they've read or learned about.

Discuss with students: Why is it important for everyone to have the opportunity to tell their own story? What happens when we tell other people's stories for them, without first hearing their voice? What is an example of this? In the example you came up with, what would be the more helpful or empathetic action to take?

TEXT TALK

Who is the "you" the speaker addresses directly in the poem?

See lines 1 and 15: The "you" is "miss rosie," who used to be called the Georgia Rose.

How has the Georgia Rose changed?

See lines 13–14: She changed from a pretty young woman into someone who looks like a wet brown paper bag.

Writer's Notebook

Connect to Essential Question: Give students time to reflect on how "miss rosie" connects to the unit's essential question, "What causes individuals to feel alienated?" by freewriting in their Writer's Notebooks.

CHECK FOR SUCCESS

If students are still struggling to respond to the prompt, ask them scaffolded questions, such as:

- What story does this poem tell?
- What relationship does the speaker of the poem have with Miss Rosie?

Reading Comprehension OPTIONAL

Have students complete the digital reading comprehension questions ✓ when they finish reading.

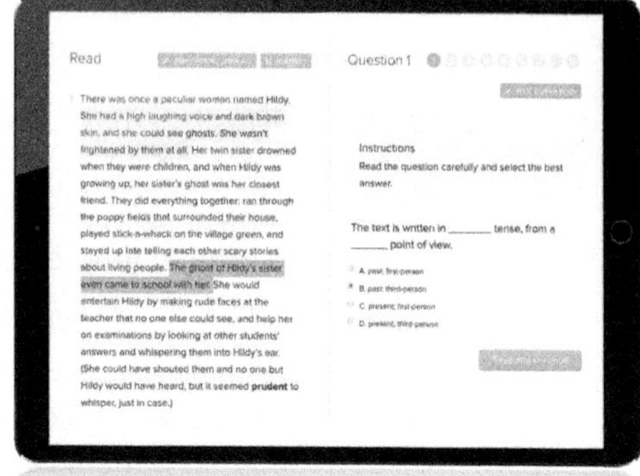

QUESTION 1: B
QUESTION 2: C
QUESTION 3: D
QUESTION 4: C
QUESTION 5: *See chart below.*

First	Second	Third	Fourth
Miss Rosie is filthy.	Miss Rosie is confused and disoriented.	The speaker thinks back to the past.	The speaker is overcome by feeling.

Connect and Extend OPTIONAL

CONNECT TO EXTENDED WRITING PROJECT

Students can find inspiration from Lucille Clifton's poem for their literary analysis essays. Have students work in groups to discuss the theme of alienation in the poem.

BEYOND THE BOOK

Writing: Copy Change Poem

Challenge students to mimic the structure of "miss rosie" as they write their own poem about a person. Tell them to fill in the blanks.

_______________ (title)

when i watch you

____

or

when i watch you

____

____

i say

when i watch you

____

i _______________

i _______________

Have students reflect by answering these questions:

- Did the copy change format make it easier or more difficult to write a poem?
- What is the theme of your poem?

Collaborative Conversation

SCAFFOLDS

Post the writing prompt to generate a discussion in small groups. Ask students to first break down the prompt before they discuss relevant ideas and textual evidence.

The poem "miss rosie" follows a dramatic structure in telling a story about a homeless woman. Write a short response in which you analyze the effect the dramatic structure has on the meaning of the poem. In your essay, consider and respond to questions such as the following: What story does this poem tell? What relationship does the speaker of the poem have with Miss Rosie? How would the story be different if Miss Rosie were telling her own story? What message is being conveyed by this story? Remember to use textual evidence to support your response.

Use the scaffolds below to differentiate instruction for your ELL English Language Learners and A Approaching grade-level learners.

ELL **BEGINNING, INTERMEDIATE** Use the discussion guide and speaking frames to facilitate the discussion with support from the teacher.

ADVANCED, ADVANCED HIGH Use the discussion guide and speaking frames to facilitate the discussion in mixed-level groups.

A **APPROACHING** Use the discussion guide to facilitate the discussion in mixed-level groups.

APPROACHING
ADVANCED, ADVANCED HIGH
BEGINNING, INTERMEDIATE

Discussion Guide	Speaking Frames
1. What story does the poem tell? How would it be different if Miss Rosie told her own story?	• The story is about ____. • The story would be different if Miss Rosie told it because ____.
2. What relationship does the speaker of the poem have with Miss Rosie? Why is this important?	• The speaker____. • This is important because ____.
3. The poem "miss rosie" tells a story about a homeless woman. How does the dramatic structure of this story in the poem affect its meaning?	• The story about her is ____. • This affects the poem's meaning because ____.

Text to World

Use the activity below to differentiate instruction for your B Beyond grade level learners.

The poem's subject, Miss Rosie, is apparently homeless and mentally ill. Have students work as a whole class to do some informal research on homelessness in their particular city.

Ask students:

- What programs does your community have to help the homeless?
- Are these programs sufficient to support the homeless?

Review Prompt and Rubric

Before students begin writing, review the writing prompt and rubric with the class.

LITERARY ANALYSIS: The poem "miss rosie" follows a dramatic structure in telling a story about a homeless woman. Write a short response in which you analyze the effect the dramatic structure has on the meaning of the poem. In your essay, consider and respond to questions such as the following: What story does this poem tell? What relationship does the speaker of the poem have with Miss Rosie? How would the story be different if Miss Rosie were telling her own story? What message is being conveyed by this story? Remember to use textual evidence to support your response.

PROMPT GUIDE

- What story does this poem tell?
- What relationship does the speaker of the poem have with Miss Rosie?
- How would the story be different if Miss Rosie were telling her own story?
- What message is being conveyed by this story?
- What effect does the dramatic structure of the story have on the poem's meaning?

Score	Literary Analysis	Language and Conventions
4	The writer clearly explains how the dramatic structure affects the meaning of the poem and responds to the questions in the prompt, using relevant textual evidence as needed.	The writer demonstrates a consistent command of grammar, punctuation, and usage conventions. Although minor errors may be evident, they do not detract from the fluency or the clarity of the essay.
3	The writer sufficiently explains how the dramatic structure affects the meaning of the poem and responds to some of the questions in the prompt, using relevant textual evidence most of the time.	The writer demonstrates an adequate command of grammar, punctuation, and usage conventions. Although some errors may be evident, they create few (if any) disruptions in the fluency of the writing or the clarity of the essay.
2	The writer begins to explain how the dramatic structure affects the meaning of the poem and respond to some of the questions in the prompt, but the explanation is incomplete. The writer uses relevant textual evidence only some of the time.	The writer demonstrates a partial command of grammar, punctuation, and usage conventions. Some distracting errors may be evident, at times creating minor disruptions in the fluency or clarity of the writing.
1	The writer attempts to explain the dramatic structure and respond to questions in the prompt, but the explanation is not successful. The writer uses little or no relevant textual evidence.	The writer demonstrates little or no command of grammar, punctuation, and usage conventions. Serious and persistent errors create disruptions in the fluency of the writing and sometimes interfere with meaning.
0	The writer does not provide a relevant response to the prompt or does not provide a response at all.	Serious and persistent errors overwhelm the writing and interfere with the meaning of the response as a whole, making the writer's meaning impossible to understand.

Write

Ask students to complete the writing assignment using text evidence to support their answers.

Use the scaffolds below to differentiate instruction for your ELL English Language Learners and A Approaching grade-level learners.

ELL **BEGINNING** With the help of the word bank, write a response using paragraph frame 1.

INTERMEDIATE With the help of the word bank, write a response using paragraph frames 1 and 2.

ADVANCED, ADVANCED HIGH Write a response of differentiated length using the sentence starters.

A **APPROACHING** Write a response of differentiated length using the sentence starters.

BEGINNING / INTERMEDIATE		INTERMEDIATE	ADVANCED, ADVANCED HIGH / APPROACHING
Word Bank	**Paragraph Frame 1**	**Paragraph Frame 2**	**Sentence Starters**
Georgia Rose structure homeless meaning garbage	The poem tells a story about a ____ woman named Miss Rosie. The speaker sees Miss Rosie and compares her to ____. The speaker knows that Miss Rosie was once a beautiful girl known as the ____. The dramatic ____ of Miss Rosie's life story conveys the poem's ____ that the prettiest girl in Georgia can fall on hard times in old age.	The speaker shifts from ____ words about Miss Rosie to ____ words at the end of the poem. This conveys the message that we should respect ____ and not judge them harshly because ____.	• The poem tells a story about . . . • The speaker sees . . . • The speaker says . . . • The speaker remembers . . . • The dramatic structure of the story affects the poem's meaning because . . . • This story conveys the poem's message that . . .

Peer Review

Students should submit substantive feedback to two peers using the review instructions below.

- How well does this response answer the prompt?
- Which of the writer's comments inspired you to think differently about the poem?
- What did the writer do well in this response? What does the writer need to work on?

Remember that your comments are most useful when they are kind and constructive.

Rate

Respond to the following with a point rating that reflects your opinion.

	1	2	3	4
Ideas	■	■	■	□
Evidence	■	■	■	■
Language and Conventions	■	■	□	□

Submit

ELL A **SENTENCE FRAMES**

- You were able to (completely / partly / almost) ____ answer the prompt.
- You could answer the prompt more completely by ____.
- I thought differently about the poem after reading ____.
- My favorite part of your response is ____.

The Idler

POETRY
Alice Dunbar-Nelson
1895

Introduction

Poet, essayist, diarist, and activist Alice Dunbar-Nelson (1875–1935) was born in New Orleans, Louisiana, the daughter of a once-enslaved Louisiana woman named Patricia Wright. Identity, family and oppression are subjects Dunbar-Nelson often explored in her work, including the groundbreaking collections *Violets and Other Tales* and *The Goodness of St. Rocque and Other Stories*. In "The Idler," the speaker observes an idler on the road who dreams all day and yet seems content.

A lingerer idles on the side of the road, gathering up his work and yawning. If he idles much longer, the load he carries will turn to dust. He doesn't care if the fast world scorns him, because he has but one mission in life: to be a happy idler, lying in the sun and dreaming. Content and without ambition, he idles and waits as time passes him by—and eventually, he dies. In the final stanza, the speaker of the poem asks whether you feel pity for this idler, reminding the reader that they will both end up in the same earth.

Proficiency-leveled summaries and summaries in multiple languages are available digitally.

Audio and audio text highlighting are available with this text.

COMPARING WITHIN AND ACROSS GENRES

"The Idler" by Alice Dunbar-Nelson has an "idle lingerer" as its central figure. The tone starkly contrasts "miss rosie" by Lucille Clifton. They are partnered with Katherine Mansfield's "A Cup of Tea," a short story which describes an encounter between a wealthy protagonist and a woman who needs money for a cup of tea.

Entry Point

As students prepare to read "The Idler," share the following information with them to provide context.

- ✓ Alice Dunbar-Nelson was born Alice Ruth Moore on July 19, 1875. Her father was Creole. The Creole people of Louisiana, and their culture, are a mixture of French, Spanish, African, and Native American. Dunbar-Nelson's mixed heritage allowed her to pass as white, but she worked to improve life for other African Americans.
- ✓ Dunbar-Nelson graduated from the teachers' training program at Straight College (now called Dillard University) and worked as a teacher throughout her literary career. She helped found the White Rose Mission, a settlement house that helped African-American women who recently arrived in New York City. Later, she taught at Howard High School in Wilmington, Delaware, and founded the Industrial School for Colored Girls in Marshalltown, Delaware.
- ✓ Dunbar-Nelson also wrote articles on teaching, such as "Is It Time for the Negro Colleges in the South to Be Put into the Hands of Negro Teachers?" and "Negro Literature for Negro Pupils."

Instructional Path

The print teacher's edition includes essential point-of-use instruction and planning tools. Complete lesson plans and program documents appear in your digital teacher account.

Independent Read: The Idler

Objectives: Closely read "The Idler" in order to participate in a collaborative conversation in response to a prompt and write a reflection on participation in the discussion.

Independent Read

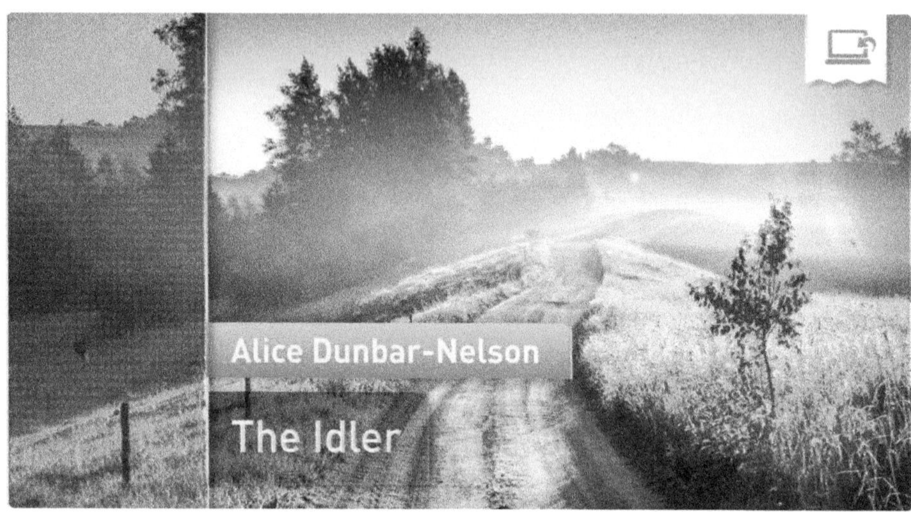

Introduce the Text

As a class, watch the video preview and have students read the introduction in pairs to make connections to the video preview.

- How do the images, words, and music in this video make you feel?
- What is one prediction you have about what you are going to read?

ELL SENTENCE FRAMES

- This video makes me feel ____.
- I predict the poem will have ____.

Access Complex Text

LEXILE: N/A **WORD COUNT:** 156

The following areas may be challenging for students, particularly ELL English Language Learners and A Approaching grade-level learners.

Purpose	Specific Vocabulary
• Some of the language in this poem usually has negative connotations, which may cause students to misinterpret the moral or theme. • Encourage students to read the poem carefully and pay attention to the context.	• Some of the words, like *tiresome*, *infantile*, *mothling*, and *infinitude*, may be unfamiliar to students. • Remind students to remove suffixes to find the roots of these words.

"To be a happy idler, to lounge and sun, And dreaming, pass his long-drawn days away."

An idle lingerer on the wayside's road,
He gathers up his work and yawns away;
A little longer, ere the tiresome load
Shall be **reduced** to ashes or to clay.

No matter if the world has marched along,
And scorned his slowness as it quickly passed;
No matter, if amid the busy **throng**,
He greets some face, **infantile** at the last.

His mission? Well, there is but one,
And if it is a mission he knows it, nay,
To be a happy idler, to lounge and sun,
And dreaming, pass his long-drawn days away.

So dreams he on, his happy life to pass
Content, without ambitions painful sighs,
Until the sands run down into the glass;
He smiles—content—unmoved and dies.

And yet, with all the pity that you feel
For this poor mothling of that flame, the world;
Are you the better for your desperate deal,
When you, like him, into **infinitude** are hurled?

Alice Ruth Moore Dunbar Nelson

NOTES

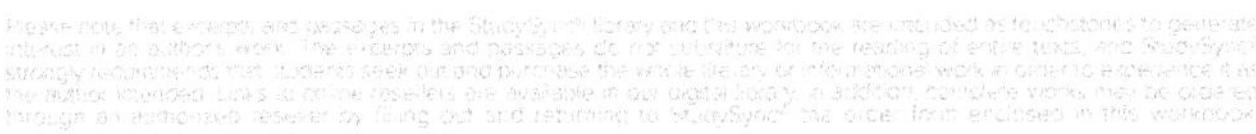

SELECTION VOCABULARY

reduce / reducir *verb* bring down to a certain condition cognate COGNATE

throng / la multitud *noun* a dense crowd

infantile / infantil *adjective* behaving like or characteristic of an infant COGNATE

content / contento/a *adjective* satisfied and happy with present conditions COGNATE

infinitude / la infinitud *noun* the state of being infinite COGNATE

Developing Background Knowledge and Cultural Awareness

1. Share with students the following quotation by Mitch Albom from *Tuesdays with Morrie*: "Maybe death is the great equalizer, the one big thing that can finally make strangers shed a tear for one another."
2. In small groups, have students discuss the quotation's meaning, and how it relates to something in their own lives or to something they've read or learned about.

Discuss with students: Do you believe there is a "correct" way to live life? For instance, do you think everyone should find a way to contribute to society, and spend time with family and friends? Have you ever met or seen someone that believes life should be lived differently? How do you think people develop these beliefs?

TEXT TALK

What is the idler's mission?

See stanza 3: The idler just wants to be happy and relaxed.

What does the speaker ask about the idler?

See stanza 5: The speaker asks if the "you" in the poem is really better than the idler, since everyone will eventually die.

How did discussing the quotation about death and how life should be lived help you better understand the poem?

Answers will vary.

Ask each Beyond grade-level student to write one additional discussion question. Then, have one or two students facilitate a discussion, using their questions to guide the conversation.

Prepare for Advanced Courses

Use the activity below to differentiate instruction for your B Beyond grade level learners.

Analyze for Enrichment

Consider the rhyme scheme in this poem.

Explain to students that poets use a wide range of sound devices in poetry to convey meaning and influence the reader's experience.

Ask students:

- Which sound device is most prevalent in this poem?
- What effect does this sound device have on the poem?

WRITE

DISCUSSION: What is the speaker's opinion of the idler's approach to life? What makes you think so? Support your interpretation with textual evidence. What are your own thoughts about the idler's way of living? Discuss with your classmates what you would want to tell him. Describe any personal experiences that led to your beliefs.

Writer's Notebook

Connect to Essential Question: Give students time to reflect on how "The Idler" connects to the unit's essential question "What causes individuals to feel alienated?" by freewriting in their Writer's Notebooks.

CHECK FOR SUCCESS

If students are still struggling to respond to the prompt, ask them scaffolded questions, such as:

- Is the idler alone or part of a community? How do you know?
- How does reading the poem make you feel? Why?

Reading Comprehension OPTIONAL

Have students complete the digital reading comprehension questions ✔ when they finish reading.

ANSWER KEY

QUESTION 1: A
QUESTION 2: D
QUESTION 3: A
QUESTION 4: C
QUESTION 5:
See chart below.

First	Second	Third	Fourth
"An idle lingerer on the wayside's road, / He gathers up his work and yawns away;"	"And scorned his slowness as it quickly passed; / No matter, if amid the busy throng,"	"To be a happy idler, to lounge and sun,"	"For this poor mothling of that flame, the world; / Are you the better for your desperate deal,"

Connect and Extend OPTIONAL

CONNECT TO EXTENDED WRITING PROJECT

Students can find inspiration from Alice Dunbar-Nelson for their literary analysis essays. Have them pose a philosophical question instead of simply describing an alienated character.

BEYOND THE BOOK

Activity: The Pursuit of Happiness

This poem shares contrasting views on what is needed to be truly happy. Students will compare and contrast their own point of view with those in the poem.

Ask students to:

- Reread the poem twice. Once to understand the speaker's perspective on what is needed for happiness and the second time to understand the idler's view on happiness.
- Use the evidence pulled from the poem to decide how each perspective is similar or different to their own perspective on happiness.
- Choose either the speaker or the idler and write a paragraph explaining how they think similarly or differently to this character.

To reflect, ask students:

- What major factors impact the quality of our lives?
- Where do our ideas for happiness come from?

Collaborative Conversation

SCAFFOLDS

Post the writing prompt to generate a discussion in small groups. Ask students to first break down the prompt before they discuss relevant ideas and textual evidence.

What is the speaker's opinion of the idler's approach to life? What makes you think so? Support your interpretation with textual evidence. What are your own thoughts about the idler's way of living? Discuss with your classmates what you would want to tell him. Describe any personal experiences that led to your beliefs.

Use the scaffolds below to differentiate instruction for your ELL English Language Learners and A Approaching grade-level learners.

ELL **BEGINNING, INTERMEDIATE** Use the discussion guide and speaking frames to facilitate the discussion with support from the teacher.

ADVANCED, ADVANCED HIGH Use the discussion guide and speaking frames to facilitate the discussion in mixed-level groups.

A **APPROACHING** Use the discussion guide to facilitate the discussion in mixed-level groups.

APPROACHING
ADVANCED, ADVANCED HIGH
BEGINNING, INTERMEDIATE

Discussion Guide	Speaking Frames
1. What does the speaker think of the idler?	• The speaker (agrees/disagrees) ____ with people who think the idler is ____. • The speaker thinks the idler is ____.
2. What evidence do you have to support this?	• In stanza ____, the poem says ____. • This shows that ____.
3. What do you think about the idler?	• I think the idler is ____. • I think this because ____.

Multiple Perspectives

Use the activity below to differentiate instruction for your B Beyond grade level learners.

Throughout the poem, the speaker describes the idler from her point of view, and imagines that she knows what he is thinking.

Direct students to consider how the idler may see himself and the speaker.

Ask students:

- How trustworthy is a wealthy person's view of a poor person?
- How might a poor person judge a wealthy person?

Review Prompt and Rubric

Before students begin writing, review the writing prompt and rubric with the class.

DISCUSSION: As you write, make sure to

- evaluate how well everyone followed the rules when making decisions affecting the group
- evaluate your own participation in the discussion
- reflect on how well you adjust your responses to the text if you find the evidence presented by others to be valid and convincing

ELL PROMPT GUIDE

A
- What does the speaker think of the idler?
- What evidence do you have to support this?
- What do you think about the idler?

Score	Reflection	Language and Conventions
4	The writer clearly reflects on his or her own participation. The writer consistently refers to specific examples from the discussion.	The writer demonstrates a consistent command of grammar, punctuation, and usage conventions. Although minor errors may be evident, they do not detract from the fluency or the clarity of the essay.
3	The writer reflects on his or her own participation. The writer refers to specific examples from the discussion most of the time.	The writer demonstrates an adequate command of grammar, punctuation, and usage conventions. Although some errors may be evident, they create few (if any) disruptions in the fluency of the writing or the clarity of the essay.
2	The writer begins to reflect on his or her own participation. The writer refers to specific examples from the discussion some of the time.	The writer demonstrates a partial command of grammar, punctuation, and usage conventions. Some distracting errors may be evident, at times creating minor disruptions in the fluency or clarity of the writing.
1	The writer attempts to reflect his or her own participation. The writer refers to few, if any, examples from the discussion.	The writer demonstrates little or no command of grammar, punctuation, and usage conventions. Serious and persistent errors create disruptions in the fluency of the writing and sometimes interfere with meaning.
0	The writer does not provide a relevant response to the prompt or does not provide a response at all.	Serious and persistent errors overwhelm the writing and interfere with the meaning of the response as a whole, making the writer's meaning impossible to understand.

Write

SCAFFOLDS

Ask students to complete the writing assignment using text evidence to support their answers.

Use the scaffolds below to differentiate instruction for your ELL English Language Learners and A Approaching grade-level readers.

ELL **BEGINNING** With the help of the word bank, write a response using paragraph frame 1.

INTERMEDIATE With the help of the word bank, write a response using paragraph frames 1 and 2.

ADVANCED, ADVANCED HIGH Write a response of differentiated length using the sentence starters.

A **APPROACHING** Write a response of differentiated length using the sentence starters.

BEGINNING / INTERMEDIATE | ADVANCED, ADVANCED HIGH / APPROACHING

Word Bank	Paragraph Frame 1	Paragraph Frame 2	Sentence Starters
state confirm analyze quote opinion ideas speaker actions	My best contribution was when I ____. I plan to ____ to my contributions in future discussions.	I think that my best contribution helped other students to ____. My goal for future discussions will help me ____.	• My best contribution to the discussion was when I . . . • To improve my contributions to future discussions, I plan to . . . • I think that my best contribution helped other students to . . . • My goal for future discussions will enable me to . . .

Peer Review

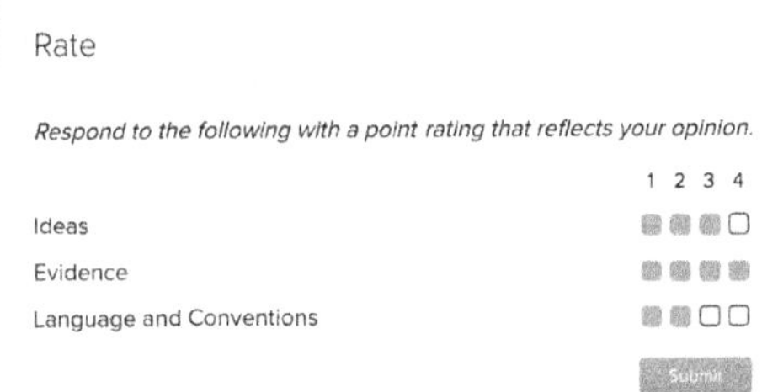

Students should submit substantive feedback to two peers using the review instructions below.

- How well does the writer refer to specific examples from the discussion?
- What does the writer do well in this reflection? What does the writer need to work on?

Remember that your comments are most useful when they are kind and constructive.

SENTENCE FRAMES

- You were able to (completely / partly / almost) ____ answer the prompt.
- You could answer the prompt more completely by ____.
- My favorite part of your response is ____.

A Cup of Tea

FICTION

Katherine Mansfield

1922

Introduction

studysync tv

Katherine Mansfield (1888–1923) was a modernist fiction writer from New Zealand who gained widespread recognition after the publication *In a German Pension*, her first collection of short stories. She soon became friends with other famous modernist writers, such as D.H. Lawrence and Virginia Woolf. The short story "A Cup of Tea" describes a not so typical day in the life of Rosemary Fell, delving into themes of class, gender, beauty, and materialism in London high society.

Although Rosemary Fell was a very rich woman, she was not very beautiful. One day, while visiting her favorite antique store, she could not bring herself to pay 28 guineas for an antique box. Outside the store, a poor woman approached Rosemary and asked for money to buy a cup of tea. Rosemary was struck with a whim and decided to take the poor girl home. Rosemary pictured how she would take care of the girl and how she would tell her friends about it later. Upstairs, the girl was very shy, but Rosemary had tea and sandwiches brought in. Then Rosemary's husband walked in and, upon seeing the girl, was shocked. In private, he told Rosemary that it was impossible for the girl to stay there, and also admitted that the girl was incredibly pretty. Now envious of the girl's looks, Rosemary abandoned her plan to keep her and sent her off with a little money. Later, Rosemary asked her husband whether he thinks she's pretty.

Proficiency-leveled summaries and summaries in multiple languages are available digitally.

Audio and audio text highlighting are available with this text.

COMPARING WITHIN AND ACROSS GENRES

A wealthy woman and an impoverished young girl meet in Mansfield's "A Cup of Tea," allowing the author to explore issues of gender, class, and materialism. Just as "miss rosie" and "The Idler" focus on what the speakers of the poems think about homeless people, Mansfield details the inner dialogue of a character who so concerned with her appearance that she has forgotten how to empathize with a person in need.

Entry Point

As students prepare to read "A Cup of Tea," share the following information with them to provide context.

- ✓ Katherine Mansfield (1888–1923) was born in New Zealand, where many of her short stories are set. Both her parents were born in Australia, and both were children of English immigrants who considered Great Britain their true home. At fifteen, Mansfield and her two older sisters attended a progressive school in London, which allowed its students more freedoms than was common at the time. She was sorry to have to return to New Zealand with her parents, whom she found tedious and intellectually inferior.
- ✓ Mansfield's stories focus on psychological conflicts, and she incorporated poetic language in her literary prose, both of which contributed to her association with the modernist literary movement.
- ✓ Mansfield returned to London to live a Bohemian life. She became an integral part of the modernist literary movement. Virginia Woolf was alternately fond and jealous of Mansfield. Mansfield died at thirty-four after several years of suffering from tuberculosis.

Instructional Path

The print teacher's edition includes essential point-of-use instruction and planning tools. Complete lesson plans and program documents appear in your digital teacher account.

First Read: A Cup of Tea

Objectives: After an initial reading and discussion of the short story, students will be able to identify and describe character traits and setting details as well as articulate the conflict that is integral to the story's plot.

Skill: Word Patterns and Relationships

Objectives: After rereading and discussing a model of close reading, students will be able to identify patterns of word changes to indicate different meanings or parts of speech.

Skill: Summarizing

Objectives: After rereading and discussing a model of close reading, students will be able to identify important details and themes in order to provide an objective summary "A Cup of Tea."

Close Read: A Cup of Tea

Objectives: After engaging in a close reading and discussion of "A Cup of Tea," students will be able to write a short response that compares and contrasts ideas and attitudes about wealth and poverty in "miss rosie," "The Idler," and "A Cup of Tea."

Progress Monitoring

Opportunities to Learn	Opportunities to Demonstrate Learning	Opportunities to Reteach
Word Patterns and Relationships		
Skill: Word Patterns and Relationships	Skill: Word Patterns and Relationships • Your Turn Close Read • Skills Focus	Spotlight Skill: Word Patterns and Relationships
Summarizing		
Skill: Summarizing	Skill: Summarizing • Your Turn Close Read • Skills Focus	Spotlight Skill: Summarizing

First Read

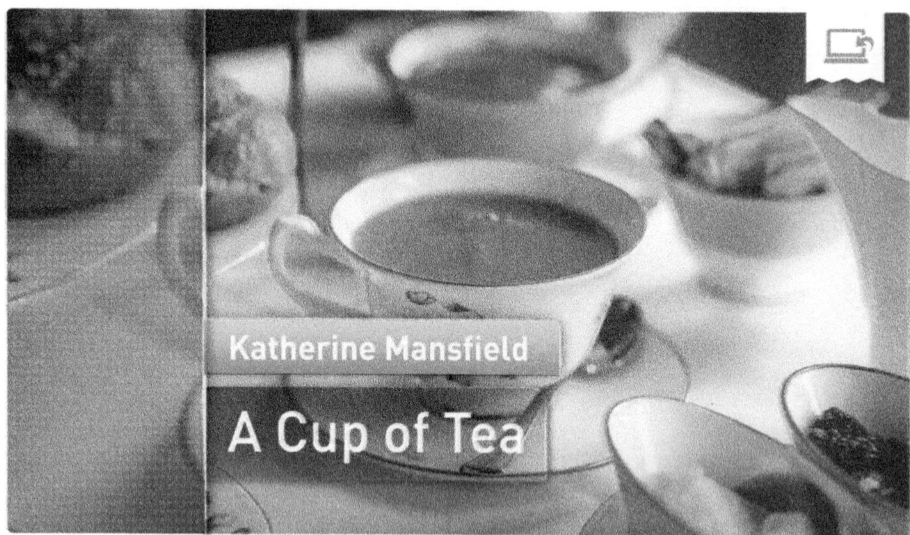

Introduce the Text

As a class, watch the video preview  and have students read the introduction in pairs to make connections to the video preview.

To activate prior knowledge and experiences, ask students:

- What part of the video stood out to you the most?
- What connections did you make between the introduction and the video?

ELL **SPEAKING FRAMES**

- The part of the video that stood out was ____.
- A connection I made between the introduction and the video was ____.

Access Complex Text

LEXILE: 620 **WORD COUNT:** 2,936

The following areas may be challenging for students, particularly ELL English Language Learners and A Approaching grade-level learners.

Connection of Ideas	Prior Knowledge
• The narrator tells the story, but doesn't comment on the events. • Readers have to draw their own conclusions about the meaning. Remind them to connect ideas to help them infer information.	• The story is set in early 20th-century Britain and includes details that reflect differences between social classes. • To fully understand this class conflict, students may need to become familiar with the historical, social, and economic context of this setting.

 SCAFFOLDS

 **ENGLISH LANGUAGE LEARNERS**  **APPROACHING GRADE LEVEL**  **BEYOND GRADE LEVEL**

These icons identify differentiation strategies and scaffolded support for a variety of students. See the digital lesson plan for additional differentiation strategies and scaffolds.

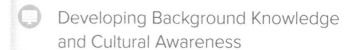

"'Philip,' she whispered, and she pressed his head against her bosom, 'am I pretty?'"

NOTES

1 Rosemary Fell was not exactly beautiful. No, you couldn't have called her beautiful. Pretty? Well, if you took her to pieces . . . But why be so cruel as to take anyone to pieces? She was young, brilliant, extremely modern, exquisitely well dressed, amazingly well read in the newest of the new books, and her parties were the most delicious mixture of the really important people and . . . artists—**quaint** creatures, discoveries of hers, some of them too terrifying for words, but others quite presentable and amusing.

Katherine Mansfield

2 Rosemary had been married two years. She had a duck of a boy. No, not Peter—Michael. And her husband absolutely adored her. They were rich, really rich, not just comfortably well off, which is odious and stuffy and sounds like one's grandparents. But if Rosemary wanted to shop she would go to Paris as you and I would go to Bond Street. If she wanted to buy flowers, the car pulled up at that perfect shop in Regent Street, and Rosemary inside the shop just gazed in her dazzled, rather exotic way, and said: "I want those and those and those. Give me four bunches of those. And that jar of roses. Yes, I'll have all the roses in the jar. No, no lilac. I hate lilac. It's got no shape." The attendant bowed and put the lilac out of sight, as though this was only too true; lilac was dreadfully shapeless. "Give me those stumpy little tulips. Those red and white ones." And she was followed to the car by a thin shopgirl staggering under an immense white paper armful that looked like a baby in long clothes . . .

3 One winter afternoon she had been buying something in a little antique shop in Curzon Street. It was a shop she liked. For one thing, one usually had it to oneself. And then the man who kept it was ridiculously fond of serving her. He beamed whenever she came in. He clasped his hands; he was so gratified he could scarcely speak. **Flattery**, of course. All the same, there was something . . .

SELECTION VOCABULARY

quaint / pintoresco/a *adjective* charming and old-fashioned

flattery / la adulación *noun* praise that is insincere

Developing Background Knowledge and Cultural Awareness

1. Share the following statement with students: "A person can never be truly selfless when helping someone else."
2. Have students raise their hands as to whether they a) agree; b) strongly agree; c) disagree; d) strongly disagree. Assign each response a corner of the room, and have students go to their respective corners to explain their positions.
3. Have one student from each group be the spokesperson to explain the group's response.

Discuss with students: According to The University of Maryland, one in four U.S. teenagers volunteered in 2015. How can we encourage more teenagers to volunteer? Is there a way to volunteer responsibly? What do you think someone should know or do when volunteering?

Summarizing

What does the reader highlight and note in paragraph 7?

The reader highlights important details which helped her have an understanding of the themes of the story. The reader also identifies some answers to the basic *who, what, when, where,* and *why* questions

NOTES

4 "You see, madam," he would explain in his low respectful tones, "I love my things. I would rather not part with them than sell them to someone who does not appreciate them, who has not that fine feeling which is so rare . . ." And, breathing deeply, he unrolled a tiny square of blue velvet and pressed it on the glass counter with his pale finger-tips.

5 To-day it was a little box. He had been keeping it for her. He had shown it to nobody as yet. An exquisite little enamel box with a glaze so fine it looked as though it had been baked in cream. On the lid a minute creature stood under a flowery tree, and a more minute creature still had her arms round his neck. Her hat, really no bigger than a geranium petal, hung from a branch; it had green ribbons. And there was a pink cloud like a watchful cherub floating above their heads. Rosemary took her hands out of her long gloves. She always took off her gloves to examine such things. Yes, she liked it very much. She loved it; it was a great duck. She must have it. And, turning the creamy box, opening and shutting it, she couldn't help noticing how charming her hands were against the blue velvet. The shopman, in some dim cavern of his mind, may have dared to think so too. For he took a pencil, leant over the counter, and his pale, bloodless fingers crept timidly towards those rosy, flashing ones, as he murmured gently: "If I may venture to point out to madam, the flowers on the little lady's bodice."

6 "Charming!" Rosemary admired the flowers. But what was the price? For a moment the shopman did not seem to hear. Then a murmur reached her. "Twenty-eight guineas[1], madam."

7 "Twenty-eight guineas." Rosemary gave no sign. She laid the little box down; she buttoned her gloves again. Twenty-eight guineas. Even if one is rich . . . She looked vague. She stared at a plump tea-kettle like a plump hen above the shopman's head, and her voice was dreamy as she answered: "Well, keep it for me – will you? I'll . . ."

Skill: Summarizing

The protagonist, Rosemary is a rich woman on a shopping trip who wants a jewelry box, but leaves it at the shop.

Rosemary doesn't say what's on her mind.

She seems more concerned about how she looks and behaves, than anything else.

8 But the shopman had already bowed as though keeping it for her was all any human being could ask. He would be willing, of course, to keep it for her for ever.

9 The **discreet** door shut with a click. She was outside on the step, gazing at the winter afternoon. Rain was falling, and with the rain it seemed the dark came too, spinning down like ashes. There was a cold bitter taste in the air, and the new-lighted lamps looked sad. Sad were the lights in the houses opposite. Dimly they burned as if regretting something. And people hurried by, hidden under their hateful umbrellas. Rosemary felt a strange pang. She pressed her muff against her breast; she wished she had the little box, too, to

1. **guineas** units of British currency until the early 19th century

TEXT TALK

What does the man show Rosemary when she visits his antique shop?

See paragraph 5: He shows her a little enamel box.

SELECTION VOCABULARY

discreet / discreto/a ***adjective*** unnoticeable or subtle COGNATE

NOTES

cling to. Of course the car was there. She'd only to cross the pavement. But still she waited. There are moments, horrible moments in life, when one emerges from shelter and looks out, and it's awful. One oughtn't to give way to them. One ought to go home and have an extra-special tea. But at the very instant of thinking that, a young girl, thin, dark, shadowy—where had she come from?—was standing at Rosemary's elbow and a voice like a sigh, almost like a sob, breathed: "Madam, may I speak to you a moment?"

10 "Speak to me?" Rosemary turned. She saw a little battered creature with enormous eyes, someone quite young, no older than herself, who clutched at her coat-collar with reddened hands, and shivered as though she had just come out of the water.

11 "M-madam," stammered the voice. "Would you let me have the price of a cup of tea?"

12 "A cup of tea?" There was something simple, sincere in that voice; it wasn't in the least the voice of a beggar. "Then have you no money at all?" asked Rosemary.

13 "None, madam," came the answer.

14 "How extraordinary!" Rosemary peered through the dusk, and the girl gazed back at her. How more than extraordinary! And suddenly it seemed to Rosemary such an adventure. It was like something out of a novel by Dostoevsky, this meeting in the dusk. Supposing she took the girl home? Supposing she did do one of those things she was always reading about or seeing on the stage, what would happen? It would be thrilling. And she heard herself saying afterwards to the amazement of her friends: "I simply took her home with me," as she stepped forward and said to that dim person beside her: "Come home to tea with me."

15 The girl drew back startled. She even stopped shivering for a moment. Rosemary put out a hand and touched her arm. "I mean it," she said, smiling. And she felt how simple and kind her smile was. "Why won't you? Do. Come home with me now in my car and have tea."

16 "You—you don't mean it, madam," said the girl, and there was pain in her voice.

17 "But I do," cried Rosemary. "I want you to. To please me. Come along."

18 The girl put her fingers to her lips and her eyes devoured Rosemary. "You're—you're not taking me to the police station?" she stammered.

19 "The police station!" Rosemary laughed out. "Why should I be so cruel? No, I only want to make you warm and to hear—anything you care to tell me."

Prepare for Advanced Courses

Use the activity below to differentiate instruction for your B Beyond grade level learners.

Author's Word Choice

Consider the the ways Rosemary describes Ms. Smith throughout the text:

a little battered creature with enormous eyes (paragraph 10)

the little captive she had netted (paragraph 21)

poor little creature (paragraph 40)

languid figure (paragraph 48)

Have students examine the author's word choice to describe Rosemary's perspective.

Ask students:

- How do Rosemary's descriptions of Ms. Smith lead the reader to the message of the text?
- How does Philip's word choice contrast with Rosemary's?

TEXT TALK

What is Rosemary thinking when she invites the girl to come home with her for tea?

See paragraph 14: Rosemary thinks it will be an adventure and something interesting to tell her friends.

Word Patterns and Relationships

What does the reader note in paragraph 23?

The reader notes that the word ending -ed suggests that the word mounted is a verb. He also notes that it sounds like the word "mountain." Combining these clues with the word's context, the reader determines the word mounted might have to do with climbing.

Skills Focus

QUESTION 2: Summary

The details about Miss Smith's hunger and Rosemary's footman and car contrast poverty and wealth. These class and power dynamics influence the plot because they are what cause Miss Smith to almost helplessly go home with Rosemary.

NOTES

20 Hungry people are easily led. The footman held the door of the car open, and a moment later they were skimming through the dusk.

21 "There!" said Rosemary. She had a feeling of triumph as she slipped her hand through the velvet strap. She could have said, "Now I've got you," as she gazed at the little captive she had netted. But of course she meant it kindly. Oh, more than kindly. She was going to prove to this girl that—wonderful things did happen in life, that—fairy godmothers were real, that—rich people had hearts, and that women were sisters. She turned impulsively, saying: "Don't be frightened. After all, why shouldn't you come back with me? We're both women. If I'm the more fortunate, you ought to expect . . ."

22 But happily at that moment, for she didn't know how the sentence was going to end, the car stopped. The bell was rung, the door opened, and with a charming, protecting, almost embracing movement, Rosemary drew the other into the hall. Warmth, softness, light, a sweet scent, all those things so familiar to her she never even thought about them, she watched that other receive. It was fascinating. She was like the rich little girl in her nursery with all the cupboards to open, all the boxes to unpack.

23 "Come, come upstairs," said Rosemary, longing to begin to be generous. "Come up to my room." And, besides, she wanted to spare this poor little thing from being stared at by the servants; she decided as they mounted the stairs she would not even ring for Jeanne, but take off her things by herself. The great thing was to be natural!

Skill: Word Patterns and Relationships

I infer that the -ed at the ending indicates mounted is a verb.

The word might have something to do with climbing because the word sounds like "mountain," and that would make sense given the context.

24 And "There!" cried Rosemary again, as they reached her beautiful big bedroom with the curtains drawn, the fire leaping on her wonderful lacquer[2] furniture, her gold cushions and the primrose[3] and blue rugs.

25 The girl stood just inside the door; she seemed dazed. But Rosemary didn't mind that.

26 "Come and sit down," she cried, dragging her big chair up to the fire, "in this comfy chair. Come and get warm. You look so dreadfully cold."

27 "I daren't, madam," said the girl, and she edged backwards.

28 "Oh, please,"—Rosemary ran forward—"you mustn't be frightened, you mustn't, really. Sit down, when I've taken off my things we shall go into the next room and have tea and be cosy. Why are you afraid?" And gently she half pushed the thin figure into its deep cradle.

2. **lacquer** shiny finish applied to furniture
3. **primrose** European flowering plant that produces flowers with small yellow petals

NOTES

29 But there was no answer. The girl stayed just as she had been put, with her hands by her sides and her mouth slightly open. To be quite sincere, she looked rather stupid. But Rosemary wouldn't acknowledge it. She leant over her, saying: "Won't you take off your hat? Your pretty hair is all wet. And one is so much more comfortable without a hat, isn't one?"

30 There was a whisper that sounded like "Very good, madam," and the crushed hat was taken off.

31 "And let me help you off with your coat, too," said Rosemary.

32 The girl stood up. But she held onto the chair with one hand and let Rosemary pull. It was quite an effort. The other scarcely helped her at all. She seemed to stagger like a child, and the thought came and went through Rosemary's mind, that if people wanted helping they must respond a little, just a little, otherwise it became very difficult indeed. And what was she to do with the coat now? She left it on the floor, and the hat too. She was just going to take a cigarette off the mantelpiece when the girl said quickly, but so lightly and strangely: "I'm very sorry, madam, but I'm going to faint. I shall go off, madam, if I don't have something."

33 "Good heavens, how thoughtless I am!" Rosemary rushed to the bell.

34 "Tea! Tea at once! And some brandy immediately!"

35 The maid was gone again, but the girl almost cried out: "No, I don't want no brandy. I never drink brandy. It's a cup of tea I want, madam." And she burst into tears.

36 It was a terrible and fascinating moment. Rosemary knelt beside her chair.

37 "Don't cry, poor little thing," she said. "Don't cry." And she gave the other her lace handkerchief. She really was touched beyond words. She put her arm round those thin, bird-like shoulders.

38 Now at last the other forgot to be shy, forgot everything except that they were both women, and gasped out: "I can't go on no longer like this. I can't bear it. I can't bear it. I shall do away with myself. I can't bear no more."

39 "You shan't have to. I'll look after you. Don't cry any more. Don't you see what a good thing it was that you met me? We'll have tea and you'll tell me everything. And I shall arrange something. I promise. Do stop crying. It's so exhausting. Please!"

40 The other did stop just in time for Rosemary to get up before the tea came. She had the table placed between them. She plied the poor little creature

Skills Focus

QUESTION 1: Word Patterns and Relationships

The word *languid* precedes the noun *figure*. It is an adjective used to describe the young woman's appearance. I think *languid* might mean she seems weak because she is described as "bird-like," and she asked for tea because she was hungry and faint.

NOTES

with everything, all the sandwiches, all the bread and butter, and every time her cup was empty she filled it with tea, cream and sugar. People always said sugar was so nourishing. As for herself she didn't eat; she smoked and looked away tactfully so that the other should not be shy.

41 And really the effect of that slight meal was marvelous. When the tea-table was carried away a new being, a light, frail creature with tangled hair, dark lips, deep, lighted eyes, lay back in the big chair in a kind of sweet **languor**, looking at the blaze. Rosemary lit a fresh cigarette; it was time to begin.

42 "And when did you have your last meal?" she asked softly.

43 But at that moment the door-handle turned.

44 "Rosemary, may I come in?" It was Philip.

45 "Of course."

46 He came in. "Oh, I'm so sorry," he said, and stopped and stared.

47 "It's quite all right," said Rosemary, smiling. "This is my friend, Miss—"

48 "Smith, madam," said the languid figure, who was strangely still and unafraid.

49 "Smith," said Rosemary. "We are going to have a little talk."

50 "Oh yes," said Philip. "Quite," and his eye caught sight of the coat and hat on the floor. He came over to the fire and turned his back to it. "It's a beastly afternoon," he said curiously, still looking at that **listless** figure, looking at its hands and boots, and then at Rosemary again.

51 "Yes, isn't it?" said Rosemary enthusiastically. "Vile."

52 Philip smiled his charming smile. "As a matter of fact," said he, "I wanted you to come into the library for a moment. Would you? Will Miss Smith excuse us?"

53 The big eyes were raised to him, but Rosemary answered for her: "Of course she will." And they went out of the room together.

54 "I say," said Philip, when they were alone. "Explain. Who is she? What does it all mean?"

55 Rosemary, laughing, leaned against the door and said: "I picked her up in Curzon Street. Really. She's a real pick-up. She asked me for the price of a cup of tea, and I brought her home with me."

SELECTION VOCABULARY

languor / la languidez ***noun*** the feeling of being pleasantly tired and relaxed COGNATE

listless / apático/a ***adjective*** characterized by a lack of energy

56 "But what on earth are you going to do with her?" cried Philip.

57 "Be nice to her," said Rosemary quickly. "Be frightfully nice to her. Look after her. I don't know how. We haven't talked yet. But show her—treat her—make her feel—"

58 "My darling girl," said Philip, "you're quite mad, you know. It simply can't be done."

59 "I knew you'd say that," retorted Rosemary. "Why not? I want to. Isn't that a reason? And besides, one's always reading about these things. I decided—"

60 "But," said Philip slowly, and he cut the end of a cigar, "she's so astonishingly pretty."

61 "Pretty?" Rosemary was so surprised that she blushed. "Do you think so? I—I hadn't thought about it."

62 "Good Lord!" Philip struck a match. "She's absolutely lovely. Look again, my child. I was bowled over when I came into your room just now. However . . . I think you're making a ghastly mistake. Sorry, darling, if I'm **crude** and all that. But let me know if Miss Smith is going to dine with us in time for me to look up *The Milliner's Gazette*[4]."

63 "You absurd creature!" said Rosemary, and she went out of the library, but not back to her bedroom. She went to her writing-room and sat down at her desk. Pretty! Absolutely lovely! Bowled over! Her heart beat like a heavy bell. Pretty! Lovely! She drew her cheque-book towards her. But no, cheques would be no use, of course. She opened a drawer and took out five pound notes, looked at them, put two back, and holding the three squeezed in her hand, she went back to her bedroom.

64 Half an hour later Philip was still in the library, when Rosemary came in.

65 "I only wanted to tell you," said she, and she leaned against the door again and looked at him with her dazzled exotic gaze, "Miss Smith won't dine with us to-night."

66 Philip put down the paper. "Oh, what's happened? Previous engagement?"

67 Rosemary came over and sat down on his knee. "She insisted on going," said she, "so I gave the poor little thing a present of money. I couldn't keep her against her will, could I?" she added softly.

4. ***The Milliner's Gazette*** Hill's Milliner's Gazette was a trade paper published in London for hatmakers, an occupation associated with prostitution

Skills Focus

QUESTION 4: Summary

Philip thinks his wife is making a mistake socializing with a poor girl off the streets because that kind of socializing "simply can't be done." He also seems aware of his wife's insecurity, and uses that knowledge to change Rosemary's mind.

Skills Focus

QUESTION 3: Theme

Rosemary wants to give Miss Smith some money, but she's also jealous of the pretty girl. In the end, Rosemary gives the girl a few pounds, which is much, much less than Rosemary would spend on some useless trinket for herself.

SELECTION VOCABULARY

crude / crudo/a *adjective* done in an unskilled or rough manner COGNATE

TEXT TALK

What does Philip notice about the girl?

See paragraphs 60–62: Philip notices the girl is very pretty.

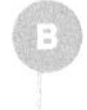

Ask each Beyond grade-level student to write one additional discussion question. Then, have one or two students facilitate a discussion, using their questions to guide the conversation.

Summarizing

What does the reader note in the conclusion of "A Cup of Tea?"

The reader notices that the author concludes the story with Rosemary inquiring about the jewelry box, which was what she wanted all along. Unable to hide her insecure nature any further, Rosemary returns to consider her own feelings and desires.

68 Rosemary had just done her hair, darkened her eyes a little and put on her pearls. She put up her hands and touched Philip's cheeks.

69 "Do you like me?" said she, and her tone, sweet, husky, troubled him.

70 "I like you awfully," he said, and he held her tighter. "Kiss me."

71 There was a pause.

72 Then Rosemary said dreamily: "I saw a fascinating little box to-day. It cost twenty-eight guineas. May I have it?"

73 Philip jumped her on his knee. "You may, little wasteful one," said he.

74 But that was not really what Rosemary wanted to say.

75 "Philip," she whispered, and she pressed his head against her bosom, "am I *pretty*?"

NOTES

Skill: Summarizing

Rosemary directs her husband's attention to her, and away from the girl. She seems insecure.

At the end of the story, Rosemary returns to what she really wanted all along.

Skills Focus

QUESTION 5: Connect to Essential Question

Rosemary's affluence and her position in society allows her to be isolated from reality others face. She temporarily seeks a connection to the girl until her husband comments on her beauty. Her alienation is compounded by the fact that she does not speak her mind.

TEXT TALK

How did the statement "A person can never be truly selfless when helping someone else" help you understand Rosemary's character?

Answers will vary.

Reading Comprehension OPTIONAL

Have students complete the digital reading comprehension questions when they finish reading.

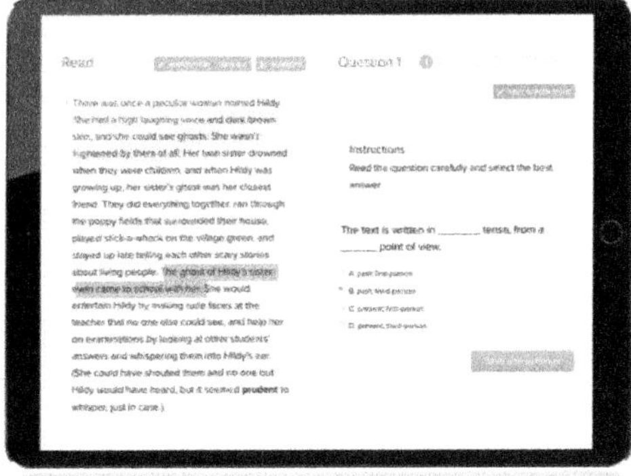

ANSWER KEY

QUESTION 1: C
QUESTION 2: B
QUESTION 3: D
QUESTION 4: A
QUESTION 5: A
QUESTION 6: B
QUESTION 7: A
QUESTION 8: D
QUESTION 9: *See first chart.*
QUESTION 10: *See second chart.*

Synonym	Word
charming	quaint
unobtrusive	discreet
rough	crude
praise	flattery
lifeless	listless

First	Second	Third	Fourth
Rosemary goes out shopping.	Rosemary asks a girl on the street to come home with her for a cup of tea.	Philip meets the girl Rosemary has brought home.	Rosemary asks the girl to leave rather than stay for dinner.

Connect and Extend OPTIONAL

CONNECT TO EXTENDED WRITING PROJECT

Students can use "A Cup of Tea" as a model for their Extended Writing Project. They may study Katherine Mansfield's methods for showing alienation through a character's inner monologue as they craft their own literary analysis essay.

BEYOND THE BOOK

Discussion: Motivations and Desires

Rosemary is adamant about looking after Ms. Smith until Philip returns home. Students will consider the motivation of Rosemary.

Ask students to:

- Break the text up into three sections; Rosemary's first meeting with Ms. Smith, bringing Ms. Smith to her home and sitting with her by the fire, Rosemary conversing with Philip and sending Ms. Smith on her way.
- In three groups discuss Rosemary's motivation and desires.
  - > What decisions is she making?
  - > Why did she make that decision?
  - > What is controlling her desires?
- Come together as a whole class to discuss major ideas shared.

To reflect, ask students to write a paragraph reflecting on what impacted Rosemary's decisions. Encourage them to draw from their conversations in their written reflections.

Think Questions

Circulate as students answer Think Questions independently. Scaffolds for these questions are shown on the opposite page.

QUESTION 1: Textual Evidence

It is not just to offer her a cup of tea. Rosemary thinks it will be "an adventure. . . like something out of a novel" that she can tell her friends to make herself appear more interesting.

QUESTION 2: Textual Evidence

The box is lovely and useless. Rosemary cares only for its superficial beauty and how it makes her own hands look "charming."

QUESTION 3: Textual Evidence

Rosemary is surprised and blushes. Rosemary gets rid of the pretty girl quickly and cheaply – she "took out five pound notes, looked at them, put two back" – because Philip's comment makes Rosemary feel insecure.

QUESTION 4: Context Clues

I think *discreet* means "quiet," or "not attracting attention" because the door shuts with a click, not a bang.

QUESTION 5: Context Clues

I think *crude* as it is used in the text means "offensive" because Philip is apologizing in case his "raw" comments offend or upset his wife.

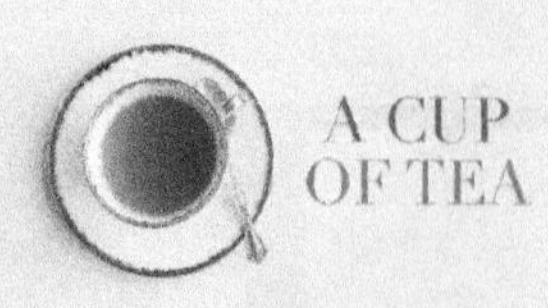

First Read

Read "A Cup of Tea." After you read, complete the Think Questions below.

THINK QUESTIONS

1. Why does Rosemary want to take the girl from the street home with her? Is it really just to offer her a cup of tea? Cite evidence from the text to support your answer.
2. Why does Rosemary like the enamel box she discovers at the antique shop? Cite evidence from the text to support your answer.
3. How does Rosemary react when Philip comments that the girl Rosemary brought home is "astonishingly pretty"? Why does she react this way? Cite evidence from the text to support your answer.
4. Which context clues helped you determine the meaning of the word **discreet** as it is used in the text? Write your definition of *discreet* here, and indicate which clues helped you figure out the meaning of the word.
5. The Latin word *crudus* means "raw or rough." With this in mind, write your best definition of the word **crude** as it is used in the text. Indicate which context clues helped you determine the word's meaning.

Think Questions

SCAFFOLDS

Use the scaffolds below to differentiate instruction for your ELL English Language Learners and A Approaching grade level readers.

ELL **BEGINNING** Write a response using the word bank and sentence frames.

INTERMEDIATE Write a response using the sentence frames.

ADVANCED, ADVANCED HIGH Write a response using the Text-Dependent Question Guide.

A **APPROACHING** Write a response using the Text-Dependent Question Guide.

BEGINNING	INTERMEDIATE	APPROACHING / ADVANCED, ADVANCED HIGH
Word Bank	**Sentence Frames**	**Text-Dependent Question Guide**
charming rough insecure door adventure surprised impolite hands quiet friends	It (is / is not) just to offer the girl a cup of tea. Rosemary thinks taking the girl home will be like an ____ and give her something interesting to tell her ____.	1. • What does the girl ask for? • How does Rosemary react? Is it positive or negative? • What two ideas help Rosemary decide to take the girl home for tea?
	Rosemary likes the box because it makes her ____ look ____.	2. • Why does Rosemary go to the antique shop? What does she like best? • Is it the box itself that Rosemary likes or something else? • What does Rosemary notice when she touches the box?
	Rosemary is ____ and blushes. Philip's comments make Rosemary feel ____.	3. • What does Rosemary say when Philip says the girl is pretty? • What does she do next? • How do Rosemary's words and actions reveal her feelings?
	Discreet means ____. It is used to describe a ____.	4. • Read: "The **discreet** door shut with a click." • Is there anything attention-getting about the door? • What does that tell me about the meaning of the word *discreet*?
	Crude means ____ or having ____ manners.	5. • Read: "Sorry, darling, if I'm **crude** and all that." • Is *crude* positive or negative? How do you know? • How does the Latin meaning help you understand why Philip might use this word to describe himself at this moment in the story?

Skill: Word Patterns and Relationships

Introduce the Skill

Watch the Concept Definition video and read the following definition with your students.

Understanding how words relate to other words is an important part of creating meaning in both reading and writing, and it can also help build vocabulary. **Cause/effect** is a relationship where one thing is the result of the other. For example, if someone is described as a catalyst for change, the reader can infer that *catalyst* means someone who causes change to happen. **Part/whole** is a relationship in which a part of something is compared to the whole. For example, the knowledge that a gearshift is a mechanism that is part of a whole automobile can help a reader define *gearshift* as well as *mechanism*. **Item/category** is a relationship in which a word can be seen to belong to larger category. For example, categorizing poodles, beagles, and schnauzers as canines shows that *canine* is another word for *dog*. Recognizing **word patterns** is another way to help you determine a word's meaning and part of speech, as when *analyze* becomes *analysis*.

Skill: Word Patterns and Relationships

Use the Checklist to analyze Word Patterns and Relationships in "A Cup of Tea." Refer to the sample student annotations about Word Patterns and Relationships in the text.

••• CHECKLIST FOR WORD PATTERNS AND RELATIONSHIPS

In order to identify patterns of word changes to indicate different meanings or parts of speech, do the following:

- ✓ determine the word's part of speech
- ✓ when reading, use context clues to make a preliminary determination of the meaning of the word
- ✓ when writing a response to a text, check that you understand the meaning and part of speech and that it makes sense in your sentence
- ✓ consult a dictionary to verify your preliminary determination of the meanings and parts of speech
- ✓ be sure to read all of the definitions, and then decide which definition, form, and part of speech makes sense within the context of the text

To identify and correctly use patterns of word changes that indicate different meanings or parts of speech, consider the following questions:

- ✓ What is the intended meaning of the word?
- ✓ Do I know that this word form is the correct part of speech? Do I understand the word patterns for this particular word?
- ✓ When I consult a dictionary, can I confirm that the meaning I have determined for this word is correct? Do I know how to use it correctly?

TURN AND TALK

1. What comes to mind when you think about word relationships?
2. How can looking at the relationships between words help you figure out the meaning of unknown words?

SPEAKING FRAMES

- When I think of word relationships ____.
- Looking at word relationships can help me ____.

SKILL VOCABULARY

cause / la causa ***noun*** something that brings about an action or effect COGNATE

effect / el efecto ***noun*** a result; that which has been brought about COGNATE

part / la parte ***noun*** a piece or fragment of something COGNATE

whole / el todo ***noun*** a complete unit or entity

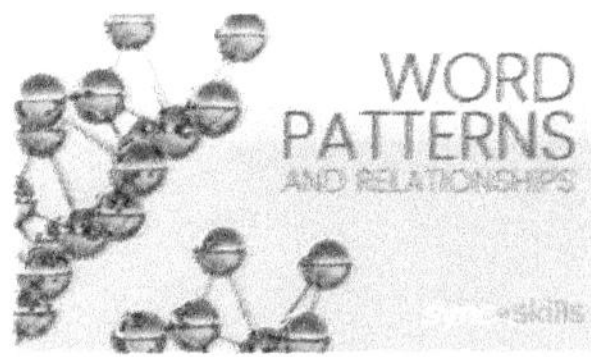

Skill: Word Patterns and Relationships

Reread paragraph 21 of "A Cup of Tea." Then, using the Checklist on the previous page, answer the multiple-choice questions below.

YOUR TURN

1. What part of speech is "impulsively"?

- A. noun
- B. verb
- C. adjective
- D. adverb

2. Given the definitions provided, what is most likely the meaning of *impulsively*?

Impulsive
/ɪmˈpʌlsɪv/
noun
1. act in the moment
2. related to electrical energy
3. a force

- A. To cause electrical energy
- B. To act without thinking
- C. To perform actions without one's consent
- D. To consider the consequences well in advance

SKILL VOCABULARY

item / el elemento ***noun*** one part or component of a group or collection

category / la categoría ***noun*** a collection of things that share a common quality COGNATE

word pattern / el patrón de las palabras ***noun*** the changes in a word depending on usage, as with the verb analyze and the noun analysis

Your Turn

Ask students to complete the Your Turn Activity.

QUESTION 1

A. Incorrect. *Impulsively* does describe a person, place or thing here.

B. Incorrect. *Impulsively* is not a state of action.

C. Incorrect. *Impulsively* is not modifying a noun here.

D. Correct. *Impulsively* directly follows the verb, *turned and describes how Rosemary's action of turning.*

QUESTION 2

A. Incorrect. There is no evidence to support this answer.

B. Correct. "To act without thinking" is the correct definition for "impulsive."

C. Incorrect. There is no evidence to support this answer.

D. Incorrect. Rather, this is the antonym for "impulsive."

Skill: Summarizing

Introduce the Skill

Watch the Concept Definition video and read the following definition with your students.

When you **summarize** a text, you briefly state the main points and most important details in your own words. Summarizing can help you organize, explain, and remember concepts in an informational text or the events that take place in a story.

To summarize, you must decide what is most important as you read. Ask the basic questions: *who, what, when, where, why,* and *how*. Using your own words, write your answers to these questions from an **objective** point of view, without inserting your own feelings and opinions.

Summarizing is sometimes confused with paraphrasing. When you **paraphrase**, you do not condense a text to its most important details. Instead, you restate the entire text in your own words. A summary is much shorter than the original text, while a paraphrase may be the same length as the original text.

Skill: Summarizing

Use the Checklist to analyze Summarizing in "A Cup of Tea." Refer to the sample student annotations about Summarizing in the text.

••• CHECKLIST FOR SUMMARIZING

In order to determine how to write an objective summary of a text, note the following:

- ✓ answers to the basic questions *who, what, where, when, why,* and *how*
- ✓ in literature or nonfiction, note how two or more themes or central ideas are developed over the course of the text, and how they interact and build on one another to produce a complex account
- ✓ stay objective, and do not add your own personal thoughts, judgments, or opinions to the summary

To provide an objective summary of a text, consider the following questions:

- ✓ What are the answers to basic *who, what, where, when, why,* and *how* questions in literature and works of nonfiction?
- ✓ Does my summary include how two or more themes or central ideas are developed over the course of the text, and how they interact and build on one another in my summary?
- ✓ Is my summary objective, or have I added my own thoughts, judgments, and personal opinions?

TURN AND TALK

1. If you were to summarize your high school experience, what would you say? What details or important points would you include?
2. Were you able to be objective, instead of inserting your feelings and biases?

SPEAKING FRAMES

- My high school experience was ____.
- Important details/points I would include are ____.
- I (was / was not) able to be objective in my summary because ____.

SKILL VOCABULARY

summarize / resumir ***verb*** to restate briefly the most important points in a text

objective / objetivo/a ***adjective*** undistorted by emotion or personal bias COGNATE

paraphrase / parafrasear ***verb*** to restate the author's words in your own words COGNATE

Skill: Summarizing

Reread paragraphs 9–13 of "A Cup of Tea." Then, using the Checklist on the previous page, answer the multiple-choice questions below.

YOUR TURN

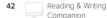

1. The following is a sentence that a student wrote to summarize this passage of the text. What feedback would you give to help improve this summary?

   "Rosemary feels sad because she can't afford the antique she feels she is entitled to, when a young girl approaches her in the street."

   - A. The summary of the passage is incomplete because it does not mention the "extra-special tea."
   - B. The summary does not provide basic information, such as Rosemary's last name or where she is shopping.
   - C. This is an analysis, not an objective summary, because the text does not explicitly say that Rosemary is sad.
   - D. The summary is not objective because the word "entitled" has negative connotations, and this is not implied in the passage.

2. If you were to write a summary of this passage, what two themes do you notice are repeated in this paragraph?

   - A. Having too much wealth and being lonely
   - B. Being homesick and knowing where you belong
   - C. Isolation in one's own world and dissatisfaction
   - D. The wealthy are hypocritical and insecurity

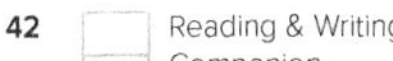

Your Turn

Ask students to complete the Your Turn Activity.

QUESTION 1

A. Incorrect. The summary does not need to include a small detail like the "extra-special tea."

B. Incorrect. In fact, a summary of this particular passage would not need to provide this information.

C. Incorrect. This is not an analysis of the text.

D. Correct. The summary is not objective because it makes a judgement about Rosemary that is not directly stated in the text.

QUESTION 2

A. Incorrect. While Rosemary Fell is wealthy, this passage does not focus on having too much of it as being a problem.

B. Incorrect. There is no evidence to support this answer.

C. Correct. Rosemary's feelings of dissatisfaction are evident in the first paragraph, "There are moments, horrible moments in life, when one emerges from shelter and looks out, and it's awful." Her social class allows her to be isolated and blind to the the struggles of the poor girl.

D. Incorrect. While these are themes in the story, these themes are not revealed or repeated in this paragraph.

Close Read

Skills Focus

QUESTION 1: Word Patterns and Relationships

See paragraph 48.

QUESTION 2: Summary

See paragraph 20.

QUESTION 3: Theme

See paragraph 63.

QUESTION 4: Summary

See paragraph 62.

QUESTION 5: Connect to Essential Question

See paragraph 68.

CHECK FOR SUCCESS

If students struggle to respond to Skills Focus Question #1, ask students the following questions:

1 What is the dialogue around paragraph 48 about?

2. What does *languid* describe?

3. Is the word a noun, verb or adjective? How do you know?

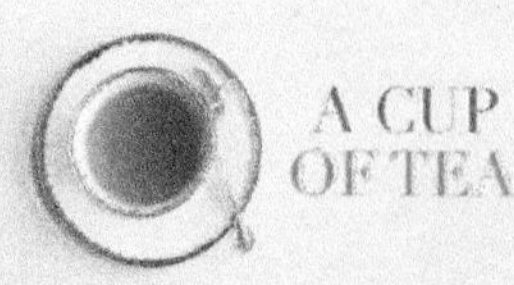

Close Read

Reread "A Cup of Tea." As you reread, complete the Skills Focus questions below. Then use your answers and annotations from the questions to help you complete the Write activity.

SKILLS FOCUS

1. Reread paragraph 48. Highlight the word *languid*, and, in your annotation, use your knowledge of word patterns and relationships to answer the following questions: What part of speech is this word? How do you know? What do you think this word means and why?

2. Identify details about the economic setting that contrast Rosemary's wealth and Miss Smith's poverty, and explain why it might be important to include these details in a summary of the story.

3. Identify a passage that shows Rosemary has conflicting feelings toward Miss Smith, and explain how these feelings contribute to the theme of materialism among the upper classes.

4. Identify a comment Philip makes about Miss Smith's beauty and explain two possible reasons why Philip discourages his wife from helping Miss Smith.

5. This story revolves around the character of Rosemary as she seeks a connection with someone or something. What details in the story help you understand why Rosemary might feel so alienated? What about her life has caused this?

WRITE

COMPARE AND CONTRAST: Write a response in which you compare and contrast the ideas and attitudes expressed about wealth and poverty in "miss rosie," "The Idler," and "A Cup of Tea." Remember to use textual evidence from "A Cup of Tea" to support your response.

Writer's Notebook

Connect to Literary Focus: Give students time to reflect on how "A Cup of Tea" demonstrates the conventions and characteristics of this unit's literary focus, Modernism, by freewriting in their Writer's Notebooks.

Beginning & Intermediate

Remind students of the unit's literary focus, Modernism. Encourage students to draw their connections or allow students to write in their native language. Circulate around the room, prompting students for their thoughts as they respond orally or through pantomime.

Advanced & Advanced High

Allow students to share their connections orally in pairs or small groups before freewriting.

StudySyncTV

Project the StudySyncTV episode and pause at the following times to prompt discussion:

studysync

1:13 Logan thinks it's significant that we meet Rosemary while she's shopping. What does this setting say about her character before we know anything else about her?

5:55 Daniela concludes that Rosemary is "out of touch" with reality based on her feelings about a box and a stranger in need. What other evidence from the text might support this claim?

7:08 Milo states that Rosemary: ". . . has so much more than Miss Smith" and therefore shouldn't be jealous of her. However, Rosemary still retracts her offer to help Miss Smith and tells her to leave. Why do you think Rosemary is blind to how privileged she is in comparison to Miss Smith?

Collaborative Conversation

SCAFFOLDS

Break students into collaborative conversation groups to discuss the Close Read prompt. Ask students to use the StudySyncTV episode as a model for their discussion. Remind them to reference their Skills Focus annotations in their discussion.

Write a response in which you compare and contrast the ideas and attitudes expressed about wealth and poverty in "miss rosie," "The Idler," and "A Cup of Tea." Remember to use textual evidence from "A Cup of Tea" to support your response.

Use the scaffolds below to differentiate instruction for your ELL English Language Learners and A Approaching grade-level learners.

ELL **BEGINNING, INTERMEDIATE** Use the discussion guide and speaking frames to facilitate the discussion with support from the teacher.

ADVANCED, ADVANCED HIGH Use the discussion guide and speaking frames to facilitate the discussion in mixed-level groups.

A **APPROACHING** Use the discussion guide to facilitate the discussion in mixed-level groups.

APPROACHING
ADVANCED, ADVANCED HIGH
BEGINNING, INTERMEDIATE

Discussion Guide	Speaking Frames
1. What ideas and attitudes about wealth and poverty are expressed in "A Cup of Tea"?	• Rosemary ____, which is important because ____. • Miss Smith ____, which is important because ____.
2. What attitude does the speaker in "miss rosie" appear to have toward poverty?	• The speaker says ____ which shows ____. • This is similar to /different from an idea in "A Cup of Tea" because ____.
3. What attitude does the speaker in "The Idler" appear to have toward the man described in the poem?	• I think the speaker's attitude is ____ because ____. • This is similar to /different from an idea in one of the other texts because ____.

Review Prompt and Rubric

Before students begin writing, review the writing prompt and rubric with the class.

COMPARE AND CONTRAST: Write a response in which you compare and contrast the ideas and attitudes expressed about wealth and poverty in "miss rosie," "The Idler," and "A Cup of Tea." Remember to use textual evidence from "A Cup of Tea" to support your response.

ELL PROMPT GUIDE

A
- What ideas and attitudes about wealth and poverty are expressed in the three texts?
- Which of these ideas are similar?
- How are some of the ideas and attitudes about wealth and poverty different?

Score	Compare And Contrast	Language and Conventions
4	The writer clearly compares and contrasts the ideas and attitudes about wealth and poverty in "miss rosie," "The Idler," and "A Cup of Tea." The writer provides exemplary analysis, using relevant textual evidence.	The writer demonstrates a consistent command of grammar, punctuation, and usage conventions. Although minor errors may be evident, they do not detract from the fluency or the clarity of the essay.
3	The writer compares and contrasts the ideas and attitudes about wealth and poverty in "miss rosie," "The Idler," and "A Cup of Tea." The writer provides sufficient analysis, using relevant textual evidence most of the time.	The writer demonstrates an adequate command of grammar, punctuation, and usage conventions. Although some errors may be evident, they create few (if any) disruptions in the fluency of the writing or the clarity of the essay.
2	The writer begins to compare and contrast the ideas and attitudes about wealth and poverty in "miss rosie," "The Idler," and "A Cup of Tea," but the analysis is incomplete. The writer uses relevant textual evidence only some of the time.	The writer demonstrates a partial command of grammar, punctuation, and usage conventions. Some distracting errors may be evident, at times creating minor disruptions in the fluency or clarity of the writing.
1	The writer attempts to compare and contrast the ideas and attitudes about wealth and poverty in "miss rosie," "The Idler," and "A Cup of Tea," but the analysis is not successful. The writer uses little or no relevant textual evidence.	The writer demonstrates little or no command of grammar, punctuation, and usage conventions. Serious and persistent errors create disruptions in the fluency of the writing and sometimes interfere with meaning.
0	The writer does not provide a relevant response to the prompt or does not provide a response at all.	Serious and persistent errors overwhelm the writing and interfere with the meaning of the response as a whole, making the writer's meaning impossible to understand.

SCAFFOLDS

Write

Ask students to complete the writing assignment using text evidence to support their answers.

Use the scaffolds below to differentiate instruction for your ELL English Language Learners and A Approaching grade level readers.

ELL **BEGINNING** With the help of the word bank, write a response using paragraph frame 1.

INTERMEDIATE With the help of the word bank, write a response using paragraph frames 1 and 2.

ADVANCED, ADVANCED HIGH Write a response of differentiated length using the sentence starters.

A **APPROACHING** Write a response of differentiated length using the sentence starters.

BEGINNING / INTERMEDIATE		INTERMEDIATE	ADVANCED, ADVANCED HIGH / APPROACHING
Word Bank	**Paragraph Frame 1**	**Paragraph Frame 2**	**Sentence Starters**
tea scorned poor Rosemary garbage	"The Idler" and "miss rosie" are both about ___ people. In "A Cup of Tea," a rich woman named ___ brings a poor girl home for ___. The speaker in "miss rosie" compares a homeless woman to ___. The speaker in "The Idler" says the world "___" the working man because he is slow and lazy.	In "A Cup of Tea," Rosemary does not understand ___. Rosemary's attitude toward poverty is ___. Rosemary ignores social conventions about ___. Rosemary could ___. But instead Rosemary ___.	• An important idea about wealth and poverty in "A Cup of Tea" is . . . • An attitude about poverty in "miss rosie" is . . . • "The Idler" is similar/different to "miss rosie" because . . . • Textual evidence that supports this is . . . • The ideas about wealth and poverty in "A Cup of Tea" are different from those in "The Idler" and/or "miss rosie" because . . .

Peer Review

Students should submit substantive feedback to two peers using the review instructions below.

- How well does this response answer the prompt?
- How well does the writer support his or her ideas with details and examples from the texts?
- Which sentence in the writer's response made you think differently about the text?
- What does the writer do well in this response? What does the writer need to work on?

Remember that your comments are most useful when they are kind and constructive

Rate

Respond to the following with a point rating that reflects your opinion.

	1	2	3	4
Ideas				
Evidence				
Language and Conventions				

Submit

ELL A **SENTENCE FRAMES**

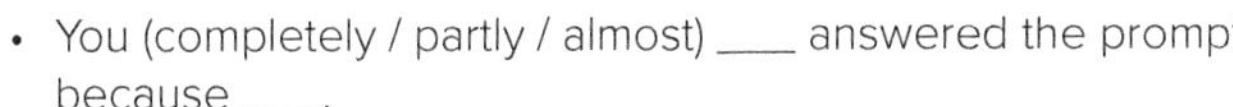

- You (completely / partly / almost) ___ answered the prompt because ___.
- You could answer the prompt more completely by ___.
- You used evidence from ___.
- One idea you expressed well is ___.
- One idea that needs clarification is ___.

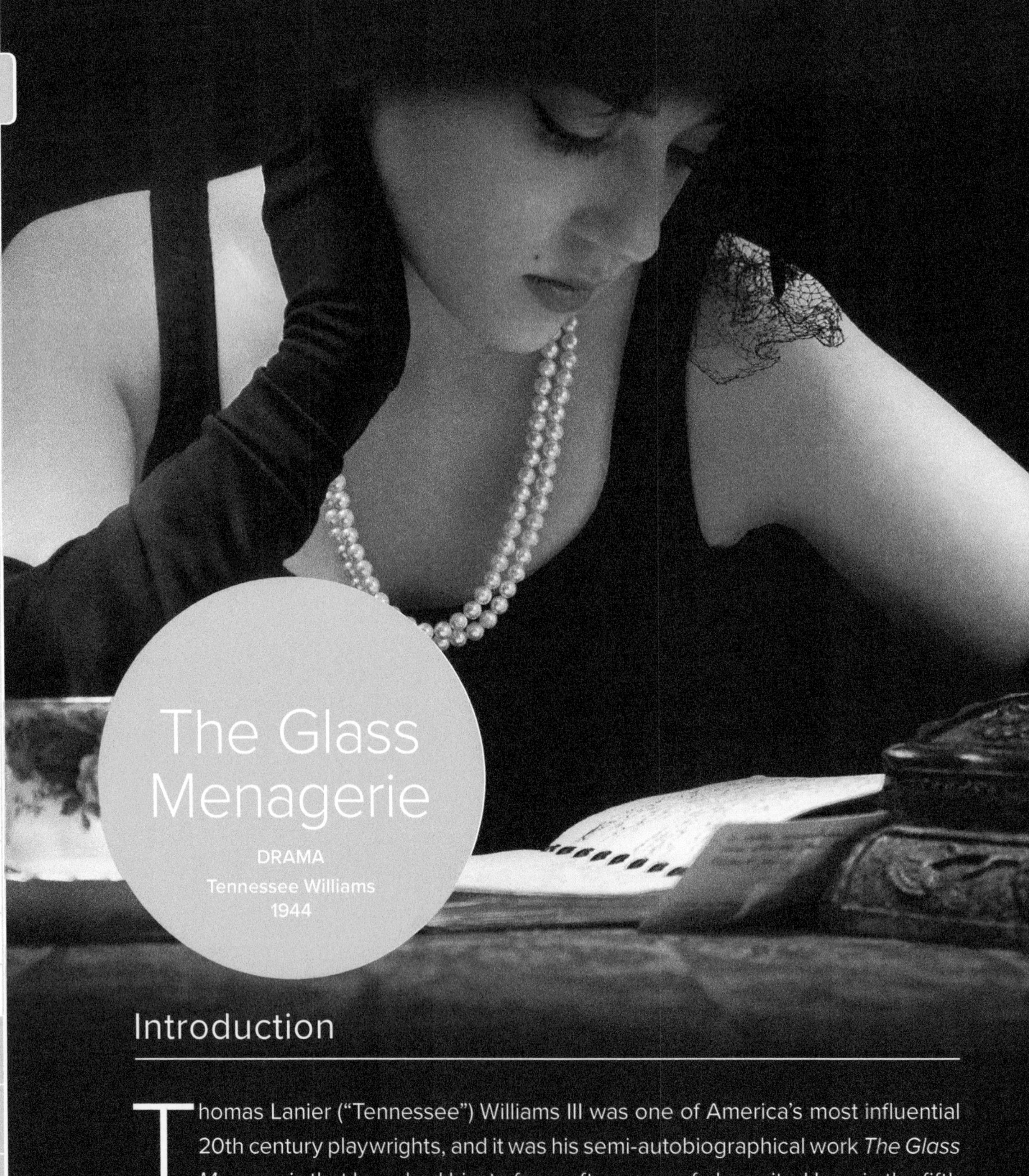

The Glass Menagerie

DRAMA

Tennessee Williams

1944

Introduction

Thomas Lanier ("Tennessee") Williams III was one of America's most influential 20th century playwrights, and it was his semi-autobiographical work *The Glass Menagerie* that launched him to fame after years of obscurity. Here, in the fifth scene from the play, frustrated would-be poet Tom Wingfield responds to his mother Amanda's inquiries about the gentleman caller he has invited over to meet Laura, his painfully shy younger sister.

Tom's mother is giving him a hard time about his smoking. He goes out on the fire escape and his mother asks him if he's made a wish over the moon this evening. She only wishes that her children find happiness. Tom informs his mother that he's invited a gentleman caller to meet Laura, his sister. Tom's mother is overjoyed and asks about this man, whose name is O'Conner. What job does he have and how much does he make? Is he homely? Does he drink too much? Tom says that O'Connor is a young man coming up in the world, but tries to temper his mom's expectations. They both love Laura because she's their kin, but she's also handicapped, not to mention eccentric, and these kinds of things tend to put men off. After Tom leaves, the mother tells Laura to make a wish on the moon. What should I wish for? She asks. For happiness, her mother tells her.

 Proficiency-leveled summaries and summaries in multiple languages are available digitally.

 Audio and audio text highlighting are available with this text.

CONNECT TO ESSENTIAL QUESTION

What causes individuals to feel alienated?

The play that made Tennessee Williams famous is now an American classic. This excerpt from Scene 5 portrays a mother's deep concern about keeping up appearances and finding a suitable husband for her daughter.

Entry Point

As students prepare to read *The Glass Menagerie*, share the following information with them to provide context.

- ✓ Thomas Lanier "Tennessee" Williams III was born in Columbus, Mississippi in 1911. His childhood was challenging: his father was known for his aggressive temper, his sister Rose was diagnosed with schizophrenia, and his mother was dissatisfied with where they lived once the family had moved to St. Louis, Missouri, causing them to move frequently. At the age of eight, Williams fell ill and spent a year recovering in bed. *The Glass Menagerie*, along with his other plays, is considered largely autobiographical.
- ✓ *The Glass Menagerie* was written first as a short story, but later changed into a stage play that premiered in 1944. Williams soon became one of the country's most respected playwrights.
- ✓ The play is now considered an American classic. It has been adapted into multiple films, radio plays, and television productions.

Instructional Path

The print teacher's edition includes essential point-of-use instruction and planning tools. Complete lesson plans and program documents appear in your digital teacher account.

First Read: The Glass Menagerie

Objectives: After an initial reading and discussion of the dramatic excerpt, students will be able to visualize details from the text to reach a deeper understanding about the play.

Skill: Dramatic Elements and Structure

Objectives: After rereading and discussing a model of close reading, students will be able to analyze how the relationships among dramatic elements develop and advance the plot in *The Glass Menagerie*.

Skill: Media

Objectives: After rereading and discussing a model of close reading, students will be able to analyze different media interpretations of an excerpt from *The Glass Menagerie*.

Close Read: The Glass Menagerie

Objectives: After engaging in a close reading and discussion of an excerpt from *The Glass Menagerie*, students will be able to compare different recorded interpretations of the play and evaluate how the interpretations differ from the source material in a short, written response.

Progress Monitoring

Opportunities to Learn	Opportunities to Demonstrate Learning	Opportunities to Reteach
Dramatic Elements and Structure		
Skill: Dramatic Elements and Structure	Skill: Dramatic Elements and Structure • Your Turn Close Read • Skills Focus • Collaborative Conversation • Write	Spotlight Skill: Dramatic Elements and Structure
Media		
Skill: Media	Skill: Media • Your Turn Close Read • Skills Focus • Write	Spotlight Skill: Media

First Read

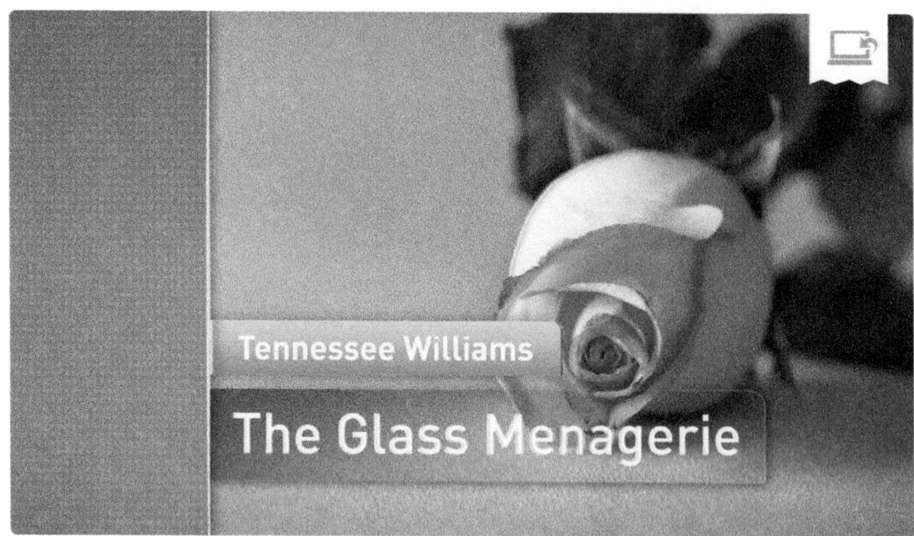

Introduce the Text

As a class, watch the video preview  and have students read the introduction in pairs to make connections to the video preview.

To activate prior knowledge and experiences, ask students:

- What key words or images from the video do you think will be most important to the play you are about to read?

ELL SPEAKING FRAMES

- The key words and images from the video that will be most important in the play are _____.

Access Complex Text

LEXILE: N/A WORD COUNT: 2,421

The following areas may be challenging for students, particularly ELL English Language Learners and A Approaching grade-level learners.

Genre	Connection of Ideas	Prior Knowledge
• Students may struggle to follow the action using only the dialogue. • Williams uses unique features, including Tom speaking to the audience, music cues, and a large screen over the stage that shows words and pictures to accompany the action.	• Students may need context to understand the excerpt. • Tom wants to be a writer but stayed home to support his mother and sister after his father abandoned them. Amanda wants to find a husband to support Laura, who dropped out of typing school.	• Students may wonder why Amanda wants Laura to find a husband rather than a job and why meeting men is limited to receiving "gentleman callers." • Explain that Amanda was raised in the South in the early 1900s and has traditional views

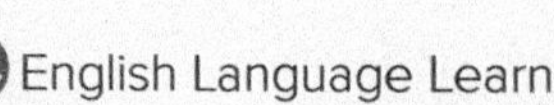

SCAFFOLDS

 ENGLISH LANGUAGE LEARNERS  APPROACHING GRADE LEVEL  BEYOND GRADE LEVEL

These icons identify differentiation strategies and scaffolded support for a variety of students. See the digital lesson plan for additional differentiation strategies and scaffolds.

"A fire escape landing's a poor excuse for a porch."

NOTES

SCENE FIVE

1 *Legend on the screen:* **"Annunciation."**

2 *Music is heard as the light slowly comes on.*

3 *It is early dusk of a spring evening. Supper has just been finished in the Wingfield apartment. Amanda and Laura, in light-colored dresses, are removing dishes from the table in the dining room, which is shadowy, their movements formalized almost as a dance or ritual, their moving forms as pale and silent as moths. Tom, in white shirt and trousers, rises from the table and crosses toward the fire escape.*

4 AMANDA [*as he passes her*]: Son, will you do me a favor?

5 TOM: What?

6 AMANDA: Comb your hair! You look so pretty when your hair is combed!

7 [*Tom slouches on the sofa with the evening paper. Its enormous headline reads: "Franco Triumphs*[1]*."*]

8 There is only one respect in which I would like you to **emulate** your father.

9 TOM: What respect is that?

10 AMANDA: The care he always took of his appearance. He never allowed himself to look untidy.

11 [*He throws down the paper and crosses to the fire escape.*]

12 Where are you going?

1. **Franco Triumphs** Eventual Spanish dictator Francisco Franco fought for the Nationalists in the Spanish Civil War, who were eventually victorious and installed him as leader from 1939 to 1975.

Developing Background Knowledge and Cultural Awareness

1. What were the expectations for women in the early 20th century? Were they different in different parts of the country (the South, urban areas, etc.)?
2. What was dating like during this time period? How did men and women meet? What role did parents play in arrangements?

Discuss with students: What traditions or expectations around dating exist today that will likely change in the future? Would these changes be positive or negative? Who benefits from the changes, and who benefits from maintaining old expectations?

Skills Focus

QUESTION 1: Dramatic Elements and Structure

See Lines 1–2. The word "Annunciation" opens the scene which hints that someone might make an important announcement. The music and lighting cue might make the audience feel comfortable looking in on someone's home life. Depending on the music, it might feel more like a noisy city apartment.

TEXT TALK

What announcement does Tom make in this excerpt? How does Amanda respond?

Tom has invited a friend from work over for dinner. Amanda makes a big "fuss" because she wants to marry Laura to the "gentleman caller."

SELECTION VOCABULARY

annunciation / la anunciación ***noun*** a formal announcement COGNATE

emulate / emular ***verb*** to imitate someone or something you admire COGNATE

Media

What does the reader notice about the beginning of the radio play?

The reader notices that the radio play starts the scene with Tom's soliloquy, instead of the dialogue or stage directions before it. Tom sets the scene, and his character is interpreted differently than the reader expected.

Skills Focus

QUESTION 5: Connect to Essential Question

Tom feels alienated from his family and the city around him. He laments that his life is unchanging because he chose to stay with Amanda and Laura after his father's departure. He is merely living through events and warns about dark events to come.

Dramatic Elements and Structure

What does the reader note about paragraph 21 and the stage directions?

The reader notes that the stage directions describe Amanda's actions on the fire escape. Amanda says she misses porches, and her actions demonstrate that she struggles to get comfortable. The stage directions that the playwright includes help develop her character and build on the dialogue.

13 TOM: I'm going out to smoke.

14 AMANDA: You smoke too much. A pack a day at fifteen cents a pack. How much would that amount to in a month? Thirty times fifteen is how much, Tom? Figure it out and you will be astounded at what you could save. Enough to give you a night-school course in accounting at Washington U.! Just think what a wonderful thing that would be for you, son!

15 [*Tom is unmoved by the thought.*]

16 TOM: I'd rather smoke. [*He steps out on the landing, letting the screen door slam.*]

17 AMANDA [*sharply*]: I know! That's the tragedy of it. . . . [*Alone, she turns to look at her husband's picture.*]

18 [*Dance music: "The World Is Waiting for the Sunrise!"*]

Skill: Media

The radio play is immediately different from the script: Tom's soliloquy sets the scene, and there is no stage direction or dialogue before it.

Tom sounds different than I imagined. He is more casual in the radio version.

19 TOM [*to the audience*]: Across the alley from us was the Paradise Dance Hall. On evenings in spring the windows and doors were open and the music came outdoors. Sometimes the lights were turned out except for a large glass sphere that the hung from the ceiling. It would turn slowly about and filter the dusk with delicate rainbow colors. Then the orchestra played a waltz or a tango, something that had a slow and sensuous rhythm. Couples would come outside, to the relative privacy of the alley. You could see them kissing behind ash pits and telephone poles. This was the compensation for lives that passed like mine, without any change or adventure. Adventure and change were imminent this year. They were waiting around the corner for all these kids. Suspended in the mist over Berchtesgaden[2], caught in the folds of Chamberlain's umbrella[3]. In Spain there was Guernica![4] But here there was only hot swing music and liquor, dance halls, bars, and movies, and sex that hung in the gloom like a chandelier and flooded the world with brief, deceptive rainbows. . . . All the world was waiting for bombardments!

Skill: Dramatic Elements and Structure

Amanda is clearly out of place in this city. The stage directions provide needed clues about who she is as a character and reveal that she is not at home in the city setting.

20 [*Amanda turns from the picture and comes outside.*]

21 AMANDA [*sighing*]: A fire escape landing's a poor excuse for a porch. [*She spreads a newspaper on a step and sits down, gracefully and demurely as if she were settling into a swing on a Mississippi veranda.*] What are you looking at?

2. **Berchtesgaden** a small German town in the Alps
3. **Chamberlain's umbrella** a figure of speech used to describe England's prime minister Neville Chamberlain's failure to appease Hitler at the Munich Conference in 1938
4. **Guernica** a large oil painting by Pablo Picasso depicting the bombing of a Spanish town during World War II

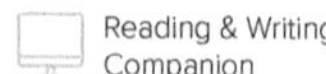

22 TOM: The moon.

23 AMANDA: Is there a moon this evening?

24 TOM: It's rising over Garfinkel's Delicatessen.

25 AMANDA: So it is! A little silver slipper of a moon. Have you made a wish on it yet?

26 TOM: Um-hum.

27 AMANDA: What did you wish for?

28 TOM: That's a secret.

29 AMANDA: A secret, huh? Well, I won't tell mine either. I will be just as mysterious as you.

30 TOM: I bet I can guess what yours is.

31 AMANDA: Is my head so transparent?

32 TOM: You're not a **sphinx**.

33 AMANDA: No, I don't have secrets. I'll tell you what I wished for on the moon. Success and happiness for my precious children! I wish for that whenever there's a moon, and when there isn't a moon, I wish for it, too.

34 TOM: I thought perhaps you wished for a gentleman caller.

35 AMANDA: Why do you say that?

36 TOM: Don't you remember asking me to fetch one?

37 AMANDA: I remember suggesting that it would be nice for your sister if you brought home some nice young man from the warehouse. I think that I've made that suggestion more than once.

38 TOM: Yes, you have made it repeatedly.

39 AMANDA: Well?

40 TOM: We are going to have one.

41 AMANDA: *What?*

Skill: Media

The audiobook is more similar to the script. The actor changes his voice to play the characters. But it sounds unnatural when he says "Um-hum", perhaps because this interpretation is meant to be an exact reading of the script.

Media

What does the reader notice about the audiobook version?

The reader observes that the actor's voice changes to accommodate different characters, that most of the stage directions are included, and that sometimes the actor sounds unnatural.

SELECTION VOCABULARY

sphinx / la esfinje *noun* an ancient mythical creature that has the body of a lion and the head of a person; a symbol of mystery

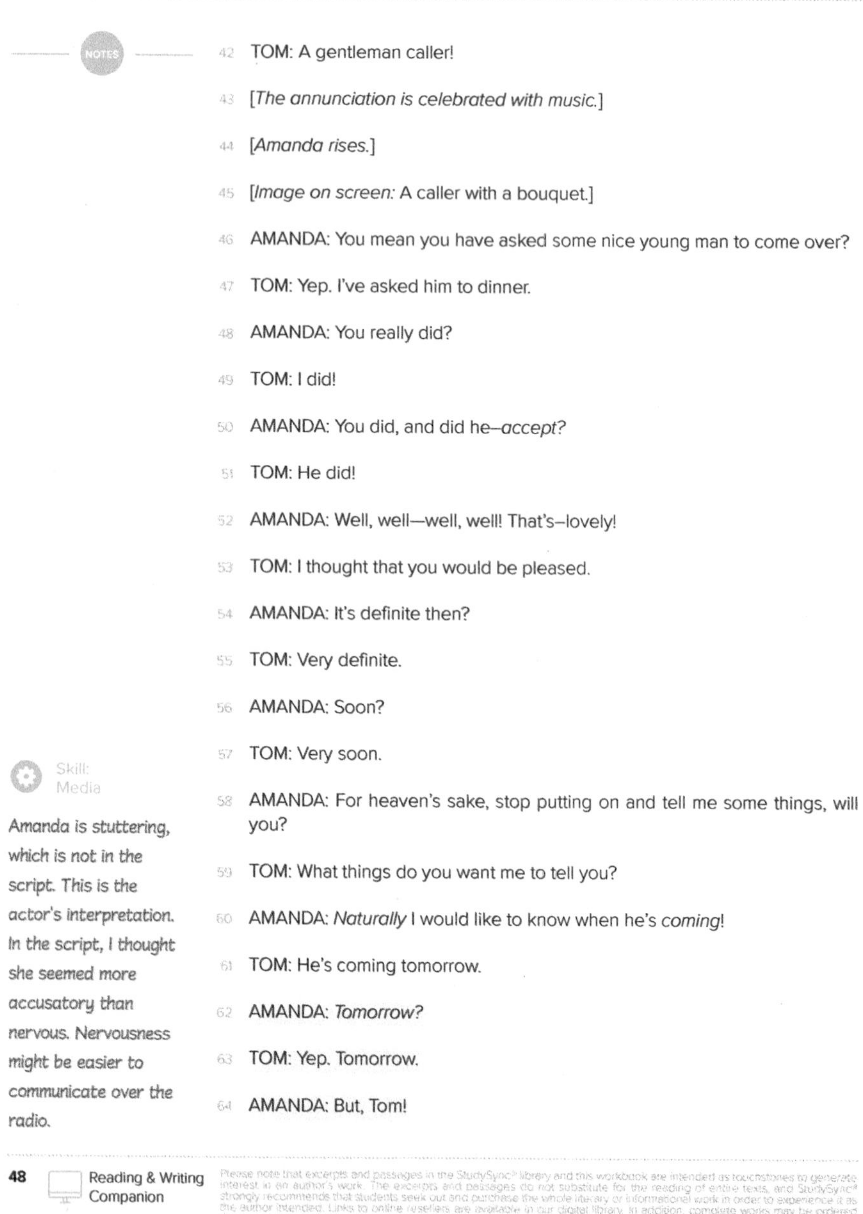

NOTES

42 TOM: A gentleman caller!

43 [*The annunciation is celebrated with music.*]

44 [*Amanda rises.*]

45 [*Image on screen:* A caller with a bouquet.]

46 AMANDA: You mean you have asked some nice young man to come over?

47 TOM: Yep. I've asked him to dinner.

48 AMANDA: You really did?

49 TOM: I did!

50 AMANDA: You did, and did he–*accept?*

51 TOM: He did!

52 AMANDA: Well, well—well, well! That's–lovely!

53 TOM: I thought that you would be pleased.

54 AMANDA: It's definite then?

55 TOM: Very definite.

56 AMANDA: Soon?

57 TOM: Very soon.

Skill: Media

Amanda is stuttering, which is not in the script. This is the actor's interpretation. In the script, I thought she seemed more accusatory than nervous. Nervousness might be easier to communicate over the radio.

58 AMANDA: For heaven's sake, stop putting on and tell me some things, will you?

59 TOM: What things do you want me to tell you?

60 AMANDA: *Naturally* I would like to know when he's *coming*!

61 TOM: He's coming tomorrow.

62 AMANDA: *Tomorrow?*

63 TOM: Yep. Tomorrow.

64 AMANDA: But, Tom!

Media

What does the reader notice about the dialogue between Tom and Amanda in the radio play?

Amanda's character stutters and this tells reader that she is interpreted differently than she expected. This offers a different but valid interpretation of the character.

NOTES

65 TOM: Yes, Mother?

66 AMANDA: Tomorrow gives me no time!

67 TOM: Time for what?

68 AMANDA: Preparations! Why didn't you phone me at once, as soon as you asked him, the minute that he accepted? Then, don't you see, I could have been getting ready!

69 TOM: You don't have to make any fuss.

70 AMANDA: Oh, Tom, Tom, Tom, of course I have to make a fuss! I want things nice, not sloppy! Not thrown together. I'll certainly have to do some fast thinking, won't I?

71 TOM: I don't see why you have to think at all.

72 AMANDA: You just don't know. We can't have a gentleman caller in a pigsty! All my wedding silver has to be polished, the monogrammed table linen ought to be laundered! The windows have to be washed and fresh curtains put up. And how about clothes? We have to *wear* something, don't we?

73 TOM: Mother, this boy is no one to make a fuss over!

74 AMANDA: Do you realize he's the first young man we've introduced to your sister? It's terrible, dreadful, disgraceful that poor little sister has never received a single gentleman caller! Tom, come inside! [*She opens the screen door.*]

75 TOM: What for?

76 AMANDA: I want to ask you some things.

77 TOM: If you're going to make such a fuss, I'll call it off, I'll tell him not to come!

78 AMANDA: You certainly won't do anything of the kind. Nothing offends people worse than broken engagements. It simply means I'll have to work like a Turk! We won't be brilliant, but we will pass inspection. Come on inside.

79 [*Tom follows her inside, groaning.*]

80 Sit down.

81 TOM: Any particular place you would like me to sit?

Skills Focus

QUESTION 3: Media

She chides Tom for having a cowlick and worries that the apartment is too much of a "pigsty" for company. She cares more about how things look than how they really are.

Skills Focus

QUESTION 4: Media

The audiobook's portrayal of Tom is similar to what I imagined when reading the script. He sounds sarcastic and confident.

In the radio play Tom seems more defensive and quick to argue with his mother.

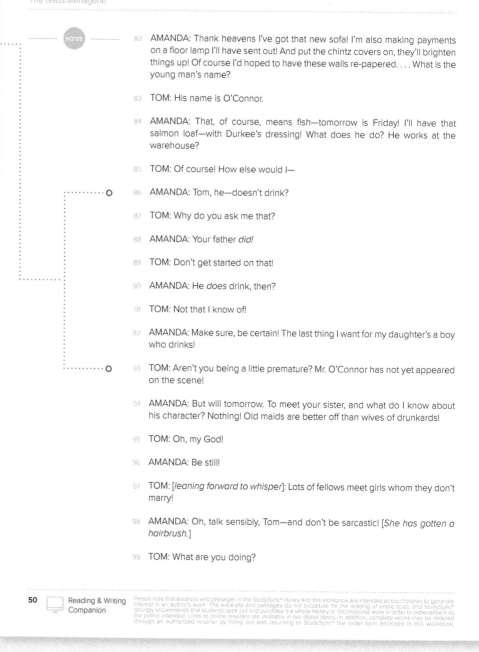

NOTES

82 AMANDA: Thank heavens I've got that new sofa! I'm also making payments on a floor lamp I'll have sent out! And put the chintz covers on, they'll brighten things up! Of course I'd hoped to have these walls re-papered. . . . What is the young man's name?

83 TOM: His name is O'Connor.

84 AMANDA: That, of course, means fish—tomorrow is Friday! I'll have that salmon loaf—with Durkee's dressing! What does he do? He works at the warehouse?

85 TOM: Of course! How else would I—

86 AMANDA: Tom, he—doesn't drink?

87 TOM: Why do you ask me that?

88 AMANDA: Your father *did!*

89 TOM: Don't get started on that!

90 AMANDA: He *does* drink, then?

91 TOM: Not that I know of!

92 AMANDA: Make sure, be certain! The last thing I want for my daughter's a boy who drinks!

93 TOM: Aren't you being a little premature? Mr. O'Connor has not yet appeared on the scene!

94 AMANDA: But will tomorrow. To meet your sister, and what do I know about his character? Nothing! Old maids are better off than wives of drunkards!

95 TOM: Oh, my God!

96 AMANDA: Be still!

97 TOM: [*leaning forward to whisper*]: Lots of fellows meet girls whom they don't marry!

98 AMANDA: Oh, talk sensibly, Tom—and don't be sarcastic! [*She has gotten a hairbrush.*]

99 TOM: What are you doing?

The Glass Menagerie

NOTES

100 AMANDA: I'm brushing that cowlick down! [*She attacks his hair with the brush.*] What is this young man's position at the warehouse?

101 TOM [*submitting grimly to the brush and interrogation*]: This young man's position is that of a shipping clerk, Mother.

102 AMANDA: Sounds to me like a fairly responsible job, the sort of a job *you* would be in if you had more *get-up*. What is his salary? Have you any idea?

103 TOM: I would judge it to be approximately eighty-five dollars a month.

104 AMANDA: Well—not princely, but—

105 TOM: Twenty more than I make.

106 AMANDA: Yes, how well I know! But for a family man, eighty-five dollars a month is not much more than you can just get by on. . . .

107 TOM: Yes, but Mr. O'Connor is not a family man.

108 AMANDA: He might be, mightn't he? Some time in the future?

109 TOM: I see. Plans and provisions.

110 AMANDA: You are the only young man that I know of who ignores the fact that the future becomes the present, the present the past, and the past turns into everlasting regret if you don't plan for it!

111 TOM: I will think that over and see what I can make of it.

112 AMANDA: Don't be **supercilious** with your mother! Tell me some more about this—what do you call him?

113 TOM: James D. O'Connor. The D. is for Delaney.

114 AMANDA: Irish on *both* sides! *Gracious!* And doesn't drink?

115 TOM: Shall I call him up and ask him right this minute?

116 AMANDA: The only way to find out about those things is to make discreet inquiries at the proper moment. When I was a girl in Blue Mountain and it was suspected that a young man drank, the girl whose attentions he had been receiving, if any girl *was*, would sometimes speak to the minister of his church, or rather her father would if her father was living, and sort of feel him out on the young man's character. That is the way such things are discreetly handled to keep a young woman from making a tragic mistake!

TEXT TALK

What announcement does Tom make in this excerpt? How does Amanda respond?

Tom has invited a friend from work over for dinner. Amanda makes a big "fuss" because she wants to marry Laura to the "gentleman caller."

SELECTION VOCABULARY

supercilious / arrogante *adjective* behaving or looking superiorly

Prepare for Advanced Courses

Use the activity below to differentiate instruction for your B Beyond grade level learners.

Analyze for Enrichment

In paragraph 134, Amanda says to Tom: "You're as eloquent as an oyster."

Ensure that students know what an oyster is. Encourage students to use context to help them understand how the word choice affects their interpretation of the scene.

Ask students:

- What does Amanda mean here? Is this a compliment, or an insult?
- How does this exchange compare to how Amanda speaks to Tom in other parts of this excerpt?

Dramatic Elements and Structure

What does the reader note about the dialogue?

The dialogue implies Tom's feelings about his sister, and invite the audience to consider how the story might unfold. Amanda seems more concerned about how Tom delivers the news than the gentleman callers' reaction to Laura.

NOTES

117 TOM: Then how did you happen to make a tragic mistake?

118 AMANDA: That innocent look of your father's had everyone fooled! He *smiled*—the world was *enchanted!* No girl can do worse than put herself at the mercy of a handsome appearance! I hope that Mr. O'Connor is not too good-looking.

119 TOM: No, he's not too good-looking. He's covered with freckles and hasn't too much of a nose.

120 AMANDA: He's not right-down **homely**, though?

121 TOM: Not right-down homely. Just medium homely, I'd say.

122 AMANDA: Character's what to look for in a man.

123 TOM: That's what I've always said, Mother.

124 AMANDA: You've never said anything of the kind and I suspect you would never give it a thought.

125 TOM: Don't be so suspicious of me.

126 AMANDA: At least I hope he's the type that's up and coming.

127 TOM: I think he really goes in for self-improvement.

128 AMANDA: What reason have you to think so?

129 TOM: He goes to night school.

130 AMANDA: [*beaming*]: Splendid! What does he do, I mean study?

131 TOM: Radio engineering and public speaking!

132 AMANDA: Then he has visions of being advanced in the world! Any young man who studies public speaking is aiming to have an executive job some day! And radio engineering? A thing for the future! Both of these facts are very illuminating. Those are the sort of things that a mother should know concerning any young man who comes to call on her daughter. Seriously or—not.

133 TOM: One little warning. He doesn't know about Laura. I didn't let on that we had dark ulterior motives. I just said, why don't you come and have dinner with us? He said okay and that was the whole conversation.

Skill: Dramatic Elements and Structure

Was Tom worried James would not come to dinner if he knew about his sister? Or does he really think these are "dark ulterior motives"?

Amanda makes fun of Tom in a kind way by calling him eloquent as an oyster.

V SELECTION VOCABULARY

homely / sencillo/a ***adjective*** plain, unattractive

134 AMANDA: I bet it was! You're eloquent as an oyster. However, he'll know about Laura when he gets here. When he sees how lovely and sweet and pretty she is, he'll thank his lucky stars he was asked to dinner.

135 TOM: Mother, you mustn't expect too much of Laura.

136 AMANDA: What do you mean?

137 TOM: Laura seems all those things to you and me because she's ours and we love her. We don't even notice she's crippled any more.

138 AMANDA: Don't say crippled! You know that I never allow that word to be used!

139 TOM: But face facts, Mother. She is and—that's not all—

140 AMANDA: What do you mean "not all"?

141 TOM: Laura is very different from other girls.

142 AMANDA: I think the difference is all to her advantage.

143 TOM: Not quite all—in the eyes of others—strangers—she's terribly shy and lives in a world of her own and those things make her seem a little peculiar to people outside the house.

144 AMANDA: Don't say peculiar.

145 TOM: Face the facts. She is.

146 [*The dance hall music changes to a tango that has a minor and somewhat ominous tone.*]

147 AMANDA: In what way is she peculiar—may I ask?

148 TOM [*gently*]: She lives in a world of her own—a world of little glass ornaments, Mother. . . .

149 [*He gets up. Amanda remains holding the brush, looking at him, troubled.*]

150 She plays old phonograph records and—that's about all—

151 [*He glances at himself in the mirror and crosses to the door.*]

152 AMANDA [*sharply*]: Where are you going?

TEXT TALK

What do readers learn about Tom and Laura's father in this excerpt?

Their father is not around and is referred to in past tense. He drank but was attractive and charming. Amanda's marriage was a "tragic mistake."

Skills Focus

QUESTION 2: Dramatic Elements and Structure

Laura may be beautiful, but introverted and cautious. She needs help doing simple tasks. This is confirmed when Laura needs help locating the moon in the sky.

153 TOM: I'm going to the movies. [*He goes out the screen door.*]

154 AMANDA: Not to the movies, every night to the movies! [*She follows quickly to the screen door.*] I don't believe you always go to the movies!

155 [*He is gone. Amanda look worriedly after him for a moment. Then vitality and optimism return and she turns from the door, crossing to the portieres.*]

156 Laura! Laura!

157 [*Laura answers from the kitchenette.*]

158 LAURA: Yes, Mother.

159 AMANDA: Let those dishes go and come in front!

160 [*Laura appears with a dish towel. Amanda speaks to her gaily.*]

161 Laura, come here and make a wish on the moon!

162 [*Screen image:* The Moon.]

163 LAURA [*entering*]: Moon—moon?

164 AMANDA: A little silver slipper of a moon. Look over your left shoulder, Laura, and make a wish!

165 [*Laura looks faintly puzzled as if called out of sleep. Amanda seizes her shoulders and turns her at an angle by the door.*]

166 Now! Now, darling, *wish!*

167 LAURA: What shall I wish for, Mother?

168 AMANDA [*her voice trembling and her eyes suddenly filling with tears*]: Happiness! Good fortune!

169 [*The sound of the violin rises and the stage dims out.*]

TEXT TALK

How does Tom describe Laura? How does Amanda respond?

Tom calls Laura "peculiar" and "crippled," which are both terms that Amanda rejects. Tom thinks Laura is "very different" from other girls.

How did discussing dating expectations and gender roles help you understand Tom and Amanda's conversation?

Answers will vary.

Ask each Beyond grade-level student to write one additional discussion question. Then, have one or two students facilitate a discussion, using their questions to guide the conversation.

Reading Comprehension OPTIONAL

Have students complete the digital reading comprehension questions ✓ when they finish reading.

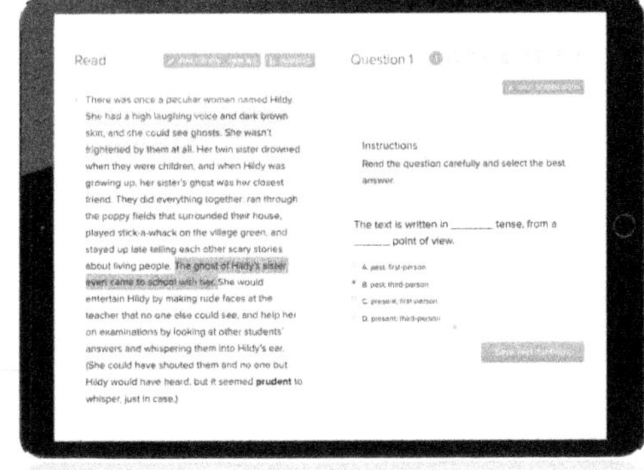

ANSWER KEY

QUESTION 1: D
QUESTION 2: A
QUESTION 3: B
QUESTION 4: C
QUESTION 5: D
QUESTION 6: B
QUESTION 7: C
QUESTION 8: A
QUESTION 9: *See first chart.*
QUESTION 10: *See second chart.*

Vocabulary Word	Definition
"[*She spreads a newspaper on a step and sits down, gracefully and demurely as if she were settling into a swing on a Mississippi veranda.*]"	Done with modesty or reserve
"All my wedding silver has to be polished, the monogrammed table linen ought to be laundered!"	A decorative design, usually a person's initials
"I see. Plans and provisions."	arrangements
"Both of these facts are very *illuminating*."	revealing

Amanda	Tom	Laura
Makes assumptions	**Discontent**	**Isolated**
"'Irish on *both* sides! *Gracious!* And he doesn't drink?'"	"'But here there was only hot swing music and liquor, dance halls, bars, and movies . . .'"	"'. . . she's terribly shy and lives in a world of her own . . .'"

Connect and Extend OPTIONAL

CONNECT TO EXTENDED WRITING PROJECT

Students can find inspiration from *The Glass Menagerie* when writing their literary analyses. Have them reflect on Tennessee William's characterization of Tom, Amanda, and Laura, and how each character experiences alienation.

BEYOND THE BOOK

Literary Period

Ask your students to combine their knowledge of early 20th-century culture with their reading of *The Glass Menagerie*. Literary modernism was frequently classified by experimentation and feelings of alienation and disillusionment.

While Tom's character is disillusioned, Amanda is more optimistic about the expectation of marriage for Laura once she learns "a gentleman caller" is coming to dinner.

Have a class discussion about how the social pressure on each character in this scene causes them to be alienated. Prompt students with questions such as:

1. What would have been the social expectations for a young man in the 1930s? How are these expectations alienating Tom and causing his disillusionment?
2. What is unusual about Amanda's marriage, and her current living situation? How might this be causing her loneliness and naive hope?
3. What would have been particularly challenging for a young woman like Laura in the 1930s? In what ways is she alienated?

Think Questions

Circulate as students answer Think Questions independently. Scaffolds for these questions are shown on the opposite page.

QUESTION 1: Textual Evidence

Tom remembers the music from the Paradise Dance Hall as "something that had a slow and sensuous rhythm." His own life is static in comparison: "This was the compensation for lives that passed like mine, without any change or adventure."

QUESTION 2: Textual Evidence

Amanda makes a wish for "success and happiness for my precious children." She seems hopeful but naive: She does not seem to take realistic actions to pursue her goals, instead relying on Tom to find a suitable "gentleman caller" for Laura.

QUESTION 3: Textual Evidence

Amanda is excited but also concerned. She asks about James's income and whether or not he drinks. She wants someone who will take her place as Laura's primary caregiver: "Those are the sort of things that a mother should know . . ."

QUESTION 4: Context Clues

Amanda says to Tom, "There is only one respect in which I would like you to emulate your father . . . The care he always took of his appearance" She wants Tom to act like his father, so the word "emulate" likely means "act like someone else."

QUESTION 5: Context Clues

Amanda asks if James is "right-down homely" after Tom says "he's not too good-looking. He's covered with freckles and hasn't too much of a nose." Readers can infer that "homely" is a way to describe a person as "unattractive."

First Read

Read *The Glass Menagerie*. After you read, complete the Think Questions below.

THINK QUESTIONS

1. What does Tom remember as he steps out onto the fire escape? Describe his memories using details from the text. What does this memory suggest about his feelings about his own life at that moment? Support your inference with a quotation from the text.

2. What ideas or feelings does the moon inspire in Amanda? What can you infer about Amanda based on the wish she expresses when seeing the moon and her behavior throughout this scene? Cite details from the text to support your inferences.

3. How does Amanda react when Tom reveals that he has invited a "gentleman caller" to dinner? What sorts of qualities does she ask about? What does her reaction suggest about her character and her relationship to her children? Support your answer with textual evidence.

4. Use context to determine the meaning of the word **emulate** as it is used in *The Glass Menagerie*. Write your definition of "emulate" here and tell how you found it.

5. Use context to determine the meaning of the word **homely** as it is used in *The Glass Menagerie*. Write your definition of "homely" here and tell how you found it.

SCAFFOLDS

Think Questions

Use the scaffolds below to differentiate instruction for your ELL English Language Learners and A Approaching grade level readers.

ELL **BEGINNING** Write a response using the word bank and sentence frames.

INTERMEDIATE Write a response using the sentence frames.

ADVANCED, ADVANCED HIGH Write a response using the Text-Dependent Question Guide.

A **APPROACHING** Write a response using the Text-Dependent Question Guide.

BEGINNING	INTERMEDIATE	APPROACHING / ADVANCED, ADVANCED HIGH
Word Bank	**Sentence Frames**	**Text-Dependent Question Guide**
caregiver wish hopeful income good looking nervous music act static suitable emulate unattractive concerned	As Tom steps out onto the fire escape, he remembers ____ from the Paradise Music Hall as "something that had a slow and sensuous rhythm." His own life ____ in comparison.	1. • What does Tom describe to the audience as he steps out on the fire escape? • What kinds of words and phrases does he use in his description? • What does that tell you about the way he is feeling? • How do you know this?
	When Amanda sees the moon, she makes a ____. Based on this action, readers can infer that Amanda is ____ but naive. She does not seem to take realistic actions to pursue her goals, instead relying on Tom to find a ____ "gentleman caller" for Laura.	2. • What is Amanda's first reaction when Tom tells her he is looking at the moon? • What does she do? • What does that action say about Amanda's character?
	When Tom reveals that he has invited over a "gentleman caller" Amanda is excited, but ____. She asks Tom about James's ____. Amanda wants someone who will be Laura's ____.	3. • What does Amanda want to do when Tom announces that James is coming for dinner? • What does that show about Amanda? • What does she want to know about James? • What does that show about her plans?
	Amanda tells Tom, "There is only one respect in which I would like you to ____ your father . . . The care he always took of his ____." Based on this context, readers can infer that Amanda wants Tom to ____ like his father, so I think that **emulate** means ____ like someone else.	4. • Read: "There is only one respect in which I would like you to emulate your father . . . " • What is Amanda talking about in this sentence? • What does *emulate* describe? • How does that help you understand the meaning of *emulate*?
	Amanda asks if James is "right-down homely" after Tom says he's not ____. Based on this context, I think **homely** means ____.	5. • What does Tom say before Amanda asks if James is "right-down homely"? • What is being described in this sentence? • What does that tell you about the meaning of *homely*?

Skill: Dramatic Elements and Structure

Introduce the Skill

Watch the Concept Definition video and read the following definition with your students.

A drama, or play, is a story performed by actors before an audience. The script of a dramatic work contains certain **dramatic elements**, such as character, setting, plot, theme, dialogue, and stage directions. The **setting** of a play is the time and place in which the events of the story unfold. The events that unfold throughout a drama are called **plot**. **Dialogue** refers to the conversation between characters in a script. **Stage directions** are the instructions written by the playwright to describe the appearance and actions of the characters as well as the sets, props, costumes, sound effects, and lighting.

Dramas are structured in acts and scenes. An **act** is a major unit of a dramatic work. A play may be divided into several acts. Acts may be further divided into **scenes**. A new act or scene may indicate a change in location or the passage of time.

Skill: Dramatic Elements and Structure

Use the Checklist to analyze Dramatic Elements and Structure in "The Glass Menagerie." Refer to the sample student annotations about Dramatic Elements and Structure in the text.

••• CHECKLIST FOR DRAMATIC ELEMENTS AND STRUCTURE

In order to determine the author's choices regarding the development of a drama, note the following:

- ✓ how character choices and dialogue affect the plot
- ✓ the stage directions and how they are used to reveal character and plot development
- ✓ the names of all the characters, and their relationships with one another
- ✓ character development, including personality traits, motivations, decisions they make, and actions they take
- ✓ the setting(s) of the story and how it influences the characters and the events of the plot

To analyze the impact of the author's choices regarding how to develop and relate elements of a story or drama, consider the following questions:

- ✓ How does the setting affect the characters and plot?
- ✓ How do the characters' actions help develop the theme or message of the play?
- ✓ How does the order of events in the play affect the development of the drama?
- ✓ How do the choices the characters make help advance the plot?

TURN AND TALK

1. What elements make a play (drama) different from a novel, short story, or poem?
2. What is your favorite movie or play? How do the dialogue and the action work together to propel the plot?

SPEAKING FRAMES

- A play is different from a story because ____.
- My favorite (movie / play) is ____. The dialogue and action work together to advance the plot by ____.

SKILL VOCABULARY

dramatic elements / los elementos del género dramático ***noun*** an essential component of a drama, such as plot, characters, theme.

stage direction / la dirección en el escenario ***noun*** an instruction written by the playwright that may describe the set, a sound effect, the lighting, or the appearance or actions of a character

dramatic conventions / las convenciones dramáticas ***noun*** rules or techniques, accepted by the audience, that an actor or playwright uses to achieve a certain dramatic effect and style COGNATE

Skill: Dramatic Elements and Structure

Reread paragraphs 152–169 of *The Glass Menagerie*. Then, using the Checklist on the previous page, answer the multiple-choice questions below.

YOUR TURN

1. What is the most likely reason that Laura is introduced at the end of the scene?

   - ○ A. To show how dialogue between Laura and Amanda differs from conversations that Amanda had with Tom.
   - ○ B. To allow the audience to finally see Laura and determine why Tom and Amanda seem so worried about her.
   - ○ C. To provide details about Laura's personality traits to the audience that show how wrong Tom and Amanda are about her.
   - ○ D. To reinforce the relationship between mother and daughter, and show that Tom is the outcast of the family.

2. Which of the following best describes the effect of the final stage direction in this scene?

   - ○ A. It uses music to add a specific emotion to the closing dialogue in the scene.
   - ○ B. It provides resolution to the scene through the character's actions.
   - ○ C. It provides background music and necessary information to the audience.
   - ○ D. It uses music to create tension so the audience wants to know what happens next.

Your Turn

Ask students to complete the Your Turn Activity.

QUESTION 1

A. Incorrect. Laura's introduction at the end of the scene is not included to show the difference in conversations amongst the characters.

B. Correct. Laura's introduction allows the audience to see why Tom and Amanda seem so worried about her.

C. Incorrect. There is no evidence in the text to support this answer.

D. Incorrect. Laura's introduction at the end of the scene does not reinforce the relationship between mother and daughter.

QUESTION 2

A. Correct. The final stage direction is included to add music and emotion to the final scene.

B. Incorrect.The final stage direction does not provide resolution in the scene.

C. Incorrect. The final stage direction does not provide needed background information to the audience.

D. Incorrect. There is no evidence to support this answer.

Skill: Media

Introduce the Skill

Watch the Concept Definition video and read the following definition with your students.

Media is the plural form of the word *medium*. A **medium** is a means of sending a communication to an intended audience. Throughout most of human history, people communicated through three main media: speech, writing, and visual arts such as drawing, painting, and sculpture. But in the 19th century media options suddenly exploded. The invention of photography, and then the telegraph and the telephone, changed the world. Within a century radio, motion pictures, and television followed.

Stories and ideas change as they are translated from one medium to another. A dialogue between two characters in a novel, for example, becomes very different when it is delivered by actors in a film—with close-ups, sound effects such as music, and other elements unique to the medium of film itself.

Today new media are being invented at a much faster pace than ever before, and each of these forms of online communication has its own "language" and creates its own experience.

The Glass Menagerie

Skill: Media

Use the Checklist to analyze Media in *The Glass Menagerie*. Refer to the sample student annotations about Media in the text.

CHECKLIST FOR MEDIA

In order to identify multiple interpretations of a story, drama, or poem, do the following:

- ✓ note the similarities and differences in different media, such as the live production of a play or a recorded novel or poetry
- ✓ evaluate how each version interprets the source text
- ✓ consider how, within the same medium, a story can have multiple interpretations if told by writers from different time periods and cultures
- ✓ consider how stories told in the same medium will likely reflect the specific objectives as well as the respective ideas, concerns, and values of each writer

To analyze multiple interpretations of a story, drama, or poem, evaluating how each version interprets the source text, consider the following questions:

- ✓ What medium is being used, and how does it affect the interpretation of the source text?
- ✓ What are the main similarities and differences between the two (or more) versions?
- ✓ If each version is from a different time period and/or culture, what does each version reveal about the author's objectives and the time period and culture in which it was written?

58  Reading & Writing Companion

TURN AND TALK

1. What are different types of media through which someone can communicate?
2. Does the media through which you choose to communicate influence what or how you communicate a story? Explain.

ELL SPEAKING FRAMES

- Different media that can be used to communicate are ____ or ____.
- In ____, I can communicate ____, because ____.

SKILL VOCABULARY

medium / el medio ***noun*** a form of communication, such as television, the Internet, and radio COGNATE

media / los medios ***noun*** the plural form of the word medium; a means of sending a communication to an intended audience

Skill: Media

Reread lines 97–114 of *The Glass Menagerie* and review the radio and audiobook clips in the digital lesson. Then, using the Checklist on the previous page, answer the multiple-choice questions below.

YOUR TURN

1. What is the most likely reason that the audiobook reads some stage directions from this passage and not others?
   - ○ A. Some stage directions were removed due to time constraints in the audiobook version of the play.
   - ○ B. Each interpretation varies given the time period and culture, and stage directions are less popular in 2018.
   - ○ C. The stage directions are read only when the audience of the audiobook version needs the additional information.
   - ○ D. The playwright omitted some stage directions because the actors did not need the instructions in the audiobook version.

2. In what way is the first line in this clip from the 1951 radio play different from the script?
   - ○ A. The radio play removes the reference to marriage that is included in the script.
   - ○ B. The radio play does not use the original words from the script in the first line.
   - ○ C. The actor does not whisper as instructed by the stage direction.
   - ○ D. The actor is devoid of emotion, unlike instructions in the script.

3. What is one effect of having a live studio audience for the radio play?
   - ○ A. The live studio audience reaction influences the actor's interpretation of the play.
   - ○ B. The playwright adjusts the script to accomodate for the audience reaction.
   - ○ C. The live studio audience sees the stage directions in action and tell the listener what is happening.
   - ○ D. The actors occasionally have to pause for the laughter to subside so that they can be heard.

Your Turn

Ask students to complete the Your Turn Activity.

QUESTION 1

A. Incorrect. There is no evidence to support this answer.

B. Incorrect. Stage directions are included to support understanding, regardless of time period or culture.

C. Correct. Stage directions are used when needed to support understanding of character action, development and plot.

D. Incorrect. Rather, stage directions are used when needed to support understanding of character action, development and plot.

QUESTION 2

A. Incorrect. There is no evidence to support this answer.

B. Incorrect. The radio play includes the original words, but they are not whispered as written in the stage directions.

C. Correct. The actor did not whisper in the radio play.

D. Incorrect. There is no evidence to support this answer.

QUESTION 3

A. Incorrect. The live studio audience is to observe and be entertained, but does not influence the interpretation of the radio play.

B. Incorrect. There is no evidence to support this answer.

C. Incorrect. While the live studio audience sees the movement of the actors, they do not see the stage directions in the performance, or communicate with the listener.

D. Correct. The live studio audience reacts with laughter or emotion to the play's content, which requires pauses in performances from time to time.

Close Read

Skills Focus

QUESTION 2: Dramatic Elements and Structure

See line 165.

QUESTION 3: Media

See line 72.

QUESTION 4: Media

See lines 86–93.

QUESTION 5: Connect to Essential Question

See line 19.

CHECK FOR SUCCESS

If students struggle to respond to Skills Focus Question #1, ask students the following questions:

1. Why are stage directions included in a play?
2. What do the stage directions tell the reader?
3. How do they help you understand character actions, decisions, or events in the play?

The Glass Menagerie

Close Read

Reread *The Glass Menagerie*. As you reread, complete the Skills Focus questions below. Then use your answers and annotations from the questions to help you complete the Write activity.

SKILLS FOCUS

1. Reread the stage directions. How do music and lighting cues contribute to the text? How do they affect your understanding of what happens in the scene and why the events are important to the story? Highlight textual evidence and make annotations to explain your choices.
2. In this scene, Williams offers indirect characterization of Laura through dialogue between Amanda and Tom. What can readers infer about Laura based on their descriptions? How do Laura's actions at the end of the scene compare and contrast with readers' expectations? Support your answer with textual evidence and make annotations to explain your answer choices.
3. Identify places in the text where Amanda shows concern about appearances. What sorts of things is she worried about and why? How does her portrayal in the radio play and in the audio book reflect the character's perspective on the importance of appearances? Highlight textual evidence and make annotations to support your explanation.
4. Compare and contrast the portrayals of Tom in the radio play and in the audiobook. How do the actors' portrayals compare to your first impressions of Tom in Williams's original text? Highlight your textual evidence and make annotations to explain your choices.
5. *The Glass Menagerie* is a "memory play" loosely based on Williams's own experiences with his mother and sister. How does the character of Tom represent feelings of alienation? What might be causing those feelings? Highlight textual evidence and make annotations to explain your ideas.

WRITE

COMPARE AND CONTRAST: Listen to the audio clips of *The Glass Menagerie*. How do these two versions differ from each other? How does each version interpret the source text of the play, making the dramatic elements work for that specific medium? Choose at least one substantial difference between the two versions, and explain and evaluate how each version interprets the source material. Support your writing with textual evidence and both audio recordings.

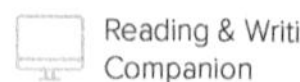

Writer's Notebook

Connect to Essential Question: Give students time to reflect on how *The Glass Menagerie* connects to the unit's essential question "What causes individuals to feel alienated?" by freewriting in their Writer's Notebooks.

Beginning & Intermediate

Read aloud the unit's essential question: "What causes individuals to feel alienated?" Encourage students to draw their connections or allow students to write in their native language. Circulate around the room, prompting students for their thoughts as they respond orally or through pantomime.

Advanced & Advanced High

Allow students to share their connections orally in pairs or small groups before freewriting.

Collaborative Conversation

SCAFFOLDS

Break students into collaborative conversation groups to discuss the Close Read prompt. Ask students to use the StudySyncTV episode as a model for their discussion. Remind them to reference their Skills Focus annotations in their discussion.

Listen to the audio clips of *The Glass Menagerie*. How do these two versions differ from each other? How does each version interpret the source text of the play, making the dramatic elements work for that specific medium? Choose at least one substantial difference between the two versions, and explain and evaluate how each version interprets the source material. Support your writing with textual evidence and both audio recordings.

Use the scaffolds below to differentiate instruction for your ELL English Language Learners and A Approaching grade-level learners.

ELL **BEGINNING, INTERMEDIATE** Use the discussion guide and speaking frames to facilitate the discussion with support from the teacher.

ADVANCED, ADVANCED HIGH Use the discussion guide and speaking frames to facilitate the discussion in mixed-level groups.

A APPROACHING Use the discussion guide to facilitate the discussion in mixed-level groups.

APPROACHING
ADVANCED, ADVANCED HIGH
BEGINNING, INTERMEDIATE

Discussion Guide	Speaking Frames
1. How is the radio play different from the text source?	• The radio play is different from the text source because ____. • Another example is ____.
2. How is the audiobook different from the text source?	• The audiobook is different from the text source because ____. • Another example is ____.
3. How do the interpretations impact the reader?	• The interpretations impact the reader by ____.

Multiple Perspectives

Use the activity below to differentiate instruction for your B Beyond grade level learners.

Look more in depth at the dialogue between Tom and Amanda in Scene 5 regarding Laura.

Direct students to determine each character's perspective on Laura and their motivation for inviting "a gentleman caller" to the house.

Ask students:

- How is Amanda's perspective on Laura different from Tom's?
- What is motivating Amanda to find a suitable "gentleman caller" for Laura?
- What does each character think will happen when the "gentleman caller" meets Laura?
- Why is each character's perspective on Laura so different?

Review Prompt and Rubric

Before students begin writing, review the writing prompt and rubric with the class.

COMPARE AND CONTRAST: Listen to the audio clips of *The Glass Menagerie*. How do these two versions differ from each other? How does each version interpret the source text of the play, making the dramatic elements work for that specific medium? Choose at least one substantial difference between the two versions, and explain and evaluate how each version interprets the source material. Support your writing with textual evidence and both audio recordings.

 PROMPT GUIDE

- How is the radio play different from the text source?
- How is the audiobook different from the text source?
- How do the interpretations impact the reader?
- How is your interpretation of the play the same or different following listening to the audio versions?

An additional rubric item for Language and Conventions appears in your digital teacher and student accounts.

Score	Media	Dramatic Elements
4	The writer clearly explains and evaluates the differences between each media interpretation. The writer provides exemplary evaluation and analysis of how each version interprets the source material and uses relevant textual evidence in the response.	The writer effectively explains how each medium adapts dramatic elements for the medium's purpose, using textual evidence to support their response.
3	The writer explains and evaluates the differences between each media interpretation. The writer provides sufficient evaluation and analysis of how each version interprets the source material and uses relevant textual evidence in the response.	The writer explains how each medium adapts dramatic elements for the medium's purpose, using textual evidence to support their response.
2	The writer begins to explain and evaluate the differences between each media interpretation, but the analysis is limited. The writer uses textual evidence to support their answer only some of the time.	The writer attempts to explains how each medium adapts dramatic elements for the medium's purpose, but there is limited textual evidence to support their response.
1	The writer attempts to explain the differences between each media interpretation, but the analysis is not successful. The writer uses little or no relevant textual evidence in the response.	The writer does not explain how how each medium adapts dramatic elements for the medium's purpose. The writer uses little or no relevant textual evidence in the response.
0	The writer does not provide a relevant response to the prompt or does not provide a response at all.	The writer does not provide a relevant response to the prompt or does not provide a response at all.

SCAFFOLDS

Write

Ask students to complete the writing assignment using text evidence to support their answers.

Use the scaffolds below to differentiate instruction for your ELL English Language Learners and A Approaching grade level learners.

ELL **BEGINNING** With the help of the word bank, write a response using paragraph frame 1.

INTERMEDIATE With the help of the word bank, write a response using paragraph frames 1 and 2.

ADVANCED, ADVANCED HIGH Write a response of differentiated length using the sentence starters.

A **APPROACHING** Write a response of differentiated length using the sentence starters.

BEGINNING | INTERMEDIATE | ADVANCED, ADVANCED HIGH | APPROACHING

Word Bank	Paragraph Frame 1	Paragraph Frame 2	Sentence Starters
stage directions similar excited exaggerated nervous silly bored entertaining	In the radio play of *The Glass Menagerie*, the characters of Tom, Laura, and Amanda were ____ to the way I imagined them when reading the play. Tom seemed ____, while Amanda sounded ____, and ____ about "a gentleman caller" with so little time to prepare. Even though the radio play did not include ____ parts such as ____, the characters felt the same as in the play. The audiobook version does not change the play at all, including the ____, but the reader's voice makes all the characters seem ____ and ____.	The stage directions, lighting cues, and images presented on the screen in are ____. In the radio play, ____. The radio play was more effective ____, even though the audiobook ____.	• In *The Glass Menagerie* . . . • The radio play . . . • The audiobook includes . . . • The audio versions were different from the *The Glass Menagerie* text because . . .

Peer Review

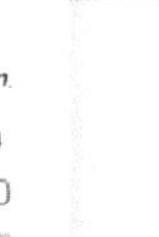

Rate

Respond to the following with a point rating that reflects your opinion

	1 2 3 4
Ideas	
Evidence	
Language and Conventions	

Submit

Students should submit feedback to two peers using the review instructions below.

- How well does the writer identify similarities and differences in each version?
- How well does the writer explain and evaluate how each version interprets the source material of the play?
- How well does the writer analyze how each medium interprets the dramatic elements of the play?

ELL A SENTENCE FRAMES

- You were able to (completely/partly/almost) identify similarities in each version.
- You explained and evaluated each version ____.
- You analyzed how each medium interpreted the dramatic elements of the play by ____.

A Room Of One's Own

ARGUMENTATIVE TEXT

Virginia Woolf

1929

Introduction

Virginia Woolf (1882–1941) was one of the most important modernist authors of the early 20th century. Best remembered for her lyrical, experimental novels, including *Mrs. Dalloway* and *To the Lighthouse*, Woolf also wrote a book-length essay entitled "A Room of One's Own," in which she muses on women as writers and as characters in fiction, describing the many challenges women face in their paths to self-actualization. In this excerpt, Woolf speculates about what might have happened if Shakespeare had had a talented and strong-willed author for a sister. Through this hypothetical scenario, Woolf illustrates the limited opportunities that had historically been available to women.

According to Virginia Woolf, Shakespeare was given the education that would have allowed him to find his way to London's theater world. If he had a sister who possessed equal amounts of genius, she mostly likely would have been forced into housework and an early marriage. If she had rebelled and ran off to London, she would have been laughed away from the theater door, perhaps finding solace in the arms of a man or killing herself. Genius did not make itself apparent among the working classes and women at the time, but Woolf believes that genius of some sort must have existed. All stories of witches, women possessed by devils, and even remarkable mothers are tales of novelists that could have been, Woolf asserts. Any woman born with a poetic gift in the sixteenth century was sure to live a painful life, torn between her own natural creativity and the culture that strove to thwart her.

ELL Proficiency-leveled summaries and summaries in multiple languages are available digitally.

Audio and audio text highlighting are available with this text.

CONNECT TO ESSENTIAL QUESTION

What causes individuals to feel alienated?

Virginia Woolf's essay *A Room of One's Own* is an important text in the history of feminism. In this excerpt, Woolf imagines what would have happened to Shakespeare's sister to argue for the necessity of giving women equal opportunities and recognizing that history has never done so.

Entry Point

As students prepare to read *A Room of One's Own,* share the following information with them to provide context.

- ✓ An early advocate of women's suffrage, or the right to vote, was Mary Wollstonecraft, who wrote *A Vindication of the Rights* of Woman in 1792. Her daughter, Mary Wollstonecraft Shelley, would write *Frankenstein*.
- ✓ By the time Woolf wrote the essay *A Room of One's Own* in 1929, England's women's suffrage movement had won substantial victories.
- ✓ In 1918 the English government extended the right to vote to all British female citizens over the age of thirty. In 1928, a year before the essay was published, the voting age for women was lowered to twenty-one. Woolf was an active supporter of the suffrage movement and other women's rights movements of the time.

Instructional Path

The print teacher's edition includes essential point-of-use instruction and planning tools. Complete lesson plans and program documents appear in your digital teacher account.

Independent Read: A Room of One's Own

Objectives: After reading *A Room of One's Own*, students will write a short response that demonstrates their understanding of Woolf's argument and determine whether it still holds true today.

Independent Read

Introduce the Text

As a class, watch the video preview and have students read the introduction in pairs to make connections to the video preview.

- What key words or images from the video do you think will be most important to the essay you are about to read?
- Have you noticed ways families treat their daughters and sons differently? How do you think that affects the children and society?

Access Complex Text

LEXILE: 1150 **WORD COUNT:** 1,116

The following areas may be challenging for students, particularly ELL English Language Learners and A Approaching grade-level learners.

Sentence Structure	Specific Vocabulary
• Woolf uses complex sentence structures with parallelisms and participles, and these long sentences with multiple sections may overwhelm readers. • Overlong sentences may require simplifying. Break down 2–3 complex sentences on the board as an example for students.	• Woolf includes proper nouns for people, such as Ovid, and places in London, such as the Elephant and Castle. She uses Anon (Anonymous) to refer to poets who chose not to sign their names to their works. • Remind students to use print or digital sources to identify the people and places Woolf mentions and consider how using those proper nouns supports Woolf's argument.

"She had no chance of learning grammar and logic, let alone of reading Horace and Virgil."

NOTES

From Chapter Three

1 Let me imagine, since the facts are so hard to come by, what would have happened had Shakespeare had a wonderfully gifted sister, called Judith, let us say. Shakespeare himself went, very probably—his mother was an heiress—to the grammar school, where he may have learnt Latin—Ovid, Virgil and Horace[1]—and the elements of grammar and **logic**. He was, it is well known, a wild boy who **poached** rabbits, perhaps shot a deer, and had, rather sooner than he should have done, to marry a woman in the neighborhood, who bore him a child rather quicker than was right. That escapade sent him to seek his fortune in London. He had, it seemed, a taste for the theatre; he began by holding horses at the stage door. Very soon he got work in the theatre, became a successful actor, and lived at the hub of the universe, meeting everybody, knowing everybody, practicing his art on the boards, exercising his wits in the streets, and even getting access to the palace of the queen. Meanwhile his extraordinarily gifted sister, let us suppose, remained at home. She was as adventurous, as imaginative, as agog to see the world as he was. But she was not sent to school. She had no chance of learning grammar and logic, let alone of reading Horace and Virgil. She picked up a book now and then, one of her brother's perhaps, and read a few pages. But then her parents came in and told her to mend the stockings or mind the stew and not moon about with books and papers. They would have spoken sharply but kindly, for they were **substantial** people who knew the conditions of life for a woman and loved their daughter—indeed, more likely than not she was the apple of her father's eye. Perhaps she scribbled some pages up in an apple loft[2] on the sly, but was careful to hide them or set fire to them. Soon, however, before she was out of her teens, she was to be betrothed to the son of a neighboring wool-stapler. She cried out that marriage was hateful to her, and for that she was severely beaten by her father. Then he ceased to scold her. He begged her instead not to hurt him, not to shame him in this matter of her marriage. He would give her a chain of beads or a fine petticoat, he said; and there were tears in his eyes. How could she disobey him? How could she

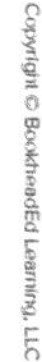

1. **Ovid, Virgil, and Horace** three of the most famous poets of ancient Rome
2. **apple loft** open second storey of a barn

Developing Background Knowledge

1. In small groups, have students do a five-minute online search about female roles in Elizabethan theater.
2. On the board, collate the various types of information students learned. Ask one student to volunteer to create an instant summary.

Discuss with students: Often, we can look back at recent history and be surprised by the inequalities that society accepted as normal. What is an example of this today that we might look back on in the future? Why do you think it is so easy for people to be "on the wrong side of history"? What insights can we gain from looking back at history that aren't available in the moment?

SELECTION VOCABULARY

logic / la lógica *noun* correct or clear reasoning COGNATE

poach / cazar furtivamente *verb* to hunt illegally

substantial / considerable *adjective* fairly large

TEXT TALK

How are Judith and William alike? How are they different?

See the beginning of paragraph 1: They have similar abilities and dreams, but Judith has fewer options.

Prepare for Advanced Courses

Use the activity below to differentiate instruction for your B Beyond grade level learners.

Author's Syntax

Reread the following sentence from paragraph 1:

But she was not sent to school.

Have students examine how the author's syntax reflects her purpose.

Ask students:

- What is the emotional impact of this shorter sentence?
- How does this short sentence among longer sentences reflect a message for the reader?

NOTES

break his heart? The force of her own gift alone drove her to it. She made up a small parcel of her belongings, let herself down by a rope one summer's night and took the road to London. She was not seventeen. The birds that sang in the hedge were not more musical than she was. She had the quickest fancy, a gift like her brother's, for the tune of words. Like him, she had a taste for the theatre. She stood at the stage door; she wanted to act, she said. Men laughed in her face. The manager—a fat, loose-lipped man—guffawed. He bellowed something about poodles dancing and women acting—no woman, he said, could possibly be an actress. He hinted—you can imagine what. She could get no training in her craft. Could she even seek her dinner in a tavern or roam the streets at midnight? Yet her genius was for fiction and lusted to feed abundantly upon the lives of men and women and the study of their ways. At last—for she was very young, oddly like Shakespeare the poet in her face, with the same grey eyes and rounded brows—at last Nick Greene the actor-manager took pity on her; she found herself with child by that gentleman and so—who shall measure the heat and violence of the poet's heart when caught and tangled in a woman's body?—killed herself one winter's night and lies buried at some crossroads where the omnibuses now stop outside the Elephant and Castle[3].

2 That, more or less, is how the story would run, I think, if a woman in Shakespeare's day had had Shakespeare's genius. But for my part, I agree with the deceased bishop[4], if such he was—it is unthinkable that any woman in Shakespeare's day should have had Shakespeare's genius. For genius like Shakespeare's is not born among labouring, uneducated, **servile** people. It was not born in England among the Saxons and the Britons. It is not born today among the working classes. How, then, could it have been born among women whose work began, according to Professor Trevelyan, almost before they were out of the nursery, who were forced to it by their parents and held to it by all the power of law and custom? Yet genius of a sort must have existed among women as it must have existed among the working classes. Now and again an Emily Bronte or a Robert Burns[5] blazes out and proves its presence. But certainly it never got itself on to paper. When, however, one reads of a witch being ducked, of a woman possessed by devils, of a wise woman selling herbs, or even of a very remarkable man who had a mother, then I think we are on the track of a lost novelist, a suppressed poet, of some mute and inglorious Jane Austen, some Emily Bronte who dashed her brains out on the moor or mopped and mowed about the highways crazed with the torture that her gift had put her to. Indeed, I would venture to guess that

3. **outside the Elephant and Castle** road and Underground transportation hub in the Southwark borough of London
4. **the deceased bishop** Woolf remembers a bishop who wrote that no woman could ever become as smart or accomplished as Shakespeare
5. **Emily Brontë or a Robert Burns** Emily Brontë (1818–1848), author of the classic novel Wuthering Heights; Robert Burns (1759–1796), national poet of Scotland, writer of "Auld Lang Syne"

TEXT TALK

How does Judith die? Why?

See the end of paragraph 1: Judith kills herself because she cannot live the life she wants for herself.

What reason does Woolf give to support the idea that it is unthinkable that any woman in Shakespeare's day would have had Shakespeare's genius?

See paragraph 2: Women were like working people, forced by the families and society into a kind of servitude.

SELECTION VOCABULARY

servile / servil ***adjective*** wanting desperately to please others, obsequious COGNATE

Anon, who wrote so many poems without signing them, was often a woman. It was a woman Edward Fitzgerald[6], I think, suggested who made the ballads and the folk-songs, crooning them to her children, beguiling her spinning with them, on the length of the winter's night.

3 This may be true or it may be false—who can say?—but what is true in it, so it seemed to me, reviewing the story of Shakespeare's sister as I had made it, is that any woman born with a great gift in the sixteenth century would certainly have gone crazed, shot herself, or ended her days in some lonely cottage outside the village, half witch, half wizard, feared and mocked at. For it needs little skill in psychology to be sure that a highly gifted girl who had tried to use her gift for poetry would have been so thwarted and hindered by other people, so tortured and pulled **asunder** by her own contrary instincts, that she must have lost her health and sanity to a certainty.

Excerpted from *A Room of One's Own* by Virginia Woolf, published by Mariner Books.

WRITE

ARGUMENTATIVE: Woolf states: "Genius like Shakespeare's is not born among labouring, uneducated, servile people." Do you think this statement still holds true today? In an essay response, discuss whether you think "genius" among the "working classes" is possible in today's society, and why or why not. How might this have been different in the time in which Woolf lived, and why?

6. **woman Edward Fitzgerald** Lady Edward FitzGerald (1809–1883), translated quatrains ascribed to the 11th century Persian poet Omar Khayyam that became very popular; later investigations strongly suggested his Rubiyat was largely of FitzGerald's own invention

TEXT TALK

What does Woolf suggest happened to gifted women in the sixteenth century?

See paragraph 3: Woolf imagines they all would have gone crazy.

How did your research about female roles in Elizabethan theater and discussion of accepted inequalities help you understand Woolf's argument in the text?

Answers will vary.

Ask each Beyond grade-level student to write one additional discussion question. Then, have one or two students facilitate a discussion, using their questions to guide the conversation.

SELECTION VOCABULARY

asunder / en pedazos *verb* to become pieces

Writer's Notebook

Connect to Essential Question: Give students time to reflect on how *A Room of One's Own* connects to the unit's essential question "What causes individuals to feel alienated?" by freewriting in their Writer's Notebooks.

CHECK FOR SUCCESS

If students are still struggling to respond to the prompt, ask them scaffolded questions, such as:

1. Who were the "labouring, uneducated, servile people" to whom Woolf refers? What was their life like?
2. Who comprises the "working classes" today? How are they different from working people in Woolf's day and age?

Reading Comprehension OPTIONAL

Have students complete the digital reading comprehension questions when they finish reading.

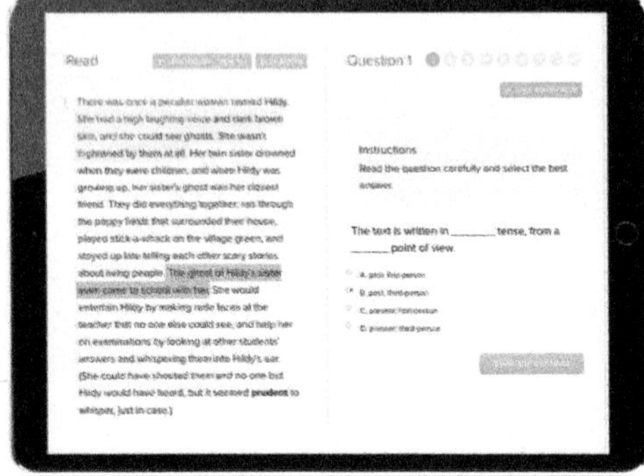

ANSWER KEY

QUESTION 1: B
QUESTION 2: D
QUESTION 3: C
QUESTION 4: B
QUESTION 5: A
QUESTION 6: B
QUESTION 7: B
QUESTION 8: C
QUESTION 9: *See chart below.*
QUESTION 10: D

Definition	Word
Of solid character or quality	substantial
Apart, into pieces	asunder
The formal study of arguments	logic
Wanting desperately to please others, obsequious	servile

Connect and Extend OPTIONAL

CONNECT TO EXTENDED WRITING PROJECT

Students can find inspiration from "A Room of One's Own" for their literary analysis. Have students review the essay and highlight and explain three pieces of textual evidence that reflects a sense of alienation, a theme common in modernist literature.

BEYOND THE BOOK

Activity: Women Accused of Witchcraft

Woolf argues that if Shakespeare had a talented sister, she could never have followed her passions given the time period. She also claims that those women who were exceptionally talented were accused of being witches. Students will research women in history accused of being witches, research their talents, and predict what they might have accomplished if given the chance.

Ask students to:

- Work in partners to identify a woman from history who was accused of witchcraft.
  - > Why were they accused of being a witch?
  - > What special talents or abilities did she possess?
  - > What do you know about this person's life?
- Given the information learned, brainstorm who this person might have become if they had not been accused of witchcraft.
- Create a magazine cover page detailing this person's accomplishments.
  - > Draw a picture or create a collage of this person surrounded by the tools of her trade.
  - > Decide on a catchy title.
  - > Write a few snippets of what articles will be inside this magazine issue.
- Share covers with classmates.

To reflect, ask students:

- Why were these women accused of witchcraft?
- What did all these women have in common?

Collaborative Conversation

Post the writing prompt to generate a discussion in small groups. Ask students to first break down the prompt before they discuss relevant ideas and textual evidence.

Woolf states: "Genius like Shakespeare's is not born among labouring, uneducated, servile people." Do you think this statement still holds true today? In an essay response, discuss whether you think "genius" among the "working classes" is possible in today's society, and why or why not. How might this have been different in the time in which Woolf lived, and why?

Use the scaffolds below to differentiate instruction for your ELL English Language Learners and A Approaching grade-level learners.

ELL **BEGINNING, INTERMEDIATE** Use the discussion guide and speaking frames to facilitate the discussion with support from the teacher.

ADVANCED, ADVANCED HIGH Use the discussion guide and speaking frames to facilitate the discussion in mixed-level groups.

A **APPROACHING** Use the discussion guide to facilitate the discussion in mixed-level groups.

APPROACHING
ADVANCED, ADVANCED HIGH
BEGINNING, INTERMEDIATE

Discussion Guide	Speaking Frames
1. What do "genius" and "working classes" mean in Woolf's statement? What are some examples?	• An example of a genius is ____ because ____. • The "working classes" include people who ____ and means ____.
2. Do you think "genius" among the "working classes" is possible in today's society? Why or why not?	• I think it (is / isn't) because ____. • An example that supports my idea is ____.
3. How might this have been different in the time in which Woolf lived?	• It was different in Woolf's time because ____. • Textual evidence that supports this is ____.

Text To World

Use the activity below to differentiate instruction for your B Beyond grade level learners.

Reread paragraph 1:

But then her parents came in and told her to mend the stockings or mind the stew and not moon about with books and papers. Have students conduct informal research about the role of men and women in the early 17th century.
Ask students:

- How do the perspectives of Judith and her parents differ?
- Why are Judith and her parents so different?

Review Prompt and Rubric

Before students begin writing, review the writing prompt and rubric with the class.

ARGUMENTATIVE: Woolf states: "Genius like Shakespeare's is not born among labouring, uneducated, servile people." Do you think this statement still holds true today? In an essay response, discuss whether you think "genius" among the "working classes" is possible in today's society, and why or why not. How might this have been different in the time in which Woolf lived, and why?

PROMPT GUIDE

- What does Woolf's statement about "'genius' among the 'working classes'" mean?
- Do you think "'genius' among the 'working classes'" is possible in today's society? Why? What examples in today's society support your idea?
- How might this have been different in Woolf's time? Why?

Score	Argumentative	Language and Conventions
4	The writer establishes a clear position. All ideas are strongly related to the position and are focused on the issue specified in the prompt. By sustaining this focus, the writer is able to create an essay that is unified and organized.	The writer demonstrates a consistent command of grammar, punctuation, and usage conventions. Although minor errors may be evident, they do not detract from the fluency or the clarity of the essay.
3	The writer establishes a clear position. Most ideas are related to the position and are focused on the issue specified in the prompt. The essay is organized, though it may not always be unified due to minor lapses in focus.	The writer demonstrates an adequate command of grammar, punctuation, and usage conventions. Although some errors may be evident, they create few (if any) disruptions in the fluency of the writing or the clarity of the essay.
2	Most ideas are generally related to the issue specified in the prompt, but the writer's position is weak or somewhat unclear. The lack of a clear, effective position or the writer's inclusion of irrelevant information interferes with the focus and organization of the essay.	The writer demonstrates a partial command of grammar, punctuation, and usage conventions. Some distracting errors may be evident, at times creating minor disruptions in the fluency or clarity of the writing.
1	Most ideas are generally related to the issue specified in the prompt, but the writer's position is missing, unclear, or illogical. The writer may fail to maintain focus on the issue, may include extraneous information, or may shift abruptly from idea to idea, weakening the organization of the essay.	The writer demonstrates little or no command of grammar, punctuation, and usage conventions. Serious and persistent errors create disruptions in the fluency of the writing and sometimes interfere with meaning.
0	The writer does not provide a relevant response to the prompt or does not provide a response at all.	Serious and persistent errors overwhelm the writing and interfere with the meaning of the response as a whole, making the writer's meaning impossible to understand.

SCAFFOLDS

Write

Ask students to complete the writing assignment using text evidence to support their answers.

Use the scaffolds below to differentiate instruction for your ELL English Language Learners and A Approaching grade level readers.

ELL **BEGINNING** With the help of the word bank, write a response using paragraph frame 1.

INTERMEDIATE With the help of the word bank, write a response using paragraph frames 1 and 2.

ADVANCED, ADVANCED HIGH Write a response of differentiated length using the sentence starters.

A **APPROACHING** Write a response of differentiated length using the sentence starters.

BEGINNING / INTERMEDIATE			ADVANCED, ADVANCED HIGH / APPROACHING
Word Bank	**Paragraph Frame 1**	**Paragraph Frame 2**	**Sentence Starters**
working class family genius gifted is	Woolf argues that ____ like Shakespeare's results when very ____ people are supported by their ____. I think genius among the working classes ____ possible today. There are scholarships that help gifted people from ____ families achieve their dreams.	In Woolf's time, the working class could not afford to ____. The working class did not have ____. They had to ____. Today, ____ helps 21st century geniuses succeed, regardless of how their family makes a living.	• When Woolf states: "Genius like Shakespeare's is not born among labouring, uneducated, servile people," she means . . . • This statement (does / does not) hold true today because. . . • In Woolf's time . . . • It's different today because . . .

Peer Review

Rate

Respond to the following with a point rating that reflects your opinion.

	1 2 3 4
Ideas	
Evidence	
Language and Conventions	

Submit

Students should submit substantive feedback to two peers using the review instructions below.

- How well does this response answer the prompt?
- Which of the author's comments inspired you to think differently about the essay?
- What does the writer do well in this response? What does the writer need to work on?

Remember that your comments are most useful when they are kind and constructive.

SENTENCE FRAMES

- You were able to (completely / partly / almost) ____ answer the prompt.
- You could answer the prompt more completely by ____.
- I thought differently about the text after reading ____.
- My favorite part of your response is ____.

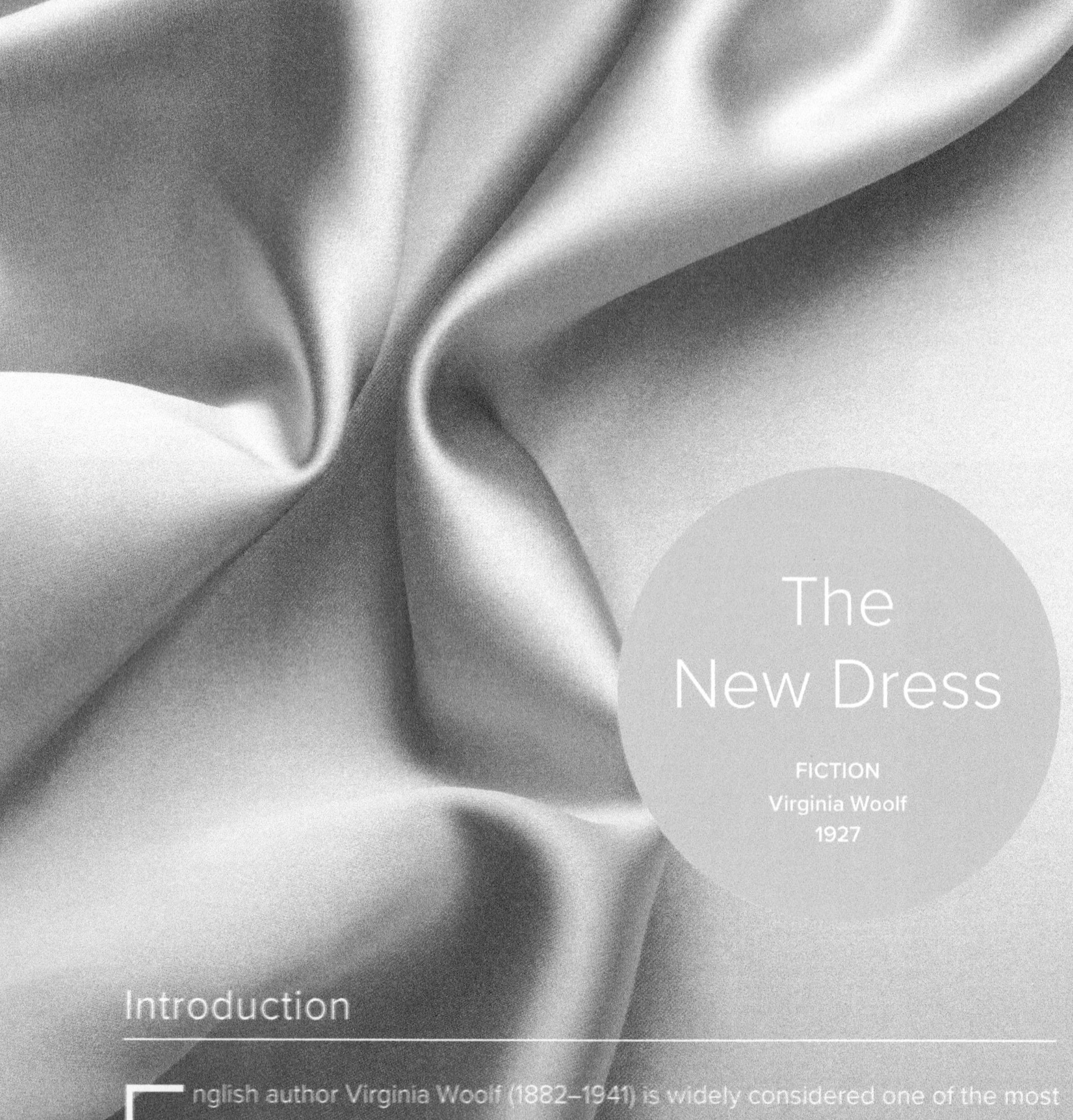

The New Dress

FICTION

Virginia Woolf

1927

Introduction

English author Virginia Woolf (1882–1941) is widely considered one of the most important literary figures of the 20th century. Woolf was a pioneer in her use of stream-of-consciousness, a narrative technique that follows a character's flow of thoughts. Her short story "The New Dress" was first published in the May 1927 issue of *Forum*, a New York City magazine. Some literary critics suspect that the short story was originally meant as a chapter for *Mrs. Dalloway*, Woolf's best-known novel. Both texts share some of the same characters and were written within three years of one another. In the story, Mabel wears a new handmade yellow dress to one of Mrs. Dalloway's cocktail parties. Deeply self-conscious, Mabel is convinced she is being mocked by the other partygoers.

Walking into the Dalloways' party wearing her new dress, Mabel Waring feels that something is wrong. Nobody says anything, but whenever Mabel catches herself in the mirror, a profound self-loathing rises within her. Everyone must be wondering why she's wearing that awful dress. Mabel wanted to rebel against the fashions of the day and, using an old Parisian fashion book for inspiration, she went to her dressmaker. She remembers being back in the fitting room and feeling that the dress was just right. Now at the party, people compliment her, but it's all just lies, she thinks to herself. Mabel can't concentrate on the conversation, thinking only of how petty social life is. She dreams about how, tomorrow, she will change her life and become a religious worker and never have to think about fashion again. Finally, Mabel gets up from the sofa and tells the Dalloways that she's had a wonderful time, but she must go home early.

 Proficiency-leveled summaries and summaries in multiple languages are available digitally.

 Audio and audio text highlighting are available with this text.

CONNECT TO ESSENTIAL QUESTION

What causes individuals to feel alienated?

This short story by Virginia Woolf was first published in a New York magazine in 1927. The story explores themes of gender, class, materialism, and beauty through Mabel's point of view, who wears a handmade dress to one of Mrs. Dalloway's famous parties.

Entry Point

As students prepare to read "The New Dress," share the following information with them to provide context.

- ✓ The term "stream of consciousness" originated with philosopher William James (1842-1910). James, a prominent figure in American psychology, was trained in medicine and coined the term to describe the changing, continuous flow of mental life. James believed that consciousness does not appear to itself "chopped up in bits," but rather flows like a river.
- ✓ Virginia Woolf uses this literary device to reflect her character's consciousness from within, as the character experiences her private thoughts. Other literary greats, including James Joyce, also used this literary device in their novels. It became a trademark of Modernism.

Instructional Path

The print teacher's edition includes essential point-of-use instruction and planning tools. Complete lesson plans and program documents appear in your digital teacher account.

Independent Read: The New Dress

Objectives: After reading "The New Dress" students will be able to compose a narrative inspired by the central character in the story.

Independent Read

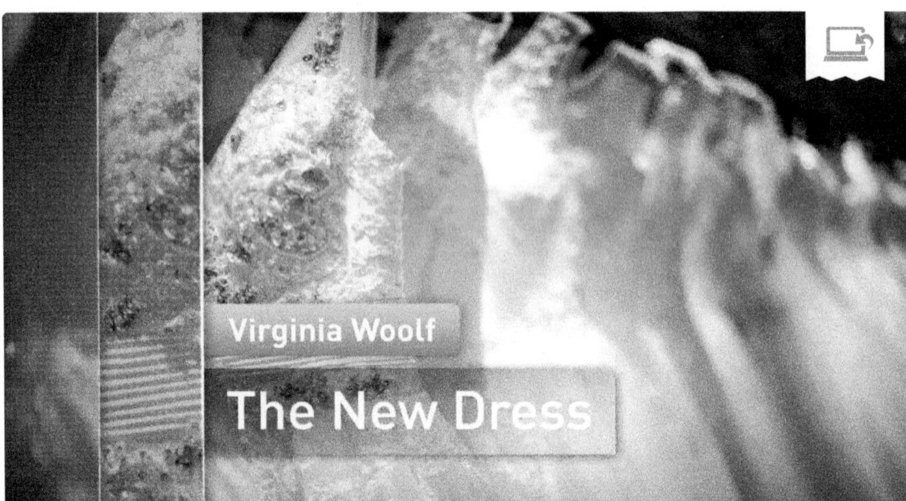

Introduce the Text

As a class, watch the video preview and have students read the introduction in pairs to make connections to the video preview.

- What two words would you use to describe this video?
- When have you regretted wearing something to school or to a party?

ELL **SPEAKING FRAMES**

- Two words that describe this video are ____ and.
- I wore ____. I regretted it because ____.

Access Complex Text

LEXILE: 1390 **WORD COUNT:** 3,205

The following areas may be challenging for students, particularly ELL English Language Learners and A Approaching grade-level learners.

Purpose	Sentence Structure
• Virginia Woolf is known for her use of the stream-of-consciousness writing style. The narrative follows Mabel's thoughts and feelings. Plot is revealed through the character's thoughts. This writing style might be challenging for students. • Have students highlight any passages they find challenging. Then work with students to paraphrase those passages.	• Woolf uses complex sentence structures with multiple phrases and clauses. • Have students highlight any long sentences they find challenging. Then have them work in groups to rewrite each long sentence into a series of shorter, more accessible sentences.

"What's Mabel wearing? What a fright she looks!"

Virginia Woolf

1 Mabel had her first serious suspicion that something was wrong as she took her cloak off and Mrs. Barnet, while handing her the mirror and touching the brushes and thus drawing her attention, perhaps rather markedly, to all the appliances for tidying and improving hair, complexion, clothes, which existed on the dressing table, confirmed the suspicion—that it was not right, not quite right, which growing stronger as she went upstairs and springing at her, with conviction as she greeted Clarissa Dalloway, she went straight to the far end of the room, to a shaded corner where a looking-glass hung and looked. No! It was not RIGHT. And at once the misery which she always tried to hide, the **profound** dissatisfaction—the sense she had had, ever since she was a child, of being inferior to other people—set upon her, relentlessly, remorselessly, with an intensity which she could not beat off, as she would when she woke at night at home, by reading Borrow or Scott[1]; for oh these men, oh these women, all were thinking—"What's Mabel wearing? What a fright she looks! What a hideous new dress!"—their eyelids flickering as they came up and then their lids shutting rather tight. It was her own appalling inadequacy; her cowardice; her mean, water-sprinkled blood that depressed her. And at once the whole of the room where, for ever so many hours, she had planned with the little dressmaker how it was to go, seemed **sordid**, repulsive; and her own drawing-room so shabby, and herself, going out, puffed up with vanity as she touched the letters on the hall table and said: "How dull!" to show off—all this now seemed unutterably silly, paltry, and provincial. All this had been absolutely destroyed, shown up, exploded, the moment she came into Mrs. Dalloway's drawing-room.

1. **Borrow or Scott** George Henry Borrow (1803–1881), travel writer, lived with English gypsies and wrote romantically about their lifestyle; Sir Walter Scott (1771–1832) author of the popular 1819 novel Ivanhoe, which presented a romanticized, unrealistic version of England in the Middle Ages

Developing Background Knowledge and Cultural Awareness

1. Share with students the following quotation from *Orlando* by Virginia Woolf: "Thus, there is much to support the view that it is clothes that wear us and not we them; we may make them take to mould of arm or breast, but they mould our hearts, our brains, our tongues to their liking."
2. In small groups, have students discuss the quotation's meaning, and how it relates to something in their own lives or to something they've read or learned about.

Discuss with students: Think of an item of clothing that you own that is significant to you. What does this clothing symbolize? What does it tell others about you? To what extent do we control the way others perceive us through the clothing we wear?

SELECTION VOCABULARY

profound / profundo/a *adjective* very great or intense COGNATE

sordid / sórdido/a *adjective* wretched, dirty, or distasteful COGNATE

TEXT TALK

What is the story's setting?

See paragraph 1: Mabel is at a party at Mrs. Dalloway's house.

Prepare for Advanced Courses

Use the activity below to differentiate instruction for your B Beyond grade level learners.

Author's Word Choice

Reread the following sentence from paragraph 6:

I feel like some dowdy, decrepit, horribly dingy old fly

Have students examine the author's use of descriptive words.

Ask students:

- How does the author's word choice achieve the purpose of the text?
- How do these words help the reader understand the character?

NOTES

2 What she had thought that evening when, sitting over the teacups, Mrs. Dalloway's invitation came, was that, of course, she could not be fashionable. It was absurd to pretend it even—fashion meant cut, meant style, meant thirty guineas at least—but why not be original? Why not be herself, anyhow? And, getting up, she had taken that old fashion book of her mother's, a Paris fashion book of the time of the Empire, and had thought how much prettier, more dignified, and more womanly they were then, and so set herself—oh, it was foolish—trying to be like them, pluming herself in fact, upon being modest and old-fashioned, and very charming, giving herself up, no doubt about it, to an orgy of self-love, which deserved to be **chastised**, and so rigged herself out like this.

3 But she dared not look in the glass. She could not face the whole horror—the pale yellow, idiotically old-fashioned silk dress with its long skirt and its high sleeves and its waist and all the things that looked so charming in the fashion book, but not on her, not among all these ordinary people. She felt like a dressmaker's dummy standing there, for young people to stick pins into.

4 "But, my dear, it's perfectly charming!" Rose Shaw said, looking her up and down with that little satirical pucker of the lips which she expected—Rose herself being dressed in the height of the fashion, precisely like everybody else, always.

5 We are all like flies trying to crawl over the edge of the saucer, Mabel thought, and repeated the phrase as if she were crossing herself, as if she were trying to find some spell to annul this pain, to make this agony endurable. Tags of Shakespeare, lines from books she had read ages ago, suddenly came to her when she was in agony, and she repeated them over and over again. "Flies trying to crawl," she repeated. If she could say that over often enough and make herself see the flies, she would become numb, chill, frozen, dumb. Now she could see flies crawling slowly out of a saucer of milk with their wings stuck together; and she strained and strained (standing in front of the looking-glass, listening to Rose Shaw) to make herself see Rose Shaw and all the other people there as flies, trying to hoist themselves out of something, or into something, meagre, insignificant, toiling flies. But she could not see them like that, not other people. She saw herself like that—she was a fly, but the others were dragonflies, butterflies, beautiful insects, dancing, fluttering, skimming, while she alone dragged herself up out of the saucer. (Envy and spite, the most detestable of the vices, were her chief faults.)

6 "I feel like some dowdy, decrepit, horribly dingy old fly," she said, making Robert Haydon stop just to hear her say that, just to reassure herself by furbishing up a poor weak-kneed phrase and so showing how detached she was, how witty, that she did not feel in the least out of anything. And, of course, Robert Haydon answered something, quite polite, quite insincere, which she

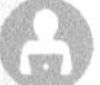

TEXT TALK

Who is Miss Milan? How does Mabel feel about her?

See paragraph 6: Miss Milan is the dressmaker who sewed Mabel's yellow dress, and Mabel is fonder of her than of anyone else in the world.

SELECTION VOCABULARY

chastise / regañar *verb* to scold

NOTES

saw through instantly, and said to herself, directly he went (again from some book), "Lies, lies, lies!" For a party makes things either much more real, or much less real, she thought; she saw in a flash to the bottom of Robert Haydon's heart; she saw through everything. She saw the truth. THIS was true, this drawing-room, this self, and the other false. Miss Milan's little workroom was really terribly hot, stuffy, sordid. It smelt of clothes and cabbage cooking; and yet, when Miss Milan put the glass in her hand, and she looked at herself with the dress on, finished, an extraordinary bliss shot through her heart. Suffused with light, she sprang into existence. Rid of cares and wrinkles, what she had dreamed of herself was there—a beautiful woman. just for a second (she had not dared look longer, Miss Milan wanted to know about the length of the skirt), there looked at her, framed in the scrolloping mahogany, a grey-white, mysteriously smiling, charming girl, the core of herself, the soul of herself; and it was not vanity only, not only self-love that made her think it good, tender, and true. Miss Milan said that the skirt could not well be longer; if anything the skirt, said Miss Milan, puckering her forehead, considering with all her wits about her, must be shorter; and she felt, suddenly, honestly, full of love for Miss Milan, much, much fonder of Miss Milan than of any one in the whole world, and could have cried for pity that she should be crawling on the floor with her mouth full of pins, and her face red and her eyes bulging—that one human being should be doing this for another, and she saw them all as human beings merely, and herself going off to her party, and Miss Milan pulling the cover over the canary's cage, or letting him pick a hemp-seed from between her lips, and the thought of it, of this side of human nature and its patience and its endurance and its being content with such miserable, scanty, sordid, little pleasures filled her eyes with tears.

7 And now the whole thing had vanished. The dress, the room, the love, the pity, the scrolloping looking-glass, and the canary's cage—all had vanished, and here she was in a corner of Mrs. Dalloway's drawing-room, suffering tortures, woken wide awake to reality.

8 But it was all so paltry, weak-blooded, and petty-minded to care so much at her age with two children, to be still so utterly dependent on people's opinions and not have principles or convictions, not to be able to say as other people did, "There's Shakespeare! There's death! We're all weevils in a captain's biscuit"—or whatever it was that people did say.

9 She faced herself straight in the glass; she pecked at her left shoulder; she issued out into the room, as if spears were thrown at her yellow dress from all sides. But instead of looking fierce or tragic, as Rose Shaw would have done—Rose would have looked like Boadicea[2]—she looked foolish and self-

2. **Boadicea** tribal queen of the indigenous Celtic Iceni, who led a rebellion against Roman occupation 60–61 A.D.

NOTES

conscious, and simpered like a schoolgirl and slouched across the room, positively slinking, as if she were a beaten mongrel, and looked at a picture, an engraving. As if one went to a party to look at a picture! Everybody knew why she did it—it was from shame, from humiliation.

10 "Now the fly's in the saucer," she said to herself, "right in the middle, and can't get out, and the milk," she thought, rigidly staring at the picture, "is sticking its wings together."

11 "It's so old-fashioned," she said to Charles Burt, making him stop (which by itself he hated) on his way to talk to some one else.

12 She meant, or she tried to make herself think that she meant, that it was the picture and not her dress, that was old-fashioned. And one word of praise, one word of affection from Charles would have made all the difference to her at the moment. If he had only said, "Mabel, you're looking charming to-night!" it would have changed her life. But then she ought to have been truthful and direct. Charles said nothing of the kind, of course. He was malice itself. He always saw through one, especially if one were feeling particularly mean, paltry, or feeble-minded.

13 "Mabel's got a new dress!" he said, and the poor fly was absolutely shoved into the middle of the saucer. Really, he would like her to drown, she believed. He had no heart, no fundamental kindness, only a **veneer** of friendliness. Miss Milan was much more real, much kinder. If only one could feel that and stick to it, always. "Why," she asked herself—replying to Charles much too pertly, letting him see that she was out of temper, or "ruffled" as he called it ("Rather ruffled?" he said and went on to laugh at her with some woman over there)—"Why," she asked herself, "can't I feel one thing always, feel quite sure that Miss Milan is right, and Charles wrong and stick to it, feel sure about the canary and pity and love and not be whipped all round in a second by coming into a room full of people?" It was her odious, weak, vacillating character again, always giving at the critical moment and not being seriously interested in conchology, etymology, botany, archeology, cutting up potatoes and watching them fructify like Mary Dennis, like Violet Searle.

14 Then Mrs. Holman, seeing her standing there, bore down upon her. Of course a thing like a dress was beneath Mrs. Holman's notice, with her family always tumbling downstairs or having the scarlet fever. Could Mabel tell her if Elmthorpe was ever let for August and September? Oh, it was a conversation that bored her unutterably!—it made her furious to be treated like a house agent or a messenger boy, to be made use of. Not to have value, that was it, she thought, trying to grasp something hard, something real, while she tried to answer sensibly about the bathroom and the south aspect and the hot water to the top of the house; and all the time she could

SELECTION VOCABULARY

veneer / la fachada *noun* a false appearance designed to mask true feelings

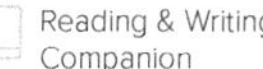

see little bits of her yellow dress in the round looking-glass which made them all the size of boot-buttons or tadpoles; and it was amazing to think how much humiliation and agony and self-loathing and effort and passionate ups and downs of feeling were contained in a thing the size of a threepenny bit. And what was still odder, this thing, this Mabel Waring, was separate, quite disconnected; and though Mrs. Holman (the black button) was leaning forward and telling her how her eldest boy had strained his heart running, she could see her, too, quite detached in the looking-glass, and it was impossible that the black dot, leaning forward, gesticulating, should make the yellow dot, sitting solitary, self-centred, feel what the black dot was feeling, yet they pretended.

15 "So impossible to keep boys quiet"—that was the kind of thing one said.

16 And Mrs. Holman, who could never get enough sympathy and snatched what little there was greedily, as if it were her right (but she deserved much more for there was her little girl who had come down this morning with a swollen knee-joint), took this miserable offering and looked at it suspiciously, grudgingly, as if it were a halfpenny when it ought to have been a pound and put it away in her purse, must put up with it, mean and miserly though it was, times being hard, so very hard; and on she went, creaking, injured Mrs. Holman, about the girl with the swollen joints. Ah, it was tragic, this greed, this clamour of human beings, like a row of cormorants, barking and flapping their wings for sympathy—it was tragic, could one have felt it and not merely pretended to feel it!

17 But in her yellow dress to-night she could not wring out one drop more; she wanted it all, all for herself. She knew (she kept on looking into the glass, dipping into that dreadfully showing-up blue pool) that she was condemned, despised, left like this in a backwater, because of her being like this a feeble, vacillating creature; and it seemed to her that the yellow dress was a penance which she had deserved, and if she had been dressed like Rose Shaw, in lovely, clinging green with a ruffle of swansdown, she would have deserved that; and she thought that there was no escape for her—none whatever. But it was not her fault altogether, after all. It was being one of a family of ten; never having money enough, always skimping and paring; and her mother carrying great cans, and the linoleum worn on the stair edges, and one sordid little domestic tragedy after another—nothing catastrophic, the sheep farm failing, but not utterly; her eldest brother marrying beneath him but not very much—there was no romance, nothing extreme about them all. They petered out respectably in seaside resorts; every watering-place had one of her aunts even now asleep in some lodging with the front windows not quite facing the sea. That was so like them—they had to squint at things always. And she had done the same—she was just like her aunts. For all her dreams of living in India, married to some hero like Sir Henry

TEXT TALK

What are Charles Burt and Rose Shaw doing by the fireplace? What does Mabel think they are doing?

See paragraph 17: They are chatting. Mabel thinks they are laughing at her.

NOTES

Lawrence[3], some empire builder (still the sight of a native in a turban filled her with romance), she had failed utterly. She had married Hubert, with his safe, permanent underling's job in the Law Courts, and they managed tolerably in a smallish house, without proper maids, and hash when she was alone or just bread and butter, but now and then—Mrs. Holman was off, thinking her the most dried-up, unsympathetic twig she had ever met, absurdly dressed, too, and would tell every one about Mabel's fantastic appearance—now and then, thought Mabel Waring, left alone on the blue sofa, punching the cushion in order to look occupied, for she would not join Charles Burt and Rose Shaw, chattering like magpies and perhaps laughing at her by the fireplace—now and then, there did come to her delicious moments, reading the other night in bed, for instance, or down by the sea on the sand in the sun, at Easter—let her recall it—a great tuft of pale sand-grass standing all twisted like a shock of spears against the sky, which was blue like a smooth china egg[4], so firm, so hard, and then the melody of the waves—"Hush, hush," they said, and the children's shouts paddling—yes, it was a divine moment, and there she lay, she felt, in the hand of the Goddess who was the world; rather a hard-hearted, but very beautiful Goddess, a little lamb laid on the altar (one did think these silly things, and it didn't matter so long as one never said them). And also with Hubert sometimes she had quite unexpectedly—carving the mutton for Sunday lunch, for no reason, opening a letter, coming into a room—divine moments, when she said to herself (for she would never say this to anybody else), "This is it. This has happened. This is it!" And the other way about it was equally surprising—that is, when everything was arranged—music, weather, holidays, every reason for happiness was there—then nothing happened at all. One wasn't happy. It was flat, just flat, that was all.

18 Her wretched self again, no doubt! She had always been a fretful, weak, unsatisfactory mother, a wobbly wife, lolling about in a kind of twilight existence with nothing very clear or very bold, or more one thing than another, like all her brothers and sisters, except perhaps Herbert—they were all the same poor water-veined creatures who did nothing. Then in the midst of this creeping, crawling life, suddenly she was on the crest of a wave. That wretched fly—where had she read the story that kept coming into her mind about the fly and the saucer?—struggled out. Yes, she had those moments. But now that she was forty, they might come more and more seldom. By degrees she would cease to struggle any more. But that was deplorable! That was not to be **endured**! That made her feel ashamed of herself!

3. **Sir Henry Lawrence** Brigadier General Sir Henry Montgomery Lawrence (1806–1857), a British colonial administrator in India who was killed at the Siege of Lucknow
4. **china egg** decorative egg made of porcelain

SELECTION VOCABULARY

endure / resistir ***verb*** to continue or survive through a difficult task or experience

19 She would go to the London Library to-morrow. She would find some wonderful, helpful, astonishing book, quite by chance, a book by a clergyman, by an American no one had ever heard of; or she would walk down the Strand and drop, accidentally, into a hall where a miner was telling about the life in the pit, and suddenly she would become a new person. She would be absolutely transformed. She would wear a uniform; she would be called Sister Somebody; she would never give a thought to clothes again. And for ever after she would be perfectly clear about Charles Burt and Miss Milan and this room and that room; and it would be always, day after day, as if she were lying in the sun or carving the mutton. It would be it!

20 So she got up from the blue sofa, and the yellow button in the looking-glass got up too, and she waved her hand to Charles and Rose to show them she did not depend on them one scrap, and the yellow button moved out of the looking-glass, and all the spears were gathered into her breast as she walked towards Mrs. Dalloway and said "Good night."

21 "But it's too early to go," said Mrs. Dalloway, who was always so charming.

22 "I'm afraid I must," said Mabel Waring. "But," she added in her weak, wobbly voice which only sounded ridiculous when she tried to strengthen it, "I have enjoyed myself enormously."

23 'I have enjoyed myself," she said to Mr. Dalloway, whom she met on the stairs.

24 "Lies, lies, lies!" she said to herself, going downstairs, and "Right in the saucer!" she said to herself as she thanked Mrs. Barnet for helping her and wrapped herself, round and round and round, in the Chinese cloak she had worn these twenty years.

NARRATIVE: Compose a brief passage of a short story focusing on a character whose outward appearance does not match his or her feelings. Use "The New Dress" as a model, because the main character in the story secretly thinks she looks hideous while she tries to put a brave face on her situation. Consider how it might affect a person to hide his or her true feelings at a party or with a single person who is important to him or her.

TEXT TALK

What kind of cloak does Mabel wear? Why is that important?

See paragraph 24: She is wearing a Chinese cloak that she's had for twenty years, which shows she doesn't buy new clothes.

How did discussing the quotation from *Orlando* deepen your understanding of "The New Dress"?

Answers will vary.

B Ask each Beyond grade-level student to write one additional discussion question. Then, have one or two students facilitate a discussion, using their questions to guide the conversation.

Writer's Notebook

Connect to Literary Focus: Give students time to reflect on how "The New Dress" demonstrates the conventions and characteristics of this unit's literary focus, Modernism, by freewriting in their Writer's Notebooks.

CHECK FOR SUCCESS

If students are still struggling to respond to the prompt, ask them scaffolded questions, such as:

1. How do Mabel's feelings and her behavior at the party embody the idea of alienation?
2. How does the characterization of Mabel break away from traditional characterizations in fiction?

Reading Comprehension OPTIONAL

Have students complete the digital reading comprehension questions ✓ when they finish reading.

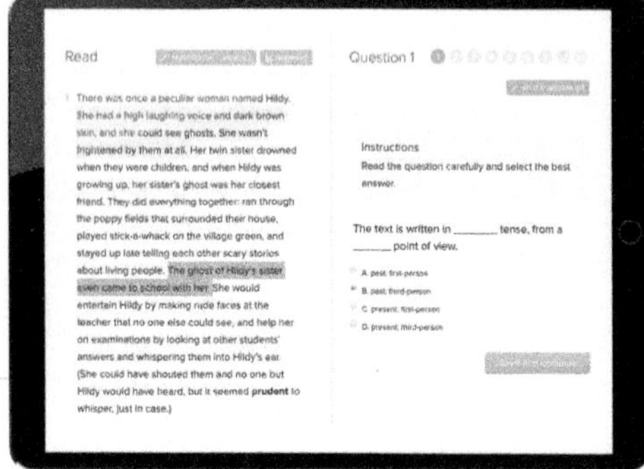

ANSWER KEY

QUESTION 1: D
QUESTION 2: A
QUESTION 3: D
QUESTION 4: B
QUESTION 5: D
QUESTION 6: C
QUESTION 7: C
QUESTION 8: A
QUESTION 9: *See first chart.*
QUESTION 10: *See second chart.*

Definition	Word
disguise	veneer
intense	profound
appalling	sordid
suffer	endure
scold	chastise

First	Second	Third	Fourth
Mabel goes to the corner to look at herself in the mirror. She feels miserable about the new dress.	Mabel interacts with other partygoers and imagines what they think about her new dress.	Mabel sits by herself on a couch and reflects on her family and her life's failures.	Mabel decides on steps she will take to transform herself and leaves the party.

Connect and Extend OPTIONAL

CONNECT TO EXTENDED WRITING PROJECT

Students can use "The New Dress"" as a mentor text for their Extended Writing Project. They may show how the story's stream of consciousness narration is effective at conveying alienation and discuss the technique in their literary analysis essay.

BEYOND THE BOOK

Performance: Same Theme

In "The New Dress," Mabel is battling her own insecurities and the fear of not fitting in with neighbors. Students will select a theme from the text to inspire an impromptu performance.

Ask students to:

- In small groups choose a theme present in "The New Dress."
- Imagine a modern-day scenario that relates to this theme.
- Create a script that presents this scenario and emphasizes the characters' emotions in this moment.
- Perform for classmates.

Have students reflect by asking them:

- Even though "The New Dress" is from a completely different generation, why can present-day readers connect with the emotions and feelings of the main character?
- How do the main character's emotions in a work of fiction lead the reader to the theme?

Collaborative Conversation

SCAFFOLDS

Post the writing prompt to generate a discussion in small groups. Ask students to first break down the prompt before they discuss relevant ideas and textual evidence.

Compose a brief passage of a short story focusing on a character whose outward appearance does not match his or her feelings. Use "The New Dress" as a model, because the main character in the story secretly thinks she looks hideous while she tries to put a brave face on her situation. Consider how it might affect a person to hide his or her true feelings at a party or with a single person who is important to him or her.

Use the scaffolds below to differentiate instruction for your ELL English Language Learners and A Approaching grade-level learners.

ELL **BEGINNING, INTERMEDIATE** Use the discussion guide and speaking frames to facilitate the discussion with support from the teacher.

ADVANCED, ADVANCED HIGH Use the discussion guide and speaking frames to facilitate the discussion in mixed-level groups.

A **APPROACHING** Use the discussion guide to facilitate the discussion in mixed-level groups.

APPROACHING
ADVANCED, ADVANCED HIGH
BEGINNING, INTERMEDIATE

Discussion Guide	Speaking Frames
1. When might a person's outward appearance not match his or her feelings?	• Sometimes a person feels ____ when he or she ____. • A person can try to hide feelings of ____ by ____.
2. In what situations might someone try to hide true feelings?	• Someone might pretend to be ____ because ____. • Someone might lie about ____ because ____.
3. How might it affect someone to hide true feelings in public or with a person who is important? Why?	• Hiding true feelings might make someone ____. • It would make a person feel ____ because ____.

Multiple Perspectives

Use the activity below to differentiate instruction for your B Beyond grade level learners.

Have students reread paragraph 14, in which Mabel has a conversation with Mrs. Holman. Readers get only Mabel's view of the conversation, but what might Mrs. Holman's perspective be?

Direct pairs of students to rewrite the encounter between Mabel and Mrs. Holman as Mrs. Holman might see it. What would Mrs. Holman's stream of consciousness reveal? Ask students:

- Why does Mrs. Holman approach Mabel? What is Mrs. Holman's opinion of Mabel?

Review Prompt and Rubric

Before students begin writing, review the writing prompt and rubric with the class.

NARRATIVE: Compose a brief passage of a short story focusing on a character whose outward appearance does not match his or her feelings. Use "The New Dress" as a model, because the main character in the story secretly thinks she looks hideous while she tries to put a brave face on her situation. Consider how it might affect a person to hide his or her true feelings at a party or with a single person who is important to him or her.

PROMPT GUIDE

- In what situations might someone try to hide true feelings?
- How might it affect someone to hide true feelings in public or with a person who is important? Why?
- What do you remember from "The New Dress" that you can use as a model?

Score	Narrative	Language and Conventions
4	The writer is able to skillfully create a believable character who is hiding his or her true feelings. Descriptive details and clear transitions contribute to the strength and unity of the narrative.	The writer demonstrates a consistent command of grammar, punctuation, and usage conventions. Although minor errors may be evident, they do not detract from the fluency or the clarity of the essay.
3	The writer is able to clearly create a believable character who is hiding his or her true feelings. Most details and transitions contribute to the strength and unity of the narrative, though there may be minor lapses in focus.	The writer demonstrates an adequate command of grammar, punctuation, and usage conventions. Although some errors may be evident, they create few (if any) disruptions in the fluency of the writing or the clarity of the essay.
2	The writer is able to create a believable character who is hiding his or her true feelings. Some details do not contribute to the narrative, which limits the unity and coherence of the narrative.	The writer demonstrates a partial command of grammar, punctuation, and usage conventions. Some distracting errors may be evident, at times creating minor disruptions in the fluency or clarity of the writing.
1	The writer is not able to create a believable character because the narrative is presented in a random or illogical way,. Many of the details and transitions do not contribute to the narrative.	The writer demonstrates little or no command of grammar, punctuation, and usage conventions. Serious and persistent errors create disruptions in the fluency of the writing and sometimes interfere with meaning.
0	The writer does not provide a relevant response to the prompt or does not provide a response at all.	Serious and persistent errors overwhelm the writing and interfere with the meaning of the response as a whole, making the writer's meaning impossible to understand.

Write

SCAFFOLDS

Ask students to complete the writing assignment using text evidence to support their answers.

Use the scaffolds below to differentiate instruction for your ELL English Language Learners and A Approaching grade-level readers.

ELL **BEGINNING** With the help of the word bank, write a response using paragraph frame 1.

INTERMEDIATE With the help of the word bank, write a response using paragraph frames 1 and 2.

ADVANCED, ADVANCED HIGH Write a response of differentiated length using the sentence starters.

A **APPROACHING** Write a response of differentiated length using the sentence starters.

BEGINNING / INTERMEDIATE | ADVANCED, ADVANCED HIGH / APPROACHING

Word Bank		Paragraph Frame 1	Paragraph Frame 2	Sentence Starters
wear school sweater hat haircut uncool confident silly	self-conscious others anxious pretend stylish new happy	(Character's name) ____ did not like ____. Still, he ____ because ____. On the inside, he felt ____. He worried that ____. Still, he tried to ____.	(Character's name) decided to ____ because ____. He felt bad because ____ and he wanted ____.	• One day, ____ wore . . . • On the inside, ____ felt . . . • Still, he / she tried to seem . . . • In the end, . . .

Peer Review

Students should submit feedback to two peers using the review instructions below.

- How well does this response answer the prompt?
- How well does the writer create a believable character is hiding his or her true feelings?
- Which sentence in the writer's response was most powerful? Why?
- What does the writer do well in this response? What does the writer need to work on?

Remember that your comments are most useful when they are kind and constructive.

Rate

Respond to the following with a point rating that reflects your opinion.

	1	2	3	4
Ideas				
Evidence				
Language and Conventions				

Submit

ELL A **SENTENCE FRAMES**

- You (completely / partly / almost) ____ answered the prompt because ____.
- You could answer the prompt more completely by ____.
- Your character (was / was not) believable because ____.
- I liked your description of ____ because ____.
- One idea you expressed well is ____.
- One idea that needs clarification is ____.

Hurricane Season

POETRY
Fareena Arefeen
2016

Introduction

In September of 2008, Hurricane Ike roared through Haiti and Cuba, traveled up the Gulf of Mexico, and barreled into Texas with increasing velocity, causing broken windows, flooded streets and numerous casualties. Houston-area poet Fareena Arefeen channels her own memories of the city's natural disasters in "Hurricane Season," an energetic meditation on her connection to Houston as a first-generation immigrant and her desire to wield language to create art. While a junior at Houston's High School for Performing and Visual Arts, Arefeen was named the city's second Youth Poet Laureate in 2016.

The speaker was born in a hurricane, where the winds are strongest, and she considers herself a low-pressure system. She's heard that children playing in Africa can start storms over the Atlantic and that immigrants in Canada can inspire poets in Texas. The speaker celebrates her ninth birthday as a hurricane arrives and floods her city. With a hurricane's strength and destructiveness, she wants to be able to use her words to bring light. Four years later, she again watches the floodwaters rushing over the bayou, and she can smell the atmospheric pressure building. The speaker thinks that brown might just be her favorite color, and observes what she sees as whirlpools embedded in her skin. By the time her seventeenth birthday arrives, so do the clouds, leaving the city fractured, looking like a mix of darkness and light. She hopes that now, with the smell of rain in her nose, she can use her words for the same effect.

Proficiency-leveled summaries and summaries in multiple languages are available digitally.

Audio and audio text highlighting are available with this text.

CONNECT TO ESSENTIAL QUESTION

What causes individuals to feel alienated?

This powerful poem was written by Fareena Arefeen, Houston's Youth Poet Laureate in 2016, about her complex relationship to the city she calls home and the natural disasters it has survived.

Entry Point

As students prepare to read "Hurricane Season," share the following information with them to provide context.

- ✓ Poet Fareena Arefeen was named Houston's Youth Poet Laureate in 2016.
- ✓ Poet laureate is an honorary office. Poet laureates are usually expected to compose poems for special occasions and to promote poetry in their communities and society. The position of Youth Poet Laureate was created by "Writers in the Schools," an organization based in Houston, Texas. The Youth Poet Laureate has a one-year term, which includes a scholarship, a book deal, and being mentored by Houston's Poet Laureate.
- ✓ Arefeen came from Bangladesh with her sister and mother. In her acceptance speech Arefeen read "Hurricane Season" aloud to the audience. She also spoke about her personal struggle to find her place and feel a sense of community.

Instructional Path

The print teacher's edition includes essential point-of-use instruction and planning tools. Complete lesson plans and program documents appear in your digital teacher account.

Independent Read: Hurricane Season

Objectives: After reading "Hurricane Season" students will write a short essay response that demonstrates their understanding of how the poet Fareena Arefeen uses hurricane imagery to express a wide variety of personal experiences.

Blast: Power to the Poets

Objectives: After exploring background information and research links about a topic, students will respond to a question with a 140-character response.

Independent Read

Introduce the Text

As a class, watch the video preview and have students read the introduction in pairs to make connections to the video preview.

- What image from the video was most powerful? Why?
- What natural phenomenon or disaster would you choose to identify with? Why?

ELL SPEAKING FRAMES

- The most powerful image was ____.
- I think I am like a ____.

Access Complex Text

LEXILE: N/A WORD COUNT: 388

The following areas may be challenging for students, particularly ELL English Language Learners and A Approaching grade-level learners.

Genre, Connection of Ideas. See the digital lesson plan for more details.

I only came into my skin after I grew into this city

NOTES

My mother tells me that I was born outside of the eye of a hurricane,
where the storm is strong and moves quickly in **radials**.
I think I am a series of low pressure systems and winds that can carry **bayous**.

I've heard that a child playing on the coast in Africa
can cause the start of a hurricane in the Atlantic and maybe
a working immigrant in Toronto can be the origin of a poet in Houston.

My ninth birthday was suspended in the space between **cyclone** and serene.
I watched my city build itself up again after Hurricane Ike and
I guess we are both having growing pains.

I've learned that my purpose is flooding.
I want to form inundacions of words and earn
the title of a Category Four[1]. Drought relief and filler of bayou banks.
Hurricanes bring heat energy from the tropics
the way I would like to bring light to the city that taught me how to hold rainwater in the form of letters.

On my thirteenth birthday, I watched the bayou
spill into this dizzy headed space city
like a push of blood to the lungs.

Inhaling **atmospheric** pressure of a tropical storm
in the eye of hurricane season felt like bayou backwash
of building Rothko[2] layers.

Maybe if I could say that brown is my favorite color,
I would finally see the whirlpools that rest in my skin and in the Buffalo Bayou.
And someday I could love the greens hidden in browns hidden in **labyrinths** of color.

1. **Category Four** hurricanes or cyclones are measured for force on a five-level scale, five being the most powerful
2. **Rothko** Mark Rothko (1903–1970), abstract expressionist painter and creator of Houston's Rothko Chapel

Developing Background Knowledge and Social Emotional Learning

1. Generate a list (on the board or on paper) of any information or ideas your students have about the use of symbolism in poetry and other literary works.
2. Have students discuss examples of symbols used in literary works, including their purpose and effects.

Discuss with students: How can metaphors help communicate feelings? Why is using something outside of yourself to represent yourself so effective? Think of a strong experience or emotion you had recently. What metaphor would help someone else understand your experience more fully?

TEXT TALK

To what does the speaker compare her growing pains?

See lines 8–9: She compares her growing pains to her city rebuilding after a hurricane.

How does the poet describe the change hurricanes can bring?

See line 12: They can create more drinking water to provide relief from drought.

SELECTION VOCABULARY

radial / el movimiento circular *noun* the movement or arrangement of a circle

bayou / el bayou *noun* in parts of the Southern U.S., an area of marshy, slow-moving water connected to a river or lake COGNATE

cyclone / el ciclón *noun* a violent rotating windstorm COGNATE

atmospheric / atmosférico/a *adjective* of or relating to the atmosphere COGNATE

labyrinth / el laberinto *noun* a complicated network of hallways or paths COGNATE

Prepare For Advanced Courses

Use the activity below to differentiate instruction for your B Beyond grade level learners.

Analyze for Enrichment

Reread lines 19–21:

Inhaling atmospheric pressure of a tropical storm in the eye of hurricane season felt like bayou backwash of building Rothko layers.

Have students close their eyes and imagine the picture described in these lines.

Ask students:

- How does the figurative language help deliver the poet's message?
- Does the use of figurative language help pinpoint the time and location of the poet?

NOTES

I only came into my skin
after I grew into this city and they both happened like storm clouds; rolling in and all at once.

Now, I find impressions of myself in the silt
as there are maps of this city pressed into my hands like footsteps on wet ground.

On my seventeenth birthday, the clouds broke light rays
the way I want to leave fractures in my city
that can be filled with the work of new artists and immigrants to take my place.

My favorite smell is rain
falling through concrete and cumin[3] because they combine homes.
I can be a drop of water falling in multiple places.

I am stuck to the city I've learned to call my own
like humidity on skin that can finally
hold its own storm.

By Fareena Arefeen, 2016. Used by permission of Fareena Arefeen.

WRITE

LITERARY ANALYSIS: Arefeen uses the image of a hurricane to express a wide variety of personal experiences; at times the speaker seems to be the hurricane itself, while at other times the speaker seems to be in the midst of experiencing a hurricane. Is the image of a hurricane in this poem creative, destructive, or both? Cite textual evidence to support your argument.

3. **cumin** a powdery spice derived from the crushed seeds of a flowering plant, commonly used in Bengali cuisine

TEXT TALK

What does speaker mean by "I only came into my skin/ after I grew into this city"?

See lines 24–25: She means she became who she is because she felt like she belonged to the city where she grew up.

Ask each Beyond grade-level student to write one additional discussion question. Then, have one or two students facilitate a discussion, using their questions to guide the conversation.

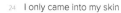

Writer's Notebook

Connect to Essential Question: Give students time to reflect on how "Hurricane Season" connects to the unit's essential question "What causes individuals to feel alienated?" by freewriting in their Writer's Notebooks.

CHECK FOR SUCCESS

If students are still struggling to respond to the prompt, ask them scaffolded questions, such as:

1. How does Arefeen's word choice reflect feelings of alienation?
2. How does the hurricane imagery in the poem make you feel? Why?

Reading Comprehension OPTIONAL

Have students complete the digital reading comprehension questions ✓ when they finish reading.

ANSWER KEY

QUESTION 1: A
QUESTION 2: C
QUESTION 3: D
QUESTION 4: A
QUESTION 5:
See chart below.

Synonym	Word
spirals	radials
twister	radials
meteorological	atmospheric
mazes	labyrinths

Connect and Extend OPTIONAL

CONNECT TO EXTENDED WRITING PROJECT

Students can draw inspiration from "Hurricane Season" in writing their literary analyses. They may consider how the author's experience of extreme weather helped her to engage more fully with the world and stave off alienation.

BEYOND THE BOOK

Writing: I Am Phenomenal

Fareena Arefeen reflects on the disaster of Hurricane Ike and compares herself to the natural disaster. Students will compare themselves to a natural phenomena.

Ask students to:

- Generate a list of their personal traits.
- Choose one trait and think of a moment in your life that best demonstrates this trait.
- Choose a natural phenomena (e.g. rainbows, specific storms, oxidation, etc.) that symbolizes this moment.
- Write a poem or short narrative using imagery inspired by a natural phenomena to write about this moment in their lives and the trait it reveals about them.
- Share with classmates.

To reflect, ask students:

- Why would a poet use a natural phenomena to explain a moment in time?
- How did connecting your moment to a natural phenomena create a visual capable of inspiring a piece of writing?

Collaborative Conversation

SCAFFOLDS

Post the writing prompt to generate a discussion in small groups. Ask students to first break down the prompt before they discuss relevant ideas and textual evidence.

Arefeen uses the image of a hurricane to express a wide variety of personal experiences; at times the speaker seems to be the hurricane itself, while at other times the speaker seems to be in the midst of experiencing a hurricane. Is the image of a hurricane in this poem creative, destructive, or both? Cite textual evidence to support your argument.

Use the scaffolds below to differentiate instruction for your ELL English Language Learners and A Approaching grade-level learners.

ELL **BEGINNING, INTERMEDIATE** Use the discussion guide and speaking frames to facilitate the discussion with support from the teacher.

ADVANCED, ADVANCED HIGH Use the discussion guide and speaking frames to facilitate the discussion in mixed-level groups.

A **APPROACHING** Use the discussion guide to facilitate the discussion in mixed-level groups.

APPROACHING
ADVANCED, ADVANCED HIGH
BEGINNING, INTERMEDIATE

Discussion Guide	Speaking Frames
1. What does the speaker say about hurricanes? How does she connect hurricanes to herself and her experiences?	• The speaker says hurricanes ____. • She says she is like a hurricane because ____.
2. What positive and negative language does the poet use to describe hurricanes?	• She uses positive language when she says ____. • She uses negative language when she says ____.
3. Think about the hurricane imagery in the poem. What do hurricanes destroy? What do they create?	• Hurricanes can destroy ____. • Hurricanes can create ____.

Multiple Perspectives

Use the activity below to differentiate instruction for your B Beyond grade level learners.

Reread lines 25 and 26:

I only came into my skin after I grew into this city and they both happened like storm clouds; rolling in and all at once.

Direct students to consider the connection she is making between her identity and a hurricane.

Ask students:

- How does Fareena Arefeen's perspective explain her self-esteem?
- How would you describe Arefeen's attitude about herself?

Review Prompt and Rubric

Before students begin writing, review the writing prompt and rubric with the class.

LITERARY ANALYSIS: Arefeen uses the image of a hurricane to express a wide variety of personal experiences; at times the speaker seems to be the hurricane itself, while at other times the speaker seems to be in the midst of experiencing a hurricane. Is the image of a hurricane in this poem creative, destructive, or both? Cite textual evidence to support your argument.

ELL PROMPT GUIDE

A

- Which examples of hurricane imagery were most powerful? Why?
- Which personal experiences does the speaker relate? How does she connect those experiences to hurricanes?
- Does the speaker think hurricanes can be creative, destructive, or both? How do you know?

Score	Literary Analysis	Language and Conventions
4	The writer establishes a cogent thesis statement. All ideas are strongly related to the thesis and are focused on the specific aspect of the text the writer must address, using relevant textual evidence most of the time. The writer is able to create an essay that is unified and organized.	The writer demonstrates a consistent command of grammar, punctuation, and usage conventions. Although minor errors may be evident, they do not detract from the fluency or the clarity of the essay.
3	The writer establishes a clear thesis statement. Most ideas are related to the thesis and are focused on the specific aspect of the text the writer must address, using relevant textual evidence some of the time. The essay is organized, though it may not always be unified.	The writer demonstrates an adequate command of grammar, punctuation, and usage conventions. Although some errors may be evident, they create few (if any) disruptions in the fluency of the writing or the clarity of the essay.
2	Most ideas are generally related to the specific aspect of the text the writer must address, but the thesis statement is weak or somewhat unclear and lacks textual evidence. The lack of a clear thesis or the inclusion of irrelevant information interferes with the focus and organization of the essay.	The writer demonstrates a partial command of grammar, punctuation, and usage conventions. Some distracting errors may be evident, at times creating minor disruptions in the fluency or clarity of the writing.
1	Some ideas are generally related to the specific aspect of the text the writer must address, but the thesis statement is missing, unclear, or illogical. The writer may fail to maintain focus on the text, may include extraneous information, or may shift abruptly between ideas.	The writer demonstrates little or no command of grammar, punctuation, and usage conventions. Serious and persistent errors create disruptions in the fluency of the writing and sometimes interfere with meaning.
0	The writer does not provide a relevant response to the prompt or does not provide a response at all.	Serious and persistent errors overwhelm the writing and interfere with the meaning of the response as a whole, making the writer's meaning impossible to understand.

Write

Ask students to complete the writing assignment using text evidence to support their answers.

Use the scaffolds below to differentiate instruction for your ELL English Language Learners and A Approaching grade level readers.

ELL **BEGINNING** With the help of the word bank, write a response using paragraph frame 1.

INTERMEDIATE With the help of the word bank, write a response using paragraph frames 1 and 2.

ADVANCED, ADVANCED HIGH Write a response of differentiated length using the sentence starters.

A **APPROACHING** Write a response of differentiated length using the sentence starters.

BEGINNING | INTERMEDIATE | ADVANCED, ADVANCED HIGH | APPROACHING

Word Bank	Paragraph Frame 1	Paragraph Frame 2	Sentence Starters
rebuilding water destructive creative growing up	The poet connects hurricane imagery with ____. The speaker compares her growing pains to her city ____ after Hurricane Ike. In this way, hurricanes can be ____. The speaker says hurricanes can bring rain and provide more drinking ____. So hurricanes can also be ____.	The hurricane imagery I found most powerful was ____. Arefeen makes her feelings about hurricanes clear when she says ____. So the image of a hurricane in this poem is ____.	• I think that the image of a hurricane in this poem is . . . • Text evidence that supports this idea is. . . • One personal experience Arefeen expresses using hurricane imagery is . . . • This examples shows the poet thinks hurricanes are . . .

Peer Review

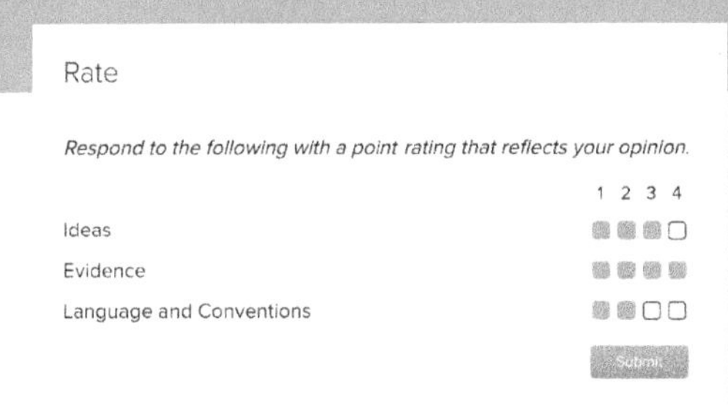

Students should submit substantive feedback to two peers using the review instructions below.

- How well does this response answer the prompt?
- Which of the writer's comments inspired you to think differently about the poem?
- What does the writer do well in this response? What does the writer need to work on?

Remember that your comments are most useful when they are kind and constructive.

ELL **SENTENCE FRAMES**

- You were able to (completely / partly / almost) ____ answer the prompt.
- You could answer the prompt more completely by ____.
- I thought differently about the poem after reading ____.
- My favorite part of your response is ____.

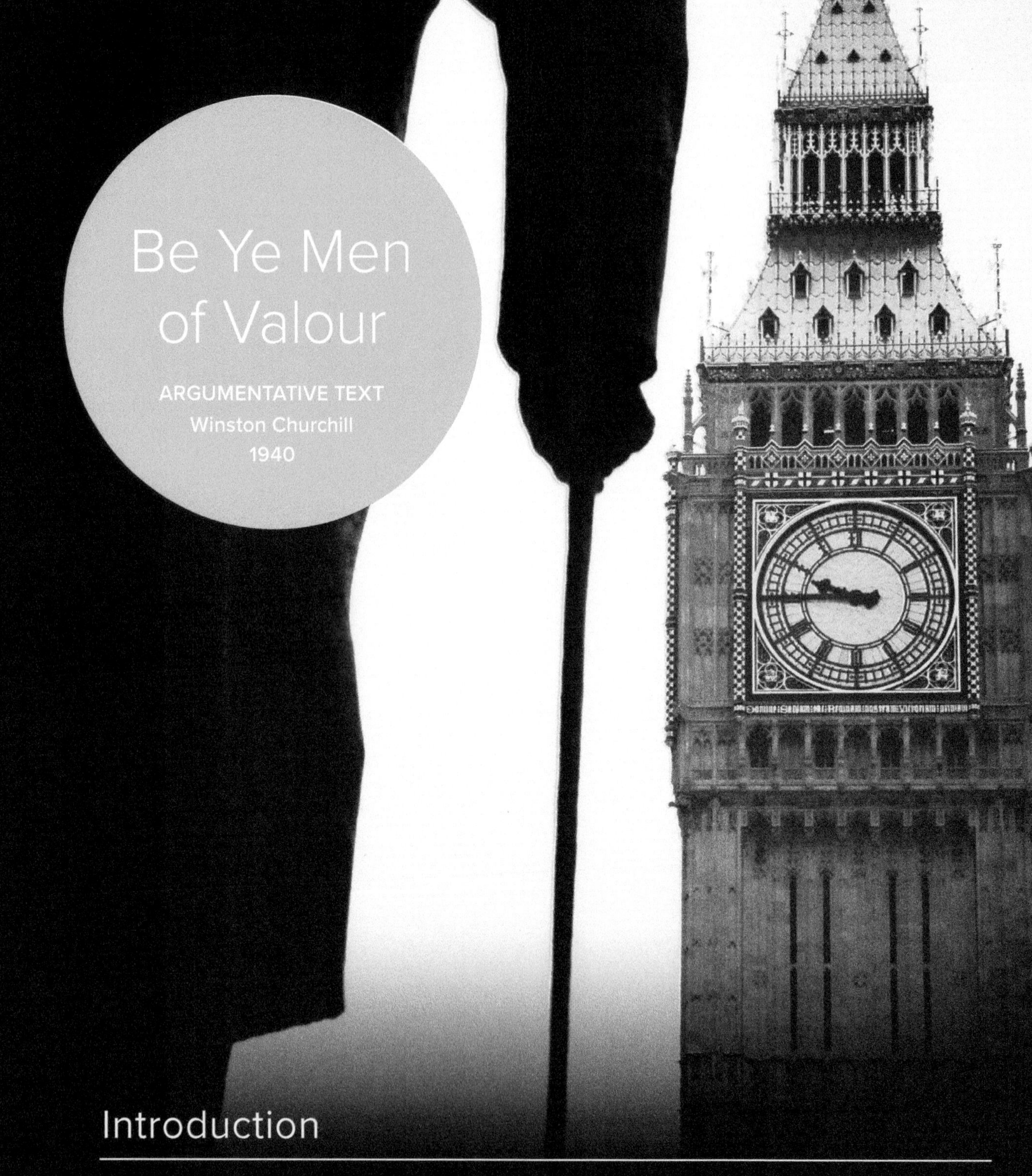

Be Ye Men of Valour

ARGUMENTATIVE TEXT
Winston Churchill
1940

Introduction

Delivered on May 19, 1940, "Be Ye Men of Valour" was Winston Churchill's (1874–1965) first radio address as British Prime Minister. In the speech, Churchill acknowledges that German military aggression would likely soon be directed at Great Britain, and tells his countrymen not to be intimidated. Instead, he urges them to prepare to do whatever is necessary to defeat a formidable adversary.

Addressing to the people of England on his first day as British prime minister, Winston Churchill acknowledges that although they will soon be engaged in fierce battle with the Germans, his countrymen should remain undaunted and prepared to defend the homeland at all costs. Churchill opens his address alerting the nation of Germany's latest military victories in France. While they need not be intimidated, his countrymen should not be foolish by dismissing the gravity of the situation. Neither should they lose courage, as the Allied forces are large, well-trained, and well-equipped to defend the country. All the while, the British planes have been marking great victories against Germany's air forces and launching nightly raids attacking German infrastructure. Still, soon enough, much of Germany's forces will be directed at England and Churchill feels confident that the nation is ready to meet the challenge. They have no choice.

Proficiency-leveled summaries and summaries in multiple languages are available digitally.

Audio and audio text highlighting are available with this text.

CONNECT TO ESSENTIAL QUESTION

What causes individuals to feel alienated?

This speech was delivered over the radio by Winston Churchill on May 19, 1940. Churchill speaks honestly of the successes and shortcomings of German military aggression in France, encouraging British citizens to be prepared, confident, and devoted to the fight for freedom.

Entry Point

As students prepare to read "Be Ye Men of Valour," share the following information with them to provide context.

- ✓ In the speech, Churchill refuses to negotiate or compromise with Adolf Hitler, the leader of the Nazi party and the leader of Germany's government since 1933.
- ✓ Initially, Churchill believed that Britain would be forced to fight the Nazis alone, with little if any assistance from France or other countries. Further complicating the situation, Hitler had signed a non-aggression pact with the Soviet Union, and the United States was not yet involved in the war.
- ✓ Churchill wrote the following about his bombing plan: "There is one thing that will bring Hitler down, and that is an absolutely devastating, exterminating attack by very heavy bombers from this country upon the Nazi homeland."

Instructional Path

The print teacher's edition includes essential point-of-use instruction and planning tools. Complete lesson plans and program documents appear in your digital teacher account.

First Read: Be Ye Men of Valour

Objectives: After an initial reading and discussion of the speech, students will be able to explain the historical background as well as identify the lines of argument that Churchill uses.

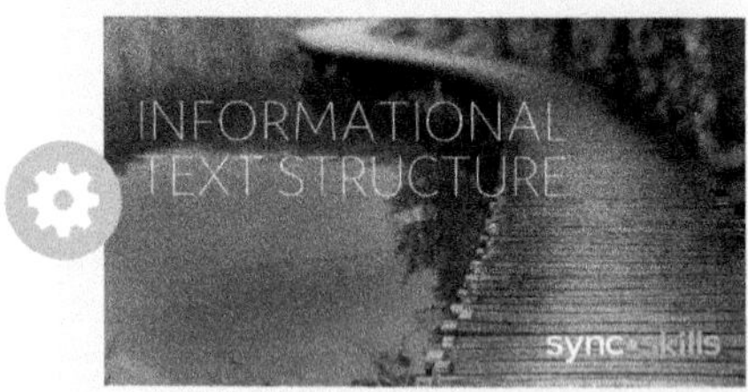

Skill: Informational Text Structure

Objectives: After rereading and discussing a model of close reading, students will be able to explain how aspects of the informational text structure determine the overall effectiveness of "Be Ye Men of Valour."

Skill: Central or Main Idea

Objectives: After rereading and discussing a model of close reading, students will be able to determine two or more central ideas in a text and analyze their development over the course of the text.

Skill: Word Meaning

Objectives: After rereading and discussing a model of close reading, students will be able to use print or digital resources to clarify and validate understanding of multiple-meaning words in a passage.

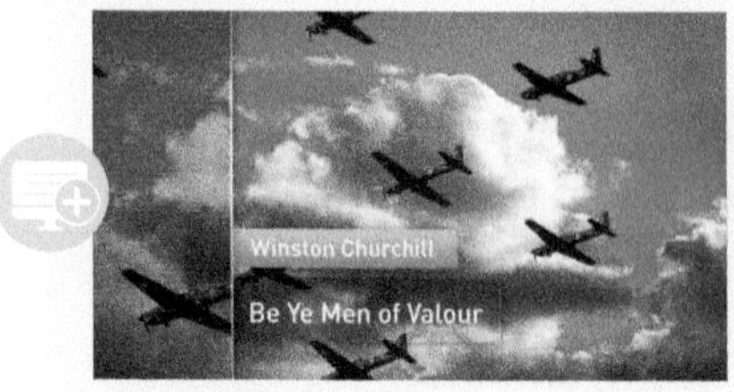

Close Read: Be Ye Men of Valour

Objectives: After engaging in a close reading and discussion of "Be Ye Men of Valour," students will be able to write a short response that summarizes and evaluates the text structure of the speech.

Progress Monitoring

Opportunities to Learn	Opportunities to Demonstrate Learning	Opportunities to Reteach
Informational Text Structure		
Skill: Informational Text Structure	Skill: Informational Text Structure • Your Turn Close Read • Skills Focus • Write	Skill: Informational Text Structure
Central or Main Idea		
Skill: Central or Main Idea	Skill: Central or Main Idea • Your Turn Close Read • Skills Focus • Write	Spotlight Skill: Central or Main Idea
Word Meaning		
Skill: Word Meaning	Skill: Word Meaning • Your Turn Close Read • Skills Focus	Spotlight Skill: Word Meaning

First Read

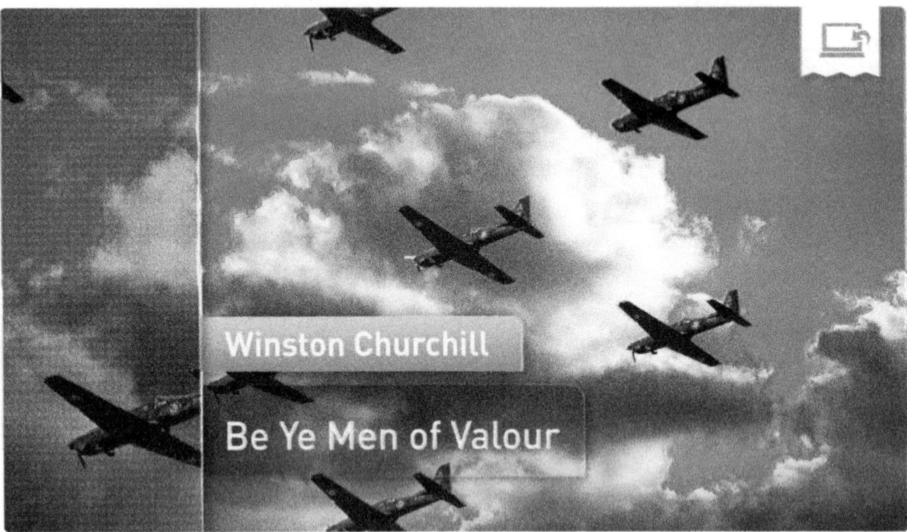

Introduce the Text

As a class, watch the video preview and have students read the introduction in pairs to make connections to the video preview.

To activate prior knowledge and experiences, ask students:

- What part of the video stood out to you the most?
- When have you been in a dangerous or desperate situation? How did you respond?

SPEAKING FRAMES

- The part of the video that stood out was ____.
- I was in danger when ____.
- I responded by ____.

Access Complex Text

LEXILE: 1350 WORD COUNT: 1,342

The following areas may be challenging for students, particularly ELL English Language Learners and A Approaching grade-level learners.

Connection of Ideas	Sentence Structure	Prior Knowledge
• In some places Churchill implies France badly needs Britain's help; in others he suggests France and Britain are equal partners. • Explain that France did need help, but Churchill feared that saying so might demoralize the British.	• Churchill's long sentences and complex syntax may confuse some readers. • Suggest that students form small groups to look up unfamiliar vocabulary and "translate" Churchill's English into modern U.S. English.	• Some readers may be unfamiliar with terms such as Flanders, the Western Front, and the Maginot Line. • Help students do research to understand these references.

SCAFFOLDS

 ENGLISH LANGUAGE LEARNERS  APPROACHING GRADE LEVEL  BEYOND GRADE LEVEL

These icons identify differentiation strategies and scaffolded support for a variety of students. See the digital lesson plan for additional differentiation strategies and scaffolds.

"Our task is not only to win the battle—but to win the war."

1 I speak to you for the first time as Prime Minister in a solemn hour for the life of our country, of our empire, of our allies, and, above all, of the cause of freedom. A tremendous battle is raging in France and Flanders[1]. The Germans, by a remarkable combination of air bombing and heavily armored tanks, have broken through the French defenses north of the Maginot Line[2], and strong columns of their armored vehicles are ravaging the open country, which for the first day or two was without defenders. They have penetrated deeply and spread alarm and confusion in their track. Behind them there are now appearing infantry in lorries[3], and behind them, again, the large **masses** are moving forward. The re-groupment of the French armies to make head against, and also to strike at, this intruding wedge has been proceeding for several days, largely assisted by the magnificent efforts of the Royal Air Force.

British prime minister Winston Churchill (1874–1965) inspects bomb damage outside the London offices of the British Equitable Assurance after a World War II air raid, 10th September 1940

2 We must not allow ourselves to be intimidated by the presence of these armored vehicles in unexpected places behind our lines. If they are behind our Front, the French are also at many points fighting actively behind theirs. Both sides are therefore in an extremely dangerous position. And if the French Army and our own Army are well handled, as I believe they will be, if the French retain that genius for recovery and counter-attack for which they have so long been famous, and if the British Army shows the dogged endurance and solid fighting power of which there have been so many examples in the past, then a sudden transformation of the scene might spring into being.

1. **Flanders** the northern area of Belgium, encompassing Brussels
2. **the Maginot Line** a line of fortifications built in the 1930s along the French border to prevent German invasion
3. **lorries** (UK) trucks

NOTES

Skill: Central or Main Idea

While there is a lot of other information here, the main idea of this first paragraph is that war is raging and Britain (Churchill's audience) is in great danger. The additional details describe what is happening with the war.

Developing Background Knowledge and Cultural Awareness

1. Share with students the following quotation by Winston Churchill: "We must expect that as soon as stability is reached on the Western Front, the bulk of that hideous apparatus of aggression which gashed Holland into ruin and slavery in a few days will be turned upon us."
2. In small groups, have students discuss the quotation's meaning and analyze this sentence as an example of persuasive diction and syntax.

Discuss with students: Why is rhetoric so powerful? Can powerful rhetoric be more persuasive than the content of a speech? Why are we more likely to follow charismatic speakers and leaders? How has this tendency shaped history?

Central or Main Idea

What are some of the details the student alludes to?

The Germans used air bombing and heavily armored tanks to break through the French defenses north of the Maginot Line. Strong columns of armored vehicles are ravaging the open country, which for the first day or two was without defenders.

SELECTION VOCABULARY

mass / la masa *noun* a large crowd of people COGNATE

formidable / temible *adjective* causing fear or dread; intimidating

TEXT TALK

According to Churchill, how have the Germans broken through the French lines?

See Paragraphs 1: They used a combination of air strikes and tanks.

Word Meaning

What does the reader do first to determine the meaning of an unfamiliar word? What does she do to begin to understand the word's meaning?

She determines that it's probably a verb due to context, and she notices a similarity with the word *grape*.

Informational Text Structure

How does the reader use informational text structure to identify and analyze Churchill's initial appeal to his audience?

The reader notices that Churchill uses words and phrases like "ruin and slavery," which suggests pathos, or an appeal to emotion.

Skills Focus

QUESTION 2: Informational Text Structure

Churchill's purpose here is to rally British citizens around the cause of supporting the war effort by producing weapons and ammunition. This text structure is an effective way of conveying the seriousness of the problem while offering a concrete and realistic solution.

TEXT TALK

What does Churchill say he expects from British men and women who are not fighting in the war?

See Paragraphs 5-6: He expects that they will work hard to build weapons, tanks, and other materials which will help win the war for Britain.

NOTES

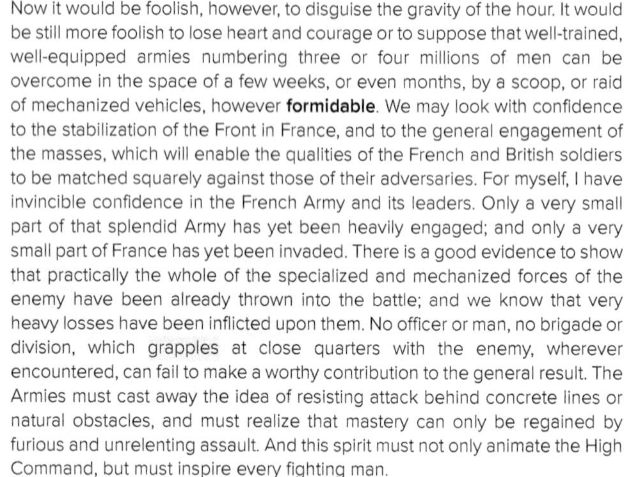
3 Now it would be foolish, however, to disguise the gravity of the hour. It would be still more foolish to lose heart and courage or to suppose that well-trained, well-equipped armies numbering three or four millions of men can be overcome in the space of a few weeks, or even months, by a scoop, or raid of mechanized vehicles, however **formidable**. We may look with confidence to the stabilization of the Front in France, and to the general engagement of the masses, which will enable the qualities of the French and British soldiers to be matched squarely against those of their adversaries. For myself, I have invincible confidence in the French Army and its leaders. Only a very small part of that splendid Army has yet been heavily engaged; and only a very small part of France has yet been invaded. There is a good evidence to show that practically the whole of the specialized and mechanized forces of the enemy have been already thrown into the battle; and we know that very heavy losses have been inflicted upon them. No officer or man, no brigade or division, which grapples at close quarters with the enemy, wherever encountered, can fail to make a worthy contribution to the general result. The Armies must cast away the idea of resisting attack behind concrete lines or natural obstacles, and must realize that mastery can only be regained by furious and unrelenting assault. And this spirit must not only animate the High Command, but must inspire every fighting man.

Skill: Word Meaning

What does grapples mean? It appears to be an action taken 'with the enemy" by a man, an officer, a brigade, or a division, so I'm guessing it's a verb. It also looks a bit like "grape," but I'm not sure about that connection.

4 In the air—often at serious odds, often at odds hitherto thought overwhelming—we have been clawing down three or four to one of our enemies; and the relative balance of the British and German Air Forces is now considerably more favorable to us than at the beginning of the battle. In cutting down the German bombers, we are fighting our own battle as well as that of France. My confidence in our ability to fight it out to the finish with the German Air Force has been strengthened by the fierce encounters which have taken place and are taking place. At the same time, our heavy bombers are striking nightly at the tap-root of German mechanized power, and have already inflicted serious damage upon the oil refineries on which the Nazi effort to dominate the world directly depends.

Skill: Informational Text Structure

Early in his speech, Churchill appeals to pathos, presenting images of "ruin and slavery . . . turned upon us." With listeners in an emotional state, he unfolds his thesis: Britain is ready to fight and will do everything to win.

5 We must expect that as soon as stability is reached on the Western Front, the bulk of that hideous apparatus of aggression which gashed Holland into ruin and slavery in a few days will be turned upon us. I am sure I speak for all when I say we are ready to face it, to endure it, and to retaliate against it to any extent that the unwritten laws of war permit. There will be many men and many women in this Island who, when the ordeal comes upon them, as come it will, will feel comfort, and even a pride, that they are sharing the perils of our lads at the Front—soldiers, sailors, and airmen—God bless them—and are drawing away from them a part at least of the onslaught they have to bear. Is not this the appointed time for all to make the utmost exertions in their power? If the battle is to be won, we must provide our men with ever-increasing quantities of the weapons and ammunition they need. We must have, and have quickly, more aeroplanes, more tanks, more shells, more guns. There is imperious need for

SELECTION VOCABULARY

abate / calmarse *verb* to lessen or weaken

these vital munitions. They increase our strength against the powerfully armed enemy. They replace the wastage of the obstinate struggle—and the knowledge that wastage will speedily be replaced enables us to draw more readily upon our reserves and throw them in now that everything counts so much.

6 Our task is not only to win the battle—but to win the war. After this battle in France **abates** its force, there will come the battle for our Island—for all Britain is, and all that Britain means. That will be the struggle. In that supreme emergency we shall not hesitate to take every step, even the most drastic, to call forth from our people the last ounce and the last inch of effort of which they are capable. The interests of property, the hours of labor, are nothing compared to the struggle for life and honor, for right and freedom, to which we have vowed ourselves.

7 I have received from the Chiefs of the French Republic, and in particular from its indomitable Prime Minister, Monsieur Reynaud, the most sacred pledges that whatever happens they will fight to the end, be it bitter or be it glorious. Nay, if we fight to the end, it can only be glorious.

8 Having received His Majesty's **commission**, I have formed an Administration of men and women of every Party and of almost every point of view. We have differed and quarreled in the past, but now one bond unites us all: to wage war until victory is won, and never to surrender ourselves to servitude and shame, whatever the cost and the agony may be. This is one of the most awe-striking periods in the long history of France and Britain. It is also beyond doubt the most sublime. Side by side, unaided except by their kith and kin in the great Dominions[4] and by the wide empires which rest beneath their shield—side by side the British and French peoples have advanced to rescue not only Europe but mankind from the foulest and most soul-destroying tyranny which has ever darkened and stained the pages of history. Behind them, behind us, behind the Armies and Fleets of Britain and France, gather a group of shattered States and bludgeoned races: the Czechs, the Poles, the Norwegians, the Danes, the Dutch, the Belgians—upon all of whom the long night of barbarism will descend, unbroken even by a star of hope, unless we conquer, as conquer we must, as conquer we shall.

9 Today is Trinity Sunday[5]. Centuries ago words were written to be a call and a spur to the faithful servants of truth and justice:

10 Arm yourselves, and be ye men of **valour**, and be in readiness for the conflict; for it is better for us to perish in battle than to look upon the outrage of our nation and our altars. As the will of God is in Heaven, even so let it be.

4. **the great Dominions** referring to the colonized lands of the British Empire in Africa, India, Southeast Asia, the Pacific and the Caribbean
5. **Trinity Sunday** the eighth Sunday after Easter in the Christian liturgical calendar, celebrating the Trinity of God, Jesus, and the Holy Spirit

NOTES

Skill: Informational Text Structure

Churchill continues his appeal to pathos here, saying "all Britain" could be lost. He then reasserts his position that Britain needs to "take every step" and that Britons will need to accept "even the most drastic" efforts.

Skill: Central or Main Idea

All the way through to the conclusion, the main ideas from the beginning are supported: Although the situation is legitimately dangerous, there is hope. But only if Britain acts with bravery and determination.

Informational Text Structure

How does the reader interpret Churchill's use of the phrase "all Britain is, and all that Britain means"?

The reader thinks that Churchill is appealing to the British people's sense of patriotism and their conviction that the British will always succeed if they put their mind to a task.

Central of Main Idea

Which ideas does Churchill maintain throughout the speech?

He maintains the ideas that the situation is grave and that there is hope as long as people are willing to sacrifice.

Skills Focus

QUESTION 5: Essential Question

The cause of division in the second passage is probably political differences. In the third passage, the cause is the invasion of Nazi Germany. Coming together is important because that is the only way Nazi Germany can be defeated.

SELECTION VOCABULARY

commission / el cargo ***noun*** a duty or title, especially in the armed forces

valour / el valor ***noun*** courage and bravery, especially in battle COGNATE

TEXT TALK

What does Churchill describe as the "foulest and most soul-destroying tyranny" in history?

See Paragraph 8: Nazism, the political ideology of the Hitler regime ruling Germany at the time.

How did discussing the power of rhetoric deepen your understanding of "Be Ye Men of Valour"?

Answers will vary.

Think Questions

Circulate as students answer Think Questions independently. Scaffolds for these questions are shown on the opposite page.

QUESTION 1: Textual Evidence

The war is not going well. Churchill's sense of urgency is based on a fear that if and when France is conquered, Germany will attack Britain ("the bulk of that hideous apparatus of aggression . . . will be turned upon us").

QUESTION 2: Textual Evidence

In paragraph 1, Churchill paints a grim picture: the Germans have "broken through the French defenses." Later, he says he has "invincible confidence" in the French armies. He is emphasizing that the situation is urgent but there is still hope.

QUESTION 3: Textual Evidence

These are countries that Germany has already defeated, such as Holland and Poland. Churchill suggests that Britain and France must preserve those nations and peoples. Britain and France are protectors, and it is up to them to defeat Germany.

QUESTION 4: Context Clues

Formidable must mean "very powerful" or "extremely dangerous." The word describes the Germans' mechanized military vehicles. Churchill says that even though they are "formidable" they cannot beat the might of the French and British militaries.

QUESTION 5: Word Meaning

A *commission* sounds like giving an order. Churchill received "His Majesty's commission." When I looked up the word, I found I was mostly correct. My dictionary defined it as "an instruction, command, or duty given to a person or a group."

First Read

Read "Be Ye Men of Valour." After you read, complete the Think Questions below.

THINK QUESTIONS

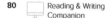

1. What is the current state of the war, and why does Churchill feel such a sense of urgency? Use details from the text to support your inferences.
2. How is what Churchill says about France in paragraph 1 different from what he says in paragraph 3? What reaction do you infer he hopes to elicit from his audience by making these two conflicting points? Support your inferences with evidence from the text.
3. Who are the "group of shattered States and bludgeoned races"? What image of Britain and France does Churchill hope to convey with this reference? Support your answer with evidence from the text.
4. Use context clues to find the definition of **formidable** as it is used in the text. Write your definition here, and explain which clues helped you arrive at it.
5. Write your definition for the word **commission** as it appears in the text. Then use a print or online dictionary to confirm the definition.

SCAFFOLDS

Think Questions

Use the scaffolds below to differentiate instruction for your ELL English Language Learners and A Approaching grade-level learners.

ELL **BEGINNING** Write a response using the word bank and sentence frames.

INTERMEDIATE Write a response using the sentence frames.

ADVANCED, ADVANCED HIGH Write a response using the Text-Dependent Question Guide.

A **APPROACHING** Write a response using the Text-Dependent Question Guide.

BEGINNING	INTERMEDIATE	APPROACHING / ADVANCED, ADVANCED HIGH
Word Bank	**Sentence Frames**	**Text-Dependent Question Guide**
Britain hopeful countries help army strong order king Holland heroes serious powerful	Germany is taking over lots of ____. Churchill thinks that the Germans will try to attack ____ next.	1. • What just happened in the war? • Is this good news or bad news for Britain? • What does Churchill think will happen next?
	Paragraph 1 says that the French need ____. In Paragraph 3, Churchill says that the French forces are still ____. Churchill wants people to know that the situation is ____ but to also stay ____.	2. • What does Churchill say about France in Paragraph 1? • What does Churchill say about France in Paragraph 3? • How do these details make the audience feel?
	The "shattered States and bludgeoned races" are small countries like ____, which the Germans have already defeated. Churchill wants to make Britain and France seem like ____ who will save such countries.	3. • What countries has Germany already taken over? • Why does Churchill call them "shattered States"? • What will happen if Britain does not fight back?
	The German ____ is *formidable*. This gives me a clue that *formidable* means something that is ____.	4. • Read: "It would be still more foolish to lose heart and courage or to suppose that well-trained, well-equipped armies numbering three or four millions of men can be overcome in the space of a few weeks, or even months, by a scoop, or raid of mechanized vehicles, however **formidable**." • What is being described as *formidable*? • What does that tell me about the meaning of the word *formidable*?
	Churchill got a *commission* from the ____. I think a *commission* means an ____ to do something.	5. • Read: "Having received His Majesty's **commission**, I have formed an Administration of men and women of every Party and of almost every point of view." • Who is "His Majesty"? • What did he give or assign to Churchill? • What did Churchill do after getting the commission? • What does that tell me about the meaning of the word *commission*?

Reading Comprehension OPTIONAL

Have students complete the digital reading comprehension questions when they finish reading.

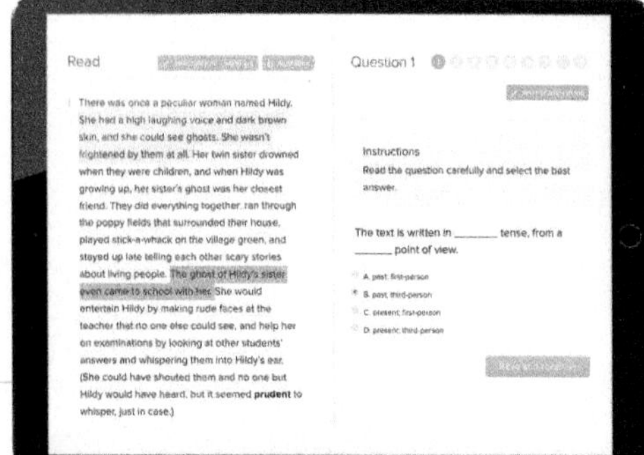

ANSWER KEY

QUESTION 1: C
QUESTION 2: C
QUESTION 3: A
QUESTION 4: D
QUESTION 5: B
QUESTION 6: A
QUESTION 7: C
QUESTION 8: D
QUESTION 9: *See first chart.*
QUESTION 10: *See second chart.*

Concept	Paragraph
Long-standing reputation of the British military	Paragraph 2
British strikes have been incredibly efficient compared to the Germans	Paragraph 4
Former political rivals have come together to focus on the war together	Paragraph 8
Citizens will proudly bear an attack knowing their military forces are doing the same	Paragraph 5

Synonym	Word
lessens	abates
bravery	valour
population	masses
intimidating	formidable
authority	commission

Connect and Extend OPTIONAL

CONNECT TO EXTENDED WRITING PROJECT

Students can use "Be Ye Men of Valour" as a model for strategic organizational structures pertaining to audience, topic, purpose, or context in their own literary analysis essays.

BEYOND THE BOOK

Speech: Embody the American Spirit

Churchill is held in high regard in part for his speeches, which embodied the British spirit and encouraged men to be courageous. Students will write a speech encouraging listeners to embody the spirit of the United States and be proud.

Ask students to:

- Form small groups and discuss the classical appeals and rhetorical devices that Churchill used in his speech.
- Brainstorm a list of ideals that embody the spirit of the United States.
- Think of a moment in history or in their lives when it was important for Americans to come together and be proud and strong.
- Write a speech, using classical appeals and rhetorical devices, to encourage the listeners to embody the American spirit.
- Practice and perform their speeches.

To reflect, ask students:

- Were there commonalities among their speeches? What were they?
- What appeals and/or rhetorical devices worked the best?

Skill: Informational Text Structure

Use the Checklist to analyze Informational Text Structure in "Be Ye Men of Valour." Refer to the sample student annotations about Informational Text Structure in the text.

••• CHECKLIST FOR INFORMATIONAL TEXT STRUCTURE

In order to determine the structure an author uses in his or her exposition or argument, note the following:

- ✓ where the author introduces and clarifies their argument
- ✓ sentences and paragraphs that reveal the text structure the author uses to frame the argument
- ✓ whether the text structure is effective in presenting all sides of the argument, and makes his or her points clear, convincing and engaging

To analyze and evaluate the effectiveness of the structure an author uses in his or her exposition or argument, including whether the structure makes points clear, convincing, and engaging, consider the following questions:

- ✓ Did I have to read a particular sentence or phrase over again? Where?
- ✓ Did I find myself distracted or uninterested while reading the text? When?
- ✓ Did the structure the author used make their points clear, convincing, and engaging? Why or why not?
- ✓ Was the author's exposition or argument effective? Why or why not?

Skill: Informational Text Structure

Introduce the Skill

Watch the Concept Definition video and read the following definition with your students.

Text structure refers to the organizational pattern authors of nonfiction use to present information. Some of the most common informational text structures include **sequential, problem and solution, cause and effect,** and **comparison and contrast.** In a sequential text structure, authors present information about events or steps in a process, in the order in which they take or have taken place. Writers who specialize in history or science topics often use a cause and effect text structure to explain how or why something happened. Many authors use a compare and contrast text structure to present information about things that are different but have something in common, such as two points of view on a subject. Or a writer may present a problem or a series of problems, and offers solutions on how to solve them.

Authors may also use text structure to organize information about multiple topics, or use more than one organizational pattern within the same text.

SKILL VOCABULARY

problem and solution text structure / el problema y la solución ***noun*** a text structure that identifies a problem and offers a solution COGNATE

cause and effect text structure / causa y efecto ***noun*** a text structure that explains how or why something happened COGNATE

compare and contrast text structure / comparar y contrastar ***noun*** a text structure that compares and contrasts two or more things COGNATE

TURN AND TALK

1. When have you heard a speaker make an argument that you found convincing?
2. How did the speaker structure, or organize, his or her argument so that it was effective and made sense?

SPEAKING FRAMES

- A speaker argued that ____.
- The argument was structured well because ____.

Your Turn

Ask students to complete the Your Turn Activity.

QUESTION 1

Part A

A. Incorrect. The defeat of the Danes is a minor part of Churchill's argument.

B. Incorrect. The size of the empires does not relate to Churchill's argument.

C. Correct. Churchill says that it is up to Britain and France to free the world of the Nazis.

D. Incorrect. Churchill does not suggest that either Britain or France abandon their principles and act tyrannically.

Part B

A. Incorrect. This may be true, but it is not Churchill's central argument.

B. Incorrect. This may be true, but it is not Churchill's central argument.

C. Incorrect. This may be true, but it is not Churchill's central argument.

D. Correct. Here, Churchill is saying that Britain and France must and will defeat the Nazis, which is his central argument.

QUESTION 2

A. Incorrect. Words like "foulest" and "soul-destroying" appeal to emotion more than to reason.

B. Correct. Words like "foulest" and "soul-destroying" are designed to embolden and outrage the audience and make them feel a deep emotional need to win the war.

C. Incorrect. Churchill recognizes that the war will be difficult to win, but he does not say it is impossible; and words such as "foulest" do not refer to the chances of winning the war.

D. Incorrect. Although Churchill emphasizes the connections between Britain and France in this passage, the phrase "foulest and most soul-destroying tyranny" refers to Nazi Germany.

Be Ye Men of Valour

Skill: Informational Text Structure

Reread paragraph 8 of "Be Ye Men of Valour." Then, using the Checklist on the previous page, answer the multiple-choice questions below.

YOUR TURN

1. This question has two parts. First, answer Part A. Then, answer Part B.

Part A: The central argument of this excerpt can best be described as—

- A. "The Danes have been soundly defeated by the Nazis."
- B. "Britain and France both have very large empires."
- C. "Britain and France must and will defeat the Nazis."
- D. "To defeat the Nazis, Britain and France must act as tyrants."

Part B: Which of the following sentences or phrases from the text best supports your answer to Part A.

- A. "This is one of the most awe-striking periods in the long history of France and Britain."
- B. "Behind them, behind us, behind the Armies and Fleets of Britain and France, gather a group of shattered States and bludgeoned races."
- C. "upon all of whom the long night of barbarism will descend, unbroken even by a star of hope"
- D. "as conquer we must, as conquer we shall"

2. In using the phrase "foulest and most soul-destroying tyranny," Churchill is most clearly—

- A. making an appeal to his audience's reason.
- B. making an appeal to his audience's emotions.
- C. explaining that Britain has no chance of winning the war.
- D. explaining that Britain and France are very close friends.

SkillsTV

Project the SkillsTV episode and pause at the following times to prompt discussion:

1:02 How do the different elements of argumentative text structure work together? Why is it important to be able to identify these elements?

1:53 How do the students know that the passage demonstrates pathos? What do the students think is the purpose of this rhetorical appeal within the larger structure of the speech?

3:18 How do the students interpret the second passage? What inferences do they make about the speech's argumentative structure and the persuasiveness of the speech?

Skill: Central or Main Idea

Introduce the Skill

Watch the Concept Definition video and read the following definition with your students.

The **central idea** of a nonfiction text is the most important point that an author makes about a **topic**. The statement of a central idea answers the question *What's it all about?* In order to find the answer, look for **supporting ideas** that help develop the central idea. Authors also include **details** as textual evidence to support the central idea about the topic. Readers **analyze** these supporting ideas or details to see what they have in common. What do they support, explain, or describe? Answering this question will help identify the central or main idea.

Skill: Central or Main Idea

Use the Checklist to analyze Central or Main Idea in "Be Ye Men of Valour." Refer to the sample student annotations about Central or Main Idea in the text.

••• CHECKLIST FOR CENTRAL OR MAIN IDEA

In order to identify two or more central ideas of a text, note the following:

- ✓ the main idea in each paragraph or group of paragraphs
- ✓ key details in each paragraph or section of text, distinguishing what they have in common
- ✓ whether the details contain information that could indicate more than one main idea in a text
  - a science text, for example, may provide information about a specific environment and also a message on ecological awareness
  - a biography may contain equally important ideas about a person's achievements, influence, and the time period in which the person lives or lived
- ✓ when each central idea emerges
- ✓ ways that the central ideas interact and build on one another

To determine two or more central ideas of a text and analyze their development over the course of the text, including how they interact and build on one another to provide a complex analysis, consider the following questions:

- ✓ What main idea(s) do the details in each paragraph explain or describe?
- ✓ What central or main ideas do all the paragraphs support?
- ✓ How do the central ideas interact and build on one another? How does that affect when they emerge?
- ✓ How might you provide an objective summary of the text? What details would you include?

TURN AND TALK

1. Think of a lecture or talk you recently heard. What was its central idea?
2. Which details were offered to support the central idea?

SPEAKING FRAMES

- A lecture or talk I recently heard was ____.
- One detail that supported its central idea was ____.

SKILL VOCABULARY

central or main idea / la idea central o principal ***noun*** the most important point an author makes about a topic or in a section of text

topic / el tema ***noun*** the subject of a literary work, usually expressed as a single word or phrase in the form of a noun

supporting idea / la idea secundaria ***noun*** a focused explanation or argument that helps develop the central idea

Your Turn

Ask students to complete the Your Turn Activity.

QUESTION 1

Part A

A. Incorrect. This is only partly true; Britain realizes it must also protect itself.

B. Correct. This is the central idea of the paragraph.

C. Incorrect. This is true but it is not the central idea of the paragraph.

D. Incorrect. Churchill does not say that it is unlikely that they will defeat Germany.

Part B

A. Incorrect. This does not adequately support the central idea.

B. Incorrect. This does not adequately support the central idea.

C. Incorrect. This does not adequately support the central idea.

D. Correct. This adequately supports the central idea.

Skill: Central or Main Idea

Reread paragraph 8 of "Be Ye Men of Valour." Then, using the Checklist on the previous page, answer the multiple-choice questions below.

YOUR TURN

1. This question has two parts. First, answer Part A. Then, answer Part B.

   Part A: Which of the following is the best restatement of the central idea of this paragraph?

   ○ A. Regardless of the cost, Britain will sacrifice everything to protect the rest of Europe from Nazi domination.
   ○ B. Regardless of the cost, France and Britain together must save humankind from the evils of Nazi domination.
   ○ C. Although Britain has had some internal strife, it is time to put all that aside and bond together to fight Nazi Germany.
   ○ D. Although it is unlikely that France and Germany will defeat Nazi Germany, they must try for the good of humankind.

   Part B: Which content from the paragraph best supports the answer to Part A?

   ○ A. "Having received His Majesty's commission, I have formed an Administration of men and women of every Party and of almost every point of view."
   ○ B. "We have differed and quarreled in the past, but now one bond unites us all . . ."
   ○ C. "This is one of the most awe-striking periods in the long history of France and Britain."
   ○ D. ". . . side by side the British and French peoples have advanced to rescue not only Europe but mankind from the foulest and most soul-destroying tyranny . . ."

SKILL VOCABULARY

detail / el detalle *noun* a fact, a description, an example, or a reason that further explains a key idea

analyze / analizar *verb* to consider in detail and discover essential features or meaning COGNATE

Skill:
Word Meaning

Use the Checklist to analyze Word Meaning in "Be Ye Men of Valour." Refer to the sample student annotations about Word Meaning in the text.

••• CHECKLIST FOR WORD MEANING

In order to find the pronunciation of a word or determine or clarify its precise meaning, do the following:

- ✓ determine the word's part of speech
- ✓ use context clues to make an inferred meaning of the word or phrase
- ✓ consult a dictionary to verify your preliminary determination of the meaning of a word or phrase
- ✓ be sure to read all of the definitions, and then decide which definition makes sense within the context of the text

In order to determine or clarify a word's part of speech, do the following:

- ✓ determine what the word is describing
- ✓ identify how the word is being used in the phrase or sentence

In order to determine the etymology of a word, or its origin or standard usage, do the following:

- ✓ use reference materials, such as a dictionary, to determine the word's origin and history
- ✓ consider how the historical context of the word clarifies its usage

To determine or clarify the etymology or standard usage of a word, consider the following questions:

- ✓ How formal or informal is this word?
- ✓ What is the word describing? What inferred meanings can I make?
- ✓ In what context is the word being used?
- ✓ Is this slang? An example of vernacular? In what other contexts might this word be used?
- ✓ What is the etymology of this word?

SKILL VOCABULARY

digital resource / el recurso digital *noun* a resource such as a map, dictionary, or encyclopedia that is found online rather than in a book COGNATE

glossary / el glosario *noun* an alphabetical list of terms or words related to a specific subject with definitions and explanations COGNATE

definition / la definición *noun* the meaning of a word or phrase COGNATE

Skill: Word Meaning

Introduce the Skill

Watch the Concept Definition video ▶ and read the following definition with your students.

When you come across a word that is unfamiliar, you can use a print or **digital resource**, such as an online dictionary or thesaurus, to find out more information about the word. Some nonfiction texts also contain a **glossary**, which is an alphabetical list of terms, or words, related to the specific subject covered in the text. A glossary includes definitions and explanations for each term. When words have multiple meanings, you can sometimes use context to confirm which meaning fits best, but a dictionary, thesaurus, or glossary can give you the following information about a word:

- the **definition** (the meaning of the word)
- the **part of speech** (the grammatical category of a word: noun, pronoun, adjective, verb, adverb, preposition, or conjunction)
- the **pronunciation** (the way the word sounds when said aloud)
- the **word's origin** (the history of the word and where it originated)

TURN AND TALK

1. What do you do when you read or hear a word you don't understand?
2. How can you use a dictionary to figure out the meaning of the word?

SPEAKING FRAMES

- When I read or hear a word I don't understand, I ____.
- I can use a dictionary to ____.

Your Turn

Ask students to complete the Your Turn Activity.

QUESTION 1

A. Incorrect. *Favorable* does not describe an action.

B. Incorrect. *Favorable* modifies the noun *balance*, not a verb, adjective, or adverb.

C. Correct. The relative balance between the two air forces had become better, or more favorable, for Britain.

D. Incorrect. *Favorable* modifies the noun *balance*, and therefore it cannot be a noun.

QUESTION 2

A. Incorrect. *Favorable* is not used to express approval or support here.

B. Incorrect. *Favorable* is not used here to show that someone is allowing something to happen.

C. Incorrect. *Favorable* is not used here to show that anyone is being given an advantage.

D. Correct. Churchill says Great Britain is winning three out of four air battles, and this suggests a good outcome.

Skill: Word Meaning

Reread the first sentence of paragraph 4 of "Be Ye Men of Valour." Then, using the Checklist on the previous page, answer the multiple-choice questions below.

YOUR TURN

1. What part of speech is the word *favorable*? How do you know?

   - ○ A. It is a verb because it describes how the British Air Force is "clawing down" three or four Germans plans for every one British plan that the Germans are shooting down.
   - ○ B. It is an adverb because it describes how the British Air Force is "clawing down" three or four Germans plans for every one British plan that the Germans are shooting down.
   - ○ C. It is an adjective because it describes the relative balance of the British and German Air Forces at the time of the speech compared with at the beginning of the battle.
   - ○ D. It is a noun because it describes the relative balance of the British and German Air Forces at the time of the speech compared with at the beginning of the battle.

2. Which of the following definitions of *favorable* is most accurate for this context?

   - ○ A. expressing approval or support
   - ○ B. giving consent; allowing something to happen
   - ○ C. giving advantage to someone or something
   - ○ D. suggesting a good outcome

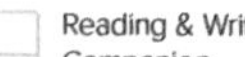

SKILL VOCABULARY

part of speech / la parte de la oración ***noun*** the grammatical category of a word

pronunciation / la pronunciación ***noun*** the way a word sounds when it is said aloud

word origin / el origen de la palabra ***noun*** a word's first use and history

Close Read

Reread "Be Ye Men of Valour." As you reread, complete the Skills Focus questions below. Then use your answers and annotations from the questions to help you complete the Write activity.

SKILLS FOCUS

1. Highlight the first sentence of Churchill's speech. What is the most likely meaning of *solemn* in this context? What part of speech is this word, and how do you know? Refer to a dictionary. What is the best definition of this word, given its usage in this passage?
2. Highlight a call to action Churchill makes to his listeners, and explain why it is an effective text structure to help him achieve his purpose.
3. Identify a passage that gives details about events in Europe. Explain how these details support the main idea of Churchill's speech.
4. Identify a passage that reveals Churchill's main idea, and explain how his word choice effectively communicates that idea to his audience.
5. Churchill's speech takes place during one of the most important turning points in modern history. Highlight two examples of Churchill discussing division and alienation, and two examples of Churchill discussing bonding and collaboration. What were the causes of the division? Why is coming together so important at this time?

WRITE

RHETORICAL ANALYSIS: Informational text structure can be used skillfully to compose ideas in a way that heightens the persuasive power of a speech or written work. Write a response in which you summarize the main argument of Churchill's speech and evaluate the structure of the speech. In your response, address the following question: Does the arrangement of ideas make the speech more persuasive? Remember to support your response with textual evidence.

Close Read

Skills Focus

QUESTION 1: Word Meaning

See paragraph 1. *Solemn* is immediately preceded by the article a and followed by the noun *hour,* so I think it's an adjective. The most appropriate definition I can find for this context is "grave and serious."

QUESTION 2: Informational Text Structure

See paragraph 5.

QUESTION 3: Central or Main Idea

See paragraph 1. Churchill's main idea here is that war is raging in Europe and that Britain is in great danger. He uses specific details (*Flanders, heavily armored tanks, Maginot Line,* etc.) to ensure that his audience understands that this is not just some vague threat.

QUESTION 4: Rhetoric

Churchill uses words with strong emotional connotations (*valour, perish, battle, outrage, God, Heaven*) to inspire his audience to be brave and determined in the face of great conflict and danger, which is his main purpose.

QUESTION 5: Essential Question

See paragraph 8.

Writer's Notebook

Connect to Literary Focus: Give students time to reflect on how "Be Ye Men of Valour" demonstrates the conventions and characteristics of this unit's literary period, Modernism, by freewriting in their Writer's Notebooks.

Beginning & Intermediate

Remind students of the unit's literary focus, Modernism. Encourage students to draw their connections or allow students to write in their native language. Circulate around the room, prompting students for their thoughts as they respond orally or through pantomime.

Advanced & Advanced High

Allow students to share their connections orally in pairs or small groups before freewriting.

Collaborative Conversation

SCAFFOLDS

Break students into collaborative conversation groups to discuss the Close Read prompt. Ask students to use the StudySyncTV episode as a model for their discussion. Remind them to reference their Skills Focus annotations in their discussion.

Informational text structure can be used skillfully to compose ideas in a way that heightens the persuasive power of a speech or written work. Write a response in which you summarize the main argument of Churchill's speech and evaluate the structure of the speech. In your response, address the following question: Does the arrangement of ideas make the speech more persuasive? Remember to support your response with textual evidence.

Use the scaffolds below to differentiate instruction for your ELL English Language Learners and A Approaching grade-level learners.

ELL **BEGINNING, INTERMEDIATE** Use the discussion guide and speaking frames to facilitate the discussion with support from the teacher.

ADVANCED, ADVANCED HIGH Use the discussion guide and speaking frames to facilitate the discussion in mixed-level groups.

A **APPROACHING** Use the discussion guide to facilitate the discussion in mixed-level groups.

APPROACHING
ADVANCED, ADVANCED HIGH
BEGINNING, INTERMEDIATE

Discussion Guide	Speaking Frames
1. What does Churchill want his listeners to know about the war?	• Churchill wants his audience to know that ____. This is good news because ____. • Churchill wants his listeners to know that ____. This is bad news because ____.
2. How does Churchill arrange ideas in his speech?	• First, Churchill tells his audience ____. • Then, Churchill ____.
3. Does this structure make the speech more persuasive? Why or why not?	• Churchill's speech is persuasive because ____. • This structure can help persuade his audience to ____.

Text to World

Use the activity below to differentiate instruction for your B Beyond grade level learners.

Reread paragraph 8.

Have students engage in conversation about war; the causes, effects, and perceptions of all parties involved. Ask students:

- What does this part of the text remind you of in the real world?
- How do you, the reader, relate to this statement?

Review Prompt and Rubric

Before students begin writing, review the writing prompt and rubric with the class.

RHETORICAL ANALYSIS: Informational text structure can be used skillfully to compose ideas in a way that heightens the persuasive power of a speech or written work. Write a response in which you summarize the main argument of Churchill's speech and evaluate the structure of the speech. In your response, address the following question: Does the arrangement of ideas make the speech more persuasive? Remember to support your response with textual evidence.

 PROMPT GUIDE

- What does Churchill want his audience to know about the war?
- How does Churchill arrange ideas in his speech?
- What is another structure Churchill could have used to compose his speech?
- Does this structure make the speech more persuasive? Why or why not?

Score	Informational Text Structure	Language and Conventions
4	The writer clearly summarizes Churchill's main argument and thoroughly evaluates whether the text structure adds to the persuasive power of the speech. The writer provides exemplary analysis, using relevant textual evidence.	The writer demonstrates a consistent command of grammar, punctuation, and usage conventions. Although minor errors may be evident, they do not detract from the fluency or the clarity of the essay.
3	The writer summarizes Churchill's main argument and evaluates whether the text structure adds to the persuasive power of the speech. The writer provides sufficient analysis, using relevant textual evidence most of the time.	The writer demonstrates an adequate command of grammar, punctuation, and usage conventions. Although some errors may be evident, they create few (if any) disruptions in the fluency of the writing or the clarity of the essay.
2	The writer begins to summarize Churchill's main argument and evaluate whether the text structure adds to the persuasive power of the speech, but the discussion is incomplete. The writer uses relevant textual evidence only some of the time.	The writer demonstrates a partial command of grammar, punctuation, and usage conventions. Some distracting errors may be evident, at times creating minor disruptions in the fluency or clarity of the writing.
1	The writer attempts to summarize Churchill's main argument and evaluate whether the text structure adds to the persuasive power of the speech, but the effort is not successful. The writer uses little or no relevant textual evidence.	The writer demonstrates little or no command of grammar, punctuation, and usage conventions. Serious and persistent errors create disruptions in the fluency of the writing and sometimes interfere with meaning.
0	The writer does not provide a relevant response to the prompt or does not provide a response at all.	Serious and persistent errors overwhelm the writing and interfere with the meaning of the response as a whole, making the writer's meaning impossible to understand.

SCAFFOLDS

Write

Ask students to complete the writing assignment using text evidence to support their answers.

Use the scaffolds below to differentiate instruction for your ELL English Language Learners and A Approaching grade level readers.

ELL **BEGINNING** With the help of the word bank, write a response using paragraph frame 1.

INTERMEDIATE With the help of the word bank, write a response using paragraph frames 1 and 2.

ADVANCED, ADVANCED HIGH Write a response of differentiated length using the sentence starters.

A **APPROACHING** Write a response of differentiated length using the sentence starters.

BEGINNING / INTERMEDIATE	BEGINNING / INTERMEDIATE	INTERMEDIATE	ADVANCED, ADVANCED HIGH / APPROACHING
Word Bank	**Paragraph Frame 1**	**Paragraph Frame 2**	**Sentence Starters**
win fight bad hope Germans persuasive structure Britain	First, Churchill gives the audience ____ news. He explains that the ____ are moving into France and may attack ____ next. Then, Churchill describes what the British can do to ____ the war. This problem-and-solution ____ makes the speech more ____ because it conveys the reality of the situation but also gives people ____. By acknowledging the difficulties of the war, Churchill inspires his audience to ____ back.	In the beginning of his speech, Churchill uses details like ____ to ____. Later, he advises his audience to ____ by saying ____. This is effective because ____.	• First, Churchill gives information about . . . • Then, Churchill describes . . . • This inspires his audience to . . . • The way Churchill arranges his ideas is effective because . . .

Peer Review

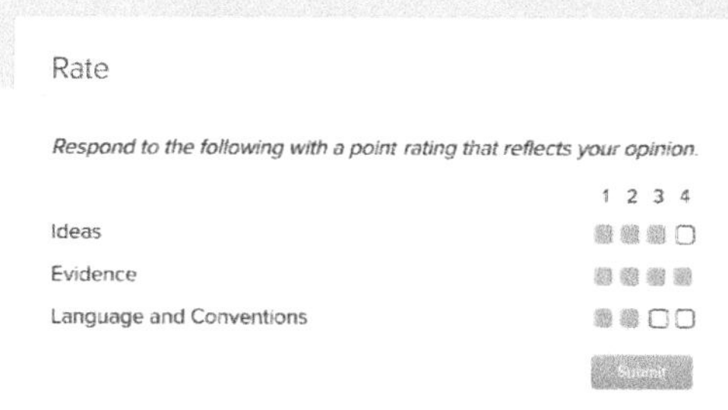

Students should submit substantive feedback to two peers using the review instructions below.

- How well does this response answer the prompt?
- How well does the writer support his or her ideas with textual evidence?
- Which sentence in the writer's response made you think differently about the text?
- What does the writer do best in this response? What should the writer continue to work on?

Remember that your comments are most useful when they are kind and constructive.

SENTENCE FRAMES

- You (completely / partly / almost) ____ answered the prompt because ____.
- You could answer the prompt more completely by ____.
- You used good evidence to show ____.
- I thought differently about the speech when I read your idea that ____.
- One idea you expressed well is ____.
- One idea that needs clarification is ____.

The Pearl Divers' Daughters

POETRY
Marci Calabretta Cancio-Bello
2016

Introduction

Marci Calabretta Cancio-Bello (b. 1989) was a John S. and James L. Knight Fellow at Florida International University before the publication of her first book, *Hour of the Ox*, which won the 2015 Donald Hall Prize for Poetry. She is a teacher and editor, and her poetry has been featured in dozens of journals and anthologies, including *Best New Poets 2015*, a collection featuring 50 up-and-coming young poets. "The Pearl Divers' Daughters" explores the lives and legacy of haenyeo, the legendary female divers of South Korea's Jeju province.

The speakers in this poem, the pearl divers' daughters, strip the ocean of its abalone scales and plant oyster seeds in each other's backs. Their mothers, with scarred wrists, carved veins into the sea while scissoring their legs into the air. The daughters name the pearl divers, whose songs blossom like sea anemones. The pearl divers press their daughters' bodies against sharks and black rays, and they trail their fingers through schools of fish. Still, the daughters are never satisfied; and so, they gnaw upon the shore. Their mothers cheer them on as cities sprout from their spines, as their eyes get used to seeing the world above water. They are the pearl divers' daughters. Their sisters walk around with coral-hemmed skirts and their brothers are lithe like eels. They cheer each other on, building their futures the way an oyster makes a pearl.

Proficiency-leveled summaries and summaries in multiple languages are available digitally.

Audio and audio text highlighting are available with this text.

CONNECT TO ESSENTIAL QUESTION

What causes individuals to feel alienated?

This poem, by Marci Calabretta Cancio-Bello, explores the lives and legacy of *haenyeo*, the legendary female divers of Korea's Jeju province. How does a parent's legacy affect a child's identity and connection with the world?

Entry Point

As students prepare to read "The Pearl Divers' Daughters," share the following information with them to provide context.

- ✓ "The Pearl Divers' Daughters" is a poem written by Marci Calabretta Cancio-Bello to describe *haenyeo*, the famous female sea divers from the Korean province of Jeju.
- ✓ The *haenyeo* dive underwater without breathing equipment looking for pearls and other treasures. These women are a symbol of female empowerment because they develop strong bodies and minds and are often the primary breadwinners for their families.

Instructional Path

The print teacher's edition includes essential point-of-use instruction and planning tools. Complete lesson plans and program documents appear in your digital teacher account.

Independent Read: The Pearl Divers' Daughters

Objectives: After reading "The Pearl Divers' Daughters," students will write a short response that demonstrates their understanding of pearl diving in the poem and how it compares to pearl diving in another culture.

Independent Read

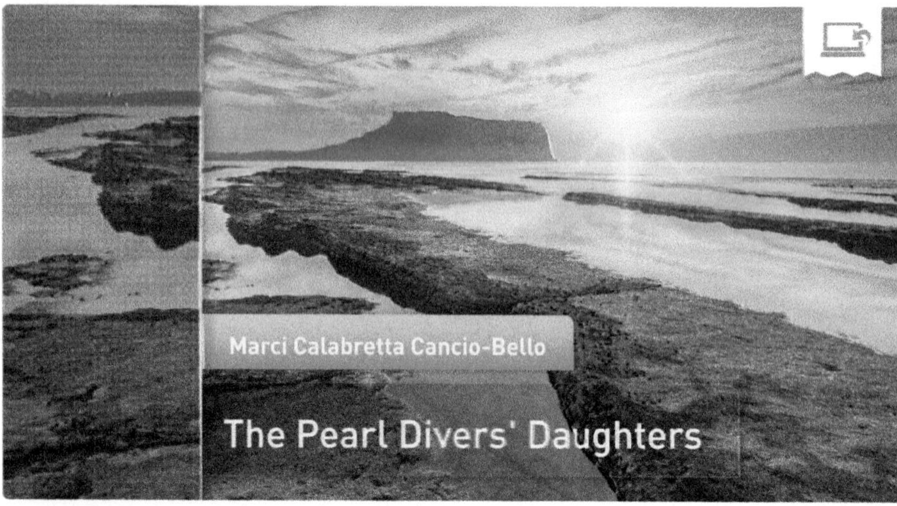

Introduce the Text

As a class, watch the video preview and have students read the introduction in pairs to make connections to the video preview.

- How does the information in this video connect to what you already know?
- Would you want to do the same job as your parent or guardian? Why or why not?

ELL SENTENCE FRAMES

- The information connects to what I already know about ____.
- My (parent / guardian) is a / an ____. I would / would not want to do that job. I think that job is ____.

Access Complex Text

LEXILE: N/A **WORD COUNT:** 177

The following areas may be challenging for students, particularly ELL English Language Learners and A Approaching grade-level learners.

Connection of Ideas	Prior Knowledge
• Though this text is a poem, it includes details about pearl diving and its important place in a culture. • Students can visualize the vivid imagery in the poem to better understand the experience of pearl diving and how it connects mothers and daughters.	• Students may not be familiar with pearl diving. • Ask if any students in the class know anything about pearls or diving. Have them share the information. Also, encourage students to closely read the poet's descriptions to understand the experience.

"... pearl divers whose songs build and blossom like barrel-fires or anemones."

NOTES

We are the pearl divers' daughters
skinning the ocean of her abalone[1] scales,
planting oyster seeds in each other's vertebrae.

Our mothers carved veins into the sea
with *reinvented* air, wrists scarred in rows and rings—
octopi and coral—legs scissoring against the sun,

the space between their thighs *profound* as trenches.
Haenyeo, we name them, pearl divers whose songs build
and blossom like barrel-fires or anemones[2].

They press our shoulders against the ribs
of whale sharks, our palms on dotted black rays.
We graze our fingers through damselfish[3] schools,

but our appetites are as *insatiate* as the sea is for land.
We gnaw the shore, legs wound in seaweed,
skin flayed by the tongues of clams, pulling, pushing.

Arirang[4], our mothers say patriotically, and cities
bloom from our spines, rooting us to *cartographies*,
thumbing our eyes into sand-locked jewels.

1. **abalone** a general name for sea snails, eaten cooked and raw all over the world
2. **anemones** sea invertebrates resembling the flowering plant for which they are named; they are sedentary or slow-moving and capture fish and marine animals for food
3. **damselfish** brightly hued fish of the family Pomacentridae, often characterized by two contrasting colors that meet horizontally along the middle of the body
4. **Arirang** traditional Korean folk song about a tragic romance that is the national anthem of both North and South Korea

Developing Background Knowledge and Cultural Awareness

1. Are humans a product of their cultural heritage?
2. Have students raise their hands as to whether they a) strongly disagree; b) disagree; c) agree; d) strongly agree. Assign each response a corner of the room, and have students go to their respective corners to explain their positions.
3. Have one student from each group be the spokesperson to explain the group's response.

Discuss with students: What is a cultural aspect that you have learned or inherited from your family, friends, or community? How can cultural artifacts, traditions or stories shape our identities and relationships? What happens when aspects of someone's culture are lost or change?

Prepare for Advanced Courses

Use the activity below to differentiate instruction for your B Beyond grade level learners.

Analyze for Enrichment

Consider the visual imagery in lines 13–15:

but our appetites are as insatiate as the sea is for land.
We gnaw the shore, legs wound in seaweed, skin flayed by the tongues of clams, pulling, pushing.

Ask students:

- Which words appeal to the senses?
- What mood is created by this imagery?

SELECTION VOCABULARY

reinvent / reinventar *verb* to create or change something so that it seems completely new COGNATE

profound / profundo/a *adjective* very great or intense COGNATE

insatiate / insaciable *adjective* impossible to satisfy COGNATE

cartography / la cartografía *noun* the art or science of map making COGNATE

hem / hacer el dobladillo *verb* to sew with a border

TEXT TALK

Why are the mothers' wrists scarred?

See stanza 2: The mothers' wrists are scarred from touching sea life as they reach for pearls.

How do the daughters feel about their future in pearl diving?

See stanzas 5–8: The daughters think pearl diving looks exciting and important.

How does your answer to question 2 help you understand the connection between mothers and daughters in the poem?

Answers will vary.

How did reflecting on cultural heritage deepen your understanding of "The Pearl Divers' Daughters"?

Answers will vary.

B Ask each Beyond grade-level student to write one additional discussion question. Then, have one or two students facilitate a discussion, using their questions to guide the conversation.

We are the pearl divers' daughters,
our sisters' skirts are *hemmed* in coral,
our brothers are cloud-eyed eels.

Arirang, we say, our futures pearled
into every empty shell, our tongues pressed
against the words until we become them.

A group of 'Haenyeo' on South Korea's southern island of Jeju. Haenyeo, or 'sea women', refers to women who use free-diving to retrieve shell fish from the sea floor.

WRITE

EXPLANATORY ESSAY: Marci Calabretta Cancio-Bello weaves references to pearl diving in the Korean province of Jeju throughout her poem "The Pearl Divers' Daughters." Analyze the images she presents to determine the actions and tasks that these pearl divers undertake as part of their job. Then, conduct informal research about pearl diving in another particular culture or time period. How do the methods and customs of pearl diving described in "The Pearl Divers' Daughters" align with or depart from those of the culture or time period you researched? Remember to use textual evidence and your research to support your response.

Writer's Notebook

Connect to Essential Question: Give students time to reflect on how "The Pearl Divers' Daughters" connects to the unit's essential question "What causes individuals to feel alienated?" by freewriting in their Writer's Notebooks.

CHECK FOR SUCCESS

If students are still struggling to respond to the prompt, ask them scaffolded questions, such as:

- How can the work of a pearl diver be isolating?
- How might the pearl divers' job connect them to a larger community?
- How does the environment shape the divers' thoughts?

Reading Comprehension OPTIONAL

Have students complete the digital reading comprehension questions ✓ when they finish reading.

ANSWER KEY

QUESTION 1: B

QUESTION 2: C

QUESTION 3: D

QUESTION 4: D

QUESTION 5: *See first chart.*

See chart below.

First	Second	Third	Fourth
"We are the pearl divers' daughters skinning the ocean of her abalone scales,"	"Our mothers carved veins into the sea with reinvented air, wrists scarred in rows and rings—"	"Arirang, our mothers say patriotically, and cities bloom from our spines, rooting us to cartographies,"	"Arirang, we say, our futures pearled into every empty shell, our tongues pressed against the words until we become them."

Connect and Extend OPTIONAL

CONNECT TO EXTENDED WRITING PROJECT

Have students explore whether they think the pearl divers are an example of physical alienation or, alternatively, one of the cultural connectedness that is lacking in modern society.

BEYOND THE BOOK

Art: Art Interpretation

In her poem, Marci Calabretta Cancio-Bello blends human and sea imagery to create emotion and meaning. Students will visualize a stanza and bring it to life through art.

Ask students to:

- Choose a stanza from the poem.
- Reread the stanza a few times while focusing on the imagery created.
- Choose an appropriate art medium that will capture the visual of the stanza.
- Using the chosen art medium, create a work that brings the stanza to life by showing how the poet blends human and sea imagery.
- Share with classmates.

To reflect, ask students to write a paragraph about how translating the stanza to a visual work changed their visualization of the poem.

Collaborative Conversation

SCAFFOLDS

Post the writing prompt to generate a discussion in small groups. Ask students to first break down the prompt before they discuss relevant ideas and textual evidence.

Marci Calabretta Cancio-Bello weaves references to pearl diving in the Korean province of Jeju throughout her poem "The Pearl Divers' Daughters." Analyze the images she presents to determine the actions and tasks that these pearl divers undertake as part of their job. Then, conduct informal research about pearl diving in another particular culture or time period. How do the methods and customs of pearl diving described in "The Pearl Divers' Daughters" align with or depart from those of the culture or time period you researched? Remember to use textual evidence and your research to support your response.

Use the scaffolds below to differentiate instruction for your ELL English Language Learners and A Approaching grade-level learners.

ELL **BEGINNING, INTERMEDIATE** Use the discussion guide and speaking frames to facilitate the discussion with support from the teacher.

ADVANCED, ADVANCED HIGH Use the discussion guide and speaking frames facilitate the discussion in mixed-level groups.

A APPROACHING Use the discussion guide to facilitate the discussion in mixed-level groups.

APPROACHING

ADVANCED, ADVANCED HIGH

BEGINNING, INTERMEDIATE

Discussion Guide	Speaking Frames
1. Which of the pearl divers' actions does the poet write about?	• Pearl divers swim in areas that are ____. • Pearl divers' tasks include ____ and ____.
2. How is the pearl diving described in the poem similar to pearl diving in another culture or time period?	• The pearl diving in the poem is similar to pearl diving from ____. • The methods of pearl diving are similar because ____.
3. How is the pearl diving described in the poem different from pearl diving in another culture or time period?	• The pearl diving in the poem is different from pearl diving from ____. • The methods of pearl diving are different because ____.

Text to World

Use the activity below to differentiate instruction for your B Beyond grade level learners.

Reread lines 1 and 2:

We are the pearl divers' daughters
skinning the ocean of her abalone scales,
Have students conduct informal research about abalone.

Ask students:

- Why would the author mention that here?
- What connections are made to the real world?

Review Prompt and Rubric

Before students begin writing, review the writing prompt and rubric with the class.

EXPLANATORY: Marci Calabretta Cancio-Bello weaves references to pearl diving in the Korean province of Jeju throughout her poem "The Pearl Divers' Daughters." Analyze the images she presents to determine the actions and tasks that these pearl divers undertake as part of their job. Then, conduct informal research about pearl diving in another particular culture or time period. How do the methods and customs of pearl diving described in "The Pearl Divers' Daughters" align with or depart from those of the culture or time period you researched? Remember to use textual evidence and your research to support your response.

ELL **PROMPT GUIDE**

A
- Which of the pearl divers' actions does the poet write about?
- How is the pearl diving described in the poem similar to pearl diving in another culture or time period?
- How is the pearl diving described in the poem different from pearl diving in another culture or time period?

Score	Explanatory	Language and Conventions
4	The writer clearly explains pearl diving in the poem and in another culture, using relevant textual evidence as needed.	The writer demonstrates a consistent command of grammar, punctuation, and usage conventions. Although minor errors may be evident, they do not detract from the fluency or the clarity of the essay.
3	The writer sufficiently explains pearl diving in the poem and in another culture, using relevant textual evidence most of the time.	The writer demonstrates an adequate command of grammar, punctuation, and usage conventions. Although some errors may be evident, they create few (if any) disruptions in the fluency of the writing or the clarity of the essay.
2	The writer begins to explain pearl diving in the poem and in another culture, but the explanation is incomplete. The writer uses relevant textual evidence only some of the time.	The writer demonstrates a partial command of grammar, punctuation, and usage conventions. Some distracting errors may be evident, at times creating minor disruptions in the fluency or clarity of the writing.
1	The writer attempts to explain pearl diving in the poem and in another culture, but the explanation is not successful. The writer uses little or no relevant textual evidence.	The writer demonstrates little or no command of grammar, punctuation, and usage conventions. Serious and persistent errors create disruptions in the fluency of the writing and sometimes interfere with meaning.
0	The writer does not provide a relevant response to the prompt or does not provide a response at all.	Serious and persistent errors overwhelm the writing and interfere with the meaning of the response as a whole, making the writer's meaning impossible to understand.

Write

SCAFFOLDS

Ask students to complete the writing assignment using text evidence to support their answers.

Use the scaffolds below to differentiate instruction for your ELL English Language Learners and A Approaching grade-level learners.v

ELL **BEGINNING** With the help of the word bank, write a response using paragraph frame 1.

INTERMEDIATE With the help of the word bank, write a response using paragraph frames 1 and 2.

ADVANCED, ADVANCED HIGH Write a response of differentiated length using the sentence starters.

A **APPROACHING** Write a response of differentiated length using the sentence starters.

BEGINNING / INTERMEDIATE	BEGINNING / INTERMEDIATE	INTERMEDIATE	ADVANCED, ADVANCED HIGH / APPROACHING
Word Bank	**Paragraph Frame 1**	**Paragraph Frame 2**	**Sentence Starters**
scars sea life generations adventure traditions	The poet explains that pearl divers in Jeju swim through waters filled with ____. As they reach for treasures, they can get ____ on their arms. In Jeju, pearl diving can connect ____ of women. In other cultures or time periods, there are different ____ surrounding pearl diving. However, pearl divers often share a passion for ____.	I researched pearl diving methods and customs in ____. The pearl divers in that culture are different from the Jeju pearl divers because ____. They are similar to the pearl divers described in the poem because ____.	• The pearl divers in the poem swim through waters that are . . . • They search for . . . • In Jeju, Pearl diving connects people because . . . • Another culture that practices pearl diving is . . . • Pearl diving in that culture is similar because . . . • Pearl diving in that culture is different because . . .

Peer Review

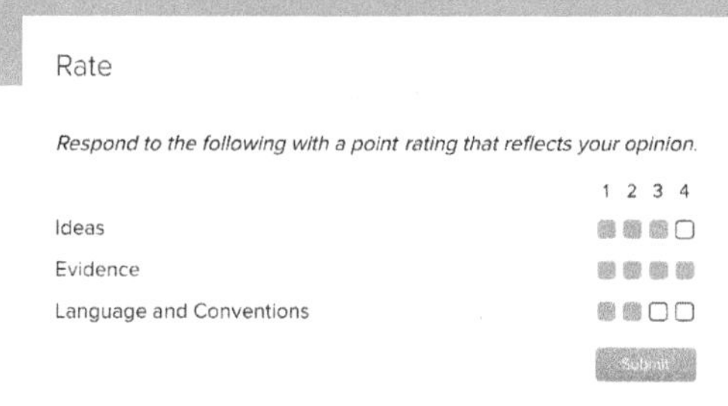

Students should submit substantive feedback to two peers using the review instructions below.

- How well does this response answer the prompt?
- Which of the writer's details caused you to learn something new about pearl diving?
- What did the writer do well in this response? What does the writer need to work on?

Remember that your comments are most useful when they are kind and constructive.

SENTENCE FRAMES

A

- You were able to (completely / partly / almost) ____ answer the prompt.
- You could answer the prompt more completely by ____.
- I learned something new after reading ____.
- My favorite part of your response is ____.

Killers Of The Dream

INFORMATIONAL TEXT
Lillian Smith
1949

Introduction

Lillian Smith (1897–1966) wrote *Killers Of The Dream*, her 1949 memoir, to challenge Southern taboos and unpack the moral and psychological costs of segregation. Written before the American civil rights movement of the 1950s and 60s, her critique of social mores about race and sin influenced those who would later stand up for racial equality. In this excerpt from the first chapter of her book, she reveals that she learned to discriminate as a child, and that these destructive lessons about maintaining white privilege were taught to her by people she loved and trusted—her own parents.

Lillian Smith grew up in witnessing racism in the South. Although every Southerner her age has tried to run away from this past, they all return to defend it out of loyalty, as if the sins committed by the South were their own. Southern whites were raised so as not to feel the pain of the people around them; and Smith recounts the conflicting messages of her childhood. While her mother taught her tenderness and compassion, she also taught Smith how to keep "Negroes in their 'place.'" Likewise, her father would remind her that all men are brothers, but would not extend that dignity to the people of color in their town. There was also an intricate system of manners, modulated through tone of voice, of things allowed and not allowed, and of ways to relate. As a child, Smith learned that Southerners were warm and hospitable to everyone except for the 13 million people amongst them who had a different skin color.

Proficiency-leveled summaries and summaries in multiple languages are available digitally.

Audio and audio text highlighting are available with this text.

COMPARING WITHIN AND ACROSS GENRES

What causes individuals to feel alienated?

Killers Of the Dream by Lillian Smith and "Shooting an Elephant" by George Orwell help students understand the power of personal narratives to convey important moments in history. The first chapter of Smith's 1949 memoir describes the confusing contradictions children learned while growing up in the segregated South.

Entry Point

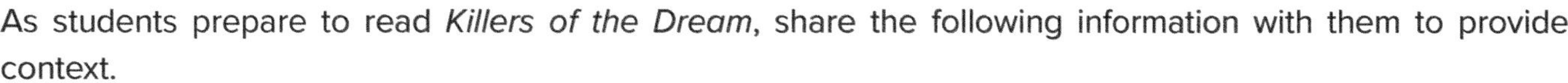

As students prepare to read *Killers of the Dream*, share the following information with them to provide context.

- ✓ Sensitive Content: This text contains racial epithets. To prepare for this lesson, please refer to the Addressing Sensitive Content section in the Grade 12 ELA Overview. It is strongly recommended that you develop a plan to address this topic with your students prior to assigning the text.
- ✓ Lillian Smith lived from 1897 to 1966. She was born to a middle class white family and grew up in Florida and Georgia. She lived during the Jim Crow era when African Americans were legally segregated from white Americans and experienced racism and discrimination in their daily lives.
- ✓ Smith was troubled by the racial segregation she witnessed. She began writing to express her frustrations and to critique Southern culture. In 1944, she published her most famous book, *Strange Fruit*, which explored interracial romance.
- ✓ Her book *Killers of the Dream* was published in 1949, years before the beginning of the Civil Rights Movement. The book is a collection of autobiographical essays that examine the damaging effects of racial injustice on the American South.

Instructional Path

The print teacher's edition includes essential point-of-use instruction and planning tools. Complete lesson plans and program documents appear in your digital teacher account.

Independent Read: Killers of the Dream

Objectives: After reading *Killers of the Dream*, students will write a short response that demonstrates their understanding of the author's claim and describes their own personal connections to this claim.

Independent Read

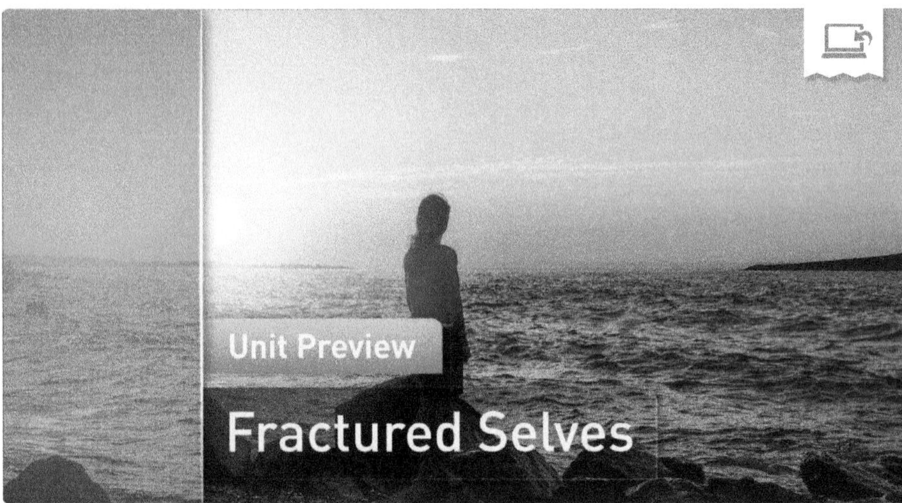

Introduce the Text

As a class, watch the video preview  and have students read the introduction in pairs to make connections to the video preview.

- What two words would you use to describe this video?
- When have you witnessed or experienced discrimination? How did it make you feel?

ELL **SENTENCE FRAMES**

- Two words I would use to describe this video are ____ and ____.
- I (witnessed/experienced) discrimination when ____. It made me feel ____.

Access Complex Text

LEXILE: 1270 **WORD COUNT:** 1,116

The following areas may be challenging for students, particularly ELL English Language Learners and A Approaching grade-level learners.

Purpose	Prior Knowledge
• The primary purpose of Lillian Smith's memoir is to inform readers about her complicated experience as a white female in the segregated South in the twentieth century. • Guide students to look for and highlight evidence that supports this purpose as they read.	• Smith explores the painful legacy of slavery in the American South in the early twentieth century. Though slavery had officially ended in the 1860s, racial discrimination against African Americans still regularly occurred. • Provide students with any historical context they may need in order to understand the main ideas in Smith's memoir.

"This haunted childhood belongs to every southerner of my age."

NOTES

1 Even its children knew that the South was in trouble. No one had to tell them; no words said aloud. To them, it was a vague thing weaving in and out of their play, like a ghost haunting an old graveyard or whispers after the household sleeps—fleeting mystery, vague menace to which each responded in his own way. Some learned to screen out all except the soft and the soothing; others denied even as they saw plainly, and heard. But all knew that under quiet words and warmth and laughter, under the slow ease and tender concern about small matters, there was a heavy burden on all of us and as heavy a refusal to confess it. The children knew this "trouble" was bigger than they, bigger than their family, bigger than their church, so big that people turned away from its size. They had seen it flash out and shatter a town's peace, had felt it tear up all they believed in. They had measured its giant strength and felt weak when they remembered.

2 This haunted childhood belongs to every southerner of my age. We ran away from it but we came back like a hurt animal to its wound, or a murderer to the scene of his sin. The human heart dares not stay away too long from that which hurt it most. There is a return journey to anguish that few of us are released from making.

3 We who were born in the South called this mesh of feeling and memory "loyalty." We thought of it sometimes as "love." We identified with the South's trouble as if we, individually, were responsible for all of it. We defended the sins and the sorrow of three hundred years as if each sin had been committed by us alone and each sorrow had cut across our heart. We were as hurt at criticism of our region as if our own name had been called aloud by the critic. We knew guilt without understanding it, and there is no tie that binds men closer to the past and each other than that.

4 It is a strange thing, this umbilical cord uncut. In times of ease, we do not feel its pull, but when we are threatened with change, suddenly it draws the wholewhite South together in a collective fear and fury that wipe our minds clear of reason and we are blocked from sensible contact with the world we live in.

Developing Background Knowledge and Cultural Awareness

Find out what your students already know about how social norms and assumptions can blind someone from seeing things as they really are.

1. Share with students the following quotation by Lillian Smith: "I broke every barrier I could to see things as they are."
2. In small groups, have students discuss the quotation's meaning, and how it relates to something in their own lives or to something they've read or learned about.

Discuss with students: How are attitudes or beliefs passed down and communicated within a family or community? Why do some people adopt similar attitudes to those around them while others do not? What causes individuals to challenge certain points of view from how they were raised?

TEXT TALK

Why did Lillian Smith know during her childhood that the South was in trouble?

See paragraph 1: She sensed the heavy burden of the past during her childhood, and she did not know how to handle her feelings.

To what did Smith compare an umbilical cord?

See paragraph 4: Smith said that the connection among white southerners was like an umbilical cord because they rejected change and outside influence.

Prepare For Advanced Courses

Use the activity below to differentiate instruction for your B Beyond grade level learners.

Analyze for Enrichment

Reread paragraph 8:

The father who rebuked me for an air of superiority toward schoolmates from the mill and rounded out his rebuke by gravely reminding me that "all men are brothers," trained me in the steel-rigid decorums I must demand of every colored male.

Ask students: How does the author present the antithesis in her father's message? What message is being sent to the audience?

5 To keep this resistance strong, wall after wall was thrown up in the southern mind against criticism from without and within. Imaginations closed tight against the hurt of others; a regional armoring that took place to ward off the "enemies" who would make our trouble different—or maybe rid us of it completely. For it was a trouble that we did not want to give up. We were as involved with it as a child who cannot be happy at home and cannot bear to tear himself away, or as a grownup who has fallen in love with his own disease. We southerners had identified with the long sorrowful past on such deep levels of love and hate and guilt that we did not know how to break old bonds without pulling our lives down. *Change* was the evil word, a shrill clanking that made us know too well our servitude. *Change* meant leaving one's memories, one's sins, one's **ambivalent** pleasures, the room where one was born.

6 In this South I lived as a child and now live. And it is of it that my story is made. I shall not tell, here, of experiences that were different and special and belonged only to me, but those most white southerners born at the turn of the century share with each other. Out of the intricate weaving of unnumbered threads, I shall pick out a few strands, a few designs that have to do with what we call color and race . . . and politics . . . and money and how it is made . . . and religion . . . and sex and the body image . . . and love . . . and dreams of the Good and the killers of dreams.

7 A southern child's basic lessons were woven of such **dissonant** strands as these; sometimes the threads tangled into a terrifying mess; sometimes **archaic**, startling designs would appear in the weaving; sometimes a design was left broken while another was completed with minute care. Bewildered teachers, bewildered pupils in home and on the street, driven by an invisible Authority, learned their lessons:

8 The mother who taught me what I know of tenderness and love and compassion taught me also the bleak rituals of keeping Negroes in their "place." The father who rebuked me for an air of superiority toward schoolmates from the mill and rounded out his rebuke by gravely reminding me that "all men are brothers," trained me in the steel-rigid **decorums** I must demand of every colored male. They who so gravely taught me to split my body from my mind and both from my "soul," taught me also to split my conscience from my acts and Christianity from southern tradition.

9 Neither the Negro nor sex was often discussed at length in our home. We were given no formal instruction in these difficult matters but we learned our lessons well. We learned the intricate system of taboos, of **renunciations** and compensations, of manners, voice modulations, words, feelings, along with our prayers, our toilet habits, and our games. I do not remember how or when, but by the time I had learned that God is love, that Jesus is His Son and came to give us more abundant life, that all men are brothers with a common

SELECTION VOCABULARY

ambivalent / indeciso/a *adjective* having mixed feelings or uncertain emotions

dissonant / disonante *adjective* discordant or clashing COGNATE

archaic / arcaico/a *adjective* old, no longer in use COGNATE

decorum / el decoro *noun* polite social behavior COGNATE

renunciation / el repudio *noun* Rejection of a thing or idea

Father, I also knew that I was better than a Negro, that all black folks have their place and must be kept in it, that sex has its place and must be kept in it, that a terrifying disaster would befall the South if I ever treated a Negro as my social equal and as terrifying a disaster would befall my family if ever I were to have a baby outside of marriage. I had learned that God so loved the world that He gave His only begotten Son so that we might have segregated churches in which it was my duty to worship each Sunday and on Wednesday at evening prayers. I had learned that white southerners are a hospitable, courteous, tactful people who treat those of their own group with consideration and who as carefully segregate from all the richness of life "for their own good and welfare" thirteen million people whose skin is colored a little differently from my own.

Excerpted from *Killers Of The Dream* by Lillian Smith, published by W.W. Norton & Company.

WRITE

PERSONAL RESPONSE: Near the beginning of the passage, Smith says "The human heart dares not stay away too long from that which hurt it most." Do you agree with this claim? Do you think people are somehow drawn back to places, events, or circumstances that have hurt them in the past? Present your response to this idea using textual evidence as well as from your own life.

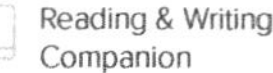

TEXT TALK

How did discussing the quotation deepen your understanding of the author's point of view?

Answers will vary.

B Ask each Beyond grade-level student to write one additional discussion question. Then, have one or two students facilitate a discussion, using their questions to guide the conversation.

Writer's Notebook

Connect to Essential Question: Give students time to reflect on how *Killers of the Dream* connects to the unit's essential question "What causes individuals to feel alienated?" by freewriting in their Writer's Notebooks.

CHECK FOR SUCCESS

If students are still struggling to respond to the prompt, ask them scaffolded questions, such as:

- How did Smith describe feeling alienated from her parents during her childhood?
- What contradictory messages did segregated churches give to southerners?

Reading Comprehension OPTIONAL

Have students complete the digital reading comprehension questions when they finish reading.

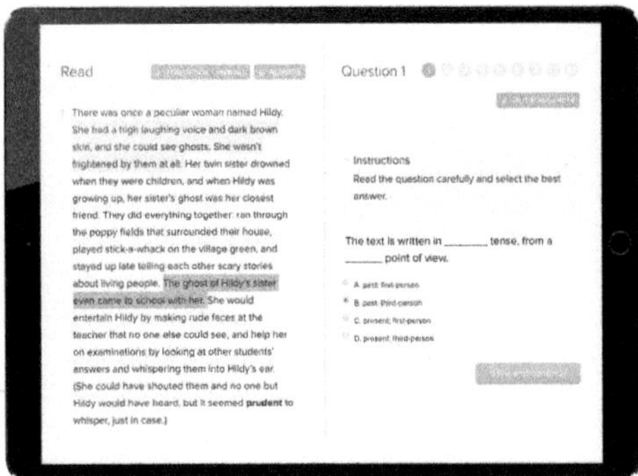

ANSWER KEY

QUESTION 1: B
QUESTION 2: A
QUESTION 3: C
QUESTION 4: C
QUESTION 5: A
QUESTION 6: C
QUESTION 7: B
QUESTION 8: D
QUESTION 9: *See first chart.*
QUESTION 10: *See second chart.*

Definition	Word
Old-fashioned and out of touch	archaic
Social conventions and expectations	decorum
Discordant or clashing	dissonant
Rejection of a thing or idea	renunciation
Possessing simultaneous, contradictory feelings	ambivalent

First	"But all knew that under quiet words and warmth and laughter, under the slow ease and tender concern about small matters, there was a heavy burden on all of us and as heavy a refusal to confess it."
Second	"Imaginations closed tight against the hurt of others; a regional armoring that took place to ward off the 'enemies' who would make our trouble different—or maybe rid us of it completely."
Third	"They who so gravely taught me to split my body from my mind and both from my 'soul,' taught me also to split my conscience from my acts and Christianity from southern tradition."
Fourth	"We were given no formal instruction in these difficult matters but we learned our lessons well. We learned the intricate system of taboos, of renunciations and compensations, of manners, voice modulations, words, feelings, along with our prayers, our toilet habits, and our games."

Connect and Extend OPTIONAL

CONNECT TO EXTENDED WRITING PROJECT

Have students analyze Smith's essay to identify of the causes and effects of her feeling of alienation from her home and family.

BEYOND THE BOOK

Game: Social Norms

The author, Lillian Smith, reflects on the negative childhood lessons she learned from her parents. Students will create a game that challenges players to think about the social and familial norms in other cultures.

Ask students to:

- Get in small groups and conduct informal research on social norms in various cultures. What are the social norms for:
  - > Interacting in public?
  - > Eating?
  - > Greeting people?
  - > Lining up?
  - > Students in school?
- Create a game that will challenge players to think about social norms from around the world.
  - > Choose the objective of the game.
  - > Decide on all the details (type of game, number of players, supplies needed, etc.).
  - > Create the game.
- Write detailed rules for the game.

Spend a class period playing all the group's games.

To reflect, ask students:

- How are social norms similar and different around the world?
- How do we learn the social norms expected of us?

Collaborative Conversation

SCAFFOLDS

Post the writing prompt to generate a discussion in small groups. Ask students to first break down the prompt before they discuss relevant ideas and textual evidence.

Near the beginning of the passage, Smith says "The human heart dares not stay away too long from that which hurt it most." Do you agree with this claim? Do you think people are somehow drawn back to places, events, or circumstances that have hurt them in the past? Present your response to this idea using textual evidence as well as from your own life.

Use the scaffolds below to differentiate instruction for your ELL English Language Learners and A Approaching grade-level learners.

ELL **BEGINNING, INTERMEDIATE** Use the discussion guide and speaking frames to facilitate the discussion with support from the teacher.

ADVANCED, ADVANCED HIGH Use the discussion guide and speaking frames to facilitate the discussion in mixed-level groups.

A APPROACHING Use the discussion guide to facilitate the discussion in mixed-level groups.

APPROACHING
ADVANCED, ADVANCED HIGH
BEGINNING, INTERMEDIATE

Discussion Guide	Speaking Frames
1. Do you agree that people are drawn to things that have caused them pain? Why or why not?	• I agree / disagree because ____. • Painful experiences shape people by ____.
2. What evidence from the text supports your ideas?	• Some text evidence that supports my ideas is ____. • It supports my ideas because ____.
3. What evidence from your own life supports your ideas?	• A story that supports my ideas is ____. • It supports my ideas because ____.

Ethical Issues

Use the activity below to differentiate instruction for your B Beyond grade level learners.

Reread paragraph 8:

They who so gravely taught me to split my body from my mind and both from my "soul," taught me also to split my conscience from my acts and Christianity from southern tradition.

Have students contemplate what they know about a scenario like this.

Ask students:

- What dilemmas or controversies are involved with exceptions to rules?
- How do Lillian Smith's ethics define who she is?

Review Prompt and Rubric

Before students begin writing, review the writing prompt and rubric with the class.

PERSONAL RESPONSE: Near the beginning of the passage, Smith says "The human heart dares not stay away too long from that which hurt it most." Do you agree with this claim? Do you think people are somehow drawn back to places, events, or circumstances that have hurt them in the past? Present your response to this idea using evidence from the text as well as from your own life.

PROMPT GUIDE

- Do you agree that people are drawn to things that have caused them pain? Why or why not?
- What evidence from the text supports your ideas?
- What evidence from your own life supports your ideas?

Score	Personal Response	Language and Conventions
4	The writer clearly explains his or her personal connection to the text, using relevant textual evidence as needed.	The writer demonstrates a consistent command of grammar, punctuation, and usage conventions. Although minor errors may be evident, they do not detract from the fluency or the clarity of the essay.
3	The writer sufficiently explains his or her personal connection to the text, using relevant textual evidence most of the time.	The writer demonstrates an adequate command of grammar, punctuation, and usage conventions. Although some errors may be evident, they create few (if any) disruptions in the fluency of the writing or the clarity of the essay.
2	The writer begins to explain his or her personal connection to the text, but the explanation is incomplete. The writer uses relevant textual evidence only some of the time.	The writer demonstrates a partial command of grammar, punctuation, and usage conventions. Some distracting errors may be evident, at times creating minor disruptions in the fluency or clarity of the writing.
1	The writer attempts to explain his or her personal connection to the text, but the explanation is not successful. The writer uses little or no relevant textual evidence.	The writer demonstrates little or no command of grammar, punctuation, and usage conventions. Serious and persistent errors create disruptions in the fluency of the writing and sometimes interfere with meaning.
0	The writer does not provide a relevant response to the prompt or does not provide a response at all.	Serious and persistent errors overwhelm the writing and interfere with the meaning of the response as a whole, making the writer's meaning impossible to understand.

Write

SCAFFOLDS

Ask students to complete the writing assignment using text evidence to support their answers.

Use the scaffolds below to differentiate instruction for your ELL English Language Learners and A Approaching grade level readers.

ELL **BEGINNING** With the help of the word bank, write a response using paragraph frame 1.

INTERMEDIATE With the help of the word bank, write a response using paragraph frames 1 and 2.

ADVANCED, ADVANCED HIGH Write a response of differentiated length using the sentence starters.

A **APPROACHING** Write a response of differentiated length using the sentence starters.

BEGINNING / INTERMEDIATE	BEGINNING / INTERMEDIATE	INTERMEDIATE	ADVANCED, ADVANCED HIGH / APPROACHING
Word Bank	**Paragraph Frame 1**	**Paragraph Frame 2**	**Sentence Starters**
healing harmful guilty conflicted school sibling friend cry sad learn	I agree / disagree that people are drawn to places, events, or circumstances that have hurt them. I think that recalling painful memories can be ____ because ____. The text says that Southerners feel ____. This reminds me of how I felt when ____. When I think about that time in my life, I ____.	Reading Smith's memoir made me realize ____. For example, when I read ____, I thought ____. This reminds me that most people ____.	• I agree / disagree with Smith because . . . • When I read . . . , I thought . . . • This memoir relates to . . . • This memoir made me realize . . .

Peer Review

Students should submit substantive feedback to two peers using the review instructions below.

- How well does this response answer the prompt?
- Which of the author's comments inspired you to think differently about the text?
- What did the writer do well in this response? What does the writer need to work on?

Rate

Respond to the following with a point rating that reflects your opinion.

	1	2	3	4
Ideas				
Evidence				
Language and Conventions				

Submit

ELL A **SENTENCE FRAMES**

- You were able to (completely / partly / almost) ____ answer the prompt.
- You could answer the prompt more completely by ____.
- I thought differently about the text after reading ____.
- My favorite part of your response is ____.

Shooting an Elephant

INFORMATIONAL TEXT
George Orwell
1936

Introduction

A British novelist, essayist and social commentator, George Orwell (1903–1950) often wrote about the complex and sometimes destructive relationship between a nation's government and its citizens. One of Orwell's most famous and influential works is *1984*, a dystopian novel set in a future where a totalitarian regime exerts almost complete control over the actions, feelings, and thoughts of its citizens. While touching on similar themes and political undertones, "Shooting an Elephant" is a short, autobiographical piece depicting Orwell's experiences living and working in Burma (known commonly today as Myanmar) in the early 1920s. These experiences would forever inform Orwell's views on imperialism, totalitarianism, and what it means to be truly free.

A young George Orwell spent five years as a police officer in Burma. One day, after an elephant had gone on a rampage in the bazaar, Orwell was called to restore order. At first, he was convinced it was a hoax, and only after finding a dead man trampled into the mud, did he call for an elephant rifle to be brought. When he came upon the elephant, peacefully eating grass from the field, Orwell had no urge to shoot it. Still he felt like he had no choice, since a crowd of over 2000 people had gathered behind him. He knew that as an Englishman in the East, he could not afford to look irresolute. So he aimed at the elephant's head and shot, sending five bullets into the body. It took over half an hour for the animal to die,; and although the owner was angry, he had no legal recourse since he was a local. On account of the dead man, Orwell faced no charges, since he did what he had to in order to restore peace.

 Proficiency-leveled summaries and summaries in multiple languages are available digitally.

 Audio and audio text highlighting are available with this text.

COMPARING WITHIN AND ACROSS GENRES

 Like Smith's *Killers Of The Dream*, the essay "Shooting an Elephant" stems from the author's first-hand experiences with confusing contradictions. George Orwell focuses on his time as a police officer in Burma (now Myanmar) in the 1920s when it was a British colony. Orwell uses a specific event to address the complexities, violence, and human costs of imperialism and oppression.

Entry Point

As students prepare to read "Shooting an Elephant," share the following information with them to provide context.

- ✓ At the time of the narrative, Britain had colonies across the globe. The holdings were so vast that Britons proclaimed "The sun never sets on the British Empire" because even as the sun went down in Britain, it was rising on British possessions elsewhere.
- ✓ Imperialism expanded British power and wealth and helped Britain gain access to new materials and markets. Burma was a particular prize. According to another essay by Orwell, Burma was "one of the richest [countries] in the world" in natural resources. Orwell named rubies, tin, petroleum, tungsten, and especially rice as valuable resources. "The British," Orwell concluded, "are robbing and pilfering Burma quite shamelessly."

Instructional Path

The print teacher's edition includes essential point-of-use instruction and planning tools. Complete lesson plans and program documents appear in your digital teacher account.

First Read: Shooting an Elephant

Objectives: After an initial reading and discussion of the autobiographical essay, students will be able to identify the narrator's conflicting thoughts about the event he describes, especially as they relate to his work as a representative of the British Empire.

Skill: Author's Purpose and Point of View

Objectives: After rereading and discussing a model of close reading, students will be able to explain and evaluate the author's purpose and point of view in "Shooting an Elephant."

Skill: Connotation and Denotation

Objectives: After rereading and discussing a model of close reading, students will be able to identify and analyze connotations and denotations.

Skill: Figurative Language

Objectives: After rereading and discussing a model of close reading, students will be able to analyze the meaning and purpose of figurative language in a text.

Close Read: Shooting an Elephant

Objectives: After engaging in a close reading and discussion of "Shooting an Elephant," students will be able to write a short response that uses an analysis of literary elements and figurative language to identify the author's point of view.

Skill: Analyzing Modernism

Objectives: After reading and discussing a model of close reading, students will be able to explain how a text from the unit reflects the literary period of Modernism.

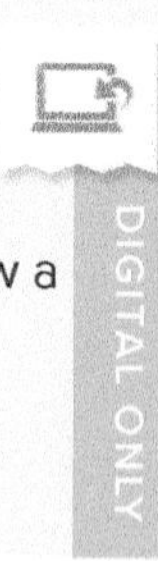

Progress Monitoring

Opportunities to Learn	Opportunities to Demonstrate Learning	Opportunities to Reteach
Author's Purpose and Point of View		
Skill: Author's Purpose and Point of View	Skill: Author's Purpose and Point of View • Your Turn Close Read • Skills Focus • Collaborative Conversation • Write	Spotlight Skill: Author's Purpose and Point of View
Connotation and Denotation		
Skill: Connotation and Denotation	Skill: Connotation and Denotation • Your Turn Close Read • Vocabulary Chart • Skills Focus • Write	Spotlight Skill: Connotation and Denotation
Figurative Language		
Skill: Figurative Language	Skill: Figurative Language • Your Turn Close Read • Vocabulary Chart • Skills Focus • Write	Spotlight Skill: Figurative Language

First Read

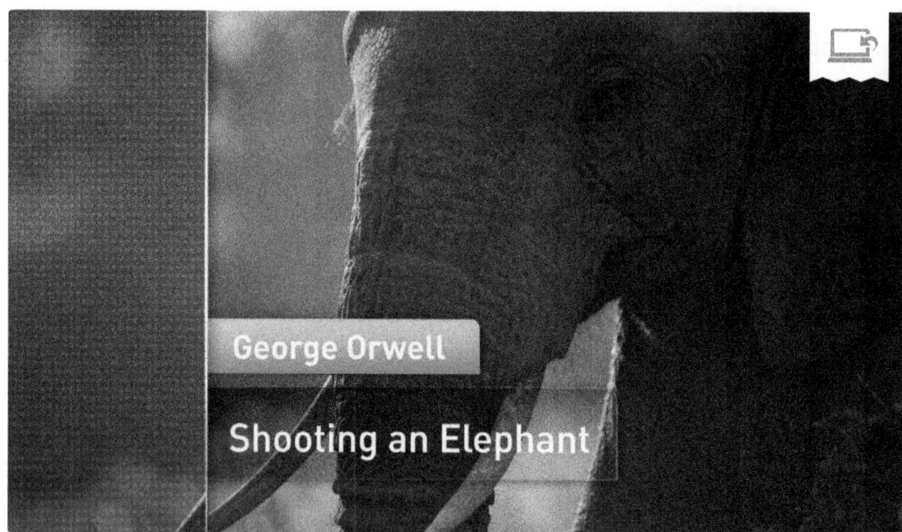

Introduce the Text

As a class, watch the video preview  and have students read the introduction in pairs to make connections to the video preview.

To activate prior knowledge and experiences, ask students:

- What was the most interesting part of the video, in your opinion?
- What choices have you made that may have seemed reasonable at the time but that you eventually came to regret?

ELL SPEAKING FRAMES

- The most interesting part of the video was ____.
- I once chose to ____. I would not do that again because ____.

Access Complex Text

LEXILE: 1070 WORD COUNT: 3,283

The following areas may be challenging for students, particularly  English Language Learners and  Approaching grade-level learners.

Connection of Ideas	Prior Knowledge
• Contemporary American readers may find it hard at times to discern Orwell's meaning; he is writing for early twentieth-century British readers familiar with topics such as imperialism and words like *sub-inspector, orderly,* and *sahib*. • Encourage students to use context clues to make inferences about words and events to be sure they understand Orwell's narrative.	• The term *imperialism* describes a system in which a country establishes colonies to increase its wealth and power. Imperial Britain colonized several countries, including India, Nigeria, Jamaica, and Burma. • Explain to students that imperial nations often establish military bases in their colonies and extract valuable resources from them.

 SCAFFOLDS  ENGLISH LANGUAGE LEARNERS  APPROACHING GRADE LEVEL  BEYOND GRADE LEVEL

These icons identify differentiation strategies and scaffolded support for a variety of students. See the digital lesson plan for additional differentiation strategies and scaffolds.

"In a job like that you see the dirty work of Empire at close quarters."

NOTES

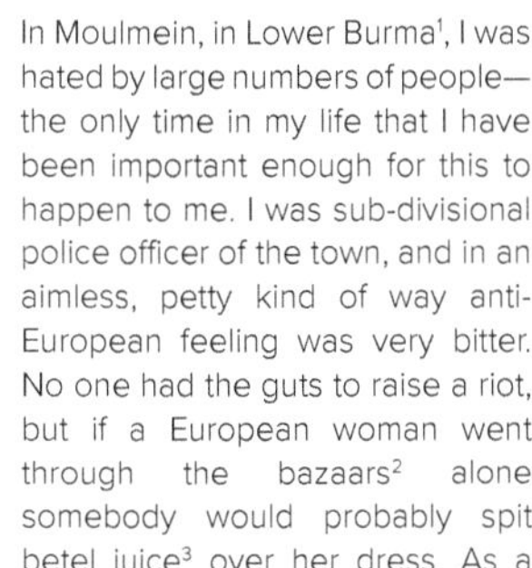

1 In Moulmein, in Lower Burma[1], I was hated by large numbers of people—the only time in my life that I have been important enough for this to happen to me. I was sub-divisional police officer of the town, and in an aimless, petty kind of way anti-European feeling was very bitter. No one had the guts to raise a riot, but if a European woman went through the bazaars[2] alone somebody would probably spit betel juice[3] over her dress. As a police officer I was an obvious target and was baited whenever it seemed safe to do so. When a nimble Burman tripped me up on the football field and the referee (another Burman) looked the other way, the crowd yelled with hideous laughter. This happened more than once. In the end the sneering yellow faces of young men that met me everywhere, the insults hooted after me when I was at a safe distance, got badly on my nerves. The young Buddhist[4] priests were the worst of all. There were several thousands of them in the town and none of them seemed to have anything to do except stand on street corners and jeer at Europeans.

Changing quarters in Upper Burma: baggage elephants arriving in camp, engraving by Paul Naumann from The Illustrated London News, No 2585, November 3, 1888.

2 All this was perplexing and upsetting. For at that time I had already made up my mind that imperialism was an evil thing and the sooner I chucked up my job and got out of it the better. Theoretically—and secretly, of course—I was all for the Burmese and all against their **oppressors**, the British. As for the job

1. **Lower Burma** the coastal area of Myanmar, formerly Burma, incorporated into the British Empire in 1852
2. **bazaars** open public markets where small producers, growers, and craftspeople sell their wares
3. **betel juice** the resulting liquid that is regularly spit out in the popular Southeast Asian habit of chewing betel leaves
4. **Buddhist** follower of Buddhism, a variety of spiritual practices based on teachings of Gautama Buddha, an Indian monk who lived between the 6th and 4th centuries B.C.

Developing Background Knowledge and Social Emotional Learning

Guide students as they find and discuss images related to the text.

1. Tell students to take a few minutes to search for images related to Burma under British rule.
2. In small groups, have students do a quick online search of images. Choose one or two to display and discuss as a class.

Discuss with students: Think of a time when what was expected or required of you conflicted with what you believed was just. How did you balance what was expected of you, and what you felt was "right"? How did you resolve the situation? After having some distance from it now, would you handle the situation differently? Why or why not?

Skills Focus

QUESTION 5: Essential Question

In the first passage, Orwell has no one to defend him—neither the crowd nor the referee—when he is tripped during a soccer game. In the second passage, Orwell describes how English people living in Asia could not even confide in each other regarding British imperialism.

SELECTION VOCABULARY

oppressor / opresor/a *noun* people or groups who use cruel or unjust power or authority over others COGNATE

TEXT TALK

Who is Orwell referring to when he uses the phrase "the evil-spirited little beasts"?

See paragraph 2: He means native Burmese who do not want the English in their country.

Author's Purpose and Point of View

How does the reader use vocabulary clues to identify Orwell's purpose in "Shooting an Elephant"?

The reader notices that the word "real" appears twice, both times in relation to imperialism, and concludes that Orwell's purpose is to show the reader the truth about the imperialist system.

Skills Focus

QUESTION 3: Figurative Language

The elephant could symbolize several things, but in this section it seems to symbolize the Burmese living under imperialism. The elephant is mostly "tame" but has the potential to lash out, just as the Burmese sometimes lash out at the British who subjugate them.

NOTES

I was doing, I hated it more bitterly than I can perhaps make clear. In a job like that you see the dirty work of Empire at close quarters. The wretched prisoners huddling in the stinking cages of the lock-ups, the grey, cowed faces of the long-term convicts, the scarred buttocks of the men who had been flogged with bamboos—all these oppressed me with an intolerable sense of guilt. But I could get nothing into perspective. I was young and ill-educated and I had had to think out my problems in the utter silence that is imposed on every Englishman in the East. I did not even know that the British Empire is dying, still less did I know that it is a great deal better than the younger empires that are going to supplant it. All I knew was that I was stuck between my hatred of the empire I served and my rage against the evil-spirited little beasts who tried to make my job impossible. With one part of my mind I thought of the British Raj[5] as an unbreakable tyranny, as something clamped down, *in saecula saeculorum*[6], upon the will of **prostrate** peoples; with another part I thought that the greatest joy in the world would be to drive a bayonet into a Buddhist priest's guts. Feelings like these are the normal by-products of imperialism; ask any Anglo-Indian official, if you can catch him off duty.

3 One day something happened which in a roundabout way was enlightening. It was a tiny incident in itself, but it gave me a better glimpse than I had had before of the real nature of imperialism— the real motives for which despotic governments act. Early one morning the sub-inspector at a police station the other end of the town rang me up on the phone and said that an elephant was ravaging the bazaar. Would I please come and do something about it? I did not know what I could do, but I wanted to see what was happening and I got on to a pony and started out. I took my rifle, an old .44 Winchester and much too small to kill an elephant, but I thought the noise might be useful *in terrorem*[7]. Various Burmans stopped me on the way and told me about the elephant's doings. It was not, of course, a wild elephant, but a tame one which had gone "must." It had been chained up, as tame elephants always are when their attack of "must" is due, but on the previous night it had broken its chain and escaped. Its mahout, the only person who could manage it when it was in that state, had set out in pursuit, but had taken the wrong direction and was now twelve hours' journey away, and in the morning the elephant had suddenly reappeared in the town. The Burmese population had no weapons and were quite helpless against it. It had already destroyed somebody's bamboo hut, killed a cow and raided some fruit-stalls and devoured the stock; also it had met the municipal rubbish van and, when the driver jumped out and took to his heels, had turned the van over and inflicted violences upon it.

Skill: Author's Purpose and Point of View

Orwell's purpose is to tell the truth about imperialism. The repetition of "real" shows he learned something he was trying to convince his readers of, too. This excerpt works because Orwell makes his intentions clear.

5. **the British Raj** the administration of the British Empire in colonial India, which consisted of the modern states of India, Pakistan, Afghanistan, Bangladesh and Myanmar (Burma) from 1858 to 1947
6. ***in saecula saeculorum*** a Latin phrase from the New Testament meaning "forever and ever"
7. ***in terrorem*** from the Latin, a threat or clause compelling someone to withdraw or avoid action

SELECTION VOCABULARY

prostrate / postrado/a *adjective* helpless or defenseless

NOTES

4 The Burmese sub-inspector and some Indian constables were waiting for me in the quarter where the elephant had been seen. It was a very poor quarter, a labyrinth of squalid bamboo huts, thatched with palmleaf, winding all over a steep hillside. I remember that it was a cloudy, stuffy morning at the beginning of the rains. We began questioning the people as to where the elephant had gone and, as usual, failed to get any definite information. That is invariably the case in the East; a story always sounds clear enough at a distance, but the nearer you get to the scene of events the vaguer it becomes. Some of the people said that the elephant had gone in one direction, some said that he had gone in another, some professed not even to have heard of any elephant. I had almost made up my mind that the whole story was a pack of lies, when we heard yells a little distance away. There was a loud, scandalized cry of "Go away, child! Go away this instant!" and an old woman with a switch in her hand came round the corner of a hut, violently shooing away a crowd of naked children. Some more women followed, clicking their tongues and exclaiming; evidently there was something that the children ought not to have seen. I rounded the hut and saw a man's dead body sprawling in the mud. He was an Indian, a black Dravidian coolie[8], almost naked, and he could not have been dead many minutes. The people said that the elephant had come suddenly upon him round the corner of the hut, caught him with its trunk, put its foot on his back and ground him into the earth. This was the rainy season and the ground was soft, and his face had scored a trench a foot deep and a couple of yards long. He was lying on his belly with arms crucified and head sharply twisted to one side. His face was coated with mud, the eyes wide open, the teeth bared and grinning with an expression of unendurable agony. (Never tell me, by the way, that the dead look peaceful. Most of the corpses I have seen looked devilish.) The friction of the great beast's foot had stripped the skin from his back as neatly as one skins a rabbit. As soon as I saw the dead man I sent an orderly to a friend's house nearby to borrow an elephant rifle. I had already sent back the pony, not wanting it to go mad with fright and throw me if it smelt the elephant.

Skill: Figurative Language

Orwell uses a simile here to help readers visualize what the dead man's back looked like. This also has the effect of demeaning the dead man and personifying the elephant, making its actions seem intentional and methodical.

5 The orderly came back in a few minutes with a rifle and five cartridges, and meanwhile some Burmans had arrived and told us that the elephant was in the paddy fields below, only a few hundred yards away. As I started forward practically the whole population of the quarter flocked out of the houses and followed me. They had seen the rifle and were all shouting excitedly that I was going to shoot the elephant. They had not shown much interest in the elephant when he was merely ravaging their homes, but it was different now that he was going to be shot. It was a bit of fun to them, as it would be to an English crowd; besides they wanted the meat. It made me vaguely uneasy. I had no intention of shooting the elephant—I had merely sent for the rifle to defend myself if necessary—and it is always unnerving to have a crowd following you. I marched down the hill, looking and feeling a fool, with the rifle over my shoulder and an ever-growing army of people **jostling** at my heels. At the bottom, when you got

8. **coolie** (derogatory) an indentured laborer

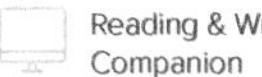

Figurative Language

How does Orwell's simile help the reader? What else does the simile do?

Orwell's simile helps the reader visualize the scene. It also demeans the dead man and personifies the elephant.

TEXT TALK

Why is Orwell reluctant to shoot the elephant at first?

See paragraph 6: Elephants are very valuable, and this elephant no longer seemed to be in a murderous rage.

SELECTION VOCABULARY

jostle / empujar *verb* to push against or collide with someone

Figurative Language

Which two things does Orwell compare the elephant to?

He compares the elephant to a costly piece of machinery and to a cow.

Connotation and Denotation

What does the student think about the meaning of *condition*?

The student is familiar with one meaning of the word but isn't sure if that's the meaning Orwell intends to convey here.

NOTES

away from the huts, there was a metalled road and beyond that a **miry** waste of paddy fields a thousand yards across, not yet ploughed but soggy from the first rains and dotted with coarse grass. The elephant was standing eight yards from the road, his left side towards us. He took not the slightest notice of the crowd's approach. He was tearing up bunches of grass, beating them against his knees to clean them and stuffing them into his mouth.

6 I had halted on the road. As soon as I saw the elephant I knew with perfect certainty that I ought not to shoot him. It is a serious matter to shoot a working elephant—it is comparable to destroying a huge and costly piece of machinery—and obviously one ought not to do it if it can possibly be avoided. And at that distance, peacefully eating, the elephant looked no more dangerous than a cow. I thought then and I think now that his attack of "must" was already passing off; in which case he would merely wander harmlessly about until the mahout came back and caught him. Moreover, I did not in the least want to shoot him. I decided that I would watch him for a little while to make sure that he did not turn savage again, and then go home.

Skill: Figurative Language

Here Orwell compares the elephant to two things: machinery and a cow. Like machinery, the elephant is very valuable in Burmese society. And like a cow, the elephant does not appear to be a threat.

7 But at that moment I glanced round at the crowd that had followed me. It was an immense crowd, two thousand at the least and growing every minute. It blocked the road for a long distance on either side. I looked at the sea of yellow faces above the garish clothes-faces all happy and excited over this bit of fun, all certain that the elephant was going to be shot. They were watching me as they would watch a conjurer about to perform a trick. They did not like me, but with the magical rifle in my hands I was momentarily worth watching. And suddenly I realized that I should have to shoot the elephant after all. The people expected it of me and I had got to do it; I could feel their two thousand wills pressing me forward, irresistibly. And it was at this moment, as I stood there with the rifle in my hands, that I first grasped the hollowness, the futility of the white man's dominion in the East. Here was I, the white man with his gun, standing in front of the unarmed native crowd—seemingly the leading actor of the piece; but in reality I was only an absurd puppet pushed to and fro by the will of those yellow faces behind. I perceived in this moment that when the white man turns tyrant it is his own freedom that he destroys. He becomes a sort of hollow, posing dummy, the conventionalized figure of a sahib[9]. For it is the condition of his rule that he shall spend his life in trying to impress the "natives," and so in every crisis he has got to do what the "natives" expect of him. He wears a mask, and his face grows to fit it. I had got to shoot the elephant. I had committed myself to doing it when I sent for the rifle. A sahib has got to act like a sahib; he has got to appear resolute, to know his own mind and do definite things. To come all that way, rifle in hand, with two thousand people marching at my heels, and then to trail feebly away, having done nothing—no, that was impossible. The crowd would laugh at me. And my whole life, every white man's life in the East, was one long struggle not to be laughed at.

Skill: Connotation and Denotation

I know condition can mean the state of something, such as how well it functions. While this meaning works here, it seems Orwell is trying to connote or denote another meaning because the previous sentence has a negative tone.

9. **Sahib** honorific term used a sign of respect in British India, derived from Arabic, meaning "young prince"

SELECTION VOCABULARY

miry / fangoso/a *adjective* soggy or muddy

NOTES

8 But I did not want to shoot the elephant. I watched him beating his bunch of grass against his knees, with that preoccupied grandmotherly air that elephants have. It seemed to me that it would be murder to shoot him. At that age I was not squeamish about killing animals, but I had never shot an elephant and never wanted to. (Somehow it always seems worse to kill a large animal.) Besides, there was the beast's owner to be considered. Alive, the elephant was worth at least a hundred pounds; dead, he would only be worth the value of his tusks, five pounds, possibly. But I had got to act quickly. I turned to some experienced-looking Burmans who had been there when we arrived, and asked them how the elephant had been behaving. They all said the same thing: he took no notice of you if you left him alone, but he might charge if you went too close to him.

9 It was perfectly clear to me what I ought to do. I ought to walk up to within, say, twenty-five yards of the elephant and test his behavior. If he charged, I could shoot; if he took no notice of me, it would be safe to leave him until the mahout came back. But also I knew that I was going to do no such thing. I was a poor shot with a rifle and the ground was soft mud into which one would sink at every step. If the elephant charged and I missed him, I should have about as much chance as a toad under a steam-roller. But even then I was not thinking particularly of my own skin, only of the watchful yellow faces behind. For at that moment, with the crowd watching me, I was not afraid in the ordinary sense, as I would have been if I had been alone. A white man mustn't be frightened in front of "natives"; and so, in general, he isn't frightened. The sole thought in my mind was that if anything went wrong those two thousand Burmans would see me pursued, caught, trampled on and reduced to a grinning corpse like that Indian up the hill. And if that happened it was quite probable that some of them would laugh. That would never do.

Skill: Author's Purpose and Point of View

I thought he would be most afraid of being "trampled on" by the elephant. Instead, he's more concerned with being humiliated than being killed. This point of view is effective because it is unexpected, which makes it memorable.

10 There was only one alternative. I shoved the cartridges into the magazine and lay down on the road to get a better aim. The crowd grew very still, and a deep, low, happy sigh, as of people who see the theatre curtain go up at last, breathed from innumerable throats. They were going to have their bit of fun after all. The rifle was a beautiful German thing with cross-hair sights. I did not then know that in shooting an elephant one would shoot to cut an imaginary bar running from ear-hole to ear-hole. I ought, therefore, as the elephant was sideways on, to have aimed straight at his ear-hole, actually I aimed several inches in front of this, thinking the brain would be further forward.

11 When I pulled the trigger I did not hear the bang or feel the kick—one never does when a shot goes home—but I heard the devilish roar of glee that went up from the crowd. In that instant, in too short a time, one would have thought, even for the bullet to get there, a mysterious, terrible change had come over the elephant. He neither stirred nor fell, but every line of his body had altered. He looked suddenly stricken, shrunken, immensely old, as though the frightful impact of the bullet had paralysed him without knocking him down. At last, after what seemed a long time —it might have been five seconds, I dare

Author's Purpose and Point of View

What does the reader conclude about Orwell's point of view?

The reader finds Orwell's point of view memorable because it is not what he expected and because he thinks that Orwell states his point of view very clearly.

Skills Focus

QUESTION 1: Summarizing

Although Orwell believes he has to shoot the elephant to avoid losing face, he believes that doing so would otherwise be pointless. This highlights the theme that it's not always easy to do the right thing.

Skills Focus

QUESTION 4: Author's Purpose and Point of View

Orwell's purpose here is to convey to the reader just how grim, even grotesque, the elephant's death is. His description is extremely effective. I almost wanted to stop reading, just as Orwell wanted to escape the experience.

Prepare for Advanced Courses

Use the activity below to differentiate instruction for your B Beyond grade level learners.

Author's Syntax

Consider the syntax in paragraph 7:

Here was I, the white man with his gun, standing in front of the unarmed native crowd—seemingly the leading actor of the piece; but in reality I was only an absurd puppet pushed to and fro by the will of those yellow faces behind.

Have students examine how Orwell"s syntax reflects his purpose.

Ask students:

- What does the dash indicate?
- How does the syntax convey voice and tone?

NOTES

say—he sagged flabbily to his knees. His mouth slobbered. An enormous senility seemed to have settled upon him. One could have imagined him thousands of years old. I fired again into the same spot. At the second shot he did not collapse but climbed with desperate slowness to his feet and stood weakly upright, with legs sagging and head drooping. I fired a third time. That was the shot that did for him. You could see the agony of it jolt his whole body and knock the last remnant of strength from his legs. But in falling he seemed for a moment to rise, for as his hind legs collapsed beneath him he seemed to tower upward like a huge rock toppling, his trunk reaching skyward like a tree. He trumpeted, for the first and only time. And then down he came, his belly towards me, with a crash that seemed to shake the ground even where I lay.

12 I got up. The Burmans were already racing past me across the mud. It was obvious that the elephant would never rise again, but he was not dead. He was breathing very rhythmically with long rattling gasps, his great mound of a side painfully rising and falling. His mouth was wide open—I could see far down into caverns of pale pink throat. I waited a long time for him to die, but his breathing did not weaken. Finally I fired my two remaining shots into the spot where I thought his heart must be. The thick blood welled out of him like red velvet, but still he did not die. His body did not even jerk when the shots hit him, the tortured breathing continued without a pause. He was dying, very slowly and in great agony, but in some world remote from me where not even a bullet could damage him further. I felt that I had got to put an end to that dreadful noise. It seemed dreadful to see the great beast lying there, powerless to move and yet powerless to die, and not even to be able to finish him. I sent back for my small rifle and poured shot after shot into his heart and down his throat. They seemed to make no impression. The tortured gasps continued as steadily as the ticking of a clock.

13 In the end I could not stand it any longer and went away. I heard later that it took him half an hour to die. Burmans were bringing dahs and baskets even before I left, and I was told they had stripped his body almost to the bones by the afternoon.

14 Afterwards, of course, there were endless discussions about the shooting of the elephant. The owner was furious, but he was only an Indian and could do nothing. Besides, legally I had done the right thing, for a mad elephant has to be killed, like a mad dog, if its owner fails to control it. Among the Europeans opinion was divided. The older men said I was right, the younger men said it was a damn shame to shoot an elephant for killing a coolie, because an elephant was worth more than any damn Coringhee coolie[10]. And afterwards I was very glad that the coolie had been killed; it put me legally in the right and it gave me a sufficient **pretext** for shooting the elephant. I often wondered whether any of the others grasped that I had done it solely to avoid looking a fool.

10. **Coringhee coolie** a laborer who has migrated from Southern India, or Coringhee

TEXT TALK

How has discussing imperialism deepened your understanding of "Shooting an Elephant"?

Answers will vary.

How did discussing moments of conflict between what is expected of you and what you know is right deepen your understanding of "Shooting an Elephant"?

Answers will vary.

B Ask each Beyond grade- level student to write one additional discussion question. Then, have one or two students facilitate a discussion, using their questions to guide the conversation.

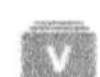

SELECTION VOCABULARY

pretext / el pretexto ***noun*** a false reason or excuse given to hide the real reason for doing something COGNATE

Reading Comprehension OPTIONAL

Have students complete the digital reading comprehension questions when they finish reading.

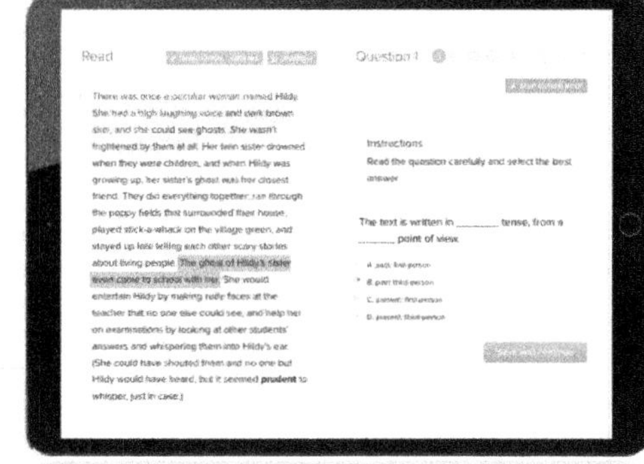

ANSWER KEY

QUESTION 1: A
QUESTION 2: C
QUESTION 3: C
QUESTION 4: B
QUESTION 5: D
QUESTION 6: B
QUESTION 7: A
QUESTION 8: A
QUESTION 9: *See first chart.*
QUESTION 10: *See second chart.*

Action	Character
Sent an orderly to bring back a more powerful weapon	The narrator
Died a slow and excruciating death	The elephant
Chased a small crowd of children away from the dead body	An old woman
Traveled in the wrong direction and was now twelve hours away	The elephant's mahout

First	Second	Third	Fourth
A sub-inspector telephones the narrator and informs him that an elephant is loose in the bazaar.	The narrator discovers a dead body half-buried in some mud.	The elephant is found in a paddy field lazily eating bunches of grass.	The narrator is cleared of any wrongdoing for his actions.

Connect and Extend OPTIONAL

CONNECT TO EXTENDED WRITING PROJECT

Students can use "Shooting an Elephant" as inspiration when writing their Extended Writing Project. As they work on their literary analysis paper, they may discuss Orwell's technique of showing alienation through a character's discomfort in a foreign land.

BEYOND THE BOOK

Infographic: Imperialism

George Orwell writes about a memory he had while working for the British in Burma. He tells the story of shooting an elephant and how it gave him insight into the nature of imperialism. Students will choose one example of imperialism to research. Ask students to:

- Form small groups.
- Choose an example of imperialism from history to research in depth.
  - When and where did this imperialism take place?
  - Who seized control, and who was controlled?
  - What motivated the country in control to seize power? What did they gain?
  - What impact did imperialization have on the culture, freedom, government, etc., of the subjugated people?
- Organize the information in an infographic that combines facts, figures, and images to explain the topic.
- Share infographics with the class. Ask students:
- What are some common political motives for imperialism?
- Can imperialism ever benefit the people who are subjugated?

Think Questions

Circulate as students answer Think Questions independently. Scaffolds for these questions are shown on the opposite page.

QUESTION 1: Textual Evidence

Orwell was hated because he was a representative of an imperialist culture who had authority over colonized people. As he writes, "As a police officer I was an obvious target and was baited whenever it seemed safe to do so."

QUESTION 2: Textual Evidence

Orwell has no one to talk to about his difficult situation. He does not trust the Burmese people, who he rightly believes do not like him or what he stands for, and he does not seem to feel supported by the British leaders who outrank him.

QUESTION 3: Textual Evidence

Although Orwell did not want to kill the elephant, he felt that the Burmese people who were watching him expected him to kill it. If the elephant had not killed someone, he would not have had as much legal right or "sufficient pretext" to do so.

QUESTION 4: Context Clues

In the sentence immediately before the one containing *oppressors*, Orwell says that "imperialism was an evil thing." In the next couple sentences, he offers examples of people in authority mistreating others. I think *oppressors* must mean "people with power who treat other people unfairly."

QUESTION 5: Word Patterns and Relationships

If *myrr* means "bog" or "swamp," then *miry* sounds like it might be an adjective form of that word and should therefore mean "like a bog or a swamp." Because bogs and swamps are muddy and wet, *miry* most likely means "land that is muddy or wet." I checked a dictionary and found that the word means "very muddy or boggy."

First Read

Read "Shooting an Elephant." After you read, complete the Think Questions below.

THINK QUESTIONS

1. According to Orwell, he was "hated by large numbers of people" during his time in Burma. Why was he so hated? Support your answer using textual evidence.
2. Referring to information that is directly stated or implied, what does Orwell mean when he says he "had to think out my problems in utter silence?"
3. In two or three sentences, explain why Orwell was "very glad" the elephant had killed someone.
4. Use context clues to determine the meaning of the word **oppressors** as it is used in the text. Write your definition of *oppressors* here and explain how you figured it out.
5. Keeping in mind that the Old Norse word *myrr* means "bog" or "swamp," determine the meaning of **miry** as it is used in the text. Write your definition of *miry* here. Then check your inferred meaning in a print or digital library.

 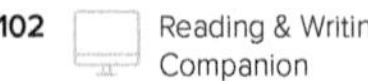

SCAFFOLDS

Think Questions

Use the scaffolds below to differentiate instruction for your ELL English Language Learners and A Approaching grade level readers.

ELL **BEGINNING** Write a response using the word bank and sentence frames.

INTERMEDIATE Write a response using the sentence frames.

ADVANCED, ADVANCED HIGH Write a response using the Text-Dependent Question Guide.

A **APPROACHING** Write a response using the Text-Dependent Question Guide.

BEGINNING	INTERMEDIATE	APPROACHING / ADVANCED, ADVANCED HIGH
Word Bank	**Sentence Frames**	**Text-Dependent Question Guide**
trust assume muddy legal glad authority feelings talk to expected imperialism	The Burmese hated Orwell because he was British and had ____ over the Burmese. The Burmese did not want the British around and made their ____ clear.	1. • What is Orwell's job? • What country is Orwell from? • Why is Orwell in Burma? • How do the Burmese people feel about the British? Why?
	Orwell means that he has no one to ____ about the problems he has. The Burmese people do not ____ him, and he does not trust the other British people in the country.	2. • How does Orwell feel about being in Burma? • Does he like and trust the Burmese people? Will he talk to them? • Does he like and trust the other British people? Will he talk to them?
	Although Orwell did not want to kill the elephant, he felt that the Burmese people who were watching him ____ Orwell to kill it. Orwell was ____ that the death of the Indian man gave Orwell the ____ right to shoot the elephant.	3. • What do the people following Orwell want him to do? • How will they feel if Orwell does not shoot the elephant? What will they do? • How will Orwell feel if the people react that way? • Why is it legally permissible for Orwell to kill the elephant?
	Orwell says that "____ was an evil thing." He also states that he is "all for the Burmese and all against their oppressors, the British." So I can ____ that being an oppressor has something in common with being evil and powerful.	4. • Read the first six sentences of paragraph two. • Who was in charge of Burma at this time? • What were the British doing to the Burmese? • Were the British acting fairly or unfairly? • What does this say about the meaning of *oppressors*?
	Myrr has to do with swamps, so *miry* probably means "____" or "wet."	5. • Read: "At the bottom, when you got away from the huts, there was a metalled road and beyond that a **miry** waste of paddy fields a thousand yards across . . ." • *Miry* comes after the consonant *a* and before the noun *waste*, so what part of speech do you think it is? • What does the Old Norse word *myrr* mean? • What does a swamp or a bog look like? • What is most important about a swamp? • What does that say about the meaning of the word *miry*?

Skill: Author's Purpose and Point of View

Introduce the Skill

Watch the Concept Definition video and read the following definition with your students.

Author's purpose is the author's reason for writing. Authors typically write for one or more of the following purposes: to entertain, to inform, to persuade, or to explain something to readers. The **author's point of view** refers to the way the author looks at a topic or a subject, and his or her attitude toward it. In order to fully understand an author's purpose for writing, it is often necessary to identify the author's point of view on the subject he or she has chosen to write about, including how it is conveyed or expressed in the text. Sometimes an author's point of view is directly stated. When it is implied, the reader will need to look at textual evidence to infer the author's point of view.

Skill: Author's Purpose and Point of View

Use the Checklist to analyze Author's Purpose and Point of View in "Shooting an Elephant." Refer to the sample student annotations about Author's Purpose and Point of View in the text.

••• CHECKLIST FOR AUTHOR'S PURPOSE AND POINT OF VIEW

In order to identify author's purpose and point of view, note the following:

- ✓ whether the writer is attempting to establish trust by citing his or her experience or education
- ✓ whether the evidence the author provides is convincing and that the argument or position is logical
- ✓ what words and phrases the author uses to appeal to the emotions
- ✓ the author's use of rhetoric, or the art of speaking and writing persuasively, such as the use of repetition to drive home a point as well as allusion and alliteration
- ✓ the author's use of rhetoric to contribute to the power, persuasiveness, or beauty of the text

To determine the author's purpose and point of view, consider the following questions:

- ✓ How does the author try to convince me that he or she has something valid and important for me to read?
- ✓ What words or phrases express emotion or invite an emotional response? How or why are they effective or ineffective?
- ✓ What words and phrases contribute to the power, persuasiveness, or beauty of the text? Is the author's use of rhetoric successful? Why or why not?

TURN AND TALK

1. Think of a nonfiction book, article, or essay you have read recently. Why do you think the author wrote it?
2. What was the main point of view the author wanted their audience to grasp? How do you know?

SPEAKING FRAMES

- I recently read ____. I think the author wrote it because ____.
- The main point of view was ____.

SKILL VOCABULARY

author's purpose / el propósito del autor ***noun*** an author's reason for writing, such as to entertain, to inform, or to persuade

author's point of view / el punto de vista del autor ***noun*** the way an author looks at a topic or subject, and his or her attitude toward it

Skill: Author's Purpose and Point of View

Reread paragraphs 12–14 of "Shooting an Elephant." Then, using the Checklist on the previous page, answer the multiple-choice questions below.

YOUR TURN

1. Orwell's point of view in paragraphs 12–13 is effective because—

   - A. it shows the reader how awful it was to watch the elephant die.
   - B. it gets the reader to understand that killing elephants requires great skill.
   - C. it explains to the reader why it was essential to kill the elephant.
   - D. it invites the reader to share Orwell's excitement upon seeing the elephant.

2. How does the information in Paragraph 14 reinforce Orwell's purpose for writing this text?

   - A. Orwell explains how the older and younger European men he talked to had different opinions about his actions.
   - B. Orwell explains how he was justified in killing the elephant because its owner had not done a good job of controlling it.
   - C. Orwell reinforces the horrible reality of colonialism by reducing the killing of the elephant to being a legal issue.
   - D. Orwell reinforces his point that Europeans and Burmans have different opinions on colonialism.

Your Turn

Ask students to complete the Your Turn Activity.

QUESTION 1

A. Correct. The details in these paragraphs all show Orwell's disgust at having to watch the elephant die slowly and in increasing agony.

B. Incorrect. Although Orwell recognizes that he was not especially skilled at shooting an elephant, that is not the purpose of these paragraphs.

C. Incorrect. Orwell has already explained why he needed to kill the elephant and does not repeat his reasoning in this section.

D. Incorrect. Orwell had seen the elephant for the first time several paragraphs earlier in the text, and he never expresses any particular excitement about seeing it.

QUESTION 2

A. Incorrect. Although there was a generational difference in the reactions of the Europeans Orwell talked to, this does not relate to the author's larger purpose about colonialism.

B. Incorrect. Orwell recognizes that the legal system justified the shooting, but this answer does not effectively relate this to Orwell's larger point of view or purpose.

C. Correct. In this paragraph, Orwell expresses his ambivalence about the entire incident, and notes that he was "legally in the right" even though his real reason for shooting was to avoid embarrassment.

D. Incorrect. This is a basic point that Orwell takes as given fact, not the purpose he is trying to convince his readers of.

Skill: Connotation and Denotation

Introduce the Skill

Watch the Concept Definition video and read the following definition with your students.

The **denotation** of a word is its dictionary definition. The **connotation** of a word is the idea or feeling that a word suggests, or that our culture or our emotions give the word. A word's connotation can be positive, negative, or neutral. For example, the words *cheap* and *affordable* both denote "inexpensive." However, *cheap* connotes something that is of low quality.

To determine the connotation of a word, readers must use **context**, such as the genre or subject of a text. They also use **context clues**, or the surrounding words that help a reader determine a word's meaning. To verify the denotation of a word and check for possible connotations, readers can consult reference materials such as dictionaries, glossaries, and thesauruses. To **analyze** an author's word choices, readers consider the emotional impact of language in the text for its potential effect on readers.

TURN AND TALK

1. Which words can you think of that have very strong positive or negative connotations?
2. Can you think of any contexts in which these words would have the opposite connotation?

SPEAKING FRAMES

- One word that has a very strong positive connotation is ____.
- One word that has a very strong negative connotation is ____.
- ____ could have the opposite connotation if ____.

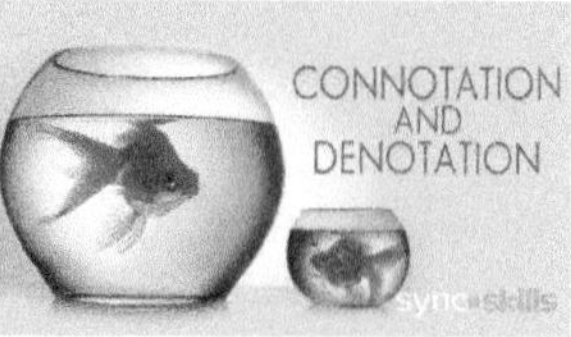

Skill: Connotation and Denotation

Use the Checklist to analyze Connotation and Denotation in "Shooting an Elephant." Refer to the sample student annotations about Connotation and Denotation in the text.

••• CHECKLIST FOR CONNOTATION AND DENOTATION

In order to identify the denotative meanings of words, use the following steps:

- ✓ first, note unfamiliar words and phrases, key words used to describe important individuals, events, or ideas, or words that inspire an emotional reaction
- ✓ next, determine and note the denotative meaning of words by consulting a reference material such as a dictionary, glossary, or thesaurus
- ✓ finally, analyze nuances in the meaning of words with similar denotations

To better understand the meaning of words and phrases as they are used in a text, including connotative meanings, use the following questions as a guide:

- ✓ What is the genre or subject of the text? Based on context, what do you think the meaning of the word is intended to be?
- ✓ Is your inference the same or different from the dictionary definition?
- ✓ Does the word create a positive, negative, or neutral emotion?
- ✓ What synonyms or alternative phrasing help you describe the connotative meaning of the word?

To determine the meaning of words and phrases as they are used in a text, including connotative meanings, use the following questions as a guide:

- ✓ What is the denotative meaning of the word? Is that denotative meaning correct in context?
- ✓ What possible positive, neutral, or negative connotations might the word have, depending on context?
- ✓ What textual evidence signals a particular connotation for the word?

SKILL VOCABULARY

denotation / la denotación *noun* the literal or dictionary meaning of a word, in contrast to the feelings or ideas that the word suggests COGNATE

connotation / la connotación *noun* an idea or feeling that a word suggests in addition to its literal or primary meaning COGNATE

context / el contexto *noun* the set of facts or circumstances that surround a situation or event COGNATE

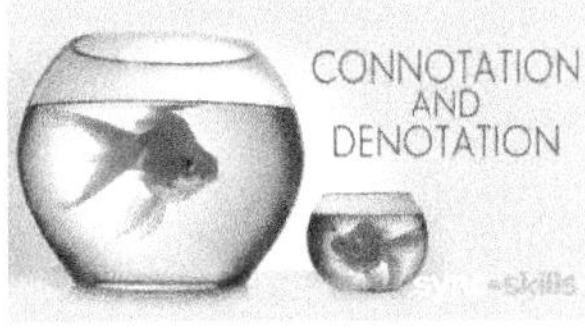

Skill: Connotation and Denotation

Reread paragraph 8 of "Shooting an Elephant." Then, using the Checklist on the previous page, answer the multiple-choice questions below.

YOUR TURN

1. What is the most likely connotation of "preoccupied grandmotherly air"?
   - ○ A. Negative: The elephant is being described as annoying.
   - ○ B. Positive: The elephant is being described as gentle and caring.
   - ○ C. Positive: The elephant is being described as wise and funny.
   - ○ D. Neutral: The elephant is being described simply as an animal.

2. What is the most likely reason Orwell uses "beast" to describe the elephant?
   - ○ A. Orwell wants to convey that the elephant could still be used to help the villagers.
   - ○ B. Orwell wants to convey that the elephant has been terribly mistreated by the mahout.
   - ○ C. After personifying the elephant, Orwell is telling the reader that it is still evil.
   - ○ D. After personifying the elephant, Orwell is reminding the reader that it is still an animal.

Your Turn

Ask students to complete the Your Turn Activity.

QUESTION 1

A. Incorrect. The phrase has a positive connotation here.

B. Correct. This is the feeling Orwell is trying to suggest.

C. Incorrect. Nothings suggests that the elephant seemed wise or funny to Orwell.

D. Incorrect. Orwell is saying more than that here.

QUESTION 2

A. Incorrect. There is no evidence that this is what Orwell is trying to convey.

B. Incorrect. There is no evidence that the mahout mistreated the elephant.

C. Incorrect. There is no evidence that Orwell thinks the elephant is evil.

D. Correct. Orwell wants the reader to know that despite the elephant's grandmotherly bearing, it is still an animal.

SELECTION VOCABULARY

context clue / la clave del contexto *noun* a hint in the surrounding text that can help a reader infer the meaning of an unfamiliar word, phrase, or description

analyze / analizar *verb* to consider in detail and discover essential features or meaning COGNATE

Skill: Figurative Language

Introduce the Skill

Watch the Concept Definition video and read the following definition with your students.

Figurative language is language used for descriptive effect, often to illustrate or imply ideas indirectly. Types of figurative language include simile, metaphor, and personification. A simile uses the words like or as to compare two seemingly unlike things. A **metaphor** directly compares two seemingly unlike things without using like or as. **Personification** is a **figure of speech** in which an animal, object, force of nature, or an idea is given human qualities.

When reading prose, and especially poetry, readers use **context**—including when and where a text was written, for example—to analyze the impact of word choice and to help determine or interpret the meaning of figurative words and phrases.

TURN AND TALK

1. What is an example of figurative language you have read or heard?

2. Why do you think a writer of an informational text would use figurative language?

SPEAKING FRAMES

- I read/heard figurative language in ____. The figurative language was ____.
- A writer of an informational text might use figurative language to ____.

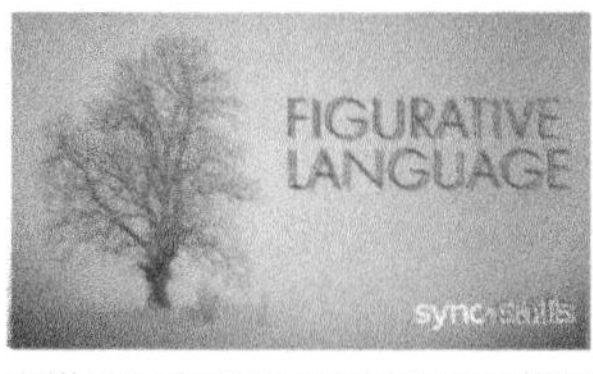

Skill: Figurative Language

Use the Checklist to analyze Figurative Language in "Shooting an Elephant ." Refer to the sample student annotations about Figurative Language in the text.

••• CHECKLIST FOR FIGURATIVE LANGUAGE

In order to determine the meaning of figurative language in context, note the following:

- ✓ words that mean one thing literally and suggest something else
- ✓ similes, metaphors, or personification
- ✓ figures of speech, including
  - paradoxes, or a seemingly contradictory statement that when further investigated or explained proves to be true, such as
    - > a character described as "a wise fool"
    - > a character stating, "I must be cruel to be kind"
  - hyperbole, or exaggerated statements not meant to be taken literally, such as
    - > a child saying, "I'll be doing this homework until I'm 100!"
    - > a claim such as, "I'm so hungry I could eat a horse!"

In order to interpret figurative language in context and analyze its role in the text, consider the following questions:

- ✓ Where is there figurative language in the text and what seems to be the purpose of the author's use of it?
- ✓ Why does the author use a figure of speech rather than literal language?
- ✓ What impact does exaggeration or hyperbole have on your understanding of the text?
- ✓ Where are there examples of paradoxes and how do they affect the meaning in the text?
- ✓ Which phrases contain references that seem contradictory?
- ✓ Where are contradictory words and phrases used to enhance the reader's understanding of the character, object, or idea?
- ✓ How does the figurative language develop the message or theme of the literary work?

SKILL VOCABULARY

figurative language / el lenguaje figurativo *noun* expressions used for descriptive or rhetorical effect that are not literally true but that express some truth beyond the literal level COGNATE

simile / el símil *noun* a figure of speech that uses the words like or as to compare two seemingly unlike things COGNATE

metaphor / la metáfora *noun* an a figure of speech that compares two seemingly unlike things but implies a comparison instead of stating it directly with the words like or as COGNATE

Skill: Figurative Language

Reread paragraph 7 of "Shooting an Elephant." Then, using the Checklist on the previous page, answer the multiple-choice questions below.

YOUR TURN

1. What is the best explanation of the simile "as they would watch a conjurer about to perform a trick"?

- A. The Burmese people are treating this experience as a kind of entertainment.
- B. The Burmese people are hoping that Orwell will make the elephant disappear.
- C. The Burmese people believe that Orwell is a kind of magician.
- D. The Burmese people believe that rifles are magical tools.

2. This question has two parts. First, answer Part A. Then, answer Part B.

Part A: What does the figurative language in this paragraph indicate the speaker is feeling at this moment?

- A. The speaker feels that the elephant is in complete control of the situation and is about to attack him.
- B. The speaker feels that he has lost control of the situation and is about to be attacked by the Burmese people.
- C. The speaker feels that the situation is in his control rather than in the control of the Burmese people.
- D. The speaker feels that the situation is in the control of the Burmese people rather than in his control.

Part B: Which simile or metaphor best supports your answer to Part A?

- A. ". . . with the magical rifle in my hands I was momentarily worth watching."
- B. ". . . the futility of the white man's dominion in the East."
- C. "Here was I, the white man with his gun, standing in front of the unarmed native crowd . . ."
- D. "I was only an absurd puppet pushed to and fro by the will of those yellow faces behind."

SKILL VOCABULARY

personification / la personificación *noun* a figure of speech in which an animal, object, force of nature, or an idea is given human form or qualities COGNATE

figure of speech / la figura literaria *noun* a word or phrase not meant to be taken literally, but rather used for effect

context / el contexto *noun* the set of facts or circumstances that surround a situation or event COGNATE

Your Turn

Ask students to complete the Your Turn Activity.

QUESTION 1

A. Correct. This is what Orwell means when he says he is "momentarily worth watching."

B. Incorrect. The Burmese people do not think Orwell can do this, nor do they want him to.

C. Incorrect. The Burmese people know that Orwell is nothing like a magician.

D. Incorrect. Orwell is using figurative language when he refers to the rifle as "magical."

QUESTION 2

Part A

A. Incorrect. Nothing in the passage indicates that the speaker feels the elephant is in control or that it will attack him.

B. Incorrect. Nothing in the passage indicates that the speaker feels he is about to be attacked by the Burmese people.

C. Incorrect. This is the opposite of what the speaker is feeling.

D. Correct. Orwell believes that the people in the crowd have more control of the situation than he does.

Part B

A. Incorrect. The term "magical rifle" is figurative, but this does not support the answer to Part A.

B. Incorrect. This contains no simile or metaphor.

C. Incorrect. This contains no simile or metaphor.

D. Correct. Puppets have no control over their actions, and this is how Orwell is feeling here.

Close Read

Skills Focus

QUESTION 1: Summarizing

See paragraph 8.

QUESTION 2: Connotation and Denotation

See paragraph 2. Orwell conveys his feelings toward imperial Britain with words such as *hatred* and *tyranny*. He describes his feelings toward the Burmese people with phrases such as *drive a bayonet into a Buddhist priest's guts*. The connotations and denotations of these words make Orwell's feelings clear.

QUESTION 3: Figurative Language

See paragraph 3.

QUESTION 4: Author's Purpose and Point of View

See paragraph 11.

QUESTION 5: Essential Question

See paragraphs 1 and 2.

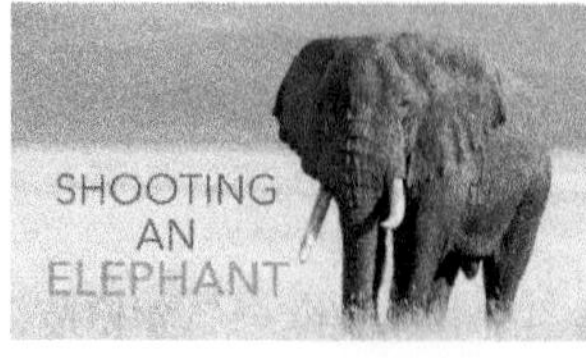

Close Read

Reread "Shooting an Elephant." As you reread, complete the Skills Focus questions below. Then use your answers and annotations from the questions to help you complete the Write activity.

SKILLS FOCUS

1. Highlight a passage in which Orwell describes the moral dilemma he is facing. Summarize the dilemma and what it reveals about the theme.
2. Identify a passage in Paragraph 2 in which Orwell describes his strong negative feelings toward both imperialism and the Burmese people. Explain how Orwell's use of language in this passage adds to the effectiveness of the text.
3. Find a section of the text in which the elephant serves as a symbol or metaphor for something else. Explain what the elephant symbolizes.
4. In Paragraph 11, highlight a description of the elephant after Orwell has shot it. Explain the point of view the author is conveying in this passage; then evaluate the effectiveness of the description in communicating that point of view.
5. Throughout the essay, Orwell describes ways in which he feels alienated and separate from everyone around him. Highlight two examples of this, and explain what is causing his alienation.

WRITE

EXPLANATORY ESSAY: What do you think is the point of view Orwell is expressing in his essay "Shooting an Elephant"? Analyze the literary elements and figurative language in the text to determine the author's point of view. Then write a short essay, responding to this question. Remember to use textual evidence to support your response.

Writer's Notebook

Connect to Literary Focus: Give students time to reflect on how "Shooting an Elephant" demonstrates the conventions and characteristics of this unit's literary focus, Modernism, by freewriting in their Writer's Notebooks.

Beginning & Intermediate

Remind students of the unit's literary focus, Modernism. Encourage students to draw pictures of their connections or allow students to write in their native language. Circulate around the room, prompting students for their thoughts as they respond orally or through pantomime.

Advanced & Advanced High

Allow students to share their connections orally in pairs or small groups before freewriting.

Collaborative Conversation

SCAFFOLDS

Break students into collaborative conversation groups to discuss the Close Read prompt. Ask students to use the StudySyncTV episode as a model for their discussion. Remind them to reference their Skills Focus annotations in their discussion.

What do you think is the point of view Orwell is expressing in his essay "Shooting an Elephant?" Analyze the literary elements and figurative language in the text to determine the author's point of view. Then write a short essay, responding to this question. Remember to use textual evidence to support your response.

Use the scaffolds below to differentiate instruction for your ELL English Language Learners and A Approaching grade-level learners.

ELL **BEGINNING, INTERMEDIATE** Use the discussion guide and speaking frames to facilitate the discussion with support from the teacher.

ADVANCED, ADVANCED HIGH Use the discussion guide and speaking frames to facilitate the discussion in mixed-level groups.

A **APPROACHING** Use the discussion guide to facilitate the discussion in mixed-level groups.

APPROACHING
ADVANCED, ADVANCED HIGH
BEGINNING, INTERMEDIATE

Discussion Guide	Speaking Frames
1. How did Orwell feel about shooting the elephant?	• Orwell felt ___ about shooting the elephant. • Orwell felt this way because ___.
2. Why did Orwell shoot the elephant?	• Orwell shot the elephant because ___ . • Orwell also shot the elephant because ___.
3. What did shooting the elephant teach Orwell about himself? How does this affect his point of view?	• Orwell learned ___ about himself because ___. • This affects his point of view by ___.

Multiple Perspectives

Use the activity below to differentiate instruction for your B Beyond grade level learners.

Orwell believes he knows what is going through the minds of the Burmese as he sets out to do something about the elephant. However, he may or may not be correct in his assumptions about what they are thinking.

Have students write a paragraph about the incident from the perspective of one of the Burmese people whose ridicule Orwell so fears. Ask students to share their paragraphs.

Review Prompt and Rubric

Before students begin writing, review the writing prompt and rubric with the class.

RHETORICAL ANALYSIS: What do you think is the point of view Orwell is expressing in his essay "Shooting an Elephant"? Analyze the literary elements and figurative language in the text to determine the author's point of view. Then write a short essay, responding to this question. Remember to use textual evidence to support your response.

PROMPT GUIDE

- What is Orwell's most important idea in the essay?
- What are some clues that help you find his most important idea?
- How do you know this is his most important idea?

Score	Author's Purpose and Point of View	Figurative Language	Language and Conventions
4	The writer analyzes literary elements and figurative language to clearly identify the author's point view. The writer provides exemplary analysis, using relevant textual evidence.	The writer clearly analyzes Orwell's use of figurative language. The writer provides exemplary analysis, using relevant textual evidence.	The writer demonstrates a consistent command of grammar, punctuation, and usage conventions. Although minor errors may be evident, they do not detract from the fluency or the clarity of the essay.
3	The writer analyzes literary elements and figurative language to identify the author's point view. The writer provides sufficient analysis, using relevant textual evidence most of the time.	The writer analyzes Orwell's use of figurative language. The writer provides sufficient analysis, using relevant textual evidence most of the time.	The writer demonstrates an adequate command of grammar, punctuation, and usage conventions. Although some errors may be evident, they create few (if any) disruptions in the fluency of the writing or the clarity of the essay.
2	The writer begins to analyze literary elements and figurative language to identify the author's point view, but the analysis is incomplete. The writer uses relevant textual evidence only some of the time.	The writer begins to analyze Orwell's use of figurative language, but the analysis is incomplete. The writer uses relevant textual evidence only some of the time.	The writer demonstrates a partial command of grammar, punctuation, and usage conventions. Some distracting errors may be evident, at times creating minor disruptions in the fluency or clarity of the writing.
1	The writer attempts to analyze literary elements and figurative language to identify the author's point view, but the analysis is not successful. The writer uses little or no relevant textual evidence.	The writer attempts to analyze Orwell's use of figurative language, but the analysis is not successful. The writer uses little or no relevant textual evidence.	The writer demonstrates little or no command of grammar, punctuation, and usage conventions. Serious and persistent errors create disruptions in the fluency of the writing and sometimes interfere with meaning.
0	The writer does not provide a relevant response to the prompt or does not provide a response at all.	The writer does not provide a relevant response to the prompt or does not provide a response at all.	Serious and persistent errors overwhelm the writing and interfere with the meaning of the response as a whole, making the writer's meaning impossible to understand.

Write

SCAFFOLDS

Ask students to complete the writing assignment using text evidence to support their answers.

Use the scaffolds below to differentiate instruction for your ELL English Language Learners and A Approaching grade level readers.

ELL **BEGINNING** With the help of the word bank, write a response using paragraph frame 1.

INTERMEDIATE With the help of the word bank, write a response using paragraph frames 1 and 2.

ADVANCED, ADVANCED HIGH Write a response of differentiated length using the sentence starters.

A **APPROACHING** Write a response of differentiated length using the sentence starters.

BEGINNING / INTERMEDIATE | ADVANCED, ADVANCED HIGH / APPROACHING

Word Bank	Paragraph Frame 1	Paragraph Frame 2	Sentence Starters
laugh calm difficult kill elephant	Orwell's main point of view in "Shooting an Elephant" is that it can be very ____ to do the right thing. When Orwell sees the elephant, he knows he should not ____ it. The elephant is ____. But the villagers want to see Orwell shoot the elephant, and Orwell thinks they might ____ if he does not. So Orwell shoots the ____ anyway, even though he would rather leave it alone.	One literary element that Orwell uses is ____. This literary element lets the reader know ____. Orwell uses other literary elements, too, such as ____. These help me identify his point of view because ____.	• Orwell uses a literary element called . . . • This literary element shows me . . . • Orwell uses figurative language, such as . . . • This figurative language shows me . . . • His main point of view is . . .

Peer Review

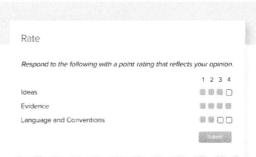

Rate

Respond to the following with a point rating that reflects your opinion.

	1	2	3	4
Ideas				
Evidence				
Language and Conventions				

Submit

Students should submit substantive feedback to two peers using the review instructions below.

- How well does this response address the prompt?
- How well does the writer support his or her ideas with textual evidence?
- Which literary elements or figurative language does the writer analyze? How does the writer analyze them?
- Which part of the writer's response was most effective? Why?

Remember that your comments are most useful when they are kind and constructive.

ELL A **SENTENCE FRAMES**

- You (completely / partly / almost) ____ answered the prompt because ____.
- You could answer the prompt more completely by ____.
- A detail you cited accurately is ____.
- One idea you expressed well is ____.
- One idea that needs clarification is ____.

Blast: Matter, Mood, and Moment

What more about the subject matter are you in the mood to read in this moment?

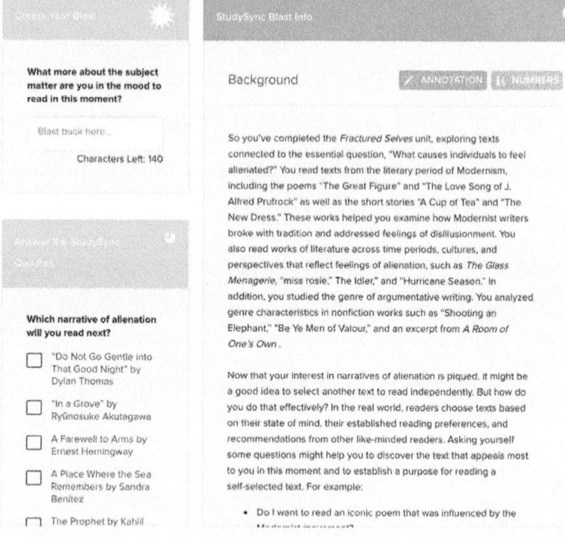

TEXT TALK

What did you think of the *Fractured Selves* unit? What is your opinion of modernism based on the unit's selections? Answers may vary.

What is one strategy you can use for self-selecting a new text? How does it work? I can ask my friends who have similar reading interests which books they recommend.

Would you be more likely to select a text related to the time period, genre, or topic of the unit? Explain. Answers may vary.

Create Your Own Blast

Ask students to write a 140-character Blast after they complete the QuikPoll.

Use the scaffolds below to differentiate instruction for your ELL English Language Learners.

ELL **BEGINNING** Write a response using the word bank to complete the sentence frame.

INTERMEDIATE Write a response using the sentence frame.

ADVANCED, ADVANCED HIGH Write a response using the sentence starter.

BEGINNING	BEGINNING / INTERMEDIATE	ADVANCED, ADVANCED HIGH
Word Bank	**Sentence Frame**	**Sentence Starter**
subject matter genre video preview time period poster	I am in the mood to read ____. The ____ made me want to read this text.	• I am in the mood to read . . . • The reasons I selected this text include . . .

Self-Selected Response

WRITE

Prompt

Self-Selected Response Prompt and Directions:

The first films were just shots of people doing ordinary things, demonstrating the new technology. Among the first to actually tell a story was *Le Voyage dans la lune*, or *A Trip to the Moon*, by Georges Méliès. It was based on a novel by Jules Verne. From the beginning of film history, writing has inspired movies.

How would you adapt a text?

Imagine you were tasked with using this text to inspire a film—it could be a movie or documentary. What would your film be about? What aspects of the text (e.g., topic, themes, characters, style, setting, etc.) would you use to inspire your film? In your response, be sure to include:

- a brief synopsis of your film, describing the genre, setting, primary characters, and other important information
- an explanation of how the text inspired the film
- an explanation of what you changed from the source material and why

Self-Selected Response

Introduce the Prompt

Read aloud the prompt. Ask students to discuss:

- What is the prompt asking you to do?
- What makes a movie adaptation successful?

Write

SCAFFOLDS

Ask students to complete the writing assignment using text evidence to support their answers.

Use the scaffolds below to differentiate instruction for your ELL English Language Learners and A Approaching grade level learners.

ELL **BEGINNING** With the help of the word bank, write a response using paragraph frame 1.

INTERMEDIATE With the help of the word bank, write a response using paragraph frames 1 and 2.

ADVANCED, ADVANCED HIGH Write a response of differentiated length using the sentence starters.

A **APPROACHING** Write a response of differentiated length using the sentence starters.

BEGINNING / INTERMEDIATE	BEGINNING	INTERMEDIATE	ADVANCED, ADVANCED HIGH / APPROACHING
Word Bank	Paragraph Frame 1	Paragraph Frame 2	Sentence Starters
romance men hero women resistance action courage war horror villain	I read the text (title) ____ by (author) ____. The main theme of the ____ is ____. The characters of my film would include ____. I think the film should be about a ____. This will be a ____ film.	I read the text (title) ____ by (author) ____. The main theme of the ____ is ____. The characters of my film would include ____. I think the film should be about a ____. This will be a ____ film. The beginning of the film would ____. The rising action will involve ____. In the climax, ____. In the falling action and resolution, ____. I think the changes I made will make the film ____.	• I read the text . . . by . . . • I want to explore the theme of . . . • Characters will include . . . and . . . as . . . • In this film, which is set in . . . , . . . • The film begins with . . . , then . . . , and finally . . . • This film is a . . . similar to . . .

Timed Writing Recommendations

Issue	Suggestion
Students don't finish their essays in the time allowed.	• Remind students of the time remaining and give suggestions of what they should be working on at that point. • Set and track writing goals for struggling students.
Students struggle to start their essays.	• Revisit and remodel the planning process. • Provide students with sentence starters for particular genres or sentence types.
Students spend too much time planning.	• Suggest students limit their planning to 5–10 minutes. • Have students identify several "buzzwords" from the prompt to use in their thesis and commentary.
Students don't understand the prompt.	• Have students rewrite the prompt using their own words. • Encourage students to use context clues to determine the meaning of unfamiliar language.
Students get nervous or stressed about writing.	• Provide students with strategies that help prevent or counter stress, such as stretching and breathing exercises, or limiting how often they look at the clock or track their peers' progress.
Students focus too much on editing and do not make progress on their writing.	• Advise students to use their knowledge of their own common errors to prioritize their editing. • Remind students to focus on specific areas, such as sentence structure or comma usage.
Students get stuck as they are writing.	• Recommend that students pause to reread the prompt and their response to that point. • Have students identify the types of challenges they encounter and brainstorm solutions to those problems that they can implement moving forward.
Your classroom spans a wide variety of abilities.	• Have several students share strategies or reflections with the rest of the class. • Create a classroom "resume" that lists each student's strengths so that students can consult with peers for their writing.

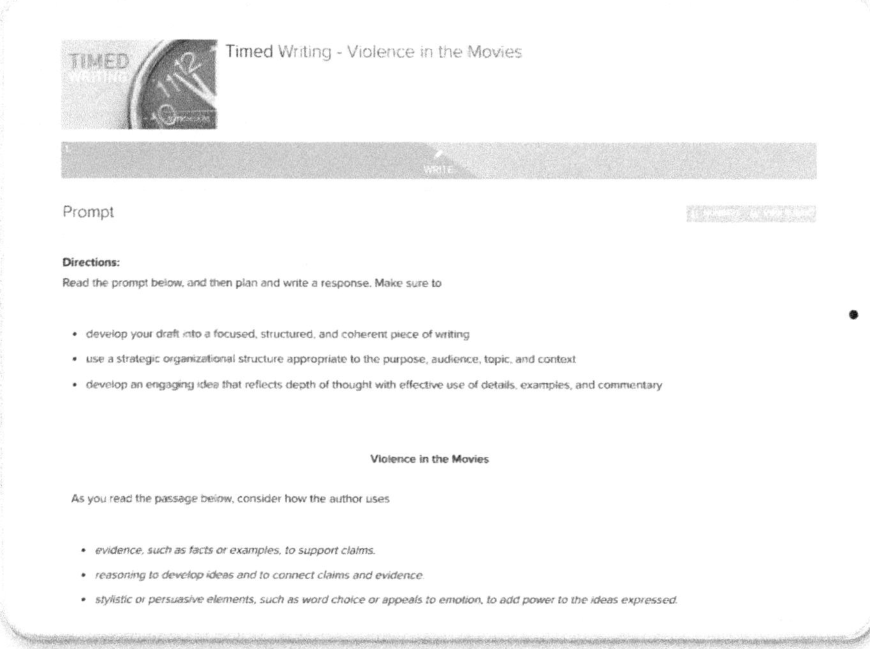
TIMED
Timed Writing - Violence in the Movies
WRITE
Prompt
Directions:
Read the prompt below, and then plan and write a response. Make sure to
• develop your draft into a focused, structured, and coherent piece of writing
• use a strategic organizational structure appropriate to the purpose, audience, topic, and context
• develop an engaging idea that reflects depth of thought with effective use of details, examples, and commentary
Violence in the Movies
As you read the passage below, consider how the author uses
• evidence, such as facts or examples, to support claims.
• reasoning to develop ideas and to connect claims and evidence.
• stylistic or persuasive elements, such as word choice or appeals to emotion, to add power to the ideas expressed.

Timed Writing

Ask students to complete the writing assignment.

Note: To replicate the testing environment, turn off scaffolds, but allow ELL students to ask clarifying questions about unknown words or phrases in the prompt before they begin writing.

ELL CLARIFYING QUESTIONS

- What does the word ______ mean in the prompt?
- I do not know what the phrase ______ means. Can you explain it to me?
- What does it mean in the instructions when it says ______?

Write

SCAFFOLDS

Use the scaffolds below to differentiate instruction for your ELL English Language Learners and A Approaching grade level learners.

ELL **BEGINNING, INTERMEDIATE, ADVANCED, ADVANCED HIGH** Use the sentence starters to organize and write your response.

A APPROACHING Write a response of differentiated length using the sentence starters.

BEGINNING, INTERMEDIATE, ADVANCED, ADVANCED HIGH

APPROACHING

Purpose of Sentence	Sentence Starters
To introduce the author's argument	• The author argues that . . . • The author presents an argument about . . .
To introduce or explain evidence from the author	• The author includes evidence from . . . • The author's claim is supported by . . .
To explain the author's reasoning	• The author's reference shows that . . . • By including ______, the author shows that . . .
To explain stylistic or persuasive elements	• The author's use of ______ is persuasive because . . . • The author's choice to ______ supports the central argument by . . .
To conclude your essay	• To summarize . . . • Overall, the author's argument is successful because . . .

Extended Writing Project

The Extended Writing Project (EWP) in Grade 12, Unit 5 focuses on literary analysis writing. Students consider the following question—Why is alienation such a common theme in modernist literature?—as they write a literary analysis about how alienation affects three characters from the texts in the unit. The unit's selections about the various ways alienation can impact people provide a context for students, and the multiple pieces of fiction in the unit serve as mentor texts for students to analyze. Specific skill lessons teach developing ideas, organization, and conventions, while other skill lessons on reasons and relevant evidence, thesis statements, and using a style guide focus on characteristics of the genre and help students develop their analyses. Directed revision leads students through the process of revising for clarity, development, organization, word choice, and sentence fluency. Throughout the EWP, students have the opportunity to practice, using created student writing, authentic texts, and their own work.

 Audio and audio text highlighting are available in select lessons in the Extended Writing Project.

CONNECT TO ESSENTIAL QUESTION

What causes individuals to feel alienated?

Alienation and identity are at the center of the texts in this unit. After reading about how various characters, narrators, and authors articulated their predicaments, students will write a literary analysis examining the effects of alienation, using three texts from the unit.

Extended Writing Project Prompt

Why is alienation such a common theme in modernist literature?

Consider all the texts you have read in this unit, and reflect on how alienation impacts those who experience it. Then, select three characters or speakers from the texts. Write a literary analysis essay to examine how the authors explore the theme of alienation through these three characters or speakers. In your conclusion, synthesize the ideas in these texts about alienation in the modern world.

These icons identify differentiation strategies and scaffolded support for a variety of students. See the digital lesson plan for additional differentiation strategies and scaffolds.

Instructional Path

The print teacher's edition includes essential point-of-use instruction and planning tools. Complete lesson plans and program documents appear in your digital teacher account.

Literary Analysis Writing Process: Plan

Objectives: After learning about genre characteristics and craft, students will analyze a sample Student Model and plan a meaningful literary analysis in response to a prompt.

Skill: Reasons and Relevant Evidence

Objectives: After reading and discussing a model of student writing, students will develop their drafts by selecting reasons and relevant evidence.

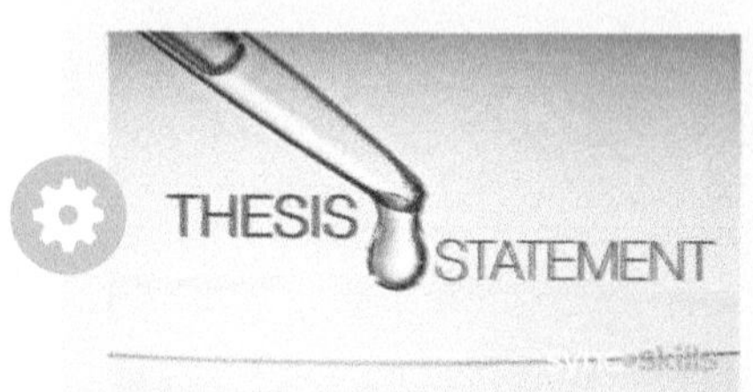

Skill: Thesis Statement

Objectives: After reading and discussing a model of student writing, students will develop their drafts by writing a thesis statement.

Skill: Organizing Argumentative Writing

Objectives: After reading and discussing a model of student writing, students will develop their drafts by organizing their argumentative literary analysis essay effectively.

Literary Analysis Writing Process: Draft

Objectives: After reading a Student Model draft and reviewing a writing checklist, students will draft a meaningful literary analysis in response to a prompt.

Skill: Introductions

Objectives: After reading and discussing a model of student writing, students will develop their drafts by improving their introductions.

Skill: Transitions

Objectives: After reading and discussing a model of student writing, students will develop their drafts by improving their transitions.

Skill: Conclusions

Objectives: After reading and discussing a model of student writing, students will develop their drafts by improving their conclusions.

Literary Analysis Writing Process: Revise

Objectives: Students will use a revision guide to revise the draft of their argumentative literary analysis essay for clarity, development, organization, style, diction, and sentence fluency.

Skill: Using a Style Guide

Objectives: After reading and discussing a model of student writing, students will develop their drafts by using a style guide, as appropriate, to improve their command of standard English conventions, syntax, and MLA citations.

Grammar: Commonly Misspelled Words

Objectives: After learning about commonly misspelled words and reading text examples, students will practice spelling the words correctly.

Grammar: Pronoun Case and Reference

Objectives: After learning about pronoun case and reference and seeing how pronouns are used in text examples, students will practice using pronouns correctly.

Literary Analysis Writing Process: Edit and Publish

Objectives: After seeing an example of editing in the Student Model and reviewing an editing checklist, students will edit and publish the final draft of their argumentative literary analysis essay.

Progress Monitoring

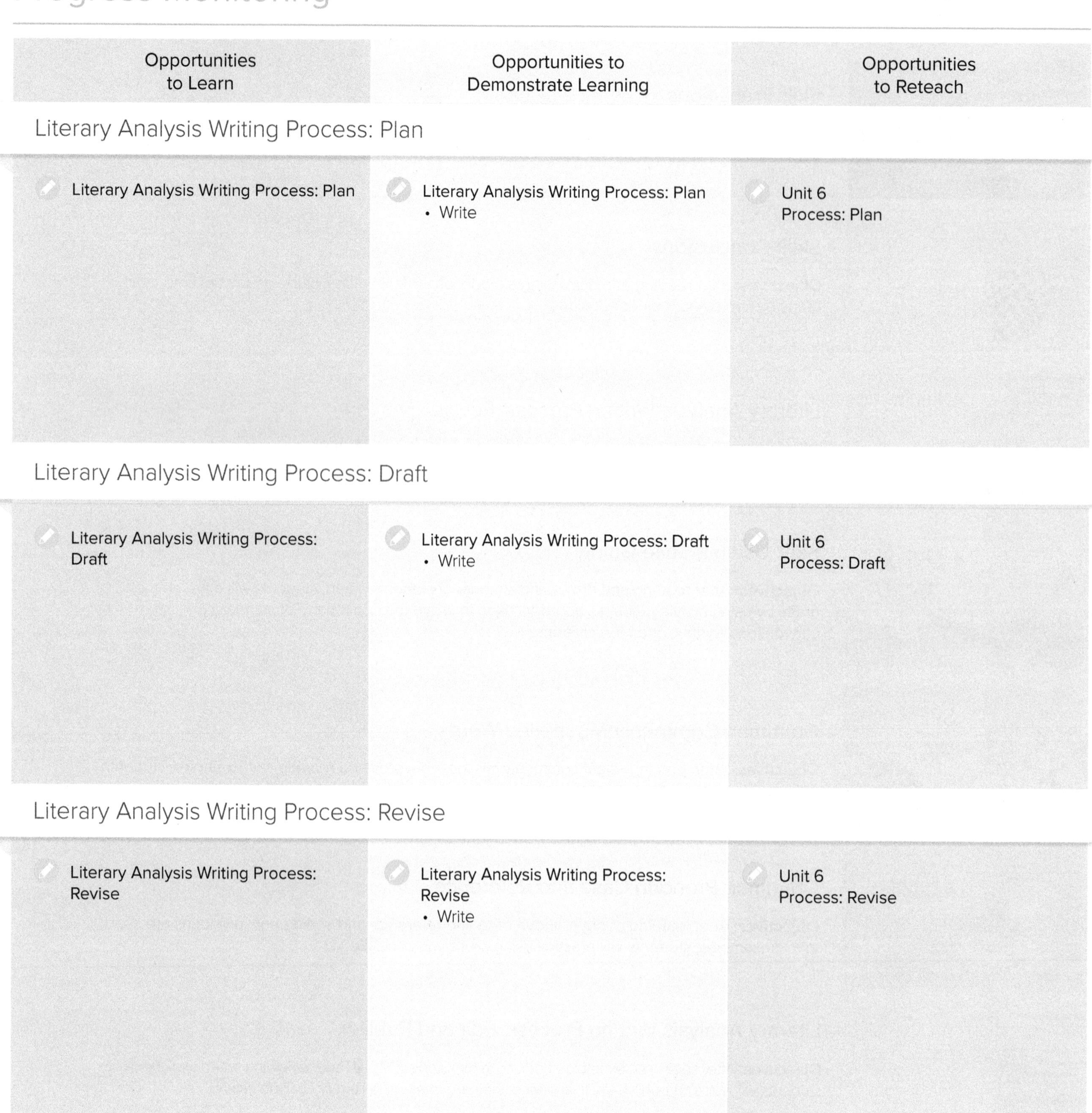

Opportunities to Learn	Opportunities to Demonstrate Learning	Opportunities to Reteach
Literary Analysis Writing Process: Plan		
Literary Analysis Writing Process: Plan	Literary Analysis Writing Process: Plan • Write	Unit 6 Process: Plan
Literary Analysis Writing Process: Draft		
Literary Analysis Writing Process: Draft	Literary Analysis Writing Process: Draft • Write	Unit 6 Process: Draft
Literary Analysis Writing Process: Revise		
Literary Analysis Writing Process: Revise	Literary Analysis Writing Process: Revise • Write	Unit 6 Process: Revise

Opportunities to Learn	Opportunities to Demonstrate Learning	Opportunities to Reteach

Literary Analysis Writing Process: Edit and Publish

Opportunities to Learn	Opportunities to Demonstrate Learning	Opportunities to Reteach
Literary Analysis Writing Process: Edit and Publish	Literary Analysis Writing Process: Edit and Publish • Write	Unit 6 Process: Edit and Present

Reasons and Relevant Evidence

Opportunities to Learn	Opportunities to Demonstrate Learning	Opportunities to Reteach
Skill: Reasons and Relevant Evidence	Skill: Reasons and Relevant Evidence • Your Turn Literary Analysis Writing Process: Draft	Unit 6 Skill: Reasons and Relevant Evidence Spotlight Skill: Reasons and Relevant Evidence

Thesis Statement

Opportunities to Learn	Opportunities to Demonstrate Learning	Opportunities to Reteach
Skill: Thesis Statement	Skill: Thesis Statement • Your Turn Literary Analysis Writing Process: Draft	Spotlight Skill: Thesis Statement

Opportunities to Learn	Opportunities to Demonstrate Learning	Opportunities to Reteach
Organizing Argumentative Writing		
Skill: Organizing Argumentative Writing	Skill: Organizing Argumentative Writing • Your Turn Literary Analysis Writing Process: Draft	Spotlight Skill: Organizing Argumentative Writing
Introductions		
Skill: Introductions	Skill: Introductions • Your Turn Literary Analysis Writing Process: Revise	Spotlight Skill: Introductions
Transitions		
Skill: Transitions	Skill: Transitions • Your Turn Literary Analysis Writing Process: Revise	Spotlight Skill: Transitions
Conclusions		
Skill: Conclusions	Skill: Conclusions • Your Turn Literary Analysis Writing Process: Revise	Spotlight Skill: Conclusions

Opportunities to Learn	Opportunities to Demonstrate Learning	Opportunities to Reteach

Using a Style Guide

Opportunities to Learn	Opportunities to Demonstrate Learning	Opportunities to Reteach
Skill: Using a Style Guide	Skill: Using a Style Guide • Your Turn Literary Analysis Writing Process: Edit and Publish	Spotlight Skill: Using a Style Guide

Commonly Misspelled Words

Opportunities to Learn	Opportunities to Demonstrate Learning	Opportunities to Reteach
Grammar: Commonly Misspelled Words	Grammar: Commonly Misspelled Words • Your Turn Literary Analysis Writing Process: Edit and Publish	Grammar: Commonly Misused Words - A While, Awhile Grammar: Commonly Misused Words - All Ready, Already

Pronoun Case and Reference

Opportunities to Learn	Opportunities to Demonstrate Learning	Opportunities to Reteach
Grammar: Pronoun Case and Reference	Grammar: Pronoun Case and Reference • Your Turn Literary Analysis Writing Process: Edit and Publish	Grammar: Pronouns - Personal and Possessive

Literary Analysis Writing Process: Plan

Introduce the Extended Writing Project

- What is the prompt asking you to do?
- Which characteristics of literary analysis writing will you need to learn more about in order to respond to the prompt?
- What are the six characteristics of literary analysis writing?
- What elements of craft do writers of literary analysis use?

DIFFERENTIATED QUESTIONS

- What does **alienation** mean?
- Who is a character or speaker in each selection that experiences alienation?
- How does alienation relate to modernism?

Literary Analysis Writing Process: Plan

PLAN | DRAFT | REVISE | EDIT AND PUBLISH

At first glance, a poem about an indecisive man, a short story about a woman wearing a new dress, and an essay about shooting an elephant might not seem to have much in common. However, each of these selections is an example of modernist literature that features themes relating to isolation and alienation.

WRITING PROMPT

Why is alienation such a common theme in modernist literature?

Consider all the texts you have read in this unit, and reflect on how alienation impacts those who experience it. Then, select three characters or speakers from the texts. Write a literary analysis essay to examine how the authors explore the theme of alienation through these three characters or speakers. In your conclusion, synthesize the ideas in these texts about alienation in the modern world. Regardless of which selections you choose, be sure your literary analysis includes the following:

- an introduction
- a thesis statement
- coherent body paragraphs
- reasons and relevant evidence
- a conclusion

Introduction to Literary Analysis Writing

A literary analysis is a form of argumentative writing that tries to persuade readers to accept the writer's interpretation of a literary text. Good literary analysis writing builds an argument with a strong claim, convincing reasons, relevant textual evidence, and a clear structure with an introduction, body, and conclusion. The characteristics of literary analysis writing include:

- an introduction
- a thesis statement
- textual evidence
- transitions
- a formal style
- a conclusion

In addition to these characteristics, writers of literary analyses also carefully craft their work through their use of a strong, confident tone and compelling syntax, or sentence structure, which help to make the text more persuasive. Effective arguments combine these genre characteristics and elements of the writer's craft to engage and convince the reader.

As you continue with this Extended Writing Project, you'll receive more instruction and practice in crafting each of the characteristics of literary analysis writing to create your own literary analysis.

Review the Rubric

Have students examine the "Literary Analysis Writing Rubric - Grade 12" grading rubric. Inform students that this is the same rubric that will be used to evaluate their completed Literary Analysis Extended Writing Project.

Read and Annotate

As students read, have them use the Annotation Tool to identify and label the genre characteristics and craft of literary analysis writing, including:

- an introduction
- a thesis statement
- textual evidence
- transitions
- a formal style
- a conclusion

When students finish reading, ask them to share their annotations in small groups.

ELL **ANNOTATION GUIDE**

Find the following quotes in the Student Model. Then, use the Annotation Tool to label each quote as an example of an introduction, a thesis statement, textual evidence, a transition, a formal style, or a conclusion. Some quotes may have more than one answer.

- In the early 20th century, the world was in flux.
- Modernist works such as "The Love Song of J. Alfred Prufrock," "The New Dress," and "A Cup of Tea" show that feelings of alienation stretched across lines of gender and class.
- Like the speaker of Eliot's poem, Mabel Waring wants to participate in society but is instead alienated by her own feelings of inadequacy.
- Later, when a fellow party guest points out that Mabel has bought a new dress, it causes her to unravel: "'Why,' she asked herself, 'can't I . . . feel sure about the canary and pity and love and not be whipped all round in a second by coming into a room full of people?'"
- Rosemary abandons Miss Smith at the first sign that their friendship could lead to a rivalry for her husband's attention.
- Alienation is a common theme in these modernist works because in a post-war, ever-changing world, it is human nature to ask, "Am I good enough?"

READ AND ANNOTATE

Pair students with on-grade-level peers to complete the annotation activity.

Before you get started on your own literary analysis, read this literary analysis that one student, Emma, wrote in response to the writing prompt. As you read the Model, highlight and annotate the features of literary analysis writing that Emma included in her literary analysis.

STUDENT MODEL

Alienation in a Post-War Society

1 In the early 20th century, the world was in flux. New technology led to destruction as war raged in Europe. At the same time, many challenged traditional norms of gender and class. For example, women's suffrage movements gained traction in both Great Britain and the United States. The world people thought they knew was changing, and as a result men and women of all levels of society felt lost. Writers and artists reacted by challenging old conventions and social norms. They created new styles and sought to represent individuals' subjective points of view. Alienation is a common theme in modernist literature because uncertainty was a by-product of the rapidly changing society. Modernist works such as "The Love Song of J. Alfred Prufrock," "The New Dress," and "A Cup of Tea" show that feelings of alienation stretched across lines of gender and class.

2 Although he was born in the United States, poet T. S. Eliot moved to England in 1914 while World War I raged in Europe. His poem "The Love Song of J. Alfred Prufrock," published the following year, reflects the disillusionment and uncertainty Europeans felt as the world changed around them. The first images in the poem create tension as a familiar scene turns ominous: "Let us go then, you and I, / When the evening is spread out against the sky / Like a patient etherized upon a table" (1–3). An evening stroll under the night sky is typically a romantic or serene image, but Eliot uses it differently. By comparing the evening to a patient about to have surgery, Eliot upends expectations. This makes readers uncomfortable because they do not know what will happen on the journey on which they are about to embark with the poem's speaker.

3 Uncertainty and alienation are also reflected in the speaker himself. He constantly doubts his own worth and place in the world. Instead of simply interacting with people, he stops to ask, "Do I dare / Disturb the universe?" (51–52). The entire poem takes place in the speaker's

TEXT TALK

Purpose

Where does Emma identify the structure and purpose of her analysis?

See paragraph 1: Emma explains that she will analyze three selections to show why feelings of alienation were common across lines of gender and class.

Focus

How does Emma focus her ideas about the selections?

See paragraphs 2–5: Emma discusses one selection at a time. In each paragraph, she discusses how the author explores the theme of alienation, through both the characters and the social context in which the character exists

NOTES

own mind. There are no outside forces preventing him from engaging with others. The speaker's own hesitancy and insecurity prevent him from participating in society. In this way, "The Love Song of J. Alfred Prufrock" shows that alienation can be a product of our own making.

4 The protagonist of Virginia Woolf's short story "The New Dress" is also a victim of her own insecurities. Like the speaker of Eliot's poem, Mabel Waring wants to participate in society but is instead alienated by her own feelings of inadequacy. Mabel is so worried that the other guests will judge her that she cannot enjoy herself at a party:

> And at once the misery which she always tried to hide, the profound dissatisfaction—the sense she had had, ever since she was a child, of being inferior to other people—set upon her, relentlessly, remorselessly, with an intensity which she could not beat off, as she would when she woke at night at home, by reading Borrow or Scott; for oh these men, oh these women, all were thinking—"What's Mabel wearing? What a fright she looks! What a hideous new dress!"—their eyelids flickering as they came up and then their lids shutting rather tight. It was her own appalling inadequacy; her cowardice; her mean, water-sprinkled blood that depressed her.

Mabel's uncertainty is directly tied to her perception of society's expectations. She worries that, as a member of a slightly lower social class, she cannot measure up to other guests' expectations, and it makes her doubt her worth. Later, when a fellow party guest points out that Mabel has bought a new dress, it causes her to unravel: "'Why,' she asked herself, 'can't I . . . feel sure about the canary and pity and love and not be whipped all round in a second by coming into a room full of people?'" Instead of enjoying her social interactions, Mabel allows a single comment to send her into a spiral of anxiety and shame. In the end, she leaves the party early, too embarrassed by her appearance to remain in the company of others. "The New Dress" shows that alienation can be a product of society's expectations.

5 Rosemary Fell, the protagonist in Katherine Mansfield's "A Cup of Tea," is the opposite of Mabel in several key ways. Rosemary is a member of London's high society and is extremely wealthy. She is also well-respected and sure of her place in the world. Yet, Rosemary

TEXT TALK

Evidence and Elaboration

Does Emma elaborate on her ideas and support them well?

Answers will vary. Sample answer: See paragraphs 2–5. Yes. I think Emma uses strong textual evidence from each of the selections to develop and support her body paragraphs.

Organization

Where does Emma use a transition to connect ideas across paragraphs?

Answers will vary. Sample answer: In paragraph 4, Emma uses the transition "like the speaker of Eliot's poem" to connect ideas across paragraphs.

Evidence and Elaboration

How does Emma use specific textual evidence to support her analysis?

Answers will vary. Sample answer: In paragraph 4, Emma quotes a long passage from "The New Dress."

Word Choice

Where do you find Emma's word choice especially strong or convincing?

Answers will vary. Sample answer: In paragraph 4, Emma uses the phrase "a spiral of anxiety and shame" to describe the character's feelings. The phrase shows a strong understanding of the character and the way the author develops the theme of alienation.

NOTES

also fails to connect with the people around her. When she decides to invite a penniless young woman, Miss Smith, home for tea, she does so in order to make herself feel like a benefactor instead of out of a genuine desire to make a friend: "She was going to prove to this girl that—wonderful things did happen in life, that—fairy godmothers were real, that—rich people had hearts, and that women *were* sisters." The class difference between the characters prevents Rosemary from seeing Miss Smith as a whole person. Instead, she views the interaction as a game to keep herself entertained on a rainy day. This becomes clear when she abruptly throws Miss Smith out after her husband, Philip, comments on the young woman's beauty. Just as the guest's comment affects Mabel in "The New Dress," this passing commentary sends Rosemary into a spiral as the words echo in her head: "Pretty! Absolutely lovely! Bowled over! Her heart beat like a heavy bell." Rosemary abandons Miss Smith at the first sign that their friendship could lead to a rivalry for her husband's attention. Later, Rosemary asks her husband to reassure her. "'Philip,' she whispered, and she pressed his head against her bosom, 'am I *pretty*?'" As the story concludes, Miss Smith has been alienated by the woman who claimed to be her benefactor, and Rosemary feels insecure in her relationship with her husband. "A Cup of Tea" shows that alienation can occur when issues relating to class and gender complicate individual relationships between two people.

6 The characters in these modernist works come from different backgrounds and have different experiences, but the results of their attempted interactions with others are similar. Hindered by their own insecurities, the speaker in "The Love Song of J. Alfred Prufrock" and the protagonists in "The New Dress" and "A Cup of Tea" are left alone and afraid. Alienation is a common theme in these modernist works because in a post-war, ever-changing world, it is human nature to ask, "Am I good enough?"

TEXT TALK

Conventions

Does Emma write her essay in the active or passive voice? Can you find an example of a verb that Emma uses in the active voice?

Answers will vary. Sample answer: Emma uses the active voice. In paragraph 5, she uses *sends* and *echo* in the active voice in the sentence "Just as the guest's comment affects Mabel in 'The New Dress,' this passing commentary sends Rosemary into a spiral as the words echo in her head: 'Pretty! Absolutely lovely! Bowled over! Her heart beat like a heavy bell.'"

Sentence Fluency

Choose one sentence that you think is really effective. Why do you think it's so strong?

Answers will vary. Sample answer: I think the sentence "'A Cup of Tea' shows that alienation can occur when issues relating to class and gender complicate individual relationships between two people" in paragraph 5 is really strong. The writer's analysis of the story and the connection to her thesis are clear.

WRITE

Writers often take notes about their ideas for a literary analysis before they sit down to write. Think about what you've learned so far about literary analysis writing to help you begin prewriting.

- **Purpose:** What selections do you want to write about, and how do they develop themes relating to alienation?
- **Audience:** Who is your audience, and what idea do you want to express to them?
- **Introduction:** How will you introduce your topic? How will you engage an audience and preview what you plan to argue in your essay?
- **Thesis Statement:** What is your claim about the selections you've chosen? How can you word your claim so it is clear to readers?
- **Textual Evidence:** What evidence will you use to support your claim? What facts, details, examples, and quotations will persuade your audience to agree with your claim?
- **Transitions:** How will you smoothly transition from one idea to another within and across paragraphs?
- **Formal Style:** How can you create and maintain a formal style and an objective tone as you build your argument?
- **Conclusion:** How will you wrap up your argument? How can you restate the main ideas in your argument without being redundant?

Response Instructions

Use the questions in the bulleted list to write a one-paragraph summary. Your summary should describe what you will argue in your literary analysis.

Don't worry about including all of the details now; focus only on the most essential and important elements. You will refer to this short summary as you continue through the steps of the writing process.

Write

Circulate as students use the questions in the bulleted list to plan their writing. See the instructions for scaffolding and differentiation that follow.

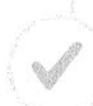

CHECK FOR SUCCESS

If students struggle to come up with answers for the questions in the lesson, work with students to provide an answer to one question and then help them build from there.

For example, start by asking students, "Which character or speaker experiences alienation?" or "How does the author show how the character or speaker is feeling?" Once students have answered one question, help them to work through a second question until they've begun to build some momentum. It may be helpful to start with a different question than the one that's listed first in the lesson.

Review Prompt and Rubric

Before students begin writing, review the writing prompt and rubric with the class.

Response Instructions

Use the questions in the bulleted list on the previous page to write a one-paragraph summary. Your summary should describe what you will argue in your literary analysis.

Don't worry about including all of the details now; focus only on the most essential and important elements. You will refer to this short summary as you continue through the steps of the writing process.

Score	Plan	Language and Conventions
4	The writer responds to the questions, and the writing is clear and focused.	The writer demonstrates a consistent command of grammar, punctuation, and usage conventions. Although minor errors may be evident, they do not detract from the fluency or the clarity of the writing.
3	The writer responds to the questions, but the writing is not always clear or focused.	The writer demonstrates an adequate command of grammar, punctuation, and usage conventions. Although some errors may be evident, they create few (if any) disruptions in the fluency or clarity of the writing.
2	The writer responds to the questions, but the writing is somewhat unclear and unfocused.	The writer demonstrates a partial command of grammar, punctuation, and usage conventions. Some distracting errors may be evident, at times creating minor disruptions in the fluency or clarity of the writing.
1	The writer responds to the questions, but the writing is very unclear and unfocused.	The writer demonstrates little or no command of grammar, punctuation, and usage conventions. Serious and persistent errors create disruptions in the fluency of the writing and sometimes interfere with meaning.
0	The writer does not provide a relevant response to the prompt or does not provide a response at all.	Serious and persistent errors overwhelm the writing and interfere with the meaning of the response as a whole, making the writer's meaning impossible to understand.

Write

Use the scaffolds below to differentiate instruction for your ELL English Language Learners and A Approaching grade-level learners.

ELL **BEGINNING, INTERMEDIATE** With the help of the word bank, write a response using the paragraph frame.

ADVANCED, ADVANCED HIGH Write a response using the sentence starters.

A **APPROACHING** Write a response using the sentence starters.

BEGINNING INTERMEDIATE		ADVANCED, ADVANCED HIGH APPROACHING
Word Bank	**Paragraph Frame**	**Sentence Starters**
"The Love Song of J. Alfred Prufrock" "The New Dress" "A Cup of Tea" *A Room of One's Own* "Shooting an Elephant" technology changes war class gender	I will write about ____, ____, and ____. The characters and speakers who experience alienation are ____, ____, and ____. Alienation is a common theme in modernism because ____. Textual evidence I will use includes ____.	• I will write about . . . • The characters and speakers who experience alienation are . . . • Some textual evidence supporting my claim is . . . • I will use transitions such as . . . • I will conclude by . . .

Peer Review

Students should submit substantive feedback to two peers using the instructions below.

- How well does this response answer the prompt?
- What part of the literary analysis are you most interested in reading?
- Are there any ideas that could be improved on? How so?

Rate

Respond to the following with a point rating that reflects your opinion.

	1	2	3	4
Ideas				
Evidence				
Language and Conventions				

ELL A **SENTENCE FRAMES**

- The response (does / does not) identify three texts the writer will write about.
- The response does a good job of addressing ____ from the prompt.
- You could improve the response by addressing ____ from the prompt.
- I am most interested in reading about ____.
- I think you could improve ____ by (adding / clarifying / describing) ____.

Skill: Reasons and Relevant Evidence

Introduce the Skill

Watch the Concept Definition video and read the following definition with your students.

An **argument** is a set of reasons designed to persuade others to adopt a certain point of view or take a certain action. The **claim** is the main idea of the argument. The structure of an argument consists of a claim and the support for that claim. Support for the claim includes reasons and evidence. **Reasons** are logical explanations that state why the author believes in his or her claim and why others should accept the claim. **Relevant evidence** consists of facts, statistics, specific examples, and expert opinions and quotations from reliable sources that uphold the claim. To be relevant and reliable, evidence for an argument must come from **credible sources** that contain verifiable information closely connected to the topic and essential to the reader's understanding of the argument.

Skill: Reasons and Relevant Evidence

CHECKLIST FOR REASONS AND RELEVANT EVIDENCE

As you determine the reasons and relevant evidence you will need to support your claim, use the following questions as a guide:

- What is my claim (or claims)? What are the strengths and limitations of my claim(s)?
- What relevant evidence do I have? Where could I add more support for my claim(s)?
- What do I know about the audience's:
  - > knowledge about my topic?
  - > concerns and values?
  - > possible biases toward the subject matter?

Use the following steps to help you develop claims fairly and thoroughly:

- establish a claim. Then, evaluate:
  - > its strengths and limitations
  - > any biases you have
  - > any gaps in support for your claim, so that your support can be more thorough
- consider your audience and their perspective on your topic. Determine:
  - > their probable prior knowledge about the topic
  - > their concerns and values
  - > any biases they may have toward the subject matter
- find the most relevant evidence that supports the claim

TURN AND TALK

Turn to a partner and use the following questions to discuss reasons and relevant evidence:

- What were some strong reasons and evidence in an argumentative text you have read recently?
- Why was the evidence convincing?

SPEAKING FRAMES

- Some strong reasons and relevant evidence in ____ were ____.
- This evidence was convincing because ____.

SKILL VOCABULARY

argument / el argumento ***noun*** a set of claims, evidence and reasons designed to persuade others to adopt a certain point of view or to take a certain action COGNATE

claim / la afirmación ***noun*** the writer's or speaker's position on a debatable issue or problem

reason / la razón ***noun*** an explanation that states why others should accept a claim

YOUR TURN

Read the quotations from "A Cup of Tea" below. Then, complete the chart by sorting the quotations into two categories: those that serve as relevant evidence to support Emma's claim and those that do not. Write the corresponding letter for each quotation in the appropriate column.

	Quotations
A	"Rosemary had been married two years. She had a duck of a boy. No, not Peter—Michael. And her husband absolutely adored her."
B	"Half an hour later Philip was still in the library, when Rosemary came in."
C	"Rosemary Fell was not exactly beautiful. No, you couldn't have called her beautiful. Pretty? Well, if you took her to pieces. . . But why be so cruel as to take anyone to pieces?"
D	"'Do you like me?' said she, and her tone, sweet, husky, troubled him."
E	"She went to her writing-room and sat down at her desk. Pretty! Absolutely lovely! Bowled over! Her heart beat like a heavy bell."
F	"The other did stop just in time for Rosemary to get up before the tea came. She had the table placed between them."

Supports Claim	Does Not Support Claim

WRITE

Use the questions in the checklist to draft your claim and select reasons and relevant evidence for your argumentative literary analysis essay.

SKILL VOCABULARY

relevant / relevante *adjective* appropriate and logically related to the topic COGNATE

evidence / la evidencia *noun* facts, examples, and expert opinions that support a claim COGNATE

credible source / la fuente confiable *noun* a source that is trustworthy and believable

Your Turn

Ask students to complete the Your Turn activity.

Supports Claim	Does Not Support Claim
C	A
D	B
E	F

Write

Ask students to complete the writing assignment.

ELL REWRITE CHECKLIST

A Prepare

- ☐ What are the requirements of the prompt?
- ☐ Which selections from the unit am I interested in writing about and are relevant to the prompt?
- ☐ What is my claim?
- ☐ What details relate to that claim?

Search for Sources

- ☐ Which selections from the unit support my claim?

Identify Reasons and Relevant Evidence

- ☐ Will this evidence help readers understand the topic?
- ☐ Does this evidence support my claim?
- ☐ What other details, examples, or quotations support my claim?

Skill: Thesis Statement

Introduce the Skill

Watch the Concept Definition video and read the following definition with your students.

In an essay, a **thesis statement** expresses the writer's main idea about a topic. The thesis statement usually appears in the **introduction**, or opening paragraph of your essay, and is often the last sentence of the introduction. The **body paragraphs** of the essay should offer a thorough explanation of the thesis statement as well as supporting details, reasons, and relevant evidence. The thesis is often restated in the **conclusion** of an essay.

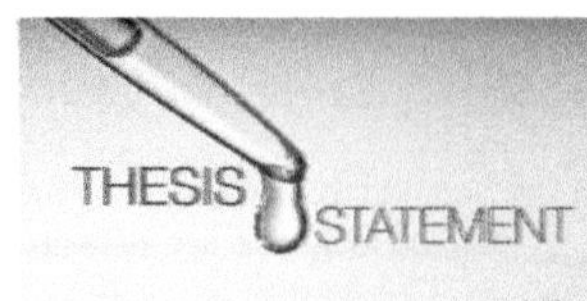

Skill: Thesis Statement

CHECKLIST FOR THESIS STATEMENT

Before you begin writing your thesis statement, ask yourself the following questions:

- What is the prompt asking me to write about?
- What claim do I want to make about the topic of this essay?
- Is my claim precise and informative?
- How is my claim specific to my topic? How does it inform the reader about my topic?
- Does my thesis statement introduce the body of my essay?
- Where should I place my thesis statement?

Here are some methods for introducing and developing a topic as well as a precise and informative claim:

- think about your central claim of your essay
  - > identify a clear claim you want to introduce, thinking about:
    - o how closely your claim is related to your topic and how specific it is to your supporting details
    - o how your claim includes necessary information to guide the reader through the topic
  - > identify as many claims as you intend to prove
- your thesis statement should:
  - > let the reader anticipate the content of your essay
  - > help you begin your essay in an organized manner
  - > present your opinion clearly
  - > respond completely to the writing prompt
- consider the best placement for your thesis statement
  - > if your response is short, you may want to present your thesis statement in the first sentence of the essay
  - > if your response is longer (as in a formal essay), you can place it at the end of your introductory paragraph

TURN AND TALK

Turn to a partner and use the following questions to discuss writing thesis statements:

- How did you come up with the thesis statement for the last essay you wrote?
- How did the thesis statement reflect the central claims of your essay?

SPEAKING FRAMES

- I came up with my thesis statement by ____.
- The thesis statement reflected my central claims because ____.

SKILL VOCABULARY

thesis statement / la presentación de la tesis ***noun*** a statement that shares the main idea of an argumentative or informative essay

introduction / la introducción ***noun*** the opening paragraph or section of an essay COGNATE

body paragraph / el párrafo del cuerpo ***noun*** a paragraph that appears between the introduction and the conclusion of an essay

conclusion / la conclusión ***noun*** the closing paragraph or section of an essay; a closing argument in an argumentative text COGNATE

YOUR TURN

Read the thesis statements below. Then, complete the chart by sorting them into two categories: effective thesis statements and ineffective thesis statements. Write the corresponding letter for each statement in the appropriate column.

	Thesis Statements
A	"The New Dress" and "A Cup of Tea" both offer harsh criticism of traditional gender roles.
B	In *A Room of One's Own*, Virginia Woolf argues that women have been negatively affected by unfair limitations.
C	"The New Dress" and "A Cup of Tea" were both written by women in the early 20th century.
D	Virginia Woolf's *A Room of One's Own* includes a long passage that hypothesizes about what might have happened if Shakespeare had had an equally talented sister.
E	T. S. Eliot's "The Love Song of J. Alfred Prufrock" is a difficult poem for most readers to understand.
F	T. S. Eliot's poem "The Love Song of J. Alfred Prufrock" warns readers that time is fleeting.

Effective Thesis Statements	Ineffective Thesis Statements

WRITE

Use the questions in the checklist to plan and write your thesis statement.

Your Turn

Ask students to complete the Your Turn activity.

Effective Thesis Statements	Ineffective Thesis Statements
A	C
B	D
F	E

Write

Ask students to complete the writing assignment.

ELL REWRITE CHECKLIST

A Topic

- ☐ What selections will you write about?
- ☐ What central ideas do you have about those selections?
- ☐ How are your central ideas related?

Clarity

- ☐ How will you let your readers know what to expect in your essay?
- ☐ How can you clearly answer the prompt?

Placement

- ☐ Will your thesis statement appear as the first sentence in your essay? Why?
- ☐ Will your thesis statement appear toward the end of your introduction? Why?
- ☐ How will the wording of your thesis statement differ based on its location?

Writer's Notebook

Project a famous speech, such as John F. Kennedy's "We Choose to Go to the Moon" or George Washington's "Farewell Address," on the board. Have students identify the author's thesis or claim and write why the author's method of communicating his or her claim is effective.

TURN AND TALK

Allow students to share their assessments of the thesis statement orally in pairs or small groups before writing.

Skill: Organizing Argumentative Writing

Introduce the Skill

Watch the Concept Definition video and read the following definition with your students.

Argumentative writing intends to convince readers of an author's position or point of view on a subject. To build an argument, authors introduce **claims**, which are arguments they will support with logical and valid reasoning and relevant evidence from reliable sources. In order to make a convincing argument, authors must distinguish their claim or claims from opposing points of view, or **counterclaims.**

When a writer is planning an argumentative essay, he or she will need to choose an organizational structure to present the argument in a logical and persuasive way. An **organizational structure** is the order or pattern that a writer uses to structure and present ideas or events. A writer of an argumentative text may do one of the following:

- discuss a claim or claims in order of importance
- compare and contrast ideas
- present cause-and-effect relationships
- list advantages and disadvantages
- describe a problem and offer a solution

Skill: Organizing Argumentative Writing

••• CHECKLIST FOR ORGANIZING ARGUMENTATIVE WRITING

As you consider how to organize your writing for your argumentative essay, use the following questions as a guide:

- What kinds of evidence could I find that would support my claim?
- Did I choose an organizational structure that establishes clear relationships between claims and supporting reasons and evidence?

Follow these steps to organize your argumentative essay in a way that logically sequences claim(s), reasons, and evidence:

- identify your precise, or specific, claim or claims and the evidence that supports them
- establish the significance of your claim
  - > find what others may have written about the topic, and learn why they feel it is important
  - > look for possible consequences or complications if something is done or is not accomplished
- choose an organizational structure that logically sequences and establishes clear relationships among claims, opposing claims or counterclaims, and the evidence presented to support the claims

TURN AND TALK

Why is it important to choose an appropriate organizational structure when writing an argumentative essay? How could using an inappropriate structure affect an essay?

SPEAKING FRAMES

- It is important to choose an appropriate structure because ____.
- Using an inappropriate structure could ____.

SKILL VOCABULARY

argumentative writing / la escritura argumentativa *noun* a genre of writing in which a writer presents a central claim and provides reasons and evidence to support that claim COGNATE

claim / la afirmación *noun* the writer's or speaker's position on a debatable issue or problem

YOUR TURN

Read the thesis statements below. Then, complete the chart by writing the organizational structure that would be most appropriate for the purpose, topic, and context of the corresponding essay, as well as the audience.

Organizational Structure Options		
order of importance	cause and effect	compare and contrast

Thesis Statement	Organizational Structure
The devastation of the world wars led to a sense of isolation among authors and readers.	
Modernists had more in common with Victorian writers than one might think.	
Many factors led Romantics to idolize nature, but the Industrial Revolution had the strongest influence.	

YOUR TURN

Complete the outline by writing an introductory statement, thesis statement, and three main ideas as well as supporting evidence for the body paragraphs of your argumentative essay. Make sure your ideas are appropriate for the purpose, topic, and context of your essay, as well as your audience.

Outline	Summary
Introductory Statement	
Thesis	
Body Paragraph 1	
Supporting Evidence 1	
Body Paragraph 2	
Supporting Evidence 2	
Body Paragraph 3	
Supporting Evidence 3	

Your Turn

Ask students to complete the Your Turn activity.

Thesis Statement 1	cause and effect
Thesis Statement 2	compare and contrast
Thesis Statement 3	order of importance

Your Turn

Ask students to complete the Your Turn activity. Answers will vary.

Introductory Statement	Early 20th-century laws and social expectations were especially harsh against women.
Thesis	Alienation is a common theme in modernist works because authors wanted to show how unfair practices had a detrimental effect on women.
Body Paragraph 1	*A Room of One's Own* argues that separate spheres would have prevented a talented woman from becoming as successful as Shakespeare.
Supporting Evidence 1	"Meanwhile his extraordinarily gifted sister, . . . Horace and Virgil."
Body Paragraph 2	"The New Dress" shows that social pressures led women to doubt their self-worth.
Supporting Evidence 2	"Mabel had her first serious suspicion . . . was not RIGHT."
Body Paragraph 3	"A Cup of Tea" demonstrates that societal expectations often pit women against each other.
Supporting Evidence 3	"'Good Lord!' Philip struck a match. . . . and all that.'"

SKILL VOCABULARY

counterclaim / el contraargumento ***noun*** an idea that is contrary to the author's position or point of view; an opposing claim

organizational structure / la estructura organizativa ***noun*** the order or pattern that a writer uses to organize information, such as cause-and-effect or compare-and-contrast COGNATE

Literary Analysis Writing Process: Draft

Write

Ask students to complete the writing assignment.

CHECK FOR SUCCESS

If students struggle to begin drafting their literary analyses, ask them the following questions:

- What is your claim?
- What reasons do you have to support your claim?
- What textual evidence best supports your reasons?
- How will the organization of your essay help readers understand your claim?

DRAFT CHECKLIST

Purpose and Focus

- ☐ Have I made my topic and claim clear to readers?

Organization

- ☐ Does the order of my ideas help make them persuasive?

Evidence and Elaboration

- ☐ Will my readers be able to easily understand the connection between my evidence and claim?

Extended Writing Project

Literary Analysis Writing Process: Draft

PLAN | DRAFT | REVISE | EDIT AND PUBLISH

You have already made progress toward writing your literary analysis. Now it is time to draft your literary analysis.

WRITE

Use your plan and other responses in your Binder to draft your literary analysis. You may also have new ideas as you begin drafting. Feel free to explore those new ideas as you have them. You can also ask yourself these questions to ensure that your writing is focused and organized and has appropriate evidence and elaboration to support your thesis:

Draft Checklist:

- ☐ **Purpose and Focus:** Have I made my topic and claim clear to readers? Have I included only relevant information and details and nothing extraneous that might confuse my readers?
- ☐ **Organization:** Is the organizational structure of my essay appropriate for my purpose, audience, topic, and context? Are my ideas presented in a way that persuades readers?
- ☐ **Evidence and Elaboration:** Will my readers be able to easily understand the connection between my ideas and supporting evidence?

Before you submit your draft, read it over carefully. You want to be sure that you've responded to all aspects of the prompt.

Peer Review

Students should submit substantive feedback to two peers using the review instructions below.

- How has the writer provided sufficient, relevant evidence to support his or her thesis? Is there any place where reasons or evidence could be added or improved?
- What suggestions can you make to help the writer improve the organization of the literary analysis?

SENTENCE FRAMES

- One piece of convincing relevant evidence is ____. A place where you could add evidence or elaborate is ____.
- I think your organization is strong because ____. I would suggest you change ____.

Here is Emma's literary analysis draft. As you read, notice how Emma develops her draft to be focused and organized, so it has relevant evidence and elaboration to support her ideas. As she continues to revise and edit her literary analysis, she will find and improve weak spots in her writing, as well as correct any language or punctuation mistakes.

STUDENT MODEL: FIRST DRAFT

Alienation in a Post-War Society

~~In the early 20th century, the world was in flux. The world people thought they knew was changing, and as a result men and women of all levels of society felt lost. Old conventions and social norms were challenged by writers and artists. They created new styles, and these same writers and artists sought to represent individuals' subjective points of view. "The Love Song of J. Alfred Prufrock," "The New Dress," and "A Cup of Tea" show that feelings of alienation can affect anyone.~~

Skill: Introductions

Emma decides to provide more context in the beginning of her introduction by adding details to show why the world was changing. She then adds a sentence about alienation to connect her introductory sentences and her thesis statement. Finally, she rephrases her thesis to give her essay a more precise focus.

In the early 20th century, the world was in flux. New technology led to destruction as war raged in Europe. At the same time, many challenged traditional norms of gender and class. For example, women's suffrage movements gained traction in both Great Britain and the United States. The world people thought they knew was changing, and as a result men and women of all levels of society felt lost. Writers and artists reacted by challenging old conventions and social norms. They created new styles and sought to represent individuals' subjective points of view. Alienation is a common theme in modernist literature because uncertainty was a by-product of the rapidly changing society. Modernist works such as "The Love Song of J. Alfred Prufrock," "The New Dress," and "A Cup of Tea" show that feelings of alienation stretched across lines of gender and class.

Poet T. S. Eliot moved to England in 1914 while World War I was going on in Europe. Although he was born in the United States. T. S. Eliot's poem "The Love Song of J. Alfred Prufrock," published in 1915, reflects the uncertainty Europeans felt as the world changed around them. The first images in the poem create tension as a familiar scene turns ominous:

> Let us go then, you and I,
> When the evening is spread out against the sky
> Like a patient etherized upon a table.

Analyze Student Model

Have students discuss the questions in the lesson as well as the Student Model draft. Ask:

- How does Emma reveal the focus of her argument in her literary analysis draft?
- How does Emma organize her draft?
- How does Emma use evidence and elaboration in her draft?
- How can you reveal your focus, organize your ideas, and ensure you use evidence and elaboration in your own literary analysis?

Encourage students to share their ideas for their own literary analysis based on the questions in the lesson.

ELL SPEAKING FRAMES

- The focus of Emma's argument is ____. This is clear because ____.
- Emma uses ____ structure to ____.
- Emma uses evidence and elaboration when she ____, which helps her ____.
- An idea that I have for my literary analysis is ____.

Introductions

Discuss the Model

1. The Model shows how Emma changed the introduction of her essay. How did she change it? She added description and details to make the introduction more appropriate for her topic, audience, and purpose.
2. How do those changes improve her introduction? Answers will vary.
3. What other revisions could Emma make to improve her introduction? Answers will vary.

ELL SPEAKING FRAMES

- Emma changed her introduction by ____.
- These changes improved her introduction because ____.
- Another revision Emma could make is ____.

Introductions

Connect to Mentor Text

Project the following example of an introduction, and discuss with your students:

Even its children knew that the South was in trouble. No one had to tell them; no words said aloud. To them, it was a vague thing weaving in and out of their play, like a ghost haunting an old graveyard or whispers after the household sleeps—fleeting mystery, vague menace to which each responded in his own way. Some learned to screen out all except the soft and the soothing; others denied even as they saw plainly, and heard. But all knew that under quiet words and warmth and laughter, under the slow ease and tender concern about small matters, there was a heavy burden on all of us and as heavy a refusal to confess it. The children knew this "trouble" was bigger than they, bigger than their family, bigger than their church, so big that people turned away from its size. (Killers of the Dream)

Ask students:

- What do you notice about this introduction?
- How does the author introduce her topic?
- What details does the author include in this introduction?

NOTES

An evening stroll under the night sky is typicaly a romantic or serene image, but Eliot uses it differently. By comparing the evening to a patient about to have surgery, Eliot goes against the reader's expectations for how natural imagery will work in the poem. This makes readers uncomfortable because they do not know what will happen on the journey on which they are about to embarck with him. Uncertainty and alienation are apparent in the speaker himself. He constantly doubts his own worth and place in the world. Instead of simply interacting with people, he stops to ask: Do I dare Disturb the universe? The entire poem takes place in the speaker's own mind. Because of insecurity, the speaker struggles to participate in society. In this way, "The Love Song of J. Alfred Prufrock" shows that alienation can be a product of our own making.

~~The person in Virginia Woolf's short story is also a victim of insecurities, like the speaker of Eliot's poem, she wants to participate in society but is instead alienated by her own feelings of inadequacy. In "The New Dress," Mabel Waring is so worried that the other guests will judge her that she cannot enjoy herself at a party:~~

> ~~And at once the misery which she always tried to hide, the profound dissatisfaction—the sense she had had, ever since she was a child, of being inferior to other people—set upon her, relentlessly, remorselessly, with an intensity which she could not beat off, as she would when she woke at night at home, by reading Borrow or Scott; for oh these men, oh these women, all were thinking—"What's Mabel wearing? What a fright she looks! What a hideous new dress!"—their eyelids flickering as they came up and then their lids shutting rather tight. It was her own appalling inadequacy; her cowardice; her mean, water-sprinkled blood that depressed her.~~

~~Later, when a fellow party guest points out that Mabel has bought a new dress, it causes her to unravel. Instead of enjoying her social interactions, Mabel allows a single comment to send her into a spiral of anxiety and shame. In the end, she leaves the party early, too embarrassed by her appearance to remain in the company of others. "The New Dress" is a story about society's expectations.~~

~~Rosemary Fell, the protagonist in Katherine Mansfield's "A Cup of Tea" is a member of London's high society and is extremely wealthy.~~

NOTES

~~She is also well-respected and sure of her place in the world. Yet, Rosemary also fails to connect with the people around her. When she decides to invite a penniless young woman home for tea, she does so in order to make herself feel like a benefactor instead of out of a genuine desire to make a friend. Rosemary is kept from seeing Miss Smith as a whole person by the class difference. Instead, she views the interaction as a game to keep herself entertained on a rainy day, which becomes clear when she abruptly throws Miss Smith out after husband, Philip, comments on the young woman's beauty. Like Mabel's experience, this sends Rosemary into a spiral as the words echo in her head, "Pretty! Absolutely lovely! Bowled over! Her heart beat like a heavy bell." Rosemary asks her husband to reassure her. "'Philip,' she whispered, and she pressed his head against her bosom, 'am I pretty?'" Rosemary abandons Miss Smith at the first sign of that their friendship could lead to a rivalry for her husband's attention. Miss Smith has been alienated by the woman who claimed to be her benefactor, and Rosemary feels insecure in her relationship with her husband.~~

Skill: Transitions

To connect her discussion of the two stories, Emma focuses on how the authors approach the same theme from different perspectives. She modifies the concluding sentence of her paragraph about "The New Dress" to summarize her analysis of this theme in the story. She then creates a transition to her discussion of "A Cup of Tea" by contrasting the two protagonists in her new topic sentence about that work.

The protagonist of Virginia Woolf's short story "The New Dress" is also a victim of her own insecurities. Like the speaker of Eliot's poem, Mabel Waring wants to participate in society but is instead alienated by her own feelings of inadequacy. Mabel is so worried that the other guests will judge her that she cannot enjoy herself at a party:

> And at once the misery which she always tried to hide, the profound dissatisfaction—the sense she had had, ever since she was a child, of being inferior to other people—set upon her, relentlessly, remorselessly, with an intensity which she could not beat off, as she would when she woke at night at home, by reading Borrow or Scott; for oh these men, oh these women, all were thinking—"What's Mabel wearing? What a fright she looks! What a hideous new dress!"—their eyelids flickering as they came up and then their lids shutting rather tight. It was her own appalling inadequacy; her cowardice; her mean, water-sprinkled blood that depressed her.

Mabel's uncertainty is directly tied to her perception of society's expectations. She worries that, as a member of a slightly lower social class, she cannot measure up to other guests' expectations, and it

Transitions

Discuss the Model

1. Emma noticed that one of her transitions between paragraphs is effective. What makes this a strong transition? Emma noticed that she used the word *also* to show how the speaker in Eliot's poem and the protagonist of Woolf's short story are connected.
2. The Model shows how Emma changed a section of her literary analysis essay. Why did she change it? Emma changed this section because she noticed that the transition between her analysis of "The New Dress" and "A Cup of Tea" was not clear and did not explain how this new text would build on her argument.
3. How did she revise her draft? She revised the final sentence of her paragraph so that it now summarizes her analysis of "The New Dress," and she also introduced a stronger transition sentence at the beginning of the next paragraph.
4. How did those changes improve her literary analysis? Answers will vary.
5. How else could Emma improve her use of transitions? Answers will vary.

ELL SPEAKING FRAMES

- Emma noticed ____, which makes it a strong transition because ____.
- Emma changed this section because ____.
- Emma revised her draft by ____.
- These changes improved her literary analysis because ____.
- Emma could change ____.

B PEER CONFERENCE

Have students choose one aspect of their writing that they would like feedback on. Ask them to design a helpful feedback question, such as "How can I ______?" Pair or group students, and allow them to read and discuss their work together, using the feedback question as a lens.

NOTES

makes her doubt her worth. Later, when a fellow party guest points out that Mabel has bought a new dress, it causes her to unravel: "'Why,' she asked herself, 'can't I . . . feel sure about the canary and pity and love and not be whipped all round in a second by coming into a room full of people?'" Instead of enjoying her social interactions, Mabel allows a single comment to send her into a spiral of anxiety and shame. In the end, she leaves the party early, too embarrassed by her appearance to remain in the company of others. "The New Dress" shows that alienation can be a product of society's expectations.

Rosemary Fell, the protagonist in Katherine Mansfield's "A Cup of Tea," is the opposite of Mabel in several key ways. Rosemary is a member of London's high society and is extremely wealthy. She is also well-respected and sure of her place in the world. Yet, Rosemary also fails to connect with the people around her. When she decides to invite a penniless young woman, Miss Smith, home for tea, she does so in order to make herself feel like a benefactor instead of out of a genuine desire to make a friend: "She was going to prove to this girl that—wonderful things did happen in life, that—fairy godmothers were real, that—rich people had hearts, and that women *were* sisters." The class difference between the characters prevents Rosemary from seeing Miss Smith as a whole person. Instead, she views the interaction as a game to keep herself entertained on a rainy day. This becomes clear when she abruptly throws Miss Smith out after her husband, Philip, comments on the young woman's beauty. Just as the guest's comment affects Mabel in "The New Dress," this passing commentary sends Rosemary into a spiral as the words echo in her head: "Pretty! Absolutely lovely! Bowled over! Her heart beat like a heavy bell." Rosemary abandons Miss Smith at the first sign that their friendship could lead to a rivalry for her husband's attention. Later, Rosemary asks her husband to reassure her. "'Philip,' she whispered, and she pressed his head against her bosom, 'am I *pretty*?'" As the story concludes, Miss Smith has been alienated by the woman who claimed to be her benefactor, and Rosemary feels insecure in her relationship with her husband. "A Cup of Tea" shows that alienation can occur when issues relating to class and gender complicate individual relationships between two people.

~~"The Love Song of J. Alfred Prufrock," "The New Dress," and "A Cup of Tea" prove that feelings of alienation were common during~~

~~Modernism. Bewildered by their own feelings, the speaker in "The Love Story of J. Alfred Prufrock" and the protagonists in "The New Dress" and "A Cup of Tea" are left alone and afraid. Alienation is a common theme in these modernist works because in a post-war, ever-changing world art, gender, and class needed redefining.~~

Skill: Conclusions

Emma strengthens her conclusion by revising the beginning and end of the paragraph. She rephrases her thesis in the first sentence. Then she adds a closing question, which helps her connect with her audience and make her idea memorable.

The characters in these modernist works come from different backgrounds and have different experiences, but the results of their attempted interactions with others are similar. Hindered by their own insecurities, the speaker in "The Love Song of J. Alfred Prufrock" and the protagonists in "The New Dress" and "A Cup of Tea" are left alone and afraid. Alienation is a common theme in these modernist works because in a post-war, ever-changing world, it is human nature to ask, "Am I good enough?"

Conclusions

Discuss the Model

1. The Model shows how Emma changed the conclusion of her essay. How did she change it?
   She rephrased her thesis statement and added a stronger concluding statement to make her conclusion more appropriate for her topic, the context of her essay, and her audience.
2. How did those changes improve her essay?
   Answers will vary.
3. What other revisions could Emma make to improve her conclusion?
   Answers will vary.

SPEAKING FRAMES

- Emma changed her conclusion by ____.
- These changes improved her essay because ____.
- Another revision Emma could make is ____.

Conclusions

Connect to Mentor Text

Project the following example of a conclusion, and discuss with your students:

Today is Trinity Sunday. Centuries ago words were written to be a call and a spur to the faithful servants of truth and justice:

Arm yourselves, and be ye men of valour, and be in readiness for the conflict; for it is better for us to perish in battle than to look upon the outrage of our nation and our altars. As the will of God is in Heaven, even so let it be. (Be Ye Men of Valour)

Ask students:

- What do you notice about this conclusion?
- What about the ending appeals to you as a reader?
- What information does the author provide in the conclusion?

Skill: Introductions

Introduce the Skill

Watch the Concept Definition video and read the following definition with your students.

The **introduction** is the opening paragraph or section of an essay or other nonfiction text. To begin an argumentative essay, writers identify the **topic**, or what the essay will be about. The most important part of the introduction in an argumentative essay is the **thesis statement**. This statement contains the writer's **claim**, or main argument, and it states something that the writer believes to be true.

In an informative/explanatory text, the introduction should provide readers with necessary information in order to introduce a topic. It should state the thesis, which in an informative/explanatory essay is a short statement that summarizes the main point of the essay and previews the ideas that will follow in the text.

In essays, many writers also include one or two sentences that are called a "hook." They are intended to engage readers' interest and grab their attention so they keep reading.

Skill: Introductions

CHECKLIST FOR INTRODUCTIONS

Before you write your introduction, ask yourself the following questions:

- What is my claim? In addition:
  - > How can I make it more precise and informative?
  - > Have I included why my claim is significant to discuss? How does it help the reader understand the topic better? What does it contribute to the conversation on my topic?
- How can I introduce my topic? Have I organized complex ideas, concepts, and information so that each new element builds on the previous element and creates a unified whole?
- How will I "hook" my reader's interest? I might:
  - > start with an attention-grabbing statement
  - > begin with an intriguing question
  - > use descriptive words to set a scene

Here are two strategies to help you introduce your precise claim and topic clearly in an introduction:

- Peer Discussion
  - > talk about your topic with a partner, explaining what you already know and your ideas about your topic
  - > write notes about the ideas you have discussed and any new questions you may have
  - > review your notes, and think about what your claim or controlling idea will be
  - > briefly state your precise and informative claim, establishing why it is important—or what ideas you are contributing to your topic—and how it is different from other claims about your topic
  - > write a possible "hook"

TURN AND TALK

Turn to a partner and use the following questions to discuss writing introductions: Imagine that you are describing your favorite movie to someone who has never seen it. How would you begin? What details would you include?

SPEAKING FRAMES

- I would begin with a description of ____.
- A detail I would include in the beginning is ____.

SKILL VOCABULARY

introduction / la introducción ***noun*** the opening paragraph or section of an essay COGNATE

topic / el tema ***noun*** the subject of a literary work, usually expressed as a single word or phrase in the form of a noun

thesis statement / la presentación de la tesis ***noun*** a statement that shares the main idea of an argumentative or informative essay

claim / la afirmación ***noun*** the writer's or speaker's position on a debatable issue or problem

- Freewriting
  - > freewrite for 10 minutes about your topic. Don't worry about grammar, punctuation, or having fully formed ideas. The point of freewriting is to discover ideas
  - > review your notes, and think about what your claim or controlling idea will be
  - > briefly state your precise and informative claim, establishing why it is important—or what ideas you are contributing to your topic—and how it is different from other claims about your topic
  - > write a possible "hook"

Writer's Notebook

Ask students to imagine that they are writing a review for the school newspaper about the last book they read. Have them write the introductory paragraph of the review. Remind them to use the questions in the checklist as a guide.

TURN AND TALK

Allow students to share their opening sentence orally in pairs or small groups before writing.

Your Turn

Ask students to complete the Your Turn activity.

A. Correct. This revision uses appropriate language and introduces the topic.

B. Incorrect. This revision uses appropriate language but does not introduce the topic.

C. Incorrect. This revision introduces the topic but does not use appropriate language.

D. Incorrect. This revision introduces the topic but does not use appropriate language.

Write

Ask students to complete the writing assignment.

ELL REWRITE CHECKLIST

A Claim

- ☐ How can I make my claim more precise and informative?
- ☐ Have I included why my claim is significant to discuss?
- ☐ How does my claim help the reader understand the topic better?

Hook

- ☐ Do I have an attention-grabbing statement?
- ☐ Should I include an intriguing question to engage the reader?
- ☐ Have I included descriptive words to help the reader visualize my topic?

Thesis Statement

- ☐ Is my main idea clear?
- ☐ Does the thesis statement allow the reader to anticipate the content that is to follow in the essay?

Relevant Evidence/Information

- ☐ Could I use a surprising piece of information to make my argument stronger and more engaging?
- ☐ What relevant evidence/information will help my reader understand the topic?

YOUR TURN

Choose the best answer to the question.

1. Below is a passage from a previous draft of Emma's introduction. The underlined sentence is inappropriate for the context of an academic essay and does not clearly introduce the topic of the paper. How should Emma revise the sentence to better suit the topic and context?

> Feeling alienated is the worst. Imagine going to a party and being ridiculed by the other guests because you are wearing a new dress, or having your husband tell you that your new friend is more beautiful than you are. How would that make you feel? Alienation is a common theme in modernist literature because writers began to fight back against the unfair social restrictions set on women during this time.

- ○ A. Women in the early 20th century faced criticism if they did not conform to societal expectations.
- ○ B. Virginia Woolf and Katherine Mansfield were modernist writers who examined societal expectations.
- ○ C. Feeling like an outsider can be a real bummer, and this was a very common feeling for modernist women.
- ○ D. Society is way more critical of women than of men, and this was definitely on Virginia Woolf's mind.

WRITE

Use the questions in the checklist to revise the introduction of your literary analysis essay.

Skill: Transitions

••• CHECKLIST FOR TRANSITIONS

Before you revise your current draft to include transitions, think about:

- the key ideas you discuss in your body paragraphs
- the relationships among your claim(s), reasons, and evidence
- the logical progression of your argument

Next, reread your current draft and note places in your essay where:

- the relationships between your claim(s), reasons, and evidence are unclear
- you could add linking words, vary sentence structure (or syntax), or use other transitional devices to make your argument more cohesive. Look for:
  > sudden jumps in your ideas
  > places where the ideas in a paragraph do not logically follow from the points in the previous paragraph
  > repetitive sentence structures

Revise your draft to use words, phrases, and clauses as well as varied syntax to link the major sections of your essay, create cohesion, and clarify the relationships between claim(s) and reasons and between reasons and evidence, using the following questions as a guide:

- Are there unifying relationships among the claims, reasons, and evidence in my argument?
- Have I clarified these relationships?
- How can I link major sections of my essay using words, phrases, clauses, and varied syntax?

Skill: Transitions

Introduce the Skill

Watch the Concept Definition video and read the following definition with your students.

Transitions are connecting words, phrases, and clauses that writers use to **clarify** the relationships among ideas and details in a text. Transitions have different functions depending on whether the text is argumentative, informative, or narrative.

In an argumentative essay, writers state claims and provide reasons and evidence for their claims. To clarify a relationship between a claim and a reason or supporting evidence, transitions such as *although* and *on the other hand* help make connections clear.

For informative essays, transitions such as *however, in addition,* and *for example* may help create **cohesion** among ideas and concepts.

In narrative writing, authors use a variety of words, phrases, and clauses to signal shifts in time, setting, and action. Transitions such as *until now, meanwhile,* and *once it was over* may make narrative events more **coherent.**

Transitions also help to connect ideas both within and across paragraphs and between major sections of text.

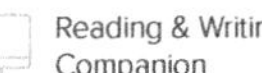

SKILL VOCABULARY

transition / la transición *noun* a connecting word or phrase that a writer may use to clarify the relationship between ideas in a text; set off with a comma COGNATE

clarify / aclarar *verb* to make clear and more comprehensible

cohesion / la cohesión *noun* the quality of parts working together as a whole COGNATE

coherent / coherente *adjective* marked by being orderly and logical; easy to understand COGNATE

TURN AND TALK

Turn to your partner and discuss the last time you had a strong reaction to something you had read. Describe the connections the author made between ideas that made the text so powerful.

SPEAKING FRAMES

- When I read ____, it made me feel ____.
- The author used ____ to connect ideas.
- A detail that caused this reaction was ____ because ____.

Your Turn

Ask students to complete the Your Turn activity.

QUESTION 1

A. Incorrect. This sentence summarizes the story. It does not improve the focus of the paragraph.

B. Incorrect. This sentence tells who the main character is. It does not improve the focus of the paragraph.

C. Correct. This sentence states the writer's main idea. It improves the focus of the paragraph.

D. Incorrect. This sentence may grab the audience's attention, but it does not improve the focus of the paragraph.

QUESTION 2

A. Incorrect. This sentence does not clearly explain how the paragraph will build on the argument.

B. Correct. This sentence creates a transition between the two paragraphs by focusing on the similarities between the characters and the way each text logically relates to the essay's argument.

C. Incorrect. This sentence continues the analysis of "The New Dress," but does not introduce "A Cup of Tea," which is what the second paragraph is about.

D. Incorrect. This sentence adds a quotation and some analysis of "The New Dress," but does not introduce "A Cup of Tea."

Write

Ask students to complete the writing assignment.

ELL **REWRITE CHECKLIST**

A
- ☐ **Introduce examples by using transitions such as:** to illustrate, including, for example, for instance
- ☐ **Compare and contrast by using transitions such as:** on the other hand, likewise, similarly, on the contrary
- ☐ **Show cause and effect by using transitions such as:** as a result, because, consequently

YOUR TURN

Choose the best answer to each question.

1. Below is a paragraph from a previous draft of Emma's argumentative literary analysis essay. The main idea of the paragraph is unclear. Which sentence should Emma add to the beginning of the paragraph to improve the focus of the paragraph?

> Once she arrives at the party, she cannot stand to look at herself: "But she dared not look in the glass. She could not face the whole horror—the pale yellow, idiotically old-fashioned silk dress with its long skirt and its high sleeves and its waist and all the things that looked so charming in the fashion book, but not on her, not among all these ordinary people." Mabel is very critical of herself.

- ○ A. The main character, Mabel, buys a new dress and goes to a party.
- ○ B. The main character in "The New Dress" is Mabel Waring.
- ○ C. Mabel's internal reflections show that she feels inadequate.
- ○ D. Have you ever felt self-conscious at a party, just like Mabel?

2. Emma wants to improve the transition between two paragraphs in a previous draft of her literary analysis essay by replacing the underlined sentence. Which sentence would be the best transition to include at the beginning of the second paragraph?

> When Mabel's confidence is shaken, she turns to others to buck up her spirits: "one word of affection from Charles would have made all the difference to her at the moment. If he had only said, 'Mabel, you're looking charming to-night!' it would have changed her life." She needs the approval of other people, and whether or not she feels affirmed can deeply impact her mood.
>
> Rosemary Fell, the protagonist of Katherine Mansfield's "A Cup of Tea" is very insecure.

- ○ A. Charles does not respond by giving Mabel a compliment, and this is very similar to what happens in Katherine Mansfield's "A Cup of Tea," which is another modernist short story.
- ○ B. Even though her economic status is different, Rosemary Fell, the protagonist of Katherine Mansfield's "A Cup of Tea," also feels alienated when she does not feel affirmed by others.
- ○ C. This brief exchange between characters is a pivotal moment in Woolf's short story, so paying close attention to the relationship between Mabel and her husband is very revealing.
- ○ D. The narrator continues, "Charles said nothing of the kind, of course. He was malice itself," emphasizing that Mabel is truly on her own and alienated from even her husband.

WRITE

Use the questions in the checklist to revise your use of transitions in a section of your literary analysis essay.

Skill: Conclusions

••• CHECKLIST FOR CONCLUSIONS

Before you write your conclusion, ask yourself the following questions:

- How can I rephrase the thesis or main idea in my conclusion? What impression can I make on my reader?
- How can I write my conclusion so that it supports and follows logically from my argument?
- How can I conclude with a memorable comment?

Below are two strategies to help you provide a concluding statement or section that follows from and supports your argument:

- Peer Discussion
  - > after you have written your introduction and body paragraphs, talk with a partner about what you want readers to remember, writing notes about your discussion
  - > review your notes, and think about what you wish to express in your conclusion
  - > do not simply restate your claim or thesis statement. Rephrase your main idea to show the depth of your knowledge and the importance of your claim
  - > write your conclusion
- Freewriting
  - > freewrite for 10 minutes about what you might include in your conclusion. Don't worry about grammar, punctuation, or having fully formed ideas. The point of freewriting is to discover ideas
  - > review your notes, and think about what you wish to express in your conclusion
  - > do not simply restate your claim or thesis statement. Rephrase your main idea to show the depth of your knowledge and the importance of your claim
  - > write your conclusion

Skill: Conclusions

Introduce the Skill

Watch the Concept Definition video and read the following definition with your students.

A **conclusion** is the closing paragraph or section of an essay, argument, or narrative. It is where the writer brings an essay to a close by restating the main idea or **thesis statement** or the **claim** in an argument. It also summarizes the evidence and research that support the claim or thesis. The conclusion should follow logically from the information, explanations, or claim that has been presented. A conclusion is a good way to suggest to your readers that you have accomplished what you set out to do. In addition, try to leave readers with an interesting final impression. This might be accomplished by closing with a quote, an anecdote, or a call to action.

In a **narrative**, a conclusion should follow logically from the events of the plot and what the characters have experienced. It might include characters reflecting on events, why they matter, and how they feel about them.

SKILL VOCABULARY

conclusion / la conclusión ***noun*** the closing paragraph or section of an essay; a closing argument in an argumentative text COGNATE

thesis statement / la presentación de la tesis ***noun*** a statement that shares the main idea of an argumentative or informative essay

claim / la afirmación ***noun*** the writer's or speaker's position on a debatable issue or problem

narrative / la narración ***noun*** a story, real or imagined, consisting of connected events

TURN AND TALK

Turn to a partner and use the following questions to discuss conclusions: Imagine that you are describing your favorite movie to someone who has never seen it. How would you describe the movie's conclusion? What details, moments, or ideas would you use in your concluding thoughts about the movie?

SPEAKING FRAMES

- I would conclude with a description of ____.
- A (detail / moment / idea) I would include in my closing thoughts about the movie is ____.

Your Turn

Ask students to complete the Your Turn activity.

A. Incorrect. This revision leaves the audience with a memorable thought but does not help the writer achieve the purpose of her literary analysis.

B. Incorrect. This revision does not help the writer achieve the purpose of her literary analysis or leave the audience with a memorable thought.

C. Correct. This revision leaves the audience with a memorable thought and helps the writer achieve the purpose of her literary analysis.

D. Incorrect. This revision does not help the writer achieve the purpose of her literary analysis or leave the audience with a memorable thought.

Write

Ask students to complete the writing assignment.

REWRITE CHECKLIST

Conclusions

- ☐ Does the conclusion effectively wrap up the main points of your literary analysis essay?
- ☐ Have you rephrased the thesis in a meaningful way, rather than simply restating it?
- ☐ How might you leave the audience with a lasting impression?

YOUR TURN

Choose the best answer to the question.

1. Below is a passage from a previous draft of Emma's conclusion. She wants to add a sentence to clarify her purpose and leave her audience with a memorable thought. Which sentence should she add?

> Taking a close look at modernist texts shows that doubt and isolation were common feelings during the early 20th century. "The Love Song of J. Alfred Prufrock," "The New Dress," and "A Cup of Tea" reflect how rapid social and political changes made people feel helpless and disconnected at this time in history.

○ A. No one likes feeling helpless and disconnected from other people, especially when so much change is happening in the world.

○ B. *The Catcher in the Rye* reveals that people still felt this way in the mid-20th century, and that the best way to fight this feeling was to find purpose in life.

○ C. While isolation was a common feeling, modernist authors collectively proved that there was nothing left to do but reimagine art, gender, and class.

○ D. Modernist authors like T. S. Eliot, Virginia Woolf, and Katherine Mansfield also developed themes that questioned social norms.

WRITE

Use the questions in the checklist to revise the conclusion of your literary analysis.

Writer's Notebook

Ask students to imagine that they are writing a review for the school newspaper about the last book they read. Have them write the concluding paragraph of the review. Remind them to use the questions in the checklist as a guide.

TURN AND TALK

Allow students to share their closing sentence orally in pairs or small groups before writing.

Extended Writing Project

Literary Analysis Writing Process: Revise

PLAN | DRAFT | REVISE | EDIT AND PUBLISH

You have written a draft of your argumentative literary analysis essay. You have also received input from your peers about how to improve it. Now you are going to revise your draft.

REVISION GUIDE

Examine your draft to find areas for revision. Use the guide below to help you review:

Review	Revise	Example
	Clarity	
Scan your body paragraphs. Annotate any sentences where the connection between your ideas is unclear.	Add details so the relationship between your ideas is clear.	The entire poem takes place in the speaker's own mind. There are no outside forces preventing him from engaging with others. ~~Because of insecurity, the speaker struggles to participate in society.~~ The speaker's own hesitancy and insecurity prevent him from participating in society.

Literary Analysis Writing Process: Revise

Review Revision Guide

Break the class into five groups, and assign each group a category of the revision guide. Ask:

- What is the purpose of this section of the guide?
- How did it improve Emma's writing?
- How will it help to improve your writing?

Allow groups to share their ideas with the class.

SPEAKING FRAMES

- I think (clarity / development / organization / word choice / sentence fluency) improved Emma's writing by ____.
- I think (clarity / development / organization / word choice / sentence fluency) will improve my writing because ____.

Revise

Students should start this activity with a copy of their drafts either printed on paper or open in a word-processing program, such as Google Docs. Allow students time to revise their drafts using the instructions in the revision guide. Once students have finished revising their essays, have them submit their work.

CHECK FOR SUCCESS

Circulate around the room to spend time with individual students. Ask:

- What category are you working on?
- Why are you revising this specific section?
- How are you revising it?
- How does this change support your purpose?
- Does this change make your writing appropriate for your audience?

If students struggle while revising their drafts, choose an exemplary revision to share with the class while the student talks through the process. You could also invite a student to share a dilemma in the revision process and allow the class to offer feedback or suggestions.

CLARITY

Find passages containing unclear connections between ideas, sentences, or paragraphs, and revise the passages to make the connections clear.

CLARITY

Tell students to revise their drafts using the revision guide, focusing on clarity. In addition, have students make revisions that focus on sentence fluency, as practiced in the previous unit.

Review	Revise	Example
Development		
Identify the reasons that support your claims. Annotate places where you feel there is not enough evidence or explanation to support your claims.	Focus on a single idea or claim and add support, such as textual evidence or explanation.	Yet, Rosemary also fails to connect with the people around her. When she decides to invite a penniless young woman, Miss Smith, home for tea, she does so in order to make herself feel like a benefactor instead of out of a genuine desire to make a friend:. "She was going to prove to this girl that—wonderful things did happen in life, that—fairy godmothers were real, that—rich people had hearts, and that women *were* sisters."
Organization		
Review your body paragraphs. Identify and annotate any sentences that don't flow in a clear and logical way.	Rewrite the sentences so they appear in a logical sequence. Include transitions that clarify the organization of your ideas. Delete details that are repetitive or not essential to support the claim.	Rosemary abandons Miss Smith at the first sign that their friendship could lead to a rivalry for her husband's attention. Later, Rosemary asks her husband to reassure her. "'Philip,' she whispered, and she pressed his head against her bosom, 'am I *pretty*?'" ~~Rosemary abandons Miss Smith at the first sign of that their friendship could lead to a rivalry for her husband's attention.~~ As the story concludes, Miss Smith has been alienated by the woman who claimed to be her benefactor, and Rosemary feels insecure in her relationship with her husband.

Review	Revise	Example
Style: Word Choice		
Identify any sentences that use informal diction. Look for everyday words and phrases that could be replaced with more formal terms.	Replace everyday language with formal, academic language.	By comparing the evening to a patient about to have surgery, Eliot ~~goes against the reader's~~ upends expectations ~~for how natural imagery will work in the poem~~.
Style: Sentence Fluency		
Read your literary analysis essay aloud. Annotate places where the sentences do not flow naturally.	Revise choppy sentences by linking them together. Shorten longer, unfocused sentences to make the key idea clear.	Instead, she views the interaction as a game to keep herself entertained on a rainy day~~, which~~ This becomes clear when she abruptly throws Miss Smith out after her husband, Philip, comments on the young woman's beauty.

WRITE

Use the revision guide, as well as your peer reviews, to help you evaluate your argumentative literary analysis essay to determine areas that should be revised.

Write

Ask students to complete their writing assignment.

ELL REVISION CHECKLIST

A Find and replace:

- ☐ vague words and phrases
- ☐ unclear or undeveloped connections between ideas
- ☐ weak transitions between paragraphs or sentences

Skill: Using a Style Guide

Introduce the Skill

Watch the Concept Definition video and read the following definition with your students.

When you write, one of your goals is to match your style to the writing discipline. A **style guide** is a manual for writing and formatting text following conventions, specifically how to apply syntax and language conventions.

Syntax refers to the orderly arrangement of words and phrases to create well-formed sentences in a language. The principles of syntax fall into two interconnected classes: parts of speech and structural elements. **Parts of speech** are types of words that have particular roles in a sentence. The most common parts of speech are nouns, pronouns, verbs, modifiers (such as adjectives and adverbs), prepositions, and conjunctions. **Structural elements** include phrases and clauses that are created by groups of words.

Language **conventions** are rules for spelling, punctuation, capitalization, grammar, sentence structure, and formatting that make writing clear and understandable.

Different disciplines, or fields of study, use different styles. Using a style guide creates consistency and helps ensure that a piece of writing meets the expectations of a particular discipline. Here are several common style guides:

- Modern Language Association (MLA): used in literature and the humanities.
- Chicago Manual of Style: used in the humanities and social sciences.
- APA (American Psychological Association): used in the social sciences.
- *A Manual for Writers* by Kate Turabian: adapts the Chicago style for students.

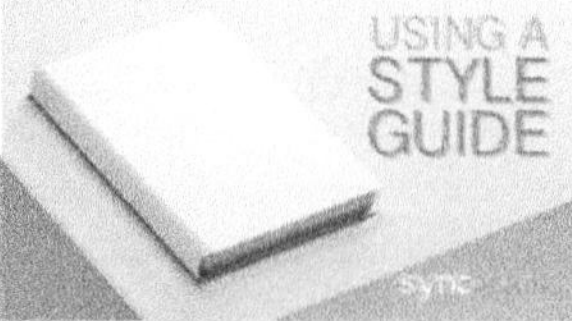

Skill: Using a Style Guide

CHECKLIST FOR USING A STYLE GUIDE

In order to ensure that your work conforms to the guidelines in a style manual, do the following:

- Determine which style guide you should use.
- Use the style guide for the overall formatting of your paper, citation style, bibliography format, and other style considerations for reporting research.
- As you draft, use an additional style guide, such as *Artful Sentences: Syntax as Style* by Virginia Tufte or William Strunk Jr.'s *The Elements of Style*, to help you vary your syntax, or the grammatical structure of sentences.
  - > Use a variety of simple, compound, complex, and compound-complex sentences to convey information.
  - > Be sure to punctuate your sentences correctly.
  - > Follow standard English language conventions to help you maintain a formal style for formal papers.

To edit your work so that it conforms to the guidelines in a style manual, consider the following questions:

- Have I followed the conventions for spelling, punctuation, capitalization, sentence structure, and formatting, according to the style guide?
- Have I varied my syntax to make my paper engaging for readers?
- Do I have an entry in my works cited or bibliography for each reference I used?
- Have I followed the correct style, including the guidelines for capitalization and punctuation, in each entry in my works cited or bibliography?

TURN AND TALK

Turn to a partner and discuss an example of a standard English convention that you need to learn more about. What is a resource you could use to clarify your understanding?

SPEAKING FRAMES

- One standard English convention that I need to learn more about is ____.
- One resource I could use to clarify my understanding is ____.

YOUR TURN

Read the style questions in the chart below. Then, complete the chart by identifying the header for a section of a style guide that would most likely contain the information needed to answer the question. Write the corresponding letter for each header in the appropriate row.

Style Guide Section Headers	
A	How to Cite Information If No Page Numbers Are Available
B	Words and Expressions Commonly Misused
C	Omit Needless Words
D	How to Cite Plays
E	Form the Singular Possessive of Nouns

Style Question	Section Header
Should I use *affect* or *effect?*	
How do I format dialogue from a drama?	
Should I write "Charles's friend" or "Charles' friend"?	
How do I cite information from a website?	
How do I make my writing more succinct?	

WRITE

Use the checklist to help you choose a convention that has been challenging for you to follow. Use a credible style guide to correct any errors related to that convention in your essay.

SKILL VOCABULARY

style guide / la guía de estilo *noun* a set of standards for the writing and formatting of documents COGNATE

syntax/ la sintaxis *noun* word order, or the way in which the elements of language (words, phrases, clauses, etc.) are arranged to create well-formed sentences COGNATE

conventions / la norma *noun* spelling, punctuation, capitalization, and grammar that help make writing and speaking clear and understandable

Your Turn

Ask students to complete the Your Turn activity.

Should I use *affect* or *effect?*	B
How do I format dialogue from a drama?	D
Should I write "Charles's friend" or "Charles' friend"?	E
How do I cite information from a website?	A
How do I make my writing more succinct?	C

Write

Ask students to complete the writing assignment.

ELL **REWRITE CHECKLIST**

A **In-Text Citation**

- ☐ How do I cite my sources in a text?
- ☐ What if the source I am using doesn't have a specific author?
- ☐ What if I am citing a television documentary as one of my sources?

Formatting a Bibliography

- ☐ Which sources do I include?
- ☐ What is the format for a source citation in a bibliography?
- ☐ How should I order my sources?

Quotation Marks

- ☐ Should I always use an open quotation mark and a close quotation mark when quoting a text?
- ☐ Should I use quotation marks if I am summarizing or paraphrasing a source?
- ☐ Should I use quotation marks for a block quote?

Varied Syntax and Sentence Structure

- ☐ Have I varied my syntax to make my essay engaging for readers?
- ☐ Have I used a style guide to confirm the rules for sentence structure and conventions?

Grammar: Commonly Misspelled Words

Introduce the Skill

Review the image and definition for commonly misspelled words as a class.

- spelling - the act of forming words from letters
- misspell - to spell incorrectly
- strategy - a plan for approaching a task or challenge
- pronunciation - the way a word sounds when it is said aloud
- visualize - to create images in your mind based on descriptions in the text

Discuss the Model

1. What should you do to learn how to spell words you have trouble with? Keep a list; use online or print dictionaries to help you spell the words; say, see, write, and check each word.
2. What are three examples of commonly misspelled words? Answers will vary but should include three words from the commonly misspelled words chart.

Grammar: Commonly Misspelled Words

By following a few simple steps, you can learn how to spell new words—even words that are unfamiliar or difficult. As you write, keep a list of words that you have trouble spelling. Refer to online or print resources for pronunciation, Latin or Greek roots, and other information that may help you remember how the words are spelled. Then, use the steps below to learn the spelling of those words.

Say it. Look at the word again, and say it aloud. Say it again, pronouncing each syllable clearly.

See it. Close your eyes. Picture the word. Visualize it letter by letter.

Write it. Look at the word again, and write it two or three times. Then, write the word without looking at the printed version.

Check it. Check your spelling. Did you spell it correctly? If not, repeat each step until you can spell it easily.

Here are some words that can sometimes confuse even strong spellers.

Commonly Misspelled Words		
abundant	accompaniment	against
apparatus	arctic	behavior
business	calendar	cemetery
circumstantial	deference	definite
exhibition	financier	forty
magnificence	metaphor	necessity
playwright	reference	repetitive
seize	sufficient	surprise
transparent	undoubtedly	unnecessary
vaccine	versatile	villain

YOUR TURN

1. How should this sentence be changed?

   No matter what the calender says today's date is, the weather feels absolutely arctic.

   ○ A. No matter what the calander says today's date is, the weather feels absolutely arctic.
   ○ B. No matter what the calendar says today's date is, the weather feels absolutely arctic.
   ○ C. No matter what the calaendar says today's date is, the weather feels absolutely artic.
   ○ D. No change needs to be made to this sentence.

2. How should this sentence be changed?

   Aunt Polly, who had gotten her degree in poetry, was always quick to seize upon a metaphor.

   ○ A. Aunt Polly, who had gotten her degree in poetry, was always quick to sieze upon a metaphor.
   ○ B. Aunt Polly, who had gotten her degree in poetry, was always quick to seise upon a metafor.
   ○ C. Aunt Polly, who had gotten her degree in poetry, was always quick to seize upon a metaphore.
   ○ D. No change needs to be made to this sentence.

3. How should this sentence be changed?

   Dr. Mason insists that the vacine against influenza is an important part of an annual checkup.

   ○ A. Dr. Mason insists that the vaccene agenst influenza is an important part of an annual checkup.
   ○ B. Dr. Mason insists that the vaccine against influenza is an important part of an annual checkup.
   ○ C. Dr. Mason insists that the vacine aggainst influenza is an important part of an annual checkup.
   ○ D. No change needs to be made to this sentence.

4. How should this sentence be changed?

   Undoubtedley in deferense to my grandfather's wishes, my family planned to hold his birthday dinner at his favorite restaurant.

   ○ A. Undoutedley in defence to my grandfather's wishes, my family planned to hold his birthday dinner at his favorite restaurant.
   ○ B. Undoubtedley in defrence to my grandfather's wishes, my family planned to hold his birthday dinner at his favorite restaurant.
   ○ C. Undoubtedly in deference to my grandfather's wishes, my family planned to hold his birthday dinner at his favorite restaurant.
   ○ D. No change needs to be made to this sentence.

Your Turn

Ask students to complete the Your Turn activities.

QUESTION 1

A. Incorrect.

B. Correct. *Calendar* is the correct spelling.

C. Incorrect.

D. Incorrect.

QUESTION 2

A. Incorrect.

B. Incorrect.

C. Incorrect.

D. Correct. All the words in the sentence are spelled correctly.

QUESTION 3

A. Incorrect.

B. Correct. *Vaccine* is the correct spelling.

C. Incorrect.

D. Incorrect.

QUESTION 4

A. Incorrect.

B. Incorrect.

C. Correct. *Undoubtedly* and *deference* are the correct spellings.

D. Incorrect.

Grammar: Pronoun Case and Reference

Introduce the Skill

Review the image and definition for pronouns as a class.

- pronoun - a word that takes the place of a noun
- personal pronoun - replaces the subject or object of a sentence
- subject, or nominative case, pronoun - serves as the subject of a sentence or clause
- object, or objective case, pronoun - serves as the object of a verb or preposition
- possessive pronoun - a pronoun showing ownership; takes the place of a noun in the possessive form

Discuss the Model

1. What are the properties and cases of pronouns? Pronouns have four properties: number, person, gender, and case. There are three cases: subject, object, and possessive.
2. What often causes writers to make pronoun-case errors? Writers often make pronoun-case errors when there are multiple subjects or multiple objects in a sentence.
3. Why are clear pronoun references important in sentences? Sentences in which pronouns don't have clear antecedents can be confusing for readers. Strong writing avoids this type of ambiguity.

Extended Writing Project

Grammar: Pronoun Case and Reference

Pronouns have four properties: number, person, gender, and case. There are three cases: subject (or nominative), object (or objective), and possessive case. Writers frequently make pronoun-case errors when there are multiple subjects (compound subjects) or multiple objects (compound objects) in a sentence.

Correctly Edited	Incorrect	Explanation
He and Joseph started a charity to help stray cats.	Him and Joseph started a charity to help stray cats.	"Him and Joseph" are the *subjects* of this sentence. "Him" is incorrect because "Him" is in the *object* case.
Read this book and tell Mr. Tannenbaum and **me** what you think.	Read this book and tell Mr. Tannenbaum and I what you think.	"Mr. Tannenbaum and I" are *objects* in this sentence. "I" is incorrect because "I" is in the *subject* case.
I know that **she** and her sister traveled through South America last year.	I know that her and her sister traveled through South America last year.	"Her and her sister" are the *subjects* in a clause. The first "her" is incorrect because "her" is in the *object* case. The second "her," however, is correct because it is in the *possessive* case, showing a relationship to the sister.

Sentences that use pronouns can become confusing for a reader if the pronouns do not have clear antecedents. Strong writing avoids ambiguity.

Correctly Edited	Incorrect	Strategy for Revision
The team captain told Karen to take **the captain's** guard position.	The team captain told Karen to take her guard position.	Replace a pronoun with a noun.
Lock the car after you put it in the garage.	When you put the car in the garage, don't forget to lock it.	Rewrite the sentence to make the antecedent clear.

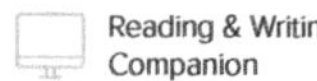

YOUR TURN

1. How should this sentence be changed?

> The committee awarded the band, the female vocalist, and him a music trophy.

- A. They awarded the band, the female vocalist, and him a music trophy.
- B. The committee awarded the band, she, and him a music trophy.
- C. The committee awarded the band, the female vocalist, and he a music trophy.
- D. No change needs to be made to this sentence.

2. How should this sentence be changed?

> The exam that Ms. Standjord is giving to us on Wednesday will be simple for you and I.

- A. The exam that Ms. Standjord is giving to we on Wednesday will be simple for you and I.
- B. The exam that Ms. Standjord is giving to us on Wednesday will be simple for you and me.
- C. The exam that Ms. Standjord is giving to us on Wednesday will be simple for she and I.
- D. No change needs to be made to this sentence.

3. How should this sentence be changed?

> Charlotte emailed Olivia, who was away on a business trip, to say that her mother had been in an automobile accident.

- A. Charlotte emailed she, who was away on a business trip, to say that her mother had been in an automobile accident.
- B. Charlotte emailed Olivia, who was away on a business trip, to say that Olivia's mother had been in an automobile accident.
- C. She emailed Olivia, who was away on a business trip, to say that her mother had been in an automobile accident.
- D. No change needs to be made to this sentence.

Your Turn

Ask students to complete the Your Turn activities.

QUESTION 1

A. Incorrect.

B. Incorrect.

C. Incorrect.

D. Correct. *Him* is an object pronoun, and it is correctly used in the sentence as an object of the verb.

QUESTION 2

A. Incorrect.

B. Correct. *I* is a subject pronoun. It should be changed to the object pronoun *me*.

C. Incorrect.

D. Incorrect.

QUESTION 3

A. Incorrect.

B. Correct. In this sentence, the possessive pronoun *her* has an unclear antecedent. Replacing *her* with *Olivia's* clarifies the meaning of this sentence.

C. Incorrect.

D. Incorrect.

Literary Analysis Writing Process: Edit and Publish

Practice with Student Model (Optional)

Provide groups with a different section of Emma's draft. Each group should practice editing Emma's Model using the checklist in the lesson. Has she:

- ☐ followed relevant rules in the style guide?
- ☐ made sure that her pronouns reflect the correct case and have clear antecedents?
- ☐ corrected any sentence fragments or run-on sentences?
- ☐ spelled everything correctly?

After the groups have finished, call on volunteers from each group to make edits until all the mistakes have been found and edited, pausing to discuss points of disagreement.

ELL **SPEAKING FRAMES**

- Emma (did/did not) follow relevant rules in the style guide when she wrote ____.
- Emma (did/did not) make sure that her pronouns reflect the correct case and have clear antecedents when she wrote ____.
- ____ is an example of a (run-on sentence/sentence fragment) that Emma (has/has not) corrected.
- ____ is spelled incorrectly. The correct spelling is ____.

Literary Analysis Writing Process: Edit and Publish

PLAN | DRAFT | REVISE | EDIT AND PUBLISH

You have revised your literary analysis based on your peer feedback and your own examination.

Now, it is time to edit your literary analysis. When you revised, you focused on the content of your literary analysis. You probably looked at your essay's claim and thesis statement, your organization, and your supporting evidence. When you edit, you focus on the mechanics of your literary analysis, paying close attention to things like grammar and punctuation.

Use the checklist below to guide you as you edit:

- ☐ Have I followed relevant rules in the style guide?
- ☐ Do my pronouns reflect the correct case and have clear antecedents?
- ☐ Do I have any sentence fragments or run-on sentences?
- ☐ Have I spelled everything correctly?

Notice some edits Emma has made:

- Fixed a spelling error
- Replaced an unclear pronoun with a noun
- Added a slash to show a line break in a quotation from a poem, and cited line numbers

By comparing the evening to a patient about to have surgery, Eliot upends expectations. This makes readers uncomfortable because they do not know what will happen on the journey on which they are about to ~~embarck~~ embark with ~~him~~ the poem's speaker.

Uncertainty and alienation are also reflected in the speaker himself. He constantly doubts his own worth and place in the world. Instead of simply interacting with people, he stops to ask:, ~~Do I dare Disturb the universe?~~ "Do I dare / Disturb the universe?" (51-52).

WRITE

Use the questions in the checklist, as well as your peer reviews, to help you evaluate your literary analysis to determine places that need editing. Then, edit your literary analysis to correct those errors.

Once you have made all your corrections, you are ready to publish your work. You can distribute your writing to family and friends, hang it on a bulletin board, or post it on your blog. If you publish online, share the link with your family, friends, and classmates.

Write

After students finish editing, suggest, if there's time, that they set their essays aside for a few minutes and that they then proofread them one more time. Once they have completed their writing, they should submit their work.

CHECK FOR SUCCESS

If students struggle to edit successfully, help them determine where edits are needed and what changes need to be made.

Direct students to the grammar lessons in this unit if they are uncertain about the rules for specific concepts.

ELL READ ALOUD

Encourage students to read their essays aloud to themselves or to a partner in order to catch any remaining mistakes.

A READ ALOUD

Encourage students to read their essays aloud to themselves or to an on-grade-level peer in order to catch any remaining mistakes.

B RETOOL YOUR WORK

Have students rewrite their piece with a different purpose in mind and/or for a different audience. For example, students could turn their essays into a blog post, an abstract for a research paper, or a series of social media posts.

English Language Learner Resources

studysync

USERS ASSIGNMENTS

GRADE 12 › UNIT

Fractured Selves

Core ELA
Grade 12
30 days

Unit Overview

Integrated Reading and Writing

Extended Writing Project

ELL Resources

Novel Study

End-of-Unit Assessment

9 10 11

Add to bookshelf

Instructional Path

Fear of Missing Out

The Ribbons

Skill: Classroom Vocabulary

After learning academic classroom vocabulary words, students will be able to recognize and use them in a variety of contexts. Words include *abstract, advanced, concrete, connection, evidence, hypothesis, interaction, issue, proficient,* and *sector.*

Teacher Resources: Lesson Plan

Assign Preview

Skill: Making Connections

After reading and discussing a model, students will be able to make a text-to-self, a text-to-text, or a text-to-world connection while reading.

Teacher Resources: Lesson Plan

Assign Preview

English Language Learner Resources

Lessons in the English Language Learner Resources section offer explicit ELL instruction. These lessons share a thematic and genre focus with all other lessons in the Core ELA unit.

The twenty ELL Resources in this section are developed around two texts and an Extended Oral Project. Each text is written at four distinct levels. For ELL's, these texts serve as structural and thematic models of authentic texts in the Integrated Reading and Writing section of the unit.

ELL lessons modify the routines used with texts in the Integrated Reading and Writing section. Explicit vocabulary instruction is emphasized, and reading and writing skills lessons focus strongly on language acquisition and reading comprehension.

The Extended Oral Project can be used in place of or as an extension to the Extended Writing Project. In this unit, students will plan and present a monologue based on a fictional character. Throughout these lessons, students will interact with texts and their peers as readers, writers, speakers, and listeners to maximize comprehension and provide multiple access points for every learner.

Focus on English Language Proficiency Levels

ADVANCED HIGH
ADVANCED
INTERMEDIATE
BEGINNING

ELL Resources provide targeted support for four levels of proficiency: Beginning, Intermediate, Advanced, and Advanced High. Instruction and scaffolds, as well as the texts themselves, are differentiated based on these levels.

Additional differentiated scaffolds include visual glossaries, speaking and writing frames, and suggested grouping for peer and teacher support. Lessons also include suggested extension activities to challenge Advanced and Advanced High students as they progress through the year.

ELL Resources

ELL TEXTS

Fear of Missing Out

- Skil: Sight Vocabulary and High-Frequency Words
- Skil: Using Prereading Supports
- First Read
- Skil: Language Structures
- Skil: Supporting Evidence
- Skil: Spelling Patterns and Rules
- Close Read

The Ribbons

- Skil: Classroom Vocabulary
- Skil: Making Connections
- First Read
- Skil: Analyzing Expressions
- Skil: Visual and Contextual Support.
- Skil: Negatives and Contractions
- Close Read

EXTENDED ORAL PROJECT

- Introduction
- Skil: Acquiring Vocabulary
- Plan
- Skil: Sentence Types
- Practice
- Present

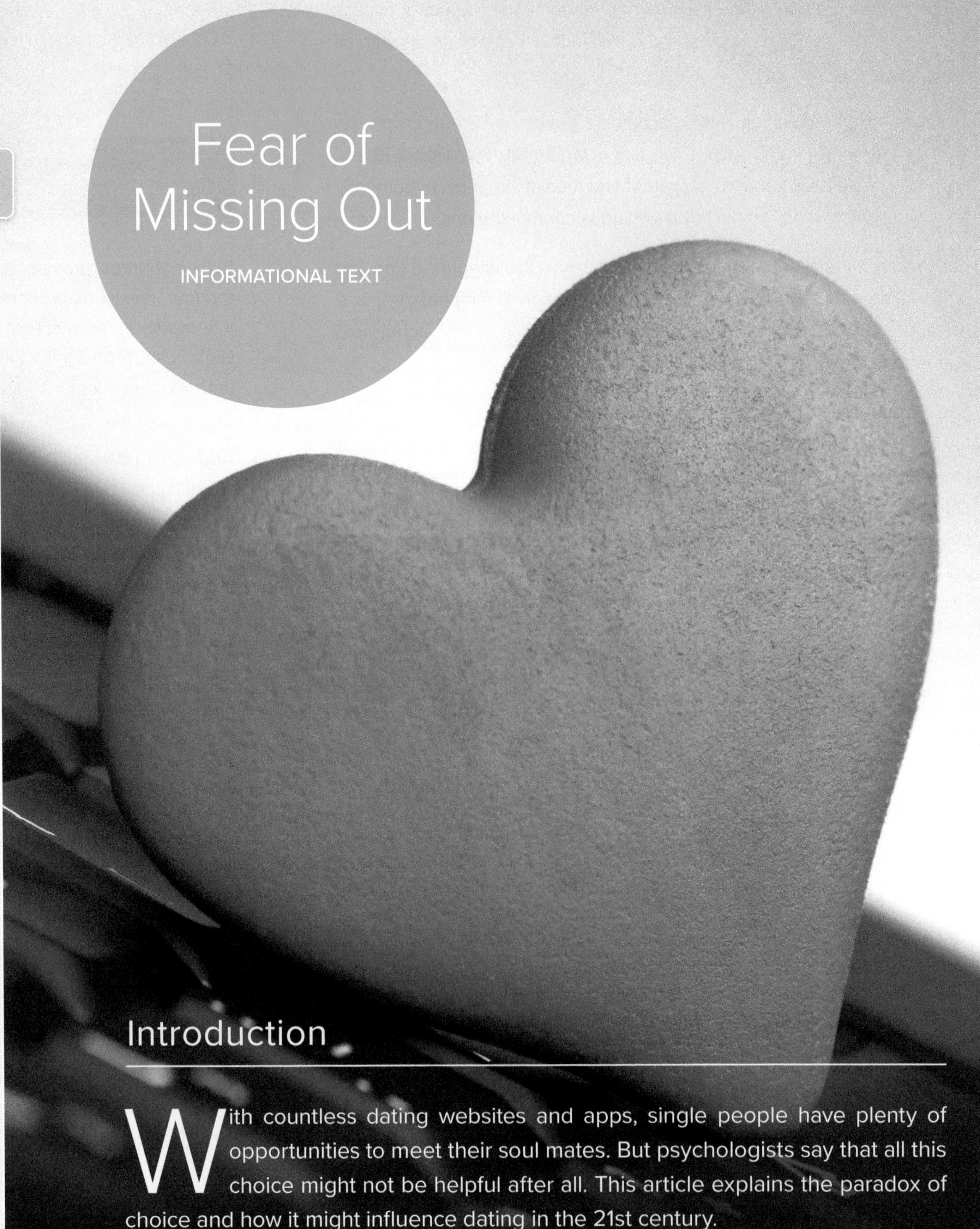

Fear of Missing Out

INFORMATIONAL TEXT

Introduction

With countless dating websites and apps, single people have plenty of opportunities to meet their soul mates. But psychologists say that all this choice might not be helpful after all. This article explains the paradox of choice and how it might influence dating in the 21st century.

This article discusses the paradox of choice involved with online dating. There are so many modern ways to meet people and there are so many people out there. The large number of options can often lead people to second-guess their choices. Two or more enticing options lead to stress and anxiety. Often, people feel unable to make any choice, fearing the other option was better. This hypothesis was supported by a Columbia University study, which concluded that having more options is not better for decision-making. Still, modern data suggests that online dating does lead to successful relationships. Between 2005 and 2012, one third of marriages began online. Some experts argue that the actual reason people go on so many online dates is because people's profiles cannot provide a full picture of their personality or compatibility. People need to go on the date to see if there's real chemistry between them.

Proficiency-leveled summaries and summaries in multiple languages are available digitally.

Audio and audio text highlighting are available with this text.

CONNECT TO ESSENTIAL QUESTION

What causes individuals to feel alienated?

One might think that high-tech dating apps would make dating easier, but this article shows how having a plethora of choices can actually be harmful to decision-making. How can having too many choices make a person feel alienated?

Core ELA Connections

Texts	Theme	Genre
The Love Song of J. Alfred Prufrock	Online dating has affected the way many people seek a relationship. This text discusses the connection between love, choice, and commitment.	The article "Fear of Missing Out" uses scholarly research to explain the paradox of choice.

Differentiated Text Levels

ELL LEVEL	BEGINNING	INTERMEDIATE	ADVANCED	ADVANCED HIGH
WORD COUNT	609	640	695	747
LEXILE	770L	900L	1010L	1110L

Instructional Path

The print teacher's edition includes essential point-of-use instruction and planning tools. Complete lesson plans and program documents appear in your digital teacher account.

Skill: Sight Vocabulary and High-Frequency Words

Objectives: Students will be able to learn and recognize sight vocabulary and high-frequency words in English.

Objectives: Students will be able to recognize sight vocabulary and high-frequency words when listening and reading, and produce sight vocabulary and high-frequency words when speaking and writing.

Skill: Using Prereading Supports

Objectives: Students will be able to learn and practice the skill of using prereading supports when reading a new text.

Objectives: Students will be able to read a new or unfamiliar text using prereading supports such as graphic organizers, illustrations, and topic vocabulary.

First Read: Fear of Missing Out

Objectives: Students will be able to perform an initial reading of a text using the strategy of using prereading supports.

Objectives: Students will be able to demonstrate comprehension of a text by responding to questions orally and in writing using textual evidence.

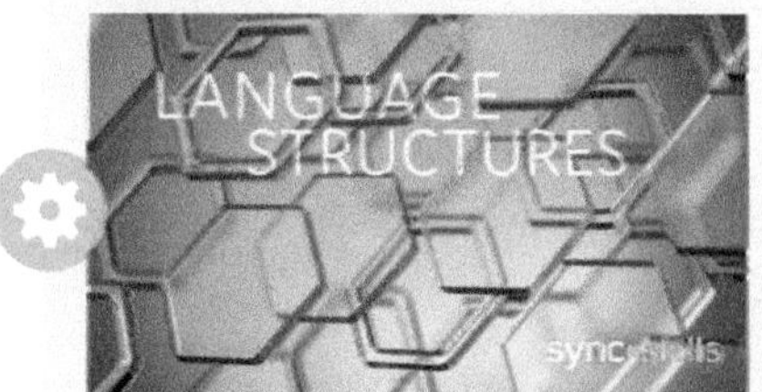

Skill: Language Structures

Objectives: Students will be able to identify how conjunctions affect the meanings of sentences.

Objectives: Students will be able to distinguish between coordinating and subordinating conjunctions and determine how they affect the meanings of sentences when reading and speaking.

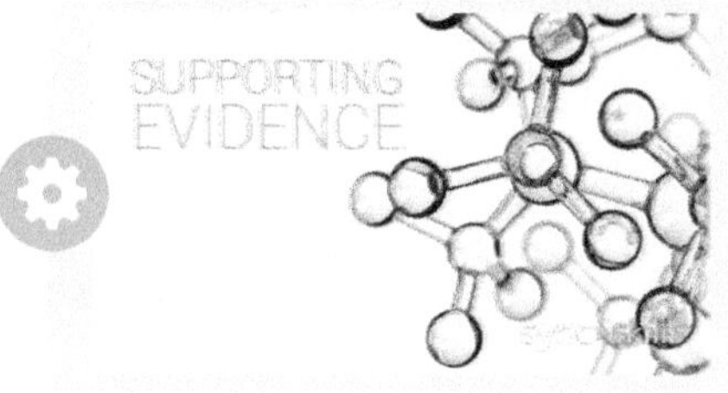

Skill: Supporting Evidence

Objectives: Students will be able to locate a claim or thesis and support it with evidence.

Objectives: After reading and discussing a model, students will be able to locate the claim or thesis and support it with evidence.

Skill: Spelling Patterns and Rules

Objectives: Students will be able to recognize and apply spelling patterns and rules.

Objectives: Students will be able to recognize spelling patterns and rules when reading and apply spelling patterns and rules when writing.

Close Read: Fear of Missing Out

Objectives: Students will be able to perform a close reading of a text in order to find and analyze supporting evidence.

Objectives: Students will be able to find and analyze supporting evidence to participate in a collaborative conversation and write a short constructed response.

Progress Monitoring

Opportunities to Learn	Opportunities to Demonstrate Learning	Opportunities to Reteach
Sight Vocabulary and High-Frequency Words		
Skill: Sight Vocabulary and High-Frequency Words	Skill: Sight Vocabulary and High-Frequency Words • Your Turn First Read • Sight Vocabulary and High-Frequency Words	Spotlight Skill: Sight Vocabulary and High-Frequency Words
Using Prereading Supports		
Skill: Using Prereading Supports	Skill: Using Prereading Supports • Your Turn First Read • Pre-Teach Vocabulary • Practice Prereading Skill	Spotlight Skill: Using Prereading Supports
Language Structures		
Skill: Language Structures	Skill: Language Structures • Your Turn Close Read • Complete Vocabulary Chart • Skills Focus • Collaborative Conversation	Spotlight Skill: Language Structures
Supporting Evidence		
Skill: Supporting Evidence	Skill: Supporting Evidence • Your Turn Close Read • Skills Focus	Spotlight Skill: Supporting Evidence
Spelling Patterns and Rules		
Skill: Spelling Patterns and Rules	Skill: Spelling Patterns and Rules • Your Turn Close Read • Write	Spotlight Skill: Spelling Patterns and Rules

First Read

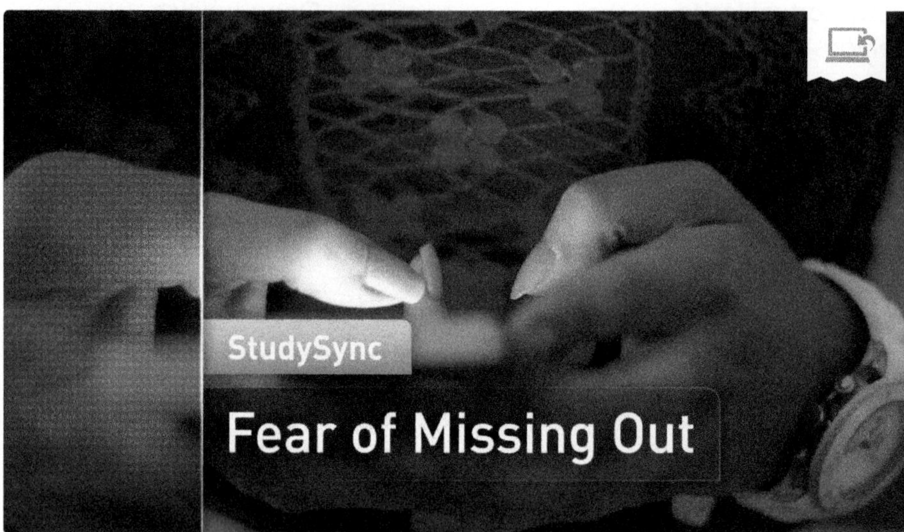

Introduce the Text

As a class, watch the video preview and have students read the introduction in pairs to make connections to the video preview. Ask students various "wh" questions such as:

- What did you see in the video? How does it make you feel?
- What do you think the text will be about?
- Is there something in the video or introduction that surprised you?

Beginning and Intermediate

SPEAKING FRAMES

- I saw ____. I feel ____.
- I think the text will be about ____.
- I was surprised by ____.

Practice Prereading Skill

Remind students that Using Prereading Supports:

Helps you prepare to read a text. By scanning the text for topic vocabulary, you can determine the topic of the text. You might stop to use context clues or look up the meaning of words that you do not know.

Have students work in small, on-level groups to scan the text and look for topic vocabulary. Remind students to use context clues or look up the meaning of any unfamiliar words.

As students are working in small groups, circulate to listen for sample phrases like:

- I notice repetition of the word . . .
- Based on this context clue . . .
- After looking up the meaning . . .

Activate Prior Knowledge and Experiences OPTIONAL

Find out what your students already know about online dating.

Have students make connections while practicing their oral language by discussing what they know about online dating. Ask students to share where their background knowledge came from. For example, did their ideas come from a movie, friend, television show, book, or family member?

 VOCABULARY

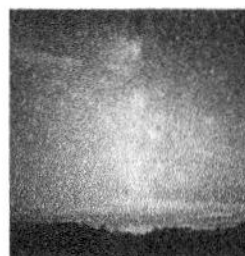

myriad
large number; multitude

paralyze
to make someone or something unable to move

anxiety
a painful or uneasy feeling about something

compatibility
the state of being able to get along without conflict

paradox
a statement that is seemingly contradictory or impossible and yet often reveals a larger truth

READ

1 Imagine you are on a date. The person is nice and attractive. You're having a good time. But you wonder if you could be having a better time with someone else. Besides, this person doesn't share your love of 90s hip-hop! Time to use that matchmaking app to find a different date for next weekend.

2 Such is the state of dating in the 21st century. There are more ways than ever to meet people, from dating sites to matchmaking services to location-based apps. That means there are always countless people out there just waiting to meet you. Why settle down when you can swipe right?

3 Making choices is hard. Not only do we struggle to choose from a **myriad** of options, but we also stress after the decision is made over whether or not it was the right one. For example, if you go to a grocery store that has only one type of breakfast cereal available, you buy it. If it's bad, then it's the store's fault for carrying only that one item. But if you buy a bad box from a store chock-full of cereal varieties, whose fault is it? Yours. And that causes **anxiety**.

 AUDIO TEXT HIGHLIGHTING

Allow students to use the audio text highlight feature to follow along as they read. Alternately, you may wish to work directly with students or group them in twos or threes for partner reading or choral reading.

Preteach Vocabulary

Model the following word and example for the class.

1. The word is *compatibility* and its meaning is "being able to get along without conflict."
2. When I hear the word *compatibility*, I think of two really good friends.
3. For example: Their shared interest in politics make Eli and Joshua's friendship *compatible*.
4. This is an example of a friendship that has *compatibility* because they get along well due to shared interests.

Continue this exercise with each word in the glossary, calling on individuals or groups of students to share out.

 **Beginning**

PRETEACH VOCABULARY

Beginning students may benefit from additional practice or visual cues that help reinforce meanings in context. Ask students multiple-choice questions with obvious correct answers such as the following:

- Which of these might be **paralyzing** to see?
  - a. a giant monster
  - b. a fluffy bunny
- Which situation might cause **anxiety**?
  - a. an essay due tomorrow that you have not started to write
  - b. a beach vacation that you have already planned
- Where might you see a **myriad** of birds?
  - a. a forest
  - b. a bedroom
- Which of these people would be a **paradox**?
  - a. a wise fool
  - b. a strong athlete

Students may also benefit from seeing images related to the correct multiple-choice responses. For example, present an image of a monster or a forest filled with birds.

Sight Vocabulary and High-Frequency Words Focus

Remind students of the sight vocabulary and high-frequency words that they studied at the beginning of the unit. Point out that some of the words may be useful as they think about and discuss the text. For example:

- object (When given a choice of *objects*, I'd choose. . .)
- known (When all the options are not *known*, people tend to . .)
- whole (On the *whole*, people prefer. . .)
- deep (*Deep* anxiety can be caused by. . .)

NOTES

4 The same goes for online dating. The sheer number of potential online matches can leave daters second-guessing their choices. They wonder if they could have done better. Having two or more equally enticing options causes stress and anxiety. Sometimes people are unable to make any choice at all. If you do choose, you live in constant fear that the other option was better. This condition is known as the **paradox** of choice.

5 Research supports the idea that choice is not always a good thing. In a famous experiment, conducted by Columbia University psychologist Sheena Iyengar, researchers set up a table in a grocery store. In two conditions, people were offered either six or 24 varieties of gourmet jam to taste and purchase. Researchers found that the number of varieties did not change how many people tasted the jam. Surprisingly, however, only three percent of people who were offered 24 varieties purchased a jar. But 30 percent of people offered six varieties purchased a jar. Researchers concluded that more options is not better for decision-making.

6 Likewise, researchers Amitai Shenhav and Randy Buckner put people in an fMRI scanner. They were asked to choose between two objects. The objects were either both high in value (for example, a camera and an MP3 player), both low in value (a bag of pretzels and a water bottle), or of opposite values (a camera and a bag of pretzels). The researchers found that when forced to choose between two high-value objects, people found the decision very hard. Afterward, they felt anxiety over whether they made the right choice.

7 And yet, online dating does lead to successful long-term relationships. According to a study from the University of Chicago, one third of U.S. couples who married between 2005 and 2012 met online. In addition, those couples were less likely to divorce. They were more likely to report being happy in their marriages.

8 Some experts use those statistics and others to show that the paradox of choice is overblown. They say that if having choices were really so **paralyzing** for people, why would we have entire aisles devoted to cereal varieties? In some cases, people seem to like having more options.

9 Some researchers theorize that the reason people go on dates with so many different online matches is not the number of available daters. Rather, it's because of the type of information on online dating profiles. It's not what potential partners really need to know for **compatibility**. A dating profile cannot realistically reflect personality. It cannot show how you interact with others. You must meet someone in person for that. A picture and a location is no substitute for chemistry.

TEXT TALK

Have students discuss the questions in small groups. Circulate around the room and check for understanding.

1. What is the text about?
2. What is the author mainly discussing?
3. What are some examples that the author gives?
4. Does the text change the way you think about the topic?

ELL All Levels

SPEAKING FRAMES

Giving Information:

- This text is about ____.
- The main idea is ____.
- Some examples the author gives about ____ include ____.
- This text makes me think ____.

Asking for Information:

- Can you explain ____?
- What do you think about ____?
- Why do you think ____?
- Do you agree with ____?

First Read

Read "Fear of Missing Out." After you read, complete the Think Questions below.

THINK QUESTIONS

1. **What is the paradox of choice? Explain in your own words. Use textual evidence to support your explanation.**

   Paradox of choice is ____

   ____.

2. **How has technology changed dating? Cite textual evidence to support your answer.**

   Technology has changed dating ____

   ____.

3. **Explain the jam study. What did researchers test, and what did they find? Support your answer with textual evidence.**

   The jam study was ____.

   Researchers tested ____.

4. **Use context to determine the meaning of the word *myriad* as it is used in "Fear of Missing Out." Write your definition of *myriad* here.**

   Myriad means ____.

   A context clue is ____.

5. **Use context to determine the meaning of the word *anxiety* as it is used in "Fear of Missing Out." Write your definition of *anxiety* here.**

   Anxiety means ____.

   A context clue is ____.

Think Questions

Circulate as students answer Think Questions independently. Answers will vary.

QUESTION 1: Comprehension

The paradox of choice is when you have many good options and you can't choose. If you do choose, "you live in constant fear that the other option was better."

QUESTION 2: Comprehension

There are so many ways to meet people, from "dating sites to matchmaking services to location-based apps." There are always other people out there.

QUESTION 3: Comprehension

In the jam study, people either choose from six or from 24 varieties of jam. Researchers were testing whether more options was a good thing. They concluded that "more options is not better" for making decisions because more people bought jam when they had six options.

QUESTION 4: Language

The paragraph talks about the stress created when "we struggle to choose from a *myriad* of options." So I think *myriad* means "a lot" of options.

QUESTION 5: Language

The text repeats the word *anxiety* many times. For example, "they felt anxiety over whether they made the right choice." So I think *anxiety* means they worried about or were unsure about their choice.

Skill: Language Structures

Introduce the Skill

Watch the Concept Definition video and read the definition for Language Structures.

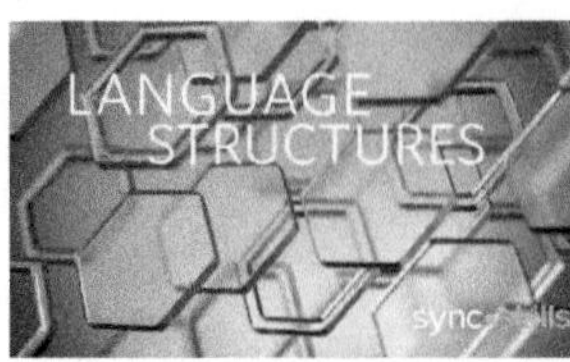

Skill: Language Structures

★ DEFINE

In every language, there are rules that tell how to **structure** sentences. These rules define the correct order of words. In the English language, for example, a **basic** structure for sentences is subject, verb, and object. Some sentences have more **complicated** structures.

You will encounter both basic and complicated **language structures** in the classroom materials you read. Being familiar with language structures will help you better understand the text.

••• CHECKLIST FOR LANGUAGE STRUCTURES

To improve your comprehension of language structures, do the following:

✓ Monitor your understanding.

- Ask yourself: Why do I not understand this sentence? Is it I do not understand some of the words? Or is it because I do not understand the way the words are ordered in the sentence?
- Pay attention to coordinating conjunctions.
  > **Coordinating conjunctions** are used to join words or groups of words that have equal grammatical importance.

  > **The Coordinating conjunctions** and *shows* that two or more things are true of a person, object, or event.
  Example: Josefina is a good athlete and **student**.

  > **The Coordinating conjunctions** or *shows* a choice between different possibilities.
  Example: Josefina can either do her homework or **go for a run**.

  > **The Coordinating conjunctions** but *shows* a contrast between people, objects, or events.
  Example: Josefina wants to run but **should** finish her homework first."
- Break down the sentence into its parts.
  > Ask yourself: What ideas are expressed in this sentence? Are there conjunctions that join ideas or show contrast?

✓ Confirm your understanding with a peer or teacher.

TURN AND TALK

1. What are language structures?
2. Which words can make a sentence structure complicated?
3. What is a conjunction?

Beginning and Intermediate

SPEAKING FRAMES
- Language structures are ____.
- ____ or ____ can make a sentence more complicated.
- A conjunction is ____.

Advanced and Advanced High

SPEAKING FRAMES
- Language structures are ____ For example, ____.
- A sentence can become complicated by adding ____. For example, ____.
- A conjunction is a word that ____ such as ____.

SKILL VOCABULARY

structure / la estructura ***verb*** the arrangement or ordering of parts COGNATE

basic / básico/a ***adjective*** relating to a base; fundamental COGNATE

complicated / complicado/a ***adjective*** composed of many different parts; difficult to understand, complex COGNATE

language structure / la estructura del lenguaje ***noun*** the order of words in a sentence

YOUR TURN

Read each sentence below from "Fear of Missing Out." Then, complete the chart by sorting the sentences into those that use coordinating conjunctions and those that use subordinating conjunctions.

	Sentences
A	They say that if having choices were really so paralyzing for people, why would we have entire aisles devoted to cereal varieties?
B	Not only do we struggle to choose from a myriad of options, but we also stress after the decision is made over whether or not it was the right one.
C	The objects were either both high in value (for example, a camera and an MP3 player), both low in value (a bag of pretzels and a water bottle), or of opposite values (a camera and a bag of pretzels).
D	If it's bad, then it's the store's fault for carrying only that one item.

Coordinating Conjunctions	Subordinating Conjunctions

Discuss the Skill Model

1. How does the student explain the subordinating conjunction in paragraph 4? She explains that the conjunction *if* "is used to show the reader a cause-and-effect relationship between ideas."
2. How does the author use the conjunction *when* in paragraph 6? The author uses the conjunction *when* to indicate another cause-and-effect relationship.
3. How does recognizing conjunctions help the student? Recognizing conjunctions helps the student break sentences down into smaller parts and helps her understand relationships between ideas.

ELL **Beginning & Intermediate**

Have students use the speaking frames and helpful terms to participate in the group discussion. If beginning students are hesitant to participate in a discussion, encourage them by prompting with *yes* or *no* questions.

Advanced & Advanced High

Have students use the speaking frames to participate in the group discussion.

SPEAKING FRAMES

- The student explains ____.
- The author uses ____ in order to ____.
- Recognizing conjunctions ____ and ____.

HELPFUL TERMS FOR DISCUSSION

- break down
- idea
- conjunction
- indicate
- help
- cause-and-effect

Your Turn

Ask students to complete the Your Turn Activity.

Coordinating Conjunctions	Subordinating Conjunctions
B	A
C	D

Skill: Supporting Evidence

Introduce the Skill

Watch the Concept Definition video and read the definition for Supporting Evidence.

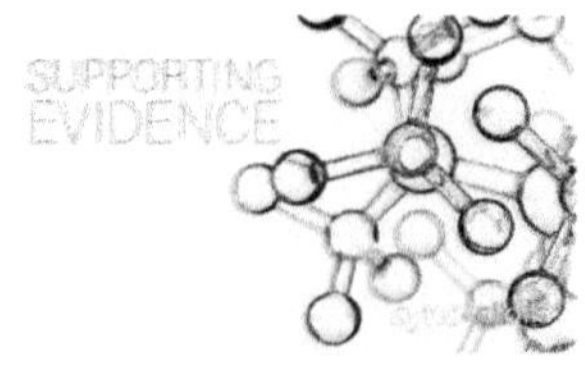

Skill: Supporting Evidence

★ DEFINE

In some informational or argumentative texts, the author may share an opinion. This **opinion** may be the author's **claim** or **thesis**. The author must then provide readers with **evidence** that supports their opinion. Supporting evidence can be details, examples, or facts that agree with the author's claim or thesis.

Looking for supporting evidence can help you confirm your understanding of what you read. Finding and analyzing supporting evidence can also help you form your own opinions about the subject.

••• CHECKLIST FOR SUPPORTING EVIDENCE

In order to find and analyze supporting evidence, do the following:

✓ Identify the topic and the author's claim or thesis.
- Ask yourself: What is this mostly about? What is the author's opinion?

✓ Find details, facts, and examples that support the author's claim or thesis.
- Ask yourself: Is this detail important? How does this detail relate to the thesis or claim?

✓ Analyze the supporting evidence.
- Ask yourself: Is this evidence strong? Do I agree with the evidence?

TURN AND TALK

1. What do we call the author's opinion in an informational or argumentative text?
2. What should you look for when looking for supporting evidence?
3. Why is it important to find and analyze supporting evidence?

ELL **Beginning and Intermediate**

SPEAKING FRAMES

- The author's opinion is called ____.
- When looking for supporting evidence, I look for ____.
- Finding and analyzing supporting evidence can help me ____.

Advanced and Advanced High

SPEAKING FRAMES

- In an informational or argumentative text, ____.
- When looking for supporting evidence, ____.
- It is important to find and analyze supporting evidence because ____.

SKILL VOCABULARY

opinion / la opinión ***noun*** a way of thinking or feeling about something, not always based on facts or knowledge COGNATE

claim / la afirmación ***noun*** the writer's or speaker's position on a debatable issue or problem

thesis / la tesis ***noun*** a statement that an author wants to discuss; the main idea or argument of an essay COGNATE

evidence / la evidencia ***noun*** facts, examples, and expert opinions that support a claim COGNATE

YOUR TURN

Read each line below from "Fear of Missing Out." Then, complete the chart by deciding if the text is a detail, a fact, or an example to support the claim.

	Lines from Text
A	The researchers found that when forced to choose between two high-value objects, people found the decision very hard.
B	The same goes for online dating. The sheer number of potential online matches can leave daters second-guessing their choices.
C	According to a study from the University of Chicago, one third of U.S. couples who married between 2005 and 2012 met online.
D	Imagine you are on a date. The person is nice and attractive. You're having a good time. But you wonder if you could be having a better time with someone else.
E	There are more ways than ever to meet people, from dating sites to matchmaking services to location-based apps.
F	It's not what potential partners really need to know for compatibility. A dating profile cannot realistically reflect personality.

Details	Facts	Examples

Discuss the Skill Model

1. Why is the opinion in the third paragraph important? The sentence "Making choices is hard" is the author's claim.
2. What type of supporting evidence does the author include in the third paragraph? The author includes a relatable example to support their claim.
3. Why is the student's second annotation considered a strong piece of supporting evidence? The evidence in the fifth paragraph is factual. Factual evidence from a university study is very convincing.

ELL **Beginning & Intermediate**

Have students use the speaking frames and helpful terms to participate in the group discussion. If beginning students are hesitant to participate in a discussion, encourage them by prompting with *yes* or *no* questions.

Advanced & Advanced High

Have students use the speaking frames to participate in the group discussion.

SPEAKING FRAMES

- The sentence "Making choices is hard" is ____.
- The author includes ____.
- The evidence is strong because ____.

HELPFUL TERMS FOR DISCUSSION

- author's claim
- example
- relatable
- convincing
- fact
- support
- detail
- factual
- study

Your Turn

Ask students to complete the Your Turn Activity.

Details	Facts	Examples
B	A	E
F	C	D

Close Read

Complete Skills Focus

To prepare students to complete the Skills Focus, remind them of the Reading Skill, Using Supporting Evidence. Tell students that one way you can find and analyze supporting evidence is to look for details, examples, and facts that support the author's claim or thesis. Direct students to the Skills Focus and remind them to track as you read aloud.

Find details, examples, and facts to support the author's claim.

Have students complete the Skills Focus in pairs. Have each pair find evidence in the text.

- Have each partner choose opposing sides of the argument from the prompt.
- Have students find evidence that supports his or her position.
- Have the partners share the evidence they found and work together to sort the evidence into facts, details, and examples.
- Have the partners work together to explain how the evidence they found supports each position.

Allow students to reread the text and mark down their ideas using the annotation tool, adding an exclamation point (!) to note things they want to remember or that surprise them, and a question mark (?) to note things that confuse them.

Prompt students to work cooperatively to complete their assigned tasks. Circulate around the room and monitor groups as they work.

Close Read

WRITE

ARGUMENTATIVE: Does online dating cause too much anxiety to be successful? Some say yes. Some say no. The article "Fear of Missing Out" explores this topic. Choose a side and write a paragraph explaining your point of view. Use evidence from the text to support your claim. Pay attention to and edit for plurals.

Use the checklist below to guide you as you write.

- ☐ Does online dating cause too much anxiety to be successful?
- ☐ What convinced you to support or disagree with the author's claim?
- ☐ What evidence supports your position?

Use the sentence frames to organize and write your personal response.

Online dating (does / does not) ____________________ cause ________________________________.

Research shows that people ____.

According to paragraph ____________, "____".

With online dating, ____.

Other research shows ____.

Overall, the paradox of choice ____.

Collaborative Conversation

Combine pairs into groups of four. Prompt groups to discuss the supporting evidence they found. Have students work together to identify the strongest lines of text evidence.

- Do you agree with the author's claim?
- Where did you find evidence to support your position?
- Did you find any more examples, details, or facts to support the author's claim?
- How did working together to discuss the evidence increase your understanding of the text?

Collaborative Conversation

SCAFFOLDS

 **BEGINNING, INTERMEDIATE** Use the word bank to participate in the group discussion.

ADVANCED Use the speaking frames to participate in the group discussion.

BEGINNING, INTERMEDIATE

Word Bank

- explain
- understand
- evidence
- position
- support
- agree
- disagree

ADVANCED

Speaking Frames

- I (agree / disagree) ____ with the author's claim that ____.
- In paragraph ____ I found ____.
- In addition, I found ____ in paragraph ____.
- Working together to discuss the evidence helped me understand ____.

Write

Personal Response

Does online dating cause too much anxiety to be successful? Some say yes. Some say no. The article "Fear of Missing Out" explores this topic. Choose a side and write a paragraph explaining your point of view. Use evidence from the text to support your ideas. Pay attention to and edit for plurals.

 **BEGINNING** Write a response using the paragraph frames and word bank.

INTERMEDIATE Write a response using the paragraph frames.

INTERMEDIATE

BEGINNING

Paragraph Frames

Online dating (does / does not) ____ cause ____. Research shows that people ____. According to paragraph ____, "____." With online dating, ____. Other research shows ____. Overall, the paradox of choice ____.

Word Bank

- anxiety
- choice
- explain
- option
- successfu

The Ribbons

FICTION

Introduction

In this fictional letter, a woman named Elizabeth tells a story of growing up in Pennsylvania in the 1820s. Her family is poor, but one day Elizabeth's mother gives her some money to spend as she likes. What will she do with this sudden windfall, and what lifelong lesson can be learned?

Elizabeth is dismayed by the behavior of Cora's niece. Cora had presented this niece with new dresses from Paris, but instead of complimenting them, she spoke only of how ugly her old dresses were. Back when Elizabeth was a child, she and her mother would spend the winters taking in sewing to earn extra money for the family. These were fond times and she neither felt the cold outside nor noticed the hours flying by. When spring came, Elizabeth's mother rewarded her with a few extra coins, telling her to buy something nice for herself. Elizabeth had never had her own money before. While shopping with her friend Mary, Elizabeth saw a spool of ribbon she liked. Mary agreed--it was much nicer than Elizabeth's old ribbons. This comment upset Elizabeth, because thinking about her previous poverty diminished the joy of getting something new. In the end, she suggests that Cora pass this advice on to her niece.

 Proficiency-leveled summaries and summaries in multiple languages are available digitally.

 Audio and audio text highlighting are available with this text.

CONNECT TO ESSENTIAL QUESTION

What causes individuals to feel alienated?

In a letter to a friend, a young woman recalls a time from her past when her perspective on a positive experience turned negative. How can other people's opinions change the way you feel about yourself and your place in the world?

Core ELA Connections

Texts	Theme	Genre
The New Dress	Elizabeth reminisces about a pivotal moment from her childhood. This piece of correspondence explores the ideas of insecurity, appearance, and inferiority.	In a letter to a close friend, the narrator of "The Ribbons" teaches the reader a valuable life lesson.

Differentiated Text Levels

ELL LEVEL	BEGINNING	INTERMEDIATE	ADVANCED	ADVANCED HIGH
WORD COUNT	288	607	676	713
LEXILE	620L	900L	980L	1100L

Instructional Path

The print teacher's edition includes essential point-of-use instruction and planning tools. Complete lesson plans and program documents appear in your digital teacher account.

Skill: Classroom Vocabulary

DIGITAL ONLY

Objectives: Students will be able to learn and recognize academic classroom vocabulary in English.

Objectives: Students will be able to recognize academic classroom vocabulary when listening and reading and produce it when speaking and writing.

Skill: Making Connections

DIGITAL ONLY

Objectives: Students will be able to learn and practice the skill of making connections when reading a new text.

Objectives: Students will be able to make text-to-self, text-to-text, and text-to-world connections while reading a new text.

First Read: The Ribbons

Objectives: Students will be able to perform an initial reading of a text using the strategy of making connections.

Objectives: Students will be able to make connections to and demonstrate comprehension of a text by responding to questions orally and in writing using textual evidence.

Skill: Analyzing Expressions

Objectives: Students will be able to analyze expressions.

Objectives: Students will be able to analyze expressions when reading.

Skill: Visual and Contextual Support

Objectives: Students will be able to use visual and contextual support to develop vocabulary.

Objectives: After reading and discussing a model, students will be able to use visual and contextual support to develop vocabulary.

NEGATIVES AND CONTRACTIONS

Skill: Negatives and Contractions

Objectives: Students will be able to recognize and use negative words and contractions.

Objectives: Students will be able to recognize negative words and contractions when reading and use them when writing.

Close Read: The Ribbons

Objectives: Students will be able to use visual and contextual supports while performing a close reading of a text.

Objectives: Students will be able to use visual and contextual support to participate in a collaborative conversation and write a short constructed response.

Progress Monitoring

Opportunities to Learn	Opportunities to Demonstrate Learning	Opportunities to Reteach
Classroom Vocabulary		
Skill: Classroom Vocabulary	Skill: Classroom Vocabulary • Your Turn First Read • Pre-Teach Vocabulary • Read and Annotate • Classroom Language Focus	Spotlight Skill: Classroom Vocabulary
Making Connections		
Skill: Making Connections	Skill: Making Connections • Your Turn First Read • Practice Prereading Skill	Spotlight Skill: Making Connections
Analyzing Expressions		
Skill: Analyzing Expressions	Skill: Analyzing Expressions • Your Turn	Spotlight Skill: Analyzing Expressions
Visual and Contextual Support		
Skill: Visual and Contextual Support	Skill: Visual and Contextual Support • Your Turn Close Read • Skills Focus • Collaborative Conversation	Spotlight Skill: Visual and Contextual Support
Negatives and Contractions		
Skill: Negatives and Contractions	Skill: Negatives and Contractions • Your Turn Close Read • Write	Spotlight Skill: Negatives and Contractions

First Read

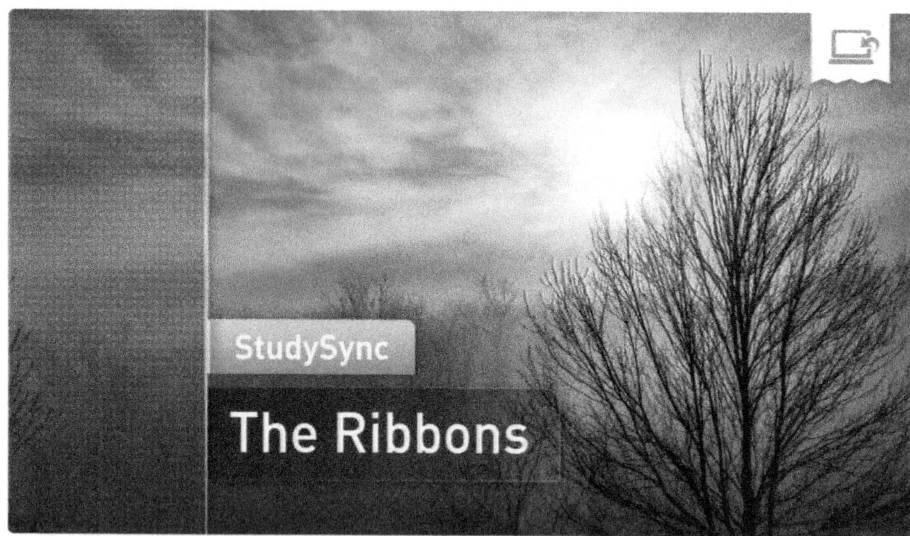

Introduce the Text

As a class, watch the video preview and have students read the introduction in pairs to make connections to the video preview. Ask students various "wh" questions such as:

- What did you see in the video? How does it make you feel?
- What do you think the text will be about?
- Is there something in the video or introduction that surprised you?

ELL **Beginning and Intermediate**

SPEAKING FRAMES

- I saw ____. I feel ____.
- I think the text will be about ____.
- I was surprised by _____.

Practice Prereading Skill

Remind students that Making Connections:

Helps you understand the text by connecting it to your own experiences or knowledge. You can connect the text to an event in your life, to something you read in another text, or to bigger ideas in the world.

Have students work in small, on-level groups to fill out their graphic organizer by listing text-to-self, text-to-text, and text-to-world connections.

As students are working in small groups, circulate to listen for sample connections like:

- This reminds me of a time when I . . .
- This reminds me of a book about . . .
- This reminds me of the news story about . . .

Activate Prior Knowledge and Experiences OPTIONAL

Find out what your students already know about appreciation.

Have students make connections while practicing their oral language by discussing what they know about appreciation. Ask students to share where their background knowledge came from. For example, did their ideas come from a movie, friend, television show, book, or family member?

VOCABULARY

dismissive
feeling or showing that something or someone is not worth consideration

frivolous
unnecessary, serving no purpose

correspond
to write to someone

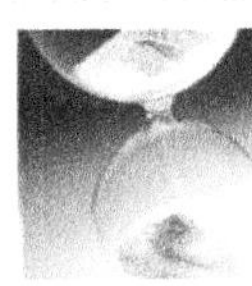

diminish
to be made smaller in size or importance

indulge
to give in to someone's whims or wishes

READ

NOTES

My dear Cora:

1 Thank you for your thoughtful and amusing letter. It brightened up an otherwise dreary day. I was especially intrigued by your story about your niece and her **dismissive** response to the new dresses that you so kindly brought her from Paris. I cannot believe she could only speak of how ugly her old dresses were without a compliment for the new ones. As you may recall, my own childhood was filled with love and laughter, but not money. What I wouldn't have given for dresses from Paris!

2 Because we have been **corresponding** for many years, you know that I love to tell stories of my youth in my small town. I am reminded of one such story now. If you **indulge** my memories, it might be of value to your churlish niece.

3 To help my family keep wood on the fire through the freezing Pennsylvania winters, my mother and I took in sewing. My brother would sit and read to us by candlelight as we sewed. On those nights, the sewing rarely felt like work,

AUDIO TEXT HIGHLIGHTING

Allow students to use the audio text highlight feature to follow along as they read. Alternately, you may wish to work directly with students or group them in twos or threes for partner reading or choral reading.

Preteach Vocabulary

Model the following word and example for the class.

1. The word is *indulge* and its meaning is "to give in to someone's whims or wishes."
2. When I hear the word *indulge*, I think of giving someone what they want.
3. For example: my grandmother *indulged* me with cookies.
4. This is an example of someone *indulging* another person by giving them something they want.

Continue this exercise with each word in the glossary, calling on individuals or groups of students to share out.

Beginning

PRETEACH VOCABULARY

Beginning students may benefit from additional practice or visual cues that help reinforce meanings in context. Ask students multiple-choice questions with obvious correct answers such as the following:

- What would be a **dismissive** action?
  a. ignoring someone who says hello
  b. opening a door for someone
- Which is a way of **corresponding** with someone?
  a. writing an email
  b. selling their house
- What are **frivolous** parts of a bicycle?
  a. wheels
  b. handlebar streamers
- What might cause your bank account to become **diminished**?
  a. buying a new gaming console
  b. winning the lottery

Students may also benefit from seeing images related to the correct multiple-choice responses. For example, present an image of bicycle wheels or an empty piggy bank.

Classroom Vocabulary Focus

Remind students of the academic vocabulary words that they studied at the beginning of the unit. Point out that some of the words may be useful as they think about and discuss the text. For example:

- connection (I can make a *connection* to . . .)
- interaction (This *interaction* shows that . . .)
- concrete (A *concrete* example of this idea is . . .)
- issue (The author addresses an *issue* about . . .)
- abstract (This idea is *abstract* because . . .)

the cold seemed distant, and the hours rushed by. One spring, when the flowers started to grow a little earlier than usual, my family no longer needed extra candles and coal. My mother allowed me to keep some of the money in gratitude for my winter of work.

4 I had never before had any money to my own name. I was filled with excitement at the possibilities. I spent days dreaming about what I should buy with my riches. After a week of rolling the coins about in my hand, I took a ride with Father into town. I grasped my coin purse like I thought it would fall right through the wood cart. The day was bright with new beginnings. I was finally going to enter a shop and choose something for myself—not flour for Mother, nor laces for Father's boots, but something **frivolous** and only for me! As I walked across the square, my friend Mary greeted me. I invited her to join me in my shopping. I thought the presence of a friend would only enhance the joy of the day. As we walked down the road together, I saw a beautiful spool of ribbon in a shop window. I instantly knew I should buy it and use it to improve my favorite hat. I pointed the ribbon out to Mary and she said, "How beautiful! Those ribbons are much prettier than the dingy ones you're wearing now. It will be such a lovely improvement."

5 At that, I felt the color rising in my cheeks. I had been so excited for the new ribbons, but Mary's careless comment hurt me deeply. I bought the ribbons, and they were quite beautiful, but I could never quite recapture the joy I felt when I first saw them in the window. Later, in thinking back on the day, I thought of a line from a book that my brother had read to us that winter. The book was *Hope Leslie* by Catharine Maria Sedgwick: "But it is unnecessary to heighten the glory of day by comparing it with the preceding twilight." The glory of my day of wealth was only **diminished** by thinking of my previous poverty, not enhanced.

6 And that, my dear friend, is what you need to remind your niece. When she is given a new dress, she should not focus on the ratty old one that preceded it. We must all focus on the glory of the present day for its own shining sake, and not think of the darkness til we must.

With love,
Elizabeth

TEXT TALK

Have students discuss the questions in small groups. Circulate around the room and check for understanding.

1. What is the story about?
2. Who are the story's characters?
3. Where does the story take place?
4. How does the story make you feel?

ELL All Levels

SPEAKING FRAMES

Giving Information:

- This story is about ____.
- The story's characters are ____.
- This story takes place in ____.
- This story makes me feel ____.

Asking for Information:

- Can you explain ____?
- What do you think about ____?
- Why do you think ____?

First Read

Read "The Ribbons." After you read, complete the Think Questions below.

THINK QUESTIONS

1. Why does Elizabeth share the story of the ribbons?

   Elizabeth shares the story about the ribbons because ______.

2. Why did Mary's comment cause Elizabeth to feel embarrassed? Support your inference with textual evidence.

   Elizabeth felt embarrassed because ______

   ______.

3. What is Cora's niece supposed to learn from this story? Support your response with textual evidence.

   Cora's niece is supposed to learn that ______

   ______.

4. Use context to determine the meaning of the word *dismissive* as it is used in "The Ribbons." Write your definition of *dismissive* here.

   Dismissive means ______.

   A context clue is ______.

5. Use context to determine the meaning of the word *correspond* as it is used in "The Ribbons." Write your definition of *correspond* here.

   Correspond means ______.

   A context clue is ______.

Think Questions

Circulate as students answer Think Questions independently. Answers will vary.

QUESTION 1: Comprehension

Cora mentioned that her niece only spoke about how ugly her old dresses were when presented with new ones. This reminds Elizabeth about a time when she felt similar to this.

QUESTION 2: Comprehension

Elizabeth feels embarrassed when she realizes how "dingy" her old ribbons are. She says "The glory of my day of wealth was only diminished by thinking of my previous poverty, not enhanced."

QUESTION 3: Comprehension

Both Cora's niece and Elizabeth thought about the past instead of being excited about the present. The niece is supposed to learn that focusing on the past will spoil the present. "We must all focus on the glory of the present day for its own shining sake, and not think of the darkness til we must."

QUESTION 4: Language

Cora's niece did not give a compliment for the new dress. Not giving a compliment after receiving a gift is rude. A synonym for *dismissive* is "rude."

QUESTION 5: Language

Cora knows that Elizabeth likes to tell stories because they have been corresponding for many years. Telling stories is part of how people communicate. *Correspond* must mean "to communicate."

Skill: Analyzing Expressions

Introduce the Skill

Watch the Concept Definition video and read the definition for Analyzing Expressions.

Skill: Analyzing Expressions

DEFINE

When you read, you may find English expressions that you do not know. An **expression** is a group of words that communicates an idea. Three types of expressions are idioms, sayings, and figurative language. They can be difficult to understand because the meanings of the words are different from their **literal**, or usual, meanings.

An **idiom** is an expression that is commonly known among a group of people. For example, "It's raining cats and dogs" means it is raining heavily. **Sayings** are short expressions that contain advice or wisdom. For instance, "Don't count your chickens before they hatch" means do not plan on something good happening before it happens. **Figurative** language is when you describe something by comparing it with something else, either directly (using the words *like* or *as*) or indirectly. For example, "I'm as hungry as a horse" means I'm very hungry. None of the expressions are about actual animals.

CHECKLIST FOR ANALYZING EXPRESSIONS

To determine the meaning of an expression, remember the following:

- ✓ If you find a confusing group of words, it may be an expression. The meaning of words in expressions may not be their literal meaning.
  - Ask yourself: Is this confusing because the words are new? Or because the words do not make sense together?
- ✓ Determining the overall meaning may require that you use one or more of the following:
  - context clues
  - a dictionary or other resource
  - teacher or peer support
- ✓ Highlight important information before and after the expression to look for clues.

TURN AND TALK

1. What is a new expression that you have heard recently?
2. Why is it important to know different types of expressions?
3. Why do people exaggerate?

ELL Beginning and Intermediate

SPEAKING FRAMES

- I heard the expression ____.
- It is important because ____.
- People exaggerate in order to ____.

ELL Advanced and Advanced High

SPEAKING FRAMES

- I heard the expression ____. I think it means ____.
- It is important because ____. For example, ____.
- Sometimes a person exaggerates because ____.

SKILL VOCABULARY

expression / la expresión ***noun*** a phrase used to express an idea COGNATE

literal / literal ***adjective*** describing the usual meaning of a word COGNATE

idiom / el modismo ***noun*** a phrase or expression used to convey a meaning that is different from its literal definition

saying / el dicho ***noun*** an expression that contains advice or wisdom

figurative / figurado/a ***adjective*** not literal; using figures of speech

YOUR TURN

Read the situations below. Then, complete the chart by matching the hyperbolic description that matches each situation.

	Hyperbolic Description
A	My brain is frozen!
B	I aged five years in that waiting room.
C	I nearly died laughing!
D	This hurts so bad that the doctor needs to remove my entire foot.

Situation	Hyperboles
You have to wait a long time at the dentist's office.	
You eat ice cream too fast and get a headache.	
You hit your little toe on a table leg.	
Someone tells you a very funny joke.	

Discuss the Skill Model

1. How does the teacher explain this type of figurative language? The teacher explains that an author uses hyperbole to exaggerate an idea. Then the teacher gives the example, "I'm dying of hunger."
2. Why does the student think that the word *riches* is an example of hyperbole? Context clues tell the student that Elizabeth only earned a small amount of money. The student thinks that Elizabeth was exaggerating to show how excited she felt.
3. How does the student explain Elizabeth's use of the word *ratty*? The student thinks that Elizabeth is using hyperbole to make a joke about how dramatic Cora's niece is.

ELL **Beginning & Intermediate**

Have students use the speaking frames and helpful terms to participate in the group discussion. If beginning students are hesitant to participate in a discussion, encourage them by prompting with *yes* or *no* questions.

Advanced & Advanced High

Have students use the speaking frames to participate in the group discussion.

SPEAKING FRAMES

- The teacher explains that ____. Then, the teacher gives the example, ____.
- Context clues tell the student ____ about Elizabeth's money. The student thinks ____.
- The student thinks that Elizabeth is using ____ to ____.

HELPFUL TERMS FOR DISCUSSION

- author
- dramatic
- emotion
- exaggerate
- hyperbole
- idea

Your Turn

Ask students to complete the Your Turn Activity.

Situation	Hyperboles
You have to wait a long time at the dentist's office.	I aged five years in that waiting room.
You eat ice cream too fast and get a headache.	My brain is frozen!
You hit your little toe on a table leg.	This hurts so bad that the doctor needs to remove my entire foot.
Someone tells you a very funny joke.	I nearly died laughing!

Skill: Visual and Contextual Support

Introduce the Skill

Watch the Concept Definition video ▶ and read the definition for Visual and Contextual Support.

Skill: Visual and Contextual Support

★ DEFINE

Visual support is an image or an object that helps you understand a text. **Contextual support** is a **feature** that helps you understand a text. By using visual and contextual supports, you can develop your vocabulary so you can better understand a variety of texts.

First, preview the text to identify any visual supports. These might include illustrations, graphics, charts, or other objects in a text. Then, identify any contextual supports. Examples of contextual supports are titles, headers, captions, and boldface terms. Write down your **observations**.

Then, write down what those visual and contextual supports tell you about the meaning of the text. Note any new vocabulary that you see in those supports. Ask your peers and your teacher to **confirm** your understanding of the text.

••• CHECKLIST FOR VISUAL AND CONTEXTUAL SUPPORT

To use visual and contextual support to understand texts, do the following:

- ✓ Preview the text . Read the title, headers, and other features. Look at any images and graphics.
- ✓ Write down the visual and contextual supports in the text.
- ✓ Write down what those supports tell you about the text.
- ✓ Note any new vocabulary that you see in those supports.
- ✓ Create an illustration for the reading and write a descriptive caption.
- ✓ Confirm your observations with your peers and teacher.

TURN AND TALK

1. What can you do if you don't understand something you read?
2. What are some examples of visual supports?
3. What are some examples of contextual supports?

Beginning and Intermediate

SPEAKING FRAMES

- If I don't understand something, I can ____.
- I can also ____.
- ____ and ____ are visual supports.
- An example of a contextual support is ____.

Advanced and Advanced High

SPEAKING FRAMES

- One method for understanding something you read is ____.
- When I don't understand something, I ____ or ____.
- ____ and ____ are example of visual supports.
- One example of a contextual support is ____, which is ____.

SKILL VOCABULARY

visual / visual *adjective* relating to the use of color, lines, and perspective in still and moving images such as illustrations and film

contextual / contextual *adjective* depending on the circumstances or situation that something is in COGNATE

support / el apoyo *noun* a person or thing that offers assistance

feature / la característica noun a prominent attribute or aspect of something

observation / la observación *noun* a statement or thought about things one hears or sees COGNATE

confirm / confirmar *verb* to establish validity; to verify, to prove COGNATE

YOUR TURN

Read the following example of correspondence. Then, complete the multiple-choice questions below.

Dear Mom and Dad,

Hello from Camp! How are you? I am doing well but I am exhausted after each long day of activities. Today we defeated the counselors in a game of beach volleyball! They have been the defending champions for the last two weeks. It feels great to win! Now I need to learn chess in order to compete in next week's mind games.

The food in the cafeteria is getting better. They actually served pizza yesterday and it tasted delicious! Can we please go out to eat when I get home in two weeks? I love your cooking, mom, but I think we all deserve a night out!

I miss you,
Charlie

1. Which is an example of a *salutation*?
   - A. Today we defeated the counselors in a game of beach volleyball!
   - B. I miss you,
   - C. Dear Mom and Dad,
2. Which sentence is part of the *body* of the letter?
   - A. Dear Mom and Dad,
   - B. Now I need to learn chess in order to compete in next week's mind games.
   - C. I miss you, Charlie
3. Which is an example of a *signature*?
   - A. It feels great to win!
   - B. I miss you, Charlie
   - C. Dear Mom and Dad,
4. Which sentence is written in *first person*?
   - A. I am so happy that we decided to send Charlie to camp this summer.
   - B. They play so many sports at summer camp.
   - C. He learned how to play chess!

Discuss the Skill Model

1. How does the student determine the meaning of the terms *correspondence* and *first person*? The student uses context clues to determine the meaning of the term *correspondence*. Then the student asks her teacher to clarify the meaning of the term *first person*.
2. Which words does the student seek to understand using contextual supports? The student uses contextual supports to understand the words *salutation*, *body*, and *signature*.
3. Where is the salutation located? Where is the signature located? The *salutation* is located at the beginning of the letter. The *signature* is located at the end of the letter.
4. How does the student organize her ideas about the contextual supports found in this letter? The student previews the text then writes her ideas in a chart.

ELL **Beginning & Intermediate**

Have students use the speaking frames and helpful terms to participate in the group discussion. If beginning students are hesitant to participate in a discussion, encourage them by prompting with *yes* or *no* questions.

Advanced & Advanced High

Have students use the speaking frames to participate in the group discussion.

SPEAKING FRAMES

- The student uses ____ to determine the meaning of ____. Then the student ____ to clarify the meaning of ____.
- The student uses contextual supports to understand the words ____, ____, and ____.
- The *salutation* is located ____. The *signature* is located ____.
- The student ____ then writes her ideas in a ____.

HELPFUL TERMS FOR DISCUSSION

• beginning	• preview	• ask
• end	• letter	• first person
• context clues	• understand	• write

Your Turn

Ask students to complete the Your Turn Activity.

QUESTION 1

C. Correct. A *salutation* addresses the person being written to.

QUESTION 2

B. Correct. This sentence ends the first body paragraph.

QUESTION 3

B. Correct. Charlie signed the letter with the phrase "I miss you."

QUESTION 4

A. Correct. The author uses the word *I*.

Close Read

Complete Skills Focus

To prepare students to complete the Skills Focus, remind them of the Reading Skill Visual and Contextual Support. Tell students that if you have trouble understanding a text, you can use visual supports, like illustrations or graphics, or contextual supports, like titles or formatting. Direct students to the Skills Focus and remind them to track as you read aloud.

Identify visual and contextual supports to develop your letter-writing vocabulary.

Have students complete the Skills Focus in pairs. Have each pair identify and analyze the text features and format of a letter.

- Have both partners label the visual and contextual supports.
- Have partners brainstorm options for each text feature, like different salutations and signatures.
- Have students brainstorm examples of visual supports that can be included in this story.

Allow students to reread the text and mark down their ideas using the annotation tool, adding an exclamation point (!) to note things they want to remember or that surprise them, and a question mark (?) to note things that confuse them.

Prompt students to work cooperatively to complete their assigned tasks. Circulate around the room and monitor groups as they work.

Close Read

 WRITE

PERSONAL NARRATIVE: The narrator in "The Ribbons" explores the memory of a lesson learned from a bittersweet experience. Write a letter to a friend or family member explaining your experience with this main idea from the text. Include specific details from your life for support. Pay attention to and edit for negatives and contractions.

Use the checklist below to guide you as you write.

- ☐ What bittersweet experience helped you learn a lesson?
- ☐ Who was involved in this experience?
- ☐ What did you learn from this experience?

Use the sentence frames to organize and write your personal narrative.

__________ __________,

How are you? I heard that you ______________________________.

Did you __________________? I learned __________________ when I__________________.

One day ______________________________said, "______________________________."

I thought, "______________________________."

Unfortunately, I __________________ and ______________________________.

It was very ______________________________.

I hope you learn from my experience!

__________ __________.

Collaborative Conversation

Regroup students so that they are in pairs with a new partner. Prompt partners to make a list of additional contextual and visual supports that they have seen in other correspondence.

- Which features do you think would improve the letter?
- What is the effect of the features you have proposed?

Collaborative Conversation

SCAFFOLDS

BEGINNING, INTERMEDIATE Use the word bank to participate in the group discussion.

ADVANCED Use the speaking frames to participate in the group discussion.

BEGINNING, INTERMEDIATE

Word Bank

- support
- appropriate
- improves it by
- visual support
- contextual support
- features

ADVANCED

Speaking Frames

- Adding ____ would improve this letter.
- I think ____ improves the letter by ____.

Write

Personal Narrative

The narrator in "The Ribbons" explores the memory of a lesson learned from a bittersweet experience. Write a letter to a friend or family member describing your experience with this main idea from the text. Include specific details from your life for support. Pay attention to and edit for negatives and contractions.

BEGINNING Write a response using the paragraph frames and word banks.

INTERMEDIATE Write a response using the paragraph frames.

INTERMEDIATE

BEGINNING

Paragraph Frames

____ ____,

How are you? I heard that you ____. Did you ____? I learned ____when I ____. One day __________ said, "____." I thought, "____." Unfortunately, I ____ and ____. It was very ____. I hope you learn from my experience!

____,

____

Word Bank

- brother
- dad
- dear
- hello
- lesson
- mother
- now
- sincerely
- sister
- your friend

In the Extended Oral Project, students plan, draft, practice, and deliver an oral presentation that ties into the theme of the unit and spans informative, argumentative, and narrative genres. Lessons provide explicit instruction to prepare students for the unique challenges of an oral presentation, and to help break down the genre characteristics of each prompt. At each step in the process, students focus in-depth on specific writing and speaking skills as they brainstorm, organize, and refine their presentation. Students also receive discussion prompts and frames to guide them in providing effective peer feedback as they practice and discuss in small group before presenting to the class on the final day.

CONNECT TO ESSENTIAL QUESTION

What causes individuals to feel alienated?

In this unit, students practiced effective collaborative communication skills as well as using prereading supports and skills needed to make connections to the text while reading and analyzing two texts about alienation and inferiority. Now students will apply those skills to write and perform a monologue.

Developing Effective Presentations

Form	Language and Conventions	Oral Language Production
Students may struggle with the creative demands of selecting a character and creating scenarios that explain that character's situation.	Students should be encouraged to experiment with more than one type of sentence to help show readers connections between their ideas and provide sentence variety.	Students may make mistakes when they transfer grammatical forms from their native languages into English. Remind students to monitor their use of adjective placement and word endings such as *-er*, *-est*, *-ing*, and *-ed*.

SCAFFOLDS

ELL ENGLISH LANGUAGE LEARNERS

Vocabulary, discussion, and peer and teacher support in the Extended Oral Project is differentiated for Beginning, Intermediate, Advanced, and Advanced High English Language Learners. See individual lesson plans for additional scaffolding and and support.

Instructional Path

All Extended Oral Project lessons lesson plans appear in your digital teacher account.

Introduction

Objectives: After learning how to identify the components of a monologue, students will plan to write and perform in response to a prompt.

Objectives: Students will be able to record ideas for a monologue in writing.

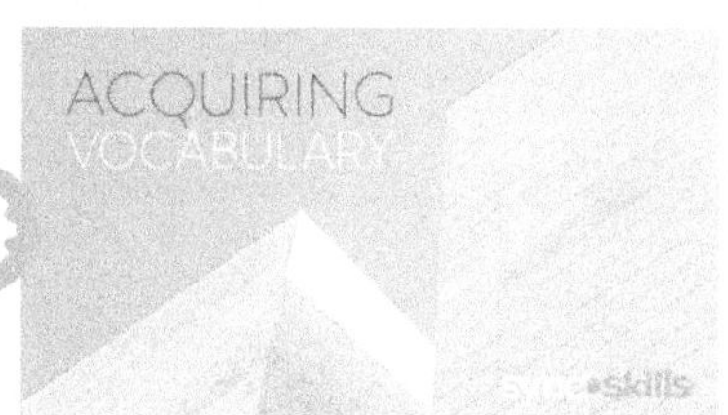

Skill: Acquiring Vocabulary

Objectives: Students will be able to use a graphic organizer to make connections between words and acquire new vocabulary for their monologue.

Objectives: Students will be able to brainstorm new words to use in writing their monologue.

Plan

Objectives: Students will be able to plan and write a first draft of their monologues.

Objectives: Students will be able to organize their first draft using an outline.

Skill: Sentence Types

Objectives: Students will be able to apply knowledge of sentence types to revise their monologues to make them more interesting and show the connections between ideas.

Objectives: Students will be able to vary sentence types orally and in writing.

Practice

Objectives: Students will be able to practice and revise their monologues based on peer feedback.

Objectives: Students will be able to practice their monologues orally and make revisions in writing.

Present

Objectives: Students will be able to observe and perform monologues in order to give and receive peer feedback.

Objectives: Students will be able to use varied sentence types in an oral presentation and give peer feedback orally and in writing.

Spotlight Skills Review

A review day before the end-of-unit assessment gives you an opportunity to review difficult concepts with students using Spotlight Skills lessons. Spotlight Skills are targeted lessons that provide you resources to reteach or remediate without assigning additional readings. Every Core ELA Skill lesson has a corresponding Spotlight Skill lesson. Spotlight Skills can be assigned at any point in the year, but the end of each unit provides a natural moment to pause, review data collected throughout the unit, and reteach skills students have not yet mastered.

Progress Monitoring

The Progress Monitoring charts that appear before every text in this unit identify standards and associated Spotlight Skills. On review day, you may want to give preference to reteaching skills that are not revisited in later units. You can see where Skills are covered again in the Opportunities to Reteach column.

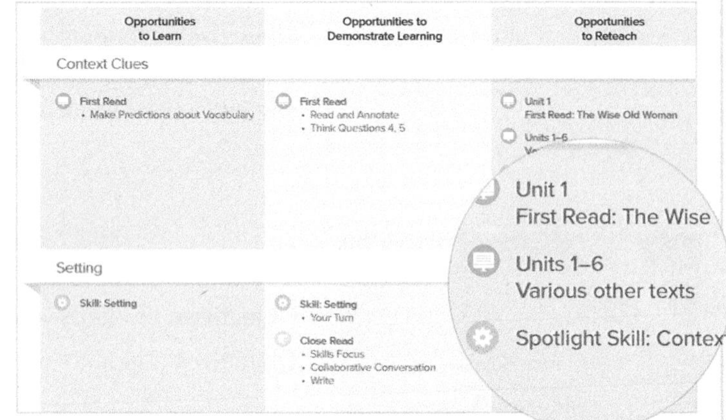

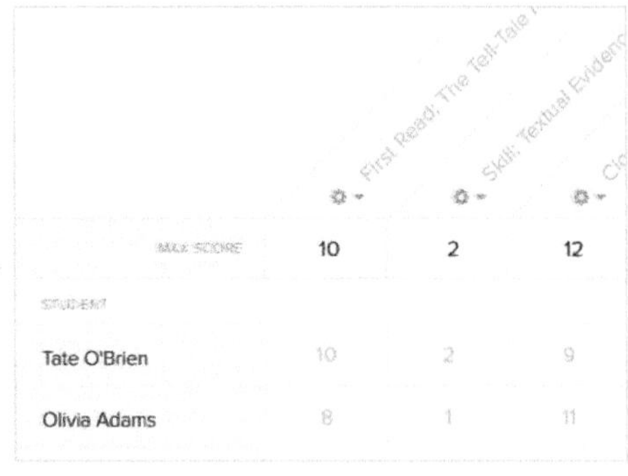

StudySync Gradebook

As students submit assignments on StudySync, their mastery of skills and standards is tracked via the gradebook. The gradebook can be sorted and viewed in a variety of ways. Sorting by assignment shows overall student performance, while sorting by standards or by Skill lessons displays student progress toward mastery goals.

Skills Library 

Spotlight Skills are located in the Skills section of the StudySync Library. You can assign Spotlight Skills to individual students or groups of students. Search tools allow you to search by Skill type or name.

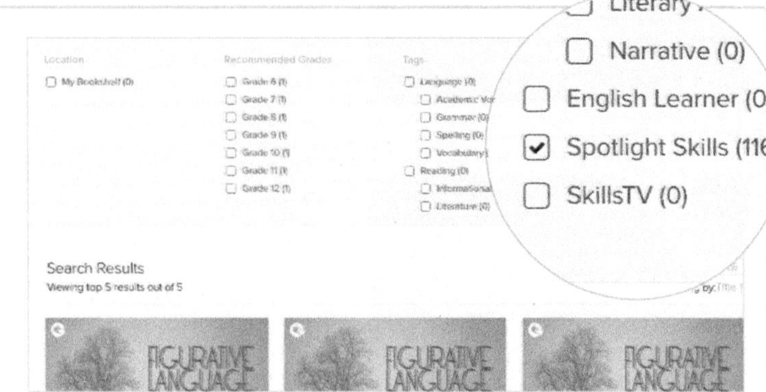

End-of-Unit Assessment

The end-of-unit assessment can be found in two places. The digital version of the assessment can be assigned from the Online Assessment tab inside your ConnectED account. The paper-based version of the assessment can be printed from the End-of-Unit Assessment tab inside this unit in your StudySync account.

Assessment Section	Content	Assessed Skills	
READING	Defying the Odds Genre: Drama Word Count: 766 Lexile: N/A	• Word Patterns and Relationships • Figures of Speech • Language, Style, and Audience	• Textual Evidence • Dramatic Elements and Structure
	The Many and the One Genre: Poetry Word Count: 99 Lexile: N/A	• Word Patterns and Relationships • Figures of Speech • Language, Style, and Audience	• Poetic Elements and Structure
	Combating Isolation of Seniors Genre: Non-fiction Word Count: 601 Lexile: 1400	• Word Meaning • Figures of Speech • Summarizing	• Connotation and Denotation • Author's Purpose and Point of View
	Kafka's Connection to "The Metamorphosis" Genre: Non-fiction Word Count: 623 Lexile: 1300	• Figures of Speech • Textual Evidence • Word Meaning • Connotation and Denotation	• Author's Purpose and Point of View • Summarizing
REVISING and **EDITING**	Student Passage #1	• Pronoun-Antecedent Agreement • Spelling	
	Student Passage #2	• Introductions • Thesis • Reasons and Relevant Evidence	• Transitions • Conclusions
WRITING	Prompt: Literary Analysis	• Literary Analysis	

What's Next?

Assessment results can be viewed by item, standard, and skill to monitor mastery and make decisions for upcoming instruction.

RETEACH skills that students have not yet mastered, using Spotlight Skills or the Test Preparation and Practice book.

REVISE your teaching plan to provide more or less explicit instruction into a skill or text, using Beyond the Book activities for enrichment.

REGROUP students and levels of scaffolding based on standards progress.

Times of Transition

How are we shaped by change?

UNIT 6

Unit Overview

Times of Transition

ESSENTIAL QUESTION

How are we shaped by change?

Heraclitus, an ancient Greek philosopher, once said that change is the only constant in life. People change their clothes, their locations, and their attitudes daily. Some changes are small and have a low impact on your life, but others can change everything.

What happens when life changes? How can outside forces change who we are inside? What can we learn from reading about how other people respond to significant changes in their own lives?

In this unit, students will think about the theme and essential question as they focus on the literary periods of postmodern and postcolonial literature. They will analyze excerpts from postmodern texts such as "The Mysterious Anxiety of Them and Us" and postcolonial works such as "A Small Place" and "Ghosts." They will also study the genre of fiction by reading the graphic short story "ARK" as well as the short stories "The Museum" and "A Temporary Matter." Students will consider how our world is changing today through the argumentative texts *Blindspot: Hidden Biases of Good People*, "News Literacy in the Misinformation Age," and "Honesty on Social Media." In addition, the speeches "Tryst with Destiny" and Zadie Smith's "Commencement Address at the New School" along with the poems "Love After Love" and "Dawn Revisited" will encourage students to think about the lasting effects of change as they read across genres.

Students will begin this unit as readers and finish it as writers and speakers, as they apply what they have learned about argumentative writing to their own argumentative oral presentations.

Unit Structure

Every StudySync unit can be taught two ways.
Pacing Guides for each option are provided on pages that follow.

Thematic Option

The thematic option provides 30 days of integrated reading and writing instruction with a series of short texts connected to a common theme.

Novel Study Option

Each novel study option provides 30 days of comparative texts with integrated reading and writing instruction.

Thematic Selections

Genre Focus
FICTION

Novel Study Choices

Death and the King's Horseman
DRAMA
Akinwande Oluwole Babatunde 'Wole' Soyinka

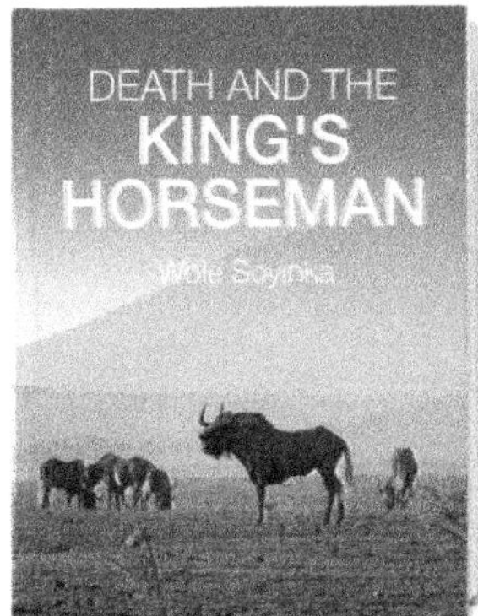

The Kite Runner
FICTION
Khaled Hosseini

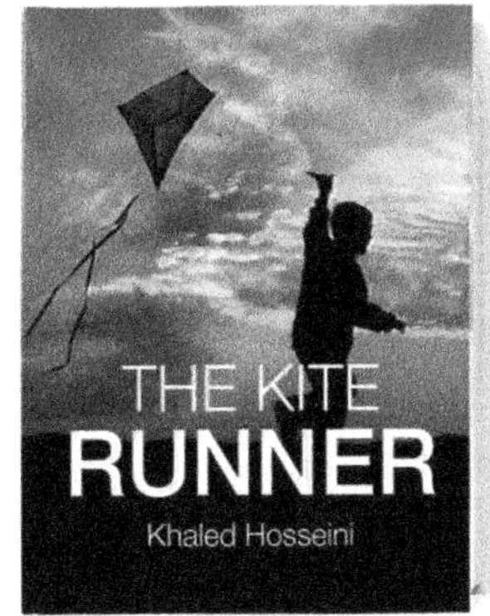

A Bend in the River
FICTION
Sir Vidiadhar Surajprasad Naipaul

Heart of Darkness
FICTION
Joseph Conrad

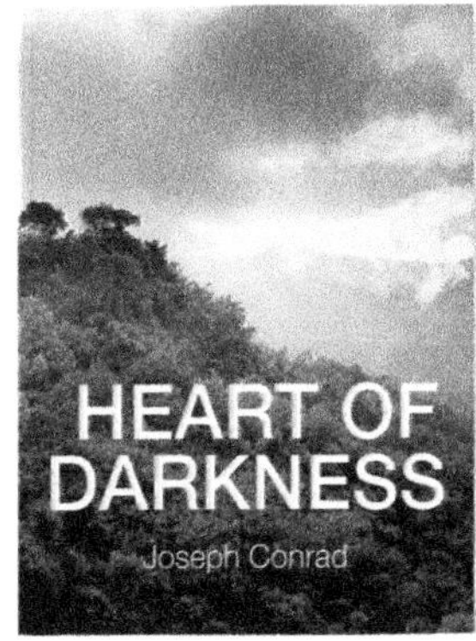

Times of Transition

tv StudySyncTV or SkillsTV Episode

Pacing Guide

Days	Readings	Skill and Standard Instruction	Skill Practice and Spiraling
1-2	Essential Question: **The Big Idea: How are we shaped by change?** p. 656	• Literary Focus: Postmodernism and Postcolonialism • Recognizing Genre: Fiction • Academic Vocabulary	
3-5	**The Mysterious Anxiety of Them and Us** p. 668	• Story Structure • Context Clues	• Language, Style, and Audience • Literary Analysis Writing
6-7	**Love After Love** p. 688		• Theme • Summarizing • Collaborative Conversations
8-11	PAIRED READINGS **The Museum** tv p. 696 **A Temporary Matter** p. 718	• Theme tv • Story Elements	• Textual Evidence • Point of View • Literary Analysis Writing • Collaborative Conversations
12-13	**Tryst with Destiny** p. 750		• Central or Main Idea • Figurative Language • Rhetorical Analysis Writing
14-16	PAIRED READINGS **A Small Place** p. 760 **Ghosts** tv p. 770	• Textual Evidence tv • Story Elements • Analyzing Postmodernism and Postcolonialism	• Theme • Comparative Writing • Collaborative Conversations

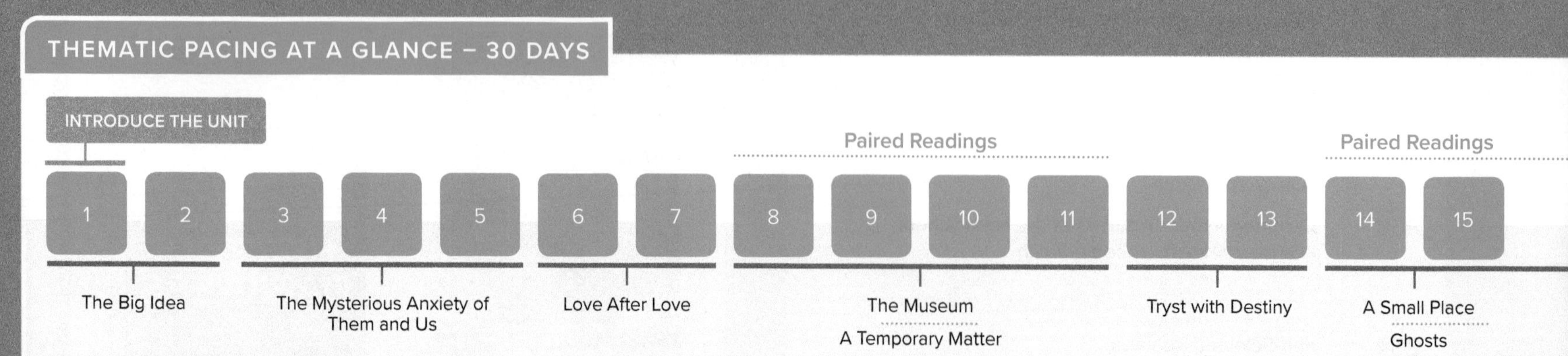

Days	Readings	Skill and Standard Instruction	Skill Practice and Spiraling
17	**ARK** p. 798		• Story Structure • Narrative Writing
18-22	PAIRED READINGS **Blindspot: Hidden Biases of Good People** p. 814 **News Literacy in the Misinformation Age** p. 824 **Honesty on Social Media** p. 838	• Informational Text Elements • Media	• Central or Main Idea • Rhetoric • Collaborative Conversations
23	**Dawn Revisited** p. 860		• Language, Style, and Audience • Narrative Writing
24-26	**Commencement Address at the New School** p. 868	• Textual Evidence • Summarizing • Language, Style, and Audience	• Informational Text Structure • Personal Response Writing
27	**Self-Selected Reading and Response** p. 894	• Independent Reading	• Personal Response Writing
28	**Timed Writing** p. 896		• Timed Writing

Review and Assessment See page 996.

Days	Review and Assessment	Skill Practice and Assessment
29	**Skills Review** p. 996	Students will have the opportunity to complete one or more Spotlight Skill lessons in order to improve understanding and further practice skills from the unit that they found most challenging.
30	**End-of-Unit Assessment** p. 997	For more details, please see the End-of-Unit Assessment information for Grade 12 Unit 6 on page 997.

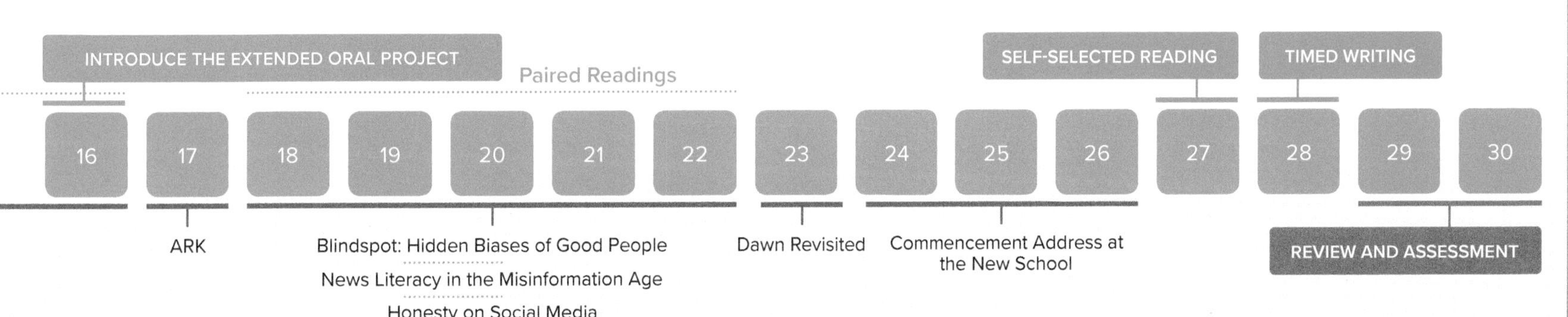

Extended Oral Project and Grammar

Pacing Guide

In the second half of the unit, students continue exploring texts that address the unit's Essential Question and begin crafting a longer composition to share their own ideas about the Essential Question in the Extended Oral Project. The writing project will take your students through the writing process to produce an argumentative oral presentation

Extended Oral Project Prompt

What do future students need to know?

As your high school years now come to a close, think back on the last several years and consider the topics you have covered in all of your subjects. Then, consider the world around you now and select a topic, issue, person, or event that is important to you, but that was not covered in your formal studies. Develop an argument to support the claim that this topic, issue, person, or event should be included in future high school instruction so that the details and significance will be heard and remembered.

Days	Extended Oral Project and Grammar	Skill and Standard Instruction	Connect to Mentor Texts
16	**Oral Presentation Process: Plan** p. 908		
17-20	**Oral Presentation Process: Draft** p. 933	• Organizing an Oral Presentation • Evaluating Sources • Considering Audience and Purpose • Persuasive Techniques	
21-24	**Oral Presentation Process: Revise** p. 950	• Sources and Citations • Communicating Ideas • Reasons and Evidence • Engaging in Discourse	• Commencement Address at the New School
25-26	**Oral Presentation Process: Edit and Publish** p. 955	• Parallel Structure • Sentence Variety: Openings	

Additional grammar lessons can be found in the StudySync Skills Library.

Research

The following lessons include opportunities for research:

Blast **The Big Idea** Research Links*

First Read **The Mysterious Anxiety of Them and Us** Developing Background Knowledge

Independent Read **Tryst with Destiny** Developing Background Knowledge

Blast **Juggling Justices** Research Links*

Independent Read **A Small Place** Developing Background Knowledge

Independent Read **A Small Place** Beyond the Book

Ghosts Beyond the Book

Independent Read **Dawn Revisited** Developing Background Knowledge

*See the teacher lesson plan online

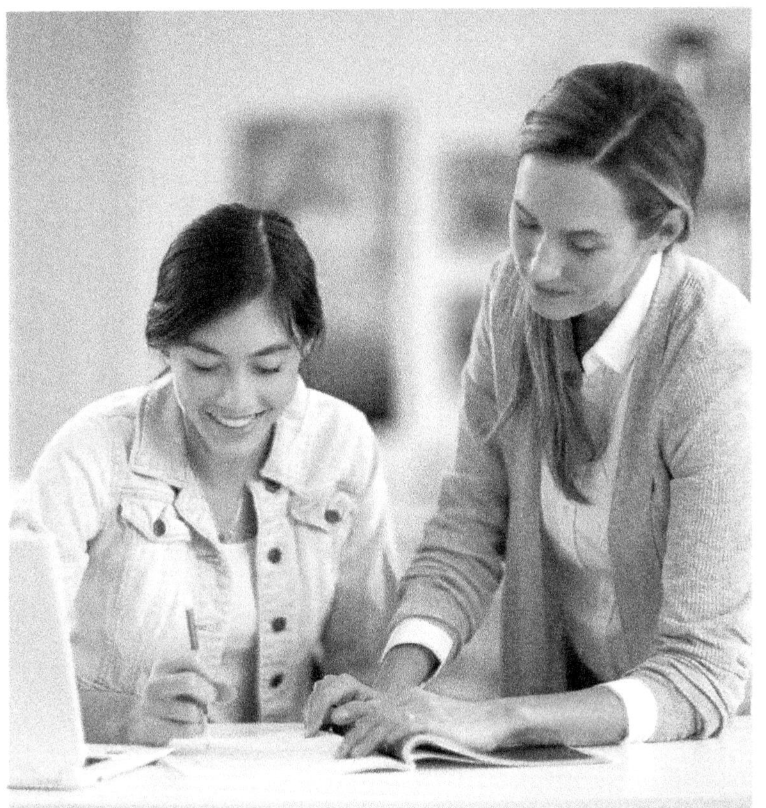

Self-Selected Reading Prompt

After reading a self-selected text, students will respond to the following informative prompt:

Have you ever noticed that the search for answers sometimes leads to more questions? In the digital world, it is easy to fall into a virtual rabbit hole, bouncing around the Internet by clicking one link after another as you learn about a topic. The same thing can happen when you read. Books, stories, poems, and essays open up new worlds for readers, and it is only natural to want to learn more about these worlds.

What else do you want to know?

What is an area you're left wondering more about after reading the selection you chose? This could be a person, time period, place, event, concept, etc. Write a response in which you propose a topic for further research.

Timed Writing Prompt

Students will respond to the following argumentative prompt:

De-Extinction

What sounds like science fiction may soon be scientific fact. De-extinction, or bringing back extinct animals and plants, is becoming increasingly possible. That is because scientists are now working to develop technology that will enable them to clone extinct species and bring them back to life. But just because we can do something, should we do it?

Think carefully about this idea.

Write an essay stating your position on whether extinct species should be brought back to life.

Unit Overview

DEATH AND THE KING'S HORSEMAN

Wole Soyinka

At-a-Glance

Author
Akinwande Oluwole Babatunde 'Wole' Soyinka

Genre
Drama

Publication Year
1975

Text Complexity
N/A

Themes & Topics

Africa

Tradition

Colonialism

Following the death of a king, Yoruban tradition mandates the king's horseman to commit ritual suicide to help guide his master through the afterlife. Horrified by this, British colonial authorities in 1940s Nigeria intervene to stop the ritual—but the break with tradition begins a spiral of destruction that ruins many more lives.

Akinwande Oluwole Babatunde 'Wole' Soyinka (b. 1934) is a Nigerian writer, teacher, and political activist. A major figure in the flowering of Nigerian theater both in London and Nigeria, Soyinka was an open critic of the Nigerian government and wrote from jail during the Biafran War of the 1960s. He holds honorary doctorates from the University of Leeds, Harvard, and Princeton, among many other honors, and won the Nobel Prize for Literature in 1986.

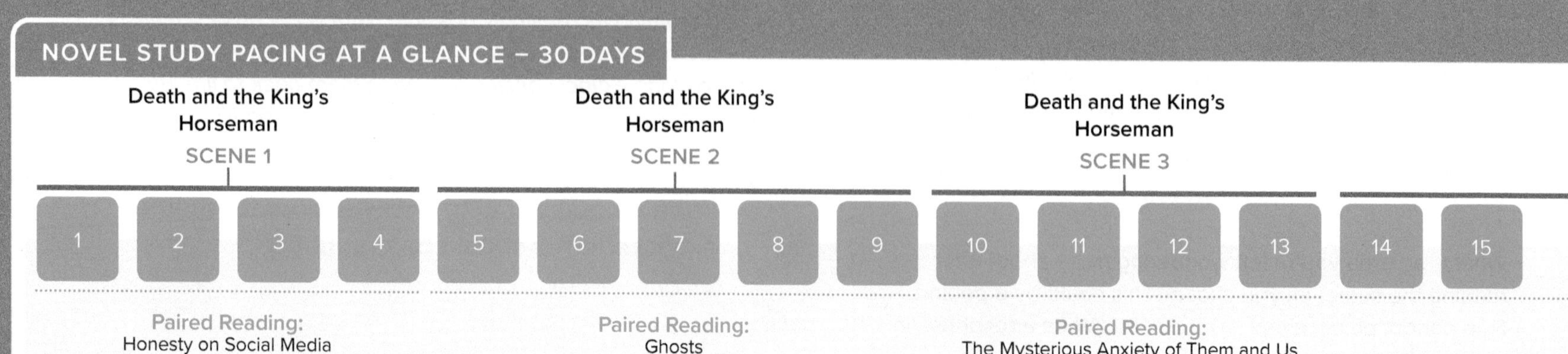

Pacing Guide: Death and the King's Horseman

Days	Readings	Paired Readings	Skill and Standard Instruction	Skill Practice and Spiraling
1-4	**Death and the King's Horseman** Scene 1	Honesty on Social Media	• Informational Text Elements • Media	• Narrative Writing • Collaborative Conversations
5-9	**Death and the King's Horseman** Scene 2	Ghosts (tv)	• Textual Evidence (tv) • Story Elements	• Comparative Writing • Collaborative Conversations
10-13	**Death and the King's Horseman** Scene 3	The Mysterious Anxiety of Them and Us	• Story Structure • Context Clues	• Language, Style, and Audience • Literary Analysis Writing
14-18	**Death and the King's Horseman** Scene 4	A Temporary Matter	• Theme (tv) • Story Elements	• Argumentative Writing • Collaborative Conversations
19-23	**Death and the King's Horseman** Scene 5	Commencement Address at the New School	• Textual Evidence • Summarizing • Language, Style, and Audience	• Informational Text Structure • Personal Response Writing
24-28	**Culminating Writing Task**	Recommended for instruction with this unit's Culminating Writing Task.	• Organizing an Oral Presentation • Evaluating Sources • Considering Audience and Purpose • Persuasive Techniques • Sources and Citations • Communicating Ideas • Reasons and Evidence • Engaging in Discourse	• Parallel Structure • Sentence Variety: Openings

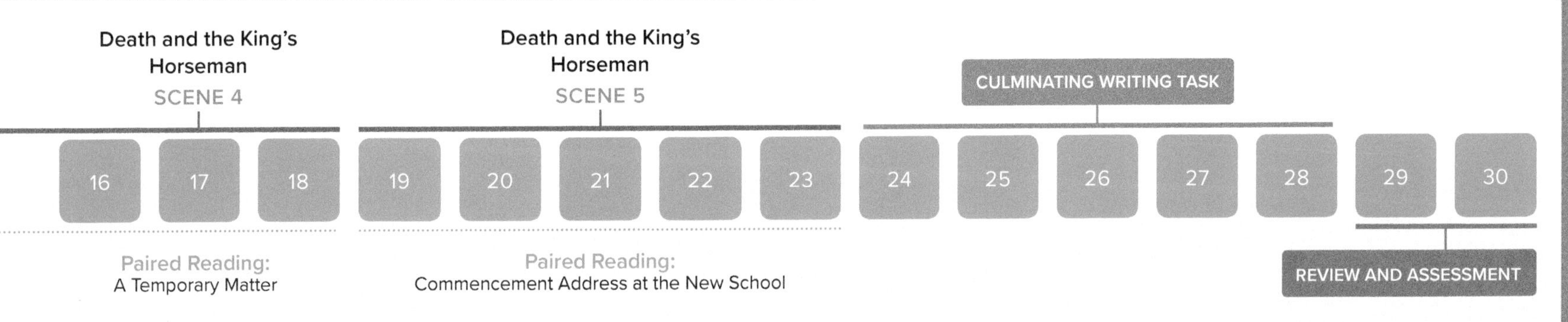

Unit Overview

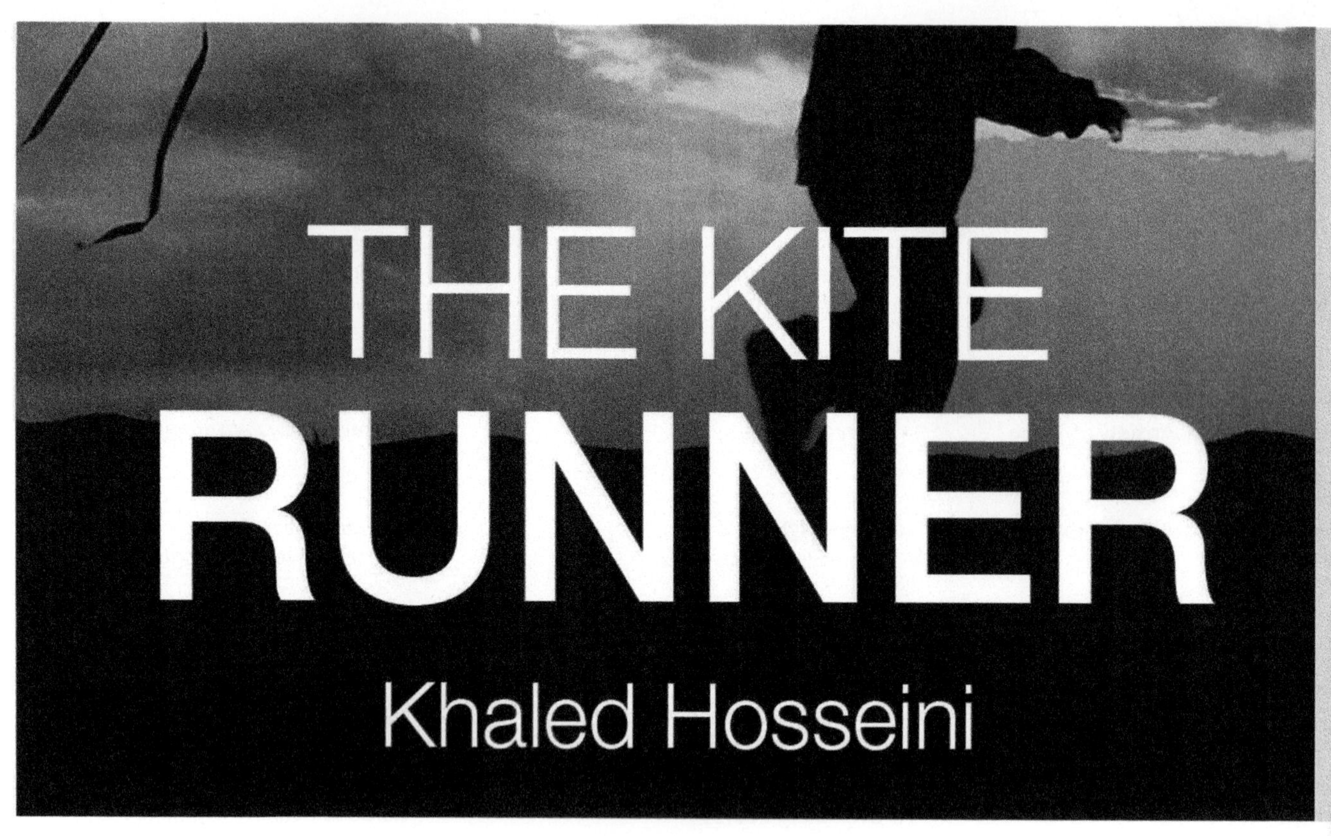

At-a-Glance

Author
Khaled Hosseini

Genre
Fiction

Publication Year
2003

Text Complexity
840L

Themes & Topics

Afghanistan

Friendship

Betrayal

In Kabul, Amir is a Pashtun boy from a wealthy family whose closest friend is Hassan, the son of his father's servant. But when Amir fails to defend Hassan from being raped, his life is irrevocably marked by guilt. *The Kite Runner* weaves decades of unrest and upheaval in Afghanistan into an intricate novel of boyhood, family, sacrifice and redemption, as Amir struggles with his actions, as well as the traditions and biases of his world.

Like the novel's characters, Khaled Hosseini (b. 1965) grew up in Kabul, Afghanistan, until age 11, when he left for Paris. Hosseini attended university in the U.S. and wrote the international bestseller *The Kite Runner* while practicing medicine. He is the author of two other novels about his homeland, *A Thousand Splendid Suns* and *And the Mountains Echoed.*

NOVEL STUDY PACING AT A GLANCE – 30 DAYS

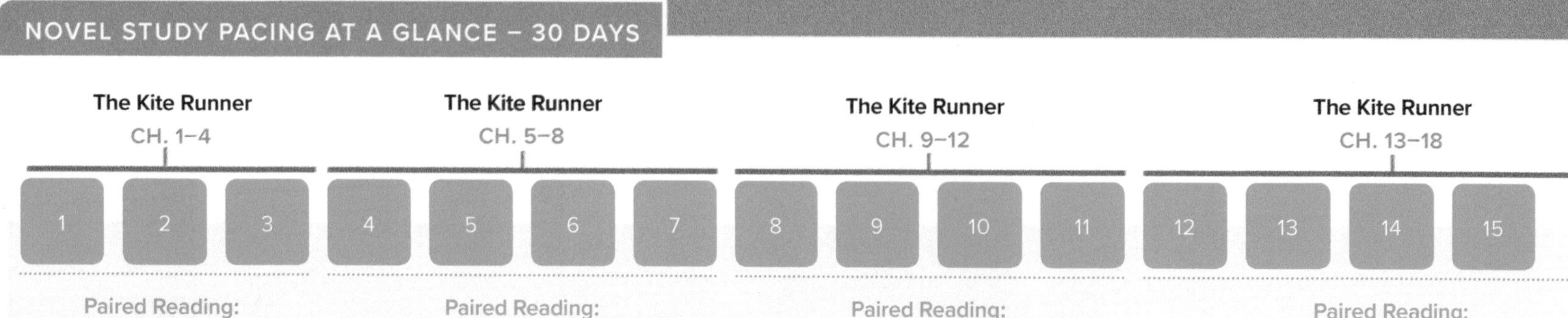

Pacing Guide: The Kite Runner

Days	Readings	Paired Readings	Skill and Standard Instruction	Skill Practice and Spiraling
1-3	**The Kite Runner** Ch. 1–4	Honesty on Social Media	• Informational Text Elements • Media	• Narrative Writing • Collaborative Conversations
4-7	**The Kite Runner** Ch. 5–8	Commencement Address at the New School	• Textual Evidence • Summarizing • Language, Style, and Audience	• Informational Text Structure • Personal Response Writing
8-11	**The Kite Runner** Ch. 9–12	The Mysterious Anxiety of Them and Us	• Story Structure • Context Clues	• Language, Style, and Audience • Literary Analysis Writing
12-16	**The Kite Runner** Ch. 13–18	A Temporary Matter	• Theme tv • Story Elements	• Argumentative Writing • Collaborative Conversations
17-21	**The Kite Runner** Ch. 19–23	Ghosts tv	• Textual Evidence tv • Story Elements	• Comparative Writing • Collaborative Conversations
22-23	**The Kite Runner** Ch. 24–25			• Textual Evidence • Writing
24-28	**Culminating Writing Task**	Recommended for instruction with this unit's Culminating Writing Task.	• Organizing an Oral Presentation • Evaluating Sources • Considering Audience and Purpose • Persuasive Techniques • Sources and Citations • Communicating Ideas • Reasons and Evidence • Engaging in Discourse	• Parallel Structure • Sentence Variety: Openings

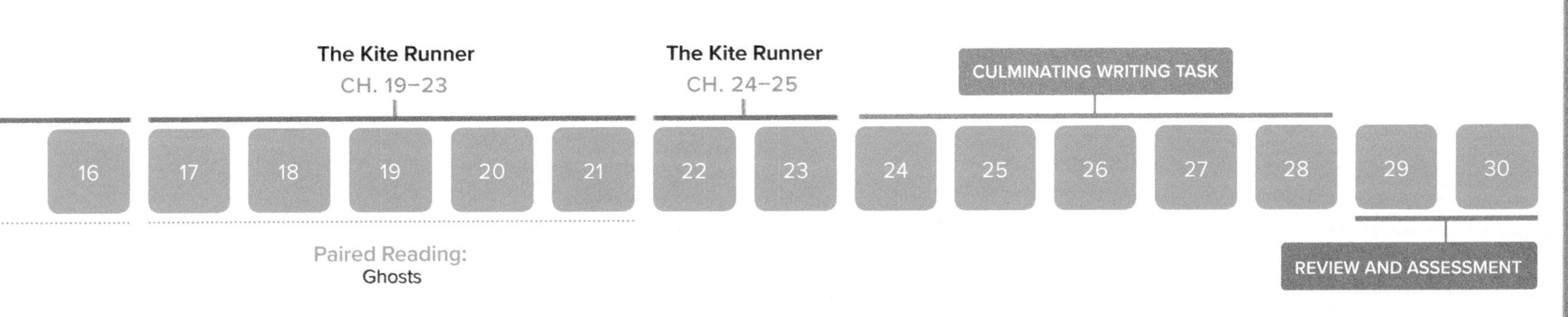

Unit Overview

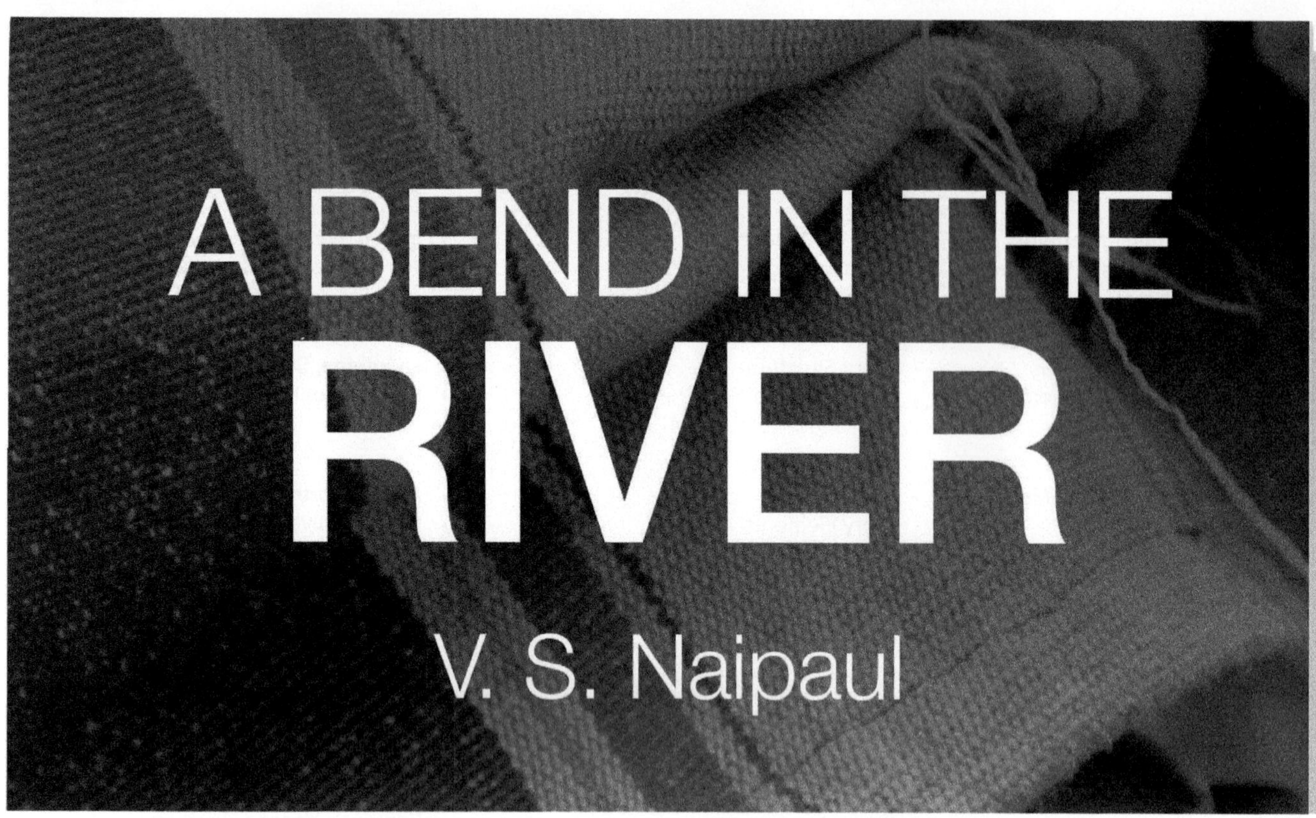

At-a-Glance

Author
Sir Vidiadhar Surajprasad Naipaul

Genre
Fiction

Publication Year
1979

Text Complexity
TK

Themes & Topics

Africa

Postcolonialism

Disillusionment

Salim is a man out of place. Growing up as an Indian Muslim in an unnamed country on the coast of Africa, he buys a shop at a riverbend in a developing area and watches a town grow around it, emblematic of the spirit of postcolonial Africa. Surrounded by white do gooders, a poacher army, and a new Bigburger franchise, Salim witnesses the hopes and challenges of a nation during a period of immense upheaval.

Sir Vidiadhar Surajprasad Naipaul (1932–2018) was a Trinidadian of Indian descent who grappled with the complications of the postcolonial world in books that blended fiction with fact—notably *A House for Mr. Biswas, In a Free State*, and *The Enigma of Arrival*—winning him the Man Booker Prize and the Nobel Prize. He was knighted by the Queen of England in 1989.

NOVEL STUDY PACING AT A GLANCE – 30 DAYS

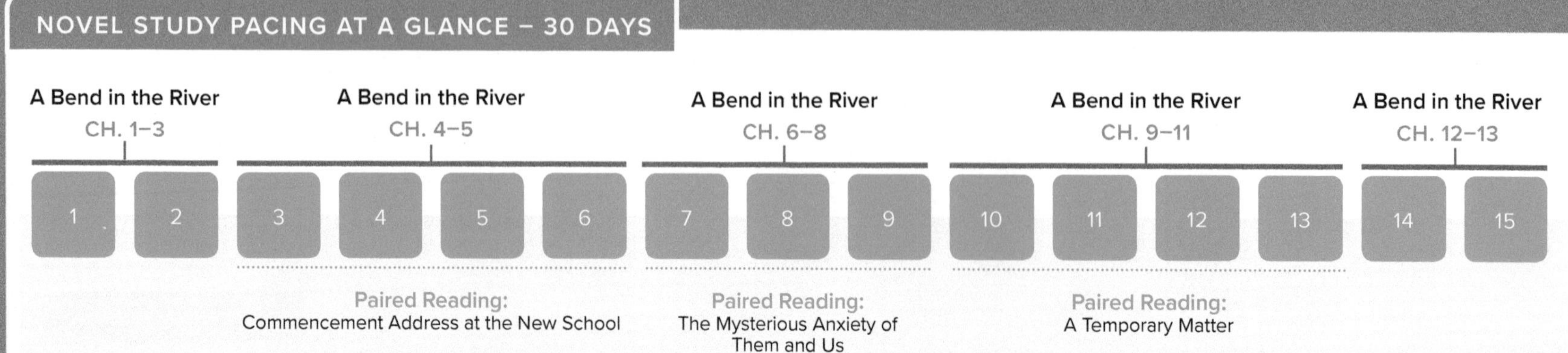

Pacing Guide: A Bend in the River

Days	Readings	Paired Readings	Skill and Standard Instruction	Skill Practice and Spiraling
1-2	**The Second Rebellion** Ch. 1–3			• Textual Evidence • Writing
3-6	**The Second Rebellion** Ch. 4–5	Commencement Address at the New School	• Textual Evidence • Summarizing • Language, Style, and Audience	• Informational Text Structure • Personal Response Writing
7-9	**The New Domain** Ch. 6–8	The Mysterious Anxiety of Them and Us	• Story Structure • Context Clues	• Language, Style, and Audience • Literary Analysis Writing
10-13	**The New Domain** Ch. 9–11	A Temporary Matter	• Theme tv • Story Elements	• Argumentative Writing • Collaborative Conversations
14-15	**The Big Man** Ch. 12–13			• Textual Evidence • Writing
16-19	**The Big Man** Ch. 14–15	Ghosts tv	• Textual Evidence tv • Story Elements	• Comparative Writing • Collaborative Conversations
20-23	**Battle** Ch. 16–17	Honesty on Social Media	• Informational Text Elements • Media	• Narrative Writing • Collaborative Conversations
24-28	**Culminating Writing Task**	Recommended for instruction with this unit's Culminating Writing Task.	• Organizing an Oral Presentation • Evaluating Sources • Considering Audience and Purpose • Persuasive Techniques • Sources and Citations • Communicating Ideas • Reasons and Evidence • Engaging in Discourse	• Parallel Structure • Sentence Variety: Openings

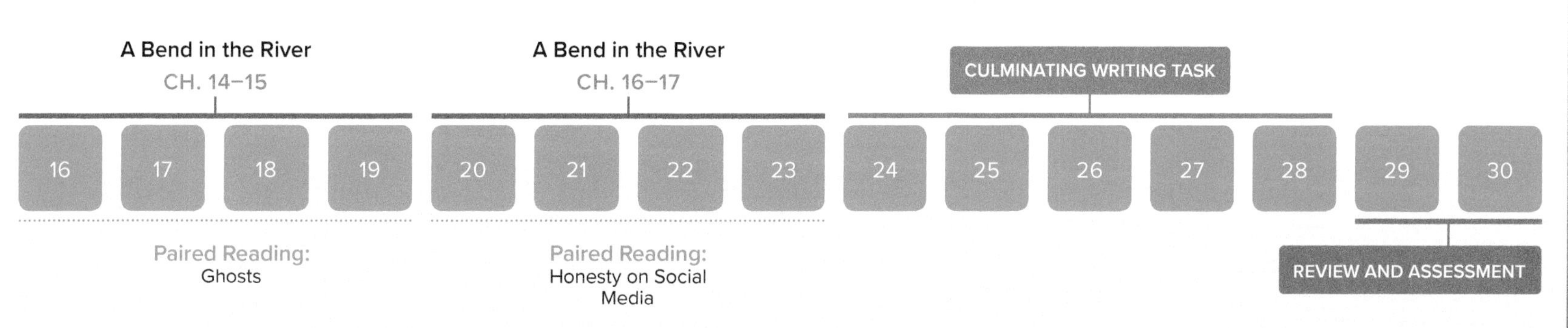

Unit Overview

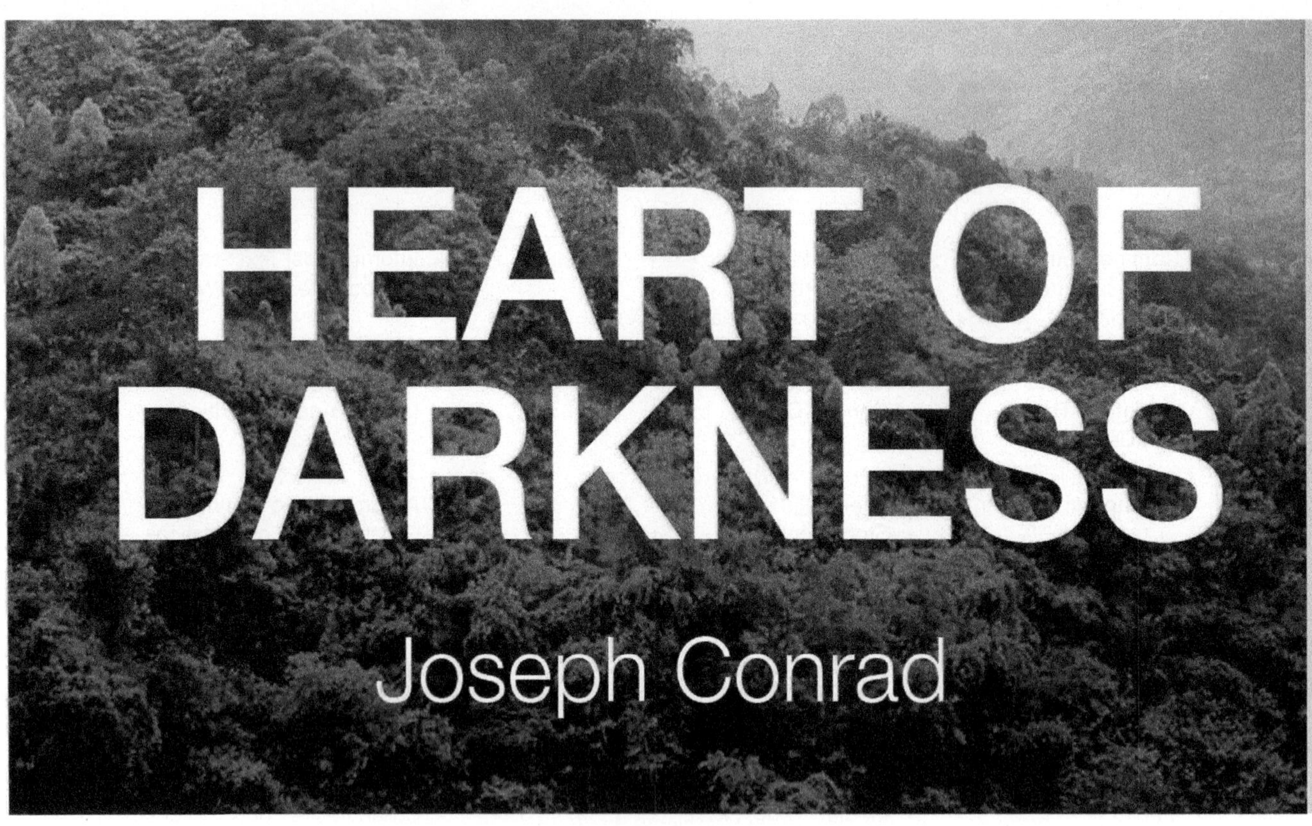

At-a-Glance

Author
Joseph Conrad

Genre
Fiction

Publication Year
1899

Text Complexity
1320L

Themes & Topics

Africa

Colonialism

Voyage

Young Marlow fulfills his dream of going upriver into the African jungle in the ivory trade. The Belgian ivory company he works for has a man in the bush, Mr. Kurtz, who was supposedly destined for greatness but is rumored to have gone mad. As Marlow's boat approaches Mr. Kurtz's camp—decorated with severed heads atop wooden posts—the colonial hero's "unsound" methods finally become clear.

Joseph Conrad (1857–1924) was born Józef Teodor Konrad Korzeniowski in his native Poland. Though he didn't learn English until adulthood, he is considered one of the most elegant stylists in the language. *Heart of Darkness* brought attention to the cruelty of Belgium's colonies in Africa and resulted in reforms, though some contemporary critics argue with its depiction of native Africans.

NOVEL STUDY PACING AT A GLANCE – 30 DAYS

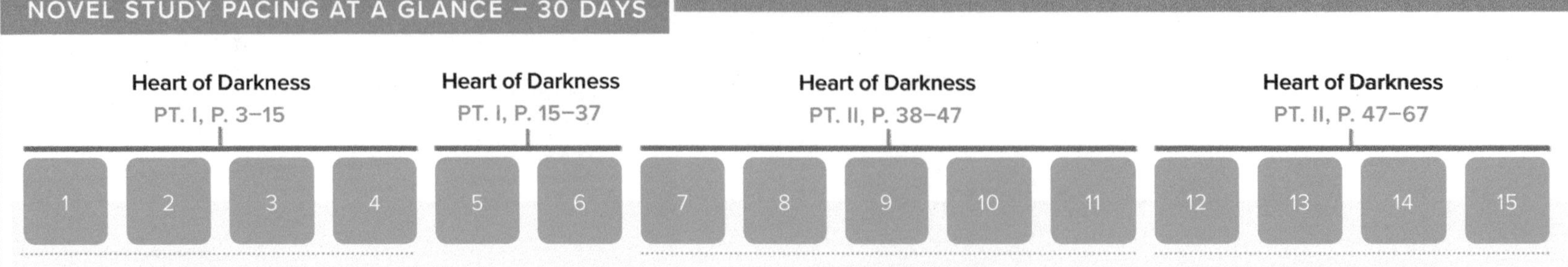

Pacing Guide: Heart of Darkness

Days	Readings	Paired Readings	Skill and Standard Instruction	Skill Practice and Spiraling
1-4	**Heart of Darkness** Part I, p. 3–15	The Mysterious Anxiety of Them and Us	• Story Structure • Context Clues	• Language, Style, and Audience • Literary Analysis Writing
5-6	**Heart of Darkness** Part I, p. 15–37			• Textual Evidence • Writing
7-11	**Heart of Darkness** Part II, p. 38–47	Commencement Address at the New School	• Textual Evidence • Summarizing • Language, Style, and Audience	• Informational Text Structure • Personal Response Writing
12-15	**Heart of Darkness** Part II, p. 47–67	Honesty on Social Media	• Informational Text Elements • Media	• Narrative Writing • Collaborative Conversations
16-19	**Heart of Darkness** Part III, p. 68–79	A Temporary Matter	• Theme tv • Story Elements	• Argumentative Writing • Collaborative Conversations
20-23	**Heart of Darkness** Part III, p. 79–96	Ghosts tv	• Textual Evidence tv • Story Elements	• Comparative Writing • Collaborative Conversations
24-28	**Culminating Writing Task**	Recommended for instruction with this unit's Culminating Writing Task.	• Organizing an Oral Presentation • Evaluating Sources • Considering Audience and Purpose • Persuasive Techniques • Sources and Citations • Communicating Ideas • Reasons and Evidence • Engaging in Discourse	• Parallel Structure • Sentence Variety: Openings

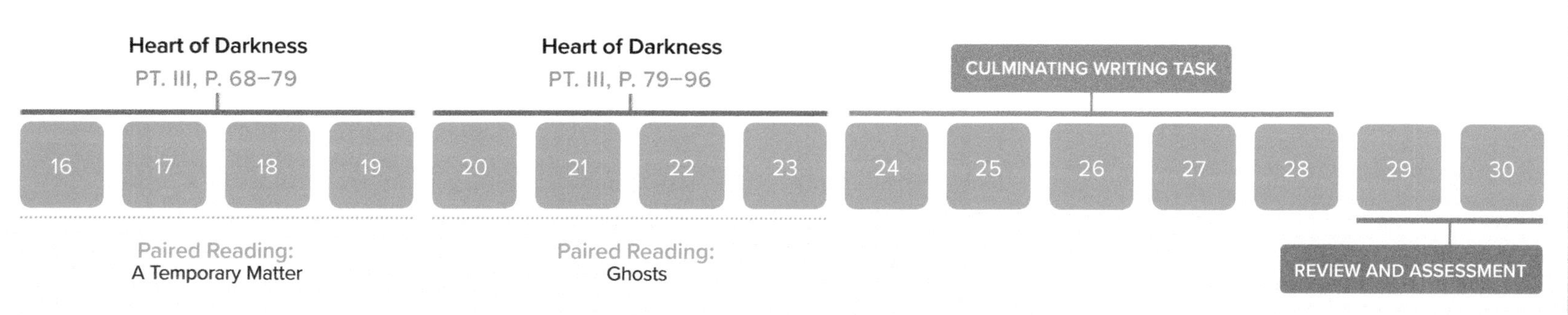

Integrated Scaffolding

ELL and Approaching grade-level students receive scaffolds for every lesson, whether in the Thematic, Novel Study or ELL Resources sections of the unit. Specific scaffolds are intentionally designed to support the needs of English Language Learners and Approaching grade-level students in the ELAR classroom. Other scaffolds exist as part of the many standard features in the StudySync digital platform and can be strategically utilized to support students' comprehension and engagement.

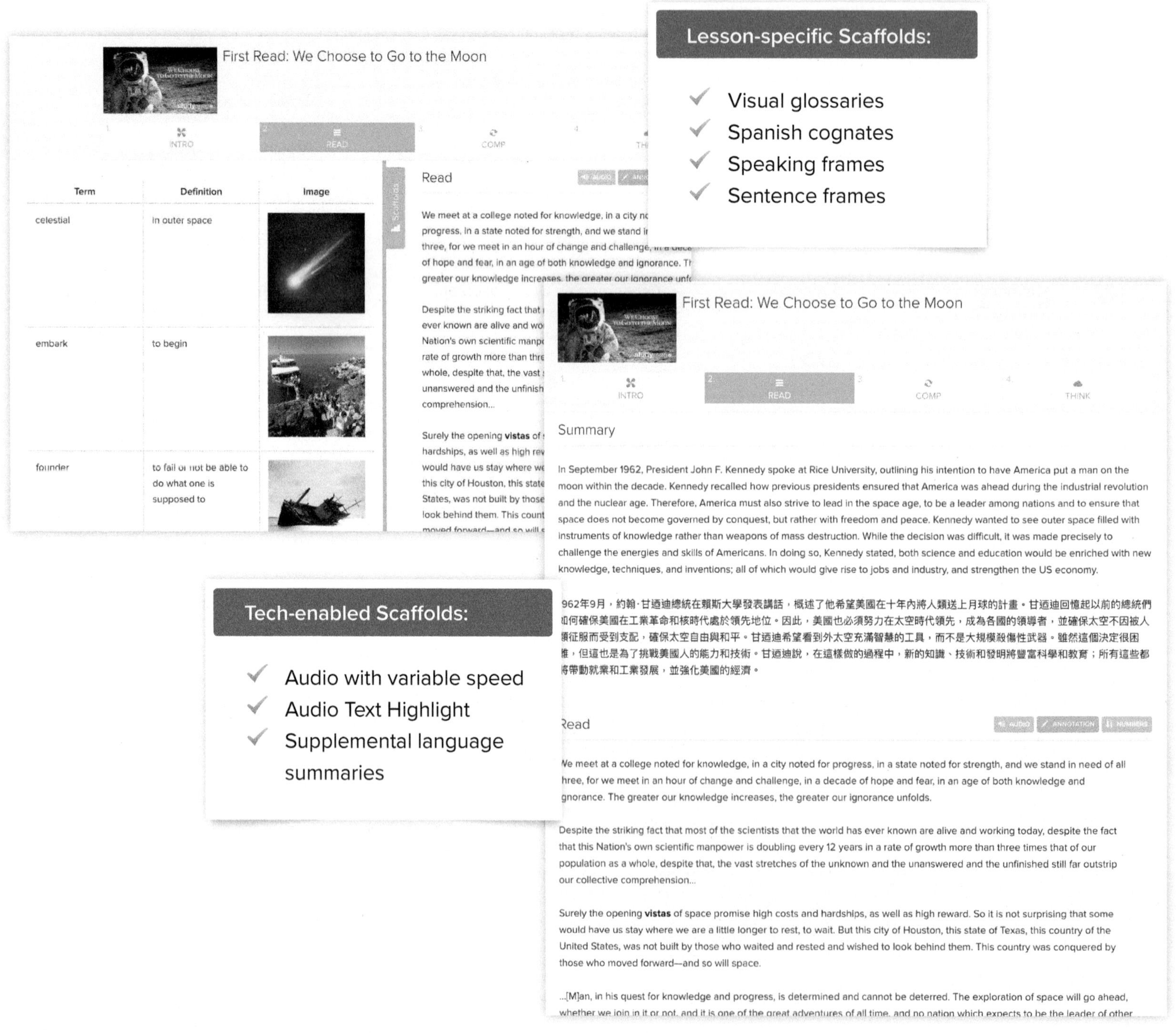

English Language Learner Resources

Both Thematic and Novel Study units include English Language Learner resources designed to match the thematic focus, text structures, and writing form of the unit. ELL resources include two leveled texts and an extended oral project.

ELL Texts	Differentiated Text Levels	Skill and Standard Instruction
	BEGINNING 680L I 970 words INTERMEDIATE 680L I 970 words ADVANCED 830L I 1248 words ADVANCED HIGH 860L I 1356 words Use this text in place of or as an extension to "Ghosts."	• Sight Vocabulary and High-Frequency Words • Environmental Print • Analyzing Expressions • Visual and Contextual Support • Pronouns and Antecedents
	BEGINNING N/A I 1013 words INTERMEDIATE N/A I 1117 words ADVANCED N/A I 1229 words ADVANCED HIGH N/A I 1242 words Use this text in place of or as an extension to "Tryst with Destiny."	• Classroom Vocabulary • Using Prior Experience • Language Structures • Developing Background Knowledge • Spelling Patterns and Rules
EXTENDED ORAL PROJECT INTRODUCTION	In this Extended Oral Project, students will write and perform a personal address. This may be assigned in place of this unit's EOP.	• Acquiring Vocabulary • Sentence Lengths

Focus on English Language Proficiency Levels

ADVANCED HIGH
ADVANCED
INTERMEDIATE
BEGINNING

ELL Resources provide targeted support for four levels of proficiency: Beginning, Intermediate, Advanced, and Advanced High. Instruction and scaffolds, as well as the texts themselves, are differentiated based on these levels.

Additional differentiated scaffolds include visual glossaries, speaking and writing frames, and suggested grouping for peer and teacher support. Lessons also include suggested extension activities to challenge Advanced and Advanced High students as they progress through the year.

Assessment

DAYS 29-30

Assessment in StudySync is built upon a recursive cycle that includes assessment, instruction, and review. Screening, placement, and benchmark assessments help teachers establish baselines and determine scaffold needs. Throughout the course of instruction, teachers regularly assess student progress using formative and summative measures, and use the individualized data from those assessments to guide choices about instruction, review, remediation, and enrichment to bring all students to standards mastery and College and Career Readiness.

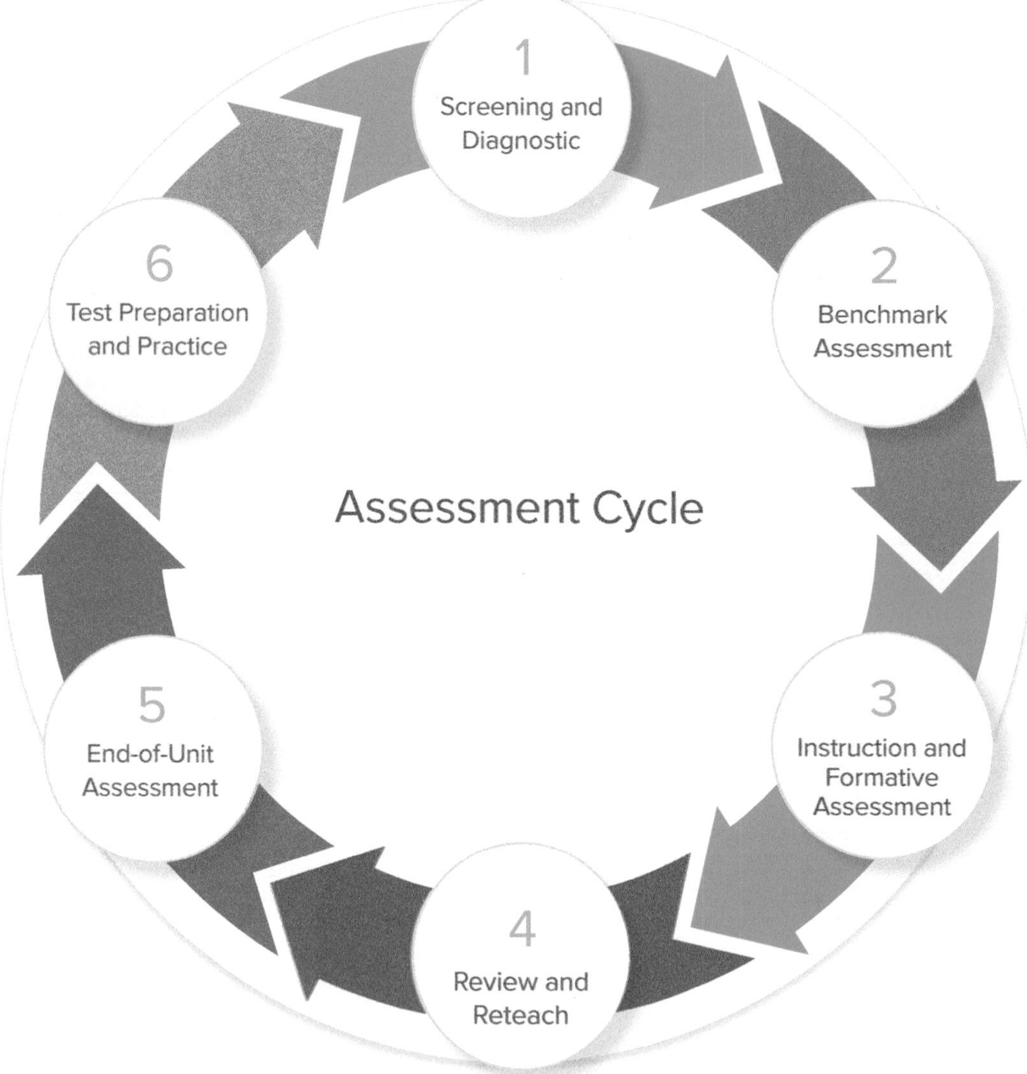

What's Next?

Assessment results can be viewed by item, standard, and skill to monitor mastery and make decisions for upcoming instruction.

- ✓ Reteach skills that students have not yet mastered, using Spotlight Skills or the Test Preparation and Practice book.
- ✓ Revise your teaching plan to provide more or less explicit instruction into a skill or text, using Beyond the Book activities for enrichment.
- ✓ Regroup students and levels of scaffolding based on standards progress.

Review

Spotlight Skills Review

A review day before the end-of-unit assessment gives you an opportunity to review difficult concepts with students using Spotlight Skills lessons. Spotlight Skills are targeted lessons that provide you resources to reteach or remediate without assigning additional readings. Every Core ELA Skill lesson has a corresponding Spotlight Skill lesson. Spotlight Skills can be assigned at any point in the year, but the end of each unit provides a natural moment to pause, review data collected throughout the unit, and reteach skills students have not yet mastered.

Progress Monitoring

The Progress Monitoring charts that appear before every text in this unit identify standards and associated Spotlight Skills. On review day, you may want to give preference to reteaching skills that are not revisited in later units. You can see where skills are covered again in the Opportunities to Reteach column.

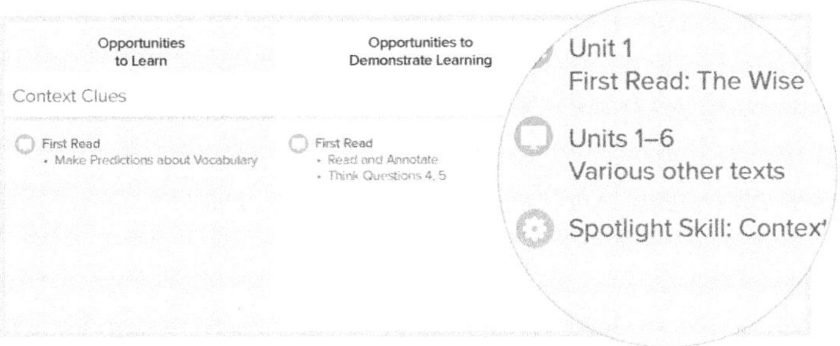

StudySync Gradebook

As students submit assignments on StudySync, their mastery of skills and standards is tracked via the gradebook. The gradebook can be sorted and viewed in a variety of ways. Sorting by assignment shows overall student performance, while sorting by standards or by skill lessons displays student progress toward mastery goals.

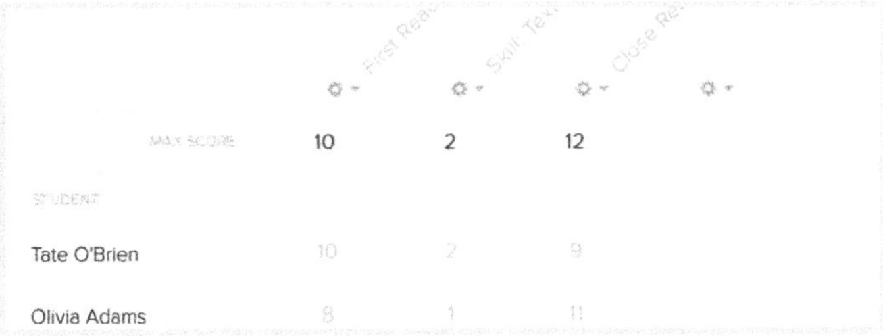

Skills Library

Spotlight Skills are located in the Skills section of the StudySync Library. You can assign Spotlight Skills to individual students or groups of students. Search tools allow you to search by skill type or name.

End-of-Unit Assessment

Assessed Reading Skills

- ✓ Character
- ✓ Context Clues
- ✓ Informational Text Elements
- ✓ Language, Style, and Audience
- ✓ Story Elements
- ✓ Story Structure
- ✓ Summarizing
- ✓ Textual Evidence
- ✓ Theme

Assessed Revising, Editing, and Writing Skills

- ✓ Parallel Structure
- ✓ Persuasive Techniques
- ✓ Sentence Variety: Openings

Unit Preview

Introduce the Unit

As a class, watch the unit preview and discuss the questions below.

- What two words would you use to describe this video?
- What key words or images from the video do you think will be most important to this unit?

Instructional Path

Big Idea Blast

Objectives: After exploring background information and research links about a topic, students will respond to a question with a 140-character response.

Literary Focus: Postmodernism and Postcolonialism

Objectives: After an initial reading about postmodernism and postcolonialism, students will be able to identify and describe characteristics of the literary period.

Skill: Recognizing Genre

Objectives: After learning about the genre of fiction, students will be able to identify and describe characteristics of stoku, realistic fiction, and graphic stories.

Skill: Academic Vocabulary

Objectives: After learning the meanings of ten academic vocabulary words, students will be able to recognize and use them in a variety of contexts.

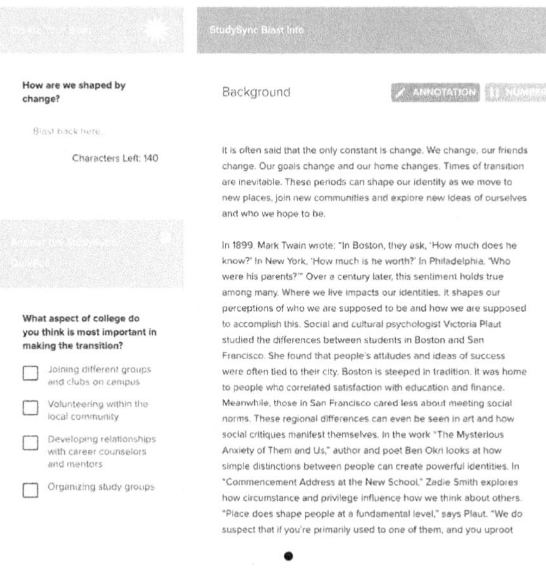

StudySync Blast Info
How are we shaped by change?
Blast back here...
Characters Left: 140
What aspect of college do you think is most important in making the transition?
Joining different groups and clubs on campus
Volunteering within the local community
Developing relationships with career counselors and mentors
Organizing study groups
Background
ANNOTATION
It is often said that the only constant is change. We change, our friends change. Our goals change and our home changes. Times of transition are inevitable. These periods can shape our identity as we move to new places, join new communities and explore new ideas of ourselves and who we hope to be.
In 1899, Mark Twain wrote: "In Boston, they ask, 'How much does he know?' In New York, 'How much is he worth?' In Philadelphia, 'Who were his parents?'" Over a century later, this sentiment holds true among many. Where we live impacts our identities. It shapes our perceptions of who we are supposed to be and how we are supposed to accomplish this. Social and cultural psychologist Victoria Plaut studied the differences between students in Boston and San Francisco. She found that people's attitudes and ideas of success were often tied to their city. Boston is steeped in tradition. It was home to people who correlated satisfaction with education and finance. Meanwhile, those in San Francisco cared less about meeting social norms. These regional differences can even be seen in art and how social critiques manifest themselves. In the work "The Mysterious Anxiety of Them and Us," author and poet Ben Okri looks at how simple distinctions between people can create powerful identities. In "Commencement Address at the New School," Zadie Smith explores how circumstance and privilege influence how we think about others. "Place does shape people at a fundamental level," says Plaut. "We do suspect that if you're primarily used to one of them, and you uproot

Blast: Times of Transition

How are we shaped by change?

TEXT TALK

What idea does Mark Twain's quote help illustrate?

It helps illustrate that where we live impacts our identities.

Why is disorientation natural during big transitions?

Disorientation is natural because of loss of routine and familiarity, new responsibilities and relationships, and adaptation to a new community, location, and lifestyle.

What are some ways to make a transition to college easier?

Students can broaden their social circles, get involved, stay organized, and use support groups if necessary.

Create Your Own Blast

SCAFFOLDS

Ask students to write a 140-character Blast after they complete the QuikPoll.

Use the scaffolds below to differentiate instruction for your ELL English Language Learners.

BEGINNING Write a response using the word bank to complete the sentence frame.

INTERMEDIATE Write a response using the sentence frame.

ADVANCED, ADVANCED HIGH Write a response using the sentence starter.

BEGINNING	BEGINNING / INTERMEDIATE	ADVANCED, ADVANCED HIGH
Word Bank	Sentence Frame	Sentence Starter
expanding, opening, breaking; horizons, experiences, traditions	Change shapes our identities by ____ our ____.	• Change shapes our identities by . . .

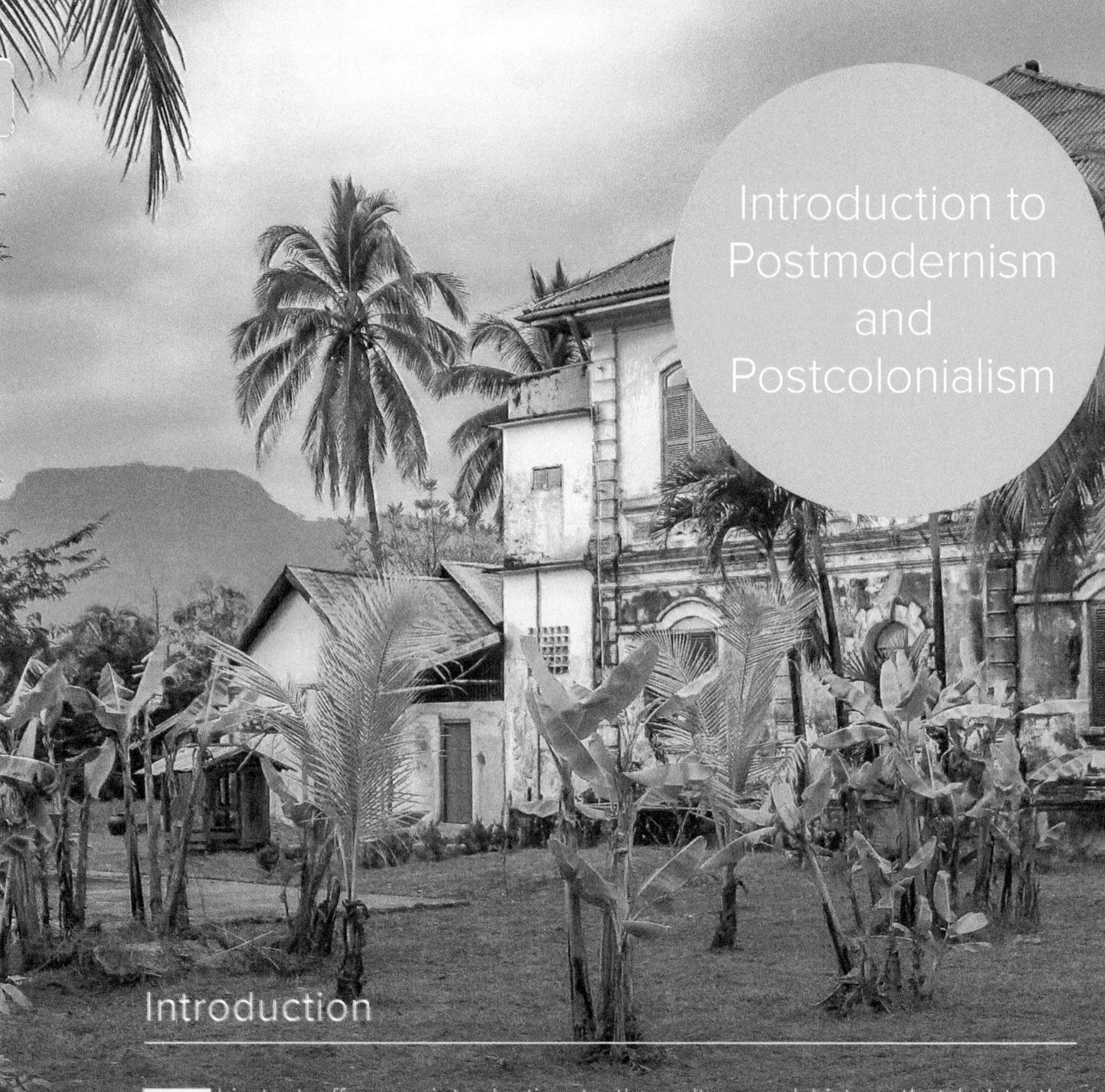

Introduction to Postmodernism and Postcolonialism

Introduction

This text offers an introduction to the culture and history that led to the movements of postmodernism and postcolonialism. Postcolonialism developed after the second World War, when British colonies all across the world gained their independence, and those living in the former colonies were left to deal with the violent consequences of years of British rule. Postcolonial writers provided necessary new perspectives in literature from people previously silenced by the dominance of colonial powers. Postmodernism was a response to the end of World War II and the modernist movement—a kind of rebellion that attempted to expand on literary tradition by imploding it from the inside.

"Colony by colony, the British Empire was dismantled."

NOTES

1 You may have heard the word *postmodern* used to describe unusual artwork, literature, music, or even experimental pop and rap stars. Another related term you may be familiar with is *postcolonialism*. Both words represent two prominent literary movements of the twentieth and twenty-first centuries. Although you may not yet have a thorough understanding of these literary periods, more than likely you have noticed that both words have one detail in common: the prefix *post-*, meaning "after." As the word parts signify, **postmodernism** came after modernism, and **postcolonialism** came after colonialism. Because both movements are reactions to previous historical, cultural, and literary events, it is important to begin by studying what led to these movements, specifically the end of modernism, British colonialism, and World War II.

British Colonialism

2 During the nineteenth and early twentieth centuries, Britain colonized large portions of the world, with the aim of total control over vast territories. Although the British Empire did build railroads, telegraphs, schools, and hospitals in these territories, colonialism was based on economic exploitation and influenced by racist attitudes. Throughout the British Empire, government administrators and Christian missionaries often came into conflict with the people under colonial rule. Later, writers would describe the devastating effects of British colonialism and the imposition of Christianity on their traditional way of life. One prominent example is Nigerian writer Chinua Achebe, who wrote the highly acclaimed and influential novel, *Things Fall Apart* (1958).

A meeting of British colonial administrators with tribal messengers from the interior in Lagos, Nigeria.

First Read

Introduce the Text

As a class, watch the video preview and have students read the introduction in pairs to make connections to the video preview. Ask students:

- What examples of postmodernism or postcolonialism did you see in the video?
- What are some examples of postmodernism or postcolonialism you have seen in media?

SPEAKING FRAMES

- In the video, I saw ____.
- I think ____ is an example of postmodernism or postcolonialism.

TEXT TALK

How did the British Empire rule over its subjects?

See paragraph 2: The British Empire oppressed the cultures it ruled over. It also compelled its subjects to learn to speak and write English.

SELECTION VOCABULARY

postmodernism / el posmodernismo ***noun*** a form of art, literature, and architecture in reaction against principles and practices of established modernism COGNATE

postcolonialism / el poscolonialismo ***noun*** a body of works in literature produced by writers of formerly colonized countries COGNATE

The End of the Empire

3 To strengthen its economy after World War II, Britain had to reduce expenses abroad and therefore, gradually agreed to many colonies' demands for independence. Colony by colony, the British Empire was dismantled. In Asia and Africa, the new nations created from former British colonies faced an array of **formidable** problems, including overpopulation, poverty, and ethnic and religious **strife.** For example, when India and Pakistan became independent in 1947, millions of people fled across new borders, with a majority of Hindus focusing on a newly free India and many Muslims streaming toward Pakistan. In the ensuing violence, more than a million people perished. In Africa, many former British colonies achieved independence during the 1950s and 1960s, but their national stability was undermined by ethnic clashes resulting often from arbitrarily drawn borders by colonial powers. When building colonial empires, Britain and other European powers had drawn up the boundaries of African nations with little regard to the inhabitants' ethnic diversity.

Postmodern and Postcolonial Literature

4 Most literary critics generally accept that the modernist movement ended when World War II ended, leading the way toward postmodernism and postcolonialism. **Postmodern literature** refers to the literature that emerged after the war in reaction to the previous modernist movement. In typical modernist works, authors presented a subjective point of view with a focus on one's inner experience, using a stream-of-consciousness narration. Modernist works dealt with themes of alienation and uncertain identity. In contrast, postmodernist works focus on the external world and may include an ironic narrator or multiple narrators offering multiple perspectives on the same event. Themes often reflect collective voices, popular culture, and multicultural experiences.

5 Although it can be difficult to define, postmodernist literature is known for its rebellious approach and willingness to test boundaries. Postmodern literary works reexamine literary tradition. For instance, such works may include a unique combination of multiple genres to comment on postmodern life or a self-awareness of the writing form through parody of other texts. One driving idea behind postmodernism is that "everything has already been done" and artists can no longer be completely original. Therefore, postmodernists take a playful approach, drawing inspiration from existing texts, combining forms, and having fun with literary experimentation.

TEXT TALK

How do postmodernists approach literature?

See paragraph 5: Postmodernists experiment with literature. They draw inspiration from existing texts and often employ multiple perspectives. They often take an ironic tone and combine texts in a spirit of experimentation.

SELECTION VOCABULARY

formidable / temible ***adjective*** causing fear or dread; intimidating

strife / la contienda ***noun*** strong, angry disagreements between individuals or groups

postmodern literature / letteratura postmoderna ***noun*** a reaction to modernism typically characterized by a return to traditional forms COGNATE

NOTES

Sotheby's unveils postmodern artist Banksy's newly-titled "Love Is in the Bin" at Sotheby's on October 12, 2018, in London, England. Originally titled "Girl with Balloon," the canvas passed through a hidden shredder seconds after it sold at Sotheby's London Contemporary Art Evening Sale on October 5, 2018, making it the first artwork in history to have been created live during an auction.

6 **Postcolonial literature** describes the genre of literature produced by writers of formerly colonized countries. Postcolonial writers describe the struggles of colonization and **decolonization** and write about the themes of identity, racism, and cultural dominance. Their writing challenges many of the assumptions of colonialism, particularly the assertion that European culture was superior and needed to spread to all corners of the earth. Many writers from former British colonies, including Chinua Achebe, Wole Soyinka, Derek Walcott, Salman Rushdie, and V. S. Naipaul, address the political and social problems that continued to plague their countries even after independence.

7 Postcolonial literature shares some similarities with postmodernism, and some postcolonial authors write in a postmodern style. For example, Indian-born author Salman Rushdie has been hailed for his innovative postmodern take on Indian history and independence in his novel *Midnight's Children* (1981). Nigerian poet and novelist Ben Okri is considered one of the foremost African authors of both postmodernism and postcolonialism, and his novel *The Famished Road* about a quest for identity won the Booker Prize in 1991.

8 Among the most obvious lasting effects of British colonialism is the large number of English speakers spread throughout the world. Postcolonial writers may have wrestled with the issue of using English, the language of their oppressors, but many choose English because it is so widely spoken and can reach large audiences. Writing in English, these authors reclaim and define their own identities and tell their own stories, from their perspectives.

TEXT TALK

What do postcolonial writers write about?

See paragraph 6: Postcolonial writers examine colonialism and its oppressive effects. They often explore themes of identity, racism, and cultural dominance.

SELECTION VOCABULARY

decolonization / la descolonización *noun* the process of changing from colonial to independent status COGNATE

Major Concepts

- **Multiple Perspectives -** Postcolonial writers express different viewpoints about colonization, history, social justice, and culture—and also challenge stereotypes.
- **Decolonization Struggles -** Postcolonial literature criticizes colonial powers but also exposes corruption in postcolonial governments.

Style and Form

- Postmodern literature experiments with different literary forms and combines existing forms to create new styles of literature. As a result, writers have created variations and innovations upon traditional forms and themes.
- Postcolonial writers may use established narrative forms and the English language, even though it may not be their native language. This has broadened the scope of English literature in both subject matter and style, offering the voices and experiences of writers from a great variety of cultures throughout the world.

9 The British Empire may have ended before the age of postmodernism and postcolonialism, but the world of literature has expanded enormously. By adding new perspectives and new voices, literature has become a platform for all narratives and literary experiments.

TEXT TALK

Do you think American literature should be considered postcolonial literature? Why or why not?

Answers will vary.

BEYOND TEXT TALK

What do modern and postmodern writers and artists have in common? What is the relationship between Modernism, postmodernism, and postcolonialism?

Reading Comprehension

Have students complete the digital reading comprehension questions when they finish reading.

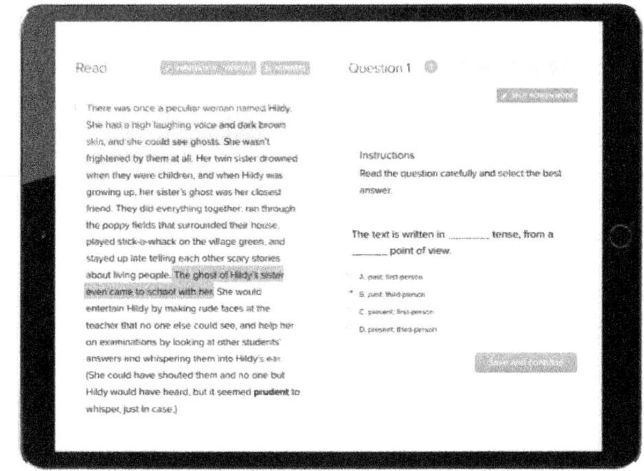

ANSWER KEY

QUESTION 1: C
QUESTION 2: C
QUESTION 3: B
QUESTION 4: A
QUESTION 5: C
QUESTION 6: B
QUESTION 7: D
QUESTION 8: D
QUESTION 9: C
QUESTION 10: *See first chart.*

Definition	Word
a movement characterized by experimentation with form and style	postmodernism
the process of withdrawal from a colony, leaving it with an independent government	decolonization
conflict or disagreement over issues	strife
relating to the aftermath of Western imperialism and occupation of colonies	postcolonialism

Think Questions

Circulate as students answer Think Questions independently. Scaffolds for these questions are shown on the opposite page.

QUESTION 1: Textual Evidence

The British Empire "built railroads, telegraphs, schools, and hospitals," but it also oppressed the cultures it colonized and caused ethnic conflicts.

QUESTION 2: Textual Evidence

Postmodernism rebels against tradition and authority because it embraces the idea that "everything has been done before." In an effort to be original, postmodernists experiment with traditional literary forms.

QUESTION 3: Textual Evidence

Because of British colonialism, people in countries spread throughout the world now speak English. This made English-language writers much more diverse. Many postcolonial writers write in English "because it is so widely spoken and can reach large audiences."

QUESTION 4: Word Patterns and Relationships

Postmodernism literally means "after modernism," and it refers to the movement that followed modernism.

QUESTION 5: Context Clues

The text says that *postcolonialism* "came after Colonialism," so the word most likely refers to all the social, literary, artistic, and political events in countries that used to be a colony of another country.

Literary Period

Read "Introduction to Postmodernism and Postcolonialism." After you read, complete the Think Questions below.

THINK QUESTIONS

1. What were the effects of imperialism? Cite evidence from the text to support your answer.
2. Why does postmodernism rebel against tradition and authority? Cite evidence from the text to support your answer.
3. What effect did British colonialism have on the English language, and why is this important to literature? Cite evidence from the text to support your answers.
4. The word *Postmodernism* contains the Latin prefix *post-*, meaning "after." With this information in mind, write your best definition of the word **Postmodernism** as it used in this text. Cite any words or phrases that were particularly helpful in coming to your conclusion.
5. Use context clues to determine the meaning of the word **Postcolonialism**. Write your best definition here, along with the words and phrases that were most helpful in determining the word's meaning. Then, check a dictionary to confirm your understanding.

Think Questions

SCAFFOLDS

Use the scaffolds below to differentiate instruction for your ELL English Language Learners and A Approaching grade level readers.

ELL **BEGINNING** Write a response using the word bank and sentence frames.

INTERMEDIATE Write a response using the sentence frames.

ADVANCED, ADVANCED HIGH Write a response using the Text-Dependent Question Guide.

A **APPROACHING** Write a response using the Text-Dependent Question Guide.

BEGINNING	INTERMEDIATE	APPROACHING / ADVANCED, ADVANCED HIGH
Word Bank	**Sentence Frames**	**Text-Dependent Question Guide**
after speak experiment followed perspectives oppressed independent colonialism original schools	Question 1 The British Empire built railroads, telegraphs, ____ and hospitals, but the empire also ____ the people it colonized.	1. • What did the British Empire build? • What do you think the British thought of imperialism? • How did the British treat the people in the colonized countries?
	Question 2 Postmodernism rebels against tradition and authority to try to be ____. Postmodernists ____ with literary forms.	2. • What does postmodernism rebel against? • What do postmodernists think "has already been done"? • How do postmodernists experiment?
	Question 3 Because of the British Empire, many people throughout the world now ____ English. Many postcolonial writers use English to tell stories from their ____.	3. • How did English become such a common language in the world? • Did colonial subjects have to learn English? • How did postcolonial writers use their knowledge of English?
	Question 4 *Postmodernism* literally means "____ modernism." It refers to the movement that ____ modernism.	4. • Read: "As the word parts signify, **postmodernism** came after modernism." • What other words start with *post-*? • What does postmodernism do?
	Question 5 The text says that postcolonialism "came after ____." The word refers to events in countries that used to be colonies but are now ____.	5. • Read: "**Postcolonial** literature describes the genre of literature produced by writers of formerly colonized countries." • Who are the writers of postcolonial literature? • What do these writers have in common?

Skill: Recognize Genre

Introduce the Genre: Fiction

Watch the Concept Definition video  and read the following definition with your students.

Fiction is writing about invented people, places, and events. It includes both long and short written works. **Novels** are long works of fiction. **Short stories**, myths, and folktales are examples of short works of fiction. Short fiction focuses on a small number of events or on just one event. You can usually read a short work of fiction in a single sitting. Short works contain the same elements as do longer works of fiction. These elements include character, plot, setting, point of view, and theme.

In addition, those elements of fiction can be endlessly transformed by the writers who use them. A change in setting can turn a story into science fiction or fantasy, and an author's choices about plot can affect whether the work is categorized as stream of consciousness or magical realism. Moreover, these choices are often influenced by the time and place in which a person writes, and a text's **subgenre**, or specific category, often reflects those influences.

However, subgenres and techniques can overlap, and texts often fit into more than one category. Categories are useful because they help us use genre characteristics to deepen our understanding of the text.

Your Turn

Ask students to complete the Your Turn activity.

Literary Subgenre	Title
Stoku	The Glory of Dawn
Realistic Fiction	How I Survived High School
Graphic Story	The Incredible Adventures of Hannah Heart

TURN AND TALK

1. Which genres or subgenres of fiction do you like to read? Why?

2. Which genres or subgenres do not interest you? Why?

 **SPEAKING FRAMES**

- I like to read ____. I like this type of fiction because ____.
- I do not like to read ____. The reason is ____.

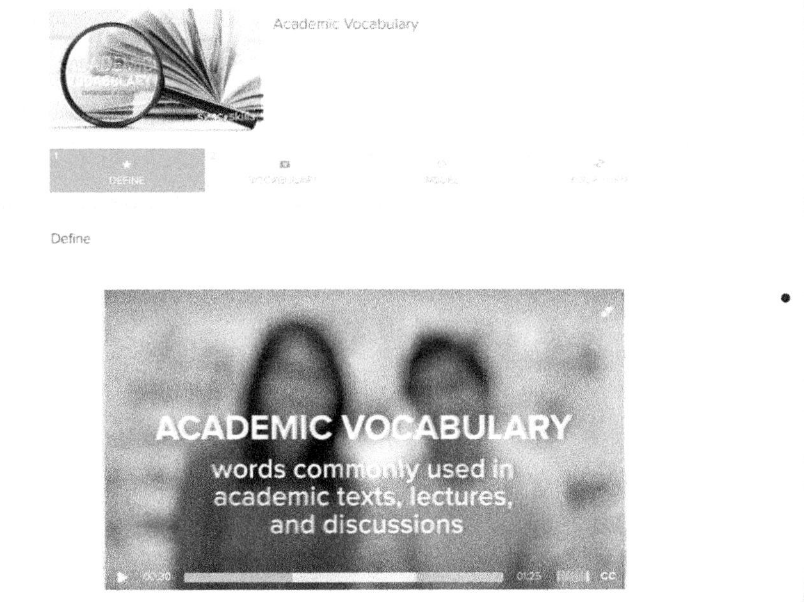

Skill: Academic Vocabulary

Introduce the Terms

cease / poner fin *verb* to put an end to a state or an activity

commence / comenzar *verb* to take the first step or steps in carrying out an action; to start or begin COGNATE

concurrently / concurrente *adjective* occurring or operating at the same time COGNATE

duration / la duración *noun* the period of time during which something continues COGNATE

eventual / final *adjective* expected to follow in the indefinite future from causes already operating

forthcoming / inminente *adjective* of the relatively near future

inevitable / inevitable *adjective* unavoidable and certain to happen COGNATE

ongoing / continuo *adjective* happening continuously; in progress

suspend / suspender *verb* to stop something for an amount of time COGNATE

temporary / temporal *adjective* only for a short time; not permanent or lasting COGNATE

Practice Using Vocabulary

Divide the vocabulary words into two lists. Pair students and give half of the list to each student. Challenge students to have a casual conversation with each other that uses every word on their list. Students should aim to insert their vocabulary words in a way that sounds natural. You may wish to turn this activity into a game, allowing partners to award each other points if they effectively use each word on their list.

Your Turn

Ask students to complete the Your Turn activities.

Your Turn 1

Word	Example	Non-Example
commence	beginning a new term at school	ending a sale after five days
duration	the period of time of an eclipse	the exact moment the band stops playing
suspend	removing the right to use a credit card until the cardholder pays the overdue amount	reactivating a library card after all past-due fines are paid
concurrent	two parades happening at the same time but following different routes	two research projects investigating the same issue but starting and ending on different dates

Your Turn 2

QUESTION 1: C **QUESTION 2:** B **QUESTION 3:** D **QUESTION 4:** A **QUESTION 5:** A

Your Turn 3

See digital teacher's edition for sample answers.

The Mysterious Anxiety of Them and Us

POETRY
Ben Okri
2006

Introduction

Ben Okri (b. 1959) is a writer of novels, poetry, short stories, and social commentary from Minna, Nigeria. During his youth, Okri was an avid reader of English literature and an avid listener to his mother's traditional African stories and myths. Okri's writing draws from both influences, often incorporating realism, folktales, mythology, as well as dream logic, or the feeling of being in a dream. In his book *Tales of Freedom*, Okri created a new form called the "stoku," which he described as "an amalgam of short story and haiku. It is a story as it inclines towards a flash of a moment, insight, vision or paradox." The invented style can be seen on full display in "The Mysterious Anxiety of Them and Us," a stoku set in a dream-like atmosphere where an arbitrary distinction engenders an almost surreal tension.

The narrator, his wife, and some friends are at a dinner party hosted by an unknown man. Before them lies a feast, but there are too many people and not enough food–the host refuses to give any instructions and the crowd grows tense. Then suddenly, those seated begin to eat, while those standing merely watch. The narrator doesn't feel guilty eating while others go hungry, but he is aware of a murmur rising up behind him. He thinks about passing some food to those standing, but doesn't know where to begin—there are too many people behind him. He rationalizes that to turn around and start passing food would be to somehow admit that they are inferior to him. After he finishes eating, the narrator turns around and, to his shock, there are only three people there. Had there only been three the whole time or had some of them wandered off? He admits that while he was eating, he was worried that someone behind him would stick a knife in his back.

Proficiency-leveled summaries and summaries in multiple languages are available digitally.

Audio and audio text highlighting are available with this text.

CONNECT TO ESSENTIAL QUESTION

How are we shaped by change?

How do changes in society affect the way people see each other? In this "stoku," a genre of the author's own invention, a nameless narrator and his wife attend a grand feast only to discover that the guests have been divided into two groups: those who are sitting at the table and those who are not.

Entry Point

As students prepare to read "The Mysterious Anxiety of Them and Us," share the following information with them to provide context.

- ✓ Ben Okri is a prominent Nigerian novelist who uses literary experimentation to represent the social and political upheaval in his country.
- ✓ Okri saw the chaos, violence, and intense human suffering caused by the Nigerian civil war (1967–1970). A grant from the Nigerian government enabled him to leave Africa to study comparative literature in England.
- ✓ Okri's best-known, award-winning novel *The Famished Road* uses magical realism to convey ideas about poverty in Africa. The book's narrator is a spirit-child named Azaro, a go-between for the human and spirit worlds, whose human parents struggle and suffer repeatedly. The story is mostly dark and tragic, with brief highlights of humor.

Instructional Path

The print teacher's edition includes essential point-of-use instruction and planning tools. Complete lesson plans and program documents appear in your digital teacher account.

First Read: The Mysterious Anxiety of Them and Us

Objectives: After an initial reading and discussion of the text, students will be able to identify and describe character traits and setting details as well as articulate the conflict that is central to the plot.

Skill: Story Structure

Objectives: After rereading and discussing a model of close reading, students will be able analyze how an author's choices concerning how to structure specific parts of a text contribute to the overall aesthetic impact and meaning in "The Mysterious Anxiety of Them and Us."

Skill: Context Clues

Objectives: After rereading and discussing a model of close reading, students will be able to use clues in the text to determine the meaning of a word or phrase and evaluate the impact of the word(s) on the overall meaning of "The Mysterious Anxiety of Them and Us."

Close Read: The Mysterious Anxiety of Them and Us

Objectives: After engaging in a close reading and discussion of "The Mysterious Anxiety of Them and Us," students will be able to write a short literary analysis that discusses the events and theme of the text.

Progress Monitoring

Opportunities to Learn	Opportunities to Demonstrate Learning	Opportunities to Reteach
Story Structure		
Skill: Story Structure	Skill: Story Structure • Your Turn Close Read • Skills Focus • Write	Spotlight Skill: Story Structure
Context Clues		
Skill: Context Clues	Skill: Context Clues • Your Turn Close Read • Vocabulary Chart • Skills Focus	Spotlight Skill: Context Clues

First Read

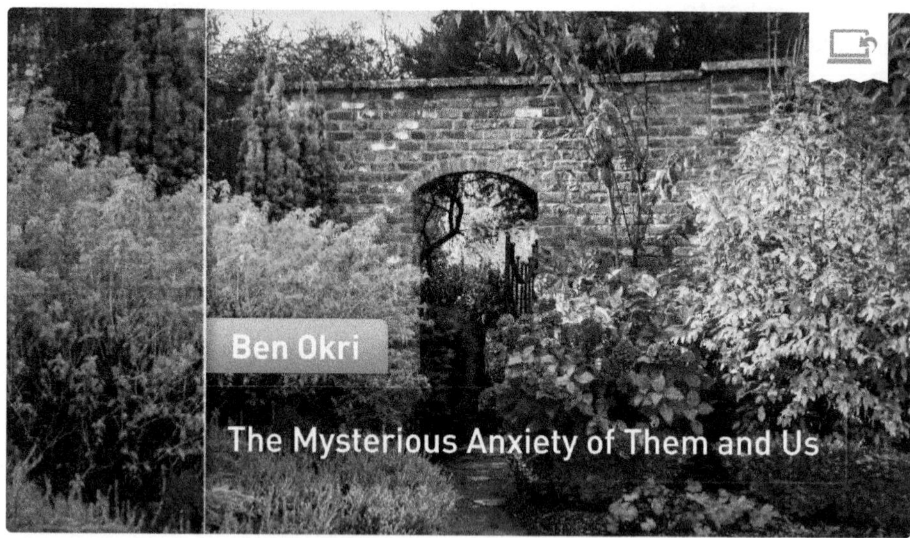

Introduce the Text

As a class, watch the video preview and have students read the introduction in pairs to make connections to the video preview.

To activate prior knowledge and experiences, ask students:

- Based on the video, how do you think this selection will make you feel?
- Can you think of an example of two rival groups? What sets them apart?

ELL SPEAKING FRAMES

- I think the selection will make me feel ____.
- Two rival groups are ____ and ____. A difference between them is ____.

Access Complex Text

LEXILE: N/A WORD COUNT: 518

The following areas may be challenging for students, particularly ELL English Language Learners and A Approaching grade-level learners.

Purpose	Genre
• Students may be confused by the mysterious setting and story that function on the allegorical level. • Explain to students that Okri was very interested in issues of social justice. Students can work in pairs or groups to figure out what the characters, conflict, and setting might represent.	• Okri explained that he was merging two genres together in what he called a stoku: "A stoku is an amalgam of short story and haiku. It is a story as it inclines towards a flash of a moment, insight, vision or paradox." • Have students discuss how this quotation helps them interpret the meaning of the story.

 SCAFFOLDS

 ENGLISH LANGUAGE LEARNERS  APPROACHING GRADE LEVEL  BEYOND GRADE LEVEL

These icons identify differentiation strategies and scaffolded support for a variety of students. See the digital lesson plan for additional differentiation strategies and scaffolds.

"While we had been eating it had often occurred to me that there was nothing to stop them from sticking knives into our backs."

1 We were in the magnificent grounds of our mysterious host. A feast had been laid out in the open air. There were many of us present. Some were already seated and some were standing behind those seated. In a way there were too many of us for the food served, or it felt like that.

Nigerian poet and novelist Ben Okri

2 There was a moment when it seemed that everyone would rush at the food and we'd have to be **barbaric** and eat with our hands, fighting over the feast laid out on the lovely tables. The moment of tension lasted a long time.

3 Our host did nothing, and said nothing. No one was sure what to do. **Insurrection** brooded in the winds. Then something strange happened. Those who were at table served themselves, and began eating.

4 We ate calmly. My wife was sitting next to me. The food was wonderful.

5 We ate with some awareness of those behind us, who were not eating, and who did not move. They merely watched us eating.

6 Did we who were eating feel guilty? It was a complex feeling. There is no way of resolving it as such. Those who were at table ate. That's it. That's all.

7 We ate a while. Then the people behind us began to murmur. One of them, in a low voice, said:

8 'The first person who offers us some food will receive . . .'

9 I was tempted to offer them some food. But how could I? Where would I start? The situation was impossible. If you turned around, you would see them all. Then your situation would be **polarized**. It would be you and them. But it was never that way to begin with. We were all at the feast. It's just that you were

Skill: Story Structure

The author uses vague descriptions to set up the allegory. This is an effective choice because it suggests that the stoku reflects abstract ideas instead of telling about concrete characters, settings, and plot events.

Skill: Context Clues

Barbaric and tension are more formal words compared to the rest of the author's diction. Perhaps the author does this to call the reader's attention to certain ideas in the story.

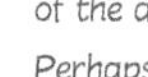

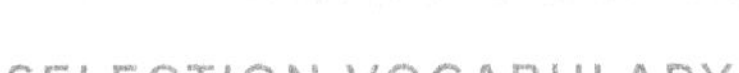

SELECTION VOCABULARY

barbaric / bárbaro/a ***adjective*** cruel; wild; uncivilized COGNATE

insurrection / la insurrección ***noun*** a violent uprising; rebellion COGNATE

Developing Background Knowledge and Cultural Awareness

Guide students as they complete a short online search.

1. In small groups, have students do a five-minute online search on the term "stoku."
2. On the board, collate the various types of information students learned. Ask one student to volunteer to create an instant summary.

Discuss with students: Reflect on the following quote by Ben Okri, the author of this story: "Beware of the stories you read or tell; subtly, at night, beneath the waters of consciousness, they are altering your world." What do you think Okri means when he says that stories are "altering your world"? How do fictional stories shape the way we think? What are the potential advantages and dangers of a story's powers to shape minds?

Story Structure

How does the reader identify and evaluate the author's use of allegory in the beginning of "The Mysterious Anxiety of Them and Us"?

The reader notices that the author includes vague descriptions of the setting, characters, and plot. She determines that this effectively signals that the text may be an allegory about abstract ideas.

Context Clues

How does the reader use context clues to determine the meaning and impact of certain words in the second paragraph?

The reader uses clues in the surrounding text to note that *barbaric* and *tension* are more formal word choices compared to the rest of the author's diction throughout the story.

Skills Focus

QUESTION 3: Language, Style, and Audience

The text suggests that a large number of people may have died, and yet the narrator seems more concerned about his own well-being, even though he is safe and fed. This makes me feel angry and helps me to see the narrator as selfish.

Skills Focus

QUESTION 4: Context Clues

Magnificent is used to describe the estate and is an adjective. Magnificent is similar to beautiful or elaborate. The author uses the term to show that the narrator is so consumed by the setting rather than the fate of the people behind him.

Skills Focus

QUESTION 5: Connect to Essential Question

The narrator has empathy for the people who are behind him. Yet, in the next paragraph he retracts feelings of empathy and makes excuses for his behavior. The narrator's change in thinking leaves me feeling frustrated that he could be so callous to their suffering.

at the table, and you began to eat. They weren't at table and they didn't eat. They did nothing. They didn't even come over, take a plate, and serve themselves. No one told them, to just stand there watching us eat. They did it to themselves.

10 So to turn around and offer them food would automatically be to see them and treat them as inferior. When in fact they behaved in a manner that made things turn out that way. And so we continued to eat, and ignored the murmurs. Soon we had finished eating. We were satisfied, and took up the invitation to visit other parts of the estate. There was still plenty of food left, as it happened. My wife and I were almost the last to leave the table. As I got up, I looked behind us. I was surprised to see only three people there. Was that all? They had seemed like more, like a crowd. Maybe there had been more of them, but they'd drifted off, given up, or died. While we had been eating it had often occurred to me that there was nothing to stop them from sticking knives into our backs. My wife and I filed out with the others, towards the gardens, in the **sumptuous** grounds of that magnificent estate. It had been a dreamy day of rich sunlight.

TEXT TALK

What is the setting?

See paragraph 1: The setting is a large outdoor feast at a magnificent estate.

What does the narrator do when people begin to eat?

See paragraph 4: The narrator begins to eat, too.

Why doesn't the narrator turn around?

See paragraph 9: The narrator does not turn around because he does not want to see the other people.

How did researching "stoku" help you understand the text?

Answers will vary.

How did discussing Ben Okri's quotation help you better understand the purpose of the stoku?

Answers may vary.

SELECTION VOCABULARY

polarized / polarizar ***verb*** to sharply divide into opposing groups COGNATE

Sumptuous / suntuoso/a ***adjective*** very expensive or impressive COGNATE

Reading Comprehension OPTIONAL

Have students complete the digital reading comprehension questions ✓ when they finish reading.

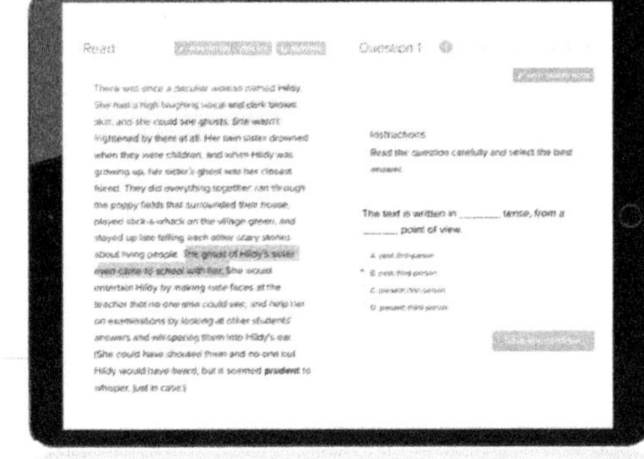

ANSWER KEY

QUESTION 1: D
QUESTION 2: C
QUESTION 3: B
QUESTION 4: D
QUESTION 5: *See chart.*

First	Second	Third	Fourth
"There was a moment when it seemed that everyone would rush at the food and we'd have to be barbaric and eat with our hands, fighting over the feast laid out on the lovely tables."	"The food was wonderful."	"I was tempted to offer them some food."	"I was surprised to find only three people there."

Connect and Extend OPTIONAL

CONNECT TO EXTENDED ORAL PROJECT

Students can use "The Mysterious Anxiety of Them and Us" as a model text for their Extended Oral Project. They can adopt the technique of telling a story to argue a point, as Ben Okri does, rather than providing only reasons and evidence. Framed as a story, their argument about what to add to the curriculum might become more engaging.

BEYOND THE BOOK

Adaptation: Dramatic Performance

Ben Okri describes a banquet where some people are eating and others choose to stand and not eat. The action is not talked about or explained and leaves those who are eating feeling guilty. Students will recreate this scene in a dramatic performance.

In small groups, ask students to:

- Reread the story through the lens of a director.
  - > What are you visualizing?
  - > How are people feeling and what would that look like?
  - > How are the scenes changing?
- Create a performance of this story that captures the mood and events.
  - > How are the people acting? Do their actions reflect how they feel?
  - > What movements are important?
  - > What colors and lighting will help create the mood?
- Share finished performances with classmates.

To reflect, ask students:

- How do performances capture the written words?
- Which performance captured the emotions of the character best? How?

Think Questions

Circulate as students answer Think Questions independently. Scaffolds for these questions are shown on the opposite page.

QUESTION 1: Textual Evidence

The people seated at the table served themselves while the people behind them "merely watched us eating." The narrator and his wife "ate calmly" but "with some awareness of those behind us," which creates tension and makes the narrator feel uneasy.

QUESTION 2: Textual Evidence

The narrator says it was "a complex feeling" and that there was "no way of resolving it," even though he could easily turn around and serve the other people. This shows that he will rationalize immoral behavior instead of correcting it.

QUESTION 3: Textual Evidence

The last line felt inconsistent with the tone. The rest of the text is tense. Descriptions like "there was nothing to stop them from sticking knives into our backs" increase the tension in the last paragraph, so the ending is not dreamy.

QUESTION 4: Context Clues

I think *insurrection* means a revolt, like when people rebel against social injustice, because the word is used to describe what might happen as a result of a tense situation where two groups of people receive unequal treatment.

QUESTION 5: Context Clues

I think *sumptuous* means "luxurious." I arrived at this meaning because of the context clue of "magnificent."

First Read

Read "The Mysterious Anxiety of Them and Us." After you read, complete the Think Questions below.

THINK QUESTIONS

1. In the middle of paragraph 3, the narrator says, "Then something strange happened." Citing evidence from the text, explain what happened. How does what occurred affect the narrator's feelings?

2. In paragraph 6, the narrator asks, "Did we who were eating feel guilty?" How does he respond to his own question? What does the way he answers tell you about him? Use examples from the text to support your answer.

3. How did you react to the last sentence, "It had been a dreamy day of rich sunlight"? Do you think it is consistent with the tone of the rest of the text? Use evidence from the text to support your answer.

4. What is the meaning of the word **insurrection** as it is used in the text? Write your best definition here, along with a brief explanation of how you arrived at its meaning.

5. Use context clues to determine the meaning of the word **sumptuous** as it is used in "The Mysterious Anxiety of Them and Us." Write your definition of *sumptuous* here, along with those words or phrases from the text that helped most. Then check a dictionary to confirm your understanding.

Think Questions

SCAFFOLDS

Use the scaffolds below to differentiate instruction for your ELL English Language Learners and A Approaching grade level readers.

ELL **BEGINNING** Write a response using the word bank and sentence frames.

INTERMEDIATE Write a response using the sentence frames.

ADVANCED, ADVANCED HIGH Write a response using the Text-Dependent Question Guide.

A **APPROACHING** Write a response using the Text-Dependent Question Guide.

BEGINNING	INTERMEDIATE	APPROACHING / ADVANCED, ADVANCED HIGH
Word Bank	**Sentence Frames**	**Text-Dependent Question Guide**
light fight tense	The people sitting at the table begin ____. The people behind ____. This makes the narrator feel ____.	1. • What do the people seated at the table do? • What do the other people do? • How does this make the narrator feel?
uneasy correcting magnificent	The narrator says the feeling is "____" and that nothing could be done about it. This shows the narrator will try to make himself feel ____ about immoral behavior instead of ____ his actions.	2. • How does the narrator describe his feeling? • Does the narrator try to resolve the situation? Why or why not? • What does this suggest about the narrator?
revolt watch better	The final sentence is / is not consistent with the tone of the text. The rest of the text is ____. The tone of the final line is ____.	3. • What feeling does the last line convey? Is it positive or negative? • Is the rest of the text positive or negative? • What are some examples from the text that support your answer?
eating complex luxurious	*Insurrection* means a ____. A clue is that one group of people is being treated unfairly, and the narrator is worried they may ____ back.	4. • Read: "**Insurrection** brooded in the winds." • Is *insurrection* a noun, a verb, an adjective, or an adverb? Is it positive or negative? • How do the narrator's thoughts in paragraph 2 provide a clue to the meaning of *insurrection?*
	Sumptuous means ____. A clue is that the "sumptuous grounds" are part of a "____ estate."	5. • Read: "My wife and I filed out with the others, towards the gardens, in the **sumptuous** grounds of that magnificent estate." • What is described as *sumptuous?* • What other descriptive word appears in the sentence? • What does that tell me about the meaning of the word *sumptuous?*

Skill: Story Structure

Introduce the Skill

Watch the Concept Definition video and read the following definition with your students.

Story structure is the framework writers use to develop the events of the **plot**. Any plot has a central problem or conflict which the story introduces, builds to a climax, and finally solves. The story may be character-driven, exploring one person's emotions, or it could be driven by suspense, with a complicated sequence of events that takes many twists and turns. The events may or may not be presented in chronological order. For example, an author who wishes to build tension may begin with a dramatic **flashback** before introducing the present situation in a story. A character-driven novel might describe events from the point of view of one character, and how the events change him or her. Whatever story structure an author chooses to use, **analyzing** how the events of a chapter or scene fit into the overall structure can help readers identify how it also contributes to the development of the **theme** and **setting**.

Skill: Story Structure

Use the Checklist to analyze Story Structure in "The Mysterious Anxiety of Them and Us." Refer to the sample student annotations about Story Structure in the text.

••• CHECKLIST FOR STORY STRUCTURE

In order to identify the choices an author makes when structuring specific parts of a text, note the following:

- ✓ the choices an author makes to organize specific parts of a text such as where to begin and end a story, or whether the ending should be tragic, comic, or inconclusive
- ✓ the author's use of any literary devices, such as:
  - pacing: how quickly or slowly the events of a story unfold
  - allegory: a story or poem that conveys a hidden meaning which is usually moral or political
- ✓ how the overall structure of the text contributes to its meaning as well as its aesthetic impact, such as
  - an allegorical story structure
  - the creation of suspense through the use of pacing

To analyze how an author's choices concerning how to structure specific parts of a text contribute to its overall structure and meaning as well as its aesthetic impact, consider the following questions:

- ✓ How does the author structure the text overall? How does the author structure specific parts of the text?
- ✓ Does the author incorporate literary elements such as allegory? How do these elements affect the overall text structure and the aesthetic impact of the text?
- ✓ What is the literal or everyday meaning of the narrative? What would the allegorical meaning of the narrative be? How do the characters, setting, and plot work together to convey this message?

TURN AND TALK

1. What is an example of a story that has a hidden social or moral meaning? How did the story say one thing and mean another?

SPEAKING FRAMES

- A story with a hidden social or moral meaning is ____.
- The story is literally about ____. The hidden meaning is ____.

SKILL VOCABULARY

story structure / la estructura de la historia ***noun*** the outline a writer uses to organize and tell a story

plot / la trama ***noun*** the sequence of events that form a story

flashback / la escena retrospectiva ***noun*** a scene in a story, play, movie, or TV show that is set in a time earlier than the events in the main story

analyze / analizar ***verb*** to consider in detail and discover essential features or meaning COGNATE

Skill: Story Structure

Reread paragraph 9 of "The Mysterious Anxiety of Them and Us." Then, using the Checklist on the previous page, answer the multiple-choice questions below.

YOUR TURN

1. What is the literal meaning of paragraph 9?
   - A. The people standing behind will eat after the people sitting are done.
   - B. The host created this situation as a test to see what the narrator would do.
   - C. The narrator thinks the best thing to do in this situation is not turn around.
   - D. The fact that some get more than others is universal and impossible to change.

2. What is the symbolic meaning of paragraph 9?
   - A. People need to take responsibility for their own life and wellbeing.
   - B. The events that happened at the feast could happen to anyone in real life.
   - C. The people standing behind have to wait their turn to eat because they arrived late.
   - D. Wealthy people avoid thinking about the poor because they do not want to feel guilty.

3. The language Okri uses to develop allegory in this paragraph is effective because it—
   - A. suggests that people are not responsible for their own actions.
   - B. reflects the way wealthy people rationalize their actions.
   - C. describes explicit conflict between two social groups.
   - D. emphasizes the struggles of people living in poverty.

SKILL VOCABULARY

theme / el tema *noun* the central idea or message of a work of literature, often expressed as a general statement about life COGNATE

setting / el escenario *noun* the time and place of the story

Your Turn

Ask students to complete the Your Turn Activity.

QUESTION 1

A. Incorrect. Readers do not know whether the people behind may or may not eat later.

B. Incorrect. The host's motivations are not described in this paragraph.

C. Correct. The narrator thinks that seeing the people behind him would make the situation worse.

D. Incorrect. This is not a literal interpretation of the events in the paragraph.

QUESTION 2

A. Incorrect. This is the opposite of the text's symbolic meaning.

B. Incorrect. What happens at the feast would not happen in real life.

C. Incorrect. This would be a literal interpretation, and it is not supported by the text.

D. Correct. The narrator's choice to keep his back turned on those behind him could be interpreted this way.

QUESTION 3

A. Incorrect. The language does not suggest that people are not responsible for their own actions.

B. Correct. Okri builds the allegory by having the narrator rationalize his behavior.

C. Incorrect. This paragraph shows an internal conflict, not an explicit conflict between the two groups.

D. Incorrect. This paragraph does not emphasize the struggles of people living in poverty.

Skill: Context Clues

Introduce the Skill

Watch the Concept Definition video and read the following definition with your students.

When readers come across words they don't know, they often use context to determine the meanings of the unfamiliar words. **Context clues** are hints in the surrounding text that a reader can use to **infer** the meaning of an unfamiliar word. Some common types of context clues include the following:

- **Definition**: an explanation of the word's meaning before or after the word appears, usually set off by a comma
- **Example**: one or more examples in a text that may demonstrate the meaning of a word
- **Comparison**: determining a word's meaning based on how it is like something else in the text
- **Contrast**: determining a word's meaning based on how it is unlike something else in the text

In addition, the genre of a text and what it is about also provide context clues for a word's meaning. Readers can verify their preliminary definitions of words or phrases by using a print or digital resource.

Skill: Context Clues

Use the Checklist to analyze Context Clues in "The Mysterious Anxiety of Them and Us." Refer to the sample student annotations about Context Clues in the text.

CHECKLIST FOR CONTEXT CLUES

In order to use context as a clue to the meaning of a word or phrase, note the following:

- ✓ clues about the word's part of speech
- ✓ clues in the surrounding text about the word's meaning
- ✓ words with similar denotations that seem to differ slightly in meaning
- ✓ signal words that cue a type of context clue, such as:
  - *comparably*, *related to*, or *similarly* to signal a comparison context clue
  - *on the other hand*, *however*, or *in contrast* to signal a contrast context clue
  - *by reason of*, *because*, or *as a result* to signal a cause-and-effect context clue

To determine the meaning of a word or phrase as they are used in a text, consider the following questions:

- ✓ What is the meaning of the overall sentence, paragraph, or text?
- ✓ How does the position of the word in the sentence help me define it?
- ✓ How does the word function in the sentence? What clues help identify the word's part of speech?
- ✓ What clues in the text suggest the word's definition?
- ✓ What do I think the word means?

To verify the preliminary determination of the meaning of the word or phrase based on context, consider the following questions:

- ✓ Does the definition I inferred make sense within the context of the sentence?
- ✓ Which of the dictionary's definitions makes sense within the context of the sentence?

TURN AND TALK

1. When have you heard someone use an unfamiliar word or phrase?
2. What are some strategies you can use when you hear someone say something you don't fully understand?

ELL SPEAKING FRAMES

- I heard someone use an unfamiliar word or phrase when ____.
- When I hear someone say something that I don't fully understand, one strategy I could use would be ____.

SKILL VOCABULARY

context clue / la clave del contexto ***noun*** a hint in the surrounding text that can help a reader infer the meaning of an unfamiliar word, phrase, or description

infer / inferir ***verb*** to determine something by using reasoning and evidence from the text COGNATE

definition context clue / la clave del contexto de definición ***noun*** text that provides a definition of a word

Skill: Context Clues

Reread paragraphs 6–8 of "The Mysterious Anxiety of Them and Us." Then, using the Checklist on the previous page, answer the multiple-choice questions below.

YOUR TURN

1. Using context clues, determine the part of speech for *murmur*.

   - A. *Murmur* is a noun.
   - B. *Murmur* is a verb.
   - C. *Murmur* is an adverb.
   - D. *Murmur* is an adjective.

2. This question has two parts. First, answer Part A. Then, answer Part B.

> **murmur**
> *noun*
>
> 1. a constant sound
> 2. condition related to issues with the heart
>
> *verb*
>
> 1. to speak in a low, soft voice
> 2. to complain
>
> **Origin:** Late Middle English: borrowed from Old French *murmure* meaning "sound of voices, from Latin, *murmur* meaning "humming" or "muttering."

Your Turn

Ask students to complete the Your Turn Activity.

QUESTION 1

A. Incorrect. *Murmur* as used in the sentence is a verb, not a noun.

B. Correct. *Murmur* is used as a verb in the sentence.

C. Incorrect. *Murmur* is used as a verb in the sentence.

D. Incorrect. *Murmur* is used as a verb in the sentence.

SKILL VOCABULARY

example context clue / la clave del contexto de ejemplo ***noun*** text that provides a clue to the meaning of a word through one or more examples

comparison context clue / la clave del contexto de comparación ***noun*** text that provides a clue to the meaning of a word through a comparison

contrast context clue / la clave del contexto de contraste ***noun*** text that provides a clue to the meaning of a word through a contrast

Your Turn

QUESTION 2

Part A

A. Incorrect. The word *murmur* in this passage does not relate to a constant sound.

B. Incorrect. The word *murmur* in this passage does not relate to a heart condition.

C. Correct. The people behind the narrator began speaking in low, soft voices.

D. Incorrect. There is no evidence to suggest that *murmur* means complaint in this passage.

Part B

A. Incorrect. This phrase does not provide the best context for *murmur* as it is used in the text.

B. Incorrect. This phrase does not provide the best context for *murmur* as it is used in the text.

C. Incorrect. This phrase does not provide the best context for *murmur* as it is used in the text.

D. Correct. This phrase is a strong context clue because it suggests that *murmur* is used to describe how the people behind the narrator were speaking.

Part A: What is the most likely definition of "murmur" given this context in this passage?

- A. Definition 1.a
- B. Definition 2.b
- C. Definition 1.b
- D. Definition 2.a

Part B: Which of the following context clues from the text **best** supports your answer to Part A?

- A. "That's it. That's all."
- B. "We ate a while"
- C. "Then the people behind us began . . ."
- D. "One of them, in a low voice, said . . ."

Close Read

Reread "The Mysterious Anxiety of Them and Us." As you reread, complete the Skills Focus questions below. Then use your answers and annotations from the questions to help you complete the Write activity.

SKILLS FOCUS

1. Identify a detail that is suggestive of a hidden meaning or abstract idea, and explain how it effectively contributes to the story's allegorical structure.
2. Identify an example of simple, plain writing in the text, and explain how the author's choice to use this diction and syntax contributes to the effectiveness of the allegory.
3. Identify a sentence that inspires readers to have an emotional response. Explain how this author's use of language effectively shapes the reader's perceptions of the narrator or events.
4. Re-read the final paragraph of the story. Using context clues, determine the part of speech and possible meaning of the word "magnificent." Then, highlight the word and in your annotation explain why the author's choice to repeat this word at the beginning and end of the story is important in the final impact of the story.
5. Throughout this allegorical short story, the narrator describes changes in thinking and in feeling about this strange situation. Highlight two instances of these changes, and in your annotation describe the impact they have on you, the reader.

WRITE

LITERARY ANALYSIS: This work is written in an allegorical, dreamlike style with little explanation of what is happening and why. What do you think is the "mysterious anxiety"? Who do you think are the "them and us"? Write a brief literary analysis that explains the events and the theme as you see them, which may not be the way your classmates see them. Tell what you think of the narrator and point out connections between the text and the real world. Support your ideas with textual evidence when you can.

Close Read

Skills Focus

QUESTION 1: Story Structure

See paragraph 2: I think the potential fight for food represents a struggle for resources. This effectively contributes to the allegory by showing that the guests at the feast symbolize all of humankind.

QUESTION 2: Language, Style and Audience

See paragraph 7: The author uses clear, informal language and a simple sentence structure to describe the moment when the people who do not have food start to protest. The allegory is effective because readers can focus on the clear distinction between the two groups.

QUESTION 3: Language, Style and Audience

See paragraph 10.

QUESTION 4: Context Clues See paragraph 10.

QUESTION 5: Connect to Essential Question

See paragraphs 9 and 10.

CHECK FOR SUCCESS

If students struggle with Question #1, ask:

- What is the narrator literally describing?
- What could be a hidden or symbolic meaning in this paragraph?
- How does the hidden or symbolic meaning connect to the allegory in the text.

Writer's Notebook

Connect to Literary Focus: Give students time to reflect on how "The Mysterious Anxiety of Them and Us" demonstrates the conventions and characteristics of this unit's literary focus, postmodernism and postcolonialism, by freewriting in their Writer's Notebooks.

ELL Beginning & Intermediate

Remind students of the unit's literary focus, postmodernism and postcolonialism. Encourage students to draw their connections or allow students to write in their native language. Circulate around the room, prompting students for their thoughts as they respond orally or through pantomime.

Advanced & Advanced High

Allow students to share their connections orally in pairs or small groups before freewriting.

Collaborative Conversation

Break students into collaborative conversation groups to discuss the Close Read prompt. Ask students to use the StudySyncTV episode as a model for their discussion. Remind them to reference their Skills Focus annotations in their discussion.

This work is written in an allegorical, dreamlike structure with little explanation of what is happening and why. What do you think is the "mysterious anxiety"? Who do you think are the "them and us"? Write a brief literary analysis that explains the events and the theme as you see them, which may not be the way your classmates see them. Tell what you think of the narrator and point out connections between the text and the real world. Support your ideas with textual evidence when you can.

Use the scaffolds below to differentiate instruction for your ELL English Language Learners and A Approaching grade-level learners.

ELL **BEGINNING, INTERMEDIATE** Use the discussion guide and speaking frames to facilitate the discussion with support from the teacher.

ADVANCED, ADVANCED HIGH Use the discussion guide and speaking frames to facilitate the discussion in mixed-level groups.

A **APPROACHING** Use the discussion guide to facilitate the discussion in mixed-level groups.

APPROACHING
ADVANCED, ADVANCED HIGH
BEGINNING, INTERMEDIATE

Discussion Guide	Speaking Frames
1. What causes anxiety in the text? Why?	• Anxiety is caused by ____. • This creates tension because ____.
2. Who is "them"? Who is "us"? How do you know?	• I think "them" is ____ because ____. • I think "us" is ____ because ____.
3. What word or phrase would you use to describe the narrator? Why?	• The narrator is ____. • I would describe the narrator this way because ____.

Text to World

Use the activity below to differentiate instruction for your B Beyond grade level learners.

Explain to students that a "social commentary" examines issues of a society and directly or indirectly states an opinion about these issues.

Have students connect the social dynamic illustrated in this text to a dynamic that exists today in the United States or abroad. Have them refer to quotes from a related news article and selections from this text to substantiate your response. Ask students:

- Is this text a social commentary? Why or why not?
- If yes, which societal norms does it appear to be evaluating?
- What do the characters' behaviors suggest about human nature (be sure to refer to the significance of the text's title in your response)?

Review Prompt and Rubric

Before students begin writing, review the writing prompt and rubric with the class.

LITERARY ANALYSIS: This work is written in an allegorical, dreamlike structure with little explanation of what is happening and why. What do you think is the "mysterious anxiety"? Who do you think are the "them and us"? Write a brief literary analysis that explains the events and the theme as you see them, which may not be the way your classmates see them. Tell what you think of the narrator and point out connections between the text and the real world. Support your ideas with textual evidence when you can.

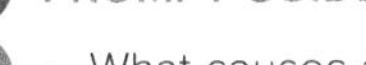

PROMPT GUIDE

- What causes anxiety in the text? Why?
- Who is "them"? Who is "us"? How do you know?
- What word or phrase would you use to describe the narrator? Why?

Score	Theme	Story Structure	Language and Conventions
4	The writer clearly analyzes and explains the events and theme in "The Mysterious Anxiety of Them and Us". The writer provides an exemplary analysis using relevant textual evidence in the response.	The writer clearly analyzes the allegory in "The Mysterious Anxiety of Them and Us", using relevant textual evidence to point out connections between the text and the real world.	The writer demonstrates a consistent command of grammar, punctuation, and usage conventions. Although minor errors may be evident, they do not detract from the fluency or the clarity of the essay.
3	The writer analyzes and explains the events and theme in "The Mysterious Anxiety of Them and Us". The writer provides a sufficient analysis using textual evidence in the response.	The writer analyzes the allegory in "The Mysterious Anxiety of Them and Us", using relevant textual evidence to point out connections between the text and the real world.	The writer demonstrates an adequate command of grammar, punctuation, and usage conventions. Although some errors may be evident, they create few (if any) disruptions in the fluency of the writing or the clarity of the essay.
2	The writer begins to analyze or explain the events and theme in "The Mysterious Anxiety of Them and Us," but the analysis is incomplete. The writer uses relevant textual evidence only some of the time.	The writer begins to analyze the allegory in "The Mysterious Anxiety of Them and Us", but the analysis is incomplete. The writer uses relevant textual evidence only some of the time.	The writer demonstrates a partial command of grammar, punctuation, and usage conventions. Some distracting errors may be evident, at times creating minor disruptions in the fluency or clarity of the writing.
1	The writer attempts to analyze or explain the events and theme in "The Mysterious Anxiety of Them and Us", but the analysis is not successful. The writer uses little or no relevant textual evidence.	The writer attempts to analyze the allegory in "The Mysterious Anxiety of Them and Us", but the analysis is not successful. The writer uses little or no relevant textual evidence.	The writer demonstrates little or no command of grammar, punctuation, and usage conventions. Serious and persistent errors create disruptions in the fluency of the writing and sometimes interfere with meaning.
0	The writer does not provide a relevant response to the prompt or does not provide a response at all.	The writer does not provide a relevant response to the prompt or does not provide a response at all.	Serious and persistent errors overwhelm the writing and interfere with the meaning of the response as a whole, making the writer's meaning impossible to understand.

Write

SCAFFOLDS

Ask students to complete the writing assignment using text evidence to support their answers.

Use the scaffolds below to differentiate instruction for your ELL English Language Learners and A Approaching grade level readers.

ELL **BEGINNING** With the help of the word bank, write a response using paragraph frame 1.

INTERMEDIATE With the help of the word bank, write a response using paragraph frames 1 and 2.

ADVANCED, ADVANCED HIGH Write a response of differentiated length using the sentence starters.

A **APPROACHING** Write a response of differentiated length using the sentence starters.

BEGINNING / INTERMEDIATE	BEGINNING / INTERMEDIATE	INTERMEDIATE	ADVANCED, ADVANCED HIGH / APPROACHING
Word Bank	**Paragraph Frame 1**	**Paragraph Frame 2**	**Sentence Starters**
food seated behavior look standing	The characters in "The Mysterious Anxiety of Them and Us" are divided into two groups: people ____ at a table and people ____. The narrator feels anxious because he worries there is not enough ____ for everyone. Instead of trying to share, the narrator refuses to ____ at the other group. The theme of the text may be that our ____, not our social standing, divides us.	The narrator wants to believe ____. For example, he says, ____. However, his actions suggest ____. The author includes details like ____ to show ____.	• The narrator's "mysterious anxiety" is . . . • The "them" is . . . • The "us" is . . . • The narrator is portrayed as . . . • The theme of the text may be . . .

Peer Review

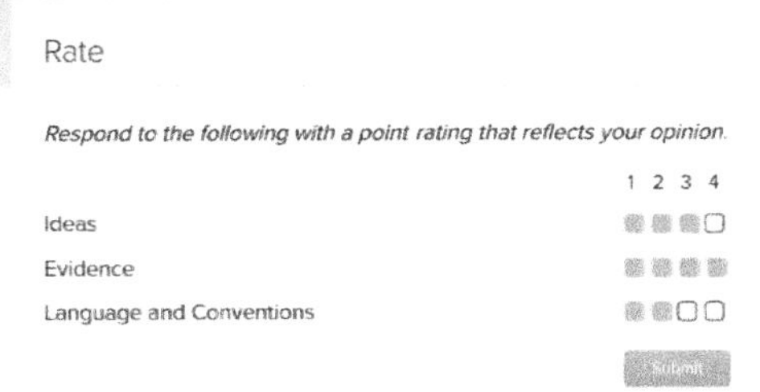

Students should submit substantive feedback to two peers using the review instructions below.

- How well does this response answer the prompt?
- How well does the writer explain the events and the theme(s) in the story?
- Did the analysis include thoughts on the narrator and point out connections between the text and the real world?
- What did the writer do well in this response? What does the writer need to work on?
- Remember that your comments are most useful when they are kind and constructive.

ELL SENTENCE FRAMES

A

- You (completely / partly / almost) ____ answered the prompt because ____.
- You could answer the prompt better by ____.
- You (completely/partly/almost) explained the events and theme(s) in the story.
- The details you included about the narrator (were/were not) helpful because ____.
- The connections you discussed between the text and the real world (were/were not) effective because ____.

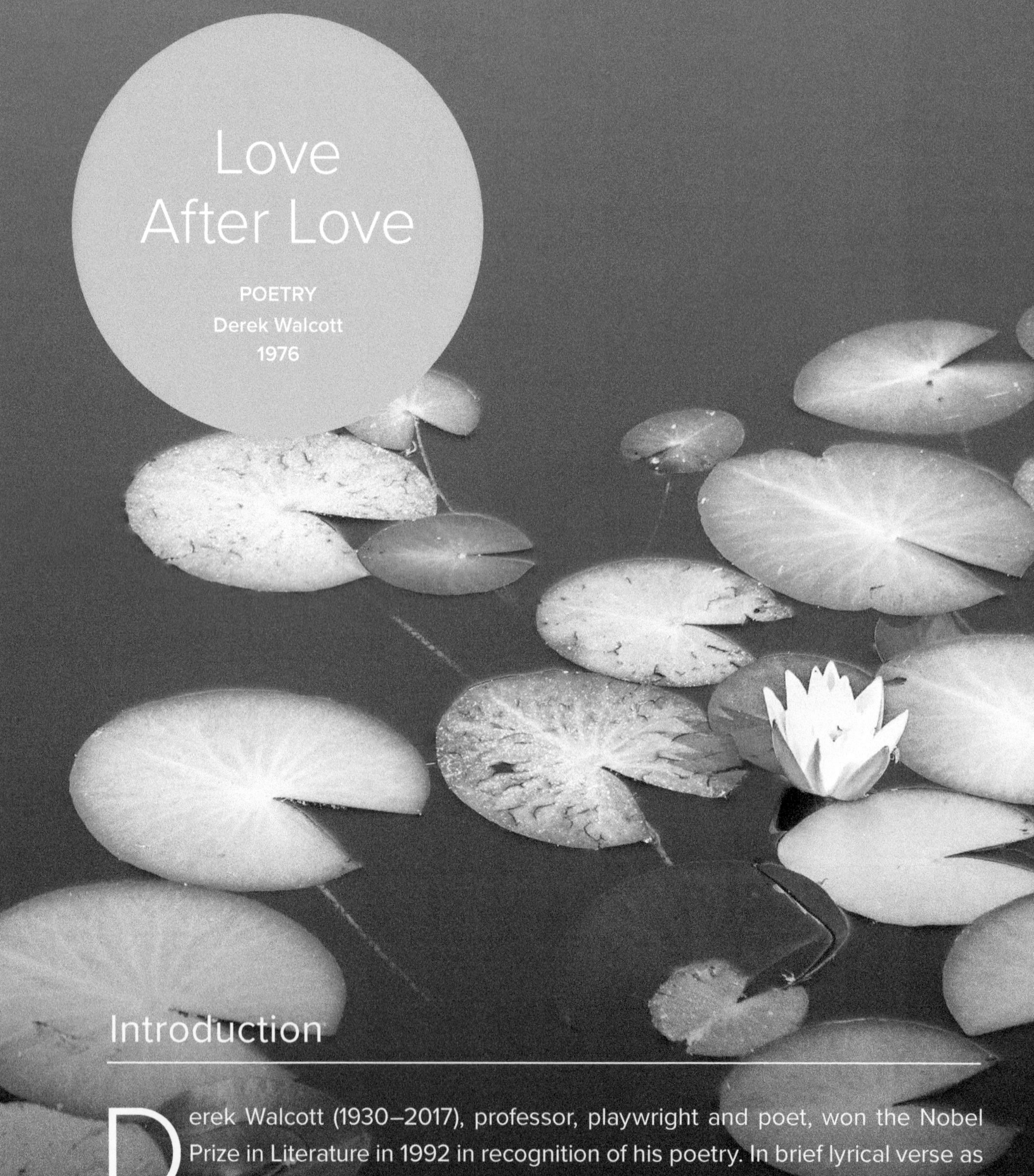

Love After Love

POETRY
Derek Walcott
1976

Introduction

Derek Walcott (1930–2017), professor, playwright and poet, won the Nobel Prize in Literature in 1992 in recognition of his poetry. In brief lyrical verse as well as epic poems, Walcott, who was born in Saint Lucia, wrote of the Caribbean experience with a perspective that shifted from one as intimate as its tiptoeing lizards to one as large-scale as the cultural scars of colonialism. "Love After Love" is one of the great 20th-century poet's most beloved works.

The speaker of the poem tells you that one day you will come home with a feeling of elation. You will be able to greet yourself at the door and smile at yourself in the mirror. You will offer yourself food and learn to love the stranger that is yourself. By feeding yourself, you will give yourself over to this strange you. The speaker talks about how all your life you've ignored yourself, even though you know yourself by heart. He asks you to fetch your old love letters and photographs. Look through them, he tells the reader, and feast upon your life.

 Proficiency-leveled summaries and summaries in multiple languages are available digitally.

 Audio and audio text highlighting are available with this text.

CONNECT TO ESSENTIAL QUESTION

How are we shaped by change?

Derek Walcott's poem "Love After Love" challenges readers to consider how love relationships change the way they see themselves. How does love transform your perspective?

Entry Point

As students prepare to read "Love After Love," share the following information with them to provide context.

- ✓ Walcott grew up in a middle-class family on the Caribbean island of Saint Lucia. The arts were valued highly in his home, and Walcott quickly developed a lasting love of language.
- ✓ As a teenager, Walcott published several poems in a local newspaper. When he was 18, he borrowed $200 from his mother to publish his first book of poetry, *25 Poems*, which was well received. His breakthrough collection, In a *Green Night: Poems 1948–1960*, showcases Walcott's mature poetic voice—one that both celebrated his Caribbean homeland and probed its scarred colonial history.
- ✓ In 1950 Walcott helped found the Saint Lucia Arts Guild, for which he wrote several plays. He has written more than 30 plays. *Ti-Jean and His Brothers* (1958) and *Dream on Monkey Mountain* (1967) are his most famous. After a long and distinguished career, Walcott won the Nobel Prize in Literature in 1992.

These icons identify differentiation strategies and scaffolded support for a variety of students. See the digital lesson plan for additional differentiation strategies and scaffolds.

Instructional Path

The print teacher's edition includes essential point-of-use instruction and planning tools. Complete lesson plans and program documents appear in your digital teacher account.

Independent Read: Love After Love

Objectives: Students will closely read "Love After Love" in order to participate in a collaborative conversation and write a reflection on their participation in the discussion.

Independent Read

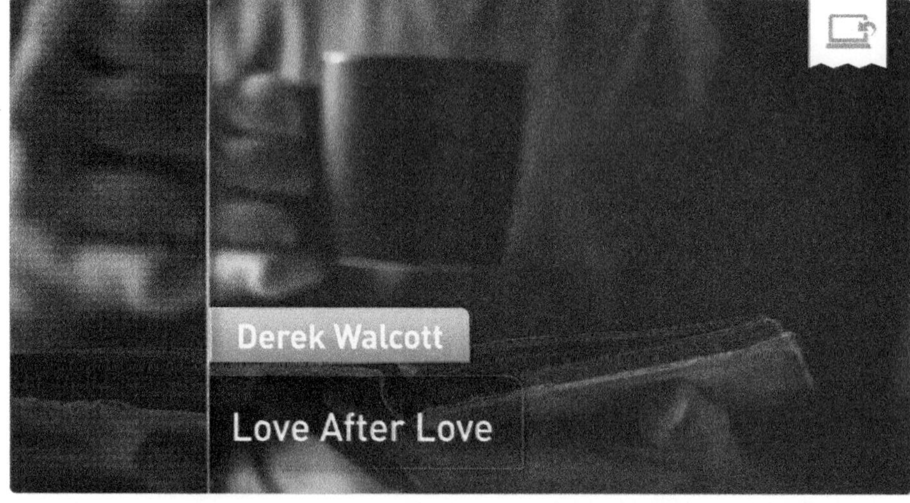

Introduce the Text

As a class, watch the video preview and have students read the introduction in pairs to make connections to the video preview.

- How do the images, words, and music in this video make you feel?
- Have you ever needed to rediscover something about yourself? What was that experience like?

ELL **SPEAKING FRAMES**

- The image, words, and music make me feel ____.
- I needed to rediscover ____. The experience was ____.

Access Complex Text

LEXILE: N/A **WORD COUNT:** 98

The following areas may be challenging for students, particularly ELL English Language Learners and A Approaching grade-level learners.

Purpose	Genre
• Explain to students that the tone of the poem matches its purpose to give advice to readers. • Have students work in groups to identify the tone of the poem and highlight words and phrases that express this tone.	• Remind students that poets use figurative language and imagery to express ideas in memorable ways. • Have students discuss the examples of figurative language and imagery in the poem and explain what makes them effective.

Love After Love

"You will love again the stranger who was your self."

NOTES

The time will come
when, with **elation**
you will greet yourself arriving
at your own door, in your own mirror
and each will smile at the other's welcome,

and say, sit here. Eat.
You will love again the stranger who was your self.
Give wine. Give bread. Give back your heart
to itself, to the stranger who has loved you

all your life, whom you ignored
for another, who knows you by heart.
Take down the love letters from the bookshelf,

the photographs, the **desperate** notes,
peel your own image from the mirror.
Sit. Feast on your life.

Derek Walcott in Saint Malo, France

"After Love" ("work") from THE POETRY OF DEREK WALCOTT 1948-2013 by Derek Walcott, selected by Glyn Maxwell

Developing Background Knowledge and Cultural Awareness

1. Share with students the following quotation by Derek Walcott: "Break a vase, and the love that reassembles the fragments is stronger than that love which took its symmetry for granted when it was whole."
2. In small groups, have students discuss the quotation's meaning, and how it relates to something in their own lives or to something they've read or learned about.

Discuss with students: St. Lucia, an island in the Caribbean and birthplace of Derek Walcott, gained freedom from British colonization in 1979, three years after this poem was published. How might the colonization of a place affect the culture of its people? How might being colonized affect one's identity or self-perception?

SELECTION VOCABULARY

elation / la euforia ***noun*** intense happiness; jubilation

desperate / desesperado/a ***adjective*** having little or no hope COGNATE

TEXT TALK

Why do you need to "give back your heart to itself"?

See lines 6–11: You need to "give back your heart to itself" because you have made yourself a stranger by ignoring your own emotional needs.

Writer's Notebook

Connect to Essential Question: Give students time to reflect on how "Love After Love" connects to the unit's essential question "How are we shaped by change?" by freewriting in their Writer's Notebooks.

CHECK FOR SUCCESS

If students are still struggling to respond to the prompt, ask them:

1. How does "Love After Love" convey a sense of change in self-perception?
2. How is the "you" in the poem shaped by change?

Reading Comprehension OPTIONAL

Have students complete the digital reading comprehension questions ✓ when they finish reading.

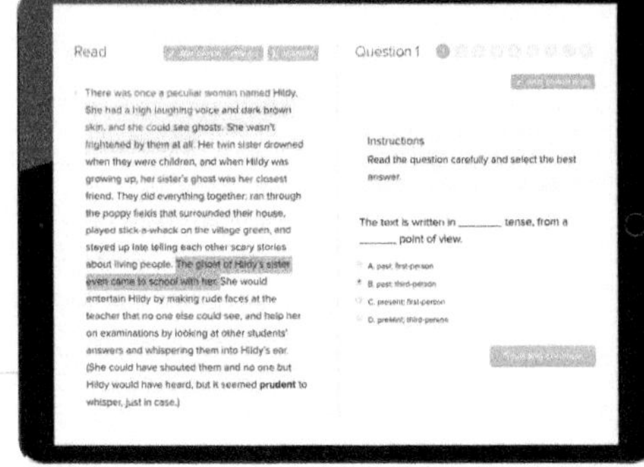

ANSWER KEY

QUESTION 1: B
QUESTION 2: A
QUESTION 3: A
QUESTION 4: B
QUESTION 5: *See chart.*

First	Second	Third	Fourth
The time will come/ when, with elation / you will greet yourself	You will love again the stranger who was your self.	Take down the love letters from the bookshelf	Sit. Feast on your life.

Connect and Extend OPTIONAL

CONNECT TO EXTENDED ORAL PROJECT

Students can find inspiration for their argumentative essays by using Walcott's poem and the advice it provides to help them reflect on themselves over the last few years.

BEYOND THE BOOK

Writing: A Letter to Future Me

Derek Walcott's poem asks readers to look back on old photographs and notes to learn more about themselves. Students will write a letter to their future selves.

Ask students to:

- Brainstorm who they are now.
  - > What are your interests?
  - > How are you doing in school?
  - > What are some recent accomplishments?
  - > What are you struggling with at the moment?
  - > What are your plans for the future?
- Write a friendly letter to themselves 5 years in the future.
- Include the letter and a current photograph and seal it in an envelope to read in five years.
- Set a calendar reminder for a date 5 years in the future and include a note to help them remember where the letter is stashed.

To reflect, ask students:

- Do you believe this letter will be interesting or relevant in five years? Why or why not?
- How can looking at your past explain events that are current?

Collaborative Conversation

Post the writing prompt to generate a discussion in small groups. Ask students to first break down the prompt before they discuss relevant ideas and textual evidence.

Derek Walcott's poem "Love After Love" is a free verse poem written in a conversational style that gives advice to readers. Work in pairs and groups to analyze the form, sound, and graphics of the poem. Notice the graphical elements of enjambment and punctuation as well as the repetition of words and phrases. Consider how these elements affect the sound of the poem. Have one volunteer read the poem aloud. Then work in pairs or as a group to change the graphical elements. For instance, you might take out the enjambment or rewrite the text to avoid a comma or period within a line. In other words, change the shape and look of the poem on the page. Then have another volunteer read aloud the revised poem. Finally, discuss the effects of a poet's choice of form and graphics on the sound of the poem and the expression of meaning.

Use the scaffolds below to differentiate instruction for your ELL English Language Learners and A Approaching grade-level learners.

ELL **BEGINNING, INTERMEDIATE** Use the discussion guide and speaking frames to facilitate the discussion with support from the teacher.

ADVANCED, ADVANCED HIGH Use the discussion guide and speaking frames to facilitate the discussion in mixed-level groups.

A **APPROACHING** Use the discussion guide to facilitate the discussion in mixed-level groups.

APPROACHING
ADVANCED, ADVANCED HIGH
BEGINNING, INTERMEDIATE

Discussion Guide	Speaking Frames
1. How do the punctuation and the short sentences affect the poem?	• The punctuation ____. • The short sentences ____.
2. How do the repeated sound of words or the free verse form affect the poem?	• The repeated sound of words ____. • The free verse form ____.
3. How do the above elements work together to affect the poem?	• These elements work together to ____. • They create ____.

Multiple Perspectives

Use the activity below to differentiate instruction for your B Beyond grade level learners.

Reread lines 8 and 9. Direct students to contemplate what the author is asking in this moment. Ask students:

- What is the poet's perspective as he speaks to his past self.
- What does the poet's perspective explain about his past?

Review Prompt and Rubric

Before students begin writing, review the writing prompt and rubric with the class.

After the discussion, write a reflection in the space below. As you write, make sure to

- evaluate how well everyone followed the rules when making decisions affecting the group
- evaluate your own participation in the discussion and promotion of civil, democratic discussions
- reflect on how well you adjust your responses to the text if you find the evidence presented by others to be valid and convincing

PROMPT GUIDE

- What are the form, sound, and graphical elements of the poem?
- How do these elements work together to express the meaning and effect of the poem?

Score	Reflection	Language and Conventions
4	The writer clearly reflects on how well he or she adjusted their responses as new evidence was presented, as well as on his or her own participation. The writer consistently refers to specific examples from the discussion.	The writer demonstrates a consistent command of grammar, punctuation, and usage conventions. Although minor errors may be evident, they do not detract from the fluency or the clarity of the essay.
3	The writer reflects on how well he or she adjusted their responses as new evidence was presented, as well as on his or her own participation. The writer refers to specific examples from the discussion most of the time.	The writer demonstrates an adequate command of grammar, punctuation, and usage conventions. Although some errors may be evident, they create few (if any) disruptions in the fluency of the writing or the clarity of the essay.
2	The writer begins to reflect on how well he or she adjusted their responses as new evidence was presented, as well as on his or her own participation. The writer refers to specific examples from the discussion some of the time.	The writer demonstrates a partial command of grammar, punctuation, and usage conventions. Some distracting errors may be evident, at times creating minor disruptions in the fluency or clarity of the writing.
1	The writer attempts to reflect on how well he or she adjusted their responses as new evidence was presented, as well as on his or her own participation in the response. The writer refers to few, if any examples from the discussion.	The writer demonstrates little or no command of grammar, punctuation, and usage conventions. Serious and persistent errors create disruptions in the fluency of the writing and sometimes interfere with meaning.
0	The writer does not provide a relevant response to the prompt or does not provide a response at all.	Serious and persistent errors overwhelm the writing and interfere with the meaning of the response as a whole, making the writer's meaning impossible to understand.

Write

SCAFFOLDS

Ask students to complete the writing assignment using text evidence to support their answers.

Use the scaffolds below to differentiate instruction for your English Language Learners and Approaching grade level readers.

ELL **BEGINNING** With the help of the word bank, write a response using paragraph frame 1.

INTERMEDIATE With the help of the word bank, write a response using paragraph frames 1 and 2.

ADVANCED, ADVANCED HIGH Write a response of differentiated length using the sentence starters.

A **APPROACHING** Write a response of differentiated length using the sentence starters.

BEGINNING / INTERMEDIATE — ADVANCED, ADVANCED HIGH / APPROACHING

Word Bank	Paragraph Frame 1	Paragraph Frame 2	Sentence Starters
state confirm analyze effects interpret think ideas form sound graphics	My best contribution was when I ____ . I plan to ____ to my contributions in future discussions.	I think that my best contribution helped other students to ____ . My goal for future discussions will help me ____.	• My best contribution to the discussion was when I . . . • To improve my contributions to future discussions, I plan to . . . • I think that my best contribution helped other students to . . . • My goal for future discussions will enable me to . . .

Peer Review

Students should submit substantive feedback to two peers using the review instructions below.

- How well does the writer refer to specific examples from the discussion?
- What does the writer do well in this reflection? What does the writer need to work on?

Remember that your comments are most useful when they are kind and constructive.

Rate

Respond to the following with a point rating that reflects your opinion.

	1	2	3	4
Ideas				
Evidence				
Language and Conventions				

ELL SENTENCE FRAMES

- You were able to (completely / partly / almost) ____ answer the prompt.
- You could answer the prompt more completely by ____.
- My favorite part of your responses is ____.

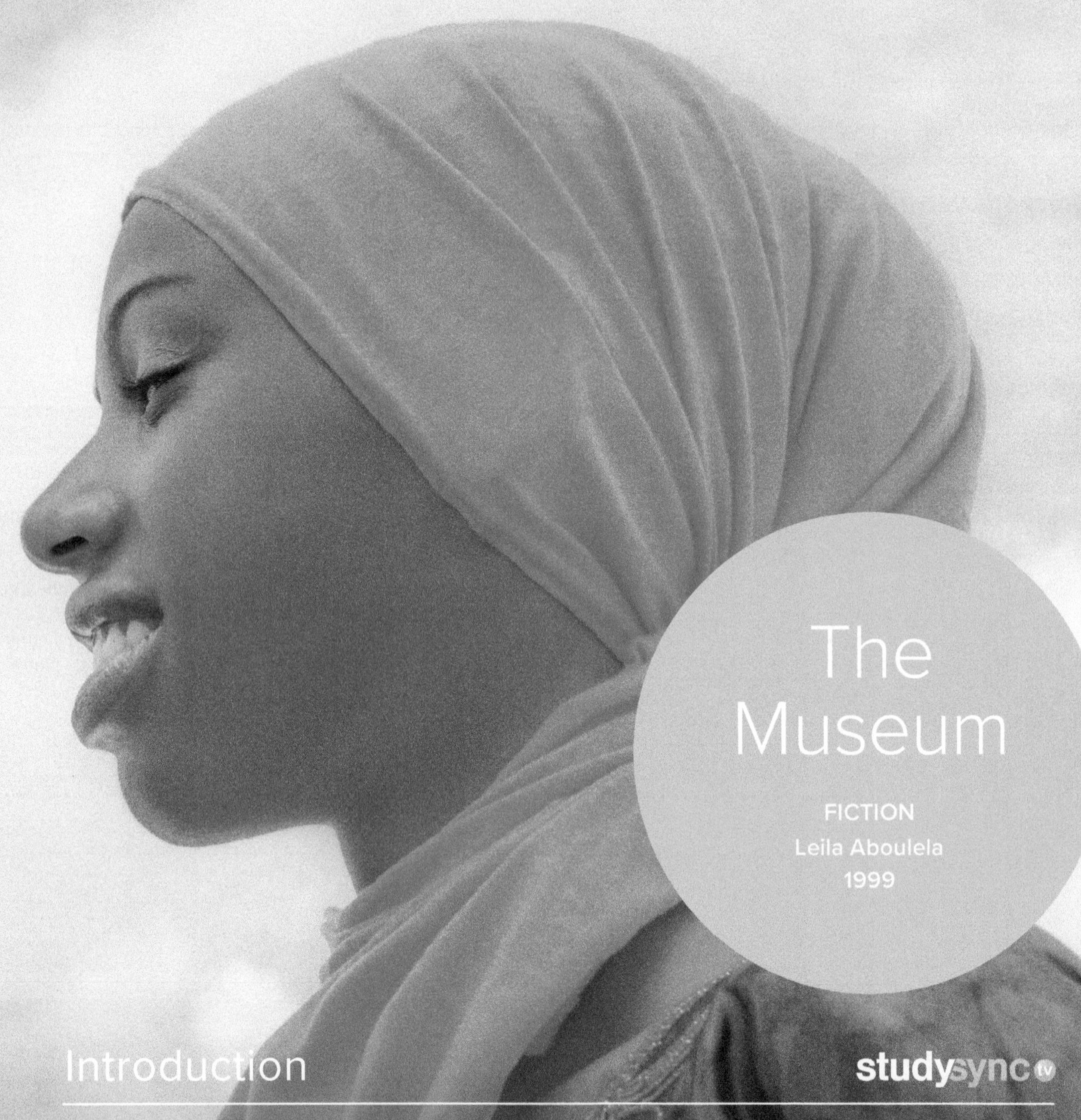

The Museum

FICTION
Leila Aboulela
1999

Introduction

studysync tv

Much like Shadia, the main character in her award-winning story "The Museum," author Leila Aboulela (b. 1964) grew up in Khartoum, the capital of Sudan, before moving as a young woman to Aberdeen, Scotland. Experiencing firsthand the cultural divide between Islam and the West would serve as the inspiration for much of Aboulela's writing, which explores issues of identity, migration, and Islamic spirituality. "The Museum" is one of her earliest published stories, yet it displays all the hallmarks of her best work, which has been translated into 14 languages and even adapted into a series of plays by BBC Radio.

Shadia has left her family and fiancé in Sudan to study at a university in Scotland. Her world is cold, grey, and she spends most of her time in her dorm room or in class, where she struggles in Statistics. Trying desperately to pass, Shadia asks a Scottish student named Bryan for his notes. In turn, Bryan asks Shadia for coffee, but she says no, because he has an earring and long hair. Meanwhile, Shadia's fiancé calls often, informing her about his plans for their house. These matters feel less and less important as Shadia begins spending more time with Bryan. He asks her questions about her life back in Sudan and tells her more about himself. Shadia is surprised to learn that she comes from a more proper family than he does and mentally, often refers to him as a silly boy. In the end, Bryan invites Shadia to an African history museum, but the colonial depictions of her country make her weep.

 Proficiency-leveled summaries and summaries in multiple languages are available digitally.

 Audio and audio text highlighting are available with this text.

COMPARING WITHIN AND ACROSS GENRES

The short story "The Museum," read in conjunction with "A Temporary Matter," leads students to consider the way relationships evolve and unspoken truths reveal themselves over time. Written by Leila Aboulela, "The Museum" focuses on an unexpected relationship between a young Sudanese woman and a classmate she meets studying abroad in Scotland. This story encourages students to consider how relationships change in response to internal and external challenges.

Entry Point

As students prepare to read "The Museum," share the following information with them to provide context.

- ✓ Leila Aboulela was born in 1964 in Cairo, Egypt, to an Egyptian mother and a Sudanese father. She moved to Sudan when she was six weeks old and lived in Khartoum until 1987.
- ✓ Although critically acclaimed as a writer, she graduated from the University of Khartoum with a degree in Economics and earned two Master's degrees in Statistics from the London School of Economics. She didn't begin writing until 1992, when she was working as a lecturer at Aberdeen College in Scotland.
- ✓ She and her family lived in Jakarta, Dubai, Abu Dhabi, and Doha before returning to Aberdeen in 2012. Much of her work focuses on identity, migration, and Islamic spirituality. Regarding her work, Aboulela says "I am interested in going deep, not just looking at 'Muslim' as a cultural or political identity but something close to the centre, something that transcends but doesn't deny gender, nationality, class and race."

BEYOND GRADE LEVEL

These icons identify differentiation strategies and scaffolded support for a variety of students. See the digital lesson plan for additional differentiation strategies and scaffolds.

Instructional Path

The print teacher's edition includes essential point-of-use instruction and planning tools. Complete lesson plans and program documents appear in your digital teacher account.

Independent Read: The Museum

Objectives: Students will closely read "The Museum" in order to participate in a collaborative conversation and write a reflection on their participation in the discussion.

Independent Read

Introduce the Text

As a class, watch the video preview and have students read the introduction in pairs to make connections to the video preview.

- What two words would you use to describe this video?
- What are some of the benefits and challenges of studying abroad?

ELL SPEAKING FRAMES

- I would describe this video as ____ and ____.
- Studying abroad can be ____, but it can also be ____.

Access Complex Text

LEXILE: 720 **WORD COUNT:** 6.272

The following areas may be challenging for students, particularly ELL English Language Learners and A Approaching grade-level learners.

Connection of Ideas	Prior Knowledge
• Students will deepen their understanding of the text if they can make connections between the events in the story and history and society. • Have students discuss the events in the story in relation to the social, cultural, and historical background of the characters and places.	• Students may benefit from developing their background knowledge about the Sudan and the colonization of Africa in general. • Have students research the term "scramble for Africa" and discuss their findings.

"We have 7UP in Africa, and some people, a few people, have bathrooms with golden taps . . ."

NOTES

1 At first Shadia was afraid to ask him for his notes. The earring made her afraid; the straight long hair that he had tied up with a rubber band. She had never seen a man with an earring and such long hair. But then she had never known such cold, so much rain. His silver earring was the strangeness of the West, another culture shock. She stared at it during classes, her eyes straying from the white scribbles on the board. Most times she could hardly understand anything. Only the notation was familiar. But how did it all fit together? How did *this* formula lead to *this*? Her ignorance and the impending exams were horrors she wanted to escape. His long hair was a dull colour between yellow and brown. It reminded her of a doll she had when she was young. She had spent hours combing that doll's hair, stroking it. She had longed for such straight hair. When she went to Paradise she would have hair like that. When she ran it would fly behind her; if she bent her head down it would fall over her like silk and sweep the flowers on the grass. She watched his ponytail move as he wrote and then looked up at the board. She pictured her doll, vivid suddenly, after years, and felt sick that she was daydreaming in class, not learning a thing.

Sudanese writer Leila Aboulela

2 The first days of term, when the classes started for the M.Sc. in Statistics, she was like someone tossed around by monstrous waves—battered, as she lost her way to the different lecture rooms, fumbled with the photocopying machine, could not find anything in the library. She could scarcely hear or eat or see. Her eyes bulged with fright, watered from the cold. The course required a certain background, a background she didn't have. So she **floundered,** she and the other African students, the two Turkish girls, and the men from Brunei. Asafa, the short, round-faced Ethiopian, said, in his grave voice—as this collection from the Third World whispered their anxieties in grim Scottish corridors, the girls in nervous giggles – 'Last year, last year a Nigerian on this very same course committed suicide. *Cut his wrists.*'

SELECTION VOCABULARY

flounder / trastabillar *verb* to stumble or struggle

Developing Background Knowledge and Cultural Awareness

1. Generate a list (on the board or on paper) of any ideas your students have about museum debates and controversies with regards to how colonization is portrayed.
2. Have students discuss what responsibilities museums have when presenting the history of colonization and other cultures.

Discuss with students: Many museums in the western world display objects that were taken from their countries of origin during colonization. Do you believe these objects should be returned to those countries? What challenges and ethical questions are at stake in this decision? Are there ethical solutions to museums keeping the objects?

Prepare for Advanced Courses

Analyze for Enrichment

Direct students to reread the first paragraph of the short story and note any examples of visual imagery.

Ask students:

- How does the author employ visual imagery to establish the mood of the text and introduce conflict? Refer to specific quotations from this paragraph in your response.

NOTES

3 Us and them, she thought. The ones who would do well, the ones who would crawl and sweat and barely pass. Two predetermined groups. Asafa, generous and wise (he was the oldest), leaned over and whispered to Shadia: 'The Spanish girl is good. Very good.' His eyes bulged redder than Shadia's. He cushioned his fears every night in the university pub; she only cried. Their countries were next-door neighbours but he had never been to Sudan, and Shadia had never been to Ethiopia. 'But we met in Aberdeen!' she had shrieked when this information was exchanged, giggling furiously. Collective fear had its **euphoria.**

4 'That boy Bryan,' said Asafa, 'is excellent.'

5 'The one with the earring?'

6 Asafa laughed and touched his own unadorned ear. 'The earring doesn't mean anything. He'll get the Distinction. He was an undergraduate here; got First Class Honours. That gives him an advantage. He knows all the lecturers, he knows the system.'

7 So the idea occurred to her of asking Bryan for the notes of his graduate year. If she strengthened her background in stochastic processes and time series, she would be better able to cope with the new material they were bombarded with every day. She watched him to judge if he was approachable. Next to the courteous Malaysian students, he was devoid of manners. He mumbled and slouched and did not speak with respect to the lecturers. He spoke to them as if they were his equals. And he did silly things. When he wanted to throw a piece of paper in the bin, he squashed it into a ball and aimed at the bin. If he missed, he muttered under his breath. She thought that he was immature. But he was the only one who was sailing through the course.

8 The glossy handbook for overseas students had explained about the 'famous British reserve' and hinted that they should be grateful, things were worse further south, less 'hospitable.' In the cafeteria, drinking coffee with Asafa and the others, the picture of 'hospitable Scotland' was something different. Badr, the Malaysian, blinked and whispered, 'Yesterday our windows got smashed; my wife today is afraid to go out.'

9 'Thieves?' asked Shadia, her eyes wider than anyone else's.

10 'Racists,' said the Turkish girl, her lipstick chic, the word tripping out like silver, like ice.

11 Wisdom from Asafa, muted, before the collective silence: 'These people think they own the world . . .' and around them the aura of the dead Nigerian student. They were ashamed of that brother they had never seen. He had weakened, caved in. In the cafeteria, Bryan never sat with them. They never

TEXT TALK

Why does Shadia decide to talk to Bryan?

See paragraphs 2–7: Shadia is struggling in class and hears that Bryan does well, so she wants to ask for his notes.

SELECTION VOCABULARY

euphoria / la euforia *noun* intense, nearly overwhelming happiness COGNATE

NOTES

sat with him. He sat alone, sometimes reading the local paper. When Shadia walked in front of him he didn't smile. 'These people are strange . . . One day they greet you, the next day they don't . . .'

12 On Friday afternoon, as everyone was ready to leave the room after Linear Models, she gathered her courage and spoke to Bryan. He had spots on his chin and forehead, was taller than her, restless, as if he was in a hurry to go somewhere else. He put his calculator back in its case, his pen in his pocket. She asked him for his notes, and his blue eyes behind his glasses took on the blankest look she had ever seen in her life. What was all the surprise for? Did he think she was an insect? Was he surprised that she could speak?

13 A mumble for a reply, words strung together. So taken aback, he was. He pushed his chair back under the table with this foot.

14 'Pardon?'

15 He slowed down, separated each word. 'Ah'll have them for ye on Monday.'

16 'Thank you.' She spoke English better than he did! How pathetic. The whole of him was pathetic. He wore the same shirt every blessed day. Grey and white stripe.

. . .

17 On the weekends, Shadia never went out of the halls and, unless someone telephoned long-distance from home, she spoke to no one. There was time to remember Thursday nights in Khartoum: a wedding to go to with Fareed, driving in his red Mercedes. Or the club with her sisters. Sitting by the pool drinking lemonade with ice, the waiters all dressed in white. Sometimes people swam at night, dived in the water—dark like the sky above. Here, in this country's weekend of Saturday and Sunday, Shadia washed her clothes and her hair. Her hair depressed her. The damp weather made it frizz up after she straightened it with hot tongs. So she had given up and now wore it in a bun all the time, tightly pulled back away from her face, the curls held down by pins and Vaseline Tonic. She didn't like this style, her corrugated hair, and in the mirror her eyes looked too large. The mirror in the public bathroom, at the end of the corridor to her room, had printed on it: 'This is the face of someone with HIV.' She had written about this mirror to her sister, something foreign and sensational like hail, and cars driving on the left. But she hadn't written that the mirror made her feel as if she had left her looks behind in Khartoum.

18 On the weekends, she made a list of the money she had spent: the sterling enough to keep a family alive back home. Yet she might fail her exams after all that expense, go back home empty-handed without a degree. Guilt was cold like the fog of this city. It came from everywhere. One day she forgot to

NOTES

pray in the morning. She reached the bus stop and then realized she hadn't prayed. That morning folded out like the nightmare she sometimes had, of discovering that she had gone out into the street without any clothes.

19 In the evening, when she was staring at multidimensional scaling, the telephone in the hall rang. She ran to answer it. Fareed's cheerful greeting: 'Here, Shadia, Mama and the girls want to speak to you.' His mother's endearments: 'They say it's so cold where you are . . .'

20 Shadia was engaged to Fareed. Fareed was a package that came with the 7UP franchise, the paper factory, the big house he was building, his sisters and widowed mother. Shadia was going to marry them all. She was going to be happy and make her mother happy. Her mother deserved happiness after the misfortunes of her life. A husband who left her for another woman. Six girls to bring up. People felt sorry for her mother. Six girls to educate and marry off. But your Lord is generous: each of the girls, it was often said, was lovelier than the other. They were clever too: dentist, pharmacist, architect, and all with the best of manners.

21 'We are just back from looking at the house.' Fareed's turn again to talk. 'It's coming along fine, they're putting the tiles down . . .'

22 'That's good, that's good,' her voice strange from not talking to anyone all day.

23 'The bathroom suites. If I get them all the same colour for us and the girls and Mama, I could get them on a discount. Blue, the girls are in favour of blue,' his voice echoed from one continent to another. Miles and miles.

24 'Blue is nice. Yes, better get them all the same colour.'

25 He was building a block of flats, not a house. The ground-floor flat for his mother and the girls until they married, the first floor for him and Shadia. When Shadia had first got engaged to Fareed, he was the son of a rich man. A man with the franchise for 7UP and the paper factory which had a monopoly[1] in ladies' sanitary towels. Fareed's sisters never had to buy sanitary towels; their house was abundant with boxes of *Pinky*, fresh from the production line. But Fareed's father died of an unexpected heart attack soon after the engagement party (five hundred guests at the Hilton). Now Shadia was going to marry the rich man himself. 'You are a lucky, lucky girl,' her mother had said, and Shadia had rubbed soap in her eyes so that Fareed would think she was weeping about his father's death.

26 There was no time to talk about her course on the telephone, no space for her anxieties. Fareed was not interested in her studies. He had said, 'I am

1. **monopoly** concentrated control over a market in one organization or group

TEXT TALK

What does Shadia's family think of her education?

See paragraph 26: Her mother wants her to have an education and career, but her fiancé, Fareed, is less supportive.

NOTES

very broad-minded to allow you to study abroad. Other men would not have put up with this . . .' It was her mother who was keen for her to study, to get a postgraduate degree from Britain and then have a career after she got married. 'This way,' her mother had said, 'you will have your in-laws' respect. They have money but you have a degree. Don't end up like me. I left my education to marry your father and now . . .' Many conversations ended with her mother bitter; with her mother say, 'No one suffers like I suffer,' and making Shadia droop. At night her mother sobbed in her sleep, noises that woke Shadia and her sisters.

27 No, on the long-distance line, there was no space for her worries. Talk about the Scottish weather. Picture Fareed, generously perspiring, his stomach straining the buttons of his shirt. Often she had nagged him to lose weight, without success. His mother's food was too good; his sisters were both overweight. On the long-distance line, listen to the Khartoum gossip as if listening to a radio play.

28 On Monday, without saying anything, Bryan slid two folders across the table towards her as if he did not want to come near her, did not want to talk to her. She wanted to say, 'I won't take them till you hand them to me politely.' But smarting, she said, 'Thank you very much.' *She* had manners. *She* was well brought up.

29 Back in her room, at her desk, the clearest handwriting she had ever seen. Sparse on the pages, clean. Clear and rounded like a child's, the tidiest notes. She cried over them, wept for no reason. She cried until she wetted one of the pages, smudged the ink, blurred one of the formulas. She dabbed at it with a tissue but the paper flaked and became transparent. Should she apologize about the stain, say that she was drinking water, say that it was rain? Or should she just keep quiet, hope he wouldn't notice? She chided herself for all that concern. *He* wasn't concerned about wearing the same shirt every day. She was giving him too much attention thinking about him. He was just an immature and closed-in sort of character. He probably came from a small town, his parents were probably poor, low-class. In Khartoum, she never mixed with people like that. Her mother liked her to be friends with people who were higher up. How else were she and her sisters going to marry well? She must study the notes and stop crying over this boy's handwriting. His handwriting had nothing to do with her, nothing to do with her at all.

30 Understanding after not understanding is a fog lifting, pictures swinging into focus, missing pieces slotting into place. It is fragments gelling, a sound vivid whole, a basis to build on. His notes were the knowledge she needed, the gap filled. She struggled through them, not skimming them with the carelessness of incomprehension, but taking them in, making them a part of her, until in the depth of concentration, in the late hours of the nights, she lost awareness of time and place, and at last, when she slept she became epsilon

NOTES

and gamma, and she became a variable, making her way through discrete space from state 'i' to state 'j'.

. . .

31 It felt natural to talk to him. As if now that she had spent hours and days with his handwriting, she knew him in some way. She forgot the offence she had taken when he had slid his folders across the table to her, all the times he didn't say hello.

32 In the computer room, at the end of the Statistical Packages class, she went to him and said: 'Thanks for the notes. They are really good. I think I might not fail, after all. I might have a chance to pass.' Her eyes were dry from all the nights she had stayed up. She was tired and grateful.

33 He nodded and they spoke a little about the Poisson distribution[2], queuing theory[3]. Everything was clear in his mind; his brain was a clear pane of glass where all the concepts were written out boldly and neatly. Today, he seemed more at ease talking to her, though he still shifted about from foot to foot, avoiding her eyes.

34 He said, 'Do ye want to go for a coffee?'

35 She looked up at him. He was tall and she was not used to speaking to people with blue eyes. Then she made a mistake. Perhaps because she had been up late last night, she made that mistake. Perhaps there were other reasons for that mistake. The mistake of shifting from one level to another.

36 She said, 'I don't like your earring.'

37 The expression in his eyes, a focusing, no longer shifting away. He lifted his hand to his ear and tugged the earring off. His earlobe without the silver looked red and scarred.

38 She giggled because she was afraid, because he wasn't smiling, wasn't saying anything. She covered her mouth with her hand, then wiped her forehead and eyes. A mistake had been made and it was too late to go back. She plunged ahead, careless now, reckless. 'I don't like your long hair.'

39 He turned and walked away.

. . .

2. **Poisson distribution** a probability distribution formula developed by French mathematician Siméon Denis Poisson (1781–1840) to predict the frequency of events in a fixed interval
3. **queuing theory** involving the mathematical study of queues, or lines

TEXT TALK

What happens after Shadia borrows Bryan's notes?

See paragraphs 34–38: He asks if she wants to get coffee, and she says she doesn't like his earring or hair.

40 The next morning, Multivariate Analysis, and she came in late, dishevelled from running and the rain. The professor, whose name she wasn't sure of (there were three who were Mc-something), smiled, unperturbed. All the lecturers were relaxed and **urbane,** in tweed jackets and polished shoes. Sometimes she wondered how the incoherent Bryan, if he did pursue an academic career, was going to transform himself into a professor like that. But it was none of her business.

41 Like most of the other students, she sat in the same seat in every class. Bryan sat a row ahead which was why she could always look at his hair. But he had cut it, there was no ponytail today! Just his neck and the collar of the grey and white striped shirt.

42 Notes to take down. *In discriminant analysis, a linear combination of variables serves as the basis for assigning cases to groups.*

43 She was made up of layers. Somewhere inside, deep inside, under the crust of vanity, in the untampered-with essence, she would glow and be in awe, and be humble and think, this is just for me, he cut his hair for me. But there were other layers, bolder, more to the surface. Giggling. Wanting to catch hold of a friend. Guess what? You wouldn't *believe* what this idiot did!

44 *Find a weighted average of variables . . . The weights are estimated so that they result in the best separation between the groups.*

45 After the class he came over and said very seriously, without a smile, 'Ah've cut my hair.'

46 A part of her hollered with laughter, sang: 'You stupid boy, you stupid boy, I can see that, can't I?'

47 She said, 'It looks nice.' She said the wrong thing and her face felt hot and she made herself look away so that she would not know his reaction. It was true though, he did look nice; he looked decent now.

. . .

48 She should have said to Bryan, when they first held their coffee mugs in their hands and were searching for an empty table, 'Let's sit with Asafa and the others.' Mistakes follow mistakes. Across the cafeteria, the Turkish girl saw them together and raised her perfect eyebrows. Badr met Shadia's eyes and quickly looked away. Shadia looked at Bryan and he was different, different without the earring and the ponytail, transformed in some way. If he would put lemon juice on his spots . . . but it was none of her business. Maybe the boys who smashed Badr's windows looked like Bryan, but with fiercer eyes, no glasses. She must push him away from her. She must make him dislike her.

 SELECTION VOCABULARY

urbane / sofisticado / a *adjective* well-mannered and self-assured

49 He asked her where she came from and when she replied, he said, 'Where's that?'

50 'Africa,' with sarcasm. 'Do you know where *that* is?'

51 His nose and cheeks under the rims of his glasses went red. Good, she thought, good. He will leave me now in peace.

52 He said, 'Ah know Sudan is in Africa, I meant where exactly in Africa.'

53 'Northeast, south of Egypt. Where are *you* from?'

54 'Peterhead. It's north of here. By the sea.'

55 It was hard to believe that there was anything north of Aberdeen. It seemed to her that they were on the northernmost corner of the world. She knew better now than to imagine suntanning and sandy beaches for his 'by the sea.' More likely dismal skies, pale, bad-tempered people shivering on the rocky shore.

56 'Your father works in Peterhead?'

57 'Aye, he does.'

58 She had grown up listening to the proper English of the BBC World Service only to come to Britain and find people saying 'yes' like it was said back home in Arabic: 'aye.'

59 'What does he do, your father?'

60 He looked surprised, his blue eyes surprised. 'Ma dad's a joiner.'

61 Fareed hired people like that to work on the house. Ordered them about.

62 'And your mother?' she asked.

63 He paused a little, stirred sugar in his coffee with a plastic spoon. 'She's a lollipop lady.'

64 Shadia smirked into her coffee, took a sip.

65 'My father,' she said proudly, 'is a doctor, a specialist.' Her father was a gynaecologist. The woman who was now his wife had been one of his patients. Before that, Shadia's friends had teased her about her father's job, crude jokes that made her laugh. It was all so sordid now.

66 'And my mother,' she blew the truth up out of proportion, 'comes from a very big family. A ruling family. If you British hadn't colonized us, my mother would have been a princess now.'

67 'Ye walk like a princess,' he said.

68 What a gullible, silly boy! She wiped her forehead with her hand and said, 'You mean I am **conceited** and proud?'

69 'No, Ah didnae mean that, no . . .' The packet of sugar he was tearing open tipped from his hand, its contents scattered over the table. 'Ah . . . sorry . . .' He tried to scoop up the sugar and knocked against his coffee mug, spilling a little on the table.

70 She took out a tissue from her bag, reached over and mopped up the stain. It was easy to pick up all the bits of sugar with the damp tissue.

71 'Thanks,' he mumbled and they were silent. The cafeteria was busy: full of the humming, buzzing sound of people talking to each other, trays and dishes. In Khartoum, she avoided being alone with Fareed. She preferred it when they were with others: their families, their many natural friends. If they were ever alone, she imagined that her mother or her sister was with them, could hear them, and she spoke to Fareed with that audience in mind.

72 Bryan was speaking to her, saying something about rowing on the River Dee. He went rowing on the weekends, he belonged to a rowing club.

73 To make herself pleasing to people was a skill Shadia was trained in. It was not difficult to please people. Agree with them, never dominate the conversation, be economical with the truth. Now, here was someone to whom all these rules needn't apply.

74 She said to him, 'The Nile is superior to the Dee. I saw your Dee, it is nothing, it is like a stream. There are two Niles, the Blue and the White, named after their colours. They come from the south, from two different places. They travel for miles over countries with different names, never knowing they will meet. I think they get tired of running alone, it is such a long way to the sea. They want to reach the sea so that they can rest, stop running. There is a bridge in Khartoum, and under this bridge the two Niles meet. If you stand on the bridge and look down you can see the two waters mixing together.'

75 'Do ye get homesick?' he asked. She felt tired now, all this talk of the river running to rest in the sea. She had never talked like this before. Luxury words, and this question he asked.

76 'Things I should miss I don't miss. Instead I miss things I didn't think I would miss. The *azan*, the Muslim call to prayer from the mosque. I don't know if you know about it. I miss that. At dawn it used to wake me up. I would hear 'prayer is better than sleep' and just go back to sleep. I never got up to pray.' She looked down at her hands on the table. There was no relief in confessions, only his smile, young, and something like wonder in his eyes.

SELECTION VOCABULARY

conceited / engreído / a *adjective* excessively vain or self-centered; narcissistic

NOTES

77 'We did Islam in school,' he said. 'Ah went on a trip to Mecca[4].' He opened out his palms on the table.

78 'What!'

79 'In a book.'

80 'Oh.'

81 The coffee was finished. They should go now. She should go to the library before the next lecture and photocopy previous exam papers. Asafa, full of helpful advice, had shown her where to find them.

82 'What is your religion?' she asked.

83 'Dunno, nothing I suppose.'

84 'That's terrible! That's really terrible!' Her voice was too loud, concerned.

85 His face went red again and he tapped his spoon against the empty mug.

86 Waive all politeness, make him dislike her. Badr had said, even before his windows got smashed, that here in the West they hate Islam. Standing up to go, she said **flippantly,** 'Why don't you become a Muslim then?'

87 He shrugged. 'Ah wouldnae mind travelling to Mecca, I was keen on that book.'

88 Her eyes filled with tears. They blurred his face when he stood up. In the West they hate Islam and he . . . She said, 'Thanks for the coffee,' and walked away, but he followed her.

89 'Shadiya, Shadiya,' he pronounced her name wrongly, three syllables instead of two, 'there's this museum about Africa. I've never been before. If you'd care to go, tomorrow . . .'

90 No sleep for the guilty, no rest, she should have said no, I can't go, no I have too much catching up to do. No sleep for the guilty, the memories come from another continent. Her father's new wife, happier than her mother, fewer worries. When Shadia visits she offers fruit in a glass bowl, icy oranges and guavas, soothing in the heat. Shadia's father hadn't wanted a divorce, hadn't wanted to leave them; he wanted two wives, not a divorce. But her mother had too much pride, she came from fading money, a family with a 'name.'

91 Tomorrow she need not show up at the museum, even though she said that she would. She should have told Bryan she was engaged to be married,

4. **Mecca** the holy city of Islam in Saudi Arabia, which Muslims face during the regular call to prayer

TEXT TALK

What does Bryan think of Islam and how does Shadia react to this?

See paragraphs 77–88: He finds it interesting and this shocks Shadia.

SELECTION VOCABULARY

flippantly / impertinentemente ***adverb*** in a manner showing disrespect or a lack of seriousness

mentioned it casually. What did he expect from her? Europeans had different rules, reduced, abrupt customs. If Fareed knew about this . . . her secret thoughts like snakes . . . Perhaps she was like her father, a traitor. Her mother said that her father was devious. Sometimes Shadia was devious. With Fareed in the car, she would deliberately say, 'I need to stop at the grocer, we need things at home.' At the grocer he would pay for all her shopping and she would say, 'No, you shouldn't do that, no, you are too generous, you are embarrassing me.' With the money she saved, she would buy a blouse for her mother, nail varnish for her mother, a magazine, imported apples.

. . .

92 It was strange to leave her desk, lock her room and go out on a Saturday. In the hall the telephone rang. It was Fareed. If he knew where she was going now . . . Guilt was like a hard boiled egg stuck in her chest. A large cold egg.

93 'Shadia, I want you to buy some of the fixtures for the bathrooms. Taps and towel hangers. I'm going to send you a list of what I want exactly and the money . . .'

94 'I can't, I can't.'

95 'What do you mean you can't? If you go into any large department store . . .'

96 'I can't, I wouldn't know where to put these things, how to send them.'

97 There was a rustle on the line and she could hear someone whispering, Fareed distracted a little. He would be at work this time in the day, glass bottles filling up with clear effervescent, the words 7UP written in English and Arabic, white against the dark green.

98 'You can get good things, things that aren't available here. Gold would be good. It would match . . .'

99 Gold. Gold toilet seats!

100 'People are going to burn in hell for eating out of gold dishes, you want to sit on gold!'

101 He laughed. He was used to getting his own way, not easily threatened. 'Are you joking with me?'

102 'No.'

103 In a quieter voice, 'This call is costing . . .'

104 She knew, she knew. He shouldn't have let her go away. She was not coping with the whole thing, she was not handling the stress. Like the Nigerian student.

105 'Shadia, gold-coloured, not gold. It's smart.'

106 'Allah is going to punish us for this, it's not right . . .'

107 'Since when have you become so religious!'

. . .

108 Bryan was waiting for her on the steps of the museum, familiar-looking against the strange grey of the city streets where cars had their headlamps on in the middle of the afternoon. He wore a different shirt, a navy-blue jacket. He said, not looking at her, 'Ah was beginning to think you wouldnae turn up.'

109 There was no entry fee to the museum, no attendant handing out tickets. Bryan and Shadia walked on soft carpets; thick blue carpets that made Shadia want to take off her shoes. The first thing they saw was a Scottish man from Victorian times. He sat on a chair surrounded by possessions from Africa: overflowing trunks, an ancient map strewn on the floor of the glass cabinet. All the light in the room came from this and other glass cabinets and gleamed on the waxed floors. Shadia turned away; there was an ugliness in the lifelike wispiness of his hair, his determined expression, the way he sat. A hero who had gone away and come back, laden, ready to report.

110 Bryan began to conscientiously study every display cabinet, to read the posters on the wall. She followed him around and thought that he was studious, careful; that was why he did so well in his degree. She watched the intent expression on his face as he looked at everything. For her the posters were an effort to read, the information difficult to take in. It had been so long since she had read anything outside the requirements of the course. But she persevered, saying the words to herself, moving her lips . . . *'During the 18th and 19th centuries, northeast Scotland made a disproportionate impact on the world at large by contributing so many skilled and committed individuals. In serving an empire they gave and received, changed others and were themselves changed and often returned home with tangible reminders of their experiences.'*

111 The tangible reminders were there to see, preserved in spite of the years. Her eyes skimmed over the disconnected objects out of place and time. Iron and copper, little statues. Nothing was of her, nothing belonged to her life at home, what she missed. Here was Europe's vision, the clichés about Africa: cold and odd.

112 She had not expected the dim light and the hushed silence. Apart from Shadia and Bryan, there was only a man with a briefcase, a lady who took down notes, unless there were others out of sight on the second floor. Something electrical, the heating of the lights, gave out a humming sound like that of an air conditioner. It made Shadia feel as if they were in an aeroplane without windows, detached from the world outside.

113 'He looks like you, don't you think?' she said to Bryan. They stood in front of a portrait of a soldier who died in the first year of the twentieth century. It was the colour of his eyes and his hair. But Bryan did not answer her, did not agree with her. He was preoccupied with reading the caption. When she looked at the portrait again, she saw that she was mistaken. That strength in the eyes, the purpose, was something Bryan didn't have. They had strong faith in those days long ago.

114 Biographies of explorers who were educated in Edinburgh; they knew what to take to Africa: doctors, courage, Christianity, commerce, civilization. They knew what they wanted to bring back: cotton—watered by the Blue Nile, the Zambezi River. She walked after Bryan, felt his concentration, his interest in what was before him and thought, 'In a photograph we would not look nice together.'

115 She touched the glass of a cabinet showing papyrus rolls, copper pots. She pressed her forehead and nose against the cool glass. If she could enter the cabinet, she would not make a good exhibit. She wasn't right, she was too modern, too full of mathematics.

116 Only the carpet, its petroleum blue, pleased her. She had come to this museum expecting sunlight and photographs of the Nile, something to relieve her homesickness: a comfort, a message. But the messages were not for her, not for anyone like her. A letter from West Africa, 1762, an employee to his employer in Scotland. An employee trading European goods for African curiosities. *It was difficult to make the natives understand my meaning, even by an interpreter, it being a thing so seldom asked of them, but they have all undertaken to bring something and laughed heartily at me and said, I was a good man to love their country so much . . .*

117 Love my country so much. She should not be here, there was nothing for her here. She wanted to see minarets[5], boats fragile on the Nile, people. People like her father. The times she had sat in the waiting room of his clinic, among pregnant women, a pain in her heart because she was going to see him in a few minutes. His room, the air conditioner and the smell of his pipe, his white coat. When she hugged him, he smelled of Listerine mouthwash. He could never remember how old she was, what she was studying; six daughters, how could he keep track. In his confusion, there was freedom for her, games to play, a lot of teasing. She visited his clinic in secret, telling lies to her mother. She loved him more than she loved her mother. Her mother who did everything for her, tidied her room, sewed her clothes from *Burda* magazine. Shadia was twenty-five and her mother washed everything for her by hand, even her pants and bras.

5. **minarets** towers in the Islamic world built specially for the *adhan*, or call to prayer, to be made

NOTES

118 'I know why they went away,' said Bryan. 'I understand why they travelled.' At last he was talking. She had not seen him intense before. He spoke in a low voice. 'They had to get away, to leave here . . .'

119 'To escape from the horrible weather . . .' She was making fun of him. She wanted to put him down. The imperialists who had humiliated her history were heroes in his eyes.

120 He looked at her. 'To escape . . .' he repeated.

121 'They went to benefit themselves,' she said, 'people go away because they benefit in some way.'

122 'I want to get away,' he said.

123 She remembered when he had opened his palms on the table and said, 'I went on a trip to Mecca.' There had been pride in his voice.

124 'I should have gone somewhere else for the course,' he went on. 'A new place, somewhere down south.'

125 He was on a plateau, not like her. She was fighting and struggling for a piece of paper that would say she was awarded an M.Sc. from a British university. For him, the course was a continuation.

126 'Come and see,' he said, and he held her arm. No one had touched her before, not since she had hugged her mother goodbye. Months now in this country and no one had touched her.

127 She pulled her arm away. She walked away, quickly up the stairs. Metal steps rattled under her feet. She ran up the stairs to the next floor. Guns, a row of guns aiming at her. They had been waiting to blow her away. Scottish arms of centuries ago, gunfire in service of the empire.

128 Silver muzzles, a dirty grey now. They must have shone prettily once, under a sun far away. If they blew her away now, where would she fly and fall? A window that looked out at the hostile sky. She shivered in spite of the wool she was wearing, layers of clothes. Hell is not only blazing fire, a part of it is freezing cold, torturous ice and snow. In Scotland's winter you have a glimpse of this unseen world, feel the breath of it in your bones.

129 There was a bench and she sat down. There was no one here on this floor. She was alone with sketches of jungle animals, words on the wall. A diplomat away from home, in Ethiopia in 1903: Asafa's country long before Asafa was born. *It is difficult to imagine anything more satisfactory or better worth taking part in than a lion drive. We rode back to camp feeling very well indeed. Archie was quite right when he said that this was the first time since we have started*

that we have really been in Africa—the real Africa of jungle inhabited only by game, and plains where herds of antelope meet your eye in every direction.

130 'Shadiya, don't cry.' He still pronounced her name wrongly because she had not told him how to say it properly.

131 He sat next to her on the bench, the blur of his navy jacket blocking the guns, the wall-length pattern of antelope herds. She should explain that she cried easily, there was no need for the alarm on his face. His awkward voice: 'Why are ye crying?'

132 He didn't know, he didn't understand. He was all wrong, not a substitute . . .

133 'They are telling lies in this museum,' she said. 'Don't believe them. It's all wrong. It's not jungles and antelopes, it's people. We have things like computers and cars. We have 7UP in Africa, and some people, a few people, have bathrooms with golden taps . . . I shouldn't be here with you. You shouldn't talk to me . . .'

134 He said, 'Museums change, I can change . . .'

135 He didn't know it was a steep path she had no strength for. He didn't understand. Many things, years and landscapes, gulfs. If she had been strong she would have explained, and not tired of explaining. She would have patiently taught him another language, letters curved like the epsilon and gamma he knew from mathematics. She would have shown him that words could be read from the right to left. If she had not been small in the museum, if she had been really strong, she would have made his trip to Mecca real, not only in a book.

WRITE

DISCUSSION: Divide yourselves into groups of four or five. Discuss these questions: How do Shadia and Bryan view each other? What is the main reason they find it so hard to communicate with each other? Support your ideas with textual evidence. Take notes as answers are suggested, and be prepared to share your group's notes with the rest of the class. If you have time, talk about your own experiences with cross-cultural friendships.

TEXT TALK

How did discussing museums help you better understand the themes of the story?

Answers will vary.

B Ask each Beyond grade-level student to write one additional discussion question. Then, have one or two students facilitate a discussion, using their questions to guide the conversation.

Writer's Notebook

Connect to Literary Focus: Give students time to reflect on how "The Museum" demonstrates the conventions and characteristics of this unit's literary focus, postmodernism and postcolonialism, by freewriting in their Writer's Notebooks.

CHECK FOR SUCCESS

If students are still struggling to respond to the prompt, ask them scaffolded questions, such as:

- How does this story defy expectations of other stories?
- What are you learning about cultural interactions?

Reading Comprehension OPTIONAL

Have students complete the digital reading comprehension questions when they finish reading.

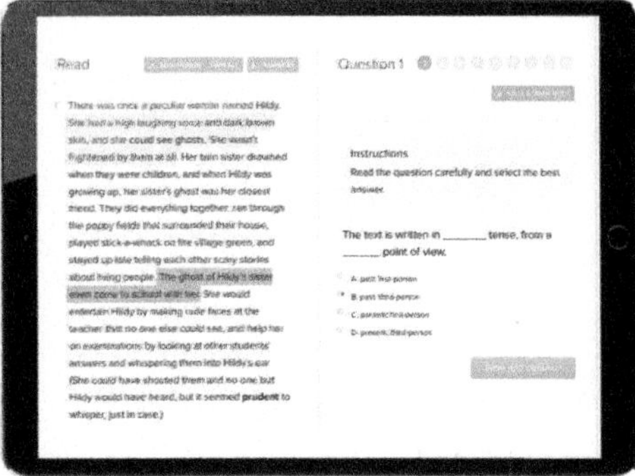

ANSWER KEY

QUESTION 1: D
QUESTION 2: A
QUESTION 3: C
QUESTION 4: A
QUESTION 5: D
QUESTION 6: B
QUESTION 7: A
QUESTION 8: D
QUESTION 9: *See first chart.*
QUESTION 10: *See second chart.*

First	Second	Third	Fourth
Shadia talks to the other students who are studying abroad.	Bryan rips off his earring in front of Shadia.	Shadia talks to Fareed on the phone about gold fixtures.	Shadia cries at the museum.

Dialogue	Character
"People are going to burn in hell for eating out of gold dishes, you want to sit on gold!"	Shadia
"It's coming along fine, they're putting the tiles down . . . "	Fareed
"Museums change, I can change . . . "	Bryan
"No one suffers like I suffer."	Shadia's mother

Connect and Extend OPTIONAL

CONNECT TO EXTENDED ORAL PROJECT

In "The Museum" Shadia is experiencing great change in her life—change of setting, status, and lifestyle. Have students analyze how these changes shape her worldview and characteristics.

BEYOND THE BOOK

Speech: Stereotypes Everyday

Shadia is caught between stereotypes people have about her and stereotypes she harbors about other groups. Students will write a speech that explains a group of people who have been stereotyped in media.

Ask students to:

- Conduct informal research on stereotypes in media (e.g. cartoons, texts, songs, commercials, etc.)
- Choose one group of people and collect facts and evidence of the stereotypes being perpetuated.
- Write a short speech that informs the general public about how this group is portrayed is nothing more than stereotypes. Make sure to include information about how they are much different than how they are portrayed.
- The speech should include a call to action.
- In small groups, give the speech and receive feedback.

To reflect, ask students:

- Are any groups of people free from being stereotyped in media?
- How are the messages we hear and see on daily basis harmful to our society?

Collaborative Conversation

SCAFFOLDS

Post the writing prompt to generate a discussion in small groups. Ask students to first break down the prompt before they discuss relevant ideas and textual evidence.

Divide yourselves into groups of four or five. Discuss these questions: How do Shadia and Bryan view each other? What is the main reason they find it so hard to communicate with each other? Support your ideas with textual evidence. Take notes as answers are suggested, and be prepared to share your group's notes with the rest of the class. If you have time, talk about your own experiences with cross-cultural friendships.

Use the scaffolds below to differentiate instruction for your ELL English Language Learners and A Approaching grade-level learners.

ELL **BEGINNING, INTERMEDIATE** Use the discussion guide and speaking frames to facilitate the discussion with support from the teacher.

ADVANCED, ADVANCED HIGH Use the discussion guide and speaking frames to facilitate the discussion in mixed-level groups.

A **APPROACHING** Use the discussion guide to facilitate the discussion in mixed-level groups.

APPROACHING
ADVANCED, ADVANCED HIGH
BEGINNING, INTERMEDIATE

Discussion Guide	Speaking Frames
1. What does Shadia think of Bryan over the course of the story?	• At first, Shadia thinks Bryan is ____. • She begins to see him as more ____ after ____.
2. What does Bryan think of Shadia over the course of the story?	• Bryan views Shadia as ____. • Bryan learns that ____.
3. Why do these characters have trouble communicating with each other?	• Shadia and Bryan are ____. • Shadia is too ____ and Bryan is too ____.

Ethical Issues

Use the activity below to differentiate instruction for your B Beyond grade level learners.

Read paragraph 16:

'Thank you.' She spoke English better than he did! How pathetic. The whole of him was pathetic. He wore the same shirt every blessed day. Grey and white stripe.

Have students consider the narrator's judgement and bias at this point in the text. Ask students:

- What are the narrator's motivations for speaking to Bryan?
- How do the narrator's initial interactions with Bryan reveal her ethics?

Review Prompt and Rubric

Before students begin writing, review the writing prompt and rubric with the class.

After the discussion, write a reflection in the space below. As you write, make sure to

- evaluate how well everyone followed the rules when making decisions affecting the group
- evaluate your own participation in the discussion
- reflect on how well you posed and responded to questions using reasons and evidence

PROMPT GUIDE

- How does Shadia view Bryan over the course of the story?
- How does Bryan view Shadia over the course of the story?
- What makes it difficult for the two characters to communicate with each other?

Score	Reflection	Language and Conventions
4	The writer clearly reflects on how well he or she posed and responded to questions using reasons and evidence as well as his or her own participation. The writer consistently refers to specific examples from the discussion.	The writer demonstrates a consistent command of grammar, punctuation, and usage conventions. Although minor errors may be evident, they do not detract from the fluency or the clarity of the essay.
3	The writer reflects on how well he or she adjusted posed and responded to questions using reasons and evidence as well as his or her own participation. The writer refers to specific examples from the discussion most of the time.	The writer demonstrates an adequate command of grammar, punctuation, and usage conventions. Although some errors may be evident, they create few (if any) disruptions in the fluency of the writing or the clarity of the essay.
2	The writer begins to reflect on how well he or she adjusted posed and responded to questions using reasons and evidence as well as his or her own participation. The writer refers to specific examples from the discussion some of the time.	The writer demonstrates a partial command of grammar, punctuation, and usage conventions. Some distracting errors may be evident, at times creating minor disruptions in the fluency or clarity of the writing.
1	The writer attempts to reflect on how well he or she adjusted posed and responded to questions using reasons and evidence as well as his or her own participation in the response. The writer refers to few, if any examples from the discussion.	The writer demonstrates little or no command of grammar, punctuation, and usage conventions. Serious and persistent errors create disruptions in the fluency of the writing and sometimes interfere with meaning.
0	The writer does not provide a relevant response to the prompt or does not provide a response at all.	Serious and persistent errors overwhelm the writing and interfere with the meaning of the response as a whole, making the writer's meaning impossible to understand.

Write

SCAFFOLDS

Ask students to complete the writing assignment using text evidence to support their answers.

Use the scaffolds below to differentiate instruction for your ELL English Language Learners and A Approaching grade level readers.

ELL **BEGINNING** With the help of the word bank, write a response using paragraph frame 1.

INTERMEDIATE With the help of the word bank, write a response using paragraph frames 1 and 2.

ADVANCED, ADVANCED HIGH Write a response of differentiated length using the sentence starters.

A **APPROACHING** Write a response of differentiated length using the sentence starters.

BEGINNING / INTERMEDIATE	BEGINNING / INTERMEDIATE	INTERMEDIATE	ADVANCED, ADVANCED HIGH / APPROACHING
Word Bank	**Paragraph Frame 1**	**Paragraph Frame 2**	**Sentence Starters**
pointed out supported trouble disputed convinced added expectations analyze give more examples make connections	My best contribution was when I ____. I plan to ____ to my contributions in future discussions.	I think that my best contribution helped other students to ____. My goal for future discussions will help me ____.	• My best contribution to the discussion was when I . . . • To improve my contributions to future discussions, I plan to . . . • I think that my best contribution helped other students to . . . • My goal for future discussions will enable me to . . .

Peer Review

Students should submit substantive feedback to two peers using the review instructions below.

- How well does the writer refer to specific examples from the discussion?
- What does the writer do well in this reflection? What does the writer need to work on?

Remember that your comments are most useful when they are kind and constructive.

Rate

Respond to the following with a point rating that reflects your opinion.

	1	2	3	4
Ideas				
Evidence				
Language and Conventions				

Submit

ELL **SENTENCE FRAMES**

- You were able to (completely / partly / almost) ____________ answer the prompt.
- You could answer the prompt more completely by ____________.
- My favorite part of your responses is ____________.

A Temporary Matter

FICTION
Jhumpa Lahiri
1999

Introduction

Pulitzer Prize-winner Jhumpa Lahiri (b. 1967) often writes about the intricacies of love and expectation among Indian American families. In "A Temporary Matter," a story from Lahiri's debut collection, *Interpreter of Maladies*, a couple confronts the sadness they've long avoided. After their baby was stillborn, Shoba and Shukumar's marriage changed. No longer intimate with one another, Shoba spends her days outside of the house, while Shukumar barely leaves. A scheduled hour-long power outage for five consecutive evenings provides the couple with a strange gift. Instead of avoiding one another, they find themselves able to talk, using the rules of a game Shoba learned from her family in India.

While Shukumar was away at an academic conference, Shoba gave birth to their stillborn child. Since then, their marriage has been troubled. Shoba leaves the house early and Shukumar often doesn't leave bed until noon. Then, a notice from the electric company informs them that their electricity will be turned off for the next five nights. The couple is forced to confront each other, and while tense at first, they soon start to notice the little familiar things they love about each other. Shoba initiates a game where each night they tell each other one secret. While these secrets are all little betrayals, they somehow give the feeling of clearing the air. By week's end, Shukumar is encouraged about the state of their marriage, but that night, Shoba comes home and tells him that she has signed a lease on a new apartment. In turn, he tries to hurt her, saying that he had a chance to hold their baby and that it was a boy.

Proficiency-leveled summaries and summaries in multiple languages are available digitally.

Audio and audio text highlighting are available with this text.

COMPARING WITHIN AND ACROSS GENRES

In Jhumpa Lahiri's short story "A Temporary Matter," a married couple trade secrets under the cover of darkness when the power company shuts off their electricity for an hour each evening. This story, read in conjunction with "The Museum," invites readers to wonder, "How can relationships change the way people see themselves?"

Entry Point

As students prepare to read "A Temporary Matter," share the following information with them to provide context.

- ✓ Jhumpa Lahiri, born in London in 1967, grew up mainly in Rhode Island and now makes her home in Brooklyn, New York. Her parents emigrated from India but maintained close identification with their Indian cultural backgrounds.
- ✓ Lahiri graduated from college in 1989 and went on to earn three master's degrees along with a doctorate in Renaissance studies. In 1999, she published her first collection of short stories, *The Interpreter of Maladies*, which won the Pulitzer Prize for fiction among many other awards.
- ✓ Lahiri's characters, like Shoba and Shukumar in "A Temporary Matter," are often Americans whose cultural roots lie in other countries. Accordingly, Lahiri is often considered a writer of "immigrant fiction." However, Lahiri dislikes that term; as she points out, "Given the history of the United States, all American fiction could be classified as immigrant fiction."

Instructional Path

The print teacher's edition includes essential point-of-use instruction and planning tools. Complete lesson plans and program documents appear in your digital teacher account.

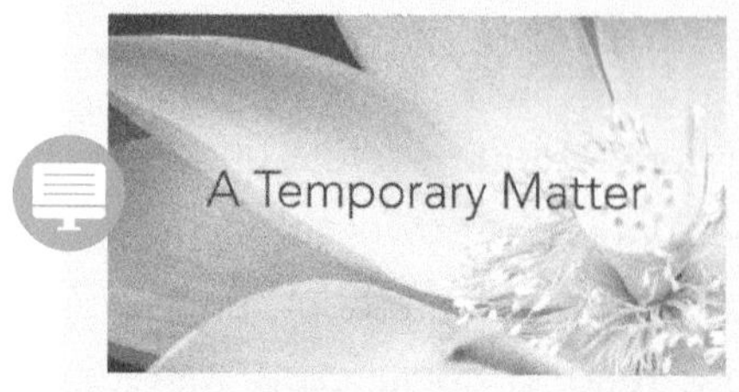

First Read: A Temporary Matter

Objectives: After an initial reading and discussion of the short story, students will be able to identify and describe character traits and the sequence of events as well as explain the conflict that is fundamental to the story's plot.

Skill: Theme

Objectives: After rereading and discussing a model of close reading, students will be able to explain how elements relating to characterization, setting, point of view, and plot build on one another to develop two or more themes in "A Temporary Matter."

Skill: Story Elements

Objectives: After rereading and discussing a model of close reading, students will be able to identify and analyze the impact of the author's choices about character, setting, and plot and how those story elements develop and connect in "A Temporary Matter."

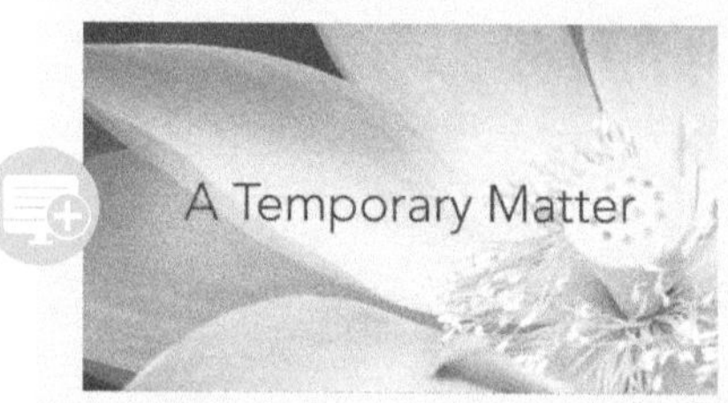

Close Read: A Temporary Matter

Objectives: After engaging in a close reading and discussion of "A Temporary Matter," students will be able to write a short response evaluating whether a critic's description of the author's work applies to this story.

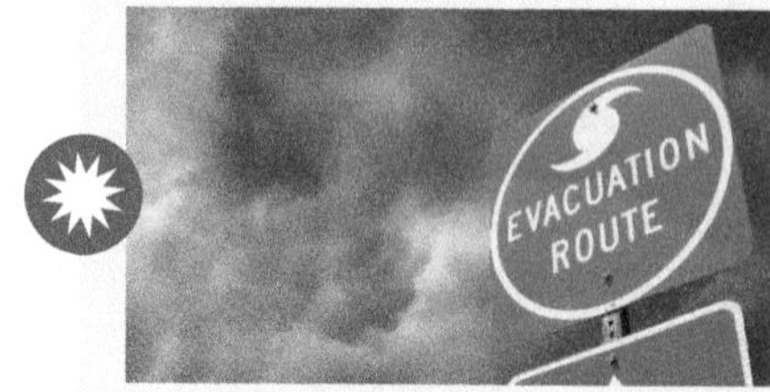

Blast: Perfect Storm

Objectives: After exploring background information and research links about a topic, students will respond to a question with a 140-character response.

Progress Monitoring

Opportunities to Learn	Opportunities to Demonstrate Learning	Opportunities to Reteach
Theme		
Skill: Theme	Skill: Theme • Your Turn Close Read • Skills Focus	Spotlight Skill: Theme
Story Elements		
Skill: Story Elements	Skill: Story Elements • Your Turn Close Read • Skills Focus • Write	Unit Skill: Story Elements- Ghosts Spotlight Skill: Story Elements

First Read

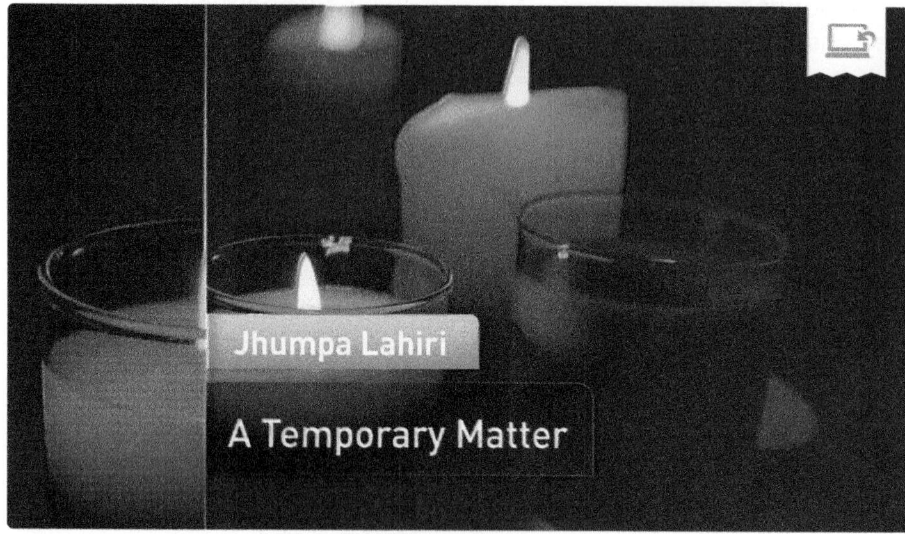

Introduce the Text

As a class, watch the video preview  and have students read the introduction in pairs to make connections to the video preview.

To activate prior knowledge and experiences, ask students:

- How does the video connect with something you already knew?
- When have you felt yourself drifting apart from a person you had once been closely connected to?

ELL SPEAKING FRAMES

- The video connected with what I already knew about ____.
- I once felt connected to ____ Now we are less connected because ____.

Access Complex Text

LEXILE: 990 WORD COUNT: 7,184

The following areas may be challenging for students, particularly ELL English Language Learners and A Approaching grade-level learners.

Organization

- The main action of the story takes place during a week in March, when Shoba and Shukumar learn that their power will be disrupted. The story also includes flashbacks about the events leading up to the death of the couple's baby six months earlier.
- Encourage students to track the order of events to support their predictions of what will happen next in the story.

Connection of Ideas

- The narrator of the story does not directly tell the reader everything about the characters. For example, nowhere does the text explicitly say that Shukumar is depressed.
- Explain that the reader needs to make inferences, based on textual evidence, to draw conclusions about the characters and the theme.

SCAFFOLDS

 ENGLISH LANGUAGE LEARNERS  APPROACHING GRADE LEVEL  BEYOND GRADE LEVEL

These icons identify differentiation strategies and scaffolded support for a variety of students. See the digital lesson plan for additional differentiation strategies and scaffolds.

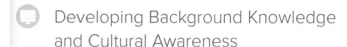

"He learned not to mind the silences."

NOTES

1 The notice informed them that it was a temporary matter: for five days their electricity would be cut off for one hour, beginning at eight P.M. A line had gone down in the last snowstorm, and the repairmen were going to take advantage of the milder evenings to set it right. The work would affect only the houses on the quiet tree-lined street, within walking distance of a row of brick-faced stores and a trolley stop, where Shoba and Shukumar had lived for three years.

Jhumpa Lahiri

2 "It's good of them to warn us," Shoba conceded after reading the notice aloud, more for her own benefit than Shukumar's. She let the strap of her leather satchel, plump with files, slip from her shoulders, and left it in the hallway as she walked into the kitchen. She wore a navy blue poplin raincoat over gray sweatpants and white sneakers, looking, at thirty-three, like the type of woman she'd once claimed she would never resemble.

3 She'd come from the gym. Her cranberry lipstick was visible only on the outer reaches of her mouth, and her eyeliner had left charcoal patches beneath her lower lashes. She used to look this way sometimes, Shukumar thought, on mornings after a party or a night at a bar, when she'd been too lazy to wash her face, too eager to collapse into his arms. She dropped a sheaf of mail on the table without a glance. Her eyes were still fixed on the notice in her other hand. "But they should do this sort of thing during the day."

4 "When I'm here, you mean," Shukumar said. He put a glass lid on a pot of lamb, adjusting it so only the slightest bit of steam could escape. Since January he'd been working at home, trying to complete the final chapters of his dissertation on agrarian revolts[1] in India. "When do the repairs start?"

1. **agrarian revolts** revolts concerning the cultivation or distribution of land

Developing Background Knowledge and Cultural Awareness

1. Share with students the following quotation by Jhumpa Lahiri: "My responsibility isn't to paint a flattering portrait; my responsibility is to paint a real portrait, a true portrait."
2. In small groups, have students discuss the meaning of the quotation, and how it relates to something they've read or learned about.

Discuss with students: Jhumpa Lahiri is a contemporary postcolonial writer who often portrays characters going about their daily lives. What do you think a "true portrait" of a character looks like? Where have you seen "true" characters? What contributed to their relatability and sense of being "true"? How does this idea of a "true portrait" relate to postcolonial literature?

NOTES

5 "It says March nineteenth. Is today the nineteenth?" Shoba walked over to the framed corkboard that hung on the wall by the fridge, bare except for a calendar of William Morris wallpaper patterns. She looked at it as if for the first time, studying the wallpaper pattern carefully on the top half before allowing her eyes to fall to the numbered grid on the bottom. A friend had sent the calendar in the mail as a Christmas gift, even though Shoba and Shukumar hadn't celebrated Christmas that year.

6 "Today then," Shoba announced. "You have a dentist appointment next Friday, by the way."

7 He ran his tongue over the tops of his teeth; he'd forgotten to brush them that morning. It wasn't the first time. He hadn't left the house at all that day, or the day before. The more Shoba stayed out, the more she began putting in extra hours at work and taking on additional projects, the more he wanted to stay in, not even leaving to get the mail, or to buy fruit or wine at the stores by the trolley stop.

8 Six months ago, in September, Shukumar was at an academic conference in Baltimore when Shoba went into labor, three weeks before her due date. He hadn't wanted to go to the conference, but she had insisted; it was important to make contacts, and he would be entering the job market next year. She told him that she had his number at the hotel, and a copy of his schedule and flight numbers, and she had arranged with her friend Gillian for a ride to the hospital in the event of an emergency. When the cab pulled away that morning for the airport, Shoba stood waving good-bye in her robe, with one arm resting on the mound of her belly as if it were a perfectly natural part of her body.

9 Each time he thought of that moment, the last moment he saw Shoba pregnant, it was the cab he remembered most, a station wagon, painted red with blue lettering. It was cavernous compared to their own car. Although Shukumar was six feet tall, with hands too big ever to rest comfortably in the pockets of his jeans, he felt dwarfed in the back seat. As the cab sped down Beacon Street, he imagined a day when he and Shoba might need to buy a station wagon of their own, to cart their children back and forth from music lessons and dentist appointments. He imagined himself gripping the wheel, as Shoba turned around to hand the children juice boxes. Once, these images of parenthood had troubled Shukumar, adding to his anxiety that he was still a student at thirty-five. But that early autumn morning, the trees still heavy with bronze leaves, he welcomed the image for the first time.

10 A member of the staff had found him somehow among the identical convention rooms and handed him a stiff square of stationery. It was only a

TEXT TALK

Why did Shukumar attend the conference in Baltimore?

See Paragraph 8: Shoba told him she would be fine and that he needed to make contacts in the academic world.

telephone number, but Shukumar knew it was the hospital. When he returned to Boston it was over. The baby had been born dead. Shoba was lying on a bed, asleep, in a private room so small there was barely enough space to stand beside her, in a wing of the hospital they hadn't been to on the tour for expectant parents. Her placenta had weakened and she'd had a cesarean[2], though not quickly enough. The doctor explained that these things happen. He smiled in the kindest way it was possible to smile at people known only professionally. Shoba would be back on her feet in a few weeks. There was nothing to indicate that she would not be able to have children in the future.

11 These days Shoba was always gone by the time Shukumar woke up. He would open his eyes and see the long black hairs she shed on her pillow and think of her, dressed, sipping her third cup of coffee already, in her office downtown, where she searched for typographical errors in textbooks and marked them, in a code she had once explained to him, with an assortment of colored pencils. She would do the same for his dissertation, she promised, when it was ready. He envied her the specificity of her task, so unlike the elusive nature of his. He was a mediocre student who had a facility for absorbing details without curiosity. Until September he had been **diligent** if not dedicated, summarizing chapters, outlining arguments on pads of yellow lined paper. But now he would lie in their bed until he grew bored, gazing at his side of the closet which Shoba always left partly open, at the row of the tweed jackets and corduroy trousers he would not have to choose from to teach his classes that semester. After the baby died it was too late to withdraw from his teaching duties. But his adviser had arranged things so that he had the spring semester to himself. Shukumar was in his sixth year of graduate school. "That and the summer should give you a good push," his adviser had said. "You should be able to wrap things up by next September."

12 But nothing was pushing Shukumar. Instead he thought of how he and Shoba had become experts at avoiding each other in their three-bedroom house, spending as much time on separate floors as possible. He thought of how he no longer looked forward to weekends, when she sat for hours on the sofa with her colored pencils and her files, so that he feared that putting on a record in his own house might be rude. He thought of how long it had been since she looked into his eyes and smiled, or whispered his name on those rare occasions they still reached for each other's bodies before sleeping.

2. **cesarean** a cesarean section, c-section, is a surgical procedure to deliver a baby through an incision in the abdomen

Skills Focus

QUESTION 1: Theme

Shoba and Shukumar live separate lives and are almost hostile toward each other. This suggests that trauma can have a negative effect on a relationship.

Skills Focus

QUESTION 5: Connect to Essential Question

The characters used to avoid each other and not confront the change in their relationship that resulted from their baby's death. While Shukumar may have hoped the change in behavior would pass, he knew the change would likely mean the demise of their relationship.

 SELECTION VOCABULARY

diligent / diligente *adjective* hardworking; showing much effort COGNATE

NOTES

13 In the beginning he had believed that it would pass, that he and Shoba would get through it all somehow. She was only thirty-three. She was strong, on her feet again. But it wasn't a consolation. It was often nearly lunchtime when Shukumar would finally pull himself out of bed and head downstairs to the coffeepot, pouring out the extra bit Shoba left for him, along with an empty mug, on the countertop.

14 Shukumar gathered onion skins in his hands and let them drop into the garbage pail, on top of the ribbons of fat he'd trimmed from the lamb. He ran the water in the sink, soaking the knife and the cutting board, and rubbed a lemon half along his fingertips to get rid of the garlic smell, a trick he'd learned from Shoba. It was seven-thirty. Through the window he saw the sky, like soft black pitch. Uneven banks of snow still lined the sidewalks, though it was warm enough for people to walk about without hats or gloves. Nearly three feet had fallen in the last storm, so that for a week people had to walk single file, in narrow trenches. For a week that was Shukumar's excuse for not leaving the house. But now the trenches were widening, and water drained steadily into grates in the pavement.

15 "The lamb won't be done by eight," Shukumar said. "We may have to eat in the dark."

16 "We can light candles," Shoba suggested. She unclipped her hair, coiled neatly at her nape during the days, and pried the sneakers from her feet without untying them. "I'm going to shower before the lights go," she said, heading for the staircase. "I'll be down."

17 Shukumar moved her satchel and her sneakers to the side of the fridge. She wasn't this way before. She used to put her coat on a hanger, her sneakers in the closet, and she paid bills as soon as they came. But now she treated the house as if it were a hotel. The fact that the yellow chintz armchair in the living room clashed with the blue-and-maroon Turkish carpet no longer bothered her. On the enclosed porch at the back of the house, a crisp white bag still sat on the wicker chaise, filled with lace she had once planned to turn into curtains.

18 While Shoba showered, Shukumar went into the downstairs bathroom and found a new toothbrush in its box beneath the sink. The cheap, stiff bristles hurt his gums, and he spit some blood into the basin. The spare brush was one of many stored in a metal basket. Shoba had bought them once when they were on sale, in the event that a visitor decided, at the last minute, to spend the night.

19 It was typical of her. She was the type to prepare for surprises, good and bad. If she found a skirt or a purse she liked she bought two. She kept the bonuses

Skills Focus

QUESTION 2: Story Elements

Shoba used to make sure the pantry was always filled. This shows that she was good at thinking ahead, shopping carefully, and being organized. The change in Shoba's behavior moves the plot forward because it deepens the conflict since this responsibility now falls on Shukumar.

NOTES

from her job in a separate bank account in her name. It hadn't bothered him. His own mother had fallen to pieces when his father died, abandoning the house he grew up in and moving back to Calcutta, leaving Shukumar to settle it all. He liked that Shoba was different. It astonished him, her **capacity** to think ahead. When she used to do the shopping, the pantry was always stocked with extra bottles of olive and corn oil, depending on whether they were cooking Italian or Indian. There were endless boxes of pasta in all shapes and colors, zippered sacks of basmati rice, whole sides of lambs and goats from the Muslim butchers at Haymarket, chopped up and frozen in endless plastic bags. Every other Saturday they wound through the maze of stalls Shukumar eventually knew by heart. He watched in disbelief as she bought more food, trailing behind her with canvas bags as she pushed through the crowd, arguing under the morning sun with boys too young to shave but already missing teeth, who twisted up brown paper bags of artichokes, plums, gingerroot, and yams, and dropped them on their scales, and tossed them to Shoba one by one. She didn't mind being jostled, even when she was pregnant. She was tall, and broad-shouldered, with hips that her obstetrician assured her were made for childbearing. During the drive back home, as the car curved along the Charles, they **invariably** marveled at how much food they'd bought.

20 It never went to waste. When friends dropped by, Shoba would throw together meals that appeared to have taken half a day to prepare, from things she had frozen and bottled, not cheap things in tins but peppers she had marinated herself with rosemary, and chutneys that she cooked on Sundays, stirring boiling pots of tomatoes and prunes. Her labeled mason jars lined the shelves of the kitchen, in endless sealed pyramids, enough, they'd agreed, to last for their grandchildren to taste. They'd eaten it all by now. Shukumar had been going through their supplies steadily, preparing meals for the two of them, measuring out cupfuls of rice, defrosting bags of meat day after day. He combed through her cookbooks every afternoon, following her penciled instructions to use two teaspoons of ground coriander seeds instead of one, or red lentils instead of yellow. Each of the recipes was dated, telling the first time they had eaten the dish together. April 2, cauliflower with fennel. January 14, chicken with almonds and sultanas. He had no memory of eating those meals, and yet there they were, recorded in her neat proofreader's hand. Shukumar enjoyed cooking now. It was the one thing that made him feel productive. If it weren't for him, he knew, Shoba would eat a bowl of cereal for her dinner.

Skill: Theme

The characters live in modern-day Boston during a week of nightly blackouts on their street. This forces them to stop avoiding each other, building suspense and suggesting a theme having to do with how relationships change.

21 Tonight, with no lights, they would have to eat together. For months now they'd served themselves from the stove, and he'd taken his plate into his study, letting the meal grow cold on his desk before shoving it into his mouth without pause, while Shoba took her plate to the living room and watched game shows, or proofread files with her arsenal of colored pencils at hand.

Theme

How does the reader use setting and plot details to draw conclusions about the theme?

The reader notices the story takes place in modern-day Boston and that scheduled blackouts force the characters to spend time together at night. This helps the reader infer that the theme may relate to relationships.

SELECTION VOCABULARY

capacity / la capacidad *noun* the ability to accomplish, learn, or perform COGNATE

invariably / invariablemente *adverb* all the time; in every case; always COGNATE

NOTES

22 At some point in the evening she visited him. When he heard her approach he would put away his novel and begin typing sentences. She would rest her hands on his shoulders and stare with him into the blue glow of the computer screen. "Don't work too hard," she would say after a minute or two, and head off to bed. It was the one time in the day she sought him out, and yet he'd come to dread it. He knew it was something she forced herself to do. She would look around the walls of the room, which they had decorated together last summer with a border of marching ducks and rabbits playing trumpets and drums. By the end of August there was a cherry crib under the window, a white changing table with mint-green knobs, and a rocking chair with checkered cushions. Shukumar had disassembled it all before bringing Shoba back from the hospital, scraping off the rabbits and ducks with a spatula. For some reason the room did not haunt him the way it haunted Shoba. In January, when he stopped working at his carrel[3] in the library, he set up his desk there deliberately, partly because the room soothed him, and partly because it was a place Shoba avoided.

23 Shukumar returned to the kitchen and began to open drawers. He tried to locate a candle among the scissors, the eggbeaters and whisks, the mortar and pestle she'd bought in a bazaar in Calcutta, and used to pound garlic cloves and cardamom pods, back when she used to cook. He found a flashlight, but no batteries, and a half-empty box of birthday candles. Shoba had thrown him a surprise birthday party last May. One hundred and twenty people had crammed into the house — all the friends and the friends of friends they now systematically avoided. Bottles of vinho verde had nested in a bed of ice in the bathtub. Shoba was in her fifth month, drinking ginger ale from a martini glass. She had made a vanilla cream cake with custard and spun sugar. All night she kept Shukumar's long fingers linked with hers as they walked among the guests at the party.

24 Since September their only guest had been Shoba's mother. She came from Arizona and stayed with them for two months after Shoba returned from the hospital. She cooked dinner every night, drove herself to the supermarket, washed their clothes, put them away. She was a religious woman. She set up a small shrine, a framed picture of a lavender-faced goddess and a plate of marigold petals, on the bedside table in the guest room, and prayed twice a day for healthy grandchildren in the future. She was polite to Shukumar without being friendly. She folded his sweaters with an expertise she had learned from her job in a department store. She replaced a missing button on his winter coat and knit him a beige and brown scarf, presenting it to him without the least bit of ceremony, as if he had only dropped it and hadn't noticed. She never talked to him about Shoba; once, when he mentioned the baby's death, she looked up from her knitting, and said, "But you weren't even there."

3. **carrel** cubicle

TEXT TALK

What had Shukumar and Shoba planned to do with the room where Shukumar now has his desk? What did Shukumar do with the room in September?

See Paragraph 22: It was going to be the baby's room. He disassembled the furniture and removed the decorations before Shoba came home.

25 It struck him as odd that there were no real candles in the house. That Shoba hadn't prepared for such an ordinary emergency. He looked now for something to put the birthday candles in and settled on the soil of a potted ivy that normally sat on the windowsill over the sink. Even though the plant was inches from the tap, the soil was so dry that he had to water it first before the candles would stand straight. He pushed aside the things on the kitchen table, the piles of mail, the unread library books. He remembered their first meals there, when they were so thrilled to be married, to be living together in the same house at last, that they would just reach for each other foolishly, more eager to make love than to eat. He put down two embroidered place mats, a wedding gift from an uncle in Lucknow, and set out the plates and wineglasses they usually saved for guests. He put the ivy in the middle, the white-edged, star-shaped leaves girded by ten little candles. He switched on the digital clock radio and tuned it to a jazz station.

26 "What's all this?" Shoba said when she came downstairs. Her hair was wrapped in a thick white towel. She undid the towel and draped it over a chair, allowing her hair, damp and dark, to fall across her back. As she walked absently toward the stove she took out a few tangles with her fingers. She wore a clean pair of sweatpants, a T-shirt, an old flannel robe. Her stomach was flat again, her waist narrow before the flare of her hips, the belt of the robe tied in a floppy knot.

27 It was nearly eight. Shukumar put the rice on the table and the lentils from the night before into the microwave oven, punching the numbers on the timer.

28 "You made *rogan josh,*" Shoba observed, looking through the glass lid at the bright paprika stew.

29 Shukumar took out a piece of lamb, pinching it quickly between his fingers so as not to scald himself. He prodded a larger piece with a serving spoon to make sure the meat slipped easily from the bone. "It's ready," he announced.

30 The microwave had just beeped when the lights went out, and the music disappeared.

31 "Perfect timing," Shoba said.

32 "All I could find were birthday candles." He lit up the ivy, keeping the rest of the candles and a book of matches by his plate.

33 "It doesn't matter," she said, running a finger along the stem of her wineglass. "It looks lovely."

NOTES

34 In the dimness, he knew how she sat, a bit forward in her chair, ankles crossed against the lowest rung, left elbow on the table. During his search for the candles, Shukumar had found a bottle of wine in a crate he had thought was empty. He clamped the bottle between his knees while he turned in the corkscrew. He worried about spilling, and so he picked up the glasses and held them close to his lap while he filled them. They served themselves, stirring the rice with their forks, squinting as they **extracted** bay leaves and cloves from the stew. Every few minutes Shukumar lit a few more birthday candles and drove them into the soil of the pot.

35 "It's like India," Shoba said, watching him tend his makeshift candelabra. "Sometimes the current disappears for hours at a stretch. I once had to attend an entire rice ceremony[4] in the dark. The baby just cried and cried. It must have been so hot."

36 Their baby had never cried, Shukumar considered. Their baby would never have a rice ceremony, even though Shoba had already made the guest list, and decided on which of her three brothers she was going to ask to feed the child its first taste of solid food, at six months if it was a boy, seven if it was a girl.

37 "Are you hot?" he asked her. He pushed the blazing ivy pot to the other end of the table, closer to the piles of books and mail, making it even more difficult for them to see each other. He was suddenly irritated that he couldn't go upstairs and sit in front of the computer.

38 "No. It's delicious," she said, tapping her plate with her fork. "It really is."

39 He refilled the wine in her glass. She thanked him.

40 They weren't like this before. Now he had to struggle to say something that interested her, something that made her look up from her plate, or from her proofreading files. Eventually he gave up trying to amuse her. He learned not to mind the silences.

41 "I remember during power failures at my grandmother's house, we all had to say something," Shoba continued. He could barely see her face, but from her tone he knew her eyes were narrowed, as if trying to focus on a distant object. It was a habit of hers.

42 "Like what?"

43 "I don't know. A little poem. A joke. A fact about the world. For some reason my relatives always wanted me to tell them the names of my friends in

4. **rice ceremony** Annaprashan, the Indian ritual of a baby's first feeding with rice

TEXT TALK

How are Shoba's recollections of India from her childhood different from Shukumar's?

See Paragraph 43: Shoba visited India often and has many memories of her time spent there, but Shukumar seldom went because he had gotten very sick there as a baby.

SELECTION VOCABULARY

extract / extraer ***verb*** to gain or remove from COGNATE

America. I don't know why the information was so interesting to them. The last time I saw my aunt she asked after four girls I went to elementary school with in Tucson. I barely remember them now."

44 Shukumar hadn't spent as much time in India as Shoba had. His parents, who settled in New Hampshire, used to go back without him. The first time he'd gone as an infant he'd nearly died of amoebic dysentery. His father, a nervous type, was afraid to take him again, in case something were to happen, and left him with his aunt and uncle in Concord. As a teenager he preferred sailing camp or scooping ice cream during the summers to going to Calcutta. It wasn't until after his father died, in his last year of college, that the country began to interest him, and he studied its history from course books as if it were any other subject. He wished now that he had his own childhood story of India.

45 "Let's do that," she said suddenly.

46 "Do what?"

47 "Say something to each other in the dark."

48 "Like what? I don't know any jokes."

49 "No, no jokes." She thought for a minute. "How about telling each other something we've never told before."

50 "I used to play this game in high school," Shukumar recalled. "When I got drunk."

51 "You're thinking of truth or dare. This is different. Okay, I'll start." She took a sip of wine. "The first time I was alone in your apartment, I looked in your address book to see if you'd written me in. I think we'd known each other two weeks."

52 "Where was I?"

53 "You went to answer the telephone in the other room. It was your mother, and I figured it would be a long call. I wanted to know if you'd promoted me from the margins of your newspaper."

54 "Had I?"

55 "No. But I didn't give up on you. Now it's your turn."

56 He couldn't think of anything, but Shoba was waiting for him to speak. She hadn't appeared so determined in months. What was there left to say to her?

NOTES

He thought back to their first meeting, four years earlier at a lecture hall in Cambridge, where a group of Bengali poets were giving a recital. They'd ended up side by side, on folding wooden chairs. Shukumar was soon bored; he was unable to decipher the literary diction, and couldn't join the rest of the audience as they sighed and nodded solemnly after certain phrases. Peering at the newspaper folded in his lap, he studied the temperatures of cities around the world. Ninety-one degrees in Singapore yesterday, fifty-one in Stockholm. When he turned his head to the left, he saw a woman next to him making a grocery list on the back of a folder, and was startled to find that she was beautiful.

57 "Okay" he said, remembering. "The first time we went out to dinner, to the Portuguese place, I forgot to tip the waiter. I went back the next morning, found out his name, left money with the manager."

58 "You went all the way back to Somerville just to tip a waiter?"

59 "I took a cab."

60 "Why did you forget to tip the waiter?"

61 The birthday candles had burned out, but he pictured her face clearly in the dark, the wide tilting eyes, the full grape-toned lips, the fall at age two from her high chair still visible as a comma on her chin. Each day, Shukumar noticed, her beauty, which had once overwhelmed him, seemed to fade. The cosmetics that had seemed superfluous were necessary now, not to improve her but to define her somehow.

62 "By the end of the meal I had a funny feeling that I might marry you," he said, admitting it to himself as well as to her for the first time. "It must have distracted me."

63 The next night Shoba came home earlier than usual. There was lamb left over from the evening before, and Shukumar heated it up so that they were able to eat by seven. He'd gone out that day, through the melting snow, and bought a packet of taper candles from the corner store, and batteries to fit the flashlight. He had the candles ready on the countertop, standing in brass holders shaped like lotuses, but they ate under the glow of the copper-shaded ceiling lamp that hung over the table.

64 When they had finished eating, Shukumar was surprised to see that Shoba was stacking her plate on top of his, and then carrying them over to the sink. He had assumed she would retreat to the living room, behind her barricade of files.

65 "Don't worry about the dishes," he said, taking them from her hands.

66 "It seems silly not to," she replied, pouring a drop of detergent onto a sponge. "It's nearly eight o'clock."

67 His heart quickened. All day Shukumar had looked forward to the lights going out. He thought about what Shoba had said the night before, about looking in his address book. It felt good to remember her as she was then, how bold yet nervous she'd been when they first met, how hopeful. They stood side by side at the sink, their reflections fitting together in the frame of the window. It made him shy, the way he felt the first time they stood together in a mirror. He couldn't recall the last time they'd been photographed. They had stopped attending parties, went nowhere together. The film in his camera still contained pictures of Shoba, in the yard, when she was pregnant.

Skill: Theme

The story is told in third-person point of view, but the narrator reveals Shukumar's thoughts. He "felt good" reflecting on memories. Sharing secrets changed him, suggesting that minor revelations can have a big impact.

68 After finishing the dishes, they leaned against the counter, drying their hands on either end of a towel. At eight o'clock the house went black. Shukumar lit the wicks of the candles, impressed by their long, steady flames.

69 "Let's sit outside," Shoba said. "I think it's warm still."

70 They each took a candle and sat down on the steps. It seemed strange to be sitting outside with patches of snow still on the ground. But everyone was out of their houses tonight, the air fresh enough to make people restless. Screen doors opened and closed. A small parade of neighbors passed by with flashlights.

71 "We're going to the bookstore to browse," a silver-haired man called out. He was walking with his wife, a thin woman in a windbreaker, and holding a dog on a leash. They were the Bradfords, and they had tucked a sympathy card into Shoba and Shukumar's mailbox back in September. "I hear they've got their power."

72 "They'd better," Shukumar said. "Or you'll be browsing in the dark."

73 The woman laughed, slipping her arm through the crook of her husband's elbow. "Want to join us?"

74 "No thanks," Shoba and Shukumar called out together. It surprised Shukumar that his words matched hers.

75 He wondered what Shoba would tell him in the dark. The worst possibilities had already run through his head. That she'd had an affair. That she didn't respect him for being thirty-five and still a student. That she blamed him for being in Baltimore the way her mother did. But he knew those things weren't

Theme

How does the reader use character details and point of view to draw conclusions about the theme?

The reader notes that the story has a third-person narrator who reveals one of the character's inner thoughts. She uses these details to explain how the character has changed as a result of the setting and plot.

Skills Focus

QUESTION 3: Story Elements

The weather has gotten much warmer after the long period of snow and cold. The thaw in the weather seems to reflect a thaw in the couple's relationship.

NOTES

true. She'd been faithful, as had he. She believed in him. It was she who had insisted he go to Baltimore. What didn't they know about each other? He knew she curled her fingers tightly when she slept, that her body twitched during bad dreams. He knew it was honeydew she favored over cantaloupe. He knew that when they returned from the hospital the first thing she did when she walked into the house was pick out objects of theirs and toss them into a pile in the hallway: books from the shelves, plants from the windowsills, paintings from walls, photos from tables, pots and pans that hung from the hooks over the stove. Shukumar had stepped out of her way, watching as she moved **methodically** from room to room. When she was satisfied, she stood there staring at the pile she'd made, her lips drawn back in such distaste that Shukumar had thought she would spit. Then she'd started to cry.

76 He began to feel cold as he sat there on the steps. He felt that he needed her to talk first, in order to reciprocate.

77 "That time when your mother came to visit us," she said finally. "When I said one night that I had to stay late at work, I went out with Gillian and had a martini."

78 He looked at her profile, the slender nose, the slightly masculine set of her jaw. He remembered that night well; eating with his mother, tired from teaching two classes back to back, wishing Shoba were there to say more of the right things because he came up with only the wrong ones. It had been twelve years since his father had died, and his mother had come to spend two weeks with him and Shoba, so they could honor his father's memory together. Each night his mother cooked something his father had liked, but she was too upset to eat the dishes herself, and her eyes would well up as Shoba stroked her hand. "It's so touching," Shoba had said to him at the time. Now he pictured Shoba with Gillian, in a bar with striped velvet sofas, the one they used to go to after the movies, making sure she got her extra olive, asking Gillian for a cigarette. He imagined her complaining, and Gillian sympathizing about visits from in-laws. It was Gillian who had driven Shoba to the hospital.

79 "Your turn," she said, stopping his thoughts.

80 At the end of their street Shukumar heard sounds of a drill and the electricians shouting over it. He looked at the darkened facades of the houses lining the street. Candles glowed in the windows of one. In spite of the warmth, smoke rose from the chimney.

81 "I cheated on my Oriental Civilization exam in college," he said. "It was my last semester, my last set of exams. My father had died a few months before. I could see the blue book of the guy next to me. He was an American guy, a

SELECTION VOCABULARY

methodically / metódicamente *adverb* in a manner that is careful and organized COGNATE

NOTES

maniac. He knew Urdu and Sanskrit. I couldn't remember if the verse we had to identify was an example of a *ghazal* or not. I looked at his answer and copied it down."

82 It had happened over fifteen years ago. He felt relief now, having told her.

83 She turned to him, looking not at his face, but at his shoes — old moccasins he wore as if they were slippers, the leather at the back permanently flattened. He wondered if it bothered her, what he'd said. She took his hand and pressed it. "You didn't have to tell me why you did it," she said, moving closer to him.

84 They sat together until nine o'clock, when the lights came on. They heard some people across the street clapping from their porch, and televisions being turned on. The Bradfords walked back down the street, eating ice-cream cones and waving. Shoba and Shukumar waved back. Then they stood up, his hand still in hers, and went inside.

85 Somehow, without saying anything, it had turned into this. Into an exchange of confessions — the little ways they'd hurt or disappointed each other, and themselves. The following day Shukumar thought for hours about what to say to her. He was torn between admitting that he once ripped out a photo of a woman in one of the fashion magazines she used to subscribe to and carried it in his books for a week, or saying that he really hadn't lost the sweater-vest she bought him for their third wedding anniversary but had exchanged it for cash at Filene's, and that he had gotten drunk alone in the middle of the day at a hotel bar. For their first anniversary, Shoba had cooked a ten-course dinner just for him. The vest depressed him. "My wife gave me a sweater-vest for our anniversary," he complained to the bartender, his head heavy with cognac. "What do you expect?" the bartender had replied. "You're married."

Skill: Story Elements

Shukumar feels disconnected from Shoba, but instead of talking to her about it, he fixates on a picture from a magazine. This dilemma shows that the conflict between the characters had already been brewing before the baby's death.

86 As for the picture of the woman, he didn't know why he'd ripped it out. She wasn't as pretty as Shoba. She wore a white sequined dress, and had a sullen face and lean, mannish legs. Her bare arms were raised, her fists around her head, as if she were about to punch herself in the ears. It was an advertisement for stockings. Shoba had been pregnant at the time, her stomach suddenly immense, to the point where Shukumar no longer wanted to touch her. The first time he saw the picture he was lying in bed next to her, watching her as she read. When he noticed the magazine in the recycling pile he found the woman and tore out the page as carefully as he could. For about a week he allowed himself a glimpse each day. He felt an intense desire for the woman, but it was a desire that turned to disgust after a minute or two. It was the closest he'd come to infidelity.

Story Elements

How did the reader analyze the effect of Shukumar's behavior on the plot of the story?

The reader notes the narrator's description of a memory that Shukumar has and how this shapes what the reader knows about this character in the story. This shows that the conflict in the plot began while Shoba was still pregnant.

NOTES

87 He told Shoba about the sweater on the third night, the picture on the fourth. She said nothing as he spoke, expressed no protest or reproach. She simply listened, and then she took his hand, pressing it as she had before. On the third night, she told him that once after a lecture they'd attended, she let him speak to the chairman of his department without telling him that he had a dab of pâté on his chin. She'd been irritated with him for some reason, and so she'd let him go on and on, about securing his fellowship for the following semester, without putting a finger to her own chin as a signal. The fourth night, she said that she never liked the one poem he'd ever published in his life, in a literary magazine in Utah. He'd written the poem after meeting Shoba. She added that she found the poem sentimental.

88 Something happened when the house was dark. They were able to talk to each other again. The third night after supper they'd sat together on the sofa, and once it was dark he began kissing her awkwardly on her forehead and her face, though it was dark he closed his eyes, and knew that she did, too. The fourth night they walked carefully upstairs, to bed, feeling together for the final step with their feet before the landing, and making love with a desperation they had forgotten. She wept without sound, and whispered his name, and traced his eyebrows with her finger in the dark. As he made love to her he wondered what he would say to her the next night, and what she would say, the thought of it exciting him. "Hold me," he said, "hold me in your arms." By the time the lights came back on downstairs, they'd fallen asleep.

89 The morning of the fifth night Shukumar found another notice from the electric company in the mailbox. The line had been repaired ahead of schedule, it said. He was disappointed. He had planned on making shrimp *malai* for Shoba, but when he arrived at the store he didn't feel like cooking anymore. It wasn't the same, he thought, knowing that the lights wouldn't go out. In the store the shrimp looked gray and thin. The coconut milk tin was dusty and overpriced. Still, he bought them, along with a beeswax candle and two bottles of wine.

90 She came home at seven-thirty. "I suppose this is the end of our game," he said when he saw her reading the notice.

91 She looked at him. "You can still light candles if you want." She hadn't been to the gym tonight. She wore a suit beneath the raincoat. Her makeup had been retouched recently.

92 When she went upstairs to change, Shukumar poured himself some wine and put on a record, a Thelonious Monk album he knew she liked.

93 When she came downstairs they ate together. She didn't thank him or compliment him. They simply ate in a darkened room, in the glow of a beeswax candle. They had survived a difficult time. They finished off the shrimp. They finished off the first bottle of wine and moved on to the second. They sat together until the candle had nearly burned away. She shifted in her chair, and Shukumar thought that she was about to say something. But instead she blew out the candle, stood up, turned on the light switch, and sat down again.

94 "Shouldn't we keep the lights off?" Shukumar asked. She set her plate aside and clasped her hands on the table. "I want you to see my face when I tell you this," she said gently.

95 His heart began to pound. The day she told him she was pregnant, she had used the very same words, saying them in the same gentle way, turning off the basketball game he'd been watching on television. He hadn't been prepared then. Now he was.

96 Only he didn't want her to be pregnant again. He didn't want to have to pretend to be happy.

97 "I've been looking for an apartment and I've found one," she said, narrowing her eyes on something, it seemed, behind his left shoulder. It was nobody's fault, she continued. They'd been through enough. She needed some time alone. She had money saved up for a security deposit. The apartment was on Beacon Hill, so she could walk to work. She had signed the lease that night before coming home.

98 She wouldn't look at him, but he stared at her. It was obvious that she'd rehearsed the lines. All this time she'd been looking for an apartment, testing the water pressure, asking a Realtor if heat and hot water were included in the rent. It sickened Shukumar, knowing that she had spent these past evenings preparing for a life without him. He was relieved and yet he was sickened. This was what she'd been trying to tell him for the past four evenings. This was the point of her game.

Skill: Story Elements

Shukumar has to decide whether or not to tell Shoba the sex of their baby. He wanted to protect Shoba, but now that she has hurt him, he wants to hurt her back. The motivation to cause Shoba pain leads to the climax of the story.

99 Now it was his turn to speak. There was something he'd sworn he would never tell her, and for six months he had done his best to block it from his mind. Before the ultrasound she had asked the doctor not to tell her the sex of their child, and Shukumar had agreed. She had wanted it to be a surprise.

100 Later, those few times they talked about what had happened, she said at least they'd been spared that knowledge. In a way she almost took pride in her decision, for it enabled her to seek refuge in a mystery. He knew that she assumed it was a mystery for him, too. He'd arrived too late from Baltimore — when it was all over and she was lying on the hospital bed. But

Skills Focus

QUESTION 4: Summarizing

Shoba has something important to say to Shukumar. She explains that she has found an apartment just for herself and that she will be moving out of their house. She explains that the separation is not the fault of either of them.

Story Elements

How did the reader analyze the effect of Shukumar's motivations on the plot of the story?

The reader pays attention to the narrator's description of Shukumar's thoughts and infers that Shukumar wants to hurt Shoba, and so he decides to tell her about the sex of the baby. This leads to the climax of the story.

TEXT TALK

What information does Shoba give Shukumar at the end of the story? What information does he then give to her?

See Paragraphs 96–100: She tells him that she is moving out, and he tells her that their baby was a boy.

Prepare for Advanced Courses

Use the activity below to differentiate instruction for your B Beyond grade level learners.

Analyze for Enrichment

Have students consider this short story's title, "A Temporary Matter."

Ask students:

- How does the title contribute to your understanding of the text?
- What is temporary in Shoba and Shukumar's past and present?
- What might author Jhumpa Lahiri have intended for readers to learn from this story about temporary experiences? Use evidence from the text to support your analysis.

NOTES

he hadn't. He'd arrived early enough to see their baby, and to hold him before they cremated him. At first he had recoiled at the suggestion, but the doctor said holding the baby might help him with the process of grieving. Shoba was asleep. The baby had been cleaned off, his bulbous lids shut tight to the world.

101 "Our baby was a boy," he said. "His skin was more red than brown. He had black hair on his head. He weighed almost five pounds. His fingers were curled shut, just like yours in the night."

102 Shoba looked at him now, her face contorted with sorrow. He had cheated on a college exam, ripped a picture of a woman out of a magazine. He had returned a sweater and got drunk in the middle of the day instead. These were the things he had told her. He had held his son, who had known life only within her, against his chest in a darkened room in an unknown wing of the hospital. He had held him until a nurse knocked and took him away, and he promised himself that day that he would never tell Shoba, because he still loved her then, and it was the one thing in her life that she had wanted to be a surprise.

103 Shukumar stood up and stacked his plate on top of hers. He carried the plates to the sink, but instead of running the tap he looked out the window. Outside the evening was still warm, and the Bradfords were walking arm in arm. As he watched the couple the room went dark, and he spun around. Shoba had turned the lights off. She came back to the table and sat down, and after a moment Shukumar joined her. They wept together, for the things they now knew.

TEXT TALK

In what way did thinking about what makes a "true portrait" deepen your understanding of "A Temporary Matter"?

Answers will vary.

B Ask each Beyond grade-level student to write one additional discussion question. Then, have one or two students facilitate a discussion, using their questions to guide the conversation.

Reading Comprehension OPTIONAL

Have students complete the digital reading comprehension questions ✓ when they finish reading.

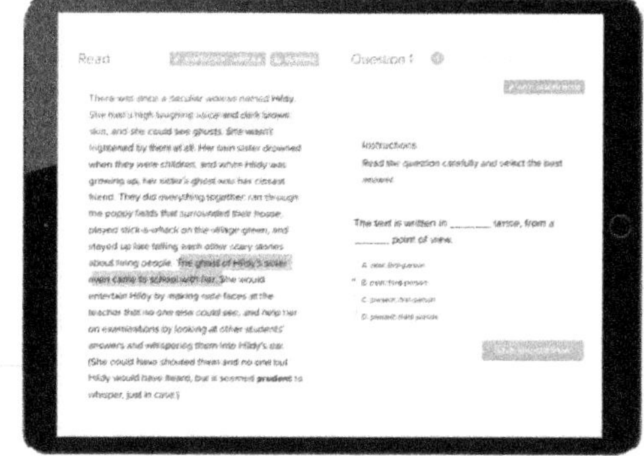

ANSWER KEY

QUESTION 1: D
QUESTION 2: B
QUESTION 3: C
QUESTION 4: A
QUESTION 5: B
QUESTION 6: C
QUESTION 7: B
QUESTION 8: C
QUESTION 9: *See first chart.*
QUESTION 10: *See second chart.*

Quote	Character
to gain or remove from	extract
to do while adhering to a specific system in place	methodically
the ability to accomplish, learn, or perform	capacity
hardworking; showing much effort	diligent
always	invariably

First	Second	Third	Fourth
Shukumar goes on a business trip to Baltimore.	Shoba and Shukumar's baby is born dead.	Shukumar and Shoba eat dinner in the dark and share their secrets with one another.	Shukumar tells Shoba their baby's gender and they both weep.

Connect and Extend OPTIONAL

CONNECT TO EXTENDED ORAL PROJECT

Students can use their written Close Read response to "A Temporary Matter" as practice for preparing and delivering a persuasive Extended Oral Project. They will get practice supporting an opinion with evidence as they craft their argumentative essay.

BEYOND THE BOOK

Performance: Life after Loss

Shukumar and Shoba navigate life together after losing their baby. Students will explore loss by creating a performance in which two people cope with and move beyond a significant loss.

Ask students to:

- Form acting troupes of four.
- Discuss loss and decide on a type of loss to focus on in their scene (e.g., loss of a friend or family member, loss of a pet, loss of a home).
- Design a scene in which the actors face this loss and use dialogue to move through the loss. The scene should explore the following questions:
  - What was lost?
  - How do each of the actors feel about the loss?
  - How are they coping with the loss?
  - What helps them navigate this hard situation?
  - What has this loss taught them about life or themselves?

To reflect, ask students:

- What are some of the ways people cope with loss? Which coping strategies are healthy and which are not?
- Why does loss sometimes divide people? How can loss bring people together?

Think Questions

Circulate as students answer Think Questions independently. Scaffolds for these questions are shown on the opposite page.

QUESTION 1: Textual Evidence

Shukumar does not have a good image of himself. He thinks he is probably a failure because he hasn't gotten launched into his career even though he is getting old; the text mentions his "anxiety that he was still a student at thirty-five."

QUESTION 2: Textual Evidence

Shoba and Shukumar begin spending their time apart after their baby dies. The text says they "had become experts at avoiding each other." These changes in their habits suggest that their relationship is starting to fall apart.

QUESTION 3: Textual Evidence

Shukumar loved and admired Shoba before the death of their baby. He was very impressed with her organizational skills, such as buying food in bulk. He also says her beauty "had once overwhelmed him."

QUESTION 4: Context Clues

The text says that Shukumar used to be "dedicated" to his work and lists time-consuming tasks like "summarizing chapters" and "outlining arguments on pads of yellow lined paper." These clues suggest that *diligent* must mean "hardworking."

QUESTION 5: Greek and Latin Roots and Affixes

I think *extract* must mean "remove." The prefix and root go together to mean "draw or pull from" or "take out of." In the text, the characters "extracted" bay leaves and cloves from the stew. They are removing spices and herbs from the stew.

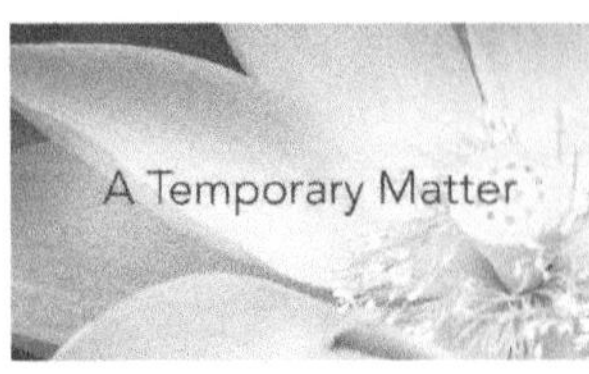

First Read

Read the short story "A Temporary Matter." After you read, complete the Think Questions below.

THINK QUESTIONS

1. How does Shukumar feel about himself? Why? Cite evidence from the story to support your answer.
2. What new habits do Shoba and Shukumar develop after the death of their baby, and what do these habits reveal about their relationship? Cite evidence from the story to support your answer.
3. How did Shukumar feel about Shoba before the death of their baby? What evidence from the text leads you to this conclusion?
4. Use context clues to determine the meaning of the word **diligent** as it is used in "A Temporary Matter." Write your definition of *diligent* here and explain which clues helped you figure it out.
5. Keeping in mind that the Latin prefix *ex-* means "from" and that the Latin root *-tract-* means "to draw or pull," determine the meaning of the word **extracted** as it is used in "A Temporary Matter." Write your definition of *extract* here and explain which clues helped you figure it out.

Think Questions

SCAFFOLDS

Use the scaffolds below to differentiate instruction for your ELL English Language Learners and A Approaching grade level readers.

ELL **BEGINNING** Write a response using the word bank and sentence frames.

INTERMEDIATE Write a response using the sentence frames.

ADVANCED, ADVANCED HIGH Write a response using the Text-Dependent Question Guide.

A **APPROACHING** Write a response using the Text-Dependent Question Guide.

BEGINNING	INTERMEDIATE	APPROACHING / ADVANCED, ADVANCED HIGH
Word Bank	**Sentence Frames**	**Text-Dependent Question Guide**
work bad notes	Shukumar feels ____ about himself. Shukumar has a hard time ____ his dissertation. Shukumar also feels bad that he is thirty-five and still a ____.	1. • How does Shukumar spend his time? • What does Shukumar worry about? • Do you think Shukumar likes his life? Why or why not?
rooms writing beautiful	After the baby dies, Shoba and Shukumar do not spend much time ____. Shukumar and Shoba eat in different ____. Shoba goes to ____ and Shukumar mostly stays ____.	2. • What do Shoba and Shukumar do together? • What do Shoba and Shukumar do separately? • Where does Shoba spend her day? Where does Shukumar spend his day?
dissertation take home	Before the baby dies, Shukumar ____ Shoba. Shukumar thinks that Shoba is ____ and ____.	3. • What did Shukumar think about the way Shoba ran the house? • What did Shukumar think about Shoba's appearance? • How did Shukumar react when he first met Shoba?
admire remove together organized	Shukumar used to spend a lot of time taking ____ about his work. This gives me a clue that *diligent* means ____.	4. • Read: "Until September he had been **diligent** if not dedicated, summarizing chapters, outlining arguments on pads of yellow lined paper." • What actions are described in the sentence? • What does that suggest about the meaning of the word *diligent*?
hardworking	*Extract* as used in the text means to ____. The characters ____ bay leaves and cloves out of the stew.	5. • Read: "They served themselves, stirring the rice with their forks, squinting as they extracted bay leaves and cloves from the stew." • What is the meaning of *ex-*? • What is the meaning of *-tract-*? • What are the characters doing?

Skill: Theme

Introduce the Skill

Watch the Concept Definition video and read the following definition with your students.

The **topic** of a literary work is the subject of the work. It is usually expressed as a noun. The **theme** is the central idea or message of a work of literature. It is often expressed as a general statement about life. For example, the topic of a literary work might be love. The theme would be what the writer suggests about love: that it is wonderful or painful or maybe both at once. A literary work may have more than one theme.

Sometimes a writer states a theme directly. More often, though, theme is revealed gradually. In short stories, novels, and dramas, theme is revealed through elements such as character, setting, and plot, what the characters do and say, and how these elements affect the events that take place. When a theme is not stated directly, a reader will have to **infer** the theme. To infer means to determine something by using reasoning and textual evidence.

Skill: Theme

Use the Checklist to analyze Theme in "A Temporary Matter." Refer to the sample student annotations about Theme in the text.

CHECKLIST FOR THEME

In order to identify two or more themes or central ideas of a text, note the following:

- ✓ the subject and how it relates to the themes in the text
- ✓ if one or more themes is stated directly in the text
- ✓ details in the text that help to reveal each theme:
  - the title and chapter headings
  - details about the setting
  - the narrator's or speaker's tone
  - characters' thoughts, actions, and dialogue
  - the central conflict, climax, and resolution of the conflict
  - shifts in characters, setting, or plot events
- ✓ when the themes interact with each other

To determine two or more themes or central ideas of a text and analyze their development over the course of the text, including how they interact and build on one another to produce a complex account, consider the following questions:

- ✓ What are the themes in the text? When do they emerge?
- ✓ How does each theme develop over the course of the text?
- ✓ How do the themes interact and build on one another?

TURN AND TALK

1. What was the theme of the last movie you watched?
2. How did the characterization, setting, point of view, and/or plot contribute to that theme?

SPEAKING FRAMES

- The theme of the last movie I watched is ____.
- The characterization / setting / point of view / plot contributed to the theme by ____.

SKILL VOCABULARY

topic / el tema ***noun*** the subject of a literary work, usually expressed as a single word or phrase in the form of a noun

theme / el tema ***noun*** the central idea or message of a work of literature, often expressed as a general statement about life COGNATE

infer / inferir ***verb*** to determine something by using reasoning and evidence from the text COGNATE

Skill:
Theme

Reread paragraphs 94–99 of "A Temporary Matter." Then, using the Checklist on the previous page, answer the multiple-choice questions below.

YOUR TURN

1. Which statement best analyzes the theme that is revealed by details like characters' thoughts, setting, and narrator's tone in this passage?
   - A. The change in the setting creates a homey feeling that becomes a safe space for Shoba to reveal her subjective point of view and prepares readers for the story's happy ending.
   - B. The shift in point of view from Shukumar's thoughts to Shoba's point of view jars the reader, mirroring the abrupt change in focus from present to past events.
   - C. The story's surprise ending is foreshadowed by the narrator's revelation of Shukumar's secret, which takes readers from the couple's home to a hospital.
   - D. The third-person limited point of view helps readers understand Shukumar's reaction to learning the truth, which is heightened by the sudden change from darkness to light.

2. This question has two parts. First, answer Part A. Then, answer Part B.

   Part A: What theme is strongly suggested by details like characterization, setting, point of view, and plot events in this passage?
   - A. People rarely keep secrets.
   - B. You cannot hide from the truth.
   - C. Bad news hurts less when revealed slowly.
   - D. Spouses sometimes need to lie to each other.

   Part B: Which evidence best supports the answer chosen in Part A?
   - A. Before the ultrasound she had asked the doctor not to tell her the sex of their child . . .
   - B. "Shouldn't we keep the lights off?" Shukumar asked. She set her plate aside and clasped her hands on the table. "I want you to see my face when I tell you this," she said gently.
   - C. He was relieved and yet he was sickened. This was what she'd been trying to tell him for the past four evenings.
   - D. ". . . and for six months he had done his best to block it from his mind."

SkillsTV

Project the SkillsTV episode and pause at the following times to prompt discussion:

1:59 What strategies do the students use to determine the theme of the text from the first paragraph? Consider the benefits of analyzing theme early in a text and discuss how this might or might not aid your understanding of a story.

3:12 How do students make a connection between characterization, setting, and plot and a shift in mood in the story?

3:35 What conclusion do the students make about the theme of the story based on what they've read so far? How should they continue to analyze theme as they read further in the story?

Your Turn

Ask students to complete the Your Turn Activity.

QUESTION 1

A. Incorrect. The story does not shift to Shoba's point of view or evoke a homey feeling.

B. Incorrect. The story does not shift to Shoba's point of view.

C. Incorrect. The surprise ending brought about by Shoba's secret is revealed before Shukumar's secret is revealed.

D. Correct. The statement best analyzes the the theme revealed by details like characters' thoughts, setting, and narrator's tone in this passage.

QUESTION 2

Part A

A. Incorrect. Rather, the characters in the story keep significant secrets from one another.

B. Correct. This theme is developed in details like characterization, setting, point of view, and plot events in the passage.

C. Incorrect. There is no evidence to support this theme.

D. Incorrect. While evidence in the text supports this theme, it is not the best answer for Part A.

QUESTION 2

Part B

A. Incorrect. This evidence does not best support the correct answer in Part A.

B. Incorrect. This evidence does not best support the correct answer in Part A.

C. Correct. Shoba initiates the game as a way to reveal the truth of her departure, and Shukumar is both relieved and sickened because he could no longer hide from the truth either.

D. Incorrect. This evidence does not best support the correct answer in Part A.

Skill: Story Elements

Introduce the Skill

Watch the Concept Definition video and read the following definition with your students.

A **story element** is something that contributes to a work of fiction or drama, one of several "building blocks" that make it effective. Story elements usually include **setting**, **character**, **plot** and **subplots**, **theme** and **point of view**. The way an author introduces each of these elements into a **narrative**, and connects them so that one has an effect on another, is what can make a story memorable. For example, the setting—a blizzard, or a raft in the middle of the ocean—can affect the events of the plot, which in turn can have an effect on the characters and their relationship to one another. This can influence the conflict the characters face and, as a result, shape the theme.

Skill: Story Elements

Use the Checklist to analyze Story Elements in "A Temporary Matter." Refer to the sample student annotations about Story Elements in the text.

••• CHECKLIST FOR STORY ELEMENTS

In order to identify the impact of the author's choices regarding how to develop and relate elements of a story or drama, note the following:

- ✓ where and when the story takes place, who the main characters are, and the main conflict, or problem, in the plot
- ✓ the order of the action
- ✓ how the characters are introduced and developed
- ✓ the impact that the author's choice of setting has on the characters and their attempt to solve the problem
- ✓ the point of view the author uses, and how this shapes what readers know about the characters in the story

To analyze the impact of the author's choices regarding how to develop and relate elements of a story or drama, consider the following questions:

- ✓ How does the author's choices affect the story elements? The development of the plot?
- ✓ How does the setting influence the characters?
- ✓ Which elements of the setting impact the plot, and in particular the problem the characters face and must solve?
- ✓ Are there any flashbacks or other story elements that have an effect on the development of events in the plot? How does the author's choice of utilizing a flashback affect this development?
- ✓ How does the author introduce and develop characters in the story? Why do you think they made these choices?

TURN AND TALK

1. What is an example of a story from a book, TV show, or movie that is complex and believable?
2. What makes a story complex and believable?
3. What choices did the creator or author likely make that impacted the development of the story?

ELL SPEAKING FRAMES

- An example of a complex, believable story is ____.
- A story is complex and believable when ____.
- The creator/author likely ____ in order to make the story complex and believable.

SKILL VOCABULARY

story elements / el elemento del cuento ***noun*** a "building block" that contributes to a work of fiction or drama, such as character or setting

setting / el escenario ***noun*** the time and place of the story

character / el personaje ***noun*** an individual in a literary work whose thoughts, feelings, actions, and reactions move the action of the plot forward

plot / la trama ***noun*** the sequence of events that form a story

Skill: Story Elements

Reread paragraph 84 of "A Temporary Matter." Then, using the Checklist on the previous page, answer the multiple-choice questions below.

YOUR TURN

1. The narrator reveals that Shukumar originally lies to Shoba about what really happened to the sweater vest because—

- ○ A. he wants Shoba to feel embarrassed about the gift.
- ○ B. he knows that Shoba would want to share the money.
- ○ C. he thinks the truth would make Shoba hurt or angry.
- ○ D. he thinks it is funny to lie to Shoba about small things.

2. How does Shukumar's decision to tell Shoba the truth affect the plot of the story?

- ○ A. It shows that Shukumar is becoming more willing to talk about difficult things with his wife.
- ○ B. It reveals that Shukumar is unloving and does not care how the truth might affect Shoba.
- ○ C. It foreshadows that Shoba may do something that will be hurtful to her husband.
- ○ D. It indicates that Shukumar regrets marrying Shoba and staying married to her.

SKILL VOCABULARY

subplot / la trama secundaria *noun* a secondary plot strand that supports the main plot, often involving secondary or minor characters

theme / el tema *noun* the central idea or message of a work of literature, often expressed as a general statement about life COGNATE

point of view / el punto de vista *noun* the standpoint, or perspective, from which a story is told COGNATE

narrative / la narración *noun* a story, real or imagined, consisting of connected events COGNATE

Your Turn

Ask students to complete the Your Turn Activity.

QUESTION 1

A. Incorrect. The opposite is true; Shukumar lies because he doesn't want Shoba to know how much he disliked her present.

B. Incorrect. There is no evidence to support this idea.

C. Correct. Shukumar lies to avoid hurting Shoba's feelings.

D. Incorrect. There is no evidence to support this idea.

QUESTION 2

A. Correct. Shukumar finds that being honest about moral questions, such as whether to tell Shoba about the sweater vest, makes him feel closer to her.

B. Incorrect. Shukumar may not love Shoba as much as he used to, but he does not tell the story to hurt her or to make her feel bad.

C. Incorrect. This story does not foreshadow Shoba's actions.

D. Incorrect. Though the bartender attributes the unwelcome gift to the fact that Shukumar is married, there is no indication that Shukumar would rather be single at this point in the story.

Close Read

Skills Focus

QUESTION 1: Theme

See paragraph 12.

QUESTION 2: Story Elements

See paragraph 19.

QUESTION 3: Story Elements

See paragraphs 69–70.

QUESTION 4: Summarizing

See paragraphs 93–96.

QUESTION 5: Connect to Essential Question

See paragraphs 11–13.

CHECK FOR SUCCESS

If students struggle to respond to Skills Focus Question #1, ask students the following questions:

1. How does Shoba spend her weekends?
2. How does Shukumar feel about Shoba after the death of their child?
3. What does this suggest about why relationships change?

Close Read

Reread "A Temporary Matter." As you reread, complete the Skills Focus questions below. Then use your answers and annotations from the questions to help you complete the Write activity.

SKILLS FOCUS

1. Identify a passage in which the third-person narrator reveals Shukumar's perspective on how the characters' daily lives have changed after the death of their child. Explain how this passage develops a theme relating to changing relationships.
2. Highlight a section of the text that describes Shoba's behavior before the death of the child. Explain how the description of this behavior contributes to the reader's understanding of Shoba's character and contributes to the plot of the story.
3. Identify details that show how the setting affects characterization. Explain which details you think are particularly effective in developing a character and why.
4. Find a scene in which Shoba tells Shukumar something that she has been keeping from him. Summarize what happens in the scene.
5. What effect does a change in routine have on the characters in "A Temporary Matter"? Does it cause them to change? Or, does it help them realize that change has already happened?

WRITE

ARGUMENTATIVE ESSAY: Critic Christopher Tayler once described Jhumpa Lahiri's stories in this way: "Unflashily written, long, almost grave in tone, her new stories patiently accumulate detail, only gradually building up a powerful emotional charge." Do you agree that "A Temporary Matter" is like this? Examine the traits named and find passages of the story that either prove or contradict Tayler's opinion.

Writer's Notebook

Connect to Essential Question: Give students time to reflect on how "A Temporary Matter" connects to the unit's essential question "How are we shaped by change?" by freewriting in their Writer's Notebooks.

Beginning & Intermediate

Read aloud the unit's essential question: "How are we shaped by change?" Encourage students to draw their connections or allow students to write in their native language. Circulate around the room, prompting students for their thoughts as they respond orally or through pantomime.

Advanced & Advanced High

Allow students to share their connections orally in pairs or small groups before freewriting.

Collaborative Conversation

SCAFFOLDS

Break students into collaborative conversation groups to discuss the Close Read prompt. Ask students to use the StudySyncTV episode as a model for their discussion. Remind them to reference their Skills Focus annotations in their discussion.

Critic Christopher Tayler once described Jhumpa Lahiri's stories in this way: "Unflashily written, long, almost grave in tone, her new stories patiently accumulate detail, only gradually building up a powerful emotional charge." Do you agree that "A Temporary Matter" is like this? Examine the traits named and find passages of the story that either prove or contradict Tayler's opinion.

Use the scaffolds below to differentiate instruction for your ELL English Language Learners and A Approaching grade-level learners.

ELL **BEGINNING, INTERMEDIATE** Use the discussion guide and speaking frames to facilitate the discussion with support from the teacher.

ADVANCED, ADVANCED HIGH Use the discussion guide and speaking frames to facilitate the discussion in mixed-level groups.

A **APPROACHING** Use the discussion guide to facilitate the discussion in mixed-level groups.

APPROACHING
ADVANCED, ADVANCED HIGH
BEGINNING, INTERMEDIATE

Discussion Guide	Speaking Frames
1. How would you describe the tone of "A Temporary Matter?" How does the author build that tone?	• The tone of the story is ____. • Details like ____ and ____ build this tone.
2. What change occurs in the story? How would you describe the change?	• A change that happens in the story is ____. • I would describe the change as ____.
3. Do you think the story fits Tayler's description? Why or why not?	• I think the story does / does not fit Tayler's description • This is my opinion because ____.

Multiple Perspectives

Use the activity below to differentiate instruction for your B Beyond grade level learners.

Reread the end of paragraph 102:

He had held him until a nurse knocked and took him away, and he promised himself that day that he would never tell Shoba, because he still loved her then, and it was the one thing in her life that she had wanted to be a surprise.

Direct students to identify Shukumar's motives in this moment. Ask students:

- How does Shukumar's decision to tell Shoba about holding their son reveal his current perspective?
- How will Shukumar's and Shoba's differing perspectives on this issue affect their relationship?

Review Prompt and Rubric

Before students begin writing, review the writing prompt and rubric with the class.

LITERARY ANALYSIS: Critic Christopher Tayler once described Jhumpa Lahiri's stories in this way: "Unflashily written, long, almost grave in tone, her new stories patiently accumulate detail, only gradually building up a powerful emotional charge." Do you agree that "A Temporary Matter" is like this? Examine the traits named and find passages of the story that either prove or contradict Tayler's opinion.

PROMPT GUIDE

- How would you describe the tone of "A Temporary Matter?" How does the author build that tone?
- What change occurs in the story? How would you describe the change?
- Do you think the story fits Tayler's description? Why or why not?

Score	Story Elements	Language and Conventions
4	The writer clearly analyzes and explains whether the story elements in "A Temporary Matter" fits Tayler's description. The writer provides exemplary analysis, using relevant textual evidence.	The writer demonstrates a consistent command of grammar, punctuation, and usage conventions. Although minor errors may be evident, they do not detract from the fluency or the clarity of the essay.
3	The writer analyzes and explains whether the story elements in "A Temporary Matter" fits Tayler's description. The writer provides sufficient analysis, using relevant textual evidence most of the time.	The writer demonstrates an adequate command of grammar, punctuation, and usage conventions. Although some errors may be evident, they create few (if any) disruptions in the fluency of the writing or the clarity of the essay.
2	The writer begins to analyze or explain whether the story elements in "A Temporary Matter" fits Tayler's description, but the analysis is incomplete. The writer uses relevant textual evidence only some of the time	The writer demonstrates a partial command of grammar, punctuation, and usage conventions. Some distracting errors may be evident, at times creating minor disruptions in the fluency or clarity of the writing.
1	The writer attempts to analyze or explain whether the story elements in "A Temporary Matter" fits Tayler's description, but the analysis is not successful. The writer uses little or no relevant textual evidence.	The writer demonstrates little or no command of grammar, punctuation, and usage conventions. Serious and persistent errors create disruptions in the fluency of the writing and sometimes interfere with meaning.
0	The writer does not provide a relevant response to the prompt or does not provide a response at all.	Serious and persistent errors overwhelm the writing and interfere with the meaning of the response as a whole, making the writer's meaning impossible to understand.

SCAFFOLDS

Write

Ask students to complete the writing assignment using text evidence to support their answers.

Use the scaffolds below to differentiate instruction for your ELL English Language Learners and A Approaching grade level readers.

ELL **BEGINNING** With the help of the word bank, write a response using paragraph frame 1.

INTERMEDIATE With the help of the word bank, write a response using paragraph frames 1 and 2.

ADVANCED, ADVANCED HIGH Write a response of differentiated length using the sentence starters.

A **APPROACHING** Write a response of differentiated length using the sentence starters.

BEGINNING | INTERMEDIATE | ADVANCED, ADVANCED HIGH | APPROACHING

Word Bank	Paragraph Frame 1	Paragraph Frame 2	Sentence Starters
unexpected hopeful closer sad avoid	"A Temporary Matter" does / does not fit Christopher Tayler's description. Overall, the tone of the story is ____, but at times it is almost ____. The way the narrator describes the way the couple ____ each other causes an emotional response in readers. However, the way the characters grow ____ as they play their nightly game hints that the ending may be happy. The story's ending is powerful because it is ____.	Another way that the story does / does not fit Tayler's description is ____. For example, ____. This shows that the tone is ____. Likewise, the changes the characters face are ____. This suggests that ____.	• The story does / does not fit the description because . . . • Tayler says ________, and I agree / disagree because . . . • One example in the story is . . . • Another example is . . .

Peer Review

Students should submit substantive feedback to two peers using the review instructions below.

- How well does this response answer the prompt?
- How well does the writer support his or her conclusion with textual evidence?
- Which sentence in the writer's response made you think differently about the text?
- What does the writer do well in this response? How could the writer improve his or her work?

Remember that your comments are most useful when they are kind and constructive.

Rate

Respond to the following with a point rating that reflects your opinion.

	1	2	3	4
Ideas				
Evidence				
Language and Conventions				

Submit

ELL A SENTENCE FRAMES

- You (completely / partly / almost) ____ answered the prompt because ____.
- You could answer the prompt more completely by ____.
- You cited the detail ____ to support your idea that ____.
- One idea you expressed well is ____.
- One idea that needs clarification is ____.

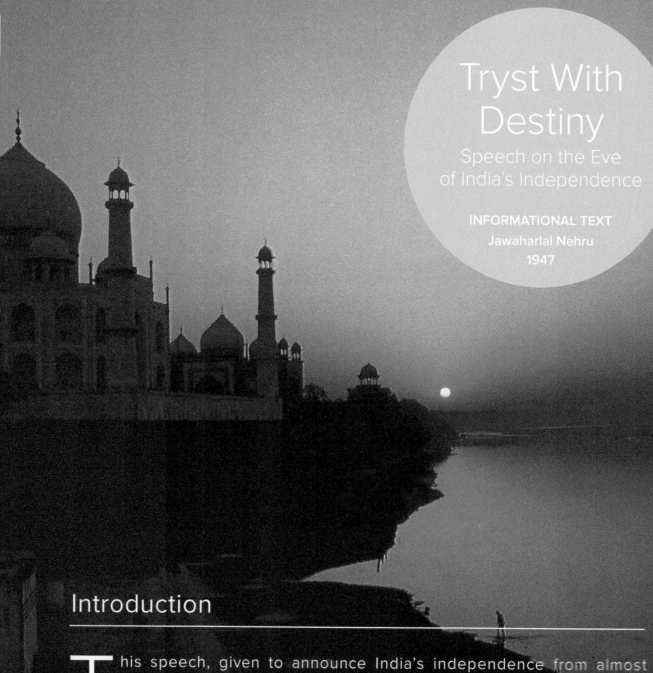

Tryst With Destiny

Speech on the Eve of India's Independence

INFORMATIONAL TEXT
Jawaharlal Nehru
1947

Introduction

This speech, given to announce India's independence from almost 200 years of British rule, was delivered to Parliament by Jawaharlal Nehru (1889-1964), the man who would become India's first prime minister. After studying law at Cambridge, Nehru returned to India, where he eventually became Mohandas Gandhi's successor. Nehru's daughter, Indira Gandhi, who later became prime minister of India, was the first and only woman to hold the post. In this triumphant address, Jawaharlal Nehru celebrates Indian victory, but also earnestly urges his fellow patriots to consider the kind of future they intend to forge for their country.

Jawaharlal Nehru states that at midnight, India will be free from British rule and will step out into a new life. With this freedom, comes great responsibility, and so, the people should strive to live up to the ideals that gave them the strength to break free. These ideals include the end of poverty, ignorance, disease, and inequality across all of India. Nehru asks the people to join him in this struggle and to have faith that all these things can be achieved. He reminds them of Ghandi's message and how the following generations will surely be guided by it. He also asks them to remember all their brothers and sisters who are not present to share in the spirit of independence. Nehru ends the speech stating that no matter what religion they belong to, everyone is a child of India and is responsible for achieving the aspirations of independence. Therefore, everyone must avoid factionalism and narrow-mindedness.

Proficiency-leveled summaries and summaries in multiple languages are available digitally.

Audio and audio text highlighting are available with this text.

CONNECT TO ESSENTIAL QUESTION

How are we shaped by change?

"Tryst with Destiny," a speech by Jawaharlal Nehru, addresses the citizens of a newly independent India. This speech helps students consider how large-scale change on a national level can affect the people of a particular country.

Entry Point

As students prepare to read "Tryst with Destiny," share the following information with them to provide context.

- ✓ Jawaharlal Nehru was a freedom fighter and an important political figure in India from the 1930s until his death in 1964. He was born into the highest Hindu social class, the Brahmin caste. His father was a lawyer and worked closely with Mohandas (Mahatma) Gandhi in the Indian independence movement.
- ✓ Nehru was tutored at home until he reached the age of 16, when he left to study in England for seven years. This experience left him feeling at home in both countries. Nehru became closer to Gandhi after Nehru's father died in 1931. The two leaders had very different approaches to politics. Gandhi maintained a religious and traditional attitude; Nehru was secular and modernist.
- ✓ The Indian Independence Act was passed by Britain's Parliament in 1947. The act created two independent nations: India and Pakistan.

These icons identify differentiation strategies and scaffolded support for a variety of students. See the digital lesson plan for additional differentiation strategies and scaffolds.

Instructional Path

The print teacher's edition includes essential point-of-use instruction and planning tools. Complete lesson plans and program documents appear in your digital teacher account.

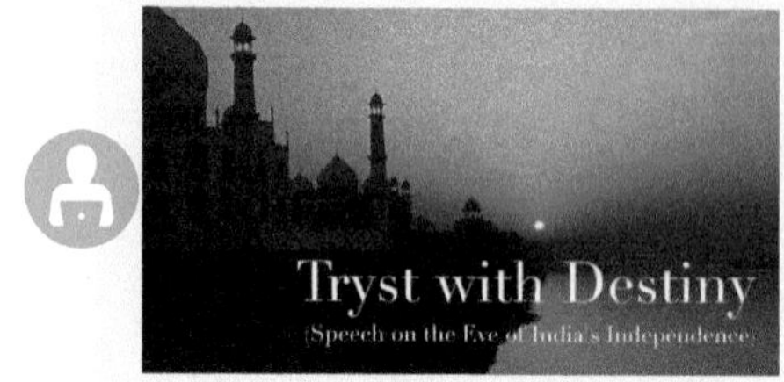

Tryst with Destiny
Speech on the Eve of India's Independence

Independent Read: Tryst with Destiny

Objectives: After reading "Tryst with Destiny," students will be able to write a short response that explains how rhetorical devices in the speech affect its audience.

Blast: Juggling Justices

Objectives: After exploring background information and research links about a topic, students will respond to a question with a 140-character response.

Independent Read

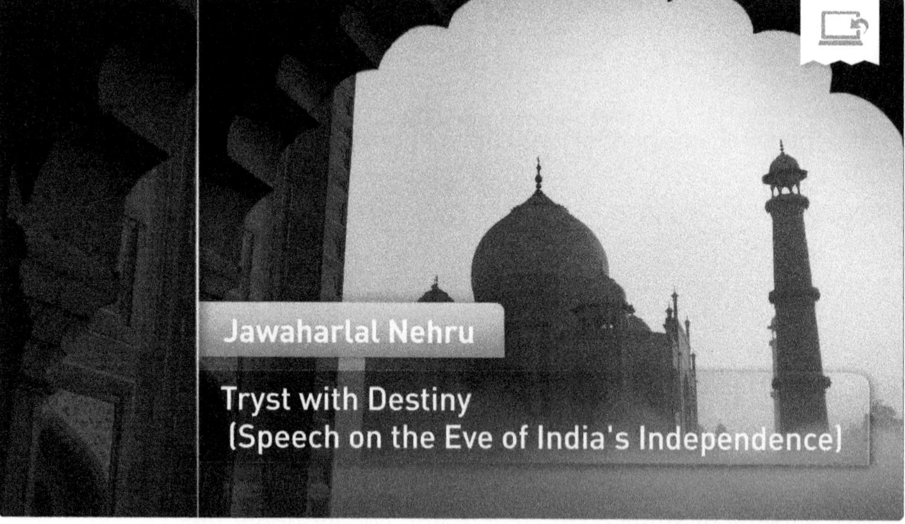

Introduce the Text

As a class, watch the video preview and have students read the introduction in pairs to make connections to the video preview.

- What part of the video stood out to you the most?
- How does the information in the introduction help you understand something about postcolonial India you didn't know before?

ELL **SPEAKING FRAMES**

- The part of the video that stood out was ____.
- The introduction helped me understand ____.

Access Complex Text

LEXILE: 1230 **WORD COUNT:** 1,096

The following areas may be challenging for students, particularly ELL English Language Learners and A Approaching grade-level learners. Connection of Ideas. Prior Knowledge.See the digital lesson plan for more details.

"We end today a period of ill fortune and India discovers herself again."

NOTES

I

School children in front of Red Fort on the 72nd Independence Day, on August 15, 2018 in New Delhi, India.

1 Long years ago we made a tryst with destiny, and now the time comes when we shall redeem our pledge, not wholly or in full measure, but very substantially. At the stroke of the midnight hour, when the world sleeps, India will awake to life and freedom. A moment comes, which comes but rarely in history, when we step out from the old to the new, when an age ends, and when the soul of a nation, long suppressed, finds **utterance**. It is fitting that at this solemn moment we take the pledge of dedication to the service of India and her people and to the still larger cause of humanity.

2 At the dawn of history India started on her unending quest, and trackless centuries are filled with her striving and the grandeur of her success and her failures. Through good and ill fortune alike she has never lost sight of that quest or forgotten the ideals which gave her strength. We end today a period of ill fortune and India discovers herself again. The achievement we celebrate today is but a step, an opening of opportunity, to the greater triumphs and achievements that await us. Are we brave enough and wise enough to grasp this opportunity and accept the challenge of the future?

3 Freedom and power bring responsibility. The responsibility rests upon this Assembly, a **sovereign** body representing the sovereign people of India. Before the birth of freedom we have endured all the pains of labour and our hearts are heavy with the memory of this sorrow. Some of those pains continue even now. Nevertheless, the past is over and it is the future that beckons to us now.

4 That future is not one of ease or resting but of **incessant** striving so that we may fulfil the pledges we have so often taken and the one we shall take

Developing Background Knowledge and Cultural Awareness

Find out what your students already know about India.

1. In small groups, have students do a five-minute online search of keywords related to India's Independence Day.
2. On the board, collate the various types of information students learned. Ask one student to volunteer to create an instant summary.

Discuss with students: In the speech, Prime Minister, Jawaharlal Nehru describes "a turning point" and explains how such a point has passed with India's Independence Day. What factors do you think led up to the turning point? What responsibilities and burdens accompany a country in the midst of a turning point?

SELECTION VOCABULARY

utterance / la mención *noun* speech, spoken words

sovereign / soberano/a *adjective* having unlimited authority

incessant / incesante *adjective* continuing, unending COGNATE

TEXT TALK

What does Nehru say will happen "at the stroke of midnight"? What does he mean?

See paragraph 1: He says, "India will awake to life and freedom." He means Indians will be independent, not British subjects.

today. The service of India means the service of the millions who suffer. It means the ending of poverty and **ignorance** and disease and inequality of opportunity. The ambition of the greatest man of our generation has been to wipe every tear from every eye. That may be beyond us, but as long as there are tears and suffering, so long our work will not be over.

5 And so we have to labour and to work, and work hard, to give reality to our dreams. Those dreams are for India, but they are also for the world, for all the nations and peoples are too closely knit together today for any one of them to imagine that it can live apart. Peace has been said to be indivisible; so is freedom, so is prosperity now, and so also is disaster in this One World that can no longer be split into isolated fragments.

6 To the people of India, whose representatives we are, we make an appeal to join us with faith and confidence in this great adventure. This is no time for petty and destructive criticism, no time for ill-will or blaming others. We have to build the noble mansion of free India where all her children may dwell.

II

7 The appointed day has come-the day appointed by destiny-and India stands forth again, after long slumber and struggle, awake, vital, free and independent. The past clings on to us still in some measure and we have to do much before we redeem the pledges we have so often taken. Yet the turning-point is past, and history begins anew for us, the history which we shall live and act and others will write about.

8 It is a fateful moment for us in India, for all Asia and for the world. A new star rises, the star of freedom in the East, a new hope comes into being, a vision long cherished materializes. May the star never set and that hope never be betrayed!

9 We rejoice in that freedom, even though clouds surround us, and many of our people are sorrowstricken and difficult problems encompass us. But freedom brings responsibilities and burdens and we have to face them in the spirit of a free and disciplined people.

10 On this day our first thoughts go to the architect of this freedom, the Father of our Nation [Gandhi], who, embodying the old spirit of India, held aloft the torch of freedom and lighted up the darkness that surrounded us. We have often been unworthy followers of his and have strayed from his message, but not only we but succeeding generations will remember this message and bear the imprint in their hearts of this great son of India, magnificent in his faith and strength and courage and humility. We shall never allow that torch of freedom to be blown out, however high the wind or stormy the tempest.

TEXT TALK

According to Nehru, who is "the Father" of India? How did he earn this honor?

See paragraph 10: Gandhi is the Father of India. He "held aloft the torch of freedom and lighted up the darkness that surrounded" India.

SELECTION VOCABULARY

ignorance / la ignorancia ***noun*** lack of knowledge about something COGNATE

NOTES

11 Our next thoughts must be of the unknown volunteers and soldiers of freedom who, without praise or reward, have served India even unto death.

12 We think also of our brothers and sisters who have been cut off from us by political boundaries and who unhappily cannot share at present in the freedom that has come. They are of us and will remain of us whatever may happen, and we shall be sharers in their good [or] ill fortune alike.

13 The future beckons to us. Whither do we go and what shall be our endeavour? To bring freedom and opportunity to the common man, to the peasants and workers of India; to fight and end poverty and ignorance and disease; to build up a prosperous, democratic and progressive nation, and to create social, economic and political institutions which will ensure justice and fullness of life to every man and woman.

14 We have hard work ahead. There is no resting for any one of us till we redeem our pledge in full, till we make all the people of India what destiny intended them to be. We are citizens of a great country on the verge of bold advance, and we have to live up to that high standard. All of us, to whatever religion we may belong, are equally the children of India with equal rights, privileges and obligations. We cannot encourage communalism[1] or narrow-mindedness, for no nation can be great whose people are narrow in thought or in action.

15 To the nations and peoples of the world we send greetings and pledge ourselves to cooperate with them in furthering peace, freedom and democracy.

16 And to India, our much-loved motherland, the ancient, the eternal and the ever-new, we pay our **reverent** homage and we bind ourselves afresh to her service.

JAI HIND

WRITE

RHETORICAL ANALYSIS: Write an essay explaining what makes this speech memorable and important. Why is it "recognized as one of the greatest of the 20th century"? Identify the audience and what the speaker wants from them. How do rhetorical devices such as personification and repetition likely affect the crowd's emotions?

1. **communalism** a system that encourages loyalty to narrower communities or identities over an allegiance to society writ large

Prepare for Advanced Courses

Use the activity below to differentiate instruction for your B Beyond grade level learners.

Analyze for Enrichment

Direct students to reread the speech and identify examples of figurative language (metaphor, personification, symbolism). Have them discuss the purposes of these instances of figurative language, using evidence in the text to support their answers.

Ask students:

- How does Nehru's use of figurative language impact your reading of the speech?
- How does the figurative language assist in conveying the speech's central message?

SELECTION VOCABULARY

reverent / reverente *adjective* showing deep respect for something or someone COGNATE

TEXT TALK

How did learning about India's Independence Day help you understand the speech?

Answers will vary.

Writer's Notebook

Connect to Literary Focus: Give students time to reflect on how "Tryst with Destiny" demonstrates the conventions and characteristics of this unit's literary focus, postmodernism and postcolonialism, by freewriting in their Writer's Notebooks.

CHECK FOR SUCCESS

If students are still struggling, ask them:

- What does Nehru say outright about colonialism in the speech? What does he imply?

Reading Comprehension OPTIONAL

Have students complete the digital reading comprehension questions ✓ when they finish reading.

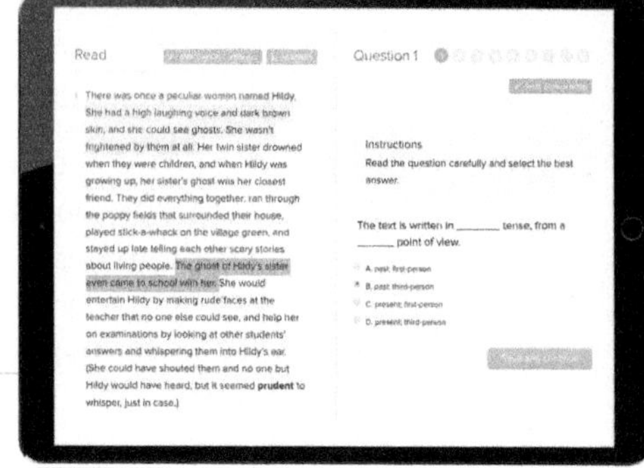

ANSWER KEY

QUESTION 1: A
QUESTION 2: D
QUESTION 3: B
QUESTION 4: B
QUESTION 5: D
QUESTION 6: C
QUESTION 7: A
QUESTION 8: C
QUESTION 9: *See first chart*
QUESTION 10: *See second chart*

Synonym	Word
unrelenting	incessant
expression	utterance
unenlightened	ignorant
respectful	reverent
autonomous	sovereign

First	Second	Third	Fourth
Nehru announces the beginning of a new independence and freedom.	Nehru discusses the responsibility of the Assembly that accompanies the freedom to self-govern.	Nehru invokes Gandhi, in order to encourage his audience to continue the leader's fight for freedom.	Nehru makes a vow to his own country to commit himself to service in its name.

Connect and Extend OPTIONAL

CONNECT TO EXTENDED ORAL PROJECT

Students can use "Tryst with Destiny" as a text that gives voice to the marginalized and ignored people of postcolonial nations to aid in reflection on what is most valuable to them in their lives today that wasn't covered, addressed, or emphasized enough in their formal studies so far.

BEYOND THE BOOK

Art: Rights and Responsibilities

Look at this line:

"But freedom brings responsibilities and burdens and we have to face them in the spirit of a free and disciplined people."

Students will discuss and analyze the connections between responsibilities and freedom.

Ask students to:

- Brainstorm a list of freedoms or rights we enjoy as U.S. citizens.
- Choose one from the list to focus on.
- In small groups, discuss the freedom or right that was chosen and the responsibilities that come with it.
    - > What is required for this right or freedom to be exercised?
    - > How does having this right create a responsibility?
    - > What is the connection between other people's rights and your responsibilities?
- Create a graphic that identifies and explains the right they have selected and outlines the responsibilities associated with that right.
- Share with classmates.

To reflect, ask students:

- What do our legal rights have to do with justice and fairness?
- To what extent do our freedoms and responsibilities reflect our society and culture?

Collaborative Conversation

SCAFFOLDS

Post the writing prompt to generate a discussion in small groups. Ask students to first break down the prompt before they discuss relevant ideas and textual evidence.

Write an essay explaining what makes this speech memorable and important. Why is it "recognized as one of the greatest of the 20th century"? Identify the audience and what the speaker wants from them. How do rhetorical devices such as personification and repetition likely affect the crowd's emotions?

Use the scaffolds below to differentiate instruction for your ELL English Language Learners and A Approaching grade-level learners.

ELL **BEGINNING, INTERMEDIATE** Use the discussion guide and speaking frames to facilitate the discussion with support from the teacher.

ADVANCED, ADVANCED HIGH Use the discussion guide and speaking frames to facilitate the discussion in mixed-level groups.

A APPROACHING Use the discussion guide to facilitate the discussion in mixed-level groups.

APPROACHING
ADVANCED, ADVANCED HIGH
BEGINNING, INTERMEDIATE

Discussion Guide	Speaking Frames
1. Who is Nehru addressing? What does he want from them?	• Nehru is addressing ____. • He wants them to ____.
2. What rhetorical devices does he use? How do they affect his audience?	• Two rhetorical devices in the speech are ____ and ____. • hey affect his audience because ____.
3. What makes this speech memorable and important?	• I think the speech is memorable because ____. • I think it is important because ____.

Text to World

Use the activity below to differentiate instruction for your B Beyond grade level learners.

Consider the main points and promises Jawaharlal Nehru makes in his speech.

Have students conduct informal research about other speeches given by leaders of newly independent countries.

Ask students:

- How do the points and promises in Nehru's compare to those made by these other leaders?

Review Prompt and Rubric

Before students begin writing, review the writing prompt and rubric with the class.

RHETORICAL ANALYSIS: Write an essay explaining what makes this speech memorable and important. Why is it "recognized as one of the greatest of the 20th century"? Identify the audience and what the speaker wants from them. How do rhetorical devices such as personification and repetition likely affect the crowd's emotions?

PROMPT GUIDE

- Who is Nehru addressing and what does he want from them?
- What rhetorical devices does he use? How do they affect the audience's emotions?
- What makes this speech memorable and important? Why?

Score	Rhetorical Devices	Language and Conventions
4	The writer clearly analyzes and explains how rhetorical devices affect the audience. The writer provides exemplary analysis, using relevant textual evidence.	The writer demonstrates a consistent command of grammar, punctuation, and usage conventions. Although minor errors may be evident, they do not detract from the fluency or the clarity of the essay.
3	The writer analyzes and explains how rhetorical devices affect the audience. The writer provides sufficient analysis, using relevant textual evidence most of the time.	The writer demonstrates an adequate command of grammar, punctuation, and usage conventions. Although some errors may be evident, they create few (if any) disruptions in the fluency of the writing or the clarity of the essay.
2	The writer begins to analyze or explain how rhetorical devices affect the audience but the analysis is incomplete. The writer uses relevant textual evidence only some of the time.	The writer demonstrates a partial command of grammar, punctuation, and usage conventions. Some distracting errors may be evident, at times creating minor disruptions in the fluency or clarity of the writing.
1	The writer attempts to analyze or explain how rhetorical devices affect the audience but the analysis is not successful. The writer uses little or no relevant textual evidence.	The writer demonstrates little or no command of grammar, punctuation, and usage conventions. Serious and persistent errors create disruptions in the fluency of the writing and sometimes interfere with meaning.
0	The writer does not provide a relevant response to the prompt or does not provide a response at all.	Serious and persistent errors overwhelm the writing and interfere with the meaning of the response as a whole, making the writer's meaning impossible to understand.

Write

SCAFFOLDS

Ask students to complete the writing assignment using text evidence to support their answers.

Use the scaffolds below to differentiate instruction for your ELL English Language Learners and A Approaching grade level readers.

ELL **BEGINNING** With the help of the word bank, write a response using paragraph frame 1.

INTERMEDIATE With the help of the word bank, write a response using paragraph frames 1 and 2.

ADVANCED, ADVANCED HIGH Write a response of differentiated length using the sentence starters.

A **APPROACHING** Write a response of differentiated length using the sentence starters.

BEGINNING / INTERMEDIATE			ADVANCED, ADVANCED HIGH / APPROACHING
Word Bank	**Paragraph Frame 1**	**Paragraph Frame 2**	**Sentence Starters**
future countries Parliament India personifies	Nehru is addressing ____, the citizens of India, and the citizens and governments of other ____ in the world. Nehru wants all of them to understand and support India's goals for the ____. He personifies India throughout the speech. Nehru also ____ the future in the title "Tryst with Destiny." Using personification in this way creates a powerful, memorable image of ____ finally achieving a goal at this moment in history.	The speech is important because ____ and also because ____. I think this speech is recognized as one of the greatest of the 20th century because ____, and also because the use of language is ____.	• The speech is important because . . . • Nehru is addressing . . . and . . . • Nehru wants the people who hear the speech to . . . • He uses the rhetorical device of . . . • The speech is memorable and important because . . .

Peer Review

Students should submit substantive feedback to two peers using the review instructions below.

- How well does this response answer the prompt?
- How well does the writer support his or her ideas with evidence from the speech?
- Which sentence in the writer's response made you think differently about the speech?
- What does the writer do well in this response? What does the writer need to work on?

Remember that your comments are most useful when they are kind and constructive.

Rate

Respond to the following with a point rating that reflects your opinion.

	1	2	3	4
Ideas				
Evidence				
Language and Conventions				

Submit

ELL A **SENTENCE FRAMES**

- You (completely / partly / almost) ____ answered the prompt because ____.
- You could answer the prompt more completely by ____.
- A detail you cited accurately is ____.
- You cited the detail ____ to support your idea that ____.
- One idea you expressed well is ____.
- One idea that needs clarification is ____.

A Small Place

INFORMATIONAL TEXT
Jamaica Kincaid
1988

Introduction

Jamaica Kincaid (b. 1949) was born Elaine Potter Richardson on the Caribbean island of Antigua. Raised in poverty, she was sent at the age of 17 to work as an au pair in New York. There, she began her writing career, eventually penning short fiction featured in publications like *The Paris Review* and becoming a long-tenured staff writer at *The New Yorker*. Much of her writing centers on themes of colonial legacy, racism, class, and power dynamics. These themes are well evident in *A Small Place*, a work of creative nonfiction that draws heavily on the author's experiences growing up in Antigua.

With a series of rhetorical questions, the narrator asks the colonialists why they only ever seem to pass on the negative parts of their culture. Imprisonment and murder, stealing the wealth of a nation, and learning how to rule as a tyrant are the only things the colonialists have taught her people. When they arrived, they murdered, robbed, and imprisoned her people; in turn, to be free of their oppressors, the colonized eventually resorted to killing some of the colonizers. She accuses them of never having grasped the message of the Age of Enlightenment, because even though they built schools and libraries, they also distorted history. She reminds them that although they think "people like her" are too dumb to think in abstractions or understand laws, bureaucracy and laws are the inventions of the colonialists, and all favor them. Lastly, she states that people like her don't want to be capitalists, because for so long, they were the capital.

Proficiency-leveled summaries and summaries in multiple languages are available digitally.

Audio and audio text highlighting are available with this text.

COMPARING WITHIN AND ACROSS GENRES

Both *A Small Place* by Jamaica Kincaid and "Ghosts," by Chimamanda Ngozi Adichie, explore the changes and struggles that take place when previously colonized countries start to rebuild. *A Small Place* reflects on the lasting impression European colonialism left on the author's Caribbean homeland, Antigua. How can an event continue to affect people long after it is over?

Entry Point

As students prepare to read *A Small Place*, share the following information with them to provide context.

- ✓ Jamaica Kincaid lived on Antigua until she moved to New York as a teenager. Kincaid is the recipient of numerous awards for her writing. She often incorporates autobiographical details in her fiction, including problematic mother-daughter relationships and her younger brother's death from AIDS.
- ✓ English settlers colonized Antigua in 1632. Tobacco and sugar were the main crops, produced using enslaved labor. Slaves were emancipated in 1834.
- ✓ Antigua remained a British colony until 1967, when it became an associated state of the United Kingdom. As an associated state, Antigua self-governed its internal affairs, and the UK governed external affairs and defense. Antigua achieved full independence in 1981. It is now a constitutional monarchy with a parliamentary government. The British monarch is head a of state, represented by a governor-general. There is a Senate and a House of Representatives, and the executive power is a Council of Ministers headed by the prime minister.

These icons identify differentiation strategies and scaffolded support for a variety of students. See the digital lesson plan for additional differentiation strategies and scaffolds.

Instructional Path

The print teacher's edition includes essential point-of-use instruction and planning tools. Complete lesson plans and program documents appear in your digital teacher account.

Independent Read: A Small Place

Objectives: After reading an excerpt from A Small Place, students will compose a correspondence protesting a great wrong.

Independent Read

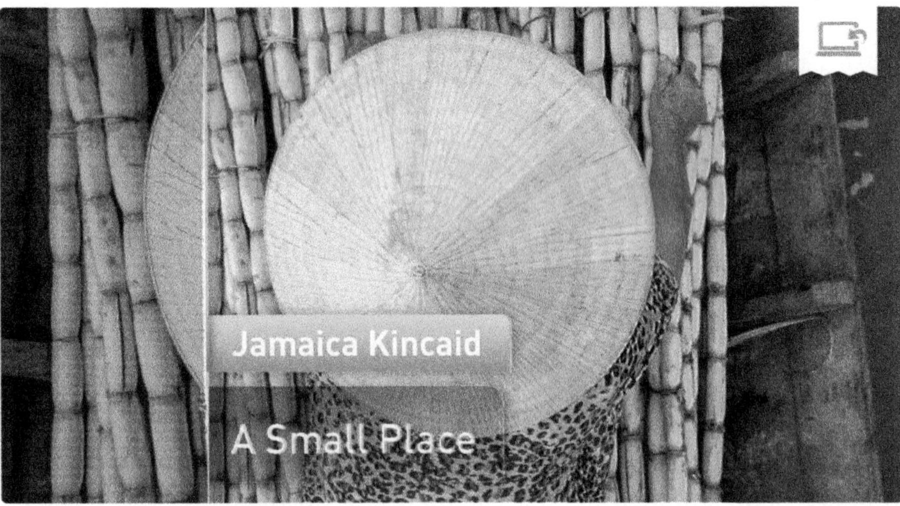

Introduce the Text

As a class, watch the video preview and have students read the introduction in pairs to make connections to the video preview.

- What two words would you use to describe this video?
- Have you ever felt like you were treated unfairly due to race, class, or power dynamics? What happened?

ELL **SPEAKING FRAMES**

- Two words that describe this video are ____ and ____.
- I was treated unfairly when ____.

Access Complex Text

LEXILE: 1360 **WORD COUNT:** 637

The following areas may be challenging for students, particularly ELL English Language Learners and A Approaching grade-level learners.

Genre	Prior Knowledge
• *A Small Place* is creative nonfiction, largely based on the author's experiences and opinions of Antigua, the small island nation where the author was born and raised. The author expresses her thoughts and feelings about Antigua's colonial past. • Students are reading a very small excerpt from the book, so some context might be helpful.	• Students will benefit from background information on the colonial and postcolonial history of Antigua. • Present the historical information provided in the Entry Point notes and support students in researching answers to any follow-up questions.

"You will have to accept that this is mostly your fault."

NOTES

1 Have you ever wondered to yourself why it is that all people like me seem to have learned from you is how to imprison and murder each other, how to govern badly, and how to take the wealth of our country and place it in Swiss bank accounts[1]? Have you ever wondered why it is that all we seem to have learned from you is how to corrupt our societies and how to be **tyrants**? You will have to accept that this is mostly your fault. Let me just show you how you looked to us. You came. You took things that were not yours, and you did not even, for appearances' sake, ask first. You could have said, "May I have this, please?" and even though it would have been clear to everybody that a yes or no from us would have been of no consequence you might have looked so much better. Believe me, it would have gone a long way. I would have had to admit that at least you were polite. You murdered people. You imprisoned people. You robbed people. You opened your own banks and you put our money in them. The accounts were in your name. The banks were in your name. There must have been some good people among you, but they stayed home. And that is the point. That is why they are good. They stayed home. But still, when you think about it, you must be a little sad. The people like me, finally, after years and years of agitation, made deeply moving and **eloquent** speeches against the wrongness of your domination over us, and then finally, after the mutilated bodies of you, your wife, and your children were found in your beautiful and spacious bungalow[2] at the edge of your rubber plantation[3]—found by one of your many house servants (none of it was ever yours; it was never, ever yours)—you say to me, "Well, I wash my hands of all of you, I am leaving now," and you leave, and from afar you watch as we do to ourselves the very things you used to do to us. And you might feel that there was more to you than that, you might feel that you had understood the meaning of the Age of Enlightenment (though, as far as I can see, it had done you very little good); you loved knowledge, and wherever you went you made sure to build a school, a library (yes, and in both of these places you distorted or erased my history and glorified your own). But then again, perhaps as you observe

1. **Swiss bank accounts** authorities have repeatedly found Swiss bank accounts held by criminal enterprises or tax evaders to take advantage of the country's financial secrecy laws
2. **bungalow** a simple, one-story type of house
3. **rubber plantation** a large-scale farm for growing and harvesting rubber from trees

SELECTION VOCABULARY

tyrant / tirano/a *noun* a cruel leader with absolute power COGNATE

eloquent / elocuente *adjective* well-spoken; capable of clear and effective use of language COGNATE

Developing Background Knowledge and Cultural Awareness

Guide students to do a brief online search for information and images related to Antigua.

1. Tell students to take a few minutes to brainstorm images related to the island of Antigua.
2. Choose one or two to project and discuss as a class.

Discuss with students: Think of a time when you were labeled or grouped due to your gender, race, class, religious, sexual orientation, etc. How did that label make you feel? In what ways did that label serve or not serve you? Why do people tend to group individuals based on labels?

TEXT TALK

Who are the "people like me" the author refers to in the text? How do you know?

See paragraph 1: "People like me" are the people of the author's country who were oppressed by the "you" in the text.

What does the author say "you" did to people?

See paragraph 1: The author says, "You murdered people. You imprisoned people. You robbed people."

What is the author's tone? How do you know?

See paragraph 1: The author is angry because she blames the colonial powers for ruining her life and country.

TEXT TALK

How did the image search and discussion of Antigua deepen your understanding of the text?

Answers will vary.

How did discussing the experience of being labeled or grouped deepen your understanding of the text?

Answers will vary.

B Ask each Beyond grade-level student to write one additional discussion question. Then, have one or two students facilitate a discussion, using their questions to guide the conversation.

the **debacle** in which I now exist, the utter ruin that I say is my life, perhaps you are remembering that you had always felt people like me cannot run things, people like me will never grasp the idea of Gross National Product[4], people like me will never be able to take command of the thing the most simpleminded among you can master, people like me will never understand the notion of rule by law, people like me cannot really think in **abstractions**, people like me cannot be **objective**, we make everything so personal. You will forget your part in the whole setup, that bureaucracy is one of your inventions, that Gross National Product is one of your inventions, and all the laws that you know mysteriously favour you. Do you know why people like me are shy about being capitalists? Well, it's because we, for as long as we have known you, *were* capital, like bales of cotton and sacks of sugar, and you were the commanding, cruel capitalists, and the memory of this is so strong, the experience is so recent, that we can't quite bring ourselves to embrace this idea that you think so much of.

Excerpted from *A Small Place* by Jamaica Kincaid, published by Farrar, Straus & Giroux.

 WRITE

CORRESPONDENCE: Like Jamaica Kincaid, write a letter protesting a great wrong done to you or a group to which you belong. Direct the letter to the person you hold responsible, such as a government official, a business executive, a criminal, or a bully. You might copy Kincaid's acid tone or other techniques she used to make her message effective, or you might deliberately choose different techniques if you think they work better. Be sure your ideas flow logically. You want to make it clear to the person you are writing to why he or she is in the wrong.

4. **Gross National Product** the total economic value generated by a country in one year

SELECTION VOCABULARY

debacle / la debacle ***noun*** a great disaster COGNATE

abstractions / la abstracción ***noun*** something that exists only as an idea or concept and not an actual person, thing, or event COGNATE

objective / objetivo/a ***adjective*** undistorted by emotion or personal bias COGNATE

Writer's Notebook

Connect to Literary Focus: Give students time to reflect on how *A Small Place* demonstrates the conventions and characteristics of this unit's literary focus, postmodernism and postcolonialism, by freewriting in their Writer's Notebooks.

CHECK FOR SUCCESS

If students are still struggling to respond to the prompt, ask them scaffolded questions, such as:

- How does the author use pronouns to show the conflict between the colonial powers and the people they oppressed?
- Which words or phrases in the text did you find surprising or shocking? How does the author use language to affect your emotions?

Reading Comprehension OPTIONAL

Have students complete the digital reading comprehension questions ✓ when they finish reading.

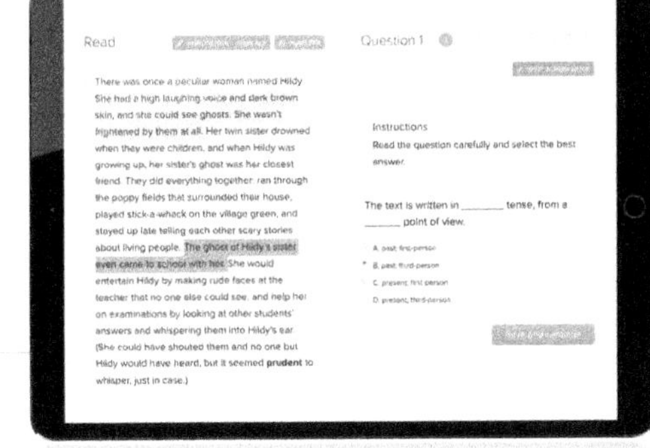

ANSWER KEY

QUESTION 1: C
QUESTION 2: D
QUESTION 3: D
QUESTION 4: C
QUESTION 5: *See chart.*

Synonym	Word
authoritarian	tyrant
articulate	eloquent
catastrophe	debacle
concept	abstraction
unbiased	objective

Connect and Extend OPTIONAL

CONNECT TO EXTENDED ORAL PROJECT

Students can use their experience drafting an explanatory correspondence to inform the techniques they will employ in their speeches. Have them work to use various argumentative techniques to express a point of view.

BEYOND THE BOOK

Research: The Effects of Privilege

Jamaica Kincaid shares how the privilege of the wealthy has wronged her and her people. Students will explore how privilege is awarded, how it affects others, and how equality could be restored.

Ask students to:

- Get into groups of three and research privilege in the United States.
  > How is privilege awarded?
  > Are the privileged aware of their station?
  > How are people on both sides—those with a lot and those with little—affected by privilege?
  > What specificities in life (e.g., education, employment, health care, etc.) are only provided to select individuals or groups?
  > What are people doing to combat the unequal treatment?
- Create a presentation that explains their research and present to classmates.

To reflect, ask students to write a plan of action for combating privilege in their community.

Collaborative Conversation

SCAFFOLDS

Post the writing prompt to generate a discussion in small groups. Ask students to first break down the prompt before they discuss relevant ideas and textual evidence.

Like Jamaica Kincaid, write a letter protesting a great wrong done to you or a group to which you belong. Direct the letter to the person you hold responsible, such as a government official, a business executive, a criminal, or a bully. You might copy Kincaid's acid tone or other techniques she used to make her message effective, or you might deliberately choose different techniques if you think they work better. Be sure your ideas flow logically. You want to make it clear to the person you are writing to why he or she is in the wrong.

Use the scaffolds below to differentiate instruction for your ELL English Language Learners and A Approaching grade-level learners.

ELL **BEGINNING, INTERMEDIATE** Use the discussion guide and speaking frames to facilitate the discussion with support from the teacher.

ADVANCED, ADVANCED HIGH Use the discussion guide and speaking frames to facilitate the discussion in mixed-level groups.

A **APPROACHING** Use the discussion guide to facilitate the discussion in mixed-level groups.

APPROACHING
ADVANCED, ADVANCED HIGH
BEGINNING, INTERMEDIATE

Discussion Guide	Speaking Frames
1. What "great wrong" was done to you or a group to which you belong?	• A great wrong I experienced was ____. • This action or behavior was wrong because ____.
2. To whom will you address your letter? Why?	• I will write a letter to ____. • I will write a letter to this person / group because ____.
3. What techniques can you use to make your letter effective?	• I can ____. • This will be effective because ____.

Ethical Issues

Use the activity below to differentiate instruction for your B Beyond grade level learners.

Reread the following:

. . . perhaps you are remembering that you had always felt people like me cannot run things, people like me will never grasp the idea of Gross National Product, people like me will never be able to take command of the thing the most simpleminded among you can master, people like me will never understand the notion of rule by law, people like me cannot really think in abstractions, people like me cannot be objective, we make everything so personal.

Have students consider the reasoning behind why the person being addressed by the narrator might make these assumptions.

Ask students:

- What component can be identified as bias, prejudice, or discrimination?
- How do the ethics of the person being addressed define who he is?

Review Prompt and Rubric

Before students begin writing, review the writing prompt and rubric with the class.

CORRESPONDENCE: Like Jamaica Kincaid, write a letter protesting a great wrong done to you or a group to which you belong. Direct the letter to the person you hold responsible, such as a government official, a business executive, a criminal, or a bully. You might copy Kincaid's acid tone or other techniques she used to make her message effective, or you might deliberately choose different techniques if you think they work better. Be sure your ideas flow logically. You want to make it clear to the person you are writing to why he or she is in the wrong.

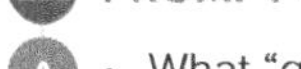

PROMPT GUIDE

- What "great wrong" was done to you or a group to which you belong?
- To whom will you address your letter? Why?
- What techniques can you use to make your letter effective?

Score	Correspondence	Language and Conventions
4	The writer composes a clear and complete correspondence protesting a great wrong, using relevant details and effective techniques.	The writer demonstrates a consistent command of grammar, punctuation, and usage conventions. Although minor errors may be evident, they do not detract from the fluency or the clarity of the essay.
3	The writer sufficiently composes a correspondence protesting a great wrong, using relevant details and effective techniques most of the time.	The writer demonstrates an adequate command of grammar, punctuation, and usage conventions. Although some errors may be evident, they create few (if any) disruptions in the fluency of the writing or the clarity of the essay.
2	The writer begins to compose a correspondence protesting a great wrong, but the response is incomplete. The writer uses relevant details and techniques only some of the time.	The writer demonstrates a partial command of grammar, punctuation, and usage conventions. Some distracting errors may be evident, at times creating minor disruptions in the fluency or clarity of the writing.
1	The writer attempts to compose a correspondence but is not successful. The writer uses little or no relevant details or techniques.	The writer demonstrates little or no command of grammar, punctuation, and usage conventions. Serious and persistent errors create disruptions in the fluency of the writing and sometimes interfere with meaning.
0	The writer does not provide a relevant response to the prompt or does not provide a response at all.	Serious and persistent errors overwhelm the writing and interfere with the meaning of the response as a whole, making the writer's meaning impossible to understand.

Write

SCAFFOLDS

Ask students to complete the writing assignment using text evidence to support their answers.

Use the scaffolds below to differentiate instruction for your ELL English Language Learners and A Approaching grade-level learners.

ELL **BEGINNING** With the help of the word bank, write a response using paragraph frame 1.

INTERMEDIATE With the help of the word bank, write a response using paragraph frames 1 and 2.

ADVANCED, ADVANCED HIGH Write a response of differentiated length using the sentence starters.

A **APPROACHING** Write a response of differentiated length using the sentence starters.

BEGINNING / INTERMEDIATE			ADVANCED, ADVANCED HIGH / APPROACHING
Word Bank	**Paragraph Frame 1**	**Paragraph Frame 2**	**Sentence Starters**
racism sexism environment help community unfair future behavior world power	To ____: People like me are angry at you because ____. It is your fault that ____. You ignored ____. You did not ____. I blame you for ____. You will have to accept it is mostly your fault because ____.	You thought ____. You felt ____. But nothing is more important than ____.	• To . . . • I blame you for . . . • You ruined . . . • I am . . . • You were in the wrong because . . .

Peer Review

Rate

Respond to the following with a point rating that reflects your opinion.

	1	2	3	4
Ideas				
Evidence				
Language and Conventions				

Submit

Students should submit substantive feedback to two peers using the review instructions below.

- How well does this response answer the prompt?
- Which of the writer's details or techniques did you find most powerful? Why?
- Which part of the writer's response inspired you to think differently about *A Small Place* or about protesting a great wrong? Why?
- What does the writer do well in this response? What does the writer need to work on?

Remember that your comments are most useful when they are kind and constructive.

SENTENCE FRAMES

- You were able to (completely / partly / almost) ____ answer the prompt.
- You could answer the prompt more completely by . . .
- I thought differently about . . . after reading . . .
- My favorite part of your response was . . .

Ghosts

FICTION
Chimamanda Ngozi Adichie
2009

Introduction

studysync tv

Many young Americans first learned of award-winning Nigerian writer Chimamanda Ngozi Adichie (b. 1977) from a speech of hers featured in a Beyoncé song, "Flawless." By that point, Adichie's dynamic body of work—three novels, numerous essays, and a collection of short stories—had already earned her a MacArthur fellowship and a spot in *The New Yorker's* "20 Under 40" series. The daughter of Nigerian academics, Adichie grew up in the same house where renowned author Chinua Achebe used to live. The story presented here, "Ghosts," weaves factual characters and events from her own history into the fictional story of a university professor, James Nwoye (Adichie's own father's name), who encounters an old colleague he'd presumed dead in the Nigerian Civil War—37 years earlier.

In a parking lot, James Nwoye meets Ikenne Okoro, a man he last saw over 30 years ago. On that day, Nwoye and his wife had been fleeing the university, which was soon to be overrun by federal soldiers. Okoro was the only one headed in the opposite direction, back to the university to retrieve some papers. Later, they'd heard that he'd been shot. Life for Nwoye had gone on—although he and his wife lost a child, they moved to California, where they had another one, and then back to Africa, where Nwoye picked up his teaching. Nowadays, his wife is deceased but visits him as a ghost at night, Nwoye believes, and his daughter is a doctor in Connecticut. His encounter with Okoro is both welcome and not, since Nwoye suspects he might be in the country peddling the fake medicine that killed his wife. Back at home, Nwoye considers how infrequently, over the past 30 years, the survivors of Biafra actually talked about the war.

Proficiency-leveled summaries and summaries in multiple languages are available digitally.

Audio and audio text highlighting are available with this text.

COMPARING WITHIN AND ACROSS GENRES

Chimamanda Ngozi Adichie's short story "Ghosts" is set in Nigeria thirty-seven years after its civil war ended. The narrator, James Nwoye, runs into an old colleague he believed had been killed during the war and reflects on how life in the country has changed over the course of the previous decades.

How can a major event, such as a civil war as described in "Ghosts" or colonialist oppression as described in Kincaid's *A Small Place,* have a lasting impact?

Entry Point

As students prepare to read "Ghosts," share the following information with them to provide context.

- ✓ The Biafran War, also known as the Nigerian Civil War, began in 1966 and lasted four years. The Hausa majority resented the better-educated and wealthier Igbo minority. They massacred 10,000 to 30,000 Igbo people in 1966, causing a million Igbo to flee to the Igbo-dominated eastern part of Nigeria. Non-Igbos were then expelled from that part of the country. Biafra seceded from Nigeria in 1967 and existed until January 1970.
- ✓ Chimamanda Ngozi Adichie says she "grew up in the shadow of Biafra." Both of her grandfathers died in the conflict, and family stories began with either "Before the war" or "After the war." Adichie writes about the war to honor her grandfathers and the collective memory of her country. Although Adichie includes many historical facts in "Ghosts" and her other stories, she focuses on complex characters who try to understand post-colonial Nigeria and its unsolved problems.

Instructional Path

The print teacher's edition includes essential point-of-use instruction and planning tools. Complete lesson plans and program documents appear in your digital teacher account.

First Read: Ghosts

Objectives: After an initial reading and discussion of the short story, students will be able to identify and describe character traits, setting details, and central ideas.

Skill: Textual Evidence

Objectives: After rereading and discussing a model of close reading, students will be able to use textual evidence to analyze explicit meanings and make inferences about a text.

Skill: Story Elements

Objectives: After rereading and discussing a model of close reading, students will be able to analyze how story elements help convey meaning.

Close Read: Ghosts

Objectives: After engaging in a close reading and discussion of "Ghosts," students will be able to write a short response that compares and contrasts the two main characters.

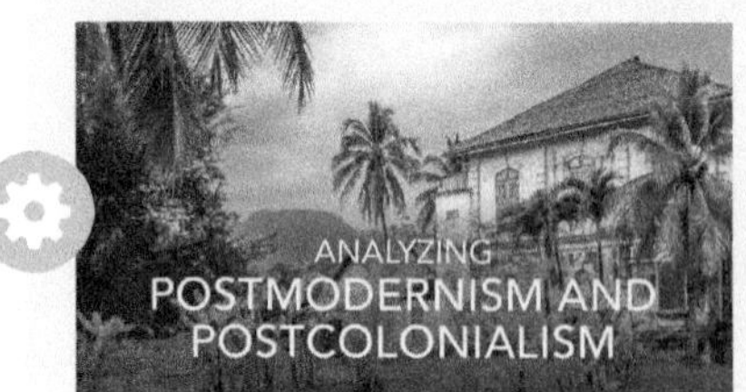

Skill: Analyzing Postmodernism and Postcolonialism

Objectives: After reading and discussing a model of close reading, students will be able to explain how a text from the unit reflects the literary period of Postmodernism and Postcolonialism.

Progress Monitoring

Opportunities to Learn	Opportunities to Demonstrate Learning	Opportunities to Reteach
Textual Evidence		
Skill: Textual Evidence	Skill: Textual Evidence • Your Turn Close Read • Skills Focus • Collaborative Conversation • Write	Unit Skill: Textual Evidence- Commencement Address at the New School Spotlight Skill: Textual Evidence
Story Elements		
Skill: Story Elements	Skill: Story Elements • Your Turn Close Read • Skills Focus • Collaborative Conversation • Write	Spotlight Skill: Story Elements

First Read

Introduce the Text

As a class, watch the video preview  and have students read the introduction in pairs to make connections to the video preview.

To activate prior knowledge and experiences, ask students:

- Which key words or images from the video do you think will be most important to the story you are about to read? Why?
- What do you know about civil wars and their impact?

ELL SPEAKING FRAMES

- An important key word / image was ____.
- Something I know about civil wars is ____.

Access Complex Text

LEXILE: 940 WORD COUNT: 5,004

The following areas may be challenging for students, particularly  English Language Learners and 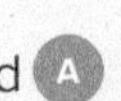 Approaching grade-level learners.

Connection of Ideas	Prior Knowledge
• The narrator's motivations and actions are implied and not explicit. • Remind students to trace details about the narrator's observations and reactions as they read and use these details to make inferences about characters and events.	• The story is set after the Nigerian Civil War, also known as the Biafran War (1967–1970). Students may be unfamiliar with the historical and cultural context of the setting. • Explain that Britain granted independence to Nigeria in 1960, resulting in ethnic conflicts a few years later that led to atrocities against the Igbo and other ethnic minorities.

  ENGLISH LANGUAGE LEARNERS  APPROACHING GRADE LEVEL  BEYOND GRADE LEVEL

These icons identify differentiation strategies and scaffolded support for a variety of students. See the digital lesson plan for additional differentiation strategies and scaffolds.

"Two men haunted by war meet again—thirty-seven years after their last encounter."

NOTES

Skill: Textual Evidence

James explicitly resists the impulse to make sure Ikenna "is not a ghost." This supports the inference that James's education separates him from "the ways of" his "people." Will the story reveal whether Ikenna is a ghost?

1 Today I saw Ikenna Okoro, a man I had long thought was dead. Perhaps I should have bent down, grabbed a handful of sand, and thrown it at him, in the way my people do to make sure a person is not a ghost. But I am an educated man, a retired professor of seventy-one, and I am supposed to have armed myself with enough science to laugh indulgently at the ways of my people. I did not throw sand at him. I could not have done so even if I had wished to, anyway, since we met on the concrete grounds of the university bursary[1].

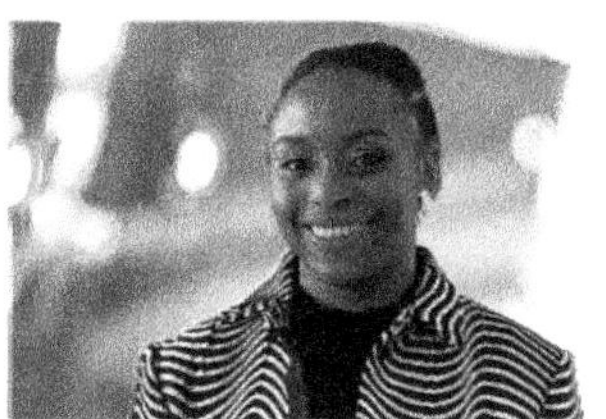

Nigerian author Chimamanda Ngozi Adichie

2 I was there to ask about my pension, yet again. "Good day, Prof," the dried-looking clerk, Ugwuoke, said. "Sorry, the money has not come in."

3 The other clerk, whose name I have now forgotten, nodded and apologized as well, while chewing on a pink lobe of kolanut. They were used to this. I was used to this. So were the tattered men who were clustered under the mango tree, talking loudly. The education minister has stolen the pension money, one fellow said. Another said that it was the vice chancellor, who deposited the money in personal high-interest accounts. When I walked up to them, they greeted me and shook their heads apologetically about the situation as if my professor-level pension is somehow more important than their messenger-level or driver-level pensions. They called me Prof, as most people do, as the hawkers sitting next to their trays under the tree did. "Prof! Prof! Come and buy good banana!"

4 I chatted with Vincent, who was our driver when I was faculty dean in the eighties. "No pension for three years, Prof. This is why people retire and die," he said.

1. **bursary** an institution's treasury

Developing Background Knowledge and Cultural Awareness

1. Have students watch Chimamanda Ngozi Adichie's TED Talk "The Danger of a Single Story."
2. In small groups, have students discuss the video's meaning and how it relates to something in their own lives or to something they've read or learned about.

Discuss with students: Part of Adichie's message in her TED talk is that single stories are common, and we tell them all the time. Reflect on your own experiences with single stories. What is a single story that you have told yourself about other people? What were the consequences of that single story? What actions might you take in the future to prevent yourself from believing in single stories?

Textual Evidence

What does the reader infer from paragraph 1?

The reader infers that James's education separates him from the beliefs of his people.

TEXT TALK

How old is the narrator? What was his job before he retired?

See paragraph 1: He is 71 and was a professor before he retired.

NOTES

5 "*O joka*," I said, although he, of course, did not need me to tell him how terrible it was.

6 "How is Nkiru, Prof? I trust she is well in America?" He always asks about our daughter. He often drove my wife, Ebere, and me to visit her at the College of Medicine in Enugu. I remember that when Ebere died, he came with his relatives for *mgbalu*[2] and gave a touching, if rather long, speech about how well Ebere treated him when he was our driver, how she gave him our daughter's old clothes for his children.

7 "Nkiru is well," I said.

8 "Please greet her for me when she calls, Prof."

9 "I will."

10 He talked for a while longer, about ours being a country that has not learned to say thank you, about the students in the hostels not paying him on time for mending their shoes, but it was his Adam's apple that held my attention; it bobbed alarmingly as if just about to pierce the wrinkled skin of his neck and pop out. Vincent must be in his early sixties—since the non-academic staff retire at sixty rather than sixty-five—but he looks older. He has little hair left. I quite remember his **incessant** chatter while he drove me to work in those days; I remember, too, that he was fond of reading my newspapers, a practice I did not encourage.

11 "Prof, won't you buy us banana? Hunger is killing us," one of the men said. He had a familiar face. I think he was Professor Eboh's gardener, next door. His tone had that half-teasing, half-serious quality, but I bought groundnuts and a bunch of bananas for them, although what they really needed was some moisturizer. Their faces and arms looked like ash. It is almost March but the Harmattan[3] is still very much here: the dry winds, the crackling static on my clothes, the gritty dust on my eyelashes. I used more lotion than usual today, and Vaseline on my lips, but still the dryness made my palms and face feel tight. Ebere used to tease me about not moisturizing properly, especially in the Harmattan, and sometimes would stop me and slowly rub her Nivea on my arms, my legs, my back. We have to take care of this lovely skin, she would say with that playful laughter of hers. She always said my complexion was the persuading trait, since I did not have any money like her other suitors. Seamless, she called it. I saw nothing particularly distinct in my dark umber tone, but I did come to preen a little with the passing years, with Ebere's massaging hands.

2. ***mgbalu*** traditional Igbo burial ceremony
3. **the Harmattan** dry wind from the Sahara blowing into West Africa that is also the name of the season when it comes, typically from November to March

SELECTION VOCABULARY

incessant / incesante *adjective* continuing, unending COGNATE

NOTES

Skill: Story Elements

James listens to the men, noticing his effect on them. Their lives are difficult, but James admires their positive attitudes: they laugh a lot and have "whole" spirits.

12 "Thank you, Prof!" the men said, and then began to mock one another about who would do the dividing.

13 I stood around and listened to their talk. I was aware that they spoke more respectably because I was there: carpentry was not going well, children were ill, more money-lender troubles. They laughed often. Of course they nurse resentment, as they well should, but it has somehow managed to leave their spirits whole. I often wonder whether I would be like them if I did not have money saved from my appointments in the Federal Office of Statistics and if Nkiru did not insist on sending me dollars that I do not need. I doubt it; I would probably have hunched up like a tortoise shell and let my dignity whittle away.

14 Finally I said good-bye to them and walked toward my car, parked near the whistling pine trees that shield the Faculty of Education from the bursary. That was when I saw Ikenna Okoro.

15 He called out to me first. "James? James Nwoye, is it you?" He stood with his mouth open and I could see that his teeth are still complete. I lost one last year. I have refused to have what Nkiru calls "work" done, but I still felt rather sour at Ikenna's full set.

16 "Ikenna? Ikenna Okoro?" I asked in the tentative way one suggests something that cannot be: the coming to life of a man who died thirty-seven years ago.

17 "Yes, yes." Ikenna came closer, uncertainly. We shook hands, and then hugged briefly.

18 We were not good friends, Ikenna and I; I knew him fairly well in those days only because everyone knew him fairly well. It was he who climbed the podium at the Staff Club, he who would speak until he was hoarse and sweating, he who handed out simplified tenets of Nyerere, the type smudgy on cheap paper. The social sciences people had too much time on their hands and worshiped radicals of all sorts who were thought by those of us in the sciences to be empty vessels. We saw Ikenna differently. I'm not sure why, but we forgave his peremptory style and did not discard his pamphlets and rather admired the erudite asperity with which he blazed through issues. He is still a shrunken man with froglike eyes and light skin that has become discolored with age. One heard of him in those days and then struggled to hide great disappointment upon seeing him, because the depth of his rhetoric somehow demanded good looks. But then my people say that a famous animal does not always fill the hunter's basket.

Skill: Story Elements

James is shocked to see Ikenna Okoro because he thought Ikenna had died. The author uses a flashback to give details about James and his family evacuating at the beginning of the war.

19 "You're alive?" I asked. I was quite shaken. My family and I saw him on the day he died, 6 July, 1967, the day we evacuated in a hurry, with the sun a strange fiery red in the sky and nearby the *boom-boom-boom* of shelling as the federal soldiers advanced. We were in my Peugeot 404. The militia waved us through the campus gates and shouted that we should not worry, that the

Skills Focus

QUESTION 2: Textual Evidence

These details support the inference that James's position as a retired professor has left him better off than most people in the country. He admires the positive attitude of the men because he believes he would not be so upbeat in their position.

Story Elements

What does the reader notice about James's observations of the men?

The reader notes that James notices his effect on them and admires their positive attitudes.

Story Elements

What does the reader note about the author's development of the plot?

The reader notes how the author uses a flashback to explain James's reaction to seeing Ikenna. The flashback also gives details about the day James and his family evacuated.

NOTES

vandals—as we called the federal soldiers—would be defeated in a matter of days and we could come back. The local villagers, the same ones who would pick through lecturers' dustbins for food after the war, were walking along, hundreds of them, women with boxes on their heads and babies tied to their backs, barefoot children carrying bundles, men dragging bicycles, holding yams. I remember that Ebere was consoling our daughter, Zik, about the doll left behind in our haste, when we saw Ikenna's green Kadet. He was driving the opposite way, back into campus. I horned and stopped. "You can't go back!" I called. But he waved and said, "I have to get some manuscripts." Or maybe he said, "I have to get some materials." I thought it rather foolhardy of him to go back in since the shelling sounded close and our troops would drive the vandals back in a week or two anyway. But I was also full of a sense of our collective invincibility, of the justness of the Biafran cause[4], and so I did not think much else of it until we heard Nsukka fell on the very day we evacuated and the campus was occupied. The bearer of the news, a relative of Professor Ezike, also told us that two lecturers had been killed. One of them had argued with the federal soldiers before he was shot. We did not need to be told this was Ikenna.

20 Ikenna laughed. "I am, I am!" He seemed to find his own response even funnier because he laughed again. Even his laughter, now that I think of it, seemed discolored, hollow, nothing like the aggressive sound that reverberated all over the Staff Club in those days.

21 "But we saw you," I said. "You remember? That day we evacuated?"

22 "Yes," he said.

23 "They said you did not come out."

24 "I did." He nodded. "I did. I left Biafra the following month."

25 "You left?" It is incredible that I felt, today, a brief flash of that deep disgust that came when we heard of saboteurs—we called them sabos—who betrayed our soldiers, our just cause, our nascent nation, in exchange for a safe passage across to Nigeria, to the salt and meat and cold water that the blockade kept from us.

26 "No, no, it was not like that, not what you think." Ikenna paused and I noticed that his gray shirt sagged at the shoulders. "I went abroad on a Red Cross plane. I went to Sweden." There was an uncertainty about him, a **diffidence** that seemed alien, very unlike the man who so easily got people to *act*. I remember how he organized the rallies after Biafra was declared, all of us

4. **the Biafran cause** referring to the political struggle of the breakaway Republic of Biafra, an area of eastern Nigeria which fought in the Nigerian Civil War for independence from 1967 until defeat in 1970

SELECTION VOCABULARY

diffidence / el retraimiento *noun* shyness or unassertiveness, due to a lack of confidence

NOTES

crowded at Freedom Square while Ikenna talked and we cheered and shouted, "Happy Independence!"

27 "You went to Sweden?" I asked.

28 "Yes."

29 He said nothing else and I realized that he would not tell me more, that he would not tell me just how he had come out of the campus alive or how he came to be on that plane; I know of the children airlifted to Gabon later in the war but certainly not of people flown out on Red Cross planes, and so early, too. The silence between us was tense.

30 "Have you been in Sweden since?" I asked.

31 "Yes. My whole family was in Abagana when they bombed it. Nobody left, so there was no reason for me to come back." He stopped to let out a harsh sound that was supposed to be laughter but sounded more like a series of coughs. "I was in touch with Doctor Anya for a while. He told me about rebuilding our campus, and I think he said you left for America after the war."

32 In fact, Ebere and I came back to Nsukka right after the war ended in 1970, but only for a few days. It was too much for us. Our books were in a charred pile in the front garden, under the umbrella tree. The lumps of calcified feces in the bathtub were strewn with pages of my *Mathematical Annals*, used as toilet paper, crusted smears blurring the formulas I had studied and taught. Our piano—Ebere's piano—was gone. My graduation gown, which I had worn to receive my first degree at Ibadan, had been used to wipe something and now lay with ants crawling in and out, busy and oblivious to me watching them. Our photographs were ripped, their frames broken. So we left for America and did not come back until 1976. We were assigned a different house on Ezenweze Avenue and for a long time we avoided driving along Imoke Street, because we did not want to see the old house; we later heard that the new people had cut down the umbrella tree. I told Ikenna all of this, although I said nothing about our time at Berkeley, where my friend Chuck Bell arranged my teaching appointment. Ikenna was silent for a while, and then he said, "How is your little girl, Zik? She must be a grown woman now."

33 He always insisted on paying for Zik's Fanta when we took her to the Staff Club on Family Day because, he said, she was the prettiest of the children. I suspect it was really because we had named her after our president, and Ikenna was an early Zikist before claiming the movement was too tame and leaving.

34 "The war took Zik," I said in Igbo. Speaking of death in English has always had for me a disquieting finality.

Skills Focus

QUESTION 3: Story Elements/Theme

James speaks in Igbo to tell Ikenna about his daughter's death. He prefers to speak about death in Igbo because the beliefs of his culture leave room for the existence of ghosts, and his science-based education, represented by speaking English, does not.

NOTES

35 Ikenna breathed deeply, but all he said was "*Ndo*," nothing more than sorry. I am relieved he did not ask how—there are not many hows anyway—and that he did not look inordinately shocked, as if war deaths are ever really accidents.

36 "We had another child after the war, another daughter," I said. But Ikenna was talking in a rush. "I did what I could," he said. "I did. I left the International Red Cross. It was full of cowards who could not stand up for human beings. They backed down after that plane was shot down at Eket as if they did not know it was exactly what Gowon wanted. But the World Council of Churches kept flying in relief through Uli. At nights! I was there in Uppsala when they met. It was the biggest operation they had done since the Second World War. I organized the fundraising. I organized the Biafran rallies all over the European capitals. You heard about the big one at Trafalgar Square[5]? I was at the top of that. I did what I could."

37 I was not sure that Ikenna was speaking to me. It seemed that he was saying what he had said over and over to many people. I looked toward the mango tree. The men were still clustered there, but I could not tell whether they had finished the bananas and groundnuts. Perhaps it was then that I began to feel submerged in hazy nostalgia, a feeling that has still not left me.

38 "Chris Okigbo died, not so?" Ikenna asked and made me focus once again. For a moment, I wondered if he wanted me to deny that, to make Okigbo a ghost-come-back, too. But Okigbo died, our genius, our star, the man whose poetry moved us all, even those of us in the sciences.

39 "Yes, the war took Okigbo."

40 "We lost a colossus in the making."

41 "True, but at least he was brave enough to fight." As soon as I said that, I was regretful. I had meant it only as a tribute to Chris Okigbo, who could have worked at one of the directorates like the rest of us university people but instead took up a gun to defend Nsukka. I did not want Ikenna to misunderstand my intention and wondered whether to apologize. He looked away. A small dust whirl was building up across the road. The wind whipped dry leaves off the trees. Perhaps because of my discomfort, I began to tell Ikenna about the day we drove back to Nsukka, about the landscape of ruins, the blown-out roofs, the houses riddled with holes that Ebere said were rather like Swiss cheese. When we got to the road that runs through Aguleri, Biafran soldiers stopped us and shoved a wounded soldier into our car; his blood dripped onto the backseat and, because the upholstery had a tear, soaked deep into the stuffing, mingled with the very insides of our car. A stranger's blood. I was not sure why I chose this particular story to tell Ikenna, but to make it seem

5. **Trafalgar Square** public square in the City of Westminster, London that is a site of major political demonstrations

TEXT TALK

What language does the narrator use when he tells Ikenna about the deaths in his family?

See paragraphs 34 and 50: He speaks in Igbo when he tells Ikenna about the deaths of his wife and daughter.

NOTES

worth his while I added that the metallic smell of the soldier's blood reminded me of him, Ikenna, because I had always imagined that the federal soldiers shot him and left him to die, left his blood to stain the street. This is not true; I neither imagined such a thing, nor did that wounded soldier remind me of Ikenna. If he thought my story strange, he did not say so. He nodded and said, "I've heard so many stories, so many."

42 "How is life in Sweden?" I asked.

43 He shrugged. "I retired last year. I decided to come back and see." He said "see" as if it meant something more that what one did with one's eyes.

44 "What about your family?" I asked.

45 "I never married."

46 "Oh," I said.

47 "And how is your wife doing? Nnenna, isn't it?" Ikenna asked.

48 "Ebere."

49 "Oh, yes, of course, Ebere. Lovely woman."

50 "Ebere fell asleep three years ago," I said in Igbo. I was surprised to see the tears that glassed Ikenna's eyes. He had forgotten her name and yet, somehow, he was capable of mourning her, or of mourning a time immersed in possibilities. I realize, now, that Ikenna is a man who carries with him the weight of what could have been.

51 "I'm so sorry," he said. "So sorry."

52 "It's all right," I said. "She visits."

Skill: Textual Evidence

James says his wife "visits" him. When Ikenna appears "perplexed" and uses a "pacifying tone," James changes the subject. This supports the inference that James is worried about what others think about him seeing his wife's ghost.

53 "What?" he asked me with a perplexed look, although he, of course, had heard me.

54 "She visits. She visits me."

55 "I see," Ikenna said with that pacifying tone one reserves for the mad.

56 "I mean, she visited America quite often; our daughter is a doctor there."

57 "Oh, is that right?" Ikenna asked too brightly. He looked relieved. I don't blame him. We are the educated ones, taught to keep tightly rigid our boundaries of what is considered real. I was like him until Ebere first visited, three weeks after her funeral. Nkiru and her son had just returned to America. I was alone. When I heard the door downstairs close and open and close again, I thought nothing of it. The evening winds always did that. But there was no rustle of leaves outside my bedroom window, no *swish-swish* of the avocado and

Skills Focus

QUESTION 5: Connect to Essential Question

The shared sense of loss unites the men. Ikenna feels genuine sorrow for the death of James's wife, and James recognizes how deeply affected Ikenna is by the possibilities that the war destroyed. The fact that Ikenna left the country during the war separates them.

Skills Focus

QUESTION 4: Language, Style, and Audience

The author uses sensory language to describe James's first encounter with his wife's ghost. This choice helps readers imagine what James heard and felt, emphasizing how real the experience had been for him.

Textual Evidence

What does the reader infer about the conversation between James and Ikenna?

The reader infers that James is worried about what Ikenna and others think about James seeing his wife's ghost.

NOTES

cashew trees. There was *no* wind outside. Yet, the door downstairs was opening and closing. In retrospect, I doubt that I was as scared as I should have been. I heard the feet on the stairs, in much the same pattern as Ebere walked, heavier on each third step. I lay still in the darkness of our room. Then I felt my bedcover pulled back, the gently massaging hands on my arms and legs and chest, and a pleasant drowsiness overcame me—a drowsiness that I am still unable to fight off. I woke up, as I still do after her visits, with my skin supple and thick with the scent of Nivea.

58 I often want to tell Nkiru that her mother visits weekly in the Harmattan and less often during the rainy season, but she will finally have reason to come here and bundle me back with her to America and I will be forced to live a life cushioned by so much convenience that it is sterile. A life littered with what we call "opportunities." A life that is not for me. I wonder what would have happened if we had won the war. Perhaps we would not be looking overseas for those opportunities, and I would not need to worry about our grandson who does not speak Igbo, who, the last time he visited, did not understand why he was expected to say "good afternoon" to strangers, because in his world one has to justify simple courtesies. But who can tell? Perhaps nothing would have changed even if we had won.

59 "How does your daughter like America?" Ikenna asked.

60 "She is doing very well."

61 "And you said she is a doctor?"

62 "Yes." I felt that Ikenna deserved to be told more, or maybe that the tension had not quite **abated,** so I said, "She lives in a small town in Connecticut, near Rhode Island. The hospital board had advertised for a doctor, and when she came they took one look at her and said they did not want a foreigner. But she is American-born—you see, we had her while at Berkeley—and so they were forced to let her stay." I chuckled, and hoped Ikenna would laugh along, too. But he did not.

63 "Ah, yes. At least it's not as bad now as it was for us. Remember what it was like schooling in *oyibo*-land[6] in the late fifties?" he asked.

64 I nodded to show I remembered, although Ikenna and I could not have had the same experience as students overseas; he is an Oxford man while I did not school in England at all.

65 "The Staff Club is a shell of what it used to be," Ikenna said. "I went there this morning."

6. ***oyibo*-land** country of Western or white people

SELECTION VOCABULARY

abated / calmarse *verb* to lessen or weaken

66 "I haven't been there in so long. Even before I retired, it got to the point where I felt too old and out of place there. These greenhorns[7] are inept. Nobody is teaching. Nobody has fresh ideas. It is university politics, politics, politics, while students buy grades with money or their bodies."

67 "Is that right?"

68 "Oh, yes. Things have fallen. Senate meetings have become personality cult battles. It's terrible. Remember Josephat Udeana?"

69 "The great dancer."

70 I was taken aback for a moment because it had been so long since I thought of Josephat as he was in those days, by far the best ballroom dancer we had on campus. "Yes, yes, he was," I said, and I felt a strange gratitude that Ikenna's memories were frozen at a time when I still thought Josephat to be a man of integrity. "Josephat was vice chancellor for six years and ran this place like his father's chicken coop. Money disappeared and then we would see new cars stamped with the names of foreign foundations that did not exist. Some people went to court, but nothing came of that. He dictated who would be promoted and who would be stagnated. In short, the man acted like a solo University Council. This present vice chancellor is following him faithfully. I have not been paid my pension since I retired, you know."

71 "And why isn't anybody doing something about all this? Why?" Ikenna asked, and for the briefest moment the old Ikenna was there, in the voice, the outrage, and I was reminded again that this was an intrepid man. Perhaps he would pound his fist on a nearby tree.

72 "Well," I shrugged. "Many of the lecturers are changing their official dates of birth. They go to Personnel Services and bribe somebody and add five years. Nobody wants to retire."

73 "It is not right. Not right at all."

74 "It's all over the country, really, not just here." I shook my head in that slow, side-to-side way that my people have perfected when referring to things of this sort, as if to say that the situation is, sadly, **ineluctable.**

75 "I was reading about fake drugs in the papers; it looks serious," Ikenna said, and I immediately thought it too convenient of a coincidence, his bringing up fake drugs. Selling expired medicine is the latest plague of our country, and if Ebere had not died the way she did, I would have found this to be a normal segue in the conversation. But I was suspicious. I wondered if Ikenna had heard how Ebere died and wanted to get me to talk about it, to exhibit a little more of the lunacy that he had already glimpsed.

7. **greenhorns** newcomers

SELECTION VOCABULARY

ineluctable / ineluctable *adjective* not capable of being avoided or prevented; inevitable COGNATE

NOTES

76 "Fake drugs are horrible," I said gravely, determined to say nothing else. But I may have been wrong about Ikenna's plot, because he did not pursue the subject. He asked me, "So what do you do these days?" He seemed curious, as if he were wondering just what kind of life I am leading here, alone, in a university town that is now a withered skin of what it used to be, waiting for a pension that never comes. I smiled and said that I am resting; is that not what one does on retiring?

77 Sometimes I drop by to visit my old friend Professor Maduewe. I take walks across the faded field of Freedom Square with the flame trees. Or along Ikejiani Avenue, where the motorcycles speed past, students perched astride, often coming too close to one another as they avoid the gaping potholes. In the rainy season, when I discover a new gully where the rains have eaten at the land, I feel a flush of accomplishment. I read newspapers. I eat well; my househelp, Harrison, comes five days a week and his onugbu soup is unparalleled. I talk to our daughter often, and when my phone goes dead every other week, I hurry to NITEL to bribe somebody to get it repaired. I unearth old, old journals in my dusty, cluttered study. I breathe in deeply the scent of the neem trees that screen my house from Professor Eboh's—a scent that is supposed to be medicinal, although I am no longer sure what it is said to cure. I do not go to church; I stopped going after Ebere first visited, because I was no longer uncertain. It is our diffidence about the afterdeath that leads us to religion. So on Sundays I sit on the veranda and watch the vultures stamp on my roof, and I imagine that they glance down in bemusement. "Is it a good life, Daddy?" Nkiru has taken to asking lately, with that faint, vaguely troubling American accent. It is not good or bad, I tell her, it is simply mine. And that is what matters.

78 I asked Ikenna to come back to my house with me, but he said he was on his way to Enugu, and when I asked if he would come by later, he made a vague motion with his hands that suggested assent. I know he will not come though. I will not see him again. I watched him walk away, this shriveled nut of a man, and I drove home thinking of the lives we might have had and the lives we did have, all of us who went to the Staff Club in those good days before the war.

79 Because of the minor scratch I had as I backed it out last week, I was careful parking my Mercedes in the garage. It is fifteen years old but runs quite well. I remember how excited Nkiru was when it was shipped back from Germany, where I bought it when I went to receive the Science Africana prize. It was the newest model. I did not know this, but her fellow teenagers did and they all came to look at it. Now, of course, everyone drives a Mercedes, imported secondhand from Cotonou. Ebere used to mock them, saying our car is old but much better than all those *tuke-tuke* things people are driving with no seatbelts. She still has that sense of humor. At her burial, when our grandson

TEXT TALK

When did the narrator stop going to church? Why?

See paragraph 77: He stopped going after his wife's ghost visited him because he was no longer uncertain about what happened to people after death.

NOTES

read his poem, "Keep Laughing, Grandma," I thought the title perfect, and the childish words almost brought me to tears, despite my suspicion that Nkiru wrote most of them.

80 I looked around the yard as I walked indoors. Harrison does a little gardening, mostly watering in this season. The rose bushes are just dried stalks, but at least the hardy cherry bushes are a dusty green. I turned the TV on. It was still raining on the screen, although Doctor Otagbu's son, the bright young man who is reading electronics engineering, came last week to fix it. My satellite channels went off after the last thunderstorm. One can stay some weeks without BBC and CNN anyway, and the programs on NTA[8] are quite good when they are not showing half-naked, dancing American teenagers. It was NTA, some days ago, that broadcast an interview with yet another man accused of importing fake drugs—typhoid fever medicine in this case. "My drugs don't actually kill people," he said, helpfully, facing the camera as if in an appeal to the masses. "It is only that they will not cure your illness." I turned the TV off because I could no longer bear to see the man's blubbery lips. But I was not offended, not as egregiously as I would have been if Ebere did not visit. I only hoped that he would not be let free to go off once again to China or India or wherever they go to import expired medicine that will not actually kill people, but will only make sure the illness kills them.

81 I am sitting now in my study, where I helped Nkiru with her difficult secondary school math assignments. The armchair leather is solid and worn. The pastel paint above the bookshelves is peeling. I wonder why it never came up, throughout the years, that Ikenna did not die. True, we did sometimes hear stories of men who had been thought dead and who walked into their compounds months, even years, after January 1970; I can only imagine the quantity of sand poured on broken men by family members suspended between disbelief and hope. But we hardly talked about the war. When we did it was with an implacable vagueness, as if what mattered were not that we crouched in muddy bunkers during air raids after which we buried corpses with bits of pink on their charred skin, not that we ate cassava peels and watched our children's bellies swell, but that we survived. It was a **tacit** agreement among all of us, the survivors of Biafra. Even Ebere and I, who had debated our first child's name, Zik, for months, agreed very quickly on Nkiru: what is ahead is better. We will look forward, forward, forward.

8. **NTA** Nigerian Television Authority

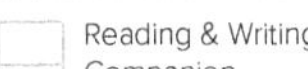

SELECTION VOCABULARY

tacit / tácito/a *adjective* understood or agreed without being stated out loud; implicit COGNATE

Prepare for Advanced Courses

Use the activity below to differentiate instruction for your B Beyond grade level learners.

Author's Word Choice

Reread the following description of Ikenna:

Even his laughter, now that I think of it, seemed discolored, hollow, nothing like the aggressive sound that reverberated all over the Staff Club in those days.

Have students examine how the author's word choice in this description informs the tone and reflects the author's purpose.

Ask students:

- How does the author's word choice help communicate a message to readers? Refer to specific words in the quote to support your response.

TEXT TALK

How did watching Chimamanda Ngozi Adichie's TED Talk "The Danger of a Single Story" help you understand "Ghosts"?

Answers will vary.

Ask each Beyond grade-level student to write one additional discussion question. Then, have one or two students facilitate a discussion, using their questions to guide the conversation.

Think Questions

Circulate as students answer Think Questions independently. Scaffolds for these questions are shown on the opposite page.

QUESTION 1: Textual Evidence

James saw Ikenna return to campus after the attack started. Later, he heard that one of the lecturers killed on campus had argued with the federal soldiers and made an assumption. He says, "We did not need to be told this was Ikenna."

QUESTION 2: Textual Evidence

Their home was destroyed. He says, "My graduation gown, which I had worn to receive my first degree at Ibadan, had been used to wipe something and now lay with ants crawling in and out." It was too much for them to bear, so they went to America.

QUESTION 3: Textual Evidence

Life in Nigeria is bleak. Details in the text show that there is corruption, the government does not pay people's pensions, people are poor and hungry, and sick people are given fake drugs instead of the medicine they need.

QUESTION 4: Context Clues

I think *diffidence* means "lack of confidence" because of the context clue "uncertainty." The text also shows that Ikenna used to be confident before the war, but now he is "unlike" that person.

QUESTION 5: Word Patterns and Relationships

I think "tacit agreement" is an unspoken understanding. *Taciturn* has to do with silence, and the survivors of Biafra do not talk about what happened and instead look ahead to the future.

First Read

Read the short story "Ghosts." After you read, complete the Think Questions below.

THINK QUESTIONS

1. Why did James Nwoye think that Ikenna Okoro was dead? Cite evidence from the text.
2. What did James and his wife see when they visited their old home, and how did it affect them? Support your response with evidence from the text.
3. What is life in Nigeria like in the aftermath of the war? Cite specific examples from the text as support.
4. The narrator says about Ikenna Okoro, "There was an uncertainty about him, a **diffidence** that seemed alien, very unlike the man who so easily got people to *act*." Using contextual clues from this passage, explain what the word *diffidence* means.
5. The adjective *taciturn* is commonly used to describe someone who is quiet or withdrawn. With this in mind, what do you think a "**tacit** agreement" might be? Explain, in your own words, the meaning of this term in the final paragraph of the story.

Think Questions

Use the scaffolds below to differentiate instruction for your ELL English Language Learners and A Approaching grade level readers.

ELL **BEGINNING** Write a response using the word bank and sentence frames.

INTERMEDIATE Write a response using the sentence frames.

ADVANCED, ADVANCED HIGH Write a response using the Text-Dependent Question Guide.

A **APPROACHING** Write a response using the Text-Dependent Question Guide.

BEGINNING	INTERMEDIATE	APPROACHING / ADVANCED, ADVANCED HIGH
Word Bank	**Sentence Frames**	**Text-Dependent Question Guide**
fake confident unspoken argued overwhelming America corrupt talk assumed uncertainty destroyed difficult	James thought Ikenna died because he heard a lecturer had ____ with soldiers before being killed. James and others ____ that was Ikenna.	1. • What was Ikenna doing the last time James saw him? • What did James hear about one of the lecturers who was killed? • Why did James assume the man was Ikenna?
	James and his wife saw that their home was ____. It was ____, so they went to ____.	2. • What happened to James's books and graduation gown? • What happened to Ebere's piano? • What did James and Ebere do after they saw their belongings?
	Life in Nigeria is ____. The government is ____. Sick people are given ____ drugs instead of the medicine they need.	3. • What does James reveal about his pension? • What does Ikenna read about in the paper about medicine? • What do these details tell readers about life after the war?
	Ikenna used to be ____ before the war, but he is now "unlike" that person. This shows that *diffidence* means ____.	4. • Read: "There was an uncertainty about him, a **diffidence** that seemed alien, very unlike the man who so easily got people to act." • Is *diffidence* a noun, a verb, an adjective, or an adverb? • Which context clues can help you understand the meaning of *diffidence*?
	People who survived the war do not ____ about what happened. I think a tacit agreement is an ____ agreement.	5. • Read "It was a **tacit** agreement among all of us, the survivors of Biafra." • Do Nwoye and Ikenna talk about the war? Why or why not? • How do the narrator's thoughts in the last paragraph explain why the survivors have this "tacit agreement"?

Reading Comprehension OPTIONAL

Have students complete the digital reading comprehension questions ✓ when they finish reading.

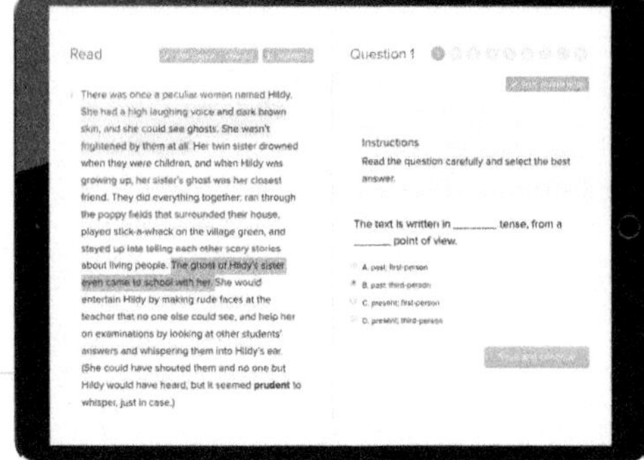

ANSWER KEY

QUESTION 1: B
QUESTION 2: A
QUESTION 3: B
QUESTION 4: A
QUESTION 5: B
QUESTION 6: C
QUESTION 7: C
QUESTION 8: A
QUESTION 9: *See first chart.*
QUESTION 10: *See second chart.*

Synonym	Word
bashfulness	diffidence
diminished	abated
implied	tacit
ceaseless	incessant
unavoidable	ineluctable

First	Second	Third	Fourth
Ikenna becomes a local leader in the movement for Biafran independence.	Ikenna disappears on July 6, 1967, and is presumed dead.	Nwoye's first daughter dies as a result of the civil war.	Nwoye's second daughter grows up to be a doctor in Connecticut.

Connect and Extend OPTIONAL

CONNECT TO EXTENDED ORAL PROJECT

Students can consider the legacy of colonialism and postcolonial inequity in "Ghosts" to inform their oral presentations on what they feel has not been given enough focus in their formal studies.

BEYOND THE BOOK

Writing: The Hidden Truth Uncovered

James Nwoye runs in to an old colleague he thought was dead, and the two men recount the events in their lives. Students will investigate a person whose death has been disputed and write an article explaining that this person is, in fact, alive and well.

Ask students to:

- Create a list of famous people whose deaths have been disputed (e.g., Elvis, Tupac, Jim Morrison, etc.).
- Choose one person and conduct informal research about the dispute and the mystery.
- Write an article to detail the discovery that this person is still alive and to explain what he or she is doing today.
  - > Why did the person disappear?
  - > Where is he or she living now?
  - > What is his or her life like today?
  - > What regrets does she or he have?
- In small groups, share the articles and receive feedback.

To reflect, ask students:

- Why is it hard for society to accept the passing of these famous people?
- How easy was it to make believe the person was still alive?

Skill:
Textual Evidence

Use the Checklist to analyze Textual Evidence in "Ghosts." Refer to the sample student annotations about Textual Evidence in the text.

••• CHECKLIST FOR TEXTUAL EVIDENCE

In order to support an analysis by citing evidence that is explicitly stated in the text, do the following:

- ✓ read the text closely and critically
- ✓ identify what the text says explicitly
- ✓ find the most relevant textual evidence that supports your analysis
- ✓ consider why an author explicitly states specific details and information
- ✓ cite the specific words, phrases, sentences, or paragraphs from the text that support your analysis
- ✓ determine where evidence in the text still leaves certain matters uncertain or unresolved

In order to interpret implicit meanings in a text by making inferences, do the following:

- ✓ combine information directly stated in the text with your own knowledge, experiences, and observations
- ✓ cite the specific words, phrases, sentences, or paragraphs from the text that led to and support this inference

In order to cite textual evidence to support an analysis of what the text says explicitly as well as inferences drawn from the text, consider the following questions:

- ✓ Have I read the text closely and critically?
- ✓ What inferences am I making about the text?
- ✓ What textual evidence am I using to support these inferences?
- ✓ Am I quoting the evidence from the text correctly?
- ✓ Does my textual evidence logically relate to my analysis or the inference I am making?
- ✓ Does evidence in the text still leave certain matters unanswered or unresolved? In what ways?

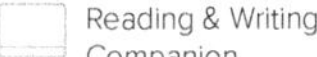

Skill: Textual Evidence

Introduce the Skill

Watch the Concept Definition video and read the following definition with your students.

Any time you're discussing a text, you need to **cite**, or point out, **textual evidence**, the details that readers use to support their ideas and opinions. Readers may cite evidence that is directly stated, or **explicit**, in the text. Other times, textual evidence may be **implicit**, which means it is suggested but not directly stated. One way to interpret implicit meanings is to **make inferences**, using clues from the text and your own experiences to make logical decisions about characters and events that are not stated directly.

Readers must also refer to textual evidence when they **analyze** and examine the different parts of a text. Analyzing specific parts of the text, such as the actions of a character or the cause-and-effect relationships between events in nonfiction, helps a reader **interpret** and explain the meaning, theme, or central idea of the text as a whole. When you cite textual evidence, someone else can look back at a particular part of a text you read and understand your analysis.

TURN AND TALK

1. When have you hinted at something instead of explicitly stating the idea?
2. Why did you choose to communicate this way?

SKILL VOCABULARY

explicit / explícito/a *adjective* precisely and clearly expressed COGNATE

implicit / implícito/a *adjective* implied but not stated directly COGNATE

analyze / analizar *verb* to consider in detail and discover essential features or meaning COGNATE

interpret / interpretar *adjective* to explain the meaning of (information, words, or actions) COGNATE

SPEAKING FRAMES

- I hinted at ___ instead of explicitly stating it.
- I chose to communicate this way because ___.

Your Turn

Ask students to complete the Your Turn Activity.

QUESTION 1

Part A

A. Incorrect. This generalization is supported explicitly in the text.

B. Incorrect. This is an explicit meaning in the text.

C. Correct. This inference is implied by the narrator's criticism of America.

D. Incorrect. This is explicit in the text.

Part B

A. Incorrect. This detail does not suggest that James likes his life in Nigeria.

B. Correct. This detail suggests that James prefers his life in Nigeria to a life in America.

C. Incorrect. This detail does not suggest that James likes his life in Nigeria.

D. Incorrect. This detail does not suggest that James likes his life in Nigeria.

Skill: Textual Evidence

Reread paragraph 58 of "Ghosts." Then, using the Checklist on the previous page, answer the multiple-choice questions below.

YOUR TURN

1. This question has two parts. First, answer Part A. Then, answer Part B.

Part A: Which inference is best supported by this paragraph?

○ A. More opportunities exist in America than Nigeria.
○ B. The narrator does not want to live in America.
○ C. The narrator loves Nigeria despite its problems.
○ D. Nkiru does not know about her mother's ghost.

Part B: Which evidence from the paragraph best supports the answer to Part A?

○ A. "I often want to tell Nkiru that her mother visits weekly in the Harmattan and less often during the rainy season . . ."
○ B. ". . . I will be forced to live a life cushioned by so much convenience that it is sterile."
○ C. "I wonder what would have happened if we had won the war."
○ D. "Perhaps we would not be looking overseas for those opportunities . . ."

SkillsTV

Project the SkillsTV episode and pause at the following times to prompt discussion:

1:39 What strategy do the students use to determine the explicit meaning of the passage? Why is this a good initial step in the process of interpreting text?

2:05 What strategy do the students use to transition from determining explicit to implicit meaning? Why is this step important in the process of interpreting text?

3:25 How do the students synthesize information from both passages? What conclusion do they reach about the implicit meaning of the text?

Skill: Story Elements

Introduce the Skill

Watch the Concept Definition video and read the following definition with your students.

A **story element** is something that contributes to a work of fiction or drama, one of several "building blocks" that make it effective. Story elements usually include **setting**, **character**, **plot** and **subplots**, **theme** and **point of view**. The way an author introduces each of these elements into a **narrative**, and connects them so that one has an effect on another, is what can make a story memorable. For example, the setting—a blizzard, or a raft in the middle of the ocean—can affect the events of the plot, which in turn can have an effect on the characters and their relationship to one another. This can influence the conflict the characters face and, as a result, shape the theme.

Skill:
Story Elements

Use the Checklist to analyze Story Elements in "Ghosts." Refer to the sample student annotations about Story Elements in the text.

••• CHECKLIST FOR STORY ELEMENTS

In order to identify the impact of the author's choices regarding how to develop and relate elements of a story or drama, note the following:

- ✓ where and when the story takes place, who the main characters are, and the main conflict, or problem, in the plot
- ✓ the order of the action
- ✓ how the characters are introduced and developed
- ✓ the impact that the author's choice of setting has on the characters and their attempt to solve the problem

To analyze the impact of the author's choices regarding how to develop and relate elements of a story or drama, consider the following questions:

- ✓ How do the author's choices affect the story elements? The development of the plot?
- ✓ How does the setting influence the characters?
- ✓ Which elements of the setting affect the plot and, in particular, the problem the characters face and must solve?
- ✓ Are there any flashbacks or other story elements that have an effect on the development of events? How does the author's choice of using a flashback affect this development?
- ✓ How does the author introduce and develop characters in the story? Why do you think the author made these choices?

TURN AND TALK

1. Who is one of your favorite characters from a novel, short story, movie, or TV show?
2. What qualities make you like this character?

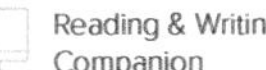

SKILL VOCABULARY

story elements / el elemento del cuento *noun* a "building block" that contributes to a work of fiction or drama, such as character or setting

setting / el escenario *noun* the time and place of the story

character / el personaje *verb* an individual in a literary work whose thoughts, feelings, actions, and reactions move the action of the plot forward

plot / la trama *noun* the sequence of events that form a story

SPEAKING FRAMES

- My favorite character is ____ from ____.
- I like this character because ____.

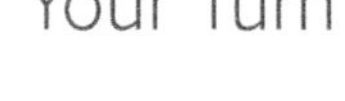

Your Turn

Ask students to complete the Your Turn Activity.

QUESTION 1

Part A

A. Correct. The author includes the details about the war setting to help the reader better understand why the characters "look forward."

B. Incorrect. The details about James's study do not help the reader better understand the characters.

C. Incorrect. The men returning after the war are not dead.

D. Incorrect. The story never explains the details of Zik's death.

Part B

A. Incorrect. This evidence does not support the correct answer to Part A.

B. Incorrect. This evidence does not support the correct answer to Part A.

C. Correct. These details show the horrors of war and best support the correct answer in Part A.

D. Incorrect. This evidence does not support the correct answer to Part A.

QUESTION 2

A. Incorrect. The paragraph does refer back to the beginning, but this does not explain why the author ended the story with this paragraph.

B. Incorrect. This paragraph does not emphasize the relationship between James and Ebere.

C. Incorrect. This detail is in the paragraph, but it does not explain why this paragraph ends the story.

D. Correct. The paragraph provides details about what the war was like for James and others, and this information segways into the final sentence of the story, which emphasizes that survivors of the war look toward the future.

Ghosts

Skill: Story Elements

Reread paragraph 81 of "Ghosts." Then, using the Checklist on the previous page, answer the multiple-choice questions below.

YOUR TURN

1. This question has two parts. First, answer Part A. Then, answer Part B.

   Part A: How do the setting details in this paragraph help the reader better understand the characters?

   - A. The details about the horrors of the war help the reader understand why the characters look toward the future instead of the past.
   - B. The details about James's study help the reader understand how much time has passed since James experienced the horrible war.
   - C. The details about dead men returning after the war help the reader understand that James is not the only character who sees ghosts.
   - D. The details about the horrors of the war help the reader understand what killed Zik and how Ikenna survived.

   Part B: Which evidence best supports the answer to Part A?

   - A. "I am sitting now in my study, where I helped Nkiru with her difficult secondary school math assignments."
   - B. "True, we did sometimes hear stories of men who had been thought dead and who walked into their compounds months, even years, after January 1970 . . ."
   - C. "When we did it was with an implacable vagueness, as if what mattered were not that we crouched in muddy bunkers during air raids after which we buried corpses with bits of pink on their charred skin . . .
   - D. Even Ebere and I, who had debated our first child's name, Zik, for months, agreed very quickly on Nkiru . . ."

2. Which statement best explains why the author ends the story with this paragraph?

   - A. The paragraph refers back to the beginning of story when James wants to throw sand at Ikenna.
   - B. The paragraph emphasizes the relationship between Ebere and James that is the focus of the story.
   - C. The paragraph explains that Ikenna is not the only one to return after so many years.
   - D. The paragraph clarifies some of James's past and his outlook on the present.

SKILL VOCABULARY

subplot / la trama secundaria *noun* a secondary plot strand that supports the main plot, often involving secondary or minor characters

theme / el tema *noun* the central idea or message of a work of literature, often expressed as a general statement about life COGNATE

point of view / el punto de vista *noun* the standpoint, or perspective, from which a story is told

narrative / la narración *noun* a story, real or imagined, consisting of connected events

Close Read

Reread "Ghosts." As you reread, complete the Skills Focus questions below. Then use your answers and annotations from the questions to help you complete the Write activity.

SKILLS FOCUS

1. Identify a detail that introduces the social and economic setting, and explain why this detail is effective in helping readers understand the theme of the story.
2. Identify James's reaction to his interaction with the men he buys groundnuts and bananas from. Infer and explain an implicit meaning evident in the textual evidence. Does anything still remain unresolved?
3. Highlight a passage in which James speaks in Igbo, and explain how the relationship between characterization and point of view in the passage helps develop a theme in the story.
4. Identify an example of vivid sensory language, and explain how it helps shape the reader's perception of characters and events in the story.
5. Reread paragraphs 42–51. In what ways has the change caused by war brought these two men closer together and helped them better understand each other? In what ways has the war separated them and increased their differences?

WRITE

COMPARE AND CONTRAST: In many ways, "Ghosts" has two main characters: James Nwoye, the narrator, and Ikenna Okoru, James's former colleague. How are the personalities and experiences of these two men different? How are they similar? What do their stories, taken together, tell you about the Nigerian Civil War and its inevitable effects on Nigeria? Support your ideas with textual evidence.

Close Read

Skills Focus

QUESTION 1: Story Elements/Theme

Paragraphs 2–3: The university does not have money to pay pensions, which is an ongoing problem. These details about the social and economic setting show that the characters are used to dealing with disappointment and corruption, which effectively introduces themes relating to struggle in a postcolonial circumstance.

QUESTION 2: Textual Evidence See paragraph 13.

QUESTION 3: Story Elements/Theme See paragraph 34.

QUESTION 4: Language, Style, and Audience

See paragraph 57.

QUESTION 5: Connect to Essential Question

See paragraphs 42–51.

CHECK FOR SUCCESS

If students struggle to respond to Skills Focus Question #1, ask students the following questions:

1. Where does the story take place?
2. What is the economic setting in that place?
3. What does this suggest about the theme of the story?

Writer's Notebook

Connect to Literary Focus: Give students time to reflect on how "Ghosts" demonstrates the conventions and characteristics of this unit's literary focus, Postmodernism and Postcolonialism, by freewriting in their Writer's Notebooks.

Beginning & Intermediate

Remind students of the unit's literary focus, Postmodernism and Postcolonialism. Encourage students to draw their connections or allow students to write in their native language. Circulate around the room, prompting students for their thoughts as they respond orally or through pantomime.

Advanced & Advanced High

Allow students to share their connections orally in pairs or small groups before freewriting.

StudySyncTV

Project the StudySyncTV episode and pause at the following times to prompt discussion:

1:06 Logan suggests that, "we have to find the different "ghosts" in the text— " How are the different types of ghosts similar in the way that they "haunt" those left behind? How are they different?

3:33 What evidence from the text could support Lia's claim that, ". . . he believes his wife's ghost is visiting him, and he's happy about that"? Is there evidence that James is troubled by these visitations?

6:39 Samrah says that, "so maybe both of their "young" selves are like ghosts," what does that suggest about the older men in the story? How much of who they are is made up of their ghosts?

Collaborative Conversation

Break students into collaborative conversation groups to discuss the Close Read prompt. Ask students to use the StudySyncTV episode as a model for their discussion. Remind them to reference their Skills Focus annotations in their discussion.

In many ways, "Ghosts" has two main characters: James Nwoye, the narrator, and Ikenna Okoru, James's former colleague. How are the personalities and experiences of these two men different? How are they similar? What do their stories, taken together, tell you about the Nigerian Civil War and its inevitable effects on Nigeria? Support your ideas with textual evidence.

Use the scaffolds below to differentiate instruction for your ELL English Language Learners and A Approaching grade-level learners.

ELL **BEGINNING, INTERMEDIATE** Use the discussion guide and speaking frames to facilitate the discussion with support from the teacher.

ADVANCED, ADVANCED HIGH Use the discussion guide and speaking frames to facilitate the discussion in mixed-level groups.

A **APPROACHING** Use the discussion guide to facilitate the discussion in mixed-level groups.

APPROACHING
ADVANCED, ADVANCED HIGH
BEGINNING, INTERMEDIATE

Discussion Guide	Speaking Frames
1. What do you know about James Nwoye's personality and experiences?	• James's personality is best described as ____ and ____. • James's experiences include ____ and ____.
2. What do you know about Ikenna Okoro's personality and experiences before and after the war?	• Ikenna was ____ before the war and ____ after the war. • Ikenna's experiences include ____ and ____.
3. How are these two characters similar? How are they different?	• One way they are similar is ____. • One way they are different is ____.

Review Prompt and Rubric

Before students begin writing, review the writing prompt and rubric with the class.

COMPARE AND CONTRAST: In many ways, "Ghosts" has two main characters: James Nwoye, the narrator, and Ikenna Okoru, James's former colleague. How are the personalities and experiences of these two men different? How are they similar? What do their stories, taken together, tell you about the Nigerian Civil War and its inevitable effects on Nigeria? Support your ideas with textual evidence.

ELL A PROMPT GUIDE

- How are the two main characters different? How are they similar?
- How did the Nigerian Civil War affect them? What does this tell you about the war?
- How did the war affect Nigeria? How do you know?

Score	Story Elements	Language and Conventions
4	The writer clearly compares and contrasts the two characters and explains what their stories reveal about the Nigerian Civil War. The writer provides exemplary analysis of the story element of character, using relevant textual evidence to show how the author's choices affect the text.	The writer demonstrates a consistent command of grammar, punctuation, and usage conventions. Although minor errors may be evident, they do not detract from the fluency or the clarity of the essay.
3	The writer compares and contrasts the two characters and explains what their stories reveal about the Nigerian Civil War. The writer provides sufficient analysis of the story element of character, using relevant textual evidence most of the time to show how the author's choices affect the text.	The writer demonstrates an adequate command of grammar, punctuation, and usage conventions. Although some errors may be evident, they create few (if any) disruptions in the fluency of the writing or the clarity of the essay.
2	The writer begins to compare and contrast the two characters and explain what their stories reveal about the Nigerian Civil War, but the analysis of the story element of character is incomplete. The writer occasionally uses relevant textual evidence to show how the author's choices affect the text.	The writer demonstrates a partial command of grammar, punctuation, and usage conventions. Some distracting errors may be evident, at times creating minor disruptions in the fluency or clarity of the writing.
1	The writer attempts to compare and contrast the two characters and explain what their stories reveal about the Nigerian Civil War, but the analysis of the story element of character is unsuccessful. Little or no relevant textual evidence is used to show how the author's choices affect the text.	The writer demonstrates little or no command of grammar, punctuation, and usage conventions. Serious and persistent errors create disruptions in the fluency of the writing and sometimes interfere with meaning.
0	The writer does not provide a relevant response to the prompt or does not provide a response at all.	Serious and persistent errors overwhelm the writing and interfere with the meaning of the response as a whole, making the writer's meaning impossible to understand.

SCAFFOLDS

Write

Ask students to complete the writing assignment using text evidence to support their answers.

Use the scaffolds below to differentiate instruction for your ELL English Language Learners and A Approaching grade level readers.

ELL **BEGINNING** With the help of the word bank, write a response using paragraph frame 1.

INTERMEDIATE With the help of the word bank, write a response using paragraph frames 1 and 2.

ADVANCED, ADVANCED HIGH Write a response of differentiated length using the sentence starters.

A **APPROACHING** Write a response of differentiated length using the sentence starters.

BEGINNING (Word Bank, Paragraph Frame 1) | INTERMEDIATE (Word Bank, Paragraph Frames 1 and 2) | ADVANCED, ADVANCED HIGH / APPROACHING (Sentence Starters)

Word Bank	Paragraph Frame 1	Paragraph Frame 2	Sentence Starters
negative loss professors uncertainty Sweden	James and Ikenna were both ____ at the university before the war. They both survived, but Ikenna fled to ____. The war has left Ikenna with feelings of guilt and ____ and James with feelings of great ____ because of his daughter. Together, their stories show that the civil war had a very ____ impact on Nigeria.	Throughout the story, James struggles with ____. For example, the text says, ____. James notices that Ikenna is ____. He says, "____." These details suggest that the war changed ____.	• James / Ikenna is . . . • Before / After the war, James / Ikenna . . . • The characters are similar because . . . • The characters are different because . . .

Peer Review

Rate

Respond to the following with a point rating that reflects your opinion.

	1	2	3	4
Ideas				
Evidence				
Language and Conventions				

Submit

Students should submit substantive feedback to two peers using the review instructions below.

- How well does this response answer the prompt?
- How well does the writer support his or her ideas with details and examples from the text?
- Which sentence in the writer's response made you think differently about the text or the characters?
- What did the writer do well in this response? What does the writer need to work on?

Remember that your comments are most useful when they are kind and constructive.

SENTENCE FRAMES

- You (completely / partly / almost) ____ answered the prompt because ____.
- The best evidence you used was ____.
- After I read your response, I thought differently about ____.
- One good point you made was ____.
- One idea that needed clarification was ____.

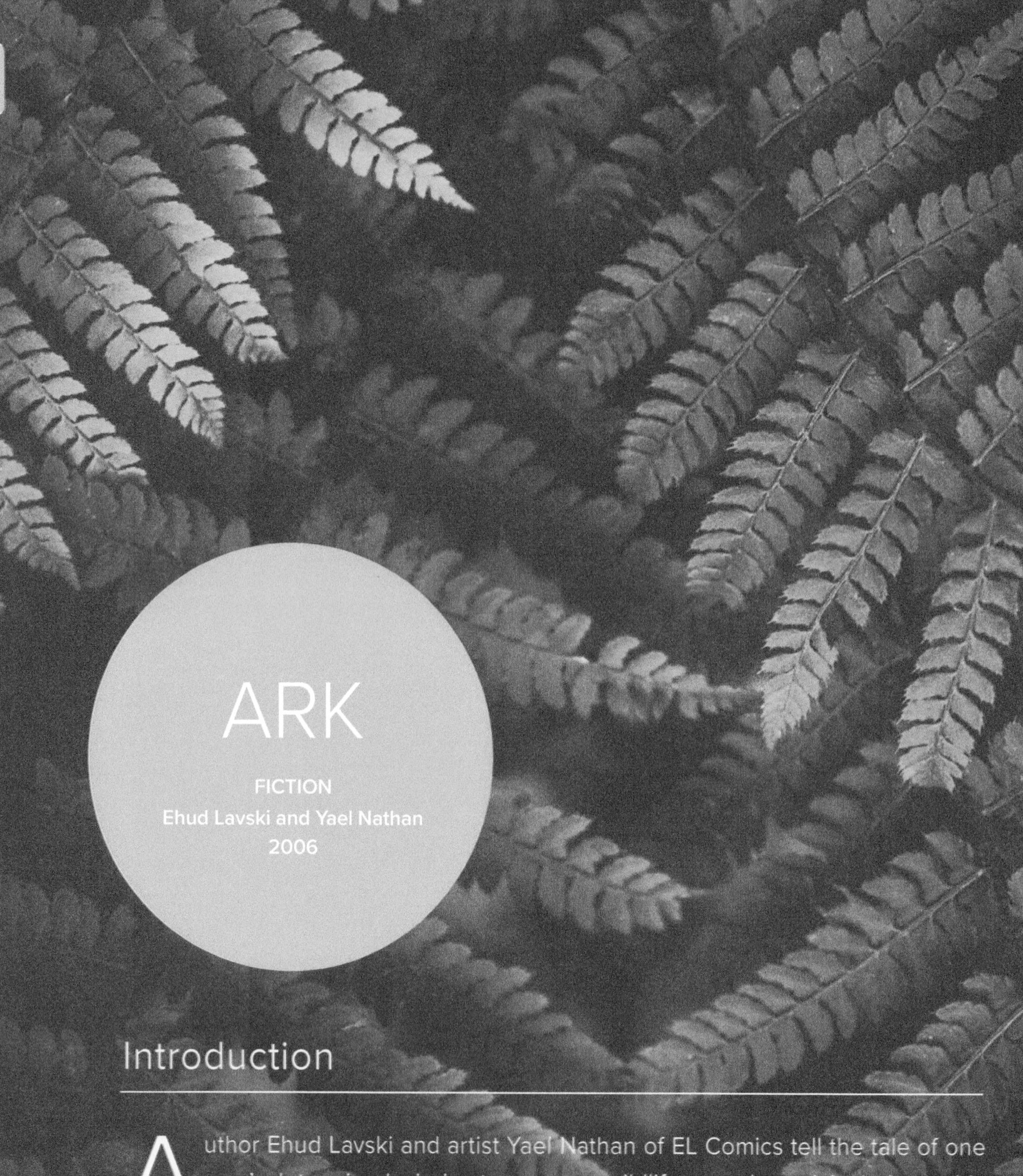

ARK

FICTION

Ehud Lavski and Yael Nathan

2006

Introduction

Author Ehud Lavski and artist Yael Nathan of EL Comics tell the tale of one man's determined mission to preserve wildlife as we know it in their graphic story "ARK." In a world plagued by mutation and illness, one man makes a determined effort to preserve wildlife—and the world—as we know it. With his body plagued by illness, will he succeed? Or will the world be irrevocably changed?

In a post-apocalyptic world, one man is on a quest to preserve un-mutated wildlife. After months of tracking, he finally manages to capture a healthy she-wolf. Suddenly, mutated members of her pack, wolves with two heads or missing skin, attack him. Luckily, he manages to fend them off and bring the she-wolf back to his lab, where he releases her into a cage with a male wolf. We see him walk through his laboratory, where cages on all sides contain healthy specimens of wildlife. He knows he doesn't have much time left, because the radiation is making him weaker by the day. Someday soon he intends to release them all back into the wild, where he hopes they'll be able to fend for themselves.

ELL Proficiency-leveled summaries and summaries in multiple languages are available digitally.

Audio and audio text highlighting are available with this text.

CONNECT TO ESSENTIAL QUESTION

How are we shaped by change?

The graphic story "ARK," created by Ehud Lavski and Yael Nathan, explores a dark, dystopian future in which one survivor strives to preserve wildlife in the face of widespread mutation and illness. How can change have a negative effect on society, and what can people do to counteract harmful consequences?

Entry Point

As students prepare to read "ARK," share the following information with them to provide context.

- ✓ The word *apocalypse* comes from early Jewish texts describing a prophesied end of the world. There is no shortage of books, films, and TV series that tell of humans attempting to survive the collapse of society, whether it be by divine punishment, nuclear armageddon, environmental catastrophe, or other disasters. It is tempting to think this genre is a new one, created by the anxiety surrounding the Cold War, but that ignores works like H. G. Wells's 1898 *War of the Worlds* and Mary Shelley's 1826 *The Last Man*, perhaps the first modern post-apocalyptic fiction.
- ✓ Some features are common in apocalyptic and post-apocalyptic fiction. The most obvious is that the stories take place during or after a catastrophe that wipes out most of humanity. The genre often has similarities to wilderness survival stories, as the characters must be self-reliant and adapt to a more primitive lifestyle.

These icons identify differentiation strategies and scaffolded support for a variety of students. See the digital lesson plan for additional differentiation strategies and scaffolds.

Instructional Path

The print teacher's edition includes essential point-of-use instruction and planning tools. Complete lesson plans and program documents appear in your digital teacher account.

Independent Read: ARK

Objectives: After reading "ARK," students will write a short comic that demonstrates their understanding of how a narrative is expressed through both text and art.

Independent Read

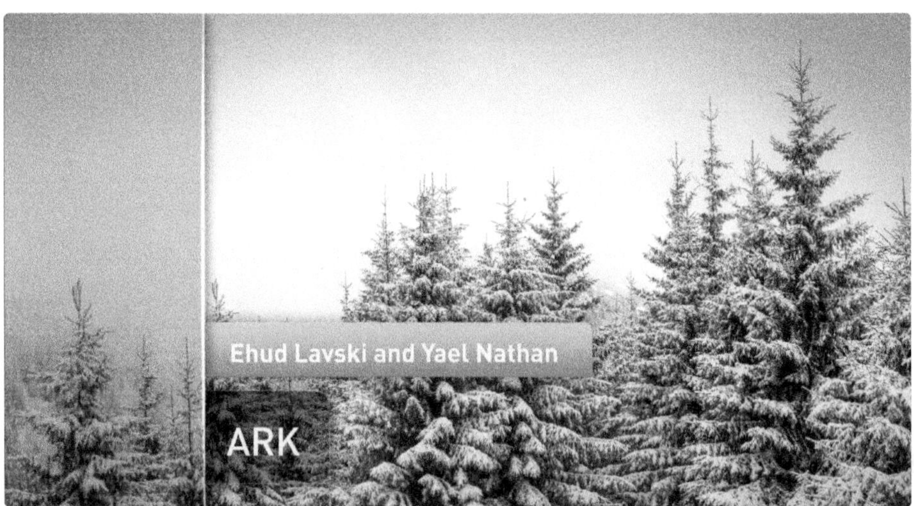

Introduce the Text

As a class, watch the video preview and have students read the introduction in pairs to make connections to the video preview.

- How do the words, images, and audio of the video all work together to convey meaning?
- If you were one of the last humans on Earth, what would you do to survive?

ELL **SPEAKING FRAMES**

- The words explain ____ and the images and audio add ____.
- If I was one of the last humans, I would ____.

Access Complex Text

LEXILE: N/A **WORD COUNT:** 192

The following areas may be challenging for students, particularly ELL English Language Learners and A Approaching grade-level learners.

Genre	Organization
• Comic strips and graphic novels can be challenging because meaning is conveyed through both the illustrations and words. Students may focus too much on the artwork and skip the narration and dialogue, or vice versa. • Encourage students to take their time reading. They should make sure they read every text bubble and study the art before moving on the next panel.	• The intended order of panels and text bubbles may be unclear or confusing to readers, especially if the reader's first language is read right-to-left. • Explain that a well-constructed comic positions the text so it can be read left-to-right, top-to-bottom. If text is placed in opposite corners of the panel, look at the art before reading the second text box.

"It's a roll of the dice every time. This time it worked."

1

Developing Background Knowledge and Cultural Awareness

Find out what your students already know about the genres of science fiction and science fantasy.

1. Generate a list (on the board or on paper) of what students know about the genres of science fiction and fantasy.
2. Have students discuss why these stories are important and how they might connect to real life.

Discuss with students: Readers tend to gravitate toward genres that they know or find relatable, sometimes avoiding science fiction or fantasy as a result. In what ways does science fiction provide an opportunity to explore and discuss issues in our society? What themes or issues might be easier to explore in science fiction as opposed to other kinds of fiction?

2

SELECTION VOCABULARY

specimen / el espécimen ***noun*** an example of a type of plant, animal, or thing COGNATE

collapse / colapsar ***verb*** to fall or fall apart; to break down COGNATE

NOTES

GRRRR
But then I hear the sound.

BLAM
BLAM
BLAM
BLAM
BLAM

Dead, but only two bullets left.
Wait. Where's the third wolf?

3

NOTES

4

TEXT TALK

What caused the mutant wolves?

See student edition page 87: The wolves were mutated by radiation from a bomb, presumably a nuclear weapon.

SELECTION VOCABULARY

generation / la generación *noun* all the people living at the same time or of approximately the same age COGNATE

mutant / el mutante *noun* an organism that has characteristics resulting from chromosomal alteration COGNATE

ARK

5

6

TEXT TALK

Why does the protagonist capture the normal wolf?

See student edition pages 88–89: He wants to breed the wolf to create a population of non-mutated wolves.

I don't know how much time I have left.

All those trips to
find new animals.

To find food
for them.

I can feel the radiation
slowly killing me.

One day, when my time comes,
I will open the gates.
Release them all into the world.

7

Prepare for Advanced Courses

Use the activity below to differentiate instruction for your B Beyond grade level learners.

Analyze for Enrichment

Direct students to describe the visual composition of the graphic novel (they might consider color, shape, perspective, proportion, texture, contrast).

Ask students:

- Do the characteristics of the illustrations change throughout the text or stay the same? Why might this be?
- What impact does the graphic novel's visual composition have on developing character and conveying the text's central message?

NOTES

I don't know if they will make it out there.
I can only hope.
But it might give this world one more chance.

8

TEXT TALK

What does the protagonist plan to do before he dies?

See student edition pages 90–91: He plans to release the animals so they can repopulate the world.

How did discussing the genres of science fiction and science fantasy contribute to your understanding of the text?

Answers will vary.

Writer's Notebook

Connect to Essential Question: Give students time to reflect on how "ARK" connects to the unit's essential question "How are we shaped by change?" by freewriting in their Writer's Notebooks.

CHECK FOR SUCCESS

If students are still struggling to respond to the prompt, ask them scaffolded questions, such as:

- What change or changes caused the protagonist to work on this task?
- What does he hope to change?

Reading Comprehension OPTIONAL

Have students complete the digital reading comprehension questions ✓ when they finish reading.

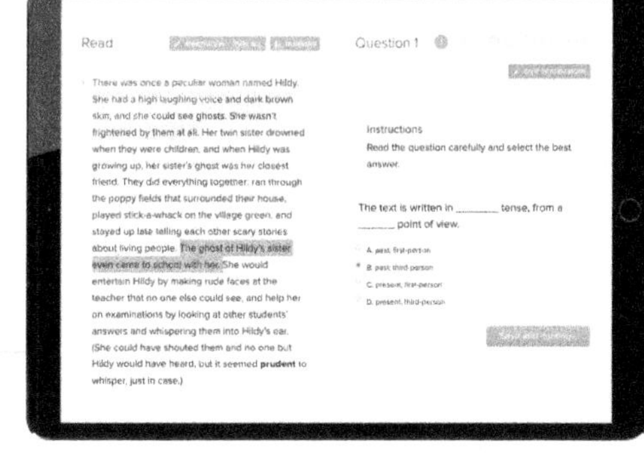

ANSWER KEY

QUESTION 1: B

QUESTION 2: D

QUESTION 3: C

QUESTION 4: D

QUESTION 5: *See chart below.*

First	Second	Third	Fourth
The narrator finds a normal wolf and tranquilizes it.	The narrator is attacked by mutant wolfs.	The narrator brings the normal wolf back to its new "home."	The narrator hopes that his efforts will help give the world another chance.

Connect and Extend OPTIONAL

CONNECT TO EXTENDED ORAL PROJECT

Students can use their experience with communicating a story through a graphic novel to inform their approach to the Extended Oral Presentation presentation. Have them reflect on the different literary and artistic devices they used to accomplish their purpose.

BEYOND THE BOOK

Graphic: History; Dystopian Style

In this story the protagonist is rescuing animals that have not been affected by radiation. Students will choose a historical story and turn it into a graphic dystopian tale.

Ask students to:

- Choose a popular historical story and outline the major events.
- Retell these events with a dystopian twist. To help develop an idea, present thinking questions:
  - > Think about technologies available and what would happen if they didn't exist or they took over in some way.
  - > Think about different government controls.
  - > Think of a global issue that can be exaggerated to harm the public.
- Create a comic that retells the historical story with a dystopian twist.
- Share with classmates.

To reflect, ask students:

- Is a dystopian society created by a sense of fear or some other source?
- How do radical ideas in text affect society?

Collaborative Conversation

SCAFFOLDS

Post the writing prompt to generate a discussion in small groups. Ask students to first break down the prompt before they discuss relevant ideas and textual evidence.

If you are familiar with graphic novels or comics, you know that each panel communicates an idea, even if there are no words on it. The art does most of the work. Create your own narrative in the form of a graphic novel, like "ARK." You don't need to write the whole story, just three panels. Alternatively, you could illustrate a story you read in class or a favorite story you read on your own time. Share your work with the class and see if they understand what is happening on the page.

Use the scaffolds below to differentiate instruction for your ELL English Language Learners and A Approaching grade-level learners.

ELL **BEGINNING, INTERMEDIATE** Use the discussion guide and speaking frames to facilitate the discussion with support from the teacher.

ADVANCED, ADVANCED HIGH Use the discussion guide and speaking frames to facilitate the discussion in mixed-level groups.

A **APPROACHING** Use the discussion guide to facilitate the discussion in mixed-level groups.

APPROACHING
ADVANCED, ADVANCED HIGH
BEGINNING, INTERMEDIATE

Discussion Guide	Speaking Frames
1. What narrative do I want to tell?	• My characters will be ____, and my narrative is set in ____. • The plot of my narrative is ____.
2. What parts of the narrative can be told with art?	• I can show ____ through the artwork. • I can show this by ____.
3. What parts of the narrative need to be told with text?	• I'll use narration to explain ____. • I'll use dialogue to show ____.

Text to World

Use the activity below to differentiate instruction for your B Beyond grade level learners.

Reread student edition redux page 87:

It's been so long since the bomb, these are third generation mutants.

Have students conduct informal research about the effects of nuclear bombs on the environment, specifically animals.

Ask students:

- How does this text relate or exaggerate events from the real world?

Review Prompt and Rubric

Before students begin writing, review the writing prompt and rubric with the class.

PERSONAL NARRATIVE: Banaji and Greenwald describe lies that people tell because they believe they more wholly represent the truth than the actual truth, even though that sounds illogical. In a narrative, describe a "blue lie" (as defined by the authors) of your own. Your narrative should include the reasoning behind your lie—such as why you believed it to be more "true" than the actual truth—whom you told it to, and what happened as a result.

ELL A

PROMPT GUIDE

- What narrative do I want to tell?
- What parts of the narrative will I express with art, and which parts will be presented through text?
- What should I put in each panel?

Score	Personal Narrative	Language and Conventions
4	The writer is able to skillfully convey the experience of telling a "blue lie" and communicate its importance or meaning.	The writer demonstrates a consistent command of grammar, punctuation, and usage conventions. Although minor errors may be evident, they do not detract from the fluency or the clarity of the essay.
3	The writer is able to clearly convey the experience of telling a "blue lie" and adequately communicate its importance or meaning.	The writer demonstrates an adequate command of grammar, punctuation, and usage conventions. Although some errors may be evident, they create few (if any) disruptions in the fluency of the writing or the clarity of the essay.
2	The writer is able to convey some sense of the experience of telling a "blue lie" but may not be able to communicate its importance or meaning.	The writer demonstrates a partial command of grammar, punctuation, and usage conventions. Some distracting errors may be evident, at times creating minor disruptions in the fluency or clarity of the writing.
1	Because the narrative is presented in a random or illogical way, the writer is not able to convey a sense of the experience of telling a "blue lie."	The writer demonstrates little or no command of grammar, punctuation, and usage conventions. Serious and persistent errors create disruptions in the fluency of the writing and sometimes interfere with meaning.
0	The writer is unable to convey a sense of the experience of telling a "blue lie," nor does he or she communicate its importance or meaning.	Serious and persistent errors overwhelm the writing and interfere with the meaning of the response as a whole, making the writer's meaning impossible to understand.

SCAFFOLDS

Write

Ask students to complete the writing assignment using text evidence to support their answers.

Use the scaffolds below to differentiate instruction for your ELL English Language Learners and A Approaching grade level readers.

ELL **BEGINNING** With the help of the word bank, write a response using paragraph frame 1.

INTERMEDIATE With the help of the word bank, write a response using paragraph frames 1 and 2.

ADVANCED, ADVANCED HIGH Write a response of differentiated length using the sentence starters.

A APPROACHING Write a response of differentiated length using the sentence starters.

BEGINNING / INTERMEDIATE		INTERMEDIATE	INTERMEDIATE	ADVANCED, ADVANCED HIGH / APPROACHING
Word Bank		**Paragraph Frame 1**	**Paragraph Frame 2**	**Sentence Starters**
man woman future past disaster	competition mountains school joke inspiration	My main character will be ____. The story is set in ____. The main event is ____. I will draw ____. The character will say ____.	In the first panel, I will ____. In the second panel, the characters will ____. In the third panel, readers will learn ____.	• My main character will be . . . • The story is set in . . . • The main event is . . . • In the first panel, I will . . . • In the second panel, the characters will . . . • In the third panel, readers will learn . . .

Peer Review

Students should submit substantive feedback to two peers using the review instructions below.

- How well does this response answer the prompt?
- How do the words and images work together to convey a theme or main idea?
- What does the writer do well in this response? What does the writer need to work on?

Remember that your comments are most useful when they are kind and constructive.

Rate

Respond to the following with a point rating that reflects your opinion.

	1	2	3	4
Ideas				
Evidence				
Language and Conventions				

Submit

SENTENCE FRAMES

A

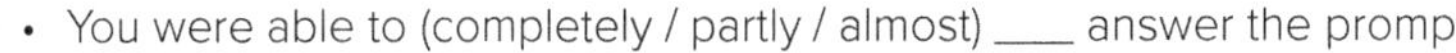

- You were able to (completely / partly / almost) ____ answer the prompt.
- You could answer the prompt more completely by ____.
- Words like ____ and images like ____ work together to convey ____.
- My favorite part of your response is ____.

Blindspot: Hidden Biases of Good People

ARGUMENTATIVE TEXT
Mahzarin R. Banaji and Anthony G. Greenwald
2013

Introduction

Two experts in the field of psychology, Mahzarin Banaji (b. 1956) and Anthony Greenwald (b. 1939), based their book, *Blindspot: Hidden Biases of Good People*, on "Project Implicit." Project Implicit details their research on how people have implicit biases that affect behavior, whether consciously or not. Their "IAT," or "implicit-association test," was collaboratively created in 1995 and has risen in popularity as people have become more open to exploring their hidden biases of gender, class, race, and culture. Banaji and Greenwald are pioneers in cognition, paving the way for deeper thought into thought itself, as seen in the following excerpt.

Even though most people think they are untruthful only rarely, we speak untruths more than we'd care to admit. When asked, "how are you" or "do I look fat in these jeans," it is usually easier not to say what is going through our heads. While not a malevolent choice, it does "reflect a diverse set of motivations," which includes hoping to avoid boring someone or hurting their feelings. Other times, people speak untruths in order to get across a deeper truth about themselves. Researchers have come to call this "impression management," finding that it even occurs with purely factual questions such as height and weight, with people skewing their answers to be more favorable. Ultimately, this is okay because if one were to practice total honesty with friends and family, one might end up alienating all of them, because our day-to-day lives require just a small amount of untruthfulness.

 Proficiency-leveled summaries and summaries in multiple languages are available digitally.

 Audio and audio text highlighting are available with this text.

COMPARING WITHIN AND ACROSS GENRES

 Most people think of themselves as honest individuals, but authors Mahzarin R. Banaji and Anthony G. Greenwald argue that people tell small lies on a daily basis in "Blindspot: Hidden Biases of Good People." Along with "News Literacy in the Misinformation Age" and "Honesty on Social Media," this text shows how honesty and truth are complicated by changes in the modern world.

Entry Point

As students prepare to read *Blindspot: Hidden Biases of Good People*, share the following information with them to provide context.

- ✓ *Blindspot: Hidden Biases of Good People* is about how people respond honestly or dishonestly to survey questions. A lot of research has gone into how to create effective survey questions that people can understand and respond to honestly.
- ✓ Researchers generally agree on a few basic points:
  - Questions should be short and written in simple language, so that people understand them and do not get bored reading them.
  - Questions should be direct, and multi-part questions should be avoided.
  - Researchers should avoid biased or leading descriptions of matters in questions.
  - Instead of yes/no answer choices, researchers should aim for a range of 5–7 answer choice options to better capture the range of people's feelings.
    - > For example: very satisfied / satisfied / somewhat satisfied / unsatisfied / very unsatisfied

These icons identify differentiation strategies and scaffolded support for a variety of students. See the digital lesson plan for additional differentiation strategies and scaffolds.

Instructional Path

The print teacher's edition includes essential point-of-use instruction and planning tools. Complete lesson plans and program documents appear in your digital teacher account.

Independent Read: Blindspot: Hidden Biases of Good People

Objectives: After reading *Blindspot: Hidden Biases of Good People,* students will demonstrate in a short, written response how to craft a personal narrative that relates to the topic of the text.

Independent Read

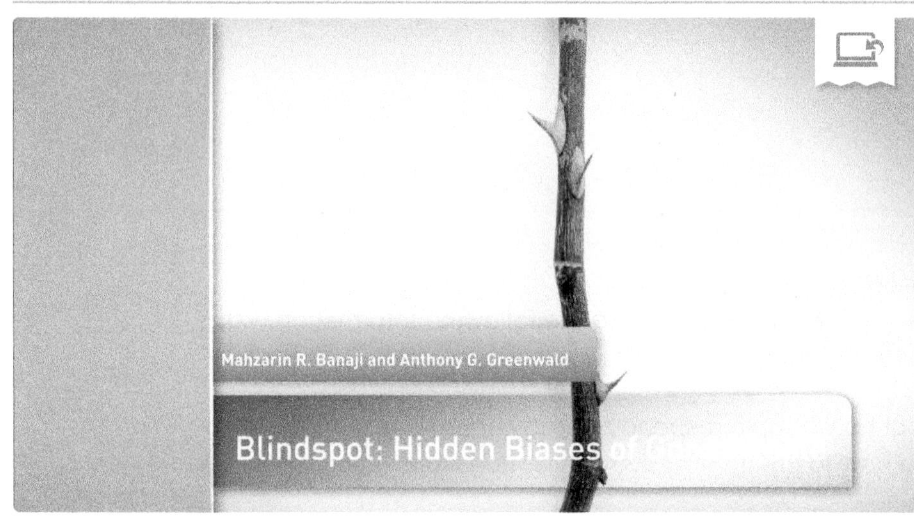

Introduce the Text

As a class, watch the video preview  and have students read the introduction in pairs to make connections to the video preview.

- What part of the video stood out to you the most?
- When have you told a lie you believed to be harmless?

ELL SPEAKING FRAMES

- The part of the video that stood out the most was ____.
- One harmless lie I told was ____.

Access Complex Text

LEXILE: 1320 **WORD COUNT:** 775

The following areas may be challenging for students, particularly ELL English Language Learners and A Approaching grade-level learners.

Organization	Purpose
• Students may not understand the intended effect of short paragraphs of questions and answers within a larger body of writing. They may assume that the questions are not meant for them. • Encourage students to engage with the text by asking them to pause when they get to a question, and then answer it to themselves as if they were a test subject in this study.	• The author does not immediately identify but instead builds up to the main idea of the text. • Coach students through the reading to point out tools that the author uses to build up from the introduction of "blue lies" and "impression management" to "the problem of distortion of survey data."

"Of course, honesty may be an overrated virtue."

Blue Lies

1 At some time, all of us will give answers that we know are untrue, for the paradoxical and totally strange reason that we actually believe the answer to be *more essentially truthful* than the actual truth. The phrase "true blue" inspired the color for this category of untruths. Some examples:

2 Q8. *Did you vote in last Tuesday's election?*

3 (Survey researcher to regular voter who neglected to vote last Tuesday but who answers yes because—"truth be told"—he or she is a "regular voter")

4 Q9. *Did you do all of the reading for the last test?*

5 (Professor to student who received a low grade on an exam and did not read the assigned texts but who answers yes)

6 Q10. *What radio station do you listen to?*

7 (Asked of a guest at an elite dinner gathering who answers "public radio," but whose car has only two preset stations, one for talk radio, the other for pop music)

8 Those who answer these three questions in known-untrue fashion may intend their answers to communicate a truth deeper than the actual facts would **indicate**, as in: *I am the type of person who votes regularly (even though I was too busy to vote last Tuesday); who always does the assigned work (but didn't last week because I had too many assignments from other courses); who shares the cultural and political values associated with public radio (but listens to it only when what's on the other stations is boring).*

9 We can justify blue lies such as these by observing that they allow others to see us as we (honestly) see ourselves. But this is a charitable view. Less charitably, these blue lies are ploys to produce favorable regard by others.

SELECTION VOCABULARY

indicate / indicar *verb* to direct attention to; to point out COGNATE

Developing Background Knowledge and Social Emotional Learning

1. Pose these questions to the whole class: "When is it wrong to lie? When is it acceptable or even preferable to lie?"
2. Ask students to write individual responses in their notebooks. Then have students share their ideas with a partner. Ask for volunteers to share their responses with the whole class.

Discuss with students: Do you believe that telling a lie can ever be a good thing? Think of times you were lied to. Was the lie meant to protect you or to hurt you? Did it have the intended effect? What was the last lie you told, and what was your motivation for telling it? Looking back, would you lie again?

TEXT TALK

How do the authors say we can justify blue lies?

See paragraph 1: We think such lies allow others to see more authentic versions of ourselves.

NOTES

Social psychologists know this ploy well, and have a telling name for it—*impression management.*

10 Impression management even comes into play when people are answering questions that do not seem to permit much wiggle room. If someone wants to know your age, height, and weight, what would you say? Although many people provide entirely accurate answers, researchers have repeatedly found that **substantial** minorities err when asked about these basic facts on survey questionnaires. And the errors are systematic: With the exception of answers provided by the very young, the very thin, and the very tall, the errors are virtually all in the direction of being younger, lighter in weight, and taller than can be verified with the aid of birth certificates, scales, and rulers.

11 Impression management has become well recognized as a problem in survey research. Survey participants will often produce less-than-true responses even when they know that their answers will just be fed into a computer and no researcher will ever see or hear them—even when they have been further assured that after their responses have been recorded, no one will be able to identify them as the source of their answers.

12 The problem of distortion of survey data by impression management is so great that survey researchers have devised a strategy to identify and weed out those survey participants who appear most likely to give responses shaped by their desire to make a favorable impression. The strategy calls for inserting some true-false catch questions such as the following into a survey.

13 Q11. *I am always courteous, even to people who are disagreeable.*

14 Q12. *I always apologize to others for my mistakes.*

15 Q13. *I would declare everything at customs, even if I knew that I could not possibly be found out.*

16 Researchers assume that many of those who answer "true" to these questions are impression managers because, for most people, full honesty should produce "false" to all three. After all, few people are *always* courteous, few people *always* apologize for mistakes, and few are so **scrupulously** honest that they would make a statement that could cost them money if they could avoid the financial penalty through a minor deception that would remain undetected. It is a more than mildly ironic comment on the **vicissitudes** of self-report survey methods that social scientists credit the person who admits to cheating at customs with greater honesty than the one who claims not to cheat.

17 If you think that you could honestly answer "true" to all three of Q11, Q12, and Q13, it is possible that you are among the very small group of completely

TEXT TALK

Why do the authors write that "honesty may be an overrated virtue?"

See paragraph 17: They believe that lies are necessary for our social lives. They make our interactions easier.

SELECTION VOCABULARY

substantial / considerable *adjective* fairly large

scrupulously / escrupulosamente *adverb* with careful attention to doing something correctly, especially in a moral sense

vicissitudes / la vicisitud *noun* a change in conditions or circumstances COGNATE

honest people on the planet. Of course, honesty may be an overrated virtue. If you decided to report all of your flaws to friends and to apply a similar standard of total honesty when talking to others about their shortcomings, you might soon find that you no longer have friends. Should you have any doubts about this, recall Q2 (*Do I look fat in these jeans?*). The white lie **typically** offered in response to Q2 can also be seen as a reflected blue lie, providing a mirror in which the questioner can find welcome agreement with his or her own too-good-to-be-true perception (that is, *I look just great*). Tamper with that self-regard at your own risk.

12 Our daily social lives demand, and generally receive, repeated lubrication with a certain amount of untruthfulness, which keeps the gears of social interaction meshing smoothly.

Excerpted from *Blindspot: Hidden Biases of Good People* by Mahzarin R. Banaji and Anthony G. Greenwald, published by Delacorte Press.

WRITE

PERSONAL NARRATIVE: Banaji and Greenwald describe lies that people tell because they believe they more wholly represent the truth than the actual truth, even though that sounds illogical. In a narrative, describe a "blue lie" (as defined by the authors) of your own. Your narrative should include the reasoning behind your lie—such as why you believed it to be more "true" than the actual truth—whom you told it to, and what happened as a result.

Prepare for Advanced Courses

Use the activity below to differentiate instruction for your B Beyond grade level learners.

Author's Word Choice

In paragraph 1, the author describes how the term "blue lie" was derived. Later, the author introduces "impression management," a term from social psychology that is related to, but not exactly the same as blue lies.

Ask students:

- What are the similarities between these terms? What are the differences? (Consider the words that are said in response to questions as well as the intention of the speaker.)
- How does the creation and use of the new term—blue lies—better serve the authors' purpose for this text?

SELECTION VOCABULARY

typically / generalmente *adverb* mostly or usually

TEXT TALK

How did reflecting on your own experiences with lies help deepen your understanding of the article?

Answers will vary.

Writer's Notebook

Connect to Essential Question: Give students time to reflect on how *Blindspot: Hidden Biases of Good People* connects to the unit's essential question "How are we shaped by change?" by freewriting in their Writer's Notebooks.

CHECK FOR SUCCESS

If students are still struggling to respond to the prompt, ask them scaffolded questions, such as:

- How do the authors view the "blue lies" that we tell? How do these lies represent both truth and falsehood?
- What does the fact that we tell "blue lies" tell us about ourselves? How does it change who we are in the eyes of others?

Reading Comprehension OPTIONAL

Have students complete the digital reading comprehension questions ✓ when they finish reading.

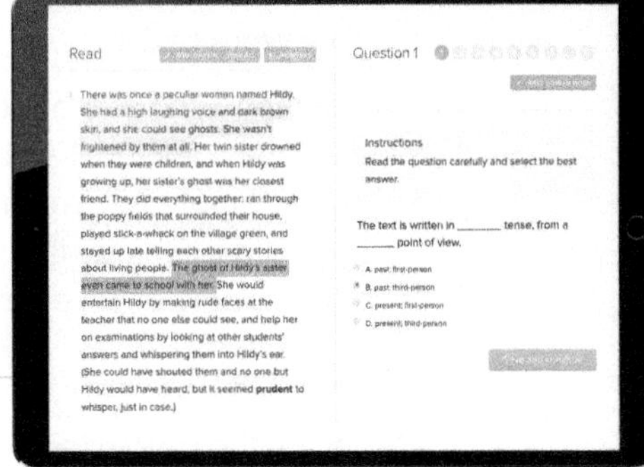

ANSWER KEY

QUESTION 1: C
QUESTION 2: B
QUESTION 3: D
QUESTION 4: A
QUESTION 5: *See chart below.*

Synonym	Word
considerable	substantial
normally	typically
meticulously	scrupulously
show	indicate
change	vicissitude

Connect and Extend OPTIONAL

CONNECT TO EXTENDED ORAL PROJECT

Students can use the concept of the "blue lie" in evaluating the resources and evidence that they are collecting for their oral presentation. In addition, the can consider the effective structure of this excerpt to help them outline their presentation.

BEYOND THE BOOK

Game: Truths and Untruths

Students will create a game that challenges players to think about truths and untruths.

Break students into small groups and ask them to:

- Generate a list of the types of untruths people tell.
  - > What types of lies do people tell because they honestly see themselves as being a certain way?
  - > What motivates different types of lying?
  - > To whom do we tell the most lies?
- Design a game that challenges players to distinguish between truths and untruths.
- Decide on the format of the game.
  - > Will it be a card game, board game, or role playing game?
  - > Will the players draw cards, roll a die, or spin a wheel?
  - > What materials will be needed?

Once students have had time to play their games, ask groups to provide each other with feedback on their game designs.

To reflect, ask students:

- After reading the text and playing the games, do you think you are now more likely to notice when you are telling an untruth?
- Is there harm in telling unconscious fibs that represent how you picture yourself?

Collaborative Conversation

SCAFFOLDS

Post the writing prompt to generate a discussion in small groups. Ask students to first break down the prompt before they discuss relevant ideas and textual evidence.

Banaji and Greenwald describe lies that people tell because they believe they more wholly represent the truth than the actual truth, even though that sounds illogical. In a narrative, describe a "blue lie" (as defined by the authors) of your own. Your narrative should include the reasoning behind your lie—such as why you believed it to be more "true" than the actual truth—whom you told it to, and what happened as a result.

Use the scaffolds below to differentiate instruction for your ELL English Language Learners and A Approaching grade-level learners.

ELL **BEGINNING, INTERMEDIATE** Use the discussion guide and speaking frames to facilitate the discussion with support from the teacher.

ADVANCED, ADVANCED HIGH Use the discussion guide and speaking frames to facilitate the discussion in mixed-level groups.

A **APPROACHING** Use the discussion guide to facilitate the discussion in mixed-level groups.

APPROACHING
ADVANCED, ADVANCED HIGH
BEGINNING, INTERMEDIATE

Discussion Guide	Speaking Frames
1. What is a blue lie? Why does it sound illogical?	• A blue lie is ____. • It sounds illogical because ____.
2. What is one blue lie you have told? To whom did you tell it?	• One blue lie I have told is ____. • I told it to ____.
3. Why did you tell your lie? What happened after you told it?	• I told this lie because ____. • After I told it, ____.

Ethical Issues

Use the activity below to differentiate instruction for your B Beyond grade level learners.

Reread paragraph 18: *Our daily social lives demand, and generally receive, repeated lubrication with a certain amount of untruthfulness, which keeps the gears of social interaction meshing smoothly.*

Ask students:

- To what extent does this quote reflect your personal code of ethics, what you value, and what you consider important in civil society?
- Do you consider it ethical to rely on "untruthfulness" in order to manage one's image and interact more comfortably with others? Provide supporting examples from your own life, literature, history, and/or current events.

Review Prompt and Rubric

Before students begin writing, review the writing prompt and rubric with the class.

PERSONAL NARRATIVE: Banaji and Greenwald describe lies that people tell because they believe they more wholly represent the truth than the actual truth, even though that sounds illogical. In a narrative, describe a “blue lie” (as defined by the authors) of your own. Your narrative should include the reasoning behind your lie—such as why you believed it to be more “true” than the actual truth—whom you told it to, and what happened as a result.

PROMPT GUIDE

- What is a blue lie? Why does it sound illogical?
- What is one blue lie you have told? To whom did you tell it?
- Why did you tell your lie? What happened after you told it?

Score	Personal Narrative	Language and Conventions
4	The writer is able to skillfully convey the experience of telling a “blue lie” and communicate its importance or meaning.	The writer demonstrates a consistent command of grammar, punctuation, and usage conventions. Although minor errors may be evident, they do not detract from the fluency or the clarity of the essay.
3	The writer is able to clearly convey the experience of telling a “blue lie” and adequately communicate its importance or meaning.	The writer demonstrates an adequate command of grammar, punctuation, and usage conventions. Although some errors may be evident, they create few (if any) disruptions in the fluency of the writing or the clarity of the essay.
2	The writer is able to convey some sense of the experience of telling a “blue lie” but may not be able to communicate its importance or meaning.	The writer demonstrates a partial command of grammar, punctuation, and usage conventions. Some distracting errors may be evident, at times creating minor disruptions in the fluency or clarity of the writing.
1	Because the narrative is presented in a random or illogical way, the writer is not able to convey a sense of the experience of telling a “blue lie.”	The writer demonstrates little or no command of grammar, punctuation, and usage conventions. Serious and persistent errors create disruptions in the fluency of the writing and sometimes interfere with meaning.
0	The writer is unable to convey a sense of the experience of telling a “blue lie,” nor does he or she communicate its importance or meaning.	Serious and persistent errors overwhelm the writing and interfere with the meaning of the response as a whole, making the writer’s meaning impossible to understand.

Write

SCAFFOLDS

Ask students to complete the writing assignment using text evidence to support their answers.

Use the scaffolds below to differentiate instruction for your ELL English Language Learners and A Approaching grade level readers.

ELL **BEGINNING** With the help of the word bank, write a response using paragraph frame 1.

INTERMEDIATE With the help of the word bank, write a response using paragraph frames 1 and 2.

ADVANCED, ADVANCED HIGH Write a response of differentiated length using the sentence starters.

A **APPROACHING** Write a response of differentiated length using the sentence starters.

BEGINNING / INTERMEDIATE	BEGINNING / INTERMEDIATE	INTERMEDIATE	ADVANCED, ADVANCED HIGH / APPROACHING
Word Bank	**Paragraph Frame 1**	**Paragraph Frame 2**	**Sentence Starters**
parent, myself, sibling, usually, friend, lied, homework, found out, chores, apologize	A blue lie I once told was ____. I told it to ____. I told the lie because ____. I believed the lie was more truthful than the actual truth because ____. In the end, ____.	After reading the excerpt from the book, I think ____. I think the authors ____ about honesty being complicated. My story shows that ____, so blue lies are ____.	• A blue lie I once told is. . . • I told the lie to . . . • I told the lie because . . . • The lie felt more true . . . • In the end . . . • After reading the excerpt, I think . . . • My story shows . . .

Peer Review

Students should submit substantive feedback to two peers using the review instructions below.

- How well does this response answer the prompt?
- How easily could you follow the story of the writer's narrative?
- What does the writer do well in this response? What does the writer need to work on?

Remember that your comments are most useful when they are kind and constructive.

Rate

Respond to the following with a point rating that reflects your opinion.

	1	2	3	4
Ideas				
Evidence				
Language and Conventions				

Submit

ELL A **SENTENCE FRAMES**

- You were able to (completely / partly / almost) ____ answer the prompt.
- You could answer the prompt more completely by ____.
- I was / was not ____ able to follow your story easily because ____.
- My favorite part of your response is ____.

News Literacy in the Misinformation Age

INFORMATIONAL TEXT
The News Literacy Project
in partnership with StudySync
2018

Introduction

This essay offers insights into the numerous types of misinformation that circulate in today's information ecosystem, and how false or misleading information often tries to exploit our biases. It also offers insight into the practice of journalism, so young people can imagine how stories they read on a daily basis come to fruition. The News Literacy Project is a nonprofit that works with schools, libraries, and media organizations to teach young people about how to navigate news and information in the current digital era. Their resources are nonpartisan and are offered online, in professional development courses, and in their weekly newsletter.

Currently, it would take multiple lifetimes to digest just a single day's news. What makes this especially challenging is learning how to distinguish credible information from raw material, as well as how to recognize fake news. Although there has never been greater access, a lot of the information we encounter has been designed to be misleading, which in turn influences the way people think and, ultimately, vote. This misinformation takes advantage of cognitive biases, often causing people to have strong emotional reactions, which make them react faster than they should. This article suggests that to be a more discerning and well-informed citizen, readers should look for unbiased and neutral reporting. Since professional journalists and news outlets are guided by a set of standards and ethos, their reporting tends to be more fair, neutral, and honest.

Proficiency-leveled summaries and summaries in multiple languages are available digitally.

Audio and audio text highlighting are available with this text.

COMPARING WITHIN AND ACROSS GENRES

How do people distinguish fact from fiction online? "News Literacy in the Misinformation Age" asks readers to think about ways they can challenge misinformation, bias, and inauthenticity on the Internet.

The article provides suggestions and guidelines for verifying whether or not information is trust-worthy, tools which students may be able to utilize even in the more personal and constant occurrences described in "Blindspot: Hidden Biases of Good People" and "Honesty on Social Media."

Entry Point

As students prepare to read "News Literacy in the Misinformation Age," share the following information with them to provide context.

- ✓ Real news should always be distinguished from fake news, but readers should also be on the lookout for satirical news. Satirical news uses humor for entertainment and to criticize its subject. Although the stories are fake, satirical news often reflects real concerns and criticisms. Fake news sites, on the other hand, present rumors as true in order to sway opinions or make money.
- ✓ Satirical news has occasionally been mistaken for real news. The Chinese website *People's Daily Online* repeated a story from *The Onion* saying that North Korean dictator Kim Jong Un was chosen as 2012's Sexiest Man Alive. A reporter from *The Washington Post* once cited satirical news site *The Daily Currant*'s claim that Sarah Palin had joined the news network Al Jazeera.

These icons identify differentiation strategies and scaffolded support for a variety of students. See the digital lesson plan for additional differentiation strategies and scaffolds.

Instructional Path

The print teacher's edition includes essential point-of-use instruction and planning tools. Complete lesson plans and program documents appear in your digital teacher account.

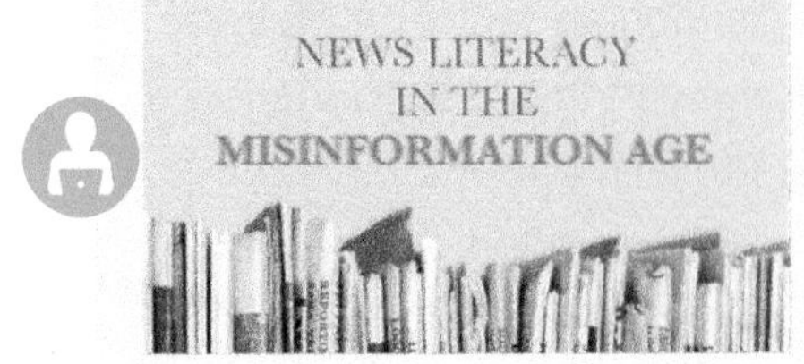

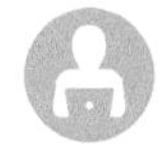

Independent Read: News Literacy in the Misinformation Age

Objectives: After reading "News Literacy in the Misinformation Age," students will write a personal response demonstrating their understanding of the production of, reaction to, and defenses against fake news.

Independent Read

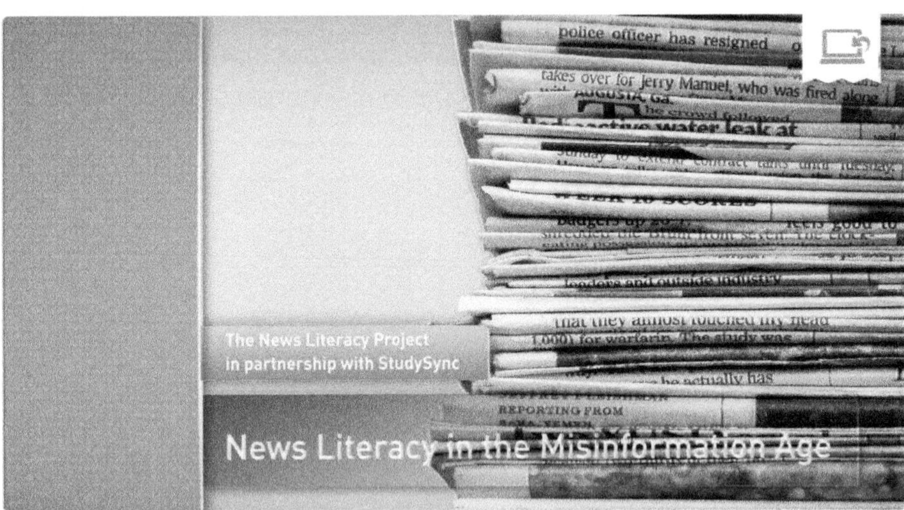

Introduce the Text

As a class, watch the video preview and have students read the introduction in pairs to make connections to the video preview.

- How does the information in this video connect to what you already know?
- Have you ever read a news story and later discovered it was not true?
- What are some methods you use for determining the legitimacy of a news story?

Access Complex Text

LEXILE: 1280 **WORD COUNT:** 2,504

The following areas may be challenging for students, particularly ELL English Language Learners and A Approaching grade-level learners.

Organization	Prior Knowledge
• This feature consists of three related articles. Students might struggle to understand the connection between the articles. • Have students identify the main idea of each article, and then discuss the relationships between the main ideas of all three articles. A graphic organizer may be useful to students.	• Students might benefit from background information on journalistic practices and the ideal of objectivity in news reporting. • Encourage students to research and discuss the core principles of journalism. Study several articles with students and discuss whether the articles meet common journalistic standards.

"Why does it matter if people create, share or believe false information?"

NOTES

The Case for News Literacy

1 If you decided to look at every single post by every single person on Facebook on a typical day — spending just one second on each post — how long do you think it would take you?

2 Let's do the math: About 1 billion status updates are made on Facebook every day. Each day is made up of 86,400 seconds — 60 seconds x 60 minutes x 24 hours. So if you did nothing else — no time for eating, no time for sleeping, no time for TV or movies, no time for school — it would take you . . . 11,574 days, or 32 years. *Thirty-two years*, just to glance through *one day's* worth of Facebook posts!

3 Now, add to this pile of status updates everything else that is created and shared in a typical day — every tweet, news report, blog post, meme, comment, photo, video and podcast — and you'd need several lifetimes to see it all. If you tried to actually read, watch, listen to and think about just one day's worth of news and information, you would need several thousand lifetimes.

4 It's not only the amount of information that's challenging; it's also the complexity of what we're reading, watching and hearing. Some of this information is, without question, credible. Some is incomplete, like raw videos, images or documents. Some is often misleading, like strong partisan opinions or branded content. And some of it is just plain fake: fake accounts on social media, faked videos, fake leaked documents, fake tweets, faked pictures, fake quotes and, of course, "fake news."

5 This avalanche of information is hitting us at a time when anyone with internet access can, in a growing number of ways, amplify his or her voice to reach a global audience. Anyone with a smartphone can document an event and share it with the world. More people than ever before have the most powerful tools in human history to search for, evaluate, comment on and spread information.

Developing Background Knowledge and Cultural Awareness

1. Present students with the following statement: Journalists can never be truly objective in their reporting of news.
2. Have students raise their hands to indicate whether they a) strongly disagree; b) disagree; c) agree; or d) strongly agree. Assign each response a corner of the room, and have students go to their respective corners to explain their positions.
3. Have one student from each group be the spokesperson to explain the group's response.

Discuss with students: Where do you and your family typically get "the news"? To what extent does the source of your news impact its reliability? What factors allow for incorrect information to spread and be believed?

Prepare for Advanced Courses

Use the activity below to differentiate instruction for your B Beyond grade level learners.

Analyze for Enrichment

In paragraph 6, the text mentions that citizens in a democracy "need accurate, reliable information about those issues, those ideas, those policies and those candidates."

Direct students to review the text, searching for the risks associated with citizens receiving and believing inaccurate and unreliable information about issues, ideas, policies, and candidates.

Ask students:

- According to the text, what are the specific consequences associated with the profusion of "fake information"?
- How effective are the examples used in this text? Which examples reveal the greatest threat to a democracy?
- Based on your own knowledge and experiences, what other examples could the authors have used to show the threat posed by fake information?

NOTES

6 Learning how to manage the challenges of this information landscape and make the most of its opportunities are essential skills for today's citizens — especially when it comes to discerning fact from fiction. After all, citizens hold the power in a democracy. They determine what form their government will take by deciding which issues they think are most important and then voting for the candidates whose ideas and policies best address those issues. To do this effectively — to truly participate — citizens need accurate, reliable information about those issues, those ideas, those policies and those candidates.

7 Here's the good news: Finding news and information has never been easier, and access is expanding to more people every day.

8 But here's the bad news: As we search for what we need, we also encounter a lot of unverified, misleading or inaccurate information — some of which is actually designed to trick us into believing and sharing things that aren't true. Those materials can cause people to make bad decisions about all kinds of things — their health, their education options, their career choices or their vote. If our neighbors or fellow citizens believe a piece of false information, their resulting votes or decisions can indirectly affect us too. And while people have been fighting false information for a long time (after all, rumors, hoaxes and propaganda are nothing new), they now need a new set of skills to help them spot falsehoods and know what's true and what's not.

9 Becoming news literate gives citizens the skills and habits they need to recognize credible information, and to spot misleading or deceptive language or images that could trick them into forming false beliefs. It helps them to evaluate the purpose of information, to understand the signs that a piece of information has been checked, and to identify when something can or cannot be trusted. And, most importantly, it enables them to make informed choices that empower their voices and that strengthen our democracy by helping it meet the needs of its people.

10 What do you think? Think about all the information you consume in a day. Do you know which pieces of information are credible? What are the most exciting — and the most challenging — aspects of today's information landscape? What is the role of credible information in a democracy?

The Misinformation Age

11 A shaky video, taken by a handheld camera, of three friends using their cell phones to pop a pile of popcorn kernels. A report that Pope Francis has endorsed Donald Trump for president. A description in a well-known newspaper of a competitive poodle-clipping event at the 1900 Olympics in Paris.

TEXT TALK

What does it mean to be "news literate"?

See paragraph 9: A news-literate person is able to recognize credible information and spot misleading or deceptive language or images.

12 Each of these seemed convincing to thousands of people, but each of them is false:

- The popcorn video was a hoax staged by an internet marketing agency hired by a maker of Bluetooth headsets. Designed to appear raw and authentic, it racked up millions of views on YouTube before it was revealed to be fake.
- The item about the pope and Trump was the most widely shared story on Facebook in the final months of the 2016 presidential campaign. It originated on WTOE5news.com (a self-described "fantasy news website" whose name sounds like it could be a local television news site) and was picked up by EndingtheFed.com, an anonymously-registered website that had several of the most widely shared items on Facebook during the campaign (all of which were fake).
- The article about poodle-clipping at the Olympics was published by The Telegraph, a well-known British news organization, as an April Fool's Day hoax, then shared by others who mistook it as real.

13 These are all examples of misinformation, a phenomenon so common on the internet that people frequently joke about it. In fact, one of the most popular memes about misinformation is the below image. See if you can get the joke:

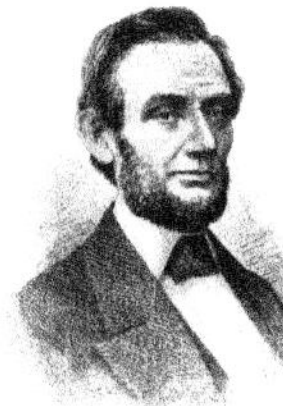

"YOU CAN'T BELIEVE EVERYTHING YOU HEAR ON THE INTERNET."
- ABE LINCOLN, 1868

14 Despite the fact that just about everyone who uses the internet (about half the world's population) knows how unreliable information found online can be, many people still get fooled every day.

15 Why does misinformation continue to thrive? The primary reason may be this: On the internet, anyone can publish anything. This is beneficial and empowering for the millions of people who have access to more than a million terabytes of information and, potentially, a global audience for their

NOTES

stories and ideas. It also means that much of the information found online has never been checked for accuracy.

16 Second, misinformation often takes advantage of our cognitive biases — our blind spots as human beings. It frequently causes us to have a strong emotional reaction — such as fear, or curiosity, or anger — that can make us feel or hope that something is true before we've taken the time to determine whether that expectation is reasonable. So we tend to filter the world of information through the biased lens of our own beliefs, noticing only those details and ideas that support what we want to believe.

17 This emotional reaction also makes us act faster than we should: We click, comment and share before we consider the stakes of sharing something we haven't verified — and most of the platforms and tools we use to engage with information make it easy to do this.

18 There's also an increasing number of free or low-cost ways to create convincing (but false) information: screenshot tools, photo- and video-editing software, graphic design tools, website hacking tools, fake tweet generators and thousands of social sharing and discussion sites and online communities where falsehoods, hoaxes and rumors can be released to specific audiences and catch fire.

19 Creating and spreading misinformation can be enormously profitable. Purveyors of "fake news" and other forms of clickbait can make tens of thousands of dollars in ad revenue a month from the traffic to their websites generates. Hoaxers and conspiracy theorists on YouTube can make significant amounts of money in the same way. Other people create or share misinformation to cause chaos, to troll others or for internet "karma" — for likes, upvotes, shares, reactions and new followers.

20 Finally, misinformation is a cheap and effective way for political activists to **alter** debates about controversial issues. And once an idea gets loose in the ether — once it starts to get shared in a variety of places and go viral — it's nearly impossible to stop it. Research even suggests that repeating a false claim as part of a fact check can sometimes strengthen it. (This is due to a cognitive bias known as the illusory truth effect: Things we see or hear enough times stick with us, and start to seem true after a while.)

21 Sometimes false information gets loose because of an innocent mistake, or as a joke. Sometimes it's created to make money. Sometimes it's a deliberate distortion of an issue for political gain. Whatever the reason, misinformation can have very real effects, causing people to form faulty beliefs, lose faith in our institutions and in the very idea that anything is true, or take misguided action that can hurt others.

TEXT TALK

How does misinformation take advantage of our emotions?

See paragraphs 16–17: Emotions like fear, curiosity, or anger can make us less skeptical and cause us to share the information faster.

SELECTION VOCABULARY

alter / alterar *verb* to change or to cause to change COGNATE

22 Luckily, as people become more and more aware of misinformation, they can also get better at **detecting** it. Here are some simple guidelines:

- Be aware when a piece of information causes you to have a strong emotional reaction. Pause and reflect on what you're feeling, and why.
- If the photo, claim or video seems too good (too outrageous, too amazing, too shocking, too terrible, or too infuriating) to be true, know that it probably isn't.
- Search for more information from credible sources. Do a quick search for the claim that is being made. Do links from fact-checking sites such as Snopes.com or FactCheck.org turn up? For an item on social media, read the comments (or, on Twitter, subsequent tweets) to see if anyone has verified it or found it to be false, and take a closer look at the account that shared it.
- Help to stop the spread of misinformation by correcting it wherever you see it being shared. Be respectful, be calm and cite high-quality sources that show why the information is false.

23 Think about what you've learned about misinformation. Think about the false information you've experienced firsthand. Why does it matter if people create, share or believe false information?

Standard Practice

24 When you read a news article, do you ever wonder what the reporter thinks or feels about the issue, event or **controversy** they are reporting on? Which political candidate do they support? Which policy do they prefer? Which sports team do they hope will win?

25 If you still have these kinds of questions after reading a news article, it means the writer is doing a good job keeping his or her personal views out of the story. Since the primary purpose of news is to inform, reporters have a duty to share information in as **unbiased** a way as possible. Even though all journalists have their own opinions, they typically strive to be as **neutral** as possible in their reporting — representing all **relevant** sides of a story without placing too much emphasis or authority where it doesn't belong.

26 How do journalists make sure they publish stories that are as neutral and fair as possible? All credible news outlets have a set of standards, or guidelines for how stories should be reported. Every newsroom's standards are different, but they share similar values, telling journalists to seek the truth and be fair and honest in reporting it.

27 When journalists report a story, they should pursue the "best **obtainable** version of the truth," as journalist Carl Bernstein puts it, by finding and verifying

SELECTION VOCABULARY

detect / detectar *verb* to discover or determine the presence or fact of COGNATE

controversy / la controversia *noun* a discussion or debate marked by opposing views COGNATE

unbiased / imparcial *adjective* without existing thoughts or opinions

neutral / neutral *adjective* having no personal preference COGNATE

relevant / relevante *adjective* appropriate and logically related to the topic COGNATE

obtainable / asequible *adjective* able to be gained or acquired

NOTES

all relevant details for their audience. This means they interview more than just one person — responsible journalists cite multiple credible sources, including documents when necessary, to get the full story.

28 For example, in reporting a workplace accident in which there are details to investigate but no clear indication of who is at fault, good journalists wouldn't just interview the person who got hurt. They would speak to eyewitnesses who saw the accident happen, they would offer the people involved an opportunity to comment on their guilt or innocence and they would contact the police for an official accident report. They would strive to treat every source fairly, giving each person a chance to respond to any allegations of wrongdoing. They would also locate and share any documents associated with the accident, which might include company memos or emails, police reports, independent reports like safety testing, chemical reports or NGO findings, relevant surveys and polls and video footage from the scene.

29 Journalists are also supposed to ensure that there are no conflicts of interest, which happen when a journalist has a strong personal connection with a group or issue that could get in the way of or compromise their ability to be fair in their reporting. In order to avoid conflicts of interest, journalists don't accept favors or gifts from sources. Most journalists also keep their political views private, and avoid participating in most political activities, such as protests or petitions. Some journalists don't even vote as a way of remaining as neutral as possible. Most news organizations also have standards, or guidelines, delineating the limitations on political activities that their journalists are expected to observe. If a conflict of interest is unavoidable, journalists should always be open and transparent about it.

30 How else do professional journalists seek to ensure accuracy and fairness in their work? They get help from other people — after a story is written, editors go through it and verify the story's facts by looking them up or double-checking the sources. These editors will also flag reporting they feel is unfair in some way, identify wording that is unclear or biased, or call attention to any critical sources or details that might be missing. Editors act as a second set of eyes, aiding reporters by showing them how their stories might be read and interpreted by other people.

31 Once an article is published, most news outlets have a way for their audience to contact them to report any errors or problems with the reporting — and credible news organizations will acknowledge their errors and correct them. Editors may read, respond to and publish these letters — whether they come in as mail, or electronically, through email or social media posts. Some news outlets also have public editors — or independent editors who point out ethical issues and problems with the reporting and publish this criticism on behalf of readers.

TEXT TALK

What are some ways journalists can ensure their stories are fair and accurate?

See paragraphs 26–30: They can find and verify all relevant details, treat their sources fairly, avoid conflicts of interest, and get help from editors.

32 Despite all the standards in place for journalists, it is still important for news consumers to seek news from a variety of high quality sources. That way, they can quickly note which details have been verified by multiple news outlets, and get a more comprehensive understanding of the news of the day.

33 What do you think? How much do you know about the checks and balances journalists go through before they publish a story? How can news consumers tell whether journalism is well-reported or poorly-reported? How can news organizations improve their standards? What journalistic standards are most important? How do you think your local news organizations do in trying to follow these guidelines? What guidelines can journalists follow to help ensure that their reporting is accurate, fair and reliable?

WRITE

PERSONAL RESPONSE: What do you think motivates certain sites or organizations to release fake news and information? What do you think makes individuals susceptible to believing fake news and information? And what measures can one take to avoid being fooled? Remember to support your ideas with textual evidence and your own background knowledge and experiences.

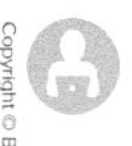

TEXT TALK

How did reflecting on your source for news articles deepen your understanding of the text?

Answers will vary.

Ask each Beyond grade-level student to write one additional discussion question. Then, have one or two students facilitate a discussion, using their questions to guide the conversation.

Writer's Notebook

Connect to Essential Question: Give students time to reflect on how "News Literacy in the Misinformation Age" connects to the unit's essential question, "How are we shaped by change?", by freewriting in their Writer's Notebooks.

CHECK FOR SUCCESS

If students are still struggling to respond to the prompt, ask them scaffolded questions, such as:

- What is fake news?
- How can you identify fake news?
- How do our behaviors have to change as a result of changes in the way we read and find news?

Reading Comprehension OPTIONAL

Have students complete the digital reading comprehension questions when they finish reading.

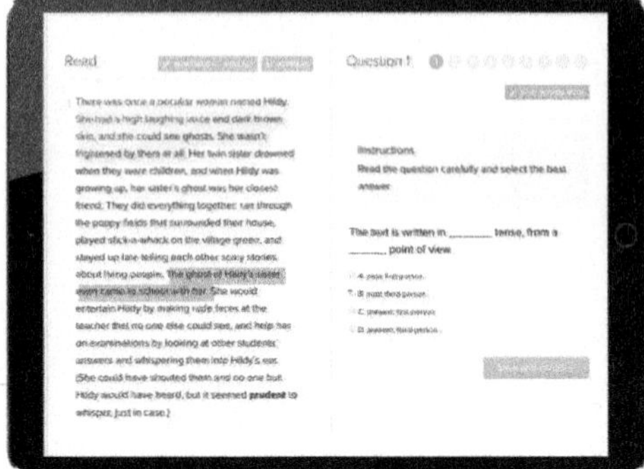

ANSWER KEY

QUESTION 1: A
QUESTION 2: D
QUESTION 3: A
QUESTION 4: B
QUESTION 5: B
QUESTION 6: C
QUESTION 7: A
QUESTION 8: D
QUESTION 9: *See first chart.*
QUESTION 10: *See second chart.*

Synonym	Word
applicable	relevant
recognize	detect
acquire	obtain
dispute	controversy
impartial	neutral

First	Second	Third	Fourth
The author describes the daunting intake of information that people encounter daily in today's world of news and technology.	The author presents the problem that young people, and people around the world, face today: the spread of misinformation.	The author offers examples of misinformation and strategies for recognizing bias and misinformation and counteracting their effects.	The author discusses the processes involved in researching, crafting, and editing a news story so that it does not contain bias or misinformation.

Connect and Extend OPTIONAL

CONNECT TO EXTENDED ORAL PROJECT

Students can learn from this selection how to support their claims with evidence, as they will have to in their extended oral presentations that share facts about an important topic that deserves more attention. To practice, have students highlight the strongest pieces of evidence in this selection.

BEYOND THE BOOK

This informational text presents strategies for reading critically and analyzing text for validity. Students will design and conduct a validity test on a news article.

Ask students to:

- Reread the text on how to analyze a text for validity.
- Design a test that any reader could use to determine validity when they come across news articles.
  - > Make sure the test is straightforward and simple (no more than five steps).
  - > The test should align to what they learned in "News Literacy in the Misinformation Age".
- Choose a current news article from social media or online.
- Exchange validity tests with other students and check articles for validity.
- Provide feedback to their partners on the effectiveness of the tests.
- Reflect, in writing, whether the tests were able to detect misinformation in their articles.

To reflect, ask students:

- Why do social media users need to evaluate the validity of online resources? What is the danger of "fake news"?
- What is your role in sharing news?

Collaborative Conversation

SCAFFOLDS

Post the writing prompt to generate a discussion in small groups. Ask students to first break down the prompt before they discuss relevant ideas and textual evidence.

What do you think motivates certain sites or organizations to release fake news and information? What do you think makes individuals susceptible to believing fake news and information? And what measures can one take to avoid being fooled? Remember to support your ideas with textual evidence and your own background knowledge and experiences.

Use the scaffolds below to differentiate instruction for your ELL English Language Learners and A Approaching grade-level learners.

ELL **BEGINNING, INTERMEDIATE** Use the discussion guide and speaking frames to facilitate the discussion with support from the teacher.

ADVANCED, ADVANCED HIGH HIGH Use the discussion guide and speaking frames to facilitate the discussion in mixed-level groups.

A **APPROACHING** Use the discussion guide to facilitate the discussion in mixed-level groups.

APPROACHING
ADVANCED, ADVANCED HIGH
BEGINNING, INTERMEDIATE

Discussion Guide	Speaking Frames
1. What motivates certain sites or organizations to release fake news and information?	• Some misinformation comes from ____. • Some people create misinformation because ____.
2. What makes individuals susceptible to believing fake news and information?	• People believe misinformation because ____. • Misinformation is more believable when ____.
3. What measures can one take to avoid being fooled by fake news?	• A person should ____. • A news literate person will

Text to World

Use the activity below to differentiate instruction for your B Beyond grade level learners.

Ask students to practice evaluating the credibility of a variety of news sources.

Ask students to:

- Review the article's bulleted list of ways to detect misinformation.
- Browse social media platforms and traditional media outlets in search of examples of both true and false information.
- Share your findings with your peers, explaining why something appears true versus false.

Review Prompt and Rubric

Before students begin writing, review the writing prompt and rubric with the class.

PERSONAL RESPONSE: What do you think motivates certain sites or organizations to release fake news and information? What do you think makes individuals susceptible to believing fake news and information? And what measures can one take to avoid being fooled? Remember to support your ideas with textual evidence and your own background knowledge and experiences.

PROMPT GUIDE

- What motivates certain sites or organizations to release fake news and information?
- What makes individuals susceptible to believing fake news and information?
- What measures can one take to avoid being fooled by fake news?

Score	Personal Narrative	Language and Conventions
4	The writer clearly answers the questions. The writer consistently supports their ideas with textual evidence, background knowledge, and experiences.	The writer demonstrates a consistent command of grammar, punctuation, and usage conventions. Although minor errors may be evident, they do not detract from the fluency or the clarity of the essay.
3	The writer answers the questions adequately. The writer supports their ideas with textual evidence, background knowledge, and experiences most of the time.	The writer demonstrates an adequate command of grammar, punctuation, and usage conventions. Although some errors may be evident, they create few (if any) disruptions in the fluency of the writing or the clarity of the essay.
2	The writer begins to reflect on his or her own participation. The writer supports their ideas with textual evidence, background knowledge, and experiences some of the time.	The writer demonstrates a partial command of grammar, punctuation, and usage conventions. Some distracting errors may be evident, at times creating minor disruptions in the fluency or clarity of the writing.
1	The writer attempts to reflect on his or her own participation. The writer rarely supports their ideas with textual evidence, background knowledge, and experiences.	The writer demonstrates little or no command of grammar, punctuation, and usage conventions. Serious and persistent errors create disruptions in the fluency of the writing and sometimes interfere with meaning.
0	The writer does not provide a relevant response to the prompt or does not provide a response at all.	Serious and persistent errors overwhelm the writing and interfere with the meaning of the response as a whole, making the writer's meaning impossible to understand.

Write

SCAFFOLDS

Ask students to complete the writing assignment using text evidence to support their answers.

Use the scaffolds below to differentiate instruction for your English Language Learners and Approaching grade level readers.

ELL **BEGINNING** With the help of the word bank, write a response using paragraph frame 1 .

INTERMEDIATE With the help of the word bank, write a response using paragraph frames 1 and 2.

ADVANCED, ADVANCED HIGH Write a response of differentiated length using the sentence starters.

A **APPROACHING** Write a response of differentiated length using the sentence starters.

BEGINNING | INTERMEDIATE | ADVANCED, ADVANCED HIGH | APPROACHING

Word Bank	Paragraph Frame 1	Paragraph Frame 2	Sentence Starters
susceptible money reflect cognitive biases political advantage true release credible sources misinformation too good to be true	Some sites and organizations are motivated to ____ fake news and information because ____. According to the reading, individuals are susceptible to believing fake news and information because ____. In my experience, ____ can make it difficult to distinguish truth from lies. To avoid being fooled, it's a good idea to ____.	It helps to know how news stories are created. Legitimate journalists should strive to ____. Reporters should avoid ____ and keep their opinions out of stories. Editors should always ____ and make sure stories are ____. In the end, it is the responsibility of readers to ____ and to expose themselves to ____.	• Some sites and organizations release fake news because . . . • According to the reading, individuals are susceptible to believing fake news and information because . . . • I have sometimes found it difficult to distinguish truth from lies due to my . . . • To avoid being fooled, people should . . . • Legitimate journalists should strive to . . . and should also . . . • Editors should alway check facts and . . . • It is the responsibility of readers to . . . • Readers should also expose themselves to . . .

Peer Review

Rate

Respond to the following with a point rating that reflects your opinion.

	1	2	3	4
Ideas				
Evidence				
Language and Conventions				

Submit

Students should submit substantive feedback to two peers using the review instructions below.

- How well does this response answer the prompt?
- How well does the writer support their ideas with textual evidence, background knowledge, and experiences?
- What does the writer do well in this reflection? What does the writer need to work on?

Remember that your comments are most useful when they are kind and constructive.

ELL A SENTENCE FRAMES

- You were able to (completely / partly / almost) ____ answer the prompt.
- You could answer the prompt more completely by ____.
- You (consistently / adequately / occasionally / rarely) ____ supported your ideas with textual evidence, background knowledge, and experiences.
- My favorite part of your response is ____.
- I think you could work on ____.

Honesty on Social Media

ARGUMENTATIVE TEXT
2018

Introduction

Social media is increasingly the domain where a larger and larger portion of human interactions take place. However, since online relationships require us to construct profiles or avatars to represent ourselves, they are inherently different from face-to-face relationships. Our online behaviors can easily lean toward deception, using anonymity to weave fantastical versions of our realities. Yet there are also aspects of the internet which hold us accountable to the truth of our offline lives. Both essays present strong opinions about the effects of social media on our interpersonal relationships. Which do you find more persuasive?

Use of social media is rising, and the first author argues that time spent on those platforms makes us more dishonest. Although 32% of people report always being honest on Facebook, between 55 and 90% of people expect that others are lying online. One reason to do this is that by making ourselves more attractive, we hope to attract an exciting partner. This kind of misrepresentation now even has a name: catfishing. So even though social media gives us a great chance to connect with others, it can also be easily manipulated and therefore threatens to normalize dishonesty. The counterpoint argues that social media actually encourages honesty because we are pursuing relationships we deem valuable. Since a lot of the connections on social media are visible to others, it behooves us to be honest, operating on very much the same social contract as in the outside world.

Proficiency-leveled summaries and summaries in multiple languages are available digitally.

Audio and audio text highlighting are available with this text.

COMPARING WITHIN AND ACROSS GENRES

As with "News Literacy in the Misinformation Age" and "Blindspot: Hidden Biases of Good People," this Point/Counterpoint article adds to the ongoing debate about honesty in society: one author argues that social media encourages people to be dishonest, while another author sets out to prove that there is a greater need for honesty in the digital era.

Entry Point

As students prepare to read "Honesty on Social Media," share the following information with them to provide context.

- ✓ Debates like this one *about* social media may be more productive than debates *on* social media. In recent Pew Research studies, only 14% of respondents said they have changed their mind about an issue based on something they saw on social media.
- ✓ But, while only 3% of U.S. adults said they place "a lot" of trust and 31% "some" trust in social media sources, nearly half of U.S. adults still get some of their news from Facebook.
- ✓ While Facebook is still the most used social media platform among most adults, it is no longer the most popular among American teens. As of 2018, it ranks fourth in popularity behind Youtube, Instagram, and Snapchat.

Instructional Path

The print teacher's edition includes essential point-of-use instruction and planning tools. Complete lesson plans and program documents appear in your digital teacher account.

First Read: Honesty on Social Media

Objectives: After reading the point/counterpoint article "Honesty on Social Media," students will be able to compare and contrast its competing viewpoints.

Skill: Informational Text Elements

Objectives: After rereading and discussing a model of close reading, students will be able to analyze a complex set of ideas and explain how these ideas interact and develop over the course of a text.

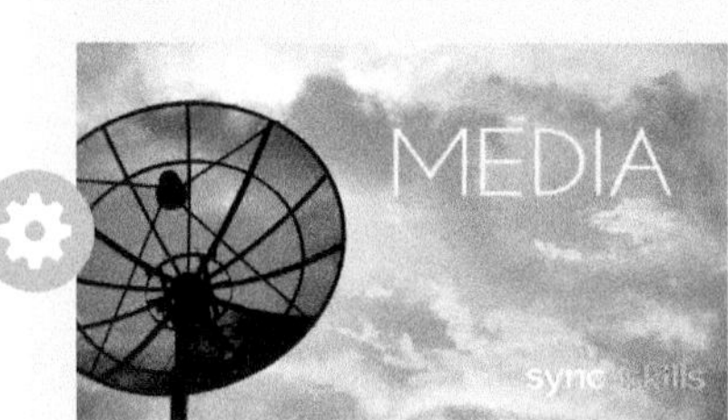

Skill: Media

Objectives: After rereading and discussing a model of close reading, students will be able to evaluate how multiple sources of information presented in different media or formats can address a question or solve a problem in a text.

Close Read: Honesty on Social Media

Objectives: After reading the point/counterpoint article "Honesty on Social Media," students will be able to evaluate each author's use of media in order to participate in a collaborative conversation in response to a prompt, and to write a reflection on their participation in the conversation.

Progress Monitoring

Opportunities to Learn	Opportunities to Demonstrate Learning	Opportunities to Reteach
Informational Text Elements		
Skill: Informational Text Elements	Skill: Informational Text Elements • Your Turn Close Read • Skills Focus • Write	Spotlight Skill: Informational Text Elements
Media		
Skill: Media	Skill: Media • Your Turn Close Read • Skills Focus • Write	Spotlight Skill: Media

First Read

Introduce the Text

As a class, watch the video preview  **and have students read the introduction in pairs to make connections to the video preview.**

To activate prior knowledge and experiences, ask students:

- What part of the video stood out to you the most?
- Do you use social media? How do you feel about how you or others you know use social media?

ELL SPEAKING FRAMES

- The part of the video that stood out most was ____.
- I (do / do not) use social media. I feel ____ about my social media use. I feel ____ about how others use social media.

Access Complex Text

LEXILE: 1370 WORD COUNT: 1,729

The following areas may be challenging for students, particularly ELL English Language Learners and A Approaching grade-level learners.

Genre	Connection of Ideas
• In reading an argumentative text, students will need to evaluate evidence and reasoning. • Assign groups of students one article. Have each group determine the strongest and weakest pieces of evidence. Have them also determine which reason is most logical and well supported, and which is least. Invite groups to discuss their evaluations with the class.	• Students will have to analyze charts and make connections between the charts and the text of each article. • Have students work in pairs to discuss the information provided in each chart and how that information relates to the article.

SCAFFOLDS

 ENGLISH LANGUAGE LEARNERS  APPROACHING GRADE LEVEL  BEYOND GRADE LEVEL

These icons identify differentiation strategies and scaffolded support for a variety of students. See the digital lesson plan for additional differentiation strategies and scaffolds.

"The more we time we spend on social media platforms, the more deceptive we become."

NOTES

Social Media: Does It Make Us More or Less Honest?

Point: Of Course We're More Deceptive on Social Media. It's Easy To Be.

Skill: Media

The author refers to a chart from a reliable source that shows the increase in social media use. This is a good way of supporting the author's purpose of visually showing the growing impact of social media on people's lives.

1 Look up from your device of choice on any bus or train, in any coffee shop, or in any place where people are made to wait, and you will most certainly find someone—and likely many people—also staring at a cell phone, tablet, laptop, or other device. A great deal of our day-to-day lives is spent engaging with technology—increasingly to access social media platforms. A survey by the Pew Research Center reports that social media usage has grown dramatically for users of all age groups, even though around 50% of users do not trust social media companies to protect their data (Rainie). Consequently, the more we time we spend on social media platforms, the more deceptive we become.

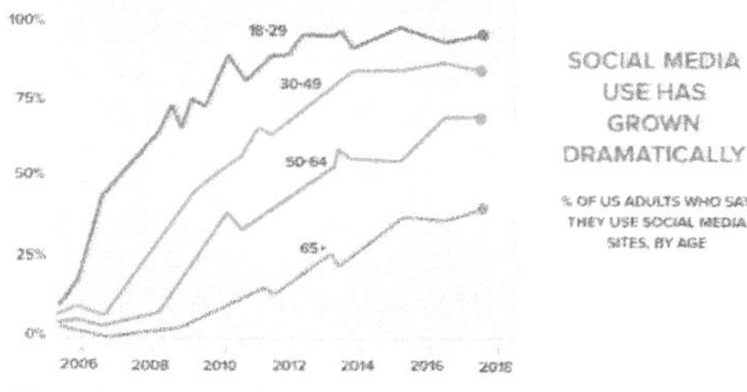

Developing Background Knowledge and Social Emotional Learning

1. Present students with the following statement: "While most people consider themselves to be honest, most of us lie to benefit ourselves."
2. Have students raise their hands to show they a) strongly disagree, b) disagree, c) agree, or d) strongly agree. Assign each response a corner of the room, and have students go to their respective corners to discuss their positions.
3. Have one student from each group be the spokesperson to explain the group's response.

Discuss with students: Think of how you present yourself on social media. How do you feel about the social media version of yourself? How is this image similar to and different from your authentic self? Why might someone create an online persona?

Media

How does the reader connect the chart to the author's purpose?

The chart shows that social media use has grown rapidly, which supports the author's purpose of showing how important social media use is to people.

Informational Text Elements

What is the paradox the student refers to?

The paradox is in the section heading. It involves being honest about lying, which seems self-contradictory at first glance, but is explained in the body paragraph.

Informational Text Elements

What supporting evidence does the student highlight?

The student highlights that 55-90 percent of participants in a Facebook study believed that other Facebook users were lying. The reader notes that this connects to the paradox in the section heading.

Skills Focus

QUESTION 2: Rhetoric

This appeal uses a quote from a scientific study to show that few people are honest online and that most people assume other users are lying. This helps readers understand the author's viewpoint that social media encourages people to be dishonest.

Skills Focus

QUESTION 3: Media

The list summarizes studies by the Pew Research Center. The bullets help the reader see there are four separate findings highlighted by the author.

Let's Be Honest: We Are All Liars

2 While most people consider themselves to be honest, most of us lie to benefit ourselves. In his book *The (Honest) Truth About Dishonesty*, behavioral economist Dan Ariely explains how people negotiate whether to be honest or dishonest: "This is where our amazing cognitive flexibility comes into play. Thanks to this human skill, as long as we cheat by only a little bit, we can benefit from cheating and still view ourselves as marvelous human beings" (27). Ariely's research shows that even within this framework, an individual's level of dishonesty can be affected by context—whether the reward is money or something that can be exchanged for money, whether there are reminders of moral standards, and whether someone within one's social group is dishonest, amongst many others.

3 People's behavior on social media, predictably, reflects this tendency to lie, but the context encourages dishonesty. In a recent study on dishonesty online, researchers found that while 32% of users on sites like Facebook reported being "always honest" in their posts, the expectations for honesty online are pretty **abysmal**: "Between 55 and 90 percent of participants believed others were lying at least some of the time about their age, gender, activities, interests, and appearance" (Misener). This belief affects users' behavior online: "[W]hen we think other people are lying online, we're more likely to lie ourselves" (Misener). This makes social media platforms spaces in which dishonesty can easily become commonplace.

Fonder Hearts Encouraged: Deception in Dating

4 One of the more common uses of social media is to attract a mate and to communicate with

5 him or her. People often manipulate how they present themselves for both purposes. There are, of course, the smaller lies—exaggerating one's height, posting only flattering or modified photos of oneself, etc. But social media can also lead to more serious deception. In fact, this practice has become so widespread that it has a name—*catfishing*, or creating fake profiles on social media sites to deceive others. One example of this was the case of Manti Te'o, the Notre Dame football player whose long-distance girlfriend—"Lennay Kekua," who apparently died during their courtship—turned out to be the machinations of a young man named Ronaiah Tuiasosopo (Zeman). Through the use of Facebook, Twitter, Instagram, phone calls, and photos of an acquaintance, Tuiasosopo managed to convince Te'o to fall in love with his imaginative creation, a feat that would have been a cumbersome, **formidable** challenge, if not impossible, had it been attempted face-to-face. But through the use of technology, including social media, Tuiasosopo managed to deceive Te'o for more than two years.

Skill: Informational Text Elements

The author introduces a paradox in the section heading, and then uses the first sentence to explain the paradox. The author then supports this idea and elaborates on it with evidence from an expert.

Skill: Informational Text Elements

The author explains how social media pushes usually honest people toward dishonesty. The author also uses data and evidence here to support this idea, and connects back to the section heading.

TEXT TALK

What does the "Point" author say about lying?

See paragraphs 2–3: Most people lie when it helps them. Most people on social media expect others to lie.

What examples does the "Point" author give of dishonesty online?

See paragraphs 4–5: The author discusses "catfishing" and deceptive marketing practices.

SELECTION VOCABULARY

abysmal / pésimo / a ***adjective*** terrible, appalling

formidable / temible ***adjective*** causing fear or dread; intimidating

Marketing and Social Media: Skilled Deception for Profit

6 The advent of social media has also opened up new ways for people and businesses to manipulate media and the public to their benefit. In his book *Trust Me, I'm Lying: Confessions of a Media Manipulator*, Ryan Holiday explains how he exploits bloggers to promote products and clients. Holiday explains that bloggers depend on traffic to generate profit and attract attention to their blogs, which they hope to use to either secure better jobs or to generate enough income so they can become self-employed. Holiday, aware that the bloggers are willing to do many things to achieve these outcomes, uses these motives to exploit them to his advantage. One way he does this is by providing them with just enough information to produce a provocative headline—and clicks, of course: "If I am giving them an official comment on behalf of a client, I leave room for them to speculate by not fully addressing the issue. . . . I trick the bloggers, and they trick their readers. This arrangement is great for the traffic-hungry bloggers, for me, and for my attention-seeking clients" (71). While this arrangement works for those who stand to make a profit from consumers' attention, it promotes **ambiguity** and scandal at the expense of informative, meaningful communication via social media.

Is It Time to Log Off?

7 While social media offers us opportunities to connect with others near and far for reasons both common and quirky—to share our lives with friends and family, to find love, or to share our love of fan fiction—it is easily manipulated. Whether we tell small lies or big ones on social media, deception does not help us create meaningful connections with one another. That presents us with an urgent and important decision as social media becomes an integral part of our lives and threatens to normalize dishonesty: Do we abandon social media, or do we relinquish our morality.

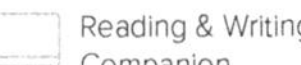

SELECTION VOCABULARY

ambiguity / la ambigüedad *noun* uncertainty or inexactness of meaning in language COGNATE

Prepare for Advanced Courses

Use the activity below to differentiate instruction for your B Beyond grade level learners.

Analyze for Enrichment

Explain to students that authors often use rhetorical appeals to persuade their readership. The three rhetorical appeals are "ethos" (persuasion through the presentation of oneself or another as a credible source of knowledge on the topic); "logos" (persuasion through the presentation of facts, figures, and logic); and "pathos" (persuasion through the stirring of readers' emotions).

Ask students:

- Which rhetorical appeals does each author employ to persuade readers—ethos, logos, and/or pathos? Use evidence from each article to support your response.
- Which rhetorical appeal—ethos, logos, or pathos—do you think most effectively persuades and why? By extension, which article do you consider most persuasive and why? Cite relevant passages from the text(s) to support your argument.

"[Social media] encourages us to be honest precisely because we are navigating a relationship."

NOTES

Counterpoint: When Everyone's Watching, It's Too Hard to Lie

8 Thirty years ago, we would have had to ask around—or wait until the next high school reunion—to reconnect with a long-lost friend; now a quick search on Facebook or Instagram will likely do the trick and, in the process, lead us to other acquaintances we used to know but may have forgotten about. Social media, like many advancements, has profoundly changed the way we engage with others, and because it allows us to establish or develop relationships, even if it is not face-to-face, it encourages us to be honest precisely because we are navigating a relationship.

Progress Is Always Imperfect

9 Some argue that social media makes us more dishonest because it establishes a connection that can be easily manipulated. Social media, like any other advancement, is not a perfect tool; some people will surely misuse it, but that does not **negate** its usefulness. People who think that the use of social media makes us more dishonest are simply clinging to romanticized notions of how we ought to engage with one another. They oppose technological advancement and only want to live in the past. Unwilling to accept virtual connections as valid, they are simply not interested in the possibilities that new technologies offer us.

 SELECTION VOCABULARY

negate / negar *verb* to deny the truth or existence of COGNATE

When We're Connected, We're More Honest

10 Social media helps us easily connect to more people—family, friends, and colleagues, sometimes on the same platform—and it is a repository of information and exchanges. As each new avenue of communication opens, the pressure to conduct oneself honestly and ethically grows. These connections and exchanges—and their visibility to others—affect our behavior. Psychologist Pamela Routledge explains the significance of this phenomenon: "Social media relationships operate with the same rules as offline ones. They are social contracts that thrive on honesty and are destroyed by deceit. . . . New media does a lot of things. One of them is that it makes it hard to keep secrets a secret. Think of that as making people accountable for their behavior."

11 Facebook is a good example of a social media platform whose popularity can help encourage honesty, at least by its users. In 2018 studies of social media by the Pew Research Center and We Are Social showed that Facebook reigned supreme among social media platforms:

- Facebook is the most popular social media platform in the world, with 2.167 billion users (Kemp).
- In the United States, Facebook is used by 68% of adults, and about 74% of those adults who use Facebook visit the site at least once a day (Smith and Anderson).
- Facebook has seen an increase of 20% in users 65 and older in the year before the study was published (Kemp).
- Of popular social media sites, Facebook has the highest percentage of users who log on at least once a day, with many users visiting several times a day (Smith and Anderson).

A MAJORITY OF FACEBOOK, SNAPCHAT AND INSTAGRAM USERS VISIT THESE PLATFORMS ON A DAILY BASIS

AMONG US ADULTS WHO SAY THEY USE _______, THE % WHO USE EACH SITE:

	SEVERAL TIMES A DAY	ABOUT ONCE A DAY	LESS OFTEN
FACEBOOK	51%	23%	26%
SNAPCHAT	49%	14%	36%
INSTAGRAM	38%	22%	39%
TWITTER	26%	20%	53%
YOUTUBE	29%	17%	55%

TEXT TALK

How does the "Counterpoint" author believe ubiquity will help with social media honesty?

See paragraphs 10–11: Since so many people use social media and are connected by it, more people can notice when someone lies.

Skills Focus

QUESTION 4: Informational Text Elements

The author connects to this idea by using the real-life example of PostSecret. The author develops this idea with the analogy of social media being like the ocean, "vast and deep and teeming with life."

Skills Focus

QUESTION 5: Essential Question

I agree more with the Counterpoint argument. Social media is a new "avenue of communication" that pressures us to be more honest and ethical both online and "in real life." The honesty and dishonesty we exhibit online affects our relationships—positively or negatively—offline.

NOTES

12 This **ubiquity**, both the increasing number of people who use the platform and the frequency of their use, is not without consequence: billions of people are using a platform that connects them to other people who know details about their lives, which creates an increasingly large pool of people who are adept at using the internet, including social media, to fact-check a post and catch users in a lie. This puts pressure on people to be careful about what they say in a space that so many people have access to.

13 LinkedIn, a professional social media platform, has a similar effect. In his research on dishonesty online, Professor Jeffrey Hancock examined people's behavior on LinkedIn and found that "LinkedIn resumes were less deceptive about claims that could be verified by people in a person's social network, such as an applicant's prior work experience and job" (281). While this did not prohibit all deception, it did deter deception about the more important elements of a resume.

When We're Honest, We're More Connected

14 Social media can also provide a space within which sharing a difficult, personal matter is easier, and that opportunity to be open and honest can help us connect with others. PostSecret, for example, allows people to anonymously share their secrets: individuals send in their secrets, and those secrets are anonymously posted on several social media platforms. This act of sharing helps both those who send in the secrets and those who read them on social media platform. Sometimes people write in to reflect upon secrets they have shared, and sometimes others who read the secrets are inspired to share something related. Even if they do not share something themselves, individuals get to connect with an experience, and that can help them feel validated or help them address a problem in their own lives. By creating a space within which people can be honest, these platforms help people connect around authentic experiences.

Social Media Helps Keeps Us Connected and Honest

15 It is easy to dismiss virtual spaces as free-for-alls where people can do their worst with anonymity and no consequences, but that is not an accurate reflection of those sort of spaces. Social media helps foster real, meaningful relationships; dishonesty within those spaces can damage those relationships just as honesty can help strengthen them. Social media is like the ocean. It is vast and deep and teeming with life, giving us opportunities to find meaning if we conduct online relationships with honesty and dependability. Online relationships are too important to risk losing them through dishonesty.

TEXT TALK

How did discussing the class's opinions on dishonesty and online personas deepen your understanding of the articles?

Answers will vary.

B Which statements from the articles do you agree or disagree with, and why?

SELECTION VOCABULARY

ubiquity / la ubicuidad *noun* the state of being everywhere at once COGNATE

Reading Comprehension OPTIONAL

Have students complete the digital reading comprehension questions when they finish reading.

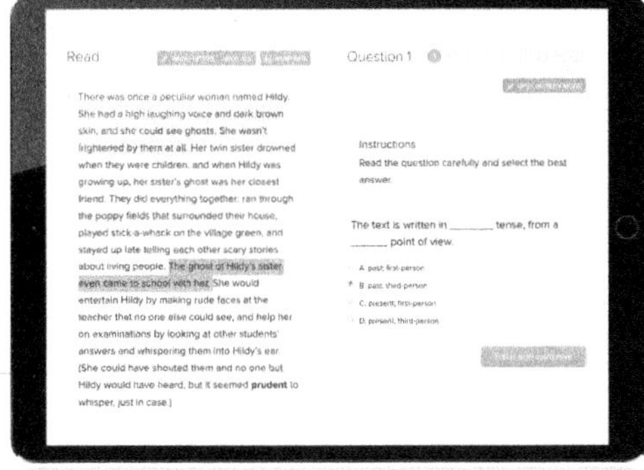

ANSWER KEY

QUESTION 1: B
QUESTION 2: C
QUESTION 3: C
QUESTION 4: D
QUESTION 5: C
QUESTION 6: C
QUESTION 7: D
QUESTION 8: B
QUESTION 9: *See first chart.*
QUESTION 10: *See second chart.*

Quote	Essay
". . . Tuiasosopo managed to convince Te'o to fall in love with his imaginative creation, a feat that would have been a cumbersome . . ."	Point
"As each new avenue of communication opens, the pressure to conduct oneself honestly and ethically grows."	Counterpoint
"Sometimes people write in to reflect upon secrets they have shared, and sometimes . . ."	Counterpoint
"While this arrangement works for those who stand to make a profit from consumers' attention, it promotes ambiguity and scandal . . ."	Point

Synonym	Word
ubiquity	omnipresence
ambiguity	nebulousness
abysmal	low
formidable	difficult
negate	refute

Connect and Extend OPTIONAL

CONNECT TO EXTENDED ORAL PROJECT

Students can use "Honesty on Social Media" as a mentor text for their Extended Writing Project. They may adopt some of the writers' methods for integrating key ideas as they construct their argumentative oral presentations.

BEYOND THE BOOK

Activity: Social Media Honesty

These two argumentative essays argue whether social media portrays honest representation of people. Students will create two different interpretations of a personal social media post.

Ask students to:

- Choose a recent event from their life.
- Analyze what happened and what emotions were involved.
- Choose a social media outlet and create two different posts for this event; one positive and one negative.
  - > How can this be a negative experience?
  - > How can this event be viewed as a positive experience?
  - > What needs to be altered to change the point of view (picture, text, etc.)
- Share with classmates.

To reflect, ask students:

- How easy was it to create a completely different slant on the same experience?
- Do you feel complete transparency is possible on social media?

Think Questions

Circulate as students answer Think Questions independently. Scaffolds for these questions are shown on the opposite page.

QUESTION 1: Textual Evidence

32% of users reported being always honest online, but 55-90% of users believed other people were lying some of the time. It affects users' behavior online because "when we think other people are lying, we're more likely to lie ourselves."

QUESTION 2: Textual Evidence

The Point author believes "the more time we spend on social media platforms, the more deceptive we become." The Counterpoint author believes that "the pressure to conduct oneself honestly and ethically grows" as more people use social media.

QUESTION 3: Textual Evidence

The author of the Counterpoint essay thinks that anonymity can be useful for making genuine connections because people can anonymously share their secrets. This can "provide a space within which sharing a difficult, personal matter is easier."

QUESTION 4: Context Clues

I think *formidable* means "difficult" because the essay says that convincing Te'o to fall in love face-to-face would have been *formidable*, "if not impossible." *Difficult* fits with the context of impossible.

QUESTION 5: Word Patterns and Relationships

Holiday says, "I leave room for them to speculate by not fully addressing the issue," which I think is the part that "promotes ambiguity" at the expense of "meaningful communication." With the Latin roots in mind, I think ambiguity means "open to both interpretations" or "vagueness." Other words I know with the root *ambo* are *ambivalent* and *ambidextrous*.

First Read

Read "Honesty on Social Media." After you read, complete the Think Questions below.

THINK QUESTIONS

1. When it comes to online interactions, the Point essay identifies a significant difference between people's assessments of their own honesty versus the honesty of others. What is this difference, and how might it affect human behavior? Explain.

2. Using information from the Point and Counterpoint essays, briefly describe how both authors believe people are affected by our increased use of social media. Cite specific evidence to support your answer.

3. What does the author of the Counterpoint essay think about the effect of anonymity on our ability to make genuine, deep connections on the internet? Explain briefly, citing evidence.

4. Based on context clues in the fourth paragraph of the Point essay, what do you think the word **formidable** means? Write your best definition of *formidable* here, explaining how you arrived at its meaning.

5. The Latin word *ambo* means "both," and the Latin word *agere* means "act" or "do." The combination of these roots gives us the noun **ambiguity.** With this in mind, try to infer the meaning of the word *ambiguity* as it is used in the fifth paragraph of the Point essay. Write your best definition of the word here, along with as many other words as you can think of that feature these Latin roots.

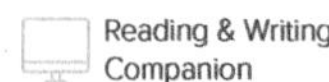

Think Questions

SCAFFOLDS

Use the scaffolds below to differentiate instruction for your ELL English Language Learners and A Approaching grade level readers.

ELL **BEGINNING** Write a response using the word bank and sentence frames.

INTERMEDIATE Write a response using the sentence frames.

ADVANCED, ADVANCED HIGH Write a response using the Text-Dependent Question Guide.

A **APPROACHING** Write a response using the Text-Dependent Question Guide.

BEGINNING	INTERMEDIATE	APPROACHING / ADVANCED, ADVANCED HIGH
Word Bank	**Sentence Frames**	**Text-Dependent Question Guide**
pressure the truth secrets honest deceptive ambivalent expectations lie difficult interpretations uncertainty	The Point essay says most people think of themselves as ____. A study found people have low ____ about other people's honesty. This affects behavior because we are more likely to ____ when we think other people are lying.	1. • Based on the Point essay, how do people view their honesty online? • According to research, do people expect other people to be honest online? • How does this difference affect people's behavior online?
	The Point author says that we become more ____ as we spend more time on social media. The Counterpoint author disagrees, saying that as our use of social media increases, the ____ to be honest grows.	2. • What does the Point author say about how spending more time on social media affects people? • What does the Counterpoint author say about it? • How do their opinions compare?
	Some apps let people share ____ anonymously, which helps people be more honest than they might be offline.	3. • What does the Counterpoint essay say people can do anonymously through social media? • Does the Counterpoint author view this as a good thing? • What are clues that the Counterpoint author feels this way?
	The context says it would be harder to trick someone in person than online, so I think *formidable* must mean ____.	4. • Read: "a feat that would have been a cumbersome, **formidable** challenge, if not impossible, had it been attempted face-to-face." • What does **formidable** have to do with "if not impossible"? • How would it be different attempted face-to-face? • What does that tell you about the meaning of **formidable**?
	The context from the summary says these people create ambiguity about ____. Since the root *ambo* means "both," I think *ambiguity* means "open to both ____" or "____." Another word with the root *ambo* is ____.	5. • Read: "While this arrangement works for those who stand to make a profit from consumers' attention, it promotes **ambiguity** and scandal at the expense of informative, meaningful communication via social media." • Given that *ambo* means "both," why is **ambiguity** at the expense of "informative, meaningful communication" ? • Do you know any other words that come from that Latin root *ambo*?

Skill: Informational Text Elements

Introduce the Skill

Watch the Concept Definition video and read the following definition with your students.

An **informational text** presents readers with information or ideas about real people, places, things, and events. In order to present information clearly, writers use a common set of **informational text elements**, or features, to link key individuals, events and ideas. Some examples of informational text include biographies, diaries, interviews, articles, letters, editorials, essays, and speeches. Many of these texts will include **supporting evidence**, or any relevant fact that an author includes to support his or her ideas, as well as **pertinent examples**. These examples have a logical connection to a subject, such as discussing the Gettysburg Address in an article on Civil War battles. To identify informational text elements, readers should look for key details in the text as well as any photographs, charts, or maps the author includes, and analyze the connections and relationships between them. Analyzing the elements of an informational text helps the reader understand how they work together to support a central idea.

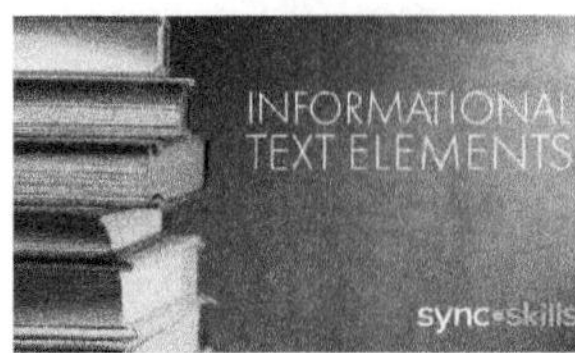

Skill: Informational Text Elements

Use the Checklist to analyze Informational Text Elements in "Honesty on Social Media." Refer to the sample student annotations about Informational Text Elements in the text.

••• CHECKLIST FOR INFORMATIONAL TEXT ELEMENTS

In order to identify a complex set of ideas or sequence of events, note the following:

- ✓ key details in the text that provide information about individuals, events, and ideas
- ✓ interactions between specific individuals, ideas, or events
- ✓ important developments over the course of the text
- ✓ transition words and phrases that signal interactions between individuals, events, and ideas, such as *because, as a consequence,* or *as a result.*
- ✓ similarities and differences of types of information in a text

To analyze a complex set of ideas or sequence of events and explain how specific individuals, ideas, or events interact and develop over the course of the text, consider the following questions:

- ✓ How does the author present the information as a sequence of events?
- ✓ How does the order in which ideas or events are presented affect the connections between them?
- ✓ How do specific individuals, ideas, or events interact and develop over the course of the text?
- ✓ What other features, if any, help readers to analyze the events, ideas, or individuals in the text?

TURN AND TALK

1. What was the last argumentative text you read? Describe it.
2. What did the author do to convince you of his/her argument?

SPEAKING FRAMES

- The last argumentative text I read was ____.
- It was about ____.
- The author convinced me of his/her argument by ____.

SKILL VOCABULARY

informational text / el texto informativo ***noun*** non-fiction writing that presents information about real people, places, things, and events COGNATE

informational text elements / los elementos del texto informativo ***noun*** characteristics of informational texts COGNATE

Skill: Informational Text Elements

Reread paragraphs 10–11 of "Honesty on Social Media." Then, using the Checklist on the previous page, answer the multiple-choice questions below.

YOUR TURN

1. Which sentence or phrase most directly supports the topic presented in the heading for this section?

   - A. "As each new avenue of communication opens, the pressure to conduct oneself honestly and ethically grows."
   - B. "'Social media relationships operate with the same rules as offline ones.'"
   - C. "'New media does a lot of things.'"
   - D. "In 2018 studies of social media by the Pew Research Center and We Are Social showed that Facebook reigned supreme among social media platforms:"

2. What idea is the evidence presented in the bulleted list intended to support?

   - A. More connections between people results in less honesty.
   - B. More connections between people results in more honesty.
   - C. Facebook is the most popular social media platform in the world.
   - D. Facebook has the highest percentage of users who log on at least once a day.

Your Turn

Ask students to complete the Your Turn Activity.

QUESTION 1

A. Correct. The author claims that we are forced to be more honest as we engage in new types of communication.

B. Incorrect. This quote does not directly mention honesty.

C. Incorrect. This quote does not directly discuss honesty or connections.

D. Incorrect. This quote does not directly discuss honesty or connections.

QUESTION 2

A. Incorrect. The opposite is true.

B. Correct. The preceding paragraph states: "Facebook is a good example of a social media platform whose popularity can help encourage honesty. . . ."

C. Incorrect. This is supporting evidence for a broader idea.

D. Incorrect. This is supporting evidence for a broader idea.

SKILL VOCABULARY

supporting evidence / la evidencia de apoyo *noun* text evidence, descriptions, examples, reasons, expert opinions, facts, and statistics that further explain key aspects of the controlling idea

pertinent example / el ejemplo pertinente *noun* a related situation that shows that what is being demonstrated is true COGNATE

Skill: Media

Introduce the Skill

Watch the Concept Definition video and read the following definition with your students.

Media is the plural form of the word *medium.* A **medium** is a means of sending a communication to an intended audience. Throughout most of human history, people communicated through three main media: speech, writing, and visual arts such as drawing, painting, and sculpture. But in the 19th century media options suddenly exploded. The invention of photography, and then the telegraph and the telephone, changed the world. Within a century radio, motion pictures, and television followed.

Stories and ideas change as they are translated from one medium to another. A dialogue between two characters in a novel, for example, becomes very different when it is delivered by actors in a film—with close-ups, sound effects such as music, and other elements unique to the medium of film itself.

Today new media are being invented at a much faster pace than ever before, and each of these forms of online communication has its own "language" and creates its own experience.

Skill: Media

Use the Checklist to analyze Media in "Honesty on Social Media." Refer to the sample student annotations about Media in the text.

••• CHECKLIST FOR MEDIA

In order to determine how to integrate and evaluate multiple sources of information presented in different media or formats, note the following:

- ✓ the key elements in each source of information
- ✓ the various elements of a particular medium and how the parts are put together
- ✓ how each media or format, such as visually or quantitatively, presents the sources of information
- ✓ what information is included or excluded in each media presentation
- ✓ the audience of each media presentation and the author's purpose
- ✓ the reliability and credibility of each presentation

To integrate and evaluate multiple sources of information presented in different media or formats as well as in words in order to address a question or solve a problem, consider the following questions:

- ✓ How is each media presentation reliable or credible?
- ✓ How can you use each media presentation?
- ✓ How can you integrate multiple sources of information presented in different media or formats to address a question or solve a problem?

TURN AND TALK

1. What does it mean to be a visual learner?
2. How can visual information make it easier for you to understand a topic?

ELL SPEAKING FRAMES

- A visual learner is someone who ____.
- Visual information, like picture and charts, can help me understand because ____.

V SKILL VOCABULARY

medium / el medio ***noun*** a form of communication, such as television, the internet, and radio COGNATE

media / los medios ***noun*** the plural form of the word medium; a means of sending a communication to an intended audience

Skill: Media

Reread paragraph 11 of "Honesty on Social Media." Then, using the Checklist on the previous page, answer the multiple-choice questions below.

YOUR TURN

1. The main purpose of the chart is to show—
   - A. which social media platforms are most popular.
   - B. which social media platforms have the best fact-checking capabilities.
   - C. how often leading social media platforms are used by social media users.
   - D. how social media platforms can help detect the percentage of users who are dishonest.

2. The main reason the author includes the chart in the essay is to support the point that—
   - A. so many people use Facebook every day that users feel pressured not to lie.
   - B. Facebook, Snapchat, and Instagram are the most popular social media platforms.
   - C. Facebook and Snapchat have better fact-checking tools than other platforms do.
   - D. more than half of the users of the top three platforms use them at least daily.

3. The author's inclusion of this graphic feature is effective because it—
   - A. shows how many different social media sites there are.
   - B. reveals the different ways people use social media.
   - C. attempts to explain why social media sites can be damaging.
   - D. reinforces the claim that social media usage is widespread.

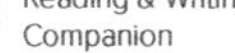

Your Turn

Ask students to complete the Your Turn Activity.

QUESTION 1

A. Correct. This information is contained in paragraph 11, which appears below the chart.

B. Incorrect. The focus of the chart is on frequency of social media use.

C. Incorrect. The chart does not include information about fact-checking tools.

D. Incorrect. The chart does show this, but this is not why the author uses the chart as support.

QUESTION 2

A. Incorrect. The chart does not show how many social media sites there are.

B. Incorrect. The chart does not help readers understand how people use social media.

C. Incorrect. The chart does not suggest that social media sites can be damaging.

D. Correct. The chart supports the idea that many people use social media frequently.

QUESTION 3

A. Incorrect. The chart does not show how many social media sites there are.

B. Incorrect. The chart does not help readers understand how people use social media.

C. Incorrect. The chart does not suggest that social media sites can be damaging.

D. Correct. The chart supports the idea that many people use social media frequently.

Close Read

Skills Focus

QUESTION 1: Central or Main Idea

See paragraph 1: The thesis is that people who use social media often are more dishonest than other people. Two reasons are that people think dishonesty online is okay because many others online are dishonest and people lie to make themselves appear more desirable on dating websites.

QUESTION 2: Rhetoric See paragraph 3.

QUESTION 3: Media See paragraph 4.

QUESTION 4: Informational Text Elements

See paragraph 14.

QUESTION 5: Essential Question

See paragraph 15.

CHECK FOR SUCCESS

- What is the topic of the first paragraph of the Point article?
- Where in the paragraph does the author make a judgment?
- In the next three paragraphs, what are two reasons the author gives to support this judgment?

Close Read

Reread "Honesty on Social Media." As you reread, complete the Skills Focus questions below. Then use your answers and annotations from the questions to help you complete the Write activity.

SKILLS FOCUS

1. Identify the thesis in the first paragraph of "Point: Of Course We're More Deceptive on Social Media. It's Easy to Be." Write two reasons that the author offers in paragraphs 2–4 to support the thesis.
2. An appeal to logos is a persuasive method that seeks to convince readers by offering reasonable and sound evidence to support an argument. Such evidence includes quotations from reliable sources. Identify an appeal to logos in "Point: Of Course We're More Deceptive on Social Media. It's Easy to Be," and explain how it affects the way the text is read and understood.
3. Identify a print feature in the first four paragraphs of "Counterpoint: When Everyone's Watching, It's Too Hard to Lie." Explain how this feature helps the reader.
4. Identify a main idea in the last two paragraphs of "Counterpoint: When Everyone's Watching, It's Too Hard to Lie" and analyze how the author makes connections to this idea and develops it.
5. How are we different, now that the world of social media has changed our relationships to one another? Do you agree more with the Point or Counterpoint arguments when it comes to the way we approach honesty on social media? Has our relationship with social media changed the way we are honest in real life?

WRITE

DISCUSSION: Which article did you find the most convincing? Do you believe we suspend our usual honesty when we are on social media? How do the graphs and media influence your opinion? Discuss how the writers' use of evidence and language contribute to the persuasiveness of the text.

Writer's Notebook

Connect to Essential Question: Give students time to reflect on how "Honesty on Social Media" connects to the unit's essential question "How are we shaped by change?" by freewriting in their Writer's Notebooks.

Beginning & Intermediate

Read aloud the unit's essential question: "How are we shaped by change?" Encourage students to draw their connections or allow students to write in their native language. Circulate around the room, prompting students for their thoughts as they respond orally or through pantomime.

Advanced & Advanced High

Allow students to share their connections orally in pairs or small groups before freewriting.

Collaborative Conversation

SCAFFOLDS

Break students into collaborative conversation groups to discuss the Close Read prompt. Ask students to use the StudySyncTV episode as a model for their discussion. Remind them to reference their Skills Focus annotations in their discussion.

Students will break up into small groups and discuss the prompt, sharing the examples they wrote down in the graphic organizer. During the discussion, students will practice the speaking/listening skills of integrating multiple sources of information to evaluate the credibility and accuracy of sources. If necessary, model the skills for students.

Use the scaffolds below to differentiate instruction for your ELL English Language Learners and A Approaching grade-level learners.

ELL **BEGINNING, INTERMEDIATE** Use the discussion guide and speaking frames to facilitate the discussion with support from the teacher.

ADVANCED, ADVANCED HIGH Use the discussion guide and speaking frames to facilitate the discussion in mixed-level groups.

A APPROACHING Use the discussion guide to facilitate the discussion in mixed-level groups.

APPROACHING
ADVANCED, ADVANCED HIGH
BEGINNING, INTERMEDIATE

Discussion Guide	Speaking Frames
1. Which article did you find more convincing? Why?	• I found the (Point / Counterpoint) article more convincing. • I found it more convincing because ____.
2. How does the author's use of evidence make the article convincing?	• One strong piece of evidence the author uses is ____. • Another good piece of evidence is ____.
3. How does the author's use of language make the article convincing?	• One of the most well-written sentences was ____ because ____.

Ethical Issues

Use the activity below to differentiate instruction for your B Beyond grade level learners.

Although the authors disagree on how social media influence honesty, both explicitly and implicitly acknowledge that deception exists on social media.

Ask students:

- What dilemmas or controversies are involved with the issue of honesty on social media? How do these issues differ from discussions of honesty in our "non-digital" lives?
- What roles, if any, should social media companies play in promoting or enforcing honesty on their own platforms?
- What roles, if any, should governments play in developing regulations regarding honesty across all social media companies?

Review Prompt and Rubric

Before students begin writing, review the writing prompt and rubric with the class.

DISCUSSION: Which article did you find the most convincing? Do you believe we suspend our usual honesty when we are on social media? How do the graphs and media influence your opinion? Discuss how the writers' use of evidence and language contribute to the persuasiveness of the text.

PROMPT GUIDE

- Why was one of the articles more convincing to you?
- Which piece of evidence did you find to be strongest?
- Which paragraph was the most well written? Why?

Score	Reflection	Language and Conventions
4	The writer clearly reflects on how well he or she evaluated the credibility and accuracy of the media used in each source, as well as his or her own participation. The writer consistently refers to specific examples from the discussion.	The writer demonstrates a consistent command of grammar, punctuation, and usage conventions. Although minor errors may be evident, they do not detract from the fluency or the clarity of the essay.
3	The writer reflects on how well he or she evaluated the credibility and accuracy of the media used in each source, as well as his or her own participation. The writer refers to specific examples from the discussion most of the time.	The writer demonstrates an adequate command of grammar, punctuation, and usage conventions. Although some errors may be evident, they create few (if any) disruptions in the fluency of the writing or the clarity of the essay.
2	The writer begins to reflect on how well he or she evaluated the credibility and accuracy of the media used in each source, as well as his or her own participation. The writer refers to specific examples from the discussion some of the time.	The writer demonstrates a partial command of grammar, punctuation, and usage conventions. Some distracting errors may be evident, at times creating minor disruptions in the fluency or clarity of the writing.
1	The writer attempts to reflect on how well he or she evaluated the credibility and accuracy of the media used in each source, as well as his or her own participation. The writer refers to few, if any examples from the discussion.	The writer demonstrates little or no command of grammar, punctuation, and usage conventions. Serious and persistent errors create disruptions in the fluency of the writing and sometimes interfere with meaning.
0	The writer does not provide a relevant response to the prompt or does not provide a response at all.	Serious and persistent errors overwhelm the writing and interfere with the meaning of the response as a whole, making the writer's meaning impossible to understand.

Write

SCAFFOLDS

Ask students to complete the writing assignment using text evidence to support their answers.

Use the scaffolds below to differentiate instruction for your ELL English Language Learners and A Approaching grade-level readers.

ELL **BEGINNING** With the help of the word bank, write a response using paragraph frame 1.

INTERMEDIATE With the help of the word bank, write a response using paragraph frames 1 and 2.

ADVANCED, ADVANCED HIGH Write a response of differentiated length using the sentence starters.

A **APPROACHING** Write a response of differentiated length using the sentence starters.

BEGINNING / INTERMEDIATE	BEGINNING / INTERMEDIATE	INTERMEDIATE	ADVANCED, ADVANCED HIGH / APPROACHING
Word Bank	**Paragraph Frame 1**	**Paragraph Frame 2**	**Sentence Starters**
integrating accuracy graphic organizers graphs and media prompt	My group discussed the ____ and shared the examples we wrote in our ____. We practiced the speaking/listening skills of ____ multiple sources of information to evaluate the credibility and ____ of sources. I added to the discussion by explaining how the ____ influenced my opinion.	I also detailed how each writer's use of ____ contributed to the ____ of their texts. While most of the other group members felt ____, I argued in favor of ____.	• My group discussed . . . and shared examples from our . . . • We practiced the speaking and listening skills of . . . in order to . . . and . . . • I added to the discussion by . . . • I also detailed how each writer's use of . . . contributed to . . . • While most of the other group members felt . . . , I . . .

Peer Review

Students should submit substantive feedback to two peers using the review instructions below.

- How well does the writer refer to specific examples from the discussion?
- How well does the writer reflect on his or her ability to respond thoughtfully to diverse perspectives during the discussion?
- How well does the writer reflect on his or her ability to evaluate the credibility and accuracy of the media used in each article?

Rate

Respond to the following with a point rating that reflects your opinion.

	1	2	3	4
Ideas				
Evidence				
Language and Conventions				

Submit

ELL A **SENTENCE FRAMES**

- You refer to specific examples from the discussion (consistently / most of the time / some of the time / rarely) ____, such as ____.
- You (clearly / begin to / attempt to) ____ reflect on your ability to respond thoughtfully to diverse perspectives during the discussion, such as ____.
- You (clearly / begin to / attempt to) ____ reflect on your ability to evaluate the credibility and accuracy of the media used in sources, such as ____.
- One thing you do well in this reflection is ____.
- One thing you could work on is ____.

Dawn Revisited

POETRY
Rita Dove
1999

Introduction

Rita Dove (b. 1952) is a widely heralded American poet, the second African American to receive the Pulitzer Prize for Poetry and the first African American ever to be named United States Poet Laureate. "Dawn Revisited" was first included in *On the Bus with Rosa Parks*, a finalist for the National Book Critics Circle Award in 1999. While most of her work contains historical elements, she imbues these events and perspectives with her own personal touch.

The speaker in this poem asks you to imagine what it would be like to wake up to a second chance. Lying there, you can see the oak tree through the window and hear the blue jay singing outside. It feels so wonderful to rise in the early morning sunlight with the smell of eggs and biscuits coming from downstairs. The sky looks like a page—blank so that you can write your future upon it. The speaker tells you to hurry up and get downstairs, to see who's cooking those eggs for you.

ELL Proficiency-leveled summaries and summaries in multiple languages are available digitally.

Audio and audio text highlighting are available with this text.

CONNECT TO ESSENTIAL QUESTION

How are we shaped by change?

Rita Dove's poem "Dawn Revisited" calls attention to the feelings a person experiences during a time of transition. Is it better to look back at where you came from or to jump ahead into the future?

Entry Point

As students prepare to read "Dawn Revisited," share the following information with them to provide context.

- ✓ Rita Dove was the youngest person to receive the highest official honor in American poetry when she was appointed Poet Laureate of the United States and Consultant in Poetry to the Library of Congress in 1993.
- ✓ Dove was born in Akron, Ohio. Her father was a research chemist who broke the race barrier in the tire industry. In 1970, Dove was invited to the White House as one of the hundred most outstanding high school graduates in the United States. After graduating from college, Dove was a Fulbright scholar at a university in Germany where she met the German writer Fred Viebahn, a fellow Fulbright scholar, whom she married in 1979.
- ✓ Dove published her first collection of poetry in 1980. She won the 1987 Pulitzer Prize for *Thomas and Beulah*, a collection of poems based on her grandparents' lives. Dove read her poetry at the White House in 1993 and in 2011.

These icons identify differentiation strategies and scaffolded support for a variety of students. See the digital lesson plan for additional differentiation strategies and scaffolds.

Instructional Path

The print teacher's edition includes essential point-of-use instruction and planning tools. Complete lesson plans and program documents appear in your digital teacher account.

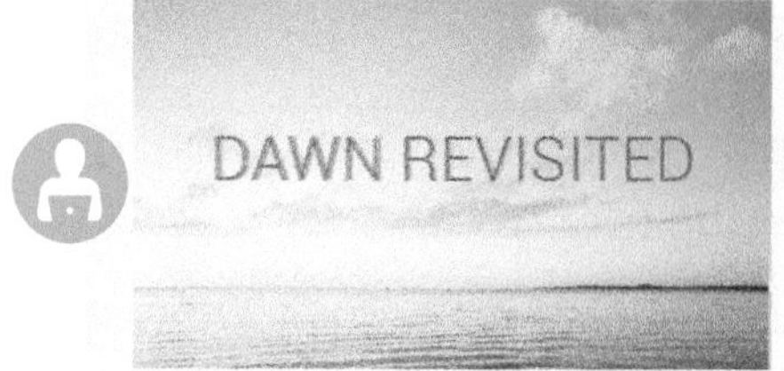

Independent Read: Dawn Revisited

Objectives: After reading "Dawn Revisited," students will write a narrative based on the idea in the poem of waking up to a new day to start a new chapter in one's life.

Independent Read

Introduce the Text

As a class, watch the video preview and have students read the introduction in pairs to make connections to the video preview.

- What image from the video was most powerful? Why?
- How do you feel when you wake up in the morning? Is it a positive or negative feeling?

ELL **SPEAKING FRAMES**

- The most powerful image in the video was ____.
- When I wake up in the morning I feel ____.

Access Complex Text

LEXILE: N/A **WORD COUNT:** 86

The following areas may be challenging for students, particularly ELL English Language Learners and A Approaching grade-level learners.

Connection of Ideas	Sentence Structure
• Students need to analyze how the poet uses figurative language in order to understand the poem's meaning and message. • Remind students to annotate descriptions or images they think are important or symbolic while they read. After reading, they can review their annotations as they infer the underlying meaning of the poem.	• The poet uses enjambment across lines and stanzas. • Have students read the poem silently to themselves as if there were no line breaks, pausing only when they reach punctuation that signals the end of an idea, and encourage them to paraphrase each complete sentence as they go.

Dawn Revisited

"How good to rise in sunlight,
in the prodigal smell of biscuits"

NOTES

Imagine you wake up
with a second chance: The blue jay
hawks his pretty **wares**
and the oak still stands, spreading
glorious shade. If you don't look back,

the future never happens.
How good to rise in sunlight,
in the **prodigal** smell of biscuits –
eggs and sausage on the grill.
The whole sky is yours

to write on, blown open
to a blank page. Come on,
shake a leg! You'll never know
who's down there, frying those eggs,
if you don't get up and see.

WRITE

NARRATIVE: Imagine you're the speaker, waking up to a new day. Write out the rest of your day as you would if you were starting a new chapter in a book. Use details from the poem to show how your past would affect your present—and your future.

Developing Background Knowledge and Social Emotional Learning

Find out what your students already know about the impact of imagery in poetry.

1. Tell students to take a few minutes to discuss the thoughts and feelings associated with different times of day and night.
2. In small groups, have students to a quick online search of images representing different points in a 24-hour cycle, such as dawn and sunset. Choose one or two to project and discuss how poets might seek inspiration and symbolism from such imagery.

Discuss with Students: Have you ever asked for a second chance? Are all people and situations worthy of a second chance? How can someone make the most of a second chance? In what ways might someone waste a second chance they've been given?

TEXT TALK

How did the image search help you understand the poem's message?

Answers will vary.

How did discussing second chances help you understand the poem's message?

Answers will vary.

SELECTION VOCABULARY

hawk / revolver *verb* to hunt

ware / la mercadería *noun* an item meant to be owned

glorious / glorioso/a *adjective* having great beauty and splendor COGNATE

prodigal / exuberante *adjective* reckless or extravagant

Writer's Notebook

Connect to Essential Question: Give students time to reflect on how "Dawn Revisited" connects to the unit's essential question "How are we shaped by change?" by freewriting in their Writer's Notebooks.

Reading Comprehension OPTIONAL

Have students complete the digital reading comprehension questions ✓ when they finish reading.

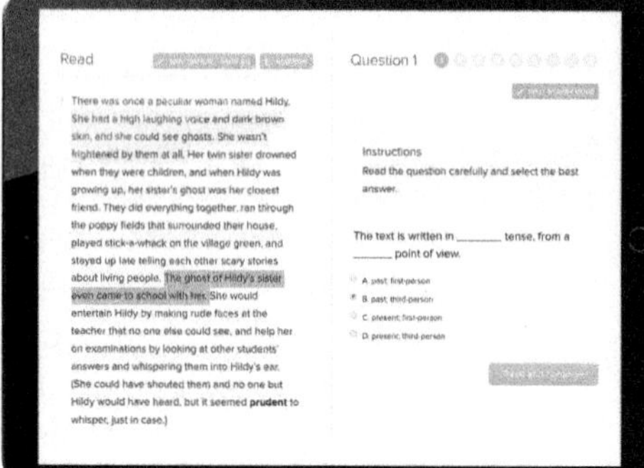

ANSWER KEY

QUESTION 1: C
QUESTION 2: C
QUESTION 3: A
QUESTION 4: D
QUESTION 5: *See chart below.*

Synonym	Word
lavish	prodigal
peddle	hawk
item	ware
magnificent	glorious

Connect and Extend OPTIONAL

CONNECT TO EXTENDED ORAL PROJECT

Students can find inspiration from Rita Dove's poem "Dawn Revisited" for their own writing. Have them think about their present lives and envision their future selves as they gather writing ideas for their personal essays.

BEYOND THE BOOK

Ask students to:

- Generate a list of fictional characters who took advantage of a new day to turn their lives around.
- Choose on character and a point of view.
- Write an editorial explaining or praising this character's choices. Make sure to include facts and information to back up statements.
- Share with classmates.

To reflect, ask students:

- What characteristics are most prevalent among the characters who took advantage of a new day?
- Is everyone who chooses to seize every moment always successful?

Collaborative Conversation

SCAFFOLDS

Post the writing prompt to generate a discussion in small groups. Ask students to first break down the prompt before they discuss relevant ideas and textual evidence.

Imagine you're the speaker, waking up to a new day. Write out the rest of your day as you would if you were starting a new chapter in a book. Use details from the poem to show how your past would affect your present—and your future.

Use the scaffolds below to differentiate instruction for your ELL English Language Learners and A Approaching grade-level learners.

ELL **BEGINNING, INTERMEDIATE** Use the discussion guide and speaking frames to facilitate the discussion with support from the teacher.

ADVANCED, ADVANCED HIGH Use the discussion guide and speaking frames to facilitate the discussion in mixed-level groups.

A **APPROACHING** Use the discussion guide to facilitate the discussion in mixed-level groups.

APPROACHING
ADVANCED, ADVANCED HIGH
BEGINNING, INTERMEDIATE

Discussion Guide	Speaking Frames
1. What does it mean to get a second chance? Why might someone need a second chance?	• A second chance is an opportunity to ____. • The blank page is a symbol for ____.
2. What connections can you make between the poem and your own life and experiences?	• This poem reminds me of the time when ____. • The poem made me think that ____.
3. What might you do if you were given a second chance? Why?	• If I had a second chance, I would ____. • I would do this because ____.

Multiple Perspectives

Use the activity below to differentiate instruction for your B Beyond grade level learners.

Reread lines 10–13:

The whole sky is yours
to write on, blown open
to a blank page. Come on,
shake a leg!

Direct students to consider Rita Dove's message. Ask students:

- Describe Dove's perspective about what each new day represents.
- How does Dove's perspective explain her personality?

Review Prompt and Rubric

Before students begin writing, review the writing prompt and rubric with the class.

NARRATIVE: Imagine you're the speaker, waking up to a new day. Write out the rest of your day as you would if you were starting a new chapter in a book. Use details from the poem to show how your past would affect your present—and your future.

PROMPT GUIDE

- What does it mean to get a second chance? Why might someone need a second chance?
- What connections can you make between the poem and your own life and experiences?
- What might you do if you were given a second chance? Why?

Score	Narrative	Language and Conventions
4	The writer is able to skillfully describe living a day as if it were the start of a new chapter. Descriptive details and clear transitions contribute to the strength and unity of the narrative.	The writer demonstrates a consistent command of grammar, punctuation, and usage conventions. Although minor errors may be evident, they do not detract from the fluency or the clarity of the essay.
3	The writer is able to clearly describe living a day as if it were the start of a new chapter. Most details and transitions contribute to the strength and unity of the narrative, though there may be minor lapses in focus.	The writer demonstrates an adequate command of grammar, punctuation, and usage conventions. Although some errors may be evident, they create few (if any) disruptions in the fluency of the writing or the clarity of the essay.
2	The writer is able to describe living a day as if it were the start of a new chapter. Some details do not contribute to the narrative, which limits the unity and coherence of the narrative.	The writer demonstrates a partial command of grammar, punctuation, and usage conventions. Some distracting errors may be evident, at times creating minor disruptions in the fluency or clarity of the writing.
1	Because the narrative is presented in a random or illogical way, the writer is not able to describe living a day as if it were the start of a new chapter. Many of the details and transitions do not contribute to the narrative.	The writer demonstrates little or no command of grammar, punctuation, and usage conventions. Serious and persistent errors create disruptions in the fluency of the writing and sometimes interfere with meaning.
0	The writer does not provide a relevant response to the prompt or does not provide a response at all.	Serious and persistent errors overwhelm the writing and interfere with the meaning of the response as a whole, making the writer's meaning impossible to understand.

Write

Ask students to complete the writing assignment using text evidence to support their answers.

Use the scaffolds below to differentiate instruction for your ELL English Language Learners and A Approaching grade-level learners.

ELL **BEGINNING** With the help of the word bank, write a response using paragraph frame 1.

INTERMEDIATE With the help of the word bank, write a response using paragraph frames 1 and 2.

ADVANCED, ADVANCED HIGH Write a response of differentiated length using the sentence starters.

A **APPROACHING** Write a response of differentiated length using the sentence starters.

BEGINNING | INTERMEDIATE | ADVANCED, ADVANCED HIGH | APPROACHING

Word Bank

future	breakfast
different	friend
past	alone
college	imagine
life	think

Paragraph Frame 1

I woke up to ____. I could smell ____. I decided I would ____. I thought about ____, but I decided I ____. That was when I realized ____.

Paragraph Frame 2

I did not have to ____. I could ____. I might even ____. I imagined ____. I felt like I ____.

Sentence Starters

- I woke up and . . .
- After breakfast I . . .
- I saw . . .
- That made me think about . . .
- I used to think . . . , but now I think . . .
- It's like I'm getting a second chance to . . .

Peer Review

Rate

Respond to the following with a point rating that reflects your opinion

	1	2	3	4
Ideas				
Evidence				
Language and Conventions				

Submit

Students should submit substantive feedback to two peers using the review instructions below.

- How well does this response answer the prompt?
- Which of the writer's descriptions inspired you to think differently about the poem or starting a new chapter in life?
- What does the writer do well in this response? What does the writer need to work on?

Remember that your comments are most useful when they are kind and constructive.

SENTENCE FRAMES

- You were able to (completely / partly / almost) ____ answer the prompt.
- You could answer the prompt more completely by ____.
- I thought differently about the poem or starting a new chapter in life after reading ____.
- My favorite part of your response is ____.

Commencement Address at the New School

ARGUMENTATIVE TEXT
Zadie Smith
2014

Introduction

Novelist and essayist Zadie Smith (b. 1975) was born and raised in London, daughter of a Jamaican mother and a white English father. Her first novel, *White Teeth*, published in 2000 when she was just 25 years old, was an international sensation, frequently appearing on lists of the best British novels of the last 50 years. In her commencement address to the 2014 graduates of the New School in New York City, she underlines the power and fulfillment of public participation over private isolation.

Speaking to the graduating class of the New School in 2014, Zadie Smith opens by recounting where she was at when she graduated college. Smith self-describes as coming from a solipsistic generation, one that was taught to chase individuality, and in pursuit of that lost touch with the communal. The generation just graduating, however, has many tough collective tasks ahead—things her generation left undone and things that can be tackled only by working together. Smith thinks their generation is up to the challenge, because even their slogans, like the "99 Percent," encompass the many. Smith echoes the importance of embracing one's place within the many, because it is a potential source of life's joy. While Smith does also believe in the importance of individuality, she reminds the graduates that it is being part of the collective that gives true meaning to our lives.

Proficiency-leveled summaries and summaries in multiple languages are available digitally.

Audio and audio text highlighting are available with this text.

CONNECT TO ESSENTIAL QUESTION

How are we shaped by change?

In her 2014 "Commencement Address at the New School," Zadie Smith draws upon the her own experiences as she encourages the graduating class to stay connected and work together. Smith invites students to consider their priorities as they prepare to enter—and possibly even change—the world after graduation.

Entry Point

As students prepare to read "Commencement Address at the New School," share the following information with them to provide context.

- ✓ Zadie Smith was born in London in 1975 to a Jamaican mother and a white English father. Her first novel, *White Teeth*, was published in 2000. The novel reflects Smith's own multicultural background and the ethnic and racial diversity of the part of London where Smith was born.
- ✓ *White Teeth* included many important themes, such as multiculturalism and the search for identity. The book won several major awards, appeared on multiple best-seller lists, and made Smith a well-known author.
- ✓ Since publishing *White Teeth*, Smith has published four novels, two essay collections, and edited and contributed to a short-story collection. She has also taught at several universities, including Harvard, Columbia, and New York University.

Instructional Path

The print teacher's edition includes essential point-of-use instruction and planning tools. Complete lesson plans and program documents appear in your digital teacher account.

First Read: Commencement Address at the New School

Objectives: After an initial reading and discussion of the speech, students will be able to identify and restate its key ideas and details.

Skill: Language, Style, and Audience

Objectives: After rereading and discussing a model of close reading, students will be able to explain how the speaker uses word choice, sentence structure, and repetition to inform and shape the perceptions of her audience.

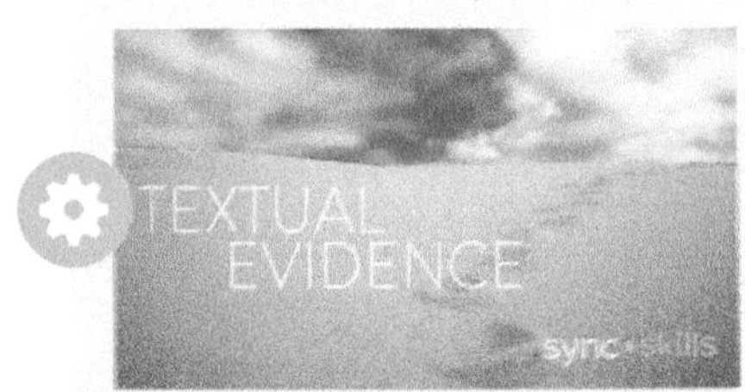

Skill: Textual Evidence

Objectives: After rereading and discussing a model of close reading, students will be able to make inferences and use relevant textual evidence to support an analysis of a text.

Skill: Summarizing

Objectives: After rereading and discussing a model of close reading, students will be able to objectively summarize a text.

Close Read: Commencement Address at the New School

Objectives: After engaging in a close reading and discussion of "Commencement Address at the New School," students will be able to write a short personal essay that responds to the main ideas of the speech.

Progress Monitoring

Opportunities to Learn	Opportunities to Demonstrate Learning	Opportunities to Reteach
Language, Style, and Audience		
Skill: Language, Style, and Audience	Skill: Language, Style, and Audience • Your Turn Close Read • Vocabulary Chart • Skills Focus	Spotlight Skill: Language, Style, and Audience
Textual Evidence		
Skill: Textual Evidence	Skill: Textual Evidence • Your Turn Close Read • Writer's Notebook • Skills Focus • Collaborative Conversation • Write	Spotlight Skill: Textual Evidence
Summarizing		
Skill: Summarizing	Skill: Summarizing • Your Turn Close Read • Skills Focus • Write	Spotlight Skill: Summarizing

First Read

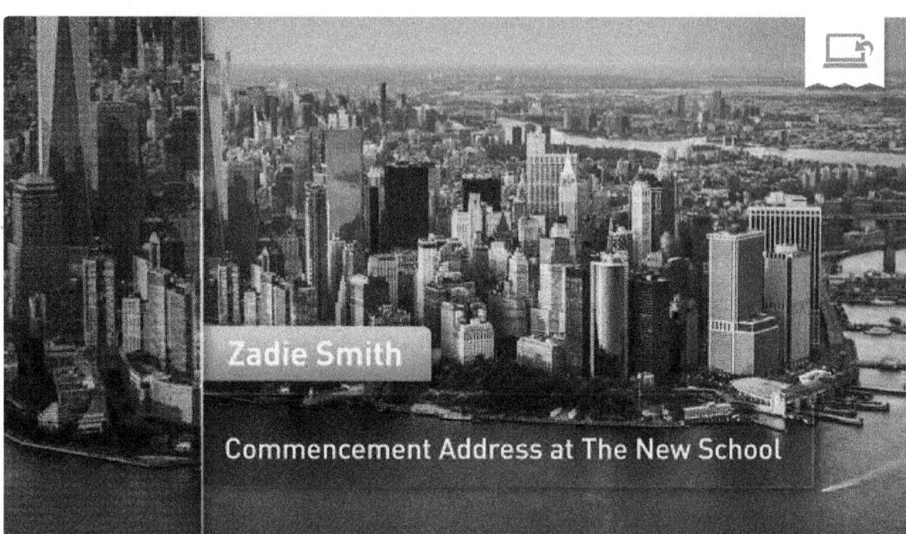

Zadie Smith
Commencement Address at The New School

Introduce the Text

As a class, watch the video preview  and have students read the introduction in pairs to make connections to the video preview.

To activate prior knowledge and experiences, ask students:

- What part of the video was most interesting to you?
- How would you describe the characteristics of your generation?

SPEAKING FRAMES

- The part of the video that I found interesting was ____.
- A characteristic of my generation is ____.

Access Complex Text

LEXILE: 970 **WORD COUNT:** 3,138

The following areas may be challenging for students, particularly 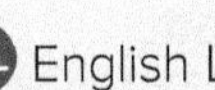 English Language Learners and  Approaching grade-level learners.

Purpose	Connection of Ideas
• Commencement speeches are given when students graduate from high school or college. These speeches typically give graduates ideas to think about as they move into the next phase of their lives. • Guide students to understand that Smith achieves this purpose by contrasting her own generation's experiences with the experiences of her audience.	• Commencement speeches often include references to multiple people and events. For instance, this speech references the author's family background and her experiences as a college student as well as the views of Margaret Thatcher. • Guide students to notice how Smith uses these events, people, and experiences to support and illustrate her ideas.

 SCAFFOLDS  ENGLISH LANGUAGE LEARNERS  APPROACHING GRADE LEVEL  BEYOND GRADE LEVEL

These icons identify differentiation strategies and scaffolded support for a variety of students. See the digital lesson plan for additional differentiation strategies and scaffolds.

"Be thankful you get to walk so close to other humans. It's a privilege."

1 Welcome graduating class of 2014 and congratulations. You did it! You made it! How do you feel?

2 I guess I can only hazard a guess which means thinking back to my own graduation in England in 1997, and extrapolate from it. Did I feel like you? I should say first that some elements of the day were rather different. I wasn't in a stadium listening to a speech. I was in an eighteenth-century hall, kneeling before the dean who spoke Latin and held one of my fingers. Don't ask me why.

3 Still the essential facts were the same.

4 Like you I was finally with my degree and had made of myself—a graduate. Like you I now had two families, the old boring one that raised me, and an exciting new one consisting of a bunch of freaks I'd met in college.

5 But part of the delightful anxiety of graduation day was trying to find a way to blend these two tribes, with their differing haircuts and political views, and hygiene standards and tastes in music. I felt like a character in two different movies. And so old! I really believed I was ancient. Impossibly distant in experience from the freshmen only three years below. I was as likely to befriend a squirrel as a freshman. Which strange relationship with time is perhaps unique to graduates and toddlers. Nowadays, at age 38, if I meet somebody who's 41, I don't **conclude** that friendship is impossible between us. But when I was 21, the gap between me and an 18-year-old felt insurmountable. Just like my four-year-old daughter, who'd rather eat sand than have a playdate with a one-year-old.

6 And what else? Oh the love dramas. So many love dramas. Mine, other people's. They take up such a large part of college life it seems unfair not to have them properly reflected in the transcript. Any full account of my university years should include the fact that I majored in English literature, with a minor in drunken discussions about the difference between loving someone and being 'in love' with that person. What can I tell you, it was the '90s. We were really into ourselves. We were into self-curation. In the '90s, we even had a thing called 'Year of Trousers' which signified any kind of ethnic or exotic

Skill: Summarizing

Zadie Smith speaks to the 2014 graduates of the New School. To understand how they feel, she will rely on how she felt as a recent college graduate 17 years earlier.

Developing Background Knowledge and Social Emotional Learning

1. Generate a list (on the board or on paper) of any information or ideas your students have about what they expect from a commencement speech.
2. Have students discuss what makes a commencement speech effective and memorable.

Discuss with students: Think of a time in your life when you were undergoing a big change. What advice or support did you receive at the time? Was it helpful? If you were to go back in time to give yourself advice, what would it be? As you prepare to graduate high school, what kind of advice would you like to hear?

Summarizing

What does the reader note about the beginning of the speech?

The reader notes specifics about the time and place and that Smith will rely on her own experiences to understand how her audience might feel.

SELECTION VOCABULARY

conclude / concluir *verb* to decide by reasoning COGNATE

TEXT TALK

What was the "Year of Trousers"? What were the trousers meant to signify?

See paragraph 6: The "Year of Trousers" refers to students wearing pants from foreign countries. The pants showed that the owner was an interesting person.

pants one brought back home from a distant (ideally third world) country. And these trousers were meant to alert to a passing stranger the fact that we'd been somewhere fascinating, and thus added further colour to our unique personalities.

7 Personally I couldn't afford the year off but I was very compelled by those trousers.

8 In short, the thing I wanted most in the world was to be an **individual**. I thought that's what my graduation signified, that I had gone from being one of the many, to one of the few. To one of the ones who would have 'choices' in life. After all my father didn't have many choices, his father had none at all. Unlike them, I had gone to university. I was a special individual. Looking back it's easy to diagnose a case of self-love. People are always accusing students of self-love, or self obsession. And this is a bit confusing because college surely encourages the habit. You concentrate on yourself in order to improve yourself. Isn't that the whole idea? And out of this process hopefully emerge strikingly competent individuals, with high self esteem, prepared for personal achievement.

9 When we graduate, though, things can get a little complicated. For how are we meant to think of this fabulous person, we've taken such care of creating? If university made me special did that mean I was worth more than my father, more than his father before him?

10 Did it mean I should expect more from life than them? Did I deserve more?

11 What does it really mean to be one of 'the few'?

12 Are the fruits of our education a sort of gift, to be circulated generously through the world, or are we to think of ourselves as pure **commodity**, on sale to the highest bidder? Well let's be honest, you're probably feeling pulled in several directions right now. And that's perfectly natural.

Skill: Summarizing

Smith explains the choice her generation faced after college: make money by working at a bank or help others. Smith now thinks that choice is funny, which means she no longer believes what she once did.

13 In the '90s, the post-graduation dilemma was usually presented to us as a straight ethical choice, between working for the banks, and doing selfless charitable work. The comic extremity of the choice I now see was perfectly deliberate. It meant you didn't have to take it too seriously. And so we peeled off from each other. Some of us, many of us, joined the banks. But those that didn't had no special cause to pat ourselves on the back. With rare exceptions, we all pursued self interest more or less. It wasn't a surprise. We'd been raised that way. Born in the seventies, we did not live through austerity, did not go to war like my father, or his father. For the most part we did not join large political or ideological movements. We simply inherited the advantages for which a previous generation had fought.

Summarizing

Why does the reader need to revise his summary?

The reader realizes he is expressing a judgement, so he revises his summary to remove bias.

SELECTION VOCABULARY

individual / el individuo *noun* a single person COGNATE

commodity / la mercancía *noun* an article of commerce; a raw or primary material or product that can be bought and sold

14 And the thing that so many of us feared was the idea of being subsumed back into the collective from which we'd come. Of being returned to the world of the many. Or doing any work at all in that world.

15 In my case this new attitude was particularly noticeable. My own mother was a social worker, and I had teachers in my rowdy state school who had themselves been educated at precisely the elite institution I would later join. But amongst my college friends, I know of no one who made that choice. For the most part, we were uninterested in what we considered to be 'unglamorous pursuits'. We valued individuality above all things. You can thank my generation for the invention of the word 'supermodel', and the popularisation of 'celebrity' and 'lifestyle', often used in conjunction with each other. Reality TV—that was us. Also televised talent shows. Also Ugg boots—you're welcome, millennials! And when the fussier amongst us detected in these visions of prestigious individuality perhaps something a little crass and commercialized, our solution was to go in some ways further down the same road, to out-individuate the celebrated individuals.

16 We became hipsters. Defined by the ways we weren't like everybody else. One amusing, much commented upon consequence of this was that we all ended up individuals of the same type. Not one-of-a-kind, but one . . . of a kind.

17 But there was another aspect I now find melancholic. We isolated ourselves. It took us the longest time to work out that we needed each other. You may have noticed that even now we seem somewhat stunned by quite ordinary human pursuits, like having children or living in a neighbourhood, or getting ill. We are always writing lifestyle articles about such matters in the Sunday papers. That's because, until very recently, we thought we were going to get through this whole life thing purely on our own steam. Even if we were no fans of the ex-British Prime Minister Margaret Thatcher, we had unwittingly taken her most famous slogan and embedded it deep within our own lives. "There is no such thing as society," she said. We were unique individuals. What did we need with society? But then it turned out that the things that have happened to everybody since the dawn of time also happened to us. Our parents got old and ill. Our children needed schools and somewhere to play. We wanted trains that ran on time. We needed each other. It turned out we were just human—like everybody.

18 Now I may have this completely backward, but I get the sense that something different is going on in your generation. Something hopeful. You seem to be smarter, sooner. Part of these smarts is surely born out of crisis. In the '90s we had high employment and a buoyant economy. We could afford to spend weeks wondering about the exact length and shape of our beards, or whether

Skill: Language, Style, and Audience

Smith mocks her generation using simple words and non-standard syntax. The sentences are brief, and the punctuation creates humorous pauses. This effectively conveys a lighthearted and informal tone.

Skill: Textual Evidence

Smith characterizes her generation as people who thought they could always succeed in life on their own. But, as they got older, they realized this wasn't possible. This textual evidence supports one of Smith's main ideas.

Language, Style, and Audience

What does the reader note about Smith's word choice?

The reader notes that Smith uses simple words.

Textual Evidence

What does the reader note about Smith's generation?

The reader notes how Smith characterizes her generation as people who thought they could do everything on their own but grew up to realize they couldn't.

Skills Focus

QUESTION 2: Summarizing

Smith's generation feared being one of the many, so they idolized individuals, which usually meant famous people. These details show how the ideals of Smith's generation affected society and how Smith began to see the flaws in what she used to value.

Textual Evidence

What does the reader say is Smith's view of the current generation?

The reader says Smith views the current generation as different from her own; they face major issues that require people working together to solve.

Skills Focus

QUESTION 5: Connect to Essential Question

Smith notes that the new generation is more aware of the need for community. Part of this is due to the relative security of the 1990s compared to the great, global crises and concerns that are prevalent now.

Skills Focus

QUESTION 4: Language, Style, and Audience

These details help the audience clearly imagine a pivotal moment in the author's life. They emphasize the author's idea that being part of a collective can be rewarding.

Skill: Textual Evidence

Smith focuses on the major issues faced by the current generation. She argues that these issues can only be solved by people working together. This textual evidence reveals how Smith sees the current generation as different from her own.

Kurt Cobain[1] was a sell-out. Your situation is more **acute**. You have so many large, collective tasks ahead, and you know that. We had them too, but paid little attention, so now I'm afraid it falls to you. The climate, the economy, the sick relationship between the individual prestige of the first world and the anonymity of the third—these are things only many hands can fix working together. You are all individuals but you are also part of a generation and generations are defined by the projects they take on together.

19 Even at the level of slogan you decided to honour the contribution of the many over the few, that now famous '99 Percent'[2]. As far as slogans go, which is not very far, yours still sounds more thoughtful to me than the slogans of my youth which were fatally infected by advertising. Be strong. Be fast. Be bold. Be different. Be you . . . be you, that was always the takeaway. And when my peers grew up, and went into advertising, they spread that message far and wide. "Just be you," screams the label on your shampoo bottle. "Just be you," cries your deodorant. "Because you're worth it." You get about fifty commencement speeches a day, and that's before you've even left the bathroom.

20 I didn't think you'd want any more of that from me. Instead I want to speak in favor of recognizing our place within 'the many'. Not only as a slogan, much less as a personal sacrifice, but rather as a potential source of joy in your life.

21 Here is a perhaps silly example. It happened to me recently at my mother's birthday. Around midnight it came time to divide up the rum cake, and I, not naturally one of life's volunteers, was press-ganged into helping. A small circle of women surrounded me, dressed in West African wraps and headscarves, in imitation of their ancestors. "Many hands make short work," said one, and passed me a stack of paper plates. It was my job to take the plated slices through the crowd. Hardly any words passed between us as we went about our collective task, but each time we set a new round upon a tray, I detected a hum of deep satisfaction at our many hands forming this useful human chain. Occasionally as I gave out a slice of cake, an older person would look up and murmur, "Oh you're Yvonne's daughter," but for the most part it was the cake itself that received the greeting or a little nod or a smile, for it was the duty of the daughter to hand out cake and no further commentary was required. And it was while doing what I hadn't realised was my duty that I felt what might be described as the exact opposite of the sensation I have standing in front of you now. Not puffed up with individual prestige, but immersed in the beauty of the crowd. Connected if only in gesture to an ancient line of practical women working in companionable silence in the

1. **Kurt Cobain** composer, singer and guitarist Kurt Cobain (1967–1994) was frontman of the Seattle post-punk band Nirvana
2. **'99 Percent'** populist term referring to percentage of the American population who are not extremely wealthy

SELECTION VOCABULARY

acute / agudo / a *adjective* describes an illness or condition that is severe but often does not last for a long time

service of their community. It's such a ludicrously tiny example of the collective action and yet clearly still so rare in my own life that even this minor instance of it struck me.

22 Anyway my point is that it was a beautiful feeling, and it was over too soon. And when I tried to look for a way to put it into this speech, I was surprised how difficult it is to find the right words to describe it. So many of our colloquial terms for this 'work of many hands' are sunk in infamy. 'Human chain' for starters; 'cog in the machine'; 'brick in the wall'. In such phrases we sense the long shadow of the twentieth century, with its brutal collective movements.

Skill: Language, Style, and Audience

The repetition of the words "collective" and "individual" draws attention to the choice Smith thinks people must make. Throughout the speech, she posits that people can focus on individual goals or work as part of a group.

23 We do not trust the collective, we've seen what submission to it can do. We believe instead in the individual, here in America, especially. Now I also believe in the individual, I'm so grateful for the three years of college that helped make more or less of an individual out of me—teaching me how to think, and write. You may well ask, who am I to praise the work of many hands, when I myself chose the work of one pair of hands, the most isolated there is.

24 I can't escape that accusation. I can only look at my own habit of self love and ask, "what is the best use I can make of this utterly human habit?" Can I make a gift of myself in some other way? I know for sure I haven't done it half as much as I could or should have. I look at the fine example of my friend, the writer and activist Dave Eggers, and see a man who took his own individual prestige and parlayed it into an extraordinary collective action—826 National[3], in which many hands work to create educational opportunities for disadvantaged kids all over this country.

25 And when you go to one of Dave's not-for-profit tutoring centres, you don't find selfless young people grimly sacrificing themselves for others. What you see is joy. Dave's achievement is neither quite charity nor simple individual philanthropy[4]. It's a collective effort that gets people involved in each other's lives.

26 I don't mean to speak meanly of philanthropy. Generally speaking, philanthropy is always better than no help at all, but it is also in itself a privilege of the few. And I think none of us want communities to rise or fall dependent upon the whims of the very rich. I think we would rather be involved in each other's lives and that what stops us, most often, is fear.

27 We fear that the work of many hands will obscure the beloved outline of our individual selves. But perhaps this self you've been treasuring for so long is

3. **826 National** a nationwide nonprofit organization founded by the writer Dave Eggers to encourage and help youth ages six to 18 interested in writing
4. **philanthropy** from Greek meaning "love of humanity," philanthropy refers to activity in financial support of humanitarian causes

Language, Style, and Audience

What does the reader notice about Smith's syntax?

The reader notes that Smith syntax is non-standard.

Skills Focus

QUESTION 3: Textual Evidence

Smith implies that philanthropy is often a rich individual giving money to those who need it. This is better than no one ever giving anyone else money, but it is not the same as people working together for the betterment of all.

TEXT TALK

What does Smith say is important about Dave Eggers?

See paragraphs 24-25: Eggers used his fame as an individual not just to benefit himself but to help others.

itself the work of many hands. Speaking personally, I owe so much to the hard work of my parents, to the educational and health care systems in my country, to the love and care of my friends.

28 And even if one's individual prestige, such as it is, represents an entirely solo effort, the result of sheer hard work, does that everywhere and always mean that you deserve the largest possible slice of the pie?

29 These are big questions, and it is collectively that you'll have to decide them. Everything from the remuneration of executives to the idea of the commons itself depends upon it. And, at the core of the question, is what it really means to be 'the few' and 'the many'. Throughout your adult life you're going to have a daily choice to throw your lot in with one or the other. And a lot of people, most people, even people without the luxury of your choices, are going to suggest to you, over and over, that only an idiot chooses to join the many, when he could be one of the few.

30 Only an idiot chooses public over private, shared over gated, communal over unique. Mrs. Thatcher, who was such a genius at witty **aphorism**, once said, "A man who beyond the age of twenty-six, finds himself on a bus, can count himself a failure."

31 I've always been fascinated by that quote. By its dark assumption that even something as natural as sharing a journey with another person represents a form of personal denigration. The best reply to it that I know is that famous line of Terence, the Roman playwright. *Homo sum, humani nihil a me alienum puto*. 'I am a human being. I consider nothing that is human alien to me.'

32 Montaigne liked that so much he had it carved into the beams of his ceiling. Some people interpret it as a call to toleration. I find it stronger than that, I think it's a call to love. Now, full disclosure, most of the time I don't find it easy to love my fellow humans. I'm still that solipsistic 21-year-old. But the times I've been able to get over myself and get involved at whatever level, well what I'm trying to say is those have proved the most valuable moments of my life.

33 And I never would have guessed that back in 1997. Oh, I would have paid lip service to it, as a noble idea, but I wouldn't have believed it. And the thing is, it's not even a question of ethics or self-sacrifice or moral high ground, it's actually totally selfish. Being with people, doing for people, it's going to bring you joy. Unexpectedly, it just feels better.

34 It feels good to give your unique and prestigious selves a slip every now and then and confess your membership in this unwieldy collective called the human race.

SELECTION VOCABULARY

aphorism / el aforismo ***noun*** a short, memorable phrase or statement that expresses a generally accepted truth COGNATE

35 For one thing, it's far less lonely, and for another, contra to Mrs Thatcher, some of the best conversations you'll ever hear will be on public transport. If it weren't for the New York and London subway systems, my novels would be books of blank pages.

36 But I'm preaching to the converted. I see you, gazing into your phones as you walk down Broadway. And I know solipsism must be a constant danger, as it is for me, as it has been for every human since the dawn of time, but you've also got this tremendous, contrapuntal force propelling you into the world.

37 For aren't you always connecting to each other? Forever communicating, rarely scared of strangers, wildly open, ready to tell anyone everything? Doesn't online anonymity tear at the very idea of a prestige individual? Aren't young artists collapsing the border between themselves and their audience? Aren't young coders determined on an all-access world in which everybody is an equal participant? Are the young activists content just to raise the money and run? No. They want to be local, grassroots, involved. Those are all good instincts. I'm so excited to think of you pursuing them. Hold on to that desire for human connection. Don't let anyone scare you out of it.

38 Walk down these crowded streets with a smile on your face. Be thankful you get to walk so close to other humans. It's a privilege. Don't let your fellow humans be alien to you, and as you get older and perhaps a little less open than you are now, don't assume that exclusive always and everywhere means better. It may only mean lonelier. There will always be folks hard selling you the life of the few: the private schools, private planes, private islands, private life. They are trying to convince you that hell is other people. Don't believe it. We are far more frequently each other's shelter and correction, the antidote to solipsism, and so many windows on this world.

39 Thank you.

Skills Focus

QUESTION 1: Informational Text Structure

Smith argues that today's young people are moved to connect with each other in a way her generation was not. Outlining the differences between the two generations helps strengthen her idea that community, rather than individual prestige, is especially important in today's society.

Prepare for Advanced Courses

Use the activity below to differentiate instruction for your B Beyond grade level learners.

Author's Syntax

Direct students to notice the author's use of questions throughout her persuasive speech.

Ask students:

- How does this choice to use rhetorical questions throughout the speech help Smith convey meaning, emotion and emphasis?

TEXT TALK

What point does Smith make when she mentions seeing students staring into their phones as they walk along the sidewalk?

See paragraphs 36-37: She sees the constant presence of phones as a symbol of the interconnectedness of the current generation.)

How did discussing the characteristics of commencement speeches deepen your understanding of "Commencement Address at the New School"?

Answers will vary.

Ask each Beyond grade-level student to write one additional discussion question. Then, have one or two students facilitate a discussion, using their questions to guide the conversation.

Think Questions

Circulate as students answer Think Questions independently. Scaffolds for these questions are shown on the opposite page.

QUESTION 1: Textual Evidence

Smith thinks her generation is "isolated" from others and obsessed with being individuals. In contrast, she envies the generations before and after hers for being more comfortable with community and focusing on "the many over the few."

QUESTION 2: Textual Evidence

Smith uses Thatcher as an example of the kind of thinking she wants her audience to avoid. Thatcher said there was no such thing as society, for instance, but Smith thinks society and community are of critical importance.

QUESTION 3: Textual Evidence

Smith distributed slices of birthday cake at her mother's party. She liked the feeling of being involved in something that felt important. She described it as a "beautiful feeling" and liked being part of "the beauty of the crowd."

QUESTION 4: Word Meaning

I think *commodity* means something bought or sold. Smith asks her audience to decide whether their education makes them a "pure commodity" or their education meant something beyond a mere business transaction.

QUESTION 5: Context Clues

I think *aphorism* means "a comment that is short and memorable." The text uses the word when it describes a short and memorable quotation from Margaret Thatcher.

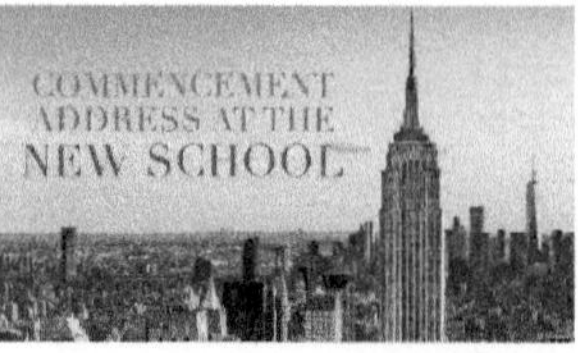

First Read

Read "Commencement Address at the New School." After you read, complete the Think Questions below.

THINK QUESTIONS

1. How does Zadie Smith evaluate her own generation's experiences, as compared to generations before and after? Explain, citing specific examples.
2. Why does Smith quote former British Prime Minister Margaret Thatcher at various points in her speech? What purpose does Thatcher serve in the address? Cite specific evidence from the text to support your answer.
3. What particular small event impressed on Smith the emotional value of shared work and contact with a community? Explain briefly, citing specific evidence from the text to support your response.
4. What is the meaning of the word **commodity** as it is used in the text? Write your best definition here. Then, check an online or print dictionary and compare your answer to the definition you find there.
5. Use context clues to determine the meaning of the word **aphorism** as it is used in the text. Write your definition here, and explain which clues helped you determine its meaning.

Think Questions

SCAFFOLDS

Use the scaffolds below to differentiate instruction for your ELL English Language Learners and A Approaching grade level readers.

ELL **BEGINNING** Write a response using the word bank and sentence frames.

INTERMEDIATE Write a response using the sentence frames.

ADVANCED, ADVANCED HIGH Write a response using the Text-Dependent Question Guide.

A **APPROACHING** Write a response using the Text-Dependent Question Guide.

BEGINNING	INTERMEDIATE	APPROACHING / ADVANCED, ADVANCED HIGH
Word Bank	**Sentence Frames**	**Text-Dependent Question Guide**
connect community disagrees said bidder statement individuals pass out opposite bought	Smith says that people in her generation wanted to be ____. However, Smith thinks that college graduates today know that it's important to ____ with each other.	1. • What does Smith say about her own generation? • What does she say about the current generation? • How are the generations different?
	Smith ____ with Thatcher. Smith hopes that her listeners will do the ____ of what Thatcher says.	2. • What does Thatcher say about society? What does she say about failure? • Does Smith agree with Thatcher? • How do the quotations relate to the main ideas in the speech?
	Smith was asked to help ____ cake at a party. Being asked to help gave Smith an idea of why ____ is so important.	3. • What happened at Smith's mother's birthday party? • Did Smith like what happened? • How did Smith feel afterward? Why?
	Smith mentions a *commodity* that is on sale to the highest ____. This gives me a clue that *commodity* means something that can be ____.	4. • Read: "Are the fruits of our education a sort of gift, to be circulated generously through the world, or are we to think of ourselves as pure **commodity,** on sale to the highest bidder?" • What happens to a *commodity*? • What does that suggest about the meaning of the word *commodity*?
	The word *aphorism* tells about things that Margaret Thatcher ____. I think an *aphorism* is a short but memorable ____.	5. • Read: "Mrs. Thatcher, who was such a genius at witty **aphorism**, once said, 'A man who beyond the age of twenty-six, finds himself on a bus, can count himself a failure.'" • What makes Thatcher seem "witty" in this sentence? • What does that suggest about the meaning of the word *aphorism*?

Reading Comprehension OPTIONAL

Have students complete the digital reading comprehension questions when they finish reading.

ANSWER KEY

QUESTION 1: C
QUESTION 2: C
QUESTION 3: A
QUESTION 4: B
QUESTION 5: D
QUESTION 6: B
QUESTION 7: C
QUESTION 8: D
QUESTION 9: B
QUESTION 10:
See second chart.

First	Second	Third	Fourth
The '90s were a time when college students' concerns for the most part were narrow.	Today's graduates live in a more serious time.	Smith's generation was surprised to find they had the same needs and life events as people have throughout history.	Smith, asked to pass out cake at a party, had a vision of how society must change.

Connect and Extend OPTIONAL

CONNECT TO EXTENDED ORAL PROJECT

Students can use "Commencement Address at the New School" as a mentor text for their Extended Oral Project. They may adopt Zadie Smith's technique of using personal experiences as evidence in her argument about how people should behave.

BEYOND THE BOOK

Activity: Quote Elaboration

Zadie Smith promotes social interaction and collaboration in her commencement speech. Students will analyze selected quotes and connect them to their own lives.

Ask students to:

- Pull a quote from Smith's speech that is powerful and speaks to them.
- Analyze the quote and connect it to their life.
  - > What does Smith mean?
  - > What is being asked of people by this quote?
  - > How does this quote make you think of your own life or events that have occurred in the world?
  - > Why is this quote powerful?
- Create a visual display of the quote and its meaning.
- Share with classmates.

To reflect, ask students to write a paragraph about how the quote they chose will shape who they become in the future.

Skill:
Language, Style, and Audience

Use the Checklist to analyze Language, Style, and Audience in "Commencement Address at the New School." Refer to the sample student annotations about Language, Style, and Audience in the text.

••• CHECKLIST FOR LANGUAGE, STYLE, AND AUDIENCE

In order to determine an author's style and possible intended audience, do the following:

- ✓ identify instances where they author uses key terms throughout the course of a text
- ✓ examine surrounding words and phrases to determine the context, connotation, style, and tone of the term's usage
- ✓ analyze how the author's treatment of the key term affects the reader's understanding of the text
- ✓ note the audience—both intended and unintended—and possible reactions to the author's word choice, style, and treatment of key terms

To analyze how an author's treatment of language and key terms affect the reader's understanding of the text, consider the following questions:

- ✓ How do the author's word choices enhance or change what is being described?
- ✓ How do the author's word choices affect the reader's understanding of key terms and ideas in the text?
- ✓ How do choices about language affect the author's style and audience?
- ✓ How often does the author use this term or terms?

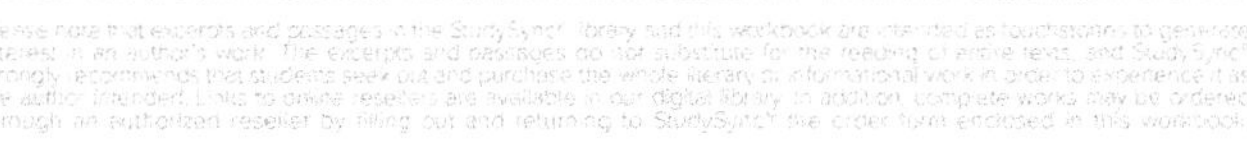

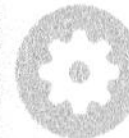

Skill: Language, Style, and Audience

Introduce the Skill

Watch the Concept Definition video and read the following definition with your students.

Authors use language to convey meaning or to affect the way their **audience** thinks and perceives. An audience is the intended reader or listener. Readers can analyze an author's style to better understand the tone and meaning of a text.

Style refers to the way an author uses language (words, sentences, paragraphs) to achieve a purpose. One element of style is word choice. **Word choice** is a technique in which writers choose specific words for precise meaning or to convey a certain tone. **Meaning** is a reader's interpretation of the text's deeper messages, themes, or ideas. **Tone** expresses a writer's **attitude** (or thoughts and feelings) toward his or her subject. Tone can be described, for example, as formal, casual, conversational, ironic, sad, bitter, humorous, or serious.

SKILL VOCABULARY

audience / la audiencia *noun* the people who read a written text, listen to an oral response or presentation, or watch a performance COGNATE

style / el estilo *noun* a way of expressing something that is characteristic of the person or time period COGNATE

word choice / la elección de palabras *noun* specific words chosen for precise meaning or to generate an emotional response

TURN AND TALK

1. What is an example of a character from a book, TV show, or movie who uses certain words or speaks a certain way?
2. What do you learn about this character based on the way he or she speaks?

SPEAKING FRAMES

- The character ____ uses words like ____.
- I think the character is ____.

Your Turn

Ask students to complete the Your Turn Activity.

QUESTION 1

A. Incorrect. Smith translates the quotation into English for listeners who do not know Latin; there is no evidence that she is trying to show off.

B. Incorrect. Smith uses the quotation to suggest that humans are connected by shared experiences.

C. Correct. Smith refers to the quotation from Terence as "the best reply" to Thatcher's ideas; she is using Terence to support her argument to the audience.

D. Incorrect. There is no evidence in the speech to support this.

QUESTION 2

A. Correct. Smith uses repetition to encourage her audience to remember that they are part of the "unwieldy collective called the human race."

B. Incorrect. Smith refutes the quote by Margaret Thatcher.

C. Incorrect. Smith does not encourage her audience to focus on their flaws.

D. Incorrect. Smith does not use a dismissive tone in this part of the speech.

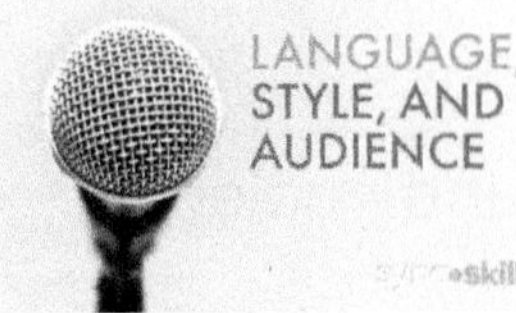

Skill: Language, Style, and Audience

Reread paragraphs 30–34 of "Commencement Address at the New School." Then, using the Checklist on the previous page, answer the multiple-choice questions below.

YOUR TURN

1. In paragraph 31, Smith's choice to quote the Roman playwright Terence effectively—

   ○ A. shows off her knowledge of Latin in order to impress her audience with her intelligence.
   ○ B. encourages her listeners to focus on their own accomplishments and ignore others.
   ○ C. provides a counterpoint to Thatcher and emphasizes her own idea of what is truly important.
   ○ D. convinces her listeners that ancient Roman culture represented a high point in world history.

2. Which statement best evaluates how Smith uses language and style to affect the reader's/listener's perception of the relationship between individualism and collectivism?

   ○ A. Smith's repetition of the words "human" and "people" strongly reminds an audience of individuals that they are also part of a large group.
   ○ B. Smith's decision to include a funny quotation by Margaret Thatcher strongly suggests that people should avoid spending too much time with others.
   ○ C. Smith's concession that she does not always like other people strongly encourages the audience to focus on one another's individual faults.
   ○ D. Smith's wit and dismissive tone strongly suggest that the audience should not take her too seriously and should instead make up their own minds.

SKILL VOCABULARY

tone / el tono *noun* the writer's or speaker's attitude toward his or her subject matter COGNATE

attitude / la actitud *noun* a state involving beliefs and feelings that causes a person to think or act in a certain way COGNATE

meaning / el significado *noun* what is meant by a word; the general message of a text or idea

Skill: Textual Evidence

Use the Checklist to analyze Textual Evidence in "Commencement Address at the New School." Refer to the sample student annotations about Textual Evidence in the text.

••• CHECKLIST FOR TEXTUAL EVIDENCE

In order to support an analysis by citing evidence that is explicitly stated in the text, do the following:

- ✓ read the text closely and critically
- ✓ identify what the text says explicitly
- ✓ find the most relevant textual evidence that supports your analysis
- ✓ consider why an author explicitly states specific details and information
- ✓ cite the specific words, phrases, sentences, or paragraphs from the text that support your analysis
- ✓ determine where evidence in the text still leaves matters uncertain or unresolved

In order to interpret implicit meanings in a text by making inferences, do the following:

- ✓ combine information directly stated in the text with your own knowledge, experiences, and observations
- ✓ cite the specific words, phrases, sentences, or paragraphs from the text that led to and support this inference

In order to cite textual evidence to support an analysis of what the text says explicitly as well as inferences drawn from the text, consider the following questions:

- ✓ Have I read the text closely and critically?
- ✓ What inferences am I making about the text?
- ✓ What textual evidence am I using to support these inferences?
- ✓ Am I quoting the evidence from the text correctly?
- ✓ Does my textual evidence logically relate to my analysis or the inference I am making?
- ✓ Does evidence in the text still leave certain matters unanswered or unresolved? In what ways?

SKILL VOCABULARY

textual evidence / la evidencia del texto *noun* details from the text that a reader can use to support his or her ideas and opinions about the text

make inferences / hacer inferencias *verb* to use your understanding of a text and your own experiences, to draw conclusions

Skill: Textual Evidence

Introduce the Skill

Watch the Concept Definition video ▶ and read the following definition with your students.

Any time you're discussing a text, you need to **cite**, or point out, **textual evidence**, the details that readers use to support their ideas and opinions. Readers may cite evidence that is directly stated, or **explicit**, in the text. Other times, textual evidence may be **implicit**, which means it is suggested but not directly stated. One way to interpret implicit meanings is to **make inferences**, using clues from the text and your own experiences to make logical decisions about characters and events that are not stated directly.

Readers must also refer to textual evidence when they **analyze** and examine the different parts of a text. Analyzing specific parts of the text, such as the actions of a character or the cause-and-effect relationships between events in nonfiction, helps a reader **interpret** and explain the meaning, theme, or central idea of the text as a whole. When you cite textual evidence, someone else can look back at a particular part of a text you read and understand your analysis.

TURN AND TALK

1. What comes to mind when you hear the word *evidence*?
2. How is textual evidence different than other types of evidence?

SPEAKING FRAMES

- The word *evidence* makes me think of ____.
- Textual evidence is different from other types of evidence because ____.

Your Turn

Ask students to complete the Your Turn Activity.

QUESTION 1

Part A

A. Incorrect. Smith does recognize that passing out cake is her unspoken duty, but this inference is not supported by the paragraph.

B. Incorrect. This inference is not supported by the paragraph.

C. Correct. Smith tells this cake story to show the power of working as part of a community.

D. Incorrect. Smith is doing a small job out of respect for her mother, but this inference is not supported by the paragraph.

Part B

A. Incorrect. This textual evidence does not support the correct answer in Part A.

B. Incorrect. This textual evidence does not support the correct answer in Part A.

C. Incorrect. This textual evidence does not support the correct answer in Part A.

D. Correct. This sentence best supports the inference that working in service of a community is better than working for individual prestige.

Skill: Textual Evidence

Reread paragraph 21 of "Commencement Address at the New School." Then, using the Checklist on the previous page, answer the multiple-choice questions below.

YOUR TURN

1. This question has two parts. First, answer Part A. Then, answer Part B.

Part A: Which inference is best supported by this paragraph?

- A. It is easy for a grown daughter to forget the duties she has toward her mother, particularly around a parent's birthday.
- B. It is important for people to honor their ancestors by continuing to respect ancient customs, such as serving cake at a birthday party.
- C. Working as part of a community creates something more beautiful and beneficial than working for individual recognition.
- D. Even when the task is seemingly minor, performing a job in honor of one's parents represents an important step in becoming an adult.

Part B: Which textual evidence from the paragraph best supports the answer to Part A?

- A. "A small circle of women surrounded me, dressed in West African wraps and headscarves, in imitation of their ancestors."
- B. "It was my job to take the plated slices through the crowd."
- C. ". . . but for the most part it was the cake itself that received the greeting or a little nod or a smile, for it was the duty of the daughter to hand out cake and no further commentary was required."
- D. "Connected if only in gesture to an ancient line of practical women working in companionable silence in the service of their community."

Skill: Summarizing

Use the Checklist to analyze Summarizing in "Commencement Address at the New School." Refer to the sample student annotations about Summarizing in the text.

••• CHECKLIST FOR SUMMARIZING

In order to determine how to write an objective summary of a text, note the following:

- ✓ answers to the basic questions *who, what, where, when, why,* and *how*
- ✓ in literature or nonfiction, note how two or more themes or central ideas are developed over the course of the text, and how they interact and build on one another to produce a complex account
- ✓ stay objective, and do not add your own personal thoughts, judgments, or opinions to the summary

To provide an objective summary of a text, consider the following questions:

- ✓ What are the answers to basic *who, what, where, when, why,* and *how* questions in literature and works of nonfiction?
- ✓ Does my summary include how two or more themes or central ideas are developed over the course of the text, and how they interact and build on one another in my summary?
- ✓ Is my summary objective, or have I added my own thoughts, judgments, and personal opinions?

Skill: Summarizing

Introduce the Skill

Watch the Concept Definition video and read the following definition with your students.

When you **summarize** a text, you concisely state the main points and most important details in your own words. Summarizing can help you organize, explain, and remember concepts in an informational text or the events that take place in a story.

To summarize, you must decide what is most important as you read. Ask the basic questions: *who, what, when, where, why,* and *how*. Using your own words, write your answers to these questions from an **objective** point of view, without inserting your own feelings and opinions.

Summarizing is sometimes confused with paraphrasing. When you **paraphrase**, you do not condense a text to its most important details. Instead, you restate the entire text in your own words. A summary is much shorter than the original text, whereas a paraphrase may be the same length as the original text.

SKILL VOCABULARY

summarize / resumir *verb* to restate briefly the most important points in a text

objective / objetivo / a *adjective* undistorted by emotion or personal bias COGNATE

paraphrase / parafrasear *verb* to restate the author's words in your own words COGNATE

TURN AND TALK

1. When you summarize someone else's words, why is it important to leave out your own feelings and opinions?
2. When is it appropriate for you to express your feelings or opinions about someone else's ideas?

SPEAKING FRAMES

- It is important to leave out your feelings and opinions because ____.
- It is appropriate to express your opinion when ____.

Your Turn

Ask students to complete the Your Turn Activity.

QUESTION 1

A. Correct. This sentence connects the ideas in these paragraphs to the main ideas of the speech.

B. Incorrect. This sentence does not accurately reflect the ideas in these paragraphs.

C. Incorrect. This sentence does not accurately reflect the ideas in these paragraphs.

D. Incorrect. This inference is somewhat supported by Smith's last sentence in paragraph 29, but this answer does not connect the main ideas in these paragraphs to the rest of the speech.

QUESTION 2

A. Incorrect. This is a biased summary.

B. Correct. This is an accurate, unbiased summary of these paragraphs.

C. Incorrect. This sentence only summarizes paragraph 27.

D. Incorrect. These sentences are not completely objective and accurate.

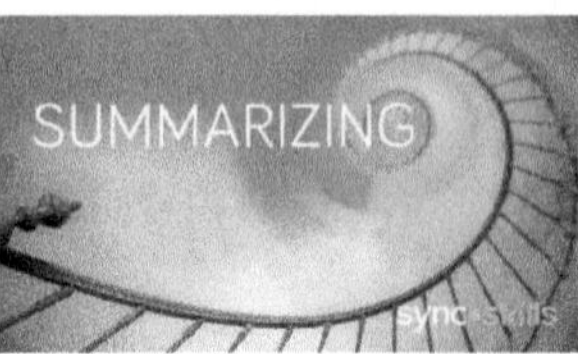

Skill: Summarizing

Reread paragraphs 27–29 of "Commencement Address at the New School." Then, using the Checklist on the previous page, answer the multiple-choice questions below.

YOUR TURN

1. How does this part of the speech build on main ideas throughout the speech?

   - ○ A. Smith argues that we all depend on family, friends, and society, and that group efforts make shared support and community possible.
   - ○ B. Smith tells her audience that they face the choice of being part of a community or part of the elite, just like Smith's generation did.
   - ○ C. Smith points out that members of the developed world, like her audience, have many more choices and options than members of the developing world.
   - ○ D. Smith argues that most people think it is a bad idea to seek to belong to a community when they could become a member of the ruling elite.

2. Which of the following is the most complete and unbiased summary of paragraphs 27–29?

   - ○ A. Smith clearly conveys the idea that people cannot rise to the top without any help and so she advocates for the value of community. However, she also recognizes that most people rightly view the choice to reject individuality as a silly one.
   - ○ B. Smith argues that we often reject working with others because of the fear of being obscured. But most people are products of collective work, and it is an important choice to strive to be an individual or part of a community, even though many believe rejecting community is best.
   - ○ C. Smith argues that successful people do not become successful completely on their own, and they owe a lot to the support of their family, friends, and society.
   - ○ D. Smith points out that even if people are able to achieve success completely on their own, it's not clear whether they deserve more than everyone else. Smith tells her audience that they will have to face the difficult choice of being poor and common or a member of the elite.

Close Read

Reread "Commencement Address at the New School." As you reread, complete the Skills Focus questions below. Then use your answers and annotations from the questions to help you complete the Write activity.

SKILLS FOCUS

1. Find a passage in which Smith uses a compare-and-contrast text structure to convey her ideas. Analyze whether the choice to use this structure helps the author make her ideas clear.
2. Highlight a passage in which Smith describes her attitude toward her generation. Summarize how details in the passage you selected develop two of the main ideas in the speech.
3. What can you infer is Zadie Smith's opinion of philanthropy? What are the positives and possible failures she sees in philanthropy? Find textual evidence to support your answer. Note where the textual evidence may leave matters unresolved.
4. Identify an example of vivid sensory language. Explain how Smith's choice to include these details effectively shapes the audience's perception of her main ideas.
5. Why is the generation graduating in 2014 so different from the class Zadie Smith graduated with in 1997? What are some of the causes that Zadie Smith identifies as the reasons things have changed so much between these generations? Cite textual evidence to support your answer.

WRITE

PERSONAL RESPONSE: Most of Smith's commencement speech is about seeing oneself as one of the few or one of the many. React to this speech in a short essay. Use the examples she gives to summarize her central idea about individualism. Tell whether you plan to be one of the few or one of the many when you leave school. Explain your choice, using examples from your own life and textual evidence from Smith's speech.

Close Read

Skills Focus

QUESTION 1: Informational Text Structure

See paragraphs 36–37.

QUESTION 2: Summarizing

See paragraphs 14–15.

QUESTION 3: Textual Evidence

See paragraphs 25–26.

QUESTION 4: Language, Style, and Audience

See paragraph 21.

QUESTION 5: Connect to Essential Question

See paragraph 18.

CHECK FOR SUCCESS

If students struggle to respond to Skills Focus Question #1, ask students the following questions:

- What does Smith say about the new generation in paragraphs 36-37?
- How is this generation different from Smith's?
- How does the compare-and-contrast structure help support Smith's main ideas?

Writer's Notebook

Connect to Essential Question: Give students time to reflect on how "Commencement Address at the New School" connects to the unit's essential question "How are we shaped by change?" by freewriting in their Writer's Notebooks.

Beginning & Intermediate

Read aloud the unit's essential question: "How are we shaped by change?" Encourage students to draw their connections or allow students to write in their native language. Circulate around the room, prompting students for their thoughts as they respond orally or through pantomime.

Advanced & Advanced High

Allow students to share their connections orally in pairs or small groups before freewriting.

Collaborative Conversation

SCAFFOLDS

Break students into collaborative conversation groups to discuss the Close Read prompt. Ask students to use the StudySyncTV episode as a model for their discussion. Remind them to reference their Skills Focus annotations in their discussion.

Most of Smith's commencement speech is about seeing oneself as one of the few or one of the many. React to this speech in a short essay. Use the examples she gives to summarize her central idea about individualism. Tell whether you plan to be one of the few or one of the many when you leave school. Explain your choice, using examples from your own life and textual evidence from Smith's speech.

Use the scaffolds below to differentiate instruction for your ELL English Language Learners and A Approaching grade-level learners.

ELL **BEGINNING, INTERMEDIATE** Use the discussion guide and speaking frames to facilitate the discussion with support from the teacher.

ADVANCED, ADVANCED HIGH Use the discussion guide and speaking frames to facilitate the discussion in mixed-level groups.

A **APPROACHING** Use the discussion guide to facilitate the discussion in mixed-level groups.

APPROACHING
ADVANCED, ADVANCED HIGH
BEGINNING, INTERMEDIATE

Discussion Guide	Speaking Frames
1. How has Smith's attitude toward individualism changed over time?	• When Smith was graduating, she thought ____. • Now Smith thinks ____.
2. What example from the text best shows Smith's central idea about individualism?	• An important example is ____. • This example suggests ____.
3. Would you rather be one of the few or one of the many? Why?	• I would rather be ____. • I choose this path because ____.

Text To World

Use the activity below to differentiate instruction for your B Beyond grade level learners.

Have students research one or two other acclaimed commencement speeches.

Ask students:

- What do you believe is the purpose of a commencement address and to what extent does Zadie Smith achieve this purpose? Is there more than one purpose? Select quotations from Smith's speech to support your response.
- How are the speeches you researched similar to or different from Smith's speech?
- Do they achieve the same purposes? Support your analysis with evidence from two or more of the speeches you researched.

Review Prompt and Rubric

Before students begin writing, review the writing prompt and rubric with the class.

PERSONAL ESSAY: Most of Smith's commencement speech is about seeing oneself as one of the few or one of the many. React to this speech in a short essay. Use the examples she gives to summarize her central idea about individualism. Tell whether you plan to be one of the few or one of the many when you leave school. Explain your choice, using examples from your own life and textual evidence from Smith's speech.

ELL A PROMPT GUIDE

- How has Smith's attitude toward individualism changed over time?
- Which example from the text best shows Smith's central idea about individualism?
- Would you rather be one of the few or one of the many? Why?

Score	Summarizing	Language and Conventions
4	The writer clearly summarizes Smith's central idea about individualism in the speech and explains his or her reaction to that idea. The writer provides exemplary analysis, using relevant textual evidence and personal experience.	The writer demonstrates a consistent command of grammar, punctuation, and usage conventions. Although minor errors may be evident, they do not detract from the fluency or the clarity of the essay.
3	The writer summarizes Smith's central idea about individualism in the speech and explains his or her reaction to that idea. The writer provides sufficient analysis, using relevant textual evidence and personal experience most of the time.	The writer demonstrates an adequate command of grammar, punctuation, and usage conventions. Although some errors may be evident, they create few (if any) disruptions in the fluency of the writing or the clarity of the essay.
2	The writer begins to summarizes Smith's central idea about individualism in the speech and explain his or her reaction to that idea, but the explanation is incomplete. The writer uses relevant textual evidence and personal experience only some of the time.	The writer demonstrates a partial command of grammar, punctuation, and usage conventions. Some distracting errors may be evident, at times creating minor disruptions in the fluency or clarity of the writing.
1	The writer attempts to summarizes Smith's central idea about individualism in the speech and explain his or her reaction to that idea, but the explanation is not successful. The writer uses little or no relevant textual evidence or personal experience.	The writer demonstrates little or no command of grammar, punctuation, and usage conventions. Serious and persistent errors create disruptions in the fluency of the writing and sometimes interfere with meaning.
0	The writer does not provide a relevant response to the prompt or does not provide a response at all.	Serious and persistent errors overwhelm the writing and interfere with the meaning of the response as a whole, making the writer's meaning impossible to understand.

Write

SCAFFOLDS

Ask students to complete the writing assignment using text evidence to support their answers.

Use the scaffolds below to differentiate instruction for your ELL English Language Learners and A Approaching grade level readers.

ELL **BEGINNING** With the help of the word bank, write a response using paragraph frame 1.

INTERMEDIATE With the help of the word bank, write a response using paragraph frames 1 and 2.

ADVANCED, ADVANCED HIGH Write a response of differentiated length using the sentence starters.

A **APPROACHING** Write a response of differentiated length using the sentence starters.

BEGINNING / INTERMEDIATE | ADVANCED, ADVANCED HIGH / APPROACHING

Word Bank	Paragraph Frame 1	Paragraph Frame 2	Sentence Starters
individual community connect few many rely work skills alone together strong help rewarding collective follow	When she was younger, Smith believed that it was better to ____. Now, she sees value in being ____. She encourages young people to ____. I agree that ____. When I leave school, I plan to ____. I feel this way because ____.	When she was younger, Smith believed that it was better to ____. An example she gives is ____. Now, she sees value in being ____. A detail that supports this idea is ____. She encourages young people to ____. I think that ____. When I leave school, I plan to ____. I feel this way because ____. When I am older, I hope to ____.	• Smith thinks that . . . • Once I worked with other people to . . . • Once I worked by myself to . . . • These experiences taught me . . . • I would prefer to be . . .

Peer Review

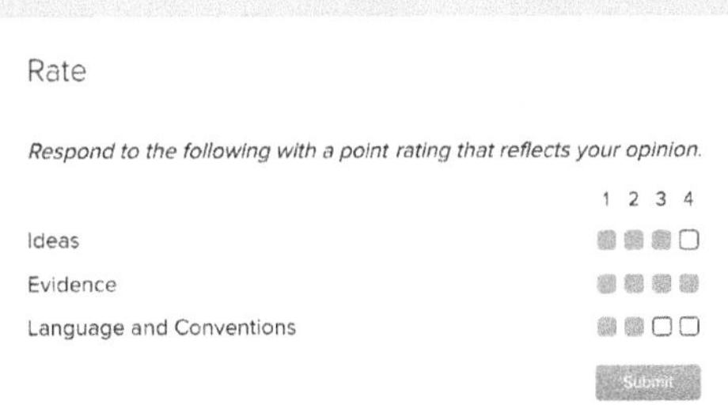

Students should submit substantive feedback to two peers using the review instructions below.

- How well does this response answer the prompt?
- How well does the writer support his or her ideas with evidence from the text and from his or her own life?
- Which part of the writer's response made you think differently about your own response?
- What did the writer do well in this response? What does the writer need to work on?

Remember that your comments are most useful when they are kind and constructive.

SENTENCE FRAMES

A

- You (completely / partly) ____ answered the prompt because ____.
- You could answer the prompt more completely by ____.
- An important detail you cited from the speech is ____.
- An important detail you cited from your own life is ____.
- One idea you expressed well is ____.
- One idea that could be clearer is ____.

Blast: Matter, Mood, and Moment

What more about the subject matter are you in the mood to read in this moment?

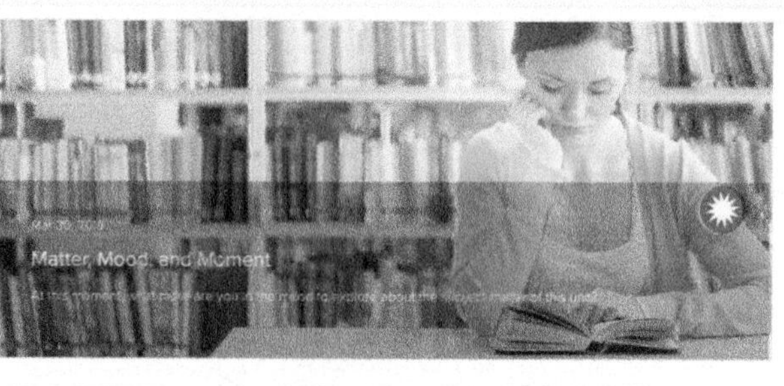

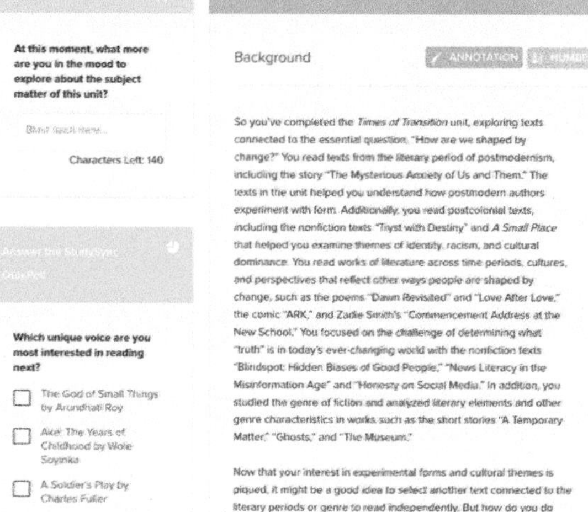

TEXT TALK

What did you think of the *Times of Transition* unit? What is your opinion of postmodernist and postcolonial literature, based on the unit's selections?
Answers will vary.

What is one strategy you can use for self-selecting a new text? How does it work?
I can ask my friends who have similar reading interests which books they recommend.

Would you be more likely to select a text related to the time period, genre, or topic of a selection in the unit? Explain.
Answers will vary.

Create Your Own Blast

SCAFFOLDS

Ask students to write a 140-character Blast after they complete the QuikPoll.

Use the scaffolds below to differentiate instruction for your ELL English Language Learners.

ELL **BEGINNING** Write a response using the word bank to complete the sentence frame.

INTERMEDIATE Write a response using the sentence frame.

ADVANCED, ADVANCED HIGH Write a response using the sentence starter.

	INTERMEDIATE	ADVANCED, ADVANCED HIGH
BEGINNING	BEGINNING	
Word Bank	**Sentence Frame**	**Sentence Starter**
subject matter genre video preview time period poster	I am in the mood to read ____. The ____ made me want to read this text.	• I am in the mood to read . . . • The main reason I selected this text is . . .

Self-Selected Response

WRITE

Prompt

Self-Selected Response Prompt and Directions:

Have you ever noticed that the search for answers sometimes leads to more questions? In the digital world, it is easy to fall into a virtual rabbit hole, bouncing around the Internet by clicking one link after another as you learn about a topic. The same thing can happen when you read. Books, stories, poems, and essays open up new worlds for readers, and it is only natural to want to learn more about these worlds.

What else do you want to know?

What is an area you're left wondering more about after reading the selection you chose? This could be a person, time period, place, event, concept, etc. Write a response in which you propose a topic for further research. In your response, be sure to include:

- a reason that explains why you want to learn more about this area
- questions inspired by the selection that you would like answered
- where you might look to find more information about the area you chose

Self-Selected Response

Introduce the Prompt

Read aloud the prompt. Ask students to discuss:

- What is the prompt asking you to do?
- Why did you choose to read the selection you chose? What did you find interesting about it?

Write

SCAFFOLDS

Ask students to complete the writing assignment using text evidence to support their answers.

Use the scaffolds below to differentiate instruction for your ELL English Language Learners and A Approaching grade level readers.

ELL **BEGINNING** With the help of the word bank, write a response using paragraph frame 1.

INTERMEDIATE With the help of the word bank, write a response using paragraph frames 1 and 2.

ADVANCED, ADVANCED HIGH Write a response of differentiated length using the sentence starters.

A **APPROACHING** Write a response of differentiated length using the sentence starters.

BEGINNING / INTERMEDIATE	BEGINNING	INTERMEDIATE	ADVANCED, ADVANCED HIGH / APPROACHING
Word Bank	**Paragraph Frame 1**	**Paragraph Frame 2**	**Sentence Starters**
culture why colonialism encyclopedia experimentation search engine who affect what familiar	I read the text (title) ____ by (author) ____. An area I would like to learn more about is ____. I find this area interesting because ____. A question I have is "____?" To find the answer to this question, I would look ____. I am also curious to learn ____. I might find more information in ____.	I read the text (title) ____ by (author) ____. An area I would like to learn more about is ____. I find this area interesting because ____. A question I have is "____?" To find the answer to this question, I would look ____. I am also curious to learn ____. I might find more information in ____. Reading the selection inspired me to learn about this area because ____. Before reading, I did not know ____. After reading, I thought ____.	• I read the text . . . by . . . • An area I would like to learn more about is . . . because . . . • I am inspired to learn more because . . . • A question I have after reading is . . . • To find the answer to this question, I would look . . .

Timed Writing Recommendations

Issue	Suggestion
Students don't finish their essays in the time allowed.	• Remind students of the time remaining and give suggestions of what they should be working on at that point. • Set and track writing goals for struggling students.
Students struggle to start their essays.	• Revisit and remodel the planning process. • Provide students with sentence starters for particular genres or sentence types.
Students spend too much time planning.	• Suggest students limit their planning to 5–10 minutes. • Have students identify several "buzzwords" from the prompt to use in their thesis and commentary.
Students don't understand the prompt.	• Have students rewrite the prompt using their own words. • Encourage students to use context clues to determine the meaning of unfamiliar language.
Students get nervous or stressed about writing.	• Provide students with strategies that help prevent or counter stress, such as stretching and breathing exercises, or limiting how often they look at the clock or track their peers' progress.
Students focus too much on editing and do not make progress on their writing.	• Advise students to use their knowledge of their own common errors to prioritize their editing. • Remind students to focus on specific areas, such as sentence structure or comma usage.
Students get stuck as they are writing.	• Recommend that students pause to reread the prompt and their response to that point. • Have students identify the types of challenges they encounter and brainstorm solutions to those problems that they can implement moving forward.
Your classroom spans a wide variety of abilities.	• Have several students share strategies or reflections with the rest of the class. • Create a classroom "resume" that lists each student's strengths so that students can consult with peers for their writing.

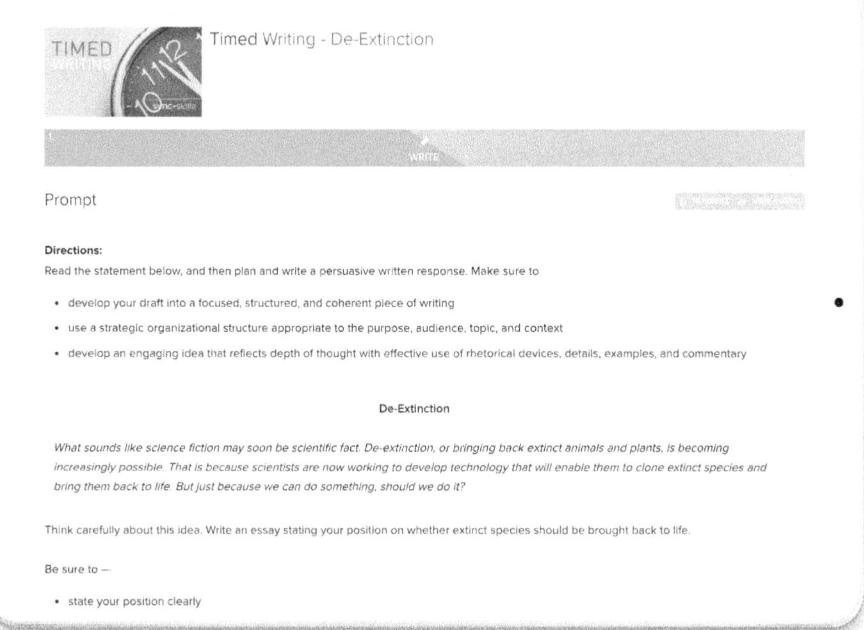

Timed Writing - De-Extinction

WRITE

Prompt

Directions:
Read the statement below, and then plan and write a persuasive written response. Make sure to

- develop your draft into a focused, structured, and coherent piece of writing
- use a strategic organizational structure appropriate to the purpose, audience, topic, and context
- develop an engaging idea that reflects depth of thought with effective use of rhetorical devices, details, examples, and commentary

De-Extinction

What sounds like science fiction may soon be scientific fact. De-extinction, or bringing back extinct animals and plants, is becoming increasingly possible. That is because scientists are now working to develop technology that will enable them to clone extinct species and bring them back to life. But just because we can do something, should we do it?

Think carefully about this idea. Write an essay stating your position on whether extinct species should be brought back to life.

Be sure to —

- state your position clearly

Timed Writing

Ask students to complete the writing assignment.

Note: To replicate the testing environment, turn off scaffolds, but allow ELL students to ask clarifying questions about unknown words or phrases in the prompt before they begin writing.

CLARIFYING QUESTIONS

- What does the word ____ mean in the prompt?
- I do not know what the phrase ____ means. Can you explain it to me?
- What does it mean in the instructions when it says ____?

Write

SCAFFOLDS

Use the scaffolds below to differentiate instruction for your ELL English Language Learners and A Approaching grade level learners.

ELL **BEGINNING, INTERMEDIATE, ADVANCED, ADVANCED HIGH** Use the sentence starters to organize and write your response.

A **APPROACHING** Write a response of differentiated length using the sentence starters.

BEGINNING, INTERMEDIATE, ADVANCED, ADVANCED HIGH
APPROACHING

Purpose of Sentence	Sentence Starters
To state your thesis or claim	• I believe ____ because I think it's important to . . . • My opinion on ____ is . . .
To introduce evidence	• For example, . . . • One reason that supports my claim is . . .
To explain your evidence	• ____ shows that . . . • This reason is important because . . .
To include a counter argument	• Some people might argue ____. However, . . . • A reason against my opinion is ____, but . . .
To conclude your essay	• To summarize . . . • Overall, the most important point to remember is . . .

Extended Oral Project

The Extended Oral Project (EOP) in Grade 12, Unit 6 focuses on writing and delivering an oral presentation. Students consider the following question—What do future students need to know?—as they write an argumentative presentation about a topic, issue, person, or event that they think should be included in future high school instruction. The unit's selections about people experiencing challenges, examining relationships, and exploring identity provide a context for students, and the multiple perspectives on the contemporary world in the unit serve as mentor texts for students to analyze and emulate. Specific skill lessons teach developing ideas, organization, and conventions, while other skill lessons on considering audience and purpose, persuasive techniques, and communicating ideas focus on characteristics of the genre and help students develop their unique voices. Directed revision leads students through the process of revising for clarity, development, organization, word choice, and sentence fluency. Throughout the EOP, students have the opportunity to practice, using created student writing, authentic texts, and their own work.

Audio and audio text highlighting are available in select lessons in the Extended Oral Project.

CONNECT TO ESSENTIAL QUESTION

How are we shaped by change?

In this unit, students read about how change can shape us. Now students will synthesize their experiences from the last several years of their schooling and write an argumentative speech about a topic, issue, person, or event that they felt was underrepresented in their education. Students will explain why this subject should be included in future curricula.

Extended Oral Project Prompt

What do future students need to know?

As your high school years now come to a close, think back on the last several years and consider the topics you have covered in all of your subjects. Then, consider the world around you now and select a topic, issue, person, or event that is important to you, but that was not covered in your formal studies. Develop an argument to support the claim that this topic, issue, person, or event should be included in future high school instruction so that the details and significance will be heard and remembered.

These icons identify differentiation strategies and scaffolded support for a variety of students. See the digital lesson plan for additional differentiation strategies and scaffolds.

Instructional Path

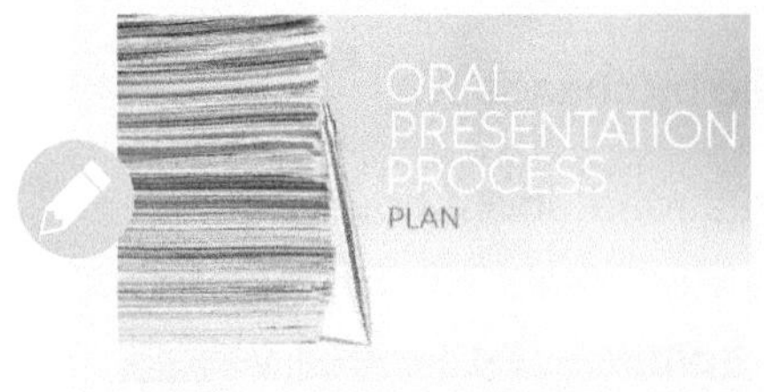

Oral Presentation Process: Plan

Objectives: After learning about genre characteristics and craft, students will analyze a sample Student Model and plan an effective argumentative oral presentation in response to a prompt.

Skill: Organizing an Oral Presentation

Objectives: After reading and discussing a model of student writing, students will prepare to give an oral presentation by structuring and organizing ideas with focus and purpose.

Skill: Evaluating Sources

Objectives: After reading and discussing a model of student writing, students will develop their oral presentation drafts by evaluating sources for accuracy, credibility and reliability.

Skill: Considering Audience and Purpose

Objectives: After reading and discussing a model of student writing, students will develop their drafts by considering their audience and purpose.

Skill: Persuasive Techniques

Objectives: After reading and discussing a model of student writing, students will develop their drafts by planning persuasive techniques.

Oral Presentation Process: Draft

Objectives: After reading a Student Model draft and reviewing a writing checklist, students will draft an effective argumentative oral presentation in response to a prompt.

The print teacher's edition includes essential point-of-use instruction and planning tools. Complete lesson plans and program documents appear in your digital teacher account.

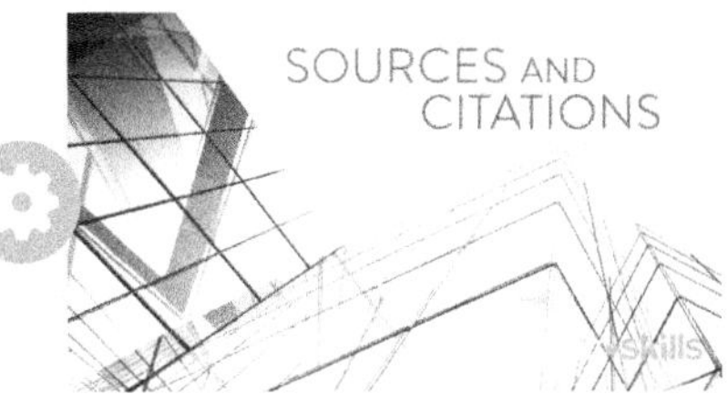

Skill: Sources and Citations

Objectives: After reading and discussing a model of a student presentation, students will develop their argumentative oral presentations by displaying academic citations and using source materials ethically.

Skill: Communicating Ideas

Objectives: Students will learn and practice strategies to communicate ideas effectively during an argumentative oral presentation.

Skill: Reasons and Evidence

Objectives: After reading and discussing a model of student writing, students will prepare to create an argumentative oral presentation using reasons and evidence.

Skill: Engaging in Discourse

Objectives: Students will learn and practice strategies for engaging effectively in meaningful and respectful discourse.

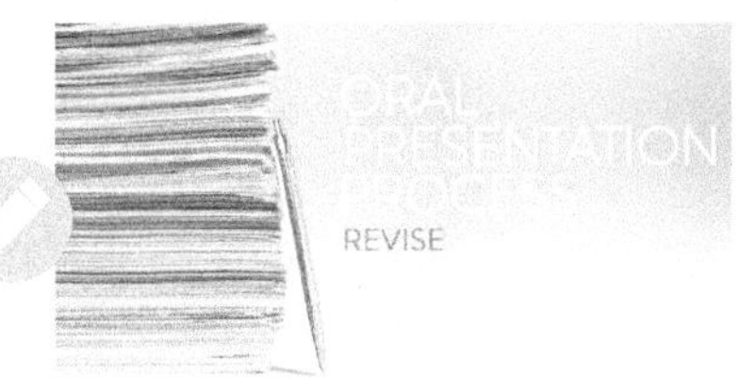

Oral Presentation Process: Revise

Objectives: Students will use a revision guide to revise the draft of their argumentative oral presentation for clarity, development, organization, style, diction, and sentence fluency.

Grammar: Parallel Structure

Objectives: After learning about parallel structure and seeing how it is used in text examples, students will practice using parallel structure correctly.

Grammar: Sentence Variety - Openings

Objectives: After learning about using varied sentence openings and seeing how they are used in text examples, students will practice using varied sentence openings correctly.

Oral Presentation Process: Edit and Present

Objectives: After seeing an example of editing in the Student Model and reviewing an editing checklist, students will edit and present the final draft of their argumentative oral presentation.

Progress Monitoring

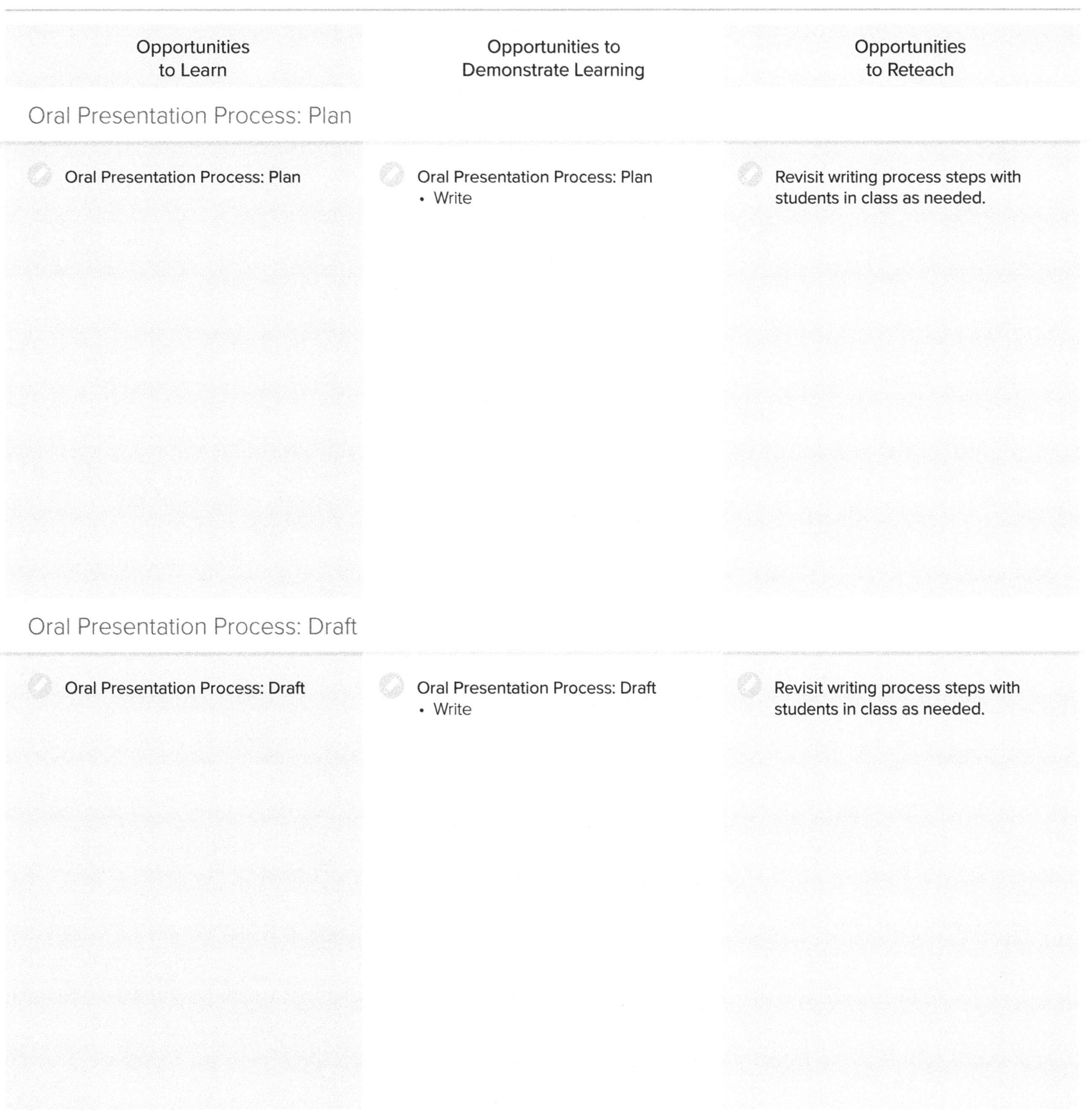

Opportunities to Learn	Opportunities to Demonstrate Learning	Opportunities to Reteach
Oral Presentation Process: Plan		
Oral Presentation Process: Plan	Oral Presentation Process: Plan • Write	Revisit writing process steps with students in class as needed.
Oral Presentation Process: Draft		
Oral Presentation Process: Draft	Oral Presentation Process: Draft • Write	Revisit writing process steps with students in class as needed.

Opportunities to Learn	Opportunities to Demonstrate Learning	Opportunities to Reteach
Oral Presentation Process: Revise		
Oral Presentation Process: Revise	Oral Presentation Process: Revise • Write	Revisit writing process steps with students in class as needed.
Oral Presentation Process: Edit and Present		
Oral Presentation Process: Edit and Present	Oral Presentation Process: Edit and Present • Write	Revisit writing process steps with students in class as needed.
Organizing an Oral Presentation		
Skill: Organizing an Oral Presentation	Skill: Organizing an Oral Presentation • Your Turn Oral Presentation Process: Draft	Spotlight Skill: Organizing an Oral Presentation

	Opportunities to Learn	Opportunities to Demonstrate Learning	Opportunities to Reteach
Evaluating Sources	Skill: Evaluating Sources	Skill: Evaluating Sources • Your Turn Oral Presentation Process: Draft	Spotlight Skill: Evaluating Sources
Considering Audience and Purpose	Skill: Considering Audience and Purpose	Skill: Considering Audience and Purpose • Your Turn Oral Presentation Process: Draft	Spotlight Skill: Considering Audience and Purpose
Persuasive Techniques	Skill: Persuasive Techniques	Skill: Persuasive Techniques • Your Turn Oral Presentation Process: Draft	Spotlight Skill: Persuasive Techniques

	Opportunities to Learn	Opportunities to Demonstrate Learning	Opportunities to Reteach
Sources and Citations			
	Skill: Sources and Citations	Skill: Sources and Citations • Your Turn Oral Presentation Process: Revise	Spotlight Skill: Sources and Citations
Communicating Ideas			
	Skill: Communicating Ideas	Skill: Communicating Ideas • Your Turn Oral Presentation Process: Revise	Spotlight Skill: Communicating Ideas
Reasons and Evidence			
	Skill: Reasons and Evidence	Skill: Reasons and Evidence • Your Turn Oral Presentation Process: Revise	Spotlight Skill: Reasons and Evidence

Opportunities to Learn	Opportunities to Demonstrate Learning	Opportunities to Reteach
Engaging in Discourse		
Skill: Engaging in Discourse	Skill: Engaging in Discourse • Your Turn Oral Presentation Process: Revise	Spotlight Skill: Engaging in Discourse
Parallel Structure		
Grammar: Parallel Structure	Grammar: Parallel Structure • Your Turn Oral Presentation Process: Edit and Present	Grammar: Sentence Structure - Complex and Compound-Complex Sentences
Sentence Variety - Openings		
Grammar: Sentence Variety - Openings	Grammar: Sentence Variety - Openings • Your Turn Oral Presentation Process: Edit and Present	Grammar: Clauses - Adjective and Adverb Clauses

Oral Presentation Process: Plan

Introduce the Extended Oral Project

- What is the prompt asking you to do?
- What are the characteristics of argumentative oral presentations?
- Which characteristics of argumentative oral presentations will you need to learn more about in order to respond to the prompt?

DIFFERENTIATED QUESTIONS

- What does **significance** mean?
- What are some topics, issues, people, or events that were important this year?
- Why were those topics, issues, people, or events so important?

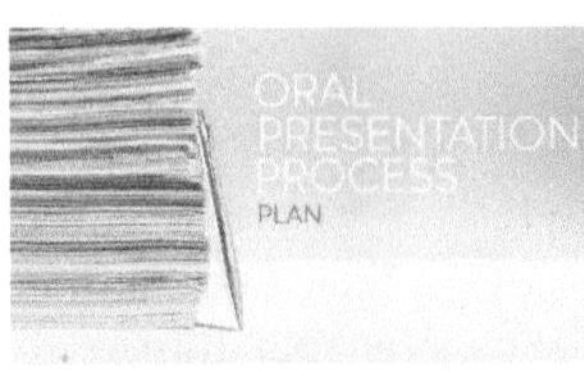

Oral Presentation Process: Plan

PLAN | DRAFT | REVISE | EDIT AND PRESENT

The four years spent in high school undoubtedly changes graduates. The experiences they have, the knowledge they gain, and the memories they make will stay with them for a lifetime. Just as high school students change, the world around them changes, too. A common life goal is to leave the world a little better than you found it, whether that world is your high school, your community, or your country, for example.

WRITING PROMPT

What do future students need to know?

As your high school years now come to a close, think back on the last several years and consider the topics you have covered in all of your subjects. Then, consider the world around you now and select a topic, issue, person, or event that is important to you, but that was not covered in your formal studies. Develop an argument to support the claim that this topic, issue, person, or event should be included in future high school instruction so that the details and significance will be heard and remembered. In order to prepare for your presentation, consider how best to meet the needs of the audience, purpose, and occasion by employing the following:

- elements of classical speeches, including an introduction, body, transitions, and a conclusion
- the art of persuasion and rhetorical devices
- the appropriate use of formal or informal language as well as purposeful vocabulary, tone, and voice
- visual aids that support the information presented, including citations and a works cited list for any information obtained from outside sources
- speaking techniques, such as eye contact, an appropriate speaking rate and volume, pauses for effect, enunciation, purposeful gestures, and appropriate conventions of language

Introduction to Oral Presentation

Compelling oral presentations use both effective speaking techniques and engaging writing to express ideas and opinions. Oral presentations can have a variety of purposes, including persuasion. The characteristics of an effective argumentative oral presentation include:

- the organizational elements of classical speeches, including an introduction, body, transitions, and a conclusion
- the art of persuasion and rhetorical devices
- the appropriate use of formal or informal language as well as purposeful vocabulary, tone, and voice
- speaking techniques, such as eye contact, an appropriate speaking rate and volume, pauses for effect, enunciation, purposeful gestures, and appropriate conventions of language

These characteristics can be organized into four major categories: context, structure, style & language, and elements of effective communication. As you continue with this Extended Oral Project, you'll receive more detailed instruction and practice in crafting each of the characteristics of argumentative writing and speaking to create your own oral presentation.

Review the Rubric

Have students examine the "EOP Rubric - Grade 12" grading rubric. Inform students that this is the same rubric that will be used to evaluate their completed Argumentative Extended Oral Project.

Read and Annotate

As students read, have them use the Annotation Tool to identify and label the genre characteristics of argumentative oral presentation writing, including:

- the organizational elements of classical speeches, including an introduction, body, transitions, and a conclusion
- the art of persuasion and rhetorical devices
- the appropriate use of formal or informal language as well as purposeful vocabulary, tone, and voice

When students finish reading, ask them to share their annotations in small groups.

ANNOTATION GUIDE

Find the following quotes in the Student Model. Then, use the Annotation Tool to label each quote as an example of an introduction, a reference to a visual aid, formal language, a counter argument, or a conclusion.

- I do admit that I use my phone a lot, but almost everything I do is online.
- I agree that parents should play a key role in teaching children how to navigate the internet, but not all parents are experts on the fast-paced digital world.
- While some people use the internet primarily to gain information, others go online to enact change.
- In addition, as Graph 3 demonstrates, social media is enabling citizens who had previously felt marginalized, including Hispanic and African American citizens, to find their voices and express their views.
- Formal lessons on living in the digital world will help future graduates become better digital citizens, be more aware of other people's experiences, and maybe even change the world.

READ AND ANNOTATE

Pair students with on-grade-level peers to complete the annotation activity.

Before you get started on your own oral presentation, read this oral presentation that one student, Josh, wrote in response to the prompt. As you read the Model, highlight and annotate the features of oral presentation writing that Josh included in his presentation.

STUDENT MODEL

NOTES

NAVIGATING THE DIGITAL WORLD

BY JOSH

Introduction—Opening

My dad often jokes that my cell phone is glued to my hand. I do admit that I use my phone a lot, but almost everything I do is online. In the past 24 hours, I bought my grandmother a birthday present, took a history quiz, streamed three episodes of my favorite television show, ordered dinner, and researched the causes and effects of air pollution—all with a device in the palm of my hand.

Introduction—Claim

There are many advantages to living in the digital world, but we need to stop and consider how being online affects individuals and our society. Because a goal of any high school curriculum is to prepare students to enter the world, a contemporary high school education is not complete without lessons on living in a digital world.

LIVING IN A DIGITAL WORLD

- We need to consider the online community's effects on individuals and society, both positive and negative.
- Schools should provide lessons on living in the digital world

Body—Counterclaim

Some might believe that it is the responsibility of parents to teach their children how to be safe and smart online. I agree that parents should play a key role in teaching children how to navigate the internet, but not all parents are experts on the fast-paced digital world. That's why including formal instruction in media literacy in schools would ensure that all students learn how to be good online citizens.

For instance, if students studied the fact-checking guidelines that journalists use, they could enhance their media literacy. If everyone is going to participate in the digital world, then we should make sure that the digital world is a good place for everyone to be.

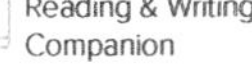

TEXT TALK

Purpose

What is Josh's purpose for speaking?

See the Introduction–Claim section: His purpose is to convince his audience that high school curricula should include lessons on living in a digital world.

Focus

What is Josh's thesis statement?

See the Introduction–Claim section: His thesis is "Because a goal of any high school curriculum is to prepare students to enter the world, a contemporary high school education is not complete without lessons on living in a digital world."

Style and Language

Where does Josh use particularly persuasive language to persuade his audience to agree with his claim?

Answers will vary. Sample answer: In the Body–Counterclaim section, Josh uses the phrase "fast-paced digital world" to emphasize that expert instruction is needed.

NOTES

NOT EVERYONE AGREES

Some believe parents should be responsible.

- Not all parents are experts.
- Schools can provide formal instruction in media literacy.
- Students can learn how to fact-check what they discover online.

Body—Elaboration

At the click of a button, users can access the thoughts, opinions, and knowledge bases of millions of other people, whether they are located across town or across an ocean. People from all over the world weigh in on a myriad of topics on social media. This all might sound great; however, it is a double-edged sword.

Sometimes it is hard to know whether or not the information you read online is accurate, authoritative, and trustworthy. It should be our duty to make the internet better, safer, and more accurate for future generations.

At the same time, aspects of the internet, such as social media, can help create online communities that help people feel safe and heard and also help them organize social action.

To accomplish this goal, schools need to teach students how to analyze and evaluate online sources and how to be responsible digital citizens. That means contributing to the digital space in a positive way, putting an end to cyberbullying, and stopping the propagation of false information.

THE ONLINE WORLD IS A DOUBLE-EDGED SWORD

- How do I know whether or not the information I read online is accurate, authoritative, and trustworthy?
- Can social media help people feel safe and heard and also help them organize toward social action?
- How can schools help students become responsible digital citizens?

TEXT TALK

Organization

Where does Josh use a transition to help his audience follow his ideas?

Answers will vary. Sample answer: In the Body–Elaboration section, Josh uses the word *however* to show a contrast between ideas.

Elements of Effective Communication/Conventions

Where does Josh use an idiom? How does that choice affect his presentation?

Answers will vary. Sample answer: In the Body–Elaboration section, Josh uses the idiom "double-edged sword." This phrase helps his audience understand that information on the internet can be both helpful and harmful.

Body—Evidence and Analysis #1

While some people use the internet primarily to gain information, others go online to enact change.

Based on data collected by the Pew Research Center, Graph 1 demonstrates that there are various ways an individual can show that they are civically active on social media. The dark blue bar at the bottom of the graph indicates that 53% of U.S. adults have taken these actions, and the light blue bars show the percentage of people who have participated in specific activities on social media.

The most popular of these actions is taking part in a group of similarly minded activists on social media.

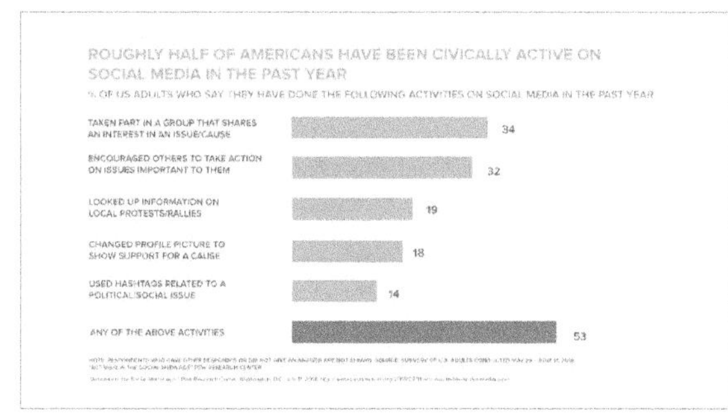

Body—Evidence and Analysis #2

My next graph indicates that people believe these actions to be effective in specific ways.

Graph 2 also represents data collected by the Pew Research Center and shows that most Americans believe that social media is important to gain the attention of politicians. If we combine the "Very" (dark blue) and "Somewhat" (blue) bars, we see that around 60% of Americans say social media platforms are at least partly effective for getting politicians to pay attention to issues, creating activist movements, and influencing policy decisions.

A MAJORITY OF AMERICANS SAY SOCIAL MEDIA ARE IMPORTANT FOR GETTING POLITICIANS TO PAY ATTENTION TO ISSUES, CREATING LONG-LASTING SOCIAL MOVEMENTS

% OF US ADULTS WHO SAY SOCIAL MEDIA ARE ______ IMPORTANT FOR ...

	VERY	SOMEWHAT	NOT VERY	NOT AT ALL
GETTING ELECTED OFFICIALS TO PAY ATTENTION TO ISSUES	23	46	20	[illegible]
CREATING SUSTAINED MOVEMENTS FOR SOCIAL CHANGE	21	46	22	[illegible]
INFLUENCING POLICY DECISIONS	15	43	29	[illegible]

NOTE: RESPONDENTS DID NOT GIVE AN ANSWER ARE NOT SHOWN. SOURCE: SURVEY OF U.S. ADULTS CONDUCTED MAY 29 - JUNE 11, 2018. "ACTIVISM IN THE SOCIAL MEDIA AGE" PEW RESEARCH CENTER

Body—Evidence and Analysis #2 (continued)

These are impressive numbers, and even our political leaders agree (watch the video in the Plan lesson on the StudySync site):

President Obama Urges Public to Use Social Media to Contact Senators

NBC News Archives Xpress

Body—Evidence and Analysis #3

In addition, as Graph 3 demonstrates, social media is enabling citizens who had previously felt marginalized, including Hispanic and African American citizens, to find their voices and express their views.

As we can see by following the legend at the top of the graph, African American and Hispanic users are more likely than their white counterparts to state that social media platforms are effective for their activism.

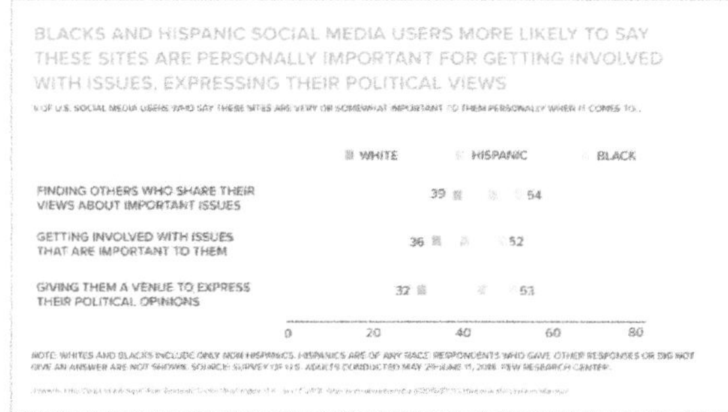

Body—Review

Although online activism can have positive effects by including a multitude of opinions, raising awareness, and promoting change, there can be many drawbacks, including people verbally attacking others and using dehumanizing speech.

Schools can help by teaching students how to evaluate the claims of online activists and how to participate effectively and respectfully in online activism.

A BRIGHTER FUTURE

- Bullying, hate speech, and misinformation are big challenges in the digital world.
- We can create a better internet by educating students to engage effectively.

Conclusion

As my classmates and I prepare to graduate from high school, we feel like experts on many topics. We've read great literature, memorized essential formulas, and repeated famous lab experiments. As a result, we are ready to move on to the next phases of our lives. While few teenagers would admit that there is something they do not know about social media, we must acknowledge that the digital world has many pitfalls. Formal lessons on living in the digital world will help future graduates become better digital citizens, be more aware of other people's experiences, and maybe even change the world.

THANK YOU

TEXT TALK

Evidence

How do Josh's visual aids contribute to his presentation?

Answers will vary. Sample answer: They are used as evidence to support Josh's points about online activism.

NOTES

WORKS CITED

Write

Circulate as students use the questions in the bulleted list to plan their writing. See the instructions for scaffolding and differentiation that follow.

CHECK FOR SUCCESS

If students struggle to come up with answers for the questions in the lesson, work with students to provide an answer to one question and then help them build from there.

For example, start by asking students, "What topics, issues, and events were particularly important in the past year?" or "Who is someone you idolize and why?" Once students have answered one question, help them to work through a second question until they've begun to build some momentum. It may be helpful to start with a different question than the one that's listed first in the lesson.

WRITE

When you write for an oral presentation, it is important to consider your audience and purpose so you can write appropriately for them. Your purpose is implied in the prompt. Reread the prompt to determine your purpose for writing and presenting.

To begin, review the questions below and then select a strategy, such as brainstorming, journaling, reading, or discussing, to generate ideas.

After generating ideas, begin the prewriting process by writing a summary of your writing plan. In your summary, respond to the following questions:

- **Purpose:** What topic, issue, person, or event will be the focus of your presentation, and what important ideas do you want to convey?
- **Audience:** Who is your audience, and what message do you want to express to your audience?
- **Thesis:** What claim will you communicate about the significance of this topic, issue, person, or event?
- **Evidence:** What facts, evidence, and details might you include to support your ideas? What research might you need to do? What anecdotes from your personal life or what background knowledge is relevant to the topic of your presentation?
- **Organization:** How can you organize your presentation so that it is clear and easy to follow?
- **Clear Communication:** How will you make sure that your audience can hear and understand what you are saying?
- **Gestures and Visual Aids:** What illustrations or other visual aids could you use during your presentation? What effect will they have on your audience? What physical gestures and body language will help you communicate your ideas?

Response Instructions

Use the questions in the bulleted list to write a one-paragraph summary. Your summary should describe what you will discuss in your oral presentation.

Don't worry about including all of the details now; focus only on the most essential and important elements. You will refer to this short summary as you continue through the steps of the writing process.

Review Prompt and Rubric

Before students begin writing, review the writing prompt and rubric with the class.

Response Instructions

Use the questions in the bulleted list on the previous page to write a one-paragraph summary. Your summary should describe what you will discuss in your oral presentation.

Don't worry about including all of the details now; focus only on the most essential and important elements. You will refer to this short summary as you continue through the steps of the writing process.

Score	Plan	Language and Conventions
4	The writer responds to the questions, and the writing is clear and focused.	The writer demonstrates a consistent command of grammar, punctuation, and usage conventions. Although minor errors may be evident, they do not detract from the fluency or clarity of the writing.
3	The writer responds to the questions, but the writing is not always clear or focused.	The writer demonstrates an adequate command of grammar, punctuation, and usage conventions. Although some errors may be evident, they create few (if any) disruptions in the fluency or clarity of the writing.
2	The writer responds to the questions, but the writing is somewhat unclear and unfocused.	The writer demonstrates a partial command of grammar, punctuation, and usage conventions. Some distracting errors may be evident, at times creating minor disruptions in the fluency or clarity of the writing.
1	The writer responds to the questions, but the writing is very unclear and unfocused.	The writer demonstrates little or no command of grammar, punctuation, and usage conventions. Serious and persistent errors create disruptions in the fluency of the writing and sometimes interfere with meaning.
0	The writer does not provide a relevant response to the prompt or does not provide a response at all.	Serious and persistent errors overwhelm the writing and interfere with the meaning of the response as a whole, making the writer's meaning impossible to understand.

Write

Use the scaffolds below to differentiate instruction for your ELL English Language Learners and A Approaching grade-level learners.

ELL **BEGINNING, INTERMEDIATE** With the help of the word bank, write a response using the paragraph frame.

ADVANCED, ADVANCED HIGH Write a response using the sentence starters.

A **APPROACHING** Write a response using the sentence starters.

BEGINNING / INTERMEDIATE		ADVANCED, ADVANCED HIGH / APPROACHING
Word Bank	**Paragraph Frame**	**Sentence Starters**
evidence context anecdote claim graph image explain	My presentation will be about ____. It / he / she is important because ____. In the beginning of the presentation, I will ____. In the middle of the presentation, I will ____. At the end of the presentation, I will ____. A visual aid I may use is ____.	• My presentation will be about . . . • It / he / she is important because . . . • First, I will . . . • Then, I will . . . • A visual aid I may use is . . .

Peer Review

Students should submit substantive feedback to two peers using the review instructions below.

- How well does this response answer the prompt?
- What part of the oral presentation are you most excited to see or hear?
- Are there any ideas that could be improved on? How so?

Rate

Respond to the following with a point rating that reflects your opinion.

	1	2	3	4
Ideas	■	■	■	□
Evidence	■	■	■	■
Language and Conventions	■	■	□	□

Submit

ELL **SENTENCE FRAMES**

- The response does a good job of addressing ____ from the prompt.
- You could improve the response by addressing ____ from the prompt.
- I would be most interested in hearing about ____.
- I think you could improve ____ by (adding / clarifying / describing) ____.

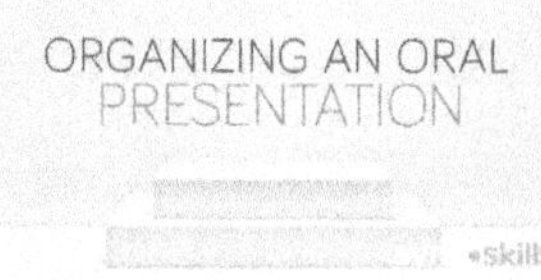

Skill: Organizing an Oral Presentation

CHECKLIST FOR ORGANIZING AN ORAL PRESENTATION

In order to present information, findings, and supporting evidence that convey a clear and distinct perspective, do the following:

- choose a style for your oral presentation, either formal or informal
- determine whether the development and organization of your presentation, as well as its substance and style, are appropriate for your purpose, audience, and task
- determine whether your presentation conveys a clear and distinct perspective so listeners can follow your line of reasoning
- make sure you address alternative perspectives that oppose your own in your presentation
- make strategic, or deliberate, use of digital media, such as textual, graphical, audio, visual, and interactive elements, to add interest and enhance your audience's understanding of the findings, reasoning, and evidence in your presentation

To present information, findings, and supporting evidence conveying a clear and distinct perspective, consider the following questions:

- Did I make sure that the information in my presentation conveys a clear and distinct perspective, so listeners can follow my line of reasoning?
- Have I presented opposing or alternative viewpoints in my presentation?
- Are the organization, development, substance, and style appropriate for my purpose and audience?
- Have I made strategic use of media to add interest and enhance my audience's understanding of my presentation?

Skill: Organizing an Oral Presentation

Introduce the Skill

Watch the Concept Definition video and read the following definition with your students.

An **oral presentation** is an address delivered to an audience. Oral presentations may be delivered to entertain, critique, inform, or persuade. Speakers identify an audience, a purpose, a genre, and a topic in order to create the content. They also choose a **style**, such as formal or informal, that uses technical language, rhetorical devices, or other language appropriate to the task.

Whether you present an argument, deliver information, or craft an entertaining speech, make sure your presentation offers facts and details in a **logical progression**. Digital media (textual, graphical, audio, visual, and interactive) in presentations can improve your audience's understanding of your findings, reasoning, and evidence.

The last task is to choose moments where you will **pause for effect**, adjust your **volume**, slow down or speed up your **rate of speech**, and make **purposeful gestures** to emphasize your points. Planning and rehearsing your delivery makes your presentation sound clear, logical, organized, and effective.

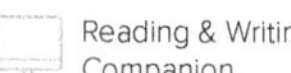

SKILL VOCABULARY

oral presentation / la presentación oral *noun* a formal address or discourse delivered to an audience COGNATE

logical progression / la progresión lógica *noun* an understandable structure COGNATE

pause for effect / la pausa efectista *noun* a pause in what someone is saying in the hope that the pause will have some kind of effect on the listener

TURN AND TALK

Turn to a partner and discuss an example of a memorable speech from a book, TV show, or movie. How did it follow (or not follow) the basic structure of oral presentations as described in the Concept Definition video?

SPEAKING FRAMES

- A memorable speech was delivered in ____.
- It (did / did not) follow the basic structure of oral presentations in the video because ____.

YOUR TURN

Read each sentence below. Then, complete the chart on the next page by determining where each sentence belongs in the outline. Write the corresponding letter for each sentence in the appropriate row.

Sentences	
A	I will acknowledge the counterclaim that forming sleep habits is complicated by early start times at school, extracurricular activities in the evening, homework, and maintaining a social life. The school schedule can prevent teenagers from getting adequate sleep, regardless of screen time. However, screens can complicate sleep schedules even more, especially when it's so hard to find the time to rest.
B	I can include a graph that shows the relationship between sleep quality and energy levels.
C	I can use words like *next, thus,* and *additionally* to support the logical flow of ideas in my argument.
D	Everybody sleeps, but some people do it better than others. I can include an anecdote about struggling with getting enough sleep because I keep my phone next to me when I sleep. My thesis will state that students should learn sleep strategies to develop good habits and support their health.
E	I believe that this topic is important because lots of people are unaware of how screen usage affects sleep patterns. I also want to explain how good sleep habits lower your risk for serious health problems and increase your ability to think clearly and get along with others.
F	In the end, I will reiterate the importance of getting solid sleep each day. I will rephrase my thesis and summarize my main points.
G	I want to convince people that students should learn about forming good sleep habits.

SKILL VOCABULARY

volume / el volumen ***noun*** the intensity, or loudness, of a sound; the level at which you speak COGNATE

rate of speech / el ritmo del habla ***noun*** the speed at which someone speaks

purposeful gesture / el gesto intencionado ***noun*** a deliberate body movement to emphasize what someone is saying, such as pointing or making a fist

Purpose	
Introduction / Thesis	
Alternative/Opposing Viewpoints	
Body	
Visual Aids	
Logical Progression	
Conclusion / Rephrasing of Thesis	

WRITE

Use the questions in the checklist to outline your oral presentation. Be sure to include a clear thesis and a logical progression of valid reasons.

Your Turn

Ask students to complete the Your Turn activity.

Purpose	G
Introduction / Thesis	D
Alternative/Opposing Viewpoints	A
Body	E
Visual Aids	B
Logical Progression	C
Conclusion / Rephrasing of Thesis	F

Write

Ask students to complete the writing assignment.

ELL **REWRITE CHECKLIST**

A **Overall Purpose**

- ☐ What am I being asked to speak about?
- ☐ What do I need to include in my presentation?

Introduction

- ☐ What is my thesis?
- ☐ How can I grab my audience's attention?

Alternative/Opposing Viewpoints

- ☐ What alternative perspectives should I include?
- ☐ What are some reasons I can use when presenting the alternative viewpoints?

Body

- ☐ What main points can I make to support my thesis?
- ☐ What reasons would support my main points?

Visual Aids

- ☐ How can I use charts or graphs to convince my audience to agree with my claim?

Logical Progression

- ☐ How can I use transition words and phrases to clearly communicate to my audience the relationships between my ideas?

Conclusion

- ☐ How can I rephrase my thesis?
- ☐ How can I summarize my main ideas?
- ☐ Is there a strong closing thought I want to include?

Skill: Evaluating Sources

Introduce the Skill

Watch the Concept Definition video and read the following definition with your students.

One important step in the research process is gathering and evaluating sources of information. Evaluating a source involves examining the source to determine whether it is reliable, credible, accurate, and useful for your purpose.

- A source is **reliable** if it provides consistently accurate and up-to-date information.
- A source is **credible** if it is trustworthy and supported by evidence.
- A source is **accurate** if its information is factual and can be verified.
- A source is useful if it directly supports your task and is suitable for your audience.

Avoid sources that contain omissions or discrepancies in the information and data provided. **Discrepancies** may mean that a source is inaccurate or biased.

If you find that a source is faulty or does not suit your purpose, you may need to adjust your search. Adding specific terms and punctuation can expand or limit your search results to provide new sources.

Skill: Evaluating Sources

CHECKLIST FOR EVALUATING SOURCES

As you reread the sources you gathered, identify the following:

- where information seems inaccurate, biased, or outdated
- where information strongly relates to your task, purpose, and audience
- where information helps you make an informed decision or solve a problem

In order to conduct advanced searches to gather relevant, credible, and accurate print and digital sources, use the following questions as a guide:

- Is the material published by a well-established source or expert author?
- Is the material up-to-date or based on the most current information?
- Is the material factual, and can it be verified by another source?
- Are there discrepancies between the information presented in different sources?
- Are there specific terms or phrases that I can use to adjust my search?

TURN AND TALK

Turn to your partner and discuss the last podcast you listened to, news clip you watched, or article you read online. How did you determine whether or not the information came from a credible source?

SPEAKING FRAMES

- The last (podcast/news clip/article) I listened to or read online was ____.
- I knew the source (was / was not) credible because ____.

SKILL VOCABULARY

reliable source / la fuente confiable ***noun*** a source that is known for providing consistently good and up-to-date information

credible source / la fuente confiable ***noun*** a source that is trustworthy and believable

accurate source / la fuente precisa ***noun*** a source based on factual information that can be verified

discrepancy / la discrepancia ***noun*** a noticeable difference or mismatch between two or more facts or sources COGNATE

YOUR TURN

Choose the best answer to each question.

1. Josh finds an article titled "A Look at 2012: How Social Media Will Bring Us Together" that was published on a website that his teacher recommended. What should Josh do to make sure he is reading a reliable source?

    - A. Josh should check all the information in the article to confirm that it is still relevant today.
    - B. Josh should check if the article contains too many counterclaims from experts on this topic.
    - C. Josh should check if he agrees with the arguments and reasons presented by the author.
    - D. Josh should check to make sure that any data and evidence presented in the article are unique.

2. Josh finds another article from 2018 titled "Social Media Will Ruin Us" published by *The Simpler Life*, a nationally distributed magazine. What should Josh consider before using this source?

    - A. The source may be outdated and contain information that is no longer relevant.
    - B. The source may be unreliable because it is printed in a nationally distributed magazine.
    - C. The source may be irrelevant to his thesis or presentation because it is about social media.
    - D. The source may be biased, given the title of the article and of the magazine in which it is published.

Your Turn

Ask students to complete the Your Turn activity.

QUESTION 1

A. Correct. The article was published years ago and may present information that is outdated.

B. Incorrect. While the source may contain numerous counterclaims, this would not necessarily indicate that the source is unreliable.

C. Incorrect. While Josh may not agree with the arguments and reasons presented by the author, this is not an indicator of whether or not a source is valid and reliable.

D. Incorrect. If a source contained data that is unique and unavailable in other sources, this may indicate that the article is not valid or reliable.

QUESTION 2

A. Incorrect. The source is from 2018 and is considered current.

B. Incorrect. A nationally distributed magazine is likely to be reliable.

C. Incorrect. The title indicates that the article could contain relevant information.

D. Correct. Josh should consider that the source may be biased and may provide only one point of view.

Writer's Notebook

Ask students to do a quick internet search on a topic of their choosing, such as their favorite band, sports team, or author. Have them identify one video or media source that they believe is credible and accurate. Have them also identify one video or media source that they believe is not credible or accurate due to bias, omission, faulty reasoning, or some other problem. Ask students to write a short paragraph to explain their reasoning.

TURN AND TALK

Allow students to share their reasons orally in pairs or small groups before freewriting.

Your Turn

Ask students to complete the Your Turn activity. Answers will vary.

Source Title and Author:	*The New York Times*: "This Is Not Fake News (but Don't Go by the Headline)" by Sydney Ember
Reliability: Has the source material been published in a well-established book or periodical or on a well-established website? Is the source material up-to-date or based on the most current information?	Yes, *The New York Times* is a well-established newspaper. Yes, the article was published in November 2017.
Accuracy: Is the source based on factual information that can be verified by another source? Are there any discrepancies between this source and others?	The article is an interview piece, but also relies on examples and statistics to back up its arguments.
Credibility: Is the source material written by a recognized expert on the topic? Is the source material published by a well-respected author or organization?	Yes, *The New York Times* is a well-respected news source. The interview with Dr. Paul Mihailidis, the Director of a new graduate program "Civic Media: Art and Practice" at Emerson College, contains the professor's opinions *and* facts.
Decision: Should I use this source in my presentation?	I might use some examples from this source because other reputable sources are referenced.

YOUR TURN

Complete the chart by filling in the title and author of a source for your presentation and answering the questions about it.

Source Title and Author: ______________________	
Reliability: Has the source material been published in a well-established book or periodical or on a well-established website? Is the source material up-to-date or based on the most current information?	
Accuracy: Is the source based on factual information that can be verified by another source? Are there any discrepancies between this source and others?	
Credibility: Is the source material written by a recognized expert on the topic? Is the source material published by a well-respected author or organization?	
Decision: Should I use this source in my presentation?	

Skill: Considering Audience and Purpose

••• CHECKLIST FOR CONSIDERING AUDIENCE AND PURPOSE

In order to present information so that listeners can follow the line of reasoning and to ensure that the organization, development, substance, and style are appropriate, note the following:

- when writing your presentation, convey and maintain a clear and distinct perspective or viewpoint.
- make sure listeners can follow your line of reasoning, or the set of reasons you have used, so that your perspective is clear.
- address any opposing or alternative perspectives.
- check the development and organization of the information in your presentation to see that they are appropriate for your purpose, audience, and task.
- determine whether the substance, or basis of your presentation, is also appropriate for your purpose, audience, and task.
- remember to adapt your presentation to your task, and if it is appropriate, use formal English and not language you would use in ordinary conversation.

To better understand how to present information so that listeners can follow the line of reasoning and to ensure that the organization, development, substance, and style are appropriate, consider the following questions:

- Have I organized the information in my presentation so that my perspective is clear?
- Did I address any opposing or alternative perspectives?
- Have I developed and organized the information so that it is appropriate for my purpose, audience, and task?
- Are the substance and style suitable?

SKILL VOCABULARY

audience / la audiencia *noun* the people who read a written text, listen to an oral response or presentation, or watch a performance COGNATE

purpose / el propósito *noun* the reason for writing or speaking COGNATE

register / el registro *noun* the use of formal or informal language COGNATE

tone / el tono *noun* the writer's or speaker's attitude toward his or her subject matter COGNATE

Skill: Considering Audience and Purpose

Introduce the Skill

Watch the Concept Definition video and read the following definition with your students.

Whether you are writing a blog post or delivering a speech, you must consider both your audience and your purpose. An **audience** consists of the people who will read your writing or listen to your speech. The **purpose** is your reason for writing or speaking. When participating in a discussion, writing to a prompt, or answering a question, you also need to consider your purpose and audience as you deliver your response.

A skilled writer and speaker needs to make thoughtful decisions about his or her register, tone, vocabulary, and voice in order to respond appropriately. **Register** refers to the use of formal or informal language. **Tone** is the writer's or speaker's attitude toward his or her topic. **Vocabulary** refers to the appropriate words for a given task. **Voice** is the distinctive use of language that conveys the personality of the writer or speaker.

TURN AND TALK

Turn to a partner and discuss the kind of language you would use to give a speech to a team you're on. Then, discuss the kind of language you would use to give a speech in class. How would the language be similar and different?

ELL SPEAKING FRAMES

- When talking to my team, I would use ____ language.
- In class, I would use ____ language.
- The language would be similar because ____. The language would be different because ____.

Your Turn

Ask students to complete the Your Turn activity.

Appropriate	Inappropriate
B	A
C	D
E	F

YOUR TURN

Read each statement below. Then, complete the chart by identifying whether the statements are appropriate for a formal presentation. Write the corresponding letter for each statement in the appropriate column.

	Statements
A	Horror movies can be real scary flicks.
B	Knowing basic first aid could help save lives.
C	Sewing not only encourages creativity, but it also improves manual dexterity.
D	My mom thinks that video games are such a waste of time, but she's wrong.
E	The history of American television reflects the values, issues, and ideals of an ever-changing nation.
F	Frank Wills, this guy who helped uncover the Watergate scandal in 1972, is somebody people should know about.

Appropriate	Inappropriate

SKILL VOCABULARY

vocabulary / el vocabulario ***noun*** words used for a specific occasion or in a particular context COGNATE

voice / la voz ***noun*** the use of language that conveys the distinctive personality of the writer or speaker, the narrator, or a particular character

YOUR TURN

Complete the chart by answering each question about your presentation.

Question	My Response
What is my purpose, and who is my audience?	
Do I plan to use formal or informal language?	
How will I organize information so that my perspective is clear?	
How will I address opposing or alternate perspectives?	
What sort of tone, or attitude, do I want to convey?	
How would I describe the voice I would like to use in my presentation?	
How will I use vocabulary and language to create that particular voice?	

Your Turn

Ask students to complete the Your Turn activity. Answers will vary.

Question	My Response
What is my purpose, and who is my audience?	My purpose is to argue that sleep habits should be taught in school. My audience is my teacher and classmates.
Do I plan to use formal or informal language?	Because this is a formal presentation, I will use formal language.
How will I organize information so that my perspective is clear?	My claim that sleep habits should be taught in school will be initially supported by anecdotal evidence to provide context and then will be supported by research and evidence from credible, reliable, and unbiased sources. This will allow for the argument to have a logical progression as well.
How will I address opposing or alternate perspectives?	I will acknowledge the counterclaim that forming sleep habits is complicated by many factors. I will use this to strengthen my claim that sleep habits and health should be taught in school.
What sort of tone, or attitude, do I want to convey?	Sleep is a serious topic that is often overlooked, so I plan to use a serious and respectful tone.
How would I describe the voice I would like to use in my presentation?	I would like my voice to be authoritative and persuasive, so my audience will be convinced.
How will I use vocabulary and language to create that particular voice?	I will use scientific language, technical terms, and rhetorical devices to develop my ideas. I plan to use correct grammar.

Skill: Persuasive Techniques

Introduce the Skill

Watch the Concept Definition video and read the following definition with your students.

Authors and speakers can use a variety of persuasive techniques to better support the arguments and claims they make.

An **appeal to logic** presents facts and logical reasoning. An **appeal to emotion** attempts to stir up positive or negative feelings. And an **appeal to ethics** aims to establish the writer's or speaker's good character and credibility.

Persuasive techniques may also include **rhetorical devices**, which are specific ways of using language to make arguments more convincing. One common rhetorical device is repetition. For example, Martin Luther King, Jr., repeated "I have a dream" eight times, making his speech one of the most powerful and memorable in American history.

Another persuasive technique is a **counter argument**, in which the writer or speaker acknowledges an opposing opinion and then attempts to disprove that opinion. A counter argument shows that the writer has considered alternatives and has tested his or her position against a different viewpoint.

Skill: Persuasive Techniques

••• CHECKLIST FOR PERSUASIVE TECHNIQUES

In order to compose argumentative texts using genre characteristics and craft, use the following steps:

1. First, consider your audience and purpose. You should ask yourself:
    - What does the audience already know or understand about my topic or argument? What possible biases does the audience hold?
    - What are the strengths and limitations of my argument?
    - What counterclaim(s) have I identified?
    - What are the strengths and limitations of each counterclaim?
2. Next, consider the following persuasive techniques and the ways you might use one or more to reach your audience and achieve your purpose:
    - Appeals to Logic
        - > What findings or supporting evidence will I use to support my claim?
        - > What is the most effective way to present factual information to persuade my audience that my argument is logically sound and reasonable?
    - Appeals to Emotion
        - > What emotions do I want my audience to feel about my topic?
        - > What words or phrases should I include to bring about those feelings in my audience?
    - Appeals to Ethics
        - > Which experts could I use to establish the credibility of my claims?
        - > What words or phrases should I include to remind my audience of our shared values about what is right, good, and fair?

TURN AND TALK

Turn to a partner and discuss your favorite commercial. Does it appeal to emotion, logic, or ethics? How do you know?

SPEAKING FRAMES

- My favorite commercial is ____.
- I like this commercial because ____.
- It appeals to (emotion / logic / ethics) because ____.

SKILL VOCABULARY

appeal to logic / apelar a la lógica *noun* a persuasive technique that appeals to logic and reasoning COGNATE

appeal to emotion / apelar a las emociones *noun* a persuasive technique that attempts to stir up emotions COGNATE

appeal to ethics / apelar a la ética *noun* a persuasive technique that aims to establish a writer's or speaker's good character or credibility COGNATE

- Rhetorical Devices or Style
  > How can I use language in artful and persuasive ways to persuade my audience to accept my position?

  > What specific rhetorical devices, such as rhetorical questions, repetition, or parallelism, do I want to use to make my argument more persuasive?
- Counterclaim
  > What is an alternative or opposing perspective that my audience might have?

  > How can I rebut that opposing perspective in a way that respects my audience and strengthens my argument?

SKILL VOCABULARY

rhetorical device / el recurso retórico *noun* a specific way of using language to make an argument more persuasive

counter argument / el contraargumento *noun* the part of an argument in which the writer considers and attempts to disprove an opposing opinion COGNATE

Your Turn

Ask students to complete the Your Turn activity.

Appeal to Logic	Appeal to Emotion	Appeal to Ethics
B	A	C
F	D	E

Write

Ask students to complete the writing assignment.

ELL REWRITE CHECKLIST

A Appeal to Logic

- ☐ What findings or supporting evidence will I use when making my claim?
- ☐ What facts support my argument?
- ☐ What other evidence would be part of a logical argument?

Appeal to Emotion

- ☐ What feelings relate to my argument?
- ☐ What words can I use to stir up those feelings in my audience?

Appeal to Ethics

- ☐ What do experts say about my topic in support of my argument?
- ☐ How does my personal credibility relate to my argument?

Rhetorical Devices or Style

- ☐ How can I use a rhetorical question?
- ☐ Which words and phrases could I repeat?

Counterclaim

- ☐ What will someone who disagrees with me likely say?
- ☐ How can I make a counterclaim to address the opposing perspective?

YOUR TURN

Read the appeals below. Then, complete the chart by placing each appeal in the appropriate category. Write the corresponding letter for each appeal in the appropriate column.

	Appeals
A	If you care about your child's safety, you will buy this car seat.
B	Cell phone use leads to 1.6 million car crashes a year.
C	Drivers have a responsibility to keep everyone safe.
D	No one wants to suffer and have his or her life cut short from a disease caused by poor diet.
E	As a pediatrician, I provide my patients information on healthy eating.
F	Unhealthy eating and inactivity cause 678,000 deaths every year.

Appeal to Logic	Appeal to Emotion	Appeal to Ethics

WRITE

Use the questions in the checklist to think about persuasive techniques that you can use in your presentation. Then, write a few sentences using persuasive techniques that you might be able to include in your presentation.

Oral Presentation Process: Draft

PLAN | DRAFT | REVISE | EDIT AND PRESENT

You have already made progress toward writing your argumentative oral presentation. Now it is time to draft your argumentative oral presentation.

WRITE

Use your plan and other responses in your Binder to draft your argumentative oral presentation. You may also have new ideas as you begin drafting. Feel free to explore those new ideas as they occur to you. You can also ask yourself these questions to ensure that your writing is focused, organized, and developed with evidence and elaboration:

Draft Checklist:

- **Focus:** Is the topic of my presentation clear to my audience? Have I included only relevant information and details about my topic? Have I avoided extraneous details that might confuse or distract my audience?
- **Organization:** Is the organization of ideas and events in my presentation logical? Have I reinforced this logical structure with transitional words and phrases to help my audience follow the order of ideas? Do the sentences in my presentation flow together naturally? Will the sentences sound choppy or long-winded when I deliver them orally?
- **Evidence and Elaboration:** Do all of my details support my thesis about why this topic, issue, person, or event should be included in high school instruction? Have I elaborated on the evidence to explain how it supports my thesis?

Before you submit your draft, read it over carefully. You want to be sure that you've responded to all aspects of the prompt.

Oral Presentation Process: Draft

Write

Ask students to complete the writing assignment.

CHECK FOR SUCCESS

If students struggle to begin drafting their presentations, ask them these questions:

- Why is your topic, issue, person, or event important?
- Why is that topic, issue, person, or event relevant to high school students?
- What evidence will best support your ideas?

DRAFT CHECKLIST

Focus

- ☐ Have I made my purpose and my thesis clear to my audience?

Organization

- ☐ Does the order of details in my presentation make sense?

Evidence and Elaboration

- ☐ Do I elaborate on the evidence to explain how it supports my thesis?

Peer Review

Students should submit substantive feedback to two peers using the review instructions below.

- Is the presentation organized in an effective way? Which details could be rearranged to make the organization more logical?
- Are the presentation's language, voice, and tone appropriate for the audience and purpose? If not, what changes would you suggest?
- Does the writer include all the elements of an argumentative oral presentation? If not, can you offer any suggestions?

SENTENCE FRAMES

- I think your organizational structure is (clear / unclear) because ____.
- You could improve your presentation overall by ____.

Analyze Student Model

Have students discuss the questions in the lesson as well as the Student Model draft. Ask:

- How does Josh organize his draft?
- How does Josh use evidence and elaboration to develop his argumentative oral presentation draft?
- How does Josh reveal the focus of his draft?
- How can you organize, develop, and reveal the focus of your own argumentative oral presentation?

Encourage students to share ideas for their own presentations based on the questions in the lesson.

ELL **SPEAKING FRAMES**

- The writer uses ____ structure to ____.
- The writer uses evidence and elaboration to develop ____, which helps him or her____.
- The focus of the writer's presentation is ____. He or she reveals this focus when ____.
- An idea that I have for my oral presentation is ____.

Reasons and Evidence

Discuss the Model

1. How does Josh's study partner respond when listening to his claim? Tyler affirms that the counterclaim and Josh's reasons are effective in developing his argument.
2. How does the listener evaluate the next section of Josh's oral presentation? Tyler hears illogical reasoning and exaggerated evidence. He explains to Josh why these are not effective supports for his argument.
3. What would you like to know from your study partner when he or she listens to you practice your own oral presentation? Answers will vary.

ELL **SPEAKING FRAMES**

- Tyler is positive about Josh's first section because ____.
- Tyler identifies a problem in Josh's next section of the presentation because ____.
- I would like to know ____ from my study partner.

Here is Josh's argumentative oral presentation draft. As you read, notice how Josh develops his draft to be focused, organized, and developed with evidence and elaboration. As he continues to revise and edit his argumentative oral presentation, he will find and improve weak spots in his writing, as well as correct any language or punctuation mistakes.

STUDENT MODEL: FIRST DRAFT

NOTES

Navigating the Digital World

My dad often jokes that my cell phone is glued to my hand. I do admit that I use my phone a lot, but almost everything I do is online. In the past 24 hours, all with a device in the palm of my hand, I bought my grandmother a birthday present, took a history quiz, streamed three episodes of my favorite television show, ordered dinner, and researched the causes and effects of air pollution. There are many advantages to living in the digital world, but we need to stop and consider how being online affects individuals and our society. Because a goal of any high school curriculum is to prepare students to enter the world, a contemporary high school education is not complete without lessons on living in a digital world.

~~Some might beleive that it is the responsibility of parents to teach their children how to be safe and smart online. I agree that parents should play a key role in teaching children how to navigate the internet. However, they cannot be the only solution. Let's be honest: parents are too out-of-touch to know everything there is to know about the fast-paced digital world. That's why including formal instruction in media literacy in schools would ensure that all students learn how to be good online citizens, for instance, if students studied the fact-checking guidelines that journalists use, they could enhance their media literacy and never fall trap to fake news again.~~

Body—Counterclaim
Some might believe that it is the responsibility of parents to teach their children how to be safe and smart online. I agree that parents should play a key role in teaching children how to navigate the internet, but not all parents are experts on the fast-paced digital world. That's why including formal instruction in media literacy in schools would ensure that all students learn how to be good online citizens.

For instance, if students studied the fact-checking guidelines that journalists use, they could enhance their media literacy. If everyone is going to participate in the digital world, then we should make sure that the digital world is a good place for everyone to be. [Show slide with bullet points.]

Skill: Reasons and Evidence

The second paragraph of Josh's draft includes exaggeration and illogical reasoning, which undermine his argument. He revises his points to ensure that his reasoning is sound.

PEER CONFERENCE

Have students determine one area of writing where they would like specific feedback. Ask them to design a helpful feedback question, such as "How can I ____?" Pair or group students, and allow them to read and discuss their work together, using the feedback question as a lens.

At the click of a button, users can access the thoughts, opinions, and knowledge bases of millions of other people, weather they are located across town or across an ocean. People from all over the world weigh in on a myriad of topics on social media. This all might sound great however, it is both a plus and a minus. Sometimes it is hard to know whether or not the information you read online is accurate, authoritative, and can be trusted. It should be our duty to make the internet better. More accurate for future generations. To accomplish this goal, schools need to teach students how to analyze and evaluate online sources and how to be responsible digital citizens.

~~As graphs 1 and 2 demonstrate, more and more Americans are using social media for the purpose of online activism and believe that social media is important to gain the attention of out-of-touch politicians. In addition, social media is enabling citizens who had previously felt marginalized to find their voices and express their views. Although online activism can have positive effects by including a multitude of opinions, raising awareness, and promoting change, there can be many bad effects, including people verbally attacking others and using dehumanizing speech. Schools can help avoid these disastrous and uncivil behaviors. [Show graphs that provide information about demographics and activities of social media users.]~~

Skill: Engaging in Discourse

Josh's partner tells him that the data in the graphs creates a strong logical appeal. He could strengthen the appeal, though, by providing a more detailed explanation of the graphs, which Josh decides to do.

Body—Evidence and Analysis #1
While some people use the internet primarily to gain information, others go online to enact change.

Based on data collected by the Pew Research Center, Graph 1 demonstrates that there are various ways an individual can show that they are civically active on social media. [Show Graph 1.] The dark blue bar at the bottom of the graph indicates that 53% of U.S. adults have taken these actions, and the light blue bars show the percentage of people who have participated in specific activities on social media.

The most popular of these actions is taking part in a group of similarly minded activists on social media.

Skill: Communicating Ideas

When Josh delivers his presentation, he'll point to the parts of the graphs that he's discussing. He'll use these gestures to focus the audience's attention on the information and help make the graphs clear.

Body—Evidence and Analysis #2
My next graph indicates that people believe these actions to be effective in specific ways. [Show Graph 2.]

Graph 2 also represents data collected by the Pew Research Center and shows that most Americans believe that social media is important to gain the attention of politicians. If we combine the "Very" (dark blue) and "Somewhat" (blue) bars, we see that around 60% of Americans say social media platforms are at least partly effective for getting politicians to pay attention to issues, creating activist movements, and influencing policy decisions.

ELL SPEAKING FRAMES

- A positive piece of feedback was ____.
- One suggestion was ____.
- Josh improved his presentation by ____.

Reasons and Evidence

Connect to Mentor Text

Project the following example of reasons and evidence from "Commencement Address at the New School":

Now I may have this completely backward, but I get the sense that something different is going on in your generation. Something hopeful. You seem to be smarter, sooner. Part of these smarts is surely born out of crisis. In the `90s we had high employment and a buoyant economy. We could afford to spend weeks wondering about the exact length and shape of our beards, or whether Kurt Cobain was a sell-out. Your situation is more acute. You have so many large, collective tasks ahead, and you know that. We had them too, but paid little attention, so now I'm afraid it falls to you. The climate, the economy, the sick relationship between the individual prestige of the first world and the anonymity of the third —these are things only many hands can fix working together. You are all individuals but you are also part of a generation and generations are defined by the projects they take on together.

Ask students:

- What stance or position does the speaker take? Is the premise based on sound, logical reasoning? Why or why not?
- What reasons and evidence does the speaker use to make a point?
- What points does the speaker choose to emphasize?

Engaging in Discourse

Discuss the Model

1. What was one positive piece of feedback Josh's partner gave him about his presentation? Josh's partner said that he provided strong evidence.
2. What was one suggestion Josh's partner gave him to improve his presentation? Answers will vary. Sample answer: Josh's partner suggested that he clarify the meaning of the phrase "citizens who had previously felt marginalized."
3. How did Josh use the feedback to improve his presentation? Answers will vary. Sample answer: Josh added an explanation of Graph 3.

Communicating Ideas

Discuss the Model

1. In the first clip, how does Ben's gesture affect the audience? Ben's gesture shows that he and Christina have a playful relationship, so it puts the audience at ease.
2. How do Ben and Christina use eye contact to connect with their audience? They look directly at the camera, which is like making eye contact with someone in real life. They also look at each other.
3. In the third clip, how does Ben draw attention to an important idea? Ben adjusts his volume, emphasis, and enunciation to stress the word *infer*.
4. How do Ben and Christina choose language that is appropriate for their task? They use clear, simple, classroom-appropriate language that will help them clarify a concept for a student audience.

ELL SPEAKING FRAMES

- Ben's gesture shows ____, which makes the audience ____.
- Ben and Christina look directly at ____ and look at ____.
- Ben adjusts his ____ and ____ to emphasize ____.
- Ben and Christina use ____ language, which is appropriate for the task of ____ because it is ____.

Sources and Citations

Discuss the Model

1. What information about the graph did Josh provide on his presentation slide? Josh indicated the title and the source, the Pew Research Center.
2. What information about the video did Josh provide on his presentation slide? Josh indicated the title and the source, NBC News Archives Xpress.
3. Why did Josh indicate the source of the graph if it was not required? Answers will vary. Sample answer: Because the Pew Research Center is easily recognizable as a trustworthy source, including it lends credibility to his presentation.

Extended Oral Project

These are impressive numbers, and even our political leaders agree: [Show video of former President Obama.]

Body—Evidence and Analysis #3
In addition, as Graph 3 demonstrates, social media is enabling citizens who had previously felt marginalized, including Hispanic and African American citizens, to find their voices and express their views. [Show graph 3.]

As we can see by following the legend at the top of the graph, African American and Hispanic users are more likely than their white counterparts to state that social media platforms are effective for their activism.

As my classmates and I preparing to gradute from high school. we feel like experts on many topics I personally loved learning about the central nervous system thought learning about how the framers wrote the Constitution was really cool. We've read great literature, memorized formulas, and famous lab experiments. We are ready to move on to the next phases of our lives. Few teenagers would admit that there is something they do not know about social media. We must acknowledge that the digital world has many pitfalls. Formal lessons on living in the digital world will help future graduates a lot.

[Show a works cited slide.]

Sources

- Pew Center Research graphs that show demographics and activities of social media users:
  - http://www.pewinternet.org/2018/07/11/public-attitudes-toward-political-engagement-on-social-media/pi_2018-07-10_social-activism_0-02/
  - http://www.pewinternet.org/2018/07/11/public-attitudes-toward-political-engagement-on-social-media/pi_2018-07-10_social-activism_0-05/
  - http://www.pewinternet.org/2018/07/11/public-attitudes-toward-political-engagement-on-social-media/pi_2018-07-10_social-activism_0-04/
  - https://www.nbcnewsarchivesxpress.com/contentdetails/214755
- **Obama video:**
  - https://www.nbcnewsarchivesxpress.com/contentdetails/214755

Skill: Sources and Citations

Josh will include a citation on each slide containing information from an outside source. At the end of his presentation, he'll include a works cited slide, listing all the sources he used.

SPEAKING FRAMES

- Josh indicated ____ and ____ for the graph.
- Josh indicated ____ and ____ for the video.
- The Pew Research Center is ____. This lends ____ to Josh's presentation.

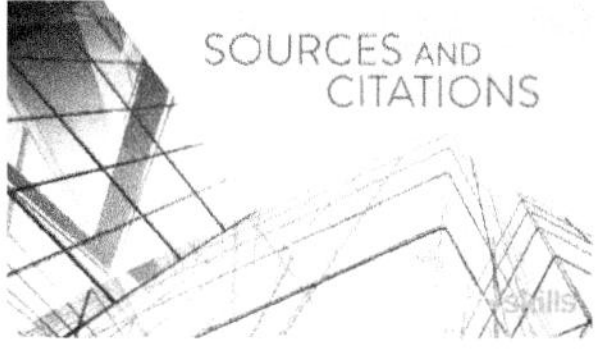

Skill: Sources and Citations

••• CHECKLIST FOR SOURCES AND CITATIONS

In your oral presentation, provide citations for any information that you obtained from an outside source. This includes the following:

- direct quotations
- paraphrased information
- tables and data
- images
- videos
- audio files

The citations in your presentation should be as brief and unobtrusive as possible. Follow these general guidelines:

- The citation should indicate the author's last name and the page number(s) on which the information appears (if the source has numbered pages), enclosed in parentheses.
- If the author is not known, the citation should list the title of the work and, if helpful, the publisher.

At the end of your presentation, include your works cited list, which should include all the texts you quote or reference directly in your presentation. Your works cited list should also follow the guidelines of a standard and accepted format, such as MLA. These are the elements and the order in which they should be listed in works cited entries, according to the MLA style:

- author (followed by a period)
- title of source (followed by a period)
- container, or the title of the larger work in which the source is located (followed by a comma)
- other contributors (followed by a comma)
- version (followed by a comma)
- number (followed by a comma)
- publisher (followed by a comma)

Skill: Sources and Citations

Introduce the Skill

Watch the Concept Definition video and read the following definition with your students.

A **source** is a person, text, or other medium from which information is obtained for research. **Primary sources** contain information that comes from first-hand accounts. **Secondary sources** are written later and are based on primary sources. Authors must give credit when using a source to avoid **plagiarism**, the practice of taking someone else's work or ideas and passing them off as one's own.

To credit sources, writers use citations. A **citation** is a reference to or a quotation from an outside source. It is required whenever authors quote another person's writing or refer to someone else's ideas. Types of citations include parenthetical citations, footnotes, and endnotes. In a **parenthetical citation** the writer gives credit to the source by using parentheses at the end of the sentence that contains the researched information. **Footnotes** are inserted at the bottom of a page, and **endnotes** are included at the end of a research paper or nonfiction book. A **bibliography** is a list of all the books and sources used to research a paper, placed at the end of the text.

SKILL VOCABULARY

source / la fuente *noun* a book or document used to provide evidence in research

primary source / la fuente primaria *noun* a source written by a person who actually experienced the event he or she recorded

secondary source / la fuente secundaria *noun* a source that summarizes, describes, or interprets primary sources

TURN AND TALK

Turn to a partner and discuss why it is important to have a common format for citations. How do citations help the audience and presenters?

SPEAKING FRAMES

- Having a common format for citations is important because ____.
- Citations help the audience ____.
- Citations help presenters ____.

- publication date (followed by a comma)
- location (followed by a comma)
- URL, without the "http://" (followed by a period)

Not all of these elements will apply to each citation. Include only the elements that are relevant for the source.

To check that you have gathered and cited sources correctly, consider the following questions:

- Did I cite the information I found using a standard format to avoid plagiarism?
- Did I include all my sources in my works cited list?

SKILL VOCABULARY

plagiarism / el plagio *noun* the taking of another person's words or ideas and presenting them as the writer's own

citation / la cita *noun* a quotation from or reference to an outside source

parenthetical citation / la documentación parentética *noun* credit given to a source in parentheses at the end of the sentence that contains the researched information COGNATE

YOUR TURN

Read the elements and examples below. Then, complete the chart by placing them in the correct order, according to the MLA style for a works cited list. Write the corresponding letter for each element and example in the appropriate column.

Elements and Examples	
A	publisher
B	"A Theatrical Moscow Trial Draws the Ire of Russia's Cultural Elite."
C	title of source
D	Atlantic Media Company,
E	URL
F	container
G	*The Atlantic,*
H	www.theatlantic.com/international/archive/2019/01/russian-artist-serebrennikov-culture-trial-moscow/580306/.
I	Nemtsova, Anna.
J	author
K	publication date
L	14 Jan. 2019,

Example	Element

Your Turn

Ask students to complete the Your Turn activity.

Example	Element
I	J
B	C
G	F
D	A
L	K
H	E

SKILL VOCABULARY

footnote / la nota al pie *noun* a note inserted at the bottom of a page, identifying a source

endnote / la nota final *noun* a note at the end of a research paper or non-fiction book, identifying a source

bibliography or works cited / la bibliografía o los trabajos citados *noun* an alphabetized list of sources that appears at the end of a research paper or nonfiction book

Write

Ask students to complete the writing assignment.

REWRITE CHECKLIST

Citation

- ☐ Is there any information from outside sources in your presentation?
- ☐ For quotations, summaries, and paraphrases: Did you include a parenthetical citation with the author and the page number, if available?
- ☐ For media: Did you identify the title and, if necessary, the publisher of the source?
- ☐ Is this citation also represented in your works cited list?

Works Cited

- ☐ Does your list follow the most up-to-date MLA guidelines?
- ☐ Do your citations vary according to the type of source (e.g., book, periodical, website)?
- ☐ Is your works cited page in the correct style and format?

WRITE

Use the information in the checklist to create or revise your citations and works cited list. Make sure to identify the source of each piece of researched information in your presentation. This will let your audience know that the information you are presenting is trustworthy. When you have completed your citations, compile a list of all your sources and write out your works cited list. Refer to the *MLA Handbook* as needed.

Writer's Notebook

Have students come up with a topic that interests them, such as the history of a particular holiday or food. Tell them to search online for one print source, one online article, and one website devoted to this topic. Then, have them consult the MLA Handbook or an online citation source, such as the Purdue Online Writing Lab (OWL)'s MLA Formatting and Style Guide, to write citations for the sources they found.

TURN AND TALK

Allow students to share the information for their citations orally in pairs or small groups before writing.

Skill: Communicating Ideas

••• CHECKLIST FOR COMMUNICATING IDEAS

Follow these steps as you rehearse your presentation:

- **Eye Contact:** Practice looking up and making eye contact while you speak. Rehearse your presentation in front of a mirror, making eye contact with yourself. Consider choosing a few audience members to look at during your presentation, but scan the audience from time to time so it doesn't seem as if you're speaking directly to only two or three people.
- **Speaking Rate:** Record yourself so you can judge your speaking rate. If you find yourself speaking too fast, time your presentation and work on slowing down your speech. In addition, you might want to plan pauses in your presentation to achieve a specific effect.
- **Volume:** Be aware of your volume. Make sure that you are speaking at a volume that will be loud enough for everyone to hear you, but not so loud that it will be uncomfortable for your audience.
- **Enunciation:** Decide which words you want to emphasize, and then enunciate them with particular clarity. Emphasizing certain words or terms can help you communicate more effectively and drive home your message.
- **Purposeful Gestures:** Rehearse your presentation with your arms relaxed at your sides. If you want to include a specific gesture, decide where in your presentation it will be most effective, and practice making that gesture until it feels natural.
- **Conventions of Language:** Make sure that you are using appropriate conventions of language for your audience and purpose.

Skill: Communicating Ideas

Introduce the Skill

Watch the Concept Definition video and read the following definition with your students.

When you communicate ideas in an oral presentation, it is important to rehearse not only what you will say but also how you will say it. Employing steady **eye contact** with one member of the audience at a time will help you keep the attention of your listeners. When a person is looking at you, they are more likely to listen and hear your message.

Speaking rate, adequate volume, and clear pronunciation can also help to convey your message. **Speaking rate** refers to how fast or slow you speak. Try not to rush through what you have to say. **Volume** is the level at which you speak. Make sure everyone can hear you. Finally, **enunciation**, or pronunciation, refers to how clearly you pronounce and emphasize your words.

Finally, it is also important to present your claims or findings in a clear and logical way, emphasizing any salient, or striking and noticeable, points.

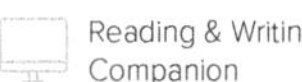

SKILL VOCABULARY

eye contact / el contacto visual *noun* the act of looking directly into one another's eyes

speaking rate / la velocidad de habla *noun* the speed at which you speak

volume / el volumen *noun* the intensity, or loudness, of a sound; the level at which you speak COGNATE

enunciation / la articulación *noun* how you pronounce and emphasize your words

TURN AND TALK

Turn to a partner and discuss how you should speak in order to communicate effectively in front of others. Describe your speaking rate, volume, and enunciation.

SPEAKING FRAMES

- If I want to speak effectively in front of others, I ____.
- My (speaking rate / volume / enunciation) is ____.

Your Turn

Ask students to complete the Your Turn activity.

Category	Example of Effective Communication	Example of Ineffective Communication
Posture	A	E
Eye Contact	H	C
Volume/Rate/ Enunciation	I	B
Gestures	D	G
Language Conventions	F	J

YOUR TURN

Read the examples of students who are communicating their ideas below. Then, complete the chart by first identifying the appropriate category for each example and then deciding whether the example illustrates effective or ineffective communication. Write the corresponding letter for each example in the appropriate place in the chart.

	Examples
A	A student stands up straight in clear view of his or her audience.
B	A student speaks very softly and rushes through the presentation, using a monotone voice.
C	A student does not look up from his or her notecards.
D	A student uses his or her hands to emphasize a particularly important point.
E	A student slouches and stands with his or her arms crossed.
F	A student begins her formal presentation by saying, "Hello. Today I will talk about rainforests."
G	A student allows his or her arms to hang limply and does not move at all.
H	A student makes eye contact with various members of the audience.
I	A student projects his or her voice, but does not shout. He or she pronounces words carefully and speaks at a slightly slower rate than used in normal conversation.
J	A student begins her formal presentation by saying, "Yo. I'mma talk about some trees."

Category	Example of Effective Communication	Example of Ineffective Communication
Posture		
Eye Contact		
Volume/Rate/Enunciation		
Gestures		
Language Conventions		

Writer's Notebook

Have students write a journal entry about a past experience of giving an oral presentation. What went well during the presentation? What will they do differently this time?

TURN AND TALK

Allow students to share their experiences orally in pairs or small groups before writing.

 WRITE

Practice delivering your presentation by yourself or in front of a partner.

As you present, do the following:

- Employ steady eye contact.
- Use an appropriate speaking rate and volume to clearly communicate your ideas.
- Use pauses and enunciation for clarity and effect.
- Use purposeful gestures to add interest and meaning as you speak.
- Maintain a comfortable, confident posture to engage your audience.
- Use language conventions appropriate for an argumentative presentation, and avoid slang or inappropriate speech.

If you are working with a partner, use the checklist to evaluate your partner's communication of ideas.

When you finish giving your argumentative oral presentation, write a brief but honest reflection about your experience of communicating your ideas. Did you make good eye contact? Did you speak too quickly or too softly? Did you maintain a comfortable, confident posture? Did you use appropriate language? Did you struggle to incorporate gestures that looked and felt natural? How can you better communicate your ideas in the future?

Write

Ask students to complete the writing assignment.

ELL REWRITE CHECKLIST

A

- [ ] I used appropriate (posture / eye contact / speaking rate / volume / gestures / enunciation / language conventions). I know this because I ____.
- [ ] I emphasized my idea of ____ by ____.
- [ ] I need to improve on (posture / eye contact / speaking rate / volume / gestures / enunciation / language conventions) by ____. I noticed this when I ____.
- [ ] I will practice by ____. This will help me get better because ____.

Skill: Reasons and Evidence

Introduce the Skill

Watch the Concept Definition video and read the following definition with your students.

An **argument** is a statement of opinion about an issue or a problem. The structure of an argument consists of a **claim** and the support for that claim. The claim is the arguable statement about what is true or should be done. Claims are most effective when they are supported with reasons and evidence. **Reasons** are logical explanations that state why the writer believes in his or her claim and why others should accept the claim. **Evidence** consists of facts, statistics or numerical data, quotations, specific examples, and expert opinions that uphold and support the claim.

Skill: Reasons and Evidence

CHECKLIST FOR REASONS AND EVIDENCE

In order to identify a speaker's point of view, reasoning, and use of evidence and rhetoric, note the following:

- the stance, or position, the speaker takes on a topic
- whether the premise, or the basis of the speech or talk, is based on logical reasoning
- whether the ideas follow one another in a way that shows clear, sound thinking
- whether the speaker employs the use of exaggeration, especially when citing facts or statistics
- the speaker's choice of words, the points he or she chooses to emphasize, and the tone, or general attitude

In order to evaluate a speaker's point of view, reasoning, and use of evidence and rhetoric, consider the following questions:

- What stance, or position, does the speaker take? Is the premise based on sound, logical reasoning? Why or why not?
- Does the speaker use facts and statistics to make a point? Are they exaggerated?
- What points does the speaker choose to emphasize?
- How does the speaker's choice of words match the tone he or she wants to establish?

TURN AND TALK

Turn to a partner and discuss whether you support your reasoning with evidence when you argue. What happens when you include evidence or fail to include evidence?

SPEAKING FRAMES

- An argument I had was ____.
- The argument I presented (was / was not) supported by evidence. For example, I said ____.
- When evidence is included in an argument, listeners say ____.
- When evidence fails to be included in an argument, listeners say ____.

SKILL VOCABULARY

argument / el argumento ***noun*** a set of claims, evidence and reasons designed to persuade others to adopt a certain point of view or to take a certain action COGNATE

claim / la afirmación ***noun*** the writer's or speaker's position on a debatable issue or problem

YOUR TURN

Read each example of reasoning from a draft of Josh's oral presentation below. Then, complete the chart by sorting the examples into two categories: those that are logical and those that are illogical. Write the corresponding letter for each example in the appropriate column.

	Examples
A	As students' access to all forms of media increases, so does their ability to navigate it responsibly.
B	A student's access to technology does not mean that the student uses it appropriately or is a good digital citizen.
C	Becoming media literacy savvy is complicated because it requires time, resources, and training.
D	We can always tell teachers to become more media literacy savvy because they use technology each day in their classrooms.
E	Living in a digital world means being inundated with both fake and legitimate news on a daily basis, but discerning fact from fiction can be tricky.
F	If a person doesn't know how to distinguish fake news from legitimate information, he or she is not trying.

Logical Reasoning	Illogical Reasoning

SKILL VOCABULARY

reason / la razón *noun* an explanation that states why others should accept a claim

evidence / la evidencia *noun* facts, examples, and expert opinions that support a claim COGNATE

Your Turn

Ask students to complete the Your Turn activity.

Logical Reasoning	Illogical Reasoning
B	A
C	D
E	F

Your Turn

Ask students to complete the Your Turn activity. Answers may vary.

Ineffective Use of Evidence	Effective Use of Evidence
Technology has made things like home security systems possible. We know that thanks to technology the world is a safer place.	There are many advantages to living in the digital world, including technological advances that make us safer, such as home security systems.
According to Nonprofit Tech for Good, 51% of wealthy donors prefer to give online. This shows that social media is so powerful that it could ensure Americans vote in every election.	Social media can even help the people in our communities that need it the most: According to Nonprofit Tech for Good, 51% of wealthy donors prefer to give online.
Studies show that most people are skeptical of the information they read on the internet. According to my father, past generations believed everything they read, heard or saw.	Consuming information in the age of the internet requires a new set of skills that previous generations may struggle to acquire.

YOUR TURN

Below are three examples of an ineffective use of evidence from a previous draft of Josh's oral presentation. In the second column, rewrite the sentences to use the evidence effectively, without exaggeration or faulty reasoning. The first row has been completed for you as an example.

Ineffective Use of Evidence	Effective Use of Evidence
Technology has made things like home security systems possible. We know that thanks to technology the world is a safer place.	There are many advantages to living in the digital world, including technological advances that make us safer, such as home security systems.
According to Nonprofit Tech for Good, 51% of wealthy donors prefer to give online. This shows that social media is so powerful that it could ensure Americans vote in every election.	
Studies show that most people are skeptical of the information they read on the internet. According to my father, past generations believed everything they read, heard, or saw.	

Writer's Notebook

Have students write a persuasive letter about or advertisement for their favorite movie or TV show. Ask them to include reasons and evidence to explain why the movie or TV show should be taught in school.

TURN AND TALK

Allow students to share their responses orally in pairs or small groups before freewriting.

Skill:
Engaging in Discourse

••• CHECKLIST FOR ENGAGING IN DISCOURSE

You and a partner will take turns practicing your argumentative oral presentations and giving feedback. The feedback you provide should be meaningful and respectful. That is, you should offer an honest assessment as well as specific tips for improvement, while using kind and considerate language.

In your feedback, make sure to evaluate and critique the speaker using these categories. Remember to always start by telling the speaker what he or she did particularly well.

Positive Points:

- What is most effective about the oral presentation?
- What strong points does the speaker make?
- Which particular phrases are well written and memorable?

Clarity:

- Does the speaker express his or her ideas in a clear, understandable way?
- What changes can the speaker make to improve the clarity of his or her message?

Evidence and Elaboration:

- Does the speaker offer a range of positions on his or her topic or issue?
- Is there an opportunity to clarify, verify, or challenge ideas and conclusions made in the argument?
- Does the speaker resolve contradictions in his or her argument?
- Does the speaker use transitions and explanations effectively to show the relationship between ideas?
- Where can the speaker add transitions or explanations to improve the logical flow of his or her message?
- What additional information or research is required to deepen his or her message?

Diction:

- Does the speaker's choice of words have an impact, or a strong effect?
- Where can the speaker improve his or her word choice to create a stronger impact?

Skill: Engaging in Discourse

Introduce the Skill

Watch the Concept Definition video and read the following definition with your students.

Discourse refers to the process of communicating content or ideas. There are several types of discourse. **Informal discourse** refers to casual, social communication. **Formal discourse** refers to communication used in professional settings. **Academic discourse** is the style of communication used in scholarly settings. Engaging in academic discourse often requires you to **evaluate** or critique the **coherence** or logic of a speaker's message. Speakers and writers must adjust their style of discourse to suit a variety of audiences and purposes.

Speakers and writers must also engage in discourse in a way that is **meaningful** (thoughtful and relevant) as well as **respectful** (polite and sincere). Responding **appropriately** (in a manner suitable to the situation) and **listening actively** (paying attention to how the speaker uses language and vocal expressions to communicate ideas) are two ways you can contribute effectively when engaged in discourse.

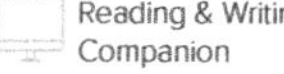

SKILL VOCABULARY

discourse / el debate *noun* the process of communicating content or ideas

informal discourse / el discurso informal *noun* casual, social communication COGNATE

formal discourse / el discurso formal *noun* communication used in professional settings COGNATE

academic discourse / el discurso académico *noun* the style of communication used in scholarly settings COGNATE

TURN AND TALK

Turn to a partner and discuss when you engage in formal discourse during a typical school day. When do you engage in informal discourse?

SPEAKING FRAMES

- I engage in formal discourse when ____.
- I engage in informal discourse when ____.

Syntax:

- Does the speaker use sentence construction to create a strong impact?
- Where can the speaker use sentence-construction techniques, such as ending a sentence with the most important idea, to improve the impact of his or her syntax?

Rhetorical Strategies:

- Does the speaker use language persuasively?
- Where can the speaker employ specific techniques, such as appeals to logic, emotion, and ethics, to improve the impact of his or her presentation?

SKILL VOCABULARY

evaluate / evaluar ***verb*** to assess or critique COGNATE

coherence / la coherencia ***noun*** clarity and logic COGNATE

meaningful / significativo/a ***adjective*** thoughtful and relevant

respectful / respetuoso/a ***adjective*** polite and sincere COGNATE

YOUR TURN

Read each example of feedback below. Then, complete the chart by placing the examples in the appropriate category. Write the corresponding letter for each example of feedback in the appropriate row. Some examples may belong in more than one category.

	Feedback
A	I'm not sure what you mean by "these strategies." Can you elaborate?
B	I think this sentence would be stronger if you moved the most important phrase to the end.
C	The wording of this sentence is a little vague. You might consider using more topic-specific vocabulary.
D	You make a good point here, but it would be stronger if you added a quote from a credible source.
E	I liked how you used an anecdote to make your opening more memorable.
F	The word *however* shows a strong connection between your ideas and evidence in this paragraph.

Category	Feedback
Positive Points	
Clarity	
Evidence and Elaboration	
Diction	
Syntax	
Rhetorical Strategy	

WRITE

Take turns reading your presentation aloud to a partner. When you finish, write a reflection about your experience of giving feedback. How did you ensure that your feedback was both meaningful and respectful? What did you do well? How can you improve in the future?

Your Turn

Ask students to complete the Your Turn activity.

Category	Feedback
Positive Points	E
Clarity	A
Evidence and Elaboration	F
Diction	C
Syntax	B
Rhetorical Strategy	D

Write

Ask students to complete the writing assignment.

ELL REWRITE CHECKLIST

A
- ☐ I did a good job of (paying attention / showing that I am listening / responding appropriately). I know this because I ____.
- ☐ I need to improve on (paying attention / showing that I am listening / responding appropriately). I noticed this when I ____.

V SKILL VOCABULARY

appropriate / apropiado/a *adjective* suitable to the situation COGNATE

active listening / escuchar atentamente *noun* the act of paying close attention to an oral presentation, focusing on a speaker's use of language and vocal expression

Oral Presentation Process: Revise

Review Revision Guide

Break the class into five groups, and assign each group a category of the revision guide. Ask:

- What is the purpose of this section of the guide?
- How did it improve Josh's writing?
- How will it help to improve your writing?

Allow groups to share their ideas with the class.

ELL SPEAKING FRAMES

- I think (clarity / development / organization / word choice / sentence fluency) improved Josh's writing by ____.
- I think (clarity / development / organization / word choice / sentence fluency) will improve my writing because ____.

Oral Presentation Process: Revise

PLAN | DRAFT | REVISE | EDIT AND PRESENT

You have written a draft of your argumentative oral presentation. You have also received input from your peers about how to improve it. Now you are going to revise your draft and prepare your presentation by creating slides and visuals to support your argument.

REVISION GUIDE

Examine your draft to find areas for revision. Keep in mind your purpose and audience as you revise for clarity, development, organization, and style. Also, examine your draft to find slides that might need additional clarification or revision. For example, when Josh revised his presentation, he paid careful attention to how the content of each slide supported his thesis and message. Use the guide below to help you review:

Review	Revise	Example
Clarity		
Highlight each sentence that connects to your thesis statement.	Make sure the claim is clear for your audience in both your introduction and conclusion. Add headings to your presentation slides to clarify your ideas and claims for your audience, and simplify your ideas by turning them into brief bullet points.	Formal lessons on living in the digital world will help future graduates ~~a lot.~~ become better digital citizens, be more aware of other people's experiences, and maybe even change the world.

Review	Revise	Example
	Development	
Identify and annotate places in your presentation where your thesis is not supported by details.	Add details that strongly support the reasons for your claim. Include images, graphs, videos, and other visual elements that support your argument in your presentation. Think about places where a visual aid might replace text.	To accomplish this goal, schools need to teach students how to analyze and evaluate online sources and how to be responsible digital citizens. That means contributing to the digital space in a positive way, putting an end to cyberbullying, and stopping the propagation of false information.
	Organization	
Syntax can help you emphasize ideas. Identify strong words and phrases that show your main ideas, and place them strategically.	Revise sentences so that the most important word or phrase comes at the end. Think about places where a visual aid might enhance a section of the presentation.	In the past 24 hours, ~~all with a device in the palm of my hand,~~ I bought my grandmother a birthday present, took a history quiz, streamed three episodes of my favorite television show, ordered dinner, and researched the causes and effects of air pollution~~.~~—all with a device in the palm of my hand.
	Style: Word Choice	
Identify key words and phrases that connect ideas across sentences. Annotate places where more precise language would strengthen the connection.	Replace vague or awkward words and phrases with precise ones that emphasize the connections between your ideas.	Although online activism can have positive effects by including a multitude of opinions, raising awareness, and promoting change, there can be many drawbacks ~~bad effects~~, including people verbally attacking others and using dehumanizing speech.

Revise

Students should start this activity with a copy of their drafts either printed on paper or open in a word-processing program, such as Google Docs. Allow students time to revise their drafts using the instructions in the revision guide. Once students have finished revising their presentations, have them submit their work.

CHECK FOR SUCCESS

Circulate around the room to spend time with individual students. Ask:

- What category are you working on?
- Why are you revising this specific section?
- How are you revising it?
- How does this change support your purpose?
- Does this change make your writing appropriate for your audience?

If students struggle while revising their drafts, choose an exemplary revision to share with the class while the student talks through the process. You could also invite a student to share a dilemma in the revision process and allow the class to offer feedback or suggestions.

STYLE

Revise your draft, focusing on style. Select informal words, phrases, or sentences, and replace or revise them to make your style more formal.

STYLE

Tell students to revise their drafts using the revision guide, focusing on style. In addition, have students make revisions that focus on clarity, as practiced in the previous unit.

Write

Ask students to complete their writing assignment

ELL REVISION CHECKLIST

A
- ☐ Find any informal words or phrases.
- ☐ Brainstorm or use a thesaurus to find a more formal synonym.
- ☐ Replace the informal word or phrase with the more formal word or phrase.

Review	Revise	Example
Style: Sentence Fluency		
Read your presentation aloud, and listen to the way the text sounds. Does it sound choppy? Or does it flow smoothly with rhythm, movement, and emphasis on important details and events?	Shorten a group of long sentences, or join shorter sentences together using conjunctions and/or dependent clauses.	~~We~~ As a result, we are ready to move on to the next phases of our lives. ~~Few~~ While few teenagers would admit that there is something they do not know about social ~~media. We~~ media, we must acknowledge that the digital world has many pitfalls.

WRITE

Use the revision guide, as well as your peer reviews, to help you evaluate your argumentative oral presentation to determine places that should be revised.

Grammar: Parallel Structure

Parallel Structure

Parallel structure, or parallelism, is the deliberate repetition of words, phrases, or other grammatical structures of equal weight or importance.

Not Parallel	Parallel
The soup was hot, wholesome, and **tasted delicious**.	The soup was hot, wholesome, and **delicious**.
After dinner, Kevin completed his Spanish homework, wrote his English essay, and **has studied** for his math test.	After dinner, Kevin completed his Spanish homework, wrote his English essay, and **studied** for his math test.
Peter opened the world almanac, **checking the index**, and identified the capital of Rwanda.	Peter opened the world almanac, **checked the index**, and identified the capital of Rwanda.

Parallelism is a rhetorical device that helps emphasize ideas, establish rhythm, and make a text or speech more memorable. The examples below are from "Be Ye Men of Valour," a speech British Prime Minister Winston Churchill delivered in 1940 at a critical time during World War II.

Text	Explanation
I speak to you for the first time as Prime Minister in a solemn hour for the life **of our country, of our empire, of our allies, and**, above all, **of the cause of freedom**. . . . I am sure I speak for all when I say we are ready **to face it, to endure it, and to retaliate against it** to any extent that the unwritten laws of war permit. . . . We must have, and have quickly, **more aeroplanes, more tanks, more shells, more guns**. Be Ye Men of Valour	Churchill uses parallelism in lists for its rhetorical effect. • Parallel prepositional phrases emphasize the gravity of the *solemn hour* Churchill cites. • The parallel series of infinitive phrases emphasizes the readiness of Churchill and the people to whom he speaks. • The deliberate repetition of *more* in the list of elements needed emphasizes the immediacy of the country's need for equipment and ammunition.

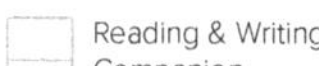

Grammar: Parallel Structure

Introduce the Skill

Review the image and definition for parallel structure as a class.

- parallel structure - repetition of similar grammatical structures, such as verbals, phrases, or clauses, within a sentence
- nonparallel structure - a series of elements in a sentence that are not in a similar grammatical form, resulting in a sentence construction error

Discuss the Model

1. What can be repeated to form parallel structure? Parallel structure repeats similar words, phrases, or other grammatical structures.
2. How can parallel structure be used as a rhetorical device? Parallel structure can emphasize ideas, establish rhythm, or make a text more memorable.

Your Turn

Ask students to complete the Your Turn activities.

QUESTION 1

A. Incorrect.

B. Incorrect.

C. Incorrect.

D. Correct. The gerunds *staying*, *eating*, and *placing* are parallel.

QUESTION 2

A. Incorrect.

B. Incorrect.

C. Correct. The past-tense verbs *set* and *lit* indicate that *waiting* should be a past-tense verb as well, so *waited* is correct.

D. Incorrect.

QUESTION 3

A. Incorrect.

B. Correct. Now there are three clauses in the list and the sentence has parallel structure, with each clause being similarly phrased.

C. Incorrect.

D. Incorrect.

QUESTION 4

A. Incorrect.

B. Correct. *The shifting wind* is parallel to the other direct objects in the sentence: *(the) parting clouds* and *(the) streaming sunlight.*

C. Incorrect.

D. Incorrect.

YOUR TURN

1. How should this sentence be changed to achieve parallel structure?

> He regretted staying up past midnight, eating an entire pizza by himself, and placing phone calls to old friends early in the morning.

- A. Replace **he regretted** with **regretting**.
- B. Replace **staying** with **stayed**.
- C. Replace **placing** with **placed**.
- D. No change needs to be made to this sentence.

2. How should this sentence be changed to achieve parallel structure?

> Sarah set the table, lit the candles, and waiting for her date to arrive.

- A. Insert **and** after **table**.
- B. Delete **lit the candles**.
- C. Replace **waiting** with **waited**.
- D. No change needs to be made to this sentence.

3. How should this sentence be changed to achieve parallel structure?

> David couldn't fall asleep because the TV was blaring, the shouting children, and the dog was barking.

- A. Replace **TV was blaring** with **blaring TV**.
- B. Replace **shouting children** with **children were shouting**.
- C. Replace **dog was barking** with **barking dog**.
- D. No change needs to be made to this sentence.

4. How should this sentence be changed to achieve parallel structure?

> She watched how the wind shifted, parting clouds, and streaming sunlight.

- A. Change **how the wind shifted** to **how the shifting wind**.
- B. Change **how the wind shifted** to **the shifting wind**.
- C. Replace **and** with **with**.
- D. No change needs to be made to this sentence.

Grammar:
Sentence Variety - Openings

Sentence Openers

Varying your syntax is one way to help a reader remain engaged. One way to vary your syntax is to use a variety of sentence openers, which help a reader more clearly understand the connection between sentences. The following strategies can help you vary the types of sentence openers you use:

Strategies	Text
Use a prepositional phrase to begin a sentence.	On the enclosed porch at the back of the house, a crisp white bag still sat on the wicker chaise, filled with lace she had once planned to turn into curtains. A Temporary Matter
Use an adverb to begin a sentence.	Generally speaking, philanthropy is always better than no help at all, but it is also in itself a privilege of the few. Commencement Address at the New School
Use a verb ending in *-ed* or *-ing* to begin a sentence.	Finding news and information has never been easier, and access is expanding to more people every day. News Literacy in the Misinformation Age
Use a very short sentence, which can help emphasize an important point or create excitement.	He looked relieved. Ghosts
Use transitional words (showing cause and effect, similarities or differences, etc.) to begin a sentence.	Consequently, the more time we spend on social media platforms, the more deceptive we become. Honesty on Social Media
Use words that correspond to time or a sequence of events to begin a sentence.	At the stroke of the midnight hour, when the world sleeps, India will awake to life and freedom. Tryst with Destiny

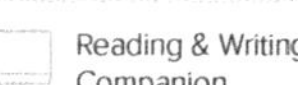

Grammar: Sentence Variety - Openings

Introduce the Skill

Review the image and definition for sentence variety - openings as a class.

- syntax - the broad term for the way in which the elements of language (words, phrases, clauses, etc.) are arranged to create well-formed sentences
- sentence opener - the words used at the beginning of a sentence
- diction - the type of language an author uses throughout a text

Discuss the Model

1. Why is varying your syntax important? It helps keep the reader engaged in what you have written.
2. Why are sentence openers important? Sentence openers clarify the relationship between sentences.

Your Turn

Ask students to complete the Your Turn activities.

QUESTION 1

A. Incorrect.

B. Correct. *As a result* is a transition that signals the effects of a specific cause or action.

C. Incorrect.

D. Incorrect.

QUESTION 2

A. Incorrect.

B. Incorrect.

C. Incorrect.

D. Correct. *Luckily* is an adverb. Using it as a sentence opener adds emphasis to the speaker's feelings.

QUESTION 3

A. Incorrect.

B. Incorrect.

C. Correct. This short statement is direct and can balance out longer sentences with more detailed pieces of information.

D. Incorrect.

QUESTION 4

A. Incorrect.

B. Incorrect.

C. Correct. *Several decades later* clarifies the sequence of events.

D. Incorrect.

 YOUR TURN

1. How should this sentence be edited to use transitional words showing cause and effect as a sentence opener?

   The new CEO took over and began to make many necessary changes.

   - A. Frighteningly, the new CEO took over and began to make many necessary changes.
   - B. As a result, the new CEO took over and began to make many necessary changes.
   - C. Behind closed doors, the new CEO took over and began to make many necessary changes.
   - D. No change needs to be made to this sentence.

2. How should this sentence be edited to use an adverb as a sentence opener?

   Luckily, I made it to the meeting on time.

   - A. I made it to the meeting on time, luckily.
   - B. I am lucky that I made it to the meeting on time.
   - C. I luckily made it to the meeting on time.
   - D. No change needs to be made to this sentence.

3. How should this sentence be edited to make the sentence opener clearer?

   People live in cities.

   - A. Cities are places where people live.
   - B. The people live in cities.
   - C. Many people live in cities.
   - D. No change needs to be made to this sentence.

4. How should this sentence be edited to use a sentence opener that corresponds to time?

   The first scholar to edit Emily Dickinson's poems collected all of them into a single edition.

   - A. The poems of Emily Dickinson were all collected into a single edition by a scholar.
   - B. Surprisingly, the first scholar to edit Emily Dickinson's poems collected all of them into a single edition.
   - C. Several decades later, the first scholar to edit Emily Dickinson's poems collected all of them into a single edition.
   - D. No change needs to be made to this sentence.

Oral Presentation Process: Edit and Present

PLAN | DRAFT | REVISE | EDIT AND PRESENT

You have revised your oral presentation based on your peer feedback and your own examination.

Now, it is time to edit your argumentative oral presentation. When you revised, you focused on the content of your oral presentation. You practiced strategies for citing your sources, communicating your ideas, presenting strong reasons and evidence, and engaging in discourse. When you edit, you focus on the mechanics of your oral presentation, paying close attention to language, syntax, and rhetorical devices that can be heard by your audience while you are talking.

Use the checklist below to guide you as you edit:

- ☐ Have I included a variety of sentence openers in my presentation?
- ☐ Have I used parallel structure to emphasize ideas, establish rhythm, and make my text or presentation more memorable?
- ☐ Have I used any language that is too informal for my presentation?
- ☐ Have I added digital media strategically to enhance my presentation?
- ☐ Do I have any sentence fragments or run-on sentences?
- ☐ Have I spelled everything correctly?

Notice some edits Josh has made:

- Edited a sentence to use transitional words as a sentence opener
- Changed a sentence to achieve parallel structure
- Corrected a sentence fragment
- Deleted a run-on sentence
- Fixed misspelled words

Oral Presentation Process: Edit and Present

Practice with Student Model (optional)

Provide groups with a different section of Josh's draft. Each group should practice editing Josh's Model using the checklist in the lesson. Has he:

- ☐ included a variety of sentence openers?
- ☐ changed a sentence to achieve parallel structure?
- ☐ used language that is appropriate for his presentation?
- ☐ added digital media strategically to enhance his presentation?
- ☐ corrected sentence fragments or run-on sentences?
- ☐ spelled everything correctly?

After the groups have finished, call on volunteers from each group to make edits until all the mistakes have been found and edited, pausing to discuss points of disagreement.

SPEAKING FRAMES

A

- Josh (did/did not) include a variety of sentence openers when he wrote ____.
- Josh (did/did not) include examples of parallel structure when he wrote ____.
- Josh (did/did not) use appropriate language when he wrote ____.
- Josh (did/ did not) add digital media strategically to enhance his presentation when ____.
- ____ is an example of a (run-on sentence/sentence fragment) that Josh (has/has not) corrected.
- ____ is spelled incorrectly. The correct spelling is ____.

Write

After students finish editing, suggest, if there's time, that they set their presentations aside for a few minutes and that they then proofread them one more time. You may suggest that students pair up and read their presentations aloud to a partner. Once they have completed their writing, they should submit their work.

CHECK FOR SUCCESS

If students struggle to edit successfully, help them determine where edits are needed and what changes need to be made.

Direct students to the grammar lessons in this unit if they are uncertain about the rules for specific concepts.

READ ALOUD

Encourage students to read their presentations aloud to themselves or to a partner in order to catch any remaining mistakes.

READ ALOUD

Encourage students to read their presentations aloud to themselves or to an on-grade-level peer in order to catch any remaining mistakes.

PREPARE FOR AN INTERVIEW

Have students imagine that they are being interviewed about their topics and are asked: What is the most important insight you gained about the writing process, preparing for a presentation, or about yourself as a writer and speaker during this Extended Oral Project? Have students consider how they might respond to those questions or what advice they would give to future students.

As my classmates and I ~~preparing~~ prepare to ~~gradute~~ graduate from high school, we feel like experts on many topics. ~~I personally loved learning about the central nervous system thought learning about how the framers wrote the Constitution was really cool.~~ We've read great literature, memorized essential formulas, and repeated famous lab experiments. As a result, we are ready to move on to the next phases of our lives.

WRITE

Use the checklist, as well as your peer reviews, to help you evaluate your oral presentation to determine places that need editing. Then, edit your presentation to correct those errors. Finally, rehearse your presentation, including both the delivery of your written work and the strategic use of the digital media you plan to incorporate.

Once you have made all your corrections and rehearsed with your digital media selections, you are ready to present your work. You may present to your class or to a group of your peers. You can record your presentation to share with family and friends or post it on your blog. If you publish online, share the link with your family, friends, and classmates.

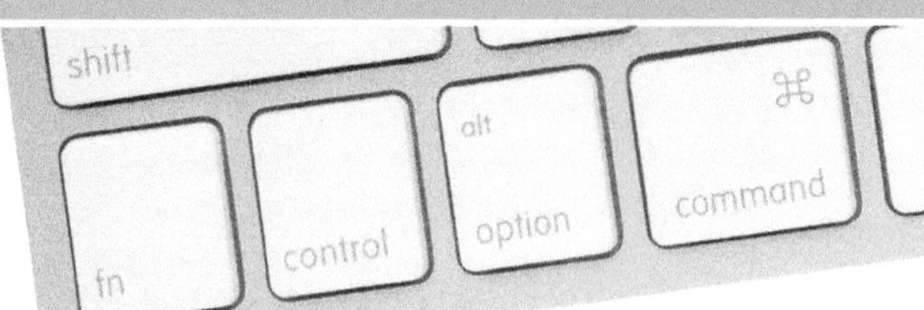

English Language Learner Resources

studysync USERS ASSIGNMENTS

GRADE 12 › UNIT

Times of Transition

Core ELA
Grade 12
30 days

Unit Overview

Integrated Reading and Writing

Extended Writing Project

ELL Resources

Novel Study

End-of-Unit Assessment

Instructional Path

Hope

When the World Sleeps

Skill: Classroom Vocabulary Words

After learning classroom vocabulary words, students will be able to recognize and use them in a variety of contexts. Words include *agree, classify, construct, demonstrate, disagree, examine, procedure, progress, research,* and *review.*

Teacher Resources: Lesson Plan

Assign Preview

Skill: Using Prior Experience

After reading and discussing a model, students will be able to use their prior experience to connect to events and ideas in the text.

Teacher Resources: Lesson Plan

USING PRIOR EXPERIENCE
WHEN THE WORLD SLEEPS
sync•skills

Assign Preview

Lessons in the English Language Learner Resources section offer explicit ELL instruction. These lessons share a thematic and genre focus with all other lessons in the Core ELA unit.

The twenty ELL Resources in this section are developed around two texts and an Extended Oral Project. Each text is written at four distinct levels. For ELL's, these texts serve as structural and thematic models of authentic texts in the Integrated Reading and Writing section of the unit.

ELL lessons modify the routines used with texts in the Integrated Reading and Writing section. Explicit vocabulary instruction is emphasized, and reading and writing Skills lessons focus strongly on language acquisition and reading comprehension.

The Extended Oral Project can be used in place of or as an extension to the Extended Writing Project. In this unit, students will plan, write, and present a personal address to a school or community leader about a local problem. Throughout these lessons, students will interact with texts and their peers as readers, writers, speakers, and listeners to maximize comprehension and provide multiple access points for every learner.

Focus on English Language Proficiency Levels

ADVANCED HIGH
ADVANCED
INTERMEDIATE
BEGINNING

ELL Resources provide targeted support for four levels of proficiency: Beginning, Intermediate, Advanced, and Advanced High. Instruction and scaffolds, as well as the texts themselves, are differentiated based on these levels.

Additional differentiated scaffolds include visual glossaries, speaking and writing frames, and suggested grouping for peer and teacher support. Lessons also include suggested extension activities to challenge Advanced and Advanced High students as they progress through the year.

ELL Resources

ELL TEXTS

Hope

- Skill: Sight Vocabulary and High-Frequency Words
- Skill: Environmental Print
- First Read
- Skill: Analyzing Expressions
- Skill: Visual and Contextual Support
- Skill: Pronouns and Antecedents
- Close Read

When the World Sleeps

- Skill: Classroom Vocabulary Words
- Skill: Using Prior Experience
- First Read
- Skill: Language Structures
- Skill: Developing Background Knowledge
- Skill: Spelling Patterns and Rules
- Close Read

EXTENDED ORAL PROJECT

- Introduction
- Skill: Acquiring Vocabulary
- Plan
- Skill: Sentence Lengths
- Practice
- Present

Hope

FICTION

Introduction

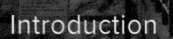

In this short story, a young girl deals with the grief she feels after a hurricane blows through her town.

A recent hurricane took many possessions from the narrator and her family, including their dog Gus. This tragedy has caused her to have nightmares every night and she can't help but draw gloomy pictures of the images in her mind. She knows this is a concern to her parents and teachers. However, she insists that drawing is the only thing that makes her feel better. One day, on their walk home from school, the narrator and her brother, Darrell, see a big black dog that is shaking and really afraid. That night, she leaves some food outside for the dog even though her parents were apprehensive. Before bed, she draws a picture of the dog surrounded by her smiling family. In the morning, she runs into the backyard to see if the dog has eaten the food that she left. The bowl was empty. When she looked up, the dog was at the top of the hill. Slowly but surely, the narrator convinces the dog to come closer and tells her she's home. That night, her family celebrates Darrell's birthday by laughing and eating too much cake. The family can't afford many presents, but it is still a happy occasion because they have a new dog. A new dog named Hope.

CONNECT TO ESSENTIAL QUESTION

How are we shaped by change?

In this short story, a young girl deals with the loss of her dog after a hurricane blows through her town. How do natural disasters change the way we see the world?

ELL Proficiency-leveled summaries and summaries in multiple languages are available digitally.

Audio and audio text highlighting are available with this text.

Core ELA Connections

Texts	Theme	Genre
Ghosts	The narrator deals with her feelings of grief following the loss of her dog. This text emphasizes the importance of family and understanding.	A short story written in the first person, "Hope" provides insight into a young girls journey of letting go.

Differentiated Text Levels

ELL LEVEL	BEGINNING	INTERMEDIATE	ADVANCED	ADVANCED HIGH
WORD COUNT	970	970	1248	1356
LEXILE	680L	680L	830L	860L

Instructional Path

The print teacher's edition includes essential point-of-use instruction and planning tools. Complete lesson plans and program documents appear in your digital teacher account.

Skill: Sight Vocabulary and High-Frequency Words

DIGITAL ONLY

Objectives: Students will be able to learn and recognize sight vocabulary and high-frequency words in English.

Objectives: Students will be able to recognize sight vocabulary and high-frequency words when listening and reading, and produce sight vocabulary and high-frequency words when speaking and writing.

Skill: Environmental Print

DIGITAL ONLY

Objectives: Students will be able to learn and practice the skill of recognizing and understanding environmental print.

Students will be able to recognize and understand various instructions, signs, drawings, logos, shapes, and pictures.

First Read: Hope

Objectives: Students will be able to perform an initial reading of a text using the strategy of recognizing and understanding environmental print.

Objectives: Students will be able to demonstrate comprehension of a text by responding to questions orally and in writing using textual evidence.

Skill: Analyzing Expressions

Objectives: Students will be able to analyze expressions.

Objectives: Students will be able to analyze expressions when reading and distinguish between literal and figurative meanings.

Skill: Visual and Contextual Support

Objectives: Students will be able to use visual and contextual supports.

Objectives: Students will be able to use visual and contextual supports to enhance their background knowledge while reading.

Skill: Pronouns and Antecedents

Objectives: Students will be able to understand and apply pronoun and antecedent agreement.

Objectives: Students will be able to recognize and apply pronoun and antecedent agreement when reading and writing.

Close Read: Hope

Objectives: Students will be able to perform a close reading of a text in order to analyze visual and contextual supports.

Objectives: Students will be able to use visual and contextual supports to participate in a collaborative conversation and write a short constructed response.

Progress Monitoring

Opportunities to Learn	Opportunities to Demonstrate Learning	Opportunities to Reteach
Sight Vocabulary and High-Frequency Words		
Skill: Sight Vocabulary and High-Frequency Words	Skill: Sight Vocabulary and High-Frequency Words • Your Turn First Read • Sight Vocabulary and High-Frequency Words	Spotlight Skill: Sight Vocabulary and High-Frequency Words
Environmental Print		
Skill: Environmental Print	Skill: Environmental Print • Your Turn First Read: • Sight Vocabulary and High-Frequency Words	Spotlight Skill: Environmental Print
Analyzing Expressions		
Skill: Analyzing Expressions	Skill: Analyzing Expressions • Your Turn	Spotlight Skill: Analyzing Expressions
Visual and Contextual Support		
Skill: Visual and Contextual Support	Skill: Visual and Contextual Support • Your Turn Close Read • Skills Focus • Collaborative Conversation	Spotlight Skill: Visual and Contextual Support
Pronouns and Antecedents		
Skill: Pronouns and Antecedents	Skill: Pronouns and Antecedents • Your Turn Close Read • Write	Spotlight Skill: Pronouns and Antecedents

First Read

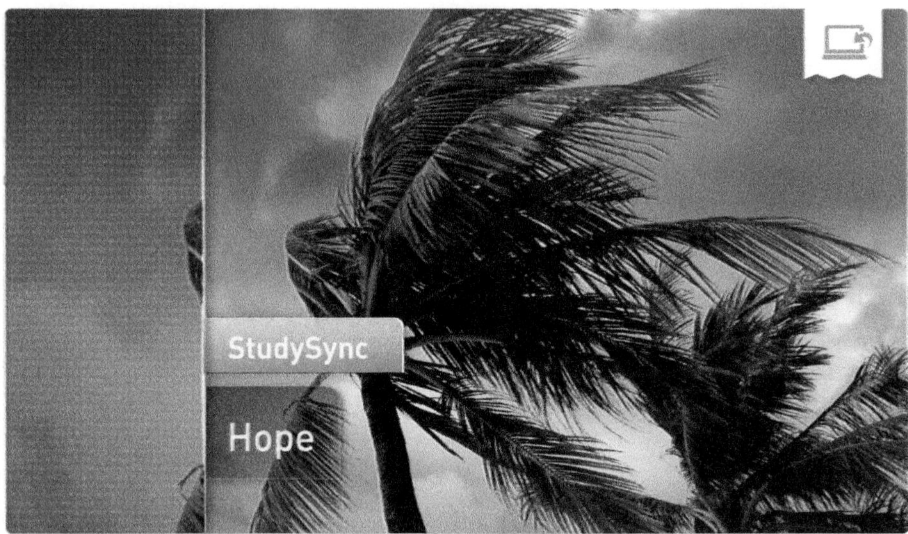

Introduce the Text

As a class, watch the video preview and have students read the introduction in pairs to make connections to the video preview: Ask students various "wh" questions such as:

- What did you see in the video? How does it make you feel?
- What do you think the text will be about?
- Is there something in the video or introduction that surprised you?

ELL **Beginning & Intermediate**

SPEAKING FRAMES

- I saw ____. • I feel ____.
- I think the text will be about ____.
- I was surprised by ____.

Practice Prereading Skill

Remind students that Making Connections:

Helps you understand the text by connecting it to your own experiences or knowledge. You can connect the text to an event in your life, to something you read in another text, or to bigger ideas in the world.

Have students work in small, on-level groups to fill out their graphic organizer by listing text to self, text to text, and text to world connections.

As students are working in small groups, circulate to listen for sample connections like:

- This reminds me of a time when I . . .
- This reminds me of a book about . . .
- This reminds me of the news story about . . .

Activate Prior Knowledge and Experiences OPTIONAL

Find out what your students already know about natural disasters.

Have students make connections while practicing their oral language by discussing what they know about natural disasters. Ask students to share where their background knowledge came from. For example, did their ideas come from a movie, friend, television show, book, or family member?

VOCABULARY

anticipate
to think of or predict what will happen in the future

enormous
very large

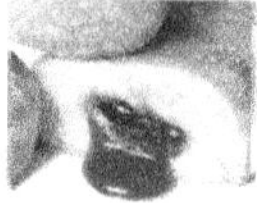

infuse
to cause to be filled with something

maybe
perhaps; possibly

draw
to create an image by making lines and marks

READ

Today I woke up before it was light out because of the nightmare I've had every night since the storm. It's about Gus drowning in the flood.

Television reporters and meteorologists track Hurricane Frances at the National Hurricane Center.

AUDIO TEXT HIGHLIGHTING

Allow students to use the audio text highlight feature to follow along as they read. Alternately, you may wish to work directly with students or group them in twos or threes for partner reading or choral reading.

Preteach Vocabulary

Model the first word and example for the class.

1. The word is *anticipate* and its meaning is "to think of or predict what will happen in the future."
2. When I hear the word *anticipate*, I think of the way I feel before my birthday. I get excited about celebrating and receiving gifts.
3. For example: Because I asked my parents for a new soccer ball, I *anticipate* that I will get one for my birthday.
4. This is an example of something that I have *anticipated* because it is a prediction of what will happen in the future.

Continue this exercise with each word in the glossary, callng on individuals or groups of students to share out.

Beginning

PRETEACH VOCABULARY

Beginning students may benefit from additional practice or visual cues that help reinforce meanings in context. Ask students multiple-choice questions with obvious correct answers such as the following:

- What supplies do you need to **draw?**
  a. a pencil and paper
  b. a bowl and a spoon
- What kind of events do people **anticipate?**
  a. past events
  b. future events
- Which animal is **enormous**?
  a. a mouse
  b. a whale
- What should you **infuse** with seasoning when cooking?
  a. meat
  b. your arm
- Which item is **maybe** a good idea to bring on a hike in case of rain?
  a. an umbrella
  b. a shovel

Students may also benefit from seeing images related to the correct multiple-choice responses. For example, present an image of a whale or an umbrella.

Sight Vocabulary and High-Frequency Words Focus

Remind students of the sight vocabulary and high-frequency words that they studied at the beginning of the unit. Point out that some of the words may be useful as they think about and discuss the text. For example:

- dry (The neighborhood is *dry*, but it used to be . . .)
- clear (It is *clear* that the narrator . . .)
- force (I think the narrator's mother wants to *force* her to feel . . .)
- less (The narrator feels *less* . . .)
- true (It is *true* that . . .)

2 It's all gone—most of our furniture, our clothes, even Darrell's lucky baseball mitt. It's funny, even though so much of our stuff was ruined or lost, I only really care about losing Gus. It sounds crazy, but sometimes I still wander outside asking, "Where are you?" I remember how he used to **anticipate** my thoughts and movements. He followed me everywhere, and he didn't even need a leash. He slept under my bed every night; every morning I'd wake up, look down, and see his front paws sticking out. When I rubbed his belly, he'd stretch out as long as possible so that the fur between his paws would open up like a flower blooming. Then, *crash*, another nightmare. I wake up from this nightmare, drenched in sweat, and Mom is there smoothing my hair. She is reminding me that Darrell's birthday is in a few days and that we need to plan a party.

Islamic Circle of North America Relief USA volunteer Shaza Cheema, right, fills bags of canned foods for Liberty City, FL residents affected by Hurricane Irma.

3 "It's important to keep celebrating our lives," Mom says, trying to **infuse** some cheer in her tone, which is heavy with melancholy. Her eyes are kind, but fill with concern when they look at me now. I know it has something to do with Mrs. Lane telling her about my drawings. They're all worried about what I **draw**, but drawing makes me happiest right now. It's the only time lately when I'm not anxious, or thinking about anything except following my hand around the sketch pad. But I get where they're coming from: the drawings *do* look kind of bad, or as they would say, *unsettling*, or sometimes even *disquieting*. Like there's one where all the trees and telephone poles are knocked down, and huge blue and black waves are so high they cover our whole house. Unfortunately, in that drawing, I drew Gus underwater like in the dream. His white curls pointing straight in different directions. Then another one is just an all black background with one jagged, skinny bolt of lightning cutting through the black sky. The lightning hits my head and splits it open like a pumpkin smashing open on the sidewalk. But I swear drawing makes me feel better.

4 Darrell walked home from school with me today. As we raced through the backyard, we both saw it at the same time: a big, shaking black dog with one white paw like it had been dipped in white paint. Darrell told me to be careful

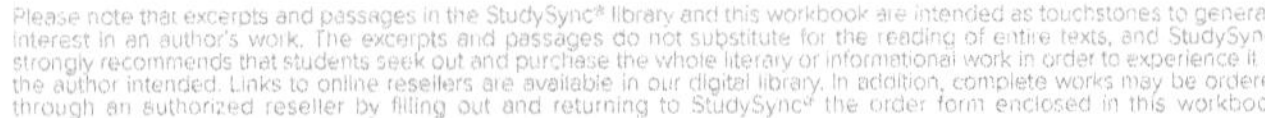

TEXT TALK

Have students discuss the questions in small groups. Circulate around the room and check for understanding.

1. What is the story about?
2. Who are the story's characters?
3. Where does the story take place?
4. How does the story make you feel?

All Levels

SPEAKING FRAMES

Giving Information:

- This story is about ____.
- The story's characters are ____.
- This story takes place in ____.
- This story makes me feel ____.

Asking for Information:

- Can you explain ____?
- What do you think about ____?
- Why do you think ____?
- Do you agree with ____?

because it looked like a potentially aggressive dog. He quickly went inside, but I stayed outside. I could tell the dog was afraid, but harmless. It looked how I feel when I wake up from one of those nightmares. So I took off my backpack and sat down on the ground, took out my pad and started drawing. I didn't want to frighten the dog, so I didn't try to move closer. I simply drew in my sketch pad.

5 That night, I told Mom all about the dog in the yard. She seemed a little worried. Dad said he wasn't sure if he was ready to replace Gus.

6 "Can I at least leave some food and water out?"

7 "How do we know it won't bite?" Mom asked. I could hear the trepidation in her voice.

8 "We don't. But he's probably really hungry. If Gus is out there, I'd want someone to make sure he's okay, too."

Rescue flights bring animal victims of Hurricane Katrina out of the flooded Gulf Coast.

9 Mom sighed, but I knew she thought I might be right. I scraped all the leftovers into Gus's old bowl and then went outside and left it right where the dog was that afternoon. I didn't see it, but I said out loud to the trees, "This could be your new home."

10 That night, I drew the black dog dipped in white paint. It was playing with a new toy, on a new bed, and there was new furniture. Darrell was playing baseball outside with his lucky mitt, and flowers and trees were exploding in the yard with color. There were tulips, **enormous** oak trees, rose bushes, and even a hammock. The sun was out, and the sky was blue. I drew Mom gardening with her peculiar-looking straw hat and Dad reading in his favorite chair. I didn't put myself in the drawing. It made me happier to look in from the outside.

11 The next day was Darrell's birthday. Mom was busy making a cake for that night before she had to leave for work.

12 "No bad dreams, honey?"

13 But I was too busy running outside to answer. I looked in the dog bowl. It was empty. I looked up the hill and saw the black dog staring at me from behind a tree. I crouched down and held my hand out. The dog inched towards me, peeking from behind trees like a turtle coming out of its shell. She was nervous, so I waited for as long as it took to build her trust. It got close enough that I could see she was a girl dog. Her tail was wagging, but she still seemed terrified. She finally sniffed my hand and then gave it a lick. Then she licked my ear over and over, which was sort of gross because I was covered in slobber, but I understood that to be a good sign.

14 "You're going to be ok. You're home. I hope you like it here." I scratched behind her floppy ear.

15 That night, the black dog celebrated with us! It wasn't a big party and I knew Mom and Dad were really anxious that Darrell would be disappointed because they couldn't buy many presents or anything. But I think we had even more fun than last year. It was a special day for everyone. My heart was still broken because I missed Gus. And I was still sad about the house and everyone's possessions. But there was a new feeling along with the sadness, a warm feeling in my chest and belly, like two very different feelings swirled together to make something new, something better than happiness **maybe**.

16 Dad gave Darrell a new mitt. We ate too much chocolate cake and played with the new dog. Dad belly laughed when the dog skidded across the floor to fetch one of Gus's old squeaky toys. I only realized then that it had been so long since I'd heard a real, big laugh from Dad. I couldn't remember the last time Mom or Dad were so elated. I gave Darrell my drawing, and I could tell he liked it because he hugged me tight. At the end of the night, the black dog was curled up sound asleep on a bunch of blankets I used to make her own bed. Her white paw was folded over her other one. She looked tender, untroubled, and really, really tired.

17 "She can finally sleep because she knows she's safe." Dad said. Mom was sitting on Dad's lap, and Darrell was on his millionth piece of cake when he asked, "So, what's her name?" We were all quiet. Then I said, "Hope. Her name is Hope."

First Read

Read "Hope." After you read, complete the Think Questions below.

THINK QUESTIONS

1. **What event did the narrator and her family experience before the start of the story?**

   Before the start of the story, the narrator and her family experienced ______________________.

2. **Write two or three sentences to describe the plot of the story.**

   The plot of the story is about ______________________.

3. **At the end of the story, how do the narrator and her family feel? Why? Include a line from the text to support your response.**

   At the end of the story, the narrator and her family feel ______________________

   because ______________________.

4. **Use context to confirm the meaning of the word *infuse* as it is used in "Hope." Write your definition of *infuse* here.**

   Infuse means ______________________.

   A context clue is ______________________.

5. **What is another way to say that something is *enormous*?**

   Something is ______________________.

Think Questions

Circulate as students answer Think Questions independently. Answers will vary.

QUESTION 1: Comprehension

The narrator and her family experienced a terrible storm.

QUESTION 2: Comprehension

The narrator's family lost their dog and many personal possessions when a hurricane flooded their town. This event causes the narrator to have nightmares and draw gloomy pictures. The family's life gets better when the narrator and her brother find another dog.

QUESTION 3: Comprehension

Answers will vary, but may include the following examples:

- "But there was a new feeling along with the sadness, a warm feeling in my chest and belly, like two very different feelings swirled together to make something new, something better than happiness maybe."
- "I only realized then that it had been so long since I'd heard a real, big laugh from Dad. I couldn't remember the last time Mom or Dad were so elated."

Student responses should explain how things are getting better for this family because now they are hopeful for the future.

QUESTION 4: Language

The narrator says that her mom tries to infuse cheer in her voice. I think that means her mom was trying to put emotion in her voice. A definition for *infuse* is "to put inside."

QUESTION 5: Language

Something is very big.

Skill: Analyzing Expressions

Introduce the Skill

Watch the Concept Definition video and read the definition for Analyzing Expressions.

Skill: Analyzing Expressions

DEFINE

When you read, you may find English expressions that you do not know. An **expression** is a group of words that communicates an idea. Three types of expressions are idioms, sayings, and figurative language. They can be difficult to understand because the meanings of the words are different from their **literal,** or usual, meanings.

An **idiom** is an expression that is commonly known among a group of people. For example, "It's raining cats and dogs" means it is raining heavily. **Sayings** are short expressions that contain advice or wisdom. For instance, "Don't count your chickens before they hatch" means do not plan on something good happening before it happens. **Figurative** language is when you describe something by comparing it with something else, either directly (using the words *like* or *as*) or indirectly. For example, "I'm as hungry as a horse" means I'm very hungry. None of the expressions are about actual animals.

••• CHECKLIST FOR ANALYZING EXPRESSIONS

To determine the meaning of an expression, remember the following:

- ✓ If you find a confusing group of words, it may be an expression. The meaning of words in expressions may not be their literal meaning.
  - Ask yourself: Is this confusing because the words are new? Or because the words do not make sense together?
- ✓ Determining the overall meaning may require that you use one or more of the following:
  - context clues
  - a dictionary or other resource
  - teacher or peer support
- ✓ Highlight important information before and after the expression to look for clues.

 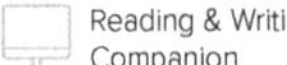

TURN AND TALK

1. What is figurative language?
2. How do you know when an author is using figurative language?
3. What can you do if you are struggling to understand the meaning of figurative language?

Beginning & Intermediate

SPEAKING FRAMES

- Figurative language is ____.
- Authors use figurative language when ____.
- I can ____ for help.

Advanced & Advanced High

SPEAKING FRAMES

- Figurative language is ____. For example, ____.
- I know that an author is using figurative language when ____.
- I can ____ or ____ for help.

SKILL VOCABULARY

expression / la expresión ***noun*** a phrase used to express an idea COGNATE

literal / literal ***adjective*** describing the usual meaning of a word COGNATE

idiom / el modismo ***noun*** a phrase or expression used to convey a meaning that is different from its literal definition

saying / el dicho ***noun*** an expression that contains advice or wisdom

figurative / figurado / a ***adjective*** not literal; using figures of speech

YOUR TURN

Choose the best answer to each question.

1. The sentence "The dog inched towards me, peeking from behind trees like a turtle coming out of its shell" suggests a comparison between—

   - A. the trees and the dog.
   - B. an inch and a turtle.
   - C. the dog and a turtle.
   - D. a turtle and its shell.

2. Which sentence contains an example of figurative language?

   - A. "But I think we had even more fun."
   - B. "My heart was still broken because I missed Gus."
   - C. "Dad gave Darrell a new mitt."
   - D. "We ate too much chocolate cake and played with the new dog."

3. Which sentence contains an example of figurative language?

   - A. "I couldn't remember the last time Mom or Dad were so elated."
   - B. "At the end of the night, the black dog was curled up sound asleep on a bunch of blankets I used to make her own bed."
   - C. "Her white paw was folded over her other one, and she looked tender, untroubled and really, really tired. "
   - D. "Mom was sitting on Dad's lap, and Darrell was on his millionth piece of cake when he asked, 'So, what's her name?'"

Your Turn

Ask students to complete the Your Turn Activity.

QUESTION: 1 C. Correct. The author uses a simile to compare the dog to a frightened turtle.

QUESTION: 2 B. Correct. This sentence contains a metaphor. The narrator's heart is not literally broken.

QUESTION: 3 D. Correct. This sentence contains an example of hyperbole. Darrell could not literally eat one million pieces of cake.

Discuss the Skill Model

1. What is the student trying to understand in the first annotation?

   The student wants to understand why the narrator is using a flower to describe her dog.

2. How does the teacher explain the figurative language in the first annotation?

   The teacher explains that the words *like* and *as* signal a simile. A simile is a type of figurative language that compares two things.

3. How does the teacher explain the figurative language in the second annotation?

   The teacher says that this example is a metaphor. A metaphor also compares two things, but it does not include the words *like* or *as*.

4. What strategies does the student use to determine the meaning of the figurative language in the text?

   Answers will vary, but should include: The student asks the teacher and looks at context clues.

ELL

Beginning & Intermediate

Have students use the speaking frames and helpful terms to participate in the group discussion. If beginning students are hesitant to participate in a discussion, encourage them by prompting with *yes* or *no* questions.

Advanced & Advanced High

Have students use the speaking frames to participate in the group discussion.

SPEAKING FRAMES

- The student wants to understand ____.
- The teacher explains ____. This type of figurative language ____.
- The teacher explains ____. This type of figurative language ____.
- The student ____.

HELPFUL TERMS FOR DISCUSSION

- simile
- describe
- metaphor
- narrator
- like
- context clues
- as
- compare
- teacher

Skill: Visual and Contextual Support

Introduce the Skill

Watch the Concept Definition video and read the definition for Visual and Contextual Support.

Skill: Visual and Contextual Support

DEFINE

Visual support is an image or an object that helps you understand a text. **Contextual support** is a **feature** that helps you understand a text. By using visual and contextual supports, you can develop your vocabulary so you can better understand a variety of texts.

First, preview the text to identify any visual supports. These might include illustrations, graphics, charts, or other objects in a text. Then, identify any contextual supports. Examples of contextual supports are titles, headers, captions, and boldface terms. Write down your **observations**.

Then, write down what those visual and contextual supports tell you about the meaning of the text. Note any new vocabulary that you see in those supports. Ask your peers and your teacher to **confirm** your understanding of the text.

CHECKLIST FOR VISUAL AND CONTEXTUAL SUPPORT

To use visual and contextual support to understand texts, do the following:

✓ Preview the text. Read the title, headers, and other features. Look at any images and graphics.

- Write down the visual and contextual supports in the text.
- Write down what those supports tell you about the text.
- Note any new vocabulary that you see in those supports.
- Create an illustration for the reading and write a descriptive caption.
- Confirm your observations with your peers and teacher.

TURN AND TALK

1. How do visual and contextual supports help a reader?
2. What are some examples of visual supports?
3. What are some examples of contextual supports?

Beginning & Intermediate

SPEAKING FRAMES

- Visual and contextual supports help ____.
- An example of a visual support is ____.
- An example of a contextual support is ____.

Advanced & Advanced High

SPEAKING FRAMES

- Visual and contextual supports help the reader ____.
- Examples of visual supports are ____, ____, and ____.
- Examples of contextual supports are ____, ____, and ____.

SKILL VOCABULARY

visual / visual *adjective* relating to the use of color, lines, and perspective in still and moving images such as illustrations and film

support / el apoyo *noun* a person or thing that offers assistance

contextual / contextual *adjective* depending on the circumstances or situation that something is in COGNATE

feature / la característica *noun* a prominent attribute or aspect of something

observation / la observación *noun* a statement or thought about things one hears or sees COGNATE

confirm / confirmar *verb* to establish validity; to verify, to prove COGNATE

YOUR TURN

Read paragraphs 5–8 from "Hope." Then, complete the multiple-choice questions below.

from "Hope"

That night, I told Mom all about the dog in the yard. She seemed a little worried, and Dad said he wasn't sure if he was ready to replace Gus.

"Can I at least leave some food and water out?"

"How do we know it won't bite?" Mom asked. I could hear the trepidation in her voice.

"We don't. But he's probably really hungry. If Gus is out there, I'd want someone to make sure he's okay, too."

1. The visual support helps readers to—
   - A. visualize what a hurricane looks like.
   - B. learn about aircraft carriers.
   - C. visualize how many animals are rescued after storms.
   - D. learn about a lesser-known recovery effort.

2. What background information does the image provide?
   - A. Many pets are killed in hurricanes.
   - B. It is dangerous for dogs to fly.
   - C. Some animals are rescued after storms.
   - D. Families are notified when their pets are rescued.

3. Based on the image and its caption, which of the following statements about the characters in the story might be true?
   - A. Gus is alive and well because he was rescued and brought to a safe location.
   - B. The narrator gave Gus away to a new family.
   - C. The black dog in the narrator's yard has been there the whole time.
   - D. The narrator's brother rescued the black dog from a shelter.

Your Turn

Ask students to complete the Your Turn Activity.

QUESTION: 1 D. Correct. The visual support shows that some pets are rescued and relocated after storms.

QUESTION: 2 C. Correct. The image shows rescue flights for animal victims.

QUESTION: 3 A. Correct. The image and caption explain that animal victims have been relocated to safety.

Discuss the Skill Model

1. What does the student notice when he previews the text?

   The student notices that the text includes several images with captions.

2. How do the first image and caption help the student build background knowledge about the text?

   The first image and caption help the student understand that hurricanes put many people in danger.

3. In his first annotation, how does the student use visual and contextual support to help understand the story?

   The student uses visual and contextual support to understand that the family in the story lost their belongings because of a hurricane.

4. How does the student use the second image and caption to answer his question about the text?

   The student realizes that the volunteers in the image are helping families have hope that they can rebuild their lives.

ELL Beginning & Intermediate

Have students use the speaking frames and helpful terms to participate in the group discussion. If beginning students are hesitant to participate in a discussion, encourage them by prompting with *yes* or *no* questions.

Advanced & Advanced High

Have students use the speaking frames to participate in the group discussion.

SPEAKING FRAMES

- The student notices ____.
- The first image and caption help the student understand ____.
- The student uses visual and contextual support to understand ____.
- The student realizes ____.

HELPFUL TERMS FOR DISCUSSION

- hurricanes
- includes
- captions
- belongings
- family
- images
- hope
- danger
- rebuild

Close Read

Complete Skills Focus

To prepare students to complete the Skills Focus, remind them of the Reading Skill Visual and Contextual Support. Tell students that visual supports, such as images, can help readers develop background knowledge to better understand the text. Direct students to the Skills Focus and remind them to track as you read aloud.

Use visual and contextual support to develop background knowledge about how natural disaster preparation and recovery can affect individuals and communities.

- Have both partners list the visual and contextual supports in the text. Students can organize their notes in a graphic organizer or outline.
- Partners should draw on their lists of visual and contextual supports to answer these questions:
  > What are some steps in preparing for natural disasters?
  > What are some ways that people help each other recover from natural disasters?
  > How are animals, such as family pets, affected by natural disasters?

Allow students to reread the text and mark down their ideas using the annotation tool, adding an exclamation point (!) to note things they want to remember or that surprise them, and a question mark (?) to note things that confuse them.

Prompt students to work cooperatively to complete their assigned tasks. Circulate around the room and monitor groups as they work.

Hope

Close Read

 WRITE

NARRATIVE: The short story "Hope" gives the reader a look at how one young girl moves on with her life after a natural disaster. Use your background knowledge about preparation and recovery efforts to write a first-person narrative from her brother's point of view. How has his life changed? How does his experience differ from his sister's experience? Include details from the short story in your writing. Pay attention to and edit for pronouns and antecedents.

Use the checklist below to guide you as you write.

☐ How is Darrell's experience of the hurricane different than his sister's experience?

☐ What happens to Darrell during the story?

☐ How does Darrell feel? How do you know?

Use the sentence frames to organize and write your narrative.

My birthday is in a few days but (I / we) ______ am ______________________

instead of happy. My family is recovering from a ______________________.

(We / They) ______________ lost most of our belongings and our dog, Gus. We had to evacuate

quickly and ______________________.

Sometimes I wish I could ______________________.

My sister has been ______________________

since the storm. (She / He) ________ misses our dog, Gus. Yesterday, we found a new dog and volunteers

gave my mom ______________________.

Maybe my birthday will be happy after all.

192 Reading & Writing Companion

Collaborative Conversation

Regroup students into groups of two or three so that they are in a group with someone who analyzed a different image than they did. Prompt students to share their insights about each of the images.

- How did using visual and contextual supports help you build background knowledge and understand the text?
- What did you learn about how natural disaster preparation and recovery affects people and communities?
- How did working with a partner help you analyze the visual and contextual supports in the text?

Collaborative Conversation

BEGINNING, INTERMEDIATE Use the word bank to participate in the group discussion.

ADVANCED Use the speaking frames to participate in the group discussion.

BEGINNING, INTERMEDIATE	ADVANCED
Word Bank	**Speaking Frames**
• helped me understand • caption • image • storm • description • preparation • recovery	• Using visual and contextual supports helped us ____. • This image and caption taught me that ____. • Working with a partner was helpful because ____.

Write

Narrative Prompt

The short story "Hope" gives the reader a look at how one young girl moves on with her life after a natural disaster. Use your background knowledge about preparation and recovery efforts to write a first-person narrative from her brother's point of view. How has his life changed? How does his experience differ from his sister's experience? Pay attention to and edit for pronouns and antecedents.

BEGINNING Write a response using the paragraph frames and word banks.

INTERMEDIATE Write a response using the paragraph frames.

INTERMEDIATE / BEGINNING	BEGINNING
Paragraph Frames	**Word Bank**
My birthday is in a few days but (I / we) ____ am ____ instead of happy. My family is recovering from a ____. (We / They) ____ lost most of our belongings and our dog, Gus. We had to evacuate quickly and ____. Sometimes I wish I could ____. My sister has been ____ since the storm. (She / He) ____ misses our dog, Gus. Yesterday, we found a new dog and volunteers gave my mom ____. Maybe my birthday will be happy after all.	• hurricane • worried • anxious • possessions • supplies • baseball mitt

When the World Sleeps

FICTION

Introduction

On June 15th, 1947, the British House of Commons passed the Indian Independence Act which divided the country into two, India and Pakistan. Their independence was to be granted by August 15th of that same year. In this short drama, a family travels through the night to find safety as India claims its independence from the British.

Anjali and her children, Santosh and Niranjan, are crammed into the back of a truck with many other strangers. It is the eve of Indian independence and they are on their way to safety. Santosh complains about leaving their hometown and does not understand the importance of independence. She says she was perfectly happy before—she could wear gold and play with her friends. Niranjan, her brother, reminds her that independence is important and chides her for only thinking about herself and not the lower castes who were really suffering. Anjali urges them not to argue. Instead, they should pray for their father's safety, because he stayed behind to arrange their affairs. Niranjan has great faith in the new India and in the new prime minister, Jawaharlal Nehru. However, they must first travel through the riots. Suddenly the truck stops and they hear shouts of jubilation outside. They have entered a free India and they have arrived at their future.

ELL Proficiency-leveled summaries and summaries in multiple languages are available digitally.

Audio and audio text highlighting are available with this text.

CONNECT TO ESSENTIAL QUESTION

How are we shaped by change?

In this short drama, a family travels through the night to find safety as India claims its independence from the British. How does freedom bring change?

Core ELA Connections

Texts	Theme	Genre
Tryst with Destiny	A family takes a leap of faith when they leave their old life behind. This text questions the true meaning of freedom and independence.	"When the World Sleeps" is a play that follows a mother, daughter, and son as they travel through the night to a safe, new world.

Differentiated Text Levels

ELL LEVEL	BEGINNING	INTERMEDIATE	ADVANCED	ADVANCED HIGH
WORD COUNT	1013	1117	1229	1242
LEXILE	N/A	N/A	N/A	N/A

Instructional Path

The print teacher's edition includes essential point-of-use instruction and planning tools. Complete lesson plans and program documents appear in your digital teacher account.

Skill: Classroom Vocabulary Words

DIGITAL ONLY

Objectives: Students will be able to learn and recognize classroom vocabulary words in English.

Objectives: Students will be able to recognize classroom vocabulary words when listening and reading, and produce classroom vocabulary words when speaking and writing.

Skill: Using Prior Experience

DIGITAL ONLY

Objectives: Students will be able to learn and practice the skill of using prior experience to connect to a text.

Objectives: Students will be able to read a new or unfamiliar text while using their prior experience to connect to events, characters, or ideas in the text.

First Read: When the World Sleeps

Objectives: Students will be able to perform an initial reading of a text using the strategy of using prior experience.

Objectives: Students will be able to use prior experience and demonstrate comprehension by responding to questions using textual evidence.

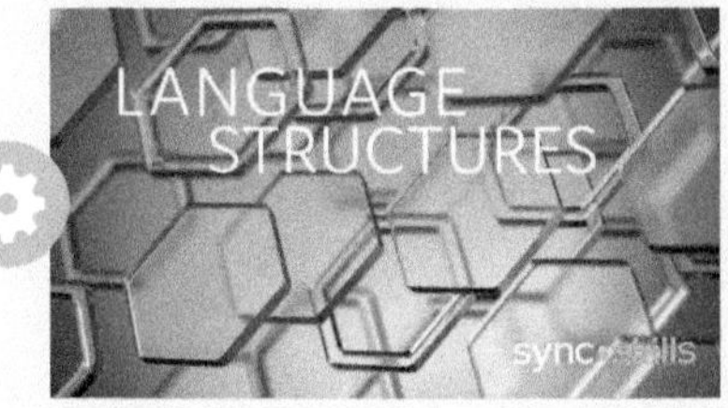

Skill: Language Structures

Objectives: Students will be able to comprehend language structures.

Objectives: Students will be able to identify and comprehend language structures involving the perfect tenses when reading.

Skill: Developing Background Knowledge

Objectives: Students will be able to develop background knowledge while reading.

Objectives: Students will be able to preview texts to develop background knowledge to better understand a wider variety of texts.

Skill: Spelling Patterns and Rules

Objectives: Students will be able to recognize and use certain homophones.

Objectives: Students will be able to recognize and use certain homophones when reading and writing.

Close Read: When the World Sleeps

Objectives: Students will be able to perform a close reading of a text in order to develop background knowledge.

Objectives: Students will be able to develop background knowledge to participate in a collaborative conversation and write a short constructed response.

Progress Monitoring

Opportunities to Learn	Opportunities to Demonstrate Learning	Opportunities to Reteach
Classroom Vocabulary Words		
Skill: Classroom Vocabulary Words	Skill: Classroom Vocabulary Words • Your Turn First Read • Read and Annotate • Classroom Language Focus • Text Talk	Spotlight Skill: Classroom Vocabulary Words
Using Prior Experience		
Skill: Using Prior Experience	Skill: Using Prior Experience • Your Turn First Read: • Introduce the Text • Practice Prereading Skill	Spotlight Skill: Using Prior Experience
Language Structures		
Skill: Language Structures	Skill: Language Structures • Your Turn Close Read • Complete Vocabulary Chart • Skills Focus • Collaborative Conversation	Spotlight Skill: Language Structures
Developing Background Knowledge		
Skill: Developing Background Knowledge	Skill: Developing Background Knowledge • Your Turn Close Read • Skills Focus • Collaborative Conversation	Spotlight Skill: Developing Background Knowledge
Spelling Patterns and Rules		
Skill: Spelling Patterns and Rules	Skill: Spelling Patterns and Rules • Your Turn Close Read • Write	Spotlight Skill: Spelling Patterns and Rules

First Read

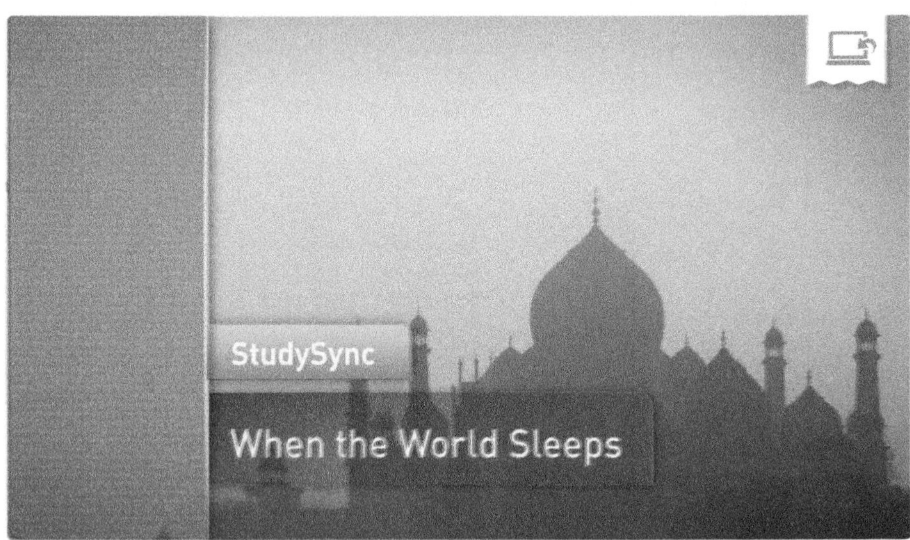

Introduce the Text

As a class, watch the video preview and have students read the introduction in pairs to make connections to the video preview. Ask students various "wh" questions such as:

- What did you see in the video? How does it make you feel?
- What do you think the text will be about?
- Is there something in the video or introduction that surprised you?

ELL **Beginning & Intermediate**

SPEAKING FRAMES

- I saw ____. • I feel ____.
- I think the text will be about ____.
- I was surprised by ____.

Practice Prereading Skill

Remind students that Using Prior Experience:

Means connecting events from your life to events in a story or play. Connecting life experiences to a text makes it easier to understand the meaning of interesting or confusing terms and phrases.

Have students work in small, on-level groups to choral read or listen to the audio of the text. Remind students to use prior experiences to understand the play.

As students are working in small groups, circulate to listen for sample statements like:

- This word means . . .
- This reminds me of . . .
- I can relate to this because . . .

Activate Prior Knowledge and Experiences OPTIONAL

Find out what your students already know about refugees.

Have students make connections while practicing their oral language by discussing what they know about refugees. Ask students to share where their background knowledge came from. For example, did their ideas come from a movie, friend, television show, book, or family member?

VOCABULARY

suffocate
to die from lack of oxygen

erupt
to burst suddenly

desperately
in a distressed or severe manner

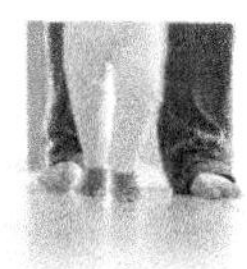

progress
to move forward toward a better outcome

illusion
an incorrect or false idea

READ

1 *It is late at night on August 14th, 1947, the night before India becomes independent from the British. A family is traveling from their old home in Lyallpur, now renamed Faisalabad, headed to the safety of India.*

2 CHARACTERS:
Santosh Singh, 19
Niranjan Singh, 15, her brother
Anjali Singh, 40, their mother

3 *Santosh, Niranjan, and Anjali are crammed in the back of a military truck. They can hear sounds but see nothing outside. Everyone is tense, hungry, and thirsty. They are aware this is a very dangerous journey to safety. Throughout the scene, the actors should be facing out, pressed shoulder to shoulder, as if there were people on all sides of them. They are talking quietly to each other, trying not to draw attention. Anjali, the mother, is seated between Santosh and Niranjan. She is perched on a small box that contains her few remaining possessions. She clutches a small framed photo in her hands.*

AUDIO TEXT HIGHLIGHTING

Allow students to use the audio text highlight feature to follow along as they read. Alternately, you may wish to work directly with students or group them in twos or threes for partner reading or choral reading.

Preteach Vocabulary

Model the following word and example for the class.

1. The word is *desperately* and its meaning is "in a distressed or severe manner."
2. When I hear the word *desperately*, I think of people who need help after a natural disaster.
3. For example: if a family has lost their home and everything they own in a hurricane, they probably need help *desperately*.
4. This is an example of people needing something *desperately* because they cannot live without it.

Continue this exercise with each word in the glossary, calling on individuals or groups of students to share out.

Beginning

PRETEACH VOCABULARY

Beginning students may benefit from additional practice or visual cues that help reinforce meanings in context. Ask students multiple-choice questions with obvious correct answers such as the following:

- What could make a person feel like he is **suffocating?**
  - a. a tight hug
  - b. an open window
- What is something that people need **desperately?**
  - a. food
  - b. concert tickets
- Who relies on **illusion** to do her job?
  - a. a teacher
  - b. a magician
- What might cause an **eruption** of laughter?
  - a. a funny joke
  - b. a pop quiz
- What shows a student's **progress?**
  - a. a late assignment
  - b. a good grade

Students may also benefit from seeing images related to the correct multiple-choice responses. For example, present an image of a person tightly hugging someone or a magician doing a trick.

Classroom Vocabulary Focus

Remind students of the classroom vocabulary words that they studied earlier in the unit. Point out that some of the words may be useful as they think about and discuss the text. For example:

- disagree (Santosh and Niranjan *disagree* about . . .)
- progress (The characters believe they will find *progress* in . . .)
- research (In order to better understand the story, I want to *research* . . .)
- review (I need to *review* the part of the story when . . .)

NOTES

4 SANTOSH: I can hardly breathe or move. I feel as if I'm **suffocating**.

5 ANJALI: Be patient. There is nothing left to do but pray to Lord Ganesha that we reach the safety of India.

6 SANTOSH: But us poor children are so thirsty!

7 NIRANJAN: How can you bellyache at a time like this? Yes, this journey may be dangerous, or uncomfortable, but these feelings are temporary. In the morning, we will be in a new, wonderful world. A free India.

8 SANTOSH: (*sharp*) How can you know that? And what if we're stopped by the rioters before we get there? What if we're killed as Ram was?

9 ANJALI: Shhh, shhh. Please, let's just pray for your father's safety, for our own.

10 NIRANJAN: Of course we can't know, but millions have risked far more than you have. And you still can complain, no matter what.

11 SANTOSH: I'm sorry, but our life was good before this need for Independence, in case you forgot. We ran and played in the streets without fear as little children. I was able to go to school with my friends and wear gold. What do we have now? I **desperately** miss my friends. We are crammed like animals to slaughter in the back of a military truck, praying not to be massacred. And this is freedom? This is the new India? You can have it.

12 ANJALI: Santosh, you have gone too far!

13 SANTOSH: I don't care.

14 *(Niranjan snorts.)*

15 NIRANJAN: Yes, sister, it was nice and comfortable for *you*, for us, perhaps. But what about the lower castes? Or do you ever think of anyone but yourself and which gold earrings to wear?

16 SANTOSH: *(tears in her eyes, soft)* You've always been so cruel to me.

17 ANJALI: Stop it, children! This is not a time for fighting! This is a time to pray for safety, hope that we make it intact across the border, and to hold each other in the light. We need to stay close, more than ever. For your father, for me, for Ram. Please! You arguing only adds to the destruction. Be sensible.

18 SANTOSH: I'm sorry, Mother. But he's being horrible!

TEXT TALK

Have students discuss the questions in small groups. Circulate around the room and check for understanding.

1. What is the play about?
2. Who are the play's characters?
3. Where does the play take place?
4. How does the play make you feel?

ELL All Levels

SPEAKING FRAMES

Giving Information:

- This play is about ____.
- The play's characters are ____.
- This play takes place in ____.
- This play makes me feel ____.

Asking for Information:

- Can you explain ____?
- What do you think about ____?
- Why do you think ____?
- Do you agree with ____?

19 NIRANJAN: I believe in Jawaharlal Nehru. If we didn't get the chance to cross over by caravan, I would have ridden over the border on horseback all by myself!

20 *(A beat. Santosh suddenly starts laughing through tears. Then they all begin to laugh.)*

21 NIRANJAN: We can have a good laugh, but it's true. I believe in Jawaharlal Nehru. I believe in the new India. You talk of how we were free to play in the streets as children. But so what? At what cost? Without independence, there is no true freedom, just the **illusion** of freedom—but the British owned us, make no mistake. The entire soul of our nation was suppressed. And you talk of wearing gold and missing your friends!

22 ANJALI: Don't be so harsh with your sister. Try to have some compassion. I am so grateful for both of your childhoods, and I always will be. It was a peaceful time.

23 NIRANJAN: If we had cared to look, we would have noticed that it was not a peaceful time for many others. Our sisters, our brothers.

24 SANTOSH: You know, for all of your self-righteousness, Mother is the one who got us a place in this caravan, while Father has stayed behind in great danger to gather our affairs! What do you do except endlessly pontificate?!

25 *(Suddenly, the caravan screeches to a stop. They hear an eruption of violence outside of the tent. Shouting, screaming, crying, gun shots. They huddle together, suddenly silent. Anjali prays, holding her children close to her. Niranjan embraces both his mother and sister with his arms, protecting them.)*

25 SANTOSH: (*whispering*) Let us not panic; let us pray together.

26 *(They wait and pray, huddled together. After a few moments, the truck begins to move again, slow and steady. The sounds of the riots slowly fade away. They all let out a big sigh of relief. Anjali clutches the small frame to her chest, her eyes closed.)*

27 ANJALI: I know he is with us; your brother is with us. For now, we are safe.

28 SANTOSH: Yes. For now we are headed to India. To the new world, to the future. Unfortunately, we don't know when we will become the victim of a bullet! Sure, you protect your relatives. But, I can't believe that this is the life we are committing to. I guess you are right, Niranjan. Because, at this point, you must be right.

29 NIRANJAN: Of course I'm right.

30 SANTOSH: Impossible, as always.

31 NIRANJAN: I wouldn't want to disappoint you.

32 *(They laugh.)*

33 ANJALI: I see a bright, new future for us! As long as I have my children, and your father . . . I am home. We will create a beautiful life in India.

34 SANTOSH: I want to have faith in the new India, in Jawaharlal Nehru. I do, we've just lost so much . . .

35 NIRANJAN: But sometimes those sacrifices are necessary, for **progress**. Letting go is an important step to becoming truly free. Look, we are all connected. Place your personal suffering on hold while we work together to end suffering for our people. Can you help this movement to end the violence so that India is a better place for all?

36 SANTOSH: *(quietly, to herself)* Yes. I can and I will.

37 *(Suddenly they hear shouts, but not of violence. Finally, shouts of joy, jubilation! All three look at each other, with light and tears in their eyes.)*

38 SANTOSH: It must be midnight; it has come.

39 NIRANJAN: India is now free. It has finally happened. We are sovereign.

40 ANJALI: The world sleeps still, but we have awakened. When the sun rises, what will we find?

41 *(Santosh takes her mother's hand. They all look out.)*

(BLACKOUT.)

First Read

Read "When the World Sleeps." After you read, complete the Think Questions below.

THINK QUESTIONS

1. **Who are the main characters in the story? What is their relationship?**

   The main characters are ______________________________.

   They are ______________________________.

2. **Write two or three sentences describing the setting of the story.**

   The setting of the story is ______________________________

   ______________________________.

3. **Why are the characters traveling? Include a line from the text to support your response.**

   The characters are traveling because ______________________________

   ______________________________.

4. **Use context to confirm the meaning of the word *illusion* as it is used in "When the World Sleeps." Write your definition of *illusion* here.**

   Illusion means ______________________________.

   A context clue is ______________________________.

5. **What is another way to say that something *erupted*?**

   Something ______________________________.

Think Questions

Circulate as students answer Think Questions independently. Answers will vary.

QUESTION 1: Comprehension

The main characters are Santosh, Niranjan, and Anjali. Santosh and Niranjan are siblings. Anjali is their mother.

QUESTION 2: Comprehension

The characters are in the back of a truck. It is the middle of the night. There are loud sounds outside.

QUESTION 3: Comprehension

Answers will vary, but may include the following examples:

- "In the morning, we will be in a new, wonderful world. A free India."
- "For now we are headed to India. To the new world, to the future."

Student responses should explain that the family is fleeing their home in order to get to safety and freedom in India.

QUESTION 4: Language

Niranjan says that independence leads to "true freedom" instead of "the illusion of freedom." A definition for *illusion* is "something that seems to be real but is not."

QUESTION 5: Language

Something exploded.

Skill: Language Structures

Introduce the Skill

Watch the Concept Definition video and read the definition for Language Structures.

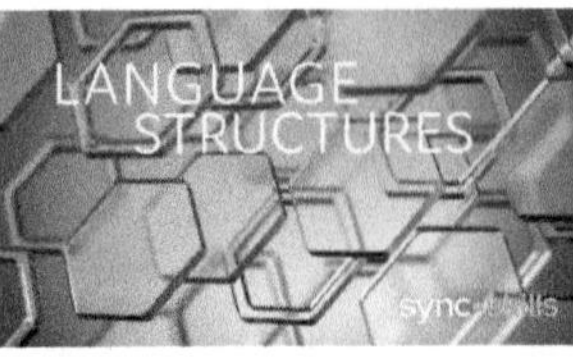

Skill: Language Structures

★ DEFINE

In every language, there are rules that tell how to **structure** sentences. These rules define the correct order of words. In the English language, for example, a **basic** structure for sentences is subject, verb, and object. Some sentences have more **complicated** structures.

You will encounter both basic and complicated **language structures** in the classroom materials you read. Being familiar with language structures will help you better understand the text.

••• CHECKLIST FOR LANGUAGE STRUCTURES

To improve your comprehension of language structures, do the following:

✓ Monitor your understanding.

- Ask yourself: Why do I not understand this sentence? Is it because I do not understand some of the words? Or is it because I do not understand the way the words are ordered in the sentence?

✓ Pay attention to **perfect tenses** as you read. There are three perfect tenses in the English language: the present perfect, past perfect, and future perfect.

- **Present perfect tense** can be used to indicate a situation that began at a prior point in time and continues into the present.
  - > Combine *have* or *has* with the past participle of the main verb.
    Example: I **have played** basketball for three years.
- **Past perfect tense** can describe an action that happened before another action or event in the past.
  - > Combine *had* with the past participle of the main verb.
    Example: I **had learned** how to dribble a ball before I could walk!

TURN AND TALK

1. What is a basic structure for sentences in English?
2. What would make a sentence structure complicated?
3. What can you do if you are struggling to understand language structures?

ELL Beginning & Intermediate

SPEAKING FRAMES

- A basic structure for sentences in English is ____.
- A complicated sentence structure would be ____.
- I can focus on ____.

Advanced & Advanced High

SPEAKING FRAMES

- A basic structure for sentences in English is ____. For example, ____.
- A complicated sentence structure would be ____. For example, ____.
- If I struggle to understand language structures, I can ____. For example, ____.

SKILL VOCABULARY

structure / la estructura ***verb*** the arrangement or ordering of parts COGNATE

basic / básico / a ***adjective*** relating to a base; fundamental COGNATE

complicated / complicado / a ***adjective*** composed of many different parts; difficult to understand, complex COGNATE

language structures / la estructura del lenguaje ***noun*** the order of words in a sentence

- **Future perfect tense** expresses one future action that will begin and end before another future event begins or before a certain time.
  - > Use *will have* or *shall have* with the past participle of a verb.
    Example: Before the end of the year, I **will have played** more than 100 games!
    Example: By the time you play your first game, I **will have played** 100 games!

✓ Break down the sentence into its parts.

- Ask yourself: What actions are expressed in this sentence? Are they completed or are they ongoing? What words give me clues about when an action is taking place?

✓ Confirm your understanding with a peer or teacher.

YOUR TURN

Read each sentence and notice the perfect tense in each one. Then, sort each sentence into the correct category by writing the letter in the Present Perfect, Past Perfect, or Future Perfect column.

	Sentences
A	My aunt has read that book.
B	They have visited Berlin.
C	The series finale will have aired by the end of the year.
D	Before next week, the student will have prepared for the exam.
E	My brother had washed the dishes before going to bed.
F	We got a sandwich after the movie had ended.

Present Perfect	Past Perfect	Future Perfect

Your Turn

Ask students to complete the Your Turn Activity.

Present Perfect	Past Perfect	Future Perfect
B	E	D
A	F	C

Discuss the Skill Model

1. Why is the student confused by the sentence in the first annotation?

   The student is confused because the meaning he knows for the word *have* does not make sense in this sentence.

2. How does the teacher use verb tenses to explain the meaning of the word *have* in this sentence?

   The teacher explains that the verb *have risked* is in the present perfect tense, which is used to talk about an event that happened at an unknown time in the past.

3. How does the student determine the meaning of the sentence in the second annotation?

   First, the student breaks down the sentence into its parts. Then, he thinks about how the present perfect tense is used in this context. This present *progressive tense* helps indicate that India recently became free and now continues to be free.

ELL

Beginning & Intermediate

Have students use the speaking frames and helpful terms to participate in the group discussion. If beginning students are hesitant to participate in a discussion, encourage them by prompting with *yes* or *no* questionns.

Advanced & Advanced High

Have students use the speaking frames to participate in the group discussion.

SPEAKING FRAMES

- The student is confused because ____.
- The teacher explains that ____.
- First, the student ____. He thinks about ____. He determines ____.

HELPFUL TERMS FOR DISCUSSION

- present perfect
- unknown time
- past perfect
- meaning
- have
- before
- tense
- breaks down
- action

Skill: Developing Background Knowledge

Introduce the Skill

Watch the Concept Definition video and read the definition for Developing Background Knowledge.

Skill: Developing Background Knowledge

★ DEFINE

Developing background knowledge is the process of gaining information about different topics. By developing your background knowledge, you will be able to better understand a wider variety of texts.

First, preview the text to determine what the text is about. To **preview** the text, read the title, headers, and other text features and look at any images or graphics. As you are previewing, identify anything that is unfamiliar to you and that seems important.

While you are reading, you can look for clues that will help you learn more about any unfamiliar words, phrases, or topics. You can also look up information in another resource to increase your background knowledge.

••• CHECKLIST FOR DEVELOPING BACKGROUND KNOWLEDGE

To develop your background knowledge, do the following:

- ✓ Preview the text. Read the title, headers, and other features. Look at any images and graphics.
- ✓ Identify any words, phrases, or topics that you do not know a lot about.
- ✓ As you are reading, try to find clues in the text that give you information about any unfamiliar words, phrases, or topics.
- ✓ If necessary, look up information in other sources to learn more about any unfamiliar words, phrases, or topics. You can also ask a peer or teacher for information or support.
- ✓ Think about how the background knowledge you have gained helps you better understand the text.

SKILL VOCABULARY

develop / desarrollar ***verb*** to work out all of the details and possibilities

background knowledge / conocimiento previo ***noun*** information gained from personal experience and prior reading

preview / hojear ***verb*** to look at or see beforehand

TURN AND TALK

1. What is background knowledge?
2. How can background knowledge improve your understanding of a text?
3. What can you do to develop your background knowledge

Beginning & Intermediate

SPEAKING FRAMES

- Background knowledge is ____.
- Background knowledge can help me ____.
- To develop background knowledge, I can ____.

Advanced & Advanced High

SPEAKING FRAMES

- Background knowledge is ____. For example, ____.
- Background knowledge can help me ____ because ____.
- To develop background knowledge, I can ____ and ____.

YOUR TURN

Read each quotation from "When the World Sleeps" below. Then, complete the chart by identifying the background knowledge that helps you understand each quotation.

	Background Knowledge Options
A	Areas formerly controlled by the British were divided into two countries: Pakistan and India.
B	The transition to independence for India was not entirely peaceful.
C	Starting in the Middle Ages, Indian society was divided into different classes called castes.

Quotation	Background Knowledge
"A family is traveling from their old home in Lyallpur, now renamed Faisalabad, headed to the safety of India."	
"But what about the lower castes?"	
"Suddenly, the caravan screeches to a stop. They hear an eruption of violence outside of the tent. Shouting, screaming, crying, gun shots."	

Your Turn

Ask students to complete the Your Turn Activity.

Quotation	Background Knowledge
"A family is traveling from their old home in Lyallpur, now renamed Faisalabad, headed to the safety of India."	A
"But what about the lower castes?"	C
"Suddenly, the caravan screeches to a stop. They hear an eruption of violence outside of the tent. Shouting, screaming, crying, gun shots."	B

Discuss the Skill Model

1. What does the student want to learn more about in the first annotation?

   The student wants to learn about Jawaharlal Nehru.

2. What does the student want to learn more about in the second annotation?

   The student wants to better understand this region and determine why they face danger on their journey.

3. What does the student do to develop her background knowledge?

   The student looks up information on the internet and asks a teacher for support.

4. How can the student develop an even better understanding of the family's journey through India?

   The student can also work together with other students to find and discuss a map of India.

5. How does developing her background knowledge help the student?

   Developing background knowledge helps the student better understand the events and characters in the play.

ELL **Beginning & Intermediate**

Have students use the speaking frames and helpful terms to participate in the group discussion. If beginning students are hesitant to participate in a discussion, encourage them by prompting with *yes* or *no* questions.

Advanced & Advanced High

Have students use the speaking frames to participate in the group discussion.

SPEAKING FRAMES

- The student wants to learn about ____.
- The student also wants to learn about ____.
- The student wants to ____ and ____.
- The student can also ____.
- Developing background knowledge helps the student ____.

HELPFUL TERMS FOR DISCUSSION

- Jawaharlal Nehru
- internet
- understand
- support
- danger
- events
- look up
- teacher
- characters

Close Read

Complete Skills Focus

To prepare students to complete the Skills Focus, remind them of the Reading Skill Developing Background Knowledge. Tell students that one way you can develop background knowledge is to look for references to real-life people, places, and events while reading. Direct students to the Skills Focus and remind them to track as you read aloud.

Use support from your classmates and teacher to gather background knowledge about Indian independence, including the partition of India and Pakistan.

Have students complete the Skills Focus in groups of three. Ask each student to choose a different character to analyze. Students can record their notes in a multiple-column table with columns labeled *Character, Evidence, Analysis,* and *Peer/Teacher Support.*

- In the *Character* column, each student writes their character's name.
- In the *Evidence* column, students record their character's actions, emotions, and dialogue that refer to real-life people, places, and events.
- In the *Analysis* column, students take notes about how their character's actions, emotions, and dialogue show his or her perspective on the historical events in the play.
- In the *Peer/Teacher Support* column, students can add to their notes by sharing information they know from reading, movies, or classwork. If any questions remain, students can ask their teacher for support.

Allow students to reread the text and mark down their ideas using the annotation tool, adding an exclamation point (!) to note things they want to remember or that surprise them, and a question mark (?) to note things that confuse them.

Prompt students to work cooperatively to complete their assigned tasks. Circulate around the room and monitor groups as they work.

Close Read

WRITE

LITERARY ANALYSIS: Santosh and her brother Niranjan view the experience of fleeing their hometown very differently. Choose one of the characters, and write a paragraph in which you explain his or her perspective and why he or she looks at this event this way. Include textual evidence to support your analysis. Pay attention to and edit for homophones.

Use the checklist below to guide you as you write.

- ☐ How does the character refer to real-life people, places, or events?
- ☐ How does the character feel about fleeing Pakistan for India?
- ☐ Why does the character feel this way?

Use the sentence frames to organize and write your literary analysis.

The character I chose is ____________________.

This character is ____________________ about Indian independence.

____________ thinks (they're / their / there) ____________ lives under British rule were ____________________.

This character believes that traveling to India is ____________________.

In the play, the character states, ____________________.

This line shows ____________________.

Collaborative Conversation

Group students into three groups, one group for each character in the play. Prompt groups to list the examples they found and explain how these details improved their background knowledge.

- What details did you find?
- What does this detail tell you about this event in history?
- How did peer and teacher support help you build background knowledge?
- How does this background knowledge improve your understanding of the play?

Collaborative Conversation

SCAFFOLDS

BEGINNING, INTERMEDIATE Use the word bank to participate in the group discussion.

ADVANCED Use the speaking frames to participate in the group discussion.

BEGINNING, INTERMEDIATE	ADVANCED
Word Bank	**Speaking Frames**
• detail • emotion • dialogue • shows • suggests • background knowledge	• An important detail is ____. • This detail shows readers ____. • Peer and teacher support helped me understand ____. • Background knowledge helps me understand the text because ____.

Write

SCAFFOLDS

Literary Analysis Prompt

Santosh and her brother Niranjan view the experience of fleeing their hometown very differently. Choose one of the characters, and write a paragraph in which you explain his or her perspective and why he or she looks at this event this way. Include text evidence to support your analysis. Pay attention to and edit for homophones.

BEGINNING Write a response using the paragraph frames and word banks.

INTERMEDIATE Write a response using the paragraph frames.

INTERMEDIATE / BEGINNING	BEGINNING
Paragraph Frames	**Word Bank**
The character I chose is ____. This character is ____ about Indian independence. ____ thinks (they're / their / there) ____ lives under British rule were ____. This character believes that traveling to India is ____. In the play, the character states, ____. This line shows ____.	• optimistic • negative • dangerous • unfair • necessary

In the Extended Oral Project, students plan, draft, practice, and deliver an oral presentation that ties into the theme of the unit and spans informative, argumentative, and narrative genres. Lessons provide explicit instruction to prepare students for the unique challenges of an oral presentation, and to help break down the genre characteristics of each prompt. At each step in the process, students focus in-depth on specific writing and speaking skills as they brainstorm, organize, and refine their presentation. Students also receive discussion prompts and frames to guide them in providing effective peer feedback as they practice and discuss in small groups before presenting to the class on the final day.

CONNECT TO ESSENTIAL QUESTION

How are we shaped by change?

In this unit, students practiced effective collaborative communication skills as well as environmental print and developing background knowledge skills while reading and analyzing two texts that deal with change and transition. Now students will apply those skills to write and deliver a personal address.

Developing Effective Presentations

Form	Language and Conventions	Oral Language Production
Students may struggle with using language efficiently in order to express the depth of the topic.	Students should be encouraged to experiment with new sentence patterns and lengths to make their dialogue sound natural and realistic.	Students may make mistakes when they transfer grammatical forms from their native languages into English. Remind students to monitor their placement of adverbs and prepositions.

SCAFFOLDS

ELL ENGLISH LANGUAGE LEARNERS

Vocabulary, discussion, and peer and teacher support in the Extended Oral Project is differentiated for Beginning, Intermediate, Advanced, and Advanced High English Language Learners. See individual lesson plans for additional scaffolding and support.

Instructional Path

All Extended Oral Project lessons lesson plans appear in your digital teacher account.

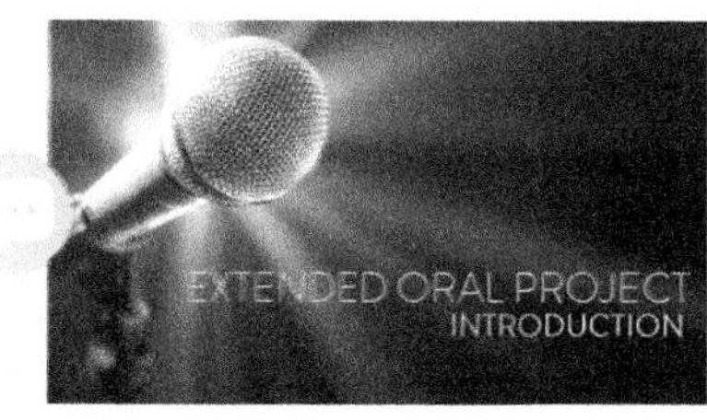

Introduction

Objectives: Students will be able to identify the components of a personal address in order to brainstorm and plan their own address.

Objectives: Students will be able to record ideas for a personal address in writing.

Skill: Acquiring Vocabulary

Objectives: Students will be able to use a graphic organizer to make connections between words and acquire new vocabulary for their oral presentation.

Objectives: Students will be able to brainstorm new words to use in drafting their oral presentation.

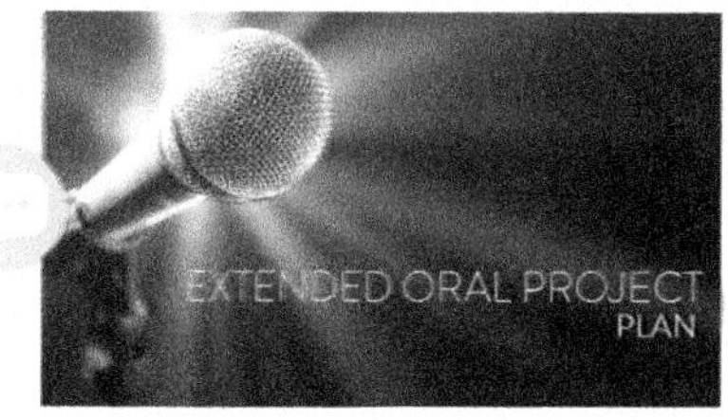

Plan

Objectives: Students will be able to plan and write a first draft of their personal address.

Objectives: Students will be able to organize their first draft using an outline.

Skill: Sentence Lengths

Objectives: Students will be able to apply knowledge of sentence lengths to revise their personal addresses.

Objectives: Students will be able to vary sentence lengths orally and in writing.

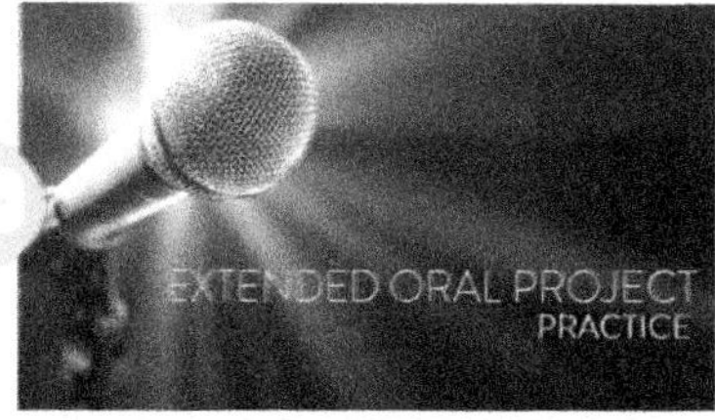

Practice

Objectives: Students will be able to practice and revise their personal address based on peer feedback.

Objectives: Students will be able to practice their personal address orally and make revisions in writing.

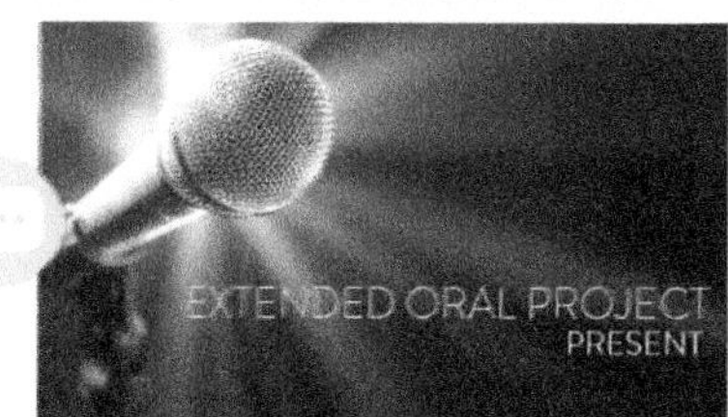

Present

Objectives: Students will be able to observe and perform a personal address in order to give and receive peer feedback.

Objectives: Students will be able to use varied sentence lengths in an oral presentation and give peer feedback orally and in writing.

Spotlight Skills Review

A review day before the end-of-unit assessment gives you an opportunity to review difficult concepts with students using Spotlight Skills lessons. Spotlight Skills are targeted lessons that provide you resources to reteach or remediate without assigning additional readings. Every Core ELA Skill lesson has a corresponding Spotlight Skill lesson. Spotlight Skills can be assigned at any point in the year, but the end of each unit provides a natural moment to pause, review data collected throughout the unit, and reteach skills students have not yet mastered.

Progress Monitoring

The Progress Monitoring charts that appear before every text in this unit identify standards and associated Spotlight Skills. On review day, you may want to give preference to reteaching skills that are not revisited in later units. You can see where Skills are covered again in the Opportunities to Reteach column.

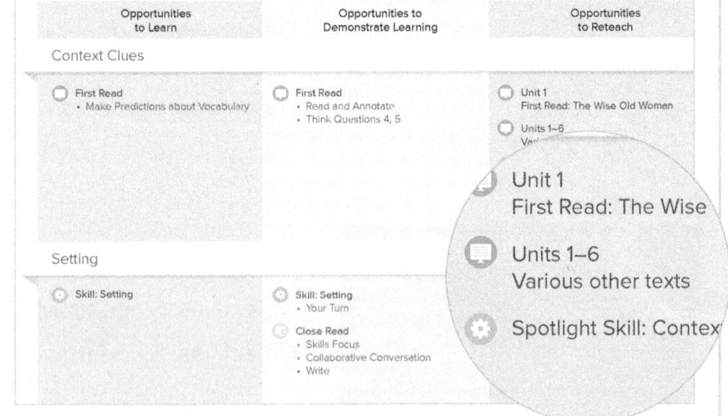

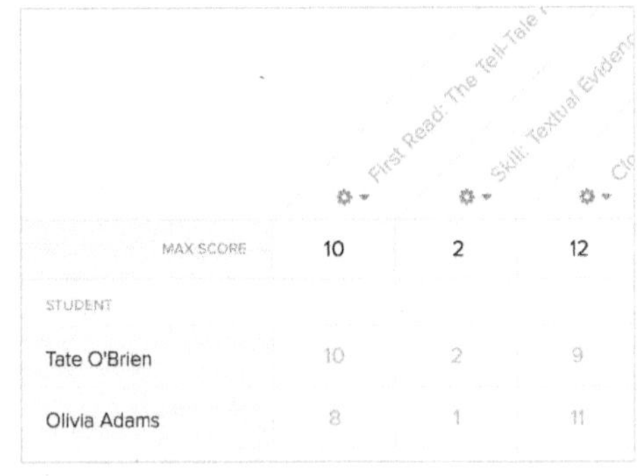

StudySync Gradebook

As students submit assignments on StudySync, their mastery of skills and standards is tracked via the gradebook. The gradebook can be sorted and viewed in a variety of ways. Sorting by assignment shows overall student performance, while sorting by standards or by Skill lessons displays student progress toward mastery goals.

Skills Library 

Spotlight Skills are located in the Skills section of the StudySync Library. You can assign Spotlight Skills to individual students or groups of students. Search tools allow you to search by Skill type or name.

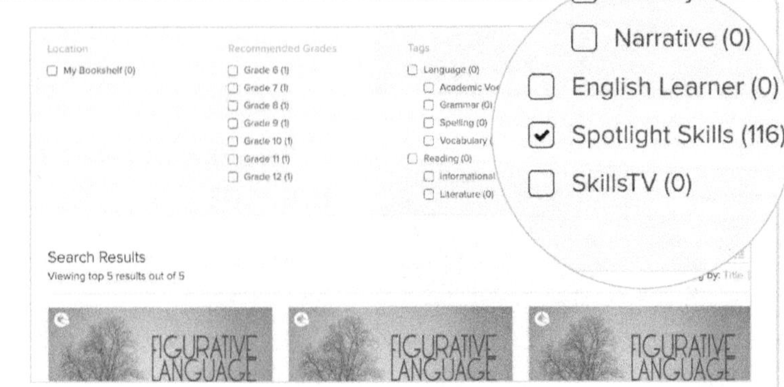

End-of-Unit Assessment

The end-of-unit assessment can be found in two places. The digital version of the assessment can be assigned from the Online Assessment tab inside your ConnectED account. The paper-based version of the assessment can be printed from the End-of-Unit Assessment tab inside this unit in your StudySync account.

Assessment Section	Content	Assessed Skills	
READING	Change Leads to Change Genre: Non-fiction Word Count: 504 Lexile: 1100	• Textual Evidence • Language, Style, and Audience	• Context Clues • Summarizing • Informational Text Elements
	Working Away from Home Genre: Fiction Word Count: 501 Lexile: 1200	• Textual Evidence • Character • Story Elements	• Context Clues • Theme • Story Structure
	Drivin' Down the Highway Genre: Non-fiction Word Count: 736 Lexile: 1300	• Informational Text Elements • Language, Style, and Audience	• Context Clues • Textual Evidence • Summarizing
	An Empty Nest Genre: Fiction Word Count: 572 Lexile: 1200	• Context Clues • Textual Evidence • Theme	• Story Elements • Story Structure
REVISING and **EDITING**	Student Passage #1	• Parallel Structure	• Syntax
	Student Passage #2	• Audience	• Communicating Ideas Clearly
WRITING	Prompt: Oral Presentation	• Oral Presentation	

What's Next?

Assessment results can be viewed by item, standard, and skill to monitor mastery and make decisions for upcoming instruction.

RETEACH skills that students have not yet mastered, using Spotlight Skills or the Test Preparation and Practice book.

REVISE your teaching plan to provide more or less explicit instruction into a skill or text, using Beyond the Book activities for enrichment.

REGROUP students and levels of scaffolding based on standards progress.

Teacher's Edition Credits

Cover, iStock.com/
Cover, iStock.com/
p. iii, iStock.com/FatCamera
p. vi, ©iStock.com/Thatpichai
p. vi, ©iStock.com/bukki88
p. vi, ©iStock.com
p. vii, ©iStock.com/urbancow
p. vii, istock.com/Mojito_mak
p. vii, iStock.com/natushm
p. vii, iStock.com/nikkytok
p. viii, Charlotte Bronte - Print Collector/Contributor/Hulton Archive/Getty Images
p. viii, Elizabeth Browning - Universal History Archive/Contributor/Universal Images Group/Getty Images
p. viii, Wanda Coleman - Sophie Bassouls/Contributor/Corbis Entertainment/Getty Images
p. viii, Charles Dickens - London Stereoscopic Company/Stringer/Hulton Archive/Getty Images
p. viii, Joan Didion - Jason Kempin/Staff/Getty Images Entertainment
p. ix, Ross Gay - Andrew Toth/Stringer/Getty Images Entertainment
p. ix, John Keats - Leemage/Contributor/Hulton Fine Art Collection/Getty Images
p. ix, Yusef Komunyakaa - Neilson Barnard/Stringer/Getty Images Entertainment
p. ix, Ursula Le Guin - Getty Images North America/Michael Buckner/Stringer
p. ix, Percy Bysshe Shelley - Art Collection 2/Alamy Stock Photo
p. ix, William Wordsworth - Hulton Archive/Stringer/Hulton Archive/Getty Images
p. 1, istock.com/francescoch
p. 3, ©iStock.com/Thatpichai
p. 3, ©iStock.com/bukki88
p. 3, ©iStock.com
p. 3, ©iStock/hanohiki
p. 7, studyync
p. 17, istock.com/Mojito_mak
p. 17, iStock.com/natushm
p. 20, istock.com/franckreporter
p. 20, ©iStock.com/vvvita
p. 20, iStock.com/hkeita
p. 21, iStock.com/hocus-focus
p. 21, iStock.com/borchee
p. 20, ©iStock.com/vvvita
p. 23, istock.com/daverhead
p. 27, ©iStock.com/cougarsan
p. 30, iStock.com/finwal
p. 30, iStock.com/borchee
p. 31, iStock.com/borchee
p. 31, iStock.com/5second
p. 34, ©iStock.com/mihtiander
p. 34, ©iStock.com/mihtiander
p. 34, ©iStock.com/mihtiander
p. 34, iStock.com/Hohenhaus
p. 34, MaFelipe/iStock.com
p. 34, Public Domain
p. 40, ©iStock.com/cougarsan
p. 48, ©iStock.com/code6d
p. 50, ©iStock.com/code6d
p. 50, istock.com/ninjaMonkeyStudio
p. 53, ©iStock.com/cougarsan
p. 58, ©iStock.com/DaveBolton
p. 58, ©iStock.com/DaveBolton
p. 60, iStock.com/Andrey_A
p. 60, iStock.com/fotogaby
p. 62, isock.com/COffe72
p. 65, ©iStock.com/cougarsan
p. 77, ©iStock.com/chuyu
p. 77, ©iStock.com/chuyu
p. 78, iStock.com/donatas1205
p. 78, iStock.com/fotogaby
p. 78, ©iStock.com/vvvita
p. 80, istock.com/Givaga
p. 86, ©iStock.com/cougarsan
p. 98, iStock.com/jmsilva
p. 100, iStock.com/jmsilva
p. 100, istock.com/schnuddel
p. 102, ©iStock.com/cougarsan
p. 106, iStock.com/Rike_
p. 108, iStock.com/Rike_
p. 108, istock.com/Yue_
p. 116, ©iStock.com/cougarsan
p. 120, iStock.com/yanukit
p. 121, istock.com/AWelshLad
p. 121, iStock.com/yanukit
p. 125, ©iStock.com/cougarsan
p. 128, ©iStock.com/MarioGuti
p. 130, ©iStock.com/MarioGuti
p. 130, istock.com/gaiamoments
p. 136, ©iStock.com/cougarsan
p. 140, ©iStock.com/GeorgesDiegues
p. 142, ©iStock.com/GeorgesDiegues
p. 142, istock.com/Kapook2981
p. 146, ©iStock.com/cougarsan
p. 150, ©iStock/hanohiki
p. 152, ©iStock/hanohiki
p. 152, iStock.com/yanukit
p. 152, istock.com/JohnnyPowell
p. 156, ©iStock.com/cougarsan
p. 160, ©iStock.com/mdmilliman
p. 162, ©iStock.com/mdmilliman
p. 162, istock.com/LPETTET
p. 166, ©iStock.com/cougarsan
p. 170, ©iStock.com/Chattrawutt
p. 172, ©iStock.com/Chattrawutt
p. 172, ©iStock.com/antoni_halim
p. 174, istock.com/alexskopje
p. 178, ©iStock.com/cougarsan
p. 186, ©iStock.com/maurusasdf
p. 188, ©iStock.com/maurusasdf
p. 188, ©iStock.com/RapidEye
p. 188, istock.com/SrdjanPav
p. 191, ©iStock.com/cougarsan
p. 196, ©iStock.com/GZeroOne
p. 198, iStock.com/GZeroOne
p. 198, iStock.com
p. 198, iStock.com/Brostock
p. 198, iStock.com/fotogaby
p. 200, istock.com/tomertu
p. 207, ©iStock.com/cougarsan
p. 222, iStock/shironosov
p. 222, iStock.com/borchee
p. 223, iStock.com/EasternLightcraft
p. 223, iStock.com/borchee
p. 225, iStock.com/franckreporter
p. 225, iStock.com/borchee
p. 226, iStock.com/hanibaram, iStock.com/seb_ra, iStock.com/Martin Barraud
p. 228, iStock.com/Martin Barraud
p. 228, ©iStock.com/koya79
p. 228, ©iStock.com/Mutlu Kurtbas
p. 228, @iStock/DNY59
p. 229, ©iStock.com/SKrow
p. 229, iStock.com/horiyan
p. 229, iStock.com/tofumax
p. 229, iStock.com/me4o
p. 229, iStock.com/Martin Barraud
p. 230, iStock.com/Customdesigner
p. 230, ©iStock.com/wingmar
p. 230, ©iStock.com/Thomas Shanahan
p. 230, iStock.com/Martin Barraud
p. 282, iStock.com/borchee
p. 282, ©iStock.com/urbancow
p. 282, iStock.com/eskymaks
p. 282, iStock.com/mukem
p. 284, istock.com/Mojito_mak
p. 286, iStock.com/blackred
p. 286, iStock.com/from2015
p. 286, istock.com/Mojito_mak
p. 286, iStock.com/BlackJack3D
p. 286, iStock.com/kyoshino
p. 286, iStock.com/eugenesergeev
p. 288, istock.com/franckreporter
p. 300, ©iStock.com/natushm
p. 301, iStock.com/nikkytok
p. 302, iStock.com/eskymaks
p. 302, iStock.com/mukem
p. 302, iStock.com/natushm
p. 302, iStock.com/Ales_Utovko
p. 302, iStock.com/AlexandrBognat
p. 302, iStock.com/m63085
p. 303, ©iStock.com/Thatpichai
p. 303, ©iStock.com/bukki88
p. 303, ©iStock.com
p. 304, istock.com/RoyFWylam
p. 306, ©iStock.com/Marco_Piunti
p. 307, ©iStock.com/Marco_Piunti
p. 317, iStock.com/juhide
p. 317, iStock.com/Aslan Alphan

Student Edition Credits

PHOTO/IMAGE CREDITS:

Cover, iStock.com/vvvita
Charlotte Bronte - Print Collector / Contributor/ Hulton Archive/ Getty Images
Elizabeth Browning - Universal History Archive / Contributor/Universal Images Group/ Getty Images
Wanda Coleman - Sophie Bassouls / Contributor/ Corbis Entertainment/ Getty Images
Charles Dickens - London Stereoscopic Company / Stringer/Hulton Archive/ Getty Images
Joan Didion - Jason Kempin / Staff/ Getty Images Entertainment
Heidi Erdrich - Chris Felver / Contributor/ Premium Archive/ Getty Images
Ross Gay - Andrew Toth / Stringer/ Getty Images Entertainment
John Keats - Leemage / Contributor/ Hulton Fine Art Collection/ Getty Images
Yusef Komunyakaa - Neilson Barnard / Stringer/ Getty Images Entertainment
Ursula Le Guin - Getty Images North America/ Michael Buckner/ Stringer
Percy Bysshe Shelley - Art Collection 2 / Alamy Stock Photo
William Wordsworth - Hulton Archive / Stringer/Hulton Archive/ Getty Images
p. 2, Public Domain Image
p. 3, Public Domain Image
p. 5, iStock.com/vvvita
p. 6, iStock.com/
p. 7, DEA / S. VANNINI/De Agostini/Getty Images
p. 8, iStock.com/
p. 9, ©iStock.com/Hohenhaus
p. 10, ©iStock.com/Hohenhaus
p. 11, iStock.com/
p. 12, ©iStock.com/code6d
p. 15, DaveBolton/iStock.com
p. 16, iStock/arogant
p. 18, DaveBolton/iStock.com
p. 19, ©iStock.com/Andrey_A
p. 20, ©iStock.com/Andrey_A
p. 21, ©iStock.com/fotogaby
p. 22, ©iStock.com/fotogaby
p. 23, DaveBolton/iStock.com
p. 24, iStock.com/chuyu
p. 25, Print Collector/Hulton Fine Art Collection/Getty Images
p. 30, iStock.com/chuyu
p. 31, ©iStock.com/donatas1205
p. 32, ©iStock.com/donatas1205
p. 33, ©iStock.com/fotogaby
p. 34, ©iStock.com/fotogaby
p. 36iStock.com/chuyu
p. 37, iStock.com/jmsilva
p. 39, iStock.com/Rike_
p. 47, iStock.com/yanukit
p. 48, Popperfoto/Popperfoto/Getty Images
p. 50, Mondadori Portfolio/Hulton Fine Art Collection/ Getty Images
p. 52, iStock.com/yanukit
p. 53, iStock.com/MarioGuti
p. 54, Time Life Pictures/The LIFE Picture Collection/Getty Images
p. 59, ©iStock.com/GeorgesDiegues
p. 60, London Stereoscopic Company/Hulton Archive/ Getty Images
p. 63, iStock.com/hanohiki
p. 64, Print Collector/Hulton Archive/Getty Images
p. 67, ©iStock.com/mdmilliman
p. 71, iStock.com/Chattrawutt
p. 73, iStock.com/Chattrawutt
p. 74, ©iStock.com/antoni_halim
p. 75, ©iStock.com/antoni_halim
p. 76, iStock.com/Chattrawutt
p. 77, iStock.com/maurusasdf
p. 80, iStock.com/GZeroOne
p. 87, iStock.com/GZeroOne
p. 88, iStock.com/
p. 89, iStock.com/
p. 91, ©iStock.com/Brostock
p. 92, ©iStock.com/Brostock
p. 94, ©iStock.com/fotogaby
p. 95, ©iStock.com/fotogaby
p. 96, iStock.com/GZeroOne
p. 97, iStock.com/hanibaram, iStock.com/seb_ra, iStock.com/Martin Barraud
p. 98, iStock.com/Martin Barraud
p. 101, "The Politics of Climate." Pew Research Center, Washington, D.C. October 4, 2016. http://www.pewresearch.org/fact-tank/2016/10/07/perceptions-and-realities-of-recycling-vary-widely-from-place-to-place/
p. 103, "The Politics of Climate." Pew Research Center, Washington, D.C. October 4, 2016. http://www.pewresearch.org/fact-tank/2016/10/07/perceptions-and-realities-of-recycling-vary-widely-from-place-to-place/
p. 108, iStock.com/koya79
p. 111, ©iStock.com/Mutlu Kurtbas
p. 114, @iStock/DNY59
p. 116, iStock.com/Martin Barraud
p. 122, ©iStock.com/
p. 124, ©iStock.com/honyan
p. 126, iStock.com/tofumax
p. 128, ©iStock.com/me4o
p. 130, iStock.com/Martin Barraud
p. 133, ©iStock.com/Customdesigner
p. 135, iStock.com/Martin Barraud
p. 137, istock.com/Mojito_mak
p. 138, iStock.com/Izabela Habur
p. 138, iStock.com/Pamela Moore
p. 138, iStock.com/Dreef
p. 138, iStock.com/Dreef
p. 138, iStock.com/
p. 140, iStock.com/
p. 141, ©iStock.com/BlackJack3D
p. 143, ©iStock.com/kyoshino
p. 146, istock.com/Mojito_mak
p. 147, iStock.com/natushm
p. 145, ©iStock.com/mangostock
p. 146, ©iStock.com/MaskaRad
p. 146, ©iStock.com/TommL
p. 146, ©iStock.com/Ilya_Starikov
p. 149, Universal Images Group/Universal Images Group/ Getty Images
p. 149, Photo 12/Universal Images Group/Getty Images
p. 151, iStock.com/natushm
p. 152, ©iStock.com/Ales_Utovko
p. 154, ©iStock.com/AlexandrBognat
p. 156, iStock.com/natushm

Teacher's Edition Credits

p. 322, ©iStock.com/Marco_Piunti
p. 323, iStock.com/ER_Creative
p. 323, iStock.com/dwleindecker
p. 323, iStock.com/urbancow
p. 335, BrianAJackson/iStock.com
p. 864, iStock.com/BilevichOlga
p. 335, iStock.com/bgwalker
p. 336, iStock.com/Ivan Bajic
p. 338, ©iStock.com/Marco_Piunti
p. 338, iStock.com/Cebas
p. 338, ©iStock.com/roman_slavik
p. 338, iStock.com/hkeita
p. 338, iStock.com/5second
p. 339, iStock.com/Cebas
p. 339, iStock.com/borchee
p. 340, iStock.com/LordRunar
p. 341, istock.com/ChamilleWhite
p. 347, iStock.com/cougarsan
p. 350, iStock.com/clu
p. 350, iStock.com/borchee
p. 351, iStock.com/borchee
p. 351, iStock.com/5second
p. 352, ©iStock.com/pastorscott
p. 352, ©iStock.com/pastorscott
p. 352, ©iStock.com/pastorscott
p. 357, iStock.com/cougarsan
p. 362, iStock.com/Peeter Viisimaa
p. 364, iStock.com/Peeter Viisimaa
p. 364, iStock.com/antoni_halim
p. 364, iStock.com/Andrey_A
p. 364, iStock.com/bernie_photo
p. 364, iStock.com/Steve Debenport
p. 366, istock.com/ShangImages
p. 371, iStock.com/cougarsan
p. 384, ©iStock.com/OGphoto
p. 386, ©iStock.com/OGphoto
p. 364, istock.com/mustafahacalaki
p. 388, iStock.com/cougarsan
p. 392, ©iStock.com/PytyCzech
p. 394, ©iStock.com/PytyCzech
p. 394, ©iStock.com/PytyCzech
p. 397, iStock.com/cougarsan
p. 402, ©iStock.com/alffalff
p. 404, ©iStock.com/alffalff
p. 404, iStock.com/Murat Göçmen
p. 404, iStock.com/Smithore
p. 404, ©iStock.com/alffalff
p. 406, iStock.com/Eva-Katalin
p. 415, iStock.com/cougarsan
p. 426, iStock.com/dem10
p. 428, iStock.com/dem10
p. 428, iStock/Spanishalex
p. 428, iStock.com/Hohenhaus
p. 430, istock.com/solidcolours
p. 441, iStock.com/cougarsan
p. 452, iStock.com/epicurean
p. 454, iStock.com/epicurean
p. 454, istock.com/BarrySheene
p. 458, iStock.com/cougarsan
p. 462, iStock.com/:kyoshino
p. 464, iStock.com/:kyoshino
p. 464, istock.com/AYOTOGRAPHY
p. 472, iStock.com/cougarsan
p. 476, ©iStock.com/ampueroleonardo
p. 476, ©iStock.com/ampueroleonardo
p. 478, Erika Goldring/Contributor/WireImage/GettyImages
p. 478, istock.com/Elen11
p. 481, iStock.com/cougarsan
p. 486, iStock.com/simonbradfield
p. 488, iStock.com/paulafrench
p. 488, iStock.com/Caval
p. 488, iStock.com/ThomasVogel
p. 488, iStock.com/janrysavy
p. 488, iStock.com/paulafrench
p. 490, iStock.com/paulafrench
p. 496, iStock.com/cougarsan
p. 508, ©iStock.com/sunara
p. 510, ©iStock.com/sunara
p. 510, iStock.com/NATA_0101
p. 513, iStock.com/cougarsan
p. 518, iStock.com/EricVega
p. 520, iStock.com/EricVega
p. 520, iStock.com/martin-dm
p. 524, iStock.com/cougarsan
p. 528, ©iStock.com/Kenneth Canning
p. 530, ©iStock.com/Kenneth Canning
p. 530, iStock.com/Brostock
p. 530, iStock.com/Orla
p. 530, iStock.com/2jenn
p. 530, ©iStock.com/roman_slavik
p. 532, iStock.com/
p. 539, iStock.com/cougarsan
p. 552, iStock.com/borchee
p. 552, iStock/shironosov
p. 553, iStock.com/borchee
p. 553, iStock.com/EasternLightcraft
p. 554, iStock.com/borchee
p. 554, iStock.com/franckreporter
p. 556, iStock.com/hanibaram, iStock.com/seb_ra, iStock.com/Martin Barraud
p. 558, iStock.com/Martin Barraud
p. 558, iStock/dem10
p. 558, iStock.com/gopixa
p. 558, iStock.com/fstop123
p. 558, iStock.com/bo1982
p. 559, iStock.com/Jeff_Hu
p. 559, iStock.com/stevedangers
p. 559, iStock.com/Martin Barraud
p. 559, iStock.com/Customdesigner
p. 559, iStock.com/efks
p. 559, iStock.com/borchee
p. 559, iStock.com/Martin Barraud
p. 602, iStock.com/borchee
p. 602, ©iStock.com/Marco_Piunti
p. 602, iStock.com/eskymaks
p. 602, iStock.com/NUMAX3D
p. 604, BrianAJackson/iStock.com
p. 606, iStock.com/blackred
p. 606, iStock.com/mukem
p. 606, BrianAJackson/iStock.com
p. 606, iStock.com/BlackJack3D
p. 606, iStock.com/BlackJack3D
p. 606, iStock.com/eugenesergeev
p. 608, istock.com/chabybucko
p. 618, iStock.com/bgwalker
p. 620, iStock.com/eskymaks
p. 620, iStock.com/NUMAX3D
p. 620, bgwalker/iStock.com
p. 620, iStock.com/Ales_Utovko
p. 620, iStock.com/AlexandrBognat
p. 620, iStock.com/Kathryn8
p. 622, istock.com/sdominick
p. 623, iStock.com/nikkytok
p. 623, iStock.com/juhide
p. 623, iStock.com/DNY59

Student Edition Credits

PHOTO/IMAGE CREDITS:

Cover, iStock.com/LordRunar
Fareena Arefeen - Credit: Used by permission of Fareena Arefeen
Winston Churchill - Fox Photos / Stringer/Hulton Archive/ Getty Images
Lucille Clifton - Afro Newspaper/Gado / Contributor/ Archive Photos/ Getty Images
Alice Dunbar Nelson - Interim Archives / Contributor/ Archive Photos/ Getty Images
T.S. Eliot - George Douglas / Stringer / Picture Post/ Getty Images
Katherine Mansfield - UniversalImagesGroup / Contributor/ Universal Images Group/ Getty Images
George Orwell - World History Archive / Alamy Stock Photo
Lillian Smith - DXPA75 Pictorial Press Ltd / Alamy Stock Photo
Tenessee Williams - RBM Vintage Images / Alamy Stock Photo
William Carlos Williams - Alfred Eisenstaedt / Contributor/ The LIFE Picture Collection
Virginia Woolf - Culture Club / Contributor/ Hulton Archive/ Getty Images
p. 2, DEA / A. C. COOPER/De Agostini/Getty Images
p. 3, DEA PICTURE LIBRARY/De Agostini/Getty Images
p. 4, Bettmann/Bettmann/Getty Images
p. 7, iStock.com/bernie_photo
p. 8, ©iStock.com/pastorscott
p. 9, Fine Art/Corbis Historical/Getty Images
p. 11, Peeter Viisimaa/iStock.com
p. 12, George Douglas/Picture Post/Getty Images
p. 16, Peeter Viisimaa/iStock.com
p. 17, iStock.com/antoni_halim
p. 18, iStock.com/antoni_halim
p. 19, iStock.com/Andrey_A
p. 20, iStock.com/Andrey_A
p. 21, iStock.com/bernie_photo
p. 22, iStock.com/bernie_photo
p. 23, Peeter Viisimaa/iStock.com
p. 24, ©iStock.com/OGphoto
p. 25, ©iStock.com/PytyCzech
p. 27, Interim Archives/Archive Photos/Getty Images
p. 29, ©iStock.com/aiffalff
p. 30, UniversalImagesGroup/Universal Images Group/ Getty Images
p. 38, ©iStock.com/aiffalff
p. 39, iStock.com/Murat Göçmen
p. 40, iStock.com/Murat Göçmen
p. 41, iStockphoto.com
p. 42, iStockphoto.com
p. 43, Peeter Viisimaa/iStock.com
p. 44, iStock.com/dem10
p. 55, iStock.com/dem10
p. 56, iStock/Spanishalex
p. 57, iStock/Spanishalex
p. 58, iStock.com/Hohenhaus
p. 59, iStock.com/Hohenhaus
p. 60, iStock.com/dem10
p. 61, iStock.com/epicurean
p. 65, ©iStock.com/kyoshino
p. 66, Culture Club/Hulton Archive/Getty Images
p. 73, ©iStock.com/ampueroleonardo
p. 76, ©iStock.com/simonbradfield
p. 77, Fox Photos/Hulton Archive/Getty Images
p. 80, ©iStock.com/simonbradfield
p. 81, iStock.com/Caval
p. 82, iStock.com/Caval
p. 83, iStock.com/ThomasVogel
p. 84, iStock.com/ThomasVogel
p. 85, iStock.com/janrysavy
p. 86, iStock.com/janrysavy
p. 87, ©iStock.com/simonbradfield
p. 88, ©iStock.com/sunara
p. 89, ED JONES/AFP/Getty Images
p. 91, iStock.com/EricVega
p. 95, ©iStock.com/Kenneth Canning
p. 96, DeA / Icas94/De Agostini/Getty Images
p. 102, ©iStock.com/Kenneth Canning
p. 103, iStock.com/Brostock
p. 104, iStock.com/Brostock
p. 105, iStock.com/Orla
p. 106, iStock.com/Orla
p. 107, iStock.com/fotogaby
p. 108, iStock.com/fotogaby
p. 109, ©iStock.com/Kenneth Canning
p. 110, iStock.com/hanibaram, iStock.com/seb_ra, iStock.com/Martin Barraud
p. 111, iStock.com/Martin Barraud
p. 117, iStock.com/Domin_domin
p. 119, iStock.com/gopixa
p. 121, iStock.com/fstop123
p. 123, iStock.com/Martin Barraud
p. 129, iStock.com/bo1982
p. 132, iStock.com/Jeff_Hu
p. 134, iStock.com/stevedangers
p. 136, iStock.com/Martin Barraud
p. 139, iStock.com/Customdesigner
p. 141, iStock.com/Martin Barraud

Teacher's Edition Credits

p. 637, ©iStock.com/Rawpixel
p. 639, ©iStock.com/bradleyhebdon
p. 639, ©iStock.com/sonnyasehan
p. 639, ©iStock.com/tzooka
p. 653, ©iStock.com/cbarnesphotography
p. 653, ©istock.com/GCShutter
p. 654, iStock.com/Ivan Bajic
p. 656, iStock.com/Konstanttin
p. 656, iStock.com/svetikd
p. 656, ©iStock.com/pawopa3336
p. 656, iStock.com/hkeita
p. 656, iStock.com/5second
p. 657, iStock.com/svetikd
p. 657, iStock.com/borchee
p. 658, ©iStock.com/pawopa3336
p. 659, 2630ben/iStock.com
p. 666, iStock.com/borchee
p. 666, iStock.com/NiseriN
p. 667, iStock.com/borchee
p. 667, iStock.com/5second
p. 668, iStock.com/borchee
p. 668, ©iStock.com/yangphoto
p. 670, ©iStock.com/yangphoto
p. 670, iStock.com/ValentinaPhotos
p. 670, iStock.com/BrianAJackson
p. 672, Ruth Craine/iStock.com
p. 675, iStock.com/cougarsan
p. 688, ©iStock.com/borchee
p. 690, ©iStock.com/borchee
p. 690, stevanovicigor/istock.com
p. 692, iStock.com/cougarsan
p. 696, iStock.com/GypsyGraphy
p. 698, iStock.com/GypsyGraphy
p. 698, mmac72/istock.com
p. 714, iStock.com/cougarsan
p. 718, iStock.com/heibaihui
p. 720, iStock.com/heibaihui
p. 720, iStock.com/Dominique_Lavoie
p. 720, iStock.com/LdF
p. 720, iStock.com/bauhaus1000
p. 722, loonara/iStock.com
p. 739, iStock.com/cougarsan
p. 750, ©iStock.com/narvikk
p. 752, mantaphoto/iStock.com
p. 752, mantaphoto/iStock.com
p. 752, iStock.com/artisteer
p. 756, iStock.com/cougarsan
p. 760, ©istock.com/shayes17
p. 762, ©istock.com/shayes17
p. 762, hadynyah/istock.com
p. 765, iStock.com/cougarsan
p. 770, ©iStock.com/peeterv
p. 772, ©iStock.com/peeterv
p. 772, iStock.com/urbancow
p. 772, iStock.com/LdF
p. 772, ©iStock.com/pawopa3336
p. 774, Fela Sanu/istock.com
p. 788, iStock.com/cougarsan
p. 798, ©istock.com/Jasmina007
p. 800, ©istock.com/Jasmina007
p. 800, Misha Kaminsky/iStock.com
p. 809, iStock.com/cougarsan
p. 814, iStock.com/Harnnarong
p. 816, iStock.com/Harnnarong
p. 816, iStock.com/Harnnarong
p. 820, iStock.com/cougarsan
p. 824, istock.com/artisteer
p. 826, istock.com/artisteer
p. 826, istock.com/artisteer
p. 834, iStock.com/cougarsan
p. 838, PeopleImages/iStock.com
p. 840, PeopleImages/iStock.com
p. 840, iStock.com/eskaylim
p. 840, iStock.com/Hohenhaus
p. 842, PeopleImages/iStock.com
p. 849, iStock.com/cougarsan
p. 860, iStock.com/spooh
p. 862, iStock.com/spooh
p. 862, MarsYu/iStock.com
p. 864, iStock.com/cougarsan
p. 868, ©istock.com/steinphoto
p. 870, ©istock.com/steinphoto
p. 870, iStock.com/antoni_halim
p. 870, iStock.com/urbancow
p. 870, ©istock.com/
p. 872, GCShutter/iStock.com
p. 882, iStock.com/cougarsan
p. 894, iStock/shironosov
p. 894, iStock.com/borchee
p. 895, iStock.com/EasternLightcraft
p. 895, iStock.com/borchee
p. 897, iStock.com/franckreporter
p. 897, iStock.com/borchee
p. 898, iStock.com/hanibaram, iStock.com/seb_ra, iStock.com/Martin Barraud
p. 900, iStock.com/Martin Barraud
p. 900, iStock.com/BilevichOlga
p. 900, iStock.com/Mutlu Kurtbas
p. 900, iStock.com/Martin Barraud
p. 900, iStock.com/DNY59
p. 901, iStock.com/tofumax
p. 901, iStock.com/polesnoy
p. 901, iStock.com/peepo
p. 901, iStock.com/SasinParaksa
p. 901, iStock.com/Martin Barraud
p. 901, iStock/Vimvertigo
p. 902, iStock.com/mooltfilm
p. 960, iStock.com/hanibaram, iStock.com/borchee
p. 960, ©iStock.com/Rawpixel
p. 960, iStock.com/eskymaks
p. 960, iStock.com/ThomasVogel
p. 962, ©iStock.com/cbarnesphotography
p. 964, iStock.com/blackred
p. 964, ©iStock.com/-Antonio-
p. 964, ©iStock.com/cbarnesphotography
p. 964, iStock.com/Ales_Utovko
p. 964, iStock.com/AlexandrBognat
p. 964, iStock.com/borzaya
p. 966, imagedepotpro/iStock.com
p. 978, ©istock.com/GCShutter
p. 980, iStock.com/eskymaks
p. 980, iStock.com/ThomasVogel
p. 980, ©istock.com/GCShutter
p. 980, iStock.com/BlackJack3D
p. 980, iStock.com/Mlenny
p. 980, iStock.com/eugenesergeev
p. 982, tunart/iStock.com
p. 995, iStock.com/nikkytok
p. 995, iStock.com/juhide
p. 995, iStock.com/Ivan Bajic

Student Edition Credits

PHOTO/IMAGE CREDITS:

Cover, ©iStock.com/pawopa3336
Leila Aboulela - Massimiliano Donati/Awakening / Contributor/ Getty Images Entertainment
Chimamanda Ngozi Adichie - Taylor Hill / Contributor/ FilmMagic/ Getty Images
Mahzarin R. Banaji - Roy Rochlin / Stringer/ Getty Images Entertainment
Rita Dove - Getty Images Europe: Barbara Zanon / Contributor
Jamaica Kincaid - Paul Marotta / Contributor/ Getty Images Entertainment
Jhumpa Lahiri - Venturelli / Contributor/ GC Images/ Getty Images
Jawaharlal Nehru - Margaret Bourke-White / Contributor/ The LIFE Picture Collection
Ben Okri - Roberto Ricciuti / Contributor/ Getty Images Entertainment
Zadie Smith - Brian Dowling / Stringer/ Getty Images Entertainment
Derek Walcott - Ulf Andersen / Contributor/ Hulton Archive
p. 1, Hulton Deutsch/Corbis Historical/Getty Images
p. 3, Tristan Fewings/Getty Images Entertainment/Getty Images
p. 5, ©iStock.com/pawopa3336
p. 6, ©iStock.com/yangphoto
p. 7, Roberto Ricciuti/Getty Images Entertainment/Getty Images
p. 9, ©iStock.com/yangphoto
p. 10, iStock.com/ValentinaPhotos
p. 11, iStock.com/ValentinaPhotos
p. 12, ©iStock/BrianAJackson
p. 13, ©iStock/BrianAJackson
p. 15, ©iStock.com/yangphoto
p. 16, ©iStock.com/borchee
p. 17, Ulf Andersen/Hulton Archive/Getty Images
p. 19, ©iStock.com/valeriebarry
p. 20, Massimiliano Donati/Awakening/Getty Images Entertainment/Getty Images
p. 35, ©iStock.com/heibaihui
p. 36, Venturelli/GC Images/Getty Images
p. 52, ©iStock.com/heibaihui
p. 53, iStock.com/Dominique_Lavoie
p. 54, iStock.com/Dominique_Lavoie
p. 55, ©iStock.com/LdF
p. 56, ©iStock.com/LdF
p. 57, ©iStock.com/heibaihui
p. 58, ©iStock.com/narvikk
p. 59, Hindustan Times/Hindustan Times/Getty Images
p. 62, ©istock.com/shayes17
p. 65, ©iStock.com/peeterv
p. 66, STEPHANE DE SAKUTIN/AFP/Getty Images
p. 77, ©iStock.com/peeterv
p. 78, iStock.com/urbancow
p. 79, iStock.com/urbancow
p. 80, ©iStock.com/LdF
p. 81, ©iStock.com/LdF
p. 82, ©iStock.com/peeterv
p. 83, ©istock.com/Jasmina007
p. 84–91, © 2016 by Ehud Lavski and Yael Nathan. Reproduced by permission of Ehud Lavski, c/o The Gotham Group.
p. 93, iStock.com/Eerik
p. 97, iStock.com/artisteer
p. 100, Public Domain
p. 105, iStock.com/PeopleImages
p. 106, istock.com/valentinrussanov
p. 109, iStock/Vladimir Vladimirov
p. 110, StudySync
p. 112, iStock.com/PeopleImages
p. 113, iStock.com/eskaylim
p. 114, iStock.com/eskaylim
p. 115, iStock.com/Hohenhaus
p. 116, iStock.com/Hohenhaus
p. 117, iStock.com/PeopleImages
p. 118, iStock.com/spooh
p. 120, ©istock.com/steinphoto
p. 128, ©istock.com/steinphoto
p. 129, iStock.com/antoni_halim
p. 130, iStock.com/antoni_halim
p. 131, iStock.com/urbancow
p. 132, iStock.com/urbancow
p. 133, iStock.com/Smithore
p. 134, iStock.com/Smithore
p. 135, ©istock.com/steinphoto
p. 136, iStock.com/hanibaram, iStock.com/seb_ra, iStock.com/Martin Barraud
p. 137, iStock.com/Martin Barraud
p. 139, StudySync
p. 140, StudySync
p. 141, StudySync
p. 141, StudySync
p. 142, StudySync
p. 143, StudySync
p. 143, NBC Universal Archives
p. 144, StudySync
p. 145, StudySync
p. 145, StudySync
p. 146, StudySync
p. 148, iStock.com/BilevichOlga
p. 151, iStock.com/Mutlu Kurtbas
p. 154, iStock.com/Martin Barraud
p. 157, iStock.com/DNY59
p. 160, iStock.com/Martin Barraud
p. 164, iStock.com/tofumax
p. 168, iStock.com/polesnoy
p. 171, iStock.com/peepo
p. 174, iStock.com/SasinParaksa
p. 177, iStock.com/Martin Barraud
p. 180, iStock.com/Martin Barraud
p. 182, ©iStock.com/cbarnesphotography
p. 183, iStock.com/Renphoto
p. 183, iStock.com/mtreasure
p. 183, iStock.com/Cecilie_Arcurs
p. 183, iStock.com/johnnorth
p. 183, iStock.com/warrengoldswain
p. 183, Jeff Greenberg/Universal Images Group/Getty Images
p. 184, Miami Herald/Tribune News Service/Getty Images
p. 185, David McNew/Getty Images News/Getty Images
p. 187, ©iStock.com/cbarnesphotography
p. 188, iStock.com/Ales_Utovko
p. 190, iStock.com/AlexandrBognat
p. 191, David McNew/Getty Images News/Getty Images
p. 192, ©iStock.com/cbarnesphotography
p. 193, ©istock.com/GCShutter
p. 194, iStock.com/davidf
p. 194, iStock.com/amriphoto
p. 194, iStock.com/mgkaya
p. 194, iStock.com/Beboy_ltd
p. 194, iStock.com/RuslanDashinsky
p. 198, ©istock.com/GCShutter
p. 199, iStock.com/BlackJack3D
p. 201, iStock.com/Mlenny
p. 203, ©istock.com/GCShutter

Text Fulfillment Through StudySync

If you are interested in specific titles, please fill out the form below and we will check availability through our partners.

ORDER DETAILS

Date:

TITLE	AUTHOR	Paperback/ Hardcover	Specific Edition *If Applicable*	Quantity

SHIPPING INFORMATION

Contact:

Title:

School/District:

Address Line 1:

Address Line 2:

Zip or Postal Code:

Phone:

Mobile:

Email:

BILLING INFORMATION

☐ *SAME AS SHIPPING*

Contact:

Title:

School/District:

Address Line 1:

Address Line 2:

Zip or Postal Code:

Phone:

Mobile:

Email:

PAYMENT INFORMATION

☐ CREDIT CARD

Name on Card:

Card Number: Expiration Date: Security Code:

☐ PO

Purchase Order Number:

StudySync Text Fulfillment, BookheadEd Learning, LLC
610 Daniel Young Drive | Sonoma, CA 95476